Snowmobile

SERVICE MANUAL ■ 11TH EDITION

The *Snowmobile Service Manual* is divided into two main service sections as follows:

A vehicle section which gives maintenance and adjustment information, exploded views and disassembly notes on specific vehicles arranged alphabetically by name.

A general service section which is further subdivided into five parts covering engine, converter (belt drive) unit, track drive, track & suspension and skis & steering. The Engine and Torque Converter sections contain specific overhaul information by make and model of component. All sections contain general operation, maintenance and service data intended to promote a more thorough understanding of the machine for more efficient service.

A table of contents is located at the beginning of each section and a heading at the top inside corner of each page will designate the sections which appear in the following order:

- *VEHICLE SERVICE SECTION*
- *ENGINE SECTION*
- *CONVERTER (BELT DRIVE) SECTION*
- *TRACK DRIVE*
- *TRACK & SUSPENSION*
- *SKIS AND STEERING*

Printed in the United States of America.
Library of Congress Catalog Card Number 91-055143
January, 2002

PRIMEDIA Business Directories & Books
P.O. Box 12901 ■ Overland Park, KS 66282-2901
Phone: 800-262-1954 Fax: 800-633-6219
www.primediabooks.com

VEHICLE SERVICE SECTION

CONTENTS

ALOUETTE

1967-1976

	Engine			Carburetor				Clutch		
Model	Make	Model	Displ.	Make	Model	Sprocket Ratio	Chain Size	Make	Shaft Center	Belt Number
					1967					
707	JLO	L292	292cc	Tillotson	HR2A	11:26	40	Salsbury		76-8
					1968					
868-1	Sachs	SA290	297cc	Tillotson	HR5A	11:26	40	Salsbury		76-8
868-2	Sachs	SA290	297cc	Tillotson	HR8A	11:26	40	Salsbury		76-8
					1969					
869-3 Custom .	Sachs	SA280	277cc	Tillotson	HL252A	11:28	40	Own		76-8
869-1 GT	Sachs	SA290	297cc	Tillotson	HR29A	11:26	40	Own		76-8
869-2 GTE	Sachs	SA290	297cc	Tillotson	HR29A	11:26	40	Own		76-8
869-4 GTO	Sachs	SA370	368cc	Tillotson	HR29A	13:28	40	Own		76-8
869-5 GTOE ...	Sachs	SA370	368cc	Tillotson	HR29A	13:28	40	Own		76-8
869-6 Cruiser ..	Sachs	SA370	368cc	Tillotson	HR29A	11:26	40	Own		76-8
					1970					
XL14	Sachs	SA280A	277cc	Tillotson	HR52A	11:26	40	Own	11.1	76-8
XL20	Sachs	SA290	293cc	Tillotson	HR52A	11:26	40	Own	11.1	76-8
XL20E	Sachs	SA290	293cc	Tillotson	HR52A	11:26	40	Own	11.1	76-8
XL26	Kohler	K399-2	399cc	Tillotson	HR52A	14:24	40	Own	11.1	76-8
XL26E	Kohler	K399-2	399cc	Tillotson	HR52A	14:24	40	Own	11.1	76-8
Big Bird	Kohler	K399-2	399cc	Tillotson	HR52A	13:26	40	Own	11.1	76-8
Big Bird E	Kohler	K399-2	399cc	Tillotson	HR52A	13:26	40	Own	11.1	76-8
GT	Sachs	SA340SS	336cc	Tillotson	HD29A	13:26	40	Own	11.1	76-8
GTO	Kohler	K440-2	440cc	Tillotson	HR52A	14:27	40	Own	11.1	76-8
					1971					
XL14	Sachs	SA280	277cc	Tillotson	HR52A	11:26	40	Own	11.1	130074
XL20	Sachs	SA290	293cc	Tillotson	HR91A	11:26	40	Own	11.1	130074
XL24	Kohler	K340-2	338cc	Tillotson	HR79A	13:28	40	Own	11.1	130074
XL28	Kohler	K399-2	399cc	Tillotson	HR79A	14:27	40	Own	11.1	130074
XL30W	Kohler	K440-2	436cc	Tillotson	HR79B	13:28	40	Own	11.1	130074
GT23	Sachs	SA290SS	293cc	Tillotson	HD29A	13:28	40	Own	11.1	130074
GT27	Sachs	SA340SS	336cc	Tillotson	HD29A	13:28	40	Own	11.1	130074
GT36	Kohler	K440-2	436cc	Tillotson	HR79B(2)	14:27	40	Own	11.1	130074
					1972					
Escort 295	Kohler	K295-1	294cc	Tillotson	HR	12:28	40	Own	11½	130301
Eliminator 295	Sachs	SA290	291cc	Tillotson	HD	12:28	40	Salsbury	11½	130302
Eliminator 340	Sachs	SA2-340	338cc	Tillotson	HD	12:28	40	Salsbury	11½	130311
Eliminator 440	Sachs	SA2-440	437cc	Tillotson	HD	19:39	35-2	Salsbury	11½	130311
Venture 440 ...	Kohler	K440-2	437cc	Tillotson	HR	14:27	40	Salsbury	11½	130302
					1973					
Mini-Brute	Tecum		209cc			11:40		Comet		
Sno Duster ...	Kohler	K295-1	294cc	Tillotson	HR147A	12:28	40	Own	11½	130301
Escort I	Kohler	K295-2AX	292cc	Tillotson	HR124A	12:28	40	Own	11½	130301
Escort II	Sachs	SA2-290	291cc	Tillotson	HR144B	12:28	40	Salsbury	11½	130311
Escort III	Sachs	SA2-340	338cc	Tillotson	HD	12:28	40	Salsbury	11½	130302
Venture 440 ...	Kohler	K440-2T	436cc	Tillotson	HR79B	14:27	40	Salsbury	11½	130302
Eliminator 295 .	Sachs	SA2-290	291cc	Tillotson	HD88A	12:28	40	Salsbury	11½	130311
Eliminator 340 .	Sachs	SA2-340	336cc	Tillotson	HD88A	12:28	40	Salsbury	11½	130311
Eliminator 440 .	Sachs	SA2-441	437cc	Tillotson	HD89A	19:36	35-2	Salsbury	11½	130302
Sno Brute 340 .	Sachs	SA2-340C	336cc	Tillotson	HD88A	12:28	40	Salsbury	11½	130302
Sno Brute 440 .	Sachs	SA2-440C	437cc	Tillotson	HD88A	19:36	35-2	Salsbury	11½	130428

Model	Engine Make	Engine Model	Engine Displ.	Carburetor Make	Carburetor Model	Sprocket Ratio	Chain Size	Clutch Make	Clutch Shaft Center	Belt Number
					1974					
Sno Duster 295	Kohler	K295-1	294cc	Tillotson	HR147A	12:28	40	Salsbury	11½	130301
Sno Duster 340	Kohler	K340-2	338cc	Tillotson	HR	12:28	40	Salsbury	11½	130301
Silver Cloud Mk II.......	Wankel		295cc	Mikuni	VM	14:27	40	Salsbury	11½	130302
Sno Brute 440.	Sachs	SA2-440C	437cc	Tillotson	HD88A	19:36	35-2	Salsbury	11½	130428
Super Brute 295........	Sachs	SA2-290	291cc	Mikuni	VM	16:35	Silent	Comet	11½	130311
Super Brute 340........	Sachs	SA2-340	338cc	Mikuni	VM	18:35	Silent	Comet	11½	130311
Super Brute 440........	Sachs	SA2-440	437cc	Mikuni	VM	20:35	Silent	Comet	11½	130302
					1975					
Sno Duster 295	Kohler	K295-1	294cc	Tillotson	HR147A	12:28	40	Salsbury	11½	130301
Sno Brute 440.	Sachs	SA2-440	437cc	Tillotson	HD88A	19:36	35-2	Salsbury	11½	130428
Super Brute 295........	Sachs	SA2-290	291cc	Mikuni	VM	16:35	Silent	Comet	11½	130311
Super Brute 340........	Sachs	SA2-340	338cc	Mikuni	VM	18:35	Silent	Comet	11½	130311
Super Brute 440........	Sachs	SA2-440	437cc	Mikuni	VM	20:35	Silent	Comet	11½	130302
					1976					
Sno Duster...	Xenoah	G34B	340cc	Mikuni	VM32	12:28	35-2	Rupp	10-7/8	36590
Sno Brute....	Kohler	K440-2AS	440cc	Mikuni	VM32	13:28	35-2	Rupp	10-7/8	36590
Brute 340.....	Xenoah	G34BWR	340cc	Mikuni	VM36	20:39	Silent		11.3	38738
Brute 440.....	Xenoah	G44BWR	440cc	Mikuni	VM38	20:35	Silent		11.3	38738
Super Brute 250........	Xenoah	G25BWR	250cc	Mikuni	VM34	15:35	Silent		11.3	38738
Super Brute 340........	Xenoah	G34BWR	340cc	Mikuni	VM36	20:39	Silent		11.3	38738
Super Brute 440........	Xenoah	G44BWR	440cc	Mikuni	VM38	20:35	Silent		11.3	38738

LUBRICATION

The engine is lubricated by oil mixed with the fuel. Correct fuel-oil ratio is 20:1 on models with JLO or Kohler engine, and 25:1 on models equipped with Sachs engine.

On Model 707 with open drive chain, the chain should be lubricated with a few drops of light oil occasionally. When vehicle is stored, remove chain and wash in kerosene or other suitable solvent. Store the chain by submerging in oil in a suitable covered pan. The spray-type chain cleaner and chain lubricant designed for motorcycle use is also effective for open chains. On 1968 and later models the drive chain is enclosed and runs in an oil bath.

The enclosed chaincase should contain 6-8 ounces of SAE 30 Motor Oil to lubricate the chain. Oil may be added through plug hole (D–Fig. 2).

On models without plug hole, tip machine on right side and remove cover (C–Fig. 3). The case should contain about ½-pint of SAE 20 engine oil.

Ski legs on Model 707 were equipped with renewable nylon bushings and were not lubricated. Later models have pressure fittings and should be lubricated occasionally with Low Temperature Alouette Grease.

Track drive axles and bogie wheels are equipped with sealed bearings and do not require lubrication.

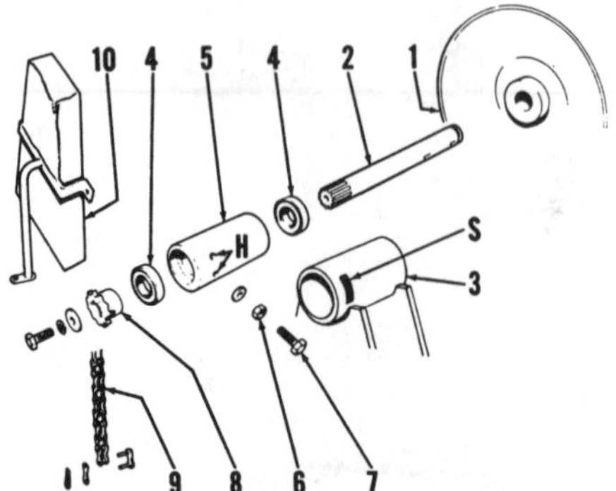

Fig. 1—Exploded view of intermediate drive shaft and associated parts used on Models 707 with open drive chain.

H. Holes
S. Slot
1. Driven sheave
2. Shaft
3. Bracket
4. Bearing
5. Eccentric housing
6. Locknut
7. Bolt
8. Drive sprocket
9. Drive chain
10. Shield

Fig. 2—View of converter drive unit, brake and chain case showing points of adjustment.

A & B. Backlash
C. Adjusting screw
D. Fill plug

ADJUSTMENT

STEERING SKIS. On early models, disconnect tie rod from left steering arm and adjust length of rod as necessary until skis are parallel when pointing straight ahead. Shorten or lengthen steering drag link if necessary, until handle bars are in normal straight driving position.

Late models are equipped with two steering rods which must be disconnected at one end for adjustment. Steering rods must be of equal length and must be installed in front hole in steering arm.

DRIVE CHAIN ADJUSTMENT. Roller drive chain should have approximately ¼-inch of free play when measured midway between sprockets.

On Model 707, free play can be directly measured and adjustment can be made by moving bolt (7–Fig. 1) downward in slot (S). If bolt bottoms in slot, remove the bolt and reinstall in the other hole (H) in eccentric housing (5).

Models with enclosed drive chain should have some slack but free play cannot be directly measured. Chain tension can be determined by measuring the backlash (A and B–Fig. 2 or A–Fig. 3) while rocking torque converter driven sheave. Adjustment is correct when backlash measures ⅜-inch at pulley rim. Adjust by loosening the locknut and turning adjusting screw (B–Fig. 2 or C–Fig. 3).

BRAKE. Model 707 and most 1972 models are equipped with a caliper type disc brake. Refer to TRACK DRIVE section of this manual for adjustment procedure.

All 1968 through 1971 and some later machines are equipped with a shoe-type brake as shown in Figs. 2, 3 and 4. Brake must not drag when hand lever is released but must fully engage before hand lever contacts handlebar grip. Wear adjustment is made at brake cable anchor housing by turning nuts (A and B–Fig. 4).

Most 1972 and 1973 machines are equipped with caliper type disc brake. First make sure that brake push pins center in valleys of actuating arm cam and that brake unit properly aligns with friction surface of driven pulley. Align if necessary by loosening the attaching bracket bolts and firmly applying brake. Center push pins by adjusting brake cable housing anchor nuts. Brake wear adjustment is made by turning actuating lever stud nut until pucks touch pulley then backing nut off approximately ½-turn.

TRACK. To adjust track tension, raise rear of vehicle until track is clear of ground. On Model 707, refer to Fig. 5. Measure the distance (A-B) from top edge of bogie wheel support shaft bracket to top edge of track midway between track axles. Distance (A-B) should be 5¾-6 inches and equal on both sides of machine.

On 1968 through 1970 models, refer to Fig. 6. Measure the distance (A) from lower edge of rear idler bearing housing to edge of frame. Distance should be 3¾-inches and equal on both sides.

Loosen the two clamp bolts (1—Fig. 5 or 6) and turn adjusting bolt (2) until tension is correct.

Fig. 4—To adjust the shoe-type brake, turn cable housing anchor adjusting screws A and B.

Fig. 5—With rear of vehicle raised, measure the distance (A - B). If distance is not 5¾ - 6 inches, loosen the two nuts (1) and turn adjusting screw (2) to adjust. Refer to text.

Fig. 3—View of converter drive unit, brake & enclosed chain case of the type used on late models, showing points of adjustment.

A. Backlash
B. Adjusting bolt
C. Side cover
L. Brake lever
S. Brake shoe

Fig. 6—With rear of vehicle raised, measure distance (A) from lower edge of rear idler bearing housing to edge of frame. Distance should be 3¾ inches and equal on both sides. Adjust by loosening clamp bolts (1) and turning adjusting bolt (2).

On models with bogie wheel suspension, loosen pivot bolt nut (A–Fig. 7) and turn adjusting bolt (B). Both sides must be adjusted alike.

On 1973 Sno Brute with slide suspension, loosen clamp screws (1–Fig. 8) and turn adjusting screws (2). Ride and weight adjustment is made by turning spring anchor nuts (3).

NOTE: Whenever track tension has been adjusted, alignment MUST be checked as outlined in TRACK SERVICE Section of this manual.

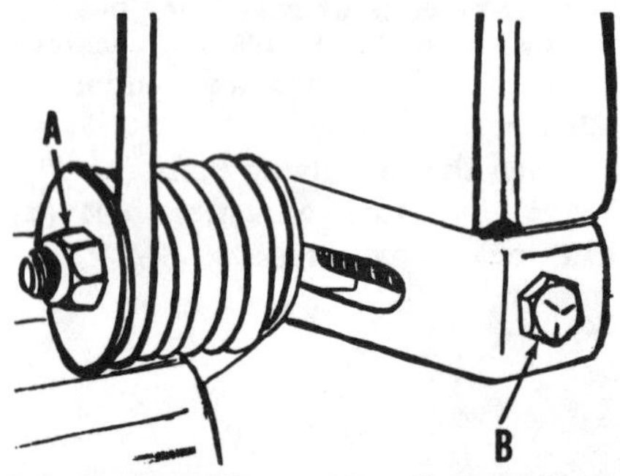

Fig. 7—On 1971 model, adjust track tension by loosening pivot bolt nuts (A) and turning adjusting bolt (B).

Fig. 8—On models with "Trail-Rider" slide suspension, tension is adjusted by loosening cap screw (1) and turning adjusting screw (2). Ride-weight adjustment is at tension nuts (3).

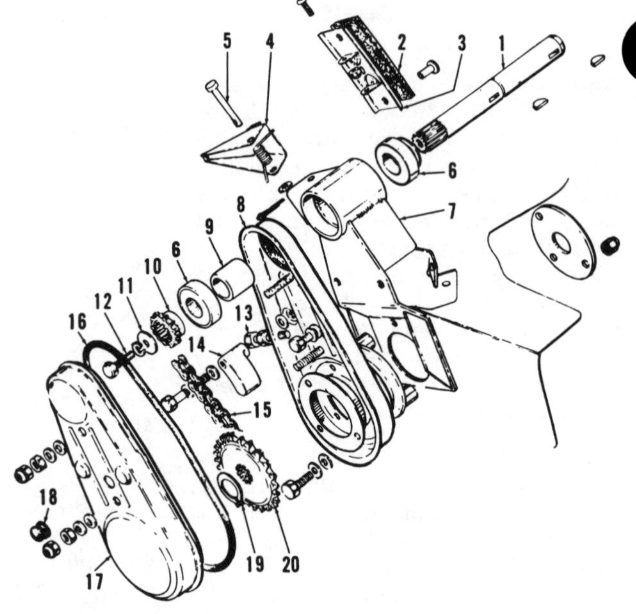

Fig. 9—Chain case, intermediate shaft and associated parts used on late models.

1. Intermediate shaft
2. Brake lining
3. Brake shoe
4. Brake arm
5. Pivot bolt
6. Bearing
7. Support
8. Chaincase
9. Spacer
10. Upper sprocket
11. Washer
12. Cap screw
13. Adjusting bolt
14. Tightener arm
15. Chain
16. Gasket
17. Cover
18. Inspection plug
19. Snap ring
20. Lower sprocket

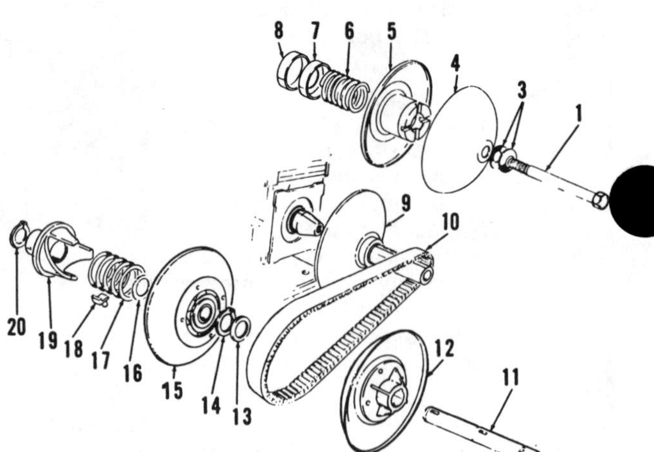

Fig. 10—Exploded view of ALOUETTE torque converter and associated parts.

1. Bolt
3. Belleville washer
4. Weight unit
5. Moving sheave
6. Spring
7. Retainer
8. Bushing
9. Fixed-sheave
10. Belt
11. Intermediate shaft
12. Fixed sheave
13. Spacer
15. Moving sheave
16. Spacer
17. Spring
18. Ramp shoe
19. Cam hub
20. Snap ring

ALSPORT

1971-1972

Model	Engine Make	Engine Model	Engine Displ.	Carburetor Make	Carburetor Model	Sprocket Ratio	Chain Size	Clutch Make	Clutch Shaft Center	Belt Number
					1971					
210	CCW	400	398cc	Tillotson	HR			Salsbury 910	11½	10102
GT15	CCW	400	398cc	Tillotson	HR			Salsbury 910	11½	10102
					1972					
Snow Sport	CCW	400	398cc	Tillotson	HR			Salsbury 910	11½	10102
SS Deluxe	CCW	440	440cc	Tillotson	HR			Salsbury 910	11½	10102
Tracker 2/10	CCW	400	398cc	Tillotson	HR			Salsbury 910	11½	10102
2 10 Deluxe	CCW	400	398cc	Tillotson	HR			Salsbury 910	11½	10102
GT15	CCW	400	398cc	Tillotson	HR			Salsbury 910	11½	10102
GT15 Deluxe	CCW	400	398cc	Tillotson	HR			Salsbury 910	11½	10102
GT Sportster	CCW	440	440cc	Tillotson	HR			Salsbury 910	11½	10102

LUBRICATION

The engine is lubricated by oil mixed with the fuel. Recommended fuel/oil ratio is 20:1 using regular gasoline and an approved snowmobile oil.

The Apex Reversing Transmission should be kept filled to level of check plug (1—Figure 1) with Automatic Transmission Fluid, Type "A" or equivalent. Add fluid if required, by removing shift bracket retaining cap screw (2).

Drive chains should be lubricated with a dry type chain lubricant once each day or oftener if necessary. Steering rack and gear should be lubricated at least once each season with Lubriplate or equivalent, or dry graphite.

Front wheels when used, should be removed and bearings packed periodically as required; or daily when used in water.

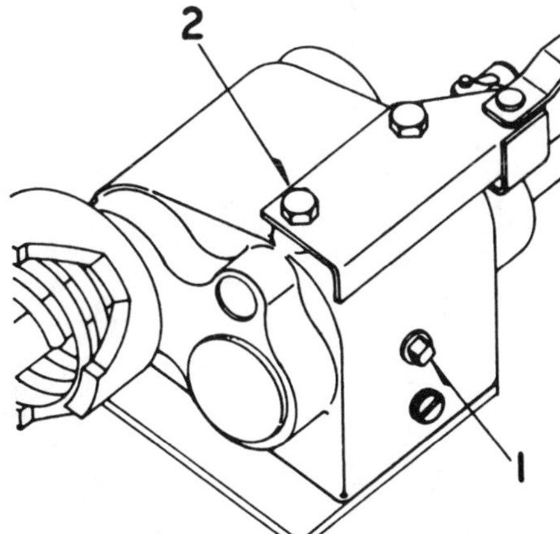

Fig. 1—The APEX reversing transmission should be kept filled to level of check plug (1). Add fluid through hole for shift bracket cap screw (2).

ADJUSTMENT

WHEELS & SKIS. Skis or front wheels should toe in a slight amount when properly adjusted. Correct toe-in should measure 5/16-⅜ inch when measured from front to rear of wheel; or ⅝-¾ inch when measured to front and rear tips of skis. Tie rod end must be disconnected from spindle to make the adjustment, and wheel must be removed if so equipped. On GT15 Models, when toe-in is adjusted, steering clutches must be checked as outlined in the following paragraph.

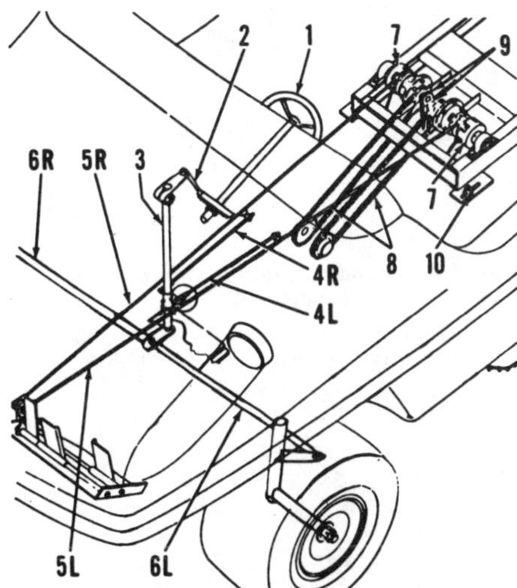

Fig. 2—On GT15, steering is synchronized with track clutches and correct adjustment is necessary for proper operation. Slight turning of front wheels should release the clutch on inside track, but a full turn should not apply the brake.

1. Steeringwheel
2. Rack tie rod
3. Steering post
4L. Control rod (left)
4R. Control rod (right)
5L. Brake rod (left)
5R. Brake rod (right)
6L. Tie rod (left)
6R. Tie rod (right)
7. "FORMSPRAG" clutch
8. Primary drive chains
9. Secondary drive chain
10. Clamp bolts

STEERING CLUTCH ADJUSTMENT. On GT15 Models, turning front wheels 2 to 5 degrees should release the clutch on inside track. Steering clutch adjustment should be checked and adjusted if necesary each time toe-in is adjusted, each time drive chain is adjusted, or any other time misadjustment is suspected.

With steering wheel carefully turned until wheels or skis are pointing EXACTLY straight ahead, steering clutch adjusting nuts should just contact brackets on brake rods without moving brake rod. Any movement of steering wheel for right or left turn should cause adjusting nut for outside track to move away from brake rod bracket. Refer to Fig. 2 and Fig. 3.

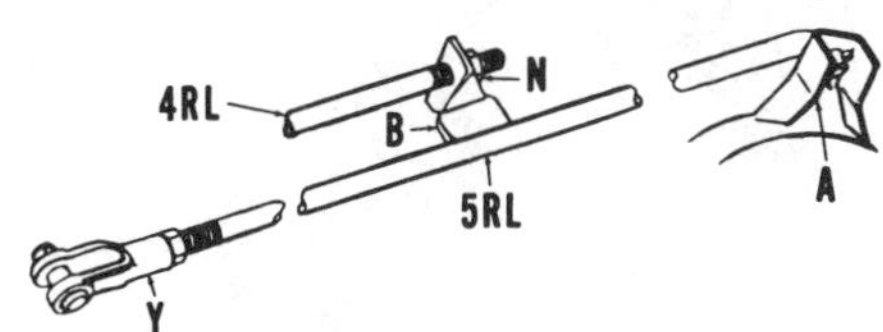

Fig. 3—Steering brake rod showing points of adjustment.

A. Actuator
B. Control rod bracket
N. Adjusting nut
Y. Adjusting yoke
4RL. Clutch control rod
5RL. Brake control rod

Adjust as necessary until proper contact is made. An operational test of steering clutches can be made as follows:

Securely support rear of machine with both tracks clear of ground or floor. With transmission in "Forward", start and run engine at moderate speed. When front wheels are turned slightly (approx. 5 degrees) in either direction, inside track should stop turning. Formsprag brake unit should not apply when steering wheel is turned to lock position in either direction. Adjust by turning nut (N—Fig. 3) as required.

DRIVE CHAINS. The 1970 Tracker and Model 210 use a single primary drive chain running from transmission output shaft to secondary shaft, and two chains running from secondary shaft, and two chains running from secondary shaft down to track drive axles. Model GT15 uses two primary and two secondary drive chains. Suggested free play on all chains is approximately ¼-inch.

Primary chain or chains can be adjusted by removing shims from beneath secondary shaft pillow block mounting bolts. Shims may be added, if necessary, beneath transmission base and upper pillow block.

Secondary chains are adjusted by loosening the four power frame mounting bolts (10—Fig. 2) and tightening anchor rod nut. Brake rods, steering clutch rods and shift linkage must be readjusted if power frame is moved.

SINGLE DISC BRAKE. 1970 models and later Model 210 are equipped with a single disc brake located on secondary drive shaft as shown in Fig. 5. To adjust the brake, proceed as follows:

Disconnect brake rod and spring (3—Fig. 4) from actuating lever. Remove cotter pin (1) and tighten adjusting nut (2) snugly, then back off until disc is free. Align cotter pin hole and reinstall cotter pin (1). Adjust brake rod yoke if necessary until pin can be installed, then reinstall spring (3). Brake link must be adjusted if powerframe is moved to adjust secondary drive chains.

NOTE: Some early models may not use return spring (3), and yoke pin will be retained by a cotter key. Spring assists in preventing weight of brake rod from partially apply brake.

MULTIPLE DISC BRAKE. On GT-15 Models, a multiple disc brake (3—Fig. 6) is a part of the FORMSPRAG control unit (CB). Individual controls are used for each track.

The clutch-brake unit does not require internal adjustment but linkage adjustment is critical. To adjust the linkage, refer to Fig. 3 and proceed as follows:

Disconnect brake rod (5RL) at forward (pedal) end. Back off nut (N) until it is free of actuating bracket on brake rod. Turn adjusting yoke (Y) as required until brake rod can just be reconnected to pedal shaft without moving actuator arm (A). Readjust steering clutch links as previously outlined after brake linkage is properly adjusted. Brake linkage must be adjusted if power frame is moved to adjust secondary drive chains.

SHIFT LEVER LINK. Shift lever link may need to be adjusted if power frame is moved to adjust secondary drive chains. or if hand lever rides either end of slot in shift plate. Refer to Fig. 8. Disconnect the rod at transmission end and turn adjustable end in or out as required until shift action is satisfactory.

TRACK. To adjust track tension, raise and block rear of machine to allow access to inside adjusting bolts. With rear of machine raised, track should just touch center bogie wheels

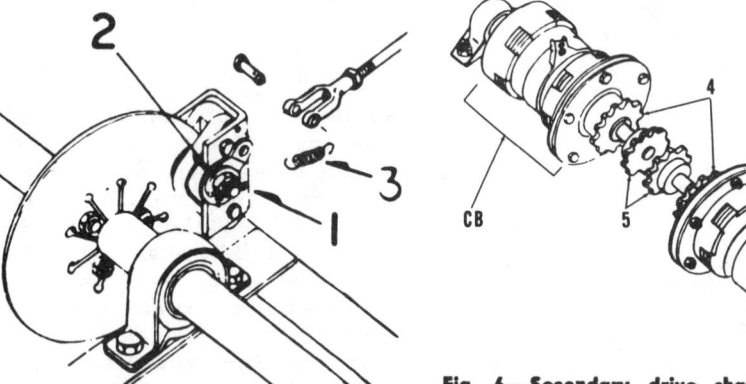

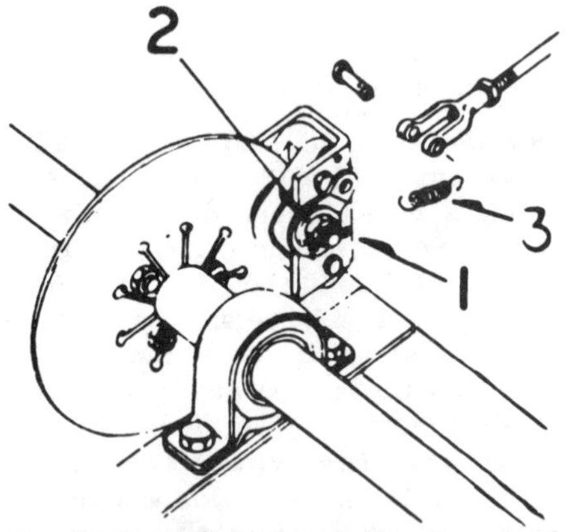

Fig. 4—To adjust the single disc clutch used on Model 210 remove cotter pin (1) and turn adjusting nut (2). Spring (3) is used on 210 but may not be present on earlier models.. Refer to text.

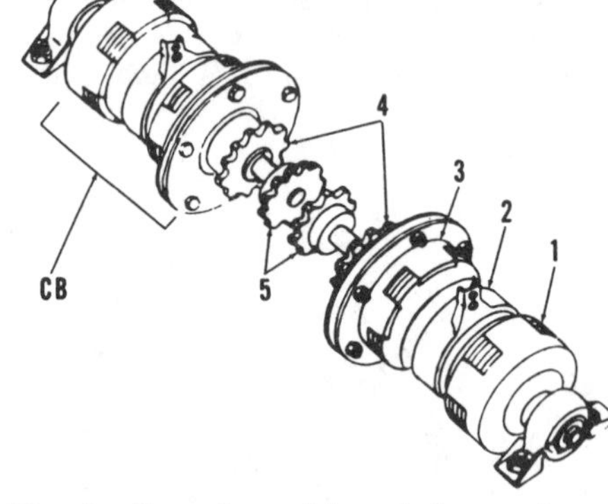

Fig. 6—Secondary drive shafts used on Model GT15.

CB. "FORMSPRAG" clutch/brake unit
1. Drive clutch
2. Actuator
3. Track brake
4. Output sprockets
5. Input sprockets

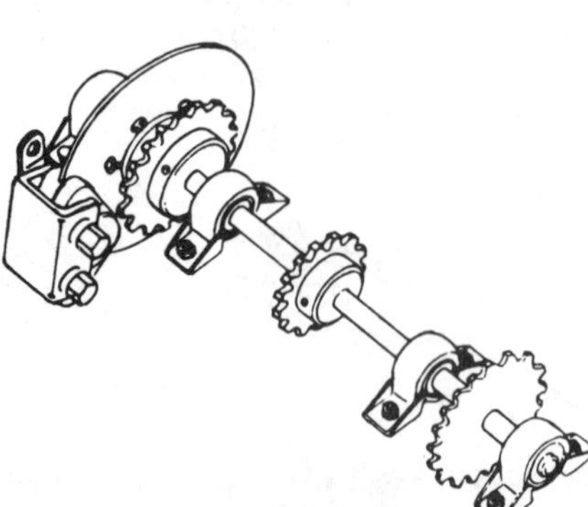

Fig. 5—Secondary drive shaft used on Model 210, showing single disc brake and sprocket location. All earlier models are similar.

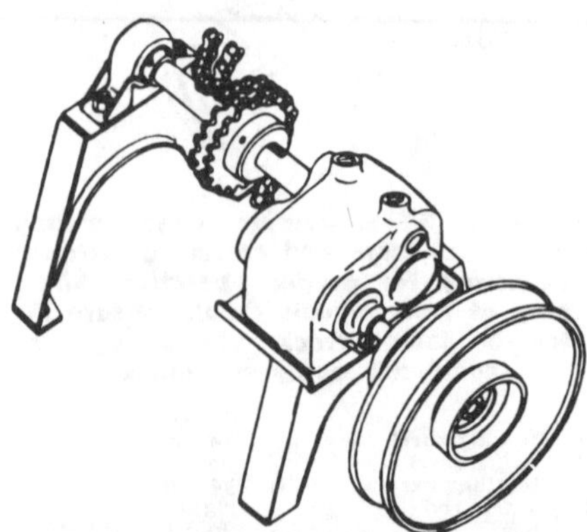

Fig. 7—Transmission unit showing the double drive sprocket used on Model GT15. Other models are similar except sprocket is single type.

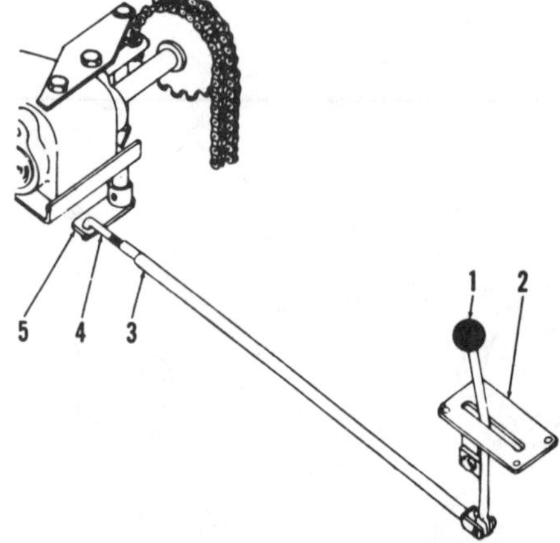

Fig. 8—Schematic view of APEX reversing transmission and shift linkage.

1. Shift lever
2. Shift plate
3. Link
4. Adjustable end
5. Shift arm

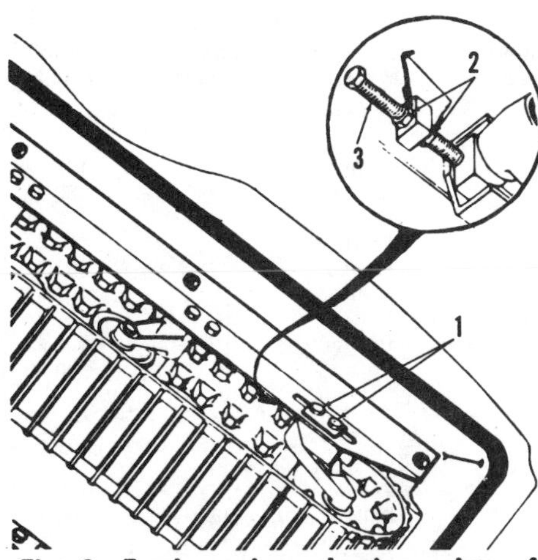

Fig. 9—Track carriage showing points of adjustment. Both sides of both tracks must be adjusted alike.

1. Clamp bolts
2. Jam nuts
3. Adjusting bolt

without moving suspension arms. Adjust by loosening clamp bolts (1—Fig. 9) and locknuts (2), then turn adjusting bolt (3) until tension is correct. Both tracks—and both sides of each track—should be adjusted alike.

NOTE: Whenever track tension has been adjusted, alignment MUST be checked as outlined in TRACK SERVICE Section of this manual.

OVERHAUL

Ski support attaches to front wheel spindle as shown in Inset, Fig. 10. Steering post, support and both tie rods are removed as a unit after removing steering wheel, shaft and rack, then disconnecting tie rods at outer ends. Silicone Rubber Sealant should be used when reinstalling support or any other parts attached to waterproof body. Front tire pressure should be 4 psi.

Engine and other units are accessible for minor service or inspection after removing rear compartment cover. Upper body half may be completely removed or tipped up for major service. Wiring harness, control cables and allied parts must be removed or disconnected for removal. To separate upper and lower body halves, first remove rubber bumper by stretching and lifting upward. Use a 3/16-inch drill to drill out pop rivets, leaving front row if body is being tipped, or until wiring is disconnected if top is being removed. When reinstalling rubber bumper, note that back portion is wider than front.

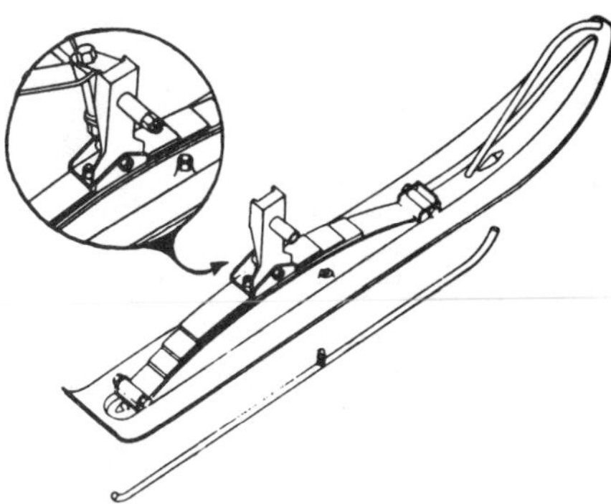

Fig. 10—Ski support slips on front wheel spindle and is secured by wheel nut as shown in inset.

ARCTIC CAT

1965-1972

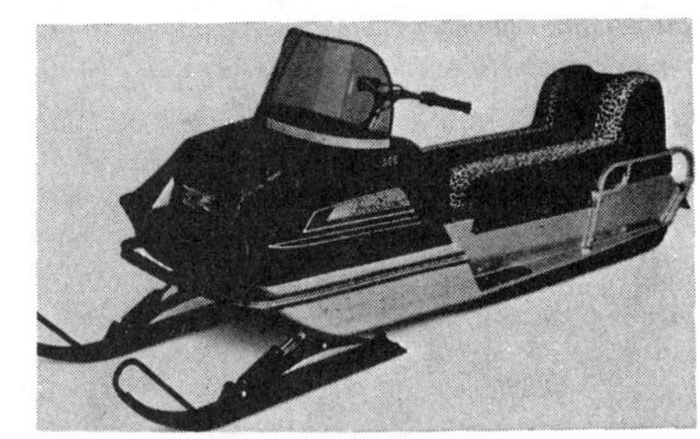

	Engine			Carburetor				Clutch		
Model	Make	Model	Displ.	Make	Model	Sprocket Ratio	Chain Size	Make	Shaft Center	Belt Number
					1965					
100	Kohler	K161	16.2ci	Carter	N	12:30		Salsbury		900043
101	Kohler	K181	18.6ci	Carter	N	12:30		Salsbury		900043
120D	Kohler	K181	18.6ci	Carter	N			Salsbury		900043
170D	Kohler	K181	18.6ci	Carter	N			Salsbury		900043
450D	Kohler	K241	23.9ci	Carter	N	12:36	50	Salsbury		900041
500D	Onan		38.8ci			15:36	50	Salsbury		RVS-28
					1966					
100	Kohler	K161	16.2ci	Carter	N	12:30		Salsbury		900043
100	Kohler	K181	18.6ci	Carter	N	12:30		Salsbury		900043
140D	Kohler	K181	18.6ci	Carter	N			Salsbury		900043
141D	Kohler	K181	18.6ci	Carter	N			Salsbury		900043
141D	Hirth	05	300cc	Tillotson	HR3A					
170D	Kohler	K181	18.6ci	Carter	N			Salsbury		900043
460D	Kohler	K301	29.1ci	Carter	N					900041
560D	Onan		38.8ci							900041
					1967					
100	Kohler	K181	18.6ci	Carter	N		35-2	Polaris	10 7/8	100-22
P-8	Kohler	K181	18.6ci	Carter	N	15:47	35-2	Polaris	10 7/8	100-22
P-12	Kohler	K301	29.1ci	Carter	N	15:47	35-2	Polaris	10 7/8	100-22
P-15	Hirth	05	300cc	Tillotson	HR3A	17:47	35-2	Polaris	10 7/8	100-22
460D	Kohler	K301	29.1ci	Carter	N		35-2	Salsbury		900041
560D	Onan		38.8ci				35-2	Salsbury		900041

	Engine			Carburetor				Clutch		
Model	Make	Model	Displ.	Make	Model	Sprocket Ratio	Chain Size	Make	Shaft Center	Belt Number
					1968					
P-12	Kohler	K301	29.1ci	Carter	N	21:47	35-2	Polaris	10⅞	100-22
P-17H	Hirth	05	300cc	Tillotson	HR12A	17:47	35-2	Polaris	11⅜	100-43
P-17J	JLO	L297	296cc	Tillotson	HD7A	17:47	35-2	Polaris	11⅜	100-43
P-20H	Hirth	016	372cc	Tillotson	HD7A	19:47	35-2	Polaris		100-32
P-25	Hirth	018	493cc	Tillotson	HR12A	19:47	35-2	Polaris	11⅜	100-32
P-35	Hirth	017	598cc	Tillotson	HR12A	21:47	35-2	Salsbury		100-42
C-8	Kohler	K181	18.6ci	Carter	N	15:47	35-2	Polaris	10⅞	100-22
C-15	JLO	L292	292cc	Tillotson	HR2A	17:47	35-2	Polaris	10⅞	100-22
C-20	Hirth	016	372cc	Tillotson	HD7A	19:47	35-2	Polaris		100-32
					1969					
P-10H	Hirth	82R4	246cc	Tillotson	HR18A	15:47	35-2	Salsbury 790	11⅜	100-22
P-12K	Kohler	K301	29.1ci	Kohler	N	21:47	35-2	Polaris	10⅞	100-66
P-17J	JLO	L297	296cc	Tillotson	HD13A	17:47	35-2	Polaris	11⅜	100-43
P-17H	Hirth	55R3	300cc	Tillotson	HR18A	17:47	35-2	Salsbury 770	11⅜	100-80
P-19K	Kohler	K309-1	309cc	Tillotson	HR22A	17:47	35-2	Polaris	11⅜	100-43
P-19J	JLO	L297	296cc	Tillotson	HD13A	17:47	35-2	Polaris	11⅜	100-43
P-19JS	JLO	L297	296cc	Tillotson	HD13A	17:47	35-2	Salsbury 770	11⅜	100-80
P-19H	Hirth	191R4E	300cc	Tillotson	HR18A	17:47	35-2	Polaris	10⅞	100-66
P-19H	Hirth	192R4E	317cc	Tillotson	HR18A	17:47	35-2	Polaris	10⅞	100-66
P-19S	Sachs	SA290	297cc	Tillotson	HR18A	17:47	35-2	Polaris	11⅜	100-43
P-19SS	Sachs	SA290	297cc	Tillotson	HR18A	17:47	35-2	Salsbury 770	11⅜	100-80
P-20W	Wankel	RC-1 18.5	303cc	Tillotson	HL263A	19:47	35-2	Polaris	10⅞	100-66
P-22J	JLO	L380	372cc	Tillotson	HD13A	19:47	35-2	Polaris	11⅜	100-43
P-22S	Sachs	SA370	368cc	Tillotson	HD23A	19:47	35-2	Salsbury 770	11⅜	100-80
P-22H	Hirth	100R4E	372cc	Tillotson	HD14A	19:47	35-2	Polaris	11⅜	100-43
P-23K	Kohler	K399-2	399cc	Tillotson	HR24A	15:39	35-2	Polaris	10⅞	100-66
P-27H	Hirth	220R4E	493cc	Tillotson	HD23A	19:39	35-2	Salsbury 770	10⅞	100-88
P-35H	Hirth	171R2	634cc	Tillotson	HD14A(Mod)	21:39	35-2	Salsbury 1195	12½	100-42
P-45J	JLO	LR760⅛2	744cc	Tillotson	HD13A	21:39	35-2	Salsbury 1195	12½	100-42
P-45H	Hirth	230R	793cc	Tillotson	HD27A	23:39	35-3	Salsbury 1195	12½	100-42
					1970					
P246H	Hirth	82R	246cc	Walbro	WR	13:39	35-2	Salsbury 770	11⅜	100-080
P292A	Kawasaki	KT150	292cc	Tillotson	HR70A	15:39	35-2	Salsbury 770	11⅜	100-080
P295J	JLO	L295	292cc	Tillotson	HD27A	15:39	35-2	Salsbury 770	11⅜	100-080
P295K	Kohler	K295-1	294cc	Tillotson	HR50A	15:39	35-2	Salsbury 770	10⅞	100-088
P303W	Wankel	RC1-18.5	303cc	Tillotson	HL263A	17:39	35-2	Salsbury 770	10⅞	100-088
P340J	JLO	L340	336cc	Tillotson	HD27A	17:39	35-2	Salsbury 770	11⅜	100-080
P340S	Sachs	SA340	336cc	Tillotson	HD27A	17:39	35-2	Salsbury 770	11⅜	100-080
P399K	Kohler	K399-2	399cc	Tillotson	HR49A	19:39	35-2	Salsbury 910	10⅞	100-092
P399H (399HP)	Hirth	210R	399cc	Tillotson	HD27A	19:39	35-2	Salsbury 770	10⅞	100-088
P440J	JLO	LR440/2	433cc	Tillotson	HD27A	17:39	35-2	Salsbury 910	10⅞	100-092
P440H	Hirth	211R	438cc	Tillotson	HD27A	17:39	35-2	Salsbury 910	10⅞	100-092
P634H	Hirth	171R	634cc	Tillotson	HD27A	21:39	35-2	Salsbury 1190	12½	100-042
P760J	JLO	LR760 2	744cc	Tillotson	HD27A	21:39	35-2	Salsbury 1190	12½	100-042
P793H	Hirth	230R	793cc	Tillotson	HD27A	21:39	35-3	Salsbury 1190	12½	100-042
					1971					
292AA-L	Kawasaki	KT150A	292cc	Tillotson	HR70A	15:39	35-2	Salsbury 770	11⅜	100-080
292AB-L	Kawasaki	KT150B	292cc	Tillotson	HR70B	17:39	35-2	Salsbury 770	11⅜	100-080
295J-L	JLO	L295	292cc	Tillotson	HD27A	15:39	35-2	Salsbury 770	11⅜	100-080
303W-L	Wankel	KM914	303cc	Tillotson	HL263A	17:39	35-2	Salsbury 770	10⅞	100-088
303W-P	Wankel	KM914	303cc	Tillotson	HL285A	17:39	35-2	Salsbury 770	10⅞	100-088
305K-L	Kohler	K181	18.6ci	Carter	N	15:39	35-2	Salsbury 770	11⅜	100-080
340H-L	Hirth	194R	338cc	Tillotson	HD27A	19:39	35-2	Salsbury 770	11⅜	100-080
340J-P	JLO	LR340/2	339cc	Tillotson	HD60A	17:39	35-2	Salsbury 770	10⅞	100-088
340J-PU	JLO	LR340/2	339cc	Tillotson	HD60A	17:39	35-2	Salsbury 770	10⅞	100-088
340A-P	Kawasaki	T1A340S1	339cc	Tillotson	HD62A	17:39	35-2	Salsbury 770	10⅞	100-088
340A-PU	Kawasaki	T1A340S1	339cc	Tillotson	HD62A	17:39	35-2	Salsbury 770	10⅞	100-088
399J-P	JLO	LR399/2	398cc	Tillotson	HD60A	19:39	35-2	Salsbury 910	10⅞	100-092
399J-PU	JLO'	LR399/2	398cc	Tillotson	HD60A	19:39	35-2	Salsbury 910	10⅞	100-092
399A-P	Kawasaki	T1A400S1	398cc	Tillotson	HD62A	19:39	35-2	Salsbury 910	10⅞	100-092
399A-PU	Kawasaki	T1A400S1	398cc	Tillotson	HD62A	19:39	35-2	Salsbury 910	10⅞	100-092
399K-P	Kohler	K399-2	399cc	Tillotson	HR105A	19:39	35-2	Salsbury 910	10⅞	100-092
399K-PU	Kohler	K399-2	399cc	Tillotson	HR105A	19:39	35-2	Salsbury 910	10⅞	100-092
440A-P	Kawasaki	T1A440S1	436cc	Tillotson	HD62A	19:39	35-2	Salsbury 910	10⅞	100-092
440A-PU	Kawasaki	T1A440S1	436cc	Tillotson	HD62A	19:39	35-2	Salsbury 910	10⅞	100-092
440J-PU	JLO	LR440/2	434cc	Tillotson	HD27A	17:39	35-2	Salsbury 910	10⅞	100-092
440S-P	Sachs	SA2/440	437cc	Walbro	WD1-1	19:39	35-2	Salsbury 910	10⅞	100-092
440S-PU	Sachs	SA2/440	437cc	Walbro	WD1-1	19:39	35-2	Salsbury 910	10⅞	100-092
634H-P	Hirth	171R	634cc	Tillotson	HD27A	21:39	35-2	Salsbury 1190	12½	100-042
634H-PU	Hirth	171R	634cc	Tillotson	HD27A	21:39	35-2	Salsbury 1190	12½	100-042
760J-P	JLO	LR760/2	744cc	Tillotson	HD27A	21:39	35-3	Salsbury 1190	12¼	100-042
290A-EXT	Kawasaki	T1A295F1	290cc	Tillotson	HR109A(2)	17:39	35-2	Salsbury 770	10⅞	100-088
340A-EXT	Kawasaki	T1A340F1	339cc	Tillotson	HR109A(2)	17:39	35-2	Salsbury 910	10⅞	100-092
399A-EXT	Kawasaki	T1A440F1	398cc	Walbro	WD2-1(2)	19:39	35-2	Salsbury 910	10⅞	100-092
440A-EXT	Kawasaki	T1A440F2	436cc	Walbro	WD2-1(2)	19:39	35-2	Salsbury 910	10⅞	100-092

	Engine			Carburetor				Clutch		
Model	Make	Model	Displ.	Make	Model	Sprocket Ratio	Chain Size	Make	Shaft Center	Belt Number
					1972					
292A-L	Kawasaki	KT150B	292cc	Tillotson	HR70B	17:39	35-2	Salsbury 770	11⅜	110-080
292A-P	Kawasaki	KT150B	292cc	Tillotson	HR70B	17:39	35-2	Salsbury 770	11⅜	100-080
303W-P	Wankel	KM914	303cc	Tillotson	HL289A	17:39	35-2	Salsbury 770	10⅞	100-088
340A-C	Kawasaki	T1A340S1B	339cc	Walbro	WDA-1	17:39	35-2	Salsbury 770	10⅞	100-088
340A-P	Kawasaki	T1A340S1B	339cc	Walbro	WDA-1	17:39	35-2	Salsbury 770	10⅞	100-088
340A-PU	Kawasaki	T1A340S1B	339cc	Walbro	WDA-1	17:39	35-2	Salsbury 770	10⅞	100-088
399A-C	Kawasaki	T1A400S1B	398cc	Walbro	WDA-1	19:39	35-2	Salsbury 910	10⅞	100-092
399A-P	Kawasaki	T1A400S1B	398cc	Walbro	WDA-1	19:39	35-2	Salsbury 910	10⅞	100-092
399A-PU	Kawasaki	T1A400S1B	398cc	Walbro	WDA-1	19:39	35-2	Salsbury 910	10⅞	100-092
440A-C	Kawasaki	T1A440S1B	436cc	Walbro	WDA-1	19:39	35-2	Salsbury 910	10⅞	100-092
440A-P	Kawasaki	T1A440S1B	436cc	Walbro	WDA-1	19:39	35-2	Salsbury 910	10⅞	100-092
440A-PU	Kawasaki	T1A440S1B	436cc	Walbro	WDA-1	19:39	35-2	Salsbury 910	10⅞	100-092

LUBRICATION

The enclosed drive chain housing should be filled to level of check plug with SAE 80 Multi-purpose gear Lubricant.

Intermediate shaft bearings on 1968 and later machies are equiped with a pressure lubrication fitting which is located in the drive chain adjusting screw. Bearings should be lubricated sparingly each 20 hours with low temperature grease. CAUTION: Be extremely careful not to damage bearing oil seals. Use a hand gun and stop pumping when resistance is felt.

The telescoping rear track support arms are equipped with grease fittings on 1969 and later models. On all models sliding support arms should be lubricated for storage and whenever necessary during use season.

ADJUSTMENT

STEERING SKIS AND LINKAGE. Turn handle bar to normal straight driving position and check to see that both skis are parallel with each other and with drive track and vehicle frame. To adjust the tie rod or drag link, disconnect the unit at one end; all tie rod ends are equipped with right-hand threads.

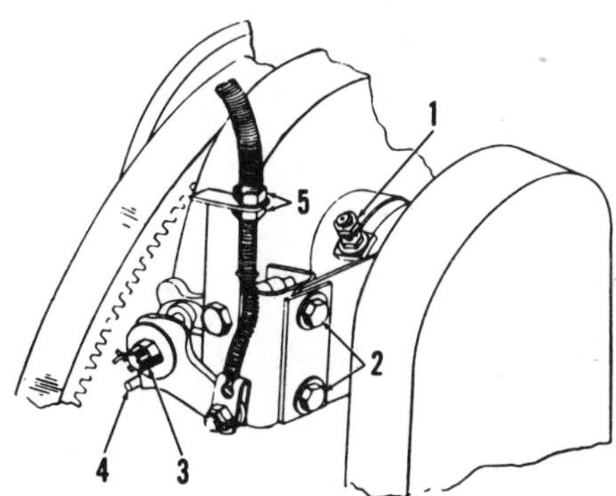

Fig. 1—View of chain case and associated parts showing point of chain adjustment and adjustment of late caliper type brake unit.

1. Clamp bolt
2. Brake mounting cap screws
3. Brake adjusting nut
4. Lever stop
5. Anchor nuts

DRIVE CHAIN. The enclosed drive chain should have some slack but deflection cannot be measured on early models. The most satisfactory method of determining chain adjustment is by backlash of driven pulley.

The eccentric bearing housing may be installed with shaft offset to front or rear and manner of installation affects method of adjustment. Rotate the eccentric in the proper direction to raise the shaft by pushing on loosened clamp bolt (1—Fig. 1) with thumb until it stops. If bolt bottoms in slot, remove and reinstall in another hole. Some models with large engines have two bearing housings; loosen and turn both the same amount at the same time to keep from cocking bearings and shaft.

On later models (with caliper type disc brake) alignment may need to be corrected after major drive chain adjustment. Loosen the two cap screws (2—Fig. 1) and compress brake lever to center brake assembly, then tighten cap screws (2) while brake is applied.

BRAKE ADJUSTMENT. On early models with shoe type brake, adjust pedal pad to clear friction surface of sheave by a slight amount but so that brake is fully applied before actuating lever touches handlebar grip. Adjustment is made by means of cable housing anchor nuts or cable clamp.

On models with caliper type disc brake, wear adjustment is made by removing cotter pin and turning adjustment nut (3—Fig. 1) until actuating lever (on handlebar) has approximately ¾-inch free travel, measured at lever end. Before adjusting the brake, first check to be sure that brake unit properly aligns with pulley face. Adjust if necessary by loosening clamp bolts (2) and applying brake to center the unit. Tighten clamp bolts (2) while brake is applied. Also check to be sure brake lever contacts stop pin (4) when brake is released. Adjust if necessary by means of housing anchor nuts (5).

TRACK ADJUSTMENT. On all models, raise rear of machine until track is clear of ground. Pull slack to center of track at bottom as shown at (S—Fig. 3); track should clear slide rails by approximately 2 inches and be equal on both sides. Adjust by turning tension adjusting screws (A—Fig. 2 or 3) until tension is correct, making sure both sides are adjusted equally.

On early models, riding characteristics are adjusted by means of turnbuckles (T—Fig. 2). Tighten for a firmer ride or loosen for softer ride,

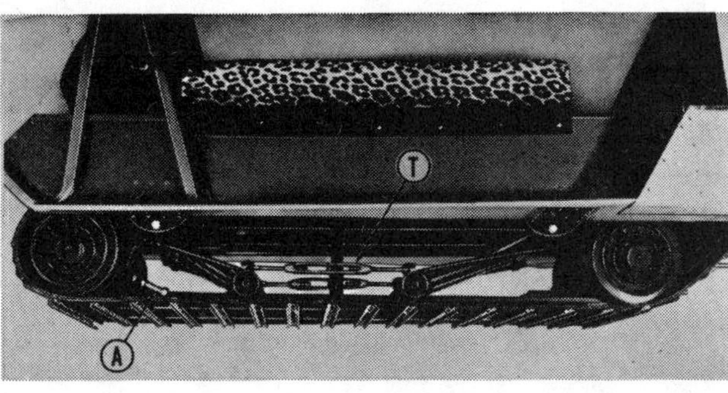

Fig. 2—Track and track suspension showing points of adjustment. Refer to text for details.

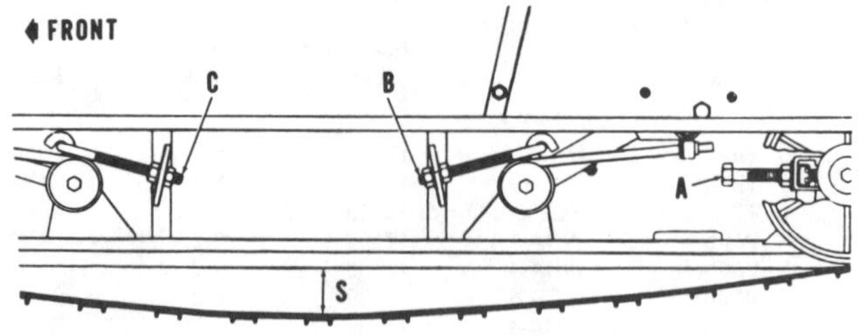

Fig. 3—View of track carriage showing points of adjustment.

A. Tension adjusting screw
B. Load adjustment
C. Traction adjustment
S. Slack

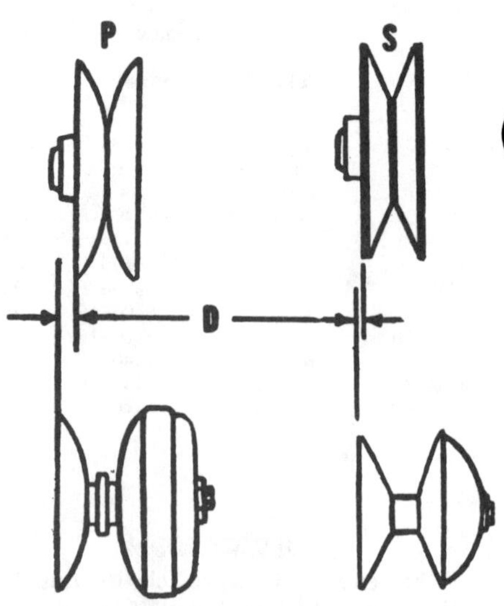

Fig. 5—Offset distance (D) should be ½-inch for Polaris Unit (P) or 13/64-inch for Salsbury Unit (S).

making sure both sides are adjusted equally. Late models have two ride adjustments. The rear eyebolt (B—Fig. 3) adjusts for weight of operator (or operator and passenger) and should be set to eliminate "bottoming out" on most bumps. Weight adjustment should be made with changes in load. The front eyebolt (C) adjusts for snow conditions. Loosen the adjustment in soft or deep snow, to improve flotation. Tighten the adjustment on packed snow or ice, to improve traction. All adjustments must be made equally on each side of machine.

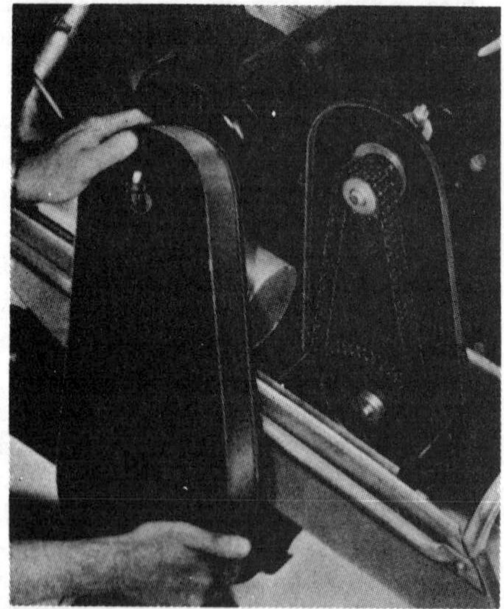

Fig. 4—View of drop case used on late models showing cover removed. An endless drive chain is also used, eliminating the master link.

NOTE: Whenever track has been adjusted, alignment MUST be checked as outlined in TRACK SERVICE Section of this manual.

OVERHAUL

SKIS. Skis, springs and spindles are interchangeable from one side of vehicle to the other. Skis are equipped with wear bars which are retained by a nut on one center stud. Wear bar can be installed either end forward, proceed as follows: Insert one end of bar in rear hole of ski. Lay a short 1-inch block behind center bolt. Guide front end of wear bar into front retaining hole moving wear bar forward by tapping on wood block. When bolt aligns with center hole, tap wood block out, allowing wear bar to snap into position. Tighten retaining nut securely.

DRIVE. Offset distance (D–Fig. 5) should be ½-inch on Polaris Type units (P) and 13/64-inch on Salsbury Type units (S). Distance can be changed by varying the shims used to position driven sheave on intermediate shaft. Shaft center distance must be accurately maintained.

Torque Sensing driven sheave spring application is as follows:

All 1969 &
1970 Models ....Standard Spring
All 1971 Models With
770 Converter ....Standard Spring
1971 Model w/JLO 440 engine &
910 Conv. ....Standard Spring
All other 1971 Models w/910
or 1190 Conv. ..Intermediate Spring

The standard spring has 5 coils and is color coded black; intermediate spring has 7 coils and is color coded yellow. Also available is a heavy duty spring which has 7 coils and is color coded black. All models use the standard 41° cam ramp.

TRACK AND SUSPENSION. "Hi-fax" plastic slides are retained to track frames by pop rivets. Slides can be examined through track without removal of frame, and should be renewed when worn to near rivet heads or when otherwise damaged or loose. Suspension should be removed for slide renewal and retaining rivets carefully drilled out.

Track belts are endless construction and all sections are available individually. In most instances a single section can be renewed at any time through the life of the track, without the necessity of complete track renewal. Straighten bent cleats as soon as possible after damage, and renew any which cannot be satisfactorily re-repaired.

ARCTIC CAT

1973-1984

Model	Engine Make	Engine Model	Engine Displ.	Carburetor Make	Carburetor Model	Sprocket Ratio	Chain Size	Clutch Make	Clutch Shaft Center	Belt Number
1973										
Kitty Cat	Kawasaki		60cc							
L-292	Kawasaki	T4B292S1A	292cc	Walbro	WRD-2	17:39	35-2	Salsbury	11-3/8	0100-080
C-340	Kawasaki	T1A340	339cc	Walbro	WDA-31	17:39	35-2	Own	10-7/8	0100-092
P-295	Wankel	KM24	294cc	Walbro	WDA-31	17:39	35-2	Own	10-7/8	0100-092
P-340	Kawasaki	T1A340	339cc	Walbro	WDA-31	17:39	35-2	Own	10-7/8	0100-092
P-400	Kawasaki	T1A400	398cc	Walbro	WDA-31	17:39	35-2	Own	10-7/8	0100-092
P-440	Kawasaki	T1A440	436cc	Walbro	WDA-31	17:39	35-2	Own	10-7/8	0100-092
PM-440	Kawasaki	T1B440S1	436cc	Walbro	WDA-31	19:39	35-2	St. Lawrence	10-7/8	0100-092
El Tigre LT-250	Kawasaki		245cc	Mikuni	VM(2)		Silent	Own		
LT-340	Kawasaki		339cc	Mikuni	VM(2)		Silent	Own		
LT-400	Kawasaki		398cc	Mikuni	VM(2)		Silent	Own		
LT-440	Kawasaki		436cc	Mikuni	VM(2)		Silent	Own		
1974										
Lynx I 292	Kawasaki		292cc					Own	11-3/8	0100-080
Lynx I 295	Wankel	KM24	294cc	Walbro	WRC-1	17:39	Silent	Own	10-7/8	0227-007
Lynx II 340	Kawasaki	TIC340	339cc	Walbro	WF-1A	19:39	Silent	Own	10-3/16	0227-007
Lynx II 440	Kawasaki	TIC440	436cc	Walbro	WF-1A	19:35	Silent	Own	10-3/16	0227-007
Cheeta 340	Kawasaki	TIC340	339cc	Walbro	WF-1A	19:39	Silent	Own	10-3/16	0227-007
Cheeta 440	Kawasaki	TIC440	436cc	Walbro	WF-1A	19:35	Silent	Own	10-3/16	0227-007
Panther 340	Kawasaki	TIC340	339cc	Walbro	WF-1A	19:39	Silent	Own	10-3/16	0227-007
Panther 440	Kawasaki	TIC440	436cc	Walbro	WF-1A	19:35	Silent	Own	10-3/16	0227-007
El Tigre 295	Kawasaki	TIC295F	292cc	Mikuni	VM(2)		Silent	Own		
El Tigre 340	Kawasaki	TIC340F	339cc	Mikuni	VM(2)		Silent	Own		
El Tigre 400	Kawasaki	TIC400F	398cc	Mikuni	VM(2)		Silent	Own		
El Tigre 440	Kawasaki	TIC440F	436cc	Mikuni	VM(2)		Silent	Own		
VIP	Kawasaki	TIC440	436cc	Walbro	WF-1A	19:35	Silent	Hydraulic Torque Converter		
1975										
Lynx	Kawasaki		246cc	Mikuni	VM			Own	11-3/8	0100-080
Cheeta 295	Wankel	KM24	294cc	Walbro	WRC-1	17:39	Silent	Own	10-7/8	0227-007
Cheeta 340	Kawasaki	TIC340	339cc	Walbro	WF-7	19:39	Silent	Own	10-3/16	0227-007
Cheeta 440	Kawasaki	TIC440	436cc	Walbro	WF-7	19:35	Silent	Own	10-3/16	0227-007
Panther 440	Kawasaki	TIC440	436cc	Walbro	WF-7	19:35	Silent	Own	10-3/16	0227-007
El Tigre 400	Kawasaki	TIC340F	339cc	Mikuni	VM(2)		Silent	Own		
El Tigre 440	Kawasaki	TIC440F	436cc	Mikuni	VM(2)		Silent	Own		
VIP 440	Kawasaki	TIC440	436cc	Walbro	WF-7		Silent	Own		
Pantera 440	Kawasaki	TIC440	436cc	Walbro	WF-7		Silent	Own		
1976										
Lynx 250	Kawasaki		246cc	Mikuni	VM					
Jag 2000	Spirit	AA28F	275cc	Mikuni	VM-30	19:39	Silent	Own	11-3/8	0227-014
Jag 3000	Spirit	AA34F3	339cc	Mikuni	VM-30	20:39	Silent	Own	11-3/8	0227-014
Cheetah 4000	Spirit	AB44A	431cc	Mikuni	VM-34	21:33	Silent	Own	10.2	0227-007
Cheetah 5000	Spirit	AB50A	500cc	Mikuni	VM-34	21:33	Silent	Own	10.2	0227-019
Panther 4000	Spirit	AB44A	431cc	Mikuni	VM-34	21:33	Silent	Own	10.2	0227-007
Panther 5000	Spirit	AB50A	500cc	Mikuni	VM-34	21:33	Silent	Own	10.2	0227-019
El Tigre 4000	Spirit	AB44F	431cc	Mikuni	2-VM-32	24:39	Silent	Own	10.2	0227-019
El Tigre 5000	Spirit	AB50F	500cc	Mikuni	2-VM-32	24:39	Silent	Own	10.2	0227-019
Pantera 5000	Spirit	AE50A	500cc	Mikuni	VM-34	18:33	Silent	Own	12.0	0227-020
1977										
Lynx 2000S	Spirit	AB25F1	250cc	Mikuni	VM30	19:39	Silent	Own	10.2	0227-007
Lynx 2000	Spirit	AA28F2	275cc	Mikuni	VM30	19:39	Silent	Own	10.2	0227-007
Jag 3000	Spirit	AA34F2	339cc	Mikuni	VM30	20:39	Silent	Own	11-3/8	0227-021
Cheetah 5000	Spirit	AB50A2	500cc	Mikuni	VM34	21:33	Silent	Own	10.2	0227-019
Panther 4000	Spirit	AC44A2	431cc	Mikuni	VM34	21:33	Silent	Own	10.2	0227-007
Panther 5000	Spirit	AB50A2	500cc	Mikuni	VM34	21:33	Silent	Own	10.2	0227-019
El Tigre 4000	Spirit	AB44F2	431cc	Mikuni	2-VM32	24:39	Silent	Own	12	0227-020
El Tigre 5000	Spirit	AD50F2	500cc	Mikuni	2-VM32	24:39	Silent	Own	12	0227-020
Pantera 5000 F/C	Spirit	AE50A1	500cc	Mikuni	VM34	18:33	Silent	Own	12	0227-020
Pantera 5000 F/A	Spirit	AC50F2	500cc	Mikuni	2-VM32	20:35	Silent	Own	12	0227-020

Model	Engine Make	Engine Model	Engine Displ.	Carburetor Make	Carburetor Model	Sprocket Ratio	Chain Size	Clutch Make	Clutch Shaft Center	Belt Number
					1978					
Lynx 2000S	Spirit	AB25F1	250cc	Mikuni	VM30	19:39	Silent	Own	10.2	0227-007
Lynx 2000T	Spirit	AA28F2	275cc	Mikuni	VM30	19:39	Silent	Own	10.2	0227-007
Jag 2000	Spirit	AA28F3	275cc	Mikuni	VM30	19:39	Silent	Own	11-3/8	0227-014
Jag 3000	Spirit	AA34F3	339cc	Mikuni	VM30	20:39	Silent	Own	11-3/8	0227-014
Cheetah 5000	Spirit	AB50A3	500cc	Mikuni	VM34	21:33	Silent	Own	10.2	0227-019
Panther 4000	Spirit	AC44A3	431cc	Mikuni	VM34	21:33	Silent	Own	10.2	0227-007
Panther 5000	Spirit	AB50A3	500cc	Mikuni	VM34	21:33	Silent	Own	10.2	0227-019
El Tigre 5000 F/A	Spirit	AD50F3	500cc	Mikuni	2-VM32	24:39	Silent	Own	10.2	0227-019
El Tigre 6000 L/C	Spirit	AF44LI	435cc	Mikuni	VM34	24:39	Silent	Own	10.2	0227-019
Pantera 5000 F/C	Spirit	AE50A2	500cc	Mikuni	VM34	18:33	Silent	Own	12.0	0227-020
Pantera 5000 F/A	Spirit	AD50F2	500cc	Mikuni	2-VM32	20:35	Silent	Own	12.0	0227-020
					1979					
Lynx 2000S	Spirit	AB25F3	250cc	Mikuni	VM30	19:39	Silent	Own	10.2	0227-007
Lynx 2000T	Spirit	AA28F4	275cc	Mikuni	VM30	19:39	Silent	Own	10.2	0227-007
Jag 2000FA	Spirit	AA28FA	275cc	Mikuni	VM30	19:39	Silent	Own	11.375	0227-014
Jag 3000FA	Spirit	AA34FA	339cc	Mikuni	VM30	20:39	Silent	Own	11.375	0227-014
Jag 3000FC	Spirit	AF34A1	339cc	Mikuni	B34	20:39	Silent	Own	11.375	0227-014
Panther 5000	Spirit	AB50A4	500cc	Mikuni	VM34	21:33	Silent	Own	10.2	0227-019
Pantera FC	Spirit	AE50A3	500cc	Mikuni	VM34	18:33	Silent	Own	12.0	0227-020
El Tigre 5000 FA	Spirit	AD50FA	500cc	Mikuni	VM32	24:39	Silent	Own	10.2	0227-027
El Tigre 6000 LC	Spirit	AF44LA	435cc	Mikuni	VM32	24:39	Silent	Own	10.2	0227-027
Trail Cat FC	Spirit	AF34A1	339cc	Mikuni	B34	20:39	Silent	Own	10.2	0227-019
					1980					
Lynx 2000S	Spirit	AB25F4	250cc	Mikuni	B34	19:39	Silent	Own	10.2	0227-007
Lynx 2000T	Spirit	AA28F5	275cc	Mikuni	B34	19:39	Silent	Own	10.2	0227-007
Jag 2000FA	Spirit	AA28F5	275cc	Mikuni	B34	19:39	Silent	Own	11.375	0227-014
Jag 3000FA	Spirit	AA34F5	339cc	Mikuni	B34	20:39	Silent	Own	11.375	0227-014
Jag 3000FC	Spirit	AF34A2	339cc	Mikuni	B34	20:39	Silent	Own	11.375	0227-014
Panther 5000	Spirit	AG44A1	431cc	Mikuni	B40	20:35	Silent	Own	10.2	0227-019
Pantera FC	Spirit	AL50A1	500cc	Mikuni	B40	18:33	Silent	Own	10.2	0227-019
El Tigre 5000 FA	Spirit	AD50F5	500cc	Mikuni	VM32	24:39	Silent	Own	10.2	0227-019
El Tigre 6000 LC	Spirit	AH50L1	500cc	Mikuni	VM38	24:35	Silent	Own	10.2	0227-027
Trail Cat 3000 FC	Spirit	AF34A2	339cc	Mikuni	B34	20:39	Silent	Own	10.2	0227-019
Trail Cat 4000 FC	Spirit	AG44A1	431cc	Mikuni	B40	24:39	Silent	Own	10.2	0227-019
					1981					
Jag 4000FC	Spirit	AG44A2	431cc	Mikuni	B40	20:35	Silent	Own	10.2	0227-014
Jag 4000LT	Spirit	AG44A2	431cc	Mikuni	B40	20:35	Silent	Own	10.2	0227-014
Panther 4000 FC	Spirit	AG44A2	431cc	Mikuni	B40	20:35	Silent	Own	10.2	0227-019
Pantera 5000 FC	Spirit	AL50A2	500cc	Mikuni	VM34	20:35	Silent	Own	10.2	0227-019
El Tigre 5000 FC	Spirit	AD50F6	500cc	Mikuni	VM32	24:39	Silent	Own	10.2	0227-030
El Tigre 6000 LC	Spirit	AH50L2	500cc	Mikuni	VM38	24:39	Silent	Own	10.2	0227-032
Trail Cat 4000 FC	Spirit	AG44A1	431cc	Mikuni	B40	24:39	Silent	Own	10.2	0227-019
					1984					
Panther	Spirit	AG44A3	431cc	Mikuni	VM34	20:35	Silent	Own	10.2	0227-019
El Tigre 6000	Spirit	AH50L3	500cc	Mikuni	VM38	24:39	Silent	Own	10.2	0227-032

LUBRICATION

The engine is lubricated by oil mixed with the fuel. In most engines a pre-mix is used; some Kawasaki engines may be equipped with oil injection. On Kawasaki engine models requiring a pre-mix, use one quart of Arctic Cat Purple Powerlube Snowmobile Oil or equivalent with five gallons of Regular gasoline. On Wankel engine models, mix one quart of Arctic Cat Rotolube, SAE 30 HD Shell Rotella T or a limited number of alternative equivalent oils with six gallons of Regular gasoline. On El Tigre 6000 with liquid cooled Spirit engine, use on quart of Spirit oil with five gallons of Regular gasoline. On other models with Spirit engine, mix 12 fluid ounces of Spirit oil with five gallons of gasoline. Premium gasoline should be used in El Tigre and Pantera 5000; Regular gasoline is usually suitable on other models with Spirit engine. Fuel:oil ratio is thus 20:1 for Kawasaki engines or Spirit liquid cooled engines; 50:1 for other Spirit engines; or 25:1 for Wankel engine using the Factory Approved Oil.

The enclosed drive chain runs in an oil bath. Check oil level once a month by removing lower (check) plug on chaincase cover. Oil level should be even with bottom of check plug hole. Recommended lubricant is Arctic Chainlube or equivalent. Lubricant should be

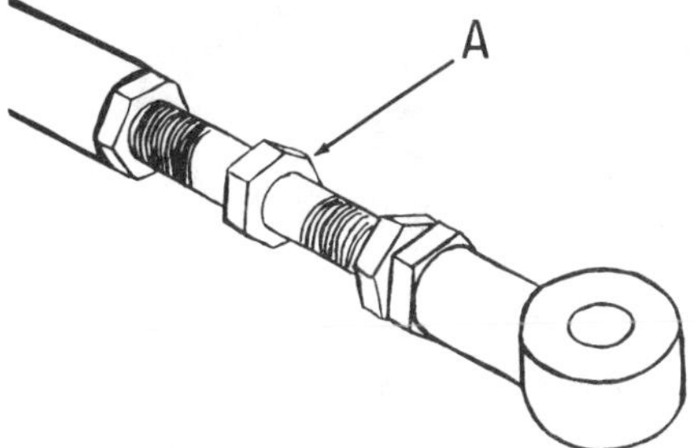

Fig. 1—In 1975 and later models, adjusting stud (A) at outer end of tie rod has right and left hand threads. Turning the stud will shorten or lengthen tie rod.

changed each 100 hours of operation or after the end of each season. To drain the lubricant, place rags beneath chaincase, remove cover and allow fluid to drain.

The driven pulley shaft bearing (chaincase upper bearing) on models with welded steel chaincase is equipped with a pressure lube fitting. Grease sparingly about once a week using a hand grease gun. Stop pumping the moment resistance is felt, to avoid rupturing seal. Rear suspension arm telescoping shafts have lube fittings and should be greased sparingly once a week. Remove excess grease with a rag or paper towel to avoid grease dropping on track.

ADJUSTMENT

STEERING SKIS AND LINKAGE. Steering skis should be parallel to each other and to track tunnel when handlebar is in a normal straight driving position. Adjustment is made by loosening the locknuts and turning adjusting bolt (turnbuckle) (A—Fig. 1) on some models; or tie rod center section on other models. Both tie rods should be adjusted as nearly as possible alike.

DRIVE CHAIN. Models with welded steel chaincase (Fig. 2) have an eccentric bearing housing carrying upper chain sprocket and periodic adjustment is required. Models with diecast chaincase (Figs. 4 and 5) are equipped with spring loaded chain tighteners and adjustment is not needed.

On models requiring adjustment, chain should have approximately ¼-inch deflection measured midway between sprockets; however, the deflection cannot be directly measured without draining chaincase and removing cover. Chain adjustment can be checked by checking the backlash measured at driven pulley rim. Chain tension can be considered correct when backlash measures 3/8-½ inch. To adjust the chain, loosen eccentric clamp bolts (A—Fig. 2) and brake anchor bolts (B). The eccentric bearing housing may be installed with shaft offset to front or rear; rotate the eccentric in the proper direction by pushing on one of the loosened clamp bolts. If any clamp bolt bottoms in adjusting slot before adjustment is correct, relocate the bolt in alternate hole which will have appeared in opposite end of slot. The housing is equipped with one hollow bolt which contains a lube fitting, and one or two additional clamp bolts. With adjustment complete and clamp bolts tightened, fully depress hand brake lever to realign brake caliper with friction surface of driven sheave, and retighten brake anchor bolts (B) while brake is applied.

On models with automatic chain tensioner, no adjustment is required. Because of the spring-loaded chain tighteners, backlash at pulley cannot be used to determine chain condition.

BRAKE. On models with pressed steel chaincase, the caliper type disc brake uses the turned rim of the driven pulley as a friction surface as shown in Fig. 3. On these models, brake caliper must be repositioned whenever brake or drive chain is adjusted. Align if necessary by loosening anchor bolts (B), fully applying brake, then tightening anchor bolts (B) while brake is applied. Actuating arm (C) must contact stop pin (P) whenever brake is released. Adjust brake cable housing anchor nuts (N) if necessary until all slack is removed from cable and actuating arm (C) starts to move away from stop pin (P) the moment brake hand lever is moved.

With preliminary adjustment made, tighten adjusting nut (A) on actuating arm stud until brake fully applies when hand lever is depressed approximately ¾-inch.

On models with diecast chaincase, brake caliper operates on a friction disc

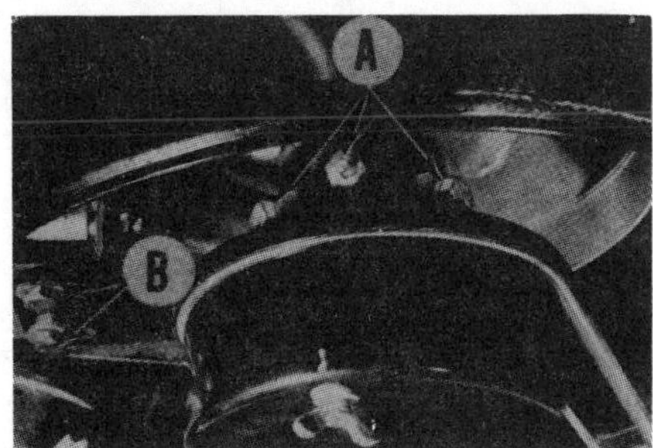

Fig. 2—On models with welded steel chain case, two or three clamp bolts (A) hold eccentric bearing housing used for chain adjustment. Adjust by loosening the bolts and moving eccentric housing. Brake anchor bolts (B) must also be loosened.

Fig. 3—View of caliper brake assembly used on models with welded chain case.

A. Adjusting nut
B. Anchor bolts
C. Actuating arm
N. Anchor nuts
P. Stop pin

Fig. 4—Left side mounted diecast chain case of the type used on some models. Drive chain is automatically tensioned. Lubricant fill plug is at (F) and fluid level check plug is at (L). The caliper type brake operates on a disc bolted to driven pulley fixed sheave as shown.

Fig. 5—Right side mounted diecast chain case of the type used on some models. Lubricant fill plug is at (F) and fluid level check plug at (L). Inset shows H-H type caliper disc brake. Refer also to Fig. 6.

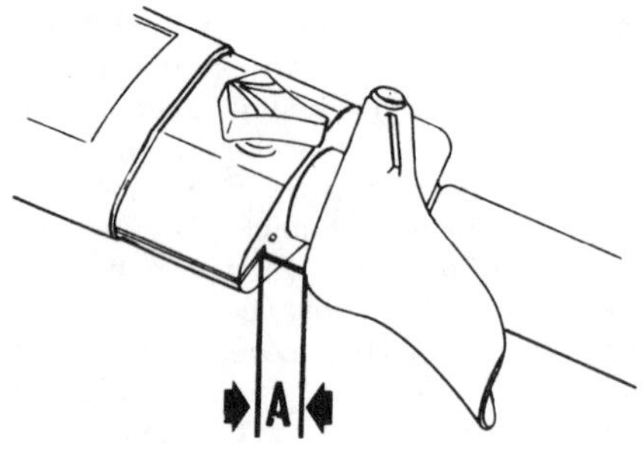

Fig. 6—With brake lever fully applied, distance (A) should measure ¼-½ inch (6.4-12.7 mm).

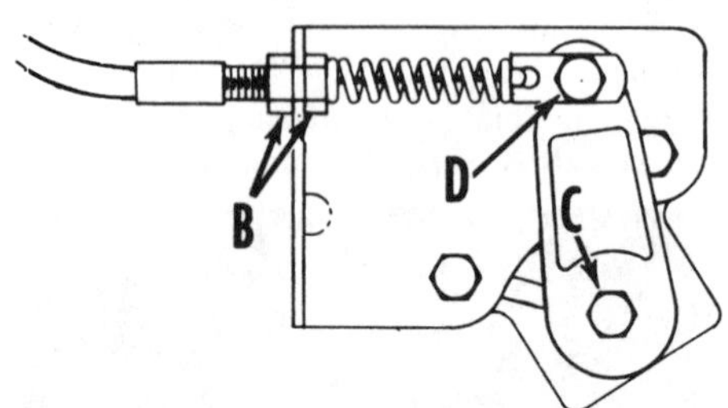

Fig. 7—Minor adjustment can be made at anchor nuts (B). For major adjustment, disconnect cable from clevis (D), loosen cap screw (C) and turn arm one notch clockwise on adjusting collar.

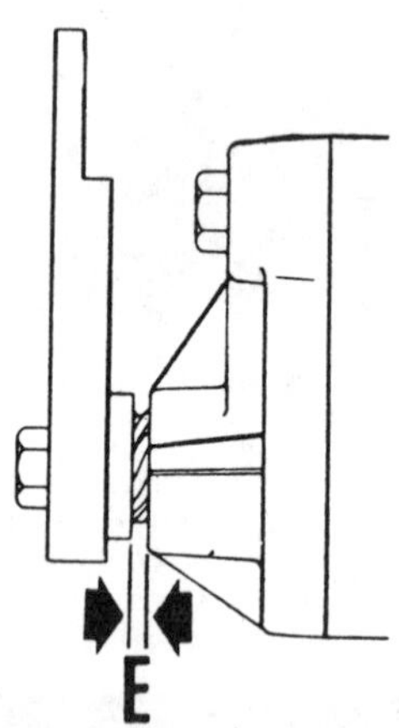

Fig. 8—Brake pucks should be renewed if distance (E) measures less than 0.040 inch (1 mm) with brake fully applied.

secured to driven pulley hub or a separate hub on cross shaft. Adjustment of H-H type disc brake is essentially the same as that outlined in the preceding paragraphs, except repositioning of brake caliper is seldom necessary except on original installation or when brake pucks are renewed. Refer also to Fig. 5.

On helix actuated dis brake of the type shown in Fig. 25 wear adjustment is accomplished by repositioning adjusting arm on actuating shaft. With brake fully applied, clearance (A—Fig. 6) between brake lever and handlebar stop should be ¼- to ½-inch (6.4-12.7 mm) Minor adjustment may be made at brake cable housing anchor nuts (B–Fig. 7); when further adjustment at this point is impossible, loosen retaining cap screw (C), disconnect cable from clevis (D) and rotate arm one notch clockwise on adjusting collar. Retighten cap screw (C) to 8 ft.-lbs. (10.9 N·m), reconnect cable to clevis (D); then readjust brake cable housing anchor nuts until clearance (A–Fig. 6) is as specified. With brake adjusted and applied, check end clearance (E–Fig. 8). If clearance with brake fully applied is less than 0.040 inch (1 mm), renew BOTH brake pucks and readjust as outlined.

Fig. 9—Adjust track tension by turning adjusting screws (A). Idler wheel must center between drive lugs (L—Inset).

Fig. 10—View of front (control) adjustment (C) and rear (load) adjustment on Lynx. On other models, adjustments are farther apart as shown in Fig. 11.

Fig. 11—View of front (control) adjustment (C) and rear (load) adjustment (L) on Panther. Refer also to Fig. 10.

TRACK. To adjust track tension, raise rear of machine until track is clear. With slack pulled to bottom center, track should clear slide rail by ¾-1 inch (19-25.4 mm) for short models (Lynx, Cheetah, El Tigre or Jag) or 1¼-1½ inches (31.8-38.1 mm) for long models (Panther or Pantera). Adjust by turning tension screws (A–Fig. 9) in front of rear idler axle. Both sides must be adjusted alike until the running track centers between internal drive lugs (L).

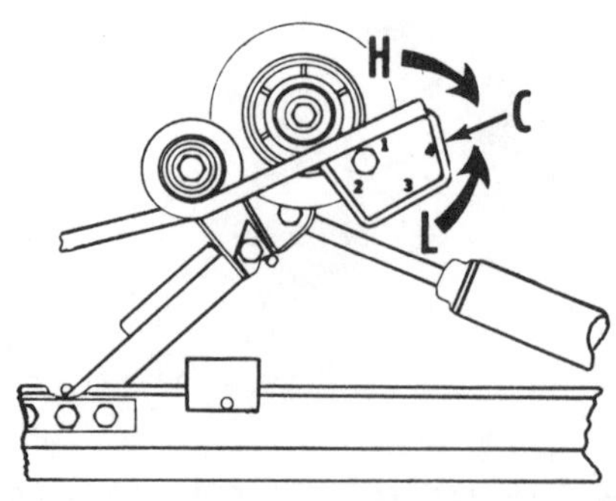

Fig. 11A—Schematic view of cam adjusted rear suspension spring used on El Tigre and Pantera FC models. Cam (C) should be turned in direction indicated by (H) for heavier loads or by (L) for lighter loads.

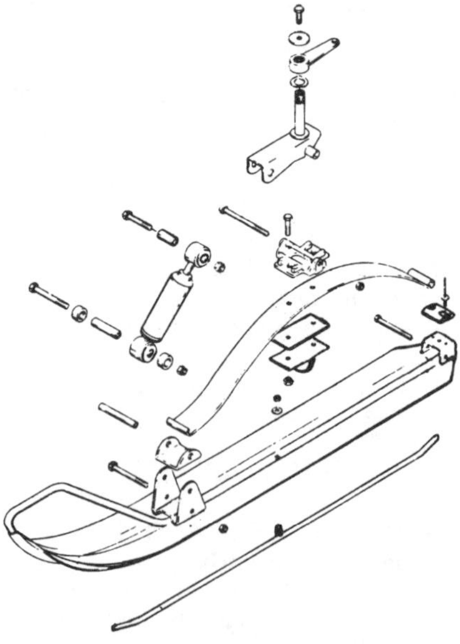

Fig. 12—Exploded view of front steering ski and associated parts similar to that used on most models. Refer also to Figs. 13, 14 and 15 for variations.

NOTE: Whenever track tension has been adjusted, alignment MUST be checked as outlined in TRACK SERVICE Section of this manual.

Rear (Load) adjustment (L—Fig. 10 or 11) should be made for weight of operator to prevent "bottoming" on all but the most severe bumps. Tighten the adjusting nuts for increased load capacity or slacken the nuts for lighter loads.

Front (Control) adjustment (C) should be made to control load distribution or handling characteristics. Increasing tension at front adjustment removes weight from skis and increases the percentage of weight borne by the track for increased traction or easier turning of the handlebar. Decreasing tension at (C) puts more weight on skis for more positive steering control. Equal adjustment must be made (at C and L) for BOTH sides of machine.

On late El Tigre models and Pantera FC, rear (Load) adjustment is cam controlled as shown in Fig. 11A. Cam can be turned using the spark plug wrench handle or other suitable tool. Turning cam to a higher number increases spring tension, to a lower number decreases tension. Cam should be turned to the next consecutive number, NEVER from 1 to 4 or 4 to 1.

SKIS AND STEERING. Skis, ski legs and associated parts are for the most part interchangeable from right to left. Separate right or left steering arms (1—Fig. 13 or 14) are used on Pantera and Lynx; and separate right or left saddles (2—Fig. 15) are used on some models. On all models, saddles must be installed with threaded spindle attaching hole to inside of machine. When assembling right or left ski unit, ALL bolts should be installed with heads to outside of the assembly.

Use suitable low temperature grease when assembling. Tighten shock assembly cap screws to 35 ft.-lbs. (47.6 N•m). Tighten spring bolts to 20-25 ft.-lbs. (27.2-34 N•m). Tighten spindle bolt to 20 ft.-lbs. (27.2 N•m) on models prior to 1979 or to 15 ft.-lbs. (20.4 N•m) on later models.

TRACK AND SUSPENSION. Track suspension may be of the general type shown in Fig. 16 or basically similar to that shown in Fig. 17 or 18. On all models, track suspension is retained by a front and rear cap screw on each side of track tunnel; however Pantera and Lynx models have a separate upper axle which also bolts to sides of track tunnel.

To remove suspension frame, suitably support rear of machine on a jack or hoist with track touching floor or support but weight removed from springs. On Pantera and Lynx, unbolt

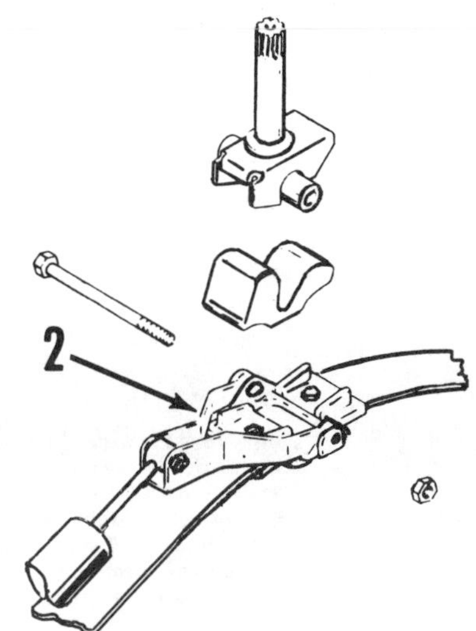

Fig. 15—Steering spindle, saddle and associated parts used on El Tigre. Saddles (2) are not interchangeable from right to left side, the correct saddle having the inside hole threaded for spindle attaching bolt.

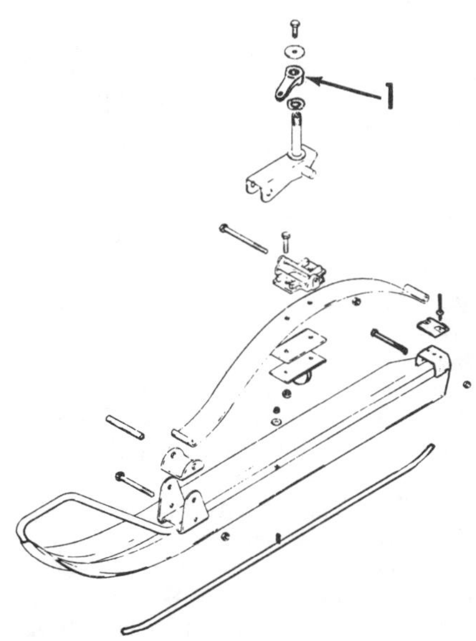

Fig. 13—Exploded view of front steering ski and associated parts used on late Lynx models. Steering arm (1) faces forward as shown and arms are not interchangeable from right to left side.

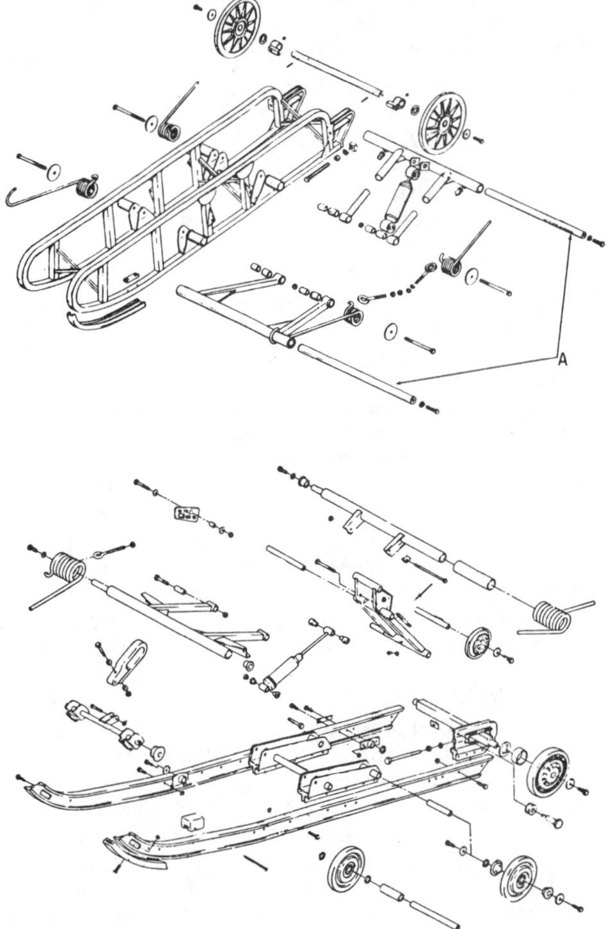

Fig. 16—Exploded view of suspension (skid) frame used on Panther. Other models are similar. The entire frame is supported on two mounting axles (A) which fasten to track tunnel.

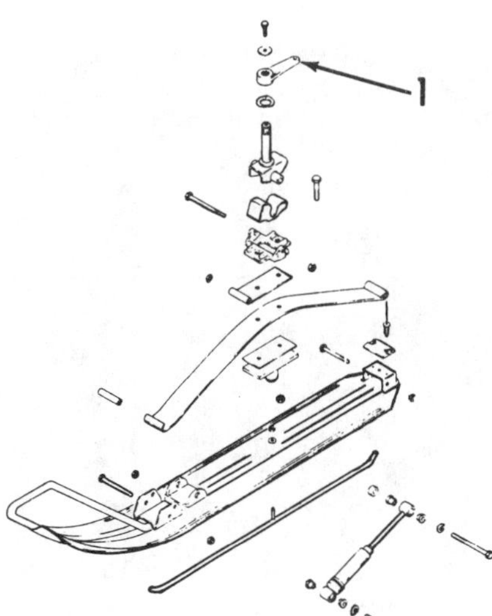

Fig. 14—Front steering ski and components used on Pantera. Different steering arms (1) are required for right or left ski.

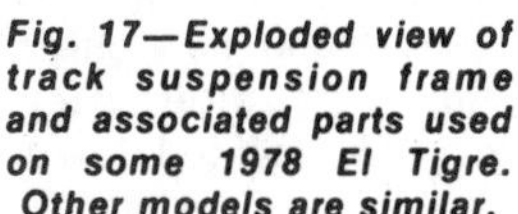

Fig. 17—Exploded view of track suspension frame and associated parts used on some 1978 El Tigre. Other models are similar.

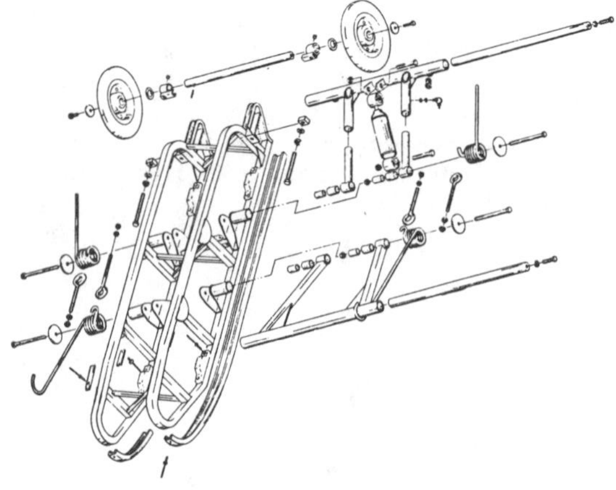

Fig. 18—Exploded view of suspension frame and associated parts used on 1978 Jag. Refer to text for details.

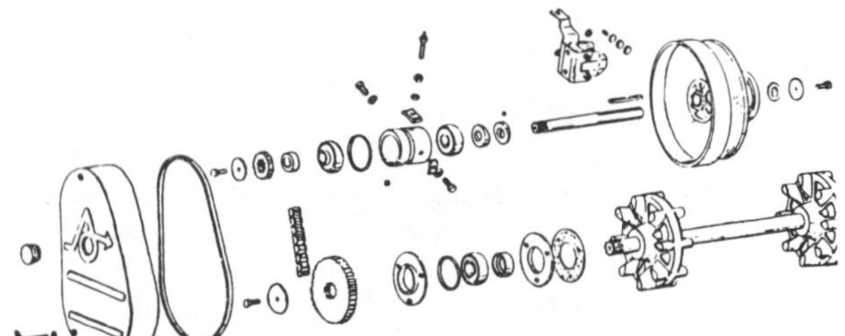

Fig. 19—Exploded view of welded chaincase cover and associated parts used on some models. Chaincase inner wall and upper bearing housing are welded to front frame.

and remove upper axle. On all models, remove the four cap screws (two on each side) retaining track frame to track tunnel, raise rear of machine until clearance exists, then withdraw skid frame assembly from either side.

Plastic slide runners (Hi-Fax Slides) must be renewed if worn to near rivet heads on frame type shown in Fig. 16 or 18; excessively worn, cracked or otherwise damaged on all models. Pantera and Lynx use an extruded, aluminum alloy rail with the Hi-Fax runner retained by three spring pins entering from the sides. Drive out the pins, then drive Hi-Fax rearward off rail using a block of wood and a suitable hammer. El Tigre models also use an extruded aluminum rail but Hi-Fax slides are retained by a machine screw and nut at forward end. Remove screw and drive slide rearward off runner. On other models, slides are retained by pop rivets; to remove the slides, cut off rivet heads using a sharp chisel, starting at rear of slide and working toward the front. Sand and repaint steel runners if necessary.

All painted metal parts should be cleaned, sanded and touched up if original surface is chipped or otherwise damaged or deteriorated. Use a rust-proofing paint on steel parts and a good primer on aluminum extrusions. Rear track idler wheels must be renewed in pairs if either wheel is damaged.

When installing new Hi-Fax slides on Pantera, Lynx or El Tigre, apply a fine spray of silicone lubricant along groove of new slide and install from rear until front end is flush with front of runner. Secure with the spring pins or machine screws used in original installation.

When installing new Hi-Fax slides on models with steel slide frame, make sure slide and frame are warmed to at least 70 degrees F. Install front pop rivet and form the slide around curve of runner, installing rivets in order and working toward the rear. After installing the last rivet, cut off any excess slide using a hacksaw.

Use a light coating of low temperature grease on suspension cross-axles and install suspension frame by reversing the removal procedure. Do not tighten any of the retaining cap screws until all are installed. It may be necessary to align some of the attaching holes using a soft mallet to position suspension frame. Tighten retaining cap screws to 20-25 ft.-lbs. (2.8-3.5 kg-m).

Drive track for most machines is composed of one center and two outer endless belts, joined by alternating ⅔-length steel cleats. If molded track drive lugs are worn and track is otherwise serviceable, track may be reversed to distribute the wear. Individual track parts may also be installed. To remove the track, first remove chaincase cover, sprockets and chain. On early models with roller chain, only the lower sprocket may need to be removed. Remove speedometer drive if so equipped. Remove suspension (skid) frame as previously outlined. Remove upper axle on Pantera or Lynx. Remove the carriage bolts securing track drive axle outboard bearing and withdraw drive axle spline from chaincase. Axle and/or track can now be removed. Install by reversing the removal procedure, being sure to align sprockets as outlined in the appropriate Chaincase Overhaul Section. Tighten outboard bearing retaining nuts to 16-18 ft.-lbs. (2.2-2.5 kg-m).

WELDED STEEL CHAINCASE. Refer to Fig. 19 for an exploded view. Secondary chain case bearing housing and inner wall are a welded part of front frame.

Upper (drive) sprocket can be removed with a two-jawed puller after removing retaining washer. Reinstall cap screw or use a shaft center, to protect shaft threads from puller bolt. Driven sheave and secondary shaft can be removed as an assembly after removing drive sprocket, drive belt and chain tightener eccentric locking screws.

Lower sprocket can be pulled from shaft using a two-jaw puller, after removing retainer washer. Reinstall cap screw or use a shaft center to protect shaft threads from puller bolt.

SPROCKET ALIGNMENT. When chaincase is reassembled, outer faces of both sprockets must be parallel to within 0.030 inch (0.8 mm) when checked with a 12-inch straightedge. Align the sprockets by sliding secondary shaft (upper sprocket shaft) in or out in bearing housing as follows: Refer to Fig. 20. Loosen the locking set screws in collars (A, B and C). Loosen the collars using a hammer and punch

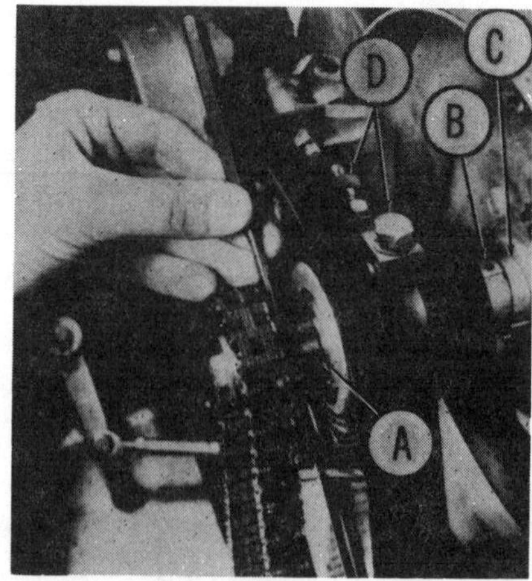

Fig. 20—View of welded chaincase with cover removed, showing bearing locking collars (A and B) and offset adjusting collar (C). Clamp screws (D) secure chain tension adjustment.

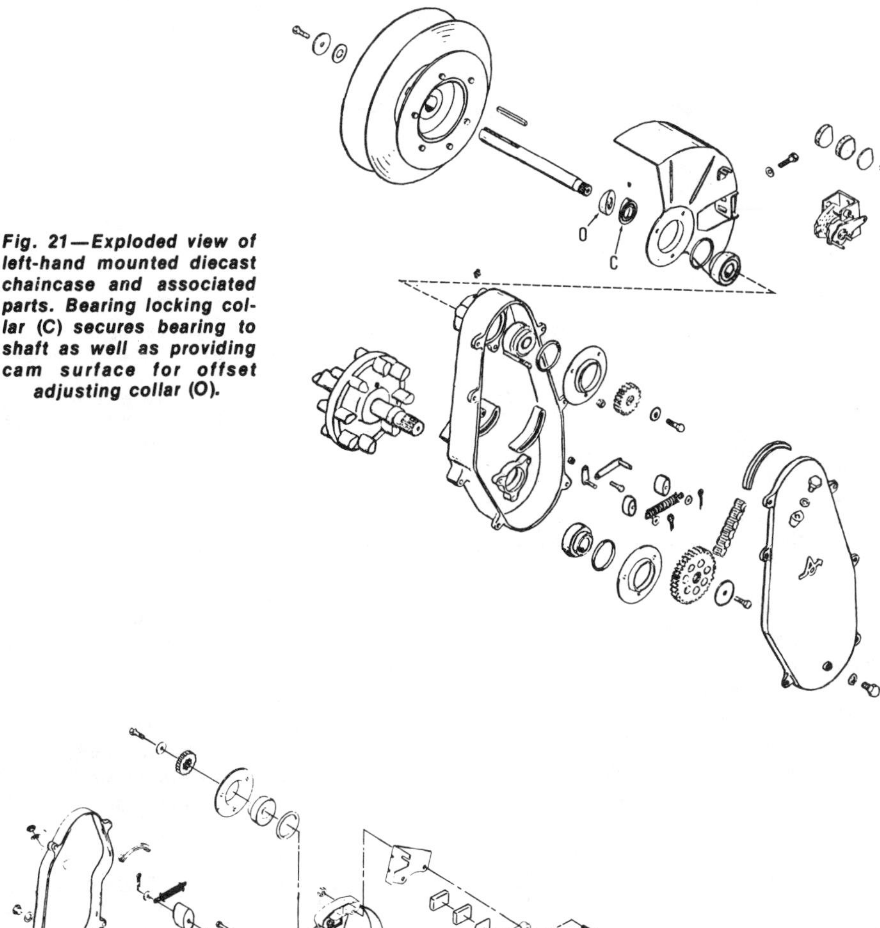

Fig. 21—Exploded view of left-hand mounted diecast chaincase and associated parts. Bearing locking collar (C) secures bearing to shaft as well as providing cam surface for offset adjusting collar (O).

Fig. 22—Exploded view of right-hand mounted diecast chaincase, secondary cross shaft and associated parts used on El Tigre. Other models are similar except that a different brake is used on some units and Lynx models have a manual chain tightener.

as shown, turning each collar in a direction opposite shaft rotation. With collars loosened, slide upper shaft in or out as required until sprocket alignment is correct. With sprocket properly aligned, tighten collar (A) on bearing by tapping it IN THE DIRECTION of normal shaft rotation. Recheck sprocket alignment, then retighten collar (B) by tapping it in direction of shaft rotation. If pulley offset remains within limits when checked as outlined in the appropriate following paragraphs, tighten collar (C), by tapping it in direction of normal shaft operation.

LEFT-HAND MOUNTED DIECAST CHAINCASE. Refer to Fig. 21 for an exploded view. Both drive chain sprockets are a light press fit on splines and can be removed with a two-jawed puller after removing retaining washer. Reinstall cap screw or use a shaft center to protect shaft threads from puller screw. Secondary (upper) shaft outer bearing seats against a shoulder on shaft and a shoulder in housing bore, and is a slip fit in both. Bearing can be withdrawn after removing upper sprocket and bearing retainer flange. Inner bearing is a press fit in housing bore and is further retained by pulley guard. Shaft is a slip fit in inner bearing and is secured by eccentric bearing collar (C).

To disassemble the secondary shaft, first remove brake assembly. Remove the cap screw in pulley end of secondary shaft, together with pulley retaining stop washer and any spacer shims which may be present. Remove chaincase cover, chain tension spring, upper sprocket and chain, together with any spacer shims which may be present behind sprocket. Remove upper bearing retainer and outer bearing. Loosen set screws in offset adjusting collars (O and C), then free collar (C) from eccentric bearing flange by tapping it in a direction opposite normal shaft rotation. Turn the collars to expose set screw contact surface on shaft and remove any burrs present using a fine file. On most engines it is necessary to remove carburetor from manifold mounting flange to obtain working clearance; fuel lines and controls need not be disconnected.

Using a soft drift and hammer and working from pulley side, tap shaft outward out of pulley hub and bearing. Lift out pulley as it is free and slide collars (O and C) from end of shaft; then withdraw the shaft to outside. If inner bearing is to be removed, unbolt and remove pulley guard; then tap bearing out of housing bore using a punch and hammer.

Assemble by reversing disassembly procedure. Make sure the cam collar (C) containing the eccentric bearing lock is installed next to bearing. Omit the square pulley key as shaft is installed. Install outer bearing and retainer, tightening the retainer locknuts to a torque of 16-18 ft.-lbs. (22-24 N•m). Bump shaft outward until outer bearing is seated against shaft shoulder. Engage lock collar (C) with cam of inner bearing and lock in place by tapping the collar in direction of normal shaft rotation until it is tight, then tighten set screw. Adjust pulley offset as outlined in the appropriate following paragraphs and sprocket alignment as follows:

SPROCKET ALIGNMENT. Upper and lower chain sprockets must be aligned within 0.030 inch (0.8 mm) when checked with a 12-inch straightedge placed against outer face of sprockets. Adjustment is made by shimming behind which ever sprocket is farther toward inside of housing. Tighten retaining cap screws to a torque of 16-18 ft.-lbs. (22-24 N•m).

Tighten chaincase cover retaining cap screws to a torque of 10 ft.-lbs. (13.6 N•m) and fill chaincase to recommended fluid level using 8 fluid ounces (235 mL) of ARCTIC CHAIN LUBE.

RIGHT-HAND MOUNTED DIE-CAST CHAINCASE. Refer to Fig. 22 for an exploded view. Chaincase is driven by a secondary cross shaft from torque converter on left side. Most models have a voltage regulator mounted on chaincase; remove and lay aside the regulator if so equipped. Machine can be tipped on left side for chaincase cover removal to prevent fluid spill. With cover off, fluid can be removed with a suction gun.

Remove cap screws retaining chain sprockets. Disconnect chain tensioner spring on all except Lynx models; fully loosen chain tension on Lynx. Lift off both sprockets and the chain as a unit, keeping separate any shims which may be installed in front of or behind either sprocket. Shims are used for sprocket alignment during assembly.

To remove the secondary cross shaft, first remove drive belt and driven pulley. Loosen the lock collar on cross shaft pulley-side bearing and remove any burrs from shaft left by lock collar set screw. Remove chaincase-side bearing, flange and "O" ring from cross shaft. Bump shaft toward left side of machine while turning shaft to prevent brake disc from binding. Remove brake disc Woodruff key when clear of brake disc hub. Slide cross shaft out chaincase side of machine after brake disc has been removed.

Assemble by reversing the disassembly procedure. Make sure brake disc is properly positioned as shaft is installed. If old shaft is reinstalled, reposition shaft in same approximate position as when removed. If a new shaft is used to install and tighten chaincase-side bearing, flange and flange retaining bolts; then temporarily install upper sprocket with removed shim pack to establish approximate proper position. Tighten locking collar on cross shaft left bearing by drifting in direction of normal shaft rotation, then tighten locking screw. Correct bearing flange retaining bolt torque is 16-18 ft.-lbs. (22-24 N·m). Adjust sprocket alignment and drive sheave alignment as outlined in the appropriate following paragraphs.

SPROCKET ALIGNMENT. Temporarily install both sprockets without the chain and check alignment with a straightedge placed against outer face of both sprockets. Alignment must be within 0.030 inch (0.8 mm). Adjust if necessary by shimming behind the sprocket fitting deeper into the crankcase. When proper alignment is obtained install both sprockets with the chain, and tighten retaining cap screws to a torque of 16-18 ft.-lbs. (22-24 N·m).

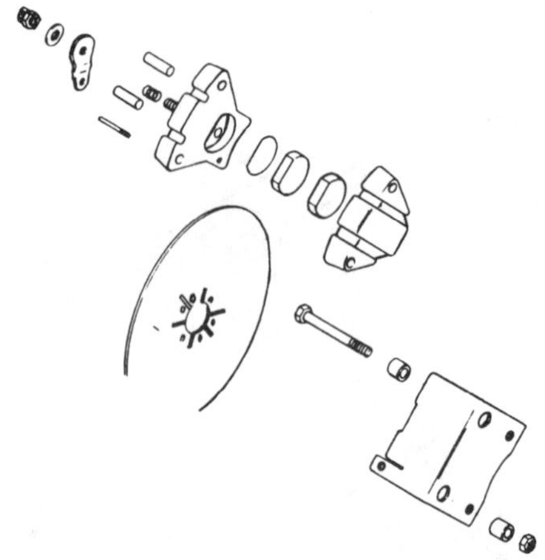

Fig. 23—Exploded view of H-H type disc brake used on some models. Units with welded chaincase use turned edge of secondary sheave fixed face as a friction surface instead of disc shown.

Fig. 25—Exploded view of helix actuated caliper disc brake used on some models. Stationary puck fits in machined pocket in chaincase casting and brake disc moves on shaft to equalize friction pressure on stationary and moving puck.

BRAKES. The H-H caliper type brake shown exploded in Fig. 23 may act on a disc attached to secondary shaft or on a drum built into the fixed face of driven sheave. On most models the brake assembly moves with engagement to equalize friction pressure on the moveable and stationary pucks. On drum mounted brakes, therefore, brake pucks must be concave and convex respectively, and are not interchangeable. On all models, brake pucks should be renewed in pairs. Check for proper alignment of mounting bracket. Check body castings for wear at mounting bolt and push pin holes. Check cam lever for wear at push pin contact points and mounting stud hole. Renew brake disc if badly worn, scored or warped. Adjust brake after assembly as outlined in previous ADJUSTMENT paragraphs.

Some late models are equipped with a helix actuated caliper disc brake of the type shown exploded in Fig. 25. Actuating helix and body are available separately but both should usually be renewed if damage or wear of helix occurs. Brake body mounts solidly and equalization of friction pressure is accomplished by movement of disc hub on secondary cross shaft. BOTH pucks should be renewed if applied clearance (E—Fig. 8) is less than 0.040 inch (1 mm) as outlined in ADJUSTMENT paragraphs. Adjust brake after assembly as previously outlined.

Fig. 24—Installed view of H-H type disc brake on model with secondary cross shaft and right-hand mounted diecast chaincase.

Most models are equipped with a plunger type brake light switch which is mounted on handlebar and actuated by brake lever. Check switch mounting, bulb, switch and wiring in logical order in the event of failure.

DRIVE BELT AND SHEAVES. Most late models are equipped with a drive belt having a top width of 1¼-inches and an outside circumference of 43¼, 45½ or 46.7 inches. Check the belt for uneven wear, frayed edges and other physical damage. Renew belt if top width is worn to 1-1/16 inch or less. The principal cause of excessive drive belt wear is incorrect offset of parallelism adjustment of drive and driven sheaves; adjust as follows:

SHEAVE ALIGNMENT. The drive belt should theoretically run true in both sheaves throughout shift range. Shaft center distance is fixed but pulley offset can be adjusted by moving driven sheave laterally on secondary shaft. Because of the cushioned engine mountings, the manufacturer also recommends that any deviation from shaft parallelism has the effect of twisting engine clockwise when viewed from above. To check or adjust sheave alignment, proceed as follows:

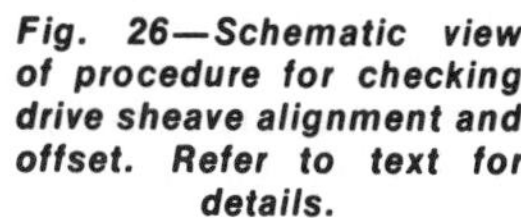

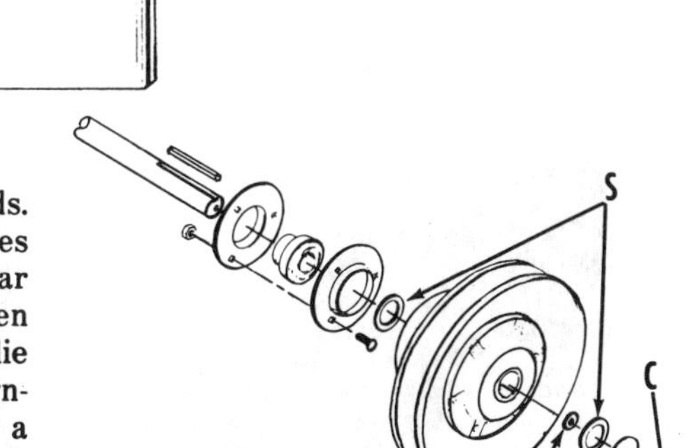

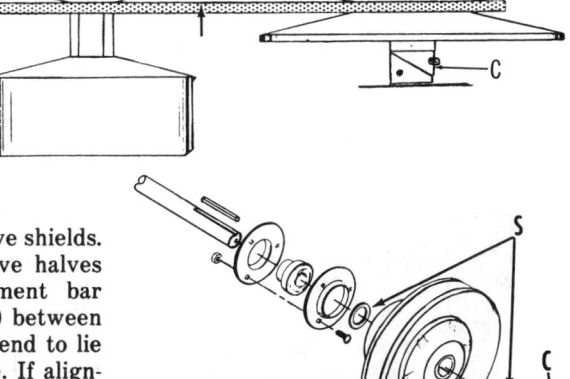

Fig. 26—Schematic view of procedure for checking drive sheave alignment and offset. Refer to text for details.

Fig. 28—View of driven pulley mounting on models with secondary cross shaft. Offset adjustment is accomplished by transferring spacer washers (S) from inside to outside sheave, adding small spacer washers (W) as required if hub of pulley extends beyond end of shaft. Retaining cap screw (C) must not apply end pressure to locked position of bearing when tightened.

Remove drive belt and sheave shields. Slightly separate driven sheave halves and place on end of alignment bar (Arctic Cat Part No. 0144-099) between sheave halves, allowing other end to lie on hub of opened drive sheave. If alignment tool is not available, use a two-foot length of STRAIGHT 7/16-inch square key stock. Offset is approximately correct if inner edge of key stock or alignment bar touches fixed face of drive sheave at the hub. To check parallelism, measure the distance from alignment bar to drive pulley rim at front and rear as shown at (A and B—Fig. 26). Front measurement (A) MUST NOT BE LESS than rear measurement (B), but must not exceed (B) by more than 1/16 inch (1.6 mm). Adjust parallelism by adding or removing shims underneath left rear motor mount as shown in Fig. 27.

To adjust offset on models with left-side mounted chaincase, refer to Fig. 26. To increase offset, loosen set screw in inner cam collar (C—Fig. 20 or 0—Fig. 21) and turn collar away from sheave hub. Remove retaining cap screw (S—Fig. 26) and stop washer (W) from inner end of secondary shaft. Install the appropriate number of 1-inch (25 mm) ID spacer washers (X) on end of shaft, then reinstall stop washer and cap screw, pushing driven sheave outward on secondary shaft. Turn cam collar (C) in direction of normal shaft rotation and lock in place by tightening set screw. Decrease offset by loosening retaining cap screw (S) and set screw in cam collar (C). Using a hammer and punch, turn cam collar (C) in direction of shaft rotation until offset is correct. Retighten set screw. Remove excess spacer washers (X) if present, then retighten cap screw (S).

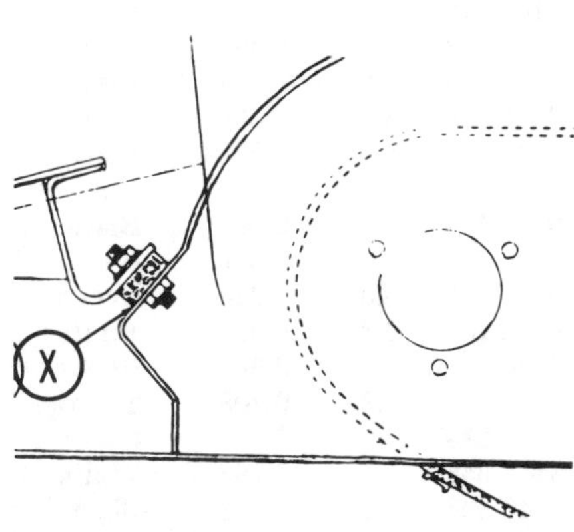

Fig. 27—Adjust sheave alignment by installing or removing shims under left rear engine mount as shown at (X).

On models with right-side mounted chaincase and secondary cross shaft, refer to Fig. 28. Adjust offset by adding or deleting spacer washers (S) on each side of sheave. If cross shaft does not extend completely through sheave hub when adjustment is correct, add small washers (W) as required so cap screw (C) will bottom on small washers and not apply excess side pressure to shaft bearings.

On all models, recheck belt alignment by observing belt operation throughout shift range while running the engine with machine blocked up until track is clear of floor. Refer also to OPERATIONAL CHECK in CONVERTER (BELT DRIVE) UNIT Section of this manual.

DRIVE CLUTCH. Fig. 29 shows an exploded view of the ARCTIC CAT Drive Clutch (except later El Tigre). Refer to CONVERTER (BELT DRIVE) UNIT Section of this manual for other models. Clutch removal requires the use of an ARTIC CAT Clutch Removal Tool (R) for the model involved. DO NOT pound on end of shaft in attempting removal, or internal engine parts may be damaged.

Because of clutch design, bushing wear can be determined by measuring backlash at a point on clutch cover as

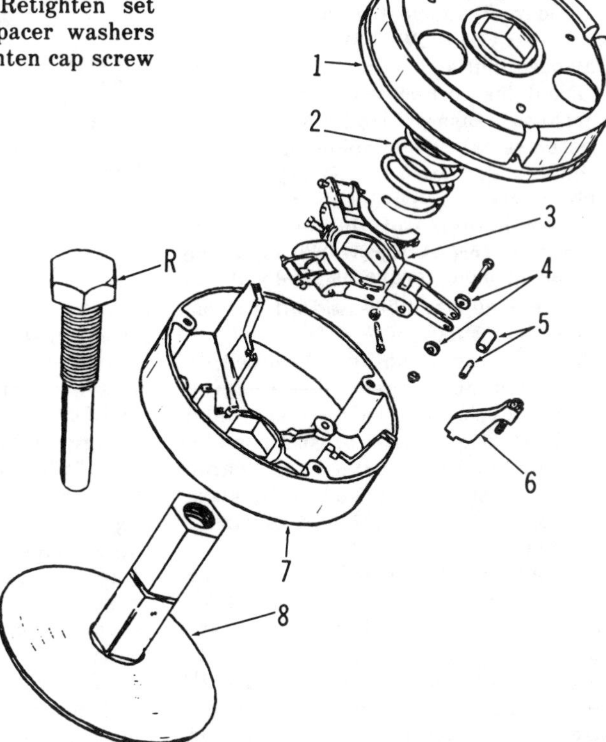

Fig. 29—Exploded view of ARCTIC CAT drive clutch showing component parts (except later El Tigre).

R. Removal tool
1. Cover
2. Spring
3. Spider
4. Weights (6 used)
5. Roller (3 used)
6. Ramp (3 used)
7. Moveable sheave
8. Stationary sheave

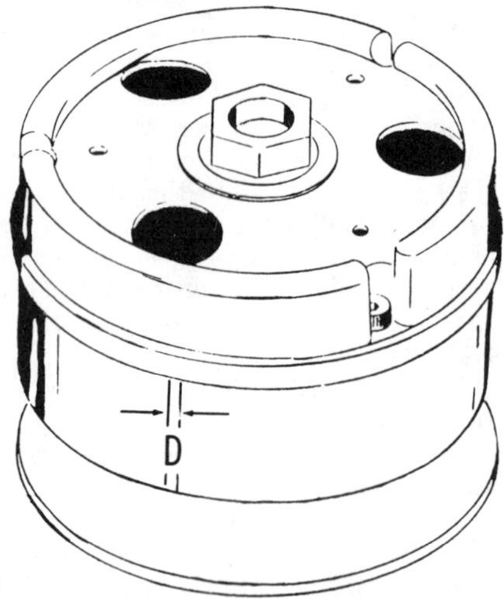

Fig. 30—Drive clutch hub bushing can be considered satisfactory if backlash (D) does not exceed 5/32-inch (4 mm).

shown at (D—Fig. 30). Condition can be considered satisfactory if backlash does not exceed 5/32-inch (4 mm). If backlash is excessive, renew moveable sheave (7—Fig. 29) or stationary sheave (8).

To disassemble the clutch unit, use a large flat washer and removal tool (R) to retain clutch cover (1). Remove the three cover retaining screws, back out removal tool (R) until spring pressure is relaxed; then remove tool (R), cover (1) and spring (2). DO NOT remove cover retaining cap screw unless cover is retained; spring (2) exerts 35-100 pounds pressure against cover, depending on strength of spring installed.

Spider (3), moveable sheave (7) and stationary sheave (8) constitute a balanced unit and these parts should be marked for correct reassembly before further disassembly is attempted. Loosen set screws in spider (3). Spider should slide down stationary sheave hub allowing removal of half-washer keepers in hub slot. If spider sticks with set screws loose, it must be drifted down until half-washer keepers are removed, then pressed off stationary sheave hub.

The Teflon bushing in moveable sheave is not renewable. Bushing should be cleaned with solvent only; DO NOT use a wire brush or metal tools on bushing surface. Moveable sheave must be renewed if backlash was excessive when checked as earlier outlined.

Ramps (6) and rollers (5) must be installed in kits consisting of three ramps and three rollers, if any are damaged. When changing rollers or weights, all bolts must be inserted with head leading and nut trailing in normal direction of clutch rotation, as shown in

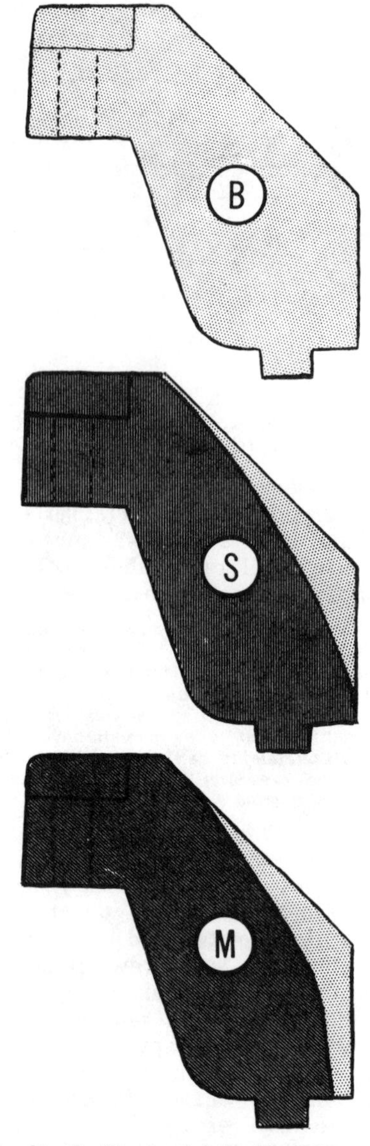

Fig. 31—Profile view of (B) Blank Ramp; (S) Standard Ramp interposed over blank ramp outline; and (M) Modified Ramp interposed over blank ramp outline. All other things being equal, the steeper the ramp angle the greater the speed required to affect shift pattern.

Fig. 29. Tighten bolt and nut to a torque of 40-45 inch-pounds (4.52-5.08 N•m) and ramp retaining cap screws to 25-30 inch-pounds (2.83-3.38 N•m).

CLUTCH ADJUSTMENT. Clutch engagement rpm and shift pattern depends on a combination of spring strength, centrifugal weight and ramp angle. It is essential, however, that all three ramps be ground to precisely the same angle, that ramp surfaces be parallel with centrifugal rollers, and that ramp surfaces be properly polished. Regrinding ramps is, therefore, not a job for the amateur or unequipped machine shop. Blank ramps are available from some sources. Fig. 31 shows the contour of a blank ramp with the outline of the standard ramp (S) and a modified ramp (M) interposed for comparison. Most normal shift patterns can be attained by changing springs, centrifugal weights or both, using the standard, factory-ground ramps.

Clutch engagement engine speed and engine speed at full upshift are both INCREASED by using a heavier spring or lighter weight kit; or DECREASED by using a lighter spring or heavier weight kit. Driven pulley adjustment will affect shift pattern but not engagement speed. Twenty-three different weights and five different clutch springs are available through parts stock. The springs are easily identifiable by color code. Weights are also color coded, but only six colors are used for the 23 weight classes, so outside diameter as well as color is used as an identifying feature. Identification and progression are as follows:

CLUTCH SPRINGS

Part No.	Compression Lbs. at 1¼ Inches	Color Code
0146-065	67.5-87.5	White (weakest)
0146-313	70-84*	Red
0146-067	145-165	Yellow
0146-005	170-190	Unpainted
0146-068	123-137*	Green (strongest)

*At 2-3/16 inches.

CENTRIFUGAL WEIGHTS

Part No.	Weight (Grams)	Outside Diameter (Inches)	Color Code
0146-227	1.0	0.400	Aluminum
0146-225	1.5	0.463	Aluminum
0146-226	2.0	0.521	Aluminum
0146-159	2.5	0.377	White
0146-108	3.06	0.406	Yellow
0146-175	3.7	0.437	Red
0146-135	4.5	0.471	Black
0146-379	4.6	0.473	Black
0146-176	4.7	0.500	Green
0146-107	5.0	0.491	White
0146-279	5.5	0.511	Black
0146-106	6.0	0.530	Red
0146-278	6.5	0.549	Black
0146-123	7.0	0.568	Yellow
0146-105	7.9	0.598	Black
0146-286	8.8	0.629	Red
0146-136	9.3	0.644	Green
0146-104	9.8	0.665	White
0146-166	10.6	0.684	Red
0146-307	11.3	0.703	Yellow
0146-314	12.0	0.723	Green
0146-345	15.0	0.798	White
0146-308	18.0	0.873	Black

Weight color coding is useful for selecting a matched set of six weights

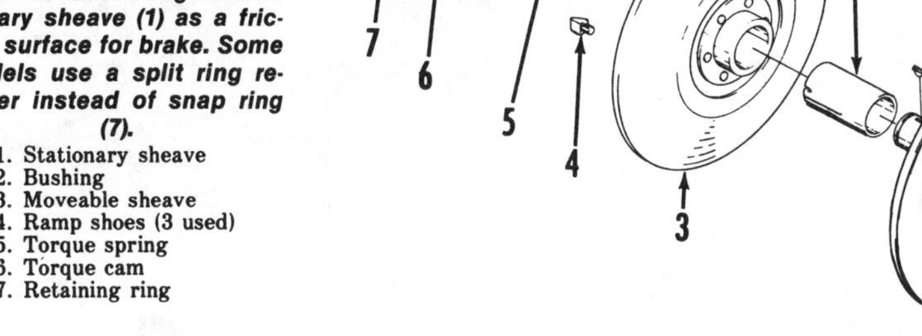

Fig. 32—Exploded view of driven pulley typical of that used on most units (except later El Tigre and Panther). Models with welded chaincase use turned edge of stationary sheave (1) as a friction surface for brake. Some models use a split ring retainer instead of snap ring (7).

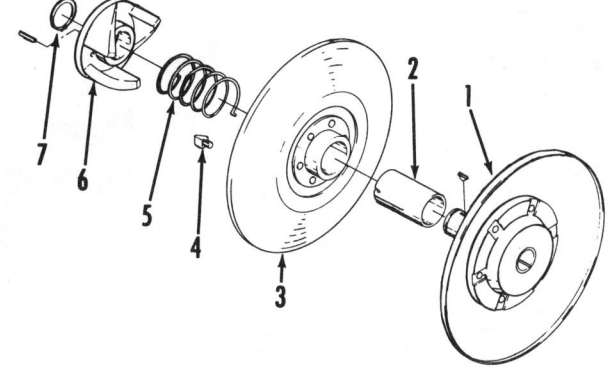

1. Stationary sheave
2. Bushing
3. Moveable sheave
4. Ramp shoes (3 used)
5. Torque spring
6. Torque cam
7. Retaining ring

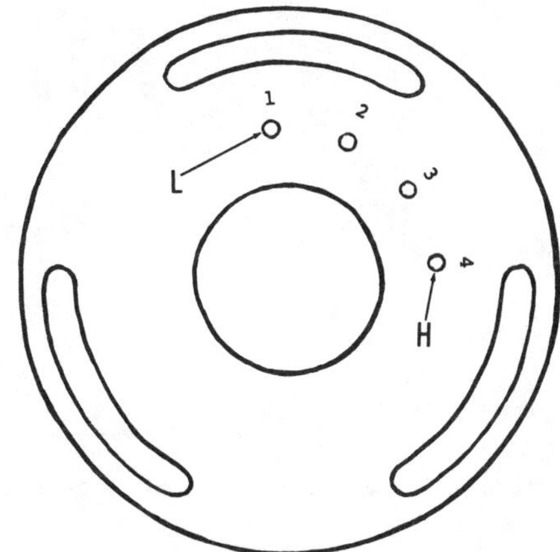

Fig. 33—Schematic view of torque cam with four spring anchor holes for torque adjustment.

H. Heavy torque L. Light torque

from a collection of optional weights. To change shift pattern, selection by size is the quickest and easiest route to progressively lighter or heavier weight options. Minor adjustment can be made by installing shim washers under the spring next to the stationary spider. As a general rule, it is usually better to hold both the weight and spring strength at the lightest level which produces the desired results. Refer also to DRIVE PULLEY ADJUSTMENT and to SPEED TUNING paragraphs of CONVERTER (BELT DRIVE) UNIT Section of this manual.

DRIVEN PULLEY (Except Later El Tigre and Panther). Fig. 32 shows an exploded view of a typical driven pulley. Models with welded chaincase use the turned edge of stationary sheave as brake friction surface. Driven pulley removal requires partial disassembly of chaincase as previously outlined.

To disassemble the removed pulley, place pulley on a clean work surface. Turn moveable sheave (3) counterclockwise until ramp shoes (4) no longer touch cam (6). Push cam down and remove snap ring (7) or retaining split ring (early models). Release cam carefully to keep spring from flying, and separate the pulley. Note installed position of torque spring (5). Recommended pre-load wrap is ⅓-turn (one ramp) and standard setting is second hole (see Fig. 33). Clean all parts with an oil base solvent only; DO NOT use a wire brush, steel wool or sharp scraping tools on friction faces of pulley. Ramp shoes (4—Fig. 32) can generally be pulled out with pliers; heat ramp brackets if necessary, to remove the shoes.

DRIVEN PULLEY ADJUSTMENT. Driven pulley torque spring (5—Fig. 32) should be pre-loaded one ramp (⅓-turn) during assembly. Most late cams (6) have four spring-anchor holes as shown in Fig. 33, to adjust torque load. Additional torque applied by moving spring anchor clockwise increases side pressure on belt, slightly increases engine speed at full upshift, and increases ability to downshift for acceleration or heavier torque load. These tendencies are multiplied when combined with lighter centrifugal weights and lighter spring in drive clutch.

Standard loading is first hole with Wankel engine and second hole with 340 or 440 engine.

ARIENS

1969-1973

	Engine			Carburetor				Clutch		
Model	Make	Model	Displ.	Make	Model	Sprocket Ratio	Chain Size	Make	Shaft Center	Belt Number
					1969					
300 III(23998-23999)......	Sachs	SA290	297cc	Tillotson	HR18A	14:33	35-2	Precico	10½	72054
					1970					
295S(23989)...	Sachs	SA290	293cc	Tillotson	HR64A	14:33	35-2	Precico	10½	72054
340S(23986-23987)......	Kohler	K335-1	335cc	Walbro	WR	14:33	35-2	Precico	10½	72054
440SS........	Kohler	K440-2	437cc	Tillotson	HR42A	17:33	35-2	Precico	10½	72054
400L(23984-23985)......	Kohler	K399-2	399cc	Tillotson	HR42A	16:33	35-2	Precico	10½	72054
					1971					
275S(923948)..	Sachs	SA280A	277cc	Tillotson	HL252A	13:33	35-2	Precico	10½	702054
300S(923947)..	Sachs	SA290	293cc	Tillotson	HR61A	14:33	35-2	Precico	10½	702054
350S(923946)..	Kohler	K340-2	338cc	Tillotson	HR79B	15:33	35-2	Precico	10½	702054
400L (923943).	Kohler	K399-2	399cc	Tillotson	HR42A	16:33	35-2	Precico	10½	702054
400SS(923945).	Kohler	K399-2	399cc	Tillotson	HR42A	16:33	35-2	Precico	10½	702054
440SX........	Sachs	SA2-440	437cc	Tillotson	HD	16:33	35-2	Precico	10½	702054
					1972					
275S.........	Sachs	SA280	277cc	Tillotson	HR252A	13:33	35-2	Precico	10½	702054
300S.........	Sachs	SA290	293cc	Tillotson	HR61A	14:33	35-2	Precico	10½	702054
350S.........	Kohler	K340-2	338cc	Tillotson	HR79B	15:33	35-2	Precico	10½	702054
400L.........	Kohler	K399-2	399cc	Tillotson	HR42A	16:33	35-2	Precico	10½	702054
400SS........	Kohler	K399-2	399cc	Tillotson	HR42A	16:33	35-2	Precico	10½	702054
350SX........	Sachs	SA2-340	338cc	Tillotson	HR			Salsbury 910	10⅜	702055
450SX........	Sachs	SA2-440	437cc	Tillotson	HD			Salsbury 910	10⅜	702055
					1973					
300S.........	Sachs	SA290	293cc	Tillotson	HR	14:33	35-2	Precico	10½	702054
350S.........	Kohler	K340-2	338cc	Tillotson	HR	15:33	35-2	Precico	10½	702054
400SS........	Kohler	K399-2	399cc	Tillotson	HR	16:33	35-2	Precico	10½	702054
400L.........	Kohler	K399-2	399cc	Tillotson	HR	16:33	35-2	Precico	10½	702054
350SX........	Sachs	SA2-340	338cc	Tillotson	HR			Salsbury 910	10⅜	702055
450SX........	Sachs	SA2-440	437cc	Tillotson	HD			Salsbury 910	10⅜	702055

LUBRICATION

The engine is lubricated by oil mixed with the fuel. Recommended fuel/oil ratio is 24:1 for models with SACHS engines or 20:1 for models with KOHLER engines. Use a good grade of Regular Gasoline and ARIENS SUPER 2-Cycle Engine Oil. Mix fuel and oil thoroughly using a separate container before pouring the mixture into fuel tank.

The enclosed chain case should be lubricated weekly with Ariens Premium Moly-Lith Grease. Remove chain case cover and add about one tablespoon of grease using a wide knife. With cover removed, lubricate upper bearing through fitting using a pressure gun. Do not over-lubricate.

Pressure fittings are located on ski legs, front drive axle, rear idler axle and bogie wheels. Lubricate sparingly with pressure gun and low temperature grease (Ariens Premium Moly-lithium). Wipe off excess grease to protect track and sprockets.

Apply light engine oil to ski mounting bolts, tie rod ends, brake & throttle cables and handle bar as required for smooth operation. Refer to Fig. 1 for lubrication chart.

ADJUSTMENT

STEERING SKIS. Steering skis should be parallel with each other and with vehicle frame when handle bar is in normal straight driving position. Tie rods are of equal length and tie rod ends are equipped with right hand and left hand threads. Adjustment is made by loosening the lock nuts and turning center section. Adjust each tie rod an equal amount.

DRIVE CHAIN. The enclosed drive chain should have ⅛-¼ inch slack measured midway between sprockets with cover removed. Adjust by loosening the nuts on bearing housing bolts (A—Fig. 2) and the two locknuts on adjusting rod (B). Rock bearing housing clockwise to tighten chain or counter-clockwise to loosen chain. Realign drive belt and check brake adjustment after drive chain has been adjusted.

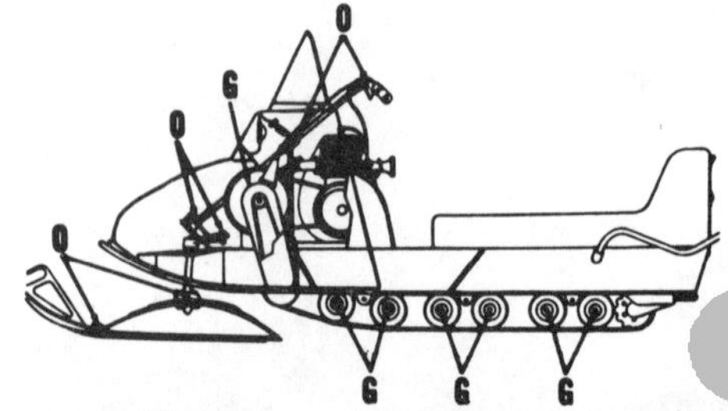

Fig. 1—Pressure gun fittings are located at points marked (G). Apply engine oil at points marked (O). Refer to LUBRICATION paragraphs.

BRAKE. The shoe type brake should just clear friction surface of driven sheave when brake lever is released, but should fully apply before lever contacts handle bar grip. Adjustment can be made at the two nuts which secure brake cable to actuating arm.

DRIVE BELT. The torque converter drive belt must be correctly aligned for proper operation and long life. Alignment must be checked whenever chain tension is adjusted, engine removed, or torque converter parts renewed.

To check drive belt adjustment, remove belt guard and lay a straightedge across inner flange of drive sheave. Measure clearance to nearest point of driven sheave rim, front and rear, as shown at (A & B—Fig. 3). Distance should be equal and measure ⅝ inch. Adjust by lengthening or shortening adjusting rod, using the two nuts (C).

TRACK. With rear of machine raised until track is clear of ground, top of track should sag ½-1 inch midway between drive and idler sprockets. To adjust track tension, loosen pivot bolt nuts (1—Fig. 4) a slight amount and turn adjustment bolts (2) equally until track tension is correct.

NOTE: Whenever track tension has been adjusted, alignment MUST be checked as outlined in TRACK SERVICE Section of this manual.

OVERHAUL

Refer to the appropriate paragraphs in the GENERAL SERVICE Sections of this manual for overhaul procedures of vehicle components.

On 1969 models, brake cable ends are looped and secured with clips (1—Fig. 5), and cable attaches to actuating arm by an eyebolt (2). Some 1970 models have a formed bar-end at lever end of cable and the eyebolt at actuating arm. Late models have a bar-end (4) at hand lever and threaded end (5) at actuating arm.

Upper drive sprocket is available in optional sizes from 13 to 20 teeth, and is interchangeable for all models.

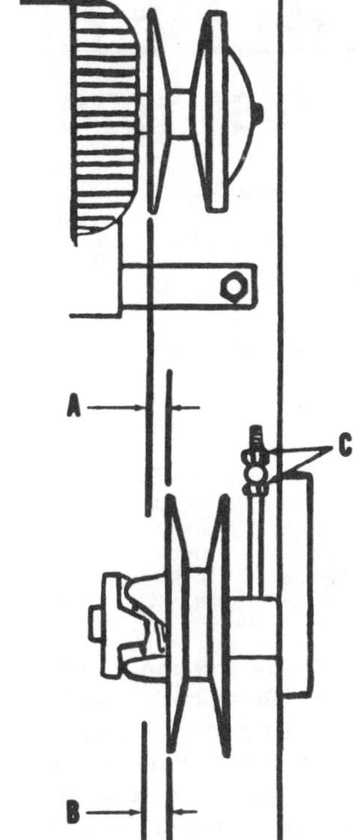

Fig. 3—To check drive belt alignment, lay a straight edge across inner rim of drive sheave and measure the distance (A & B) to driven sheave. (A & B) should be equal and measure ⅝ inch. Align by repositioning brace nuts (C).

Fig. 2—To adjust drive chain, loosen the nuts on three bearing housing bolts (A) and brace anchor (B; then turn bearing housing until correct chain tension is obtained.

Fig. 4—To adjust track tension, loosen the two pivot bolt nuts (1) and turn adjusting screws (2) until top of track sags ½-1 inch with rear of machine raised. Refer to text.

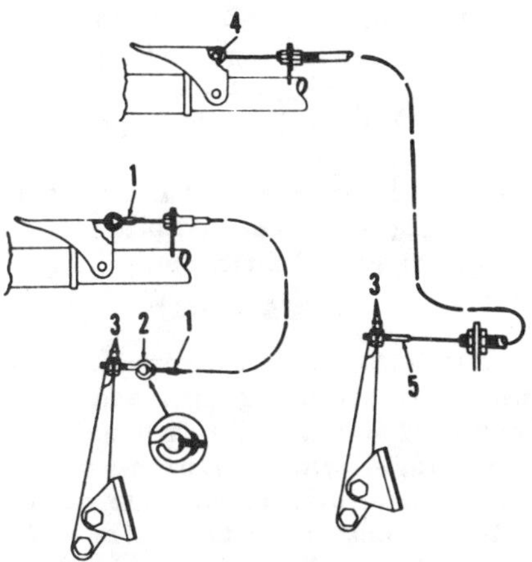

Fig. 5—Early type brake cable connections are shown at lower left, late type at upper right. Refer to text.

1. Cable clip
2. Eyebolt
3. Adjusting nuts
4. Bar end
5. Threaded end

ARLBERG

1969-1970

	Engine			Carburetor				Clutch		
Model	Make	Model	Displ.	Make	Model	Sprocket Ratio	Chain Size	Make	Shaft Center	Belt Number
					1969					
20	Sachs	SA290	297cc	Tillotson	HR29A	11:26	40	Featherw't	11.1	76-8
20E	Sachs	SA290	297cc	Tillotson	HR29A	11:26	40	Featherw't	11.1	76-8
25	Sachs	SA370	368cc	Tillotson	HR29A	13:28	40	Featherw't	11.1	76-8
25E	Sachs	SA370	368cc	Tillotson	HR29A	13:28	40	Featherw't	11.1	76-8
25EWT	Sachs	SA370	368cc	Tillotson	HR29A	11:26	40	Featherw't	11.1	76-8
					1970					
15	Sachs	SA280	277cc	Tillotson	HR52A	11:26	40	Featherw't	11.1	76-8
20	Sachs	SA290	293cc	Tillotson	HR52A	11:26	40	Featherw't	11.1	76-8
25WT	Kohler	K399-2	399cc	Tillotson	HR52A	13:26	40	Featherw't	11.1	76-8
25EWT	Kohler	K399-2	399cc	Tillotson	HR52A	13:26	40	Featherw't	11.1	76-8
Magnum 340	Sachs	SA340SS	336cc	Tillotson	HD29A	14:27	40	Featherw't	11.1	76-8

LUBRICATION

The engine is lubricated by oil mixed with the fuel. Recommended fuel-oil ratio is 25:1, using regular gasoline and a reputable Heavy Duty SAE30 or SAE40 Motor Oil.

The drive chain is enclosed and runs in an oil bath. Tip machine on right side and remove cover (C—Fig. 1). The chain case should contain about ½-pint of SAE 20 Motor Oil.

Ski legs are equipped with pressure fittings and should be lubricated occasionally with Low Temperature Grease.

Track drive axles and bogie wheels are equipped with sealed bearings and do not require lubrication.

ADJUSTMENT

STEERING SKIS. Disconnect tie rod from left steering arm and adjust length of rod as necessary until skis are parallel when pointing straight ahead. Steering arms are interchangeable and both have two holes at free (rear) end. Tie rod must be installed in forward hole of both steering arms. Drag link attaches to rear hole of right steering arm. Shorten or lengthen drag link if necessary, until handle bar is in normal straight driving position with both skis pointing straight ahead.

DRIVE CHAIN. The roller drive chain should have a minimum amount of slack but no tension. Adjustment can be measured by checking the backlash (A—Fig. 1) at pulley rim. Adjustment is correct when backlash (A) is approximately ⅜-inch. Adjust by loosening the locknut and turning idler adjusting screw (B) until backlash is correct.

BRAKE. A shoe-type brake is used as shown in Fig. 1. Brake is adjusted at cable housing anchor as shown in Fig. 2. Make sure brake does not drag when lever is released but is fully engaged before lever contacts handlebar grip.

TRACK. To adjust track tension, raise rear of vehicle until track is clear of ground. Refer to Fig. 3 and measure the distance (A-B) from lower edge of rear idler bearing housing to edge of frame. Distance should be 3¾ inches and equal on both sides. To adjust the track, loosen the two clamp bolts (1) and turn adjusting bolt (2) until tension is correct.

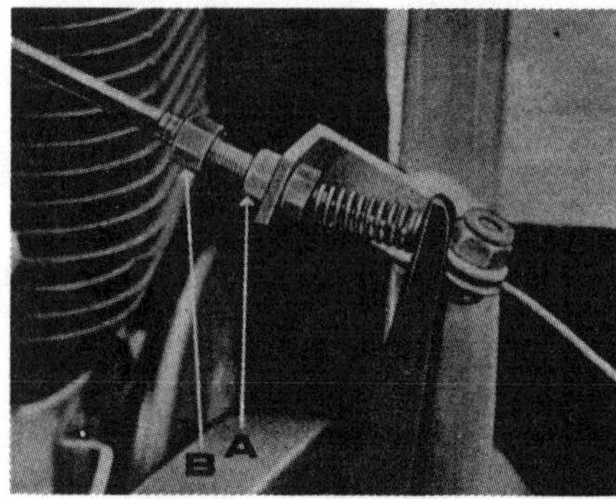

Fig. 2—To adjust the brake, loosen locknut (A) and turn connector (B).

Fig. 1—View of converter unit, brake & enclosed chain case showing points of adjustment.

A. Backlash
B. Adjusting bolt
C. Side cover
L. Brake lever
S. Brake shoe

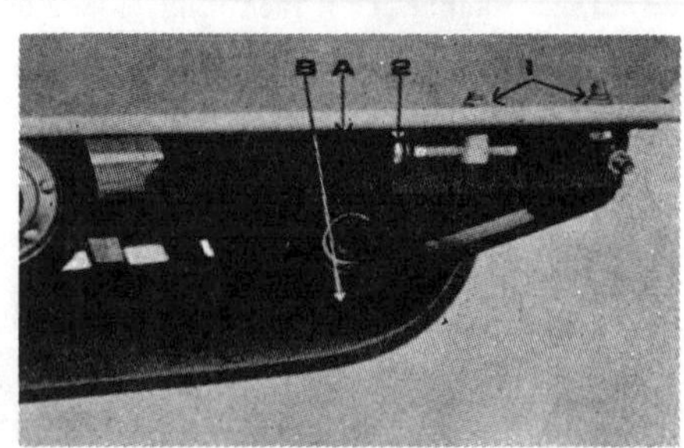

Fig. 3—With rear of vehicle raised, measure distance (A-B) from lower edge of rear idler bearing housing to edge of frame. Distance should be 3¾ inches and equal on both sides. Adjust by loosening clamp bolts (1) and turning adjusting bolt (2).

AUTO SKI

1971-1975

	Engine			Carburetor				Clutch		
Model	Make	Model	Displ.	Make	Model	Sprocket Ratio	Chain Size	Make	Shaft Center	Belt Number
					1971					
Mini Jet	CCW	225	226cc	Tillotson or	Keihin	13:33	35-2	St. Law.	10½	460000
Midjet	Sachs	SA280	277cc	Tillotson or	Keihin	13:33	35-2	St. Law.	10½	460000
Bonanza	Sachs	SA290	293cc	Tillotson or	Keihin	13:33	35-2	St. Law.	10¼	460000
Camaro	Sachs	SA340	336cc	Tillotson or	Keihin	13:33	35-2	St. Law.	10½	460000
Spitfire	Sachs	SA2-440	437cc	Tillotson or	Keihin	15:33	35-2	St. Law.	10½	460000
Avenger	Sachs	SA2-340	338cc	Tillotson or	Keihin	15:33	35-2	St. Law.	10½	460000
Avenger	Sachs	SA2-440	437cc	Tillotson or	Keihin	15:33	35-2	St. Law.	10½	460000
Avenger	Sachs	SA2-740C	735cc	Tillotson or	Keihin	15:33	35-2	St. Law.	10¼	460000
					1972					
Midget "S"	CCW	225	226cc	Tillotson	HR	14:33	35-2	St. Law.	10½	460000
Midget "DL"	CCW	225	226cc	Tillotson	HR	14:33	35-2	St. Law.	10½	460000
Bonanza	Sachs	SA290	283cc	Tillotson	HR	15:33	35-2	St. Law.	10½	460000
Bonanza	CCW	292	290cc	Tillotson	HR	15:33	35-2	St. Law.	10½	460000
Camaro	Sachs	SA2-340	338cc	Tillotson	HD	15:33	35-2	St. Law.	10½	460000
Torino	CCW	440	398cc	Tillotson	HR	15:33	35-2	St. Law.	10½	460000
Spitfire	Sachs	SA2-440	437cc	Tillotson	HD	15:33	35-2	St. Law.	10¼	460000
Avenger 340	Sachs	SA2-340	338cc	Tillotson	HD	15:33	35-2	St. Law.	10½	460000
Avenger 400	CCW	400	398cc	Tillotson	HR	15:33	35-2	St. Law.	10½	460000
Avenger 440	Sachs	SA2-440	437cc	Tillotson	HD	15:33	35-2	St. Law.	10½	460000
					1973					
Midget 225	CCW	225	226cc	Tillotson	HR	13:36	35-2	St. Law.	10½	SV-135HP
Midget 290SGL	Sachs	SA290	293cc	Tillotson	HR	14:36	35-2	St. Law.	10½	SV-135HP
Midget 290TW	CCW	290/2	290cc	Tillotson	HR	14:36	35-2	St. Law.	10½	SV-135HP
Bonanza 290	CCW	290/2	290cc	Tillotson	HR	14:36	35-2	St. Law.	10½	SV-135HP
Bonanza 340	Sachs	SA2-340	338cc	Tillotson	HD	14:36	35-2	St. Law.	10½	SV-135HP
Bonanza 440	Sachs	SA2-440	437cc	Tillotson	HD	16:36	35-2	St. Law.	10½	SV-135HP
Spitfire 290	CCW	290/2	290cc	Tillotson	HR	14:36	35-2	St. Law.	10½	SV-135HP
Spitfire 340	Sachs	SA2-340	338cc	Tillotson	HD	14:36	35-2	St. Law.	10½	SV-135HP
Spitfire 440	Sachs	SA2-440	437cc	Tillotson	HD	16:36	35-2	St. Law.	10½	SV-135HP
Spitfire SS	Sachs	SA2-440C	437cc	Tillotson	HD	16:40	35-2	Comet		9815-3150
Mach 340	Sachs	SA2-340RX	338cc	Tillotson	HD	15:40	35-2	Comet		9815-3150
Mach 440	Sachs	SA2-440RX	431cc	Tillotson	HD	16:40	35-2	Comet		9315-3150
Mach 650	Sachs	SA3-650RX	647cc	Tillotson	HD	18:40	35-2	Comet		9315-3150
					1974					
Bonanza	Kohler	K295-1	294cc	Tillotson	HR	14:36	35-2	Drummond 700		
Bonanza	Kohler	K295-2AX	292cc	Walbro	WD	14:36	35-2	Drummond 700		
Bonanza	Kohler	K340-2AX	338cc	Walbro	WD	14:36	35-2	Drummond 700		
Bonanza	Kohler	K440-2AX	436cc	Walbro	WD	16:36	35-2	Drummond 700		
Spitfire	Kohler	K340-2AX	338cc	Walbro	WD	14:36	35-2	Drummond 700		
Spitfire	Kohler	K440-2AX	436cc	Walbro	WD	16:36	35-2	Drummond 700		
SS Free Air	Kohler	K339-2SS	398cc	Mikuni	VM(2)	16:36	35-2	Drummond 700		
					1975					
Spitfire 290	Kohler	K295-2AX	290cc	Walbro	WD	14:36	35-2			
Spitfire 340	Kohler	K340-2AX	338cc	Walbro	WD	14:36	35-2			
Spitfire 440	Kohler	K440-2AX	436cc	Walbro	WD	16:36	35-2			
SS440	Kohler	K440-2AS	436cc	Mikuni	VM(2)	16:36	35-2			
FA340	Kohler	K340-2RS	339cc	Mikuni	VM(2)	14:36	35-2			
FA440	Kohler	K440-2RS	436cc	Mikuni	VM(2)	15:36	35-2			

LUBRICATION

The engine is lubricated by oil mixed with the fuel. The manufacturer recommends using one quart of snowmobile oil to 5 gallons of regular gasoline (20:1).

Suspension wheels (bogie wheels) are equipped with pressure fittings and should be lubricated after each 50 hours, or oftener under adverse driving conditions. Steering linkage and handlebar bushing should be lubricated twice a month using low temperature type grease. Chaincase lubricant should be checked at least once a week.

ADJUSTMENT

STEERING SKIS. Steering skis should be parallel with each other and with vehicle frame when handle bar is in normal straight driving position.

DRIVE CHAIN. The roller drive chain should have approximately ⅛-¼ inch free play measured midway between sprockets. The need for adjustment can be determined by rocking the driven pulley and noting free movement (backlash).

Adjustment is made by loosening the locknut on adjusting bolt (A—Fig. 1) and moving the bolt in slotted hole. If bolt bottoms in slot before correct adjustment is obtained, remove the bolt

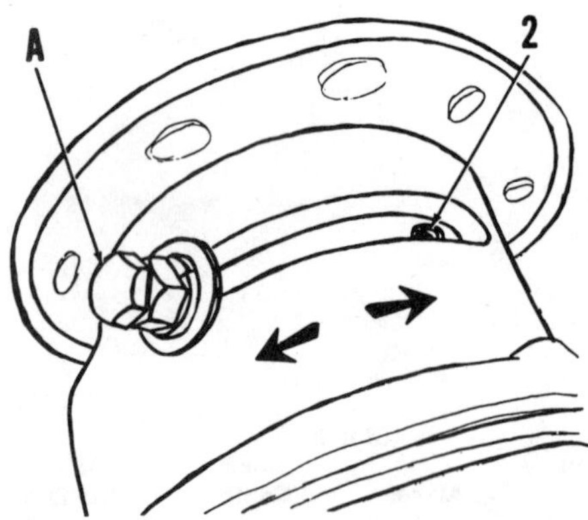

Fig. 1–To adjust the enclosed drive chain loosen jam nut and move adjusting bolt (A) in slotted hole. If adjusting bolt bottoms, move bolt to alternate hole (2) at opposite end of slot.

and reinstall in optional hole (2) which will have appeared in opposite end of slot. Tighten locknut securely when correct adjustment is obtained.

Brake alignment may need to be corrected after drive chain is adjusted. Loosen the two brake unit anchor bolts and fully compress brake lever on handlebar. Retighten anchor bolts while holding brake applied. Readjust brake if necessary.

BRAKE. The caliper type disc brake uses driven pulley fixed face as a braking surface. First make sure brake is properly aligned, then apply brake while retightening anchor bolts.

Brake adjustment should normally be made by tightening the actuating lever stud nut until brake pucks lightly contact sheave face, then backing off 1/6 turn.

BELT ALIGNMENT. The torque converter drive belt can be adjusted, if necessary, by loosening the engine mounting bolts and sliding engine to align belt.

To check the alignment, slightly separate the driven sheave and insert a ¼-inch spacer between sheave halves; then using a straightedge, align right edge of both pulleys.

TRACK. To adjust track tension, raise machine until track is clear, then measure clearance between track and center bogie wheels. Clearance should be 1-inch; or just enough to allow hand to slip into opening. Adjust by loosening clamp screws (1—Fig. 2) and turning adjusting bolt (2) as required. Both sides must be adjusted alike.

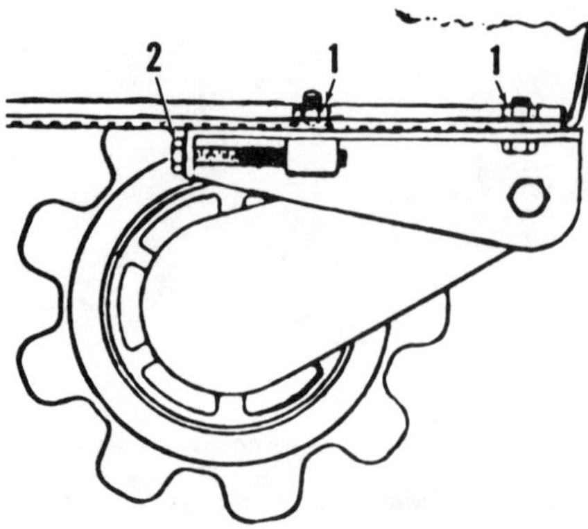

Fig. 2–To adjust track tension, loosen clamp bolts (1) and turn adjusting bolt (2) as required.

NOTE: Whenever track tension has been adjusted, alignment MUST be checked as outlined in TRACK SERVICE Section of this manual.

OVERHAUL

Refer to the appropriate paragraphs in GENERAL SERVICE sections of this manual for overhaul specifications and procedures.

BOA SKI

1968-1972

	Engine			Carburetor				Clutch		
Model	Make	Model	Displ.	Make	Model	Sprocket Ratio	Chain Size	Make	Shaft Center	Belt Number
					1968					
A-1	Hirth	54R	300cc	Tillotson	HR8A	10:21	40	Own		540
A-2	Hirth	54R	300cc	Tillotson	HR8A	10:21	40	Own		540
A-3	Hirth	54R	300cc	Tillotson	HR8A	10:21	40	Own		540
A-4	Hirth	160R	371cc	Tillotson		10:21	40	Own		540
A-5	Hirth	160R	371cc	Tillotson		10:21	40	Own		540
A-6	Hirth	170R	600cc	Tillotson		11:21	40	Own		540
					1969					
Standard 15	Hirth	55R	300cc	Tillotson	HR18A	10:21	40	Own		358
Standard 19	Hirth	191R	300cc	Tillotson	HR18A	10:21	40	Own		358
Deluxe 15	Hirth	55R	300cc	Tillotson	HR18A	10:21	40	Own		358
Deluxe 19	Hirth	191R	300cc	Tillotson	HR18A	10:21	40	Own		358
Deluxe 23	Hirth	200R	372cc	Tillotson	HD13A	10:21	40	Own		358
Deluxe 28	Hirth	220R	493cc	Tillotson	HD13A	10:21	40	Own		358
Deluxe 36	Hirth	171R	634cc	Tillotson	HD13A	11:21	40	Own		358
					1970					
Mark I	Hirth	82R	246cc	Tillotson	HR18A	10:23	40	Own		540HD
Mark II	Hirth	193R	292cc	Tillotson	HR35A	10:23	40	Own		540HD
Mark II	Hirth	192R	317cc	Tillotson	HR35A	10:23	40	Own		540HD
Mark II	Hirth	210R	399cc	Tillotson	HD13A	10:21	40	Own		540HD
Mark II	Hirth	211R	438cc	Tillotson	HD13A	10:21	40	Own		540HD
Mark II	Hirth	220R	493cc	Tillotson	HD13A	10:21		Own		540HD
Mark II	Hirth	194R	338cc	Tillotson	HR18A	10:21		Own		540HD
Mark II	Hirth	171R	634cc	Tillotson	HD13A	11:21		Own		540HD
Cobra	Hirth	210R	299cc	Tillotson	HR35A	10:21		Own		540HD
Cobra	Hirth	211R	438cc	Tillotson	HR35A	10:21		Own		540HD
Cobra	Hirth	194R	338cc	Tillotson	HR35A	10:21		Own		540HD
Cobra	Hirth	171R	634cc	Tillotson	HR35A	11:21		Own		540HD
Cobra	Hirth	230R	793cc	Tillotson	HR35A	11:21		Own		540HD
					1971					
Mk I	Hirth	193R	292cc	Tillotson		17:38	35-2	Own		540HD
Mk I	JLO	L295	292cc	Tillotson		17:38	35-2	Own		540HD
Mk II	Hirth	193R	292cc	Tillotson		17:38	35-2	Own		540HD
Mk II	JLO	L295	292cc	Tillotson		17:38	35-2	Own		540HD
Mk II	Hirth	194R	338cc	Tillotson		18:38	35-2	Own		540HD
Mk II	JLO	LR340/2	339cc	Tillotson		18:38	35-2	Own		540HD
Mk II	Hirth	211R	438cc	Tillotson		18:38	35-2	Own		540HD
Mk II	Hirth	220R	493cc	Tillotson		18:36	35-2	Own		540HD
Mk II	Hirth	171R	634cc	Tillotson		18:36	35-2	Own		540HD
Cobra	Hirth	211R	438cc	Tillotson		18:38	35-2	Own		540HD
Cobra	Hirth	220R	493cc	Tillotson		18:36	35-2	Own		540HD
Cobra	Hirth	171R	634cc	Tillotson		18:36	35-2	Own		540HD
					1972					
Mk O	CCW	225	226cc	Tillotson		10:23	40	Own		540HD
Mk I	Hirth	193R	292cc	Tillotson		17:38	35-2	Own		540HD
Mk I	Hirth	194R	338cc	Tillotson		18:38	35-2	Own		540HD
Mk I	Hirth	211R	438cc	Tillotson		18:38	35-2	Own		540HD
Mk I	Hirth	220R	493cc	Tillotson		18:36	35-2	Own		540HD
Mk II R/T	Kohler	K340-2	338cc	Tillotson		17:38	35-2	Salsbury 780		540HD
Mk R/T	Kohler	K440-2	437cc	Tillotson		18:38	35-2	Salsbury 910		540HD
Mk II W/T	Kohler	K440-2	437cc	Tillotson		18:38	35-2	Salsbury 910		540HD

LUBRICATION

The engine is lubricated by oil mixed with the fuel; the manufacturer recommends the use of BOA-SKI Two Cycle oil at the ratio of 20:1.

The enclosed chain case on 1969 models contains 8 ounces of lubricant and any low temperature grease is recommended. On 1970 Models, 8 Fluid Ounces of BOA-SKI Chain Lubricant should be used.

The rear axle bearings should be lubricated weekly during operation and before storage, using low temperature grease.

Torque converter driven unit shaft (countershaft) bearings require seasonal lubrication at fitting (L—Fig. 2). Use any good quality low temperature lubricant.

On 1970 models, the centrifugal weight unit of the converter drive sheave contains ½ ounce (1 Table spoon) of Automatic Transmission Fluid, Type "A". Fluid can be added if necessary, after removing cap screw and cover assembly.

ADJUSTMENT

STEERING SKIS. With handlebar in normal straight driving position, both skis should point straight ahead and center-to-center distance should be the same at front and rear of skis. Each drag link must be adjusted separately after disconnecting outer end.

DRIVE CHAIN. The roller drive chain should have a free play of ¼-inch. To check the adjustment, tip machine to right and remove chain case cover. On 1969 machines, adjust tension by tightening or loosening the two adjustment screws (A—Fig. 2). On 1970 machines, loosen the three bearing bolt nuts (1—Fig. 3) and turn adjusting screw (2).

BRAKE. The shoe type brake should clear fixed face of driven sheave when brake is released, but should be fully applied before hand lever contacts handlebar grip. To adjust the brake on all models, loosen cable lock screw (B—Fig. 2) and reposition brake lever arm on cable.

TRACK. On 1968 machines, distance (A—Fig. 4) from running board to lowest point of track idler bearing housing should measure 2⅞-3⅛ inches with rear of machine raised until track is clear of ground.

On later machines, tension is checked with machine resting on track. Upper section of track should deflect 1-1½ inches midway between sprockets when tested with fingers or a rule.

On all models, tension is adjusted by loosening clamp bolts (1—Fig. 4) and turning adjusting screw (2). Both sides must be adjusted alike.

NOTE: When track tension has been adjusted, alignment MUST be checked as outlined in TRACK SERVICE Section of this manual.

CONVERTER ADJUSTMENT. If slippage or excessive wear becomes apparent on drive belt, tighten converter spring by removing roll pin and slipping cam off shaft until it clears sliding plate. Turn sliding plate one ramp (⅓-turn) toward the rear to increase spring tension, then reinstall cam and roll pin.

OVERHAUL

SKIS AND STEERING. Skis, springs, steering arms and drag links are interchangeable from right to left but ski legs (spindles) are not. Skis are equipped with renewable wear bar and ski legs with renewable bushings.

ENGINE AND DRIVE. Refer to the appropriate general service section elsewhere in this manual for service on engine, torpue converter, track and brake assemblies and associated parts.

Drive (upper) sprockets are available with 9, 10, 11, 12, 13 and 14 teeth and driven sprockets with 20, 21 or 23 teeth. Sprockets can be changed to change drive ratio.

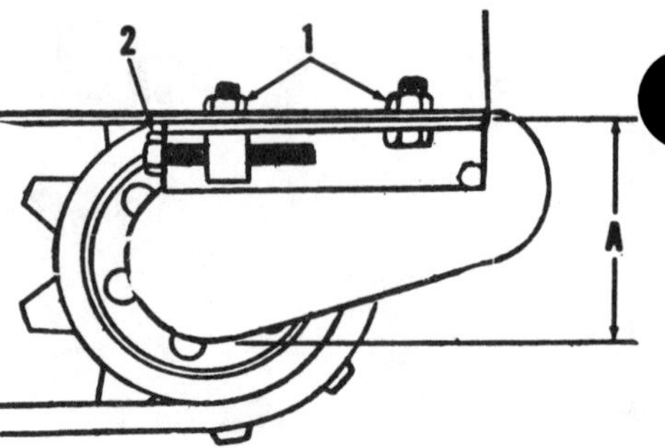

Fig. 4—To adjust track tension, loosen clamp screws (1) and turn adjusting screw (2). On 1968 models, distance (A) should measure 2⅞-3⅛ inches with rear of machine raised. On later models upper section of track should deflect 1-1½ inches with machine resting on track.

TORQUE CONVERTER. In 1970, drive unit is equipped with a "Safety Oiled" clutch cover which should contain ½ ounce of Automatic Transmission Fluid, Type "A" when unit is assembled.

Driven unit is torque sensing and should be pre-loaded two cams (⅔-turn) when unit is assembled. If excessive belt wear or slippage occurs, drive out the roll pin and turn outer cam an additional ⅓ turn.

Fig. 2—View of converter unit, brake and associated parts used on 1969 models, showing points of adjustment.

A. Adjusting screws
B. Brake cable lock screw
L. Lube fitting
W. Wingnut

Fig. 3—To adjust chain tension on 1970 machines, loosen the three bearing nuts (1) and turn adjusting screw (2).

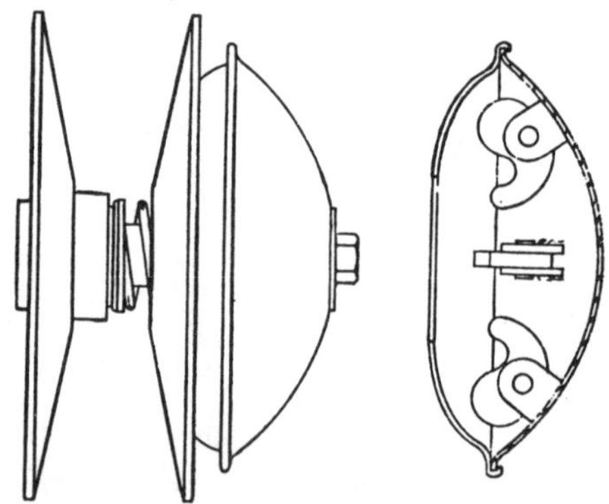

Fig. 5—Schematic view of BOA SKI "Safety Oiled" drive sheave used on 1970 models. Weight unit contains approximately ½ ounce of Type "A" Automatic Transmission Fluid.

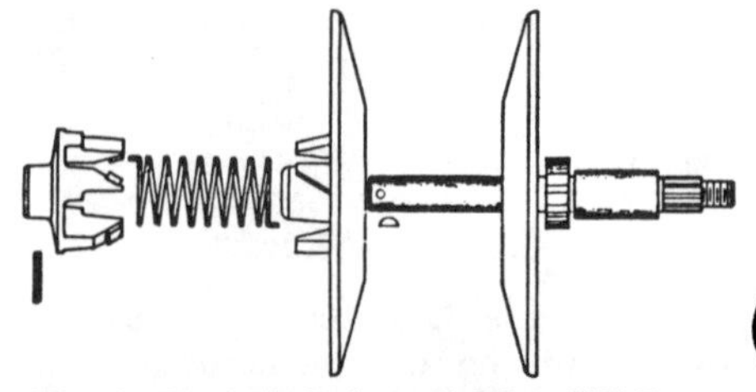

Fig. 6—Exploded view of BOA SKI Torque Sensing driven sheave.

BOA SKI

1973-1976

Model	Engine Make	Engine Model	Engine Displ.	Carburetor Make	Carburetor Model	Sprocket Ratio	Chain Size	Clutch Make	Clutch Shaft Center	Belt Number
					1973					
Mk I	Hirth	193R	292cc	Tillotson	HR88A	17:38	35-2	Own		S0901040
Mk I	Hirth	261R	291cc	Walbro	WD	17:38	35-2	Own		S0901040
Mk II R/T	Kohler	K340-2	338cc	Walbro	WD	17:38	35-2	Salsbury		S0901040
Mk II R/T	Kohler	K440-2	437cc	Walbro	WD	18:38	35-2	Salsbury		S0901040
					1974					
Mk 230	JLO	L230	223cc	Tillotson	HR88A	15:38	35-2	Own		S09-01-040
Mk I 292T	Kohler	K295-2T	292cc	Walbro	WD	16:38	35-2	Own		S09-01-040
Mk I 295	JLO	L295	292cc	Tillotson	HR88A	17:38	35-2	Own		S09-01-040
Mk II 292T	Kohler	K295-2T	292cc	Walbro	WD	16:38	35-2	Own		S09-01-040
Mk II 340T	Kohler	K340-2AX	338cc	Walbro	WD	17:38	35-2	Own		S09-01-040
Mk II 440T	Kohler	K440-2AX	437cc	Walbro	WD	18:38	35-2	Own		S09-01-040
S S 340T	Kohler	K340-2AS	338cc	Mikuni	VM	18:36	35-2	Comet C100		S09-04-040
S S 440T	Kohler	K440-2AS	437cc	Mikuni	VM	19:36	35-2	Comet C100		S09-04-040
					1975					
Mk I 292	Kohler	K295-2AX	292cc	Walbro	WRD33	17:38	35-2	Own		S09-01-040
Mk I 340	Kohler	K340-2AX	338cc	Walbro	WRD33	18:38	35-2	Own		S09-01-040
Mk II 292	Kohler	K295-2AX	292cc	Walbro	WRD33	17:38	35-2	Own		S09-01-040
Mk II 340	Kohler	K340-2AX	338cc	Walbro	WRD33	18:38	35-2	Own		S09-01-040
Mk II 440	Kohler	K440-2AX	437cc	Walbro	WDA-48	19:38	35-2	Own		S09-01-040
SS 340	Kohler	K340-2AS	338cc	Mikuni	VM(2)	18:36	35-2	Comet		S09-04-040
SS 440	Kohler	K440-2AS	437cc	Mikuni	VM(2)	19:36	35-2	Comet		S09-04-040
					1976					
Mk I 292	Kohler	K295-2AX	292cc	Walbro	WRD33	16:38	35-2	Own		S09-01-040
Mk I 340	Kohler	K340-2AX	338cc	Walbro	WRD33	16:38	35-2	Own		S09-01-040
Mk II 292	Kohler	K295-2AX	292cc	Walbro	WRD33	16:38	35-2	Own		S09-01-040
Mk II 340	Kohler	K340-2AX	338cc	Walbro	WF19	17:38	35-2	Own		S09-01-040
Mk II 440	Kohler	K440-2AX	437cc	Walbro	WF19	18:38	35-2	Comet 102C		S09-04-040
SS 340	Kohler	K340-2AS	338cc	Mikuni	36mm	18:36	35-2	Comet 102C		S09-04-040
SS 440	Kohler	K440-2AS	436cc	Mikuni	36mm	19:36	35-2	Comet 102C		S09-04-040

LUBRICATION

The engine is lubricated by oil mixed with the fuel. On KOHLER engines, use Premium Grade gasoline and an approved Snowmobile Oil mixed at a ratio of 40:1. On other engines, use Regular gasoline and Snowmobile Oil mixed at 20:1. A quality Air-Cooled, Two-Stroke Engine Oil can be substituted for Snowmobile Oil; do not use Outboard Motor Oil or Automotive Motor Oil as a substitute except for a short time in extreme emergency.

The enclosed chaincase should be lubricated at the end of each use season with low temperature, semi-fluid pressure gun grease as follows: Remove chaincase cover and gasket and wipe out excess grease using clean towels or rags. Thoroughly wash grease and dirt from chain and sprockets using a suitable solvent and air dry. Recoat chain and sprocket with new grease and place an additional pound of grease in housing and cover; then reinstall cover and gasket.

Rear track idler bearings, drive clutch hub, secondary shaft bearings, ski legs and speedometer cables contain pressure gun fittings on some models. Those points should be lubricated with Lithium type low temperature grease about once a week. Do not over-lubricate.

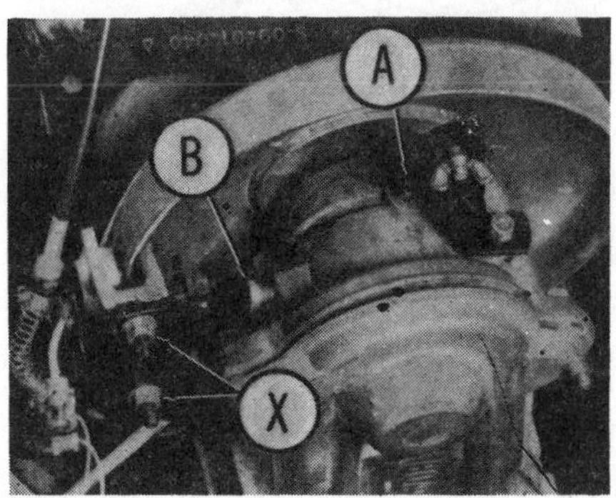

Fig. 1—View of chain case on Mk I and Mk II units showing points of adjustment.

A. Adjusting screw
B. Clamp screw
X. Brake caliper screws

ADJUSTMENT

STEERING SKIS. Steering skis should toe in 1/8-¼ inch when handlebar is in a normal straight driving position. Tie rods must be disconnected at one end to change tie rod length. Equalize the adjustment between the two tie rod ends and adjust both tie rods an equal amount.

DRIVE CHAIN. To adjust drive chain on Mk I and Mk II units, refer to Fig. 1. Chain tension can be considered satisfactory when backlash measured at driven sheave rim is 3/16-½ inch. If adjustment is required, loosen adjusting screw (A), clamp screw (B) and the two brake caliper mounting screws (X). Push screw (A) counter-clockwise in slotted hole until backlash is satisfactory, then tighten screws (A and B). Fully apply hand brake lever to realign caliper with pulley rim, then retighten caliper mounting screws (X).

On SS Models, refer to Fig. 2. The roller drive chain should have all measureable slack removed but should not be pre-loaded. To adjust the tension, remove case cover and loosen chain idler clamp screw (A), then turn tensioner screw (B) until tension is correct. Retighten clamp screw (A) and reinstall cover after adding lubricant as required. Chaincase is located on right side of engine compartment. Drive chain adjustment does not affect brake adjustment on these models.

BRAKE. On Mk I and Mk II units, the mechanical caliper type brake uses the fixed face of driven sheave as a friction surface. Caliper must properly align with friction surface and alignment is altered whenever drive chain is adjusted. To properly align caliper unit, refer to Fig. 1. Slightly loosen the two caliper retaining cap screws (X), fully apply the brake; then retighten cap screws (X) with brake applied. Check to see that caliper actuating lever contacts stop pin when operating lever is released and starts to move away from pin when operating lever is depressed. Adjust if necessary at brake cable housing anchor nuts. Brake wear adjustment is made by turning castellated nut on actuating lever stud.

SS models use brake disc mounted on cross shaft and a handlebar mounted hydraulic master cylinder. No adjustment is required. Keep master cylinder filled to within ¼-inch of top with automotive type brake fluid.

TRACK. With rear of machine raised until track is clear, approximately ½-inch of clearance should exist between track and center bogie, or track and center of slide. This amount of clearance will permit easy insertion of fingers as shown in Fig. 3. On models with bogie wheel suspension, track tension is adjusted by loosening clamp nuts (1—Fig. 4) and turning adjusting screw (2). Both sides must be adjusted alike.

On slide rail models, loosen locknut (1—Fig. 5) and turn adjusting bolts (2) to adjust track tension. Both sides must be adjusted alike.

On all models, track alignment MUST be checked after tension is adjusted, as outlined in TRACK & SUSPENSION Section elsewhere in this manual.

On slide rail suspension models only, adjustments are provided for ride and load control; refer to Fig. 6. Tightening upper eyebolt nuts (C) removes weight from skis and increases the percentage of load borne by the track. This results in increased traction at the expense of better steering control with the skis. Tightening lower eyebolt nuts (L) stiffens the suspension and prevents "bottoming" under heavy loads. The nuts should be tightened for heavier loads or loosened for lighter loads. Equal adjustment MUST be made at (C) and (L) for BOTH sides of machine.

OVERHAUL

Refer to the individual component SERVICE SECTIONS elsewhere in this manual for overhaul data and specifications of major components.

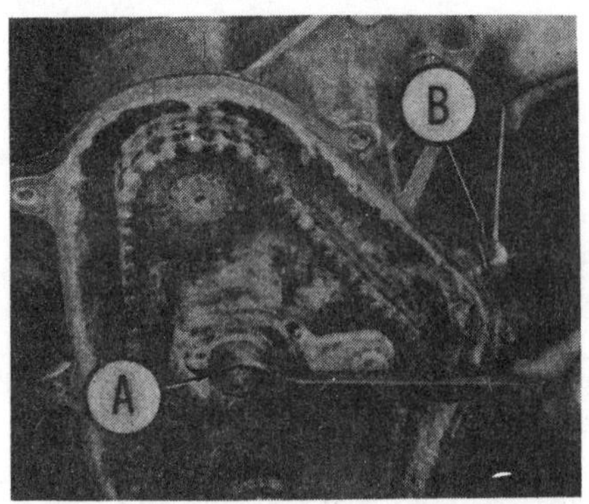

Fig. 2—View of Model SS chain case with cover removed, showing idler clamp screw (A) and adjusting screw (B). Chain case is on right side, driven by a cross shaft from torque converter driven sheave.

Fig. 3—Track tension is correct when clearance midway at bottom of track is approximately ½-inch. This clearance permits snug insertion of fingers as shown between track and center bogie wheel or track and slide rail.

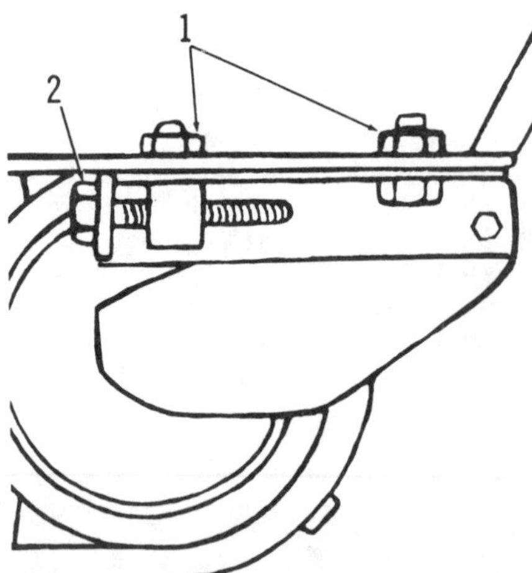

Fig. 4—To adjust track tension on bogie wheel models, loosen clamp nuts (1) and turn adjusting screw (2).

Fig. 5—To adjust track tension on slide rail models, loosen locknuts (1) and turn adjusting bolts (2) to tighten or loosen track.

Fig. 6—Eyebolt nuts (C and L) adjust for control and load. Upper nuts (C) determine weight distribution between front of track and skis, while lower nuts (L) are adjusted for weight of load. Refer to text.

BOATEL (GRAND PRIX)

1965-1972

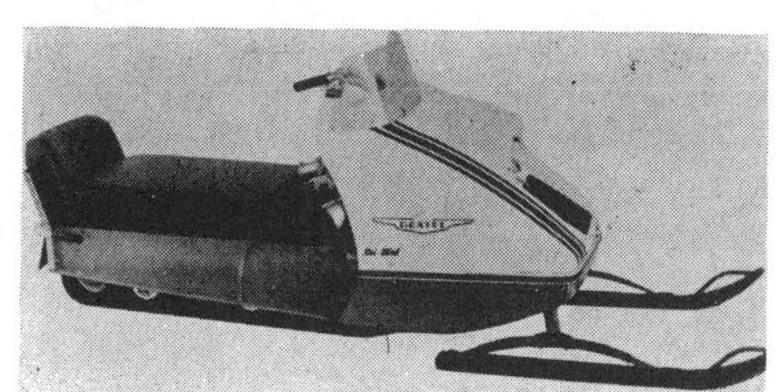

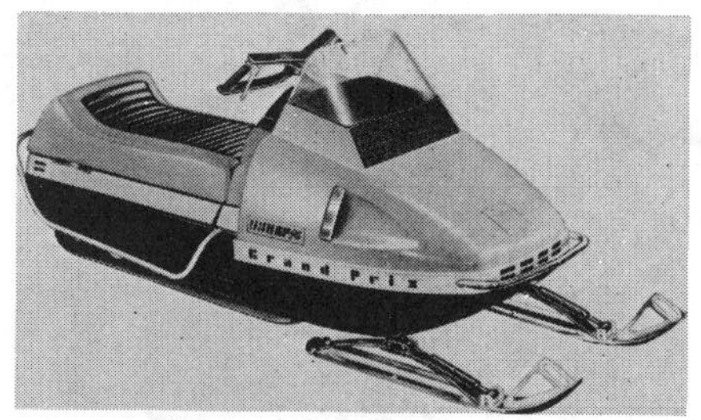

Model	Engine Make	Engine Model	Engine Displ.	Carburetor Make	Carburetor Model	Sprocket Ratio	Chain Size	Clutch Make	Clutch Shaft Center	Belt Number
					1965					
Trailmaker....	Kohler	K141	16.2ci	Carter	N			Salsbury		900043
Trailmaker....	Kohler	K181	18.6ci	Carter	N			Salsbury		900043
					1966					
Bulldog 8.....	Kohler	K181	18.6ci	Carter	N					11838
Bulldog 13....	Hirth	05	300cc	Tillotson						11838
Ski-Bird 8....	Kohler	K181	18.6ci	Carter	N					11838
Ski-Bird 13...	Hirth	05	300cc	Tillotson						11838
					1967					
Trailmaker 8..	Kohler	K181	18.6ci	Carter	N			Salsbury		900043
Trailmaker 13.	Hirth	05	300cc	Tillotson	HR8A					11838
Ski-Bird 8....	Kohler	K181	18.6ci	Carter	N			Borg Warner		135
Ski-Bird 11...	Hirth	82R	246cc	Tillotson	HR3A			Borg Warner		135
Ski-Bird 15...	Hirth	05	300cc	Tillotson	HR3A			Borg Warner		135
Ski-Bird 17...	JLO	L372	372cc	Tillotson	HD14A			Borg Warner		135
Ski-Bird XL...	Hirth	05	300cc	Tillotson	HR3A			Borg Warner		135
					1968					
Ski-Bird 246..	Hirth	82R2	246cc	Tillotson	HR3A			Salsbury		702698
Ski-Bird......	Hirth	05	300cc	Tillotson	HR3A			Salsbury		702698
Ski-Bird 371..	Hirth	016	372cc	Tillotson	HD6A			Salsbury		702698
Ski-Bird 494..	Hirth	018	493cc	Tillotson	HR3A(2)					
Ski-Bird 600..	Hirth	017	598cc	Tillotson	HR3A(2)			Salsbury		702874
					1969					
150 Deluxe....	Hirth	82R2	246cc	Tillotson	HR3A			Own		
200 Deluxe....	Hirth		300cc	Tillotson	HR19A			Salsbury 790	10¼	702698
250 Deluxe....	Hirth	160R	372cc	Tillotson	HD14A			Salsbury 790	10¼	702698
200 XL.......	Hirth	190R	300cc	Tillotson	HR19A			Salsbury 790	10¼	702698
250 XL.......	Hirth	160R	372cc	Tillotson	HD14A			Salsbury 790	10¼	702698
380 XL.......	Hirth	017	598cc	Tillotson	HR3A(2)			Salsbury 1195	12½	702874
					1970					
440..........	JLO	LR440/2	434cc	Tillotson	HR	18:37	35-2	Salsbury 910	10¼	02109
760..........	JLO	LR760/2	744cc	Tillotson	HD	22:37	35-2	Salsbury 910	10¼	02109
					1971					
400..........	CCW	400	398cc	Tillotson	HR94A	18:37	35-2	Salsbury 910	10¼	02109
					1972					
Mk II.........	CCW	400	398cc	Tillotson	HR94A	18:37	35-2	Salsbury 910	10¼	02109
Mk III........	CCW	440	436cc	Tillotson	HD	18:37	35-2	Salsbury 910	10¼	02109

LUBRICATION

In Kohler engine, oil level must be maintained at full mark on dipstick. Two cycle engines are lubricated by oil mixed with the fuel. The vehicle manufacturer recommends a fuel-oil ratio of 20:1 for the first 20 hours and 25:1 thereafter, using a good quality two cycle, two stroke or outboard motor oil.

The drive chain should be lubricated every 10 hours with 10W oil or STP lubricant. Do not over lubricate, but do not allow chain to run dry.

Drive and suspension parts of machine are equipped with self-lubricating bearings or bushings and do not require attention.

The transmission or chain case should contain approximately ½ pint of Automatic Transmission Fluid Type A, or SAE 10W Motor Oil.

Steering shaft and bushings should be lubricated with a few drops of engine oil occasionally. Track bearings are sealed type and do not require lubrication.

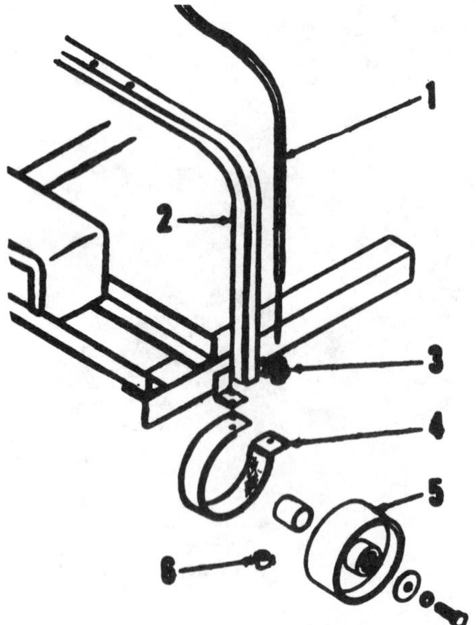

Fig. 1—Exploded view of band type brake. Drum (5) mounts on end of track drive shaft.

1. Brake cable
2. Engine frame
3. Adjuster
4. Band
5. Drum
6. Clamp

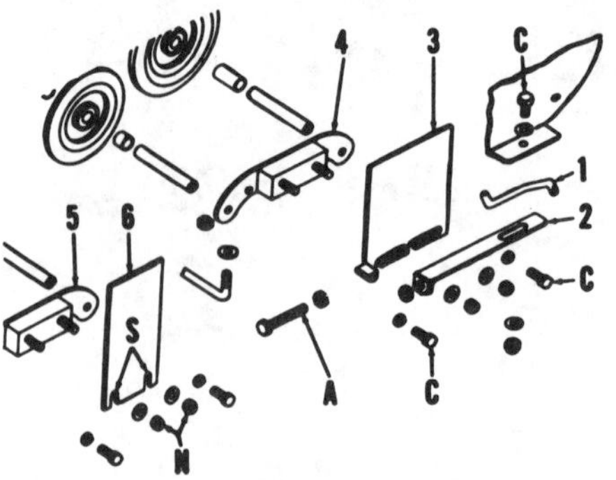

Fig. 2—Exploded view of track suspension. Bogie wheel hangers (5) can be moved up and down in slots (S).

A. Adjusting screws
C. Capscrews
N. Nuts
S. Slots
1. Torsion bar
2. Bracket
3. Rear plate
4. Rear Hanger
5. Front plate
6. Front plate

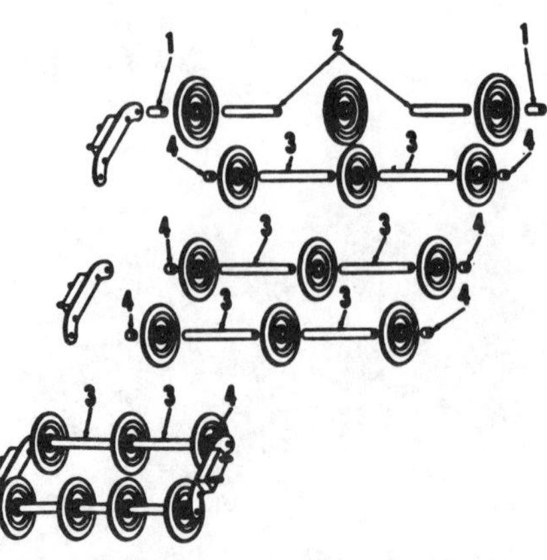

Fig. 3—Exploded view of bogie wheels and associated parts. Front spacers are 4⅜ and 5 22/32 inches in length. Other spacers are as follows.

1. 1⅝ in.
2. 6$\frac{11}{16}$ in.
3. 8 5/32 in.
4. ¼ in.

ADJUSTMENT

STEERING SKIS. A toe-in of ¼-inch, measured at tips of skis, is recommended. Tie rods can be adjusted after disconnecting either end. Because both tie rods should be adjusted to equal length, disconnecting at the common center end is recommended.

DRIVE BELT. The torque converter drive belt tension should be adjusted so that, by squeezing the belt midway between pulleys, the two sides will come within 1½-2 inches of touching. Adjust by loosening the four engine mounting bolts and sliding engine. Be sure pulleys are parallel and belt centers aligned after adjustment has been made.

DRIVE CHAIN. On models with reversing transmission, the drive chain is not adjustable. On other models, adjustment is provided by slotted holes in bearing plate on pulley side of case. Chain tension is correct when deflection is approximately ½-inch midway between sprockets or backlash is ½-¾ inch, measured at driven pulley rim.

BRAKE. The band type brake contracts around an external drum mounted on left end of track drive axle as shown in Fig. 1. Drum should be completely free to turn when brake is released, but should be fully applied before operating lever contracts steering grip. Adjust the brake at the two nuts securing lower cable housing anchor.

The shoe type brake uses the fixed flange of torque converter driven sheave as a friction face. Brake shoe should clear sheave by approximately 1/16 inch. Adjustment is made at cable housing anchor. Refer also to BRAKE paragraph in TRACK DRIVE section of this manual.

TRACK. On models before 1970, raise rear of machine so that track is clear of ground, track should clear center bogie wheels 1½-2 inches. Adjust by loosening the two nuts on each side which secure rear track axle hanger brackets, then turning the adjusting screws until adjustment is correct. Both sides must be adjusted alike.

On 1970, 1971 and 1972 models, suspend rear of machine so that track is clear of ground. Track should not sag more than ¼-inch. Adjust by loosening the clamp screws securing rear bogie assembly to frame and tightening adjusting screws equally.

Track suspension unit frames are rubber mounted, solidly bolted to vehicle frame. Mounting holes for rear unit are horizontally slotted for track adjustment. The two front units mount in vertical slots; refer to Fig. 2. The slotted holes are primarily for ease in assembly. They also provide some adjustment for vehicle control. The recommended normal adjustment is to adjust the two front suspension units to a plane even with skis and rear idler wheels when unloaded vehicle is setting on a level surface. (This adjustment is attained when mounting bolts are at top of slots on 1971 machine, slightly below top in earlier sleds). Lowering the front suspension units will remove some weight from steering skis and may improve the machine's ability to operate in deep snow.

NOTE: On all models whenever track has been adjusted, alignment MUST be checked as outlined in TRACK SERVICE section of this manual.

OVERHAUL

Except for ski legs (spindles), steering parts are interchangeable from right to left. The Tillotson carburetor is equipped with a maximum speed limiting screw which may be set to limit throttle opening.

Bogie wheel spacers are of six different widths as shown in Fig. 3. Suspension frame units can be removed by loosening track tension and loosening the four clamping nuts.

Power-Pack frame assembly can be removed as a unit or parts may be removed individually. Refer to the appropriate Service Sections elsewhere in this manual for service on engine and drive parts.

Refer to the appropriate paragraphs in GENERAL SERVICE sections of this manual for overhaul specifications and procedures of vehicle components.

BOLENS

1964-1968

Model	Engine Make	Engine Model	Engine Displ.	Carburetor Make	Carburetor Model	Sprocket Ratio	Chain Size	Clutch Make	Clutch Shaft Center	Belt Number
					1964					
200	JLO	L152	148cc	Tillotson						
400	JLO	L252	247cc	Tillotson						
					1965					
Hus-Ski 200A	JLO	L152	148cc	Tillotson	HL167A			Own		H-706
Hus-Ski 444	JLO	L252	247cc	Tillotson	HL186A	9:36		Salsbury	10¼	54516
					1966					
Hus-Ski 444	JLO	L252	247cc	Tillotson	HL186A	9:36		Salsbury	10¼	54516
					1967					
Hus-Ski 444	JLO	L252	247cc	Tillotson	HL186A	9:36		Salsbury	10¼	54516
Diablo Rouge 500	Hirth	54R3	300cc	Tillotson	HR3A	9:26		Own		180-1047
					1968					
Diablo Rouge 502	Hirth	54R3	300cc	Tillotson	HR3A	9:26		Own		180-1047
Diablo Rouge 503	Hirth	54R3	300cc	Tillotson	HR3A	9:26		Own		180-1047

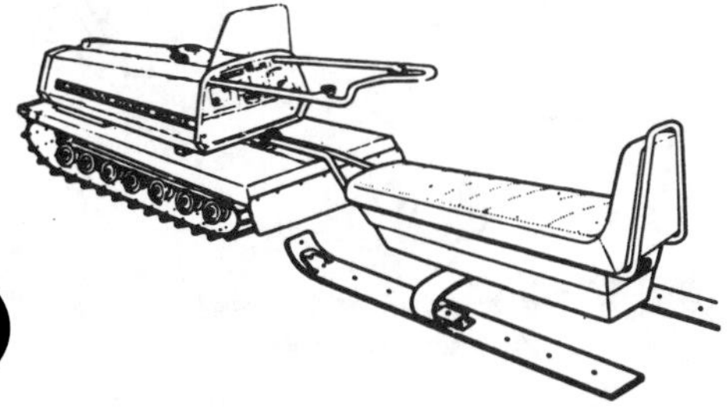

Fig. 1—Hus-Ski units consist of a powered prime mover and trailing sled as shown.

LUBRICATION

The engine is lubricated by oil mixed with the fuel.

Models 500, 502 and 503 Diablo Rouge are equipped with a chain case which must be filled to level of plug hole (P—Fig. 4) with SAE 10W Motor Oil. On all other models, the main drive chain is in the open and should be lubricated occasionally with a few drops of light oil. On models with open drive chain, it is recommended that when vehicle is stored the chain be removed, washed in kerosene or other suitable solvent, and stored separately by submerging in oil in a covered pan.

Track and drive bearings are sealed type and do not require lubrication.

ADJUSTMENT

DRIVE CHAIN. On models with open drive chain, refer to Figs. 2 and 3. Shaft bearing housing (3) pivots on support bolt (5) and is positioned by adjusting screw (4). To adjust the chain, loosen the nuts on support bolt and adjusting screw and turn adjusting screw until drive chain deflection is ½-inch, measured midway between sprockets.

On Diablo Rouge, refer to Fig. 4. Drive chain is adjusted by moving idler roller (4) into closer contact with drive chain (3), and adjustment cannot be directly measured. To make the adjustment, loosen locking nut (12) and slide axle bolt inward in slot until slack is removed.

BRAKE. Model 444 and Diablo Rouge are equipped with caliper type disc brakes as shown in Figs. 3 and 4. To adjust the brakes, remove the cotter pin and turn castellated nut (26) until pucks (14) are almost touching brake disc (16).

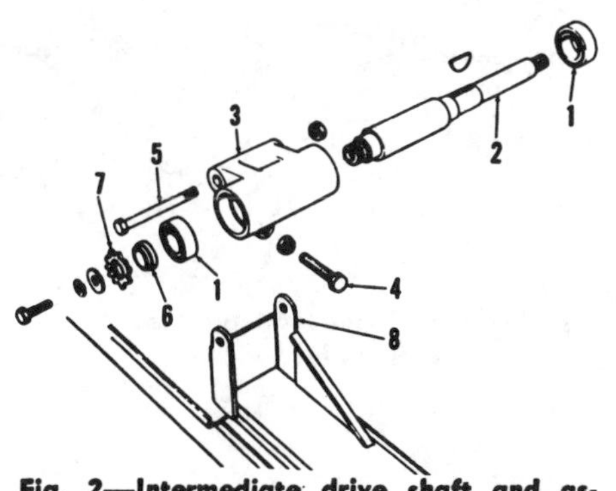

Fig. 2—Intermediate drive shaft and associated parts used on Model 600.

1. Bearing
2. Intermediate shaft
3. Bracket
4. Adjusting bolt
5. Pivot bolt
6. Spacer
7. Drive sprocket
8. Main frame

Some early models are equipped with a shoe and lever type brake which uses the back face of driven sheave fixed flange as a friction surface. Shoe brakes are not adjustable.

TRACK. Track adjustment is made at front on Diablo Rouge and at rear on other models. Both sides must be adjusted exactly alike, with some slack but not enough that track can easily be pushed upward into contact with deck pan. If track rubs side of drive or idler sprockets while in operation, tighten the opposite adjuster slightly until track centers on the sprockets.

OVERHAUL

Refer to the exploded views as a guide when removing or installing vehicle components, and to the appropriate service section elsewhere in this manual for overhaul procedures.

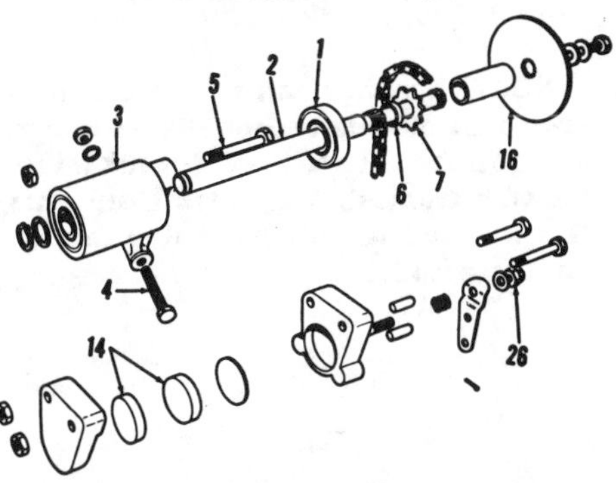

Fig. 3—Model 444 is similar to Model 600 except caliper type disc brake is added. Refer to Figs. 2 and 4 for parts identification.

Fig. 4 — Intermediate drive shaft, chain housing and brakes used on Diablo Rouge.

1. Cover
2. Spacer
3. Chain
4. Tightener
5. Gasket
6. Housing
7. Tightener nut
8. Drive sprocket
9. Spacer
10. Bearing
11. Intermediate shaft
12. Nut
13. Caliper housing
14. Brake puck
15. Spacer
16. Brake disc
17. Retaining ring
18. Washer
19. Cam housing
20. Push pin
21. Return spring
22. Return spring
23. Bracket
24. Adjusting cam
25. Clevis
26. Adjusting nut

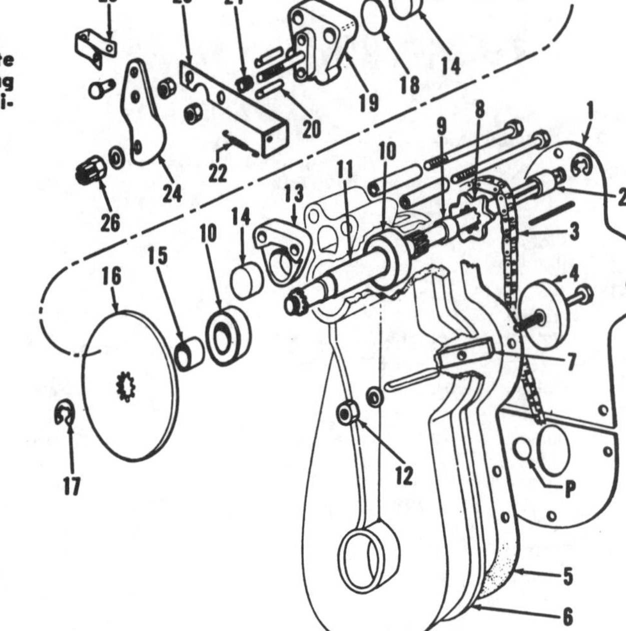

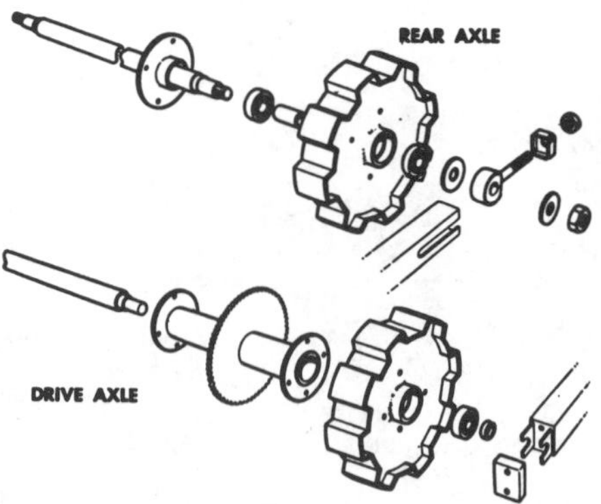

Fig. 8—Track axles and associated parts of the type used on Model 444.

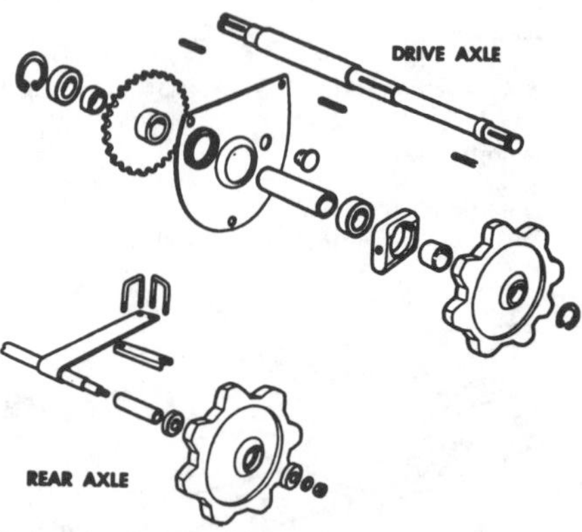

Fig. 9—Track axles and associated parts used on Diablo Rouge.

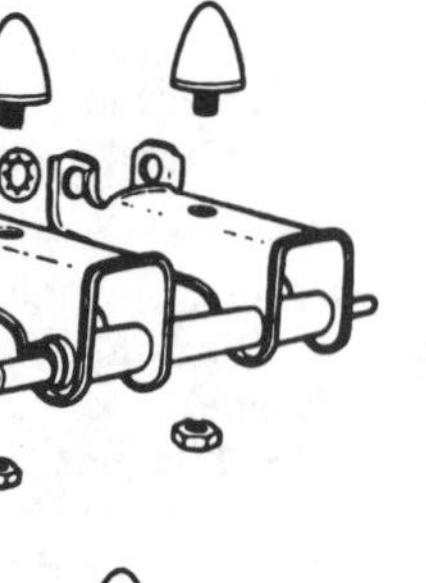

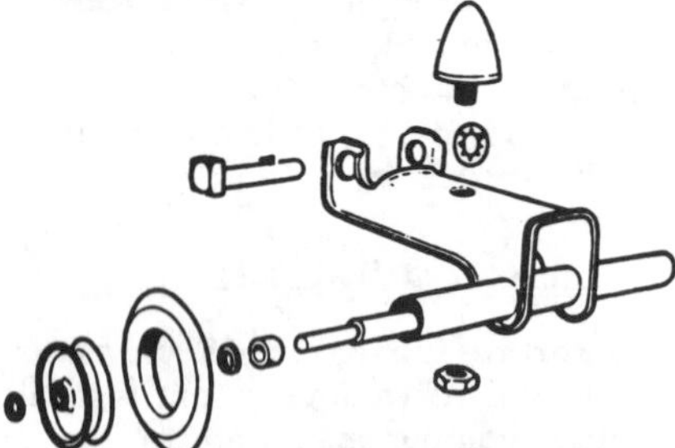

Fig. 5—Exploded view of bogie wheels used on Diablo Rouge.

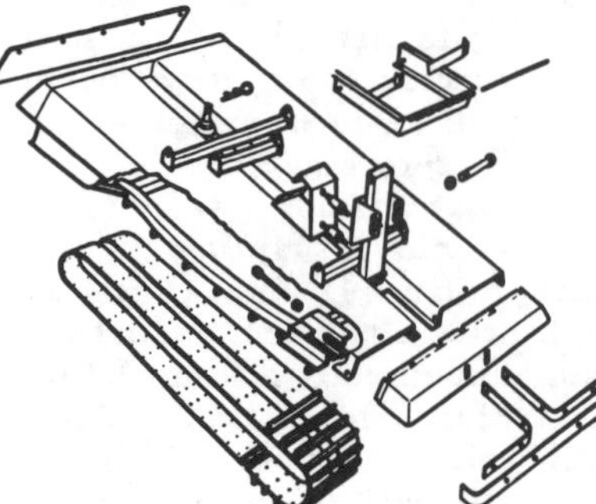

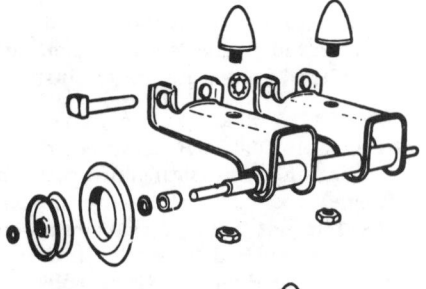

Fig. 6—Main frame and associated parts used on Diablo Rouge.

Fig. 10—Engine and drive compartment on DIABLO-ROUGE.

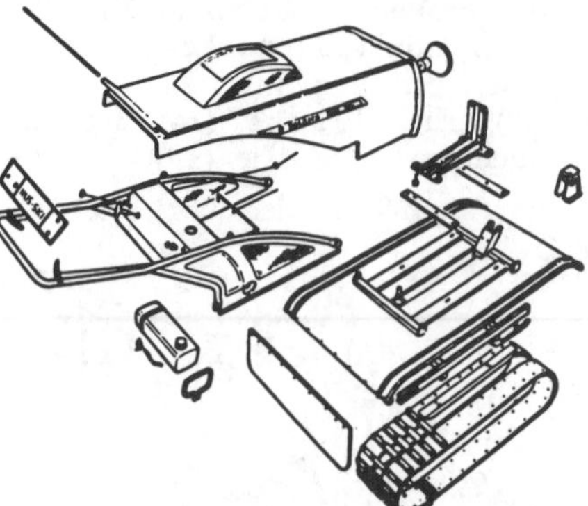

Fig. 7—Main frame and associated parts used on Model 444.

NOTE: Engines and torque converters on all models except Diablo Rouge are counter-rotating (clockwise, viewed from drive end). Keep this fact in mind when performing service on these units.

BOLENS

1969-1972

Model	Engine Make	Engine Model	Engine Displ.	Carburetor Make	Carburetor Model	Sprocket Ratio	Chain Size	Clutch Make	Clutch Shaft Center	Belt Number
1969										
Diablo Rouge 503	Hirth	54R3	300cc	Tillotson	HR3A	9:26		Own		180-1047
Sprint 620	JLO	L297	296cc	Tillotson	HR28A	12:30		Own		1805-306
Sprint 621	JLO	L297E	296cc	Tillotson	HR28A	12:30		Own		1805-306
Sprint 624	Bolens	2Z15	310cc	Tillotson	HR28A	12:30		Own		1805-306
1970										
S-295	JLO	L297	296cc	Tillotson	HR28A	12:30		Own		1805-306
TW315	Bolens	2Z15	310cc	Tillotson	HL279A(2)	14:30		Own		1805-306
S-340	JLO	L340	336cc	Tillotson	HR57A	14:30		Own		180-5306
TW-399	Kohler	K399-2	399cc	Tillotson	HR42A	18:35		Own		180-5306
TW-400	Kohler	K399-2	399cc	Tillotson	HR42A	18:35		Own		180-5306
1971										
TW-292 (80292-01)	Bolens	2Z15.70	310cc	Tillotson	HL279A(2)	12:28	35-2	Bolens		1805306
TW-295 (80295-01)	Bolens	2Z300	292cc	Tillotson	HR89A	14:30	35-2	Bolens		1805306
TW-340 (80340-01)	Bolens	2Z340	336cc	Tillotson	HR89A	14:30	35-2	Bolens		1805306
TR-399 (80399-01)	Bolens	3Z400	396cc	Tillotson	HR89A	17:35	35-2	Bolens		1805550
TR-440 (80440-01)	Bolens	3Z440	438cc	Tillotson	HR89A	18:35	35-2	Bolens		1805550
1972										
83293	Bolens	2Z300	292cc	Tillotson	HR89A	14:30	35-2	Salsbury		1806790
83295	Bolens	2Z300	292cc	Tillotson	HR89A	14:30	35-2	Salsbury		1806790
83340	Bolens	2Z340	336cc	Tillotson	HR89A	14:30	35-2	Salsbury		1806790
83433/WT	Kiekhaefer	440S	433cc	Tillotson	HD95			Salsbury		1807135
83440/WT	Kiekhaefer	440S	433cc	Tillotson	HD95			Salsbury		1807135
83440/SS	Kiekhaefer	440S	433cc	Tillotson	HD94A			Salsbury		1807135

LUBRICATION

The engine is lubricated by oil mixed with the fuel. Correct fuel-oil ratio is 20:1. Only regular gasoline and a branded Air Cooled Two Cycle Engine Oil is recommended.

Some models use a guarded, open drive chain which is automatically lubricated by a tube leading from crankcase bleed valve. Chain should be spray lubricated after storage and inspected regularly to see that end of tube is directly above center groove of lower chain sprocket and that tube is open and clean.

On models with enclosed chain case, fluid level should be maintained at lower housing plug opening using SAE 50 engine oil. SAE 90 Multipurpose Gear Oil may be substituted if SAE 50 oil is not available.

Ski legs (spindles) are equipped with pressure gun fittings and should be lubricated after each 25 hours with low temperature grease.

Drive train and track are equipped with self aligning sealed bearings which do not require lubrication.

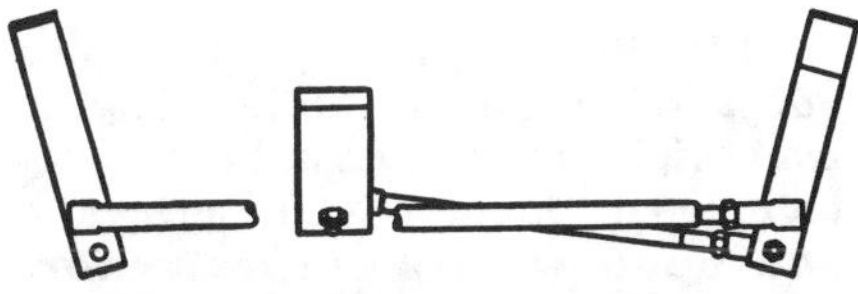

Fig. 2—Schematic view of steering arms, tie rods and drag link (early models) showing proper method of attachment. Later models use two identical tie rods and ski link (steering arm) has only one attaching hole; refer to Fig. 3.

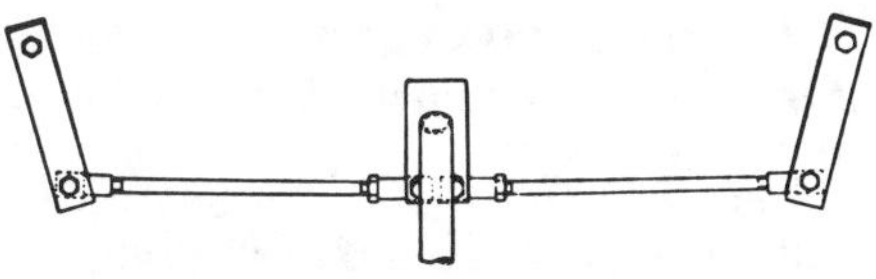

Fig. 3—Schematic view of steering arms and associated parts used on late models.

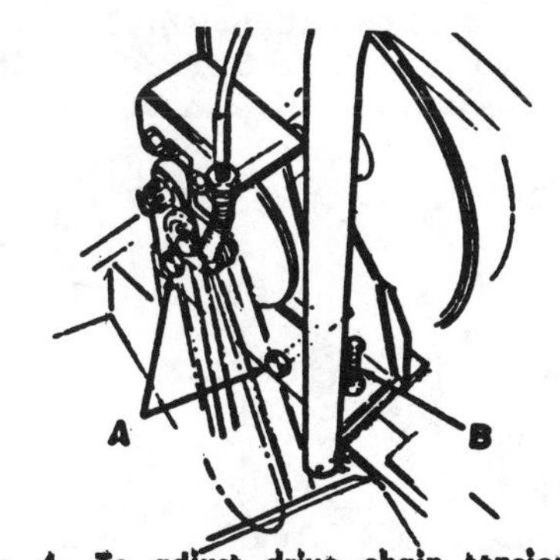

Fig. 4—To adjust drive chain tension on models with open chain, loosen the two bolts (A) and turn adjusting bolt (B) until tension is correct.

ADJUSTMENT

STEERING SKIS. Steering skis should be parallel with each other and with vehicle frame when handle bar is in a normal straight driving position.

Tie rod or drag link can be adjusted after disconnecting either end and steering arms are interchangeable from left to right side. On 1969 models, refer to Fig. 2. Connect tie rod to inner hole of both steering arms, and drag link to outer hole of right steering arm as shown.

On later models, two interchangeable tie rods are used as shown in Fig. 3. With handle bar properly positioned, disconnect either tie rod as required and adjust to correct length making sure threads are equalized on both ends of rod.

DRIVE CHAIN. Drive chain should have ¼-⅜ inch deflection measured from a straight edge midway between upper and lower sprockets. To adjust the open drive chain on models so equipped, loosen the two bolts (A—Fig. 4) and turn adjusting screw (B) until tension is correct. Retighten bolts (A) after completing the adjustment.

On models with enclosed drive chain, remove large plug (A—Fig. 5) to check tension and adjust by loosen-

Fig. 5—View of engine compartment on late machine showing points of adjustment.

A. Chaincase cover B. Adjusting screw C. Brake unit

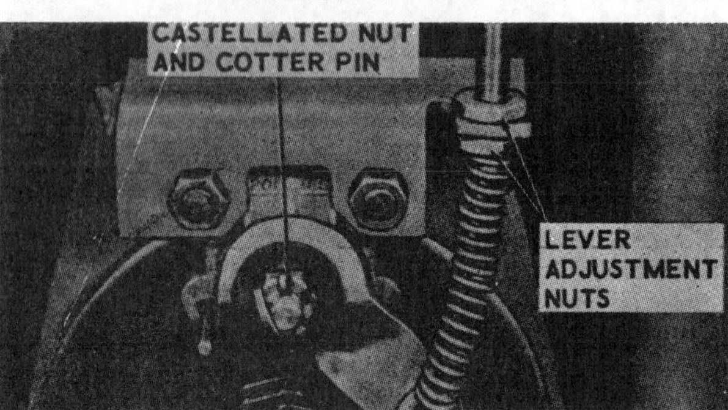

Fig. 6—Brake lever position is adjusted at cable anchor nuts. Wear adjustment is obtained by removing cotter pin and turning castellated nut to compensate for wear.

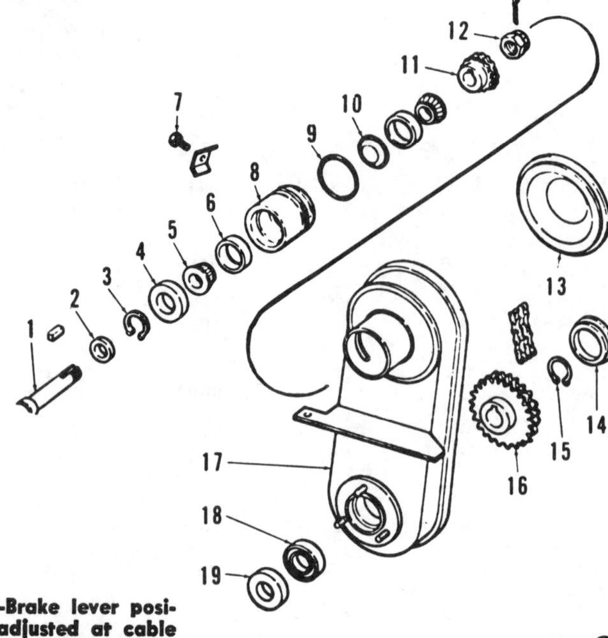

Fig. 8—Exploded view of chain case and associated parts used on models with enclosed chain.

1. Intermediate shaft
2. Spacer
3. Snap ring
4. Oil seal
5. Bearing cone
6. Bearing cup
7. Adjusting screw
8. Eccentric housing
9. O-ring
10. Disc
11. Drive sprocket
12. Nut
13. Upper cover
14. Lower cover
15. Snap ring
16. Driven sprocket
17. Chaincase
18. Bearing
19. Oil seal

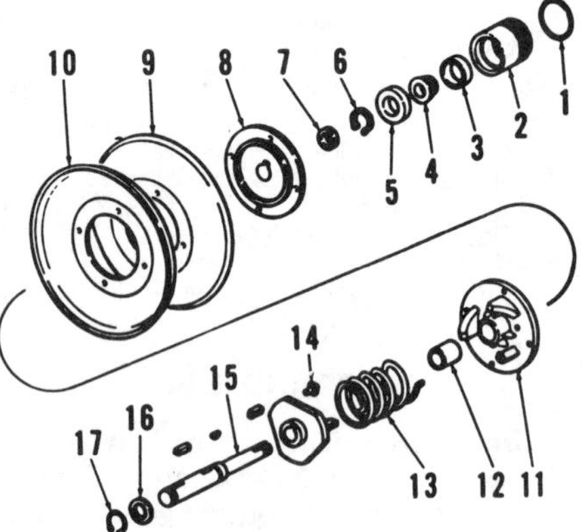

Fig. 10—Exploded view of torque sensing driven sheave.

1. O-ring
2. Eccentric housing
3. Bearing cup
4. Bearing cone
5. Oil seal
6. Snap ring
7. Spacer
8. Hub
9. Fixed flange
10. Moving flange
11. Floating hub
12. Bushing
13. Torque spring
14. Nylon shoe
15. Intermediate shaft
16. Thrust washer
17. Snap ring

ing cap screw (B) in eccentric housing. Push cap screw down in slot to tighten chain, or up to loosen. If cap screw bottoms in slot before slack is removed, install bolt in alternate threaded hole which has appeared at top of slot. Tighten cap screw securely and reinstall plastic plug when tension is correct.

BRAKE. Friction disc for the caliper type disc brake is combined with the main drive (upper) sprocket. on early models (see Fig. 6). Late models use fixed face of driven sheave as friction surface as shown at (C—Fig. 5).

Brake should not drag when released but should fully engage before hand lever touches handlebar grip. To adjust for wear, remove cotter pin (Fig. 6) and turn castellated nut until there is a slight drag on brake disc, back off one notch and reinstall cotter pin. Hand lever travel is adjusted at the two anchor nuts.

Fig. 7—To adjust track tension, raise rear of machine and loosen clamp screw nuts (1). Turn adjusting screws (2) equally until distance (D) is as outlined in text.

TRACK. To adjust track tension, raise rear of machine until track is clear of ground, then measure distance between running board and lowest point of swing arm as shown at (D—Fig. 7). Measurement should be 3-3½ inches for 1969 models; four inches for 1970 models and as follows for 1971 machines:

Models 295 & 340 ....4⅜ in.
Model 292 ....$4\frac{15}{16}$ in.

To adjust the track, loosen the two clamp bolts (1) and turn adjusting bolt (2) until measurement is correct.

NOTE: Whenever track tension has been adjusted, alignment MUST be checked as outlined in TRACK SERVICE Section of this manual.

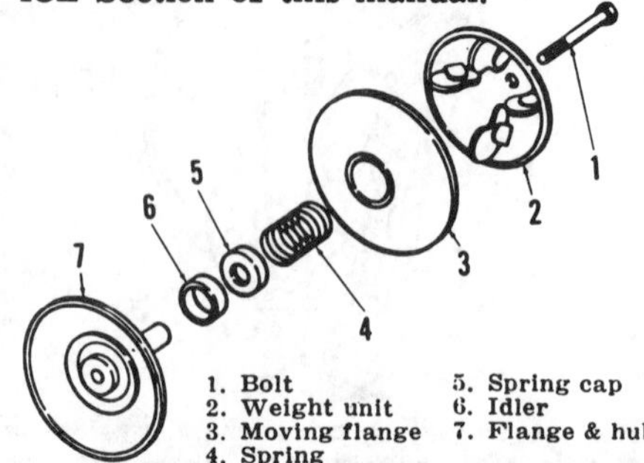

1. Bolt
2. Weight unit
3. Moving flange
4. Spring
5. Spring cap
6. Idler
7. Flange & hub

Fig. 9—Exploded view of centrifugal drive sheave used on BOLENS Sprint.

OVERHAUL

SKIS. Steering skis, spindles and associated parts are interchangeable from right to left. Skis have renewable wear runners. Ski springs are equipped with a conical rubber bumper which should be installed to rear.

IMPORTANT: DO NOT tighten locknut on bumper stud tight against spring leaf, or action of the spring will be restricted.

TORQUE CONVERTER. Refer to Fig. 9 for an exploded view of torque converter drive sheave and to Fig. 10 for driven sheave. Torque spring (13—Fig. 10) should be preloaded ⅓ turn (one cam) when unit is assembled.

CHAPARRAL

1968-1974

	Engine			Carburetor				Clutch		
Model	Make	Model	Displ.	Make	Model	Sprocket Ratio	Chain Size	Make	Shaft Center	Belt Number
					1968					
Chaparral	Hirth	55R	300cc	Tillotson	HR8A			Salsbury 790	10½	D100
Chaparral	Hirth	160R	372cc	Tillotson	HD7A			Salsbury 790	10½	D100
Firebird	Hirth	170R	600cc	Tillotson	HR2A(2)			Salsbury 1195	10½	D100
					1969					
Chaparral	Kohler	K309-1	309cc	Tillotson	HR22A	13:36	35-2	Salsbury 790	10½	D100S
Chaparral	Hirth	200R	372cc	Tillotson	HD7AX	13:36	35-2	Salsbury 790	10½	D100S
Chaparral	Kohler	K618-2	618cc	Tillotson	HR35A		35-2	Salsbury 1195	10½	D100FB
Firebird	Hirth	200R	372cc	Tillotson	HD7AX	13:36	35-2	Salsbury 790	10½	D100S
Firebird	Hirth	170R	600cc	Tillotson	HR2A(2)		35-2	Salsbury 1195	10½	D100FB
Snowgoer	Kohler	K618-2	618cc	Tillotson	HR35A		35-2	Salsbury 1195	10¼	D100FB
					1970					
300	Kohler	K309-1	309cc	Tillotson or	Keihin	15:36	35-2	Salsbury	10½	10542-1
300	Hirth	200R	372cc	T or K		15:36	35-2	Salsbury 770	10½	10542-1
Firebird	Sachs	SA340	336cc	T or K		15:36	35-2	Salsbury 770	10½	10542-1
Firebird	Hirth	210R	399cc	T or K		15:36	35-2	Salsbury 910	10½	10542-2
Firebird	Hirth	211R	438cc	T or K		15:36	35-2	Salsbury 910	10½	10542-2
Firebird	Hirth	220R	493cc	T or K		17:36	35-2	Salsbury 910	10½	10542-2
Firebird	Hirth	171R	634cc	T or K		17:36	35-2	Salsbury 1190	10½	10542-3
Executive	Kohler	K399-2	399cc	T or K		15:36	35-2	Salsbury 910	10½	10542-2
Executive	Hirth	210R	399cc	T or K		15:36	35-2	Salsbury 910	10½	10542-2
Executive	Hirth	211R	438cc	T or K		17:36	35-2	Salsbury 910	10½	10542-2
Executive	Hirth	220R	493cc	T or K		17:36	35-2	Salsbury 910	10½	10542-2
Executive	Hirth	171R	634cc	T or K		17:36	35-2	Salsbury 1190	10¼	10542-3
					1971					
Skylark	Hirth	193R	292cc	Tillotson	HR	15:36	35-2	Salsbury 770	10½	31650-1
Skylark	Hirth	194R	338cc	Tillotson	HD	15:36	35-2	Salsbury 770	10½	31650-1
Skylark	Hirth	200R	372cc	Tillotson	HD	15:36	35-2	Salsbury 770	10¼	31650-1
Firebird	Hirth	194R	338cc	Tillotson	HD	15:36	35-2	Salsbury 770	10½	31650-1
Firebird	JLO	LR340/2	339cc			15:36	35-2	Salsbury 770	10½	31650-1
Firebird	CCW	340	339cc	Keihin	406	15:36	35-2	Salsbury 770	10¼	31650-1
Firebird	JLO	LR399/2	398cc			17:36	35-2	Salsbury 910	10½	31650-2
Firebird	CCW	400	398cc	Keihin	406	17:36	35-2	Salsbury 910	10½	31650-2
Firebird	Hirth	211R	438cc	Keihin	407	17:36	35-2	Salsbury 910	10¼	31650-2
Firebird	Sachs	SA2-440	437cc	Keihin	407	17:36	35-2	Salsbury 910	10½	31650-2
Firebird	CCW	440	436cc	Keihin	407	17:36	35-2	Salsbury 910	10½	31650-2
Firebird	Hirth	220R	493cc	Keihin	407	17:36	35-2	Salsbury 910	10½	31650-2
Firebird	Hirth	171R	635cc	Keihin	407	19:36	35-2	Salsbury 910	10½	31650-2
Executive	JLO	LR340/2	339cc			15:36	35-2	Salsbury 770	10½	31650-1
Executive	CCW	340	339cc	Keihin	406	15:36	35-2	Salsbury 770	10½	31650-1
Executive	JLO	LR399/2	398cc			17:36	35-2	Salsbury 910	10½	31650-2
Executive	CCW	400	398cc	Keihin	406	17:36	35-2	Salsbury 910	10½	31650-2
Executive	Hirth	211R	438cc	Keihin	407	17:36	35-2	Salsbury 910	10½	31650-2
Executive	Sachs	SA2-440	437cc	Keihin	407	17:36	35-2	Salsbury 910	10½	31650-2
Executive	CCW	440	436cc	Keihin	407	17:36	35-2	Salsbury 910	10½	31650-2
Executive	Hirth	220R	493cc	Keihin	407	17:36	35-2	Salsbury 910	10½	31650-2
Executive	Hirth	171R	634cc	Keihin	407	19:36	35-2	Salsbury 910	10½	31650-2
					1972					
Skylark	CCW	248	249cc	Tillotson	HR	15:36	35-2	Salsbury 770	10½	41650
Skylark	Hirth	193R	292cc	Tillotson	HR	15:36	35-2	Salsbury 770	10½	41650
Firebird	Hirth	260R	338cc	Walbro	WR	17:36	35-2	Salsbury 770	10¼	41650
Firebird	CCW	340	339cc	Keihin	406	17:36	35-2	Salsbury 770	10½	41650
Firebird	Chaparral	400	394cc	Keihin	407	17:36	35-2	Salsbury 910	10½	31650-2
Firebird	CCW	400	398cc	Keihin	406	17:36	35-2	Salsbury 910	10½	31650-2
Firebird	Hirth	270R	438cc	Walbro	WD	17:36	35-2	Salsbury 910	10½	31650-2
Firebird	Chaparral	440	432cc	Keihin	407	17:36	35-2	Salsbury 910	10½	31650-2
Firebird SS	Hirth	261R	292cc	Walbro	WR	15:36	35-2	Salsbury 770	10½	41650
Firebird SS	Hirth	260R	338cc	Walbro	WD	17:36	35-2	Salsbury	10½	41650
Firebird SS	Hirth	271R	399cc	Walbro	WD	17:36	35-2	Salsbury 910	10½	31650-2
Firebird SS	Chaparral	400	394cc	Keihin	407	17:36	35-2	Salsbury 910	10½	31650-2
Firebird SS	Sachs	SA2-440	437cc	Keihin	407	17:36	35-2	Salsbury 910	10½	31650-2
Firebird SS	Hirth	270R	438cc	Walbro	WD	17:36	35-2	Salsbury 910	10½	31650-2
Firebird SS	Chaparral	440	432cc	Keihin	407	17:36	35-2	Salsbury 910	10½	31650-2
Firebird SS	Hirth	280R	649cc	Walbro	WD	19:36	35-2	Salsbury 910	10½	31650-2
Thunderbird	Hirth	260R	338cc	Walbro	WD	17:36	35-2	Salsbury 910	10½	31650-2
Thunderbird	Chaparral	400	394cc	Keihin	407	17:36	35-2	Salsbury 910	10½	31650-2
Thunderbird	Chaparral	440	432cc	Keihin	407	17:36	35-2	Salsbury 910	10½	31650-2
Thunderbird	Hirth	280R	649cc	Walbro	WD	19:36	35-2	Salsbury 910	10½	31650-2

	Engine			Carburetor				Clutch		
Model	Make	Model	Displ.	Make	Model	Sprocket Ratio	Chain Size	Make	Shaft Center	Belt Number
					1973					
Firebird......	Chaparral	248	249cc	Mikuni	38mm	15:36	35-2	Own*	Fixed	
Firebird......	Chaparral	295	292cc	Keihin	CD 42	15:36	35-2	Own*	Fixed	
Firebird......	Chaparral	340	338cc	Keihin	CD 42	17:36	35-2	Own*	Fixed	
Firebird......	Chaparral	400	398cc	Keihin	CD 42	17:36	35-2	Own*	Fixed	
Firebird......	Chaparral	440	432cc	Keihin	CD 42	17:36	35-2	Own*	Fixed	
SS III........	Chaparral	295SS	292cc	Keihin	CD 42	15:36	35-2	Own*	Fixed	
SS III........	Chaparral	340SS	338cc	Keihin	CD 42	17:36	35-2	Own*	Fixed	
SS III........	Chaparral	400SS	394cc	Keihin	CD 50	19:36	35-2	Own*	Fixed	
SS III........	Chaparral	440SS	432cc	Keihin	CD 50	19:36	35-2	Own*	Fixed	
Thunderbird...	Chaparral	340	338cc	Keihin	CD 42	17:36	35-2	Own*	Fixed	
Thunderbird...	Chaparral	440	432cc	Keihin	CD 42	19:36	35-2	Own*	Fixed	

*Asymetric Clutch. Recommended replacement is Salsbury 850 on 10½ center using Chaparral 31650-2 Belt.

	Engine			Carburetor				Clutch		
Model	Make	Model	Displ.	Make	Model	Sprocket Ratio	Chain Size	Make	Shaft Center	Belt Number
					1974					
Firebird 292...	Chaparral		292cc	Mikuni	BND 42	15:36	35-2	Salsbury 815	10½	741-650
Firebird 340...	Chaparral		338cc	Mikuni	BNO 42	17:36	35-2	Salsbury 815	10½	741-650
Thunderbird 440	Chaparral		432cc	Mikuni	BNO 42	19:36	35-2	Salsbury 815	10½	741-650
SSX 340	Chaparral		338cc	Mikuni	BNO 38(2)	19:36	35-2	Salsbury 815	10½	741-650
SSX 440......	Chaparral		432cc	Mikuni	BNO 42(2)	21:36	35-2	Salsbury 815	10½	741-650

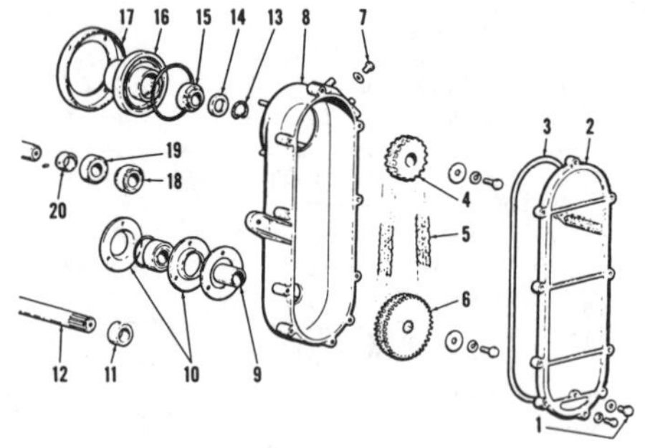

Fig. 1—Exploded view of "CHAPARRAL" chain case used on 1971 models and 1972 SKYLARK. 1970 model chaincase is similar.

1. Check plug
2. Cover
3. Gasket
4. Upper sprocket
5. Chain
6. Lower sprocket
7. Fill plug
8. Chain case
9. Spacer
10. Flangette bearing
11. Lock collar
12. Track drive shaft
13. Snap ring
14. Nut
15. Roller bearing
16. Eccentric housing
17. Lock ring
18. Roller bearing
19. Seal
20. Sleeve

LUBRICATION

The engine is lubricated by oil mixed with the fuel. The manufacturer recommends the use of Two Cycle Motor Oil at the ratio of 20:1.

The enclosed chain case on 1968 and 1969 models should be filled to level of check plug with Automatic Transmission Fluid, Type "A", and should be checked occasionally or when leakage is apparent.

All other parts are self lubricated and require attention only when service is needed.

On 1970, 300 Models, remove fill plug at top of chain case and insert a stiff wire to touch the bottom. Add Automatic Transmission Fluid, Type A, as necessary to bring fluid level to between 1 and 2 inches from chaincase bottom. On 1970 Executive and Firebird models, remove lower chaincase cover and add fluid if necessary, until level is ½-inch below cover opening.

On late models with "Chaparral" gearcase, check fluid level at plug (1—Fig. 1) and fill to level of plug opening at upper plug (7). Use automatic transmission fluid, type A.

The steering column on 1970, 300 Models has two lubrication fittings; Firebird and Executive have one lube fitting on steering column. All other parts are self lubricated and require attention only when service is needed.

ADJUSTMENT

STEERING SKIS. With handlebar in normal straight driving position, skis should be parallel with each other and with vehicle frame. Steering arms are splined to spindle and both arms should point straight to rear.

On early models all tie rod ends have right hand threads and adjustment is made by disconnecting one end. Late models have R.H. and L.H. threads and adjustment can be made by loosening locknut and turning rod center section.

DRIVE CHAIN. Drive chain should have ¼-½ inch free play. Chain can be inspected by removing chain

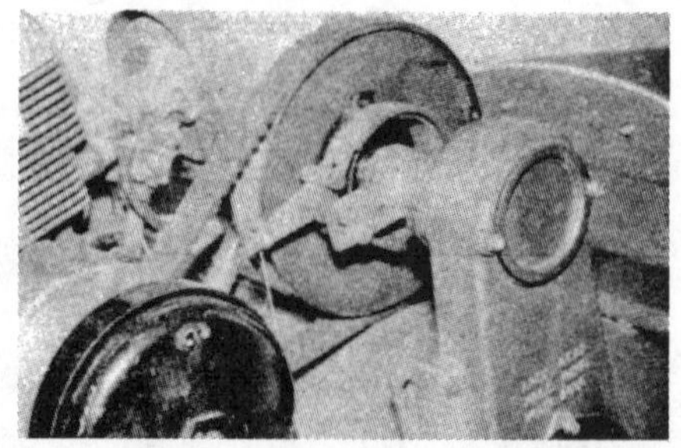

Fig. 2—View of torque converter drive unit, brake & chain case with hood removed.

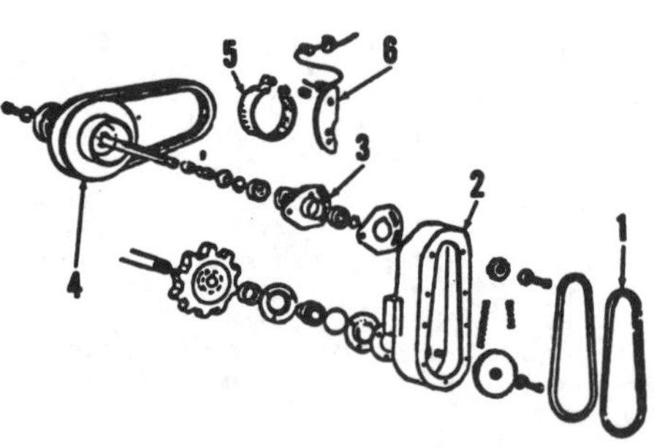

Fig. 3—Exploded view of chain case and associated parts used in 1969.

1. Cover
2. Chaincase
3. Bearing
4. Driven sheave
5. Brake band
6. Anchor plate

case inspection cover. Adjust the chain on 1969 models by loosening the stud nuts retaining upper shaft housing (3—Fig. 3) to chain case (2) and moving shaft housing in the slotted holes.

On 1970 and 1971 machines and 1972 Skylark, upper shaft housing (16—Fig. 1) is secured in chain case by clamp ring (17) but housing is not slotted and no inspection cover is provided. Loosen clamp screws and turn housing to reduce backlash to a minimum, then retighten nuts. Backlash can be measured at pulley rim.

On other 1972 models, turn adjusting stud (1—Fig. 4) until a backlash of ¼ inch can be measured at pulley rim.

NOTE: On late models with caliper type brakes, alignment must be checked after drive chain is adjusted.

BRAKE. The band type brake is shown in Fig. 2 and 3. Band should just clear drum when brake is releasesd but should fully engage before hand lever contacts handlebar. Adjust by loosening cable clamp at actuating lever and pulling cable

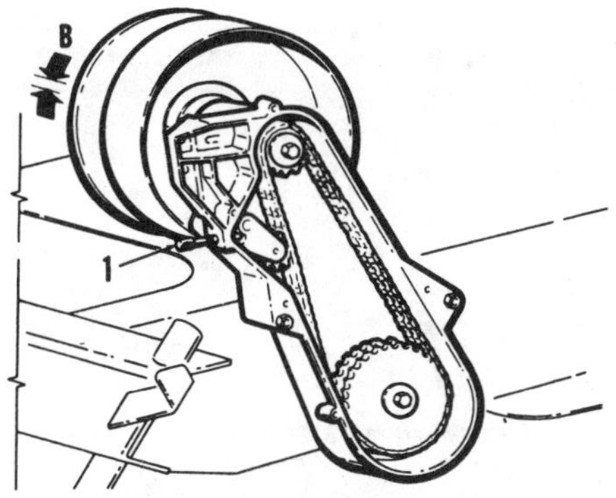

Fig. 4—View of "CHAPARRAL" chain case used on 1972 models except SKYLARK. Turn adjusting stud (1) until backlash (B) is ¼-inch. Relative position of brake unit will not be changed by chain adjustment on these models.

through lever.

On models with caliper type disc brake, adjustment is made by removing cotter pin and turning slotted nut on actuating arm stud. First make sure that caliper is properly aligned on sheave rim and that push pins center the valleys in actuating arm. Tighten nut until resistance is felt, back off one full turn, then reinstall cotter pin. Actuating arm can be re-aligned if necessary, by repositioning the cable housing anchor nuts.

Brake unit must be properly aligned with braking flange on driven pulley, and alignment on some models will be changed when drive chain is adjusted. Readjust by loosening the two bolts clamping brake housing to mounting bracket, fully applying the brake then retightening clamp bolts while brake is applied. Actuating arm may need to be repositioned after alignment.

TRACK. With rear of machine raised so that track is clear of ground, track should have some slack but must not be excessively loose. Adjust by loosening the screws on each side which secure rear track hanger brackets, then turning adjusting screws until excessive slack is removed. Both

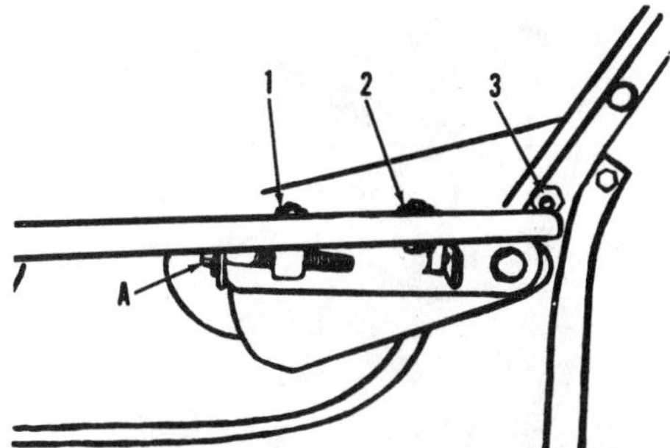

Fig. 5—To adjust track tension, loosen clamp bolts (1, 2 & 3) and turn adjusting screw (3) until tension is correct. Some early models have only two clamp screws.

sides must be adjusted alike. Refer to Fig. 5.

NOTE: Whenever track has been adjusted, alignment MUST be checked as outlined in TRACK SERVICE Section of this manual.

Snowgoer 600 is equipped with two 18-inch tracks. Adjustment is as outlined above except that each track must be adjusted individually.

COLUMBIA

1972-1975

	Engine			Carburetor				Clutch		
Model	Make	Model	Displ.	Make	Model	Sprocket Ratio	Chain Size	Make	Shaft Center	Belt Number
					1972					
C300 (351-900)	Sachs	SA290	293cc	Tillotson	HR	15:32	35-2	Salsbury	12½	754-152
C340T (351-910)	JLO	LR340/2	339cc	Walbro	WD	15:32	35-2	Salsbury	12½	754-152
C400T (351-920)	JLO	LR399/2	398cc	Walbro	WD	15:32	35-2	Salsbury	12½	754-160
C440T (351-930)	JLO	LR440/2	434cc	Walbro	WD	15:32	35-2	Salsbury	12½	754-160
SST340 (351-940)	JLO	LR340/2	339cc	Walbro	WD	15:32	35-2	Salsbury	12½	754-152
SST400 (351-950)	JLO	LR399/2	398cc	Walbro	WD	15:32	35-2	Salsbury	12½	754-160
SST440 (351-960)	JLO	LR440/2	434cc	Walbro	WD	15:32	35-2	Salsbury	12½	754-160
					1973					
C-340	JLO	LR340/2	339cc	Walbro	WDA30	15:32	35-2	Salsbury	12½	754-152
C-400	JLO	LR399/2	398cc	Walbro	WDA30	15:32	35-2	Salsbury	12½	754-160
C-440	JLO	LR440/2	428cc	Walbro	WDA30	15:32	35-2	Salsbury	12½	743-160
					1974					
C-340	JLO	2F-340-5	339cc	Walbro	WDA39	16:33	35-2	Salsbury 780	12	754-174
C-400	JLO	2F-400-7	398cc	Walbro	WDA39	17:33	35-2	Salsbury 850	12	754-172
C-440	JLO	2F-440-8	428cc	Walbro	WDA39	19:33	35-2	Salsbury 850	12	754-172
					1975					
C-340	JLO	2F-340-5	339cc	Walbro	WDA39	16:33	35-2	Salsbury 780	12	754-174
C-400	JLO	2F-400-7	398cc	Walbro	WDA39	17:33	35-2	Salsbury 850	12	754-172
C-440	JLO	2F-440-8	428cc	Walbro	WDA39	19:33	35-2	Salsbury 850	12	754-172

LUBRICATION

The engine is lubricated by oil mixed with the fuel. The vehicle manufacturer recommends the use of regular gasoline and SAE 40 or 50 Motor Oil or a known brand of Snowmobile Oil, mixed at a ratio of 20:1 for JLO engines or 25:1 for Sachs engines.

The enclosed chaincase should be filled to just above bottom of lower inspection cover opening with Automatic Transmission Fluid, Type A. Tip

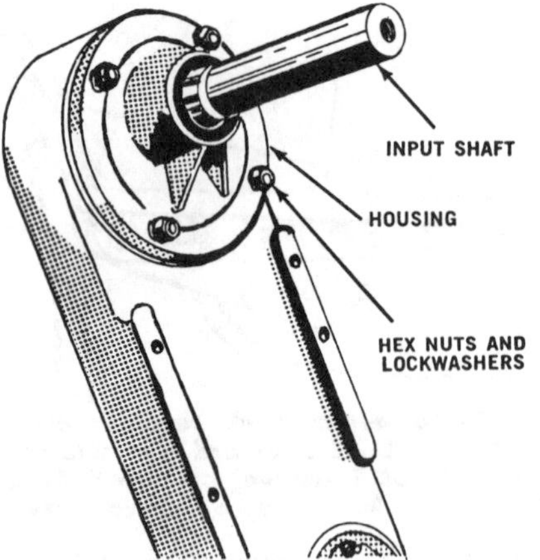

Fig. 1—Inside view of chain case showing eccentric bearing housing for chain adjustment.

Fig. 2—View of driven pulley showing points of brake adjustment.

1. Anchor nuts
2. Adjusting nut
3. Alignment screws
4. Light switch

Fig. 3—View showing procedure for checking track slack.

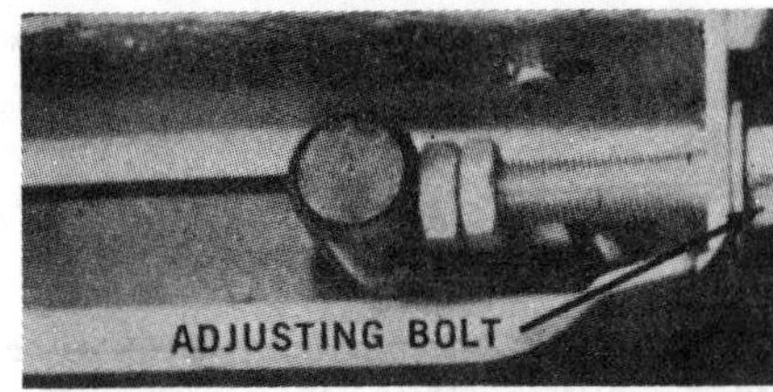

Fig. 4—Adjust track tension by loosening jam nuts and turning adjusting bolt.

machine to right side about 40 degrees when removing cover to prevent loss of lubricant.

ADJUSTMENT

SKIS AND STEERING. Turn handlebar to normal straight driving position and check to see that skis are parallel with each other and with drive track and vehicle frame. To adjust, loosen both locknuts on each tie rod and turn the tie rods until proper alignment is attained. Tie rods are equal in length and interchangeable.

DRIVE CHAIN. The enclosed drive chain should have approximately ¼-inch free play midway between sprockets. Free play cannot be measured directly but can be checked by measuring backlash of input shaft at torque converter driven pulley rim. Free play can be considered satisfactory when backlash measures ¾-1 inch.

To adjust the chain refer to Fig. 1. Loosen the four hexagon nuts retaining input shaft bearing housing clamp. Also loosen the two cap screws retaining brake caliper mounting bracket to support. Turn the eccentric housing in chaincase until chain adjustment is correct and tighten clamp. Apply the brake to align caliper unit to pulley rim, then tighten retaining cap screws.

BRAKE. The caliper type brake uses the turned rim of driven pulley as a friction surface. Brake must fully apply before hand lever contacts handlebar grip and fully release when hand pressure is relaxed. Brake light switch (4—Fig. 2) must close when brakes are applied.

Brake unit must properly align with driven pulley. Alignment can be corrected by loosening the two cap screws (3) which secure caliper bracket to support, firmly applying the brake, then retightening cap screws with brake applied.

Brake push pins must rest in valleys of actuating arm cam when brake is released. Adjust by turning the nuts (1) on brake cable housing anchor if adjustment is required. Brake wear adjustment is made by turning the self-locking nut (2) securing actuating lever. Tighten nut until pucks barely clear friction drum with brake released.

TRACK. The drive track should be comfortably snug without slack when machine is sitting still. With rear of vehicle raised until track is clear and all slack pulled to center as shown in Fig. 3, there should be just room enough to slip hand between track and center bogie wheels (or slide rails) as shown. Adjust by loosening jam nuts and turning adjusting bolt (Fig. 4) on each side of machine. Both sides must be adjusted alike.

DAUPHIN

1970-1971

	Engine			Carburetor				Clutch		
Model	Make	Model	Displ.	Make	Model	Sprocket Ratio	Chain Size	Make	Shaft Center	Belt Number
					1970					
D1150	Hirth	82R	246cc	Keihin	406	13:33	35-2	Eastern	10½	508
D1500	Hirth	56R	292cc	Keihin	406	13:33	35-2	Eastern	10½	508
D1900	Hirth	193R	292cc	Keihin	406	13:33	35-2	Eastern	10½	508
D2400	Hirth	211R	438cc	Keihin	407	14:33	35-2	Eastern	10½	508
D2800	Hirth	220R	493cc	Keihin	407	14:33	35-2	Eastern	10½	508
D3600	Hirth	171R	634cc	Keihin	407	15:33	35-2	Eastern	10½	508

	Engine			Carburetor				Clutch		
Model	Make	Model	Displ.	Make	Model	Sprocket Ratio	Chain Size	Make	Shaft Center	Belt Number
					1971					
115	Hirth	82R	246cc	Tlt'sn	HR19A	13:34	...	*	10½"	...
150	Hirth	56R	292cc	Tlt'sn	HR19A	13:34	...	*	10½"	...
190	Hirth	193R	292cc	Tlt'sn	HR19A	13:34	...	*	10½"	...
190E	Hirth	193R	292cc	Tlt'sn	HR19A	13:34	...	*	10½"	...
SS399	Hirth	210R	399cc	Keihin	407	14:34	...	*	10½"	...
240	Hirth	211R	438cc	Keihin	407	14:34	...	*	10½"	...
240E	Hirth	211R	438cc	Keihin	407	14:34	...	*	10½"	...
280	Hirth	220R	493cc	Keihin	407	14:34	...	*	10½"	...
280E	Hirth	220R	493cc	Keihin	407	14:34	...	*	10½"	...
360	Hirth	171R	634cc	Keihin	407	15:34	...	*	10½"	...
360E	Hirth	171R	634cc	Keihin	407	15:34	...	*	10½"	...

*St. Lawrence or Drummond converters – Drive belt is interchangeable.

LUBRICATION

The engine is lubricated by oil mixed with the fuel. The manufacturer recommends the use of regular gasoline and a known brand Snowmobile Oil at the ratio of 20:1. Do not use Outboard Oil, straight mineral oil or Multi-Viscosity Oil.

The chain case should contain a generous amount ½-1 cup of low temperature grease. Lubricant can be checked (and/or added) by removing the chain case cover or through lubrication fitting on rear edge of case. Add two or three shots of lubricant when lubricating bogie wheels, track axle and converter shaft bearing.

Pressure gun fittings are located on each bogie wheel hub, track axle bearing and converter shaft bearing. Lubricate each fitting with low temperature grease each 16 hours of machine operation.

Ski legs (spindles) are equipped with oilite bushings and handlebar with Teflon bearings, neither of which require regular lubrication.

ADJUSTMENT

STEERING SKIS. Steering skis should be parallel with each other and with vehicle frame when handle bar is in normal straight driving position. On 1970 models, disconnect tie rod ends at center; on 1971 models, loosen locknut and turn tie rod center section. Both tie rods should be adjusted alike.

DRIVE CHAIN. The roller drive chain should have ¼-inch deflection measured midway between sprockets. To adjust the chain remove chaincase cover. Loosen the three nuts (B—Fig. 1) securing converter shaft bearing housing to chain case. Loosen the two nuts (A—Fig. 2) securing chain case long support to frame bracket and rock the bearing housing in two slotted holes until chain adjustment is correct, then tighten the nuts (B—Fig. 1). Adjust drive belt and brake as outlined in the appropriate following paragraphs before releasing machine for service.

BRAKE. Brake wear adjustment is made by removing the cotter pin and turning the castellated nut (1—Fig. 2). Before brake can be adjusted, it must first be determined that brake properly aligns with friction surface of torque converter driven sheave and that actuating pins are centered in valleys of actuating lever when hand lever is released.

Align brake with driven sheave by loosening the two brake unit mounting bolts and shifting unit as required. Center the actuating lever on push pins after realigning brake unit by adjusting brake cable housing anchor nuts. With brake properly aligned, turn castellated nut (1) until brake is fully engaged when end of hand lever is ⅜-inch away from handlebar grip.

DRIVE BELT. The same drive belt (Dayco GTS744) is used on Eastern Industries, Drummond or St. Lawrence converter. Belt (shaft) center distance is 10½ inches with all units. Engine may be shifted sideways to obtain pulley alignment, and center distance is adjusted by anchor nuts (A—Fig. 2) on chaincase long support rod. Centerlines of drive and driven sheave must align as outlined in CONVERTER (BELT DRIVE) UNIT Section elsewhere in this manual.

TRACK. With rear of machine raised until track is clear of ground, press down on track in area of center bogie wheel. There should be just enough slack to allow hand to pass between bogie wheel and track without compressing suspension spring. Adjust by loosening pivot bolt nut (1—Fig. 3) and turning adjusting bolt (2). Both sides must be adjusted alike.

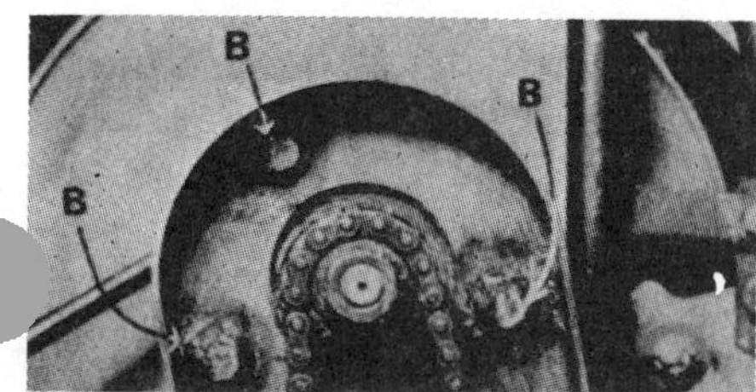

Fig. 1—To adjust drive chain, remove chaincase cover and loosen the three nuts (B). Refer also to Fig. 2.

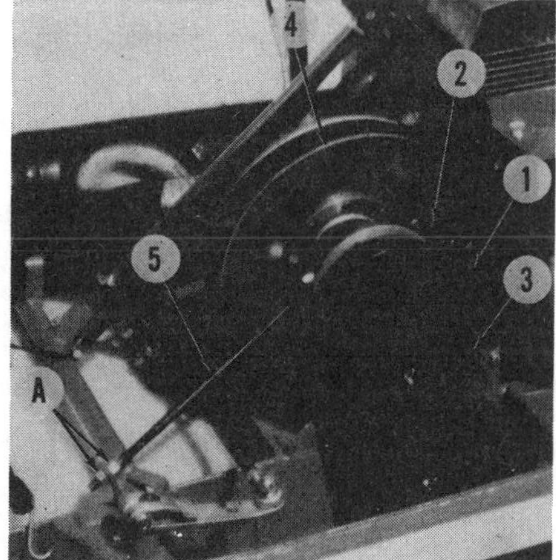

Fig. 2—View of chain case, torque converter driven sheave and associated parts of the type used.

1. Brake adjusting nut
2. Brake mounting bracket
3. Chain case
4. Driven sheave
5. Support rod
A. Adjusting nuts

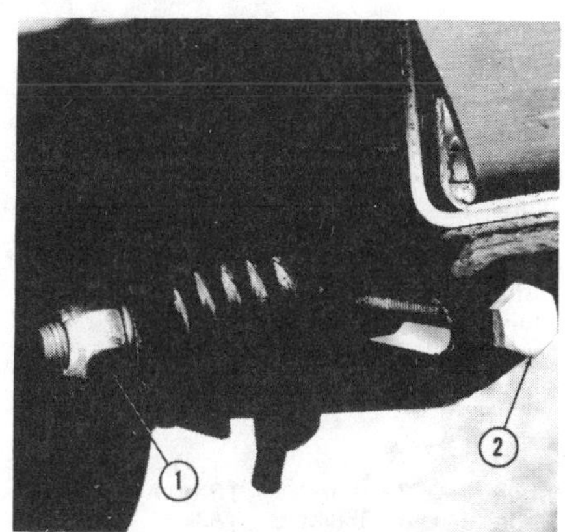

Fig. 3—To adjust track tension, loosen pivot bolt nut (1) and turn adjusting bolt (2). Both sides must be adjusted alike.

JOHN DEERE
1972-1982

Model	Engine	Engine Model	Displ.	Carb	Carb Model	Gear Ratio	Chain	Clutch		Belt
1972										
400	CCW	KEC340	339cc	Walbro	WR7-5	16:35	35-2	Salsbury 780	11.5	M63123
500	CCW	KEC440	436cc	Walbro	WD8-5	16:35	35-2	Salsbury 910	11.5	M63124
1973										
400	CCW	KEC340	339cc	Walbro	WR7-5	16:35	35-2	Salsbury 780	11.5	M63911
500	CCW	KEC440	436cc	Walbro	WD8-5	16:35	35-2	Salsbury 850	11.5	M63912
600	CCW	KEC440	436cc	Walbro	WD	16:35	35-2	Salsbury 850	11.5	M63912
JDX4	Kohler	K295-2AX	292cc	Walbro	WR	16:35	35-2	Salsbury 780	11.5	M63911
JDX8	CCW	440/21	438cc	Walbro	WD	16:35	35-2	Salsbury 850	11.5	M63912
1974										
300	Kohler	K295-2AX4	292cc	Walbro	WDA31	16:35	35-2	Salsbury 780	11.5	M64549
400	CCW	KEC340/5	339cc	Bendix	1612	16:35	35-2	Comet 100C	11.5	M64550
JDX4-Special	CCW	KEC340/5	339cc	Bendix	1612	16:35	35-2	Comet 100C	11.5	M64550
JDX6	CCW	KEC400/22	399cc	Walbro	WRA31	18:37	35-2	Comet 100C	11.5	M64550
500	CCW	KEC440/5	436cc	Bendix	1612	16:35	35-2	Comet 100C	11.5	M64550
600	CCW	KEC440/5	436cc	Bendix	1612	16:35	35-2	Comet 100C	11.5	M64550
JDX8	CCW	KEC440/22	438cc	Walbro	WRA31	18:37	35-2	Comet 100C	11.5	M64550
1975										
300	Kohler	K295-2AX4	292cc	Walbro	WDA31	16:39	35-2	Salsbury 780	11.5	M64549
400	Kioritz	KEC340/5	339cc	Bendix	1612	16:35	35-2	Comet 101	11.5	M64550
600	Kioritz	KEC440/5	436cc	Bendix	1612	16:35	35-2	Comet 101	11.5	M64550
800	Kioritz	KEC440/22	438cc	Walbro	WRA31	16:35	35-2	Comet 101	11.5	M64550
JDX4	Kioritz	KEC340/22	339cc	Walbro	WRA31	16:35	35-2	Comet 101	11.5	M64550
JDX6	Kioritz	KEC400/22	399cc	Walbro	WRA31	18:37	35-2	Comet 101	11.5	M64550
JDX8	Kioritz	KEC440/22	438cc	Walbro	WRA31	18:37	35-2	Comet 101	11.5	M64550
1976										
300	Kohler	K295-2AX	292cc	Walbro	WDB31	16:39	35-2	Salsbury 780	11.5	M64549
400	Kioritz	KEC340/22A	339cc	Walbro	WRA31	16:35	35-2	Comet 102C	11.5	M64550
Cyclone 340 .	Kioritz	KEC340/22A	339cc	Mikuni	VM34-83	21:39	Silent	Comet 102C	11.5	M66345
Cyclone 440 .	Kioritz	KEC440/22A	438cc	Mikuni	VM34-84	24:40	Silent	Comet 102C	11.5	M66345
Liquifire 340 .	Kioritz	KEC340/23LC	339cc	Mikuni	VM34-79	21:39	Silent	Comet 102C	11.5	M66345
Liquifire 440 .	Kioritz	KEC440/23LC	438cc	Mikuni	VM34-80	24:40	Silent	Comet 102C	11.5	M66345
JD295/S	Kioritz	KEC295RS/2	295cc	Mikuni	VM34-55	16:39	35-2	Comet 101C	11.5	M64550
JD340/S	Kioritz	KEC340RS/2	339cc	Mikuni	VM34-68		Silent	Comet 102C	13	M65703
1977										
300	Kohler	K295-2AXY	292cc	Walbro	WDB31	16:39	35-2	Salsbury	11.5	M64549
400	Kioritz	340/22A	339cc	Walbro	WRA31	16:35	35-2	Deere/Comet	11.5	M63911
Cyclone 340 .	Kioritz	340/22B	339cc	Mikuni	VM34	21:39	Silent	Deere/Comet	11.5	M66345
Cyclone 440 .	Kioritz	440/22B	438cc	Mikuni	VM34	24:40	Silent	Deere/Comet	11.5	M66345
Liquifire 340 .	Kioritz	340/23ALC	339cc	Mikuni	VM34	21:39	Silent	Deere/Comet	11.5	M66345
Liquifire 440 .	Kioritz	440/23ALC	438cc	Mikuni	VM34	24:40	Silent	Deere/Comet	11.5	M66345
1978										
Spitfire 340 ..	Kohler	K340-2FA	338cc	Mikuni	2-VM28	Direct	None	Comet 94D	10.5	M66345
Cyclone 340 .	Kioritz	KEC340/22B	339cc	Mikuni	VM34	21:39	Silent	Comet 102CS	11.5	M66345
Cyclone 440 .	Kioritz	KEC440/22B	438cc	Mikuni	VM34	24:40	Silent	Comet 102CS	11.5	M66345
Liquifire 340 .	Kioritz	KEC340/23ALC	339cc	Mikuni	VM34	21:39	Silent	Comet 102CS	11.5	M66345
Liquifire 440 .	Kioritz	KEC440/23ALC	438cc	Mikuni	VM34	24:40	Silent	Comet 102CS	11.5	M66345
1979										
Spitfire	Kohler	K-340-2FA	338cc	Mikuni	VM-28 or B34/32-2	Direct	None	Comet 94C	10.5	M66345
Trailfire 340 ..	Fireburst	TA340A	339cc	Mikuni	VM-34	21:39	Silent	Comet 94C	11.5	M66345
Trailfire 440 ..	Fireburst	TA440A	436cc	Mikuni	VM-34	25:39	Silent	Comet 102C	11.5	M66345
Sportfire	Fireburst	TA440B	436cc	Mikuni	VM-34	21:39	Silent	Comet 102C	11.5	M66345
Liquifire	Fireburst	TC440A	436cc	Mikuni	VM-36	22:35	Silent	Comet 102C	11.5	M68715
1980										
Spitfire	Fireburst	TB340-A	338cc	Mikuni	B34/32-1	Direct	None	Comet 94C	10.8	M66345
Trailfire 340 ..	Fireburst	TA340-A	339cc	Mikuni	VM-34	17:35	Silent	Comet 102C	11.5	M66345
Trailfire 440 ..	Fireburst	TA440-A	436cc	Mikuni	VM-34	21:39	Silent	Comet 102C	11.5	M66345
Sportfire	Fireburst	TA440-B	436cc	Mikuni	VM-34	21:39	Silent	Comet 102C	11.5	M66345
Liquifire	Fireburst	TC440-A	436cc	Mikuni	VM-36	22:35	Silent	Comet 102C	11.5	M68715
1981										
Spitfire	Fireburst	TB340-A	338cc	Mikuni	B34/32-1	Direct	None	Comet 94C	10.8	M66345
Trailfire 340 ..	Fireburst	TA340-A	339cc	Mikuni	VM-34	17:35	Silent	Comet 102C	11.5	M66345
Trailfire 440 ..	Fireburst	TA440-A	436cc	Mikuni	VM-34	21:39	Silent	Comet 102C	11.5	M66345
Sportfire	Fireburst	TA440-B	436cc	Mikuni	VM-34	21:39	Silent	Comet 102C	11.5	M66345
Liquifire	Fireburst	TC440-A	436cc	Mikuni	VM-36	22:35	Silent	Comet 102C	11.5	M68715

	Engine			Carburetor				Clutch		
Model	Make	Model	Displ.	Make	Model	Sprocket Ratio	Chain Size	Make	Shaft Center	Belt Number
					1982					
Spitfire	Fireburst	TB340-A	338cc	Mikuni	B34/32-1	Direct	None	Comet 94C	10.8	M66345
Trailfire 340	Fireburst	TA-340-A	339cc	Mikuni	VM-34	17:35	Silent	Comet 102C	11.5	M66345
Trailfire LX	Fireburst	TA-440-A	436cc	Mikuni	VM-34	21:39	Silent	Comet 102C	11.5	M66345
Sportfire	Fireburst	TA-440-B	436cc	Mikuni	VM-34	24:40	Silent	Comet 102C	11.5	M66345
Liquifire	Fireburst	TC-440-A	436cc	Mikuni	VM-36	21:39	Silent	Comet 102C	11.5	M69170

LUBRICATION

The engine is lubricated by oil mixed with the fuel. Use John Deere Snowmobile Oil or a suitable BIA equivalent. Use Regular or Premium gasoline, 90 octane or better on early models and Regular or Non-Leaded gasoline, 88 octane or better on later models. Recommended fuel:oil ratio is 20:1 for units 1974 or earlier, and 50:1 for later models without oil injection.

For models with oil injection, gasoline and oil should be mixed to a 50:1 ratio before installing fuel in tank when weather temperature is −40 degrees F or below. Oil injection system may not operate properly at −40 degrees F or below.

The pressed steel chaincase should contain SAE 30 engine oil to a level ¼-½ inch below inspection plug hole after removing lower rubber plug as shown in Fig. 1.

Models with right-hand mounted diecast chaincase should be filled to level of lower plug (L – Fig. 2) with SAE 90 gear oil. Add oil if needed through upper fill plug (F). Old oil should be removed using a suction gun at lower plug hole every 200 hours, 2 years or 1000 miles and new oil put in to bring fluid to correct level.

Except for using light oil on hinges or pivots whenever necessary to prevent binding, all other parts are self lubricating and do not require periodic attention.

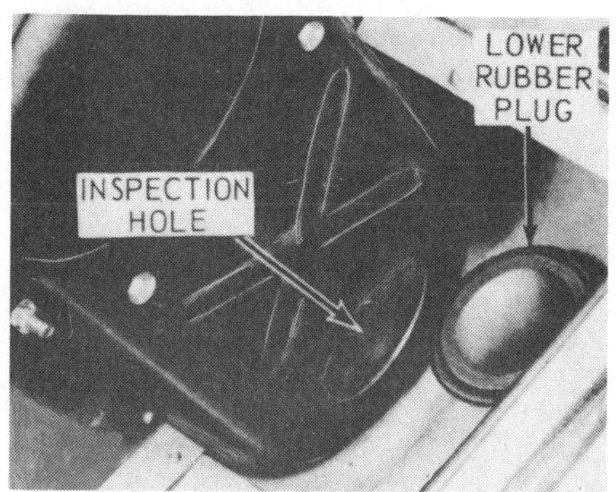

Fig. 1 – Chain case lubricant level should be just below lower inspection hole after removing lower rubber plug.

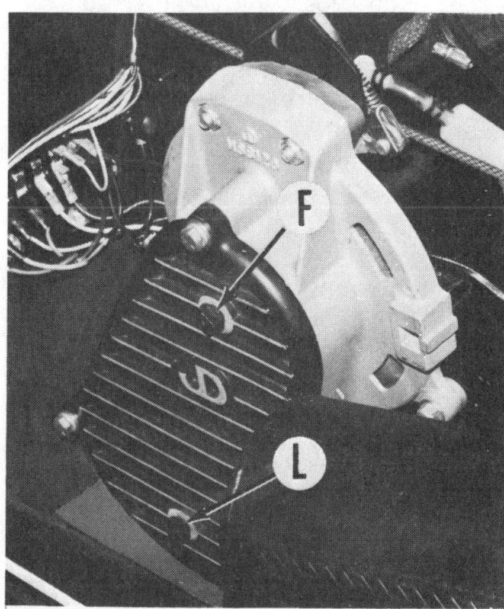

Fig. 2 – View of right-hand mounted diecast chaincase showing fill plug (F) and check plug (L).

ADJUSTMENT

STEERING AND SKIS. Steering skis should be parallel to each other and with vehicle frame when handlebar is in normal straight driving position.

On models with two tie rods, tie rods are adjusted by turning center section after loosening locknuts. For early models, nominal length of each tie rod is 11.87 inches and 13.25 inches on later models. Both tie rods should be adjusted alike.

Adjust steering system as follows for early models with a single tie rod (T – Fig. 3) and drag link (D). Exhaust silencer must be removed on most models for access to tie rod ends. Loosen locknuts and turn center tube or tie rod until distances (A and B) measured at ski wear bar nuts are equal. Adjust drag link (D) until handlebars are straight when skis point straight ahead. Extended length adjuster (M) must not exceed two inches (50 mm). Late models (Fig. 3A) are adjusted same as early models with exception of drag link (D). Adjust drag link by loosening jam nuts

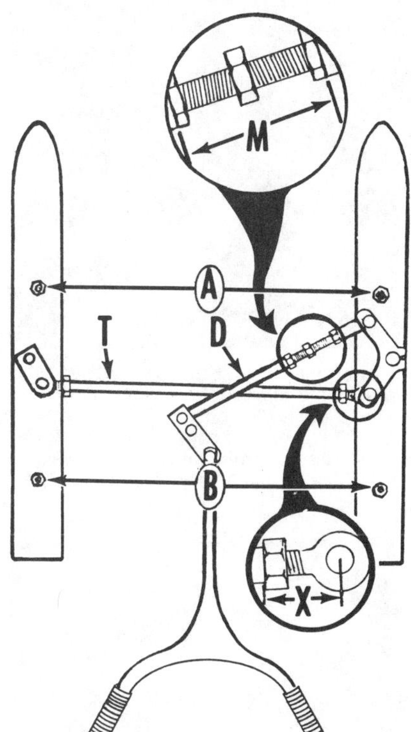

Fig. 3-View of steering system used on early single tie rod models. Distances (A and B) measured at wear bar studs on skis should be equal. Final installed length of drag link adjuster (M) should not exceed two inches (50 mm). Final installed length of tie rod end (X) should not exceed 1-5/16 inches (33 mm).

D. Drag link
T. Tie rod

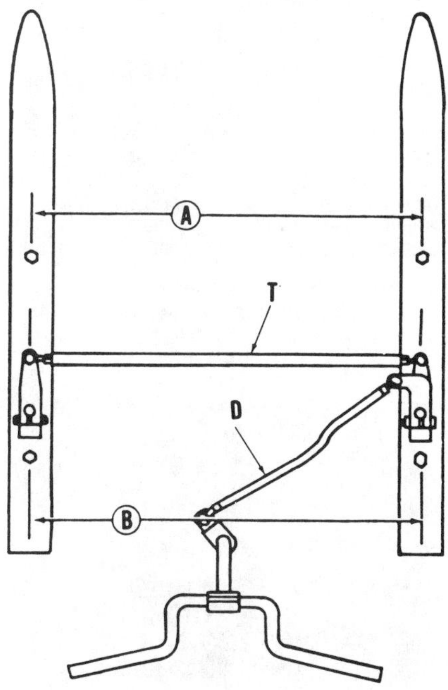

Fig. 3A – View showing late model steering system. Refer to Fig. 3 for identification of parts and measurements.

on rod ends and turning center sleeve. Adjust sleeve until handlebars are straight ahead when skis point straight ahead, then retighten jam nuts.

Extended length of tie rod ends (X–Fig. 3) on both early and late models must not exceed 1-5/16 inches (33 mm).

DRIVE CHAIN. Early models used a 35-2 roller drive chain while all late models have silent type chain. All models are equipped with spring-loaded nylon tighteners and no adjustment is provided. If excessive backlash is noted, remove inspection plug or side cover and examine chain, sprockets and tighteners for wear or other damage.

BRAKE (Band Type). The band type brake should fully apply when free end of hand lever is approximately one inch from handlebar grip. To adjust the brake refer to Fig. 4 and reposition brake cable housing anchor by turning jam nuts. If end of threads is reached before proper adjustment is attained, withdraw brake band anchor pin and reposition in rear hole of attaching boss.

Brake light switch (Fig. 5) is normally closed but is held open by brake linkage when brake is released. With brake in released position, loosen front jam nut and tighten rear nut until brake light comes on, then reverse the procedure until light just goes out. Recheck to be sure brake light comes on when actuating lever is depressed but stays off with lever released. Light switch may need to be repositioned when brake linkage is adjusted.

(Disc Type). On early models with disc type brake, refer to Fig. 6. Adjust cable housing anchor nuts (1) if necessary, until push pins center in valleys of actuating arm with brake released; then tighten actuating stud nut (2) until brake fully applies with one inch (25 mm) clearance remaining between end of brake hand lever and handlebar grip.

For later models refer to Fig. 6A. Loosen cable locknut (top arrow) and adjust actuating lever (bottom arrow) parallel with track tunnel, then tighten cable locknut. Pull brake lever back and measure distance between lever and handlebar, distance should be 1-1½ inches. If adjustment is needed loosen jam nut (1) and turn adjusting bolt (2) until correct adjustment is reached, then retighten jam nut.

Check to be sure brake light comes on when brakes are applied and goes out when lever pressure is released. Brake light switch is not adjustable.

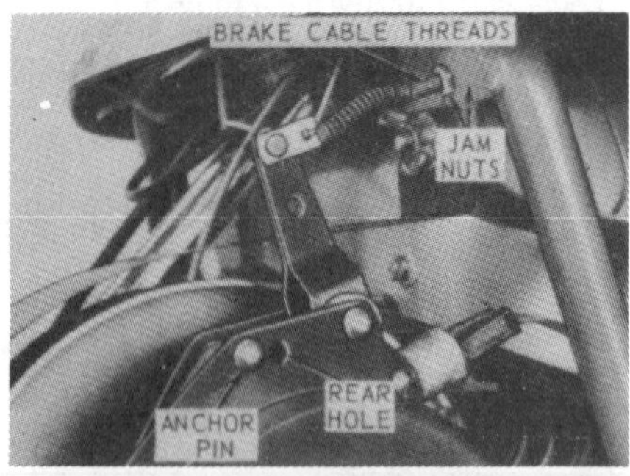

Fig. 4—Normal brake adjustment is made by turning jam nuts toward end of brake cable threads. Reposition anchor pin in rear hole if end of threads is reached.

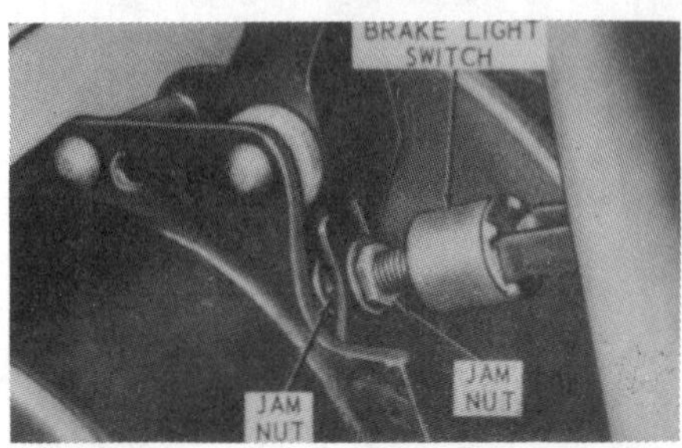

Fig. 5—Make sure brake light switch closes when brake is applied by repositioning jam nuts.

Fig. 6—For early type disc brake, adjust cable housing anchor nuts (1) if necessary until push pins (inset) center in valleys of actuating arm; then adjust stud nut (2) until brake fully applies with one inch (25 mm) clearance remaining on hand lever.

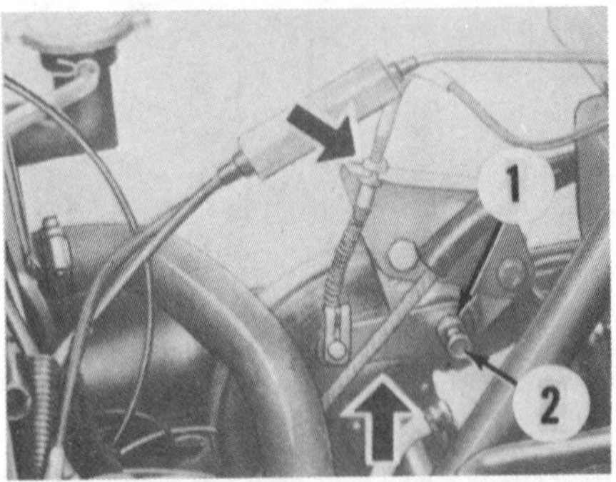

Fig. 6A—View showing cable locknut (top arrow), actuating lever (bottom arrow), brake pad adjusting bolt (2) and jam nut (1) for adjusting brake system on late model disc brake.

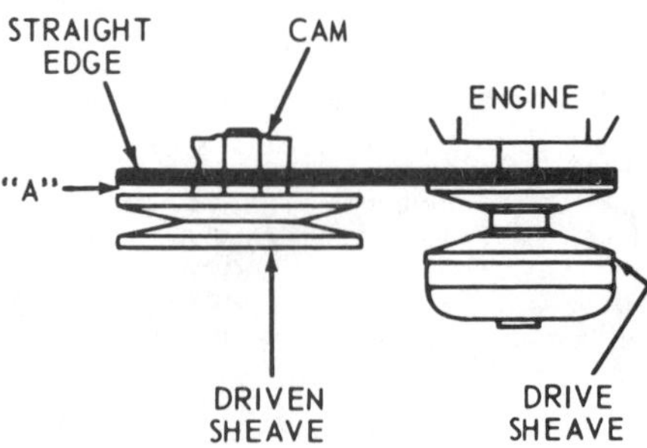

Fig. 7—Distance "A" should be equal at front and rear of driven sheave rim and 9/32-inch on Model 400 or ¼-inch on Model 500.

DRIVE BELT ALIGNMENT (Early Models). With drive belt removed and engine not running, place a straightedge along engine side of drive sheave as shown in Fig. 7; then measure clearance (A) between straightedge and nearest rim of driven sheave. Distance should be equal at front and rear and measure 9/32-inch on Model 400 or ¼-inch on Model 500. No adjustment of shaft center distance is provided.

(Late Models). On all models with cross shaft except Liquifire refer to Fig. 8. Engine can be moved forward or rearward to adjust shaft centers, refer to **CONDENSED SERVICE DATA** for shaft center distance. Centerline adjustment is provided by adding or removing washers (W–Fig. 8) which are available in thicknesses of 0.018 and 0.060 inch (0.5 and 1.5 mm). The recommended method of adjusting center distance and offset is by use of the appropriate John Deere Special Tool as shown at (T); proceed as follows:

Remove driven sheave, key and spacer washers (W) from cross shaft. Slip hub of tool over cross shaft and drop free end over drive sheave fixed face as shown. Loosen engine mounting bolts and slide engine forward or rearward as required until welded lugs of tool encompass drive sheave rim. Slide tool inward until it contacts base of flange, then measure the clearance between inner end of tool hub and cross shaft bearing to determine required thickness of

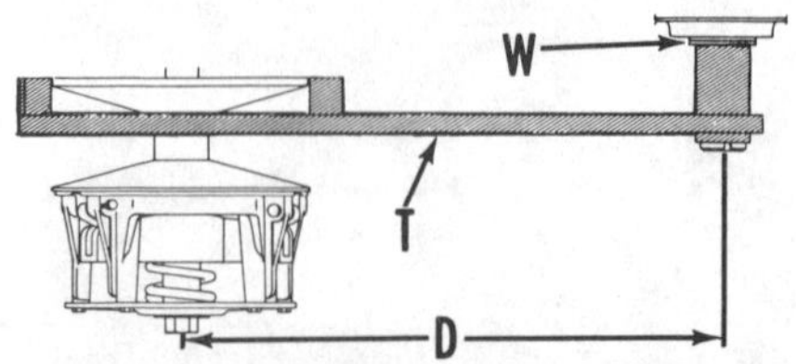

Fig. 8—Special tool (T) permits quick and simple adjustment of late model torque converter. Shaft center distance (D) is adjusted by loosening motor mounts. Washers (W) adjust offset.

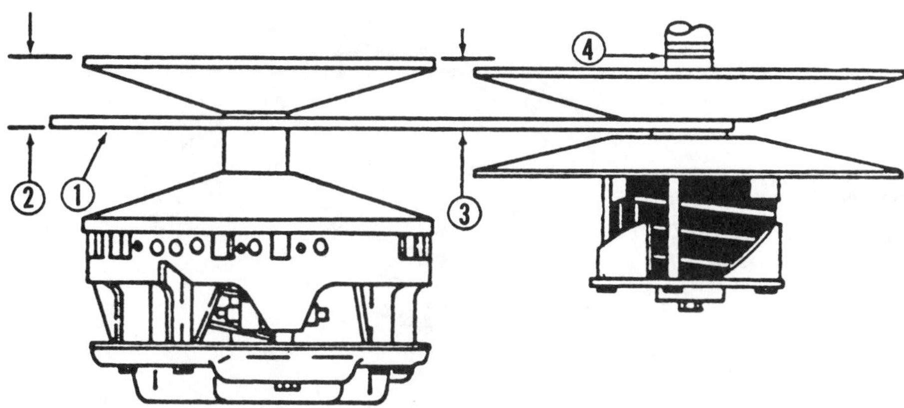

Fig. 8A – View showing Liquifire drive belt alignment components, refer to text for checking and adjusting.

1. Key stock (3/8-inch x 20 inches) 2. Measured distance 3. Measured distance 4. Shims

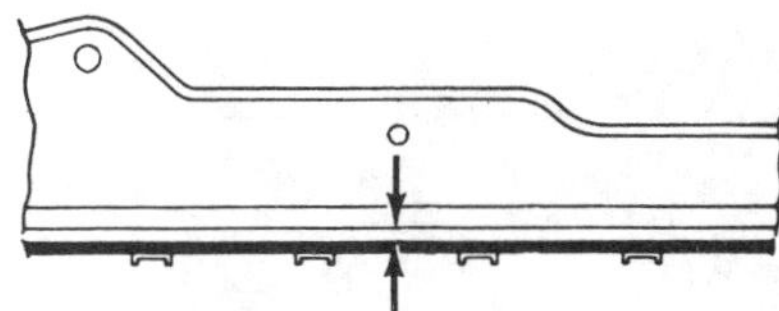

Fig. 11 – On 1976 and 1977 riveted track models, track should not clear slide more than 1/4-inch (6 mm) measured beneath lower shock absorber mount as shown by arrows.

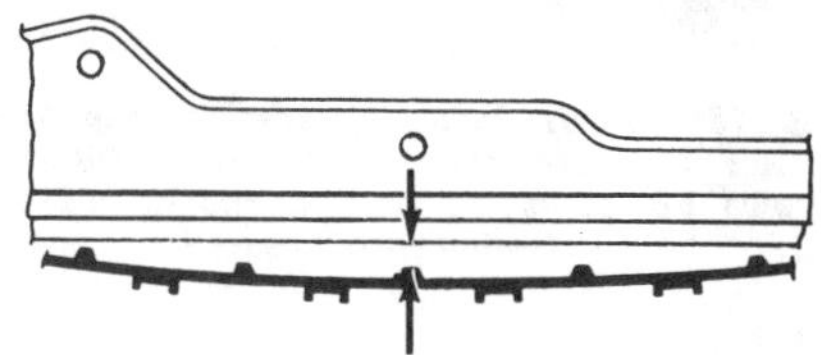

Fig. 12 – On 1976 and 1977 models with molded track, top of drive lug should not clear slide by more than 3/8 inch (10 mm) measured beneath lower shock mount as shown by arrows.

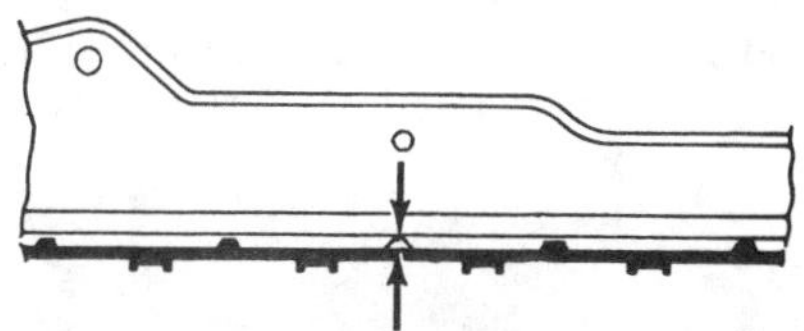

Fig. 13 – On 1978 models, inside of track must not clear slide by more than 1/4-inch (6 mm) measured beneath lower shock mount as shown by arrows.

shim pack (W). Install the required shim pack, coat exposed end of cross shaft with "NEVER-SEEZ COMPOUND", then reinstall driven sheave and key. Tighten retaining cap screw to a torque of 20 ft.-lbs. (2.8 kg-m).

On Liquifire models refer to Fig. 8A. Shaft center distance is non-adjustable, only clutch offset may be adjusted. To check and adjust offset remove drive belt; then use a 3/8-inch x 20 inches long piece of key stock and place between clutches as shown at 1 – Fig. 8A. Measure distance two (2) and three (3) – Fig. 8A, add distances together and divide the total by two (2). The answer will give you the pulley offset. On early models offset should be between 1.26-1.30 inches, later models 1.44-1.48 inches. If offset is not within specification, add or remove shims (4) from between driven sheave and secondary shaft. For early models, shims are available in 0.018 or 0.060-inch thickness and 0.018, 0.031 or 0.049-inch thickness on later models. After adjustment reinstall driven sheave and check pulley alignment, then install drive belt.

Fig. 9 – With machine unloaded, approximately half of rear flange screw (S) should appear below edge of bracket as shown in inset. Adjust by loosening clamp screws (C) and turning adjusting screw (A). When end of threads is reached, move clamp screws to rear holes (H).

Fig. 10 – Tension bolt (arrow) adjusts track tension on slide suspension models.

TRACK TENSION (Bogie Wheel Models). With machine unloaded, approximately half of rear bearing flange screw (S – Fig. 9) should appear below edge of adjustment bracket as shown in inset. Adjust by loosening the two clamp screws (C) and turning adjusting screw (A) on each side of machine an equal amount.

NOTE: Whenever track tension has been adjusted, alignment MUST be checked as outlined in TRACK SERVICE Section of this manual.

(Slide Suspension Models). On 1976 and 1977 models with slide suspension, track may be of one-piece construction with full length grouser bars molded in; or three piece belt design with 2/3-length riveted grouser bars.

On all models, track is adjusted by a tension bolt on each side of rear idler axle as shown by arrow, Fig. 10. Raise rear of machine until track is clear. On early models with riveted track, inside of track belt must not clear slide by more than 1/4-inch (6 mm), measured beneath lower shock absorber mount as shown in Fig. 11. On models with molded track, top of drive lug should not clear slide rail by more than 3/8-inch (10 mm), measured beneath lower shock mount as shown in Fig. 12. On 1978 models, inside of track must not clear slide by more than 1/4-inch (6 mm) as shown in Fig. 13. On all 1979-1982 models except Liquifire, track to slide clearance is 1/4-inch (6 mm) measured below lower shock mount. For Liquifire models, track to slide clearance is 1/2-inch (12 mm) measured below lower shock mount. A track that is either too loose or too tight will affect performance.

All slide suspension models have a means of independently adjusting spring rate. Increasing or decreasing spring strength at rear compensates for a heavier or lighter load. Increasing spring strength at front of track will decrease ski effectiveness but permit operation in deep or fluffy snow. Decreasing front spring strength will transfer more weight to skis for better steering control on packed snow or ice. Refer to Figs. 14 through 18 for adjustment points.

Fig. 14 – Arrows show suspension spring adjusting screws used on 1976 and 1977 models. Tighten front screws for a firm ride, loosen for a soft ride. Tighten rear screws to prevent bottoming according to load.

Fig. 15—Arrows indicate steering response screws on 1976 and 1977 models. Turning screws out gives lift to skis and decreases steering response.

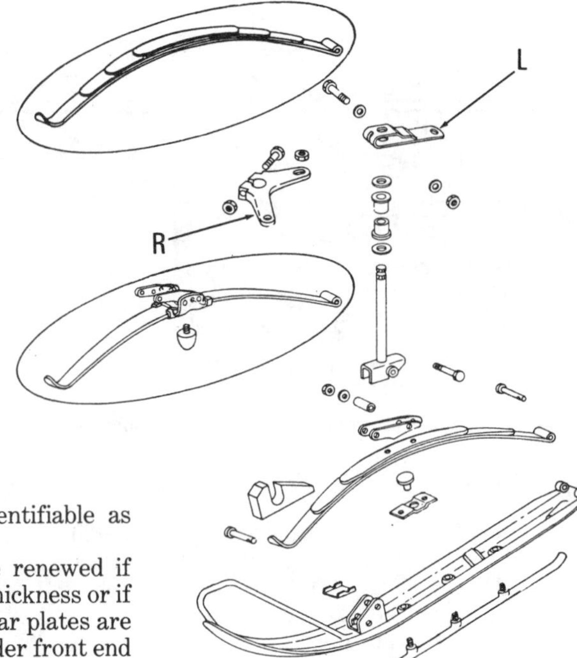

Fig. 19—Exploded view of steering skis and associated parts used on a typical single tie rod model. Right steering arm is shown at (R), left steering arm at (L).

OVERHAUL

SKIS AND STEERING. Skis, ski legs and springs are interchangeable from left to right. Steering arms on models with two tie rods are marked "R" and "L" for proper installation. Models with single tie rod are identifiable as shown in Fig. 19.

Ski wear bars should be renewed if worn to half their original thickness or if otherwise damaged. Ski wear plates are provided for installation under front end of spring. Wear plates should be renewed if badly worn. Early models used one, three and four-leaf springs as shown in Fig. 19. Late models use only a single spring assembly. Spring leaves are renewable only as a complete spring assembly which includes spring saddles and bumpers, but saddles are renewable individually on three and four leaf springs, and bumpers are renewable individually on all models. Refer to Fig. 20 or 21.

When installing steering linkage on models with two tie rods, adjust length of each tie rod (Fig. 22) to 11⅞ inches on early models and 13¼ inches on later models measured from center to center of attaching bolt holes on steering arms. After adjustment attach steering arms to tie rods. Point both skis straight ahead, then attach steering arms to ski legs. Inner end of right tie rod must be installed below steering post; inner end of left tie rod installed above steering

Fig. 16—On 1976 Liquifire only, a second hole (arrow) is provided for maximum ski lift.

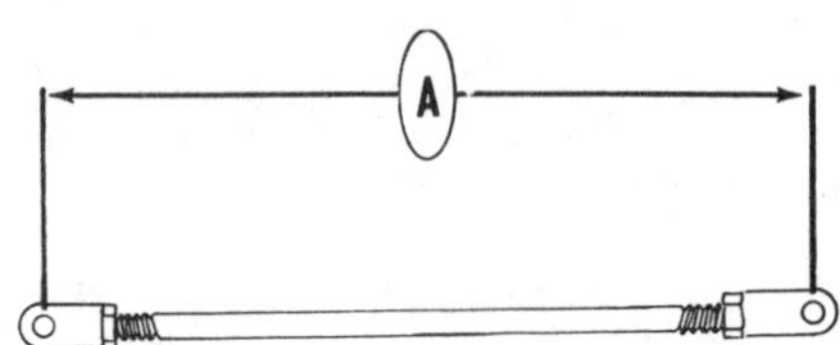

Fig. 22—On models with two tie rods, each one should be adjusted until distance (A) equals 11-⅞ inches (302 mm) on early models and 13¼ inches (336.6 mm) on late models.

Fig. 17—Load adjustment on 1978-1982 models consists of alternate anchors for rear springs. Move spring end to upper anchor for heavier load.

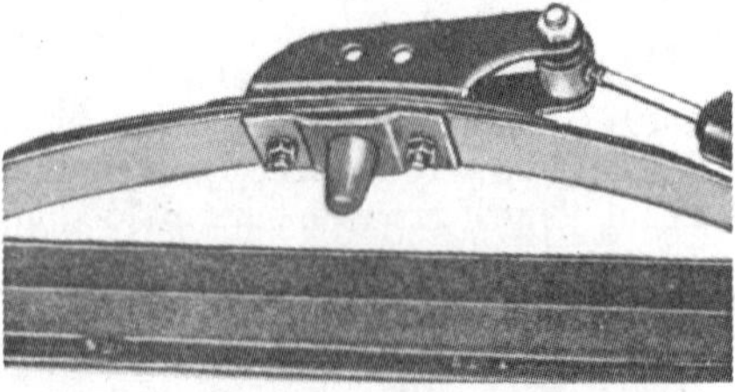

Fig. 20—On three or four-leaf springs, saddles or bumpers can be renewed individually by removing retaining nuts and bolts.

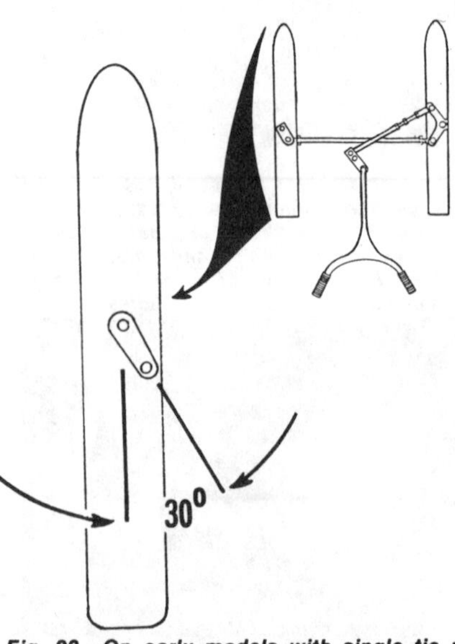

Fig. 23—On early models with single tie rod, steering arms must be installed to ski legs at a 30 degree inward angle as shown.

Fig. 18—Steering response on 1978-1982 models so equipped is accomplished by tightening or loosening front spring adjustment. Tightening the adjustment provides more ski lift and less steering response.

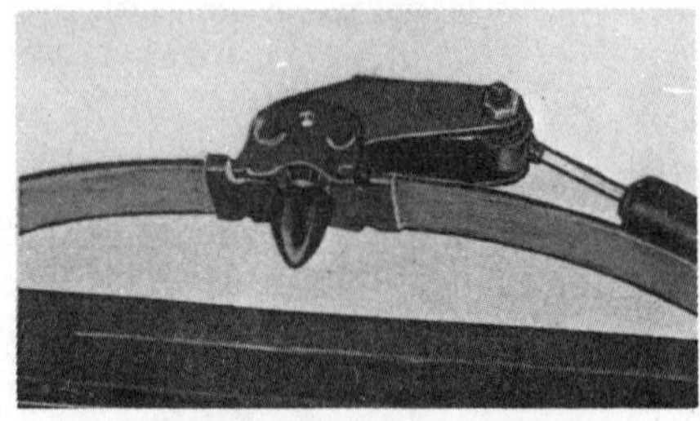

Fig. 21—On one-leaf springs, bumper only can be renewed by unscrewing from spring mount.

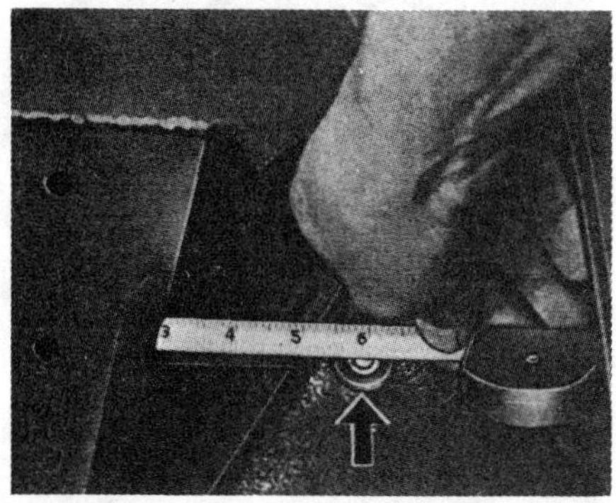

Fig. 24—With skis pointing straight ahead, measure from snowmobile frame to center of tie rod end as shown. Distance should measure 6 inches (150 mm) ± ⅛ inch.

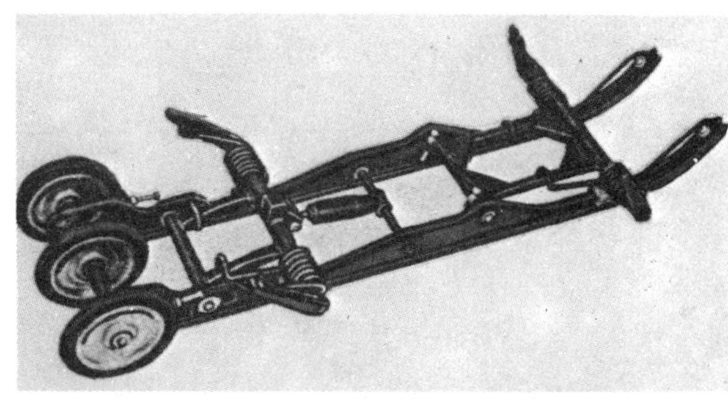

Fig. 28—Suspension frame used in 1976 and 1977 models.

Fig. 29—Typical suspension frame used on 1978-1982 models.

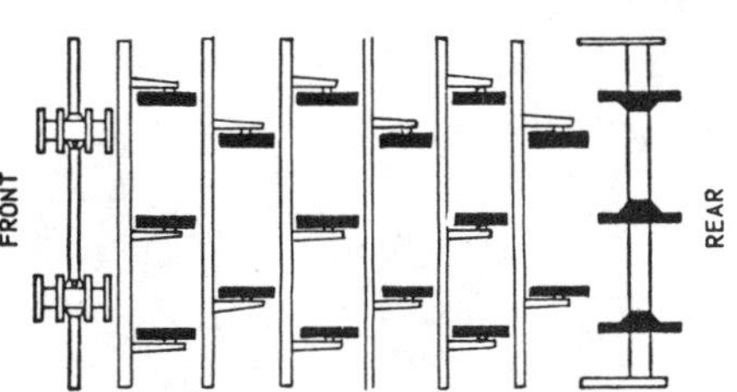

Fig. 25—Exploded view of trailing arm bogie system used on early models.

post. Make minor ski alignment adjustments after linkage is assembled.

On early models with a drag link and tie rod, both steering arms should angle inward about 30 degrees as shown in Fig. 23. With skis pointing straight ahead, measure from vehicle frame to center of tie rod attaching hole in steering arm as shown in Fig. 24. Distance should be 6 inches (150 mm) plus or minus ⅛-inch (3 mm). Late model steering arms should be adjusted to where they are parallel with vehicle frame when skis are pointed straight ahead. Exhaust silencer must be removed for access to steering arms.

TRACK AND SUSPENSION. Early models are equipped with a trailing arm bogie suspension system. Bogie wheels have sealed ball bearings and are renewable individually by removing the mounting bolt. Six bogie support axles are used. Units must be installed as shown in Fig. 26 to prevent interference. Refer to Fig. 27 for attaching procedure for bogie clamps and springs.

Renew bogie wheel assemblies if tires or bearings are damaged or worn. Renew bogie support tubes if bent to the point where they bind, or if bogie wheels do not run true and straight.

Refer to Fig. 28 for suspension frame used on 1976 and 1977 models, and to Fig. 29 for a typical frame unit used on 1978-1982 models.

To remove early frame unit, invert the snowmobile and loosen track tension.

NOTE: Empty fuel tank and chaincase and remove battery on models so equipped, to prevent fluid leakage.

Use a 1¼-inch end wrench or Crescent wrench on shaft end of anchor arm (A–Fig. 30) to relieve spring pressure, and unbolt outer end of arm. With spring pressure released on both sides, remove retaining screws securing frame to track tunnel and lift out the frame.

To remove the polyethylene slide rail wear bars, remove the retaining nut and bolt at front end of slide rail. On models so equipped remove the stop from rear of rail, then use a hammer and chisel to drive the wear bar rearward out of slide rail slot.

NOTE: If difficulty is encountered in loosening bar, drill a ⅜-inch hole in exact center of wear bar about 18 inches from the rear, and insert a ⅜ x ¾-inch cap screw to drive against, as shown in Fig. 32.

Some rail slots are narrow. Measure slot width by sliding a 7/16-inch drill bit or rod the full length of the slot. Pry slot open if gage rod is snug at any point.

Lubricate rail with grease and install new wear bar from rear, using a soft mallet to bump wear bar into position.

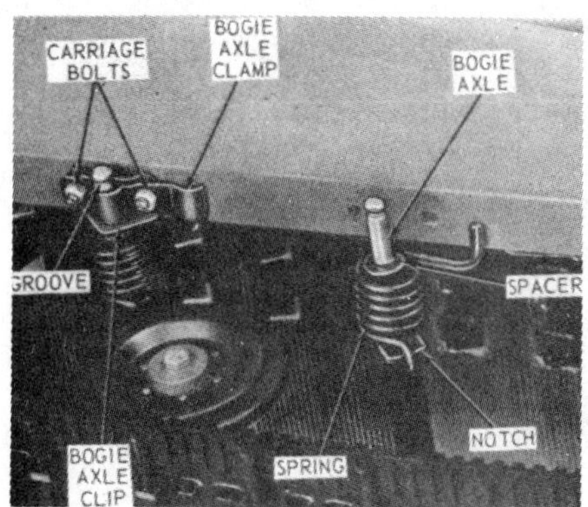

Fig. 26—Bogie suspension units must be installed as shown to prevent interference.

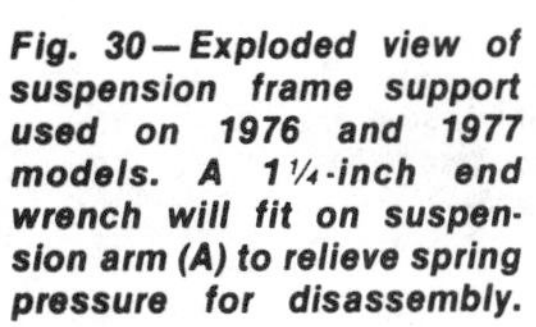

Fig. 27—Attaching detail for bogie support tubes and springs.

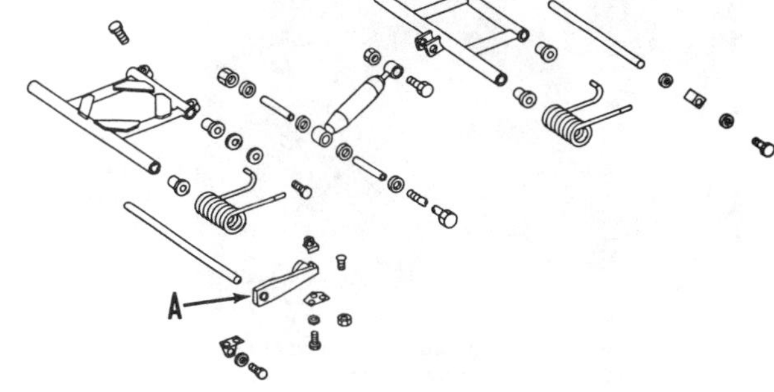

Fig. 30—Exploded view of suspension frame support used on 1976 and 1977 models. A 1¼-inch end wrench will fit on suspension arm (A) to relieve spring pressure for disassembly.

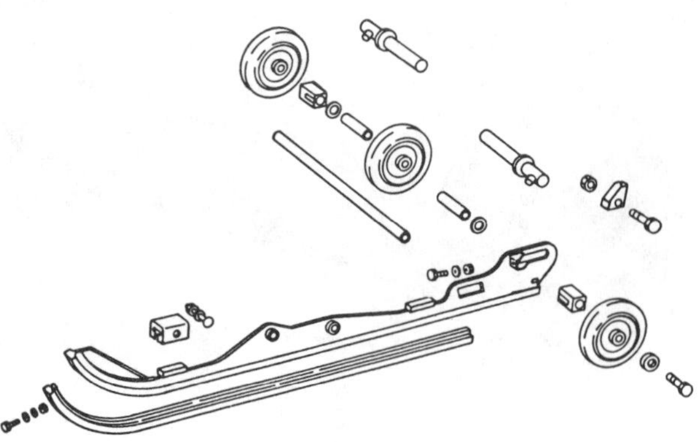

Fig. 31 — Slide rail frame and associated parts used on 1976 and 1977 models.

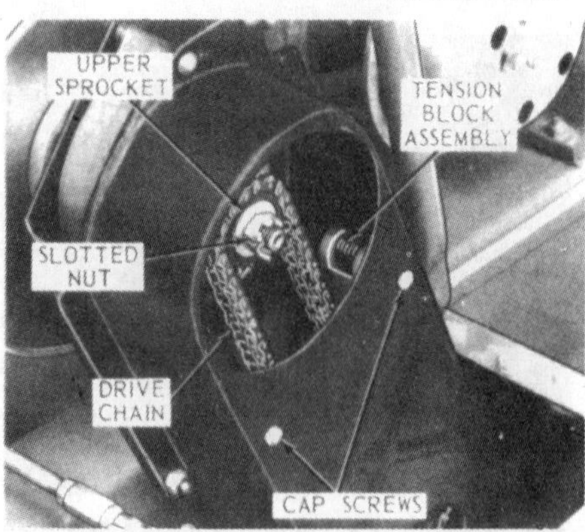

Fig. 36 — Removing chain and sprockets from models with welded steel chain case.

Install front retaining bolt and nut, and rear stop if so equipped.

To remove suspension frame on 1978-1982 models, remove two hex head cap screws (Fig. 32A) on each side of track tunnel which secure suspension. Turn vehicle over on its right side, then withdraw suspension unit from track.

NOTE: Fluids should be drained or siphoned out to prevent spillage when vehicle is turned on its side.

Slide rail wear bars are retained by a stop (S – Fig. 33) at rear of rail and a cap (C) at front. To remove the wear bar, remove stop (S) and drive wear bar rearward out of slide rail slot using a wooden block and hammer. Inspect and repair slot for burrs, bends or rust, then lubricate slot and install new wear bar from front using a soft mallet. Be careful not to damage surface of slide during installation.

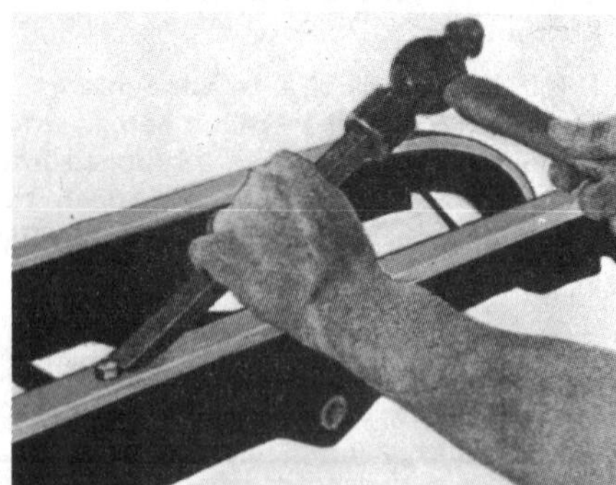

Fig. 32 — A sticking wear bar can be removed by drilling a hole and installing a bolt to drive against as shown.

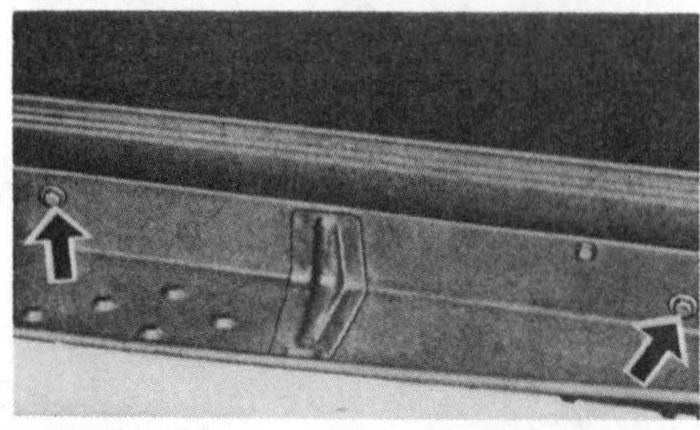

Fig. 32A — View showing cap screws used to bolt suspension to tunnel frame.

Most slide rail models have riveted polyethylene wear bars in top of track tunnel which are renewable. Remove seat and suspension as outlined earlier in section. Continue to turn vehicle over on its top side and place track over front of vehicle. Drill out rivets and cut heads off using a sharp chisel and hammer. Renew wear bars and install rivets from wear bar side.

On all models, install slide suspension by reversing removal procedure, then adjust as previously outlined.

WELDED STEEL CHAINCASE. Refer to Fig. 35 for an exploded view. Refer to CONDENSED SERVICE DATA tables for standard sprocket ratio for each model. Automatic spring-loaded chain tensioners are used and adjustment is not required.

The 35-2 endless chain is renewable only as a unit and repair links are not provided. To remove the chain, remove the two rubber access plugs, remove the two cap screws securing the chain tensioner blocks and lift out tensioner units. Work drive chain off lower sprocket and lift chain out through upper access plug hole. Refer to Fig. 36.

Upper chain sprocket can be slipped off of secondary shaft splines after

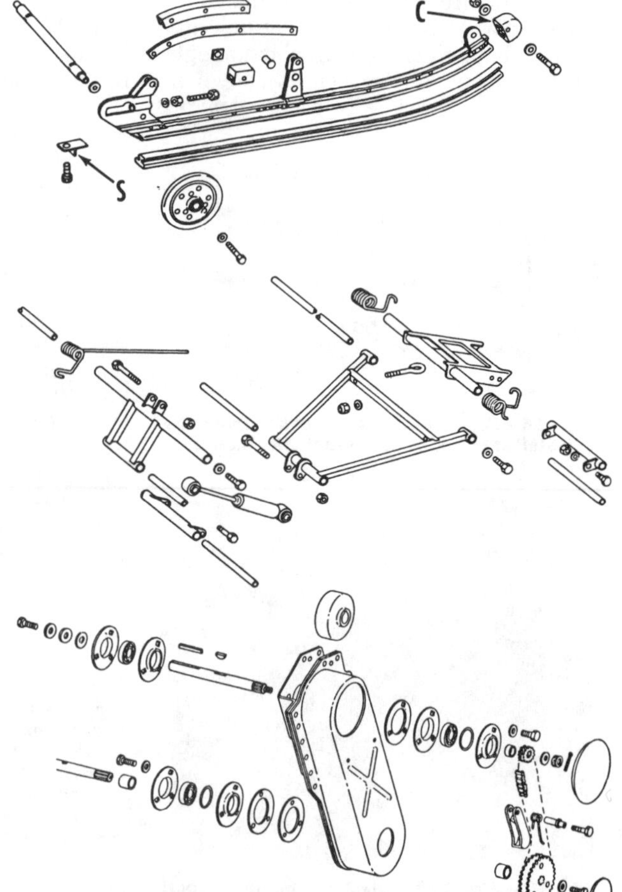

Fig. 33 — Slide rail frame and associated parts used on most 1978-1982 models. Wear bar is retained by cap (C) at front end and stop (S) at rear.

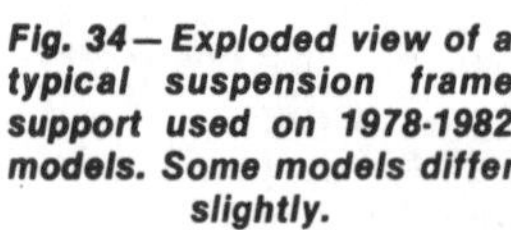

Fig. 34 — Exploded view of a typical suspension frame support used on 1978-1982 models. Some models differ slightly.

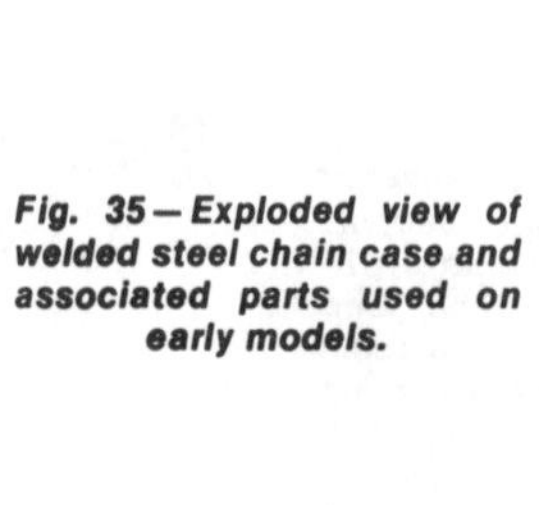

Fig. 35 — Exploded view of welded steel chain case and associated parts used on early models.

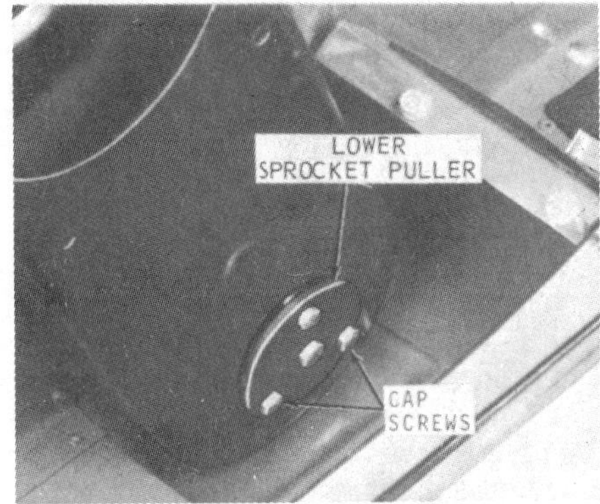

Fig. 37—A special puller (JDM-13) is required to remove lower chain sprocket.

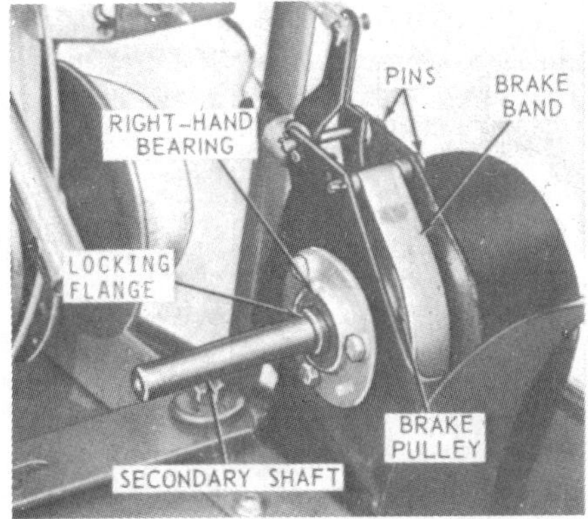

Fig. 38—Secondary shaft and brake is used on models with welded steel chain case.

removing cotter pin and slotted nut. Removal of lower sprocket requires the use of a special puller (JDM-13) as shown in Fig. 37. Remove sprocket through upper access hole after sprocket is pulled from track drive shaft splines.

To remove the secondary shaft, brake mechanism or secondary shaft bearings, first remove drive belt. Disconnect

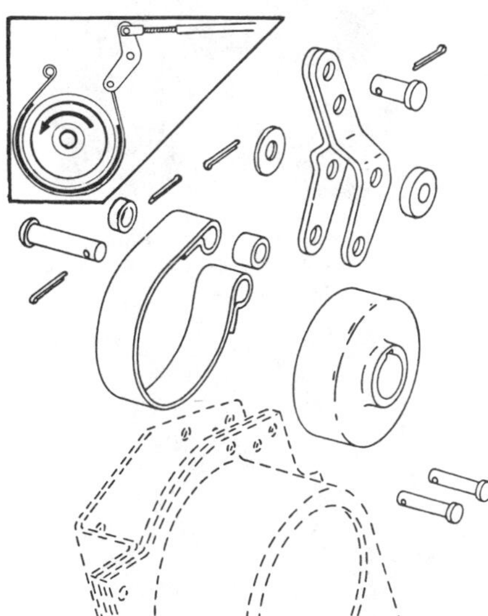

Fig. 39—Exploded view of band type brake used on models with welded steel chain case.

Fig. 40—Chain case can be removed by removing two bolts after attaching components are removed.

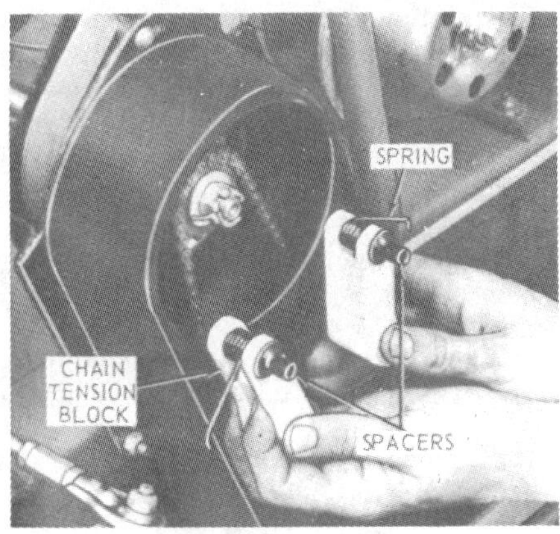

Fig. 41—Removed view of chain tension blocks used on models with welded chain case.

steering column from steering post and slide steering column up about six inches to provide clearance; then remove driven pulley. Remove drive chain and upper sprocket as previously outlined.

Loosen the locking flange on right-hand bearing (Fig. 38) by driving top side rearward, then remove the bearing. Loosen the locking flange on left-hand bearing and slide secondary shaft out of left-hand bearing, brake drum and gearcase unit.

Refer to Fig. 39 for an exploded view of brake assembly. The drum can be renewed after removing secondary shaft as previously outlined. The bonded type brake band can be renewed when drum is out or by rolling the band around drum with secondary shaft and drum installed.

Drive chain and lower sprocket must be removed before track drive shaft can be removed. Raise rear of machine, loosen track and remove rear track idler. Remove lubricant from chaincase using a suction pump. Unbolt right-hand bearing flange and speedometer drive. Loosen locking flange on left-hand bearing. Loosen the three flange bolts on gearcase side to allow bearing outer race to turn; move opposite end of track drive shaft until drive wheels clear tunnel wall, then withdraw the shaft, drive wheels and right bearing as an assembly.

Gearcase can be unbolted and removed after drive axle and secondary shaft are out, by removing the two bolts shown in Fig. 40. When installing gearcase, leave the two bolts (Fig. 40) loose until track drive shaft is installed and flange bolts tightened.

Assemble gearcase components by reversing the disassembly procedure. Tighten cap screw retaining lower sprocket to 30-35 ft.-lbs. (4.2-4.8 kg-m). Paint secondary shaft in area of brake drum and driven sheave with NeverSeez and install secondary shaft, brake, upper sprocket and sprocket nut BEFORE tightening the cap screw retaining driven sheave. Tighten the sheave retaining cap screw to a torque of 20 ft.-lbs. (2.8 kg-m).

Install chain tension blocks as shown in Fig. 41 and tighten retaining cap screws to 100 inch-pounds (1.2 kg-m). Fill chaincase with five ounces of SAE 30 engine oil when unit is assembled.

RIGHT-HAND MOUNTED DIE-CAST CHAINCASE. Refer to Fig. 42 for an exploded view and to CONDENSED SERVICE DATA tables for standard sprocket ratios. Silent chain with automatic tensioner unit is used.

To remove chain and sprockets, loosen cover screws and allow fluid to drain, then remove cover. Remove sprocket retaining cap screws. On 1976 models, remove chain tension assembly (A), both sprockets and chain as a unit. On 1977

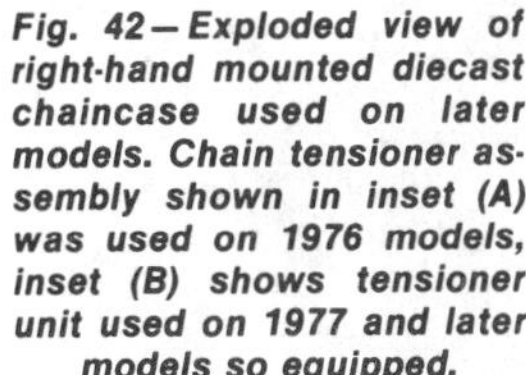

Fig. 42—Exploded view of right-hand mounted diecast chaincase used on later models. Chain tensioner assembly shown in inset (A) was used on 1976 models, inset (B) shows tensioner unit used on 1977 and later models so equipped.

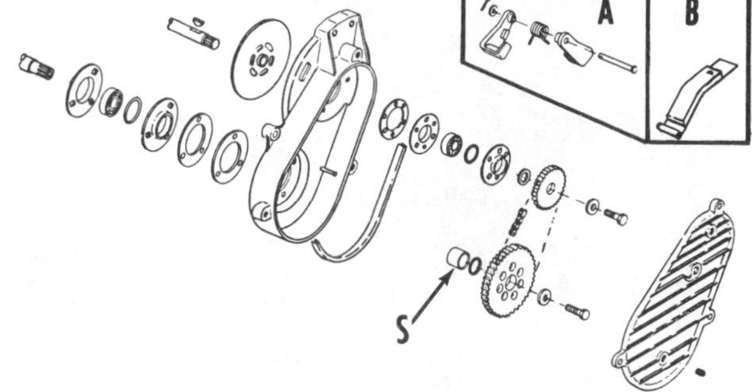

and later models except Liquifire, withdraw chain tension block (B–Fig. 42) from pin; then remove chain and both sprockets as an assembly. On Liquifire models loosen chain tensioner (Fig. 42A) adjusting screw and remove tensioner, sprockets and chain.

On all models except Liquifire, chain is available as an endless assembly only; in 62, 66 and 68 pitch lengths. Correct length for standard and optional drive ratios are as follows:

Speed Ratio	Upper Sprocket	Lower Sprocket	Chain Length
1.56:1	25	39	62
1.67:1	24	40	68
1.72:1	22	38	66
1.86:1	21	39	66
2.06:1	17	35	62
2.47:1	17	42	66

On Liquifire models, chain is available as an endless assembly only; in 66, 68 and 70 pitch lengths. Correct length for standard and optional drive ratios are as follows:

Speed Ratio	Upper Sprocket	Lower Sprocket	Chain Length
1.56:1	25	39	70
1.59:1	22	35	66
1.67:1	24	40	70
1.77:1	22	39	68
1.86:1	21	39	68
1.91:1	22	42	70
1.96:1	20	39	66
2.05:1	19	39	66

Fig. 42A—View of chain tensioner used on Liquifire models.

Fig. 43—Using a straightedge to check sprocket alignment. Refer to text for details.

Do not intermix sprocket or chain combinations other than those listed.

NOTE: Changing to a slower (higher) speed ratio does not necessarily mean that top speed will be reduced. Actual ground speed results from a COMBINATION of drive ratio, load, engine torque and drive clutch setting.

On all models except Liquifire, the 38-tooth lower sprocket requires a different spacer (S–Fig. 42) than any of the other sprocket sizes. When changing to or from the 1.72:1 ratio, the optional spacer must be obtained. Note and record the total number of shims installed behind each of the two sprockets when gearcase is disassembled. Shims control sprocket alignment and permit sprockets to be tightly installed (without end float). Sprockets must align within 0.010-inch (0.25 mm) and shaft ends must be recessed in sprocket hubs when properly installed. A maximum of three 0.018-inch (0.457 mm) shims may be used between spacer and sprocket on lower shaft. A maximum of ten 0.010-inch (0.25 mm) shims may be used between bearing and sprocket on upper shaft.

When checking sprocket alignment, install sprockets without the chain as shown in Fig. 43. When shim pack thickness is determined; remove sprockets leaving shim packs installed, then reinstall chain and both sprockets. On 1976 models, tightener assembly must be installed with the chain, with special tool (JDM-82) assisting in holding tensioner as shown in Fig. 44.

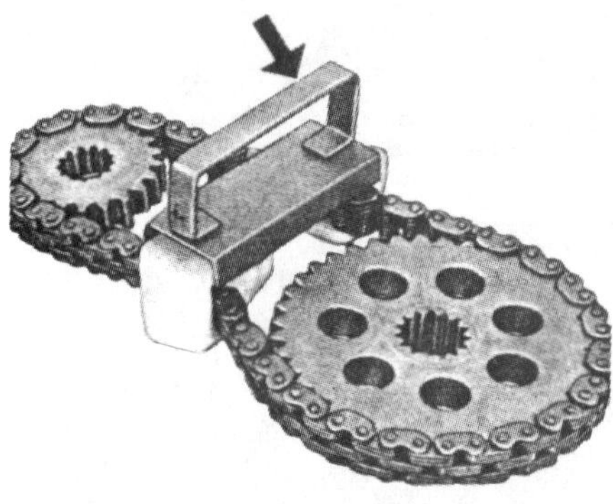

Fig. 44—Tensioner tool (JDM-82) installed (arrow) to assist in assembling sprockets in 1976 model chain case.

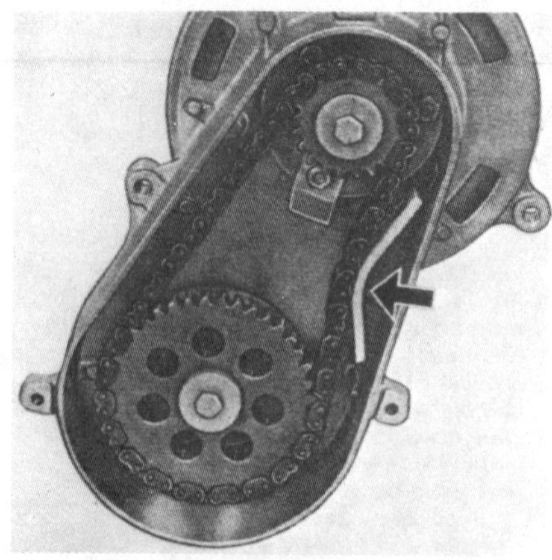

Fig. 45—View of chain tensioner used on 1977 and later models.

On later models except Liquifire the tensioner (Arrow–Fig. 45) is slipped into position after chain and sprockets are installed. Use LOCTITE on sprocket retaining screw threads on final assembly.

On Liquifire models chain tensioner (Arrow–Fig. 42A) adjusting screw must be adjusted to set tension on chain. Loosen jam nut and turn screw in until tensioner is snug on chain. Turn driven sheave ½-turn forward and check adjustment, then repeat. Back off adjusting screw ¼-turn, then tighten jam nut. Use LOCTITE on sprocket retaining screw threads on final assembly.

On early models with split cover gasket, install gasket ends at eleven o'clock as shown at Arrow–Fig. 46. End gap should be 1/16 to 3/16-inch (2-5 mm). If later endless gasket is installed on early chaincase, drill a 1/16-inch hole in upper plug to provide a vent.

To remove secondary shaft, brake mechanism or secondary shaft bearings, first raise belt guard and remove drive belt. Remove retaining cap screw and washer, then slide driven sheave from secondary shaft. Retrieve and save adjusting shim pack from behind driven sheave. Remove chain and sprockets as previously outlined. On some models air intake silencer assembly and hose will need to be removed. On models so equipped, locking collar (Fig. 46A) will need

Fig. 46—On early models with split cover gasket, install gasket ends at eleven o'clock as shown by arrow.

Fig. 46A—View showing locking collar and set screw used on models so equipped.

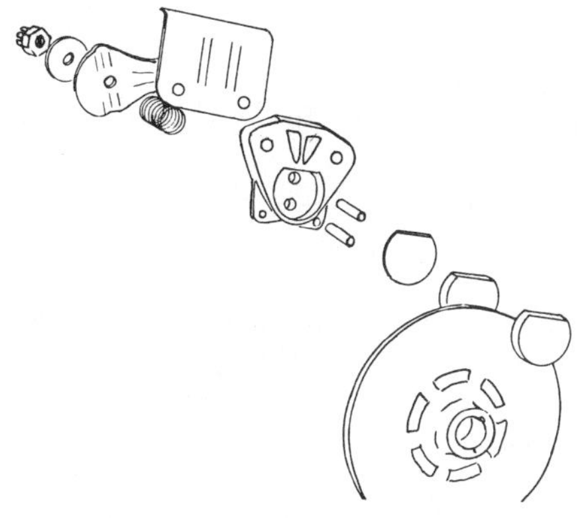

Fig. 47 — Exploded view of early type disc brake assembly used on models with diecast chaincase.

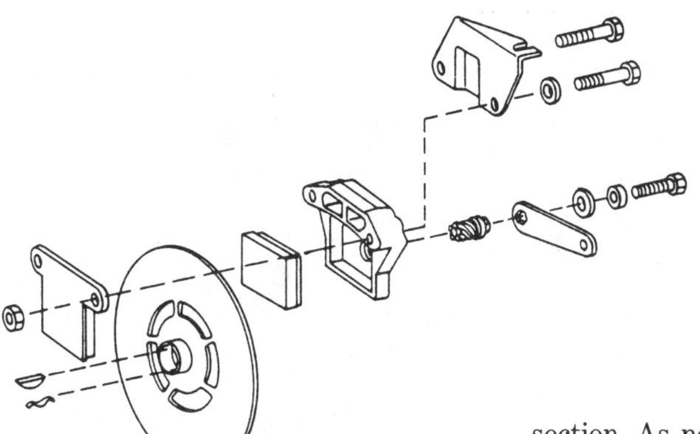

Fig. 47A — View showing late model disc brake assembly.

to be removed. To remove collar, turn set screw out of housing, then loosen collar by tapping it clockwise. Remove left (pulley end) bearing and flanges, then slide secondary shaft to left and out of chaincase side bearing and brake disc.

Refer to Fig. 47 for an exploded view of an early type disc brake assembly and Fig. 47A for an exploded view of a late type disc brake assembly. With secondary shaft removed, unbolt cable bracket and brake puck body from chaincase, then lift out brake disc.

Pucks and/or brake disc can be renewed at this time. If brake disc is warped or pucks are cracked, install heavy duty brake kit. On early model (Fig. 47) brake assembly, stationary puck is installed in chaincase with LOCTITE. Heat puck to 400 degrees F to break the LOCTITE seal and loosen the puck. Degrease housing recess and coat new puck with LOCTITE or two-part epoxy when assembling. On late model brake assembly, renew pucks with reference to Fig. 47A. When assembling outside housing be sure to position puck with metal part facing the actuating screw; not brake disc.

Coat secondary shaft in brake disc hub area with NEVER-SEEZ when assembling. Brake disc must be free to slide on shaft or brakes will not work properly.

Adjust brake engagement system after assembly by referring to DISC BRAKE ADJUSTMENT section.

DRIVE SHAFT (Direct Drive). Remove muffler, outer brake body, brake puck, brake disc, shaft key, driven sheave and spacer shims. Remove two suspension mounting bolts from each side of tunnel. Drain fluids as needed to prevent spillage, then tip vehicle onto right side and withdraw suspension assembly. Continue to turn vehicle over on its top side. Remove bolt securing right-hand drive wheel to shaft and slide drive wheel over to left side. Remove right-hand bearing assembly mounting bolts and nuts, then withdraw bearing from shaft and tunnel. Slide drive shaft assembly to right-hand side of tunnel, remove left-hand bearing assembly mounting bolts and nuts and then withdraw shaft assembly from tunnel.

Inspect drive shaft, bearings and drive wheels for excessive wear or any other damage. Renew all parts as needed. Reassemble in reverse order of disassembly. Adjust brake assembly and track tension as outlined in earlier sections.

(Chain and Sprocket Drive). All models except Liquifire use two drive wheels, Liquifire models use three drive wheels.

To remove track drive shaft, first empty fuel tank. Remove battery on electric start models. Loosen chaincase cover retaining screws and allow fluid to drain. Remove cover, chain and sprocket as outlined in earlier section. Remove two suspension mounting bolts from each side of tunnel. Tip vehicle onto right side and withdraw suspension assembly. Continue to turn vehicle over on its top side. On models with two drive wheels, remove the two bolts securing drive wheels to track drive axle and slide wheels toward center as shown in Fig. 48. On all models, remove cap screws securing drive shaft bearing flanges to track tunnel. Slide track drive shaft toward chaincase side, lift opposite end of shaft and withdraw shaft, drive wheels and bearings from track tunnel and track.

Inspect drive shaft, bearings and drive wheels for excessive wear or any other damage. Renew all parts as needed. On late model Liquifire, drive wheels are pressed on track drive shaft. If renewal is needed, shaft and wheels must be renewed as a complete unit. Reassemble in reverse order of disassembly. Refill fluids to proper levels. Adjust brake assembly and track tension as outlined in preceding sections.

CHAINCASE. To remove chaincase, first remove chaincase cover, drive chain and sprockets as outlined in earlier section. As needed remove muffler, air intake silencer and hose. Remove upper and lower bearing flange nuts, then remove drive belt, driven sheave and secondary shaft as previously outlined. Remove brake cable from brake lever and bracket. Remove two nuts (Arrows – Fig. 49) securing chaincase to outside of track tunnel, and lift off chaincase with brake assembly.

Reassemble by reversing removal procedures. Locking flanges on both track drive shaft bearings must face toward chaincase side. Install a new gasket between track drive shaft bearing flange and chaincase, and a new "O" ring on chaincase side bearing. Adjust brake cable and refill chaincase to proper level with recommended gear oil.

Fig. 48 — View of track drive shaft with drive wheels slid to middle for shaft removal.

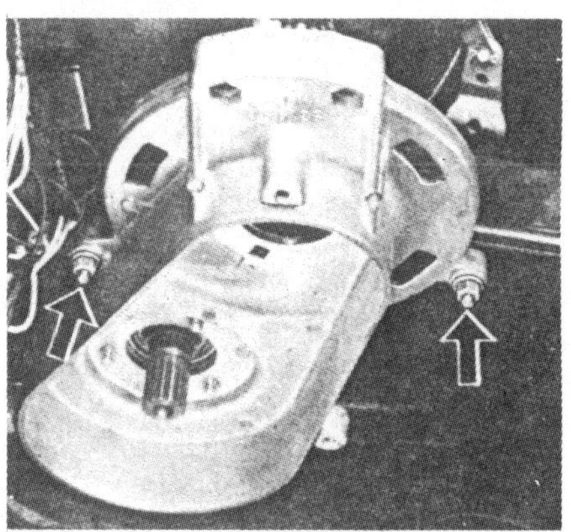

Fig. 49 — To remove the diecast chain case, remove the two nuts (arrows) and upper and lower bearing flange nuts.

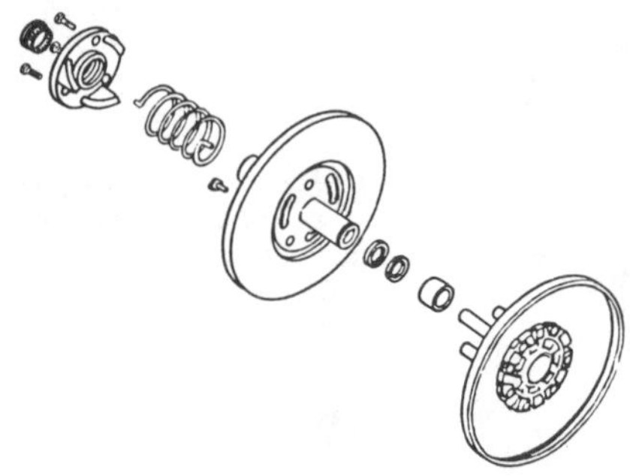

Fig. 50-Exploded view of driven clutch and associated parts used on late models.

DRIVE BELT AND SHEAVES. Refer to CONDENSED SERVICE DATA tables for belt and converter application, and to the appropriate components section for unit overhaul.

Late model machines with John Deere/Comet drives can be adjusted for engagement speed and governed speeds. Clutch engagement speed is adjusted by changing springs and weights in drive clutch. Modifications in drive clutch will also affect maximum speed, however, upshift can be independently altered by changing spring setting in driven sheave.

Fig. 51—To remove John Deere driven pulley remove retaining cap screw (arrow) and washer.

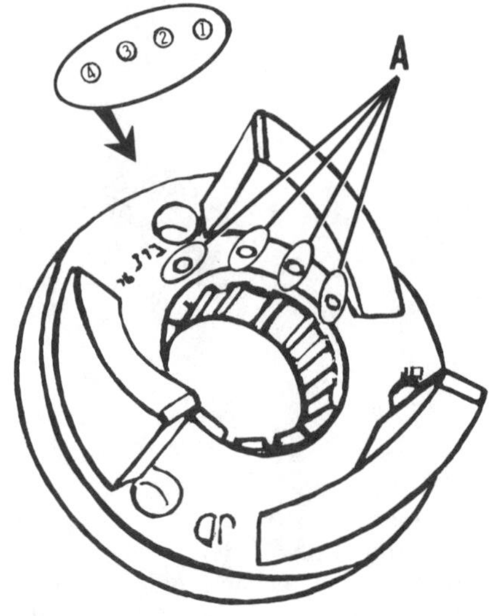

Fig. 52—View of John Deere clutch cam removed showing torque spring anchor holes (A) which are numbered right to left as shown in inset.

JOHN DEERE DRIVEN SHEAVE. Refer to Fig. 50 for an exploded view. The John Deere driven unit is unique in that the actuating spring and torque cam are on the fixed face side of pulley.

To remove the driven pulley, raise belt shield and remove the drive belt. Remove cap screw (Arrow – Fig. 51) and washer and slide pulley unit off of shaft.

Remove the three cap screws securing cam to moving face studs and lift off cam and spring. Note positioning of torque spring anchor in cam face as pulley is disassembled. Cam is equipped with four anchor holes as shown at (A – Fig. 52) which are numbered counter-clockwise as shown in inset. The correct hole for most applications is No. 2. Moving spring anchor to a higher numbered hole **increases** spring tension and engine top speed.

NOTE: When spring anchor is moved to No. 4 hole, cam must be turned clockwise TWO ramps (140 degrees). In all other anchor hole positions, correct preload is ONE ramp.

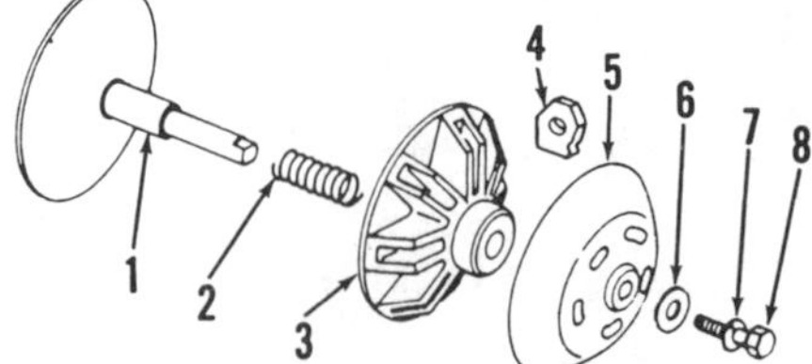

Fig. 52A—Exploded view of Model 94C drive sheave.

1. Fixed face hub
2. Spring
3. Moveable face
4. Wedge
5. Cover plate
6. Flat washer
7. Lockwasher
8. Cap screw

Inspect Nylon ramp shoes in fixed face for wear or damage. If removal is indicated, break off ramp shoe, then CAREFULLY drill out shoe shank using a 15/64 inch drill. Do not enlarge hole in ramp post. Install new ramp shoes with epoxy, and tap into place with a soft hammer.

Bushings in moveable hub and cam are renewable. Bushing in hub must be pressed out and new bushing pressed in until flush with hub bore. Cam bushing can be driven out with a hammer and punch, and new bushing pushed in by hand.

Use NEVER-SEEZ lubricant sparingly when assembling on shaft and both bushings. Make sure the removed spacers are installed between sheave halves.

Recheck belt alignment when installing sheave, as previously outlined.

JOHN DEERE DRIVE SHEAVE. Clutch Models 94C and 102C are manufactured for John Deere by Comet Industries. Refer to COMET CONVERTER section for disassembly and repair procedures. Refer to accompanying tables for making altitude adjustments. For identification of components listed in tables refer to Fig. 52A for Model 94C and Fig. 52B for Model 102C.

Trailfire 340—94C Clutch (Black Cover)

Altitude	Clutch Engagement (rpm)	Governed Speed (rpm)	Primary Sheave No. of Weights	Primary Sheave Hole Size	Primary Sheave Spring	Driven Sheave Spring Pos.	Driven Sheave Cam (Degrees)	Chaincase Sprocket Teeth	Chaincase Chain (Pitch)
Sea Level to 3000 Ft.	4000 to 4300	6000 to 6500	9	7/8 in.	White	No. 2	44	21/39	66
3000 to 6000 Ft.	4000 to 4300	6000 to 6500	6 3	7/8 in. 1 in.	White	No. 2	44	17/35	62
Above 6000 Ft.	4000 to 4300	6000 to 6500	3 6	7/8 in. 1 in.	White	No. 2	44	17/35	62

Trailfire 340—94C Clutch (Silver Cover)

Altitude	Clutch Engagement (rpm)	Governed Speed (rpm)	Primary Sheave No. of Weights	Primary Sheave Hole Size	Primary Sheave Spring	Driven Sheave Spring Pos.	Driven Sheave Cam (Degrees)	Chaincase Sprocket Teeth	Chaincase Chain (Pitch)
Sea Level to 3000 Ft.	3200 to 3500	6000 to 6500	9	¾ in.	White	No. 2	44	21/39	66
3000 to 6000 Ft.	3300 to 3600	6000 to 6500	6 3	¾ in. ⅞ in.	White	No. 2	44	17/35	62
Above 6000 Ft.	3400 to 3700	6000 to 6500	9	⅞ in.	White	No. 2	44	17/35	62

Spitfire—94C Clutch (Prior to 1980)

Altitude	Primary Sheave No. of Weights	Primary Sheave Hole Size	Primary Sheave Spring	Driven Sheave Spring Pos.	Driven Sheave Cam (Degrees)
Sea Level to 3000 Ft.	9	¾ in.	White	No. 2	44
3000 to 6000 Ft.	9	¾ in.	White	No. 2	44
6000 to 9000 Ft.	3 6	¾ in. ⅞ in.	White	No. 2	44
Above 9000 Ft.	9	1 in.	White	No. 2	44

Fig. 52B—Exploded view of Model 102C drive sheave.

1. Fixed face hub
2. Steel washer
3. Arm
4. Bushing
5. Moveable face hub
6. Bearing
7. Washer
8. Plug
9. Pin
10. Washers
11. Roller
12. Spider
13. Spring
14. Cover plate
15. Washer
16. Washer
17. Lockwasher
18. Cap screw

Spitfire—94C Clutch (1980 and later)

Altitude	Primary Sheave No. of Weights	Primary Sheave Hole Size	Primary Sheave Spring	Driven Sheave Spring Pos.	Driven Sheave Cam (Degrees)
Sea Level to 3000 Ft.	9	¾ in.	White	No. 2	44
3000 to 6000 Ft.	6 3	¾ in. ⅞ in.	White	No. 2	44
6000 to 9000 Ft.	9	⅞ in.	White	No. 2	44
Above 9000 Ft.	9	1 in.	White	No. 2	44

Fig. 53—View showing knock-out plug removed from frame and special John Deere JDM-41-1 puller used to remove drive sheave.

Trailfire 340—102C Clutch

Altitude	Clutch Engagement (rpm)	Governed Speed (rpm)	Primary Sheave Arm Kit	Primary Sheave Spacers	Primary Sheave Spring	Driven Sheave Spring Pos.	Driven Sheave Cam (Degrees)	Chaincase Sprocket Teeth	Chaincase Chain (Pitch)
Sea Level to 4000 Ft.	3600 to 3800	6200 to 6700	55159	2	Silver	No. 2	38	17/35	62
Above 4000 Ft.	4300 to 4500	6200 to 6700	54287	2	Silver	No. 2	Compound AM55127	17/35	62

Trailfire 440 and LX—102C Clutch

Altitude	Clutch Engagement (rpm)	Governed Speed (rpm)	Primary Sheave Arm Kit	Primary Sheave Spacers	Primary Sheave Spring	Driven Sheave Spring Pos.	Driven Sheave Cam (Degrees)	Chaincase Sprocket Teeth	Chaincase Chain (Pitch)
Sea Level to 4000 Ft.	3600 to 3800	6200 to 6700	54281	2	Silver	No. 2	44	21/39	66
Above 4000 Ft.	3700 to 3900	6200 to 6700	54920	2	Silver	No. 2	44	21/39	66

Sportfire 440—102C Clutch

Altitude	Clutch Engagement (rpm)	Governed Speed (rpm)	Primary Sheave Arm Kit	Primary Sheave Spacers	Primary Sheave Spring	Driven Sheave Spring Pos.	Driven Sheave Cam (Degrees)	Chaincase Sprocket Teeth	Chaincase Chain (Pitch)
Sea Level to 4000 Ft.	3800 to 4000	6700 to 7200	55195	2	Silver	No. 2	Compound AM55127	21/39	66
Above 4000 Ft.	4300 to 4500	6700 to 7200	54287	2	Silver	No. 1	Compound AM55127	21/39	66

Liquifire—102C Clutch

Altitude	Clutch Engagement (rpm)	Governed Speed (rpm)	Primary Sheave Arm Kit	Primary Sheave Spacers	Primary Sheave Spring	Driven Sheave Spring Pos.	Driven Sheave Cam (Degrees)	Chaincase Sprocket Teeth	Chaincase Chain (Pitch)
Sea Level to 4000 Ft.	4400 to 4600	8000 to 8200	55172	2	Purple	No. 2	44	22/35	66
4000 to 8000 Ft.	5000 to 5200	8000 to 8200	55112	2	Green	No. 2	44	22/42	70
Above 8000 Ft.	5200 to 5400	8200 to 8400	55112	2	Gold	No. 2	44	22/42	70

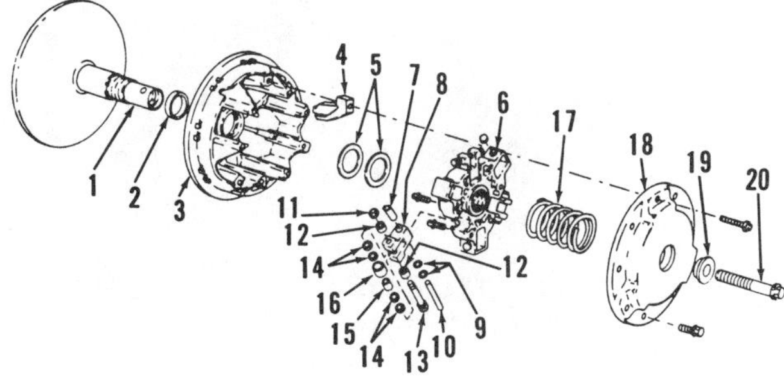

Fig. 54—Exploded view of Model TR800 drive sheave.

1. Fixed face hub
2. Bushing
3. Moveable face hub
4. Ramp
5. Washer
6. Spider
7. Bushing
8. Arm
9. Washer
10. Pin
11. Locknut
12. Weight
13. Bolt
14. Washer
15. Sleeve
16. Bushing
17. Spring
18. Cover plate
19. Washer
20. Cap screw

(Model TR800). Drive sheave assembly is centrifugally operated. As engine speed increases, arms (8–Fig. 54) swing out against ramps (4) on moveable face (3) forcing moveable face half in towards face hub (1). Clutch spring, weight kit and ramp kit is available to make altitude change adjustments on clutch.

To remove drive sheave, raise belt shield and remove drive belt. Remove knock-out plug from side of pan (Fig. 53), then remove drive sheave retaining cap screw and washer. Using special John Deere puller JDM-41-1 (Fig. 53) or suitable equivalent withdraw drive sheave from crankshaft.

To disassemble sheave refer to Fig. 54 for parts breakdown and identification. Press down on cover plate (18) and remove retaining screws equally. Caution should be used during removal as cover plate is under spring pressure. Remove cover plate, spring and ramps (4). Remove locknut (11) and withdraw bolt (13) from arm (8). Complete disassembly of arm (8) by removing weights (12), washers (14), sleeve (15) and bushing (16). Use suitable tools and turn spider assembly (6) off hub (1). Inspect all parts for wear, cracks, pitting or any other damage and renew as needed.

Reassemble sheave assembly in reverse order of disassembly. Ridge on arm (R–Fig. 55) must be aligned with square (S) to insure proper operation of arm. Arrow (1–Fig. 56) on spider should be aligned with arrow (2) on moveable face during assembly to insure proper balance of sheave assembly. Complete reassembly with reference to Fig. 54. Install drive sheave on crankshaft and tighten retaining cap screw and washer to 50 ft-lbs. Install drive belt and check operation of unit.

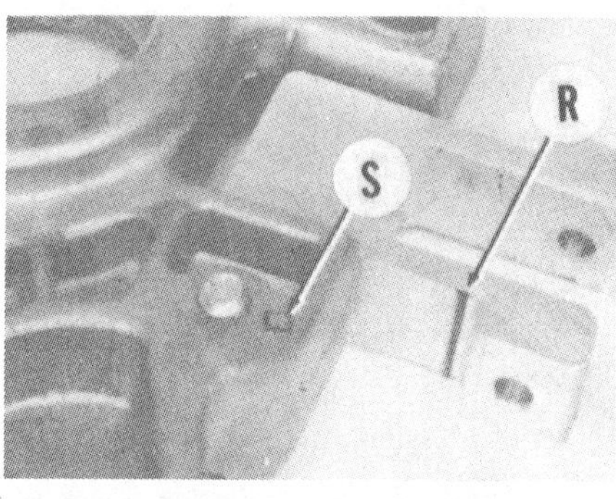

Fig. 55—View showing alignment ridge (R) on arm and square (S) on spider.

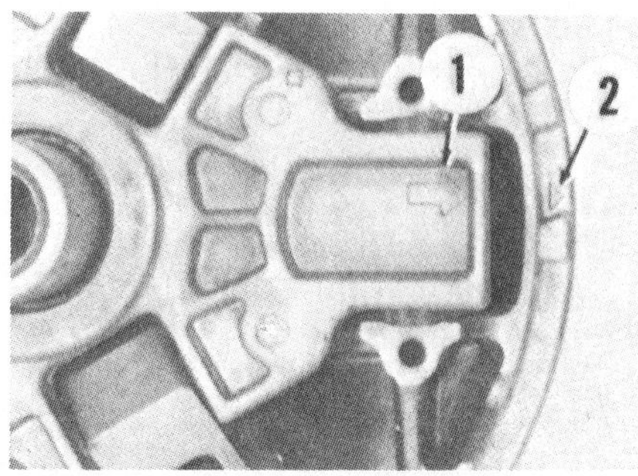

Fig. 56-View showing alignment arrows on spider (1) and moveable face hub (2).

Refer to table shown below for making altitude adjustments. Refer to Fig. 54 for identification of drive sheave components listed in table.

Altitude	Clutch Engagement (rpm)	Governed Speed (rpm)	TR800 Drive Sheave				Secondary Sheave		Chaincase	
			Spacers	Clutch Spring	Weight Kit	Ramp Kit	Spring Position	Cam	Sprocket Teeth	Chain (Pitch)
Sea Level to 4000 Ft.	4400 to 4600	8000 to 8200	2	Green	6-AM55476	No. 1 AM55477	No. 2	44	21/39	68
4000 to 8000 Ft.	5100 to 5300	8000 to 8200	2	Red	3-AM55476 3-AM55478	No. 2 AM55479	No. 2	44	20/39	66
8000 Ft. and Above	5100 to 5300	8000 to 8200	2	Red	3-AM55476 3-AM55478	No. 2 AM55479	No. 2	44	19/39	66

ESKIMO

1969-1971

Model	Engine Make	Engine Model	Engine Displ.	Carburetor Make	Carburetor Model	Sprocket Ratio	Chain Size	Clutch Make	Clutch Shaft Center	Belt Number
					1969					
LX	Sachs	SA280	277cc	Tillotson	HL	12:33		Drummond	10½	13440300
MX	Sachs	SA290	297cc	Tillotson	HR18A	13:33		Drummond	10½	13440300
MXE	Sachs	SA290E	297cc	Tillotson	HR18A	13:33		Drummond	10½	13440300
QX	Sachs	SA370	368cc	Tillotson	HR18A	13:33		Drummond	10½	13440301
					1970					
270M	Sachs	SA280	277cc	Tillotson	HL	12:33		Drummond	10½	13440300
290M	Sachs	SA290	293cc	Tillotson	HR18A	13:33		Drummond	10½	13440300
290E	Sachs	SA290	293cc	Tillotson	HR18A	13:33		Drummond	10½	13440300
440M	JLO	LR440/2	434cc	Tillotson	HR18A(2)	15:33		Drummond	10½	13440301
440E	JLO	LR440/2	434cc	Tillotson	HR18A(2)	15:33		Drummond	10½	13440301
RT-1	Sachs	SA340	336cc	Keihin	407	16:33		Drummond	10½	13440301
RT-2	Sachs	SA440/2	438cc	Tillotson	HD	16:33		Drummond	10½	13440301
RT-3	Sachs	SA740/2	735cc	Tillotson	HD	18:33		Drummond	10½	13440302
RT-1S	Sachs	SA340C	336cc	Tillotson	HD	16:33		Drummond	10½	13440301
					1971					
280M	Sachs	SA280	277cc	Tillotson	HL	12:33		Drummond	10½	13440300
290M	Sachs	SA290	293cc	Tillotson	HR18A	13:33		Drummond	10½	13440300
290E	Sachs	SA290E	293cc	Tillotson	HR18A	13:33		Drummond	10½	13440300
436M	Sachs	SA2-440	437cc	Tillotson	HD	15:33		Drummond	10½	13440301
436E	Sachs	SA2-440	437cc	Tillotson	HD	15:33		Drummond	10½	13440301
R/T 1	Sachs	SA340SS	336cc	Tillotson	HD	16:33		Drummond	10½	13440301
R/T S	Sachs	SA290SS	293cc	Tillotson	HD	15:33		Drummond	10½	13440300
R/T 2	Sachs	SA2-440	437cc	Tillotson	HD	16:33		Drummond	10½	13440301
R/T 3	Sachs	SA2-740C	735cc	Tillotson	HD (2)	18:33		Drummond	10½	13440302

LUBRICATION

The engine is lubricated by oil mixed with the fuel. Use HD40 Motor Oil, Air Cooled Two Cycle Oil or Snowmobile Oil at a ratio of 25:1.

The enclosed drive chain case should contain approximately 1 cup (8-10 oz.) of low temperature grease. Turn machine on right side and remove chain case cover to check and/or add lubricant.

Pressure gun fittings are located on lower side of ski legs (spindles), right end of track drive shaft and both ends of track idler shaft. Use a small quantity of low-temperature grease about twice a month or oftener if necessary. Do not overlubricate track axle bearings.

Lubricate brake and throttle cables, tie rod ends and converter moveable sheaves periodically with a small amount of light oil, being careful not to allow oil to coat sheave faces or brake contact area. Bogie wheels are equipped with sealed bearings and lubrication is not required at this point.

ADJUSTMENT

STEERING SKIS AND LINKAGE. Steering skis should have ¼-⅜ inch toe-in measured at tips of skis (front and rear). With handle-bar in a straight ahead position, adjust each tie-rod equally by loosening nuts (N—Fig. 1) and turning rod center tube (R).

DRIVE CHAIN. The roller drive chain should have approximately ⅜ inch free play measured midway between sprockets after removing chain case cover. To adjust the tension, back out adjusting screw (1—Fig. 2) on front side of eccentric bearing housing and push the screw upward in slot (direction of heavy arrow) until free play is correct. If adjusting screw reaches top of slot before excess play is removed, transfer the screw to the other hole (3) which has then appeared in bottom of slot.

BRAKE. The caliper type disc brake uses the fixed flange of torque con-

Fig. 1 — Loosen locknut (N) and turn center tube (R) to adjust toe-in, which should be ¼-⅜ inch, measured at ends of skis. (L) shows lube fitting on ski leg which is accessible from above.

Fig. 2—Chain tightening slot is located in front side of bearing housing as shown. Tighten chain by moving lock bolt (1) in direction of arrow.

1. Lock bolt
2. Locknut
3. Threaded hole

verter driven sheave as a friction face. Brake wear adjustment should be made by removing the cotter pin and tightening castellated nut (N—Fig. 3) until resistance is felt; then backing off the nut ½-turn and reinstalling cotter pin. Make sure brake puck push pins center the valley in actuating arm (A) when lever is released by readjusting cable housing anchor.

TRACK. With rear of machine raised so that track is clear of ground, track should have some slack but

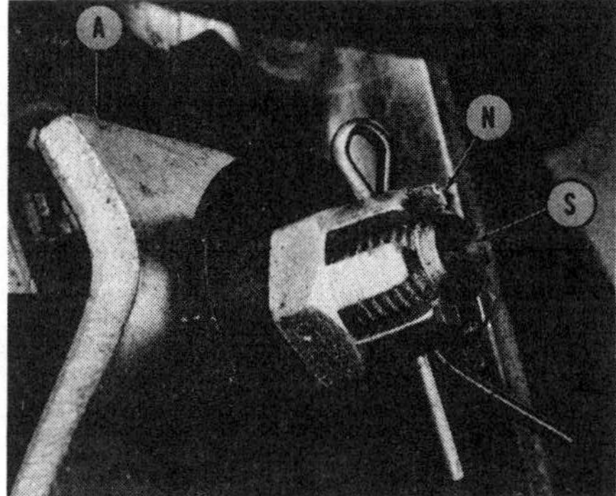

Fig. 3—Brake wear adjustment is made by tighening slotted nut (N).

A. Actuating arm
N. Nut
S. Pivot stud

must not be excessively loose. Tension is correct if distance (A—Fig. 5) from running board to lowest point of swing arm measures $2\frac{15}{16}$ inches. If adjustment is required, loosen pivot bolt nut (1—Fig. 6) and turn adjustment screw (2) until measurement is correct.

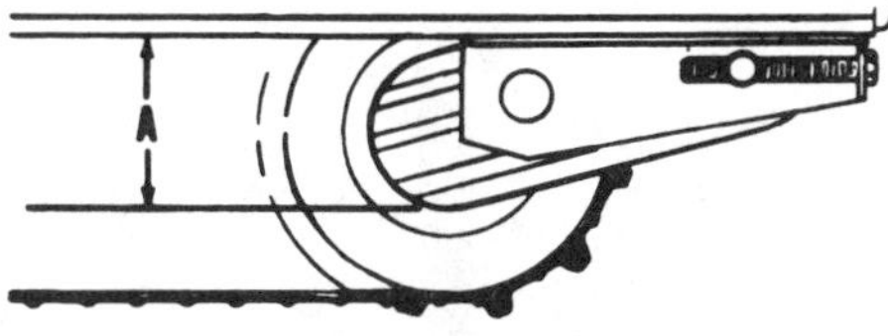

Fig. 5—With rear of machine raised until track is clear, distance (A) should measure $2\frac{15}{16}$ inches.

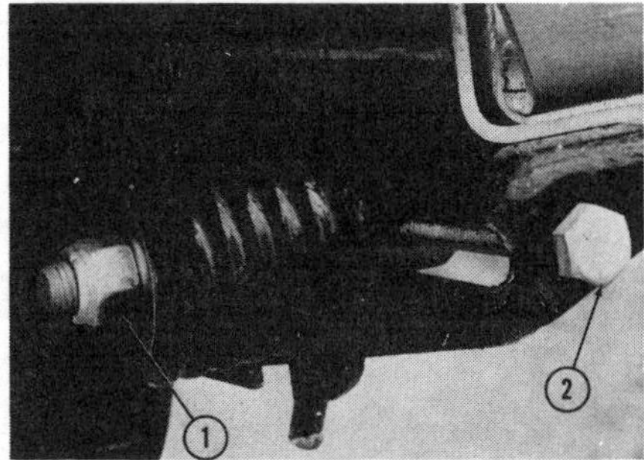

Fig. 6—To adjust track tension, loosen pivot bolt nut (1) and turn adjusting screw (2).

NOTE: Whenever track tension has been adjusted, alignment MUST be checked as outlined in TRACK SERVICE Section of this manual.

OVERHAUL

Refer to the appropriate paragraphs in GENERAL SERVICE sections of this manual for overhaul specifications and procedures of vehicle components.

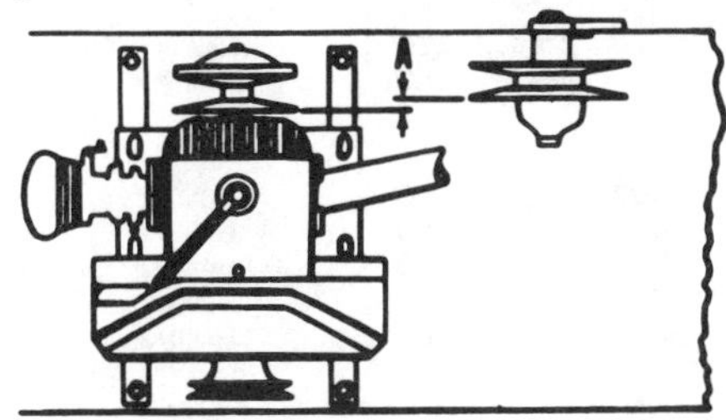

Fig. 7—Driven sheave should be offset 5/16 inch when measured as shown at (A).

FOX TRAC

1966-1972

	Engine			Carburetor				Clutch		
Model	Make	Model	Displ.	Make	Model	Sprocket Ratio	Chain Size	Make	Shaft Center	Belt Number
					1966					
RT-10	JLO	L252	247cc	Tillotson	HL228	9:28	40	Own	12¼	250-712
					1967					
RT-250	JLO	L252	247cc	Tillotson	HR2A	9:28	40	Own	12¼	250-712
RT-300	JLO	L292	292cc	Tillotson	HR2A	10:28	40	Own	12¼	250-712
RT-X40	JLO	L372	372cc	Tillotson	HD7A	10:28	40	Own	12¼	250-712

Model	Engine Make	Engine Model	Engine Displ.	Carburetor Make	Carburetor Model	Sprocket Ratio	Chain Size	Clutch Make	Clutch Shaft Center	Belt Number
					1968					
RT-250	JLO	L252	247cc	Tillotson	HR9A	9:28	40	Own	12¼	250-712
RT-300	JLO	L292	292cc	Tillotson	HR9A	10:28	40	Own	12¼	250-712
RT-350	JLO	L372	372cc	Tillotson	HR8A	11:28	40	Own	12¼	250-712
RT-400	JLO	L372	372cc	Tillotson	HD7A	12:28	40	Own	12¼	250-712
WT-450	JLO	L297	296cc	Tillotson	HR8A	10:28	40	Own	12¼	250-712
WT-500	JLO	L372	372cc	Tillotson	HD7A	11:28	40	Own	12¼	250-712
					1969					
Special	JLO	L292	292cc	Tillotson	HR20A	10:28	40	Own	12¼	250-712
Futura	JLO	L227	223cc	Tillotson	HR21A	10:28	40	Own		250-808
Futura	JLO	L297	296cc	Tillotson	HR20A	10:28	40	Own		250-808
Futura	JLO	L300	296cc	Tillotson	HR20A	10:28	40	Own		250-808
Futura	JLO	L380	372cc	Tillotson	HD14A	10:28	40	Own		250-808
Centura	JLO	L297	296cc	Tillotson	HR20A	10:28	40	Own		250-808
Centura	JLO	L380	372cc	Tillotson	HD14A	10:28	40	Own		250-808
					1970					
Special	JLO	L227	223cc	Tillotson	HR21A	10:28	40	Own	12¼	204-236
Futura	JLO	L295	292cc	Tillotson	HR20A	10:28	40	Own	12¼	204-236
Futura	JLO	L340	336cc	Tillotson	HD14A	10:28	40	Own	12¼	204-236
Futura	Kohler	K399-2	399cc	Tillotson	HR32A	10:28	40	Own	12¼	204-236
Centura	JLO	L340	336cc	Tillotson	HD14A	10:28	40	Own	12¼	204-236
Centura	Kohler	K399-2	399cc	Tillotson	HR32A	10:28	40	Own	12¼	204-236
Centura	JLO	LR440/2	433cc	Tillotson	HD27A	10:28	40	Own	12¼	204-236
Spoiler	Kohler	K399-2	399cc	Tillotson	HR32A	10:28	40	Own	12¼	204-236
Spoiler	JLO	LR440/2	433cc	Tillotson	HD27A	10:28	40	Own	12¼	204-236
Spoiler	JLO	LR760/2	744cc	Tillotson	HD27A	10:28	40	Own	12¼	204-236
					1971					
Special	JLO	L227	223cc	Tillotson	HR21A	10:28	40	Own	12¼	204-236
Futura 340	JLO	L340	336cc	Tillotson	HD14A	10:28	40	Own	12¼	204-236
Futura 399	JLO	LR399/2	398cc			10:28	40	Own	12¼	204-236
					1972					
4222	JLO	LR340/2	339cc	Walbro	WD	14:38	35-2	Salsbury 770		205-753
4232	JLO	LR399/2	398cc	Walbro	WD	18:38	35-2	Salsbury 910		205-854
4242	JLO	LR440/2	434cc	Walbro	WD	18:38	35-2	Salsbury 910		205-854
4312	JLO	LR399/2	398cc	Walbro	WD	16:38	35-2	Salsbury 910		205-854
4322	JLO	LR440/2	434cc	Walbro	WD	18:38	35-2	Salsbury 910		205-854

LUBRICATION

The engine is lubricated by oil mixed with the fuel. The manufacturer recommends that only a good air-cooled, two cycle oil such as SNO-BIL OIL, Chain Saw Oil or Motorcycle Oil be used. Recommended fuel is regular gasoline and recommended fuel-oil ratio is 20:1.

Ski legs (spindles) are equipped with lube fittings at upper end. Lubricate handle bar bushings, tie rod ends and ski hinge points with oil can. Lubricate main drive chain occasionally with a few drops of oil. When vehicle is stored for short periods, remove and clean the chain and immerse in oil for complete lubrication. The manufacturer recommends KLEEN-LUBE or other moly base chain oil.

Track and drive bearings are self-aligning sealed type and do not require lubrication.

ADJUSTMENT

STEERING SKIS AND LINKAGE. With handle bars in normal straight driving position, both skis should point straight ahead and center-to-center distance should be the same at front and rear of skis. Each drag link must be adjusted separately by disconnecting either end of link.

DRIVE CHAIN. The open final drive chain should have approximately ¼-inch deflection measured midway between sprockets. To adjust the chain, loosen the nut on adjusting bolt (9—Fig. 3) and push down on bolt, rotating eccentric housing (8) until adjustment is correct.

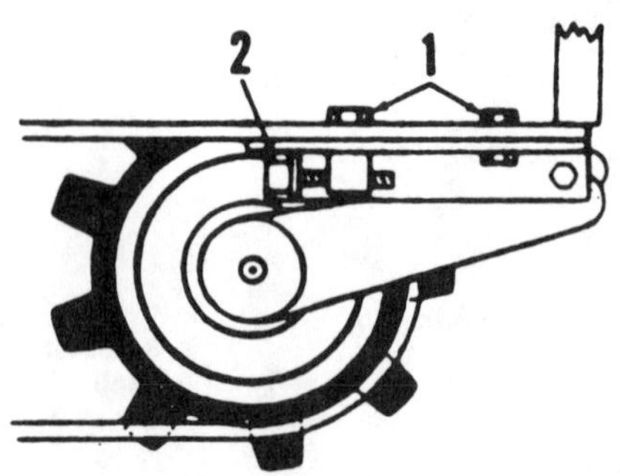

Fig. 2—To adjust track tension, loosen the two clamp bolts (1) and turn adjusting screw (2). Refer to text for details.

BRAKE. On early models, the caliper type disc brake (4—Fig. 3) floats in mounting holes on bracket (6) to apply friction to brake disc (3) which is rigidly attached to pulley shaft. On

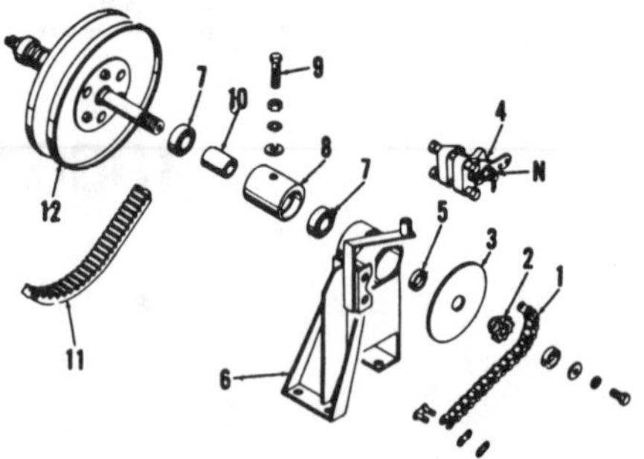

Fig. 3 — Exploded view of intermediate drive shaft and associated parts.

N. Adjusting nut
1. Drive chain
2. Drive sprocket
3. Brake disc
4. Brake caliper
5. ¼-inch spacer
6. Bracket
7. Bearing
8. Eccentric housing
9. Adjusting bolt
10. Spacer
11. Drive belt
12. Driven sheave

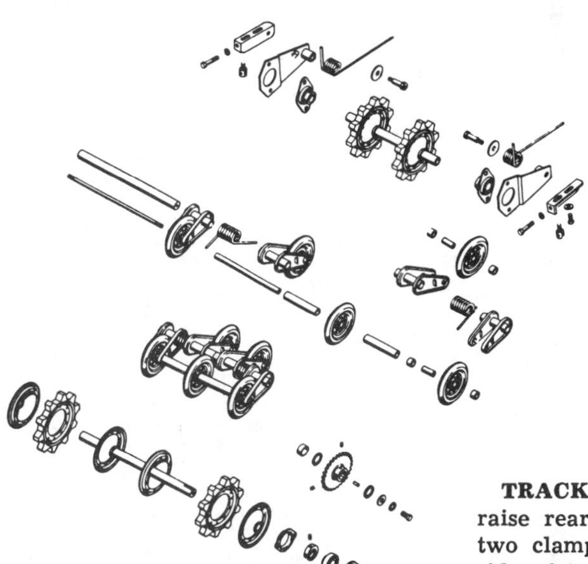

Fig. 4—Exploded view of track suspension and drive axles.

late models, brake is rigidly mounted and disc floats, otherwise action is the same. To adjust the brake, remove cotter pin and turn nut (N) until pucks almost touch shaft but do not drag.

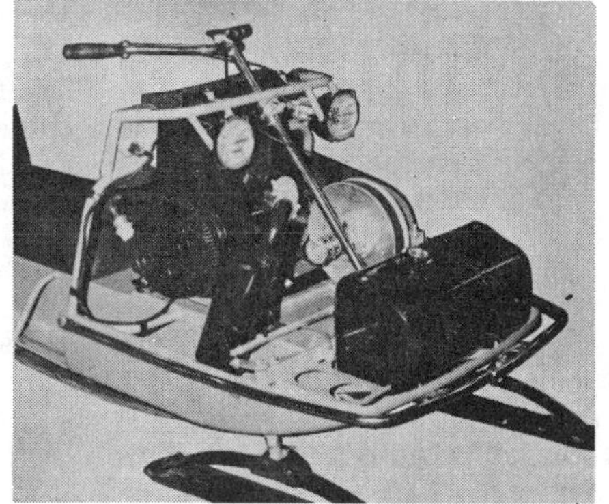

Fig. 5—View of engine and drive unit of 1969 machine with cowl removed.

TRACK. To adjust track tension, raise rear of vehicle and loosen the two clamp nuts (1—Fig. 2) on each side of track frame. Tighten the two adjusting screws (2) evenly until all slack is removed but track is not under tension.

NOTE: When track tension has been adjusted, alignment MUST be checked as outlined in TRACK SERVICE Section of this manual.

OVERHAUL

SKIS & STEERING. Ski legs (spindles) are built into vehicle frame and not available separately. Skis and springs are interchangeable from right to left. Skis are equipped with renewable runners which are retained to skis with one nut on a center stud. Runner can be installed either end forward.

TORQUE CONVERTER. On Fox driven sheave, turn adjusting nut (9—Fig. 7) to compress spring (7) for higher horsepower units, operation on packed snow; or to correct belt slipping. Back nut off for deep snow or where required to obtain desired vehicle performance.

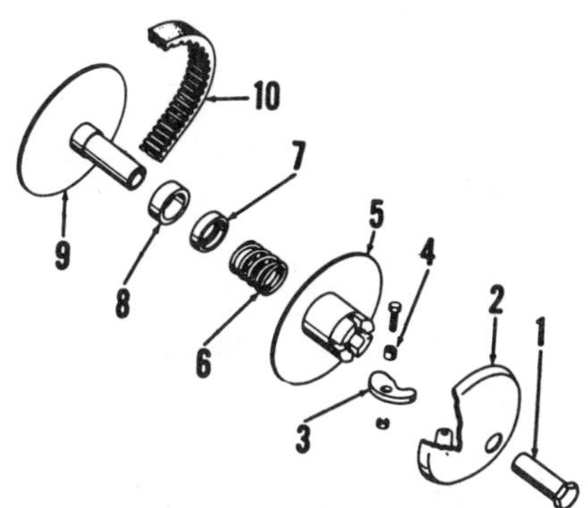

1. Nut
2. Weight housing
3. Weight
4. Spacer
5. Moving flange
6. Spring
7. Spring seat
8. Idler
9. Drive flange
10. Drive belt

Fig. 6—Exploded view of FOX drive sheave unit.

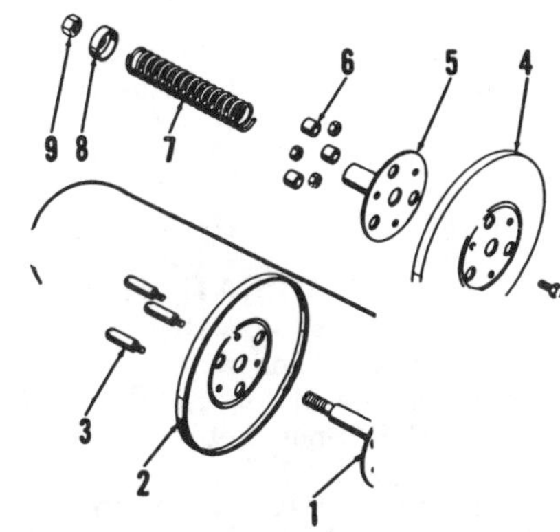

1. Shaft & flange
2. Fixed flange
3. Torque pin
4. Moving flange
5. Slide tube
6. Bushing
7. Spring
8. Spring seat
9. Adjusting nut

Fig. 7 — Exploded view of FOX driven sheave unit.

FREDERICK-WILLYS

1969

Model	Engine Make	Engine Model	Engine Displ.	Carburetor Make	Carburetor Model	Sprocket Ratio	Chain Size	Clutch Make	Clutch Shaft Center	Belt Number
1969										
Galaxy 289....	Kohler	K181	18.6ci	Kohler	N		40	Salsbury		A2117
Galaxy 3129...	JLO	L227	223cc	Tillotson	HR21A		40	Salsbury		A2118
Galaxy 4189...	Kohler	K309-1	309cc	Tillotson	HR23A		35-2	Salsbury		A2215
Galaxy 5189...	Kohler	K309-1	309cc	Tillotson	HR23A		35-2	Salsbury		A2215
Galaxy 6239...	Kohler	K399-2	399cc	Tillotson	HR24A		35-2	Salsbury		A2215

GILSON

1971-1973

Model	Engine Make	Engine Model	Engine Displ.	Carburetor Make	Carburetor Model	Sprocket Ratio	Chain Size	Clutch Make	Clutch Shaft Center	Belt Number
					1971					
420	Kohler	K295-1	294cc	Tillotson	HR78A	15:33	35-2	Salsbury 780	13⅛	16971
431	Kohler	K335-1	335cc	Kohler	BDL	12:32	35-2	Salsbury 780	13⅛	16971
422	Kohler	K309-1	309cc	Tillotson	HR78A	15:33	35-2	Salsbury 780	13⅛	16971
432	Kohler	K399-2	399cc	Tillotson	HR79B	15:33	35-2	Salsbury 780	13⅛	16971
434	Kohler	K440-2	437cc	Tillotson	HR79B	15:33	35-2	Salsbury 910	12-15 16	17609
					1972					
420	Kohler	K295-1	294cc	Tillotson	HR78A	15:33	35-2	Salsbury 780	13⅛	16971
431	Kohler	K335-1	335cc			12:32	35-2	Salsbury 780	13⅛	16971
422	Kohler	K399-2	399cc	Tillotson	HR79B	15:33	35-2	Salsbury 780	13⅛	16971
434	Kohler	K440-2	437cc	Tillotson	HR79B	15:33	35-2	Salsbury 910	12-15 16	17609
					1973					
420	Kohler	K295-1	294cc	Tillotson	HR78A	15:33	35-2	Salsbury 780	13⅛	16971
431	Kohler	K335-2	335cc			12:32	35-2	Salsbury 780	13⅛	16971
432	Kohler	K399-2	399cc	Tillotson	HR79B	15:33	35-2	Salsbury 780	13¼	16971
434	Kohler	K440-2	437cc	Tillotson	HR79B	15:33	35-2	Salsbury 910	12-15 16	17609
435	Kohler	K440-2	437cc	Tillotson	HR79B	15:33	35-2	Salsbury 910	12-15 16	17609

LUBRICATION

The engine is lubricated by oil mixed with the fuel. The manufacturer recommends the use of regular gasoline and SAE 30 Snowmobile Oil mixed at the rate of 20:1.

The drive chain runs in an enclosed chain case which should be filled to level of check plug with approximately 4 fluid ounces of Automatic Transmission Fluid, Type A (Dextrone). Fill plug is located at top of chain case as shown in Fig. 1.

Ski legs (spindle shafts) are equipped with pressure gun fittings which are accessible from engine compartment after raising hood. Lubricate occasionally with low temperature grease.

Lightly lubricate ski pivot bolt and spring mount front bracket with SAE 30 oil periodically for smoother operation and longer life.

Fig. 1–View of engine compartment showing points of adjustment and service.

Track carriage and associated parts are equipped with self-aligning sealed bearings which do not require lubrication.

ADJUSTMENT

STEERING SKIS. Steering skis should be parallel to each other and to vehicle frame when handle bar is in normal straight driving position. Tie rods should be equal in length and adjustment can be made after disconnecting either end.

DRIVE CHAIN. The roller drive chain should have all slack removed but must not be under tension. Because the idler sprocket adjustor is located on the chaincase cover, the adjustment cannot be directly observed. The adjustment may be considered to be correct when the rim of the driven sheave has a free movement of not less than ⅛-inch nor more than ⅜-inch. Refer to Fig. 1.

To adjust the chain, loosen the clamp bolt and move chain adjusting lever (2) down to tighten chain, or up to loosen chain.

BRAKE. The caliper type disc brake uses the fixed flange of the torque converter driven sheave as a friction face. Brake wear adjustment should be made by removing the cotter pin securing the castellated nut to lever arm stud. Tighten the nut until resistance is felt, then back off ½-turn and reinstall cotter pin. Make sure brake puck push pins center in valleys of actuating arm when adjustment is made. Lever arm can be centered by adjusting cable housing anchor nuts.

TRACK. With rear of machine raised until track is clear of ground, center of track should measure 4¾-4⅞ inches from bottom of frame as shown in Fig. 2. Make sure swing arms (support arms) are free and that measurement is made immediately below center bogie support as shown. Both sides must be adjusted alike. Make the adjustment by loosening the jam nut and turning adjustment screw.

NOTE: Whenever track tension has been adjusted, alignment MUST be checked as outlined in TRACK SERVICE Section of this manual.

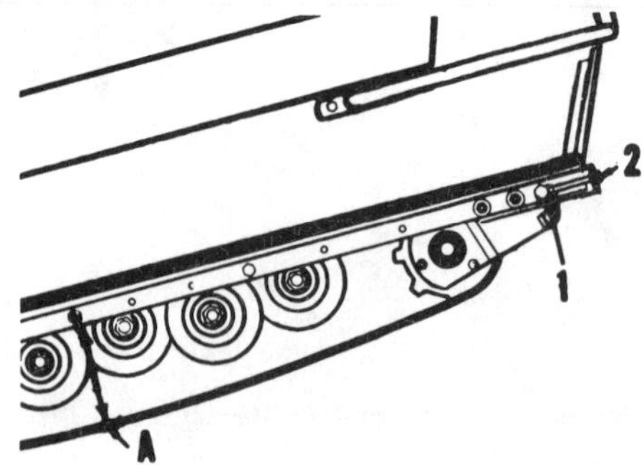

Fig. 2–To adjust track tension, raise rear of machine and loosen nuts on pivot bolts (1). Turn adjusting screw (2) until distance (A) measures 4¾ inches.

HARLEY-DAVIDSON

1972-1975

	Engine			Carburetor				Clutch		
Model	Make	Model	Displ.	Make	Model	Sprocket Ratio	Chain Size	Make	Shaft Center	Belt Number
					1972					
Y, Manual	Own		398cc	Tillotson	HD77A	16:36	35-2	Own	11-15/16	HD-36394-67
Y, Electric	Own		398cc	Tillotson	HD77A	16:36	35-2	Own	11-15/16	HD-36394-67
					1973					
398CC	Own	398/2	398cc	Tillotson	HD77A	15:34	35-2	Own	11-15/16	HD-36394-67
440CC	Own	440/2	433cc	Tillotson	HD77A	16:34	35-2	Own	11-15/16	HD-36394-67
					1974					
Y398	Own	398/2	398cc	Tillotson	HD141A	17:32	35-2	Own	12½	HD-34959-74
Y440	Own	440/2	433cc	Tillotson	HD139A	18:32	35-2	Own	12½	HD-34959-74
					1975					
Y398 Manual	Own	398/2	398cc	Tillotson	HD141A	17:32	35-2	Own	12½	HD-34959-74
Y398 Electric	Own	398/2	398cc	Tillotson	HD141A	17:32	35-2	Own	12½	HD-34959-74
Y440 Manual	Own	440/2	433cc	Tillotson	HD139A	18:32	35-2	Own	12½	HD-34959-74
Y440 Electric	Own	440/2	433cc	Tillotson	HD139A	18:32	35-2	Own	12½	HD-34959-74

LUBRICATION

The engine is lubricated by oil mixed with the fuel. The manufacturer recommends the use of Harley-Davidson Sno Oil and leaded gasoline at the ratio of 20:1. Regular grade gasoline is suitable for Y398, while Y440 requires Premium Fuel. The use of No-Lead, Low-Lead or gasolines containing phosphorous are not recommended.

The torque converter primary drive clutch should be kept filled to bottom of filler plug hole when filler plug is in its lowermost position as shown in Fig. 1, using Harley-Davidson Transmission Lubricant (Part No. 99890-61). Once each season, drain the clutch by removing drive clutch cover, then refill using 12 fluid ounces of Transmission Lubricant.

The enclosed chaincase should be filled to level of sight glass (early models) or fluid level plug (late models) using 6 fluid ounces of Harley-Davidson Transmission Lubricant (99890-61). Drain and refill annually by removing chaincase cover.

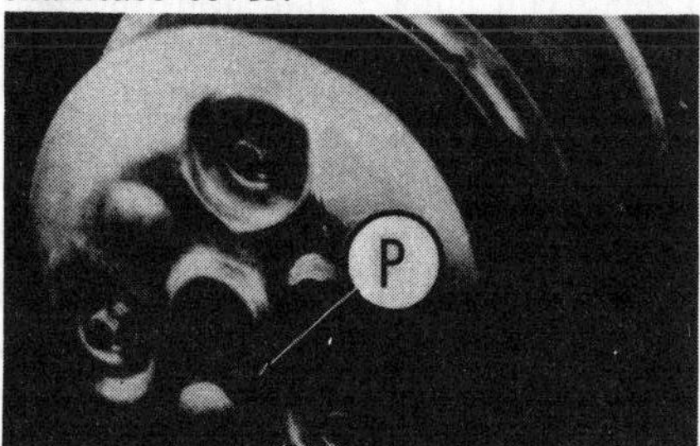

Fig. 1—Primary drive clutch should be kept filled to bottom of plug hole (P) when plug is turned to lowermost position. Recommended fluid is Harley-Davidson Transmission Lubricant 99890-61.

Also annually, lubricate steering spindles and bushings by partially withdrawing ski legs; and track suspension by partially withdrawing slide unit or bogie wheel pivot shafts. Use General Electric VERSI-LUBE No. G-322-L or equivalent high temperature grease.

Other points requiring periodic lubrication with VERSI-LUBE are brake actuating pins and cam; speedometer cable and drive; driven clutch cam pads and bushing; and similar parts.

ADJUSTMENT

STEERING SKIS. Steering skis should be parallel with each other and with vehicle frame when handlebar is in normal straight driving position. A ¼-inch toe-out at front of skis is permissible. Toe-in is normally correct when EACH tie-rod measures 12¼ to 12½ inches center-to-center of ball joints and is equal for both tie-rods. Adjustment is made by loosening jam nuts and turning tie-rod center section.

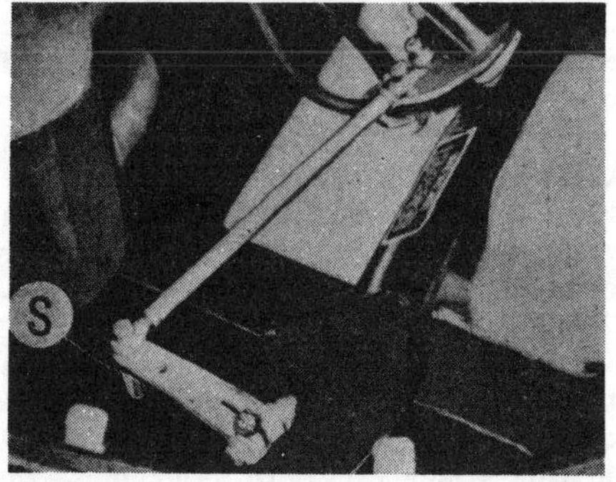

Fig. 2—On 1973 and earlier models, steering stop (S) should contact track tunnel at extreme turn.

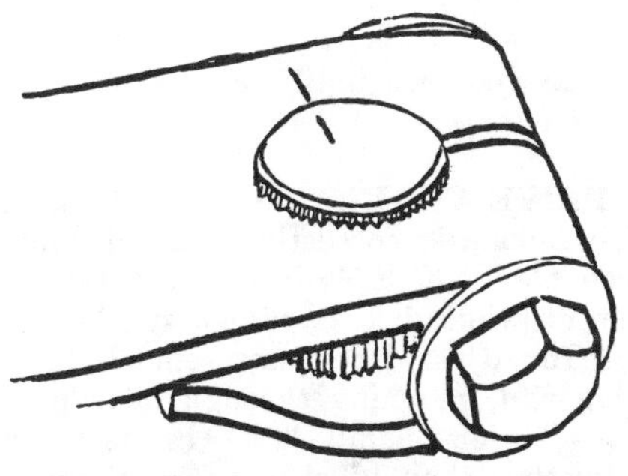

Fig. 3—Scratch-mark top end of ski spindle and steering arm before disassembly.

On 1973 and earlier models, one steering stop (S—Fig. 2) at rear of each steering arm should contact track tunnel at extreme turn in either direction. Shorten drag link if necessary, to accomplish this condition. On later models the positive steering stops bolt to frame casting but adjustment is the same.

Steering arms attach to upper end of ski legs with mini-splines as shown in Fig. 3. There is no master spline and installation position is not marked. Major adjustments may be accomplished by repositioning steering arm on ski leg after marking installed location and removing clamp bolt. Use a small screwdriver or chisel as a spreading wedge when removing or installing the arm.

On 1973 and earlier models, a "Shock Absorber" type steering damper attaches to lower end of steering column and no adjustment is required. Late models use an adjustable "Friction Disc" type damper at steering column lower support. Tighten or loosen Star

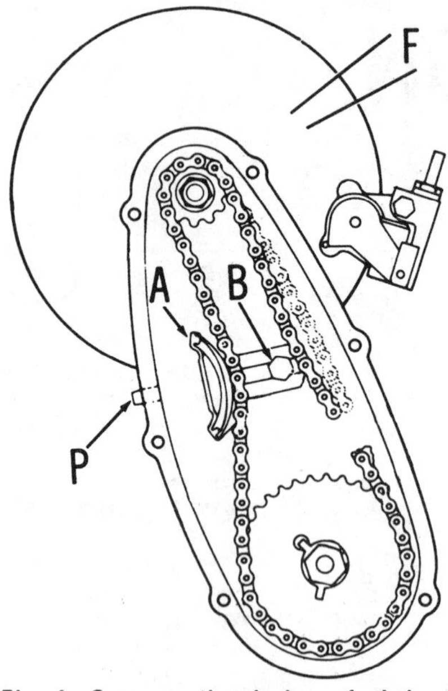

Fig. 4—Cross sectional view of chain case and associated parts showing chain adjustment procedure.

A. Adjusting shoe
B. Clamp bolt
F. Free play (½-inch)
P. Access hole plug

Nut as required until steering action is satisfactory.

DRIVE CHAIN. The enclosed main drive chain is correctly adjusted when free play equals ½-inch, measured at rim of brake disc as shown at (F—Fig. 4). To adjust free play remove filler plug and, reaching through filler plug hole loosen clamp bolt (B) securing adjusting shoe to chain case. Remove access hole plug (P) and working through access hole, bump adjusting shoe inward until free play is correct.

Upper sprocket is optionally available with 13, 14, 15, 16, 17 or 18 teeth and lower sprocket is available with 32, 34 or 36 teeth. This results in a possible optional chain ratio of 1.77:1 to 2.77:1.

Fig. 5—Brake lever should contact stop pin (P) when brakes are released. Wear adjustment is made by removing cotter pin and turning castellated nut (N).

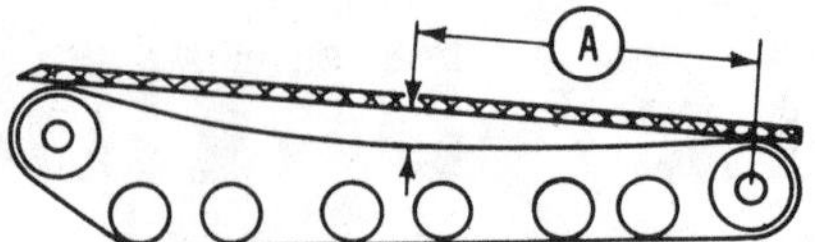

Fig. 6—On bogie wheel models, track tension is correct when top of track sags ¾ inch measured 24 inches ahead of rear idler shaft as shown at (A).

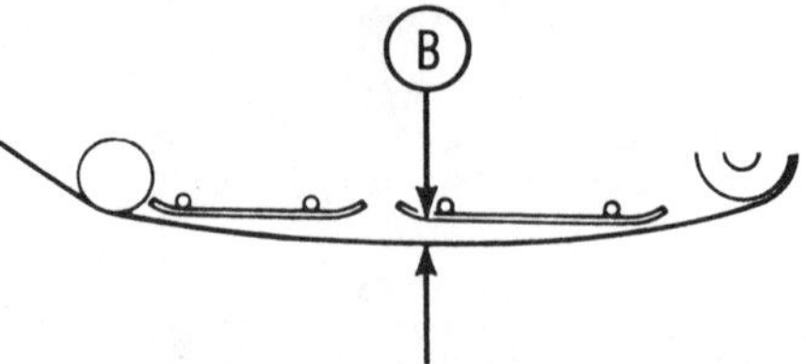

Fig. 7—On slide rail models, track should sag 5/8—1-1/8 inch below front of rear shoe as shown at (B).

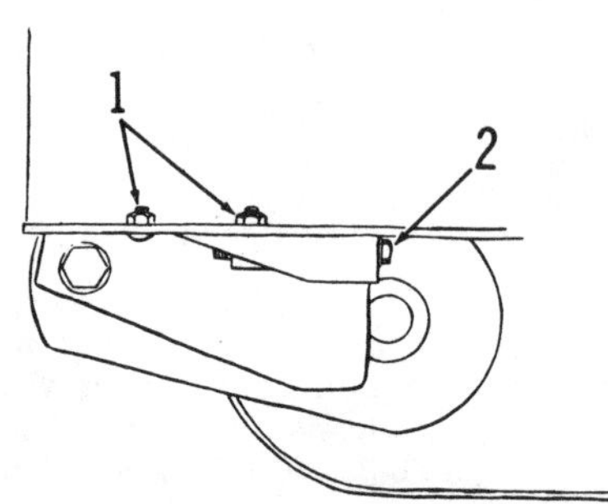

Fig. 8—To adjust track tension on early models, loosen the two clamp nuts (1) and turn adjusting screw (2).

BRAKE. The caliper type disc brake should be adjusted by removing cotter pin and turning castellated nut (N—Fig. 5) until brake pads just clear brake disc when lever is released. Brake lever must contact stop pin (P). On 1973 and later models, make sure brake light switch contacts close when brake is applied. The brake must fully apply before hand lever touches handlebar grip.

TRACK TENSION. To check track tension on models with bogie wheel suspension, place snowmobile on a flat, level surface. With snowmobile resting on track without load, measure sag of track using a straightedge as shown in Fig. 6. Track should sag ¾-1½ inches measured 24 inches forward of rear idler sprocket shaft as shown at (A). Sag should be equal on both sides of machine.

On models with slide rail suspension, track should sag 5/8—1-1/8 inches below front of rear slider shoe when machine is supported with track clear of floor or ground as shown at (B—Fig. 7).

On 1973 and earlier models, adjust track tension by loosening the two clamp bolts (1—Fig. 8) and turning adjusting screw (2). Both sides must be adjusted equally and track alignment MUST be checked as outlined in TRACK SERVICE Section of this manual.

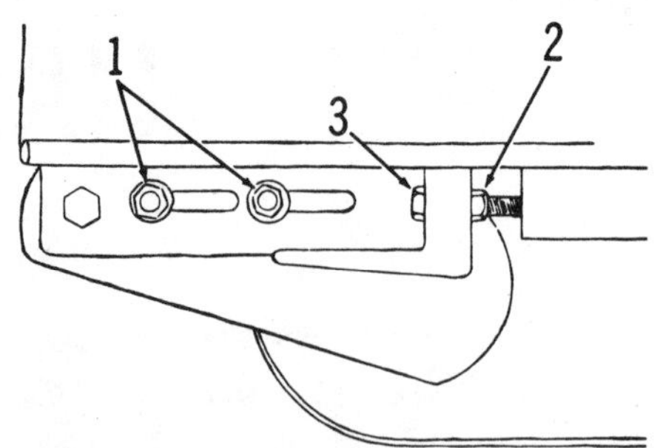

Fig. 9—To adjust track tension on late models, loosen clamp nuts (1) and slightly loosen jam nut (2); then turn jam nut and adjusting bolt (3) at the same time using two wrenches.

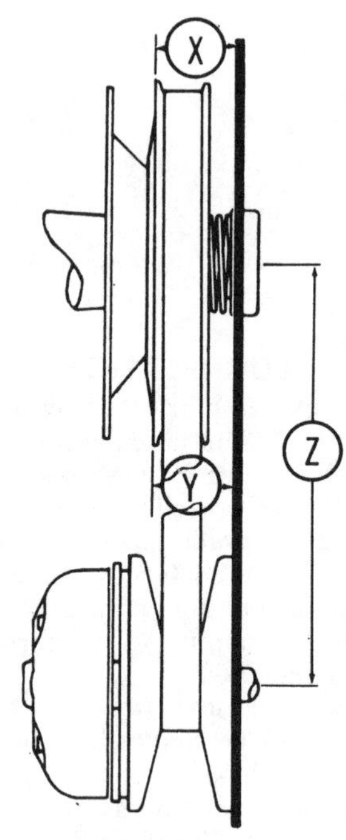

Fig. 10—Offset distance (X & Y) when measured from straightedge should be equal; correct distance is given in text. Shaft center distance (Z) is also given in text and in tables at beginning of this section.

On 1974 and later models, adjust track tension by loosening the two nuts (1—Fig. 9) and jam nut (2); then turning jam nut (2) and adjusting bolt (3) at the same time using TWO end wrenches. Both sides must be adjusted alike and track alignment must be checked after adjustment as outlined in TRACK SERVICE Section of this manual.

DRIVE BELTS & SHEAVES. New belt width is approximately 1-3/16 inches. Recommended method of measuring sheave alignment is shown in Fig. 10. Place a straightedge against inner (fixed) rim of drive sheave, then measure offset distance to inner (fixed) rim of secondary sheave at front and

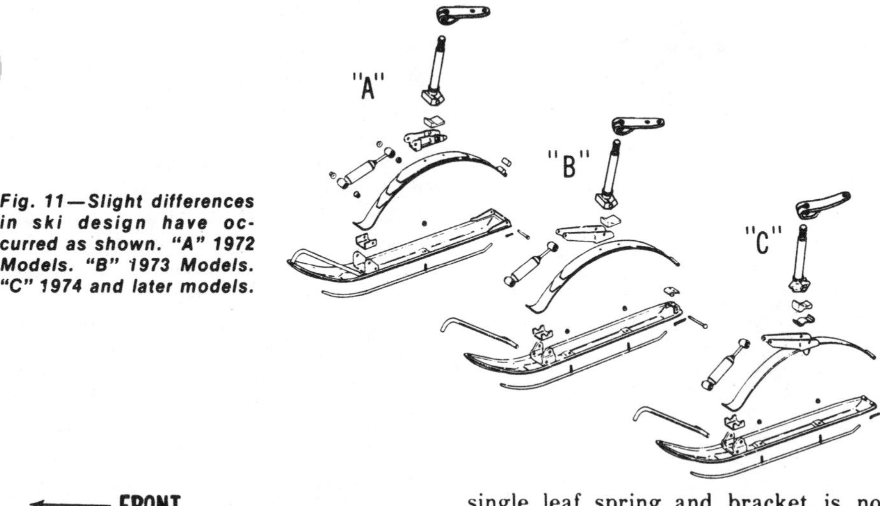

Fig. 11—Slight differences in ski design have occurred as shown. "A" 1972 Models. "B" 1973 Models. "C" 1974 and later models.

← FRONT

Fig. 12—On 1973 and later models the molded track is directional and is marked with an arrow on inside of track which points in direction of TRACK ROTATION. If arrow is missing, make sure vertical side of cleat upon which machine rests is toward FRONT OF MACHINE.

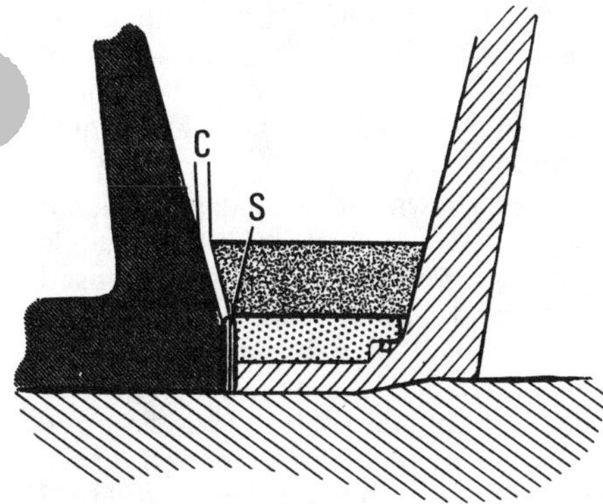

Fig. 13—When machine is not running, side clearance (C) of drive belt in drive clutch sheave should not be less than 0.040 inch [1 mm] nor more than 0.060 inch [1.5 mm]. Clearance is adjusted by adding or removing shims (S).

rear as shown at (X and Y). The distance should be equal and 2¼ inches for 1973 and earlier models; or 2-9/32 inches for 1974 and later machines. Shaft center distance (Z) should be 11-15/16 inches on earlier models with HD-36394-67 drive belt or 12½ inches on later models with HD-34959-74 drive belt. Refer to the separate CONVERTER (BELT DRIVE) UNIT Section elsewhere for operating fundamentals.

OVERHAUL

SKIS. Skis, ski legs, shock absorbers and steering arms are interchangeable from left to right. Multiple leaf springs are interchangeable but the late model single leaf spring and bracket is not. Refer to Fig. 11 for parts identification.

Mark steering arm and ski leg for convenience in realignment before disassembly. Tighten steering arm clamp bolt to a torque of 25-30 ft.-lbs. (3.45-4.25 kg/m) and spring to ski leg retaining bolt to 100-110 ft.-lbs. (13.8-15.2 kg/m).

All 1973 and earlier models used a steering damper (shock absorber) at lower end to dampen steering action. Steering damper is not interchangeable with ski shocks.

TRACK & SUSPENSION. To remove bogie wheels or slide rail suspension units block up rear of machine and completely loosen track tension. Remove the capscrews retaining bogie wheel or slide rail frame support shafts and lift out suspension units. Unbolt rear idler suspension brackets from sides of track tunnel, lower track to shop floor and withdraw rear idler shaft and brackets as a unit.

Place a shallow drain pan beneath chain case and remove chaincase cover. Loosen clamp bolt securing chain adjusting shoe to chain case and completely loosen chain. On 1972 models, remove nut and tab washer securing lower sprocket to drive axle; on later models, remove snap ring and washer. On all models, remove lower sprocket from drive axle splines.

Remove the three locknuts securing drive axle right-hand bearing housing or speedometer drive adapter, then remove the housing by prying out the oil seal. Remove the three lock nuts securing left hand bearing retainer flange to chain case. Drop right end of drive axle to obtain clearance then withdraw to the right until splined end of drive axle clears chain case, then remove the unit.

When reinstalling slide rail suspension unit, note that the four front suspension springs have a narrower angle than the four rear springs. Note also that rear support cross shaft is made of a different material than the three front shafts and is identified by a spot of paint on one end. Springs and rear shaft must always be installed in the proper location.

On 1973 and later models, the molded track is directional and **is marked with an arrow on inside of track which points in direction of TRACK ROTATION, not direction of** snowmobile travel. If arrow is missing, install track so slanted edge of track cleat is first to contact snow as track spins. Refer also to Fig. 12.

DRIVE BELT AND SHEAVES. Most work on the primary drive clutch can be performed without removing fixed sheave from crankshaft. Before attempting to disassemble primary drive clutch install a new drive belt if necessary and use a feeler gage to measure belt side clearance as shown at (C—Fig. 13). Side clearance must not be less than 0.040 inch (1 mm) and should not be more than 0.060 inch (1.5 mm). If side clearance is excessive, decide whether shims (S) should be removed or if a new (unworn) drive belt should be installed. Shims (S) are available in thicknesses of 0.007, 0.020 and 0.060 inch (0.18, 0.5 and 1.5 mm). If belt side clearance is less than specified, shims MUST be added before unit is returned to service. Refer also to Fig. 14.

The first step in disassembling or removing the primary drive clutch is to remove the three lock nuts and drive cup cover (1—Fig. 15). If cover sticks, bump around edge with a plastic hammer or carefully blow compressed air through oil level plug hole to force off the cover.

NOTE: Cup cover is sealed with O-ring but spring pressure tends to force cover off. Cover also contains a small amount of lubricant which must be wiped up when cover is off.

Withdraw springs, guides and retainers. Use the special holding tool as

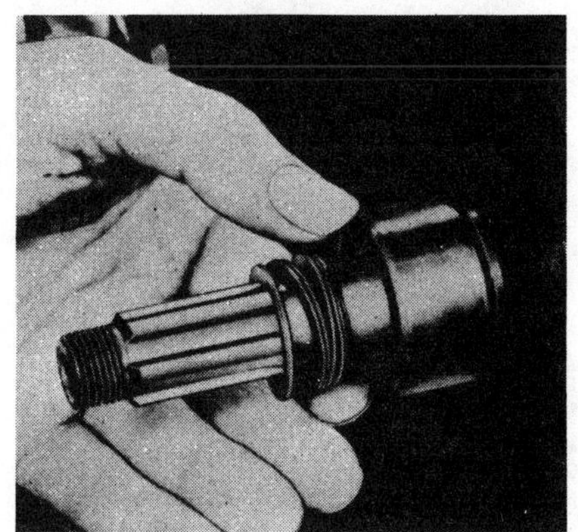

Fig. 14—View of crankshaft with drive clutch outer face removed, showing adjusting shim pack.

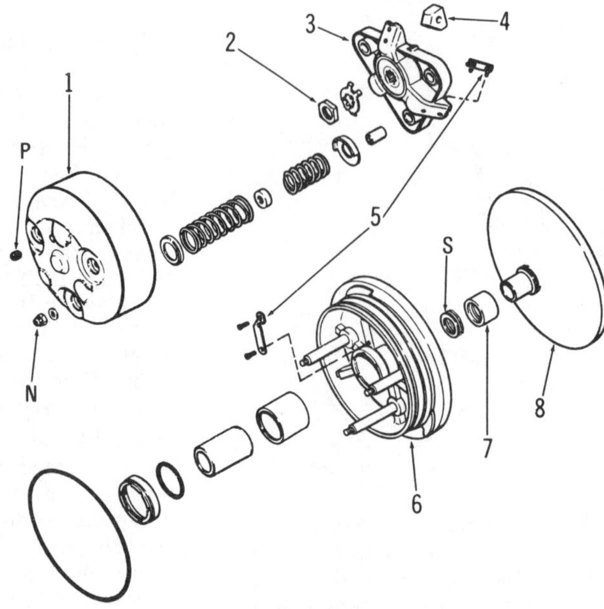

Fig. 15—Exploded view of primary drive clutch, showing component parts.

N. Nut
P. Oil level plug
S. Adjusting shims
1. Drive cup cover
2. Crankshaft nut
3. Drive cup
4. Centrifugal weights
5. Slide strips
6. Floating flange
7. Belt idler
8. Fixed flange

shown in Fig. 16 or other suitable means to keep crankshaft from turning and remove crankshaft nut (2—Fig. 15), lockwasher if used, drive cup (3), weights (4), floating flange (6) and associated parts from crankshaft and fixed flange (8).

To remove fixed flange from crankshaft taper, first lift off shims (S) and belt idler (7). Install a knife-edge puller attachment in groove in pulley hub and use a screw-puller as shown in Fig. 17. It may be necessary to bump end of forcing screw with slight pressure applied to loosen fixed flange from shaft.

Fig. 16—A special tool is available to hold shaft from turning while removing crankshaft nut.

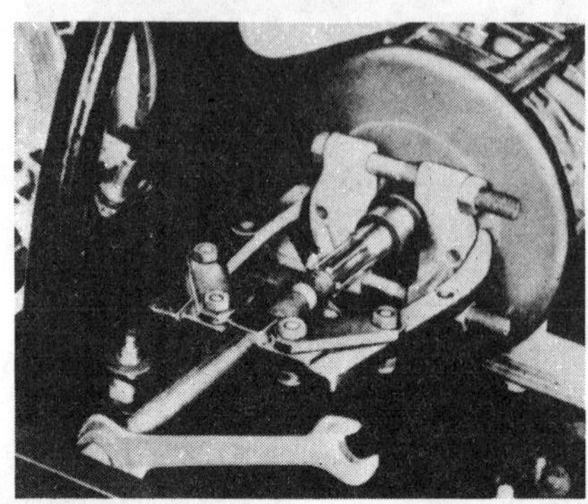

Fig. 17—Remove fixed flange from crankshaft taper by tightening a knife-edge attachment in disassembly groove as shown.

Fig. 18—Pushing secondary shaft and driven sheave from chain case using a jaw puller.

Check belt contact surfaces of both sheave halves for grooving, scoring, heat discoloration or other damage. Check slide strips (5—Fig. 15) in drive cup (3) and on floating flange (6). Renew slide strips in sets if worn or damaged. The flat slide strip on floating flange is retained by self-tapping screws and renewal procedure is evident. Slide strips in drive cup are riveted. Center punch and drill off peened ends if renewal is indicated and back up the new strip on a 5/8-inch brass rod or formed shoe to prevent damage to new part during riveting operation.

If bushings are worn in hub of floating flange (6) or drive pin holes of driving cup (3), install new bushings using LOCTITE after removing old bushings and degreasing bore. Use LOCTITE on crankshaft nut on late models not equipped with tab washer. Tighten crankshaft nut (2) to a torque of 65-75 ft.-lbs. (9.0-10.4 kg/m) on early models using tab washer or 95-105 ft.-lbs (13.0-14.5 kg/m) on late models without tab washer. Tighten drive cup cover locknuts to 85-95 inch pounds (98-109 kg/cm). Refill drive cup cover with Harley Davidson Transmission Lubricant (12 fluid ounces) to bottom of fill plug hole when hole is in lowermost position.

Fig. 19 shows the secondary (driven) sheave used in 1973 and earlier models while Fig. 21 shows driven sheave used on 1974 and later machines. To remove either secondary drive unit first remove drive belt, place a drain pan under chaincase well and remove chaincase cover. Fully loosen drive chain adjuster. Remove lock nut (1972 models) or cotter pin and castle nut (later models) retaining upper drive shaft sprocket to secondary drive shaft splines. Remove lower sprocket locknut

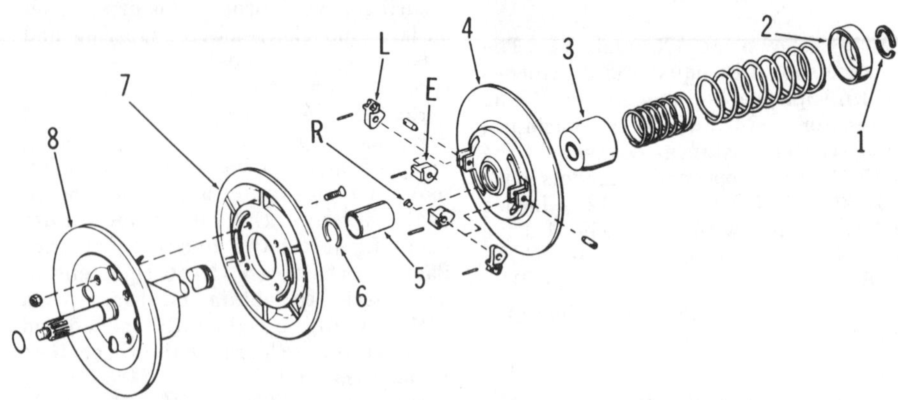

Fig. 19—Exploded view of driven sheave used in 1973 and earlier models.

E. Ramp shoe (early)
L. Ramp shoe (late)
1. Retainers
2. Spring cup
3. Spring cup
4. Floating flange
5. Bushing
6. Snap ring
7. Fixed flange
8. Brake disc & shaft

(1972 models) or snap ring and thrust washer (later models) and remove both sprockets and drive chain as an assembly.

Remove the two cap screws retaining brake assembly to bracket and move brake unit out of the way. If engine is not to be removed, unbolt chain case from its mounting position on track tunnel. Remove the three bolts securing drive axle left bearing retainer to chain case; move case until secondary drive sheave clears cylinder block and press secondary drive shaft from chain case bearing using a two-jaw puller as shown in Fig. 18.

To disassemble the early secondary drive sheave (Fig. 19), first put match marks on both rims of secondary sheave halves using a file or other permanent means. (Drive unit is dynamically balanced and balance must be maintained.) Clamp secondary drive shaft in a soft-jawed vise, spring end up. Depress spring cup (2) by hand as shown in Fig. 20 and remove half-moon retainers (1—Fig. 19). Release spring pressure carefully and lift off spring cup (2), both springs, inner spring cup (3) if used, and floating flange (4). Do not separate brake disc and shaft assembly (8) from fixed flange (7) except on 1972 model where one part must be renewed. The two parts are not available separately on 1973 model. On 1973 model, floating flange bushing (5) is available and renewable, and can be pressed into flange hub after old bushing is removed. Reverse ramp shoes (R) can be pried out with a blade screwdriver if renewal is indicated. Forward ramp shoes (E or L) are retained by a spring pin and shoe axle, and can be removed after driving out spring pins and extracting axle pins.

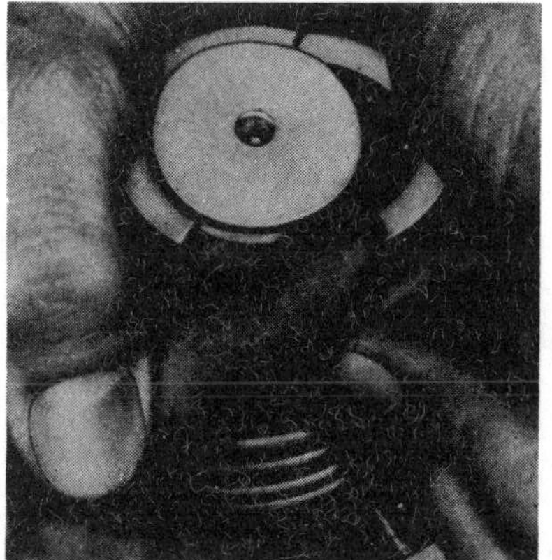

Fig. 20—Depress spring cup (2—Fig. 19) by hand and install half moon retainers (1) as shown.

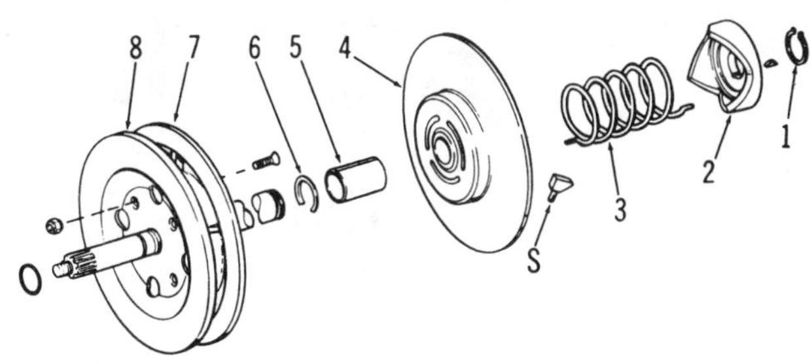

Fig. 21—Exploded view of driven sheave of type used on 1974 and later machines.

S. Ramp shoe
1. Snap ring
2. Cam
3. Spring
4. Floating flange
5. Flange bushing
6. Snap ring
7. Fixed flange
8. Brake disc & shaft

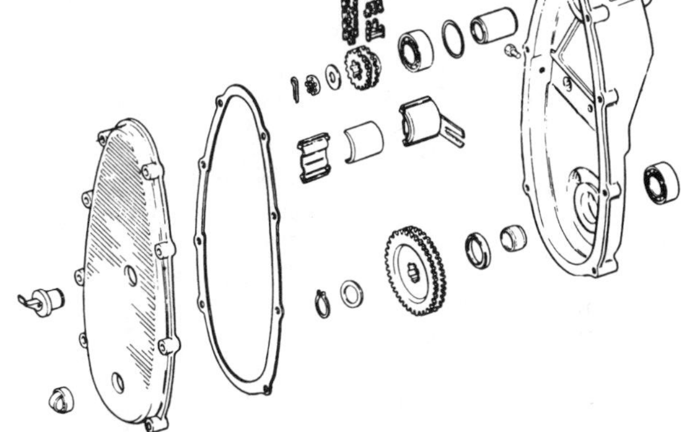

Fig. 22—Exploded view of chain case showing component parts.

Check belt contact surfaces of flanges for wear using a straightedge. If flange face is cupped or grooved more than 1/32-inch, parts should be renewed for best performance. Assemble by reversing the disassembly procedure, using General Electric VERSALUBE No. G-322-L sparingly on ramp shoes and ramps.

Outer cam (2—Fig. 21), spring (3) and associated parts can be removed from 1974 and later models without removing secondary drive sheave or disassembling chain case. Before disassembling spring and cam, first remove drive belt. Pull rearward on top of floating flange rim and check to see that shoe (S) moves away from ramp of cam (2) readily but returns without binding when hand pressure is relaxed. Also note position of tang on flange-end of spring, relative to the three torque holes in flange. Depress outer cam (2), then unseat and remove snap ring (1). Slowly release spring pressure while supporting floating flange rim lightly with other hand. When cam ramp clears Nylon shoes (S), flange rim should unwind less than 1/3-turn. Remove outer cam and spring. When installing spring and cam, preload spring (3) one cam by pulling top of flange rim rearward about 1/3-turn after ends of spring engage holes in flange and cam. Normal spring hole in flange is the one which allows the least torque wrap. Increase torque wrap for faster down-shift under load and quicker engine response to throttle. To renew ramp shoes (S), break off cam contact pad using suitable pliers and drive stem downward with a suitable pin punch. Install new pads using epoxy cement.

CHAIN CASE AND CHAIN. An exploded view of chain case and associated parts is shown in Fig. 22. Chain is double row #35. Upper sprocket is available with 13, 14, 15, 16, 17 or 18 teeth and lower sprocket is available with 32, 34 or 36 teeth. Sprockets are completely interchangeable and can be intermixed to provide a wide range of gear ratios. Chain adjuster shoe is provided with a renewable liner and liner retainer.

HERTER'S

1968-1972

Model	Engine Make	Engine Model	Engine Displ.	Carburetor Make	Carburetor Model	Sprocket Ratio	Chain Size	Clutch Make	Clutch Shaft Center	Belt Number
1968										
10 HP	JLO	L252	247cc	Tillotson	HL186B	9:26		Salsbury 790	11½	25297115
17.5 HP	JLO	L297	292cc	Tillotson	HD6B	9:26		Salsbury 790	11½	25297115
20 HP	JLO	L372	372cc	Tillotson	HD6B	9:26		Salsbury 795	11½	372-125
1969										
Sitka	JLO	L227	223cc	Tillotson	HR22A	9:26		Salsbury 790	11½	25297115
Yakutat	JLO	L300	296cc	Tillotson	HD14A	9:26		Salsbury 790	11½	25297115
Seward	JLO	L300	296cc	Tillotson	HD14A	9:26		Salsbury 790	11½	25297115
Kodiak	JLO	L380	372cc	Tillotson	HD14A	9:26		Salsbury 795	11½	372-125
Yukon	JLO	L380	372cc	Tillotson	HD14A	9:26		Salsbury 795	11½	372-125
Barrow	Kohler	K399-2	399cc	Tillotson	HR21A	9:26		Salsbury 795	11½	372-125
1970										
Sitka 15	JLO	L295	292cc	Tillotson	HD14A	9:26		Salsbury 780	10½	780-10.5
Sitka 18	JLO	L295	292cc	Tillotson	HD14A	9:26		Salsbury 780	10½	780-10.5
Yakutat 15	JLO	L340	336cc	Tillotson	HD14A	9:26		Salsbury 780	10½	780-10.5
Yakutat 18	JLO	L340	336cc	Tillotson	HD14A	9:26		Salsbury 780	10½	780-10.5
Seward 15	JLO	L395	396cc	Tillotson	HD14A	9:26		Salsbury 910	10½	910-10.5
Seward 18	JLO	L395	396cc	Tillotson	HD14A	9:26		Salsbury 910	10½	910-10.5
Kodiak 18	JLO	L440 2	433cc	Tillotson	HD14A	9:26		Salsbury 910	10½	910-10.5
Yukon 18	JLO	L440 2	433cc	Tillotson	HD14A	9:26		Salsbury 910	10½	910-10.5
Barrow 18	Kohler	K339-2	399cc	Tillotson	HR21A	9:26		Salsbury 910	10½	910-10.5
Nome 15	Lloyd	LS400	386cc	Tillotson	HD14A	9:26		Salsbury 780	10½	780-10.5
Nome 18	Lloyd	LS400	386cc	Tillotson	HD14A	9:26		Salsbury 780	10½	780-10.5
Nitro G	JLO	L295	292cc	Tillotson	HD13A	9:26		Salsbury 910	10½	910-10.5
Nitro G I	JLO	L340	336cc	Tillotson	HD13A	9:26		Salsbury 910	10½	910-10.5
Nitro G II	JLO	LR760 2	744cc	Tillotson	HD13A	9:26		Salsbury 1190	10½	702890
1971										
Sitka	JLO	L295	292cc	Tillotson	HR61A	14:35	35-2	Salsbury 780	10½	780-10.5
Yakutat	JLO	L340	338cc	Tillotson	HD63A	16:35	35-2	Salsbury 780	10½	780-10.5
Kodiak	Sachs	SA2-440	436cc	Tillotson	HD64A	19:35	35-2	Salsbury 910	10½	910-10.5
Yukon	Kohler	K340-2	339cc	Tillotson	HR79A	16:35	35-2	Salsbury 910	10½	910-10.5
Barrow	Kohler	K399-2	399cc	Tillotson	HR79A	18:35	35-2	Salsbury 910	10½	910-10.5
Nitro G	Sachs	SA290SS	293cc	Tillotson	HD29A	16:35	35-2	Salsbury 910	10½	910-10.5
Nitro G	Sachs	SA340	336cc	Tillotson	HD27A	17:35	35-2	Salsbury 910	10½	910-10.5
Nitro G	Sachs	SA2-440	436cc	Tillotson	HD64A	16:35	35-2	Salsbury 910	10½	910-10.5
1972										
Yukon	Kohler	K340-2	339cc	Tillotson	HR79B	16:35	35-2	Salsbury 780	10½	780-10.5
Kodiak	Sachs	SA2-440	436cc	Tillotson	HD64A	19:35	35-2	Salsbury 910	10½	910-10.5
Klondike	Kohler	K440-2	436cc	Tillotson	HR42	19:35	35-2	Salsbury 910	10½	910-10.5
Nome	Kohler	K440-2	436cc	Tillotson	HR42	19:35	35-2	Salsbury 910	10½	910-10.5
Nitro G I	Kohler	K340-2	339cc	Tillotson	HR79B.	16:35	35-2	Salsbury 780	10½	780-10.5
Nitro G II	Kohler	K440-2	436cc	Tillotson	HR42	19:35	35-2	Salsbury 910	10½	910-10.5
Nitro G III	Sachs	SA2-440	436cc	Tillotson	HD64A	19:35	35-2	Salsbury 910	10½	910-10.5

LUBRICATION

The engine is lubricated by oil mixed with the fuel.

The enclosed drive chain housing should be filled to level of check plug (1968 models) or just below track drive shaft (1969 models), using SAE 80 EP gear oil.

All models have three lube fittings on steering gear. 1968 models have fittings at rear track idler shaft bearings. Fittings should be lubricated periodically using low temperature grease.

The remainder of the track carriage is equipped with sealed bearings and does not require lubrication.

ADJUSTMENT

STEERING SKIS AND LINKAGE. Steering skis should be parallel to each other and to vehicle frame when handle bar is in a normal straight driving position. Tie rod can be adjusted by disconnecting either end. Drag link is not adjustable.

DRIVE CHAIN. The enclosed drive chain should have not more than ¼-inch play midway between sprockets. Tension can be estimated by removing top access cover from chain case. To adjust the chain, loosen the jam nut on adjusting screw (5—Fig. 2) and move the screw downward in its slot. If screw bottoms in slot, remove the screw and install in the next threaded hole which has appeared in top of slot. Tighten jam nut securely when adjustment is correct.

BRAKE. The shoe-type brake (early models) uses the fixed flange of driven torque converter sheave as a friction face. Brake shoe should clear sheave by approximately $\frac{1}{16}$ inch. Adjustment is made at cable housing anchor. Refer also to BRAKE paragraphs in TRACK DRIVE section of this manual.

On 1970-71 models, an external brake band contracts on a drum

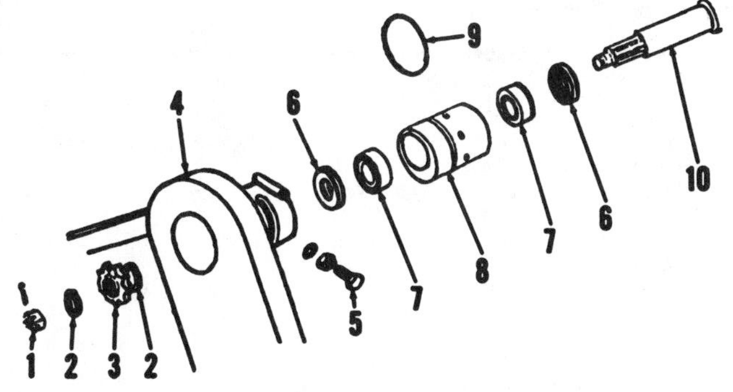

Fig. 2—Exploded view of intermediate shaft bearings and associated parts showing eccentric housing (8) which is turned to adjust chain tension.

1. Nut
2. Spacer washers
3. Sprocket
4. Chain case
5. Adjusting screw
6. Oil seal
7. Bearing
8. Eccentric housing
9. O-ring
10. Intermediate shaft

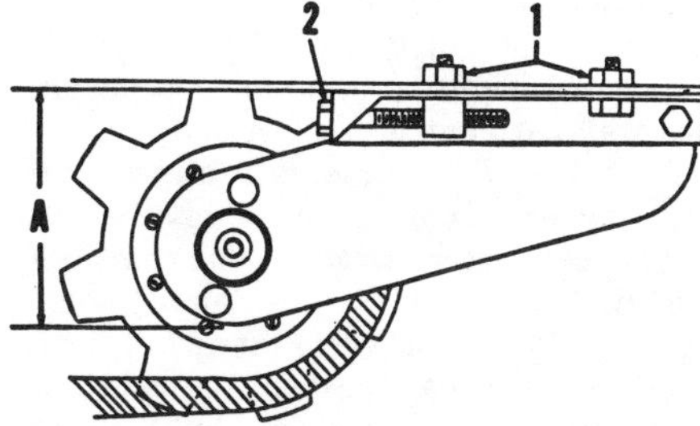

Fig. 3—Schematic drawing of rear swing arm and associated parts used on 1968 models showing track adjustment procedure. Distance (A) should measure 2½-3 inches with track clear of ground and adjustment is made by loosening the two nuts (1) and turning adjusting screw (2).

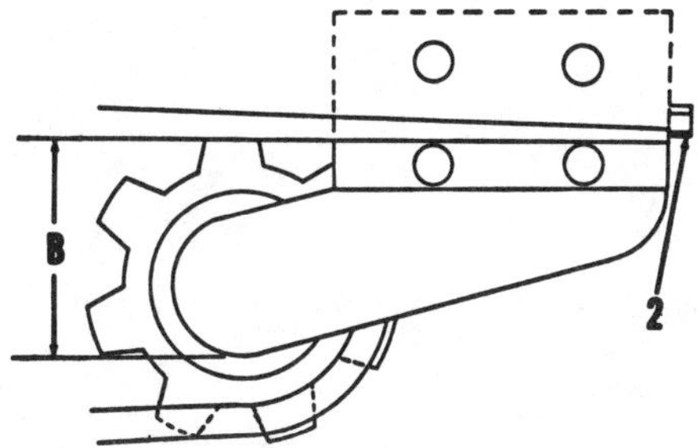

Fig. 4—On 1969 models, distance (B) should measure 2¾-3¼ inches with track clear of ground and adjustment is made by turning adjusting screw (2). Refer also to Fig. 3.

riveted to fixed face of driven sheave. Band should be free when lever is released but should be fully engaged before lever contacts handle bar grip.

TRACK. With rear of machine raised so that track is clear of ground, (A—Fig. 3) on 1968 models should measure 2½-3 inches; or (B—Fig. 4) on 1969 models should measure 2¾-3¼ inches. Adjust by loosening the clamp bolts (1) (1968 models) and turning adjusting screw (2) Both sides must be adjusted alike.

On 1970-71 models, track tension should be as loose as possible—just tight enough to keep track from riding up or slipping on drive sprocket.

NOTE: Whenever track has been adjusted, alignment MUST be checked as outlined in TRACK SERVICE section of this manual.

OVERHAUL

SKIS & STEERING. Skis are equipped with wear bars which are renewable. Skis, springs, spindles and steering arms are interchangeable between right and left side.

POWER TRAIN. Salsbury torque converters are used. Refer to the separate section elsewhere in this manual for service procedures. The intermediate drive shaft (10—Fig. 2) rolls on tapered roller bearings which should be adjusted to provide a very slight rolling torque. If adjustment is required, remove main drive belt and disconnect main drive chain. Remove the cotter pin and tighten the castellated nut (1) a slight amount until adjustment is correct.

TRACK. In 1968, the molded rubber track was equipped with spring steel stays which were riveted in place, and renewable wear clips at drive sprocket holes.

On later models the track is one-piece molded construction and is repairable if returned to the vehicle manufacturer.

HERTER'S

1973-1975

	Engine			Carburetor				Clutch		
Model	Make	Model	Displ.	Make	Model	Sprocket Ratio	Chain Size	Make	Shaft Center	Belt Number
					1973					
Snow Tiger	Kohler	K340-2AX	338cc	Walbro	WD1	15:35	35-2	Salsbury	10¼	910-10.5
Snow Leopard	Kohler	K440-2AX	436cc	Walbro	WD1	16:35	35-2	Salsbury	10¼	910-10.5
Nitro I	Kohler	K340-2AX	338cc	Walbro	WD1	15:35	35-2	Salsbury	10¼	910-10.5
Nitro II	Kohler	K440-2AX	436cc	Walbro	WD1	16:35	35-2	Salsbury	10¼	910-10.5
Yukon	Kohler	K340-2AX	338cc	Walbro	WD1	15:35	35-2	Salsbury	10¼	910-10.5
Klondike	Kohler	K440-2AX	436cc	Walbro	WD1	16:35	35-2	Salsbury	10¼	910-10.5
					1974					
Yukon	Kohler	K340-2AX	339cc	Walbro	WDI-1	15:35	35-2	Salsbury	10¼	910-10.5
Klondike	Kohler	K440-2AX	436cc	Walbro	WDI-1	16:35	35-2	Salsbury	10¼	910-10.5
Nome	Kohler	K440-2AX	436cc	Walbro	WDI-1	16:35	35-2	Salsbury	10¼	910-10.5
Nitro G I	Kohler	K340-2AX	339cc	Walbro	WDA-6	16:35	35-2	Salsbury	10¼	910-10.5
Nitro G II	Kohler	K440-2AX	436cc	Walbro	WDA-6	19:35	35-2	Salsbury	10¼	910-10.5
Snow Leopard	Kohler	K340-2AX	339cc	Walbro	WDA-6	15:35	35-2	Salsbury	10¼	910-10.5
Snow Tiger	Kohler	K440-2AX	436cc	Walbro	WDA-6	16:35	35-2	Salsbury	10¼	910-10.5

Model	Engine Make	Engine Model	Engine Displ.	Carburetor Make	Carburetor Model	Sprocket Ratio	Chain Size	Clutch Make	Clutch Shaft Center	Belt Number
					1975					
Snow Wolf....	Kohler	K340-2AX	339cc	Walbro	WD	15:35	35-2	Salsbury	10¼	910-10.5
Snow Master..	Kohler	K440-2AX	436cc	Walbro	WD	16:35	35-2	Salsbury	10¼	910-10.5
Snow Leopard.	Kohler	K340-2AX	339cc	Walbro	WDA	15:35	35-2	Salsbury	10¼	910-10.5
Snow Tiger...	Kohler	K440-2AX	436cc	Walbro	WDA	16:35	35-2	Salsbury	10¼	910-10.5
Nitro G I.....	Kohler	K340-2AX	339cc	Walbro	WDA-6	16:35	35-2	Salsbury	10¼	910-10.5
Nitro G II.....	Kohler	K440-2AX	436cc	Walbro	WDA-6	19:35	35-2	Salsbury	10¼	910-10.5
Snow Falcon I	Kohler	K340-2AS	339cc	Mikuni	VM(2)		35-2			
Snow Falcon II	Kohler	K440-2AS	436cc	Mikuni	VM(2)		35-2			

LUBRICATION

The engine is lubricated by oil mixed with the fuel. Refer to the appropriate engine section elsewhere in this manual for details of engine lubrication. Use HUDSON BAY 2 Cycle Motor Oil or equivalent high performance, low ash oil.

The enclosed drive chain housing should be filled to just below level of track drive shaft using SAE 80 EP gear oil. Lube fitting for intermediate shaft bearings (in drive chain adjusting bolt) should receive about four strokes with a hand grease gun about once a month or every 40 hours. Do not over-lubricate or oil seal will be damaged. Lube fittings are also located on each ski leg (spindle) and lower handlebar bushing. Lubricate periodically using low temperature grease. Remainder of machine is equipped with sealed bearings and does not require lubrication.

ADJUSTMENT

STEERING SKIS. Steering skis should be parallel with each other and with vehicle frame when handlebar is in normal straight driving position. Both tie rods should be adjusted alike and adjustment can be made by turning center section.

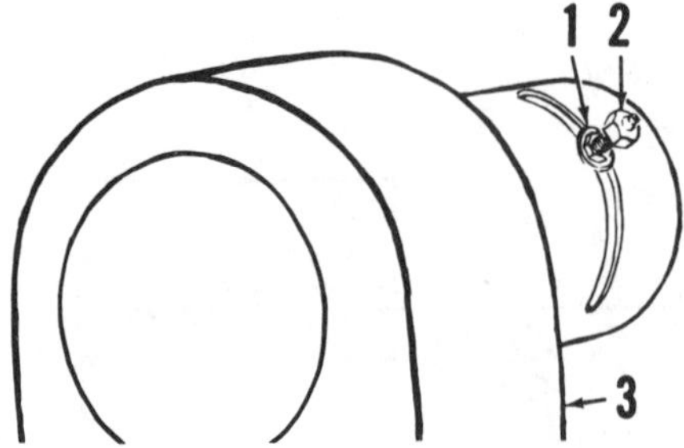

Fig. 1—View of chaincase showing points of adjustment.

1. Jam nut
2. Adjusting bolt
3. Chain case

DRIVE CHAIN. The enclosed drive chain should have not more than ¼-inch side play midway between sprockets. Adjustment can be estimated by removing upper access cover from chain case.

To adjust the chain, loosen jam nut (1—Fig. 1) and move adjusting bolt down in slot to tighten chain. Secure by tightening jam nut. If adjusting bolt bottoms in slot, transfer to the second threaded hole which has appeared in upper end of slot then continue the adjustment. Tighten jam nut securely when adjustment is correct.

BRAKE. The external band-type brake contracts on a drum riveted to torque converter driven pulley. Brake should fully apply before hand lever contacts handlebar grip and fully release when hand pressure is relaxed. Wear adjustment is made by turning anchor nuts on brake cable housing.

TRACK. The manufacturer recommends that track be run as loose as possible without slipping or jumping under fast acceleration or heavy load. Adjust by loosening clamp nuts and turning track adjusting bolts at rear of track tunnel on either side. Both sides must be adjusted alike, so that track centers in track tunnel with machine in motion.

NOTE: Whenever track tension has been adjusted, alignment MUST be checked as outlined in TRACK SERVICE Section of this manual.

HOMELITE

1969-1970

Model	Engine Make	Engine Model	Engine Displ.	Carburetor Make	Carburetor Model	Sprocket Ratio	Chain Size	Clutch Make	Clutch Shaft Center	Belt Number
					1969					
Ranger.......	Husqvarna	SM150	147cc	Tillotson	HL269A	10:45	40	Salsbury 500	7	3211010
Forester......	JLO	L297	296cc	Tillotson	HR	11:38	40	Polaris	10¾	3211001
Explorer......	JLO	L300	296cc	Tillotson	HD7A	13:36	40	Polaris	10¾	3211001
					1970					
Ranger II.....	Polaris	EC16P	164cc	Mikuni	VM26	11:39	35-1	Polaris	11.1	3211006
Ranger II.....	Polaris	EC17P	175cc	Mikuni	VM26	11:39	35-1	Polaris	11.1	3211006
Forester II....	JLO	L380	372cc	Tillotson	HD14A	15:39	35-2	Polaris	11.1	3211004
Forester II....	Hirth	220R	493cc	Tillotson	HD14A	15:39	35-2	Polaris	11.1	3211004
Explorer II....	Hirth	220R	493cc	Tillotson	HD14A	15:39	35-2	Polaris	11.1	3211004

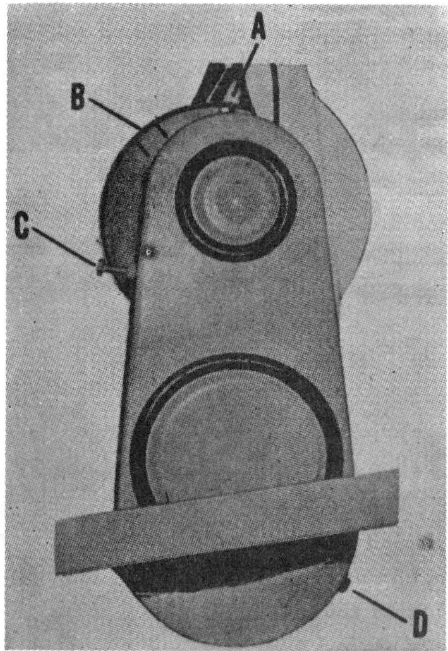

Fig. 2—View of chain case showing oil level plug (D) and fill plug (A). Chain tension is correct when backlash (B) of driven sheave is ½-inch measured at rim as shown. Adjust by tightening or loosening adjusting screw (C).

LUBRICATION

The engine is lubricated by oil mixed with the fuel. Recommended fuel-oil mixture is 20:1 for all models except Forester II and Explorer II equipped with Hirth engine. Recommended mixture for Hirth engine is 25:1. The vehicle manufacturer recommends the use of regular gasoline and HOMELITE Motor Oil. If HOMELITE Oil is not available a high quality, SAE 30 Two Cycle motor oil or a good non-detergent SAE 30 Motor Oil may be used.

The closed chain case should be filled to the level of check plug (D—Fig. 2 or 17—Fig. 7) with SAE 10W non-detergent engine oil.

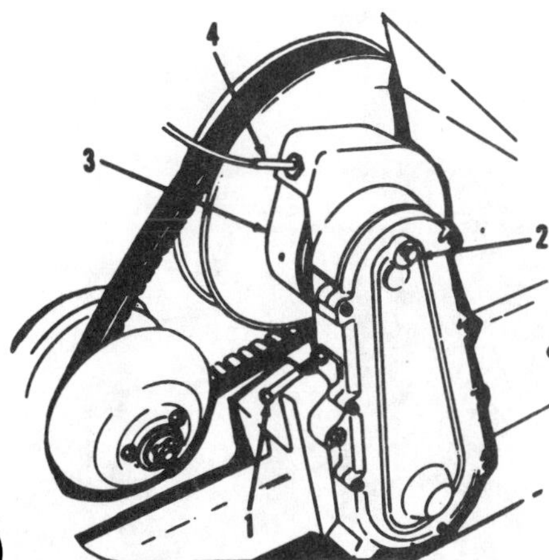

Fig. 3—View of late chain case. Chain idler adjusting screw is shown at (1) and filler plug at (2). Brake band (3) is adjusted by adjusting anchor nuts of cable housing (4).

Fig. 4—To adjust track tension, loosen the three clamp bolts (A) and turn adjusting screw (B). Refer to text.

Throttle and brake cables and steering bushings should be lubricated occassionally with light engine oil. Oil these parts also before machine storage.

Drive train and track are equipped with self-aligning, sealed type bearings which do not require lubrication.

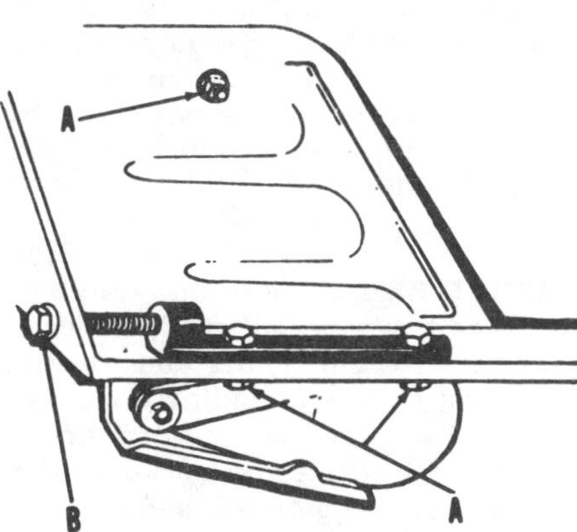

Fig. 5 — To adjust track tension, loosen clamp nuts (A) and turn adjusting screw (B).

ADJUSTMENT

STEERING SKIS. Steering skis should be parallel with each other and with vehicle frame when handle bar is in normal straight driving position. To adjust either drag link, it is necessary to disconnect the link at one end.

DRIVE CHAIN. To check the free play of the roller drive chain, refer to Fig. 2 and proceed as follows:

With engine not running, rock the torque converter driven sheave and measure backlash of intermediate shaft at rim of sheave as shown at (B). Backlash should be not more than ½-inch. To make the adjustment loosen the locknut on chain tightener adjusting screw (C) and turn the screw until backlash is correct.

BRAKE. The band type brake operates on a flat pulley mounted on the intermediate shaft between torque converter driven sheave and upper drive chain sprocket. Wear adjustment is made at brake cable anchor. Adjustment is correct when brake band is free of pulley with brake released but brake is fully engaged before lever contacts handle bar grip. Refer also to BRAKE paragraph in TRACK DRIVE Section of this manual.

TRACK. To check track tension, make sure vehicle is setting on a level surface and sight along top section of track from rear of machine. If track sags more than two inches, adjust by loosening clamp bolts (A—Fig. 4) and tightening adjusting screw (B) an equal amount for both sides of frame.

NOTE: When track tension has been adjusted, alignment MUST be checked as outlined in TRACK SERVICE Section of this manual.

OVERHAUL

SKIS & STEERING. Skis, ski legs (spindles) and associated parts are interchangeable from right to left. Spindle housings are equipped with bushings which are renewable.

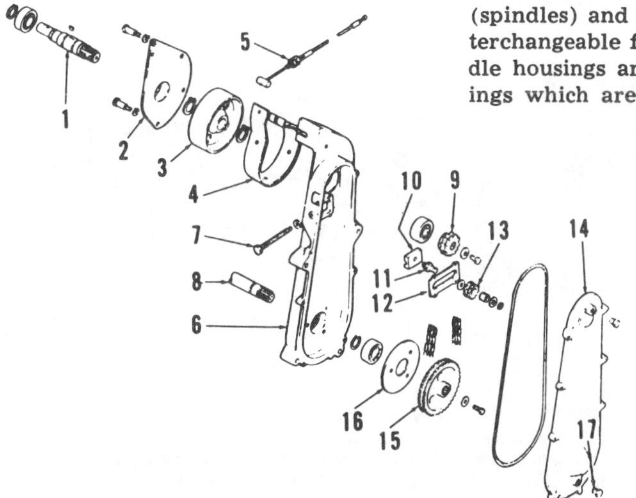

Fig. 7—Exploded view of chain case and associated parts used on most 1970 models.

1. Intermediate shaft
2. Cover
3. Brake drum
4. Brake band
5. Brake cable
6. Chain case
7. Adjusting screw
8. Drive axle
9. Drive sprocket
10. Idler slide
11. Idler stud
12. Retainer plate
13. Idler sprocket
14. Cover
15. Driven sprocket
16. Cover
17. Level check plug

HUSTLER-RUSTLER
1968-1970

	Engine			Carburetor				Clutch		
Model	Make	Model	Displ.	Make	Model	Sprocket Ratio	Chain Size	Make	Shaft Center	Belt Number
					1968					
Hustler	JLO	L297	296cc	Tillotson	HR8A	10:32		Salsbury 790	11¼	50826
Rustler	JLO	L297	296cc	Tillotson	HR8A	10:32		Salsbury 790	11¼	50826
					1969					
Hustler	JLO	L380	372cc	Tillotson	HD13A	13:32		Salsbury 795	10¾	S-4450
Rustler	JLO	L297	296cc	Tillotson	HR18A	10:32		Salsbury 790	10¾	S-4450
					1970					
Rustler	JLO	L297	296cc	Tillotson	HR18A	10:32		Salsbury 790	10¾	702695

LUBRICATION

The engine is lubricated by oil mixed with the fuel. Correct fuel-oil mixture is 20:1. The vehicle manufacturer recommends a good grade of regular gasoline and Esso EASY MIX or Shell QUICK MIX, SAE 40 oil or equivalent.

The closed chain case should be filled to a depth of 1½ inches with Esso MARVELUBE EP9-F or equivalent.

Sealed ball bearings and nylon sleeve bearings are used elsewhere throughout the machine and regular lubrication is not required.

ADJUSTMENT

STEERING SKIS. Skis should be parallel at front and rear. A slight toe-out is permissible. Drag link must be disconnected from steering arm or handlebar if adjustment is required. Steering arms are clamped to splined sections of spindle and installed position is not marked. Steering arms must be set at same angle when skis are pointed straight ahead to maintain correct steering geometry. Punch marks may be used for disassembly and assembly if desired.

DRIVE CHAIN. The enclosed drive chain should have some slack but deflection cannot be measured on early models. On 1969 and 1970 models, chain case cover can be removed as shown in Fig. 1. On all models, loosen screw in slotted hole in bearing housing and move screw downward to tighten chain. Measured slack as shown by arrows should be ½-inch on 1969 and 1970 models. On 1968 models, move screw downward until it stops, then up in slot approximately $\frac{1}{16}$-inch to obtain the required slack. If adjusting bolt bottoms in slot, remove the bolt and reinstall in the next threaded hole which has appeared in top of slot. Tighten the locknut when adjustment is correct.

DRIVE BELT. The torque converter drive belt can be adjusted, if necessary, by loosening the four engine mounting bolts and sliding engine on frame. Be sure drive and driven sheaves are perfectly parallel after adjustment is completed, and that belt centers the vee in each sheave.

BRAKE. On 1968 models, brake hand lever should have approximately ½-inch free play when measured as shown at (B—Fig. 2). On later models, brake lever should have approximately ⅛-inch free movement. Adjust by turning the brake housing anchor nuts at forward end of cable.

TRACK. To adjust the track tension, raise machine until track is clear of ground; then measure the clearance between center bogie wheels and track. Clearance should be 1-1½ inches and should be equal on both sides. To make the adjustment, loosen the two screws (A & B—Fig. 3) on sides of track tunnel. Loosen locknut (C) and turn adjusting bolt (D) until track tension is correct and equal on both sides.

NOTE: Whenever track tension has been adjusted alignment MUST be checked as outlined in TRACK SERVICE section of this manual.

OVERHAUL

Refer to the appropriate paragraphs in GENERAL SERVICE sections of this manual for overhaul specifications and overhaul procedures of vehicle components.

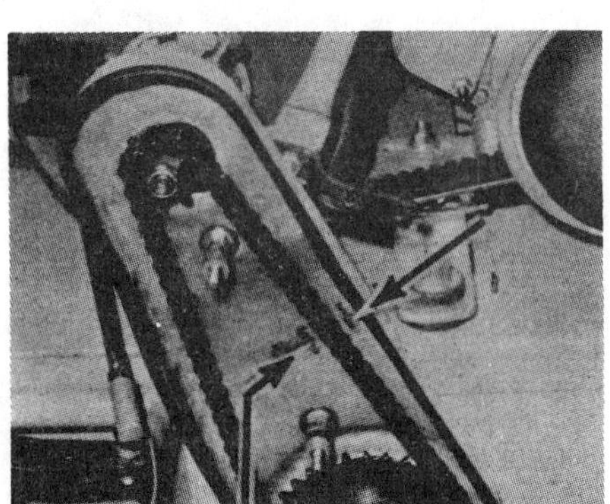

Fig. 1—Chain case cover can be removed as shown on late models for checking drive chain tension.

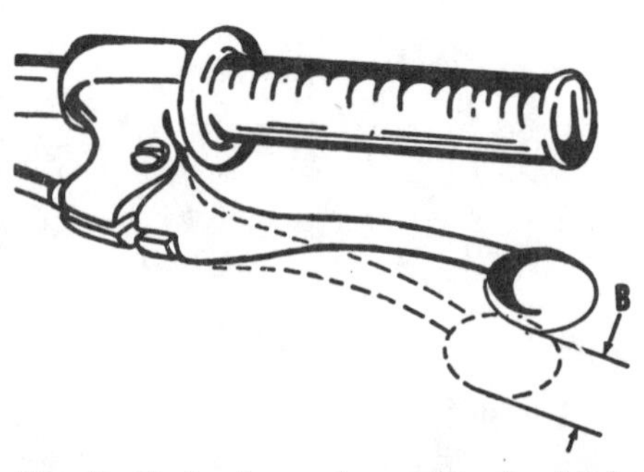

Fig. 2—Brake lever free play should be approximately ½-inch on 1968 models or ⅛-inch on later models when measured as shown at (B).

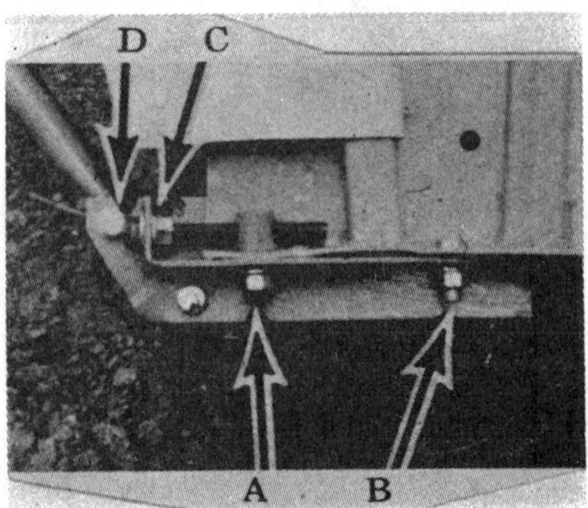

Fig. 3—To adjust the track, raise machine and loosen nuts (A, B & C) then turn adjusting bolt (D) until tension is correct.

JAC-TRAC
1971-1973

Model	Engine Make	Engine Model	Engine Displ.	Carburetor Make	Carburetor Model	Sprocket Ratio	Chain Size	Clutch Make	Clutch Shaft Center	Belt Number
					1971					
200	CCW	312	312cc	Walbro			35-2	Salsbury 780	10¼	702695
340S	CCW	340	339cc	Walbro			35-2	Salsbury 780		151
340L	CCW	340	339cc	Walbro			35-2	Salsbury 780		151
399S	CCW	400	399cc	Walbro			35-2	Salsbury 910	11⅝	SV-165
399L	CCW	400	399cc	Walbro			35-2	Salsbury 910	11⅝	SV-165
					1972					
340	CCW	340	339cc	Walbro			35-2	Salsbury 910	11⅝	SV-165
399	CCW	400	399cc	Walbro			35-2	Salsbury 910	11⅝	SV-165
440	CCW	440	436cc	Walbro			35-2	Salsbury 910	11⅝	SV-165
440WT	CCW	440	436cc	Walbro			35-2	Salsbury 910	11⅝	SV-165
					1973					
290	CCW	290	290cc	Walbro			35-2	Salsbury 910	11⅝	SV-165
399	CCW	400	398cc	Walbro			35-2	Salsbury 910	11⅝	SV-165
440	Kohler	K440-2	437cc	Walbro			35-2	Salsbury 910	11⅝	SV-165
LTD Wide Track	CCW	400	398cc	Walbro			35-2	Salsbury 910	11⅝	SV-165
LTD Wide Track	Kohler	K440-2	437cc	Walbro			35-2	Salsbury 910	11⅝	SV-165

LUBRICATION

The engine is lubricated by oil mixed with the fuel. Correct fuel/oil ratio is 20:1 using regular gasoline and SAE 30, Two Cycle Air Cooled engine oil (or Snowmobile Oil).

The drive chain runs in an enclosed housing which contains oil to approximately the level of lower inspection cover opening. Approximately ½-pint of SAE 30 Non-Detergent Motor Oil or Automatic Transmission Fluid, Type "A" is required.

Sealed or self-lubricating bearings are used elsewhere and periodic lubrication is not required.

ADJUSTMENT

SKIS. Toe-in should be ¼-inch measured at ends of skis. Toe-in can be adjusted by disconnecting tie rod at either end.

DRIVE CHAIN. The enclosed drive chain should have approximately ¼-½ inch deflection measured midway between sprockets. To adjust the chain, loosen the three stud nuts securing upper shaft bearing housing to chain case and rotate housing in the two slotted holes. Tighten nuts securely when adjustment is correct.

Brake alignment may need to be corrected after drive chain is adjusted. Loosen the two brake caliper anchor cap screws and fully compress brake lever on handlebar, then retighten cap screws while brake is applied.

BRAKE. The caliper type disc brake uses the fixed face of driven pulley as a friction surface. Brake must fully apply before hand lever touches handlebar grip and fully release when hand pressure is relaxed.

First be sure brake alignment is correct by loosening brake caliper anchor screws then fully applying brake, retightening the screws with brake applied. Make sure brake push pins center in valleys of actuating lever cam, adjusting if necessary at cable housing anchor jam nuts. Make wear adjustment as required by tightening the self-locking adjusting nut on actuating arm stud until lever action is correct.

TRACK. To adjust the track, raise rear of machine until track is clear. Track should sag below center bogie wheels approximately ⅛-¼ inch. Adjust by slightly loosening the rear axle hanger pivot bolt nut on each side and turning adjusting screws an equal amount.

NOTE: Whenever track tension has been adjusted, alignment MUST be checked as outlined in TRACK SERVICE Section of this manual.

JETSTAR

1970-1972

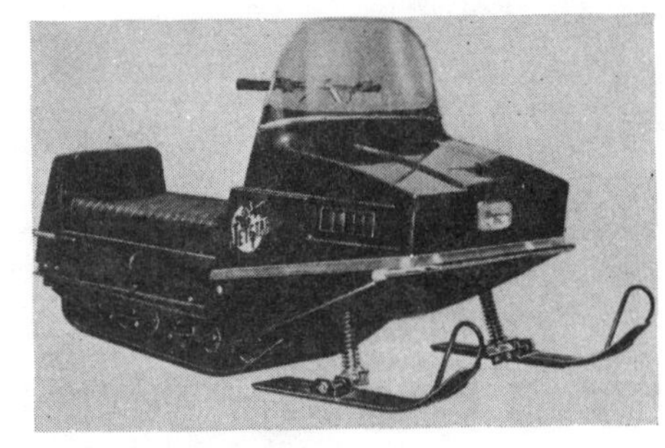

Model	Engine Make	Engine Model	Engine Displ.	Carburetor Make	Carburetor Model	Sprocket Ratio	Chain Size	Clutch Make	Clutch Shaft Center	Belt Number
1970										
170	Chrysler	820	149cc	Tillotson				Salsbury 500	7	900390
220	JLO	L230	223cc	Keihin	406	15:37	35-2	Salsbury 780	11.47	702391
327	JLO	L295	292cc	Keihin	406	15:37	35-2	Salsbury 780	11.47	702391
330	JLO	L230	223cc	Keihin	406	15:37	35-2	Salsbury 780	11.47	702391
440	JLO	L295	292cc	Keihin	406	15:37	35-2	Salsbury 780	11.47	702391
550	JLO	L380	372cc	Keihin	407	15:37	35-2	Salsbury 780	11.47	702391
TT770	JLO	L295	292cc	Walbro	WD1	15:37	35-2	Salsbury 780	11.47	702391
TT880	JLO	L380	372cc	Walbro	WD1	15:37	35-2	Salsbury 780	11.47	702391
1971										
220	JLO	L230	223cc	Keihin	406	15:37	35-2	Salsbury 780	11.5	702391
327	JLO	L295	292cc	Keihin	406	15:37	35-2	Salsbury 780	11.5	702391
330	JLO	L230	223cc	Keihin	406	15:37	35-2	Salsbury 780	11.5	702391
440	JLO	L295	292cc	Keihin	406	15:37	35-2	Salsbury 780	11.5	702391
527	JLO	L380	372cc	Keihin	407	15:37	35-2	Salsbury 780	11.5	702391
550	JLO	L380	372cc	Keihin	407	15:37	35-2	Salsbury 780	11.5	702391
627T	JLO	LR340 2	339cc	Walbro	WD6	15:37	35-2	Salsbury	12-3/16	38
660T	JLO	LR340 2	339cc	Walbro	WD6	15:37	35-2	Salsbury	12-3/16	38
727T	JLO	LR399 2	398cc	Walbro	WD6	15:37	35-2	Salsbury 910	12½	75
770T	JLO	LR399 2	398cc	Walbro	WD6	15:37	35-2	Salsbury 910	12½	75
1972										
330	JLO	L230	223cc	Keihin	406	15:37	35-2	Salsbury 780	11.5	702391
440	JLO	L295	292cc	Walbro	WDS	15:37	35-2	Salsbury 780	11.5	702391
660T	JLO	LR340 2	339cc	Walbro	WD6	15:37	35-2	Salsbury	12-3/16	38
770T	JLO	LR399 2	398cc	Walbro	WD6	15:37	35-2	Salsbury 910	12½	75
880T	JLO	LR399 2	398cc	Walbro	WDA	15:37	35-2	Salsbury 910	12½	75

LUBRICATION

The engine is lubricated by oil mixed with the fuel. The manufacturer recommends CASTROL SNOWMOBILE OIL or other good quality two-stroke engine oil. Recommended fuel-oil ratio is 20:1.

The enclosed chain case should be filled to approximately the level of lower chain case opening with Automatic Transmission Fluid. Inspection and filling can be accomplished by removing chaincase lower cover.

Track carriage and associated parts are equipped with sealed or self-lubricated bearings and do not require lubrication.

NOTE: Optional front wheels are equipped with bushings. Hub is equipped with a pressure gun fitting and whels should be lubricated periodically as required.

ADJUSTMENT

STEERING SKIS. Steering skis should toe out approximately ¾-inch measured at extreme ends when skis are in normal straight driving position. Tie rod ends are right hand and left hand threaded and adjustment can be made by loosening locknuts and turning center section (Tie Rod). Tie rods should be equal in length.

DRIVE CHAIN. The roller drive chain should have ⅜-½ inch total deflection, measured midway between sprockets. Adjustment can be observed by removing inspection covers. To adjust the chain, loosen the four stud

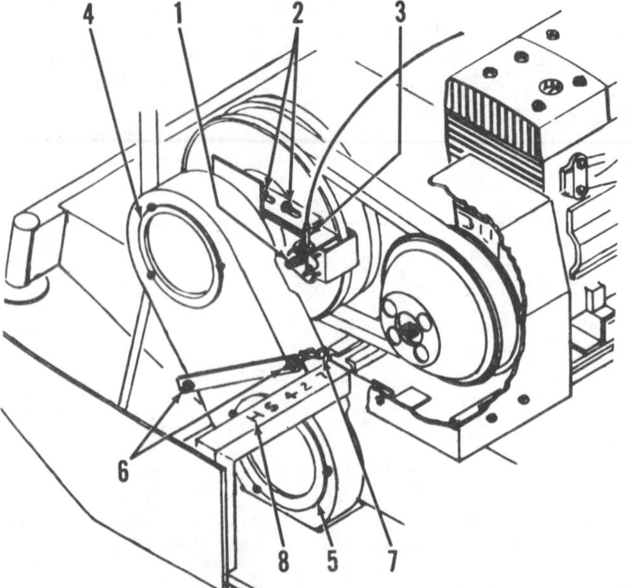

Fig. 1—View of chain case and associated parts showing points of adjustment.

1. Brake adjusting nut
2. Brake alignment bolts
3. Cable anchor nuts
4. Chaincase upper cover
5. Chaincase lower cover
6. Clamp nuts
7. Locating bolt
8. Serial number

nuts holding upper bearing housing clamp ring and rotate housing in chain case until adjustment is correct.

NOTE: Whenever chain is adjusted, brake must be realigned with friction surface of driven sheave as outlined in BRAKE ADJUSTMENT paragraph. Also major adjustment of eccentric shaft (such as changing sprocket ratio, etc.) may change belt center distance. Refer to BELT ADJUSTMENT paragraph for procedure and to tables for specifications.

On some models, clamp ring stud nuts are inaccessible because of driven pulley clearance. The manufacturer suggests the following procedure on these units:

Spread torque converter driven unit by pulling rearward on right sheave half while pushing lower, forward portion of belt into center of sheave.

Remove cap screw and washer from right end of chain case upper shaft. Remove cap screws (2—Fig. 1) securing brake assembly to chain case bracket. Slide driven sheave away from chain case two or three inches to provide clearance, loosen clamping ring stud nuts and adjust drive chain. Check belt alignment and brake as outlined in the appropriate following paragraphs, when unit is reassembled.

BRAKE ADJUSTMENT. Before adjusting the brake, first check to make sure caliper unit properly aligns with angled friction face of driven sheave. Loosen the two cap screws (2—Fig. 1) retaining brake unit to mounting bracket; fully apply the brake, then retighten screws with brake applied.

Brake caliper push pins must be centered in valleys of actuating lever with brake released. Adjust if necessary, at brake cable housing anchor (3).

Brake wear adjustment is made by removing cotter pin and turning adjusting nut (1). Adjustment should only be made with unit properly aligned and lever centered. Brake should be free with lever released but should fully apply before hand lever contacts handlebar grip.

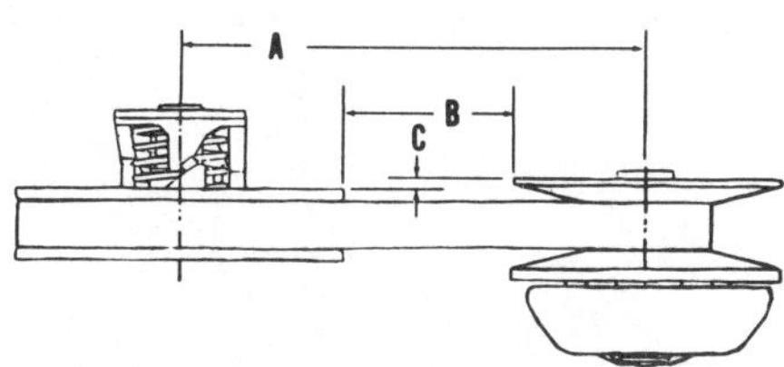

Fig. 2—Belt center distance (A) can be more easily determined by measuring distance (B) between nearest points of pulley rims. Offset (C) should be ¼-inch for single cylinder models and 340 twin; or 5/16-inch for larger models.

BELT ADJUSTMENT. The engine will slide sideways on mounting frame but front to rear position is fixed. Drive and driven pulleys must be initially adjusted for shaft center distance (A—Fig. 2) and offset (C). Major adjustments of driven sheave shaft (such as changing sprocket size) may necessitate checking and/or readjustment of shaft centers.

Offset (C) should not change unless engine mounting bolts are loosened, or unless chain case is sprung or upper shaft worn or damaged. Belt should ideally be removed for checking offset which should be ¼-inch for single cylinder models or 340cc twin; or 5/16-inch for larger twins. Adjustment is made by loosening mounting bolts and sliding engine.

Belt center distance is adjusted by loosening the two gear case clamp nuts (6—Fig. 1) and rotating top of gear case forward to increase center distance. If center distance is to be decreased, it will first be necessary to back out locating bolt (7) to allow top of case to move rearward. Tighten clamp nuts (6) and turn locating bolt (7) in to touch case after adjustment is complete. (Do not attempt to move gear case forward by tightening locating bolt (7) or parts may be damaged). Belt center distance (A—Fig. 2) is given in condensed service data tables. A more convenient method of adjustment is to measure the distance (B) between nearest points on rim of drive and driven sheaves. Shaft center distance is correct when (B) measures:

Model 170	9/16-inch
Other single cylinder models	3¼-inch
Models 627T & 660T	3 15/16-inch
Models 727T & 770T	3¾-inch

TRACK ADJUSTMENT. With rear of machine raised until track is clear, forward bogie wheel of rear unit should clear ½ to 1 inch as shown in Fig. 3. Adjust by loosening carriage bolts and turning track tightener nut. Both sides must be adjusted alike.

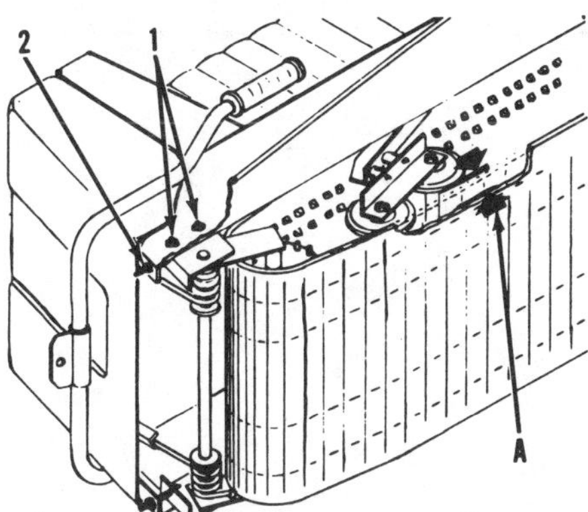

Fig. 3 — Track tension is correct when front bogie wheel of rear suspension arm clears ½-1 inch as shown at (A). Adjust by loosening carriage bolts (1) and turning tightener nut (2).

NOTE: Whenever track tension has been adjusted, alignment MUST be checked as outlined in TRACK SERVICE Section of this manual.

OVERHAUL

Refer to the appropriate paragraphs in the GENERAL SERVICE Sections of this manual for overhaul procedures of vehicle components.

Ski legs (spindles) are equipped with coil, rather than leaf springs. See Fig. 4. The optional automotive type shock absorbers (5) attach to rear hole in steering arm (4) and bracket (6) on forward arch. Steering arms (4) are splined to ski legs (2) and must be installed with front end pointing outward 13-15 degrees from ski centerline as shown in Fig. 5.

On models equipped with Salsbury 780 converter, the standard spring has five coils and is color coded black. The Model 910 converter is normally equipped with intermediate spring which has 7 coils and is color coded yellow. The 41° cam is standard on all models.

Upper drive sprocket is available in 17, 19 and 21 tooth size as well as the standard 15 tooth. Lower (driven) sprocket is available in 32 tooth option in addition to the standard 37 tooth unit.

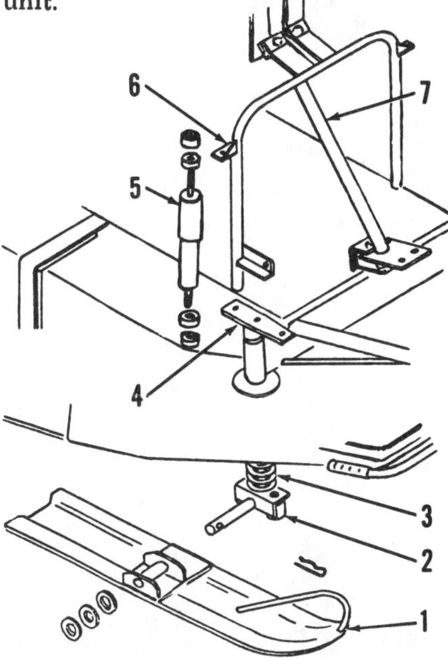

Fig. 4—Front coil spring suspension showing optional shock absorbers (5) which are installed between upper bracket (6) and rear hole in steering arm (4). Steering arms have no master spline, but front end should point outward 13-15 degrees from ski centerline.

KAWASAKI

CONDENSED SERVICE DATA

	Engine			Carburetor				Clutch		
Model	Make	Model	Displ.	Make	Model	Sprocket Ratio	Chain Size	Make	Shaft Center	Belt Number
					1977					
Astro 340	Kawasaki	340	339cc	Mikuni	VM34	2.05:1	Silent	Artic	10.3	59011-3503
Astro 440	Kawasaki	440	436cc	Mikuni	VM34	1.89:1	Silent	Artic	10.3	59011-3503
SST 340	Yamaha	340	338cc	Mikuni	VM34	2.05:1	Silent	Kawasaki	10.3	59011-3503
SST 440	Yamaha	440	433cc	Mikuni	VM36	1.89:1	Silent	Kawasaki	10.3	59011-3503
					1978					
Inviter	Kawasaki	340	339cc	Mikuni	VM34	2.06:1	Silent	Artic	10.3	59011-3503
Intriguer	Kawasaki	440	436cc	Mikuni	VM34	1.68:1	Silent	Artic	10.3	59011-3503
Invader 340	Kawasaki	340	339cc	Mikuni	VM32	2.06:1	Silent	Kawasaki	12.0	59011-3502
Invader 440	Kawasaki	440	436cc	Mikuni	VM36	1.86:1	Silent	Kawasaki	12.0	59011-3502
Intruder 440	Kawasaki	440	436cc	Mikuni	VM32	1.86:1	Silent	Kawasaki	12.0	59011-3502
					1979					
Drifter 340	Kawasaki	340	339cc	Mikuni	VM32	2.24:1	Silent	Artic	10.3	59011-3503
Drifter 440	Kawasaki	440	436cc	Mikuni	VM32	1.81:1	Silent	Artic	10.3	59011-3503
Invader 340	Kawasaki	340	339cc	Mikuni	VM32	2.06:1	Silent	Kawasaki	12.0	59011-3502
Invader 440	Kawasaki	440	436cc	Mikuni	VM36	1.86:1	Silent	Kawasaki	12.0	59011-3502
Intruder 440	Kawasaki	440	436cc	Mikuni	VM32	1.86:1	Silent	Kawasaki	12.0	59011-3502
					1980					
Drifter 340F/A	Kawasaki	340	339cc	Mikuni	VM28	2.24:1	Silent	Artic	10.3	59011-3503
Drifter 340	Kawasaki	340	339cc	Mikuni	VM32	2.24:1	Silent	Artic	10.3	59011-3503
Drifter 440	Kawasaki	440	436cc	Mikuni	VM32	1.81:1	Silent	Artic	10.3	59011-3503
Intruder 440	Kawasaki	440	436cc	Mikuni	VM32	1.86:1	Silent	Kawasaki	12.0	59011-3502
Invader 340	Kawasaki	340	339cc	Mikuni	VM32	2.06:1	Silent	Kawasaki	12.0	59011-3502
Invader 440	Kawasaki	440	436cc	Mikuni	VM36	1.86:1	Silent	Kawasaki	12.0	59011-3502
Invader LTD	Kawasaki	440	436cc	Mikuni	VM36	1.81:1	Silent	Kawasaki	12.0	59011-3502
					1981					
Drifter 340	Kawasaki	340	339cc	Mikuni	VM32	2.24:1	Silent	Kawasaki	10.3	59011-3503
Drifter 440	Kawasaki	440	436cc	Mikuni	VM32	1.81:1	Silent	Kawasaki	10.3	59011-3503
Invader 340	Kawasaki	340	339cc	Mikuni	VM32	2.06:1	Silent	Kawasaki	12.0	59011-3502
Invader 440	Kawasaki	440	436cc	Mikuni	VM32	1.86:1	Silent	Kawasaki	12.0	59011-3502
Invader LTD	Kawasaki	440	436cc	Keihin	BD40-36	1.73:1	Silent	Kawasaki	12.0	59011-3502
Intruder 440	Kawasaki	440	436cc	Mikuni	VM32	1.86:1	Silent	Kawasaki	12.0	59011-3502
					1982					
Intruder 440	Kawasaki	440	436cc	Mikuni	VM32	1.86:1	Silent	Kawasaki	12.0	59011-3502
LTD 440	Kawasaki	440	436cc	Keihin	BD40-36	1.73:1	Silent	Kawasaki	12.0	59011-3502
Interceptor 550	Kawasaki	550	530cc	Keihin	BD42-38	1.68:1	Silent	Kawasaki	12.0	59011-3502

NOTE: Production Discontinued

KOMETIK

1970-1975

	Engine			Carburetor				Clutch		
Model	Make	Model	Displ.	Make	Model	Sprocket Ratio	Chain Size	Make	Shaft Center	Belt Number
					1970					
Mark II	CCW	225	225cc	Keihin	406	11:25	40	St. Law.	10½	3602
					1971					
Mark II	CCW	225	225cc	Keihin	406	11:25	40	St. Law.	10½	3602
MK III	CCW	225	225cc	Keihin	406	11:25	40	St. Law.	10½	3602
Mk III	CCW	312	312cc	Keihin	406	11:25	40	St. Law.	10½	3602
Mk III	CCW	CCW340	339cc	Keihin	406	17:33	35-2	St. Law.	10½	3602
Mk III	CCW	CCW400	398cc	Keihin	407	17:33	35-2	St. Law.	10½	3602
					1972					
Mk II-225	CCW	225	225cc	Keihin	CD-	11:25	40	St. Law.	10½	3602
Mk III-225	CCW	225	225cc	Keihin	CD-	11:25	40	St. Law.	10½	3602
Mk III-340	CCW	CCW340	339cc	Keihin	CD-	17:33	35-2	St. Law.	10½	3602
Mk III-400	CCW	CCW400	398cc	Keihin	CD-	17:33	35-2	St. Law.	10½	3602
Mk III-440	CCW	CCW440 2	436cc	Keihin	CD-	17:33	35-2	St. Law.	10½	3602
					1973					
Mk II-225	CCW	225	225cc	Keihin	CD-	11:25	40	St. Law.	10½	3602
Mk III-295	Kohler	K295-1T	294cc	Keihin	CD-	11:25	40	St. Law.	10½	3602
Mk III-340	CCW	CCW340	339cc	Keihin	CD-	17:33	35-2	St. Law.	10½	3602
Mk III-340	Kohler	K340-2AX	338cc	Walbro	WD	17:33	35-2	St. Law.	10½	3602
Mk III-440	Kohler	K440-2AX	436cc	Walbro	WD	18:33	35-2	St. Law.	10½	3602
					1974					
Mk II	CCW	225	226cc	Keihin	CD	11:25	40	St. Law.	10½	3602
Mk III	Kohler	K295-1T	294cc	Keihin	CD	11:33	35-2	St. Law.	10½	3602
Mk III	Kohler	K340-2AX	338cc	Walbro	WD	17:33	35-2	St. Law.	10½	3602
Mk III	Kohler	K440-2AX	436cc	Walbro	WD	18:33	35-2	St. Law.	10½	3602
					1975					
Mk III-295	Kohler	K295-1T	294cc	Walbro	WR	17:33	35-2	St. Law.	10½	SV-135
Mk III-340	Kohler	K340-2AX	338cc	Walbro	WD	17:33	35-2	St. Law.	10½	SV-135
Mk III-440	Kohler	K440-2AX	436cc	Walbro	WD	18:33	35-2	St. Law.	10½	SV-135

LUBRICATION

The engine is lubricated by oil mixed with the fuel. Recommended fuel/oil ratio is 20:1 using regular gasoline and an approved snowmobile oil.

The enclosed drive chain case should contain approximately ½-pint of low temperature grease. Replenish the supply as necessary when checking drive chain tension.

Lubricate bogie wheel bearings, track axle bearings and intermediate shaft bearings once a week and before storage with low temperature grease. All other metal parts where movement exists should be lubricated periodically as necessary to prevent binding, sticking or scoring.

ADJUSTMENT

STEERING SKIS. Tie rods can be adjusted by loosening lock nuts and turning center section. Adjustment is correct when tie rods are of equal length and toe-in is 1/8-inch measured at tips of skis.

DRIVE CHAIN. The roller drive chain should be adjusted to provide approximately ½-inch side play measured midway between sprockets. Adjust by loosening the four bolts securing top bearing housing to chain case and moving housing in slotted holes. Remove chain case cover for checking and adjusting the chain and add lubricant at that time if necessary.

On Mk III models with caliper type brake, adjustment may be affected when drive chain is adjusted. Realign by loosening cap screws (2—Fig. 2) securing mounting bracket to chain case. Firmly apply the brake and retighten cap screws (2) with brake applied.

BRAKE. Mark II machines are equipped with a pivot lever type brake which uses fixed face of driven pulley as a friction surface as shown in Fig. 1. Mark III uses a caliper type brake as shown in Fig. 2.

On all models, brake should fully apply before hand lever touches handlebar grip and fully release when lever is

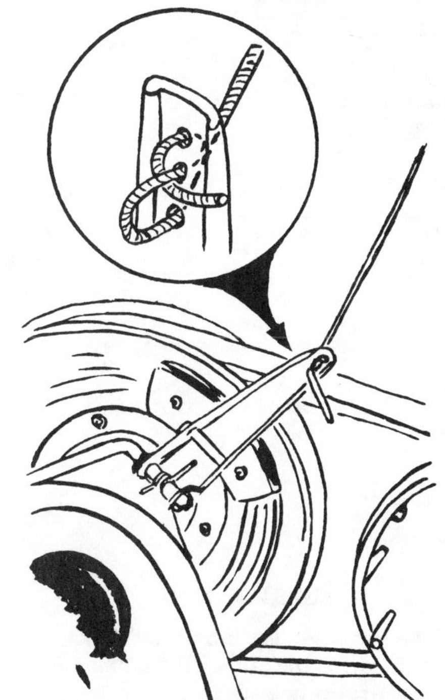

Fig. 1—View of pivot lever type brake used on Mark II. Inset shows correct lacing technique.

released. On Mk II models refer to Inset—Fig. 1 for correct lacing technique and remove slack from cable at pivot lever end.

On MK III models, wear adjustment is made by turning adjustment nut (3—Fig. 2) until actuating hand lever has approximately ¾-inch free travel measured at lever end. Before adjusting the brake, first check to make sure that brake unit properly aligns with pulley face. Adjust if necessary by loosening the two bracket bolts (2) and firmly applying brake to center the unit. Tighten bracket bolts (2) while brake is applied. Also check to be sure actuating lever contacts stop pin (4) with brake released. Adjustment can be made at cable housing anchor nuts (5).

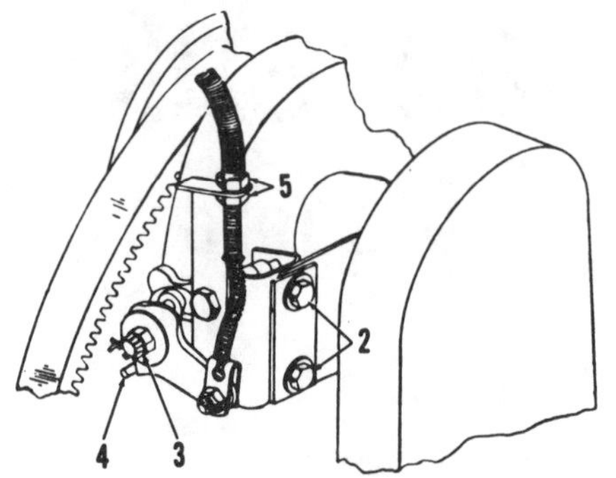

Fig. 2—Schematic view of caliper type brake used on Mark III.

2. Bracket bolts
3. Adjustment nut
4. Stop pin
5. Anchor nuts

TRACK. To adjust track tension, raise rear of machine until track is clear, then measure slack which should be approximately two inches at center. Adjust by loosening the two rear track hanger clamp screws on each side of machine, then turning adjusting screws until slack is removed. Both sides must be adjusted alike.

NOTE: Whenever track tension is adjusted, alignment MUST be checked as outlined in TRACK SERVICE Section of this manual.

DRIVE BELT. Clutch alignment and offset can be obtained by shifting engine in slotted mounting brackets. Shaft center adjustment is given in CONDENSED SERVICE DATA tables.

OVERHAUL

Refer to the appropriate paragraphs in the GENERAL SERVICE Sections of this manual for overhaul procedures of vehicle components.

LARSON

1966-1969

	Engine			Carburetor				Clutch		
Model	Make	Model	Displ.	Make	Model	Sprocket Ratio	Chain Size	Make	Shaft Center	Belt Number
					1966					
Falcon	JLO	L252	247cc	Tillotson	HS216A	11:38	40	Polaris	10¾	11210
Eagle	JLO	L252	247cc	Tillotson	HR2A	11:38	40	Polaris	10¾	11211
Powerhawk ...	JLO	L372	372cc	Tillotson	HD	11:38	40	Polaris	10¾	11211
					1967					
Falcon	JLO	L252	247cc	Tillotson	HL216A	11:38	40	Polaris	10¾	121001
Falcon	Daihatsu		305cc	Tillotson	HR3A	11:38	40	Polaris	10¾	121004
Hawk	JLO	L292	292cc	Tillotson	HR2A	11:38	40	Polaris	10¾	121001
Hawk	JLO	L372	372cc	Tillotson	HD6A	13:36	40	Polaris	10¾	121001
Eagle	JLO	L292	292cc	Tillotson	HR2A	11:38	40	Polaris	10¾	121001
Eagle	JLO	L372	372cc	Tillotson	HD6A	13:36	40	Polaris	10¾	121001
					1968					
Falcon	JLO	L292	292cc	Tillotson	HR2A	11:38	40	Polaris	10¾	121001
Hawk	JLO	L297	296cc	Tillotson	HD7A	11:38	40	Polaris	10¾	121001
Eagle	JLO	L372	372cc	Tillotson	HD7A	13:36	40	Polaris	10¾	121001
					1969					
Falcon Mk 1 ..	JLO	L292	292cc	Tillotson	HR2A	11:38	40	Polaris	10¾	121001
Hawk Mk 2 ...	JLO	L297	296cc	Tillotson	HD7A	11:38	40	Polaris	10¾	121001
Eagle Mk 3 ...	JLO	L372	372cc	Tillotson	HD7A	13:36	40	Polaris	10¾	121001

LUBRICATION

The engine is lubricated by oil mixed with the fuel. Recommended fuel-oil ratio is 20:1.

The drive chain runs in an enclosed chain housing which contains oil to the level of inspection plug located near bottom of housing. A filler plug is located at the top. Recommended lubricant is SAE 10 Motor oil. Lubricant should be changed every year.

Ski-legs and handle bar bracket are equipped with grease fittings and should be lubricated with low-temperature type grease about once each week while vehicle is in use.

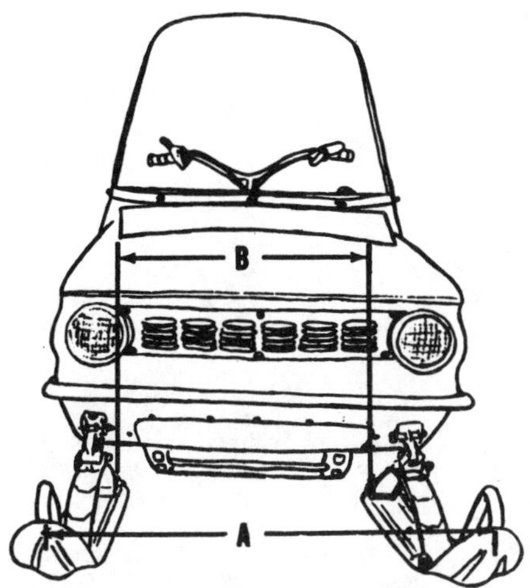

Fig. 1—Skis should toe out approximately one inch when measured as shown. Refer to text for details.

Bogie wheels and track axles are equipped with self aligning, sealed type bearings which do not require lubrication.

ADJUSTMENT

STEERING SKIS. Steering skis are properly aligned when skis toe out approximately one inch with handle bars in a straight ahead driving position. Refer to Fig. 1. Center to center distance (A) measured at front of skis should be approximately 27 inches. Distance (B) measured at rear should be approximately 26 inches. Tie rods must be disconnected at one end to make the adjustment.

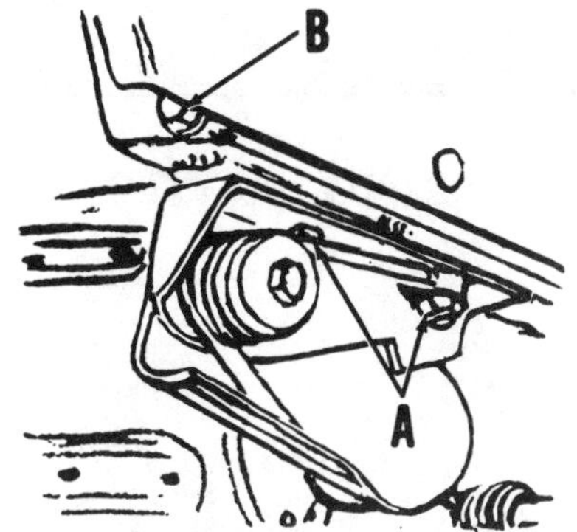

Fig. 3—Rear track axle support used on EAGLE, showing points of adjustment.

A. Clamp bolts
B. Adjusting screw

DRIVE CHAIN. The roller drive chain should have all slack removed without being under tension. A chain tightener block is located inside chain housing and adjusted by a cap screw on front wall. Before attempting to adjust the chain, first remove both chain housing access covers so the proper adjustment can be determined. Covers are retained by the soft rubber sealing rings and can be pried out with a small screwdriver.

BRAKE. The brake is wedge-shape band type which rides in a vee pulley mounted on torque converter driven pulley shaft. To adjust the brake, loosen band anchor bolt and slide band upward in slotted hole until slack is eliminated but be sure band does not drag in pulley.

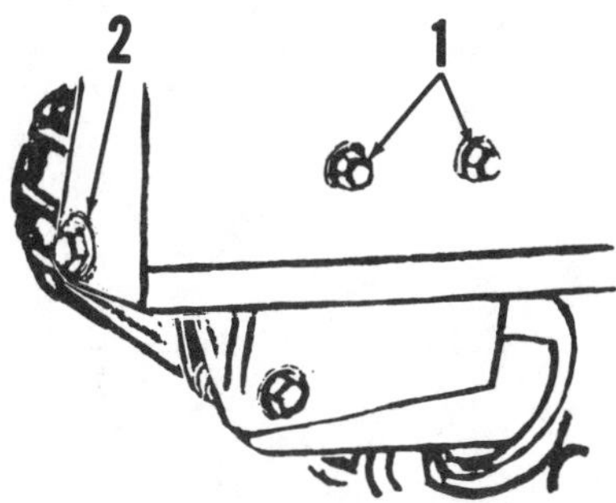

Fig. 4—On FALCON and HAWK, loosen the two bolts (1) and turn adjusting screw (2) to adjust track tension. Refer to text for details.

TRACK. To adjust track tension, raise rear of vehicle until track is clear of ground. With load removed, there should be some clearance between center bogie wheels and track surface.

On Eagle, loosen the two clamp bolts (A—Fig. 3) and turn the adjusting screw (B). On other models, loosen cap nuts (1—Fig. 4) and turn adjusting screw (2).

NOTE: On all models, when track tension is adjusted, alignment must be checked as outlined in TRACK SERVICE Section of this manual.

MALLARD

1968-1971

	Engine			Carburetor				Clutch		
Model	Make	Model	Displ.	Make	Model	Sprocket Ratio	Chain Size	Make	Shaft Center	Belt Number
					1968					
155	JLO	L292	292cc	Tillotson	HR18A			Salsbury	10¾	702695
180	JLO	L297	296cc	Tillotson	HR18A			Salsbury	10¾	702695
					1969					
155	JLO	L292	292cc	Tillotson	HR18A			Salsbury	10¾	702695
180	JLO	L297	296cc	Tillotson	HR18A			Salsbury	10¾	702695
					1970					
B295	JLO	L295	292cc	Tillotson				Salsbury 780	12.0	751176
B399	Kohler	K399-2	399cc	Tillotson				Salsbury 780	13	751177
					1971					
B295	JLO	L295	292cc	Tillotson				Salsbury 780	12	751176
B399	Kohler	K399-2	399cc	Tillotson				Salsbury 780	13	751177

MERCURY

1969-1970

	Engine			Carburetor				Clutch		
Model	Make	Model	Displ.	Make	Model	Sprocket Ratio	Chain Size	Make	Shaft Center	Belt Number
1969										
220M	Own		399cc	Tillotson	MD	13:29		Own	12¼	D5753520
220E	Own		399cc	Tillotson	MD	13:29		Own	12¼	D5753520
220ER	Own		399cc	Tillotson	MD	13:29		Own	12¼	D5753520
1970										
200M	Hirth	193R	292cc	Tillotson	HR66A	13:29		Salsbury 780	11½	D5757113
220M	Own		399cc	Tillotson	MD	13:29		Own	12¼	D5753520
220E	Own		399cc	Tillotson	MD	13:29		Own	12¼	D5753520
220ER	Own		399cc	Tillotson	MD	13:29		Own	12¼	D5753520
250M	Own		439cc	Tillotson	MD147A1	15:29		Own	12¼	D5756039
250E	Own		439cc	Tillotson	MD147A1	15:29		Own	12¼	D5756039
250ER	Own		439cc	Tillotson	MD147A1	15:29		Own	12¼	D5756039

Models 200M, 220M and 250M are equipped with manual starting. Other models have electric start; in addition, Models 220ER and 250ER are reversing models in which the engine is stopped then restarted in reverse rotation to obtain the reversal. CAUTION: Engine should not be operated or idled for prolonged periods in reverse rotation as cooling capacity is reduced and engine could overheat.

LUBRICATION

The engine is lubricated by oil mixed with the fuel. Correct fuel/oil ratio is 20:1. Only Quicksilver Formula Four Motor Oil, SAE 30 is recommended by the manufacturer.

The enclosed chain case should be filled to level of inspection plug hole using Quicksilver Formula Four Motor Oil, SAE 20. Oil may be added or chain inspected by removing inspection cover. Refer to Fig. 2.

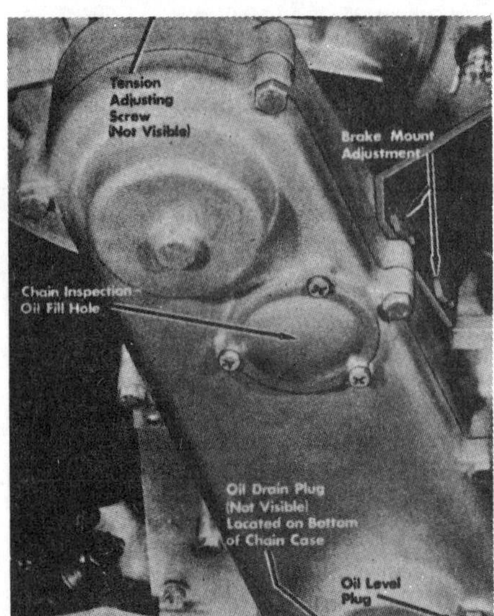

Fig. 2—View of enclosed chain case showing points of lubrication, inspection and adjustment. Refer to text.

The torque converter drive and driven sheaves are both equipped with fittings and should be lubricated sparingly each 25 hours with a light, low temperature lubricant. Lightly oil steering parts, brake and throttle controls, etc, as needed. Track drive mechanism and bogie wheels are equipped with sealed bearings and nylon bushings and do not require lubrication.

ADJUSTMENT

STEERING SKIS. Steering skis should be parallel with each other and with track channel when handlebar is in normal straight driving position. Tie rods may be adjusted by turning the center tube after loosening the locknuts. The normal method of making minor adjustment, however, is by slightly loosening "Screw A" and "Screw B", Fig. 4 and shifting ski on pivot plate.

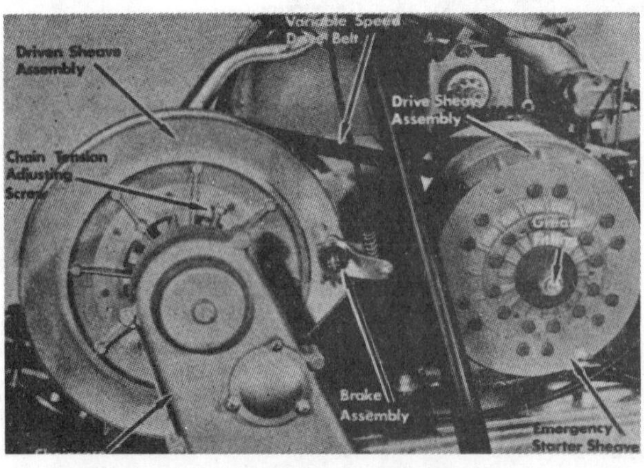

Fig. 3—Torque converter and brake, showing points of lubrication and adjustment.

DRIVE CHAIN ADJUSTMENT. The enclosed drive chain should have all slack removed but should not be under tension. Adjustment can be checked by removing inspection cover (Figs. 2 & 3). Chain can be adjusted by loosening the locknut on chain tension adjusting screw and moving the

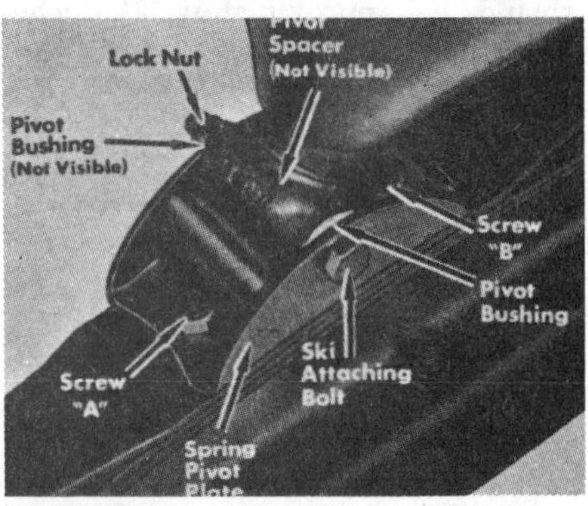

Fig. 4—Minor ski alignment can be accomplished by loosening the screws and moving ski spring on pivot plate. Refer to text.

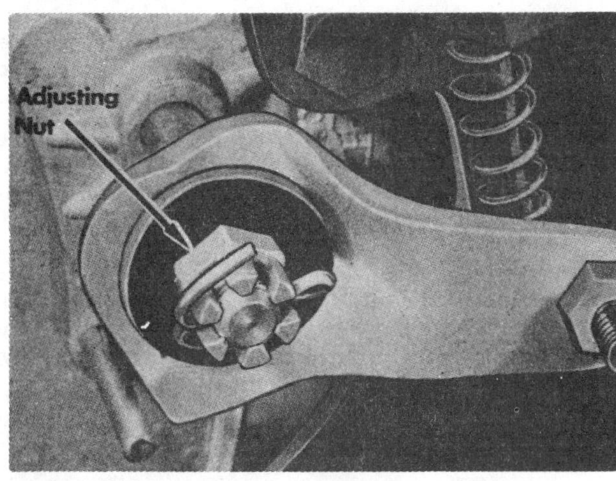

Fig. 5—Adjust for brake wear by removing the cotter pin and turning the adjusting nut.

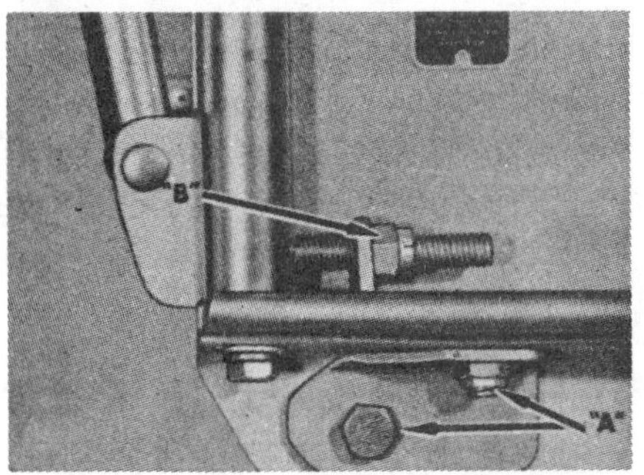

Fig. 6—To adjust track tension, loosen anchor screws (A) and turn adjusting nut (B).

screw toward the rear to tighten chain, or toward the front to loosen chain.

NOTE: Whenever chain tension has been changed, brake assembly may need to be repositioned on driven sheave as outlined in the following BRAKE ADJUSTMENT paragraph.

BRAKE ADJUSTMENT. The caliper type disc brakes use the fixed flange of the driven sheave as the friction surface. Whenever the drive chain adjustment is changed, the position of brake unit on sheave face should be checked, and adjusted if necessary, by loosening the brake mount adjustment screws. Refer to Fig. 2.

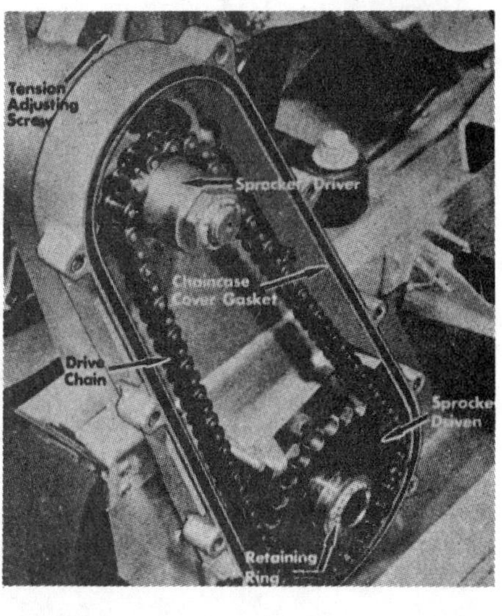

Fig. 9—View of chain case with cover removed. When renewing chain, retaining (snap) ring must be removed from lower shaft and chain tension completely loosened, then lower sprocket slipped from shaft splines.

With brake unit properly positioned, remove the cotter pin and turn adjusting nut (Fig. 5) until brake discs contact sheave face; back nut off ½-turn and reinstall cotter pin.

TRACK TENSION. With machine stopped and supported by the track, top portion of track should sag ½-inch midway between front and rear drive shafts. Adjust by loosening anchor screws (A—Fig. 6) and turning adjusting nut (B) until tension is correct. Both sides must be adjusted alike.

NOTE: Whenever track tension is adjusted, alignment MUST be checked as outlined in TRACK SERVICE section of this manual.

Fig. 7—On direct reversing models, lockout tool must be used when removing drive belt. Refer to text.

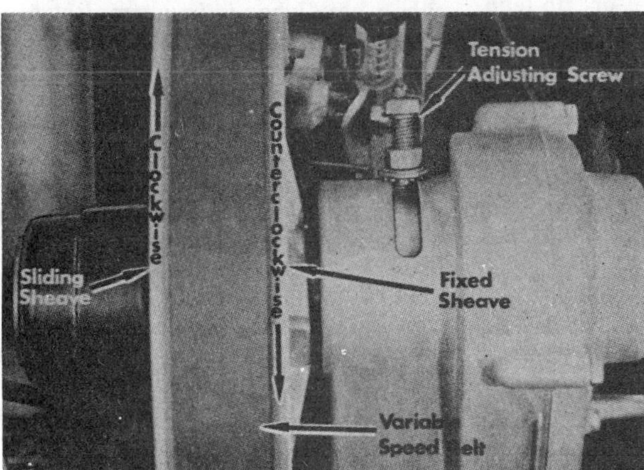

Fig. 8—Turn shave halves as shown to spread the sheaves for belt removal.

OVERHAUL

SKIS. Skis, ski legs, spindle arms, tie rods and associated parts are interchangeable from right to left. Nylon or rubber bushings are used throughout.

DRIVE BELT. The torque converter drive belt should be renewed if worn to less than $1\frac{3}{16}$ inches in width or when otherwise damaged. Belt can be removed or installed after spreading the two halves of the driven sheave.

NOTE: Reversing models are equipped with locking bars which prevent the driven sheave assembly from opening when machine is operated in reverse direction. Reverse locking bars must be held in neutral position in order to spread the driven sheave; proceed as follows:

Refer to Fig. 7, remove Reverse Lockout Tool from tool kit, bend and install in hub of driven sheave as shown. With reverse locking bars held in neutral position, proceed as outlined for all models.

On all models, refer to Fig. 8 and proceed as follows. Standing in front of machine, hold fixed sheave from turning while pushing rearward (clockwise) on sliding sheave. When the sheave is spread apart, belt will drop farther into the vee relieving belt tension. A suitable block of wood or other object may be inserted between sheave halves to hold them apart while belt is being installed.

Remove spacer block and, on Reversing Models, Reverse Lockout Tool before returning machine to service.

DRIVE CHAIN. To renew or inspect the enclosed drive chain, first remove drain plug and lubricant, then unbolt and remove chaincase cover. Refer to Fig. 9. Remove retaining (snap) ring from lower shaft splines and completely loosen chain and tension. Slip driven sprocket from shaft splines and lift off chain and sprocket. The drive chain has no master link.

MERCURY

1971-1972

	Engine			Carburetor				Clutch		
Model	Make	Model	Displ.	Make	Model	Sprocket Ratio	Chain Size	Make	Shaft Center	Belt Number
					1971					
Merc 200	Hirth	193R	292cc	Tillotson	HR66A	13:29	40	Salsbury 780	11½	D5757113
Rocket	CCW	340	339cc	Tillotson	HR84A	11:29	40	Salsbury 910		D5758703
Lightning	CCW	400	398cc	Tillotson	HR84A	11:29	40	Salsbury 910		D5758703
Merc 250	Own		439cc	Tillotson	MD147A	15:29	40	Own	12¼	D5756039

NOTE: Merc 250 is available in Manual Start; or Electric Start—Direct Reverse.

Model	Make	Model	Displ.	Make	Model	Sprocket Ratio	Chain Size	Make	Shaft Center	Belt Number
					1972					
Rocket	CCW	340	339cc	Tillotson	HR84A	11:29	40	Salsbury 910		D5758703
Lightning	CCW	400	339cc	Tillotson	HR113A	11:29	40	Salsbury 910		D5758703
Hurricane.....	Own		644cc	Tillotson	OM40A	15:36	35-2	Salsbury 910		D5759630

Fig. 2–View of chain case used on all models except Hurricane.

1. Clamp bolt
2. Lever
3. Fill plug
4. Inspection cover
5. Level plug
6. Adjusting nut

LUBRICATION

The engine is lubricated by oil mixed with the fuel. Quicksilver Winter Formula 25 is recommended, if not available, Quicksilver Formula 50 may be used but ONLY AT 25:1 ratio. Regular gasoline is the specified fuel. The manufacturer specifically cautions against the use of most "lead-free" or "no-lead" gasolines except those containing no phosphorus additives.

The enclosed chain case should be filled to level of inspection plug hole using Automatic Transmission Fluid Type A, AA or Dextron. Inspection plug is shown at (5—Fig. 2). Hurricane chain case differs but plug location is similar.

On Model 250, torque converter drive and driven sheaves are both equipped with fittings which should be lubricated sparingly each 25 hours with a light, low temperature grease.

Lightly oil steering parts as needed. Track drive mechanism and bogie wheels are equipped with sealed bearings and nylon bushings and do not require lubrication.

ADJUSTMENT

Steering skis should be parallel with each other and with track channel when handlebar is in normal straight driving position. Tie rods may be adjusted by loosening locknuts and turning center section but tie rods are not easily accessible. The recommended procedure for minor adjustment is by loosening the two bolts (B—Fig. 3) which secure ski pivot to spring, and turning ski on ski leg. Tighten the bolts (B) to a torque of 25-30 ft.-lbs.

DRIVE CHAIN. On all models except HURRICANE, refer to Fig. 2. Recommended drive chain free play of 3/16-5/16 inch can be checked after removing inspection cover (4). Adjust

Fig. 3–Ski alignment can normally be achieved by loosening pivot bolts (B) and repositioning skis.

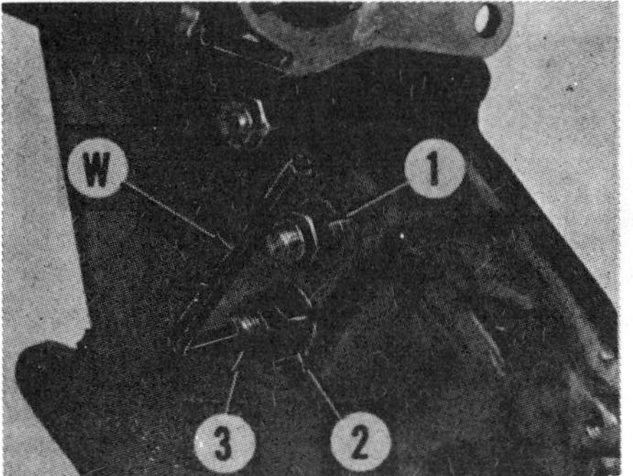

Fig. 4–To adjust drive chain on Hurricane, loosen idler clamp nut (1) and crank nut (2). Insert 7/32-inch Allen wrench (W) in idler crank stud (3) and turn the stud until backlash is correct.

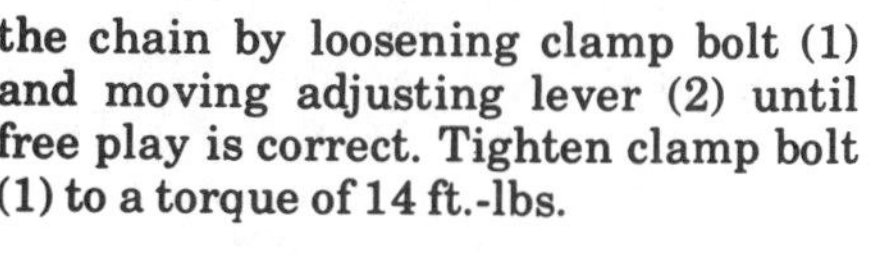

the chain by loosening clamp bolt (1) and moving adjusting lever (2) until free play is correct. Tighten clamp bolt (1) to a torque of 14 ft.-lbs.

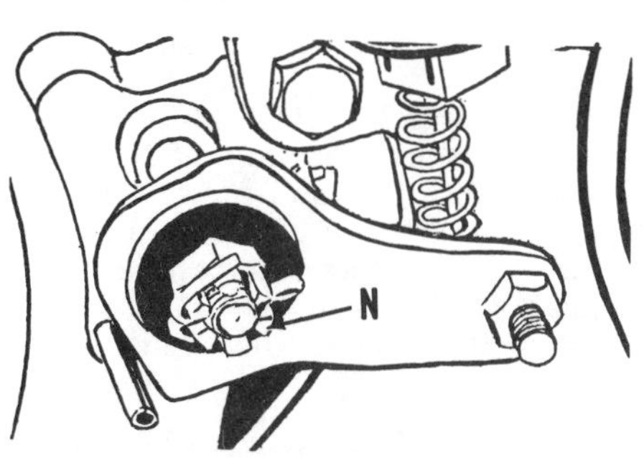

Fig. 5–Brake wear adjustment is made by turning adjusting nut (N) on actuating arm stud.

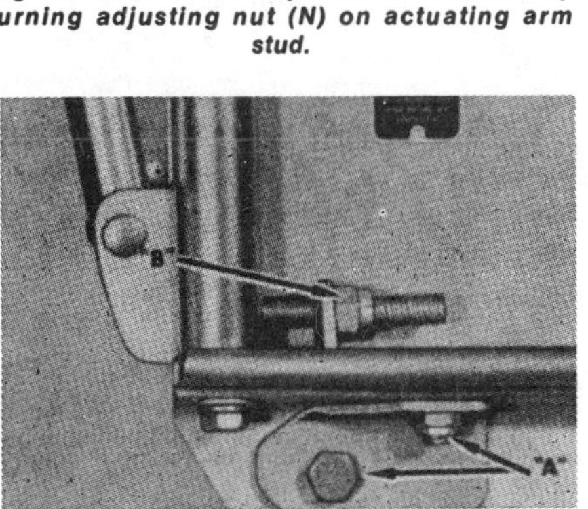

Fig. 6–Adjust track tension on Model 250, loosen clamp nuts (A) and turn adjusting screw (B).

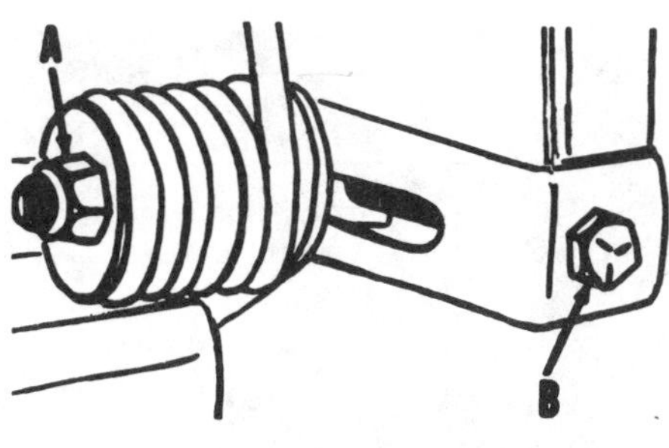

Fig. 7–On 200, Rocket and Lightning, adjust track tension by loosening pivot bolt nut (A) and turning adjusting screw (B).

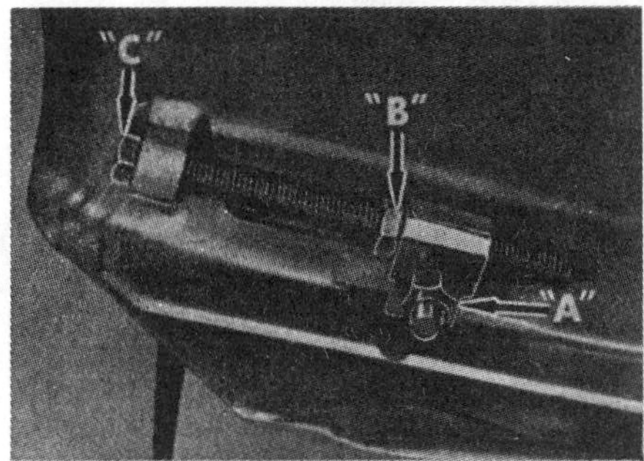

Fig. 8–On Hurricane, adjust track tension by loosening clamp nut (A) and jam nut (B), then turning adjusting screw (C).

NOTE: Whenever chain tension has been changed on these models, brake assembly may need to be realigned with friction face of driven sheave as outlined in BRAKE ADJUSTMENT paragraph.

On HURRICANE models refer to Fig. 4. Drive chain free play can be considered satisfactory when backlash measured at driven pulley rim is ⅛-⅜ inch. To adjust the chain, loosen idler clamp nut (1) and crank nut (2) on inside wall of chain case, insert a 7/32-inch Allen wrench (W) in idler crank stud (3) and move the stud counterclockwise to decrease backlash or clockwise to increase backlash. Tighten both nuts securely when adjustment is correct.

BRAKE. The caliper type brake uses a turned drum on driven sheave (Hurricane Models) or fixed face of driven sheave (other models) as the friction surface. On all models, brake must properly align with friction surface. To correct misalignment, loosen the two screws securing caliper unit to support bracket and firmly apply the brake; then retighten the screws while brake is applied. Also check to be sure that actuating lever contacts stop pin when released. Adjust at cable housing anchor nuts.

Brake wear adjustment is made by turning the nut (N—Fig. 5) on actuating arm stud until brake pucks contact friction face of sheave, then backing off ½ turn.

TRACK. With machine stopped and supported on track on an even surface, top portion of track should sag approximately ¼-inch midway between front and rear drive shafts.

On Model 250, adjust by loosening anchor screws (A—Fig. 6) and turning adjusting nut (B). On 200, Rocket and Lightening, loosen pivot screw nuts (A—Fig. 7) and turn adjusting screws (B). On Hurricane, loosen nuts (A & B—Fig. 8) and turn adjusting screws (C). On all models, both sides must be adjusted alike.

NOTE: Whenever track tension has been adjusted, alignment MUST be checked as outlined in TRACK SERVICE Section of this manual.

OVERHAUL

SKIS. Skis, ski legs, spindle arms, tie rods and associated parts are interchangeable from right to left. Nylon or rubber bushings are used throughout.

DRIVE BELT. On Model 250, the torque converter drive belt is 1⅜-

Fig. 9–On direct reversing models, lockout tool must be used when removing drive belt.

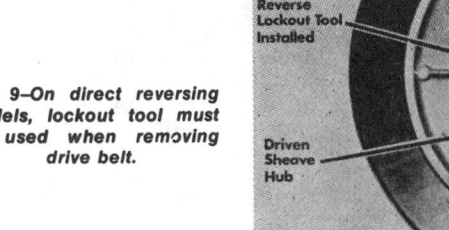

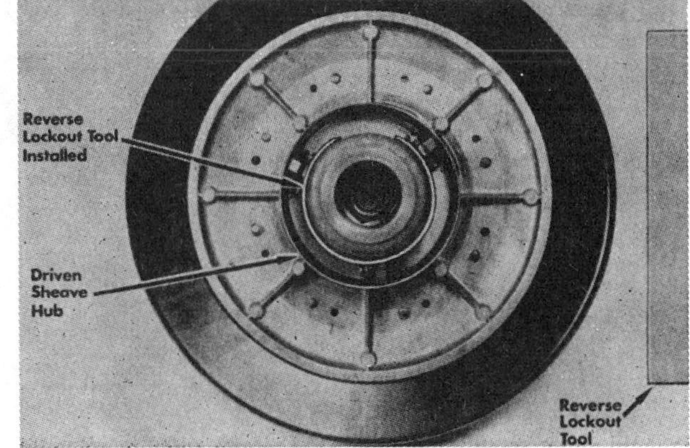

Fig. 10–Turn sheave halves as shown to spread for belt removal.

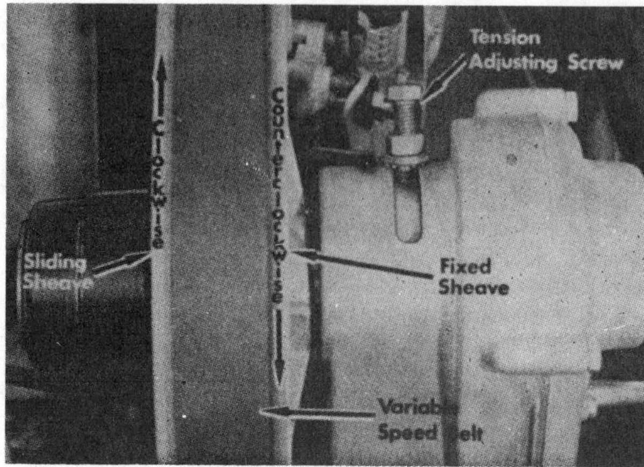

inches wide when new, and belt should be renewed when worn to 1 3/16-inches or less. On other models, new belt width is 1 3/16 inches and wear to 1 1/16 inches is permissible.

NOTE: Direct reversing models are equipped with locking bars which prevent the driven sheave assembly from opening when machine is operated in reverse direction. Reverse locking bars must be held in neutral position in order to spread the driven sheave. Refer to Fig. 9 and remove Reverse Lockout Tool from tool kit. Bend and install the tool as shown.

With reverse lockout neutralized, or on models without direct reverse, refer to Fig. 10. Stand in front of machine and hold fixed sheave from turning while pushing rearward (clockwise) on sliding sheave. With sheave spread, belt will drop farther into the vee relieving belt tension and permitting removal of the belt. A suitable block of wood or other object may be inserted between sheave halves to hold them apart for belt installation. Remove spacer block and Reverse Lockout Tool before returning machine to service.

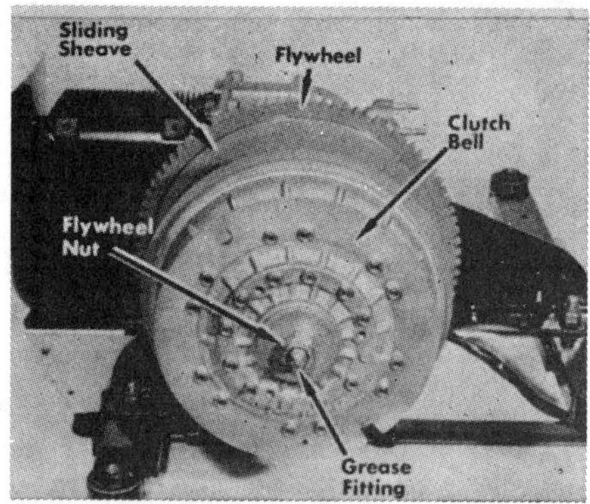

Fig. 11–To remove or disassemble drive pulley on Model 250, first remove grease fitting and flywheel nut, then attach a puller as shown in Fig. 12.

Fig. 12–Attach a suitable puller to the three threaded holes to remove clutch bell and associated parts.

Fig. 13–Double nut and remove retaining stud as shown.

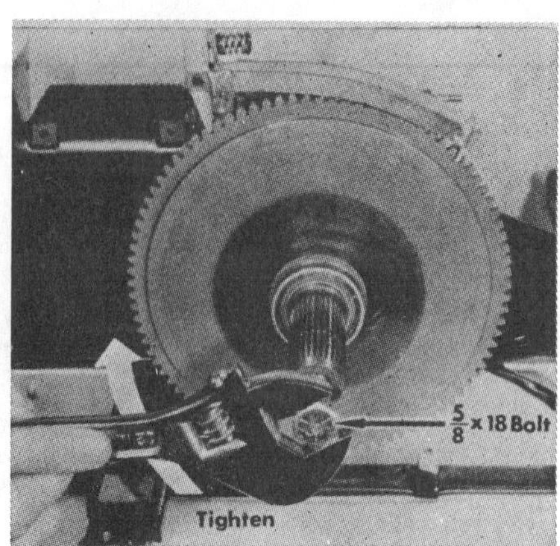

Fig. 14–Use a ⅝-inch puller bolt to remove flywheel.

Fig. 15–Adjust clutch weight side clearance to 0.015 using a feeler gage as shown.

CONVERTER UNITS. Refer to SALSBURY paragraphs of CONVERTER UNIT Section for overhaul of converters except those used on Model 250.

On Model 250, the drive unit fixed sheave is part of the flywheel and carries the starter ring gear and alternator rotor magnets. To remove or disassemble the drive unit, first remove drive belt, flywheel nut and grease fitting (Fig. 11). Using a suitable puller and stud protector, remove clutch bell as shown in Fig. 12. Retaining stud may be removed by double nutting as shown in Fig. 13 and using a suitable protector for end of crankshaft, remove flywheel using a ⅝-18 bolt as shown in Fig. 14.

Clutch weights and bushings can be removed after removing 24 No. 10-32 self-locking nuts and bolts which secure the retainers and emergency starting disc. When reinstalling, adjust clutch weight side clearance to 0.015 and tighten the retaining nuts to 60 inch-pounds.

Lubricate clutch weights, idler bearing and clutch splines sparingly with low temperature grease. Install flywheel stud using LOCTITE and tighten retaining stud nut to 60-65 ft.-lbs.

To remove driven sheave first remove drive belt and disassemble and remove brake unit. Check to see if fixed and sliding sheaves have index marks on spring side as shown in Fig. 16. Mark if necessary. Remove spring and sliding sheave and wedge off the fixed sheave half using special tool C-91-60215A1 as shown in Fig. 17. Intermediate shaft is slightly tapered at sheave hub and once loosened, fixed sheave can be easily withdrawn.

Check sliding sheave cams for burrs or other damage which could cause

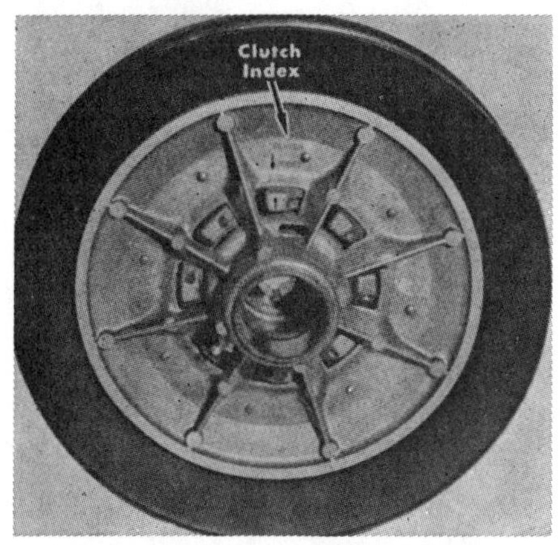

Fig. 16–Examine driven pulley for index marks as shown.

sheave to bind. Bronze bushing in sliding sheave hub is not serviced separately; if worn, sliding half should be renewed. Plastic wear plates on fixed sheave are renewable in sets only. Wear plates are a tight press fit on fixed sheave; cement with a suitable epoxy if necessary when installing. Wear plate configuration has been changed slightly to reduce the possibility of binding and late style plate is to be used on all models when renewing. When assembling driven sheave on direct reversing models, reverse lockout tool must be installed before installing sliding half. Tighten shaft nut to a torque of 75-100 ft.-lbs. when unit is assembled.

Fig. 17–Driven pulley can be removed using the special wedge tools (C-91-60215A1) and a hammer as shown.

Fig. 18–Examine sliding sheave cams for burrs or other damage and bushing for wear or scoring. Bushing is not renewable.

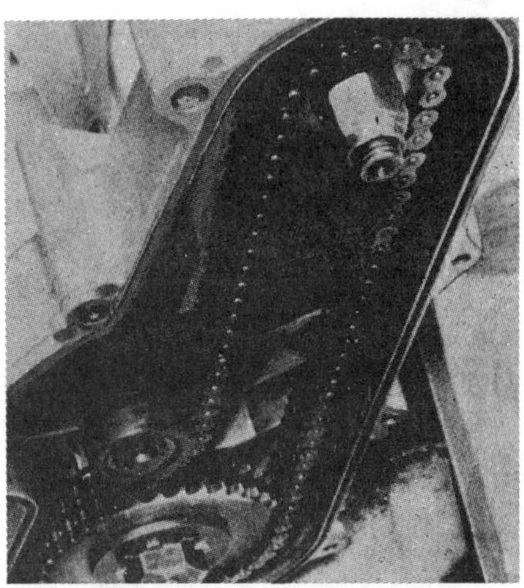

Fig. 19–Hurricane chain case with cover removed showing chain, sprockets and idler.

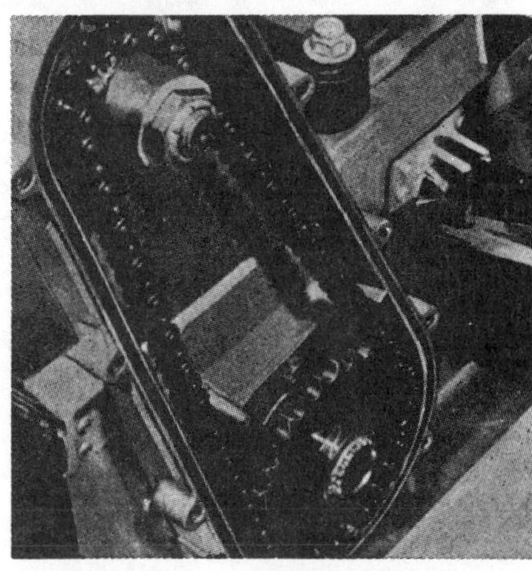

Fig. 20–Chain and sprockets used on all models except Hurricane shown assembled with cover removed.

DRIVE CHAIN. To renew or inspect enclosed drive chain or sprockets, first remove drain plug and lubricant, then unbolt and remove chain case cover.

On Hurricane models, refer to Fig. 19 and loosen chain idler. Remove upper sprocket retaining nut and lower sprocket retaining screw, then slip both sprockets and the chain as a unit from chain case. A 15-tooth upper sprocket and 36-tooth lower sprockets are standard. The High Altitude Accessory Kit contains an optional 40-tooth lower sprocket and chain which may be installed to obtain a lower drive ratio.

On other models refer to Fig. 20. To remove chain and lower sprocket, completely loosen chain tension and remove lower sprocket retaining snap ring. Disengage chain from upper sprocket and lift off chain and lower sprocket as a unit. Upper sprocket may be removed with a suitable puller after removing upper shaft nut. Tighten the nut to a torque of 75-100 ft.-lbs. when reinstalling. Optional upper sprockets are available in 9, 10, 11, 13, 14, 15 and 16 tooth size.

MERCURY

1973-1976

	Engine			Carburetor				Clutch		
Model	Make	Model	Displ.	Make	Model	Sprocket Ratio	Chain Size	Make	Shaft Center	Belt Number
					1973					
440 Max......	CCW	440	436cc	Tillotson	HD115A	17:35	35-2	Salsbury 850		D5763353
Hurricane Mk I	Own		644cc	Tillotson	OM41A	16:36	35-2	Salsbury 850		D5763353
Hurricane Mk II	Own		644cc	Tillotson	HD127A(2)	17:36	35-2	Salsbury 850		D5765427
					1974					
440 Max......	CCW	440/22	438cc	Walbro	WDA-47	17:36	35-2	Salsbury 850	12	57-65427
440 SR.......	CCW	440/22	438cc	Walbro	WDA-47	17:36	35-2	Salsbury 850	12	57-65427
Mark II.......	Own		644cc	Walbro	WRA-35(2)	16:36	35-2	Salsbury 850	12	57-65427
400 S/T......	Kohler	K400-2RS	398cc	Mikuni	VM36(2)	15:34	35-2	Comet 100C	11¾	57-67941-1
					1975					
340 S/R......	Kohler	K340-2AX	338cc	Walbro	WDA50	15:36	35-2	Salsbury 850	12	57-67633
440 S/R......	Kioritz	440/22	438cc	Walbro	WDA47	18:28	35-2	Own	12	57-70854
440 M/X......	Kioritz	440/22	438cc	Walbro	WDA47	17:36	35-2	Salsbury 850	12	57-67633
Mark II.......	Own		644cc	Walbro	WRA35(2)	16:36	35-2	Salsbury 850	12	57-67633
340 S/T......	Kohler	K340-2RS	339cc	Mikuni	36134(2)	14:34	35-2	Arctic Cat	11¾	57-67941-1
440 S/T......	Kohler	K440-2RS	429cc	Mikuni	36144(2)	15:34	35-2	Arctic Cat	11¾	57-67941-1
440 S/T......	Kohler	K440-2RS	436cc	Mikuni	VM36(2)	17:34	35-2	Salsbury 850	11¾	57-67941-1
					1976					
340 T/T......	Kohler	K340-2AS	339cc	Mikuni	VM32	17:34	35-2	Arctic	11¾	57-74294
440 T/T......	Kohler	K440-2AS	436cc	Mikuni	VM36	18:34	35-2	Arctic	11¾	57-74294
250 S/T......	Kohler	K250-RLC	250cc	Mikuni	VM34	14:34	35-2	Arctic	11¾	57-74294
B40 S/T......	Kohler	K340-RLC	339cc	Mikuni	VM36	15:34	35-2	Arctic	11¾	57-74294
440 S/T......	Kohler	K440-RLC	436cc	Mikuni	VM38	16:34	35-2	Arctic	11¾	57-74294

LUBRICATION

The engine is lubricated by oil mixed with the fuel. Quicksilver Winter Formula 25 is recommended. Regular gasoline is the specified fuel for all models except Sno Twister and Trail Twister models, which require Automotive Premium Gasoline. Recommended fuel:oil ratio is 20:1 for Sno-Twister. Recommended fuel:oil ratio for other models is 50:1 for normal operation or 25:1 for severe service. The manufacturer specifically cautions against the use of most "lead-free" or "no-lead" gasolines except those containing no phosphorus additives.

The enclosed chaincase should be filled to level of inspection plug hole using Automatic Transmission Fluid Type A, AA or Dextron. Inspection plug is shown at (3—Fig. 1). Other chaincases differ, but plug location is similar.

Lightly oil steering parts as needed. Track drive mechanism and bogie wheels are equipped with sealed bearings and nylon bushings and do not require lubrication.

ADJUSTMENT

STEERING SKIS. Steering skis should be parallel with each other and with track channel when handlebar is in normal straight driving position. Tie rods may be adjusted by loosening locknuts and turning center section or (on some models) the short adjusting studs.

DRIVE CHAIN. To adjust the roller drive chain on 440 Max, 340 S/R, 440 S/R and 440 M/X, refer to Fig. 2. Check the backlash, measured at driven pulley rim as shown at (A). Backlash should be within the limits of 1/8-3/8 inch (3-10 mm); if it is not, loosen nut on clamp bolt (1—Fig. 1) and slide the bolt in slotted hole until backlash is correct.

NOTE: On some models, brake uses fixed face of driven sheave as a friction surface. Other models have a separate brake disc. On models using driven sheave for braking, brake must be realigned with sheave after chain adjustment. Loosen brake bracket mounting screws (S—Fig. 2) and fully apply the brake; then retighten screws with brake applied.

On Sno-Twister and Trail Twister models, chaincase is on right side of machine. To adjust the chain, remove access plug (P—Fig. 3). Loosen tensioner adjusting bolt (A), then carefully tighten

Fig. 1—Installed view of chaincase used on 440 Max, 340 S/R, 440 S/R and 440 M/X.

1. Clamp bolt 2. Fill plug 3. Level plug

until all slack is JUST removed from chain when checked through access plug hole. Do not overload the chain by over-tightening.

On Hurricane, Mk I and Mk II models, refer to Fig. 5. Chain adjustment can be considered satisfactory when 1/8-3/8 inch (3-10 mm) backlash exists, measured at driven pulley rim. To adjust chain, loosen idler clamp nut (1) and crank nut (2), then turn idler crank stud (3) using a 7/32-inch Allen wrench as shown. Tighten both nuts securely when adjustment is correct.

Fig. 2—View of chaincase and brake used on 440 Max. Chain tension is correct when backlash (A) measured at pulley rim is 1/8-3/8 inch (3-10 mm).

A. Backlash
P. Stop pin
S. Cap screws
1. Adjusting nut
2. Anchor nuts
3. Switch anchor

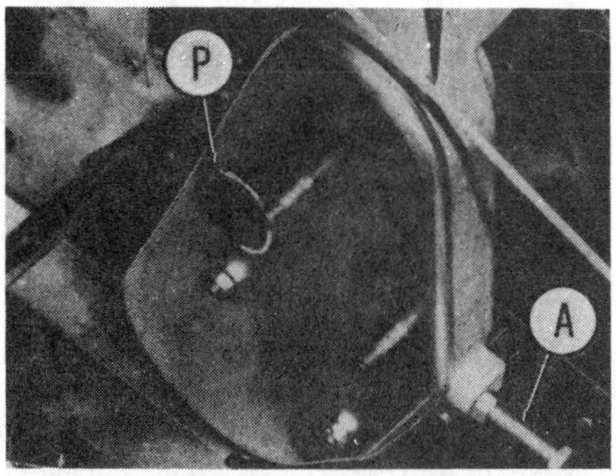

Fig. 3—To adjust drive chain on Sno-Twister models and 440 Trail-Twister, remove access plug (P). Back off adjusting screw (A), then retighten until ALL slack is just removed.

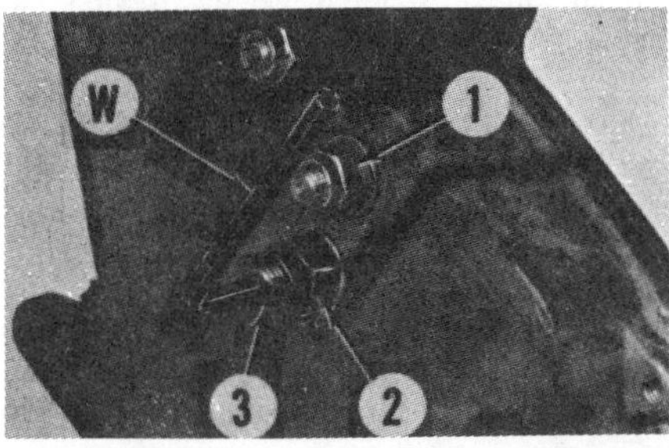

Fig. 4—View of Sno-Twister chain case with cover removed.

BRAKE. The caliper type disc brake uses a turned drum on driven sheave (Mk I and Mk II), fixed face of driven sheave; or a separate brake disc as the friction surface. On all models, brake must properly align with friction surface. To correct misalignment, loosen the two screws securing caliper unit to support bracket and firmly apply the brake; then retighten screws while brake is applied. Check to be sure that actuating lever contacts stop pin (P—Fig. 2) when brake is released, and adjust if necessary by turning cable housing anchor nuts (2). Brake lights must light when brakes are applied and go out when brakes are released. Adjust brake light switch by turning the stop switch mounting nuts (3).

Fig. 5—To adjust drive chain on Hurricane, Mk I and Mk II models, loosen idler clamp nut (1) and crank nut (2). Insert 7/32-inch Allen wrench (W) in idler crank stud (3) and turn the stud until backlash is correct.

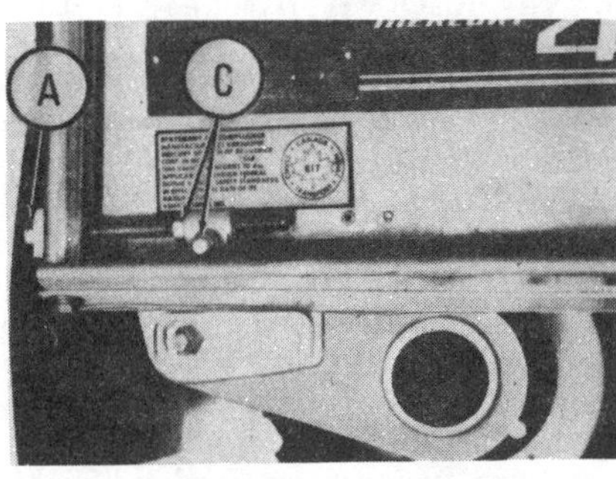

Fig. 6—On 440 Max and & 440 M/X models, track tension is adjusted by loosening clamp nuts (C) and turning adjusting screw (A) on both sides of machine.

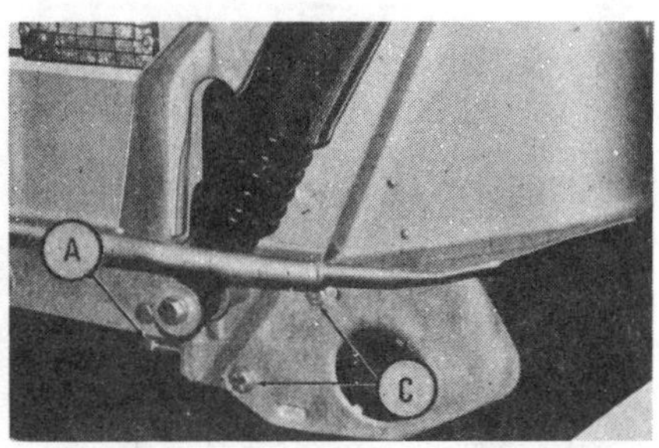

Fig. 7—On Mk I and Mk II, loosen clamp bolts (C) and turn adjusting screw (A) to adjust track tension. Both sides must be adjusted alike.

Brake wear adjustment is made by removing cotter pin and turning actuating stud nut (1) until brake pucks clear friction surface when hand lever is released but fully apply before lever contacts handlebar grip.

TRACK. On bogie wheel suspension models, track tension is measured at top of track with snowmobile resting on track. On slide rail suspension units, track tension is measured at bottom with rear of machine suspended until track is clear.

On 440 Max and 440 M/X, loosen nuts (C—Fig. 6) and turn adjusting screw (A) until track sags ½-1 inch (12-25 mm) midway between drive axle and rear idler axle. On Mk I and Mk II, loosen the two clamp bolts (C—Fig. 7).

Loosen locknut on adjusting screw (A) and turn the screw until track sag is ½-1 inch (12-25 mm). On all models, both sides must be adjusted alike and track must center between idler arms when running.

On 340 S/R and 440 S/R, refer to Figs. 8 and 9. Suspend rear of machine until track is clear. Pull out the slack and measure clearance between track and slide midway of track just behind front shock absorber rear mounting bracket as shown. Clearance should be 1/8-3/8 inch (3-10 mm), if it is not,

Fig. 8—On 340 S/R and 440 S/R, measure track clearance as shown with rear of machine suspended. Adjust at (A—Fig. 9).

Fig. 9—On 340 S/R and 440 S/R, adjust track tension by loosening locknuts and turning adjusting screws (A).

loosen jam nuts and turn rear idler axle adjusting bolts (A—Fig. 9) as shown. On Sno-Twister and Trail-Twister models, suspend rear of machine until track is clear and measure slack between track and slide midway of track as shown in Fig. 10. Clearance should be 1-inch (25 mm). Adjust by loosening the jam nuts and turning rear idler axle adjusting screws (A—Fig. 11). On all models, both sides must be adjusted alike and track must center in track tunnel when running.

OVERHAUL

SKIS. Skis, ski legs, spindle arms and associated parts are interchangeable from right to left. Ski pivot and spring mounting cap screws should be tightened to a torque of 30 ft.-lbs. (4.1 kg-m). Ski shock absorber mounting bolts should be torqued to 50 ft.-lbs. (6.9 kg-m). Nylon bushings are used on ski legs and pivots.

ENGINE. To remove the engine on Hurricane Mk I and Mk II models, first remove hood, battery cables and battery. Remove drive belt and drive clutch. Mark wiring if necessary for correct reassembly, then disconnect engine controls, fuel lines and wiring. Remove the four engine mount nuts and lift out engine. Install by reversing the removal procedure. Tighten the four nuts securing engine mounts to frame to a torque of 235 inch-pounds (270 kg-cm) then check clearance of rubber bumper at left rear corner of engine and adjust to 1/32-1/16 inch (0.8-1.6 mm). Tighten drive clutch retaining cap screw to 55 ft.-lbs. (7.6 kg-m).

To remove engine on 440 Max, 340 S/R, 440 S/R and 440 M/X, first open hood. Remove belt guard and drive belt. If drive clutch will need to be removed, remove clutch at this time. Mark and disconnect necessary wiring and controls, then unbolt and remove engine dash and windshield. Remove air silencer housing if so equipped, unbolt and remove carburetor, then lift off the insulating air baffle between carburetor and engine. Disconnect ground wire from recoil starter housing mounting screw. Remove the four bolts and nuts securing engine mounting plate to mounting rails and lift out engine and mounting plate as an assembly. Install by reversing removal procedure. If engine mounting plate is removed, it must be installed with stamped "X" up and to exhaust side of crankcase. Most models are equipped with spacers between crankcase and mounting plate. Spacers must be reinstalled if present. Tighten all mounting plate screws to a torque of 30 ft.-lbs. (4.1 kg-m). Tighten drive clutch retaining cap screw to 55 ft.-lbs. (7.6 kg-m) and carburetor to manifold screws to 150 inch-pounds (170 kg-cm).

On Sno-Twister models, engine is forward mounted and Free-Air Cooled, and much engine service can be performed without removing engine from frame. To remove the engine, first remove top cowl and carburetor air intake chute. Disconnect throttle controls, fuel lines and engine wiring. Remove belt guard, drive belt and drive clutch. If flywheel is to be removed for future work, remove flywheel at this time. Remove the four locknuts which secure engine mounting plate to front frame and lift out engine and mounting plate as an assembly. Keep spacers and shim washers identified for reinstallation under the correct mounting positions; shim washers control belt adjustment. When installing engine, be sure engine is installed correctly on mounting plate. Spacers are used under some models. Tighten engine to mounting plate screws to a torque of 230 inch-pounds (265 kg-cm), mounting plate nuts to 50 ft.-lbs. (6.9 kg-m), drive sheave to crankshaft bolt to 55 ft.-lbs. (7.6 kg-m) and flywheel nut to 90 ft.-lbs. (12.4 kg-m). Check belt tension adjustment as follows:

With drive belt installed and engine not running, check to see that drive clutch is fully open (clutch released) and that driven sheave is fully closed. Lay a suitable straightedge across top of belt where it rests on both pulleys, then measure belt slack midway between the two pulleys. Measurement should be 1½ inches (38 mm). If belt is too tight, add shim washers underneath front engine mounts or remove shim washers underneath rear engine mounts. Add shim washers at rear or remove at front, if belt is too loose. It is preferable to leave belt slightly tight rather than too loose. Plain 7/16 inch washers can be modified as shown in Fig. 12 to be used as adjusting shims without completely loosening all engine mounts. Tighten mounting plate nuts to recommended torque when adjustment is correct.

CONVERTER UNITS. Salsbury, Comet or Arctic Cat units are used. Specified clutch engagement speed for early 440 Max (before Serial No. 3447392) is 3000-3500 rpm. Specified clutch engagement speed for late 440 Max, 340 S/R, 440 S/R and 440 M/X is 3300-3600 rpm. Specified clutch engagement speed for Mark I is 2700-3000 rpm; early Mk II (before Serial No. 3591478), 3200-3500 rpm; late Mk II, 3200-3400 rpm, Trail-Twister, 3400-3600; and all Sno-Twister models, 3800-4000 rpm.

CHAIN CASE AND CHAIN. Fig. 13 shows a view of drive chain and sprockets used on Models 440 Max, 340 S/R, 440 S/R and 440 M/X. Both sprockets are a slip fit on shaft splines and a puller is not normally required in disassembly. Chain and both sprockets should be removed together as follows: On models using fixed face of driven sheave as a brake friction surface,

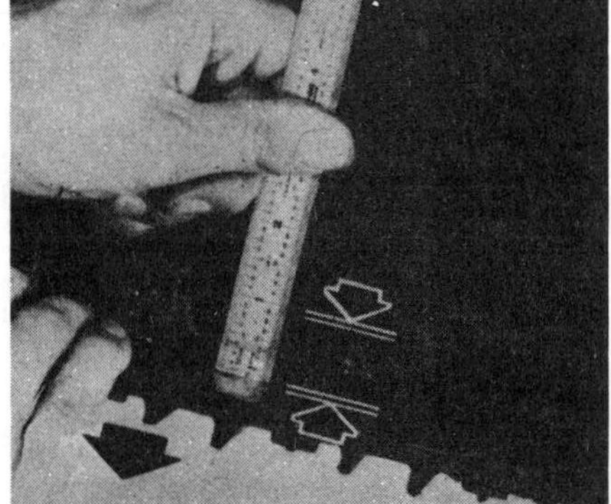

Fig. 10—On Sno-Twister and Trail-Twister models, measure track clearance midway of slide with rear of machine suspended. Refer also to Fig. 11.

Fig. 11—On Sno-Twister and Trail-Twister models, loosen locknuts and turn adjusting screws (A) to adjust track tension.

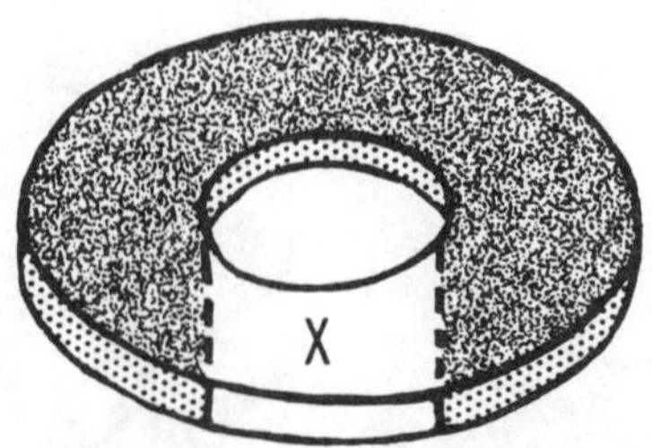

Fig. 12—Plain 7/16-inch washers can be modified by cutting out a slotted portion (X) to adjust belt tension on Sno-Twister models.

Fig. 13—View of chaincase with cover removed, showing drive chain and sprockets.

Fig. 14—Remove chain and sprockets as a unit as shown, after removing retaining cap screws.

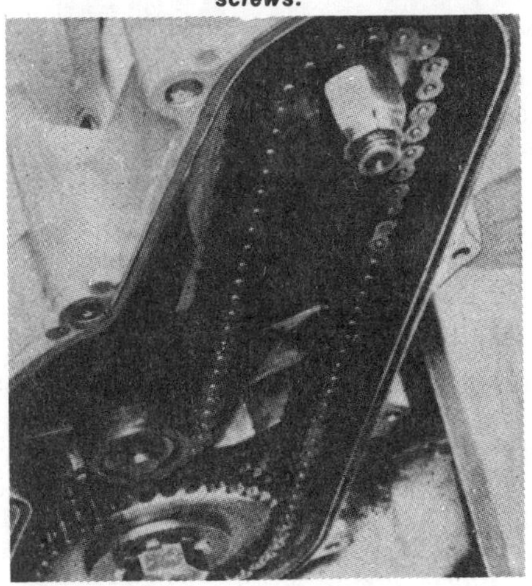

Fig. 15—Mk II chaincase with cover removed, showing chain, sprockets and idler. Chain and sprockets are interchangeable with other models.

Fig. 16—View of Sno-Twister chaincase with cover removed. Chaincase is mounted on right side of machine, with a drive shaft running across the frame to the left mounted torque converter.

loosen brake caliper mounting screws so brake is free to move, then completely loosen chain tension. Remove retaining screws and washers and slide sprockets from shaft splines as shown in Fig. 14. Sprockets are interchangeable for all Mercury models; upper sprockets are available with 12, 13, 14, 15, 16 or 17 teeth and lower sprocket is available with 34 or 36 teeth. Tighten upper sprocket retaining cap screw to a torque of 30 ft.-lbs. (4.1 kg-m) and lower sprocket screw to 40 ft-lbs. (5.5 kg-m).

Fig. 15 shows Mark II chaincase with cover removed. Chain and sprockets are interchangeable with 340 and 440 models, and removal procedure and tightening torques are the same.

On Sno-Twister models, the chaincase is mounted on right side of frame and driven by a cross shaft from the driven sheave. Chain and sprockets are interchangeable with other models.

MONTGOMERY WARD
1968-1972

Model	Engine Make	Engine Model	Engine Displ.	Carburetor Make	Carburetor Model	Sprocket Ratio	Chain Size	Clutch Make	Clutch Shaft Center	Belt Number
					1968					
Caribou	Sachs	SA280	277cc	Tillotson	HR3A	10:32	40	Scorpion	10½	11121
					1969					
Caribou	Sachs	SA280	277cc	Tillotson	HR3A	10:32	40	Scorpion	10½	11121
					1970					
Mini 99	JLO	L99	100cc	Tillotson	HL270B	(Centrifugal clutch & 8:1 double chain reduction. No converter)				
Snowmobile 370	Sachs	SA370	368cc	Tillotson	HR30A	12:32	40	Scorpion	10½	11121
					1971					
300	Kohler	K295-1	294cc	Tillotson	HR41A	15:33	35-2	Salsbury 780	13⅛	16971
450	Kohler	K440-2	437cc	Tillotson	HR79B	15:33	35-2	Salsbury 910	12-15/16	17609
					1972					
300	Kohler	K295-1	294cc	Tillotson	HR41A	15:33	35-2	Salsbury 780	13⅛	16971
450	Kohler	K440-2	437cc	Tillotson	HR79B	15:33	35-2	Salsbury 910	12-15/16	17609

LUBRICATION

The engine is lubricated by oil mixed with the fuel. The manufacturer recommends the use of regular gasoline and SAE 30 Snowmobile Oil mixed at the rate of 20:1.

The drive chain runs in an enclosed chain case which should be filled to level of check plug with approximately 4 fluid ounces of Automatic Transmission Fluid, Type A (Dextrone). Fill plug is located at top of chain case as shown in Fig. 1.

Ski legs (spindle shafts) are equipped with pressure gun fittings which are accessible from engine compartment after raising hood. Lubricate periodically with low temperature grease.

Fig. 1—View of engine compartment showing points of adjustment and service.

1. Clamp screw
2. Adjusting lever
3. Filler plug
4. Brake adjusting nut
5. Housing anchor nuts
6. Lube fitting

Lightly lubricate ski pivot bolt and spring mount front bracket with SAE 30 oil periodically for smoother operation and longer life.

Track carriage and associated parts are equipped with self-aligning, sealed bearings and do not require lubrication.

ADJUSTMENT

STEERING SKIS. Steering skis should be parallel to each other and to vehicle frame when handle bar is in normal straight driving position. Tie rods should be equal in length and adjustment can be made after disconnecting either end.

DRIVE CHAIN. The roller drive chain should have all slack removed but must not be under tension. Because the idler sprocket adjustor is located on the chaincase cover, the adjustment cannot be directly observed. Adjustment may be considered to be correct when rim of driven sheave has a free movement of not less than ⅛-inch nor more than ⅜-inch. Refer to Fig. 1.

To adjust the chain, loosen the clamp bolt and move chain adjusting lever (2) down to tighten, or up to loosen chain.

BRAKE. The caliper type disc brake uses the fixed flange of torque converter driven sheave as a friction face. Brake wear adjustment should be made by removing the cotter pin securing castellated nut to lever arm stud. Tighten the nut until resistance is felt, then back off ½-turn and reinstall cotter pin. Make sure brake puck push pins center in valleys of actuating arm when adjustment is made. Lever arm can be centered by adjusting cable housing anchor nuts.

TRACK. With rear of machine raised until track is clear of ground, center of track should measure 4¾-4⅞ inches from bottom of frame as shown at (A—Fig. 2). Make sure swing arms (support arms) are free and that measurement is made immediately below center bogie support as shown. If adjustment is required, loosen nuts on clamp bolts (1) and turn adjusting bolts (2). Both sides must be adjusted alike.

NOTE: Whenever track tension has been adjusted, alignment MUST be checked as outlined in TRACK SERVICE Section of this manual.

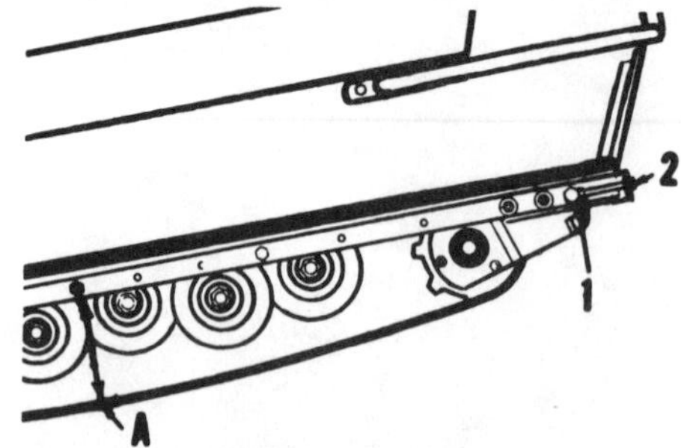

Fig. 2—To adjust track tension, raise rear of machine and loosen nuts on pivot bolts (1). Turn adjusting screw (2) until distance (A) measures 4¾ inches.

1. Clamp screw
2. Adjusting lever
3. Filler plug
4. Brake adjusting nut
5. Housing anchor nuts
6. Lube fitting

MOTO-SKI

1965-1972

					1965					
100	JLO	L252	247cc	Tillotson	HL187A	10:36	40	Own	10-15/16	7409
300	Hirth	53R	300cc	Tillotson	HL192A	11:36	40	Own	10-15/16	7409
					1966					
Cadet	Hirth	81R	246cc	Tillotson	HL187A	11:36	40	Own	10-15/16	7409
Capri	Hirth	54R	300cc	Tillotson	HL207A	11:36	40	Own	10-15/16	7409
Zephyr	Hirth	54R	300cc	Tillotson	HL207A	11:36	40	Own	10-15/16	7409
					1967					
Capri 151H ...	Hirth	55R	300cc	Tillotson	HR3A	12:36	40	Own	10-15/16	7409
Capri 202H ...	Hirth	55R	300cc	Tillotson	HR3A	12:36	40	Own	10-15/16	7409
					1968					
Cadet	Hirth	82R	246cc	Tillotson	HR13A	10:30	40	Own	10-15/16	7409
Capri	Hirth	55R	300cc	Tillotson	HR16AX	11:30	40	Own	10-15/16	9409
Zephyr	Hirth	55R	300cc	Tillotson	HR16AX	11:30	40	Own	10-15/16	9409
Zephyr	Hirth	160R	372cc	Tillotson	HD7AX	12:30	40	Own	10-15/16	9409
MS-18........	Hirth	55R	300cc	Tillotson	HR16AX	10:25	40	Own	10-15/16	9409
					1969					
Cadet	Hirth	82R	246cc	Tillotson	HR16	10:30	40	Own	10-15/16	7409
Capri	Hirth	192R	317cc	Tillotson	HR25A	12:30	40	Own	10-15/16	MO409L
Capri	Hirth	200R	372cc	Tillotson	HD17A	13:30	40	Own	10-15/16	MO409L
Zephyr	Hirth	192R	317cc	Tillotson	HR25A	12:30	40	Own	10-15/16	MO409L
Zephyr	Hirth	200R	372cc	Tillotson	HD17A	12:30	40	Own	10-15/16	MO409L
MS-18........	Hirth	200R	372cc	Tillotson	HD17A	11:25	40	Own	10-15/16	MO409L
MS-18........	Hirth	220R	493cc	Tillotson	HD17A	12:25	40	Own	10-15/16	MO409L
MS-18........	Hirth	171R	634cc	Tillotson	HD17A	15:25	40	Own	10-15/16	MO409L
					1970					
Cadet	JLO	L295	292cc	Tillotson	HR44A	11:30	40	Own	10-15/16	9757
Capri	Hirth	191R	300cc	Tillotson	HR44A	11:30	40	Own	10-15/16	9757
Capri	Hirth	194R	338cc	Tillotson	HD25A	11:30	40	Own	10-15/16	9757
Capri	JLO	L380	372cc	Tillotson	HD25A	13:30	40	Own	10-15/16	9757
Zephyr	Hirth	192R	317cc	Tillotson	HR44A	11:30	40	Own	10-15/16	9757
Zephyr	Hirth	194R	338cc	Tillotson	HD17A	11:30	40	Own	10-15/16	9757
Zephyr	Hirth	200R	372cc	Tillotson	HD17A	13:30	40	Own	10-15/16	9757
Zephyr	JLO	L380	372cc	Tillotson	HD17A	13:30	40	Own	10-15/16	9757
MS-18........	JLO	L380	372cc	Tillotson	HD17A	11:25	40	Own	10-15/16	9757
MS-18........	Hirth	220R	493cc	Tillotson	HD17A	13:25	40	Own	11½	9756
MS-18........	Hirth	171R	634cc	Tillotson	HE17A	14:25	40	Own	11½	9756
Grand Prix....	Hirth	194R	338cc	Tillotson	HD17A	11:30	40	Own	10-15/16	9757
Grand Prix....	Sachs		340cc	Tillotson	HD17A	11:30	40	Own	10-15/16	9757
Grand Prix....	Hirth	211R	438cc	Tillotson	HD17A	14:30	40	Own	11½	9756
Grand Prix....	Hirth	171R	634cc	Tillotson	HD17A	16:30	40	Own	11½	9756
					1971					
Mini Sno	JLO	L223	223cc	Keihin	406	10:30	40	Own	10-15/16	0020005
Capri	JLO	L295	292cc	Keihin	406	11:30	40	Own	10-15/16	0020003
Capri	Hirth	194R	338cc	Tillotson	HR	12:30	40	Own	10-15/16	0020003
Capri	JLO	LR399/2	398cc	Tillotson	HR	13:30	40	Own	10-15/16	0020003
Zephyr	Hirth	194R	338cc	Tillotson	HD	12:30	40	Own	10-15/16	0020003
Zephyr	JLO	LR399/2	398cc	Tillotson	HD	13:30	40	Own	11½	0020004
Grand Prix....	JLO	LR340/2	339cc	Tillotson	HD	12:30	40	Own	10-15/16	0020003
Grand Prix....	JLO	LR399/2	398cc	Tillotson	HD	13:30	40	Own	11½	0020004
Grand Prix....	Hirth	171R	634cc	Tillotson	HD	16:30	40	Own	11½	0020004
MS-18........	JLO	LR399/2	398cc	Tillotson	HD	13:30	40	Own	11½	0020004
MS-18........	Hirth	171R	634cc	Tillotson	HD	16:30	40	Own	11½	0020004
					1972					
Mini Sno	JLO	L223	223cc	Keihin	406	10:30	40	Own	10-15/16	0020005
Cadet 250	BSE	250	248cc	Tillotson	HR117A	11:30	40	Own	10-15/16	700027
Capri 295.....	Hirth	193R	292cc	Tillotson	HR44A	11:30	40	Own	10-15/16	700027
Capri 340.....	Hirth	194R	338cc	Tillotson	HD25A	12:30	40	Own	10-15/16	700027
Capri 340.....	JLO	LR340/2	339cc	Tillotson	HD53B	11:30	40	Own	10-15/16	700027
Capri 400.....	JLO	LR399/2	398cc	Tillotson	HD53B	13:50	40	Own	11½	700027
Zephyr 340....	BSE	340	336cc	Tillotson	HR118A	13:30	40	Own	10-15/16	700027
Zephyr 440....	BSE	440	435cc	Tillotson	HD86A	15:30	40	Own	11½	700027
MS-18 400	JLO	LR399/2	398cc	Tillotson	HD53B	12:30	40	Own	11½	700027
Grand Prix....	BSE	340	336cc	Tillotson	HR126A	13:30	40	Own	10-15/16	700027
Grand Prix....	BSE	440	435cc	Keihin	CD42	15:30	40	Own	11½	700027

LUBRICATION

The engine is lubricated by oil mixed with the fuel. The vehicle manufacturer recommends the use of "VEEDOL" Two Stroke Oil at the ratio of 16:1.

Grease fittings are located on ski spindles, each bogie wheel, each side of rear track axle and top flange of drive chain guard. Lubricate as required with "MOTO-SKI" grease or equivalent low temperature grease.

On models with enclosed chain case, lubricate the chain at regular intervals with "MOTO-SKI" Low Temperature Grease. On older models, spray or brush lubricate the chain regularly with a suitable oil or chain lubricant.

ADJUSTMENT

STEERING SKIS. Disconnect tie rod from left steering arm and adjust length of rod as necessary until skis are parallel when pointing straight ahead. Shorten or lengthen steering drag link if necessary, until handle bars are parallel when skis are straight.

Fig. 1—View of chain case, brake and associated parts on late model with caliper disc brake.

1. Chain adjusting bolt
2. Anchor nuts
3. Adjusting nut
4. Brake light switch

Fig. 2—Driven sheave, brake and enclosed chain case used on 1970 models.

B. Brake anchor nuts
C. Chain adjusting bolt

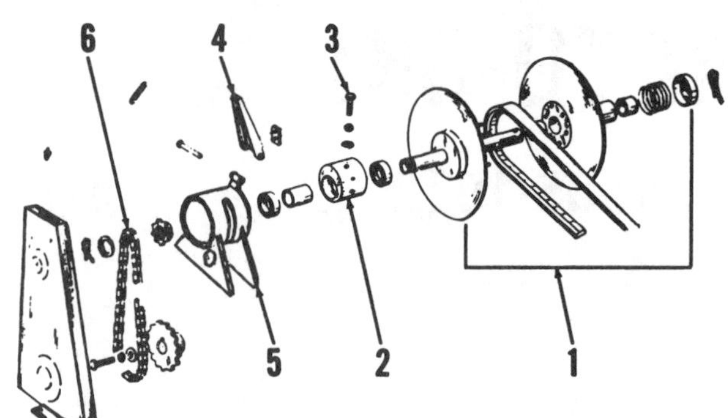

Fig. 3—Exploded view of intermediate drive shaft and associated parts used on early models with open chain case. Intermediate shaft is part of torque converter driven sheave.

1. Driven sheave
2. Eccentric housing
3. Adjusting bolt
4. Brake lever
5. Bracket
6. Drive chain

DRIVE CHAIN. The roller drive chain (6—Fig. 3) on models with open chain should have approximately ½-inch of free play, measured midway between sprockets. Adjustment is by means of eccentric bearing housing (2). To adjust the chain, back off the locknut and push down on jam bolt (3) until tight, then raise bolt approximately $\frac{1}{16}$-inch and tighten locknut. Check and readjust if necessary.

On later models, direct measurement of free play is less convenient but adjustment is the same. Move adjusting bolt (C—Fig. 2) down until it stops, then up approximately $\frac{1}{16}$ inch. If adjusting bolt bottoms in slot, move bolt to next threaded hole which has appeared at top of slot. Tighten locknut when adjustment is correct.

The enclosed drive chain should have ⅛-⅜ inch free play measured midway between sprockets. On earlier models free play can be directly measured by removing inspection cover; on late models free play can be estimated by checking backlash of driven pulley. On all models, adjust drive chain by loosening tensioner bolt (1–Fig. 1) and sliding the bolt in slotted hole.

NOTE: If bolt bottoms in slot, remove and then reinstall in threaded hole which will have appeared in opposite end of slot.

BRAKE. On models with drum or pivot lever type brake 1/16-inch clearance should exist between lining and friction surface of drum or pulley with brake released. Adjust by relocating brake cable housing anchor nuts until correct clearance is obtained.

On models with caliper type disc brake, adjust cable housing anchor nuts (2–Fig. 1) if necessary until brake push pins center in valleys of actuating lever cam with brake released; then make wear adjustment by turning the adjusting nut (3). Be sure brake light switch (4) closes when brake is applied but opens (light goes out) with brake released.

On all models brake should fully apply before hand lever contacts handlebar grip but should be free with lever released.

TRACK. To adjust track tension, raise rear of machine until track is clear. Bottom of track should clear center bogie wheel by 1½-2 inches. Adjust by loosening clamp bolts on rear axle adjusting brackets and turning adjusting screws until tension is correct. Refer to Fig. 4. Measure the distance (A) from running board flange of frame to lower edge of adjuster link plate. Distance should be equal for both sides and within the limits of 2¾-3¼ inches; if it is not, loosen the two clamp bolts (1) and turn adjusting bolt (2) until measurement is correct.

NOTE: When track tension has been adjusted, alignment MUST be checked as outlined in the TRACK SERVICE section of this manual.

OVERHAUL

SKIS. Skis are fitted with wear bars which are retained by a nut on one center stud. Wear bar can be installed either end forward. Skis, springs, spindle, spindle arm and associated parts are interchangeable for either side of vehicle.

TRACK. On all models, track cleats are riveted to the special endless track belts and can be renewed if necessary, if cleats are bent, worn or otherwise damaged.

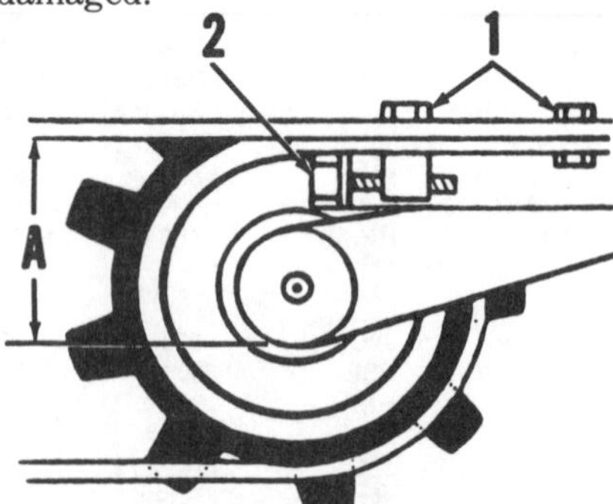

Fig. 4—With rear of vehicle raised, distance (A) should measure 2¾ - 3¼ inches. Adjust by loosening clamp bolts (1) and turning adjusting screw (2).

MOTO-SKI

BOMBARDIER CORPORATION
4505 West Superior Street
Duluth, MN 55806

1973-1982

CONDENSED SERVICE DATA

	Engine			Carburetor				Clutch		
Model	Make	Model	Displ.	Make	Model	Sprocket Ratio	Chain Size	Make	Shaft Center	Belt Number
					1973					
Cadet	BSE	250	247cc	Tillotson	HR139A	10:25	40	Own		700050
Capri 295	BSE		294cc	Tillotson	HR139A	11:30	40	Own		700036
Capri 340	BSE	340	336cc	Tillotson	HR145A	13:30	40	Own		700036
Capri 440	BSE	440	435cc	Tillotson	HD121A	14:30	40	Own		700036
Zephyr 340	BSE	340	336cc	Tillotson	HR139A	13:30	40	Own		700036
Zephyr 440	BSE	440	435cc	Tillotson	HD121A	14:30	40	Own		700036
"F" 295	BSE		294cc	Tillotson	HR139A	10:30	40	Own		700036
"F" 340	BSE	340	336cc	Tillotson	HR145A	12:30	40	Own		700036
"F" 440	BSE	440	437cc	Tillotson	HD121A	13:30	40	Own		700036
"S" 400	BSE	400	399cc			13:30	40	Own		
"S" 440	BSE	440	437cc			13:30	40	Own		
					1974					
Cadet 250	BSE	250M	247cc	Tillotson	HR156A	10:25	40	Own	10⅝	061442
Capri 295	BSE	296	294cc	Tillotson	HR159A	11:30	40	Own	11-11/16	700027
Futura 295	BSE	296	294cc	Tillotson	HR159A	11:30	40	Own	11-11/16	061378
Futura 340	BSE	340T	339cc	Walbro	WDB30	12:30	40	Own	10⅝	061378
Futura 440	BSE	440T	436cc	Walbro	WDB30	13:30	40	Own	11-11/16	061442
Grand Sport 440	BSE	440T	436cc	Walbro	WDB30	13:30	40	Own	11-11/16	061443
Grand Sport TS400	BSE	399	399cc	Tillotson	HD122BM	11:30	40	Own	10⅝	061442
Chimo 440	BSE	440T	436cc	Walbro	WDB30	13:30	40	Own	10⅝	061442
					1975					
Cadet 250	BSE	250M	247cc	Tillotson	HR156A	10:25	40	Own	10⅝	061442
Nuvik 300	Rotax	305	295.1cc	Tillotson	HR139A	13:38		Bomb.	10½	061378
Nuvik 340	Rotax	343	339.2cc	Tillotson	HR152A	15:34		Bomb.	10½	061378
Futura 440	Rotax	440	436.6cc	Tillotson	HD138A	13:30	40	Own	11-11/16	061442
Chimo 440	BSE	440	436cc	Walbro	WDB30	13:30	40	Own	11-11/16	061442
Grand Sport 440	BSE	440	436cc	Walbro	WDB30	13:30	40	Own	11-11/16	061443
TS400	BSE	399	399cc	Tillotson	HD122BM	11:31	40	Own	11-11/16	061442
Sonic	Rotax	345	336.7cc	Mikuni	VM38(2)	18:40	35-3	Bomb.	10½	414-2277
					1976					
Spirit 250	Rotax	247	246.8cc	Tillotson	HR	10:25	40	Bombardier	1¾*	570-0411-00
Nuvik 300	Rotax	305	295.1cc	Tillotson	HR	16:35	35-2	Bombardier	1⅜*	414-2327
Nuvik 340	Rotax	343	339.2cc	Tillotson	HR	17:34	35-2	Bombardier	1⅜*	414-2327
Futura 440	Rotax	440	436.6cc	Tillotson	HD	21:38	35-3	Bombardier	1⅜*	570-0414
Sonic 250	Rotax	245	247.3cc	Mikuni	VM34(2)	16:40	35-2	Bombardier	1⅜*	414-2277
Sonic 340	Rotax	345	336.7cc	Mikuni	VM38(2)	18:40	35-3	Bombardier	1⅜*	414-2277
*Pulley Rim Clearance.										
					1977					
Spirit 250	Rotax	247	246.8cc	Tillotson	HR-173A	10:25	40	Bombardier	1¾*	570-04400
Nuvik 300	Rotax	305	295.1cc	Mikuni	VM-30-90	15:34	35-2	Bombardier	1⅜*	414-232-700
Nuvik 340	Rotax	343	339.2cc	Mikuni	VM-30-91	16:33	35-2	Bombardier	1⅜*	414-232-700
Nuvik 440	Rotax	440	436.6cc	Mikuni	VM-32-113	17:33	35-3	Bombardier	1⅜*	414-241-700
Futura 400	Rotax	402	398.6cc	Mikuni	VM-30-92	18:34	35-2	Bombardier	1⅜*	414-241-700
Futura 440	Rotax	440	436.6cc	Mikuni	VM-34-110	21:38	35-3	Bombardier	1⅜*	414-241-700
Sonic 340	Rotax	345	336.7cc	Mikuni	VM-34-135(2)	18:38	35-3	Bombardier	1⅜*	414-227-700
*Pulley Rim Clearance.										

	Engine			Carburetor				Clutch		
Model	Make	Model	Displ.	Make	Model	Sprocket Ratio	Chain Size	Make	Shaft Center	Belt Number
					1978					
Spirit 250	Rotax	247	246.8cc	Tillotson	HR-173A	10:25	40	Bombardier	10¾	5700411
Nuvik 340	Rotax	343	339.2cc	Mikuni	VM30-91	17:34	35-2	Bombardier	10-9/16	4142327
Futura 400	Rotax	402	398.6cc	Mikuni	VM30-92	18:34	35-2	Bombardier	10-9/16	4142417
Futura 440	Rotax	440	436.6cc	Mikuni	VM34-165	21:38	35-3	Bombardier	10-9/16	4142417
Futura 444L/C	Rotax	444	436.6cc	Mikuni	VM34-150	20:34	35-3	Bombardier	10-9/16	4142277
Sonic 340	Rotax	345	336.7cc	Mikuni	VM34-135(2)	18:38	35-3	Bombardier	10-9/16	4142277
					1979					
Spirit 250	Rotax	247	246.8cc	Tillotson	HR173A	10:25	½-1	Own	1¾*	570-0411-00
Mirage 300	Rotax	294	293.5cc	Mikuni	VM30-104	17:33	⅜-2	Own	1-7/16*	414-2327-00
Nuvik 340	Rotax	343	339.2cc	Mikuni	VM30-98	17:33	⅜-2	Own	1-7/16*	414-2327-00
Futura 400	Rotax	402	398.6cc	Mikuni	VM30-92	18:34	⅜-2	Own	1-7/16*	414-2417-00
Futura 440	Rotax	440	436.6cc	Mikuni	VM34-165	21:38	⅜-3	Own	1-7/16*	414-2417-00
Futura 444LC	Rotax	444	436.3cc	Mikuni	VM34-150	20:34	⅜-3	Own	1-7/16*	414-2277-00
Grand Prix Special	Rotax	503	496.7cc	Mikuni	VM34-203	21:38	⅜-3	Own	1⅜*	414-2277-00
Super Sonic LC	Rotax	354	339.2cc	Mikuni	VM34-184	19:38	⅜-3	Own	1-7/16*	414-2277-00
*Pulley Rim Clearance.										
					1980					
Spirit	Rotax	247	250.4cc	Mikuni	VM28-242	10:25	½-1	Own	1¾*	570-0411-00
Mirage I	Rotax	277	268.7cc	Mikuni	VM34-228	15:34	⅜-2	Own	Fixed	414-3945-00
Mirage II	Rotax	377	368.3cc	Mikuni	VM34-229	16:33	⅜-2	Own	Fixed	414-3945-00
Mirage Special	Rotax	377	368.3cc	Mikuni	2XVM30-111	18:34	⅜-2	Own	Fixed	414-3945-00
Futura 500	Rotax	503	496.7cc	Mikuni	VM36-83	19:40	⅜-3	Own	1⅜*	414-3758-00
Futura LC	Rotax	464	462.8cc	Mikuni	VM34-227	17:34	⅜-3	Own	1⅜*	414-3758-00
Grand Prix Special	Rotax	503	496.7cc	Mikuni	2XVM34-203	21:38	⅜-3	Own	1⅜*	414-3758-00
Super Sonic	Rotax	354	339.2cc	Mikuni	MAG: VM34-230 PTO: VM34-233	17:38	⅜-3	Own	1⅜*	414-3758-00
Ultra Sonic	Rotax	454	436.6cc	Mikuni	MAG:VM36-86 PTO:VM36-88	19:40	⅜-3	Own	1⅜*	414-3758-00
*Pulley Rim Clearance.										
					1981					
Spirit	Rotax	247	250.4cc	Mikuni	VM28-242	10:25	½-1	Own	1¾*	570-0411-00
Mirage I	Rotax	277	268.7cc	Mikuni	VM34-255	15:34	⅜-2	Own	Fixed	414-3945-00
Mirage II	Rotax	377	368.3cc	Mikuni	VM34-256	16:33	⅜-2	Own	Fixed	414-3945-00
Mirage Special	Rotax	377	368.3cc	Mikuni	2XVM34-257	18:34	⅜-2	Own	Fixed	414-3945-00
Futura 500	Rotax	503	496.7cc	Mikuni	VM36-104	19:40	⅜-3	Own	1⅜*	414-3758-00
Futura LC	Rotax	464	462.8cc	Mikuni	VM34-227	17:34	⅜-3.	Own	1⅜*	414-3758-00
Grand Prix Special	Rotax	503	496.7cc	Mikuni	2XVM34-203	21:38	⅜-3	Own	1⅜*	414-3758-00
Super Sonic	Rotax	354	339.2cc	Mikuni	2XVM34-230	17:38	⅜-3	Own	1⅜*	414-3758-00
Ultra Sonic	Rotax	454	436.6cc	Mikuni	MAG:VM36-86 PTO:VM36-88	19:40	⅜-3	Own	1⅜*	414-3758-00
*Pulley Rim Clearance.										
					1982					
Spirit 250	Rotax	247	250.4cc	Mikuni	VM28-242	10:25	½-1	Own	1¾*	570-0411-00
Mirage I	Rotax	277	268.7cc	Mikuni	VM34-255	15:34	⅜-2	Own	1⅝*	414-3945-00
Mirage II	Rotax	377	368.3cc	Mikuni	VM34-276	16:33	⅜-2	Own	1⅝*	414-3945-00
Mirage Special	Rotax	377	368.3cc	Mikuni	2XVM34-277	17:35	⅜-2	Own	1⅝*	414-3945-00
Ultra Sonic	Rotax	454	436.6cc	Mikuni	MAG:VM36-118 PTO:VM36-119	20:39	⅜-3	Own	1⅜*	414-3758-00
Sonic	Rotax	503	496.7cc	Mikuni	2XVM34-203	19:40	⅜-3	Own	1⅜*	414-3758-00
Futura 300	Rotax	377	368.3cc	Mikuni	VM34-276	14:35	⅜-3	Own	1⅝*	414-3758-00
Futura LC	Rotax	464	462.8cc	Mikuni	VM34-227	17:34	⅜-3	Own	1⅜*	414-3758-00
Futura 500	Rotax	503	496.7cc	Mikuni	VM36-114	19:40	⅜-3	Own	1⅜*	414-3758-00
*Pulley Rim Clearance.										

LUBRICATION

The engine for models without oil injection is lubricated by mixing oil with the fuel. Mix fuel and oil thoroughly in a separate container before pouring mixture into fuel tank. Bombardier concentrated 50:1 oil should be mixed with recommended fuel at a ratio of one pint of oil to six gallons of gasoline. If Bombardier oil is not available, USE ONLY a good quality recognized brand snowmobile oil or two-cycle oil and mix at fuel:oil ratio recommended by oil manufacturer. For cold weather blending, pre-mix the oil with a small amount of gasoline and shake thoroughly until mixture is liquid, then blend with remainder of fuel. Do not use kerosene or fuel oil for pre-mixing.

Normally the engine on models with oil injection will be adequately lubricated

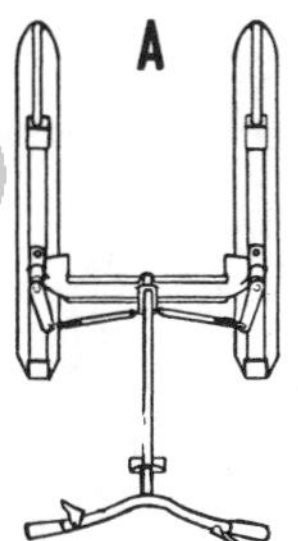

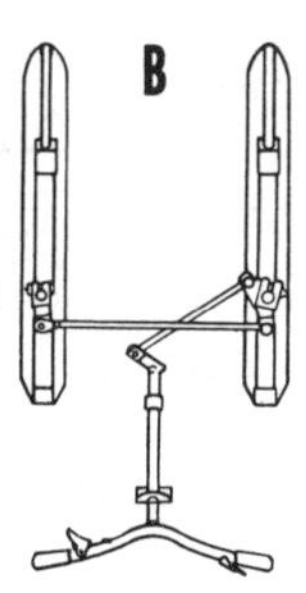

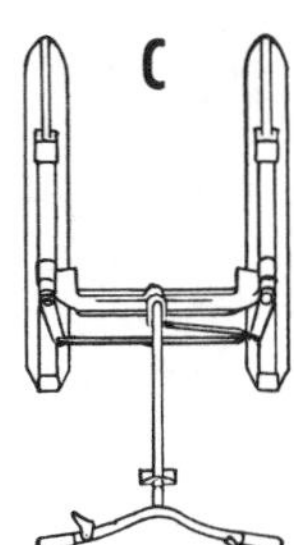

Fig. 1—Schematic view of three steering types used on Moto Ski units. (A) Separate drag links from handlebar to each ski leg. (B) Tie rod and drag link to front of right steering arm. (C) Tie rod and drag link to rear of right steering arm.

by oil delivered and metered by the oil injection pump. In extremely cold weather, the oil injection system may not pump correctly. Below −20 degrees F. (−29 degrees C.), mix one pint of oil with each six gallons of gasoline to supplement oil injection pump to insure proper lubrication.

Individual bogie wheels on models so equipped have pressure gun fittings as do drive axle bearing and idler wheels on single sprocket drive models. Idler axle bearings on most units also have pressure gun fittings. Suspension system, drive fittings and ski legs should be lubricated sparingly with low temperature grease in a hand grease gun each 50 hours.

ADJUSTMENT

STEERING SKIS. Steering skis should be parallel to 1/8-inch toe-in for 1974 and earlier models except Chimo, Grand Sport and Futura, which should have 1/4-inch toe-in. All late models and late Futura units should be adjusted so skis toe out 1/8-inch. Pull front ski tips together to take up the slack when measuring toe-in. On models (A—Fig. 1) having two drag links, adjust both links an equal amount to keep handlebar straight. On other models, shorten or lengthen tie rod to adjust toe-in, then adjust drag link until handlebar is straight.

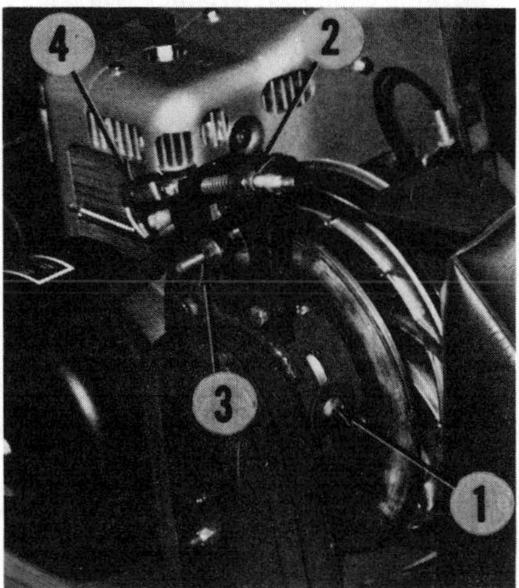

Fig. 2—View of chaincase, brake and associated parts on model with eccentric chain tightener and caliper disc brake.

1. Chain adjusting bolt
2. Anchor nuts
3. Adjusting nut
4. Brake light switch

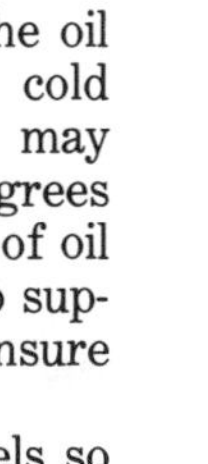

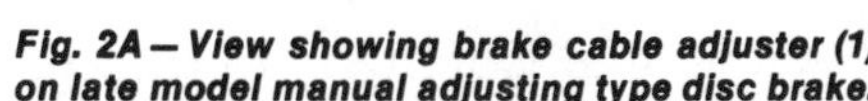

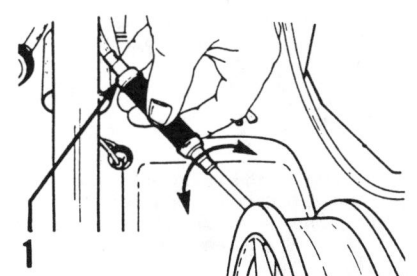

Fig. 2A—View showing brake cable adjuster (1) on late model manual adjusting type disc brake.

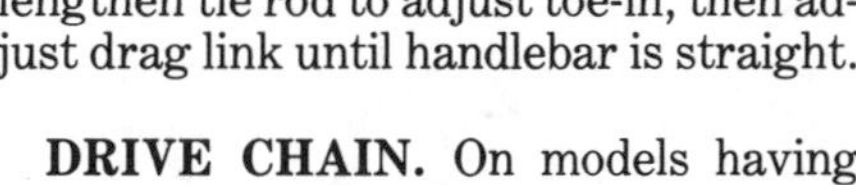

DRIVE CHAIN. On models having an eccentric chain tightener (1—Fig. 2), chain should have approximately 1/4-inch free play, measured midway between sprockets. Free play can be estimated by checking backlash at driven pulley rim. Some movement must exist, but backlash should not exceed 1/2-inch. Models without the eccentric chain tightener have spring-loaded tensioners and adjustment is not required.

BRAKE. On models with drum or pivot lever type brake, 1/16-inch clearance should exist between lining and friction surface of drum or pulley with brake released. Adjust by relocating brake cable housing anchor nuts until correct clearance is obtained.

On early models with manual adjusting caliper type disc brake, refer to Fig. 2. Adjust cable housing anchor nuts (2) until brake push pins center in valleys of actuating lever cam with brake released; then make wear adjustment by turning the adjusting nut (3) until brake pucks just clear friction surface of disc. Be sure brake light switch (4) closes when brake is applied but opens (light goes out) with brake released.

On late models with manual adjusting type disc brake, refer to Fig. 2A. Adjust cable by turning adjuster (1) counterclockwise until disc pucks are tight against brake disc, then back off adjuster 1½ turns. Brake should fully apply when hand lever is approximately 1/2-inch from handlebar grip.

On models equipped with self-adjusting brake types, wear adjustment is not required.

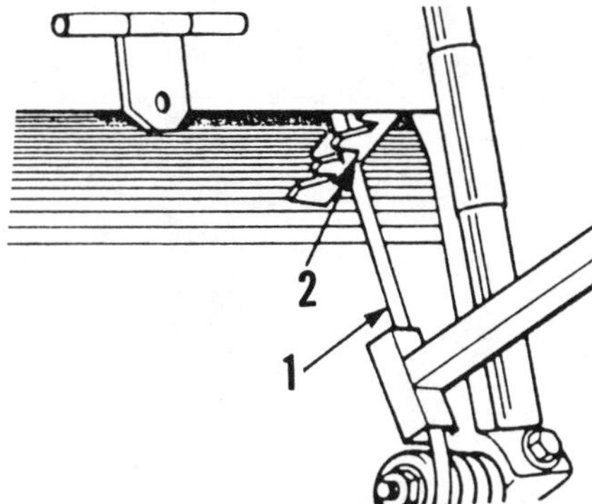

Fig. 2B—View showing link plate springs (1) and slotted anchors (2) for late model Spirits.

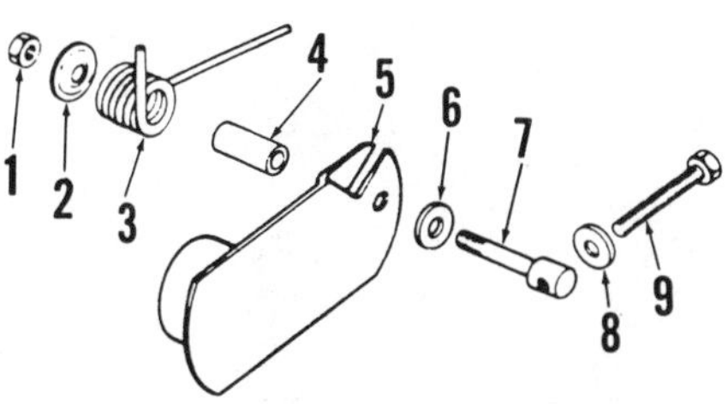

Fig. 2C-View showing track tension adjustment components for late model Spirit. Left and right components are the same.

1. Locknut
2. Retaining washer
3. Spring
4. Sleeve
5. Link plate
6. Washer
7. Eye bolt
8. Washer
9. Adjuster bolt

TRACK. To adjust track tension on early bogie wheel models, raise rear of machine until track is clear. Bottom of track should clear center bogie wheel by 1½-2 inches. Adjust by loosening clamp bolts on rear axle adjusting brackets and turning adjusting screws until tension is correct. Both sides must be adjusted alike.

On late model Spirits, first place all link plate springs (1—Fig. 2B) in middle position (2) of three position slotted anchors. Raise rear of vehicle off ground, then measure track deflection at top of middle set of bogie wheels. Track deflection should be 1⅜ inches between top inside edge and bottom of foot board. To adjust track tension, loosen locknut (1—Fig. 2C) on left and right side. Turn adjuster bolts (9) clockwise to tighten track tension and counter-clockwise to loosen track tension. Turn adjuster bolts equal amounts on both sides. Retighten locknuts after adjustment, then check track alignment. Distance between link plate (5) and edge of track must be equal on both sides.

On slide suspension models, raise rear of machine until track is clear. On 1975 Futura, Grand Sport, Chimo and TS-400, measure clearance between slide rail and inner side of track **cleat** as shown in Fig. 3. Clearance should be one inch and equal on both sides. Adjust

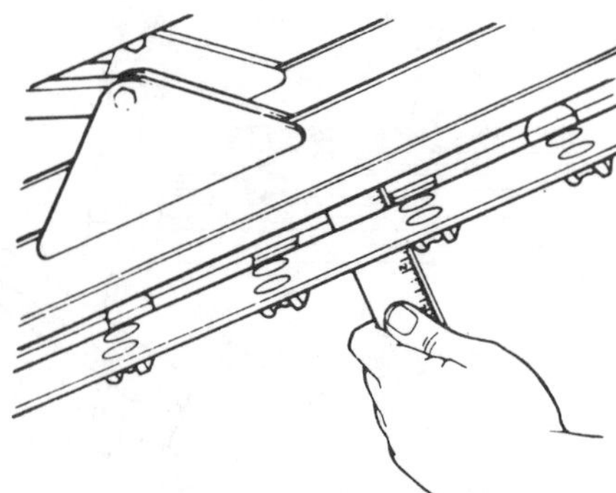

Fig. 3—Measuring track adjustment on earlier models with slide suspension.

Fig. 4—Loosen the locknut and turn adjusting screw (A) on each side of machine to adjust track tension.

tension at adjuster bolts at front of idler axle as shown in Fig. 4. With track tension adjusted, set machine on level ground with skis straight, and measure running board height at rear idler axle. Now place driver in normal operating position and again measure running board height at same position. If loaded drop is not ½-inch, tighten or loosen ALL FOUR eyebolt nuts equally until ½-inch loaded drop is obtained.

On all Nuvik models, clearance (C–Fig. 5) measured from inside of track to slide rail midway between idler wheels should be ⅜-½ inch. Clearance should be ¾-inch on early Futura and Sonic models. On all later models clearance should be ½-inch measured between slide rail shoe and bottom inside of track. On all models, adjust by turning adjusting bolts (A–Fig. 4) at each end of idler axle.

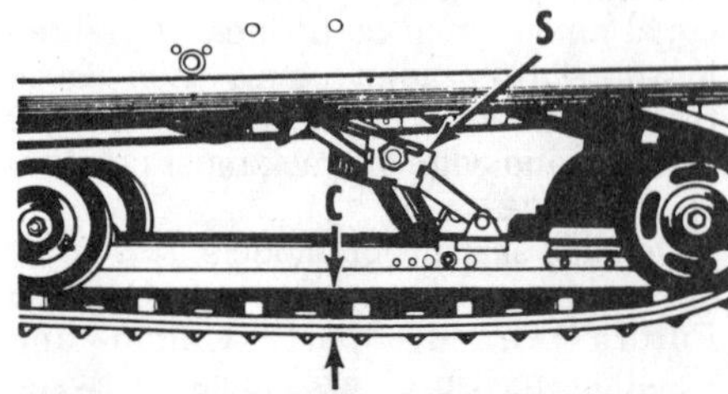

Fig. 5—View of "Torque Reaction" slide suspension used on some models. Measure clearance at (C). Suspension cams (S) adjust ride.

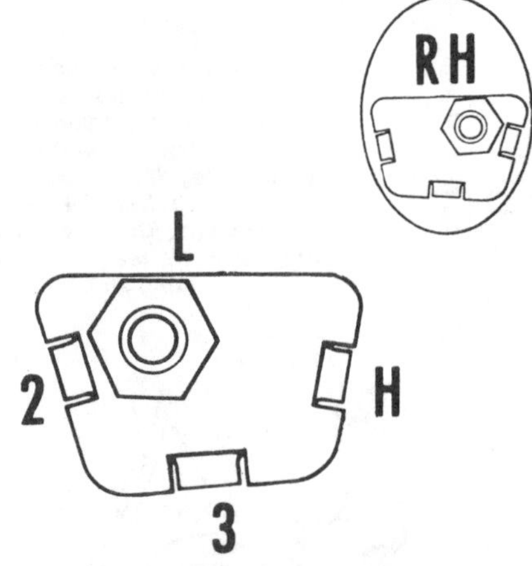

Fig. 6—View of left-hand adjusting cam showing low (L), high (H) and two intermediate positions (2 and 3). Right hand cam (RH) is a mirror image of left cam as shown.

On all models with Torque Reaction Slide Suspension, cams (S–Fig. 5) provide a ride adjustment for varying load and snow conditions. Front and rear cams may be adjusted independently but right and left cams must be adjusted the same.

NOTE: Right cam is a mirror image of left cam as shown in inset, Fig. 6. Front cams adjust for snow conditions, rear cams for load. Cams have four lift positions as shown in Fig. 6.

NOTE: Do not attempt to turn cam directly from low (L) to high (H) position or vice versa. Always adjust through the intermediate positions (2 and 3) when raising or lowering cam setting. Always turn left side adjuster cams clockwise and right side adjuster cams counterclockwise.

Front cams should be at lowest (L) position for deep snow. Turn to a higher position to increase steering response. Rear cams should be adjusted to provide 4½-5½ inches clearance between rear of footrest and snow surface when carrying normal load. A spark plug wrench fits the adjusting hex on cams.

On MX suspension models, front suspension is adjusted by cams as outlined in previous paragraphs. Rear suspension is adjusted by turning cam (C–Fig. 6A) on rear shocks to set desired tension on shock spring. There are three adjustment positions on cam, they are: First position (lowest step) for passenger/driver weight of 0-150 pounds; second position (middle step) for passenger/driver weight of 150-180 pounds and third position (highest step) for passenger/driver weight of 180 pounds and up. Be sure to adjust both sides on same step of cam.

A snubber strap (Fig. 7) on front slide support limits torque lift of front of

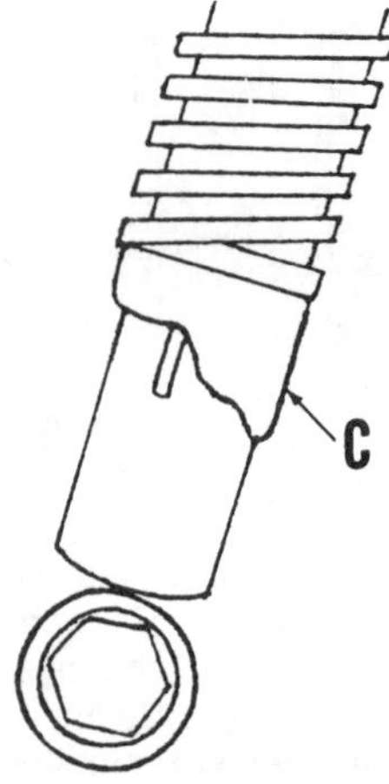

Fig. 6A—View showing rear shock adjustment cam (C) on MX suspension models. Refer to text for adjustment settings.

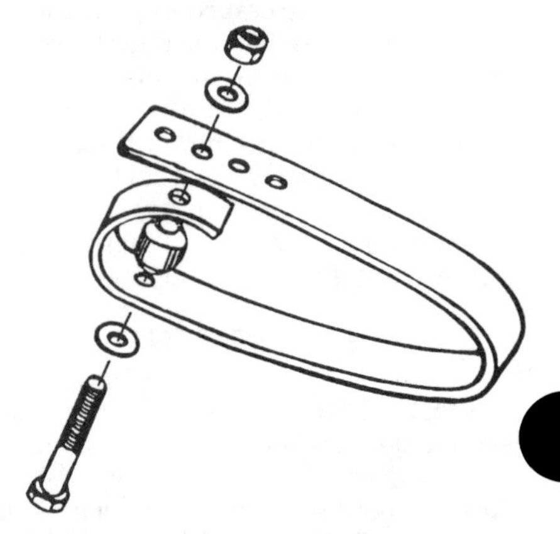

Fig 7—Snubber strap used on front slide support is normally adjusted in second hole as shown. Shortening strap limits torque lift of skis during acceleration.

machine during acceleration. Normal snubber adjustment is in second hole from outer end as shown. Lengthening snubber strap permits greater acceleration lift while shortening the strap prevents ski lift and provides greater ski control at acceleration.

DRIVE BELT AND SHEAVES. To check drive belt alignment on 1975 Sonic and Nuvik, remove drive belt shield and belt and refer to Fig. 8. Spread driven sheave and insert a ½-inch "Simulator"

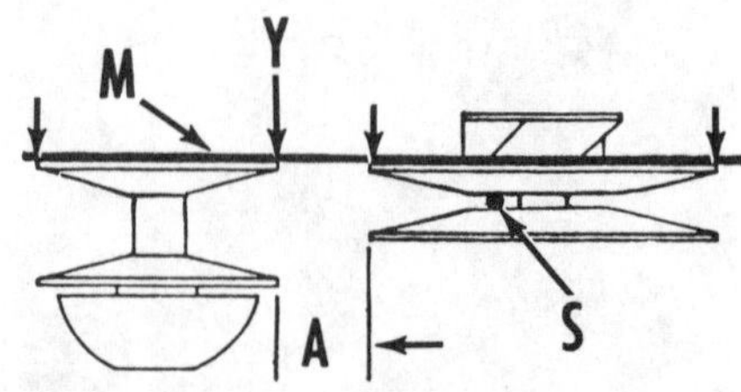

Fig. 8—Method of checking belt alignment on 1975 Sonic and Nuvik. Refer to text for details.

A. Rim clearance
M. Straightedge
S. Simulator
Y. Near rim

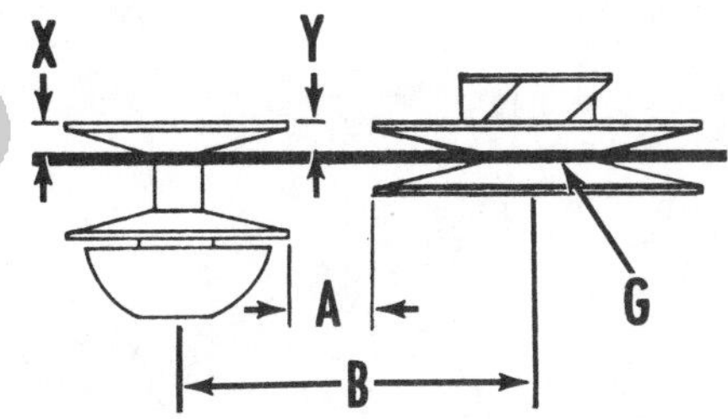

Fig. 9—Method of checking belt alignment on most models. Refer to text for details.

A. Rim clearance
B. Shaft center
G. Gage bar
X. Far rim clearance
Y. Near rim clearance

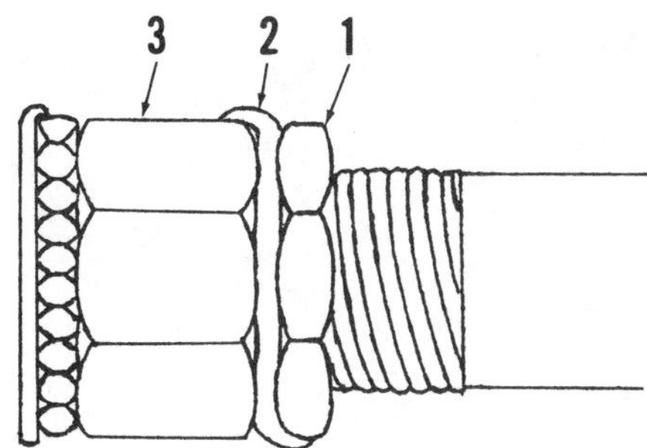

Fig. 9A—View showing thin nut (1), locking tab (2) and adjuster nut (3) used for adjusting driven clutch offset on late Futura 300 and Mirage models.

(S) (such as a rod, bolt or drill bit) between sheave halves to hold pulley open; then lay a straightedge (M) along inner rims of both sheaves as shown. Straightedge should touch both sheave rims at two places but may clear near rim of drive sheave (Y) by not more than 1/16-inch. Far edge of drive sheave MUST touch straightedge.

If drive pulley is too far in, remove drive pulley and ADD shims at crankshaft shoulder; or REMOVE shims between chaincase and track tunnel. Not more than five (5) shims may be used on crankshaft.

If drive pulley is too far out, REMOVE shims behind drive pulley at crankshaft shoulder; or ADD shims between chaincase and track tunnel.

Pulley rim clearance (A) should be 1⅜ inches (35 mm) on 1975 Sonic or 1⅞ inches (41 mm) on 1975 Nuvik.

To check drive belt alignment on other models, remove belt guard and drive belt and refer to Fig. 9. Slightly spread rims of driven sheave and insert a ⅜x19 inch gage bar (G) between pulley halves as shown, then measure distance between far edge of gage bar and inner edge of drive sheave rim as shown at (X) and (Y). The two measured distances should be equal except that (X) may exceed (Y) by **UP TO** 1/16-inch. Distance (Y) **MUST NEVER** exceed (X). Nominal measured distance on early models should be 13/16-inch. Measured distance

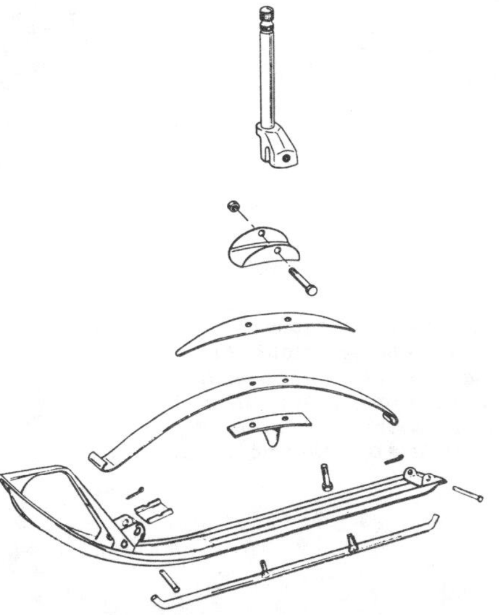

Fig. 10—Exploded view of steering ski and associated parts used on Spirit models. Some models use three springs.

on 1979 models should be 1-5/16 - 1⅜ inches, 1-11/32 inches on 1980 models, 1-5/16 inches on 1981 models except Spirit and Mirage models which should be 1-11/32 inches and 1-11/32 inches on 1982 models except all Sonic and Futura models which should be 1-9/32 inches.

NOTE: Futura and Sonic models are equipped with a floating type driven pulley. Pulley must be pushed against bearing flange before measuring distance.

To adjust pulley offset on early models with BSE engines, loosen engine mounting bolts and slide engine sideways.

On all models with ROTAX engines except late Futura 300 and Mirage models adjust pulley offset as follows. Remove drive pulley and add shims to crankshaft shoulder or remove shims from behind chaincase to DECREASE offset distance; remove shims from crankshaft shoulder or add shims behind chaincase to INCREASE offset distance.

CAUTION: Never use more than five shims on crankshaft shoulder.

On late Futura 300 and Mirage models adjust drive pulley by adding or removing shims. To adjust driven pulley offset refer to Fig. 9A. Straighten locking tab ears (2), then loosen thin nut (1). Turn adjuster nut (3) until correct distance is reached. While holding adjuster nut tighten thin nut to 48 ft.-lbs., then bend locking tab ears down.

Drive sheave rim clearance (A – Fig. 9) or shaft center distance (B) is given in CONDENSED SERVICE DATA tables. Adjust by either loosening engine mounting bolts and sliding the engine, loosening chaincase mounts and reposi-

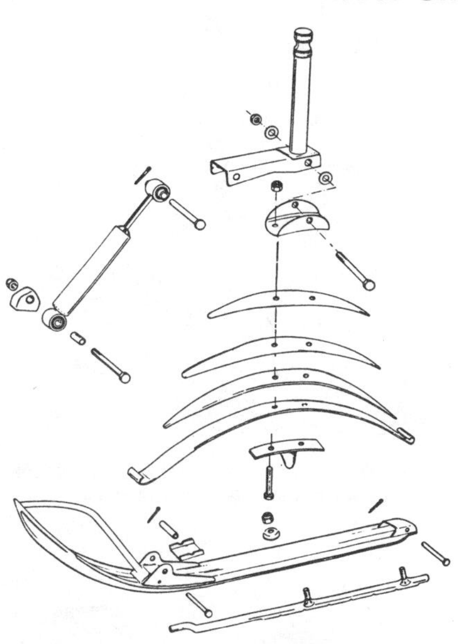

Fig. 11—Typical view of steering skis and associated parts used on most models except Futura LC and Sonic models.

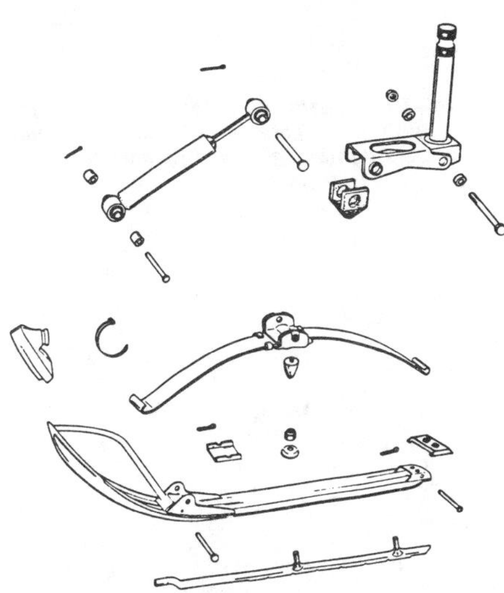

Fig. 12—Exploded view of steering skis and associated parts used on Sonic and Futura LC.

tioning chaincase to correct position or by adding or removing shim between the two driven pulley halves as recommended.

OVERHAUL

SKIS AND STEERING. Skis, spring assemblies, ski legs and steering arms are interchangeable from left to right on most models except Sonic MX, skis cannot be interchanged from side to side. Refer to Figs. 10, 11, 12 and 13 for views of front skis and suspension set-ups typical of most models. Ski wear bars should be renewed when worn to one-half or less of their original thickness or if otherwise damaged.

Tab locks on tie rod and drag link ends should be renewed if machine is so equipped. Use LOCTITE on nuts of tie

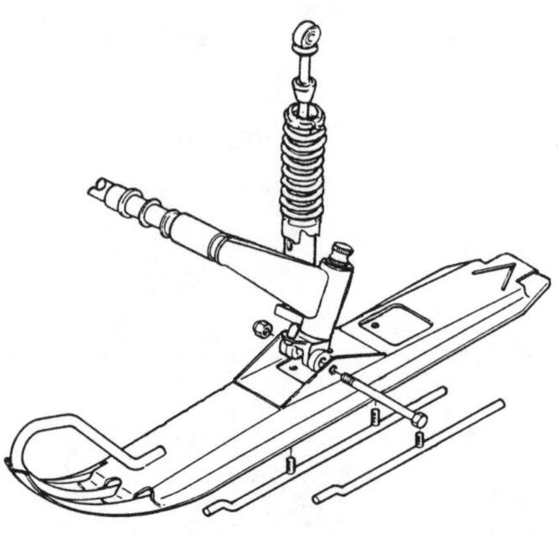

Fig. 13 – View showing MX steering and suspension used on Sonic MX models.

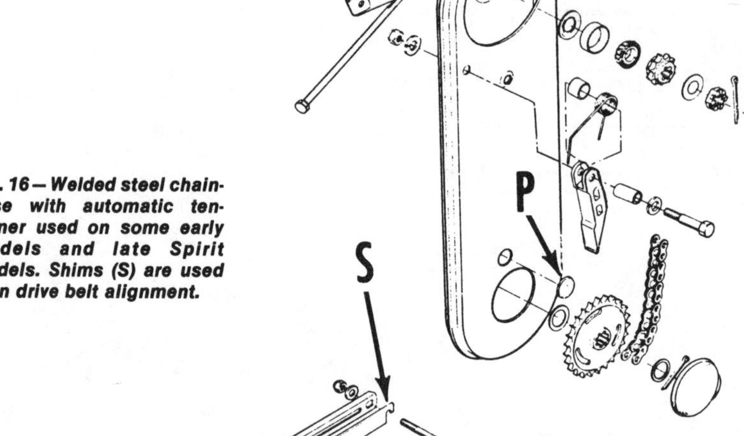

Fig. 16 – Welded steel chaincase with automatic tensioner used on some early models and late Spirit models. Shims (S) are used in drive belt alignment.

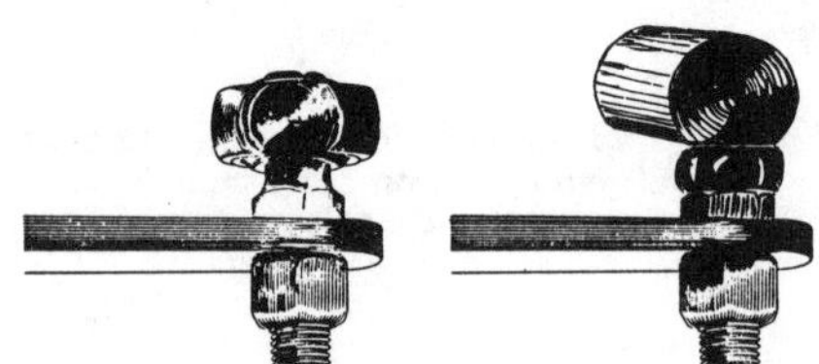

Fig. 14 – On models with ball linkage, align socket until it is parallel with steering arm before tightening adjusting locknut.

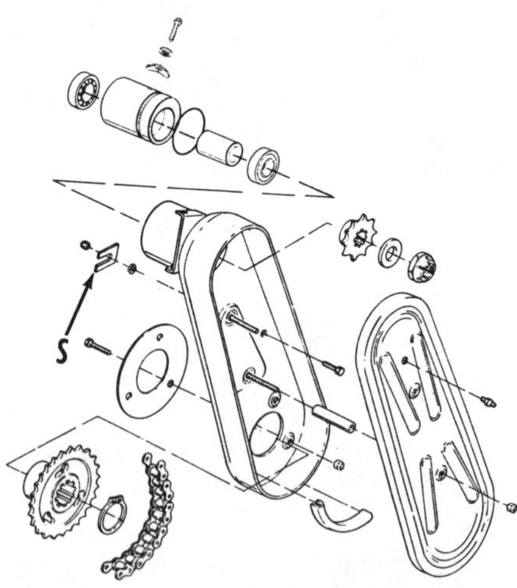

Fig. 15 – Welded steel chaincase and associated parts on models with eccentric chain tightener. Shims (S) are used in drive belt alignment.

rod and drag link ends not equipped with tab locks. On all models with ball linkage, align socket until it is parallel with steering arm as shown in Fig. 14 when tightening locknut.

CHAINCASE. Refer to Fig. 15 for an exploded view of steel chaincase with eccentric chain tensioner. Chaincase and driven pulley can be removed as an assembly after removing drive belt, brake cable, chaincase cover, drive chain and lower sprocket. Note and record the number and location of shims (S) between chaincase and track tunnel. Shims must be reinstalled at assembly to correctly align the drive belt. Put approximately eight ounces of low temperature grease in chaincase before reinstalling cover.

Steel chaincase with automatic chain tensioner used on some early models and late Spirit models is shown in Fig. 16. Chain and sprockets can be removed through upper access opening after removing lower sprocket from track drive axle.

To remove the chaincase and driven pulley as a unit, first remove drive belt and disconnect brake. Drain chaincase and remove track drive shaft. Remove bracket braces and U-bolts, then using two screwdrivers as shown in Fig. 17, pry chaincase from its mounting position on track tunnel. Save shim pack (S – Fig. 16) if used, for installation during reassembly. Fill chaincase to level plug (P) with Bombardier Chaincase Oil after reassembly.

Figure 18 shows diecast aluminum chaincase used on most early models and late Mirage models. Chain and sprockets can be renewed after removing chaincase cover and tensioner. To remove chaincase and driven pulley as a unit, remove pulley guard, drive belt and disconnect brake. Remove chaincase cover, lower sprocket and spacer. Pry oil seal from chaincase, then unbolt and lift off chaincase and driven pulley unit. Save shims (S) for reinstallation if any are present. Shims provide correct belt alignment. If secondary (upper) shaft bearing cup and oil retainer ring is to be removed, heat chaincase to 150 degrees

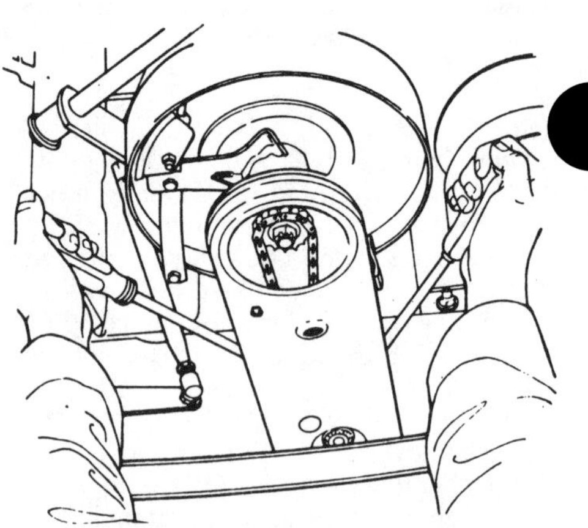

Fig. 17 – Removing chaincase and driven pulley as an assembly.

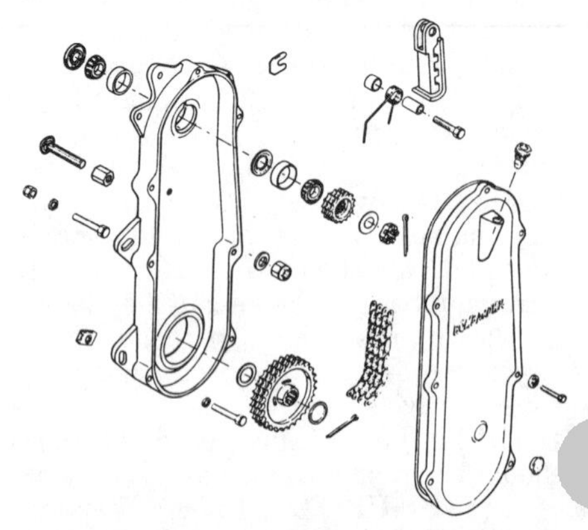

Fig. 18 – Exploded view of diecast aluminum chaincase used on most early models and late Mirage models.

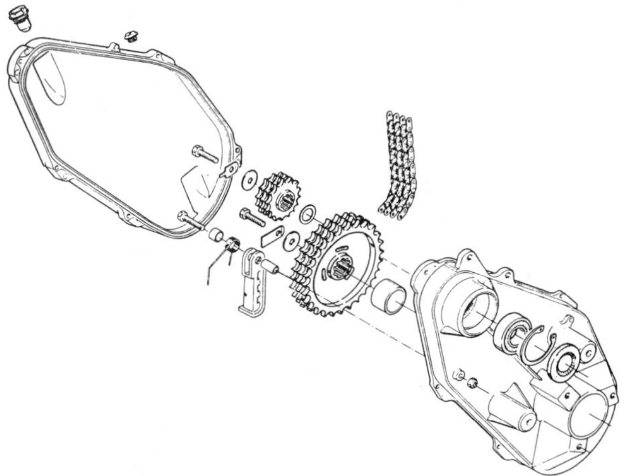

Fig. 18A—Exploded view of chaincase used on late Grand Prix Special, Futura and Sonic models.

F. Fill chaincase to level of sight glass using Bombardier Chaincase Oil.

Figure 18A shows chaincase used on late Grand Prix Special, Futura and Sonic models. To renew chaincase proceed as follows. Remove rear suspension system as outlined in TRACK AND SUSPENSION section. Remove outer chaincase cover and drain oil. Loosen end bearing housing cap screws on drive axle and pry oil seal out of chaincase housing. Bend ears on locking tabs away from sprocket retaining cap screws. Loosen chain tension, then remove retaining cap screws, washers, sprockets and chain. Remove chaincase mounting bolts and nuts, then withdraw chaincase from frame.

Inspect all parts for excessive wear, cracks, roughness or any other damage. Renew oil seals and all other parts as needed. Reinstall and assemble chaincase in reverse order of disassembly. Be sure to bend locking tab ears up against cap screws. Renew locking tabs if ears are damaged. Reinstall chaincase cover and fill chaincase with Bombardier Chaincase Oil.

TRACK AND SUSPENSION. To remove bogie wheels on models so equipped, raise rear of machine and loosen track tension, then unhook rear suspension springs from track tunnel. Tag bogie wheel units for reinstallation in correct location. Remove center bogie axle first, by removing the two cap screws on outside of track tunnel. If cross shaft turns after one cap screw is removed, wedge a screwdriver between cross shaft and bogie wheel support as show in Fig. 19.

Bogie wheel bearings are a tight press fit on wheel supports. Bogie wheels are factory riveted, but may be disassembled for service by drilling out rivets using a 3/16-inch drill bit. Reassemble using bolts and nuts, tightening in a criss-cross pattern. Bearing should be installed on wheel support shielded side first, until outer edge is flush with end of support.

On some machines, bogie wheel suspension springs are not interchangeable. On models where one set of bogies has heavier springs, the heavy set should be installed at rear. Clean and lubricate each cross shaft using low temperature grease, then install by reversing removal procedure. Install center set last. Lubricate each bogie wheel until new grease appears, then wipe off excess grease.

Standard slide suspension used on most early models is shown exploded in Figs. 21 and 22. To remove suspension system, raise rear of machine and release track tension. Loosen spring tension eyebolts and remove the four cap screws securing cross shafts to track tunnel, then remove suspension assembly. If cross shaft turns after one cap screw is removed, wedge a small screwdriver between cross shaft and suspension frame as shown in Fig. 19. Slide rail wear bars must be renewed if worn to where rivets are flush, or if otherwise damaged. To remove wear bars, drill rivet head using a 3/16-inch drill bit and punch out rivets, using care not to dam-

Fig. 19—Using a screwdriver to keep suspension cross shaft from turning. Refer to text.

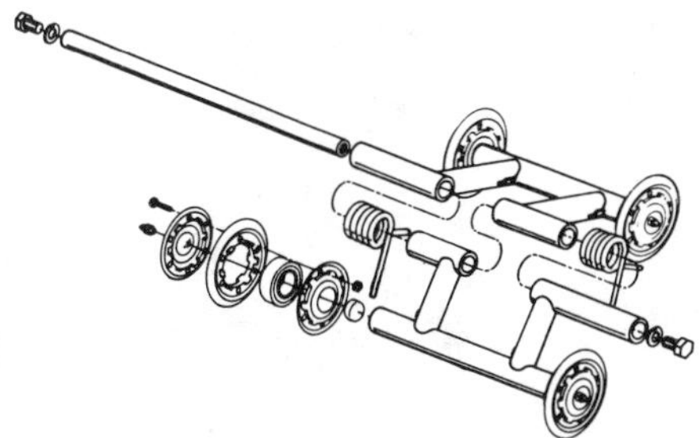

Fig. 20—Exploded view of bogie wheel suspension using two springs. Some models use a single spring.

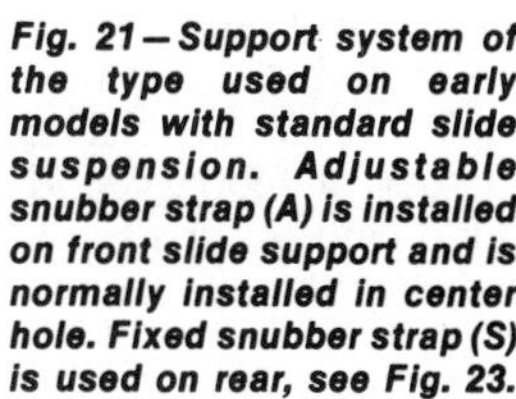

Fig. 21—Support system of the type used on early models with standard slide suspension. Adjustable snubber strap (A) is installed on front slide support and is normally installed in center hole. Fixed snubber strap (S) is used on rear, see Fig. 23.

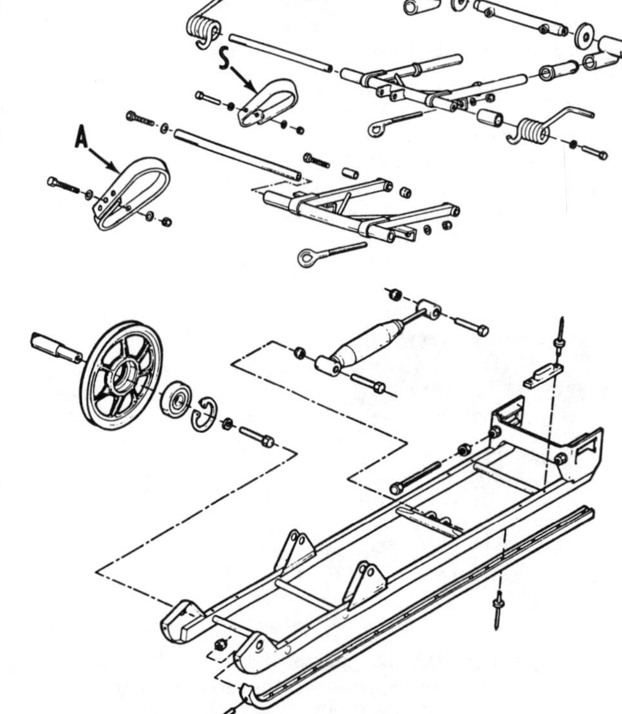

Fig. 22—Standard slide rail and associated parts used on early models so equip ped.

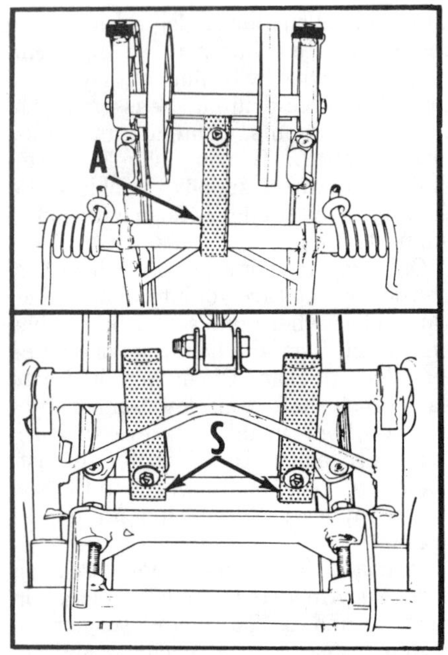

Fig. 23—Schematic view of standard slide suspension showing front snubber strap (A) and rear snubber straps (S) correctly installed. Shortening front snubber (A) transfers greater share of load to skis for better steering control, while lengthening front snubber transfers more weight to track for improved performance in deep snow.

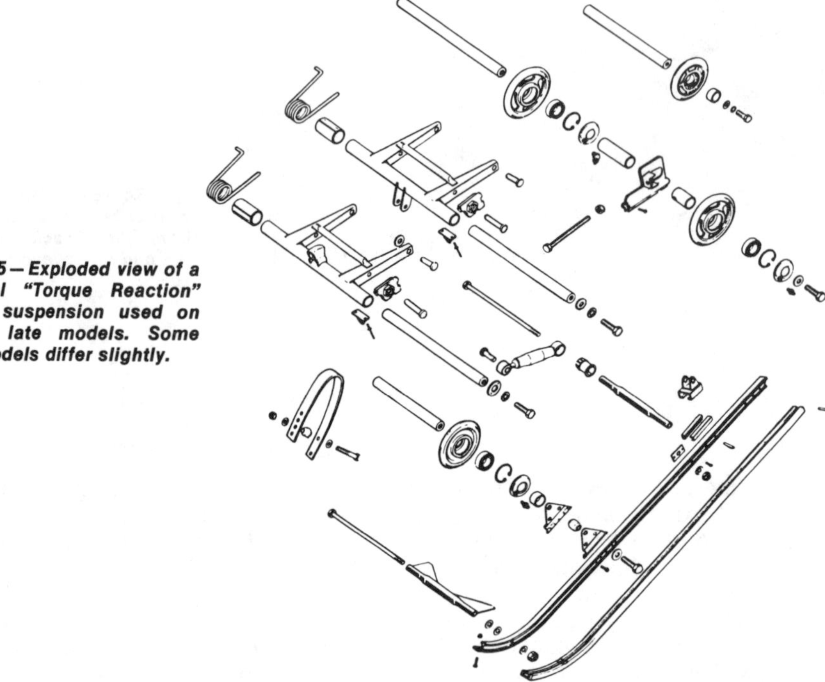

Fig. 25—Exploded view of a typical "Torque Reaction" slide suspension used on most late models. Some models differ slightly.

age rivet holes in metal rail. Remove bolt at front of wear bar and lift off wear bar. When installing new wear bars, use a spacer sleeve over countersunk rivet stem to properly tighten rivet (Fig. 24).

All 1975 Sonic and Nuvik models and most 1976 and later models except Sonic MX have a Torque Reaction type slide suspension system similar to that shown exploded in Fig. 25. To remove the suspension system, first raise rear of machine and release track tension. Turn suspension cams to low (L) position (Fig. 26). Remove the four cap screws securing suspension cross shafts to track tunnel and lift out the suspension assembly. If cross shaft turns after one bolt is removed, wedge a small screwdriver between cross shaft and suspension frame as shown in Fig. 19. To renew slide rail wear bar, remove cap screw at front and spirol pin at rear of wear bar and slide wear bar rearward off of runner.

Note that coil diameter of front suspension springs is smaller than rear springs. Front and rear cross shafts differ on some models. Snubber strap (Fig. 27) on front slide support limits torque lift of front of machine during acceleration. Normal snubber strap adjustment is in second hole from end as shown. Shortening snubber strap limits ski lift and provides greater ski control during acceleration. Turning front cams to a higher position increases steering response; to a lower position increases traction in deep snow. Rear cams adjust for load. Recommended adjustment when loaded, will provide 4½-5½ inches clearance between rear of footrest and ground. Right and left cams on the same support mode must be adjusted alike.

Some two-sprocket drive axles must be timed. Timing marks may be dots or arrows, located on inside of sprocket as shown in Fig. 28. When installing, align timing marks as shown in inset. Sprocket teeth MUST be in plane as shown by arrows.

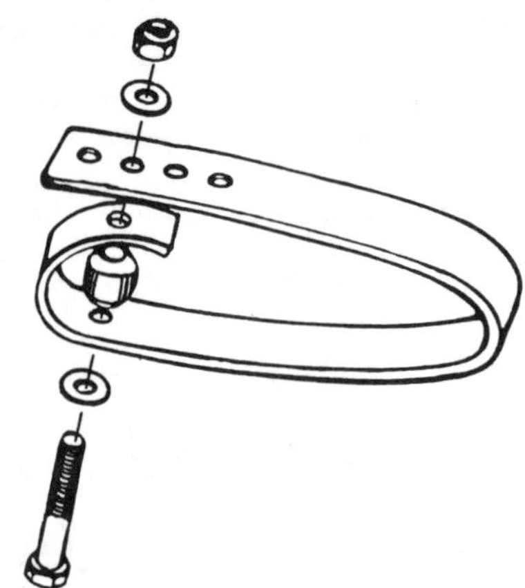

Fig. 27—Snubber strap used on front slide support is normally adjusted in second hole as shown. Shortening strap limits torque lift of skis during acceleration.

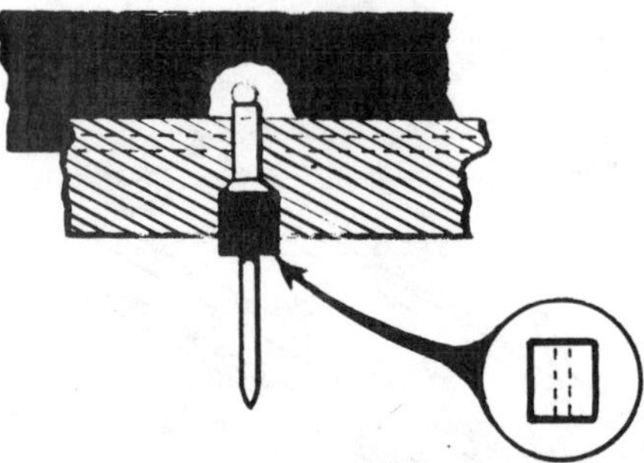

Fig. 24—A suitable sleeve may be required to apply proper pressure to pop rivet head when installing slider wear bars.

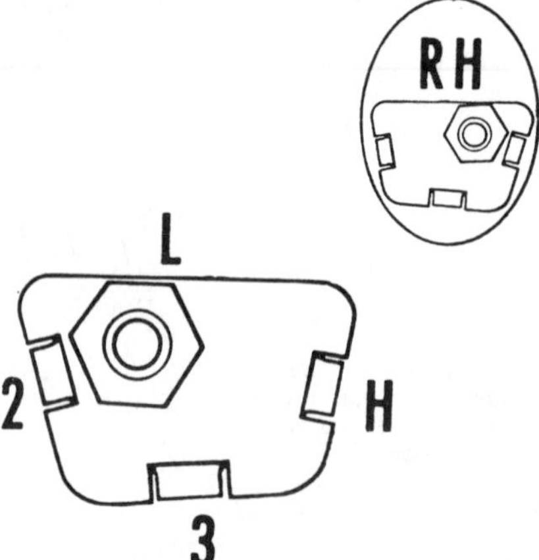

Fig. 26—View of left hand adjusting cam showing low (L), high (H) and two intermediate positions (2 and 3). Right hand cam (RH) is a mirror image of left cam as shown.

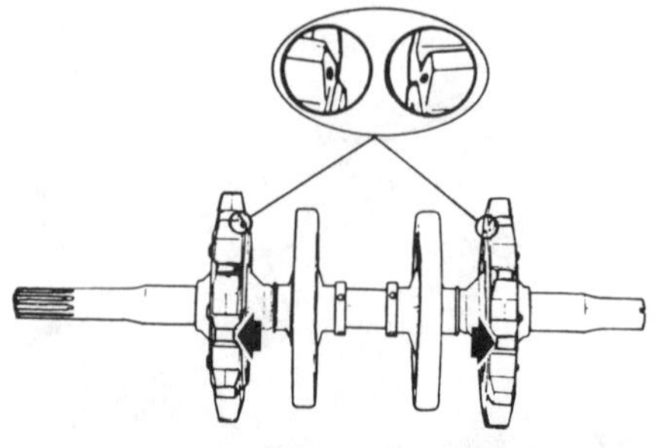

Fig. 28—Some two-sprocket drive axles must be timed as shown in inset. Sprocket teeth MUST align as shown by arrows.

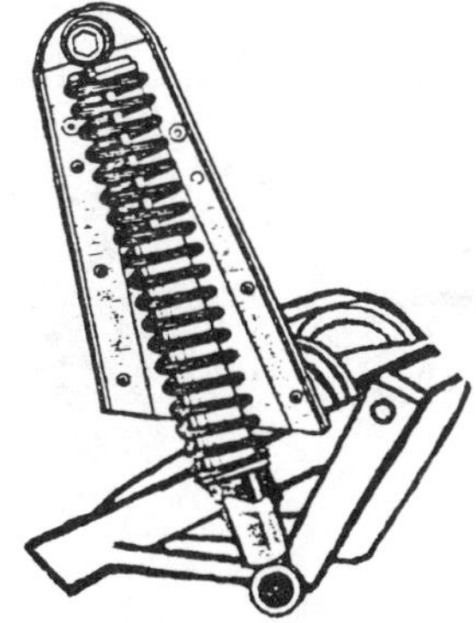

Fig. 28A — View shows rear shock absorber set-up used on MX suspension systems.

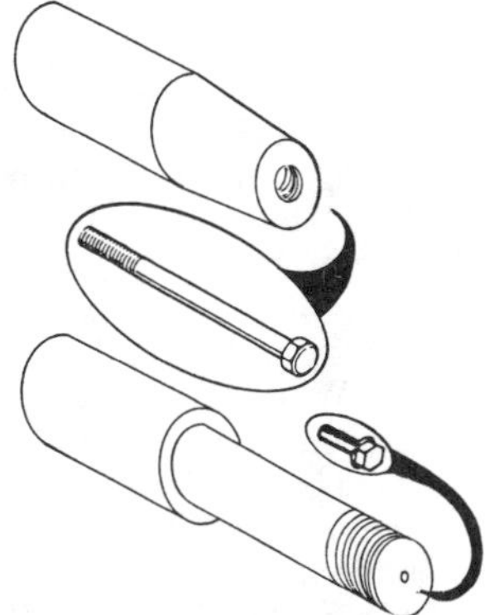

Fig. 29 — Pto end of crankshaft may have 20 degree taper as shown in upper view or be a shouldered straight shaft as shown in lower view. Shaft type may be identified by type of drive clutch retaining screw as shown by insets.

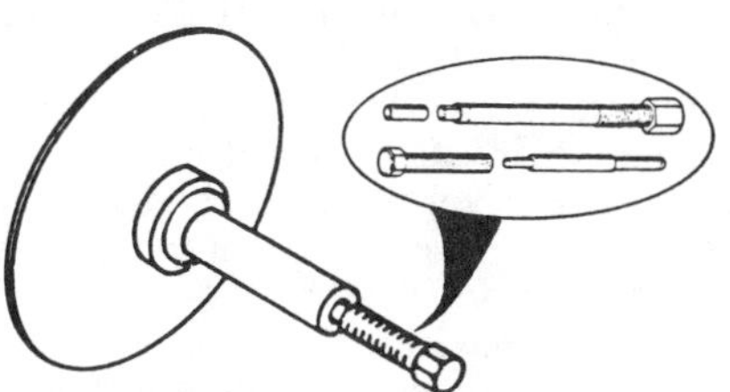

Fig. 30 — Puller screws used to remove drive sheave hub from most units with taper shaft are shown in inset.

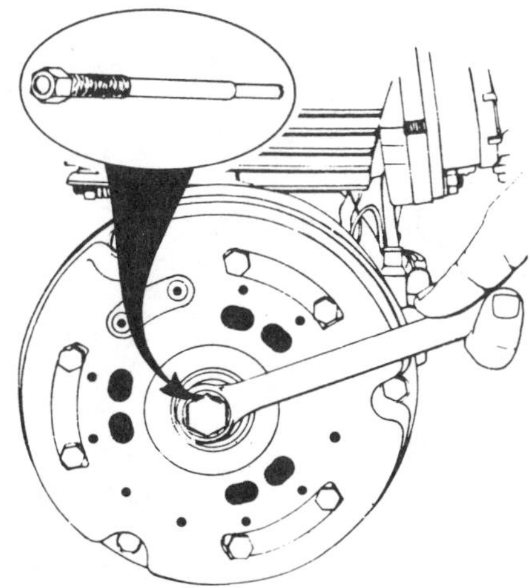

Fig. 31 — Removing high performance drive clutch from model with taper shaft.

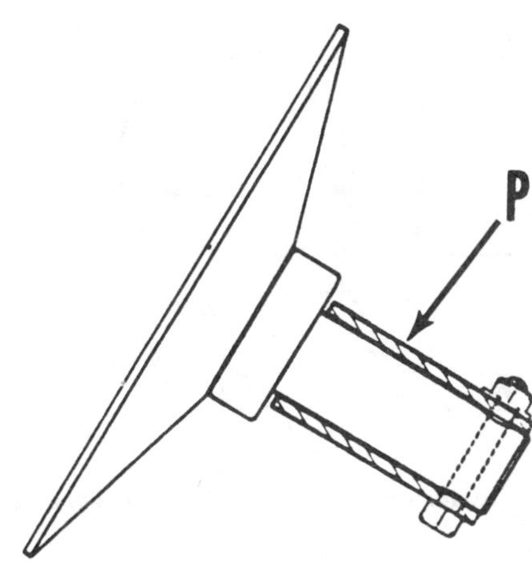

Fig. 32 — A pipe spacer-protector (P) may be installed on round shaft models, permitting use of pipe wrench to remove clutch hub from shouldered shaft.

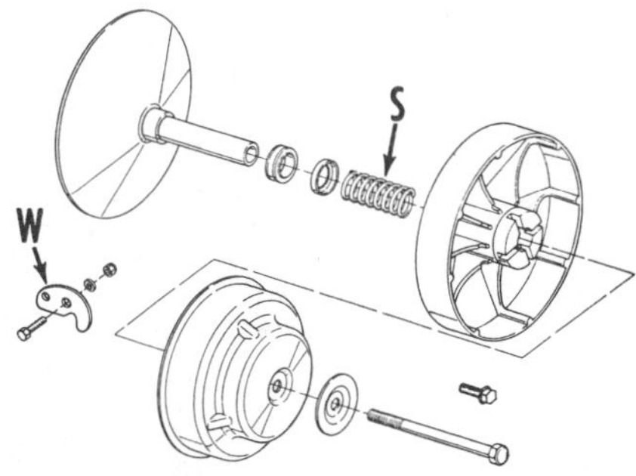

Fig. 33 — Exploded view of pressure lever type drive clutch of the type used on most early models. Counterweight (W) acts centrifugally against spring (S) to control engagement setting.

Late Sonic MX models use a MX suspension system. Suspension system is similar to "Torque Reaction" models except uses rear shock set-up as shown in Fig. 28A. To remove the suspension system, first raise rear of machine and release track tension. Turn two front suspension cams to low (L) position (Fig. 26). Remove two lower shock absorber mounting cap screws. Remove the four cap screws securing suspension cross shafts to track tunnel and lift out the suspension assembly. If cross shaft turns after one bolt is removed, wedge a small screwdriver between cross shaft and suspension frame as shown in Fig. 19. To renew slide rail wear bar, remove cap screw at front and spirol pin at rear of wear bar and slide wear bar rearward off of runner.

Inspect all parts for cracks, breaks, or any other damage, check rear shock absorbers for binding, seizing or oil leakage. Renew all parts as needed. Reassemble and install suspension assembly in reverse order of disassembly.

Adjust front cams to a higher position to increase steering response and to a lower position to increase traction in deep snow. Cams on rear shock absorbers adjust for carrying load. Adjusting cam to higher step will increase carrying load. Right and left cams on the same support mode must be adjusted alike.

DRIVE BELT AND SHEAVE. Units with BSE engines and some ROTAX engines have a 20 degree taper pto shaft as shown in upper view, Fig. 29. Other ROTAX engines have a male-threaded, shouldered, straight shaft as shown in lower view. If type of shaft is not known, refer to drive clutch retaining screw as shown in inset. Taper shaft requires a long screw which threads into crankshaft, while shouldered shaft uses a short screw which threads only into clutch hub.

To remove the drive clutch from engines with taper shaft, first remove belt shield and drive belt. Remove retaining cap screw from end of crankshaft.

CAUTION: Outer weight cover is under spring pressure, hold pressure against cup when removing retaining cap screw.

On all models except clutch used on early TS400 remove outer weight cover, sheave half and spring. Thread the appropriate puller screw (Insert-Fig. 30) into hub of drive pulley and tighten puller screw. Rap head of puller screw lightly if necessary, to loosen pulley hub from tapered shaft. On early TS400 models outer clutch components do not come apart when retaining cap screw is removed. With the appropriate puller screw, remove assembled drive clutch as shown in Fig. 31.

To remove the drive clutch on engines with shouldered shaft, first remove belt guard and drive belt. Lock crankshaft into position by either using a crankshaft locking tool on later models or remove spark plug from pto (drive) side cylinder and turn crankshaft clockwise until piston passes TDC about ¼-turn. Feed a length of Nylon starter rope into spark plug hole until cylinder is full, then turn crankshaft counter-clockwise until the shaft is locked. Remove retaining cap screw, weight cover, sliding sheave and spring. On models with square shaft hub, use a 1-1/8 inch open end wrench or large adjustable wrench and unscrew drive pulley fixed face and hub unit from crankshaft. Remove and save the shims found on crankshaft shoulder. Shim pack is used to align pulley offset. On roundshaft models, slide a length of steel pipe over the hub shaft as shown at

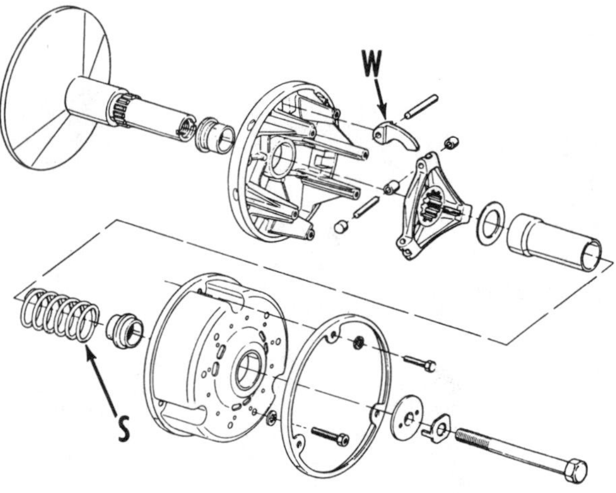

Fig. 34—Exploded view of high performance drive clutch used on TS400. Centrifugal counterweights are at (W) and reaction spring is at (S).

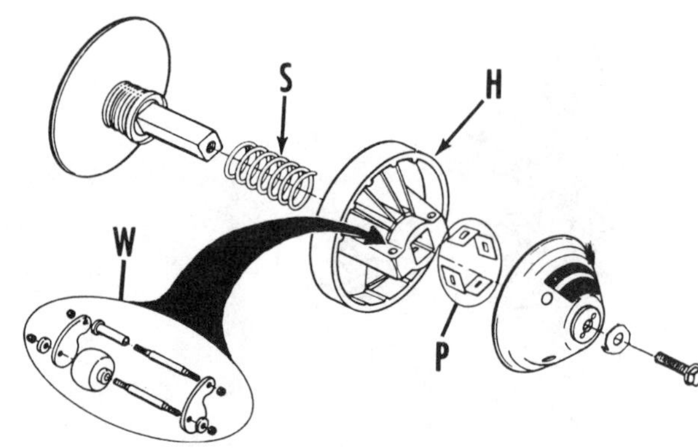

Fig. 38—Exploded view of Roller Square Shaft drive clutch of the type used on some models.

H. Sliding hub
P. Wear pads
S. Spring
W. Counterweight

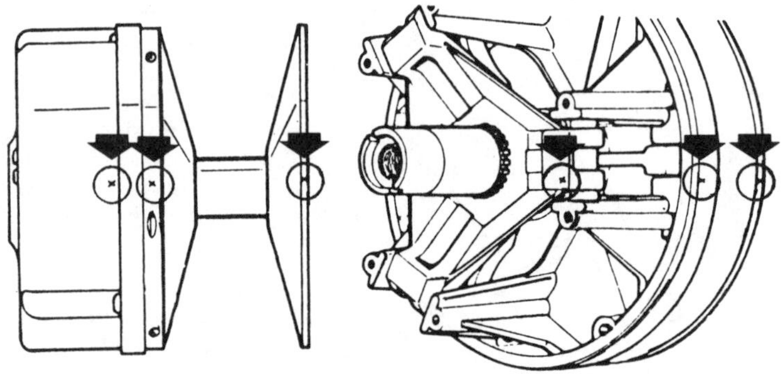

Fig. 35—When assembling high performance clutch, balance marks (Arrows) must be aligned as shown.

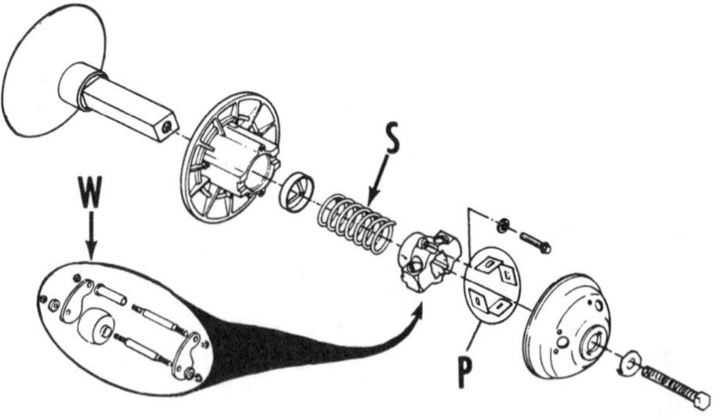

Fig. 36—Exploded view of Roller Square Shaft drive clutch with hub plug used on 1975 Sonic and other models so equipped.

P. Wear pads
S. Spring
W. Counterweight

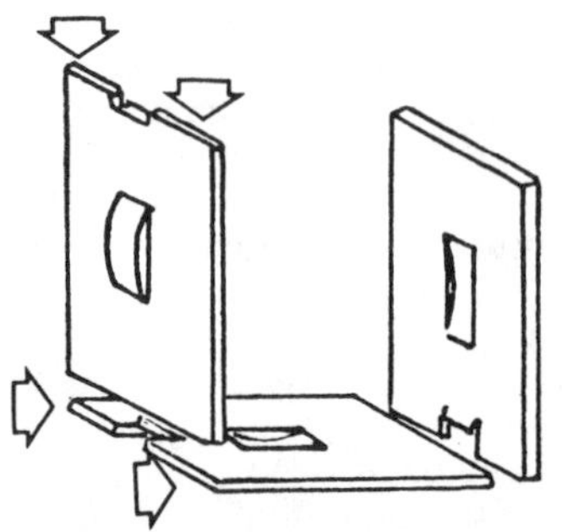

Fig. 37—Teflon coated wear pads snap into place as shown and are retained by raised center tab on one end which interlocks with opposite end of adjoining pad.

(P–Fig. 32) and secure with a 5/16-inch bolt and nut. Unscrew fixed face assembly from crankshaft using a pipe wrench on the protected shaft. Check for and save any shims located on crankshaft shoulder as outlined for square shaft models.

All 1975 models except TS400 and Sonic use a drive pulley of the type shown in Fig. 33. On Cadet, Nuvik and Futura 340, counterweight (W) is identified as No. 3. On all 440 models, counterweight is identified as No. 1 with two rivets. An aluminum colored (medium weight) spring (S) is used on Cadet 250. A lightweight (Violet) spring is used on Nuvik, Futura 340, Grand Sport and Chimo 440 and Gold colored (heavyweight) spring is used on Futura 440.

The 1975 TS400 uses a High Performance drive clutch of the type shown exploded in Fig. 34. Counterweight (W) is identified with an "A" and spring (S) is color coded White. A pressure of 50-55 lbs. is required to compress spring one inch. Be sure balance marks are aligned as shown (Arrows–Fig. 35) when clutch is reassembled.

The 1975 Sonic 340 and some machines manufactured around 1975 use a square shaft drive clutch of the type shown in Fig. 36. Counterweights (W) are identified "A-3" on Sonic 340 and spring (S) is color coded Gold. Spring should require a pressure of 95-100 lbs. to compress it one inch. Teflon wear pads (P) should be renewed if Teflon coating is worn through to the steel backing. Pads can be pried out with a small screwdriver and must be snapped in so that the raised center of tab on one end of pad interlocks the solid end of adjoining pad. See Fig. 37. Counterweight is available only as a complete unit and should not be disassembled unless renewal is planned. Self-locking nuts and shouldered pins are damaged in disassembly and must not be reinstalled.

Some early units use a Roller Square Shaft drive clutch of the type shown in Fig. 38. Condition of wear pads (P) can be checked without disassembly by rocking the sliding half (H) on its hub. If total movement exceeds 1/8-inch, wear pads should be renewed. Pry out old wear pads using a small screwdriver. When installing, raised center tab on one end of pad must interlock with solid end of adjoining pad as shown in Fig. 37.

Figure 39 shows the Roller Round Shaft type drive clutch used on 1976 and later Spirit models. Sliding hub and weight unit (H) is available as an assembly or weight units (W) are available separately. Weight unit on early models is identified "D-2" and later models

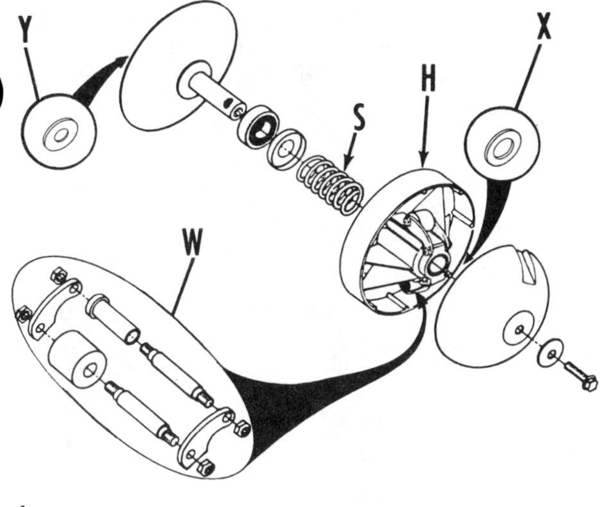

Fig. 39—Exploded view of Roller Round Shaft type drive clutch used on late Spirit models. Tapered model is similar in construction.

H. Sliding hub
S. Spring
W. Counterweight

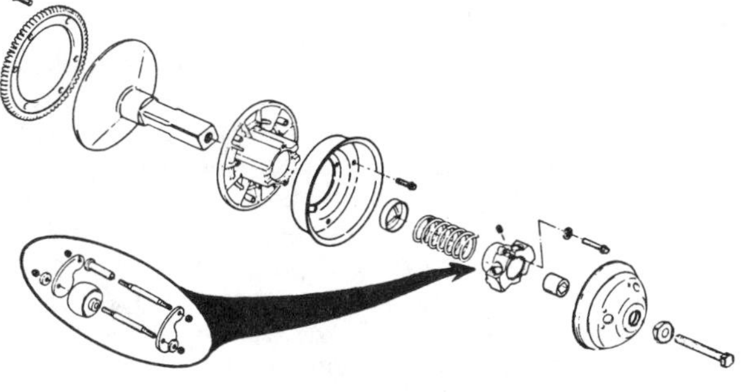

Fig. 40—Exploded view of hub plug type drive clutch with Duralon bushing used on many late models.

"E-4". Spring (S) is color coded Blue on early models and Bronze on later models. Weight cover retaining cap screw should be torqued to 45 ft.-lbs. on later models.

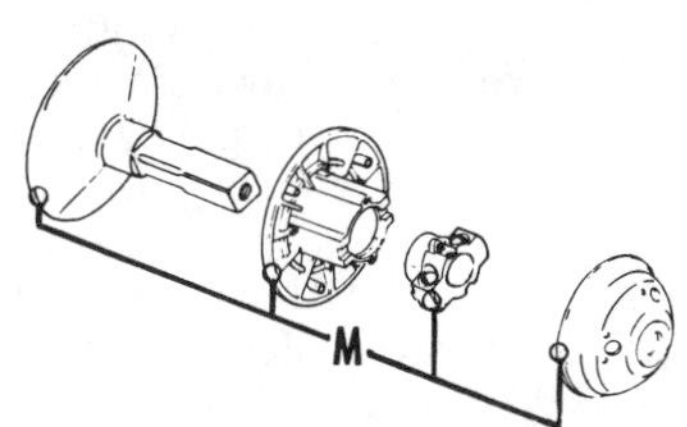

Fig. 41—Timing marks (M) should be present or affixed if missing, and aligned when unit is assembled.

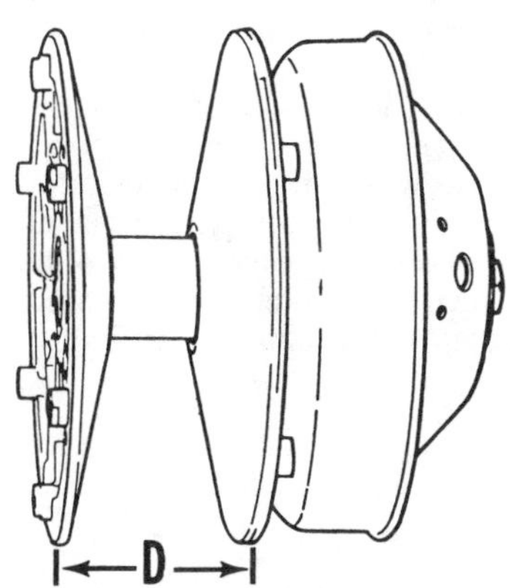

Fig. 42—After assembly of drive clutch shown in Fig. 40, measure distance (D), which should be 75 mm (2-15/16 inches) on early models and 76 mm (3 inches) on later models. If measurement is incorrect, shaft end is not properly seated in governor cup and malfunction may result.

Some later Mirage models use a drive pulley that is similar in construction to the Roller Round Shaft (Fig. 39). The drive pulley fits onto a tapered crankshaft instead of a shoulder crankshaft.

Figure 40 shows an exploded view of hub plug type drive clutch with Duralon bushing used on many late models. Some pulleys are match-marked for balance as shown in Fig. 41. If components are not marked, affix suitable marks before disassembly. The assembly bolts in drive clutch are installed with LOCTITE and an impact wrench or moderate heat are advised for removal.

The Duralon bushing in hub plug is made of fiberglass with a bearing surface of Teflon impregnated cloth. Bushing should be renewed if bearing surface is badly worn or fiberglass backing shows through. Remove set screw and use a press to push bushing from the hub. Set screw dimple in bushing is offset toward outer side when reinstalling.

Do not remove counterweights unless removal is indicated. Counterweights are available only as an assembly kit and removed units cannot be reinstalled. On earlier models refer to the following.

Nuvik models so equipped, counterweights are identified as "C-3-L", spring is color coded Light Blue and tests 40 lbs. when compressed to a height of 3.68 inches. On 1976 Futura, counterweights are identified as "C-4-L"; spring is color coded Black (cut) and tests 35 lbs. when compressed to a height of 3-1/8 inches. On later Futura, counterweights are "C-4-L" and spring is color coded Pink. On 1976 Sonic 250, counterweights are identified as "A-2"; spring is color coded Gold and should test 100 lbs. when compressed to a height of 1-15/16 inches. On 1976 Sonic 340, counterweights are identified "A-3"; spring is color coded Violet and should test 110 lbs. when compressed to a height of 1.9 inches. On later Sonic, counterweights are "A-3" and spring is color coded Red.

Refer to chart shown below for counterweight kit and spring identification on 1979-1982 models.

Model	Counter-weight Kit	Spring
	1979	
Mirage	A3S	Light Blue
Nuvik	C3L	Light Blue
Futura 400	C3L	Light Blue
Futura 440	C4L	Pink
Futura 444 LC	C7L	Yellow
Grand Prix Special	C8M-H	Light Blue
	1980	
Mirage Special	A-3-S-H	Orange
Futura 500/E	C-6-L-H	Gold
Futura LC	C-7-L-H	Light Blue
Grand Prix Special	C-6-L-H	Light Blue

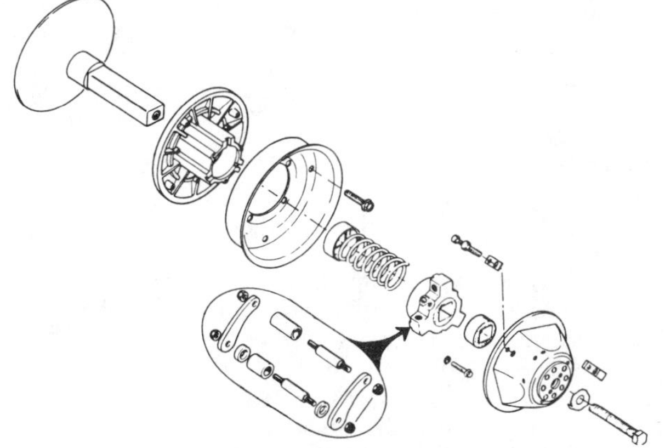

Fig. 42A—Exploded view of a Roller Square Shaft drive pulley with three ramps.

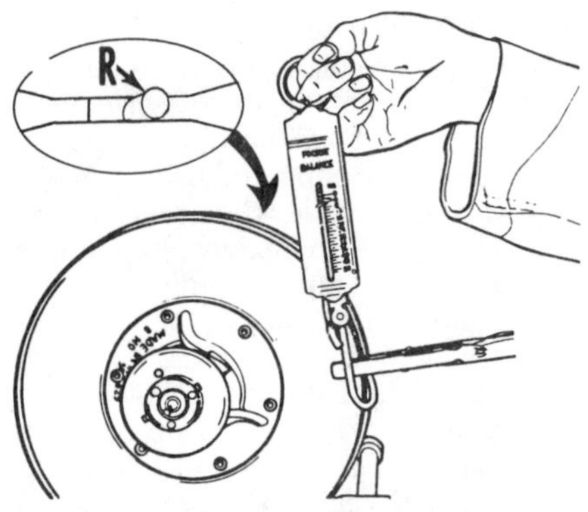

Fig. 43—Using vise grip and spring scale to check torque tension of driven clutch spring. Insert a short piece of 1/8 inch rod (R) between pulley halves to provide rolling friction.

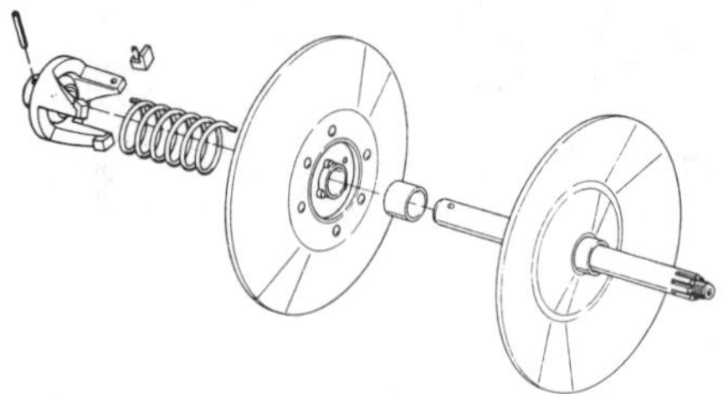

Fig. 44—Exploded view of driven pulley used on Cadet 250.

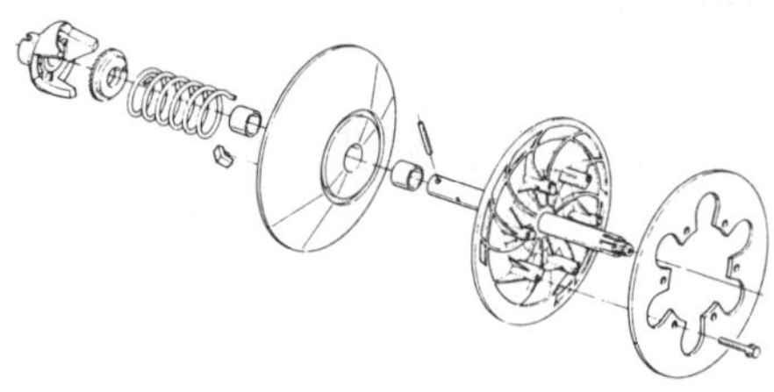

Fig. 45—Exploded view of driven pulley of the type used on most early models.

Model	Counter-weight Kit	Spring
	1981	
Mirage Special	A-3-S-H	Yellow
Futura 500/E	C-6-L-H	Gold
Futura LC	C-7-L-H	Light Blue
Grand Prix Special	C-7-L-H	Light Blue
Grand Prix MX	C-7-L-H	Light Blue
	1982	
Mirage II	B-E-K-S-H	Yellow
Futura 300	B-3-K-S-H	Yellow
Futura 500/E	C-6-L-H	Gold
Futura LC	C-7-L-H	Light Blue
Sonic	C-7-L-H	Orange

Fig. 42A shows exploded view of Roller Square Shaft with three ramps. Pulley components should be marked for proper assembly. If components are not marked, affix suitable marks before disassembly. To remove drive sheave use starter rope to block pto piston at TDC. Bend tab down from around weight cover retaining cap screw and remove screw. Use caution when removing screw. Remove fixed hub by using a suitable jack screw.

The Duralon bushing in hub is made of fiberglass with a bearing surface of Teflon impregnated cloth. Bushing should be renewed if bearing surface is badly worn or fiberglass backing shows through. Remove set screw and use a suitable pushing tool against bushing, then remove and/or reinstall bushing by using a hammer or press.

Do not remove counterweights unless removal is indicated. Counterweights are available only as an assembly kit.

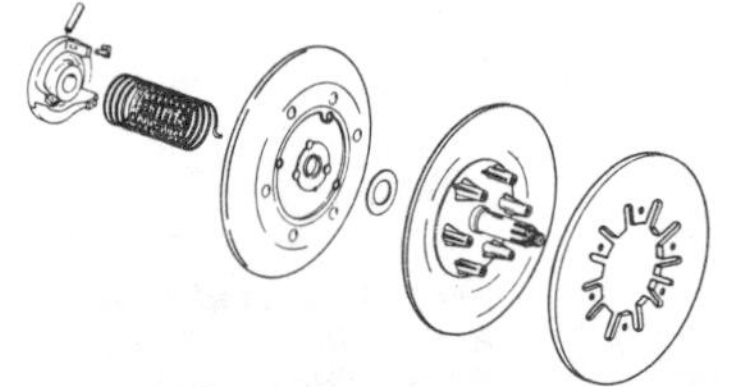

Fig. 46—Exploded view of driven pulley of the type used on Nuvik model so equipped.

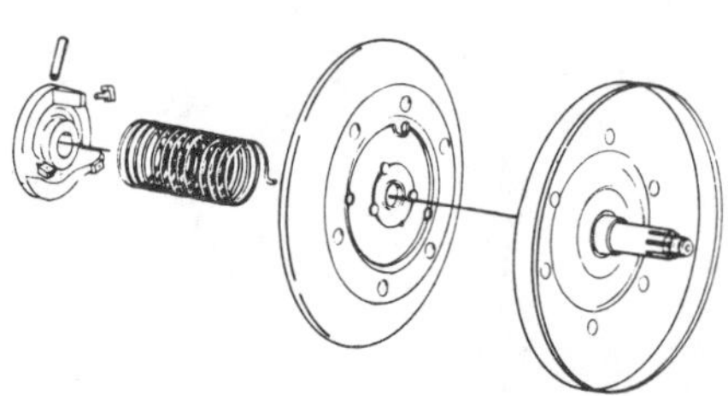

Fig. 47—Exploded view of driven pulley used on early Spirit models.

Fig. 47A—Exploded view of driven pulley used on late Spirit models.

Refer to chart shown below for counterweight kit and spring identification on 1979-1982 models.

Model	Counter-weight Kit	Spring
1979		
Super Sonic	A3S	Brown
Super Sonic Cross Country	A6S	Light Blue
1980		
Super Sonic	A3S	Purple
Ultra Sonic	A3S	Purple
1981		
Super Sonic	A3S	White
Ultra Sonic	A3S	White
1982		
Ultra Sonic	A6S	Brown

To check torque load of driven pulley spring on all models, first slightly spread pulley halves and insert a short piece of 1/8-inch rod (R–Fig. 43) to provide rolling friction to any movement of sliding half. Clamp vise-grip pliers to pulley rim to serve as a pull scale anchor and use a pull scale to measure the force necessary to move friction shoes away from cam. Recommended torque load and method of adjustment is given in individual driven pulley paragraphs.

Figure 44 shows an exploded view of driven pulley of the type used on Cadet 250. Torque load should be 17-19 lbs. and adjustment is made by changing torque wrap of cam or renewing spring.

Figure 45 shows driven pulley used on most 1974 and 1975 models. Torque load is adjusted by a ratchet type tensioner at anchor end of spring which can be turned with a screwdriver. Torque tension should be 10-13 lbs. on TS400 and 13-15 lbs. on other models.

Figure 46 shows driven pulley used on Nuvik model so equipped. Torque load can be adjusted by repositioning spring end in sliding pulley half or by changing torque wrap of cam. Torque tension should be 6-10 lbs.

Figure 47 shows driven pulley used on early Spirit models and Figure 47A shows view of driven pulley used on later models. Torque tension should be 6-10 lbs. on early models and 8 lbs. on later models. Adjust by repositioning spring end of sliding pulley half or by changing torque wrap of cam.

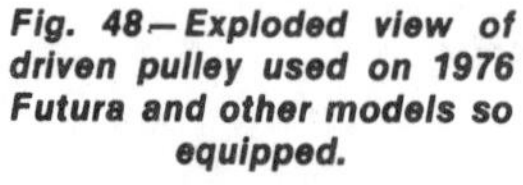

Fig. 48—Exploded view of driven pulley used on 1976 Futura and other models so equipped.

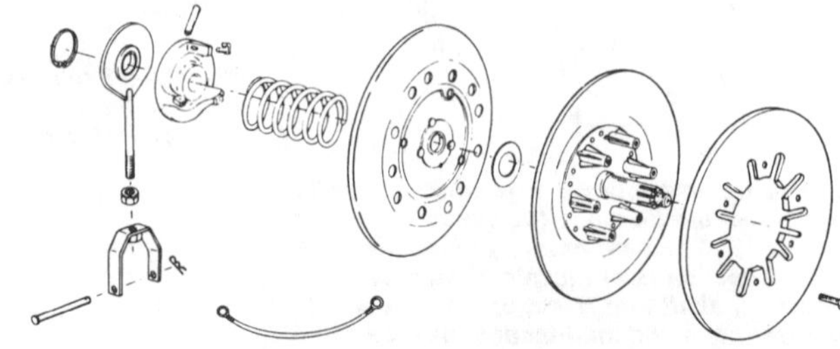

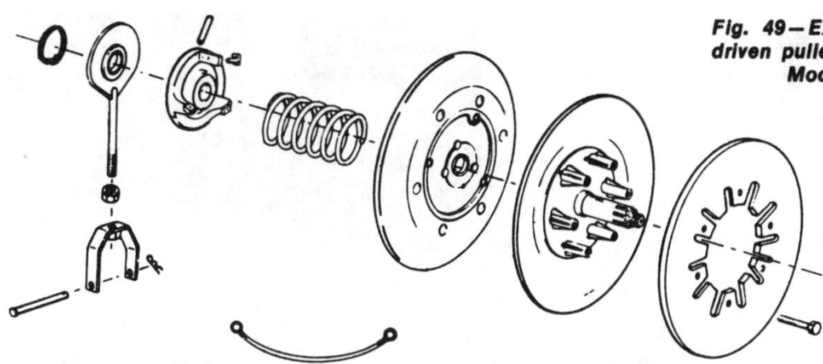

Fig. 49—Exploded view of driven pulley used on early Model Sonic.

Figure 48 shows driven pulley used on 1976 Futura and other models so equipped. Torque tension should be 6-10 lbs. and adjustment is accomplished by relocating spring end in sliding pulley half or changing torque wrap of cam.

Figure 49 shows driven pulley used on early Model Sonic. Torque tension should be 11-15 lbs. Adjust by repositioning spring end of sliding pulley half or by changing torque wrap of cam.

Figure 50 shows driven pulley used on Mirage models so equipped. Torque tension should be 8 lbs. and adjustment is accomplished by relocating spring end in sliding pulley half or changing torque wrap of cam.

Figure 51 shows driven pulley used on Mirage models so equipped, Grand Prix Special and later Futura and Sonic models. Torque tension should be 13 lbs. and adjustment is accomplished by relocating spring end in sliding pulley half or changing torque wrap of cam.

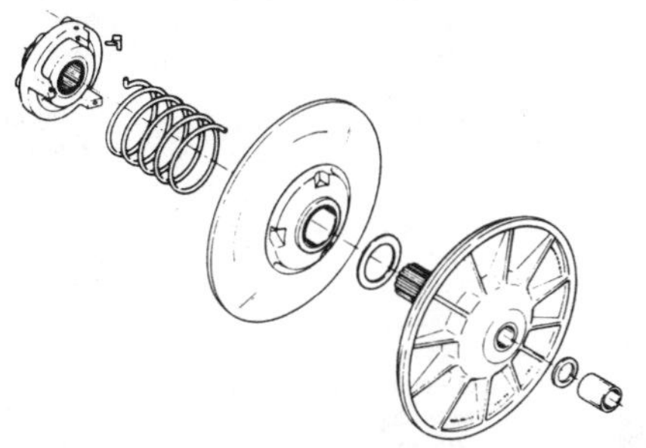

Fig. 50—Exploded view of driven pulley used on Mirage and Futura 300 models so equipped.

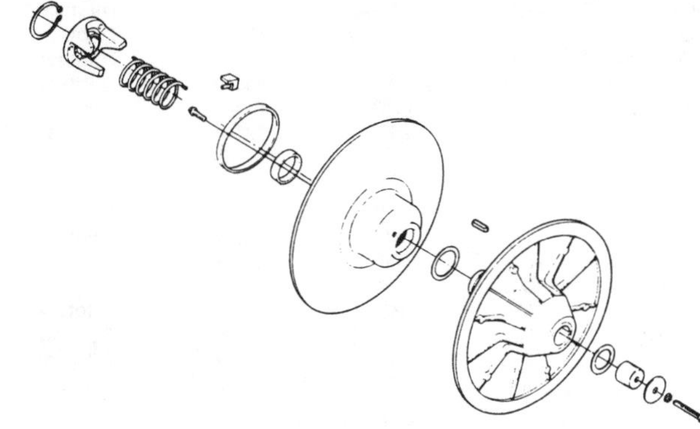

Fig. 51—Exploded view of driven pulley used on Grand Prix Special and later Futura and Sonic models so equipped.

NORTHWAY

1970-1974

	Engine			Carburetor				Clutch		
Model	Make	Model	Displ.	Make	Model	Sprocket Ratio	Chain Size	Make	Shaft Center	Belt Number
1970										
GO-20	Sachs	SA280A	277cc	Tillotson	HL	13:33		Precico	10½	1032-M
GO-30	Sachs	SA280	277cc	Tillotson	HR	13:33		Precico	10½	1032-M
GO-45	Sachs	SA290	293cc	Tillotson	HR	15:33		Precico	10½	1032-M
GO-60	Sachs	SA340	336cc	Tillotson	HR	17:33		Precico	10½	1032-M
GO-60	Sachs	SA340SS	336cc	Tillotson	HR	18:33		Precico	10½	1032-M
GO-75	JLO	LR440/2	433cc	Tillotson	HD	18:33		Precico	10½	1032-M
GO-90	JLO	LR440/2	433cc	Tillotson	HD	19:33		Precico	10½	1032-M
Mach-1	Sachs	SA2-340	338cc	Tillotson	HD	18:33		Precico	10½	1032-M
Mach-2	JLO	LR760/2	744cc	Tillotson	HD	19:33		Precico	10½	1032-M
Mach-3	Hirth	230R	793cc	Tillotson	HD	22:33		Precico	10½	1032-M
1971										
N-250						13:33	35-2	Precico	10½	1032-M
N-300	Sachs	SA290	293cc	Tillotson	HR	14:33	35-2	Precico	10½	1032-M
N-340	CCW	340	339cc	Tillotson	HR	15:33	35-2	Precico	10½	1032-M
N-400	CCW	400	398cc	Tillotson	HR	17:33	35-2	Precico	10½	1032-M
N-440	CCW	440	436cc	Tillotson	HD	18:33	35-2	Precico	10½	1032-M
W-340	CCW	340	339cc	Tillotson	HR	14:33	35-2	Precico	10½	1032-M
W-400	CCW	400	398cc	Tillotson	HR	15:33	35-2	Precico	10½	1032-M
W-440	CCW	440	436cc	Tillotson	HD	17:33	35-2	Precico	10½	1032-M
W-600	Hirth	171R	634cc	Tillotson		20:33	35-2	Precico	10½	1032-M
1972										
N-300	CCW	290/2	290cc	Tillotson	HR119A	16:33	35-2	Precico	10½	1626-1004
N-340	CCW	340/1	339cc	Tillotson	HR99A	16:33	35-2	Precico	10½	1626-1004
N-340S	CCW	340/3	339cc	Tillotson	HR120A	17:33	35-2	Precico	10½	1626-1004
N-400	CCW	400/2	398cc	Tillotson	HR100A	18:33	35-2	Precico	10½	1626-1004
N-440	CCW	440/2	436cc	Walbro	WD6-5	19:33	35-2	Precico	10½	1626-1004
N-440S	Sachs	SA2-440	437cc	Walbro	WD6-5	20:33	35-2	Precico	10½	1626-1004
N-440K	Kiekhaefer	440S	433cc	Tillotson	HD95A	20:33	35-2	Precico	10½	1626-1004
W-300	CCW	290/2	290cc	Tillotson	HR119A	16:33	35-2	Precico	10½	1626-1004
W-340	CCW	340/1	339cc	Tillotson	HR99A	15:33	35-2	Precico	10½	1626-1004
W-400	CCW	400/2	398cc	Tillotson	HR100A	17:33	35-2	Precico	10½	1626-1004
W-440	CCW	440/2	436cc	Walbro	WD6-5	18:33	35-2	Precico	10½	1626-1004
W-440S	Sachs	SA2-440	437cc	Walbro	WD6-5	19:33	35-2	Precico	10½	1626-1004
W-440K	Kiekhaefer	440S	433cc	Walbro	WD6-5	19:33	35-2	Precico	10½	1626-1004
1973										
Explorer 15	CCW	340	339cc	Tillotson	HR	16:33	35-2	N W-SK	10½	1626-1004
Explorer 15	CCW	400	398cc	Tillotson	HD	17:33	35-2	N W-SK	10½	1626-1004
Explorer 15	CCW	440	436cc	Walbro	WD6	18:33	35-2	N W-SK	10½	1626-1004
Explorer 15	Sachs	SA2-441	437cc	Walbro	WD6	18:33	35-2	N W-SK	10½	1626-1004
Explorer 15	Kiekhaefer	440	433cc	Tillotson	HD95A	18:33	35-2	N W-SK	10½	1626-1004
Interceptor 15	CCW	340	339cc	Walbro	WR6	16:33	35-2	St. Law.	10½	1626-1004
Interceptor 15	Hirth	260R	338cc	Walbro	WRD6	16:33	35-2	St. Law.	10½	1626-1004
Interceptor 15	CCW	440	436cc	Walbro	WD6	18:33	35-2	St. Law.	10½	1626-1004
Interceptor 15	Hirth	211R	438cc	Walbro	WDA43	18:33	35-2	St. Law.	10½	1626-1004
Explorer 18	CCW	340	339cc	Tillotson	HR120A	15:33	35-2	St. Law.	10½	1626-1004
Explorer 18	CCW	400	398cc	Walbro	WD6	17:33	35-2	St. Law.	10½	1626-1004
Explorer 18	CCW	440	436cc	Walbro	WD6	18:33	35-2	St. Law.	10½	1626-1004
Explorer 18	Sachs	SA2-441	437cc	Walbro	WD6	18:33	35-2	St. Law.	10½	1626-1004
Explorer 18	Kiekhaefer	440S	433cc	Tillotson	HD95A	18:33	35-2	St. Law.	10½	1626-1004
Interceptor 18	CCW	340	339cc	Walbro	WDA41	16:33	35-2	St. Law.	10½	1626-1004
Interceptor 18	Hirth	260R	338cc	Walbro	WRD43	16:33	35-2	St. Law.	10½	1626-1004
Interceptor 18	CCW	440	436cc	Walbro	WD12	18:33	35-2	St. Law.	10½	1626-1004
Interceptor 18	Hirth	211R	438cc	Walbro	WD43	18:33	35-2	St. Law.	10½	1626-1004
Interceptor 18	Hirth	231R	647cc	Walbro	WDA44	18:33	35-2	St. Law.	10½	1626-1004
1974										
Explorer	Opt.		340cc	Walbro	WR-6-12		35-2	St. Law.	10½	1626-3004
Explorer	Opt.		400cc	Walbro	WR-6-12		35-2	St. Law.	10½	1626-3004
Explorer	Opt.		440cc	Walbro	WD12		35-2	St. Law.	10½	1626-3004
Explorer DeLuxe	Opt.		440cc	Walbro	WD12		35-2	St. Law.	10½	1626-3004
Interceptor 340	Opt.		340cc	Walbro	WD33		35-2	St. Law.	10½	1626-3004
Interceptor 440	Opt.		440cc	Walbro	WD33		35-2	St. Law.	10½	1626-3004
Interceptor DeLuxe	Opt.		340cc	Walbro	WD33		35-2	St. Law.	10½	1626-3004
Interceptor DeLuxe	Opt.		440cc	Walbro	WD-40-41		35-2	St. Law.	10½	1626-3004

Optional Engines Are CCW, Kohler, Hirth.

LUBRICATION

The engine is lubricated by oil mixed with the fuel. Use only regular gasoline and a good quality snowmobile oil mixed at a ratio of 40:1 for Kohler engines; of 25:1 for Hirth or Sachs engines; or 20:1 for CCW or Kiekhaefer engines.

The enclosed drive chain should be lubricated with a good quality low temperature grease. Check monthly by tipping machine on its side and removing chaincase cover. Check chain adjustment at the same time on all except Interceptor models equipped with self-tensioning adjuster.

Ski legs and bogie wheels are equipped with pressure gun fittings. Lubricate once a month or oftener with a hand grease gun and lower temperature grease.

Ski pivot bolt, ski springs and steering tie rods should be lightly oiled with SAE 30 engine oil once a month or oftener as necessary.

ADJUSTMENT

STEERING SKIS. Steering skis should be parallel with vehicle frame and toe in approximately 1/8-inch when handlebar is in normal straight driving position. On later models, adjustment can be made by loosening locknuts and turning tie rod center section. On earlier models it is necessary to disconnect tie rod at one end in order to adjust.

DRIVE CHAIN. The enclosed roller drive chain on Interceptor models is equipped with a spring-loaded nylon idler arm and is self-adjusting. On all other models the chain should have 5/16-3/8 inch slack measured midway between sprockets and adjustment should be checked at lubrication periods. To adjust the chain, loosen the two jam nuts (1—Fig. 1) and back out the two adjusting bolts (2); then move adjusting bolt either way in housing until adjustment is correct. If screw bottoms in slot, remove screw and transfer to threaded hole which has appeared in opposite end of slot. Tighten both screws and jam nuts when adjustment is correct.

Fig. 1—View of chain housing showing points of adjustment.

1. Jam nuts 2. Adjusting screws

Fig. 2—Brake wear adjustment is made by turning stud nut (1). Cable housing anchor nuts (2) can be used to properly align actuating arm.

BRAKE. Brake wear adjustment is made by turning the self-locking nut (1—Fig. 2) on brake actuating arm stud. Tighten nut until resistance is felt then back off 1/2-turn. If brake still drags, back nut off a slight amount until puck clears friction surface when brake is released. Push pins must center in valleys of actuating arm when brake is released. Turn brake housing anchor nuts (2) if necessary to properly position brake arm.

On models before 1973, brake used driven pulley fixed face as a friction surface and realignment may be required after adjusting drive chain. On later models a separate brake disc is used.

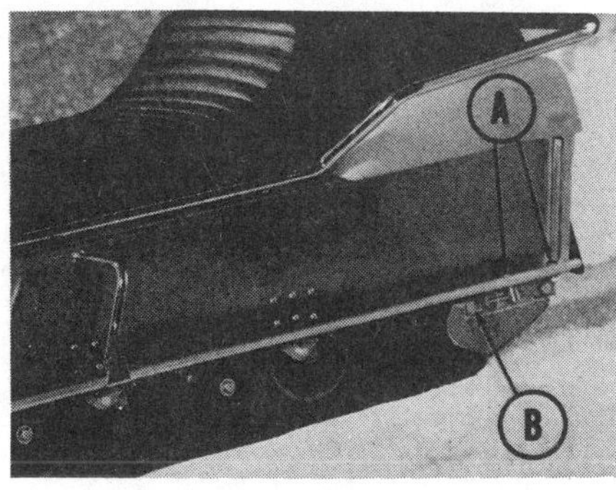

Fig. 3—To adjust track tension, loosen clamp screws (A) and turn adjusting screw (B).

TRACK. With rear of machine raised until track is clear, vertical distance between bottom of footrest and lower edge of track should be 4½-5 inches measured at center bogie support. Adjust by loosening clamp bolts (A—Fig. 3) and turning adjusting screws (B). Both sides must be adjusted alike.

NOTE: When track tension has been adjusted, alignment MUST be checked as outlined in TRACK SERVICE Section of this manual.

On models with slide suspension, rear eyebolt (R—Fig. 4) on each side controls softness or firmness of ride; while front eyebolt (F) controls load distribution. Both sides must be adjusted alike. Normal adjustment for rear (R) is made for weight of operator (and passenger) to eliminate bottoming on all but the most severe conditions. Increasing tension on front adjustment removes weight from skis and increases percentage of weight borne by track for increased traction. Decreasing tension at (F) puts more weight on skis for better steering control.

OVERHAUL

Refer to the appropriate paragraphs in the GENERAL SERVICE Sections of this manual for overhaul data and procedures.

Optional upper sprockets are available with from 13 to 22 teeth. A 31-tooth lower sprocket is also available for use in place of the standard 33-tooth unit, thus permitting almost unlimited variation of drive ratio.

Fig. 4—On models with slide suspension, front adjusting nuts (F) control load distribution; rear nuts (R) control load.

OUTBOARD MARINE CORPORATION

1965-1972

Model	Engine Make	Engine Model	Engine Displ.	Carburetor Make	Carburetor Model	Sprocket Ratio	Chain Size	Clutch Make	Clutch Shaft Center	Belt Number
EVINRUDE			**SKEETER BOBCAT**	**TRAILBLAZER NORSEMAN**						
					1965					
E1400	OMC		362cc	Carter	N	14:49	35-2	Own		111496
					1966					
E1560	OMC		362cc	Carter	N	16:49	35-2	Own		111496
E2060	OMC		362cc	Carter	N	16:49	35-2	Own		111496
E2063	OMC		362cc	Carter	N	16:49	35-2	Own		111496
					1967					
E1570	OMC		362cc	Carter	N	16:42	35-2	Own		112634
E2070	OMC		362cc	Carter	N	14:42	35-2	Own		112634
E2075	OMC		362cc	Carter	N	14:42	35-2	Own		112634
					1968					
E1580	OMC		362cc	Bendix		16:42	35-2	Own		113291
E2080	OMC		362cc	Bendix		14:42	35-2	Own		113291
E2085	OMC		362cc	Bendix		14:42	35-2	Own		113291
					1969					
3090 Bobcat	JLO	L297	296cc	Tillotson	HD18A	13:35	35-2	Salsbury		113532
3890 Bobcat	JLO	L380	372cc	Tillotson	HD13A	13:30	35-2	Salsbury		113532
1592 Skeeter	OMC		362cc	Bendix		16:42	35-2	Own		113532
2093 Skeeter	OMC		362cc	Bendix		14:42	35-2	Own		113532
2096 Skeeter	OMC		362cc	Bendix		14:42	35-2	Own		113532
1590 Skeeter	OMC		437cc	Tillotson	HD	18:42	35-2	Own		113291
2090 Skeeter	OMC		437cc	Tillotson	HD	18:42	35-2	Own		113291
2095 Skeeter	OMC		437cc	Tillotson	HD	18:42	35-2	Own		113291
					1970					
E250 Bobcat	OMC		437cc	Tillotson	HD	13:30	35-2	Own		405182
1500 Skeeter	OMC		437cc	Tillotson	HD	16:42	35-2	Own		113532
2000 Skeeter	OMC		437cc	Tillotson	HD	18:42	35-2	Own		113532
2001 Skeeter	OMC		437cc	Tillotson	HD	18:42	35-2	Own		113532
					1971					
E250C	OMC		437cc	Tillotson	HD37B	13:30	35-2	Own	11¾	405182
E251C	OMC		437cc	Tillotson	HD37B	13:30	35-2	Own		113532
E251M	OMC		437cc	Tillotson	HD37B	16:30	35-2	Own		113532
E251HP	OMC		437cc	Tillotson	HD37B	18:30	35-2	Own		113532
E2005	OMC		437cc	Tillotson	HD37B	18:42	35-2	Own		113532
E2015	OMC		437cc	Tillotson	HD37B	16:42	35-2	Own		113532
E2010	OMC		437cc	Tillotson	HD37B	16:42	35-2	Own		113532
					1972					
E252HP (Bobcat)	OMC		437cc	Tillotson	HD37B	16:30	35-2	Own	11¾	405182
E252 HPE (Bobcat)	OMC		437cc	Tillotson	HD37B	16:30	35-2	Own	11¾	405182
E1521 (Norseman)	OMC		437cc	Tillotson	HD37B	16:30	35-2	Own	11¾	405182
E1522 (Norseman)	OMC		399cc	OMC	Float Type	13:33	35-2	Own	11¾	405182
E1523 (Bobcat)	OMC		399cc	Tillotson	HD37B	16:30	35-2	Own	11¾	405182
E2020A (Trailblazer)	OMC		437cc	Tillotson	HD37B	16:42	35-2	Own	10¼	113896
E2025A (Trailblazer)	OMC		437cc	Tillotson	HD37B	16:42	35-2	Own	10½	113896

JOHNSON

SKEE-HORSE CHALLENGER RAMPAGE

Model	Engine Make	Engine Model	Engine Displ.	Carburetor Make	Carburetor Model	Sprocket Ratio	Chain Size	Clutch Make	Clutch Shaft Center	Belt Number
					1965					
Skee Horse 1400	OMC		362cc	Carter	N	14:49	35-2	Own		111496
					1966					
J1560	OMC		362cc	Carter	N	16:49	35-2	Own		111496
J2060	OMC		362cc	Carter	N	16:49	35-2	Own		111496
J2063	OMC		362cc	Carter	N	16:49	35-2	Own		111496
					1967					
J1570	OMC		362cc	Carter	N	16:42	35-2	Own		112634
J2070	OMC		362cc	Carter	N	14:42	35-2	Own		112634
J2075	OMC		362cc	Carter	N	14:42	35-2	Own		112634
					1968					
J1580	OMC		362cc	Bendix		16:42	35-2	Own		113291
J2080	OMC		362cc	Bendix		14:42	35-2	Own		113291
J2085	OMC		362cc	Bendix		14:42	35-2	Own		113291
					1969					
Challenger 227	JLO	L227	223cc	Tillotson	HR20A	12:39	35-2	Salsbury		113532
Challenger 297	JLO	L297	296cc	Tillotson	HR18A	13:37	35-2	Salsbury		113532
Challenger 300	JLO	L300	296cc	Tillotson	HD18A	13:35	35-2	Salsbury		113532
Challenger 380	JLO	L380	372cc	Tillotson	HD13A	13:30	35-2	Salsbury		113532
Skee Horse 1592	OMC		362cc	Bendix		16:42	35-2	Own		113532
Skee Horse 2093	OMC		362cc	Bendix		14:42	35-2	Own		113532
Skee Horse 2096	OMC		362cc	Bendix		14:42	35-2	Own		113532
Skee Horse 1590	OMC		437cc	Tillotson	HD	18:42	35-2	Own		113291
Skee Horse 2090	OMC		437cc	Tillotson	HD	18:42	35-2	Own		113291
Skee Horse 2095	OMC		437cc	Tillotson	HD	18:42	35-2	Own		113291
					1970					
C227	JLO	L227	223cc	Tillotson	HR	12:39	35-2	Salsbury		113532
C297	JLO	L297	296cc	Tillotson	HR	13:37	35-2	Salsbury		113532
C300	JLO	L300	296cc	Tillotson	HD	13:35	35-2	Salsbury		113532
C380	JLO	L380	372cc	Tillotson	HD	13:30	35-2	Salsbury		113532
J250	OMC		437cc	Tillotson	HD	13:30	35-2	Own		405182
25-200R	OMC		437cc	Tillotson	HD	18:42	35-2	Own		113532
25-200RC	OMC		437cc	Tillotson	HD	18:42	35-2	Own		113532
25-200RS	OMC		437cc	Tillotson	HD	18:42	35-2	Own		113532
					1971					
J250	OMC		437cc	Tillotson	HD37B	13:30	35-2	Own	11¾	405182
J251	OMC		437cc	Tillotson	HD37B	16:30	35-2	Own	11¾	405182
J251HP	OMC		437cc	Tillotson	HD37B	18:30	35-2	Own		113532
J200R	OMC		437cc	Tillotson	HD37B	18:42	35-2	Own		113532
J200RS	OMC		437cc	Tillotson	HD37B	18:42	35-2	Own		113532
J201R	OMC		437cc	Tillotson	HD37B	16:42	35-2	Own	10½	113896
J201RS	OMC		437cc	Tillotson	HD37B	16:42	35-2	Own	10½	113896
					1972					
J21-152C (Challenger)	OMC		399cc	OMC	Float Type	13:33	35-2	Own	11¾	405182
J27-152M (Challenger)	OMC		437cc	Tillotson	HD37B	16:30	35-2	Own	11¾	405182
J30-152HP (Rampage)	OMC		399cc	Tillotson	HD37B	16:30	35-2	Own	11¾	405182
J32-252HP (Rampage)	OMC		437cc	Tillotson	HD37B	16:30	35-2	Own	11¾	405182
J32-252HPE (Rampage)	OMC		437cc	Tillotson	HD37B	16:30	35-2	Own	11¾	405182
J30-202RS (Skeehorse)	OMC		437cc	Tillotson	HD37B	16:42	35-2	Own	10½	113896

SNOW CRUISER

	Engine			Carburetor				Clutch		
Model	**Make**	**Model**	**Displ.**	**Make**	**Model**	**Sprocket Ratio**	**Chain Size**	**Make**	**Shaft Center**	**Belt Number**
					1966					
C1560	OMC		362cc	Carter	N	16:49	35-2	Own		111496
C2060	OMC		362cc	Carter	N	16:49	35-2	Own		111496
C2065	OMC		362cc	Carter	N	16:49	35-2	Own		111496
					1967					
C1570	OMC		362cc	Carter	N	16:42	35-2	Own		112634
C2070	OMC		362cc	Carter	N	14:42	35-2	Own		112634
C2075	OMC		362cc	Carter	N	14:42	35-2	Own		112634
					1968					
C1580	OMC		362cc	Bendix		16:42	35-2	Own		113291
C2080	OMC		362cc	Bendix		14:42	35-2	Own		113291
C2081	OMC		362cc	Bendix		14:42	35-2	Own		113291
C2085E	OMC		362cc	Bendix		14:42	35-2	Own		113291
					1969					
C189	Kohler	K309-1	309cc	Tillotson	HR31A	13:35	35-2	Salsbury 790		113532
C1592	OMC		362cc	Bendix		16:42	35-2	Own		113532
C2092	OMC		362cc	Bendix		14:42	35-2	Own		113532
C2096	OMC		362cc	Bendix		14:42	35-2	Own		113532
C1590	OMC		437cc	Tillotson	HD	18:42	35-2	Own		113291
C2090	OMC		437cc	Tillotson	HD	18:42	35-2	Own		113291
C2095	OMC		437cc	Tillotson	HD	18:42	35-2	Own		113291
					1970					
C200	Kohler	K309-1	309cc	Tillotson	HR31A	13:35	35-2	Salsbury 790		113532
C200E	Kohler	K309-1	309cc	Tillotson	HR31A	13:35	35-2	Salsbury 790		113532
C260	Kohler	K399-2	399cc	Tillotson	HR43A	13:35	35-2	Salsbury 780		405485
C1500	OMC		437cc	Tillotson	HD	20:42	35-2	Own		113532
C2000	OMC		437cc	Tillotson	HD	18:42	35-2	Own		113532
C2005	OMC		437cc	Tillotson	HD	18:42	35-2	Own		113532
					1971					
C201	Kohler	K309-1	309cc	Tillotson	HR	13:30	35-2	Own		113532
C201E	Kohler	K309-1	309cc	Tillotson	HR	13:30	35-2	Own		113532
C281	Kohler	K399-2	399cc	Tillotson	HR	13:30	35-2	Own		405485
C321	Kohler	K399-2	399cc	Tillotson	HR(2)	13:30	35-2	Own		405485
C361	Kohler	K440-2	437cc	Tillotson	HR(2)	13:30	35-2	Own		405485
C2011	OMC		437cc	Tillotson	HD37B	18:42	35-2	Own		113532
C2016	OMC		437cc	Tillotson	HD37B	16:42	35-2	Own	10½	113896

NOTE: 1972 and later Models are Johnson or Evinrude.

LUBRICATION

The engine is lubricated by oil mixed with the fuel. Correct fuel-oil ratio is 16:1 for 1965 and 1966 models or 24:1 for later OMC engnes. On JLO and Kohler engines, use 20:1 mixture.

The primary drive sheave on OMC clutch contains a grease fitting which is accessible through a port in transmission guard alongside the "NEUTRAL SHIFT" knob. Turn crankshaft slowly until fitting is aligned with port, and pump in two or three shots of low temperature grease such as Texaco ALL-TEMP, each 15-20 hours of operation. CAUTION: Do not over-lubricate, or belt damage and malfunction could result.

Lubricate steering linkage with light engine oil every 25 hours and ski columns (spindles) annually with Texaco ALL-TEMP or equivalent.

The drive chain on models with open chain is automatically oiled by a tube leading from crankcase bleeder valve. Be sure that tube is open and clean, and that end of tube is properly aligned with drive chain. On models with enclosed chain case, maintain lubricant at level of lowest cover screw using Automatic Transmission Fluid, Type "A". Track bearings are sealed type and do not require lubrication.

Fig. 1 — Reversing transmission pedestal showing fill, drain and vent plugs.

On models with reversing transmission, the transmission pedestal (Fig. 1) should be filled to level of fill plug with Automatic Transmission Fluid, Type "A". Reservoir capacity is 70 cc (approx. 2⅓ fluid ounces). Fluid level should be checked every 25 hours or oftener if leakage is evident.

ADJUSTMENT

STEERING SKIS. Steering skis should be parallel with each other and with vehicle frame when handle bar is in normal straight driving position. To adjust the steering gear, first remove engine shroud (vehicle hood), then disconnect steering tie rod at either end.

DRIVE CHAIN. Roller drive chain should have ¼-½ inch deflection when measured midway between sprockets. To check the adjustment on open drive chain, it is necessary

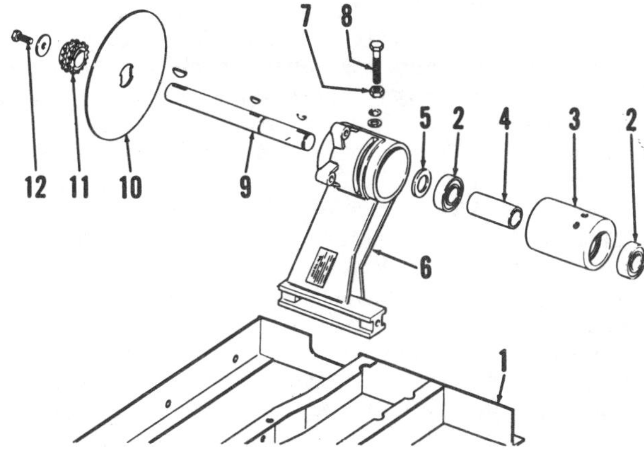

Fig. 2—Exploded view of intermediate drive shaft showing principal components.

1. Engine frame
2. Bearing
3. Eccentric housing
4. Spacer
5. Washer
6. Pedestal
7. Jam nut
8. Bolt
9. Shaft
10. Brake disc
11. Drive sprocket
12. Cap screw

to remove left foot rest and chain guard. Adjustment for models prior to 1968 is by means of eccentric bearing housing for shaft which carries upper chain sprocket and driven pulley; refer to Fig. 2. To make the adjustment, loosen locknut (7) and move eccentric screw (8) down to tighten chain or up to loosen chain.

On 1968 and later models with open chain an idler sprocket is used and tension is adjusted by sliding the idler bracket in slotted holes.

On 1969 Challenger and Bobcat, chain is tightened by loosening the three nuts (N—Fig. 3) and by shifting intermediate shaft in slotted holes. Adjustment is determined by checking backlash of secondary sheave(s).

On most models with enclosed chain case, the idler sprocket mounts on an eccentric housing which clamps to outside of chain case (See Fig. 4). To adjust the chain, loosen the clamps and remove upper chaincase cover as shown. Turn main drive sheave forward (clockwise) to eliminate slack in back flight of chain, then turn eccentric housing counter-clockwise until chain adjustment is correct. Tighten clamps and reinstall top cover.

Fig. 3—View of intermediate shaft showing secondary sheave (S) and nuts (N) which retain housing to chain case.

On some later models, the enclosed chain case uses an eccentric chain tightener of the type shown in Fig. 2.

BRAKE. To adjust the caliper type disc brake on early models with clamp type adjuster, loosen the locknut and tighten clamp adjusting screw until it stops; then back out approximately ½-turn and tighten locknut.

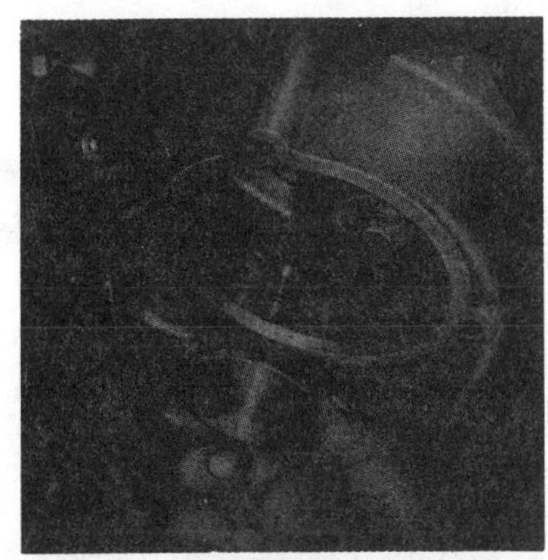

Fig. 4—View of chain case with cover removed showing eccentric housing which carries chain idler. Clamps do not need to be removed for chain adjustment.

Fig. 5—Late type brake unit. Adjust brake clearance by removing cotter pin and turning castellated nut (N).

1. Nut
2. Anchor screw
3. Clamp screw
10. Brake disc

On late models, brake body is housed in a pressed steel bracket as shown in Fig. 5. To adjust the brake, remove cotter pin and turn nut (N) until there is a slight drag on brake disc (10); then back off nut to the first castellation and insert cotter pin.

On all models, check to see that parking latch can be engaged before releasing vehicle for service. Travel of hand lever can be adjusted by loosening jam nut (1) and turning cable housing anchor screw (2); or by loosening clamp screw (3) and repositioning brake cable on actuating arm.

NEUTRAL CONTROL. On 1967 and earlier models a neutral shift knob was located on the primary (drive) sheave hub and was accessible through belt guard.

On 1968 models a neutral control knob is located on instrument panel. Pulling the knob out:

(1) Retards ignition timing.

(2) Locks primary sheave in neutral.

(3) Opens compression release valves.

(4) Sets throttle speed.

Any of the adjustments can be made independently, however if ignition timing adjustment must be made, the other adjustments will need to be changed. Proceed as follows:

Disconnect magneto advance arm from bell crank actuator arm as shown in Fig. 6 and push down on advance arm until it stops. With neutral control knob pushed in and detent engaged, loosen locknut (Fig. 7) and shorten or lengthen neutral control rod until magneto advance arm can be reconnected to bell crank actuator arm without moving magneto away from advance stop. Tighten the

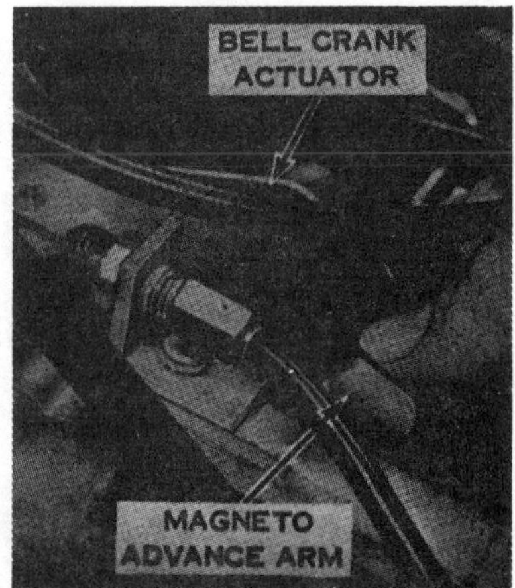

Fig. 6—Disconnect magneto advance arm and push down as shown to fully advance the timing.

locknut when adjustment is completed.

With neutral control knob remaining at "IN" (Operating) position, check the clearance between neutral control knob and button on primary drive sheave as shown in Fig. 8. Clearance should be 1/16-inch as shown. If it is not, adjust at control cable housing nuts, at point where cable housing attaches to engine frame.

With neutral control knob "IN", check for 1/16-inch free play at compression release cables as shown in Fig. 9. Adjust at cable housing bracket fittings as shown.

Refer to Fig. 10. Loosen the locknut on "L" shaped throttle rod and back rod out of ball joint several turns. Pull out on neutral control knob until it snaps into neutral detent position; then turn "L" shaped rod into ball joint until idle compensator cam contacts its stop on high speed needle boss and short hooked end of rod contacts idle control lever. Tighten locknut when adjustment is completed.

On 1969 and 1970 models so equipped, Neutral Control Arm should clear stop plunger by ⅛-inch with engine stopped and Neutral Control Knob pushed in. Refer to Fig. 11. Adjust at anchor nuts for control cable housing. Decompression releasse is independent of Neutral Control on these models and recommended adjustment is shown in Fig. 12.

REVERSING TRANSMISSION LINKAGE ADJUSTMENT. To adjust the reverse shift linkage on Wide Track models so equipped, proceed as follows:

Pull out on reverse shifter lever and refer to Fig. 13. Actuating clevis and lock plates should snap over-center as shown and clevis eye should touch pinion shaft actuating link. If clevis eye does not touch and linkage does not snap over-center, shorten linkage at clevis eye. If linkage is straight and link eye does not touch, lengthen the linkage. When linkage is correctly adjusted, shorten or lengthen operating rod until dash panel locknut (Fig. 14) JUST TOUCHES dash with lever moved to forward position.

TRACK. To adjust track tension, raise rear of vehicle until track is clear of ground.

On 1967 and earlier models, track tension is correct when distance (A—Fig. 15) between top of track and center truck (bogie) wheels is ¾-inch.

To make the adjustment, loosen the three clamp bolts (1—Fig. 16) and locknut (2) on each side of vehicle, then turn adjusting screw (3) until measurement is correct.

On later models with spring loaded bogie wheels, refer to Fig. 17 and proceed as follows. With track clear of ground, loosen nuts on clamp bolts (1) and turn adjusting bolts (2) until distance (A) measures as follows:

Models 1580, J1580 .... 2 9/16 in.
Models 2080, J2080, 2085, J2085, E2093, J2093 .... 2⅞ in.
All other Models .... 2¼ in.

NOTE: When track tension has been adjusted, alignment MUST be checked as outlined in the TRACK SERVICE section of this manual.

OVERHAUL

SKIS. In 1965, a two-leaf spring was used and ski was not equipped with a detachable runner. Later models use a three-leaf spring. In 1966, two different skis were used and runners were not interchangeable; measure runner length to be sure the correct part is ordered when renewal is indicated.

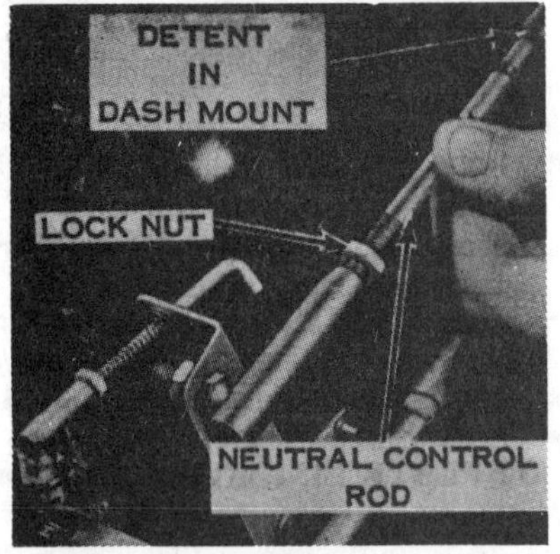

Fig. 7—Adjust the length of neutral control rod until magneto advance arm can be reconnected. Refer to text.

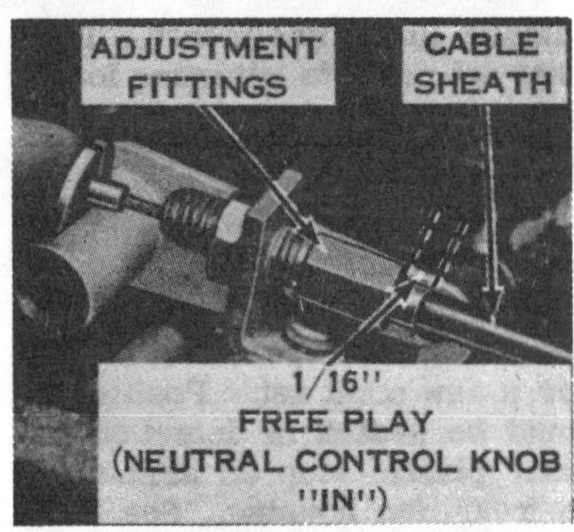

Fig. 9—Both compression release cables should have 1/16 inch clearance as shown.

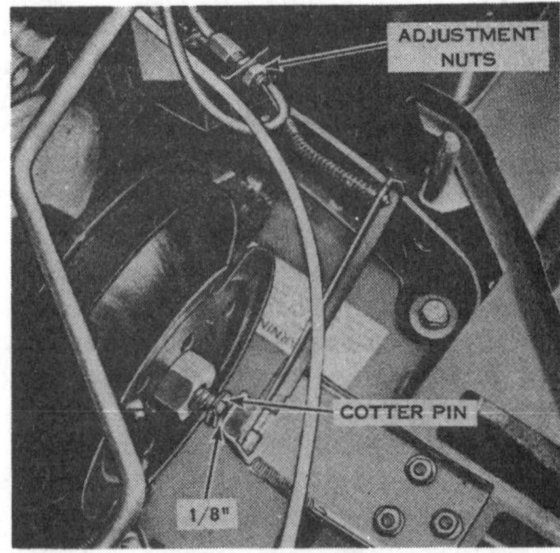

Fig. 11—Turn anchor (adjustment) nuts as required until Neutral Control Arm Clears stop plunger ⅛-inch as shown.

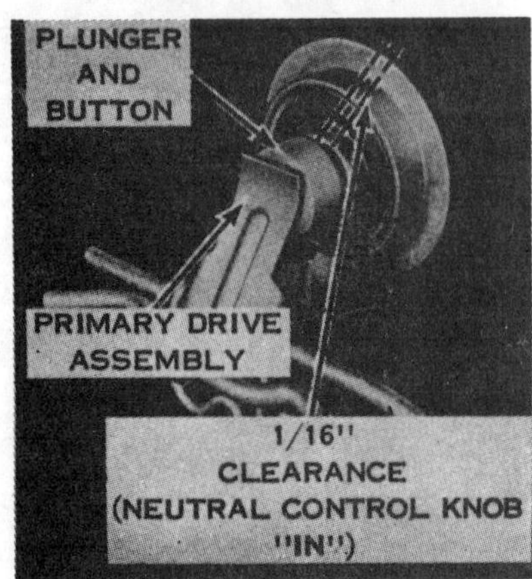

Fig. 8—In running position, lockout linkage should have 1/16 inch clearance as shown.

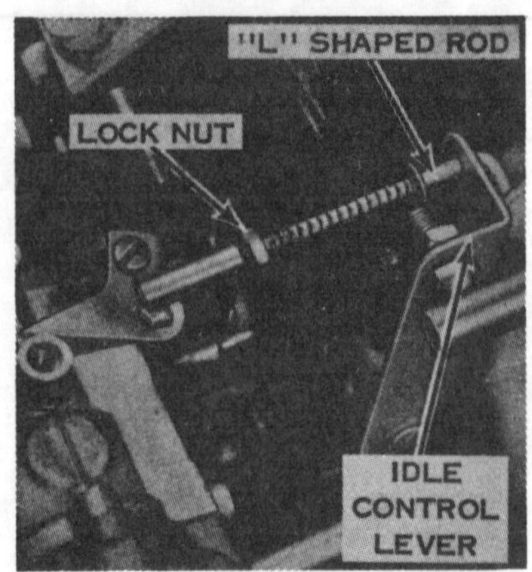

Fig. 10—View of throttle linkage with control knob in "NEUTRAL" position.

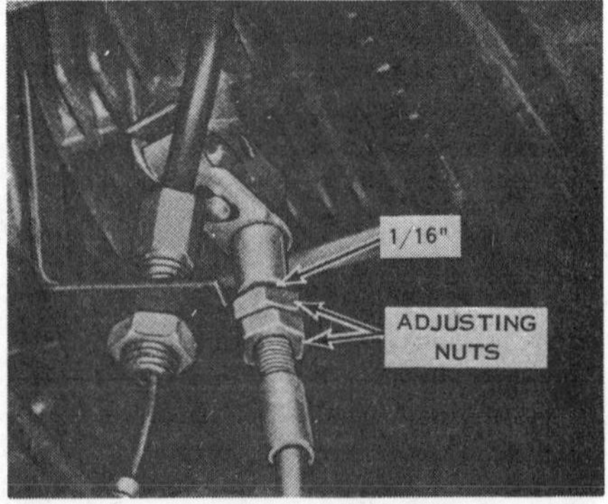

Fig. 12—To adjust compression release, push knob in and turn adjusting nuts until clearance is 1/16-inch as shown.

Ski columns (spindles) are not interchangeable right to left. Spindles must be installed with flat for taper pin (7—Fig. 18) forward and ski attaching point horizontal. Early type spindle is shown at (12), late type at (12A).

ENGINE & DRIVE. Engine and drive unit is mounted on a separate frame and can be removed as a unit after removing engine shroud (hood), drive chain, and brake and throttle controls. Refer to Figs. 18 and 19 for exploded views.

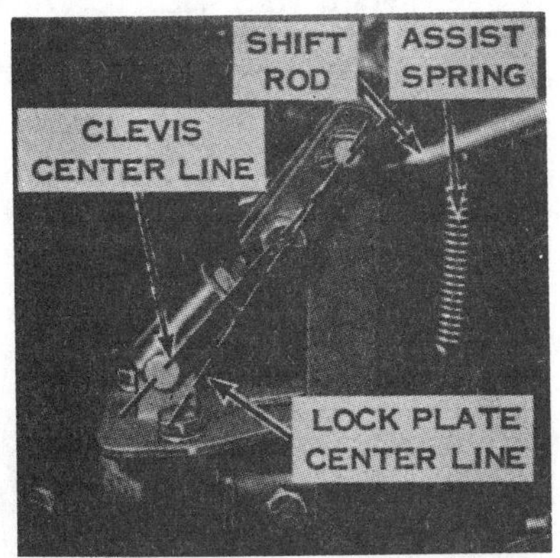

Fig. 13—Reverse shift linkage should snap over-center as shown, to hold lever in reverse position.

Fig. 14—Dash panel locknut should contact instrument panel in forward position.

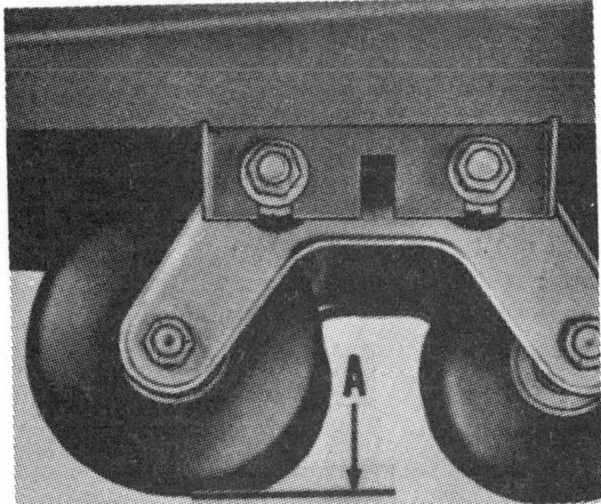

Fig. 15—Track should sag about ¾-inch when measured from center bogie wheel as shown at (A).

The recoil starter ratchet mount is provided with a holding hole (Arrow—Fig. 20). When removing the transmission (torque converter) drive sheave, first remove starter and insert a suitable holding bar through the hole to keep crankshaft from turning. Turn drive sheave in normal direction of engine rotation to unscrew the sheave.

Fig. 16—Adjust track tension by loosening clamp bolts (1) and locknut (2) and turning adjusting screw (3). Both sides must be adjusted alike, see text.

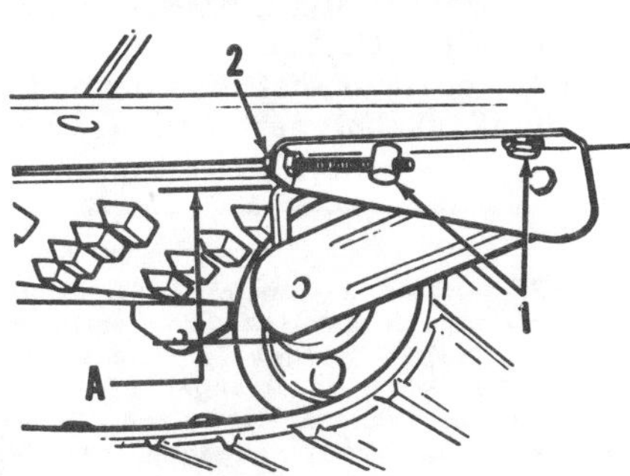

Fig. 17—To adjust track tension on 1968 models, loosen nuts on clamp screws (1) and turn adjusting screw (2) until distance (A) measures as indicated in text.

Fig. 18 — Main vehicle frame showing steering components exploded. Ski leg (12A) and bushing (13A) are used on late models.

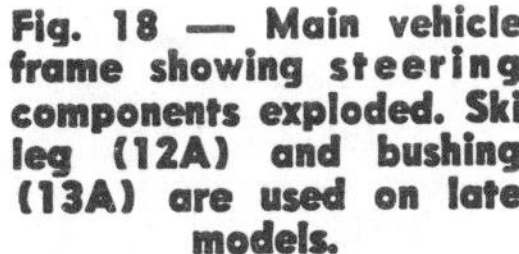

1. Fuel tank
2. Drain line
3. Handlebar
4. Drag link
5. Drag link
6. Steering arm
7. Taper pin
8. Main frame
9. Bracket
10. Spring
11. Ski
12. Ski leg
13. Thrust washer

REVERSING TRANSMISSION. On models so equipped, the reversing transmission serves as the mounting pedestal for the torque converter secondary (driven) sheave and main drive chain drive sprocket. Refer to Fig. 21.

The two upper views (F) show the transmission engaged in forward gear. The spring loaded dog clutch (4) connects the input shaft (2) and output shaft (3). Reverse pinion (6) is pulled back from both shaft gears, and both shafts turn together as a unit.

The two lower views (R) show the transmission engaged in reverse gear. Action of the shift linkage moves the reverse pinion (6) into engagement with the input and output shaft gears. The wedge-shaped shifter clevis (7) moves the dog clutch (4) out of engagement with input shaft (2) and shafts turn in opposite directions through the reversing action of the gears. The transmission has no neutral position.

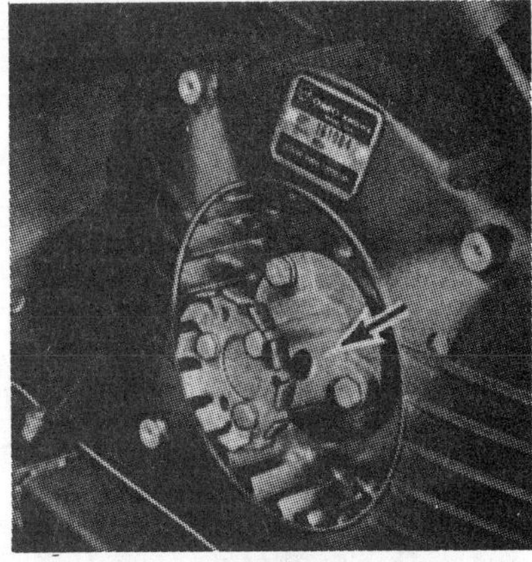

Fig. 20—View of engine with recoil starter removed. Hole (Arrow) in ratchet mount is for holding crankshaft for drive sheave removal.

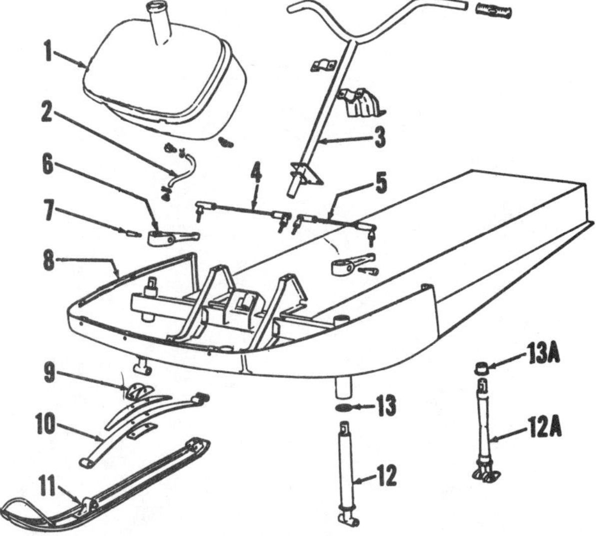

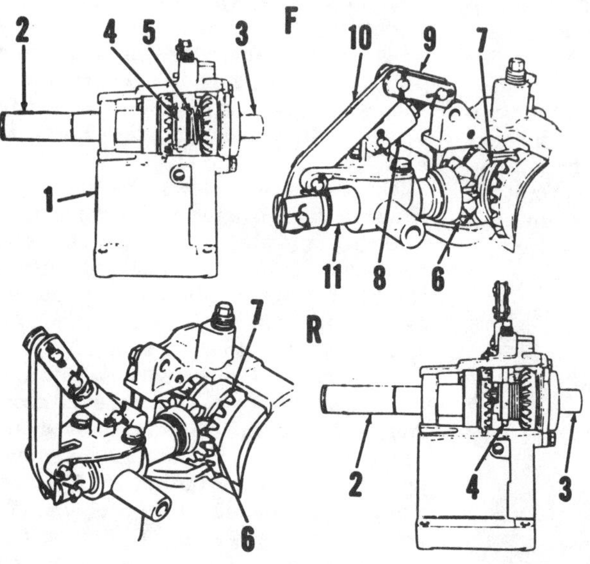

Fig. 21—Schematic view of assembled reversing transmission showing principal components. Upper views (F) are in forward gear, lower views (R) in reverse.

1. Pedestal
2. Input shaft
3. Output shaft
4. Clutch dog
5. Spring
6. Reverse pinion
7. Shifter clevis
8. Actuating clevis
9. Lock plates
10. Actuating link
11. Reverse spindle

To disassemble the removed transmission, first shift the linkage to "Reverse" position and unbolt and remove end cap from output side of housing. Withdraw output shaft and gear.

Remove the socket head screw retaining shifter clevis (7) to inner end of reverse pinion spindle, then remove shifter clevis, reverse pinion and reverse pinion thrust bearing. Input shaft and gear can now be removed.

NOTE: Shims may be used between reverse pinion thrust bearing and pinion spindle shoulder to reduce gear backlash to a minimum without binding. Shims are available in thicknesses of 0.002, 0.003, 0.004 and 0.005.

Use LOCTITE Bearing Lock on ID and OD of input shaft bearing and on ID of output shaft gear when reassembling the transmission. Use LOCTITE Stud Lock on socket head screw retaining shifter clevis to reverse pinion spindle. Fill transmission housing with 70 cc (2⅓ oz.) of Automatic Transmission Fluid, Type "A", and adjust shifter linkage as outlined in the previous ADJUSTMENT paragraphs.

TORQUE CONVERTER

Models **Skee Horse and Skeeter**
Drive Ratio
Low 3:1
High 1:1
Belt Face Width (In.) 1*
*Minimum allowable
Engagement Speed (RPM).......2000

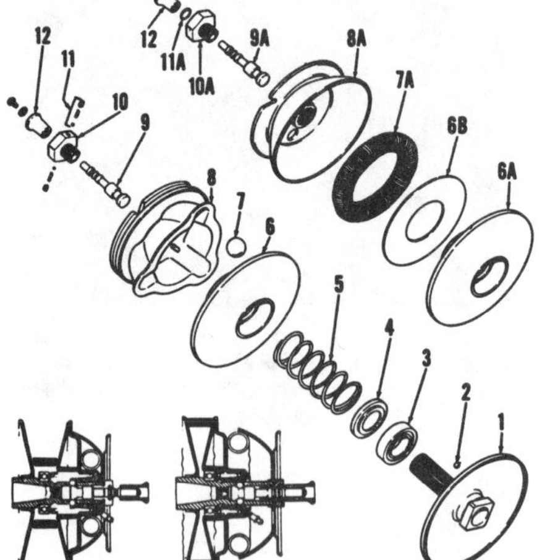

Fig. 22—Exploded view of OMC Primary (drive) sheave used on Skee-Horse and Skeeter. Parts 6 through 11 were used on early units, parts 6A through 11A on late units. Cross sectional views show neutral position with lockout engaged, and high speed position.

1. Fixed flange
2. Lockout ball
3. Idler bearing
4. Spring seat
5. Spring
6. Moving flange (early)
6A. Moving flange (late)
6B. Primary disc
7. Weight ball
7A. Garter spring
8. End cap (early)
8A. End cap (late)
9. Lockout plunger
9A. Lockout plunger
10. Nut
10A. Nut
11. Detent assy
11A. Garter spring
12. Lockout knob

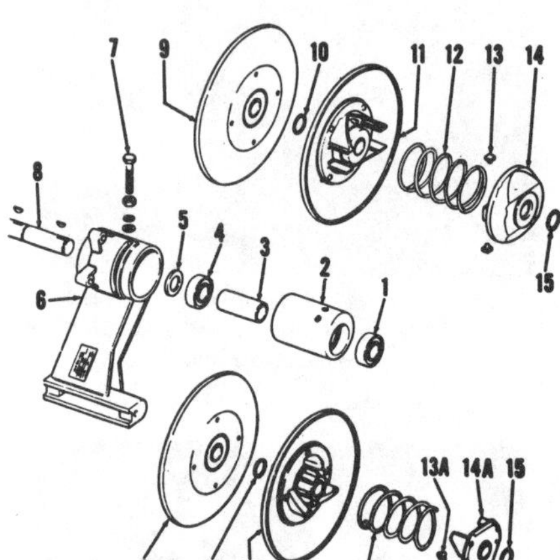

Fig. 23—Exploded view of OMC Secondary (driven) sheave used on Skee-Horse and Skeeter. The speed-sensing early unit is shown in upper right (9 through 15). Parts 11A through 14A in lower right are used in the torque-sensing late unit. Spring (12A) must be pre-stressed by turning end cap (14A) approximately ⅓-turn clockwise after engaging hooked ends of spring in moving sheave (11A) and end cap (14A).

OUTBOARD MARINE CORPORATION

1973-1975

EVINRUDE

Model	Engine Make	Engine Model	Engine Displ.	Carburetor Make	Carburetor Model	Sprocket Ratio	Chain Size	Clutch Make	Clutch Shaft Center	Belt Number
1973										
1532	Own		399cc	OMC	Float Type	13:33	35-2	Own	11-9/32	
1531	Own		437cc	Tillotson	HD37B	16:30	35-2	Own	11¾	405182
1533	Own		399cc	Tillotson	HD37B	16:30	35-2	Own	11¾	405182
1534	Own		437cc	Tillotson	HD37B	16:30	35-2	Own	11¾	405182
E253E	Own		437cc	Tillotson	HD37B	16:30	35-2	Own		
E2035	Own		437cc	Tillotson	HD37B	16:42	35-2	Own		
TW-30-Q	Own		437cc	Own		16:42	35-2	Own		
RC-35-Q	Own	RC	528cc							
1974										
Skimmer 400	Own	M242	399cc	Tillotson	HD130A	17:39	Silent	Own	10½	114271
Skimmer 440	Own	M243	436cc	Tillotson	HD130A	19:39	Silent	Own	10½	114271
Skimmer 650	Own	M244	646cc	Tillotson	HD129A	19:39	Silent	Own	10½	114271
Quiet Flite	Own	M245E	437cc	Bendix	136-74	16:42	35-2	Own	10½	114271
Trailblazer 35	Own RC	385600	528cc	Own	386614	16:42	35-2	Own	11	114272
Trailblazer 45	Own RC	386202	528cc	Own	386435	17:39	Silent	Own	11	114272
1975										
Skimmer 400	Own	M247	399cc	Tillotson	HD130B	17:39	Silent	Own 443		114617
Skimmer 440	Own	M248	436cc	Tillotson	HD130B	19:39	Silent	Own 443		114617
Skimmer 650	Own	M249	646cc	Tillotson	HD129B	19:39	Silent	Own 443		114617
Skimmer 650S	Own	M249	646cc	Tillotson	HD129C	19:39	Silent	Own 443		114617
Rotary 35	Own	386200	528cc	Own	Float	16:42	35-2	Own 507	11	114272
Rotary 45	Own	386202	528cc	Own	Float	17:39	Silent	Own 507	11	114272

JOHNSON

Model	Engine Make	Engine Model	Engine Displ.	Carburetor Make	Carburetor Model	Sprocket Ratio	Chain Size	Clutch Make	Clutch Shaft Center	Belt Number
1973										
Reveler 153C	Own		399cc	OMC	Float Type	13:33	35-2	Own	11-9/32	
Reveler 153M	Own		437cc	Tillotson	HD37B	16:30	35-2	Own	11¾	405182
Reveler 153HPE	Own		437cc	Tillotson	HD37B	16:30	35-2	Own	11¾	405182
J30-153HP	Own		399cc	Tillotson	HD37B	16:30	35-2	Own	11¾	405182
J32-153HP	Own		437cc	Tillotson	HD37B	16:30	35-2	Own	11¾	405182
Skee-Horse	Own		437cc	Tillotson	HD37B	16:42	35-2	Own		
Golden Ghost	Own		437cc							
Phantom	Own	RC	528cc							
1974										
JX400	Own	M242	399cc	Tillotson	HD130A	17:39	Silent	Own 443	10½	114271
JX440	Own	M243	436cc	Tillotson	HD130A	19:39	Silent	Own 443	10½	114271
JX650	Own	M244	646cc	Tillotson	HD129A	19:39	Silent	Own 443	10½	114271
Golden Ghost 30	Own	M245E	437cc	Bendix	136-74	16:42	35-2	Own 507	10½	114271
Phantom 35	Own RC	385600	528cc	Own	386614	16:42	35-2	Own 507	11	114272
Phantom 45	Own RC	386202	528cc	Own	386435	17:39	Silent	Own 507	11	114272
1975										
JX400	Own	M247	339cc	Tillotson	HD130B	17:39	Silent	Own 443		114617
JX440	Own	M248	436cc	Tillotson	HD130B	19:39	Silent	Own 443		114617
JX650	Own	M249	646cc	Tillotson	HD129B	19:39	Silent	Own 443		114617
JX650S	Own	M249	646cc	Tillotson	HD129C	19:39	Silent	Own 443		114617
Rotary Powered 35	Own RC	386200	528cc	Own	Float	16:42	35-2	Own 507	11	114272
Rotary Powered 45	Own RC	386202	528cc	Own	Float	17:39	Silent	Own 507	11	114272

LUBRICATION

The engine is lubricated by oil mixed with the fuel. Recommended fuel/oil ratio is 50:1, using a good grade of Regular gasoline and an approved motor oil. Johnson or Evinrude 50/1 Two Cycle Oil is recommended for piston engines and Johnson or Evinrude 50/1 Rotary Combustion Snowmobile Oil is specified for RC engines.

The enclosed chaincase should be filled to level of check plug (L—Fig. 1) using Dexron ATF Fluid or equivalent. The reversing transmission on models so equipped should be filled to level of check plug (R) using same fluid.

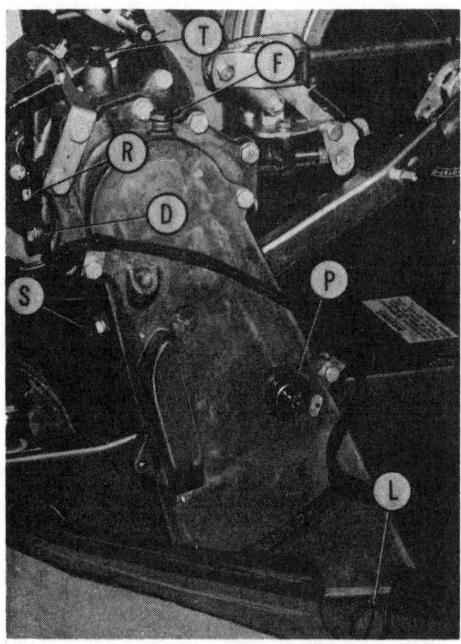

Fig. 1—Chain case and reversing transmission used on models so equipped.

D. Transmission drain plug
F. Trans. fill plug
L. Chaincase level plug
P. Chaincase fill plug
R. Trans. level plug
S. Idler adjusting screw
T. Trans. breather plug

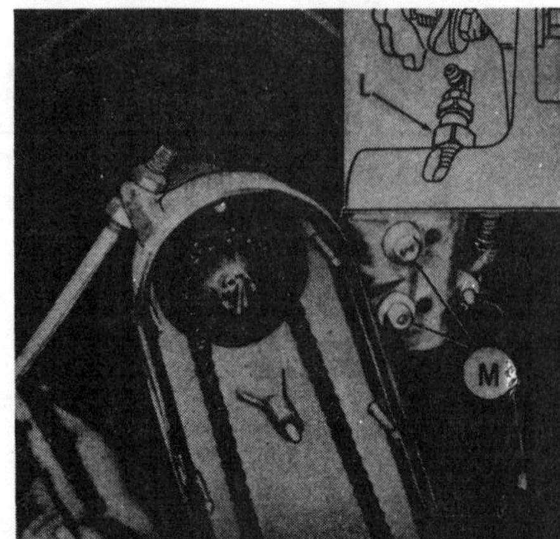

Fig. 2—Chain case (with cover removed) used on models with eccentric chain adjuster.

L. Adjusting bolt locknut
M. Brake mounting bolts

Some models may have lube fittings on ski legs. Lubricate sparingly with a pressure gun about once a week during use periods. On all models, lubricate spring shackles and ski pivots with light engine oil about once a week. Once a season in normal use or oftener under heavy use, disassemble drive and driven sheaves and lightly coat moving parts with Lubriplate, being sure the grease does not reach belt area.

ADJUSTMENT

SKIS. Steering skis should be parallel with each other and with vehicle frame when handlebar is in normal straight driving position. To adjust the steering gear it is necessary to disconnect tie rod at either end.

DRIVE CHAIN. On models with eccentric chain adjustment (Fig. 2), chain free play measured midway between sprockets should be 3/16-5/16 inch. Chaincase cover should be removed to measure free play. To adjust the chain, loosen eccentric adjusting bolt locknut (L) and move adjusting bolt DOWNWARD in slot to tighten chain, or UPWARD in slot to loosen chain. With chain correctly adjusted, slightly loosen brake caliper mounting nuts (M) and firmly apply the brake to align caliper with friction face. Tighten nuts (M) with brake applied. Refill chaincase to proper level with OMC SEA LUBE or DEXRON ATF Fluid.

NOTE: To prevent chain lubricant loss, machine may be tipped on right side before chaincase cover is removed.

On models with reversing transmission, refer to Fig. 1. Shift transmission to FORWARD position and check drive chain free play as follows: Remove chaincase inspection cover plug (P) and rock secondary sheave clockwise until all slack is gathered to rear of chain. At this time, outside edge of chain should align with front edge of inspection plug hole. Adjust the chain by loosening locknut and turning idler adjusting screw (S) as required. DO NOT overtighten.

Models with silent chain are equipped with automatic chain tensioners and adjustment is not required.

BRAKE. The caliper type disc brake should fully release when hand lever is released and fully apply before lever touches handlebar grip. On models with eccentric drive chain adjustment, align caliper with friction face of secondary sheave by loosening mounting bolt nuts (M—Fig. 2) and firmly applying brake; then retightening nuts.

Be sure stop boss on actuating arm (A—Fig. 3) contacts stop pin (P), adjusting if necessary at cable housing anchor (H). Adjust for wear by carefully tightening actuating lever stud nut (N). On models with parking brake lock (Fig. 4), retaining pawl should drop into position as shown at (B) when hand brake is fully applied.

Adjust brake light switch anchor nuts (S—Fig. 3) if necessary until brake light comes on when brake is applied but goes off when brake lever is released.

REVERSING TRANSMISSION LINKAGE. To adjust the reverse shift linkage on models so equipped, pull shift lever into reverse position as shown in Fig. 5. Actuating linkage should snap over-center as shown by broken lines and clevis eye should touch shift lever link. If linkage is

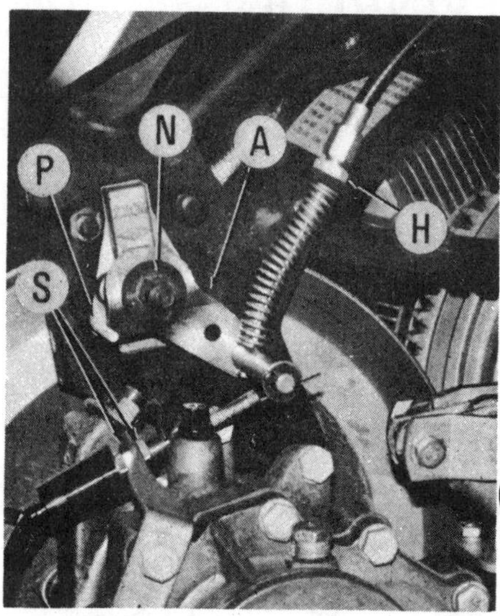

Fig. 3—Installed view of caliper type disc brake showing points of adjustment.

A. Actuating arm
H. Cable housing anchor
N. Adjusting nut
P. Stop pin
S. Stoplight switch anchor nuts

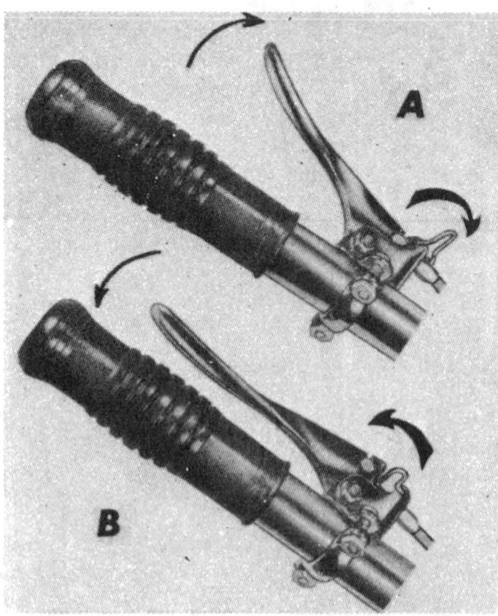

Fig. 4—Some models have a parking brake lock located on hand lever mounting bracket. Brake is released in view (A) and applied in view (B).

Fig. 5—When shift linkage is moved to REVERSE position, actuating linkage should snap over-center as shown by broken lines.

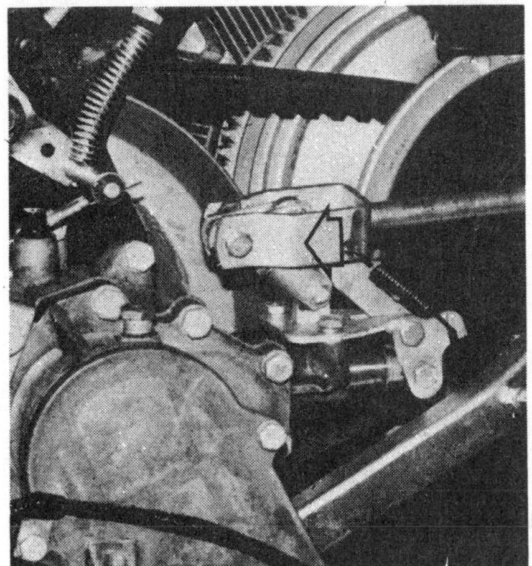

Fig. 6—View of reversing transmission actuating linkage shifted to FORWARD position. Refer also to Fig. 5.

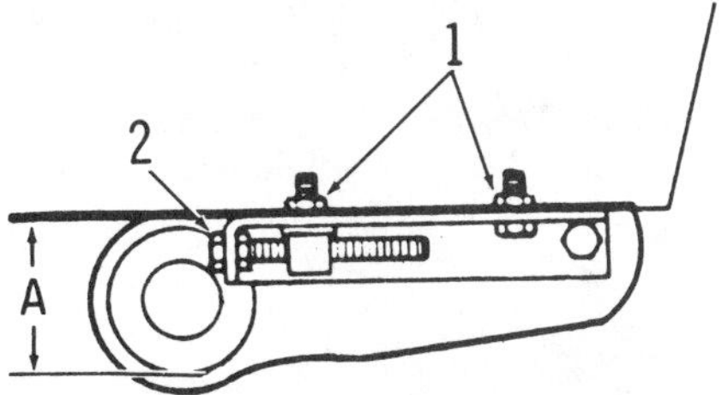

Fig. 7—Schematic view of track adjusting mechanism used on early narrow track models. Distance (A) should measure 2¾ inches with track clear of ground.

1. Clamp bolts
2. Adjusting screw

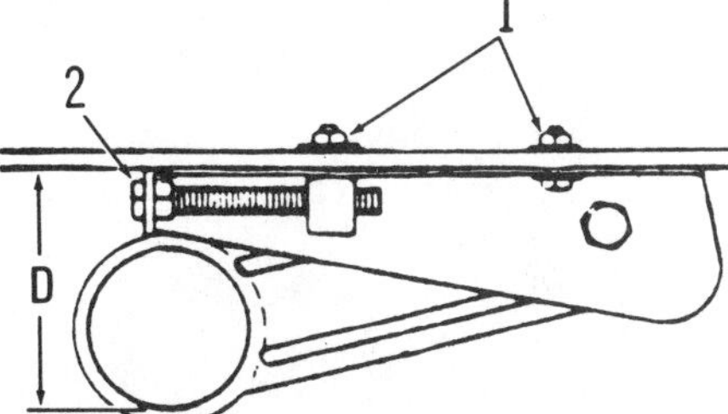

Fig. 8—Schematic view of track adjusting mechanism used on Wide Track models. Distance (D) should measure 3-1/8 inches. Refer also to Fig. 7.

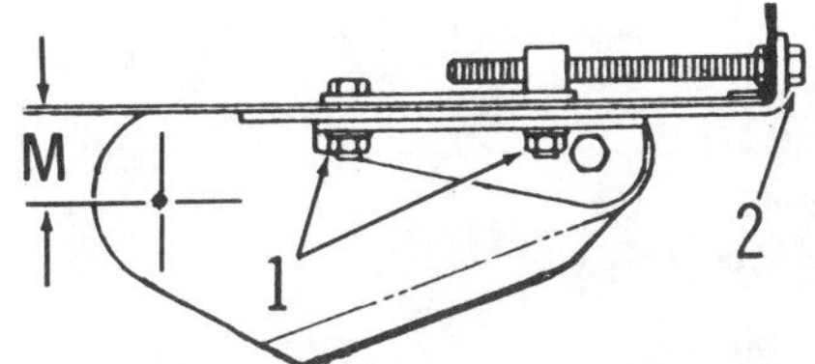

Fig. 9—View of track adjusting mechanism used on late bogie wheel models. Distance (M) should measure 1½ inches. Refer also to Fig. 7.

Fig. 10—View of track adjusting mechanism used on slide rail models. Track should clear center of slide by about ½ inch when correctly adjusted.

either too short or too long, unit will not lock and stay in reverse. Adjust by removing lever pin, loosening eyebolt locknut and shortening or lengthening the link.

When adjustment is correct, shorten or lengthen operating rod if necessary, until dash panel locknut JUST TOUCHES dash when lever is moved to forward position.

TRACK. On all models, track tension is checked and adjustment made with rear of machine suspended until track is free. Suitably support the machine and refer to the appropriate following paragraphs for procedure.

BOGIE WHEEL MODELS. On early narrow track models, refer to Fig. 7. Track tension is correct when distance (A), measured from bottom of pivot bearing bore to underside of running board is 2-3/4 inches.

On Wide Track models, refer to Fig. 8. Track tension is correct when distance (D) measured from bottom of pivot bearing bore to underside of running board is 3-1/8 inches.

On late bogie wheel models, refer to Fig. 9. Track tension is correct when distance (M) measured from center dimple on pivot arm shield to underside of chassis rail is 1½ inches.

On all models, adjustment is made by loosening clamp bolt nuts (1) and turning adjusting screw (2). Both sides must be adjusted alike and free length of adjusting bolt (2) on each side of machine must be equal to within 1/32 inch.

NOTE: Whenever track tension has been adjusted, alignment MUST be checked as outlined in TRACK SERVICE Section of this manual.

SLIDE RAIL MODELS. On models with slide rail suspension, track tension is correct when inside center of track clears slide about ½-inch, measured at middle of slide.

To adjust track tension, loosen track idler axle nut and the jam nuts on adjusting screws (Fig. 10). Turn adjusting screws on each side of machine an equal amount until track tension is correct. Both sides must be adjusted alike and distance from bolt heads to bracket on both sides must be equal.

NOTE: Whenever track tension has been adjusted, alignment MUST be checked as outlined in TRACK SERVICE Section of this manual.

Slide rail suspension units are adjustable for operating conditions and load. The single set of torsion springs controls ski pressure through leverage on front control link while rear link is directly controlled by spring main adjustment. Refer to Fig. 11. Normal setting of front control link is shown in (Inset A) for models with slotted reaction arm or at (M) for models with multi-hole arm. Normal setting of

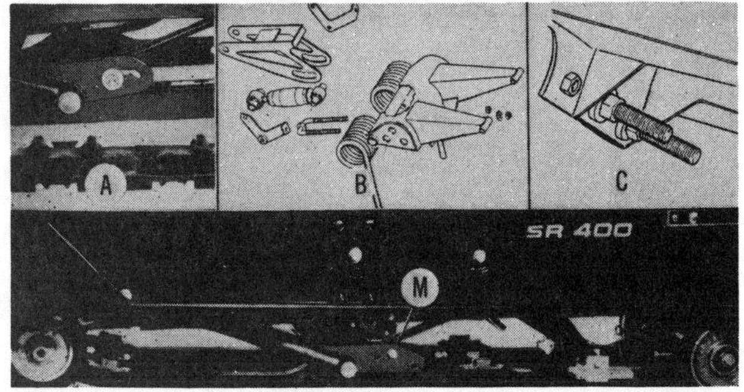

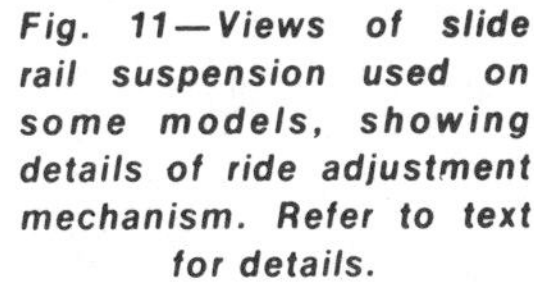

Fig. 11—Views of slide rail suspension used on some models, showing details of ride adjustment mechanism. Refer to text for details.

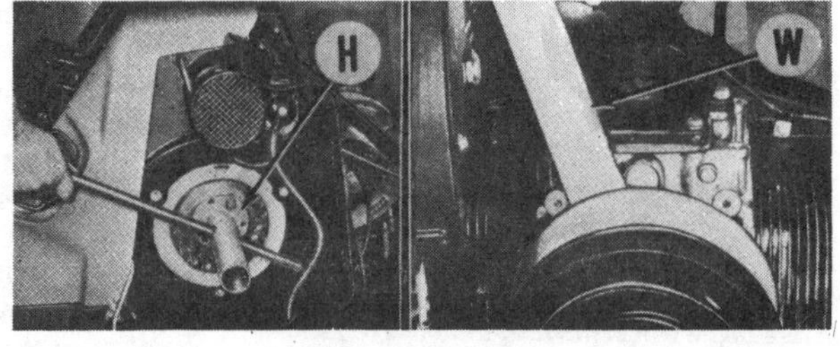

Fig. 12—Special tools are provided for drive clutch removal on opposed cylinder engines.

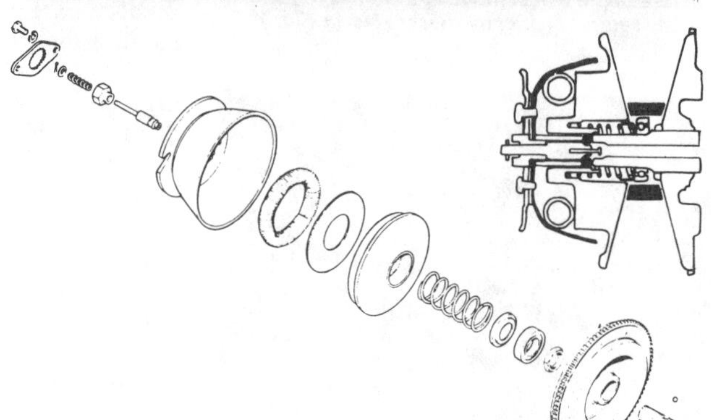

Fig. 13—Exploded view of drive clutch typical of that used on most models.

spring tension U-bolt is with 2 inches of threads exposed as shown in (Inset C). Tightening U-bolt nuts increases total spring tension while loosening the nuts decreases tension. Moving spring pivot rearward to outer end of reaction arm increases the load carried on front portion of track and lightens load carried on skis. This results in increased traction and decreased steering control. Before attempting to move spring pivot on front link reaction arm, it is first necessary to completely loosen main tension U-bolt (Inset C); then retighten to desired setting after front adjustment is changed.

Fig. 14—Use the special clamp to secure sliding sheave when disassembling drive clutch.

Fig. 15—View of drive clutch partially exploded showing compression spring and the centrifugally actuated garter spring.

OVERHAUL

ENGINE AND DRIVE. On all models, engine and drive clutch can be removed as a unit after removing hood, dash panel, wiring, controls, belt guard, drive belt, fuel lines and muffler or connections. Before unbolting engine frame from chassis, scribe alignment marks on frame and support to aid in belt alignment when engine is reinstalled.

On rotary combustion engines and alternate firing twins, flywheel is combined with drive clutch fixed face and is an essential part of engine. On opposed twins, the splined main clutch shaft threads onto crankshaft and special tools are needed for clutch removal as shown in Fig. 12. Remove starter and ratchet mount, then attach holding tool (H) to threaded holes of flywheel. The flat, open-end wrench (W) fits machined flat on rear of fixed sheave. Break primary sheaves loose by striking wrench handle with a short mallet, then unscrew clutch from flywheel.

Fig. 13 shows an exploded view of drive clutch typical of that used on all models, although neutral lockout is not always used. Drive clutch can be disassembled without removal of engine. Clutch is spring loaded and spring should be compressed and secured by clamping as shown in Fig. 14, before retaining nut is removed. When sliding sheave is withdrawn, be sure to catch and save the lockout balls in shaft. The manufacturer recommends the use of Trichlorethylene as a cleaning agent. Be careful, however, as the vapors are harmful. Be sure neutral lockout balls are correctly reinstalled if so equipped.

Check belt friction faces for cupping or wear. Check springs for distortion and splines for wear or scoring. Renew any parts which are questionable. Lightly coat shaft splines with LUBRIPLATE and reassemble by reversing disassembly procedure. Tighten cap nut to a torque of 90-100 ft.-lbs. (12.5-13.8 kg-m). Lock plate serrations are positioned so that plate can be turned over to double available locking positions. Wipe excess lubricant from clutch hub before installing drive belt.

SECONDARY DRIVE. Refer to Figs. 16 and 17 for exploded views of

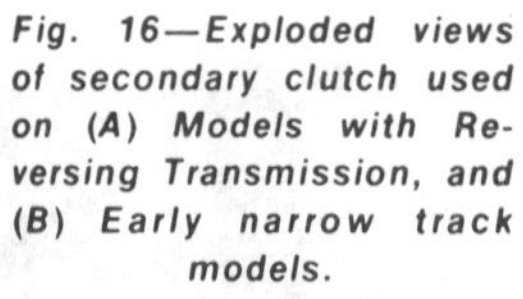

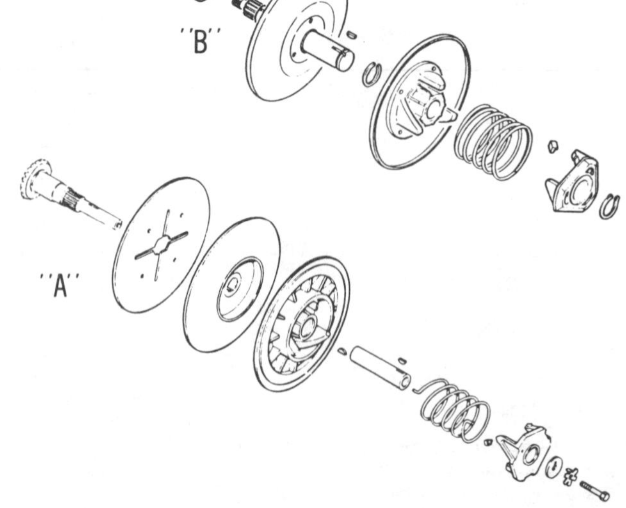

Fig. 16—Exploded views of secondary clutch used on (A) Models with Reversing Transmission, and (B) Early narrow track models.

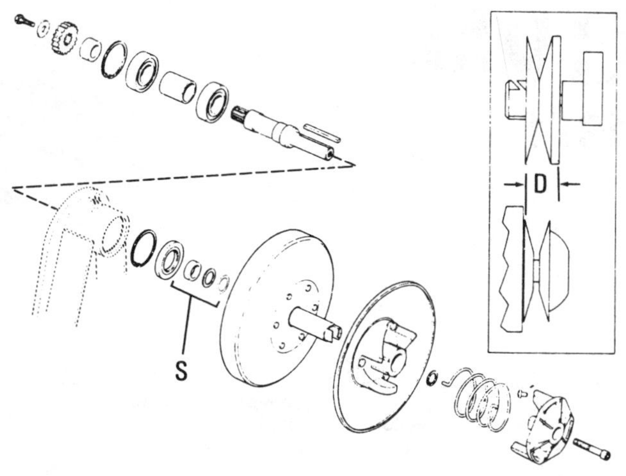

Fig. 17—Exploded view of secondary clutch used on late models. Spacer package (S) controls offset which should be 3.56 inches (90.4 mm) measured from outside edges of fixed flanges as shown at (D).

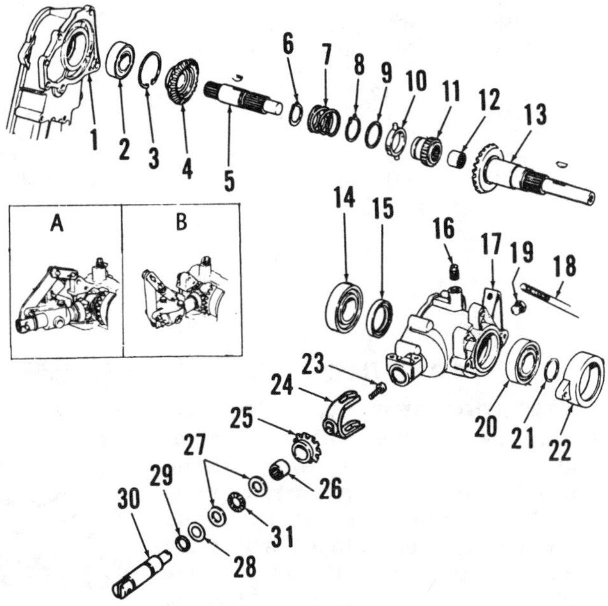

Fig. 18—Exploded view of reversing transmission showing component parts. Insets show forward gear engaged at "A" and reverse gear at "B".

1. Chain case
2. Bearing
3. Snap ring
4. Output gear
5. Output shaft
6. Snap ring
7. Spring
8. Snap ring
9. O-ring
10. Cradle
11. Coupling
12. Needle bearing
13. Input shaft
14. Bearing
15. Seal
16. Plug
17. Gear housing
18. Support rod
19. Plug
20. Bearing
21. Snap ring
22. Bearing housing
23. Cap screw
24. Shift fork
25. Reverse idler
26. Needle bearing
27. Thrust races
28. Shims
29. Retaining ring
30. Pinion shaft
31. Thrust bearing

secondary (driven) pulley units. On all models, torsion spring is pre-loaded one ramp (1/3 turn).

On opposed twin models, sheaves are aligned and offset accomplished by loosening engine frame mounting bolts. On late, alternate firing twin models, alignment is not adjustable and offset is controlled by spacer set (S—Fig. 17) which consists of one 0.36 inch (9.1 mm) spacer and 0.030 and 0.010 inch (0.75 & 0.25 mm) shims as required to establish the specified 3.56 inch (90.4 mm) distance between outside edges of fixed flanges as shown at (D).

REVERSING TRANSMISSION. On models so equipped, the reversing transmission serves as the secondary drive shaft. Refer to Fig. 18 for an exploded view.

In forward gear, pinion shaft (30), gear (25), fork (24) and associated parts move outward from housing as shown at (A), and fork (24) moves coupling (11) on output shaft (5) into engagement with input shaft (13) providing a direct drive through the unit. In reverse (View B), shift fork disengages coupling (11) and reverse idler (25) meshes with the bevel gear on input shaft (13) and with the gear (4) which is splined to output shaft (5) driving output shaft in reverse direction. The only adjustment required, except for linkage, is adjustment of pinion (25) to zero backlash with input gear when retaining ring (29) contacts housing (17). Adjust by adding or removing shims (28) which are available in thicknesses of 0.002, 0.003, 0.004 and 0.005 inch (0.05, 0.08, 0.1 and 0.13 mm).

DRIVE CHAIN. Number 35-2 roller chain is used in all earlier models, while most later models use silent chain. Either chain should be renewed when stretch exceeds 3%, or 3/8 inch per foot of new chain length. A new chain should also be installed whenever sprockets are renewed. Standard sprocket sizes and chain types are given in condensed service data tables.

TRACK AND SUSPENSION. Bogie wheel bearings are sealed type and are pressed into bogie wheel hubs. The molded runners of side rail models fit over a T-shaped rail and are retained by a single bolt at forward end. Renew runners if worn to less than 3/8 inch in thickness at any point.

Metal track cleats on models so equipped can be individually renewed. Cleats are provided in a kit which includes one cleat and the eight rivets necessary for installation. Original track cleats are bonded to track. Cut the bond along sides and ends of cleat using a sharp knife, being careful not to cut into track material. Starting at one end, squirt a small amount of Methyl Ethyl Ketone Solvent into cut while applying hand pressure to separate the parts. Use new track cleat as a template and drill eight 3/16 inch holes for new rivets, then rivet cleat to track using rivets provided.

PHANTOM

1970-1971

	Engine			Carburetor				Clutch		
Model	Make	Model	Displ.	Make	Model	Sprocket Ratio	Chain Size	Make	Shaft Center	Belt Number
					1970					
269295	JLO	L295	292cc	Keihin	407	13:37		Salsbury 780	12½	GTS-720
269340	JLO	L340	336cc	Keihin	407	13:37		Salsbury 780	12½	GTS-720
269395	JLO	L395	396cc	Keihin	407	15:37		Salsbury 910	12½	GTS-752
269440	JLO	LR440/2	433cc	Keihin	407	15:37		Salsbury 910	12½	GTS-752
					1971					
270295	JLO	L295	292cc	Walbro	WD	13:37		Salsbury 780	12½	GTS-720
270340	JLO	L340	336cc	Walbro	WD	13:37		Salsbury 780	12½	GTS-720
270399	Kohler	K399-2	399cc	Walbro	WD	15:37		Salsbury 910	12½	GTS-752
270440	Kohler	K440-2	437cc	Walbro	WD	15:37		Salsbury 910	12½	GTS-752

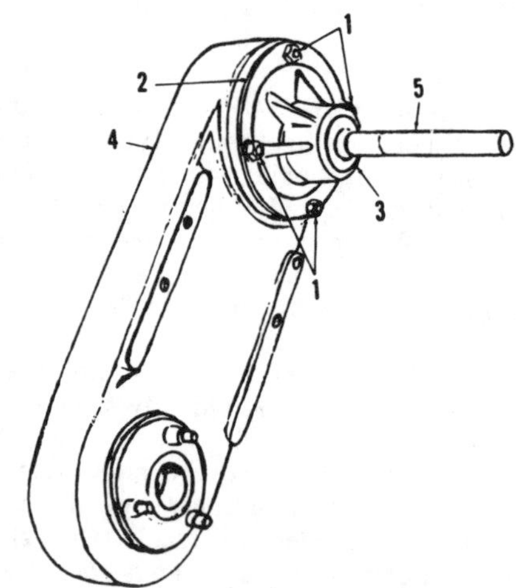

Fig. 1—View of chain case showing points of adjustment.

1. Clamp nuts
2. Clamp ring
3. Housing
4. Chain case
5. Jackshaft

LUBRICATION

The engine is lubricated by oil mixed with the fuel. Use only regular gasoline and a recognized, branded Snowmobile Oil in the ratio of 20:1.

The enclosed drive chain should be covered to a depth of ½-inch using Automatic Transmission Fluid, Type A. Level can be checked, and unit refilled if necessary, after removing lower inspection cover.

Drive train and track carriage are equipped with sealed type, self aligning bearings and do not require lubrication.

ADJUSTMENT

STEERING SKIS. Steering skis should be parallel with each other and with vehicle frame when handle bar is in normal straight driving position. Tie rods are of equal length and tie rod ends are equipped with right hand and left hand threads, so adjustment can be made by turning center section. Adjust each tie rod an equal amount when making adjustments.

DRIVE CHAIN. The enclosed drive chain should not have more than ¼-inch slack measured midway between sprockets, but must not be under tension. Chain deflection can be checked after removing upper inspection cover. If adjustment is required, slightly loosen the four stud nuts securing upper drive shaft housing clamp (2) to chain case (4) and move the housing until all slack is removed.

BRAKE. The caliper type disc brake uses the fixed flange of torque converter driven sheave as a friction face. Brake wear adjustment should be made by removing the cotter pin securing castellated nut to lever arm stud. Tighten nut until resistance is felt, then back off ½-turn and reinstall cotter pin. Make sure brake puck push pins center valleys in actuating arm when lever is released and adjustment is made. Lever arm can be centered by adjusting cable housing anchor.

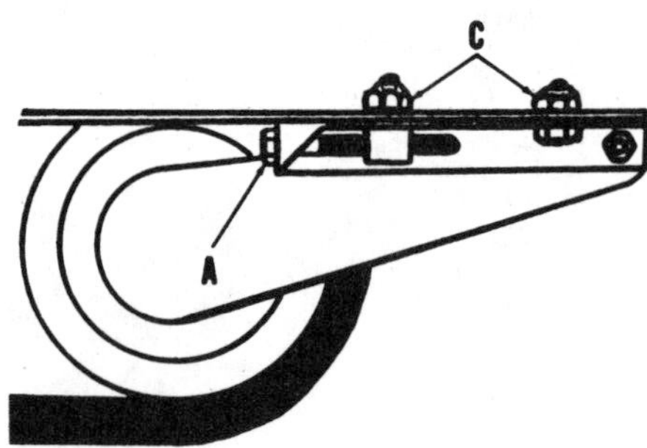

Fig. 2 — To adjust track tension, loosen clamp screws (C) and turn adjustment screw (A) until tension is correct. Both sides must be adjusted alike. Refer to text.

TRACK. With rear of machine raised until clear of ground, track should be just snug beneath center bogie assembly. To adjust track tension, loosen the two clamp nuts (C—Fig. 2) on each side of machine and turn adjusting bolts (B) evenly until tension is correct.

NOTE: Whenever track tension has been adjusted, alignment MUST be checked as outlined in TRACK SERVICE Section of this manual.

OVERHAUL

Refer to the appropriate paragraphs in the GENERAL SERVICE Sections of this manual for overhaul procedures of vehicle components.

POLARIS

1965-1972

Model	Engine Make	Engine Model	Engine Displ.	Carburetor Make	Carburetor Model	Sprocket Ratio	Chain Size	Clutch Make	Clutch Shaft Center	Belt Number
1965										
Lil' Andy	JLO	L152	148cc	Tillotson	HL158AX		40	Salsbury	10¼	900392
Mustang KA80H	Kohler	K181	18.6ci	Carter	N		40	Polaris	10¾	11211
Mustang J90H	JLO	L252	247cc	Tillotson	HL187A		40	Polaris	10¾	11211
Mustang H12H	Hirth	52R	300cc	Tillotson	HL184A		40	Polaris	10¾	11211
1966										
Colt	JLO	L252	247cc	Tillotson	HL211B		40	Polaris	10¾	11211
Mustang 900	JLO	L252	247cc	Tillotson	HL211B		40	Polaris	10¾	11211
Mustang 1000	JLO	L252	247cc	Tillotson	HL211B		40	Polaris	10¾	11211
Mustang 1400	JLO	L372	372cc	Tillotson	HD6A		40	Polaris	10¾	11211
1967										
Colt 80	Kohler	K181	18.6ci	Carter	N	11:38	40	Polaris	10¾	11211
Colt 100	JLO	L252	247cc	Tillotson	HL211B	11:38	40	Polaris	10¾	11211
Colt 130	JLO	L292	292cc	Tillotson	HR2A	11:38	40	Polaris	10¾	11211
Colt 140	Hirth	54R	300cc	Tillotson	HR3A	11:38	40	Polaris	10¾	11211
Colt 150	JLO	L372	372cc	Tillotson	HD6A	13:36	40	Polaris	10¾	11211
Mustang 1300	JLO	L292	292cc	Tillotson	HR2A	11:38	40	Polaris	10¾	11211
Mustang 1400	Hirth	54R	300cc	Tillotson	HR3A	11:38	40	Polaris	10¾	11211
Mustang 1500	JLO	L372	372cc	Tillotson	HD6A	13:36	40	Polaris	10¾	11211
Voyager 2300	JLO	L292	292cc	Tillotson	HR2A	11:38	40	Polaris	10¾	11211
Voyager 2400	Hirth	54R	300cc	Tillotson	HR3A	11:38	40	Polaris	10¾	11211
Voyager 2500	JLO	L372	372cc	Tillotson	HD6A	11:38	40	Polaris	10¾	11211
1968										
Colt 127500	Sachs	SA280A	277cc	Tillotson	HR3B	11:38	40	Polaris	10¾	3211002
Colt 129200	JLO	L292	292cc	Tillotson	HR2A	11:38	40	Polaris	10¾	3211002
Colt 227500	Sachs	SA280A	277cc	Tillotson	HR3B	11:38	40	Polaris	10¾	3211002
Colt 229700	JLO	L297	296cc	Tillotson	HD7A	11:38	40	Polaris	10¾	3211002
Colt 237100	Hirth	160R	372cc	Tillotson	HD7A	13:36	40	Polaris	10¾	3211002
Colt 237200	JLO	L372	373cc	Tillotson	HD7A	13:36	40	Polaris	10¾	3211002
Colt 230000	Wankel	RC18-1	303cc	Tillotson	HD252A	11:38	40	Polaris	10¾	3211002
Mustang 329700	JLO	L297	296cc	Tillotson	HD7A	11:38	40	Polaris	10¾	3211002
Mustang 337100	Hirth	160R	372cc	Tillotson	HD7A	13:36	40	Polaris	10¾	3211002
Mustang 337200	JLO	L372	372cc	Tillotson	HD7A	13:36	40	Polaris	10¾	3211002
Mustang 330000	Wankel	RC18-1	303cc	Tillotson	HL252A	11:38	40	Polaris	10¾	3211002
Voyager 437100	Hirth	160R	372cc	Tillotson	HD7A			Polaris	13½	5-1630
Voyager 437200	JLO	L372	372cc	Tillotson	HD7A			Polaris	13½	5-1630
Voyager 460005	Hirth	160R	600cc	Tillotson	HD7A			Polaris	13½	5-1630
Voyager 459405	JLO	LB600/2	592cc	Tillotson	HD7A			Polaris	13½	5-1630
1969										
Charger 127500	Sachs	SA280A	277cc	Tillotson	HR3B	11:38	40	Polaris	11.1	3211006
Charger 129800	Sachs	SA290	297cc	Tillotson	HR18A	11:38	40	Polaris	11.1	3211006
Charger 130000	JLO	L300	296cc	Tillotson	HD7A	11:38	40	Polaris	11.1	3211006
Charger 131700	Hirth	192R	317cc	Tillotson		11:38	40	Polaris	11.1	3211006
Charger 137200	Polaris		372cc	Mikuni	VM	13:36	40	Polaris	11.1	3211006
Charger 138000	JLO	L380	372cc	Tillotson	HD14A	13:36	40	Polaris	11.1	3211006
Charger 139900	Kohler	K399-2	399cc	Tillotson	HR24A	13:36	40	Polaris	11.1	3211006
Charger 150000	Hirth	220R	493cc	Tillotson	HD14A	13:36	40	Polaris	11.1	3211006
Charger 163400	Hirth	171R	634cc	Tillotson				Polaris	11.1	3211007
Colt 229800	Sachs	SA290	297cc	Tillotson		11:38	40	Polaris	11.1	3211006

	Engine			Carburetor				Clutch		
Model	Make	Model	Displ.	Make	Model	Sprocket Ratio	Chain Size	Make	Shaft Center	Belt Number
1969 Cont.										
Colt 230000 . . .	JLO	L300	296cc	Tillotson		11:38	40	Polaris	11.1	3211006
Colt 230300 . . .	Wankel	RC18-1	303cc	Tillotson	HL252A	11:38	40	Polaris	11.1	3211006
Colt 231700 . . .	Hirth	192R	317cc	Tillotson		11:38	40	Polaris	11.1	3211006
Colt 238000 . . .	JLO	L380	372cc	Tillotson	HD14A	13:36	40	Polaris	11.1	3211006
Colt 239900 . . .	Kohler	K399-2	399cc	Tillotson	HR24A	13:36	40	Polaris	11.1	3211006
Colt 250000 . . .	Hirth	220R	493cc	Tillotson	HD14A	13:36	40	Polaris	11.1	3211006
Colt 263400 . . .	Hirth	171R	634cc	Tillotson				Polaris	11.1	3211007
Mustang 330300	Wankel	RC18-1	303cc	Tillotson	HL252A	11:38	40	Polaris	11.1	3211006
Mustang 338000	JLO	L380	372cc	Tillotson	HD14A	13:36	40	Polaris	11.1	3211006
Mustang 339900	Kohler	K399-2	399cc	Tillotson	HR24A	13:36	40	Polaris	11.1	3211006
Mustang 350000	Hirth	220R	493cc	Tillotson	HD14A	13:36	40	Polaris	11.1	3211006
Mustang 363400	Hirth	171R	634cc	Tillotson				Polaris	11.1	3211007
1970										
Playmate	Husqvarna	SM150	147cc	Tillotson	HL269A	10:42	35-1	Salsbury 770	11.1	3211006
Playmate	Polaris	EC16P	164cc	Mikuni	B21	12:42	35-1	Drummond	11.1	3211006
Playmate	Polaris	EC17P	175cc	Mikuni	B21	12:42	35-1	Drummond	11.1	3211006
Charger	Hirth	56R	292cc	Tillotson	HR	13:39	35-2	Polaris	11.1	3211006
Charger	Sachs	SA290	293cc	Tillotson	HR	13:39	35-2	Polaris	11.1	3211006
Charger	JLO	L340	336cc	Tillotson	HD14A	13:39	35-2	Polaris	11.1	3211006
Charger	JLO	L380	372cc	Tillotson	HD14A	13:39	35-2	Polaris	11.1	3211006
Charger	Polaris	EC40P	398cc	Mikuni	VM30	15:39	35-2	Polaris	11.1	3211006
Charger	Polaris	EC44P	436cc	Mikuni	VM30	15:39	35-2	Polaris	11.1	3211006
Charger	Polaris	EC50P	488cc	Mikuni	VM30	17:39	35-2	Polaris	11.1	3211006
Mustang	Polaris	EC40P	398cc	Mikuni	VM30	13:39	35-2	Polaris	11.1	3211006
Mustang	JLO	LR440/2	433cc	Tillotson	HD14A	13:39	35-2	Polaris	11.1	3211006
Mustang	Polaris	EC50P	488cc	Mikuni	VM30	15:39	35-2	Polaris	11.1	3211006
Voyager	Polaris	EC50P	488cc	Mikuni	VM30	15:39	35-2	Polaris	13¼	5-1630
TX Playmate . .	Sachs	SA290	293cc	Tillotson	HR	15:39	35-2	Polaris	11.1	3211006
TX Playmate . .	Polaris	FAEC29P	294cc	Mikuni	VM26	15:39	35-2	Polaris	11.1	3211006
TX Playmate . .	Polaris	FAEC35P	335cc	Mikuni	VM26	15:39	35-2	Polaris	11.1	3211006
TX Charger . . .	Polaris	FAEC29P	294cc	Mikuni	VM26	13:39	35-2	Polaris	11.1	3211006
TX Charger . . .	Polaris	FAEC35P	335cc	Mikuni	VM26	13:39	35-2	Polaris	11.1	3211006
TX Charger . . .	Polaris	FAEC40P	398cc	Mikuni	VM30	15:39	35-2	Polaris	11.1	3211006
TX Charger . . .	Polaris	FAEC44P	436cc	Mikuni	VM30	15:39	35-2	Polaris	11.1	3211006
TX Charger . . .	Hirth	171R	634cc	Keihin	417	19:39	35-2	Salsbury 910	11.1	3211007
TX Colt.	Hirth	171R	634cc	Keihin	417	19:39	35-2	Salsbury 910	11.1	3211007
1971										
Playmate	Polaris	EC17P	175cc	Mikuni	VM24	12:42	35	Drummond	11.1	3211006
Charger	Polaris	EC29P	294cc	Mikuni	VM26(2)	13:39	35-2	Polaris	11.1	3211006
Charger	Polaris	EC34P	335cc	Mikuni	VM26(2)	13:39	35-2	Polaris	11.1	3211006
Charger	Polaris	EC40P	398cc	Mikuni	VM30(2)	15:39	35-2	Polaris	11.1	3211006
Charger	Polaris	EC44P	432cc	Mikuni	VM30(2)	15:39	35-2	Polaris	11.1	3211006
Charger	Polaris	EC50P	488cc	Mikuni	VM30(2)	17:39	35-2	Polaris	11.1	3211006
Mustang	Polaris	EC40P	398cc	Mikuni	VM30(2)	13:39	35-2	Polaris	11.1	3211006
Mustang	Polaris	EC50P	488cc	Mikuni	VM30(2)	15:39	35-2	Polaris	11.1	3211006
Voyager	Polaris	EC50P	488cc	Mikuni	VM30(2)	13:39	35-2	Polaris	13¼	5-1630
Charger TX . . .	Polaris	EC29PF	294cc	Mikuni	VM26(2)	13:39	35-2	Polaris	11.1	3211006
Charger TX . . .	Polaris	EC34PF	335cc	Mikuni	VM26(2)	13:39	35-2	Polaris	11.1	3211006
Charger TX . . .	Polaris	EC40PF	398cc	Mikuni	VM30(2)	15:39	35-2	Polaris	11.1	3211006
Charger TX . . .	Polaris	EC44PF	432cc	Mikuni	VM30(2)	15:39	35-2	Polaris	11.1	3211006
Charger TX . . .	Polaris	EC65PF	649cc	Tillotson	HD40B(3)	19:39	35-2	Polaris	11.1	3211007
Charger TX . . .	Polaris	EC79PF	795cc	Tillotson	HD40B(3)	21:39	35-2	Polaris	11.1	3211007
1972										
Colt 72C1700 . .	Polaris	EC17P	175cc	Mikuni	VM24	12:35	35-2	Polaris	11.1	3211021
Colt 72C2500 . .	Polaris	EC25P	244cc	Mikuni	VM30	13:35	35-2	Polaris	11.1	3211021
Colt 72C2900 . .	Polaris	EC29P	294cc	Mikuni	VM26(2)	13:35	35-2	Polaris	11.1	3211021
Colt SS	Polaris	EC29PF	294cc	Mikuni	VM26(2)	13:35	35-2	Polaris	11.1	3211021
Charger 7212900	Polaris	EC29P	294cc	Mikuni	VM26(2)	13:39	35-2	Polaris	12.15	3211031
Charger 7214000	Polaris	EC40P	398cc	Mikuni	VM30(2)	15:41	35-2	Polaris	12.15	3211031
Charger 7215400	Polaris	EC54P	530cc	Mikuni	VM32(2)	17:41	35-2	Polaris	12.15	3211031
Mustang 7234000	Polaris	EC40P	398cc	Mikuni	VM30(2)	13:39	35-2	Polaris	11.1	3211021
Mustang	Polaris	EC54PF	530cc	Mikuni	VM32(2)	15:39	35-2	Polaris	11.1	3211021
Charger SS . . .	Polaris	EC40PF	398cc	Mikuni	VM30(2)	15:41	35-2	Polaris	12.15	3211031
Charger SS . . .	Polaris	EC54PF	530cc	Mikuni	VM32(2)	17:41	35-2	Polaris	12.15	3211031
ATX	Polaris	EC34PS	335cc	Mikuni	VM30(2)	13:39	35-2	Polaris	13	3211026
ATX	Polaris	EC51PS	500cc	Mikuni	VM30(3)	17:39	35-2	Polaris	13	3211026

Fig. 1—View of chain housing used on models with die cast housing. Backlash should be ½-inch when measured at sheave rim as shown at (B). Adjust by turning screw (C). Chain case filler plug is at (A), level plug at (D).

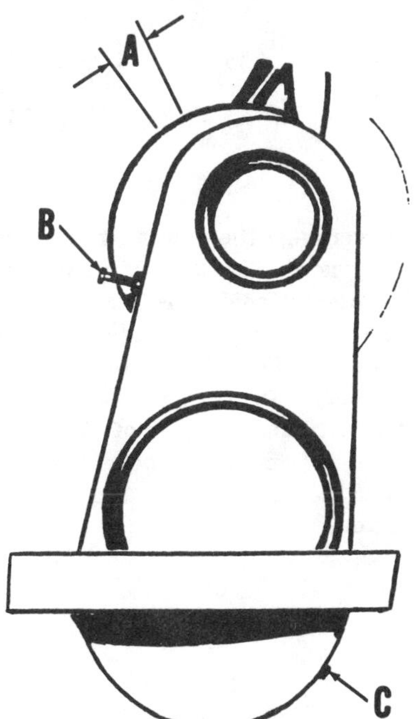

Fig. 2—View of chain housing (early Models) showing points of reference for drive chain adjustment.

A. Backlash (½-inch)
B. Adjusting screw
C. Oil level plug

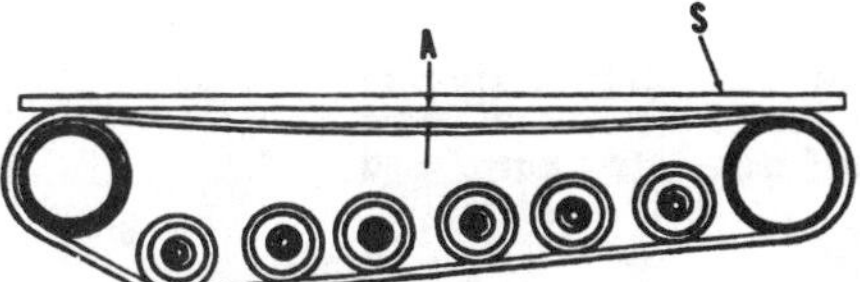

Fig. 3—Using a straight-edge (S) to check track tension. Sag (A) should not exceed ½-inch. Refer to text.

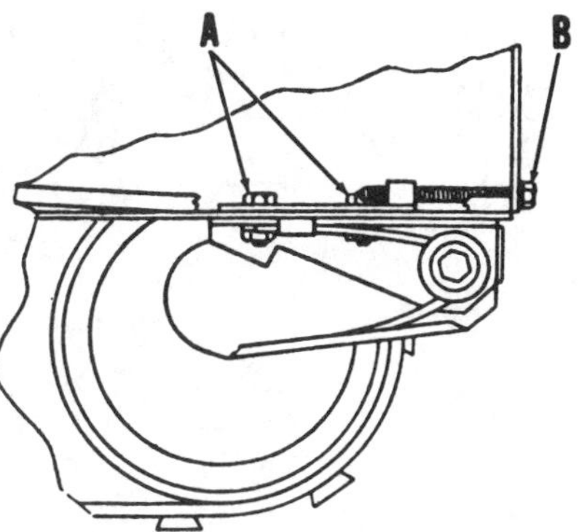

Fig. 4—To adjust track tension on early models, loosen the two clamp screws (A) and turn adjusting screw (B). Refer to Fig. 3 and to text.

LUBRICATION

The drive chain runs in an enclosed chain case which contains oil to the level of inspection plug (D—Fig. 1 or C—Fig. 2). A filler plug is located in top of housing. Recommended lubricant is SAE 10W Motor Oil.

Drive train and track are equipped with self-aligning, sealed type bearings which do not require lubrication.

ADJUSTMENT

STEERING SKIS. Steering skis should be parallel with each other and with vehicle frame when handle bar is in normal straight driving position. To adjust either drag link, it is necessary to disconnect the link at one end.

DRIVE CHAIN. To check the free play of the roller drive chain, refer to Fig. 1 or 2 and proceed as follows. With engine running, rock the torque converter driven sheave back and forth and measure the amount of backlash of intermediate shaft at rim of sheave as shown at (B—Fig. 1 or A—Fig. 2). Backlash should not be more than ½-inch. To make the adjustment, loosen locknut on chain tightener adjusting screw (B) and turn the screw until backlash is correct.

Fig. 5—On late models with bogie suspension system, loosen the three clamp nuts (1) and turn adjusting screw (2) to adjust track tension.

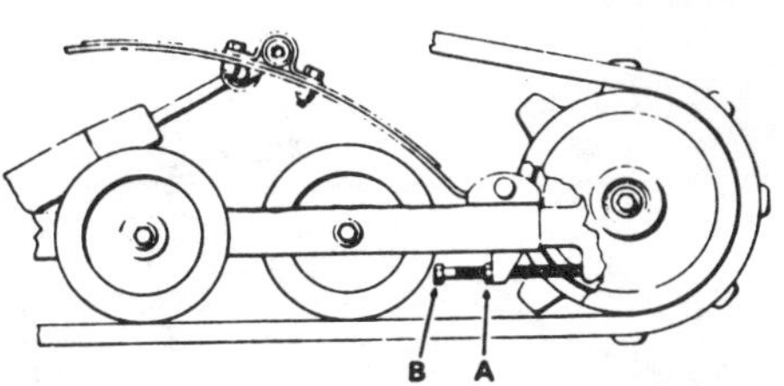

Fig. 6—On models with "Drift Skipper" suspension, adjust track tension by loosening locknuts (A) and turning adjusting screws (B).

BRAKE. The wedge type shoe brake (early models), or band brake (late units), is located between the torque converter driven sheave and final drive chain housing on intermediate shaft. Wear adjustment is made at brake cable anchor. Refer to Fig. 8 or 9 for exploded view. Refer also to BRAKE paragraph in TRACK DRIVE Section of this manual.

TRACK. To check track tension, on early models make sure the vehicle is setting on a level surface and lay a suitable straight-edge over idlers at extreme outer edges of track as shown in Fig. 3. Sag (A) should not exceed ½-inch midway between track axles and should be equal on both sides. To adjust the track, refer to Fig. 4 or 5 and adjust as indicated. Do not operate with track so loose a slapping noise is heard, but track must be loose enough to turn freely.

On "Drift Skipper" models raise rear of machine until track is clear of ground. Free play of track measured at center bogie wheels should be about one inch. To adjust the track, loosen locknuts (A—Fig. 6) on each side and turn adjusting screw (B). Ride adjustment is provided moving from end of suspension link to upper end of suspension link to upper hole for normal operation or lower hole to transfer additional weight to track, which improves trac- but reduces steering effectiveness. (NOTE: Use the two forward holes in bracket only. Bracket is interchangeable on both sides of machine).

On "Power Slide" suspension raise rear of machine or tip machine on side. Attach spring scale to side of

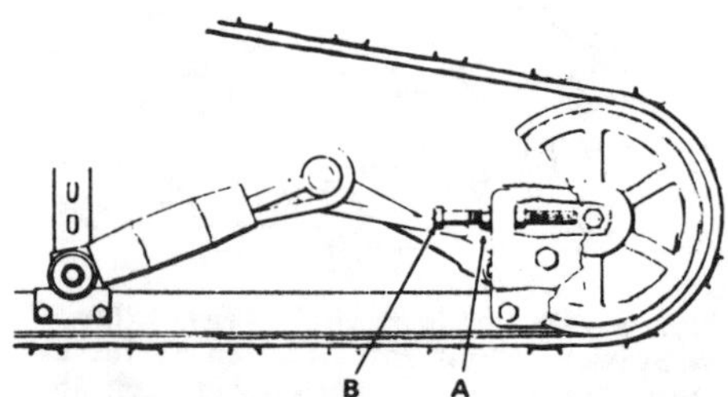

Fig. 7—On TX Models with "Power Slide" suspension, loosen locknuts (A) and turn adjusting screws (B) to adjust track tension.

track midway of slide. With 15 pounds pull, track should clear slide rail by about one inch. Adjust by loosening locknut (A—Fig. 7) and turning adjusting screw (B). Both sides of track must be adjusted alike. A firmer ride can be obtained by hooking front end of suspension spring in upper hooks on slide frame.

NOTE: When track tension has been adjusted, alignment MUST be checked as outlined in TRACK SERVICE Section of this manual.

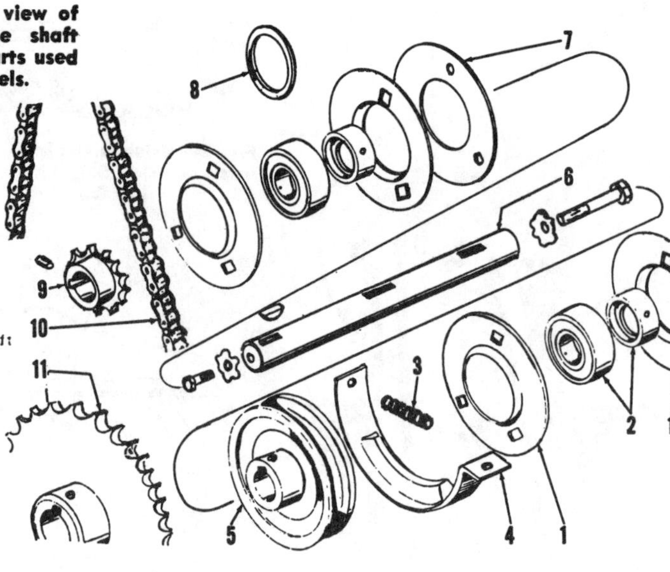

Fig. 8—Exploded view of intermediate drive shaft and associated parts used on early models.

1. Flange
2. Bearing
3. Return spring
4. Brake band
5. Brake pulley
6. Intermediate shaft
7. Gasket
8. Gasket
9. Drive sprocket
10. Drive chain
11. Driven sprocket

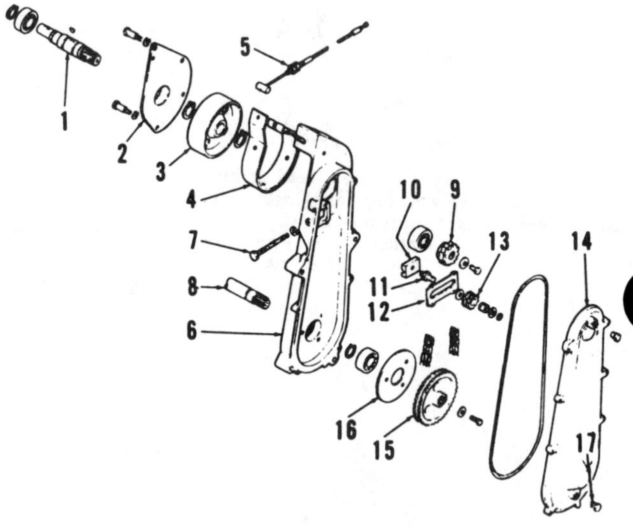

Fig. 9—Exploded view of diecast chain housing, drum type brake and associated parts used on most late models.

1. Intermediate shaft
2. Rear cover
3. Brake drum
4. Brake band
5. Brake cable
6. Chaincase
7. Adjusting screw
8. Drive axle
9. Drive sprocket
10. Idler slide
12. Retainer plate
13. Idler sprocket
14. Cover
15. Driven sprocket
16. Retainer plate

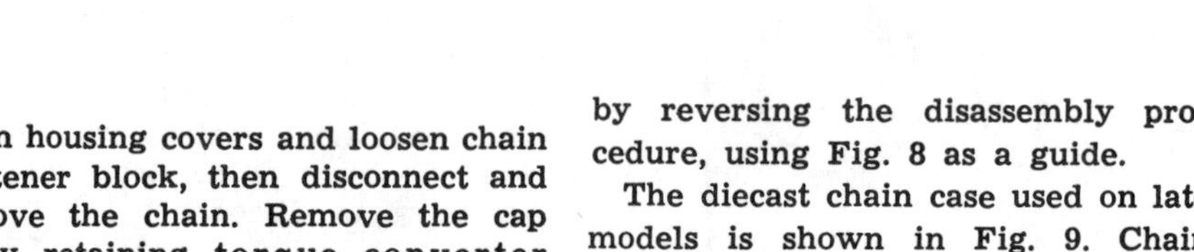

OVERHAUL

SKIS & STEERING. Ski legs (spindles), skis and associated parts are interchangeable from right to left. Skis are equipped with renewable runners which are retained to skis with one nut on a center stud. Runner (skag) can be installed either end forward.

CHAIN HOUSING. The chain housing on early models is part of the vehicle main frame. The intermediate shaft (6—Fig. 8) is carried on two sealed bearings (2) housed in the chain case and contains the drive sprocket (9) and brake pulley (5) in addition to the torque converter driven sheave. Pulley (5) and sprocket (9) are keyed to shaft and retained by set screws. Bearings (2) are retained by locking collars. To remove shaft and/or bearings, first remove chain housing covers and loosen chain tightener block, then disconnect and remove the chain. Remove the cap screw retaining torque converter driven sheave, loosen the set screws retaining brake pulley and bearing locking collars; then unlock the collars. Tap the shaft toward outside of vehicle, removing Woodruff keys as they clear sheave bores. Assemble by reversing the disassembly procedure, using Fig. 8 as a guide.

The diecast chain case used on late models is shown in Fig. 9. Chain tightener slide (10) is retained by plate (12). Drive sprocket (9) is available in size options of 13, 15, 17, 19 and 21 teeth. Sprocket can be matched to engine size and type of operation.

POLARIS

POLARIS INDUSTRIES INC.
1225 N. County Road 18
Minneapolis, MN 55441

1973-1986

CONDENSED SERVICE DATA

	Engine			Carburetor				Clutch		
Model	Make	Model	Displ.	Make	Model	Sprocket Ratio	Chain Size	Make	Shaft Center	Belt Number
					1973					
Colt 175	Polaris	EC17P	175cc	Mikuni	VM24	12:35	35-2	Polaris	11.1	3211021
Colt 250	Polaris	EC25P	244cc	Mikuni	VM30	13:35	35-2	Polaris	11.1	3211021
Colt 295	Polaris	EC29P	294cc	Mikuni	VM26(2)	13:35	35-2	Polaris	11.1	3211021
Colt SS 295	Polaris		294cc							
Colt SS 340	Polaris		335cc							
Charger 295	Polaris	EC29P	294cc	Mikuni	VM26(2)	13:39	35-2	Polaris	12.15	3211031
Charger 400	Polaris	EC40P	398cc	Mikuni	VM30(2)	15:41	35-2	Polaris	12.15	3211031
Charger 530	Polaris	EC54P	530cc	Mikuni	VM32(2)	17:41	35-2	Polaris	12.15	3211031
Mustang 400	Polaris	EC40P	398cc	Mikuni	VM30(2)	13:39	35-2	Polaris	11.1	3211021
Mustang 530	Polaris	EC54P	530cc	Mikuni	VM32(2)	15:39	35-2	Polaris	11.1	3211021
					1974					
Colt 175	Polaris	EC17PM	175cc	Mikuni	VM24	12:35	35-2	Polaris	11.1	3211021
Colt 250	Polaris	EC25PS	244cc	Mikuni	VM30	13:35	35-2	Polaris	11.1	3211021
Colt 295	Polaris	EC29PF	294cc	Mikuni	VM26(2)	13:35	35-2	Polaris	11.1	3211021
Colt SS 250	Polaris	EC25PC	250cc	Mikuni	VM26(2)	13:35	35-2	Polaris	11.1	3211021
Colt SS 336	Polaris	EC34PC	335cc	Mikuni	VM26(2)	15:35	35-2	Polaris	11.1	3211021
Custom II 250	Polaris	EC25PS	244cc	Mikuni	VM30	13:39	35-2	Polaris	12.15	3211031
Custom II 398	Polaris	EC40PM	398cc	Mikuni	VM30(2)	15:39	35-2	Polaris	12.15	3211031
Custom II 530	Polaris	EC54PM	530cc	Mikuni	VM32(2)	17:39	35-2	Polaris	12.15	3211031
Electra 340	Polaris	EC34PQ	336cc	Mikuni	VM32	13:39	35-2	Polaris	12.15	3211031
Electra 432	Polaris	EC44PQ	432cc	Mikuni	VM38	15:39	35-2	Polaris	12.15	3211031
TC175	Polaris	EC17PM	175cc	Mikuni	VM24	14:39	35-2	Polaris	9.5	3211039
TC250	Polaris	EC25PS	244cc	Tillotson	HR163A	14:39	35-2	Polaris	9.5	3211039
TX250	Polaris	EC25PT	250cc	Mikuni	VM30(2)	13:39	35-2	Polaris	13	3211028
TX340	Polaris	EC34PS	335cc	Mikuni	VM30SC(2)	15:39	35-2	Polaris	13	3211028
TX440	Polaris	EC44PT	432cc	Mikuni	VM38SC(2)	17:39	35-2	Polaris	13	3211028
TX500	Polaris	EC51PT	500cc	Mikuni	VM32SC(2)	19:39	35-2	Polaris	13	3211028
					1975					
TC175	Polaris	EC17PM	175cc	Mikuni	VM24SH	14:39	35-2	Polaris	9.5	3211039
TC244	Polaris	EC25PS	244cc	Mikuni	VM30SH	14:39	35-2	Polaris	9.5	3211039
Colt 250	Polaris	EC25PC	250cc	Mikuni	VM26SC(2)	15:35	35-2	Polaris	11.1	3211021
Colt 340	Polaris	EC34PC	336cc	Mikuni	VM26SC(2)	15:35	35-2	Polaris	11.1	3211021
Colt SS 250	Polaris	EC25PC	250cc	Mikuni	VM26SC(2)	15:35	35-2	Polaris	11.1	3211021
Colt SS 340	Polaris	EC34PC	336cc	Mikuni	VM26SC(2)	15:35	35-2	Polaris	11.1	3211021
Electra 250	Polaris	EC25PS	244cc	Mikuni	VM30SH	13:39	35-2	Polaris	12.15	3211031
Electra 340	Polaris	EC34PQ	336cc	Mikuni	VM30SC(2)	15:39	35-2	Polaris	12.15	3211031
Electra 440	Polaris	EC44PQ	439cc	Mikuni	VM30SC(2)	17:39	35-2	Polaris	12.15	3211031
TX250	Polaris	EC25PT	250cc	Mikuni	VM30SC(2)	13:39	35-2	Polaris	13	3211028
TX340	Polaris	EC34PT	335cc	Mikuni	VM32SC(2)	15:39	35-2	Polaris	13	3211028
TX440	Polaris	EC44PT	432cc	Mikuni	VM38SC(2)	17:39	35-2	Polaris	13	3211028
TX500	Polaris	EC51PT	500cc	Mikuni	VM32SC(3)	19:39	35-2	Polaris	13	3211028
					1976					
Colt 175	Star	EC17PM	175cc	Mikuni	VM24SH	12:35	35-2	Polaris	11.1	3211021
Colt 250	Star	EC25PS	244cc	Mikuni	VM30SH	13:35	35-2	Polaris	11.1	3211021
Colt 250	Star	EC25PC	250cc	Mikuni	VM26SC	15:35	35-2	Polaris	11.1	3211021
Colt 340	Star	EC34PC	336cc	Mikuni	VM26SC	15:35	35-2	Polaris	11.1	3211021
Colt SS 250	Star	EC25PC	250cc	Mikuni	VM26SC	15:35	35-2	Polaris	11.1	3211021
Colt SS 340	Star	EC34PC	336cc	Mikuni	VM26SC	15:35	35-2	Polaris	11.1	3211021
Electra 250	Star	EC25PS	244cc	Mikuni	VM30SH	13:39	35-2	Polaris	12.1	3211031
Electra 340	Star	EC34PQ	339cc	Mikuni	VM30SC	15:39	35-2	Polaris	12.1	3211031
Electra 440	Star	EC44PQ	433cc	Mikuni	VM30SC	17:39	35-2	Polaris	12.1	3211031
TX250	Star	EC25PT-06	250cc	Mikuni	VM32SC	14:39	Silent	Polaris	12.0	3211042
TX340	Star	EC34PT-05	336cc	Mikuni	VM32SC	17:39	Silent	Polaris	12.0	3211042
TX440	Star	EC44PT-05	433cc	Mikuni	VM34SC	19:39	Silent	Polaris	12.0	3211042
250 Starfire	Star	EC25PT-05	250cc	Mikuni	VM32SC	14:39	Silent	Polaris	12.0	3211042
340 Starfire	Star	EC34PT-06	336cc	Mikuni	VM34SC	15:39	Silent	Polaris	12.0	3211042

Engine				Carburetor				Clutch		
Model	Make	Model	Displ.	Make	Model	Sprocket Ratio	Chain Size	Make	Shaft Center	Belt Number
					1977					
Colt 244	Star	EC25PS	244cc	Mikuni	VM30SH	13:35	35-2	Polaris	11.1	3211021
Colt 250	Star	EC25PC	250cc	Mikuni	VM26SS	15:35	35-2	Polaris	11.1	3211021
Colt SS 250	Star	EC25PM-01	244cc	Mikuni	VM26SS(2)	15:35	35-2	Polaris	11.1	3211021
Colt SS 340	Star	EC34PM-03	333cc	Mikuni	VM26SS(2)	17:35	35-2	Polaris	11.1	3211021
Electra 250	Star	EC25PS	244cc	Mikuni	VM30SH	13:39	35-2	Polaris	12.1	3211031
Electra 340	Star	EC34PQ	339cc	Mikuni	VM30SS	15:39	35-2	Polaris	12.1	3211031
Electra 440	Star	EC44PQ	339cc	Mikuni	VM30SS	17:39	35-2	Polaris	12.1	3211031
TX250	Star	EC25PT-07	249cc	Mikuni	VM30SS	15:39	Silent	Polaris	12.0	3211042
TX340	Star	EC34PT-05	336cc	Mikuni	VM32SS	17:39	Silent	Polaris	12.0	3211042
TX440	Star	EC44PT-05	433cc	Mikuni	VM34SS	19:39	Silent	Polaris	12.0	3211042
TX340	Star	EC34PL-01	333cc	Mikuni	VM38SS	19:39	Silent	Polaris	12.0	3211042
					1978					
Colt 244	Star	EC25PS	244cc	Mikuni	VM30SH	13:35	35-2	Polaris	11.1	3211021
Colt 250	Star	EC25PC	250cc	Mikuni	VM26SS	15:35	Silent	Polaris	11.1	3211021
S/S 340	Star	EC34PM-03/04N	333cc	Mikuni	VM26SS	15:35	Silent	Polaris	11.1	3211021
Cobra 340	Star	EC34PM-04	333cc	Mikuni	VM26SS(2)	15:35	Silent	Polaris	12.0	3211042
Cobra 440	Star	EC44PM-01	432cc	Mikuni	VM34SS(2)	17:33	Silent	Polaris	12.0	3211042
TX250	Star	EC25PT-07	249cc	Mikuni	VM30SS	15:39	Silent	Polaris	12.0	3211042
TX340	Star	EC34PT-05	336cc	Mikuni	VM32SS	17:39	Silent	Polaris	12.0	3211042
TX440	Star	EC44PT-05	432cc	Mikuni	VM34SS	19:39	Silent	Polaris	12.0	3211042
TX-L340	Star	EC34PL-02	333cc	Mikuni	VM38SS	19:39	Silent	Polaris	12.0	3211042
					1979					
Gemini	Fuji	EC25PS	244cc	Mikuni	VM30SH	13:35	35-2	Polaris	11.1	3211021
Gemini	Fuji	EC25PM-01	244cc	Mikuni	VM26SS	15:35	Silent	Polaris	11.1	3211021
Apollo	Fuji	EC34PM-03	333cc	Mikuni	VM26SS	18:35	Silent	Polaris	11.1	3211021
Cobra	Fuji	EC34PM-04	333cc	Mikuni	VM26SS	15:35	Silent	Polaris	12.0	3211042
Cobra	Fuji	EC44PM-01	432cc	Mikuni	VM34SS	17:33	Silent	Polaris	12.0	3211042
TX	Fuji	EC25PT-07	249cc	Mikuni	VM30SS	15:39	Silent	Polaris	12.0	3211042
TX	Fuji	EC34PT-05	336cc	Mikuni	VM32SS	17:39	Silent	Polaris	12.0	3211042
TX	Fuji	EC44-PT-05	432cc	Mikuni	VM34SS	19:39	Silent	Polaris	12.0	3211042
TX-L	Fuji	EC34PL-02	333cc	Mikuni	VM38SS	19:39	Silent	Polaris	12.0	3211042
Centurion	Fuji	EC51PL-01	500cc	Mikuni	VM34SS	19:35	Silent	Polaris	12.0	3211042
					1980					
Gemini	Fuji	EC25PS	244cc	Mikuni	VM30SS	13:35	35-2	Polaris	11.1	3211021
Gemini	Fuji	EC25PM-01	244cc	Mikuni	VM26SS	15:35	Silent	Polaris	11.1	3211021
Apollo	Fuji	EC34PM-03	333cc	Mikuni	VM26SS	18:35	Silent	Polaris	11.1	3211044
Galaxy	Fuji	EC34PM-01	333cc	Mikuni	VM26SS	15:35	Silent	Polaris	12.0	3211042
Galaxy	Fuji	EC44PM-01	432cc	Mikuni	VM34SS	17:33	Silent	Polaris	12.0	3211042
TX	Fuji	EC34PT-07	336cc	Mikuni	VM32SS	17:39	Silent	Polaris	12.0	3211042
TX	Fuji	EC44PT-05	432cc	Mikuni	VM34SS	19:39	Silent	Polaris	12.0	3211042
TX-C	Fuji	EC34PT-07	336cc	Mikuni	VM32SS	17:39	Silent	Polaris	12.0	3211042
TL-L	Fuji	EC34PL-02	333cc	Mikuni	VM38SS	19:39	Silent	Polaris	12.0	3211042
Centurion	Fuji	EC51PL-02	500cc	Mikuni	VM34SS	19:35	Silent	Polaris	12.0	3211042
TX-L Indy	Fuji	EC34PL-05	333cc	Mikuni	VM38SS	19:39	Silent	Polaris	12.0	3211042
					1981					
Gemini	Fuji	EC25PS	244cc	Mikuni	VM30SS	13:35	35-2	Polaris	11.1	3211021
Galaxy	Fuji	EC44PM-02	432cc	Mikuni	VM34SS	17:33	Silent	Polaris	12.0	3211042
Cutlass	Fuji	EC34PM-03	333cc	Mikuni	VM26SS			Polaris	11.5	3211043
Cutlass SS	Fuji	EC44-2PM-3100	432cc	Mikuni	VM38SS			Polaris	11.5	3211043
TX-C	Fuji	EC44-2PM-1100	432cc	Mikuni	VM34SS	19:35	Silent	Polaris	11.1	3211044
TX-L	Fuji	EC34PL-05	333cc	Mikuni	VM38SS	19:39	Silent	Polaris	12.0	3211042
TX-L Indy	Fuji	EC34PL-05	333cc	Mikuni	VM38SS	19:39	Silent	Polairs	12.0	3211042
Centurion Indy	Fuji	EC51PL-02	500cc	Mikuni	VM34SS	19:35	Silent	Polaris	12.0	3211042
					1982					
Cutlass SS	Fuji	EC44-2PM-3100	432cc	Mikuni				Polaris	11.5	3211046
TX-C	Fuji	EC44-2PM-1100	432cc	Mikuni	VM34SS	19:35	Silent	Polaris	11.1	3211044
TX-L	Fuji	EC34PL-05	333cc	Mikuni	VM38SS	19:39	Silent	Polaris	12.0	3211042
TX-L Indy	Fuji	EC34PL-05	333cc	Mikuni	VM38SS	19:39	Silent	Polaris	12.0	3211042
Centurion Indy	Fuji	EC51PL-02	500cc	Mikuni	VM34SS	19:35	Silent	Polaris	12.0	3211042
					1983					
Gemini	Fuji	EC25PS	244cc	Mikuni	VM30SS	13:35	35-2	Polaris	11.1	3211021
Star	Fuji	EC25PS	244cc	Mikuni	VM30SS			Polaris	12.0	3211042
Sport	Fuji	EC44-2PM-5100	432cc	Mikuni	VM30SS			Polaris	11.5	3211046
SS	Fuji	EC44-2PM-3100	432cc	Mikuni	VM34SS			Polaris	11.5	3211046
IndyTrail	Fuji	EC44-2PM-2100	432cc	Mikuni	VM34SS	19:35	Silent	Polaris	12.0	3211042
Cross Country	Fuji	EC34PL-05	333cc	Mikuni	VM38SS	19:39	Silent	Polaris	12.0	3211042
Indy 600	Fuji	EC60PL-01	597cc	Mikuni	VM38SS	25:35	Silent	Polaris	12.0	3211042
Long Track	Fuji	EC44-2PM-5000	432cc	Mikuni	VM30SS	19:39	Silent	Polaris	12.0	3211042

	Engine			Carburetor				Clutch		
Model	Make	Model	Displ.	Make	Model	Sprocket Ratio	Chain Size	Make	Shaft Center	Belt Number
1984										
Star	Fuji	EC25PS	244cc	Mikuni	VM30SS			Polaris	12.0	3211042
SS	Fuji	EC44-2PM-3100	432cc	Mikuni	VM34SS			Polaris	11.5	3211046
Indy Trail	Fuji	EC44-2PM-2100	432cc	Mikuni	VM34SS	19:35	Silent	Polaris	12.0	3211042
Indy 600	Fuji	EC60PL-02	597cc	Mikuni	VM38SS	19:35	Silent	Polaris	12.0	3211042
Long Track	Fuji	EC44-2PM-5000	432cc	Mikuni	VM30SS	19:39	Silent	Polaris	12.0	3211042
Long Track	Fuji	EC25PS-05	244cc	Mikuni	VM30SS	16:39	Silent	Polaris	12.0	3211042
1985										
Star	Fuji	EC25PS-06	244cc	Mikuni	VM30SS			Polaris	12.0	3211042
SS	Fuji	EC44-2PM-3100	432cc	Mikuni	VM34SS			Polaris	11.5	3211046
Indy Trail	Fuji	EC44-2PM-2100	432cc	Mikuni	VM34SS	19:35	Silent	Polaris	12.0	3211042
Indy 400	Fuji	EC40PL-02	398cc	Mikuni	VM34SS	19:35	Silent	Polaris	12.0	3211042
Indy 600	Fuji	EC60PL-02	597cc	Mikuni	VM38SS	19:35	Silent	Polaris	12.0	3211042
Long Track	Fuji	EC44-2PM-5000	432cc	Mikuni	VM30SS	19:39	Silent	Polaris	12.0	3211042
1986										
Star	Fuji	EC25PS-06	244cc	Mikuni	VM30SS			Polaris	12.0	3211042
Sprint	Fuji	EC34-2PM-01	339cc	Mikuni	VM30SS			Polaris	12.0	3211042
SS	Fuji	EC44-2PM-3100	432cc	Mikuni	VM34SS			Polaris	11.5	3211046
Indy Trail	Fuji	EC50-PM-01	488cc	Mikuni	VM34SS	21:35	Silent	Polaris	12.0	3211042
Indy 400	Fuji	EC40PL-02	398cc	Mikuni	VM34SS	19:35	Silent	Polaris	12.0	3211042
Indy 600	Fuji	EC60PL-02	597cc	Mikuni	VM38SS	21:35	Silent	Polaris	12.0	3211042
Long Track	Fuji	EC44-2PM-5100	432cc	Mikuni	VM30SS	19:39	Silent	Polaris	12.0	3211042

LUBRICATION

Polaris snowmobile engines are lubricated by either an oil injection pump or a fuel premixture of oil and gasoline. Recommended oils are Polaris Injection Oil on oil injected models and Polaris Snowmobile Oil on premixture models. Recommended fuel grade is regular leaded or premium unleaded gasoline.

New or overhauled engines require additional lubrication during break-in. On oil injected models, the first tank of fuel must contain a 40:1 fuel:oil premixture in conjunction with oil injection to ensure adequate lubricaton. On premixture models, increase fuel:oil ratio to 20:1 for the first tank of fuel. After break-in, recommended fuel:oil ratio for normal operation is 40:1 on all premixture models.

Mix fuel and oil thoroughly in a separate container before pouring mixture into fuel tank. Fuel should preferably be mixed at normal room temperature. For outdoor mixing at cold temperatures, mix the oil with a small amount of gasoline until oil is fluid, then add remainder of fuel and remix. **DO NOT** use kerosene or diesel fuel as a blending agent.

The enclosed chaincase should be kept filled to level of check plug with Polaris Chaincase Lubricant.

NOTE: SAE 10W motor oil may be substituted for models with ROLLER chain only.

TC models are equipped with an open drive chain. Lubricate the chain about once a week or after driving in wet (sloppy) snow with a foam-type motorcycle chain cleaner/lubricant. Remove chain during periods of storage and submerge in a good rust-preventive oil. DO NOT overlubricate, causing excess lubricant to be thrown on brake or drive belt.

Drive train and track are equipped with self-aligning sealed type bearings which do not require lubrication.

ADJUSTMENT

STEERING SKIS. Steering skis should be parallel with each other and with vehicle frame when handlebar is in normal straight driving position. Adjustment is made by turning rod after loosening locknuts.

Fig. 1 — Steering stop bolt (S) should be adjusted to prevent steering overtravel and permit equal movement in each direction.

Early models are equipped with steering stop bolts (S – Fig. 1) which should be adjusted to prevent steering overtravel and provide equal steering in both directions. Late models have an adjustable steering stop (S – Fig. 2). Turn handlebar in either direction until clearance (C) between end of steering arm and nearest part of nosepan equals ½-inch (12.7 mm), then adjust OPPOSITE stop (S) until it touches steering arm. Both stops must be adjusted alike.

On models with independent front suspension, toe and camber must be adjusted correctly to ensure optimum handling. To check settings, raise ma-

Fig. 2 — Steering stop (S) on OPPOSITE side should contact steering arm when clearance (C) between steering arm and nosepan equals ½ inch (12.7 mm).

chine off floor 1 to 2 inches (25.4-50.8 mm). Remove skis, pivot bushings and disconnect torsion bar linkage. Using alignment bar, slide bar through one of the spindles and into the opposite spindle. Bar should slide through opposite spindle with very low resistance. If bar does not slide through spindle easily check the following settings: Distance from chassis center to spindles should be equal to or within 1/8-inch (3.1 mm). Refer to Fig. 3. Spindle-to-spindle center distance should be 36½ inches (927 mm) or within 1/8-inch (3.1 mm). Refer to Fig. 4. If measurements are not within specifications then adjust radius rod length accordingly.

To adjust toe loosen tie rod sleeve lock nuts, then turn sleeve as needed to allow alignment bar to slide through spindles without dragging.

Camber setting should be true vertical or zero degree position. To adjust camber loosen lower radius rod jam nut, then remove radius rod cap screw. Adjust radius rod length to obtain correct setting. Be sure alignment bar slides easily through spindles.

To center handlebars, install alignment bar through spindles. Loosen jam nuts on drag link, then adjust drag link length until handlebar is centered.

Reassemble steering linkage and suspension in reverse of disassembly. Tighten radius rod cap screws to 25 ft. lbs., (33.9 N·m), torsion bar linkage to 15 ft. lbs. (20.3 N·m) and pivot bushing bolts to 25 ft. lbs. (33.9 N·m).

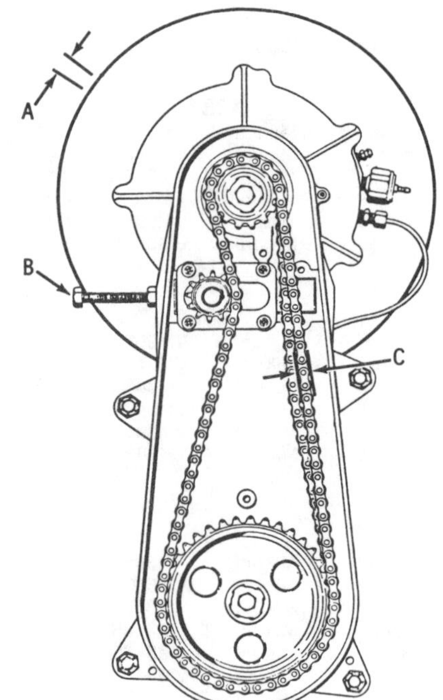

Fig. 5 — View of left-hand chaincase showing points of adjustment.

A. Backlash
B. Adjusting screw
C. Deflection

DRIVE CHAIN. To check free play of roller drive chain, refer to Fig. 5 and proceed as follows: With engine not running, rock the torque converter driven sheave and measure the backlash (A) measured at sheave rim. Slight backlash should exist but total movement should not exceed ½-inch (12.7 mm). To adjust chain, it is recommended that chaincase cover be removed. Loosen locknut and turn adjusting screw (B) until chain deflection (C) is approximately 3/8-inch (9.5 mm), with all slack pulled to rear chain flight. Reinstall cover and refill chaincase to level of check plug hole with Polaris Chaincase Oil or SAE 10W Motor Oil. On models with silent chain, adjustment and adjusting method is identical to that outlined for roller chain units.

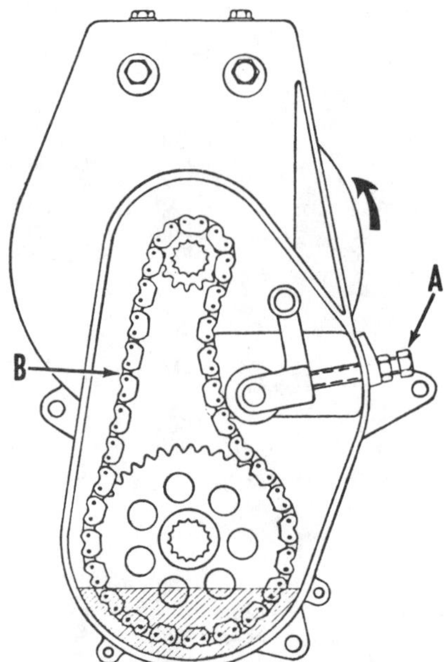

Fig. 6 — On right-hand mounted chaincase, chain deflection at (B) should equal ¼ to 3/8 inch (6.3-9.5 mm). Adjust at (A) after removing chaincase cover.

On models with right-hand mounted chaincase, remove chaincase cover and refer to Fig. 6. Apply slight tension to

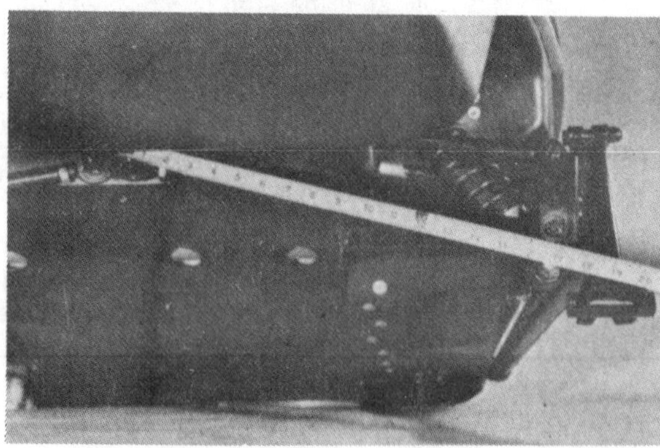

Fig. 3 — View showing procedure for checking distance from chassis center to spindles.

Fig. 4 — View showing procedure for checking spindle-to-spindle center distance.

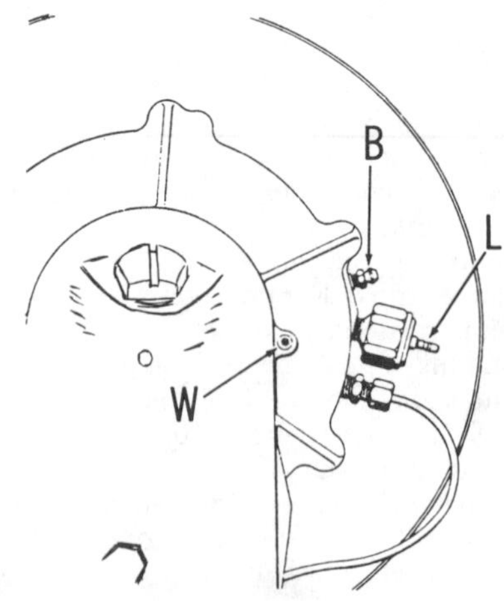

Fig. 7 — Brake wear adjustment is accomplished by turning screw (W) in until brake is locked, then backing screw out ¼ turn. Bleed screw is at (B) and brake light switch at (L).

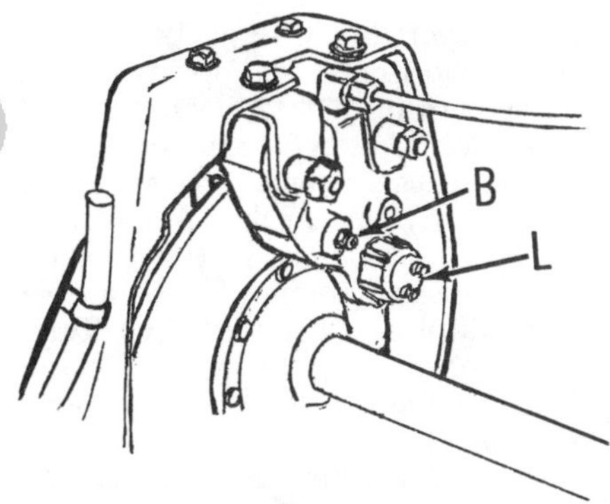

Fig. 8—On right-hand mounted chaincase, hydraulic brake is self-adjusting. Bleed screw is at (B), light switch at (L).

idler side of chain by turning cross shaft in direction indicated by arrow and measure chain deflection at (B). Deflection should be 1/4 to 3/8-inch (6.3-9.5 mm). Adjust by loosening locknut and turning idler adjusting screw (A) until deflection is correct. Reinstall chaincase cover and add 3 oz. (88.7 mL) of Polaris Chaincase Lubricant through fill plug hole in cover.

TC models with open drive chain are equipped with a rub block type automatic chain tensioner and adjustment is not required.

BRAKES. Types one, two and three brake assemblies are equipped with a manual hydraulic disc brake built into chaincase housing and actuated by a master cylinder mounted on handlebar. Type four, five and TC models are cable operated.

Brake wear adjustment on type one models with left-hand chaincase is accomplished by turning wear adjustment screw (W–Fig. 7) in (clockwise) until brake is locked; then backing screw out 1/4 turn. Brake should be free when released, but solidly apply with minimum lever movement.

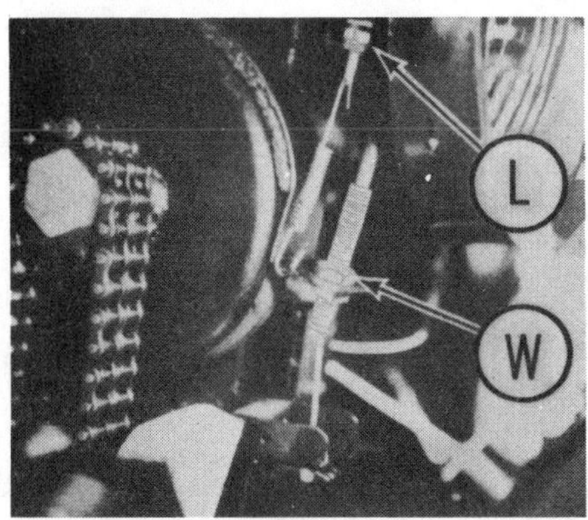

Fig. 9—On TC series, band type mechanical brake is adjusted by turning cable anchor nuts (W). Brake light switch anchor (L) can be adjusted if necessary.

Type two models with right-hand mounted chaincase are similar to type one except for location of brake caliper unit (see Fig. 8) and absence of wear adjustment screw which is not used, brakes are self-adjusting. It is important however, to check fluid reservoir level periodically as fluid level drops as brake linings wear.

Type three model (see Fig. 16A) is used on 1979-current TX, TX-C, TX-L, Centurion, TX-L Indy and Centurion Indy models. There is no wear adjustment screw as brakes are self-adjusting.

Type four model (see Fig. 24) is used on 1981 Cutlass and 1981-current Cutlass SS and type five (see Fig. 25) is used on 1983-1986 Long Track Models. Brake pads are applied using an actuating lever that is operated by a brake cable. Brake should be adjusted to where there is a slight drag on a 0.015-inch (0.38 mm) feeler gage when slid between brake disc and brake pad. To adjust, bend lock tab (12–Fig. 24) away from jam nut (13) and loosen nut. Turn adjusting bolt (15) in or out to obtain proper clearance. Tighten jam nut and bend lock tab back to original position. Recheck clearance and check for proper application and release of brake pads.

On TC models with mechanical band-type brake, wear adjustment is made at cable housing anchor nuts (W–Fig. 9). Tighten adjustment until a slight drag exists with brake released, then loosen until drag just disappears and band is free. Adjust brake light switch anchor (L) if necessary. Light should come on when brake is applied but go off when hand lever is released.

Master cylinder reservoir should be kept filled to within 1/8-inch (3.1 mm) of top of reservoir with Polaris silicone brake fluid or Motor Vehicle brake fluid. To bleed brakes, slip a bleeder hose on fitting (B–Fig. 8) and place other end of hose in a clean container. Depress brake lever and open, then close bleeder valve. Repeat the operation until a solid stream of fluid with no evidence of air bubbles emerges from bleeder hose. Keep master cylinder full at all times.

NOTE: Do not spill or splash brake fluid on painted surfaces or paint may be damaged. Refill reservoir to proper level after bleeding operation is completed.

TRACK AND SUSPENSION. There are three different models of suspensions used, they are: Glass rail; Stamped Steel (Types I, II, III); Extruded Aluminum (Types I through XV). Refer to the table shown below for suspension application.

SUSPENSION MODELS	APPLICATION MODELS
Glass Rail	1972 TX; 1972-1973 Charger, Charger SS, Mustang and Custom
Stamped Steel Type I	1972-1978 Colt; 1972-1977 Colt SS Shock Accessory on Some Models
Stamped Steel Type II (E Slot)	1973-1974 TX; 1974 Custom II; 1975 TX with Rear Spring Tensioner; 1974-1977 Electra
Stamped Steel Type III (Front Limiter Strap and Rear Spring Tensioner)	1978 S/S 340 Cobra (Has Pivoting Front Limiter); 1979 Cobra; 1979-1980 Apollo; 1979-1981 Gemini
Extruded Aluminum Type I	1976 Starfire; 1976-1979 TX
Extruded Aluminum Type II	1977-1978 TX-L
Extruded Aluminum Type III	1979 TX-C, TX-L and Centurion
Extruded Aluminum Type IV	1980 Galaxy and TX (Cleated Track)
Extruded Aluminum Type V	1980-1981 Galaxy (Rubber Track)
Extruded Aluminum Type VI	1980 Centurion; 1980-1982 TX-C and TX-L
Extruded Aluminum Type VII	1980-1983 Indy Models
Extruded Aluminum Type VIII	1981 Cutlass; 1981-1982 Cutlass SS; 1983 Gemini and Sport; 1983-1984 SS; 1983-1985 Star

SUSPENSION MODELS	APPLICATION MODELS
Extruded Aluminum Type IX	1983-1984 Long Track Models
Extruded Aluminum Type X	1984 Indy Models
Extruded Aluminum Type XI	1985 Indy Models
Extruded Aluminum Type XII	1985 SS
Extruded Aluminum Type XIII	1986 Star and Sprint
Extruded Aluminum Type XIV	1986 SS
Extruded Aluminum Type XV	1986 Indy Models

Track tension on all models except 1983-1984 Long Track models is checked by suspending a 10 lb. (4.5 kg) weight approximately 16 inches (406.4 mm) from center of rear idler wheel; as shown in Fig. 10. Track tension specification is shown in table below.

TRACK TENSION

MODEL
1972 TX; 1972-1973 Charger, Charger SS, Mustang and Custom; 1976 Starfire; 1976-1980 TX and 1980 Galaxy.

TOLERANCE (With a 10 lb. [4.5 kg] Weight)
½ inch (12.7 mm) between cleat and hi-fax

MODEL
1972-1978 Colt; 1972-1977 Colt SS; 1973-1975 TX; 1974 Custom II; 1974-1977 Electra; 1978 S/S 340; 1978-1979 Cobra; 1979-1980 Apollo and 1979-1981 Gemini

TOLERANCE (WIth 10 lb. [4.5 kg] Weight)
⅜-¾ inch (9.5-19.0 mm) between cleat and hi-fax

MODEL
1977-1978 TX-L

TOLERANCE (With 10 lb. [4.5 kg] Weight)
⅛-¼ inch (3.1-6.3 mm) between track clip and hi-fax

MODEL
1979-1982 TX-C and TX-L; 1979-1980 Centurion; 1980-1981 Galaxy; 1980-1986 Indy models; 1981 Cutlass; 1981-1982 Cutlass SS; 1983 Gemini and Sport; 1983-1986 SS; 1983-1986 Star and 1986 Sprint

TOLERANCE (With 10 lb. [4.5 kg] Weight)
⅜-½ inch (9.5-12.7 mm) between track clip and hi-fax

MODEL
1983-1984 Long Track Models

TOLERANCE (Free Hanging)
¾-1 inch (19.0-25.4 mm) free hanging between track clip and hi-fax as measured at rear of front hi-fax.

For all models, track tension is adjusted by turning adjusting screw (B – Fig. 11). To adjust tension loosen jam nut (A) and turn adjusting screw in to tighten track tension or out to loosen track tension. Retighten jam nut after adjustment. Be sure to check track alignment after performing tension adjustment. A misaligned track will make tension tighter on one side than on the other.

On Glass Rail models, the rear spring tension is the only suspension adjustment. Adjust by raising spring leading end to one of the upper notches when adding carrying weight or wanting a firmer ride. Lower spring tension when a softer ride is wanted or when machine is carrying less weight.

Stamped Steel model Type I has no suspension adjustments. Type II is equipped with adjustment for ski pressure and driver/passenger load. Move spring anchor stud (C – Fig. 12) forward in lower horizontal slot to transfer a greater percent of total vehicle weight to front skis. To compensate for greater driver/passenger weight, move anchor stud upward in any of the three vertical slots. Be sure to adjust both sides alike. Type II is also equipped with a rear spring adjustment cap screw (D). Turning cap screw clockwise provides softer ride and more ski lift during acceleration; counterclockwise adjustment is for firmer rides and less weight transfer. Rear spring anchor adjustment modifies E-Slot adjustment (C). Type III model uses all adjustments used by Type II plus front limiter adjustments. Refer to Fig. 10 and to the following:

E. Torque arm pivot can be positioned in upper hole (U) which provides increased ski pressure, or lower hole (L) which decreases the pressure.

F. Limiter bracket is provided with an upper hole (1) which provides increased ski pressure and decreased ski lift on acceleration, and a lower hole (2) which decreases ski pressure but increases acceleration lift.

G. Lower limiter bracket can be installed in normal position (N) which provides maximum lift on acceleration; or reversed position (R) which provides more ski pressure.

The standard adjustment for general trail use is E(U), F(2) and G(N).

Standard adjustment for grass drag racing is E(L), F(2) and G(N).

Variations from the standard can be made on a trial and error basis using the criteria outlined in previous paragraphs and reference to Fig. 10.

Extruded Aluminum models Type I and II suspension system is designed to carry and distribute the load and the many adjustments individually tailor the suspension for specific riding, load and track conditions. Refer to Fig. 13 and to the following:

A, B AND C. Front suspension anchor can be raised or lowered to adjust ski pressure. Lower hole (C) is normally best suited for average conditions. Upper hole (A) applies high ski pressure for high performance riding on hard-packed snow or ice, while center hole (B) applies moderate ski pressure.

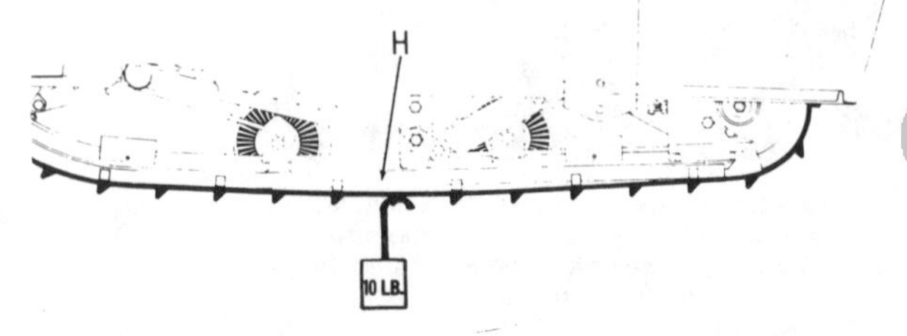

Fig. 10 – View showing procedure for checking track tension. Hi-Fax is rail shown at (H).

D AND E. Rear suspension anchor works in conjunction with front suspension anchor to distribute the weight between skis and track. Upper hole (D) is normally used for general riding while lower hole (E) may improve performance when climbing or running in deep snow.

F and G. Rear spring anchor adjusts for load. Lower position (G) is for normal loads while upper position (F) provides a firmer ride or additional support for loads in excess of 200 lbs. (889.6 N). A center hole midway between F and G may be used by moving upper anchor bolt down.

H AND I. Front torque arm pivot independently controls ski pressure and acceleration lift. Lower position (H) provides more ski pressure during acceleration and is the standard setting for normal driving. Upper position (I) provides greater ski lift at acceleration and works well for deep snow driving or hill climbing.

J, K AND L. Front Spring Anchor is factory set and not normally changed, having less effect on performance or stance than adjustments "A, B, C, H and I". Moving spring anchor to upper hole (K) on models so equipped or tightening adjustment (J) will have some effect in firming suspension, increasing acceleration lift or reducing ski pressure.

Extruded Aluminum suspension models Types III, IV, V, VI, VII, IX, X, XI, XII, XIII, XIV and XV have three to four suspension adjustments. Type VIII suspension system has only two. Adjustment of the suspension system is as follows:

REAR SPRING **(Type III, IV, V, VI, VII, X, XI, XII, XIV and XV).** To adjust rear spring tension turn eyebolt (E–Fig. 14) retaining nut. Adjust tension to where there is approximately ½-1 inch (12.7-25.4 mm) drop on Type III suspension and 1½ inch (38.1 mm) drop on Types IV, V, VI, VII, X, XI, XII, XIV and XV from normal unloaded loaded vehicle height when weight of driver/passenger is on the machine. Be sure to adjust eyebolts equally.

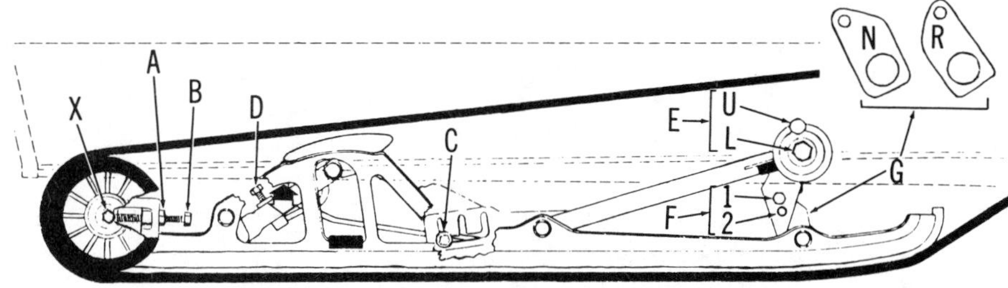

Fig. 12—View of a Typical Stamped Steel Side Rail Assembly. Refer to text for application of adjustments.

A. Locknut
B. Adjusting bolt
C. E-Slot adjustment
D. Rear anchor screw
E. Torque arm pivot
F. Upper limiter bracket
G. Lower limiter bracket
L. Lower hole
N. Normal profile
R. Reversed profile
U. Upper hole
X. Cross axle nut
1. Upper hole
2. Lower hole

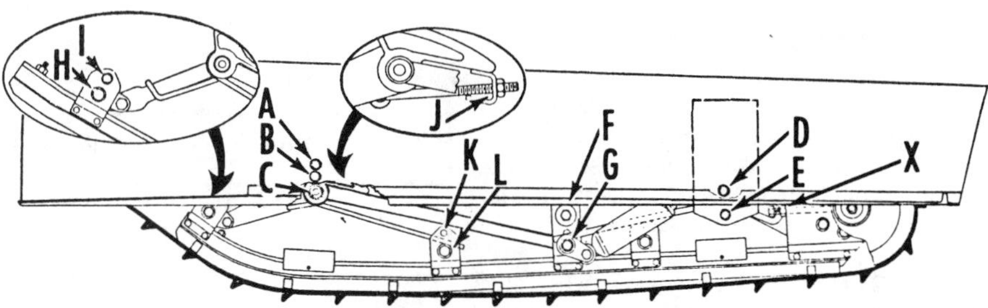

Fig. 13—View of Extruded Aluminum Track Types I and II suspension and adjustments. Refer to text for adjustment procedures.

A. Upper anchor (high ski pressure)
B. Center anchor (moderate ski pressure)
C. Lower anchor (standard setting)
D. Upper anchor (standard setting)
E. Lower anchor (deep snow)
F. Upper position (firm ride)
G. Lower position (standard setting)
H. Standard setting
I. Greater ski lift at acceleration
J. Spring anchor adjustment
K. Upper setting
L. Standard setting
X. Tension adjusting screw

(Type VIII, IX and XIII). Rear spring adjustment is accomplished by releasing spring leg (1–Fig. 15) from carrier wheel (3) and then repositioning spring leg (2) in a higher or lower retaining hook. Rehook spring leg (1) over carrier wheel (3) after adjusting tension leg (2). Raising spring leg (2) will increase spring tension and lowering it will decrease tension.

FRONT SPRING **(Type IV and V).** Adjustment of front spring pressure is accomplished by repositioning spring legs (S–Fig. 16) in a higher or lower adjustment slot. Adjust both springs equally. Raising spring legs to highest position will decrease ski to ground pressure. Lowering spring legs to lowest

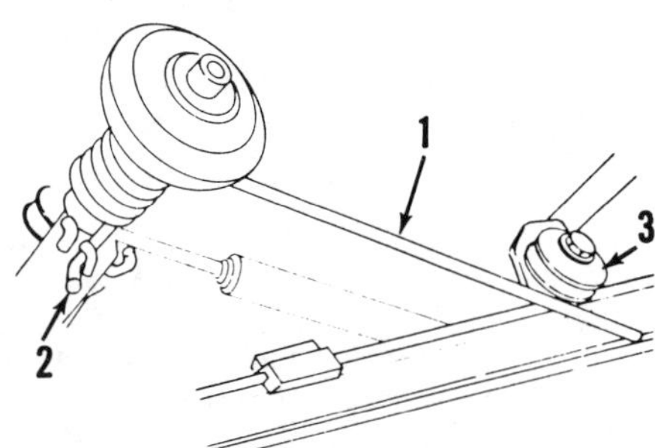

Fig. 15—View showing spring legs (1 and 2) and carrier wheel (3) used for adjusting rear spring tension on Type VIII.

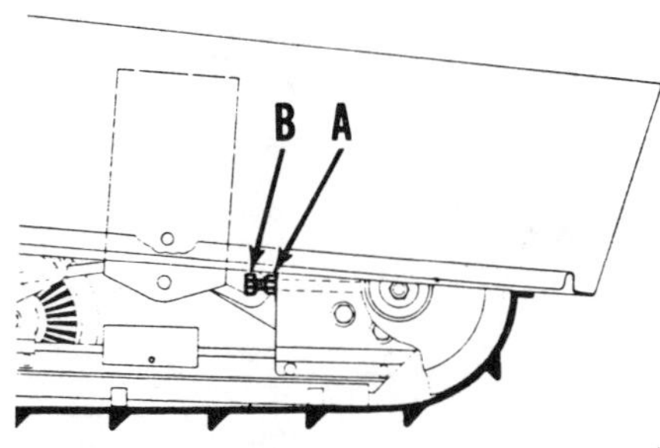

Fig. 11—View showing track tension adjusting screw (B) and jam nut (A).

Fig. 14—View showing rear spring tension adjustment nut (E) for Types III, IV, V, VI and VII.

Fig. 16—View showing adjustment slots (S) for adjusting front spring pressure on Types IV and V.

position will increase ski to ground pressure, which will cause a more harsh ride. If machine pitches upward at high speeds when hitting bumps, springs should be adjusted to a higher or softer position.

(Type III, VI and VII). To adjust ski pressure turn adjustment cam on bottom of front shock (C–Fig. 17). Adjustment to highest step on cam will increase ski to ground pressure. If front ski pressure is too severe, then machine will pitch upward when hitting bumps at high speeds. Spring adjustment cam should be adjusted to a lower step or softer ride.

(Type XI and XV). Adjustment of front shock position is recommended if ride is too firm or too soft. The shock has two top mounting positions. Place shock in the lower position to decrease travel firmness or place shock in upper position to increase travel firmness.

LIMITER STRAP **(Type III, VI, VII, VIII, IX, X, XI, XII, XIII, XIV and XV).** The length of the limiter strap (S–Fig. 17) will effect the amount of pressure applied by the skis to the ground. A higher pressure will result by shortening the limiter strap travel. Placing strap in longest position will decrease pressure. For a softer ride place strap in longest position.

REAR SHOCK **(Type III, VI, VII, XI and XV).** Adjustment of rear shock position is recommended if ride is too firm or too soft. Adjustment of shock position changes usable angle which will either increase or decrease firmness. Place shock in a higher position to decrease firmness and lower shock position to increase firmness.

SUSPENSION ASSEMBLY **(Type XI and XV).** Type XI and XV suspensions are used on 1985-1986 Indy models. The suspension assembly can be raised or lowered within the vehicle tunnel to adjust ski pressure. There are four positions available for front suspension mount, but the uppermost and lowermost positions should never be used as extensive track damage may result. Two positions are available for rear suspension mount. The suspension mounting position will also determine what of the three limiter strap lengths can and cannot be used. Refer to the illustration and chart in Fig. 18. The manufacturer originally locates the suspension assembly at positions (B and E).

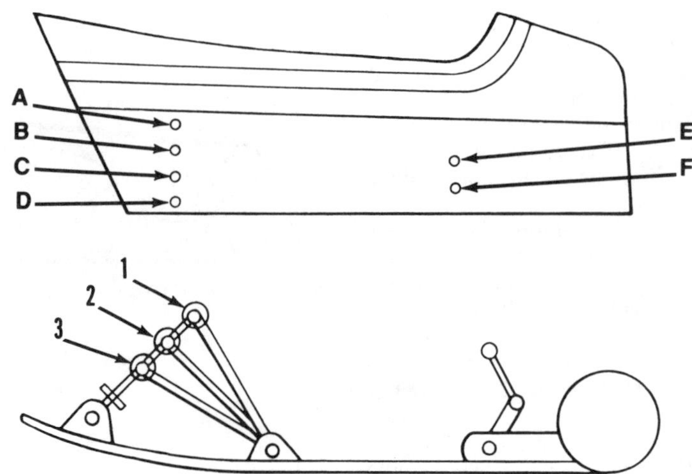

Front Mount	Rear Mount	Limiter Strap Length
B	E	1,2,3,
B	F	1,2,3,
C	E	3
C	F	2,3

Fig. 18—On Type XI and XV suspensions (1985-1986 Indy models), use the top views in conjunction with the table to determine acceptable suspension mounting positions and limiter strap lengths. Refer to text.

Fig. 17—View showing adjustment cam (C) for Types III, VI and VII and limiter strap (S) for Types III, VI, VII and VIII, both used for adjusting front ski to ground pressure.

OVERHAUL

ENGINE. Refer to the POLARIS engine section elsewhere in this manual for overhaul data on engines.

BRAKE. Refer to Fig. 19 for an exploded view of a molded velox master cylinder and Fig. 20 for an exploded view of a cast aluminum master cylinder. On some molded velox master cylinder models only one piston return spring is used.

Actuating lever pivot on molded velox moldel is riveted on original assembly. Rivet must be drilled out for overhaul and a pin (part 7661615) and C-Ring (part 7710401) installed upon reassembly.

Upon disassembly inspect cylinder bore for scratches, etching or corrosion and renew master cylinder as a unit if cylinder cannot be satisfactorily cleaned up. Cylinder must be absolutely clean when reassembling. Do not use mineral oil solvent for cleaning. Denatured alcohol is satisfactory, but alcohol based antifreeze may contan an antirust solution and should not be used. Dip all internal parts in clean brake fluid. Use a new cover gasket to prevent leakage.

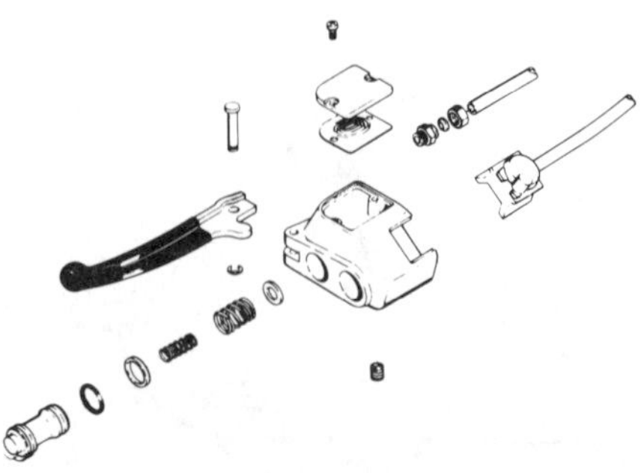

Fig. 19—Exploded view of handlebar mounted molded velox brake master cylinder.

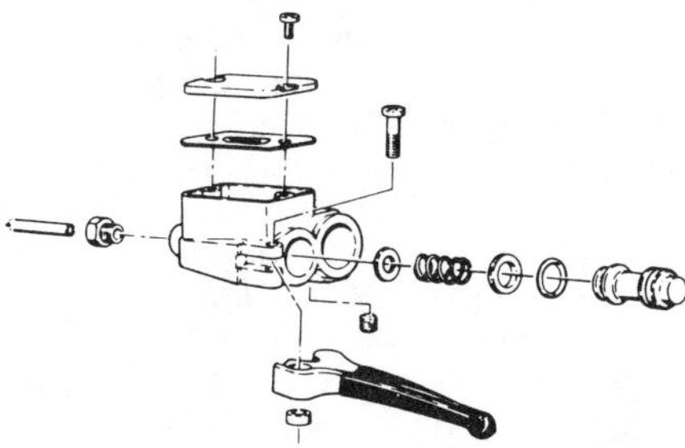

Fig. 20—Exploded view of a cast aluminum master cylinder.

To service brake actuating cylinder, caliper assembly or brake pads and associated parts; refer to Fig. 21 for Type I (Slave Cylinder), Fig. 22 for Type II, Fig. 23 for Type III, Fig. 24 for Type IV and Fig. 25 for Type V.

To remove Type I for disassembly and repair remove air box, driven clutch, hydraulic brake hose, brake light switch wiring and five cap screws retaining chaincase rear cover. If cover bearing is seized on shaft heat will need to be applied around bearing area in order to withdraw rear cover from shaft. Remove rear cover and slave cylinder. Disassemble slave cylinder with reference to Fig. 21. Inspect piston and bore for roughness and corrosion. A small amount of roughness maybe cleaned up by using fine crocus cloth and alcohol. Upon reassembly dip new "O" rings in clean brake fluid before installation. Reassemble brake assembly in reverse order of disassembly.

Bleed out and adjust brake system as outlined in **BRAKE ADJUSTMENT** section.

To remove Type II caliper assembly for repair or renewal of brake pads use following procedure.

Remove hydraulic brake line, caliper halves mounting bolts and nuts and four bracket mounting cap screws. Compress piston with a suitable tool and renew brake pads. If caliper assembly is to be repaired disassemble caliper with reference to Fig. 22. Inspect piston and bore for roughness and corrosion. Clean up and renew parts if there is severe roughness as piston and "O" ring will not seal.

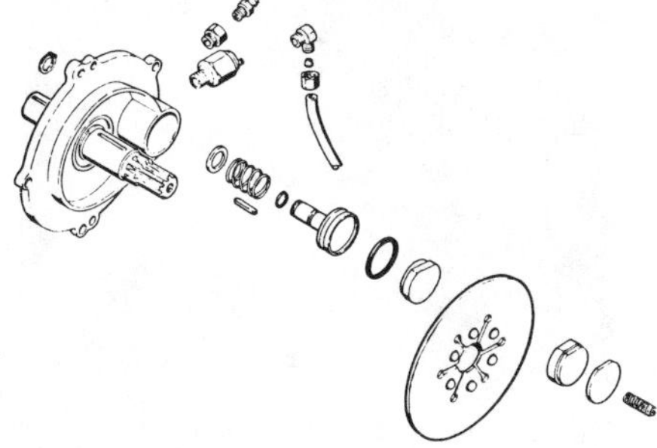

Fig. 21—Exploded view of Type I brake disc, actuating cylinder and associated parts.

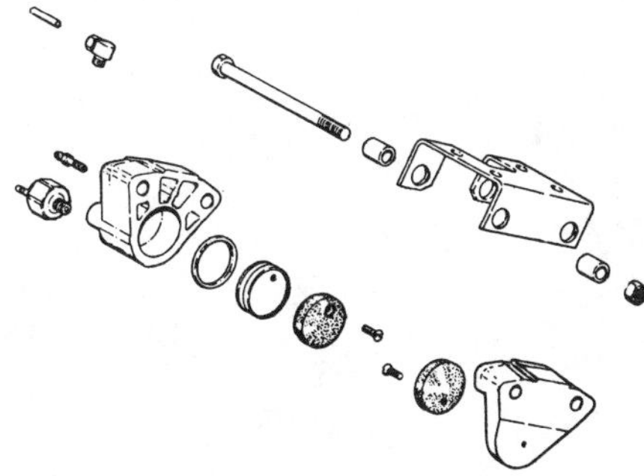

Fig. 22—Exploded view of Type II caliper brake used on models with right-hand chaincase.

Upon reassembly dip new "O" ring in clean brake fluid before installation. Reassemble brake assembly in reverse order of disassembly.

Bleed out brake system as outlined in **BRAKE ADJUSTMENT** section.

Remove and disassemble Type III caliper assembly with reference to Fig. 23. Remove two bolts (14), spacers (15) and nuts (17). Remove four bracket (16) mounting cap screws. Withdraw caliper assembly from chaincase housing. If only caliper pads are to be renewed then open bleeder screw (9) and using a suitable tool compress piston back into caliper housing. Close bleeder valve screw. Remove clips (8) from pad retaining pins (7), then withdraw pins. Remove and renew friction pads.

If caliper assembly is to be overhauled refer to Fig. 23 for parts breakdown and identification. Clean all parts and wipe dry with a lint-free cloth. If an air hose is available blow out all fluid passages. Inspect all parts for pitting, corrosion or any other damage and renew as needed. During reassembly apply clean brake fluid on seal (10). Reassemble in reverse order of disassembly. Caliper bolts (14) should be torqued to 30 ft.-lbs. (40.6 N·m) and bracket cap screws to 8 ft.-lbs. (10.8 N·m)

Bleed out system as outlined in **BRAKE ADJUSTMENT** section and check for proper application and release of brake pads. Reservoir fluid level should be keep within 1/8-inch (3.1 mm) of top.

To remove and disassemble Type IV proceed as follows and refer to Fig. 24. Open locking tab (12), loosen jam nut (13) and remove adjusting bolt (15). Remove actuating lever (11) and return spring (16). Remove caliper mounting

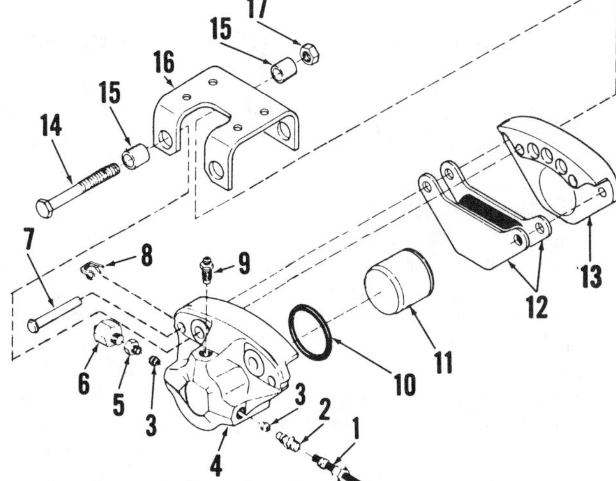

Fig. 23—Exploded view of Type III brake caliper assembly used on 1979-current TX, TX-C, TX-L, Centurion, TX-L Indy and Centurion Indy.

1. Brake line & fittings
2. Male adapter
3. Seat insert
4. Piston housing
5. Brass adapter
6. Brake light switch
7. Pad retaining pin
8. Spring clip
9. Bleeder screw
10. Piston "O" ring
11. Piston
12. Brake pads
13. Carrier housing
14. Bridge bolt
15. Spacer bushing
16. Bracket
17. Nut

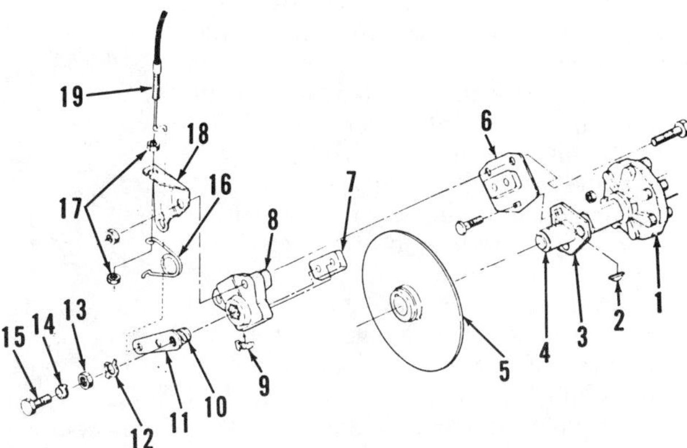

Fig. 24—Exploded view of Type IV brake caliper assembly used on 1981 Cutlass and 1981-current Cutlass SS.

1. Front drive sprocket
2. Woodruff key
3. Bearing flange
4. Front drive shaft
5. Brake disc
6. Stationary pad assy.
7. Moveable pad assy.
8. Caliper housing
9. Brake pad retainer
10. Helix shaft
11. Actuating lever
12. Locking tab
13. Jam nut
14. Bolt stop
15. Adjusting bolt
16. Return spring
17. Jam nut
18. Cable bracket
19. Brake cable

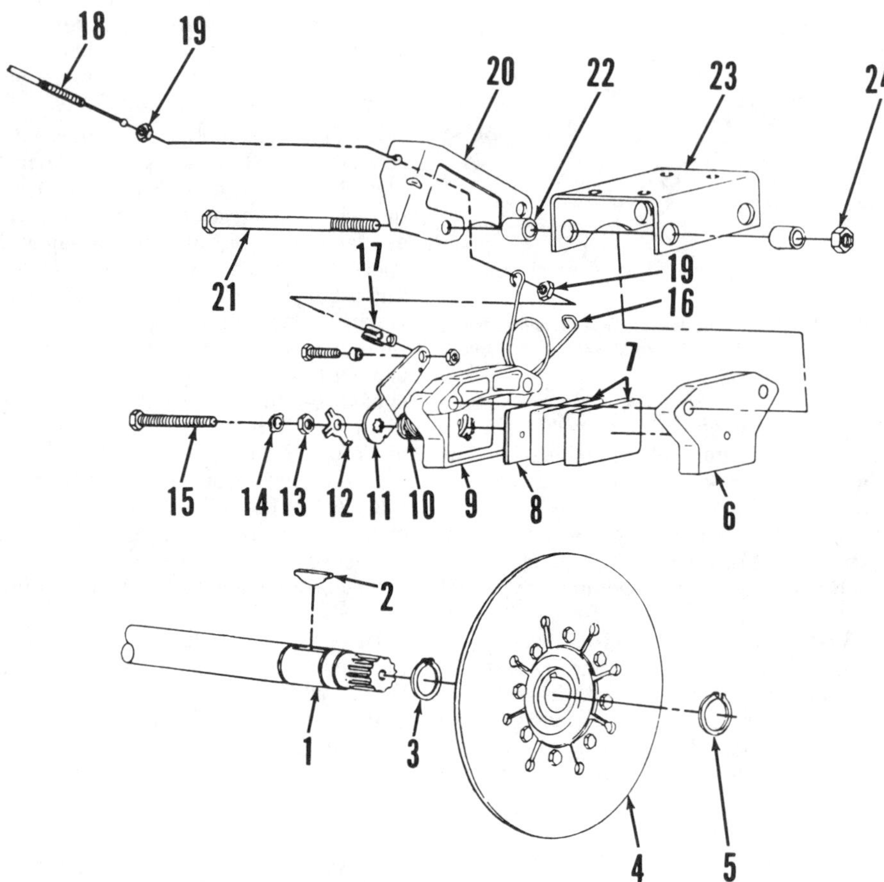

Fig. 25 — Exploded view of Type V brake caliper assembly used on 1983 and later Long Track models.

1. Jack shaft
2. Woodruff key
3. Snap ring
4. Brake disc
5. Snap ring
6. Caliper housing
7. Brake pads
8. Backing plate
9. Caliper housing
10. Helix shaft
11. Actuating lever
12. Locking tab
13. Jam nut
14. Bolt stop
15. Adjusting bolt
16. Return spring
17. Cable clevis
18. Brake cable
19. Adjusting nuts
20. Cable bracket
21. Bolt
22. Spacer
23. Bracket
24. Nut

nuts and withdraw cable mounting bracket and caliper assembly. Remove brake disc (5), then remove carriage bolt and nut as to renew brake pad (6).

Inspect all parts for excessive wear, breaks, scoring or any other damage. Renew parts as needed.

Reassemble in reverse order of disassembly. Clean drive shaft and install a light coat of antiseize on shaft. Install brake disc, then install caliper assembly with new pad. Install cable bracket and torque retaining nuts to 30 ft.-lbs. (40.6 N•m). Depress brake lever on handlebar, then bottom out helix shaft (10) in caliper housing. Install actuating level (11), lock tab (12), jam nut (13) and adjusting bolt (15). Place a 0.015-inch (0.38 mm) feeler gage between brake pad and brake disc. Release brake lever and install actuating lever return spring. Turn adjusting bolt in until feeler gage cannot be slid between pad and disc easily, then back bolt out until there is a light drag when feeler gauge is moved between pad and disc. Tighten jam nut and bend locking tab into place. Check for proper application and release of brake pads.

To remove and disassemble Type V brake system, proceed as follows and refer to Fig. 25. Loosen brake cable adjusting nuts (19) and disconnect cable (18) at clevis (17). Open locking tab (12), loosen jam nut (13) and remove adjusting bolt (15). Remove actuating lever (11) and return spring (16). Remove two bolts (21), spacers (22) and nuts (24). Remove four cap screws securing bracket (23). Withdraw caliper assembly from chaincase housing.

Inspect all parts for excessive wear, breaks, scoring or any other damage. Renew parts as needed.

Reassemble in reverse order of disassembly. Depress brake lever on handlebar, then bottom out helix shaft (10) in caliper housing. Install actuating lever (11), lock tab (12), jam nut (13) and adjusting bolt (15). Place a 0.015-inch (0.38 mm) feeler gage between brake pad and brake disc. Release lever and install actuating lever return spring. Turn adjusting bolt in until there is a light drag when feeler gage is moved between pad and disc. Tighten jam nut and bend locking tab into place. Check for proper application and release of brake pads.

On TC models with band brake, band can be removed without major disassembly. Renew band if badly worn and renew or relubricate actuating cable as required. Use only an approved low temperature lubricant if cable is oiled.

LEFT MOUNTED CHAINCASE. To remove the chaincase, drain reservoir and remove chaincase cover. Loosen chain tension and remove both sprockets and the chain as an assembly as shown in Fig. 26. Remove drive belt and disconnect brake hydraulic line. Disconnect brake light wire. Remove driven clutch. Remove the four nuts securing chaincase to track tunnel and lift off chaincase. When reinstalling chaincase, use CONDENSED SERVICE DATA tables as a guide and readjust drive pulley shaft center distance as required before tightening retaining nuts. Adjusting stop bolt is at (E, Inset – Fig. 27) for 1974 models and at (D) for later models.

Roller drive chain should be renewed when a 32-pitch length measures 12¼ inches (311.1 mm) or more, when otherwise damaged, or when sprockets are renewed. Thirty-two pitches of new chain measures 12 inches (304.8 mm). A similar amount of stretch (about 3%) is

Fig. 26 — Drive chain and sprockets can be removed as an assembly as shown, after removing chaincase cover.

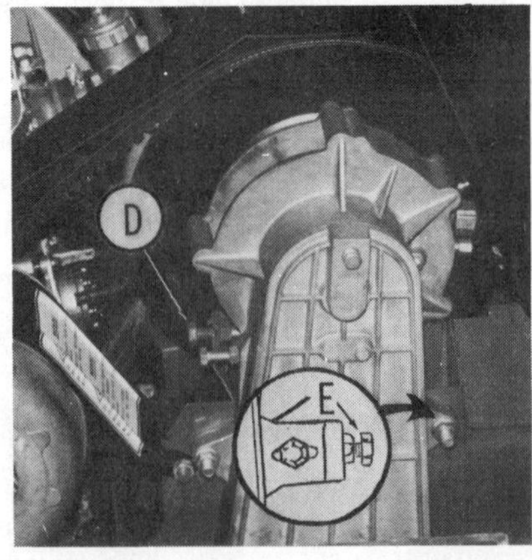

Fig. 27 — Chaincase can be shifted on its mounting to provide correct pulley shaft center adjustment. Stop screw is shown at (D) for later models or (E) for early units.

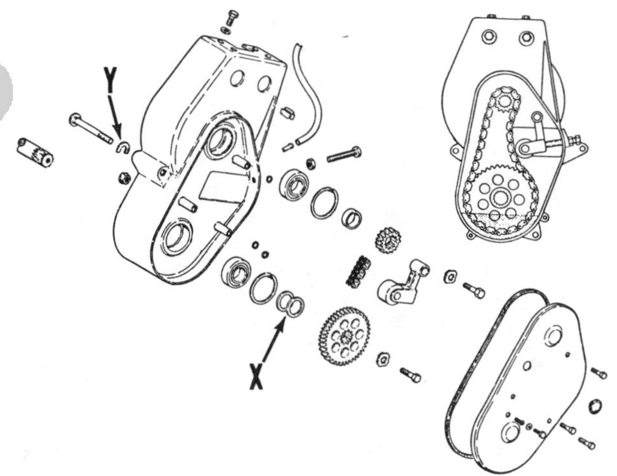

Fig. 28—Exploded view of right mounted chaincase showing sprocket alignment shims (X) and jackshaft alignment shims (Y).

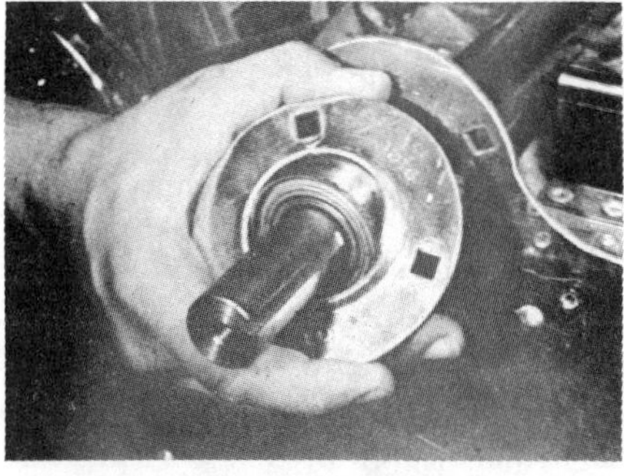

Fig. 31—Installing left jackshaft bearing.

Fig. 32—Using a straightedge (arrow) to check for support plate movement. Refer to text.

allowable with silent chain and similar criteria for renewal apply. Refer to CONDENSED SERVICE DATA tables for standard sprocket ratios.

RIGHT MOUNTED CHAINCASE. Refer to Fig. 28 for an exploded view. Chain and sprockets can be removed after removing cover and allowing chaincase to drain. Loosen tension screw and remove sprocket retaining cap screws, then slide both sprockets and chain from shaft splines as an assembly. Remove and set aside shim pack (X) on lower shaft behind sprocket. Shims provide sprocket alignment adjustment to permit chain to run true.

To remove chaincase with chain and sprockets out, remove the four cap screws securing brake caliper to housing and the three nuts retaining housing to track tunnel; then work the housing bearings from shafts. Note presence and location of shims (Y) which may be found on any of the three mounting bolt locations. Shims align chaincase with jackshaft left bearing.

To install and align the chaincase, temporarily bolt chaincase into position and install Jackshaft Alignment Tool (Polaris part 2870399) on sprocket end of jackshaft as shown in Fig. 29. Install a flangette on left jackshaft bearing mount as shown in Fig. 30. Jackshaft should be fully centered in flange as shown. If it is not; loosen chaincase mounting bolts and insert shims between flanges and track tunnel as required until shaft properly centers when mounting bolts are tightened.

Apply a light coating of grease to clamping surfaces of bearing flanges, then install locking collar, flanges and bearing as shown in Fig. 31. Turn shaft slowly as flange nuts are tightened, to assist in centering bearing as flanges tighten. Check alignment by laying a straightedge along support plate as shown by arrow, Fig. 32, then continuing to turn shaft. Movement of plate while shaft is turning indicates misalignment. Loosen mounting bolts slightly and gently tap the flanges as shaft is turned, until movement ceases indicating proper alignment.

The silent drive chain should be renewed when a 32-pitch length measures 12⅜ inches (314.3 mm) or more. Chain should also be renewed when sprockets are renewed. When assembling, install both sprockets without the chain but including removed shim pack (X–Fig. 28) behind lower sprocket, and install and tighten retaining cap screws; then using a straightedge, measure alignment of sprocket faces which must be parallel within 0.040 inch (1 mm). Align if necessary, by adding or removing shims (X) as required.

Install cover and fill chaincase to lower check plug hole using three ounces of Polaris Chaincase Lubricant.

DRIVEN CLUTCH. Refer to Fig. 33 for exploded view of driven clutch used on all early models except TX and TX-L. To remove the driven clutch, first remove belt guard and drive belt. On most models it is necessary to remove carburetor air silencer. On some models left-hand carburetor should be unbolted from mounting flange and moved to the

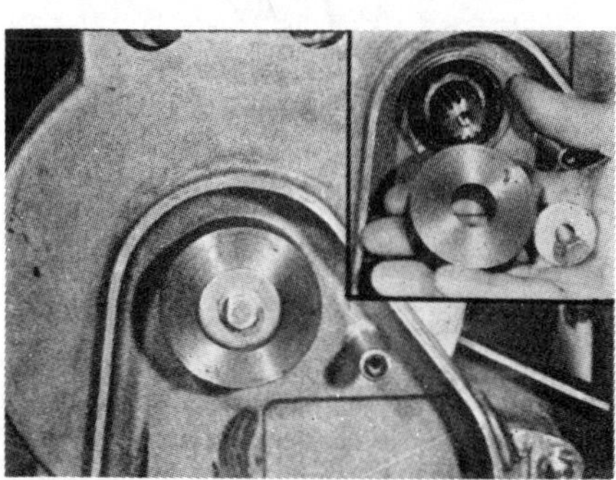

Fig. 29—Installation view of jackshaft alignment tool (Polaris part 2870399). Tool is shown removed in inset.

Fig. 30—Left jackshaft bearing flangette installed to check jackshaft alignment. Shaft should be centered in flange as shown.

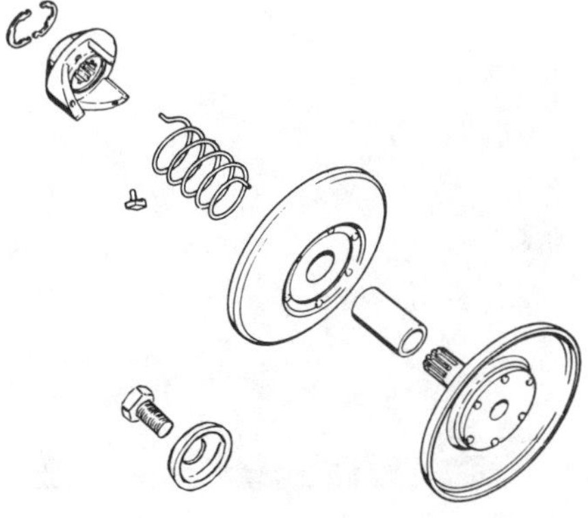

Fig. 33—Exploded view of driven clutch of type used on all early models except TX and TX-L.

right to obtain clearance. Remove retaining cap screw and washer and slide driven clutch unit to right off its keyed position on secondary shaft.

To disassemble driven clutch, slightly depress outer cam and remove split retaining ring using a blade screwdriver or knife. Slowly release spring pressure and lift off cam. To remove broken or worn ramp shoes, heat vertical side of ramp with a torch. Ramp shoe can now be withdrawn or broken portion pried out with an ice pick or similar tool. Check friction faces of both sheave halves for nicks or excessive wear in any one place. Also check for bent hub or rim which would cause runout of the rotating member.

When reassembling, insert spring ends in anchor holes in sliding sheave and fixed cam and push cam down until points almost touch; then turn sliding sheave one full cam (1/3 turn) in direction to wind the spring. Push cam down over splines until retaining ring grooves are exposed and install retaining rings in place using pliers.

Driven clutch on early TX and TX-L models and all later models can be removed after removing belt guard, belt and retaining cap screw. To disassemble the removed driven clutch, apply slight down pressure to torque cam (3–Fig. 34) and remove snap ring (1), washer (2) and cam. Note anchor position of torque spring in series of holes in cam as shown in Fig. 35. Lift off spring and sliding sheave, being careful not to lose the two thrust washers located on hub between sheave halves. Inspect nylon ramp buttons and bushings in sliding sheave for wear or damage and renew as indicated. To renew broken or worn ramp shoes, heat ramp with a torch then withdraw broken portion or pry out with an ice pick. Check sheave holes for nicks, wear or other damage. When assembling, note that spring end should be installed in hole (1–Fig. 35) on TX 340 and in hole (2) for all other models. Moving spring anchor to a higher number hole increases spring windup tension and results in increased upshift delay during acceleration. Preload the spring one ramp (1/3 turn) by turning sliding sheave counterclockwise after spring is connected, then complete the assembly by reversing disassembly procedure.

Fig. 34—To disassemble later model driven clutch, remove snap ring (1), spacer washer (2) and cam (3). Refer to text.

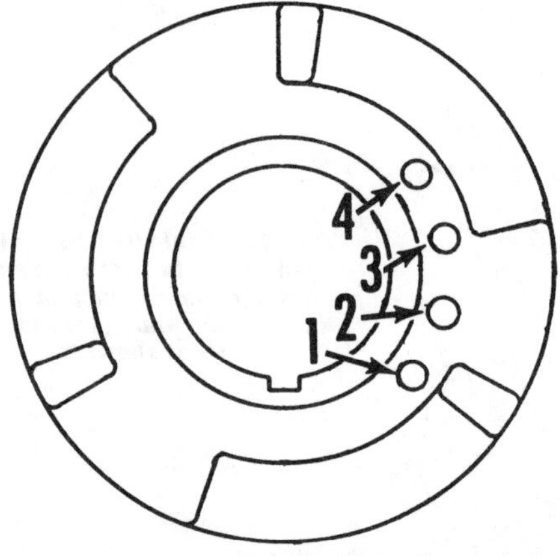

Fig. 35—Four spring anchor holes in later model driven clutch cam permit adjustment of torque load. Refer to text.

When installing driven clutch, offset distance (A–Fig. 36) should be 5/8-inch (16 mm) on all models with aluminum clutch, all Cobra models and all Galaxy models. Offset (A) should be 9/16-inch (14 mm) on all other models except electric start models with starter ring gear attached to drive clutch which should have a 1 inch (25.4 mm) offset. Primary adjusting method is by sliding engine in slotted mounts, but one or two spacer washers may be used on jackshaft behind driven clutch. Check and adjust offset when driven clutch is installed.

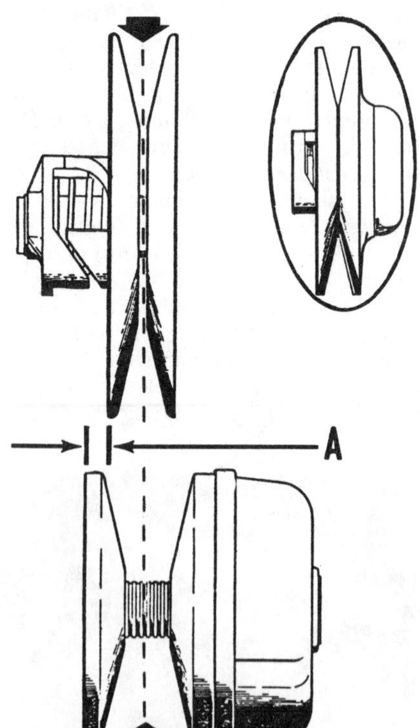

Fig. 36—Offset distance (A) should be 5/8 inch (15.8 mm) on all models with aluminum clutch, all Cobra models and all Galaxy models. Offset for all other models should be 9/16 inch (14.3 mm).

Shaft center distance (D–Fig. 37) is adjusted on models with left-mounted chaincase by loosening chaincase mounting bolts and turning positioning screw (E) for early models or (L) for late models until center distance is correct. Adjusting gage tool (T) is identified by Polaris part 2870207 and can be used on most models.

DRIVE CLUTCH. Early drive clutches were supplied only as factory rebuilt units. Late model clutches can be rebuilt, but manufacturer recommends that overhaul be attempted by experienced personnel with the proper training and tools.

Refer to Figs. 38, 39 and 40 for exploded views of standard, high performance and P-85 high performance drive clutches respectively. To remove the clutch, first remove drive belt. Use a strap wrench (Polaris part 2870336) or equivalent to hold fixed pulley rim and remove clutch retaining bolt, then use puller (Polaris part 2870030 for steel clutch or 2870130 for aluminum clutch) tightening puller screw until clutch pops loose from tapered shaft.

Before installing drive clutch, manufacturer recommends trueing clutch bore with tapered reamer (Polaris part 2870576). Clamp reamer in a vise and apply cutting oil. Position the clutch on the reamer and turn by hand in a clockwise direction only. Do not remove more material than is necessary to true clutch bore.

Install drive clutch by reversing the strap wrench and using a torque wrench to tighten retaining cap screw to 40-45 ft.-lbs. (54.2-61.0 N·m) as shown in Fig. 41.

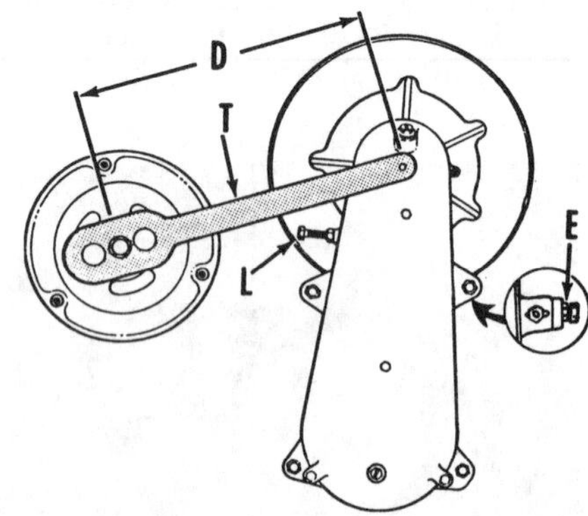

Fig. 37—View showing method of adjusting shaft centers on models with left-hand mounted chaincase.

D. Distance
E. Adjustment (early)
I. Adjustment (late)
T. Tool (2870207)

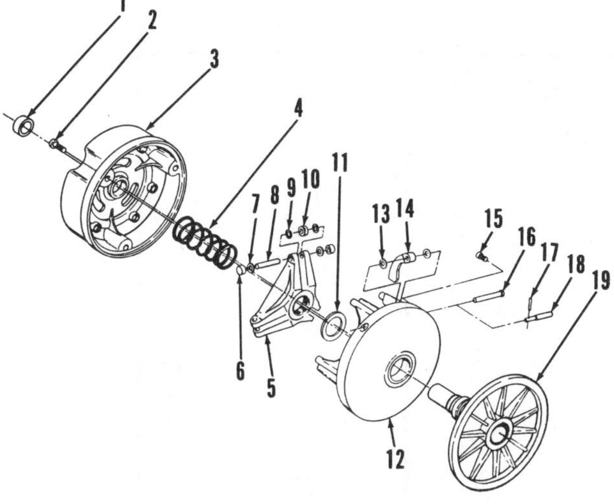

Fig. 38—Exploded view of standard drive clutch assembly. Refer to Fig. 39 for parts identification.

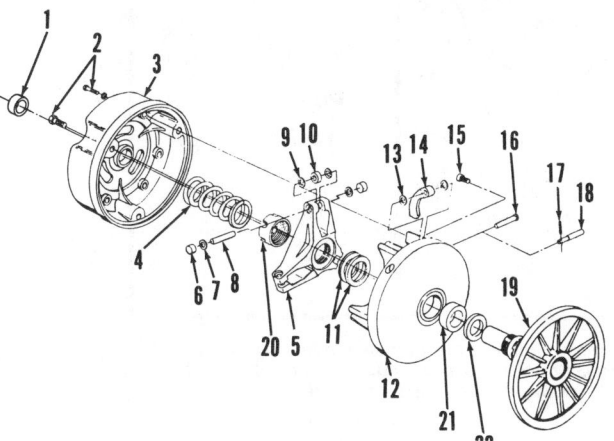

Fig. 41—Using Strap Wrench (part 2870336) to hold clutch while torquing cap screw.

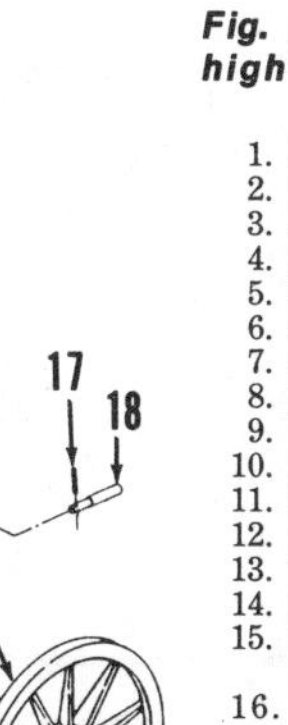

Fig. 39—Exploded view of high performance drive clutch assembly.

1. Engagement spacer
2. Cover cap screws
3. Clutch cover
4. Spring
5. Spider
6. Cap
7. Shim
8. Pin
9. Washer
10. Roller
11. Shims
12. Sliding sleeve
13. Washer
14. Centrifugal weight
15. Weight pin cap screw (1984 models)
16. Weight pin (1984 models)
17. Spring pin (1983 models)
18. Weight pin (1983 models)
19. Fixed pulley & hub
20. Jam nut
21. Bushing
22. Bushing retainer

Fig. 42—Place alignment marks on cover and sliding flange as shown, before removing cover.

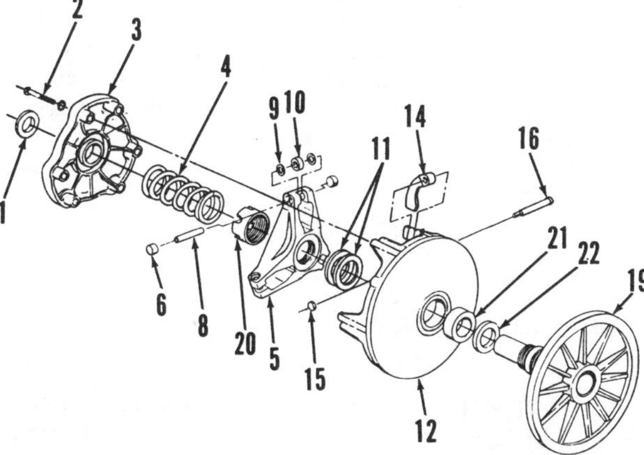

Fig. 40—Exploded view of P-85 drive clutch assembly. Refer to Fig. 39 for parts identification except for nut (15).

Fig. 43—X-mark top of spider leg to correspond with marks on sliding sheave, inside of cover and under surface of spider. Spider jam nut is used on high performance and P-85 models only.

NOTE: DO NOT use an impact wrench when installing clutch retaining cap screw, or spider may loosen on clutch hub.

On high-performance and P-85 clutch units, before starting disassembly, pull a NEW drive belt tightly into hub and against one flange, then measure belt clearance from other flange using a feeler gage. Record the clearance for future reference during assembly.

To disassemble the removed clutch, attach the clutch to disassembly tool (Polaris part 2870461) as shown in Fig. 42 and using a marking pen, place alignment marks on sliding sheave and cover as shown. Keeping in mind the fact that cover is spring loaded, remove the cover.

On standard clutch units, cover is retained by three 1/4-20x3/4 inch screws. On high performance clutch units, cover is retained by three 1/4-20x3/4 inch screws and either six #10-32x3/4 inch screws or six #10-32x1 inch screws. On P-85 clutch units, cover is retained by six 1/4-20x2 1/4 inch screws.

When cover and spring are lifted off, note the "X" balance marks on inside of cover and inside of sliding sheave, and make a corresponding mark on the outside of the aligned spider leg as shown in Fig. 43. (Aligning mark on spider is on inside and hard to see with unit assembled). The clutch used on high-performance and P-85 models has a jam nut (20—Fig. 39 or Fig. 40) as shown in Fig. 43. Use Spider Spanner Nut Driver (Polaris part 2870338) and a suitable wrench to loosen jam nut as shown in Fig. 44.

Fig. 44 — Removing spider jam nut using special tool (part 2870338).

Fig. 45 — Spider Tool (part 2870341) in position for spider removal.

Weights	Springs
03, U, Y	BLUE/GOLD
W, K1, B, P1	GOLD
B, J1, M1, A	SILVER
A/P, 08, 01, 02	RED
06, 10, 0, 09	RED/WHITE
10, N1, 07, ⓪	BROWN
05, 15, 04	ORANGE
	PINK
	YELLOW
	GREEN
	PURPLE
	WHITE
	PLAIN
	BLACK

HEAVY ↑ ↓ LIGHT

Fig. 46 — Optional weight kits are letter coded from 03 (32.5 grams) to 04 (57.5 grams). Springs are color coded from light to heavy as shown. Refer to text and TABLE 1.

Use Spider Tool (Polaris part 2870341) (Fig. 45) and spanner nut driver to remove spider on all models. On high-performance and P-85 models when spider is off, remove and measure the shim pack (11 – Fig. 39 or Fig. 40) between sliding sheave (2) and spider (3). Shim pack thickness determines drive belt to sheave clearance in disengaged position. Shims are available in thicknesses of 0.020, 0.032 and 0.050-inch (0.5, 0.8 and 1.3 mm). Use measured clearance before disassembly plus removed shim pack thickness to determine proper shim pack thickness for use in reassembly. Minimum disengaged clearance without dragging should be established.

Fourteen color-coded engagement springs (4 – Figs. 38, 39 or 40) and twenty six different shift weight kits provide a wide range of engagement and shift pattern possibilities. Refer to chart shown in Fig. 46. Weight kits vary from 32.5 grams (03) to 57.5 grams (04) by letter code. Weights are provided as a kit only, consisting of a set of three weights and retaining pins, plus necessary attaching parts.

Changing to a stronger spring or lighter weight kit increases engagement speed and upshift rpm, although upshift speed is also affected by torque wrap of spring in driven clutch. So many factors are involved that it is difficult to forecast a pattern change, and trial and error is the only practical means of fine tuning. TABLE 1 gives standard and high altitude settings for drive clutch on late models. Variations can be estimated for other models or conditions by referring to TABLE 1 and Fig. 46.

TABLE 1-POLARIS DRIVE CLUTCH DATA

MODEL	ENGINE	STANDARD WT. CODE	SETTING SPRING COLOR	6500 FT. WT. CODE	ALTITUDE SPRING COLOR
1976 Models					
Colt 175cc	EC17PM	A	Black	....	....
Colt 244cc	EC25PS	G	Black	....	....
Colt 250cc	EC25PC	U	Unpainted	....	....
Colt 340cc	ED34PC	W	Unpainted	....	....
Electra 244cc	EC25PS	B	Unpainted	....	....
Electra 339cc	EC34PQ	B	Unpainted	....	....
Electra 433cc	EC44PQ	B	Unpainted	....	....
TX250cc	EC25PT-06	G	Orange	....	....
TX336cc	EC34PT-05	A	Brown	....	....
TX433cc	EC44PT-05	A	Purple	....	....
Starfire 250cc	EC25PT-05	W	Silver	....	....
Starfire 336cc	EC34PT-06	Y	Brown	....	....

TABLE 1—Continued

MODEL	ENGINE	STANDARD WT. CODE	SETTING SPRING COLOR	6500 FT. WT. CODE	ALTITUDE SPRING COLOR
1977 Models					
Colt 244	EC25PS	G	Purple	G	Orange
Colt 250	EC25PC	W	Purple	W	Purple
Colt SS250	EC25PM-01	G	Orange	G	Silver
Electra 250	EC25PS	B	Purple	B	Orange
TX250	EC25PT-07	W	Silver	U	Orange
Colt SS340	EC34PM-03	A	Orange	B	Orange
Electra 340	EC34PQ	B	Purple	B	Orange
TX340	EC34PT-05	B	Pink	G	Pink
TX-L340	EC34PL-01	G	Pink	W	Pink
Electra 440	EC44PQ	B	Purple	B	Orange
TX440	EC44PT-05/06	A	Orange	B	Purple
1978 Models					
Colt 244	EC25PS	G	Purple	G	Orange
Colt 250	EC25PC	W	Purple	G	Silver
TX250	EC25PT-07	W	Silver	U	Pink
S/S 340	EC34PM-03/04	A	Orange	B	Orange
Cobra 340	EC34PM-04	A	Purple	A	Silver
TX340	EC34PT-05	B	Pink	G	Red
TX-L340	EC34PL-02	G	Red	W	Red
Cobra 440	EC44PM-01	OO	Black	OO	Purple
TX440	EC44PT-05	A	Orange	A	Orange
1979 Models					
Gemini 244	EC25PS	G	Purple	G	Orange
Gemini 250	EC25PM-01	G	Orange	W	Red
Apollo 340	EC34PM-03	A	Orange	B	Orange
Cobra 340	EC34PM-04	A	Purple	A	Silver
Cobra 440	EC44PM-01	OO	Black	OO	Purple
TX250	EC25PT-07	W	Silver	U	Pink
TX340	EC34PT-05	B	Yellow	G	Red
TX440	EC44PT-05	A/P	Yellow	A	Orange
TX-L340	EC34PL-02	B	Silver	W	Red
Centurion	EC51PL-01	A	Red	B	Red
1980 Models					
Gemini	EC25PS	G	Purple	G	Orange
Gemini	EC25PM-01	G	Orange	W	Red
Apollo	EC34PM-03	A	Orange	B	Orange
Galaxy	EC34PM-04	A	Purple	A	Silver
Galaxy	EC44PM-01/02	OO	Black	OO	Purple
TX/TX-C	EC34PT-07	B	Yellow	G	Red
TX	EC44PT-05	A/P	Yellow	A	Orange
TX-L/TX-L Indy	EC34PL-02/05	B	Silver	W	Red
Centurion	EC51PL-02	A	Orange	A	Red
1981 Models					
Gemini	EC25PS	G	Purple	G	Orange
Galaxy	EC44PM-02	OO	Black	OO	Purple
Cutlass	EC34PM-03	O	Orange	O	Blue
Cutlass SS	EC44-2PM-3100/3300	02	White	02	Silver
TX-C	EC44-2PM-1100	01	Purple	02	Silver
TX-L/TX-L Indy	EC34PL-05	B	Silver	03	White
Centurion Indy	EC51PL-02	A	Orange	A	Red
1982 Models					
Cutlass SS	EC44-2PM-3100	02	White	02	Orange
TX-C	EC44-2PM-1100	01	Purple	02	Silver
TX-L/TX-L Indy	EC34PL-05	B	Silver	03	White
Centurion Indy	EC51PL-02	A	Orange	A	Red

(Continued on Page 140)

Spring can be changed by removing drive clutch cover, without removing clutch from engine. Mark cover and sliding sheave before unbolting cover, and reinstall with marks aligned to maintain balance. Measure clutch cover retaining screws to determine correct tightening torque.

Tightening torques for clutch cover cap screws are as follows: 1/4-20x3/4 inch screws—80-100 in.-lbs. (9.0-11.2 N·m); 1/4-20x2 1/4 inch screws—100 in.-lbs. (11.2 N·m); 10-32x3/4 inch screws—25-30 in.-lbs. (2.8-3.3 N·m); and 10-32x1 inch screws 40-50 in.-lbs. (4.5-5.6 N·m).

If only weight kits are to be changed and overhaul is not required, spider will not need to be removed from clutch hub. Install clutch on fixture and mark and remove cover and spring. Block sliding sheave in wide-open position using a suitable length of split radiator hose as shown in Fig. 47. (Blocking sheave open eliminates the danger of spreading guide towers while removing weight pins).

On 1983 and earlier standard and high performance clutch units, remove spring pin (Inset—Fig. 47) from end of weight pin and drive weight pin out in direction of arrow using Weight Pin Punch (Polaris part 2870507). On 1984 and later standard and high performance clutch units, weight pin is retained by a cap screw while on P-85 clutch units, weight pin is retained by nut threaded to end of pin.

Discard the removed weights and pins. Install new weight kit by reversing removal procedure. The complete weight kit MUST be installed. On 1983 and earlier standard and high performance clutch units, be sure to turn weight pin so spring pin hole is accessible; see inset Fig. 47. Install spring pin on models so equipped, using Spring Pin Punch (Polaris part 2870402). On 1984 and later standard and high performance clutch units, carefully examine weight pin retaining cap screw threads prior to installation. If threads are pull-

Fig. 47—Weight pin must be driven out in direction indicated by arrow. Retaining spring pin hole (inset) must be properly turned when weight pin is installed.

TABLE 1—Continued

MODEL	ENGINE	STANDARD WT. CODE	SETTING SPRING COLOR	6500 FT. WT. CODE	ALTITUDE SPRING COLOR
1983 Models					
Gemini	EC25PS	G	White	G	Orange
Star	EC25PS	B	Purple	G	Silver
Sport	EC44-2PM-5100	04	Brown	04	Silver
SS	EC44-2PM-3100	02	White	02	Orange
Indy Trail	EC44-2PM-2100	M1 Mod.	Green	M1 Mod.	Purple
Indy Cross Country	EC34PL-05	B	Silver	03	White
Indy 600	EC60PL-01	N1-Mod	Silver	02	Red
Long Track	EC44-2PM-5000	04	Yellow	04	Orange
1984 Models					
Star	EC25PS-05	B	Purple	G	Silver
SS	EC44-2PM 3100	02	White	02	Orange
Indy Trail	EC44-2PM 2100	M1 Mod.	Green	M1 Mod.	Purple
Indy 600	EC60PL-02	05	Gold	06	Red
Star LT	EC25PS-05	A	Yellow	B	Orange
Long Track	EC44-2PM 5000	04	Yellow	04	Orange
1985 Models					
Star	EC25PS-06	08	Brown	08	Brown
SS	EC44-2PM 3100	07	White	07	Orange
Indy Trail	EC44-2PM 2100	N1 Mod.	Brown	N1 Mod.	Gold
Indy 400	EC40PL-02	N1 Mod.	Gold	P1	Red
Indy 600	EC60PL-02	05	Gold	06	Blue
Long Track	EC44-2PM 5000	04	Yellow	04	Orange
1986 Models					
Star	EC25PS-06	08	Brown	08	Red/White
Sprint	EC34-2PM-01/02	05	Gold	05	Blue/Gold
SS	EC44-2PM 3100	07	White	07	Orange
Indy Trail	EC50PM-01	10	Red/White	M1 Mod.	Orange
Indy 400	EC40PL-02	10 Mod.	Blue/Gold	M1 Mod.	Gold
Indy 600	EC60PL-02	15	Blue/Gold	06	Blue/Gold
Long Track	EC44-2PM-5100	04	Yellow	04	Orange

ed or damaged, renew the complete set with P-85 weight pins and nuts. If threads are satisfactory, install and tighten weight pin retaining cap screws to 60 in.-lbs. (6.7 N·m) torque. On P-85 clutch units, tighten weight pin retaining nuts to 25 in.-lbs. (2.8 N·m) torque.

Spider pin and roller kit is interchangeable for all models but guide buttons differ for High-Performance and P-85 units. A Roller Pin Gage Block (Polaris part 2870310) is available for centering the pin during installation on standard spider units, as shown in Fig. 48. On High-Performance and P-85 spider, it is necessary to center the roller pin using special Roller Pin Centering Punch (Polaris part PN2870401). If pins are not properly centered, guide buttons will bind on sides of guide towers and shifting will be erratic.

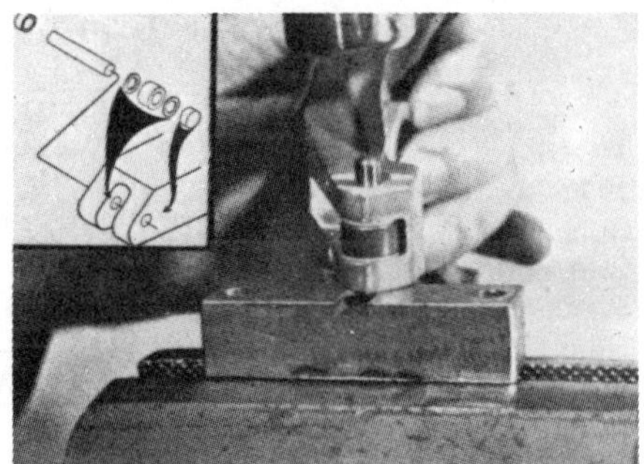

Fig. 48—Weight roller pin exploded (inset) and installed. Gage Block (part 2870310) centers pin for proper operation.

Clean all parts thoroughly and lubricate weights, rollers and hubs with WD-40, SPL-2 or similar spray lubricant. Align balance marks on sliding hub and spider as spider is threaded to hub. Tighten spider to 200 ft.-lbs. (271.16 N·m) using Spider Tool (2870341) and Spanner Nut Driver (2870338). On High-Performance and P-85 models, tighten spider jam nut to a torque of 235 ft.-lbs. (319 N·m). Complete the assembly and installation by reversing removal and disassembly procedure.

TRACK AND SUSPENSION. The slide rail track suspension is retained to track tunnel by two cap screws on each side. To remove suspension, completely loosen track tension. Remove the four retaining cap screws. Turn machine on its side, swing frame and track out of track tunnel and lift the assembled frame unit out of track. Install by reversing the removal procedure.

On the bogie wheel suspension used on TC models, bogie wheels are attached to track tunnel brackets by cap screws and rear track idler is separate. Normal service can be performed by completely loosening track tension, then removing retaining cap screws at each end of rear idler axle. When reinstalling bogie wheel, note that the three idler wheels of front bogie set go toward the front of machine to provide solid support for front of track contact area.

DRIVE AXLE. On all models except direct drive, remove track drive axle as follows: Completely loosen track tension. Drain chaincase and remove drive chain and sprockets. Turn machine on chaincase side and disconnect drive axle bearing flange on right side of track tunnel. Remove speedometer drive if so equipped. Loosen set screw in right bearing retaining collar, using a punch tap collar opposite normal direction of shaft rotation to loosen collar. Remove right bearing. Slip right end of shaft out of opening in track tunnel and withdraw shaft and drive sprockets to right out of bearing on chaincase end of shaft. Install by reversing removal procedure.

On direct drive models; remove drive belt, driven clutch and spacer washers. Remove caliper assembly and actuating components. Withdraw brake disc and half moon key from front drive shaft. Remove suspension mounting cap screws, turn machine on its side and swing unit clear of track tunnel. Loosen lock collar Allen head set screw, then using a punch and hammer loosen bearing lock collar located on brake end of drive shaft. Remove brake side bearing flange attaching bolts and nuts. Slide drive shaft toward brake side until driven clutch end is clear of bearing. Drive shaft and track may now be removed. Inspect drive shaft, sprockets and bearings; renew as needed. Reassemble in reverse order of disassembly.

To renew plastic slide, remove retaining bolt from front end of runner and drive slide rearward using a hammer and suitable block of wood. Plastic side slide should be renewed when worn to less than 1/8-inch (3.1 mm) at any point.

POLORON

1970-1972

		Engine		Carburetor				Clutch		
Model	Make	Model	Displ.	Make	Model	Sprocket Ratio	Chain Size	Make	Shaft Center	Belt Number
					1970					
Cyclone 704	Kohler	K295-1	295cc	Tillotson	HR78A	13:36	35-2	Salsbury 780	10¾	703074
Tornado 805	Kohler	K399-2	399cc	Tillotson	HR79A	19:39	35-2	Salsbury 910	10¾	703040
					1971					
Cyclone 704J	JLO	L295	292cc	Tillotson	HR78A	17:37	35-2	Salsbury 780	10¾	100120
Cyclone 705K	Kohler	K295-1	294cc	Tillotson	HR78A	17:37	35-2	Salsbury 780	10¾	100120
Tornado 804K	Kohler	K399-2	399cc	Tillotson	HR79A	17:37	35-2	Salsbury 910	10¾	100121
Tornado 805K	Kohler	K399-2	399cc	Tillotson	HR79A	17:37	35-2	Salsbury 910	10¾	100121
					1972					
Cyclone 704J	JLO	L295	292cc	Tillotson	HR78A	17:37	35-2	Salsbury 780	10¾	100120
Cyclone 705K	Kohler	K295-1	294cc	Tillotson	HR78A	17:37	35-2	Salsbury 780	10¾	100120
Tornado 804K	Kohler	K399-2	399cc	Tillotson	HR79B	17:37	35-2	Salsbury 910	10¾	100121
Tornado 805K	Kohler	K399-2	399cc	Tillotson	HR79B	17:37	35-2	Salsbury 910	10¾	100121
Tornado 806K	Kohler	K340-2	338cc			17:37	35-2	Salsbury 780	10¾	100120

LUBRICATION

The engine is lubricated by oil mixed with the fuel. Correct fuel-oil ratio is 20:1. Too much oil will cause carbon deposits. Too little oil will cause insufficient lubrication. Fuel and oil should be mixed thoroughly in a separate container at a temperature above freezing. Use only a good grade of SAE 30 Two Cycle Engine Oil. Do not use light duty oils or multi-viscosity oils. Use a good grade of regular gasoline.

On 1970 models the enclosed chain case should be filled to level of check plug using SAE 80 EP Gear Oil. Filler plug is located at (F—Fig. 2) on top of chain case. On 1971 models, fluid level should be maintained approximately ¼-inch below level of lower inspection cover (L—Fig. 1).

Lubricate tie rod ends with light machine oil periodically. Lube fittings on the two front shock housings should be greased occasionally with low temperature grease. Bogie wheels are equipped with sealed ball bearings which do not require lubrication.

Fig. 1—View of chain case and drive used on 1971 models.

A. Brake mounting screws
B. Slotted nut
C. Upper cover
L. Lower cover
M. Backlash
N. Anchor nuts

ADJUSTMENT

STEERING SKIS & LINKAGE. Turn handle bar to normal straight driving position and check to see that both skis are parallel with each other and with drive track and snowmobile frame. To adjust either tie rod, disconnect at spindle end.

DRIVE CHAIN. Tension of the enclosed drive chain cannot be directly measured on 1970 models. On all models, adjustment is correct when ½-inch of free movement (backlash) exists, measured at rim of driven sheave as shown at (M—Fig. 1 or 2). To adjust the chain on 1970 machines loosen locknut and turn chain adjusting bolt (C—Fig. 2) until backlash is correct. On 1971 models, adjust chain tension by loosening the three nuts securing upper bearing housing to chain case and turning housing to adjust the chain. Adjustment may be checked by removing upper cover (C—Fig. 1).

NOTE: Whenever chain tension is adjusted on 1971 machines, realign brake unit by loosening the two cap screws (A).

BRAKE. Brake band on 1970 machines should be free of drum when lever is released but should fully engage before hand lever contacts handlebar grip. Adjustment is made at the two brass nuts (B—Fig. 2) which secure cable housing to brake housing anchor.

On 1971 models, brake wear adjustment is made by removing cotter pin and turning castellated nut (B—Fig. 1) on lever stud. Tighten nut until resistance is felt, then back off one turn and reinstall cotter pin. Brake must be properly aligned with sheave rim and push pins must center in valleys in actuating arm when ad-

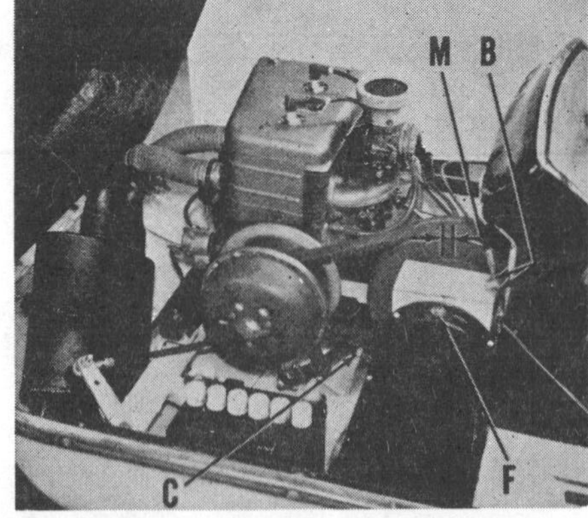

Fig. 2—View of chain case and drive unit with cowl opened. Drive chain tension is determined by measuring backlash (M) at driven pulley rim. Turn chain adjusting screw (C) until backlash measures ½-inch. Brake is adjusted by turning the two cable housing anchor nuts (B). Chaincase filler plug is shown at (F).

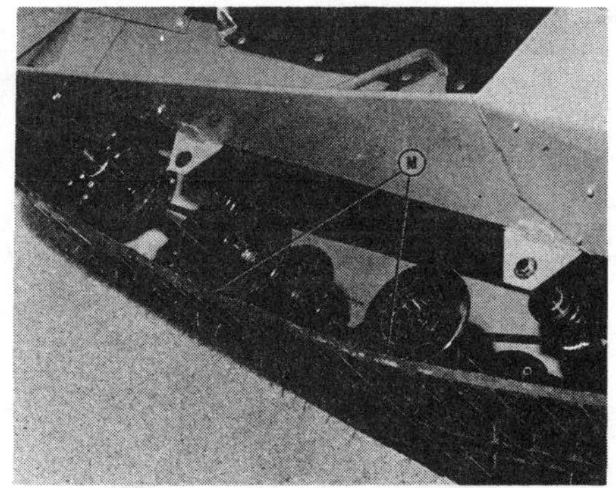

Fig. 3—With rear of machine raised until track is clear of ground, clearance (M) between center bogie wheel and track should measure ½-inch.

justment is made. Arm is centered by adjusting nuts (N) on cable housing.

TRACK. With rear of machine raised so that track is clear of ground, track should clear center bogie wheels by approximately ½-inch (M—Fig. 3). To adjust the track, loosen the two clamp bolts (A—Fig. 4) and turn adjusting screw (B) equally on each side of machine. Both sides must be adjusted alike.

NOTE: When track tension has been adjusted, alignment MUST be checked as outlined in the special TRACK SERVICE Section of this manual.

OVERHAUL

SKIS AND STEERING. Skis, ski spindles, steering arms and tie rod ends are interchangeable for right or left side. Skis are fitted with wear bars which may be renewed if worn or damaged.

DRIVE. Refer to the appropriate service section elsewhere in this manual for service on torque converter, track, brakes and related parts. Torque converter driven sheave on all models is equipped with standard spring and 41° cam ramps.

Fig. 4 — On 1971 models loosen clamp screws (A) and turn adjusting screws (B) to adjust track tension.

RAIDER

1972-1975

	Engine			Carburetor				Clutch		
Model	Make	Model	Displ.	Make	Model	Sprocket Ratio	Chain Size	Make	Shaft Center	Belt Number
					1972					
Raider 290	CCW		290cc	Walbro	WR6	13:29	40	Salsbury 770	10½	RA-1261
Raider 340	CCW		340cc	Walbro	WR6	15:29	40	Salsbury 770	10½	RA-1262
Raider 400	CCW		400cc	Walbro	WD6	16:29	40	Salsbury	10½	RA-1422
Bandit 290	Hirth		290cc	Walbro	WR5(2)	13:29	40		11½	RB-1540
Bandit 340	Hirth		340cc	Walbro	WR5(2)	15:29	40		11½	RB-1540
Bandit 440	Hirth		440cc	Walbro	WR5(2)	17:29	40		11½	RB-1540
Raider 440	Hirth		440cc	Walbro	WR5(2)	16:29	40		11½	RB-1540
					1973					
34TT	CCW		398cc	Walbro	WDA38	18:37	35-2		10.83	1603-R-3000
44TT	CCW	KEC440-4	436cc	Walbro	WDA38	20:37	35-2		10.83	1603-R-3000
44TT	CCW	KEC440-21	437.7cc	Walbro	WDA38	20:37	35-2		10.6	1603-R-3000
					1974					
Hawk	CCW		339cc	Walbro	WR-27	13:29	40	Salsbury 770	10.83	1603-R-4001
Eagle	CCW		398cc	Walbro	WDA-38	18:37	35-2	Salsbury 850	10.83	1603-R-3000
Eagle	CCW	KEC440-4	436cc	Walbro	WDA-38	20:37	35-2	Salsbury 850	10.6	1603-R-3000
Double Eagle	CCW	KEC440-21	437.7cc	Walbro	WRA-34	15:31	40	Salsbury 850	12.6	1603-R-4000
Double Eagle	CCW	KEC440-22	437.7cc	Walbro	WRA-34	15:31	40	Salsbury 850	12.6	1603-R-4000
					1975					
Eagle	Kohler	K340-2AS	339cc	Walbro	WDA-38	13:29	40	Salsbury 780	12.6	6008
Double Eagle	Kohler	K440-2AS	436cc	Walbro	WRA-34(2)	15:31	428	Salsbury 850	12.6	6038

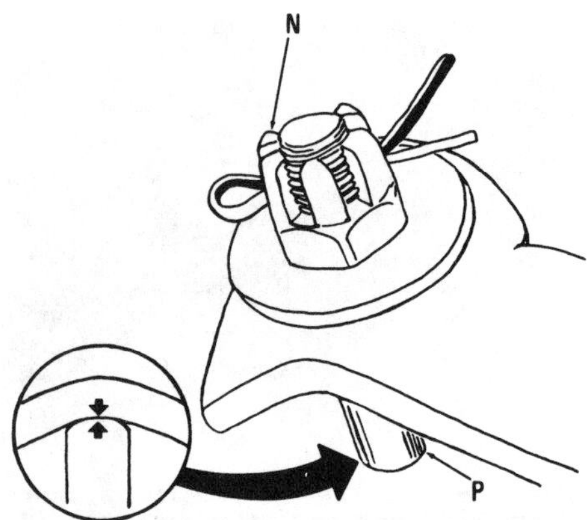

Fig. 1—Brake caliper adjustment is made by tightening or loosening actuating lever stud nut (N). When brake lever is released, push pins (P) must center in valleys on lever as shown in inset.

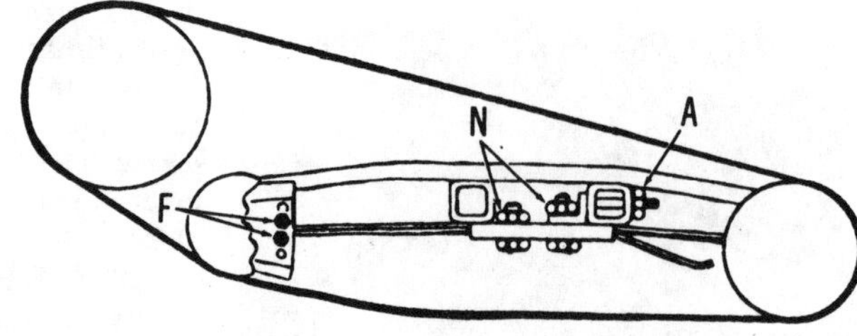

Fig. 2—Schematic view of leaf type spring track suspension used on some models. To adjust track tension, loosen the two spring clamp nuts (N) and turn adjusting bolt nut (A). Front spring anchor bolts (F) can be adjusted to any of three positions to vary load carried on skis.

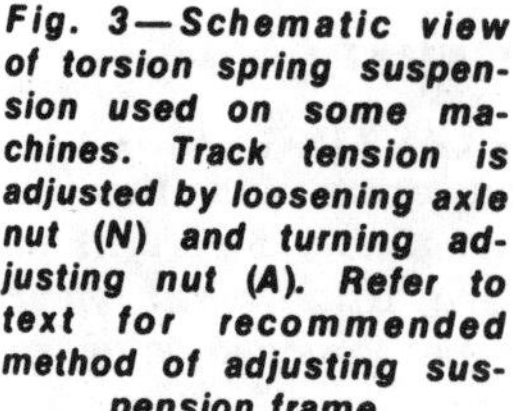

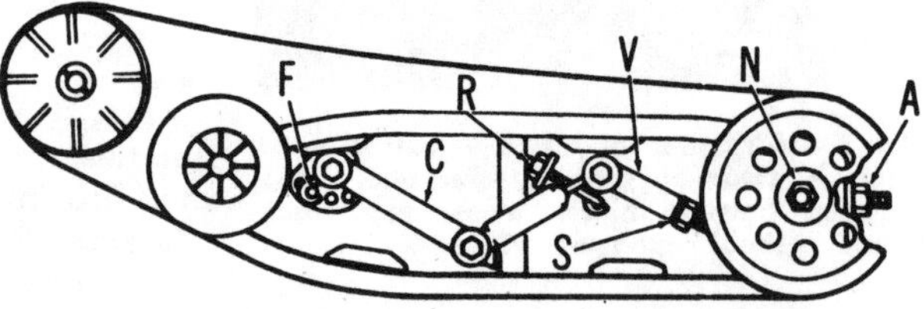

Fig. 3—Schematic view of torsion spring suspension used on some machines. Track tension is adjusted by loosening axle nut (N) and turning adjusting nut (A). Refer to text for recommended method of adjusting suspension frame.

A. Adjusting nut
C. Front control link
F. Front spring adjustment
N. Axle nut
R. Rear spring adjustment
V. Variable control link

LUBRICATION

The engine is lubricated by oil mixed with the fuel. Recommended fuel:oil mixture for models equipped with Hirth or CCW engines is 20:1 using Regular Gasoline and a recognized, branded Snowmobile Oil. On machines equipped with Kohler engines, recommended mixture is 40:1 using Premium Gasoline and Snowmobile Oil. Low Lead or No-Lead gasolines should not be used.

The enclosed chaincase should be filled to within ¼-inch below fill plug opening or not more than level with fill plug opening. Recommended lubricant is SAE 90 EP gear oil and gearcase capacity is approximately 9 fl.-oz.

No other periodic lubrication is required, however, all joints should be lubricated when needed with engine oil or spray lubricant.

ADJUSTMENT

STEERING SKIS. Toe-in should be 1/8-inch, measured at ends of skis when handlebar is in normal straight driving position. Adjustment is made by disconnecting tie rod at one end, and adjustment should be equalized between tie rods.

DRIVE CHAIN. The enclosed drive chain is self-adjusting and spring loaded tighteners are used on both sides of the chain.

BRAKE. Brake hand lever should have approximately 1/16-inch free play before brake begins to apply. Adjustment should be made at castellated nut (N—Fig. 1) on actuating lever stud rather than at cable housing anchor nuts. Caliper unit must be correctly aligned with friction surface of driven sheave fixed face, and alignment can be accomplished by loosening mounting bolts, applying brake; then retightening mountings while brakes are applied.

Push pins (P) must center in valleys of actuating lever when brake is released as shown in inset. Alignment can be accomplished by adjusting anchor nuts on cable housing until positioning is correct.

TRACK. Track tension is correct when top run of track sags approximately ½-inch midway between sprockets when bare machine is setting on a level surface.

To adjust track tension on models with leaf type springs, loosen the two clamp bolt nuts (N—Fig. 2) and turn adjusting bolt nut (A) until tension is correct. Retighten clamp bolt nuts when adjustment is correct. Both tracks must be adjusted alike.

On models with torsion bar suspension, refer to Fig. 3. To adjust track tension, loosen axle locknut (N) and turn adjusting bolt nut (A). Adjust both sides alike.

On all models with leaf springs, front spring anchor (F—Fig. 2) can be adjusted to any of three positions to vary the load carried on steering skis. Moving anchor to the two upper holes puts maximum pressure on skis; moving bolts to the two lower holes lessens ski pressure.

On models with torsion bar suspension, front control link (C) is a fixed link while rear control link (V) is not only adjustable but capable of lengthening automatically to allow maximum track contact over uneven terrain. Recommended method of adjusting suspension frame is as follows: Place the bare machine on a hard, level surface. Loosen the locknuts and turn both rear control link inner sleeves (S) out until track below front of slide rails begins to lift off the floor. Turn sleeves in until 7-9 track cleats touch the floor, then lock in place by tightening locknuts. Front torsion spring anchor (F) and rear torsion spring anchor (R) adjusts for weight of load. Normal adjustment is made at rear adjusting nut (R), with further adjustment at (F) as required.

NOTE: Be sure both tracks are adjusted exactly alike when machine is put back in service. If you have reason to believe that adjustment is unequal when machine is received, completely loosen the adjustments and bring both sides up together.

ROLL-O-FLEX

1971-1974

Model	Engine Make	Engine Model	Engine Displ.	Carburetor Make	Carburetor Model	Sprocket Ratio	Chain Size	Clutch Make	Clutch Shaft Center	Belt Number
					1971					
Apache 312 . . .	CCW	CCW312	312cc	Keihin	CD34-406	14:36	35-2	Eastern	10½	SV1354-2
Apache 340 . . .	CCW	CCW340/1	339cc	Keihin	CD34-406	14:36	35-2	Eastern	10½	SV1354-2
Apache 400 . . .	CCW	CCW400/1	398cc	Keihin	CD34-406	15:36	35-2	Eastern	10½	SV1354-2
Apache 440 . . .	CCW	CCW440/1	436cc	Keihin	CD34-406	16:36	35-2	Eastern	10½	SV1354-2
Comanche 295	CCW	CCW290/1	290.1cc	Keihin	CD34-406	14:36	35-2	Eastern	10½	SV1354-2
Comanche 340	CCW	CCW340/1	339cc	Keihin	CD34-406	15:36	35-2	Eastern	10½	SV1354-2
Comanche 400	CCW	CCW400/1	398cc	Keihin	CD34-406	16:36	35-2	Eastern	10½	SV1354-2
Comanche 440	CCW	CCW440/1	436cc	Keihin	CD34-406	17:36	35-2	Eastern	10½	SV1354-2
Cherokee 340 .	CCW	CCW340/1	339cc	Keihin	CD34-406	14:36	35-2	Eastern	10½	SV1354-2
Cherokee 400 .	CCW	CCW400/1	398cc	Keihin	CD34-406	15:36	35-2	Eastern	10½	SV1354-2
Cherokee 440 .	CCW	CCW440/1	436cc	Keihin	CD34-406	16:36	35-2	Eastern	10½	SV1354-2
					1972					
Comanche 292Y	Yamaha	SL292	292cc	Keihin	CD34-406	14:36	35-2	Yamaha	10¾-11	7148-2
Comanche Chf	Yamaha	SL292	292cc	Keihin	CD34-406	14:36	35-2	Yamaha	10¾-11	7148-2
Apache 292Y . .	Yamaha	SL292	292cc	Keihin	CD34-406	14:36	35-2	Yamaha	10¾-11	7148-2
Apache 338Y . .	Yamaha	338	338cc	Keihin	CD42-38	15:36	35-2	Yamaha	10¾-11	7148-2
Apache 396Y . .	Yamaha	396	396cc	Keihin	CD42-38	16:36	35-2	Yamaha	10¾-11	7148-2
Apache 433Y . .	Yamaha	433	433cc	Keihin	CD42-38	16:36	35-2	Yamaha	10¾-11	7148-2
Cherokee 396Y	Yamaha	396	396cc	Keihin	CD42-38	16:36	35-2	Yamaha	10¾-11	7148-2
Cherokee 433Y	Yamaha	433	433cc	Keihin	CD42-38	16:36	35-2	Yamaha	10¾-11	7148-2
GT292SS	Yamaha	292	292cc	Keihin	CD42-38	14:36	35-2	Yamaha	10¾-11	7148-2
GT338SS	Yamaha	338	338cc	Keihin	CD34-406(2)	16:36	35-2	Yamaha	10¾-11	7148-2
GT433SS	Yamaha	433	443cc	Keihin	CD34-406(2)	17:36	35-2	Yamaha	10¾-11	7148-2
					1973					
Comanche 292Y	Yamaha	292	292cc	Keihin	CD34-406	14:36	35-2	Yamaha	10¾-11	7148-2
Apache 338Y . .	Yamaha	338	338cc	Keihin	CD42-38	15:36	35-2	Yamaha	10¾-11	7148-2
Apache 396Y . .	Yamaha	396	396cc	Keihin	CD42-38	16:36	35-2	Yamaha	10¾-11	7148-2
Apache 433Y . .	Yamaha	433	433cc	Keihin	CD42-38	16:36	35-2	Yamaha	10¾-11	7148-2
Cherokee 396Y	Yamaha	396	396cc	Keihin	CD42-38	15:36	35-2	Yamaha	10¾-11	7148-2
Cherokee 433Y	Yamaha	396	396cc	Keihin	CD42-38	16:36	35-2	Yamaha	10¾-11	7148-2
GT292SS	Yamaha	292	292cc	Keihin	CD42-38	14:38	35-2	Yamaha	10¾-11	7148-2
GT338SS	Yamaha	338	338cc	Keihin	CD42-38	16:36	35-2	Yamaha	10¾-11	7148-2
GT433SS	Yamaha	433	433cc	Keihin	CD42-38	17:36	35-2	Yamaha	10¾-11	7148-2
					1974					
Apache.	Yamaha	338Y	339cc	Keihin	407	15:36	35-2	Yamaha	11-11¼	1204-03033A
Apache.	Yamaha	396Y	396cc	Keihin	407	16:36	35-2	Yamaha	11-11¼	1204-03033A
Apache.	Yamaha	433Y	433cc	Keihin	407	16:36	35-2	Yamaha	11-11¼	1204-03033A
G.T.	Yamaha	292S	292cc	Keihin	407	14:36	35-2	Yamaha	11-11¼	1204-03033A
G.T.	Yamaha	338S	338cc	Keihin	407	16:36	35-2	Yamaha	11-11¼	1204-03033A
G.T.	Yamaha	433S	433cc	Keihin	407	17:36	35-2	Yamaha	11-11¼	1204-03033A
Comanche	Yamaha	292S	292cc	Keihin	407	14:36	35-2	Yamaha	11-11¼	1204-03033A
Wild One	Kohler	K340-2AS	338cc	Dual Mikuni		16:36	35-2	Comet	11-11¼	

RUPP

1966-1972

Model	Engine Make	Engine Model	Engine Displ.	Carburetor Make	Carburetor Model	Sprocket Ratio	Chain Size	Clutch Make	Clutch Shaft Center	Belt Number
					1966					
SS II	JLO	L252	247cc	Tillotson	HL187A	10:30	35-2	Salsbury	11½	11831-4
SS III	Hirth	53R	300cc	Tillotson	HL214A	11:30	35-2	Salsbury	11½	11831-4
					1967					
SS250	JLO	L252	247cc	Tillotson	HL187A	11:26	40	Own	2⅛*	12047
SS300	Hirth	53R	300cc	Tillotson	HR3A	11:26	40	Own	2⅛*	12047
					1968					
Sport 281	Sachs	SA280	277cc	Tillotson	HL207B	12:28	35-2	Own	2⅛*	12754
GT300	Sachs	SA290	297cc	Tillotson	HR8A	12:28	35-2	Own	2⅛*	12754
					1969					
S281	Sachs	SA280	277cc	Tillotson	HR18A	12:28	35-2	Own	2⅛*	12754
GT300	Sachs	SA290	297cc	Tillotson	HR30A	12:28	35-2	Own	2⅛*	12754
GT370	Sachs	SA370	368cc	Tillotson	HD14A	13:28	35-2	Own	2⅛*	12754
					1970					
Sprint 29	Sachs	SA290	293cc	Tillotson		12:28	35-2	Own	2⅛*	12754
Sprint 34	Sachs	SA340	336cc	Tillotson		13:28	35-2	Own	2⅛*	12754
Sprint 44	Hirth	211R	438cc	Tillotson		14:28	35-2	Own	2⅛*	12754
Wide Track 44	Hirth	211R	438cc	Tillotson		14:28	35-2	Own	2⅛*	12754
Wide Track 634	Hirth	171R	634cc	Tillotson		15:28	35-2	Own	2⅛*	12754
*Rim Clearance.										
					1971					
S-23	JLO	L230	223cc	Walbro	BDC	11:28	35-2	Own	2⅛*	12754
S-29	Sachs	SA290	293cc	Tillotson	HD38A	12:28	35-2	Own	2⅛*	12754
S-34	CCW	340	339cc	Tillotson	HD38A	13:28	35-2	Own	2⅛*	12754
American 30	Rupp	TR340	337cc	Keihin	407	13:28	35-2	Own	2⅛*	12754
S-44	Rupp	TR440	438cc	Keihin	407	14:28	35-2	Own	2⅛*	12754
WT-440	Rupp	TR440	438cc	Keihin	407	14:28	35-2	Own	2⅛*	12754
WT-634	Hirth	171R	634cc	Tillotson	HD38A	15:28	35-2	Own	2⅛*	12754
M-400N	Rupp	TR400S	399cc	Keihin	407	15:28	35-2	Own	2⅛*	12754
M-440N	Rupp	TR440S	438cc	Keihin	407	15:28	35-2	Own	2⅛*	12754
M-440W	Rupp	TR440S	438cc	Keihin	407	15:28	35-2	Own	2⅛*	12754
M-600	Rupp	TR600SR	598cc	Keihin	407(3)	14:26	35-3	Salsbury	10½	18189
M-800	Hirth	230R	793cc	Tillotson	HD38A(3)	17:26	35-3	Salsbury 1190	10½	17602
*Rim Clearance.										
					1972					
Rogue 15	JLO	L230	223cc	Walbro	BDC	11:28	35-2	Own	2⅛*	12754
Rogue 25	Rupp	TR295	294cc	Keihin	407	13:28	35-2	Own	2⅛*	12754
Yankee 25	Rupp	TR295	294cc	Keihin	407	13:28	35-2	Own	2⅛*	12754
Yankee 30	Rupp	TR340	337cc	Keihin	407cc	13:28	35-2	Own	2⅛*	12754
Yankee 40	Rupp	TR440-2	438cc	Keihin	407	14:28	35-2	Own	2⅛*	12754
American 30	Rupp	TR340	337cc	Keihin	407	13:28	35-2	Own	2⅛*	12754
American 40	Rupp	TR440-2	438cc	Keihin	407	14:28	35-2	Own	2⅛*	12754
American 50	Rupp	TR650	644cc	Keihin	407	16:28	35-2	Own	2⅛*	12754
Nitro 295	Rupp	TR295S	294cc	Keihin		13:28	35-2	Own	2⅛*	12754
Nitro 340	Rupp	TR340S	337cc	Keihin		13:28	35-2	Own	2⅛*	12754
Nitro 400	Rupp	TR400S-2	399cc	Keihin	407	13:28	35-2	Own	2⅛*	12754
Nitro 440	Rupp	TR440S-2	438cc	Keihin	407	14:28	35-2	Own	2⅛*	12754
*Rim Clearance.										

LUBRICATION

The engine is lubricated by oil mixed with the fuel. Recommended fuel-oil ratio is 20:1.

The manufacturer recommends that the following chassis and drive train points be lubricated each 25 hours or two weeks of use, which ever occurs first.

Steering linkage & handle bar bushings—Low temp. grease

Torque Converter Driven Sheave (shaft & pins)—Low temp. grease

On models with enclosed drive chain, oil level should be maintained at level of check plug opening with Automatic Transmission Fluid, (Dexron or equivalent). On models with open drive chain, keep chain clean and well oiled using Rupp Lubricant or equivalent.

Track bearings are self-aligning sealed type which do not require lubrication.

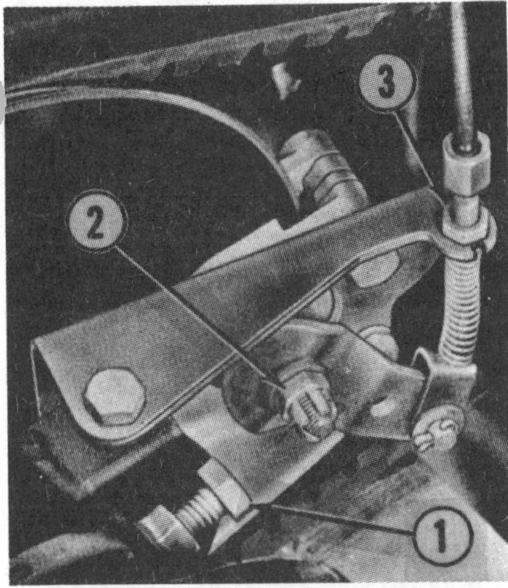

Fig. 2—Drive chain is adjusted by moving eccentric bearing housing bolt (1) in slotted hole. To adjust the disc type brake, remove cotter pin and turn castellated nut (2) until brake puck just clears sheave rim. Brake actuating lever height can be adjusted at cable housing nuts (3).

Fig. 4—A special tool is available to properly adjust torque converter offset as shown.

Fig. 6—On most 1972 models, remove chaincase cover and loosen retaining nuts (shown) to adjust drive chain.

ADJUSTMENT

STEERING SKIS. Turn handle bar to normal straight driving position and check to see that both skis are parallel with each other and with drive track and vehicle frame. If adjustment is required, remove the bolt securing both tie rods to handle bar and shorten or lengthen tie rods as needed.

DRIVE BELT ADJUSTMENT. On 1967 and 1968 models with Rupp Torque Converter, drive belt should be snug in idle position but not depressed into groove of driven sheave. On 1969 models, distance (A—Fig. 3) between sheave rims should measure 2⅛ inches. On models with Salsbury torque converter, center distance of converter sheave hubs should be 11½ inches. Adjust by loosening the four engine mounting screws and sliding engine on frame as required.

On 1970 and later machines, center distance is not adjustable but engine mounting frame can be moved side-

Fig. 3—On 1969 models, torque converter sheave spacing is correct when distance (A) equals 2⅛ inches.

Fig. 5—Some models have a rubber inspection plug which may be removed as shown for checking drive chain tension.

ways to adjust pulley alignment. The manufacturer provides a special gage (Rupp Part No. 15012) to assist in alignment as shown in Fig. 4. If the special tool is not available, carefully align sheave centerlines as outlined in CONVERTER (BELT DRIVE) Section tion elsewhere in this manual.

DRIVE CHAIN ADJUSTMENT. Drive chain tension is correct when a deflection of ⅜-½ inch exists, measured midway between sprockets. Adjustment on all except some 1972 models is by means of eccentric bearing housing for upper sprocket shaft. Refer to Fig. 2.

Eccentric adjusting bolt (1) may be toward rear (early models) or front (1970 & 1971 Models and 1972 Rogue). Pushing down on bolt normally tightens the chain, pulling up loosens chain. If bolt bottoms in adjusting slot, remove and reinstall in threaded hole in opposite end of slot for additional adjustment. Chain tension can be checked on some models by removing rubber inspection plug as shown in Fig. 5.

On 1972 models except ROGUE it is necessary to remove chaincase cover as shown in Fig. 6. Tip the machine on rght side to keep lubricant from running out, then remove the cover. Loosen the three retaining nuts and move (rotate) bearing housing as required.

On those models using fixed face of driven sheave as a brake friction surface, brake adjustment and alignment must be checked after drive chain is adjusted.

TRACK ADJUSTMENT. To adjust track tension on early models raise rear of vehicle on track stand. With track clear of ground, measure the distance (A—Fig. 7) from running board to underside of bearing bracket on both sides of vehicle. Distance (A) should be 3½ inches on early models and 3¼ inches on late models. Both sides should be equal. To adjust the track, loosen the clamp bolts and turn adjusting screws until measurement is correct.

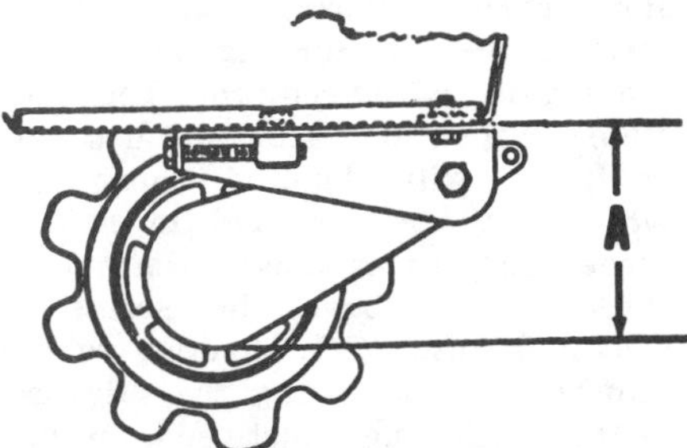

Fig. 7—With track clear of ground, distance (A) from running board to furthest part of swing arm should be 3½ inches on early models or 3¼ inches on late models.

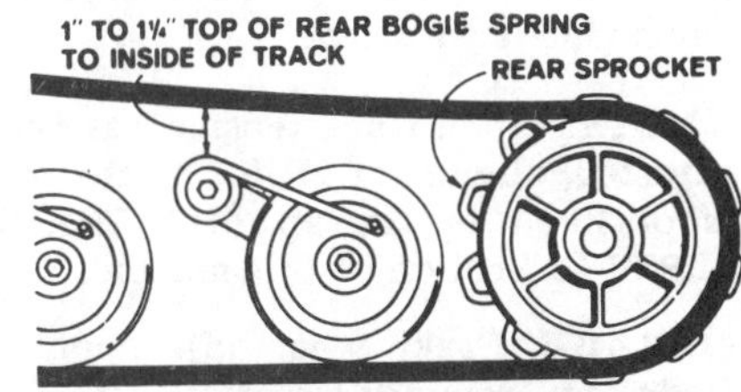

Fig. 8—On 1970 and 1971 models, track tension is correct when track clears rear bogie spring 1-1½ inches when setting on ground without operator.

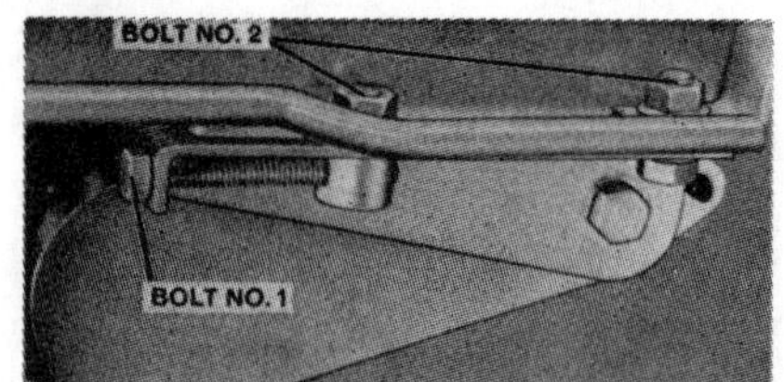

Fig. 9—To adjust track tension on 1970 and 1971 models and Rogue, Yankee or American for 1972, loosen clamp bolts (2) and turn adjusting bolt (1).

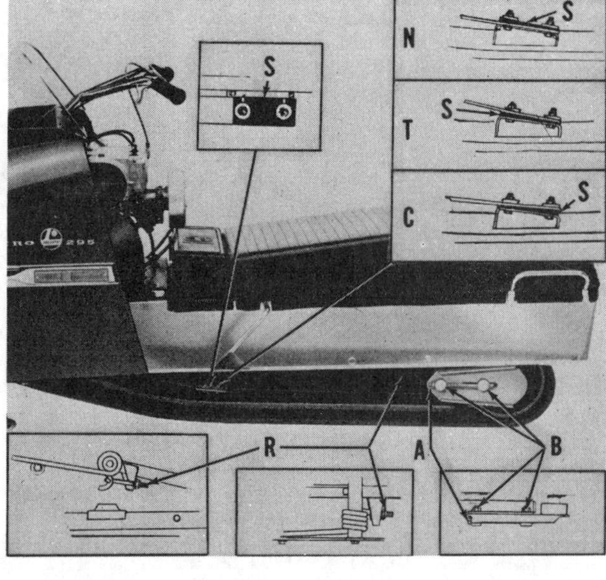

Fig. 10—On 1972 Nitro with Slider Suspension, track tension is adjusted by loosening clamp bolts (B) and turning adjusting bolt (A). Turning nut (R) on rear tension springs adjusts for weight of operator. Shim (S) can be installed in three positions as shown for differing operating conditions.

C. Increased steering control
N. Normal
T. Increased traction

On 1970 and 1971 models, adjust track tension with machine setting on even surface without operator. Upper run of track should clear rear bogie spring by 1-1¼ inches as shown in Fig. 8. Adjust by loosening clamp bolts. (2—Fig. 9) and turning adjusting screws (1).

On 1972 Rogue, Yankee and American, track tension is adjusted as shown in Fig. 9. Tension is correct when top run of track sags 1-1¼ inches with machine setting on even surface without operator.

On 1972 Nitro with slider suspension, track tension is correct when sag of top run of track is 1-inch, machine setting on even surface with normal load of operator. Adjust track tension by loosening the two clamp nuts (B—Fig. 10) and tightening adjusting bolts (A). On Nitro Models, two additional adjustments are provided; rear spring tension should be adjusted to provide approximately 2½-inches deflection (D) at rear of machine while standing with normal load. Adjustment is made by turning ride adjustment nuts (R) as required. The front slide suspension leaf springs are equipped with tapered shims (S) which may be installed in any of three positions as shown. Normal installation is above the spring as shown in inset (N). Traction can be improved by installing the shim beneath the spring, thick end forward as shown at (T). Steering control is improved by installing shim beneath the spring, thin end forward as shown at (C). Shim can be withdrawn and moved by loosening the clamp bolts, which should be tightened securely when ride is adjusted.

NOTE: When track tension has been adjusted, alignment MUST be checked as outlined in the special TRACK SERVICE Section of this manual.

BRAKE. Brake wear adjustment is made by removing cotter pin and turning castellated nut (2—Fig. 2) until brake is applied. On models using fixed face of driven sheave as a friction surface, brake must be properly aligned and alignment may change with drive chain adjustment. Loosen brake housing anchor bolts and apply the brake to align the unit. Turn cable housing anchor nuts (3) as required to align brake push pins with valleys in actuating lever.

OVERHAUL

SKI WEAR BARS. Skis are fitted with wear bars which are retained by a nut on one (or two) center studs. Wear bar can be installed either end forward when renewal is indicated.

FIBERGLASS NOSE. To remove the fiberglass nose on early models, it is first necessary to remove skis and ski spindles. Remove fuel tank cap and remove or disconnect headlamp. Nose must be removed for access to fuel tank. Most other service on vehicles can be performed without removing nose piece.

Fig. 11—On late models, upper sprocket is retained by nut and cotter pin, and lower nut by snap ring. Optional sprocket sizes are available.

DRIVE CHAIN. The lower (driven) sprocket on early models is retained to track drive (secondary) shaft by a taper lock bushing and ¼-inch square key. To remove the sprocket, remove one of the Allen head set screws and loosen other screw several turns. Thread the removed screw in third hole (opposite split in taper hub) and use as forcing screw to loosen hub in sprocket bore. When hub is loose, slide hub and sprocket as an assembly from shaft. Upper sprocket on models SS250 and SS300 is threaded on torque converter driven shaft. To remove the sprocket, hold driven sheave and loosen jam nut, then unscrew nut and sprocket from shaft. Chain is ½-inch pitch (No. 40) steel roller chain.

On models with enclosed chain case, a ⅜-inch pitch double (35-2) chain is used. On 1969 models, lower sprocket must be removed through upper access opening after first removing the splined, track drive axle.

On 1970 and later models, chaincase is equipped with a full cover as shown in Fig. 11. Upper sprocket is retained by a nut and cotter pin and lower sprocket by a snap ring. Sprockets are fully interchangeable; upper sprocket is available in all sizes from 11 to 18 teeth and lower sprocket in 28 or 32 tooth size. Tighten upper sprocket nut to a torque of 50 ft.-lbs. when reinstalling.

RUPP

1973-1978

	Engine			Carburetor				Clutch		
Model	Make	Model	Displ.	Make	Model	Sprocket Ratio	Chain Size	Make	Shaft Center	Belt Number
1973										
Sport 25	Rupp	TR295	294cc	Tillotson	HR141A	13:28	35-2	Own	2-1/8*	12754
Sport 30	Rupp	TR340	337cc	Tillotson	HR141A	13:28	35-2	Own	2-1/8*	12754
American 30	Rupp	TR340	337cc	Tillotson	HR141A	13:28	35-2	Own	2-1/8*	12754
American 40	Rupp	TR438	438cc	Tillotson	HD119A	14:28	35-2	Own	2-1/8*	12754
Nitro 295	Rupp	TR295S	294cc	Tillotson	HR141A	13:28	35-2	Own	2-1/8*	12754
Nitro 340	Rupp	TR340S	337cc	Tillotson	HR141A	13:28	35-2	Own	2-1/8*	12754
Nitro 400	Rupp	TR400S-2	399cc	Tillotson	HD119A	14:28	35-2	Own	2-1/8*	12754
Nitro 440	Rupp	TR440S-2	438cc	Tillotson	HD119A	14:28	35-2	Own	2-1/8*	12754
Yankee 30	Rupp	TR340	337cc	Tillotson	HR141A	13:28	35-2	Own	2-1/8*	12754
Yankee 40	Rupp	TR440	438cc	Tillotson	HD119A	14:28	35-2	Own	2-1/8*	12754
*Rim Clearance.										
1974										
Sport 25	Rupp	TR295	292cc	Tillotson	HR141A	13:28	35-2	Own	10.87	12754
Sport 30	Rupp	TR340	338cc	Tillotson	HR141A	13:28	35-2	Own	10.87	12754
American 30	Rupp	TR340	338cc	Tillotson	HR141A	13:28	35-2	Own	10.87	12754
American 40	Rupp	TR440	438cc	Tillotson	HD119A	14:28	35-2	Own	10.87	12754
Nitro II	Kohler	SK340-2AS	339cc	Mikuni	VM32-2	12:28	35-2	Own	10.87	36590
Nitro II	Kohler	K440-2AS	436cc	Mikuni	VM32-2	13:28	35-2	Own	10.87	36590
1975										
Sport 25	Rupp	TR295	292cc	Tillotson	HR141A	13:28	35-2	Own	10.87	12754
Sport 30	Rupp	TR340	338cc	Tillotson	HR141A	13:28	35-2	Own	10.87	12754
American 30	Rupp	TR340	338cc	Tillotson	HR141A	13:28	35-2	Own	10.87	12754
American 40	Rupp	TR440	438cc	Tillotson	HD119A	14:28	35-2	Own	10.87	12754
Nitro 340	Kohler	SK340-2AS	339cc	Mikuni	VM32-2	12:28	35-2	Own	10.87	36590
Nitro 440	Kohler	K440-2AS	436cc	Mikuni	VM32-2	13:28	35-2	Own	10.87	36590
Nitro F A340	Kohler	K340-2RS	339cc	Mikuni	VM36-2	14:28	35-2	Own	10.87	36590
Nitro F A440	Kohler	K440-2RS	429.4cc	Mikuni	VM38-2	15:28	35-2	Own	10.87	36590
1976										
Sport 340	Rupp	G34B	338cc	Mikuni	VM32	12:28	35-2	Own	10.88	36590
Rally 440	Kohler	K4402AS	436cc	Mikuni	VM32	13:28	35-2	Own	10.88	36590
Nitro 340	Rupp	G34BWR	338cc	Mikuni	VM36	20:39	Silent	Arctic	11.30	38738
Nitro 440	Rupp	G44BWR	432cc	Mikuni	VM38	20:35	Silent	Arctic	11.30	38738
Magnun 250	Rupp	G25BWR	248cc	Mikuni	VM34	15:35	Silent	Arctic	11.30	39839
Magnum 340	Rupp	G34BWR	338cc	Mikuni	VM36	20:39	Silent	Arctic	11.30	38738
Magnum 440	Rupp	G44BWR	432cc	Mikuni	VM38	20:35	Silent	Arctic	11.30	38738
1977										
Nitro 250	Xenoah	G25BWR	248cc	Mikuni	VM34	15:35	Silent	Arctic	11.3	38738
Nitro 440	Xenoah	G44BWR	432cc	Mikuni	VM34	20:35	Silent	Arctic	11.3	38738
1978										
Nitro 440	Xenoah	G44BWR	432cc	Mikuni	VM38	19:35	Silent	Arctic	11.3	38738
Rally	Xenoah	G50B	484cc	Mikuni	VM36	14:28		Comet	...	36590

LUBRICATION

The engine is lubricated by oil mixed with the fuel. Recommended fuel:oil ratio is 20:1 for models equipped with early RUPP engines and KOHLER Free Air racing engines. Models with KOHLER Axial Fan cooled engines use 40:1 fuel:oil ratio except on models equipped with automatic oil injection. Recommended fuel:oil ratio for Xenoah engines is 30:1.

The manufacturer recommends that the following chassis and drive train points be lubricated each 25 hours or two weeks of use, which ever occurs first.

Steering linkage and handlebar bushings—Low temperature grease.

Torque Converter Driven Sheave (shaft and pins)—Low temperature grease.

Chaincase oil level should be maintained at level of check plug opening with Automatic Transmission Fluid (Dextron or equivalent).

Track bearings are self-aligning sealed type which do not require lubrication.

ADJUSTMENT

STEERING SKIS. Turn handlebar to normal straight driving position and check to see that both skis are parallel with each other and with drive track and vehicle frame. If adjusting is required, remove the bolt securing both tie rods to handlebar and shorten or lengthen tie rods as needed.

DRIVE BELT ADJUSTMENT. Center distance is not adjustable on early models but engine mounting frame can be moved sideways to adjust pulley alignment. The manufacturer provides a special gage (Rupp Part No. 15012) to assist in alignment as shown in Fig. 1. If the special tool is not available, carefully align sheave centerlines as outlined in CONVERTER (BELT DRIVE) Section elsewhere in this manual.

On late models using Arctic Enterprises clutch, engine can be shifted front to rear as well as sideways. Shaft center distance (A—Fig. 2) should be 11.3 inches (287 mm) and offset (B) should be ½-inch (6.5 mm). Adjustment is made by moving engine.

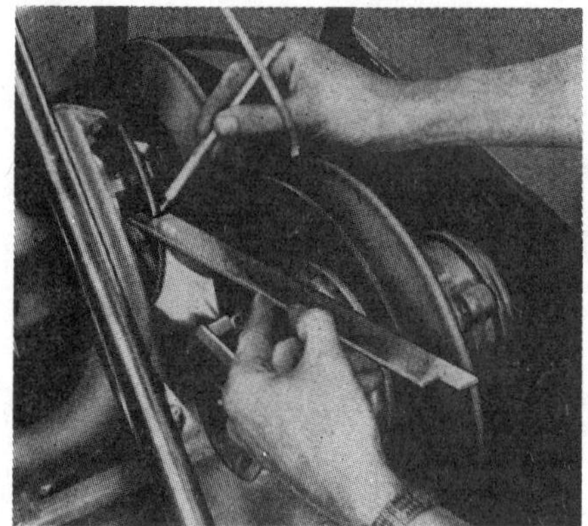

Fig. 1—A special tool is available to properly adjust torque converter offset on some models.

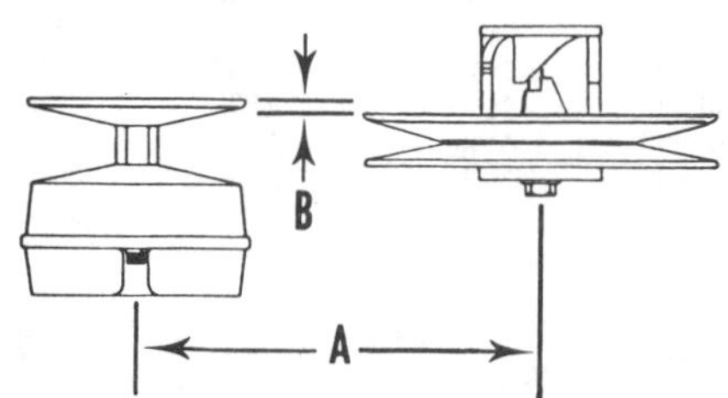

Fig. 2—Shaft center distance (A) should measure 11.3 inches and offset (B) 7/16 inch.

Fig. 3—Some models have a rubber inspection plug which may be removed as shown for checking drive chain tension.

DRIVE CHAIN ADJUSTMENT. On early models, drive chain tension is correct when a deflection of 3/8-½ inch exists, measured midway between sprockets. Adjustment is checked by removing rubber inspection plug from chaincase cover as shown in Fig. 3. On models having a chaincase cover of the type shown in Fig. 4, adjustment is made by loosening locknut on eccentric adjusting bolt (E) and moving bolt in slotted hole until correct slack is obtained. On models having a chaincase of the type shown in Fig. 6, tip machine on right side to prevent lubricant loss, remove chaincase cover, loosen the three clamping retaining nuts shown in Fig. 5 and turn eccentric housing as required until correct slack is obtained. On models not requiring removal of chaincase cover, check the slack by reaching through inspection plug hole.

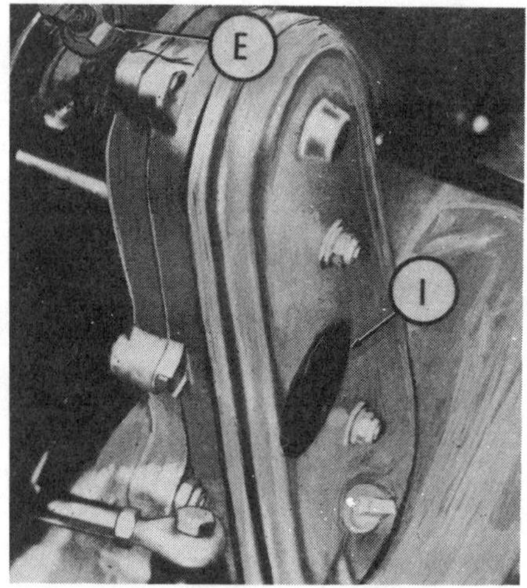

Fig. 4—View of chaincase used on some models. Chain tension is checked through opening for inspection plug (I) and adjusted at eccentric locking bolt (E). Chain deflection should be 3/8-½ inch (10-12 mm).

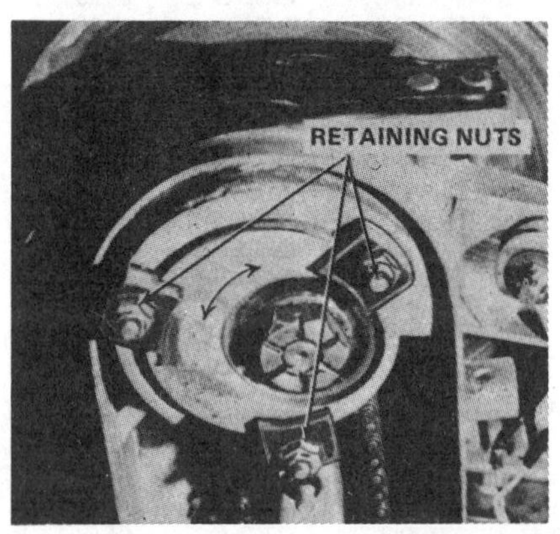

Fig. 5—Remove chaincase cover and loosen retaining nuts (shown) to adjust drive chain.

On models using fixed face of driven sheave as a brake friction surface instead of a separate disc, brake must be realigned and adjusted after drive chain is adjusted.

On late models using a cross shaft and right-hand mounted chaincase, drive chain tensioning is automatic. Because of the spring-loaded chain tighteners, backlash at pulley cannot be used to determine chain condition.

BRAKE ADJUSTMENT. On early models with self-adjusting brakes, adjust brake cable housing anchor nuts (AN—Fig. 6) until actuating cam push pins (P—Fig. 7) center in valleys of actuating arm as shown in inset. Also be sure that ratchet pawl arm moves freely on actuating cable clevis and that pawl properly engages teeth on adjusting nut.

On models without self-adjusting brakes, make sure push pins (P) center in valleys of actuating arm as shown in inset, and tighten actuating stud nut (N) until brake is free when released, but fully applies before hand brake lever touches handlebar grip.

On models using fixed face of secondary sheave as a friction surface, caliper pads must be parallel with braking surface of sheave. If realign-

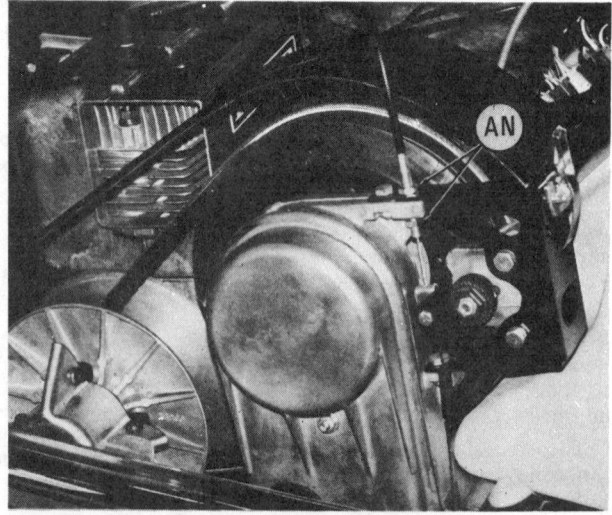

Fig. 6—View of drive unit, chaincase and self-adjusting caliper brake used on some models. Brake push pins should center in valleys of actuating cam when brake is released; adjust by repositioning brake cable housing anchor nuts (AN).

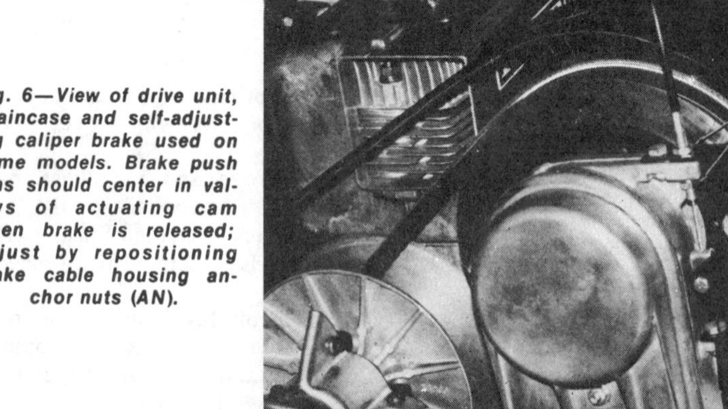

ment is required, loosen mounting screws and fully apply the brake, then retighten mounting screws with brake applied. Readjust brake clearance after alignment has been corrected.

On late models with helix actuated caliper disc brakes, wear adjustment is accomplished by repositioning adjusting arm on actuating shaft. With brake fully applied, clearance between hand brake lever and handlebar stop should be ¼- to ½-inch. Minor adjustment may be made at brake cable housing anchor nuts (B—Fig. 8); when further adjustment at this point is impossible, loosen retaining cap screw (C), disconnect cable from clevis (D) and rotate arm one notch clockwise on adjusting collar. Retighten cap screw (C) to 8 ft-lbs. (1 kg-m), reconnect cable to clevis (D) then readjust brake cable housing anchor nuts (B) until clearance at hand lever is as specified. With brake adjusted and applied, check end clearance (E—Fig. 9). If clearance with brake fully applied is less than 0.040 inch (1 mm), renew BOTH brake pucks and readjust as outlined.

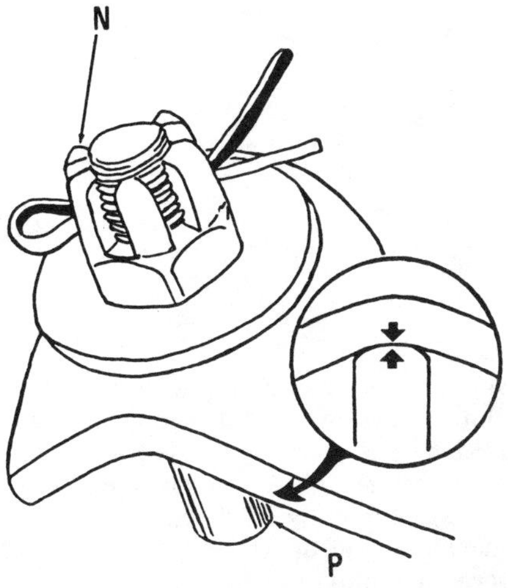

Fig. 7—Schematic view of caliper type disc brake actuating mechanism. Actuating push pins (P) must center in valleys of actuating cam (inset) when brake is released. Wear adjustment is accomplished by turning stud nut (N).

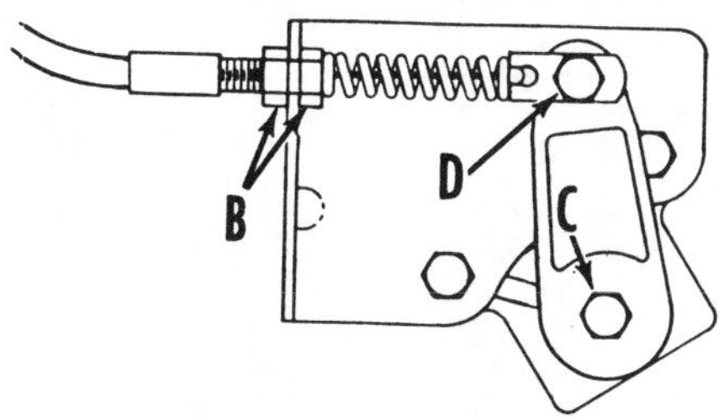

Fig. 8—Adjust brake by repositioning brake cable housing anchor nuts (B). When additional adjustment is required, disconnect cable from actuating arm (D), loosen helical shaft cap screw (C) and move actuating arm one notch clockwise on helical shaft. Retighten cap screw (C) and reconnect cable; then readjust at cable housing anchor nuts (B).

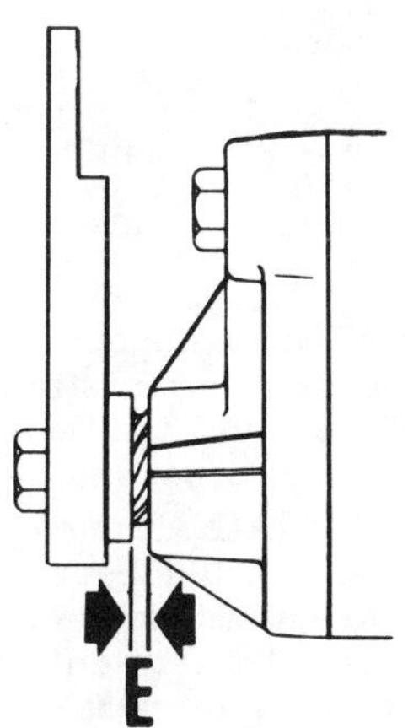

Fig. 9—If clearance (E) between actuating arm collar and brake housing is less than 0.040 inch (1 mm) with brake fully applied, renew both brake pucks.

TRACK ADJUSTMENT. Adjust track tension with machine setting on even surface without operator. Upper run of track should clear rear bogie spring by 1-1¼ inches as shown in Fig. 10. Adjust by loosening clamp bolts, (2—Fig. 11) and turning adjusting screws (1).

On models with slider suspension, track tension is correct when sag at top run of track is 1-inch, machine setting on even surface with normal load of operator. Adjust track tension by loosening the two clamp nuts (B—Fig. 12) and tightening adjusting bolts (A). On Nitro models, two additional adjustments are provided; rear spring tension should be adjusted to provide approximately 2½-inches deflection (D) at rear of machine while standing with normal load. Adjustment is made by turning ride adjustment nuts (R) as required. The front slide suspension leaf springs are equipped with tapered shims (S) which may be installed in any of three positions as shown. Normal installation is above the spring as shown in inset (N). Traction can be improved by installing the shim beneath the spring, thick end forward as shown at (T). Steering control is improved by installing shim beneath the spring, thin end forward as shown at (C). Shim can be withdrawn and moved by loosening the clamp bolts, which should be tightened securely when ride is adjusted.

NOTE: When track tension has been adjusted, alignment MUST be checked

Fig. 10—Track tension is correct when track clears rear bogie spring 1-1½ inches when setting on ground without operator.

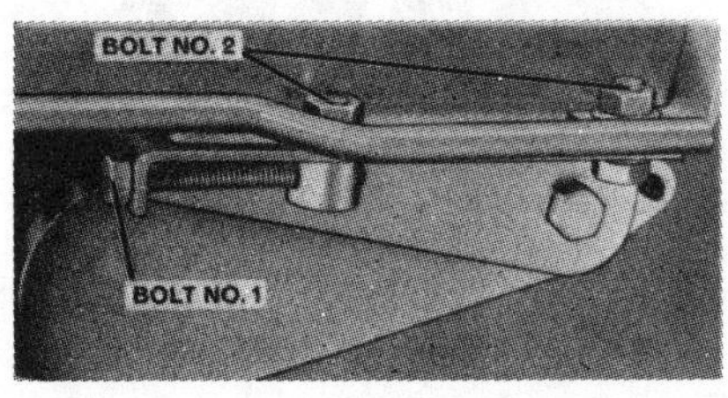

Fig. 11—To adjust track tension on bogie wheel models loosen clamp bolts (2) and turn adjusting bolt (1).

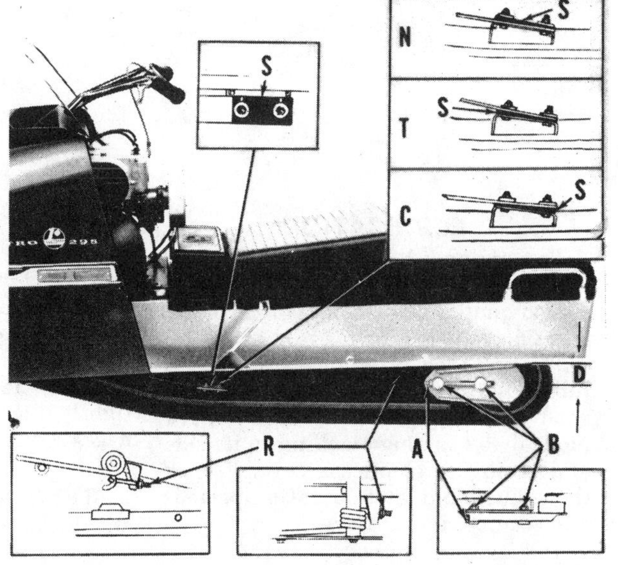

Fig. 12—Models with Slider Suspension, track tension is adjusted by loosening clamp bolts (B) and turning adjusting bolt (A). Turning nut (R) on rear tension springs adjusts for weight of operator. Shim (S) can be installed in three positions as shown for different operating conditions.

C. Increased steering control
N. Normal
T. Increased traction

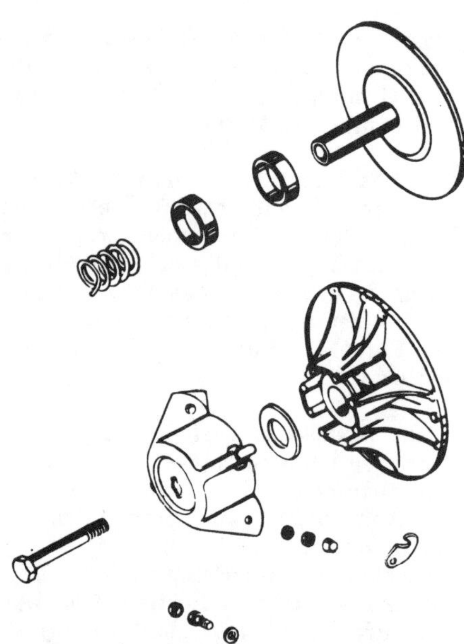

Fig. 13—Exploded view of RUPP drive clutch showing component parts. Optional weights and springs are available to alter engagement and shift patterns. Weight retaining bolt head should always be installed on clockwise as shown.

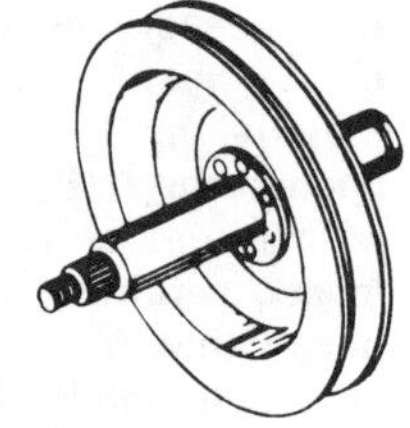
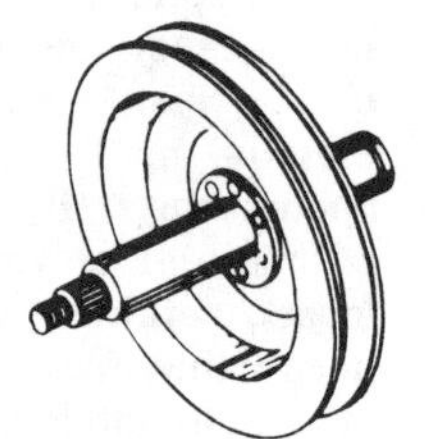
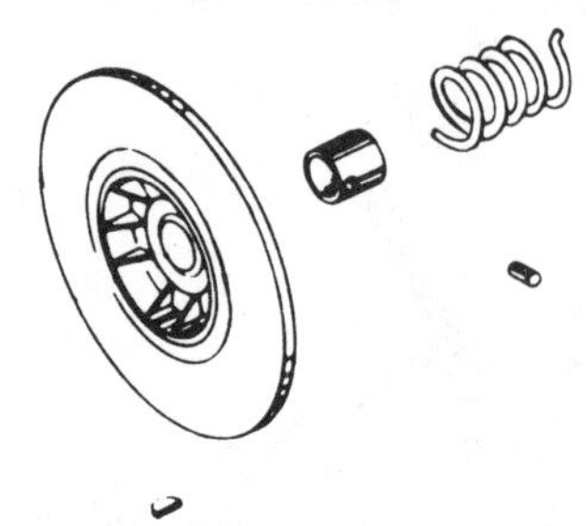
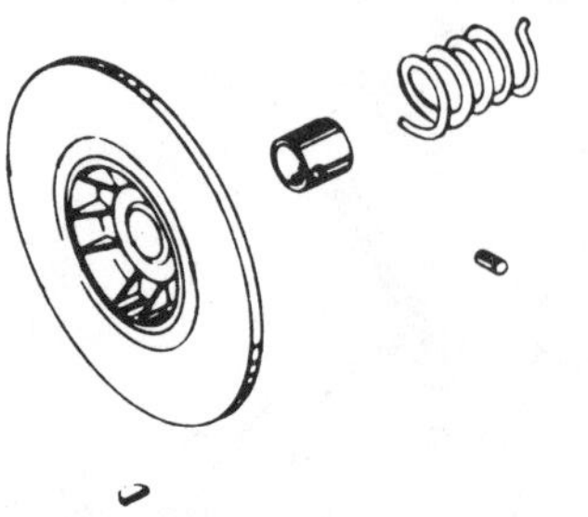

Fig. 14—Exploded view of RUPP driven clutch. Torsion spring should be preloaded ⅓-turn when unit is assembled.

as outlined in the special TRACK SERVICE Section of this manual.

OVERHAUL

ENGINE. Refer to the appropriate service sections elsewhere in this manual for service specifics on engine and components.

TORQUE CONVERTER. Figure 13 shows an exploded view of RUPP Drive Clutch and Fig. 14 an exploded view of driven unit. Optional drive clutch weights and springs are available for adapting clutch to different engine sizes; check with parts supply source for proper application. Driven clutch torsion spring should be preloaded one cam 120 degrees when clutch is assembled. Engagement speed is approximately 3000 rpm for family machines and up to 3800 rpm for performance units.

Clutch components should be kept clean and dry, and lubricated with a dry-type spray lubricant such as WD-40, LPS-2, etc.

Refer to ARCTIC CAT section for Arctic drive clutch and to CONVERTER section for COMET unit.

SABRE

1972-1973

	Engine			Carburetor				Clutch		
Model	Make	Model	Displ.	Make	Model	Sprocket Ratio	Chain Size	Make	Shaft Center	Belt Number
					1972					
340T	JLO	LR340 2	339cc	Walbro	WD6-6	16:33	35-2	Precico	10¾	16261004
400T	JLO	LR399 2	398cc	Walbro	WD6-6	17:33	35-2	Precico	10¾	16261004
400T	JLO	LR440 2	428cc	Walbro	WD6-6	18:33	35-2	Precico	10¾	16261004
					1973					
340T	JLO	LR340/2	339cc	Walbro	WD-6	16:33	35-2	Precico	10¾	16261004
400T	JLO	LR399/2	398cc	Walbro	WD-6	17:33	35-2	Precico	10¾	16261004
440T	JLO	LR440/2	428cc	Walbro	WD-6	18:33	35-2	Precico	10¾	16261004

LUBRICATION

The engine is lubricated by oil mixed with the fuel. Use regular gasoline and a good quality snowmobile oil mixed at a ratio of 20:1.

The enclosed drive chain should be lubricated with FIBREX EP7 or other good low temperature grease. Check monthly by tipping machine on its side and removing chaincase cover. Check the adjustment at lubrication periods and readjust if necessary.

Ski legs, bogie wheel bearings and secondary drive shaft bearings are equipped with grease fittings and should be lubricated as necessary with low temperature grease.

Ski pivot bolt, ski springs and steering tie rod ball joints should be lightly oiled with SAE 30 engine oil as necessary.

ADJUSTMENT

STEERING SKIS. Steering skis should be parallel with vehicle frame and toe in approximately ⅛-inch when handlebar is in normal straight driving position. To adjust the tie rods, disconnect the rod at either end.

DRIVE CHAIN. The enclosed roller drive chain should have 5/16-⅜ inch slack measured midway between sprockets. Adjustment should be checked during lubrication periods. To adjust the chain, loosen the two jam nuts (1—Fig. 1) and back out the two adjusting bolts (2); then move adjusting bolt either way in housing slot until adjustment is correct. If screw bottoms in slot, remove screw and transfer to threaded hole which has appeared in opposite end of slot. Tighten adjusting screws and jam nuts when adjustment is complete.

BRAKE. Brake wear adjustment is made by turning the self-locking nut (1—Fig. 2) on brake actuating arm stud. Tighten nut until slight resistance is felt then back off ½-turn. If brake still drags, back nut off an additional amount until brake is free.

Push pins must center in valleys of actuating arm when brake is released. Turn brake housing anchor nuts (2) if necessary to properly position brake arm. Fixed face of driven pulley is used as friction surface and alignment may be altered when drive chain is adjusted. Realign if necessary by loosening mounting bolts then applying brake.

TRACK. With rear of machine raised until track is clear, vertical distance between bottom of footrest and lower edge of track should be 4½—5 inches measured at center bogie support. Adjust by loosening clamp bolts (1—Fig. 3) and turning adjusting screws (2). Both sides must be adjusted alike.

NOTE: When track tension has been adjusted, alignment MUST be checked as outlined in TRACK SERVICE Section of this manual.

OVERHAUL

Upper sprocket is available in optional sizes from 13 to 22 teeth and lower sprocket is available in an optional 31 tooth size.

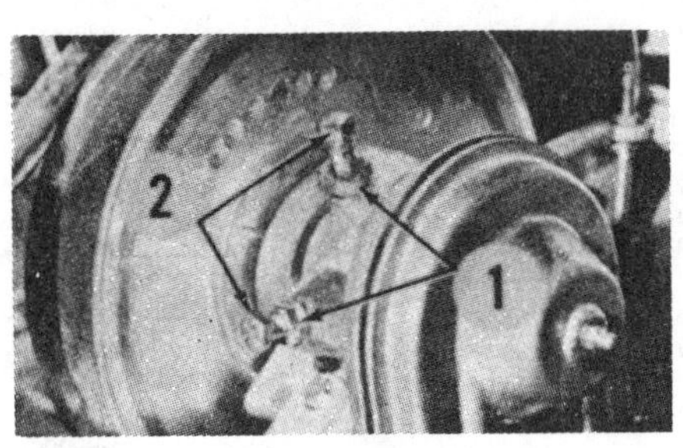

Fig. 1—To adjust drive chain, loosen the two jam nuts (1) and back out adjusting screws (2), then move rear bolt in slotted hole.

Fig. 2–Adjust for brake wear by turning actuating stud nut (1). Reposition actuating arm if necessary, at cable housing anchor nuts (2).

Fig. 3–To adjust track tension, loosen clamp nuts (1) and turn adjusting screws (2) on each side at rear of machine. Both sides must be adjusted alike.

SAFARI

1970-1972

	Engine			Carburetor				Clutch		
Model	Make	Model	Displ.	Make	Model	Sprocket Ratio	Chain Size	Make	Shaft Center	Belt Number
					1970					
295	Kohler	K295-1	295cc	Tillotson	HR41A	15:33	35-2	Salsbury 780	10¼	510684
309	Kohler	K309-1	309cc	Tillotson	HR41A	15:33	35-2	Salsbury 780	10¼	510684
335	Kohler	K335-1	335cc	Tillotson	HR48A	15:33	35-2	Salsbury 780	10¼	510684
399	Kohler	K399-2	399cc	Tillotson	HR43A	15:33	35-2	Salsbury 780	10¼	510684
440	Kohler	K440-2	437cc	Tillotson	HR43A	15:33	35-2	Salsbury 910	10¼	510906
309W	Kohler	K309-1	309cc	Tillotson	HR41A	15:33	35-2	Salsbury	10¼	510975
					1971					
295	Kohler	K295-1	295cc	Tillotson	HR41A	15:33	35-2	Salsbury 780	10¼	510684
309	Kohler	K309-1	309cc	Tillotson	HR41A	15:33	35-2	Salsbury	10¼	510684
335	Kohler	K335-1	335cc	Tillotson	HR48A	15:33	35-2	Salsbury 780	10¼	510684
399	Kohler	K399-2	399cc	Tillotson	HR43A	15:33	35-2	Salsbury 780	10¼	510684
440	Kohler	K440-2	437cc	Tillotson	HR43A	15:33	35-2	Salsbury 910	10¼	510906
309W	Kohler	K309-1	309cc	Tillotson	HR41A	15:33	35-2	Salsbury	10¼	510975
					1972					
335	Kohler	K335-1	335cc	Kohler	34-053-10	15:33	35-2	Salsbury 780	10¼	510684
399	Kohler	K399-2	399cc	Kohler	37-053-01	15:33	35-2	Salsbury 780	10¼	510684
399W	Kohler	K399-2	399cc	Kohler	37-052-01	15:33	35-2	Salsbury 780	10¼	510684

SCORPION

1966-1972

	Engine			Carburetor				Clutch		
Model	Make	Model	Displ.	Make	Model	Sprocket Ratio	Chain Size	Make	Shaft Center	Belt Number
					1966					
TAS-J252	JLO	L252	247cc	Tillotson	HL207B	10:32	40	Own	10½	989900
TAS-H300	Hirth	53R	300cc	Tillotson	HL192A	10:32	40	Own	10½	989900
					1967					
J252	JLO	J252	247cc	Tillotson	HL207B	10:32	40	Own	10½	989900
J292	JLO	L292	292cc	Tillotson	HR2A	10:32	40	Own	10½	989900
S280	Sachs	SA280	277cc	Tillotson	HR3A	10:32	40	Own	10½	989900
J292L	JLO	L292	292cc	Tillotson	HR2A	10:32	40	Own	10½	989900
S280L	Sachs	SA280	277cc	Tillotson	HR3A	10:32	40	Own	10½	989900
					1968					
Mark II	Sachs	SA280	277cc	Tillotson	HR3A	10:32	40	Own	10½	989900
Mark II	Sachs	SA290	297cc	Tillotson	HR3A	11:32	40	Own	10½	989900
Mark II	Hirth	160R	372cc	Tillotson	HD7A	12:32	40	Own	10½	989900
Mark II	JLO	L372	372cc	Tillotson	HD7A	12:32	40	Own	10½	989900
Mark III	Sachs	SA280	277cc	Tillotson	HR3A	10:32	40	Own	10½	989900
Mark III	Sachs	SA290	297cc	Tillotson	HR3A	11:32	40	Own	10½	989900
Mark III	Hirth	160R	372cc	Tillotson	HD7A	12:32	40	Own	10½	989900
Mark III	JLO	L372	372cc	Tillotson	HD7A	12:32	40	Own	10½	989900
Mark III	Wankel	RC18-1	303cc	Tillotson	HL252A	12:32	40	Own	10½	989900
					1969					
Mark I	Sachs	SA280	277cc	Tillotson	HR19A	10:32	40	Own	10½	989900
Mark II	Sachs	SA280	277cc	Tillotson	HR19A	10:32	40	Own	10½	989900
Mark II	Sachs	SA290	297cc	Tillotson	HR19A	11:32	40	Own	10½	989900
Mark II	Sachs	SA370	368cc	Tillotson	HR30A	12:32	40	Own	10½	989900
Mark II	Wankel	RC18-1	303cc	Tillotson	HL252A	12:32	40	Own	10½	989900
Mark II	Hirth	171R	634cc	Tillotson	HD	18:32	40	Own	10½	989900
Mark III	Sachs	SA290	297cc	Tillotson	HR19A	11:32	40	Own	10½	989900
Mark III	Sachs	SA370	368cc	Tillotson	HR30A	12:32	40	Own	10½	989900
Mark IV	Sachs	SA370	368cc	Tillotson	HR30A	12:32	40	Own	10½	989900
Mark IV	Hirth	171R	634cc	Tillotson	HD	18:32	40	Own	10½	989900
					1970					
Mark I	Sachs	SA280	277cc	Tillotson	HR19A	10:32	40	Own	10½	989900
Mark II	Sachs	SA290	293cc	Tillotson	HR95A	12:32	40	Own	10½	989900
Mark II	CCW	340-1	339cc	Tillotson	HD	11:32	40	Own	10½	989900
Mark II	Hirth	56R	292cc	Tillotson	HR	11:32	40	Own	10½	989910
Mark II	Sachs	SA340	336cc	Tillotson	HR	11:32	40	Own	10½	989910
Mark II	Hirth	210R	399cc	Tillotson	HD	13:32	40	Own	10½	989910
Mark II	Hirth	211R	438cc	Tillotson	HD	14:32	40	Own	10½	989910
Mark II	Hirth	220R	493cc	Tillotson	HD	15:32	40	Own	10½	989910
Mark II	Hirth	171R	634cc	Tillotson	HD	18:32	40	Own	10½	989910
Mark II	Hirth	230R	793cc	Tillotson	HD	18:32	40	Own	10½	989910
Mark III	Sachs	SA370	368cc	Tillotson	HR	12:32	40	Own	10½	989900
Mark III	CCW	400-1	398cc	Tillotson	HD	13:32	40	Own	10½	989910
Mark III	Kohler	K440-2	437cc	Tillotson	HD	14:32	40	Own	10½	989910
Mark IV	Kohler	K440-2	437cc	Tillotson	HD	14:32	40	Own	10½	989910
					1971					
Mark I	Sachs	SA280	277cc	Tillotson	HR95A	11:32	40	Own	10½	989900
Mark II	Sachs	SA290	293cc	Tillotson	HR95A	12:32	40	Own	10½	989900
Mark II	CCW	340	339cc	Tillotson	HR95A	12:32	40	Own	10½	989900
Mark II	CCW	400	398cc	Tillotson	HR98A	14:32	40	Own	10½	989910
Mark III	Sachs	SA370	368cc	Tillotson	HR95A	12:32	40	Own	10½	989900
Stinger II	Sachs	SA290	293cc	Tillotson	HR95A	13:32	40	Own	10½	989900
Stinger II	CCW	290	290cc	Tillotson	HR95A	13:32	40	Own	10½	989900
Stinger II	CCW	340	339cc	Tillotson	HR95A	13:32	40	Own	10½	989900
Stinger II	CCW	400	398cc	Tillotson	HR98A	15:32	40	Own	10½	989910
Stinger II	Sachs	SA2-440	437cc	Tillotson	HD56A	21:43	35-2	Own	10½	989910
Stinger II	CCW	440	440cc	Tillotson		21:38	35-2	Own	10½	989910
Stinger III	CCW	400	398cc	Tillotson	HR98A	14:32	40	Own	10½	989910
Stinger III	Sachs	SA2-440	437cc	Tillotson	HD56A	20:43	35-2	Own	10½	989910
					1972					
Stingeroo	Sachs	SA280	277cc	Tillotson	HR115A	11:32	40	Own	10½	989901
Stinger I	Sachs	SA290	293cc	Tillotson	HR116A	12:32	40	Own	10½	989900
Stingerette	CCW	290	290cc	Tillotson	HR121A	13:32	40	Own	10½	989900
Stinger II	Sachs	SA340SS	336cc	Tillotson	HD85A	13:32	40	Own	10½	989900
Stinger II	CCW	400	398cc	Walbro	WDA-2	18:38	35-2	Own	10½	989910
Stinger II	JLO	2F440/3	428cc	Walbro	WDA-4	19:38	35-2	Own	10½	989910
Stinger III	CCW	400	398cc	Walbro	WDA-2	17:38	35-2	Own	10½	989910
Stinger III	JLO	LR440/2	428cc	Walbro	WDA-4	18:38	35-2	Own	10½	989910

LUBRICATION

The engine is lubricated by oil mixed with the fuel. The vehicle manufacturer recommends a fuel-oil ratio of 20:1 using a good grade of regular gasoline and SCORPION Engine oil or other good Snowmobile Oil, Do not use outboard motor oil, multi-viscosity oil or light duty oil.

The drive chain runs in an enclosed housing which should contain SAE 10 engine oil to level of lower chain sprocket (early models), or to level of check plug, late models.

Handle bar and ski legs (spindles) are equipped with oilite bushings and should be lubricated occasionally with engine oil.

Idler needle bearing in drive pulley should be lightly oiled about every 10 hours of running time. Be careful not to over-oil or allow oil to get on drive belt.

Track axles and bogie wheels are equipped with sealed bearings. The manufacturer recommends disassembly and repacking with lithium base grease before vehicle is stored for the season.

ADJUSTMENT

STEERING SKIS. With handle bars in normal straight driving position, both skis should point straight ahead and center-to-center distance should be the same at front and rear of skis.

On early models with two drag links, each drag link must be adjusted separately after disconnecting either end of link. Late models have a drag link and tie rod, either can be adjusted after removing the bolt connecting both to the right steering arm.

DRIVE CHAIN. The roller drive chain should have approximately ¼-inch free play when measured midway between sprockets. Adjustment is by means of eccentric bearing housing for intermediate shaft which carries upper chain sprocket and torque converter driven sheave. To tighten the chain, loosen the locknut and push bolt (D—Fig. 2) down in slot in housing until it stops, then back up about 1/16-inch and tighten locknut. If bolt bottoms in slot, remove then reinstall in alternate hole which has appeared in opposite end of slot.

BRAKE. Early models were equipped with a shoe type brake which used the fixed face of driven sheave as a friction surface. Late models use a disc brake with brake disc bolted to driven sheave hub. Adjustment is made at brake cable housing anchor for both types. Free travel, measured at end of brake lever, should be approximately ½-inch.

TRACK. To adjust track tension, raise rear of vehicle until track is clear of ground. On 1966 and 1967 models, track tension is correct when track clears rear bogie wheels 1-1½ inches when bogie is set parallel to track. On later models, track should clear center bogie wheels by ¼-inch. To adjust the tension, loosen the two side bolts (B—Fig. 3) on each side of frame. Loosen locknuts on adjusting bolts (C) and adjust both sides equally.

NOTE: When track tension has been adjusted, alignment MUST be checked as outlined in the special TRACK SERVICE section of this manual.

OVERHAUL

SKIS AND STEERING. Skis, ski legs (spindles), bushings and steering arms are interchangeable from right to left. Skis are fitted with wear bars which are retained by a nut on one center stud. Wear bar can be installed either end forward.

Fig. 2—View of driven clutch and chain case on 1969 model, showing points of chain adjustment.

A. Lower cover
B. Upper cover
C. Locknut
D. Adjusting bolt

Fig. 3—View of rear of machine showing points of track adjustment and alignment.

A. Suspension plate
B. Clamp bolts
C. Adjusting screws
D. Locknuts

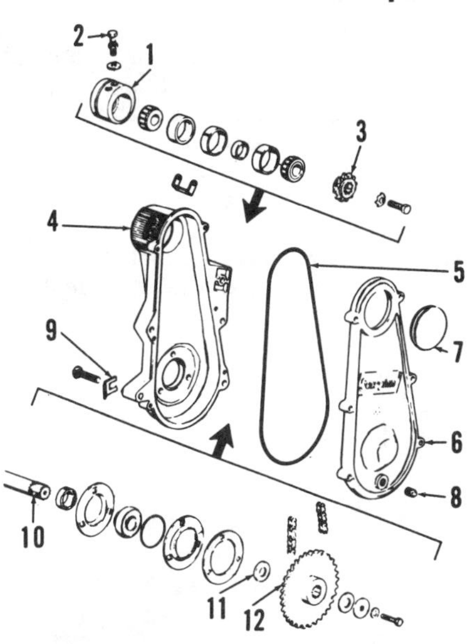

Fig. 4 — Exploded view of diecast chain case and associated parts used on most late models. Shims (9) are used to properly align torque converter sheaves if necessary, and their location should be noted if service is performed.

1. Eccentric housing
2. Adjusting cap
3. Upper sprocket screw
4. Chaincase
5. Gasket
6. Cover
7. Upper boot
8. Oil level plug
9. Alignment shims
10. Front drive shaft
11. Spacer washer
12. Lower sprocket

Fig. 5—Exploded view of rear track idler suspension assembly showing component parts.

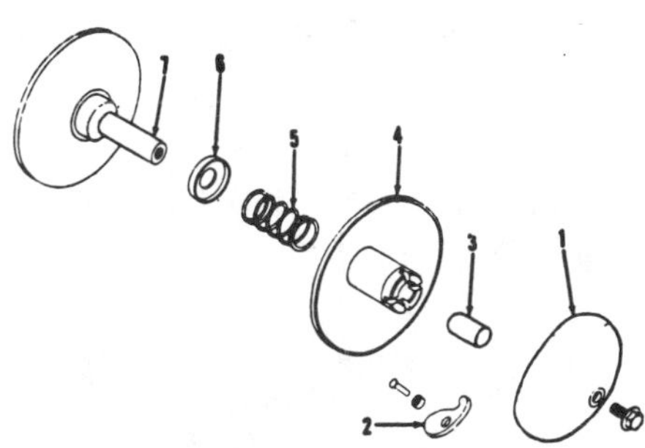

Fig. 6—Exploded view of drive unit used on Scorpion before 1969.

1. Drive cover
2. Weight
3. Bushing
4. Moving flange
5. Spring
6. Spring cap
7. Fixed flange

DRIVE. Refer to the appropriate service section elsewhere in this manual for service on torque converter, track, brake and associated parts.

Drive sprocket on early models is threaded on to intermediate shaft. To remove the sprocket, remove upper chain housing cover, block the track from turning; then turn torque converter driven sheave in normal (forward) direction of rotation until sprocket has started to unscrew from shaft. Disconnect drive chain on early models or loosen chain tension (late models) and remove the sprocket. Late models use an endless chain (no master link) and sprocket is splined to shaft and retained by a slotted nut and cotter pin or by a cap screw as shown in Fig. 4. Sprocket ratio should be specified when buying chain.

TORQUE CONVERTER. Scorpion snowmobiles manufactured before the 1969 Model Year used the drive and driven sheaves shown in Figs. 6 and 7. Nut (1—Fig. 7) should be tightened for higher horsepower, packed snow or ice; or to correct for belt slipping. Loosen the nut for deep snow, to improve slow speed performance or for use with low horsepower engines.

1969 and 1970 models use the "High-Torque" units shown in Figs. 8 & 9. The splined "Nylatron" insert used in drive sheave sliding unit has left hand threads and is renewable. Drive ratio is 3:1 at low range and 1:1 at high range. Driven sheave and eccentric shaft can be removed as an assembly after removing handle bars and upper sprocket; or removed from shaft after removing cotter pin and slotted nut. Sheave spring is under tension when sheave is assembled, to disassemble use a suitable press or the special tool (Manufacturer's Part No. 903910).

Beginning in 1971 model year alternate drive and driven clutch are used; refer to Figs. 10 & 11. The "Nylatron" insert (10—Fig. 10) is splined to fixed sheave shaft and driven sheave. Parts (1 through 8) are interchangeable on both clutch types except that stationary sheave (1) must be selected to fit the engine. Hub and sheave faces (3, 4 & 5—Fig. 11) are interchangeable on torque sensing and speed sensing driven unit. Items (6 through 11) are used on torque sensing unit and items (12 through 16) in speed sensing unit. Bushing (7) is interchangeable in both sliding hubs (6 & 12) as shown.

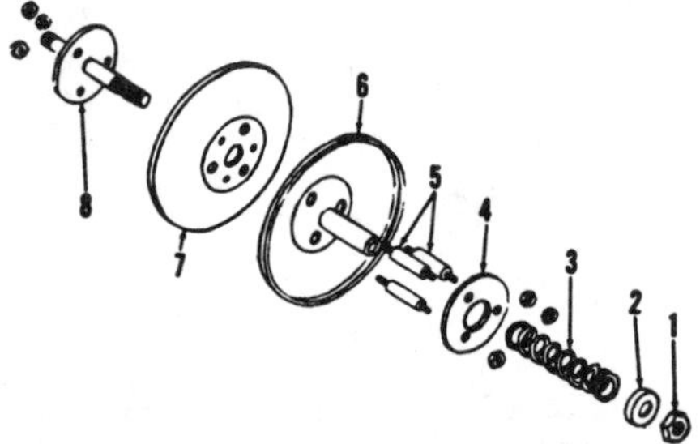

Fig. 7—Exploded view of driven sheave used on Scorpion before 1969.

1. Adjusting unit
2. Spring cap
3. Spring
4. Stop ring
5. Dowel pins
6. Moving flange
7. Fixed flange
8. Shaft and flange

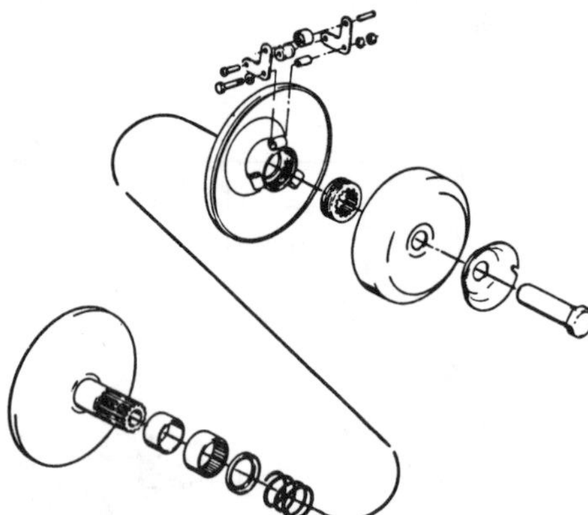

Fig. 8—Exploded view of drive unit used on 1969 models. Moving flange contains a screw-in plastic insert.

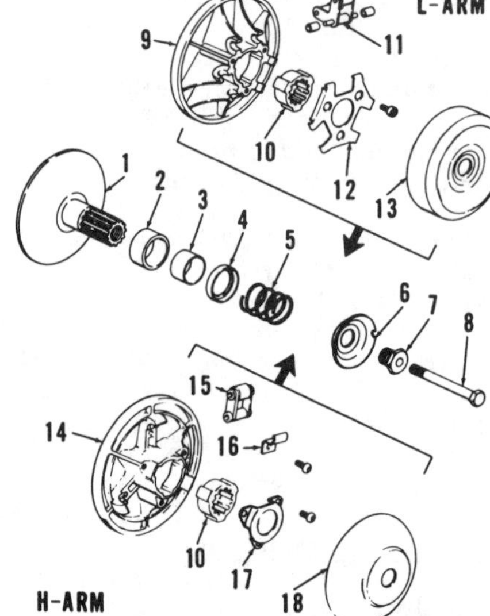

Fig. 10—Exploded view of torque converter drive clutch used on late models. Items (1 through 8) interchange on "L-Arm Clutch" and "H-Arm Clutch"; the other items are identified according to model.

1. Stationary sheave
2. Idler bearing
3. Sleeve
4. Spring cup
5. Spring
6. Starting rope drum
7. Bell retainer bolt
8. Cap screw
9. Moveable sheave
10. Torque plug
11. Weight arm
12. Retainer
13. Bell housing
14. Moveable sheave
15. Weight arm
16. Arm retainer
17. Plug retainer
18. Bell housing

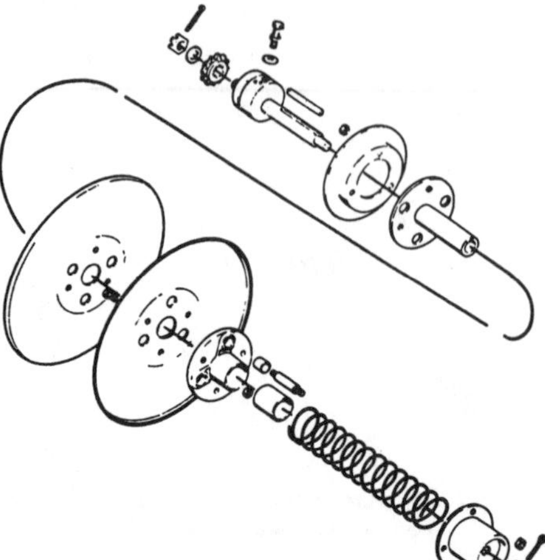

Fig. 9 — Exploded view of secondary (driven) sheave used on some models.

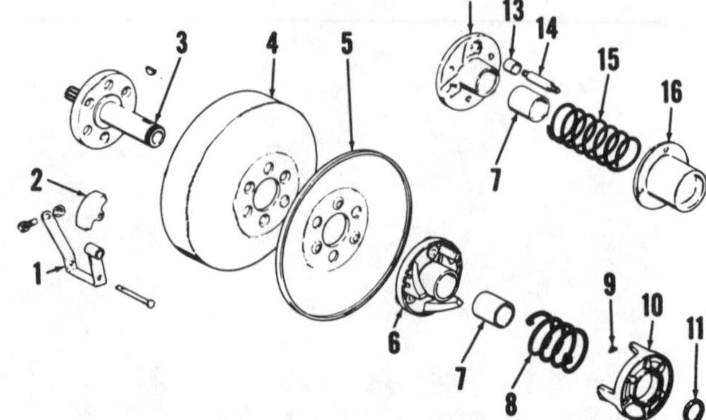

1. Brake lever
2. Brake shoe
3. Shaft & hub
4. Stationary sheave
5. Moveable sheave
6. Cam hub
7. Bushing
8. Torque spring
9. Nylon shoe
10. Fixed cam
11. Snap ring
12. Spring hub
13. Bushing
14. Dowel pin
15. Spring
16. Retainer

Fig. 11—Exploded view of late type torque converter driven clutch. Items (6 through 11) are used on torque sensing (Cam Clutch) unit and items (12 through 16) on speed sensing (Spring Clutch) type.

SCORPION

1973-1978

Model	Engine Make	Engine Model	Engine Displ.	Carburetor Make	Carburetor Model	Sprocket Ratio	Chain Size	Clutch Make	Clutch Shaft Center	Belt Number
					1973					
Stinger 290ET	CCW	290-2	290cc	Walbro	WR	16:38	35-2	Own	10½	989910
Stinger 290AB	CCW	290-2	290cc	Walbro	WR	16:38	35-2	Own	10½	989910
Stinger 340AE	CCW	340-4	339cc	Walbro	WR	16:38	35-2	Own	10½	989910
Stingerette AC	CCW	290-2	290cc	Walbro	WR	16:38	35-2	Own	10½	989910
Super Stingerette	CCW	340-4	339cc	Walbro	WR	16:38	35-2	Own	10½	989910
Super Stinger 400RV	CCW	440-4	436cc	Walbro	WD	18:38	35-2	Own	10½	989910
Super Stinger 400TK	JLO	2F-400	398cc	Walbro	WD	18:38	35-2	Own	10½	989910
Super Stinger 440	JLO	2F-440	428cc	Walbro	WD	18:38	35-2	Own	10½	989910
					1974					
Stinger 290	Rockwell	2F-295	285cc	Walbro	WR	16:38	35-2	Own	10½	989910
Stinger 440	Rockwell	2F-440	428cc	Walbro	WDA	18:38	35-2	Own	10½	989910
Super Stingerette	Rockwell	2F-340	339cc	Walbro	WRA	16:38	35-2	Own	10½	989910
Super Stinger 340	Rockwell	2F-340	339cc	Walbro	WRA	16:38	35-2	Own	10½	989910
Super Stinger 440	Rockwell	2F-440	339cc	Walbro	WDA	18:38	35-2	Own	10½	989910
					1975					
Super Stinger 290	Rockwell	2F-295	285cc	Walbro	WRA	16:38	35-2	Own	10½	989910
Super Stinger 340	Rockwell	2F-340	339cc	Walbro	WRA	16:38	35-2	Own	10½	989910
Super Stinger 400	Rockwell	2F-400	398cc	Walbro	WDA	18:38	35-2	Own	10½	989910
Super Stinger 440	Rockwell	2F-440	428cc	Walbro	WDA	18:38	35-2	Own	10½	989910
Whip 340	Rockwell	2F-340	339cc	Walbro	WF10	16:38	35-2	Own	10½	989910
Whip 400	Rockwell	2F-400	398cc	Walbro	WF11	18:38	35-2	Own	10½	989910
Whip 400	Rockwell	2F-400	398cc	Walbro	WF11	18:38	35-2	Own	10½	989910
Whip 440	Rockwell	2F-440	428cc	Walbro	WF11	18:38	35-2	Own	10½	989910
Brut 340	Brooten	LC34	336cc	Mikuni	VM32-2	17:39	35-2	Own	12-3/8	766938
Brut 440	Brooten	LC44	439cc	Mikuni	VM34-3	19:39	35-2	Own	12-3/8	766938
					1976					
Lil' Whip	Cuyuna	290	294cc	Walbro	WRA37	14:32	40	Own	10½	989900
Range Whip	Cuyuna	400	399cc	Walbro	WF17	17:37	35-2	Own	10½	989910
Whip 340	Cuyuna	340	338cc	Walbro	WF15	18:38	35-2	Own	10½	989910
Whip 440	Cuyuna	440	428cc	Walbro	WF14	19:38	35-2	Own	10½	989910
					1977					
Lil' Whip	Cuyuna	290	294cc	Walbro	WF21	14:32	40	Own	10½	989900
Range Whip	Cuyuna	400	399cc	Walbro	WF24	18:38	35-2	Own	10½	989910
Sting	Cuyuna	440	428cc	Walbro	WF23	21:38	35-2	Own	10½	989910
Whip	Cuyuna	340	339cc	Walbro	WF17	18:38	35-2	Own	10½	989910
Whip	Cuyuna	440	428cc	Walbro	WF22	19:38	35-2	Own	10½	989910
					1978					
Lil' Whip	Cuyuna	290	294cc	Walbro	WF21	14:32	40	Own	10½	989910
Whip	Cuyuna	340	339cc	Walbro	WF17	18:38	35-2	Own	10½	989910
Whip	Cuyuna	440	428cc	Walbro	WF22	19:38	35-2	Own	10½	989910
Range Whip	Cuyuna	400	399cc	Walbro	WF24	19:38	35-2	Own	10½	989910
Sting	Cuyuna	440	428cc	Walbro	WF23	20:38	35-2	Own	10½	989914

LUBRICATION

The engine is lubricated by oil mixed with the fuel. Recommended fuel:oil ratio is 20:1 using Premium gasoline and an approved, branded snowmobile oil. Lead-free fuel should not be used.

The enclosed chaincase should be filled to level of check plug hole with Automatic Transmission Fluid or 10W Motor Oil.

ADJUSTMENT

STEERING SKIS. With handlebars in normal straight driving position, both skis should point straight ahead and center-to-center distance should be the same at front and rear of skis.

DRIVE CHAIN. The roller drive chain should have approximately ¼-inch free play when measured midway between sprockets. Adjustment on early models is by means of eccentric bearing housing for intermediate shaft which carries upper chain sprocket and torque converter driven sheave. To tighten the chain, loosen the locknut and push bolt (D—Fig. 1) down in slot in housing until it stops, then back up about 1/16-inch and tighten locknut. If bolt bottoms in slot, remove then reinstall in alternate hole which has appeared in opposite end of slot.

Fig. 1—View of chaincase and associated parts showing points of adjustment.

A. Cover
B. Adjusting slots
C. Jam nut
D. Adjusting bolt

Fig. 2—Most late models have automatic chain tensioners on both sides of chain as shown.

NOTE: Whenever drive chain is adjusted, brake must be checked and readjusted if necessary. Brake drum may move toward or away from friction shoe because of movement of eccentric shaft.

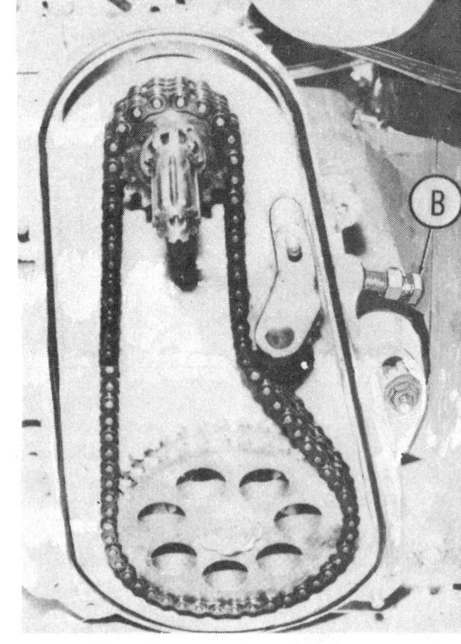

Fig. 3—To adjust chain tension on BRUT, back off locknut, tighten adjusting screw (B) to 10 in.-lbs. (12 kg-cm) USING A TORQUE WRENCH; then back off exactly ½-turn and tighten locknut.

Later models except BRUT have automatic chain tensioners as shown in Fig. 2. On Scorpion BRUT models, chaincase is mounted on right side of track tunnel and driven by a cross shaft which reaches across engine compartment to secondary driven sheave. To adjust chain tension on BRUT models, back off jam nut on chain tension bolt (B—Fig. 3). Make sure bolt threads are clean and lubricated and that bolt turns freely in housing threads; then tighten adjusting bolt to a torque of 10 inch-pounds (12 kg-m), back bolt out exactly ½-turn and tighten jam nut.

BRAKE. The shoe-type brake should have about ½-inch free play measured at end of brake hand lever. Adjustment is made by turning brake cable housing anchor nuts (1—Fig. 4).

On Scorpion BRUT the caliper type disc brake is mounted on outside of chaincase cover on right side of machine as shown in Fig. 5. Adjust actuating cable housing anchor nuts (H) if necessary until push pins (P) center in valleys of actuating lever as shown in inset; then turn actuating lever stud nut (N) as required until end of hand brake lever has approximately ¾-inch (20 mm) free travel before brake is fully applied.

On models so equipped, check brake light and readjust if necessary after brake adjustment.

Fig. 4—Shoe type brake adjustment is made at cable housing anchor nuts (1).

TRACK. To adjust track tension, raise rear of vehicle until track is clear. On early machines with bogie wheel suspension, track should clear center bogie wheels by ¼-inch and both sides should be adjusted equally. To adjust the track, loosen the two side bolts (B—Fig. 6) on each side of frame, loosen locknuts on adjusting bolts (C) and turn adjusting bolts until adjustment is correct.

On Lil' Whip, track should clear second bogie wheel from front by approximately one inch (25 mm) with ten pounds pressure exerted to push track away from bogie wheels. The manufacturer makes available a "Track Jack" (Scorpion Part No. 901736) to apply the required tension as shown in Fig. 6A. Adjust Track Jacks to one inch and position as shown; green ring on each jack should align with lip of cylinder. To adjust track tension, loosen pivot bolts (1—Fig. 7) and sliding bolts (2), then turn pull bolts (3) as required, until tension is correct. Retighten the loosened bolts securely. Rear track idler suspension springs can be repositioned in four anchor positions to compensate for heavier or lighter passenger load. Be sure both sides are adjusted alike.

On models with Para-Rail suspension, a pressure of ten pounds should depress track until a clearance of 1¼ inches (32 mm) exists between track and center bogie wheel. If "Track Jacks" are used, adjust jacks to 1¼ inches and position jacks as center bogie wheels; green ring on each jack should align with lip on cylinder. To adjust track tension, loosen rear suspension mounting screws (X—Fig. 8) and locknuts on adjusting screws (Y). Turn each adjusting screw until tension is correct, then retighten mounting screws and locknuts. Rear eye-bolt nuts (Z) provide adjustment to compensate for passenger load. Tighten the nuts for heavier load or firmer ride, or loosen the nuts for lighter load. Measure nut position on eye-bolt and adjust both sides alike. Normal adjustment for a particular passenger load is made by having passenger(s) sit on machine on a hard, level surface, then measuring distance from rear bottom of running board to ground. Adjust the distance to 4½-6 inches (9-12 mm) on 1976 and earlier models; or 6½-7½ inches (13-15 mm) on 1977 and later models. Adjustment is made by turning eyebolt nuts (see Fig. 9) on each side of rear suspension frame until correct distance is obtained.

NOTE: If normal passenger load will equal or exceed 300 lbs. a heavy duty spring kit (Scorpion Part No. 902135) should be installed.

On models with Para-Slide suspension, a pressure of ten pounds should depress track until a clearance of 1¼ inches (32 mm) exists between top of track cleat and bottom of slide rail at midpoint of slide. If "Track Jacks" (Scorpion Part No. 901736) are used,

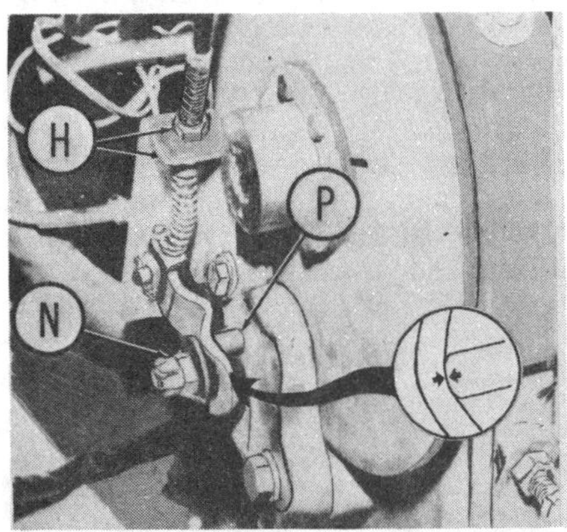

Fig. 5—On BRUT, adjust cable housing anchor nuts (H) until push pins (P) center in valleys of actuating arm as shown in inset; then tighten anchor stud nut (N) until clearance is correct.

Fig. 6—View of rear of machine showing points of track adjustment and alignment.

A. Suspension plate
B. Clamp bolts
C. Adjusting screws
D. Locknuts

Fig. 6A—"Track Jacks" (J) can be used to properly adjust track tension. Refer to text.

Fig. 7—To adjust bogie wheel track on Lil' Whip, loosen pivot bolts (1) and sliding bolt nuts (2); then turn pull bolts (3) as required until tension is correct.

Fig. 8—To adjust track tension on Para Rail suspension, loosen pivot screws (X) and locknuts on adjusting bolts (Y), then turn adjusting bolts until tension is correct. Eyebolt nuts (Z) adjust rear springs for passenger load.

Fig. 9—Adjust rear spring anchor nuts (Z) until running board height at rear is 4½-6 inches with normal load. Both sides must be adjusted alike.

Fig. 10—Track jacks (J) can be used to properly adjust track tension. Refer to text.

adjust tracks to 1¼ inches and position jacks between slide rail and metal cleat midway of slide rail as shown at (J—Fig. 10). Green ring on track jack should align with lip on cylinder. To adjust track tension, loosen rear suspension mounting screws on each side of track tunnel (X—Fig. 8) and jam nuts on each adjusting screw (A—Fig. 11). Turn each adjusting screw (A) until tension is correct, then retighten mounting screws and locknuts.

Rear eye-bolt nuts (Z—Fig. 9) provide adjustment to compensate for passenger load. Tighten the nuts for heavier load or firmer ride, or loosen nuts for softer ride. Measure nut position on eye-bolt and adjust both sides alike. Normal adjustment for a particular passenger load is made by having passenger(s) sit on machine on a firm, level surface, then measuring distance from rear bottom of running board to ground. Adjust the distance to 4½-6 inches by turning nuts (Z).

NOTE: On all models, when track tension has been adjusted, alignment MUST be checked as outlined in TRACK SERVICE Section of this manual.

OVERHAUL

DRIVE CLUTCH. Retaining bolt and clutch hub stud are both right-hand thread. To remove the clutch, first remove engine cover and clutch guard. Be sure ignition system is grounded and turn crankshaft in normal direction of rotation until one piston is against compression; then using an impact wrench (preferred method) remove clutch retaining cap screw. If an impact wrench is not available sharp hammer blows against wrench handle will loosen screw if carefully done. A steady pull against wrench handle will turn crankshaft instead of loosening screw. (Refer to Fig. 12.) On BRUT models, check for index marks (M—Fig. 13) on the three clutch components to make sure they are present and aligned.

On all models, remove clutch hub stud using the same procedure used for retaining cap screw. Lift off clutch cover, weight unit, movable sheave and spring.

To remove fixed face and hub unit, use the clutch hub stud and a suitable ¾-inch (18 mm) diameter plug as shown in Fig. 15. Plug must be 3¼-inches (82.5 mm) long for Brut; 2-13/16-inches (66.7 mm) long for other models before 1977; or 3¾ inches (95 mm) for late models. Insert plug in hub and reinstall stud to use as a forcing screw to loosen hub on tapered portion of shaft. Applied heat can sometimes free the hub if plug is not available.

The BRUTANZA clutch (used on BRUT) is torque sensing in the drive as well as driven unit. The drive unit compression spring is indexed (I—Fig. 16 and 17) at both ends and ramps (R—Fig. 16) transmit positive or negative torque to clutch. Weight unit cap screws (C—Fig. 18) should always be installed with head at trailing edge as shown by arrow. Shoulder of weight bushing (B) should always be installed on nut-end of cap screw, with nylon washer (N) at head end of cap screw.

Fig. 11—Track tension adjusting bolt is shown at (A). Both sides must be adjusted alike.

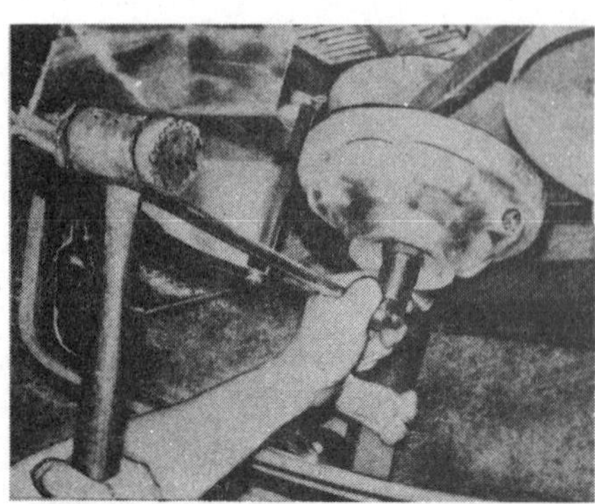

Fig. 12—A sharp blow will loosen clutch retaining cap screw better than a steady pull. An impact wrench is recommended.

Fig. 13—Match marks (M) should be aligned on BRUTANZA drive clutch.

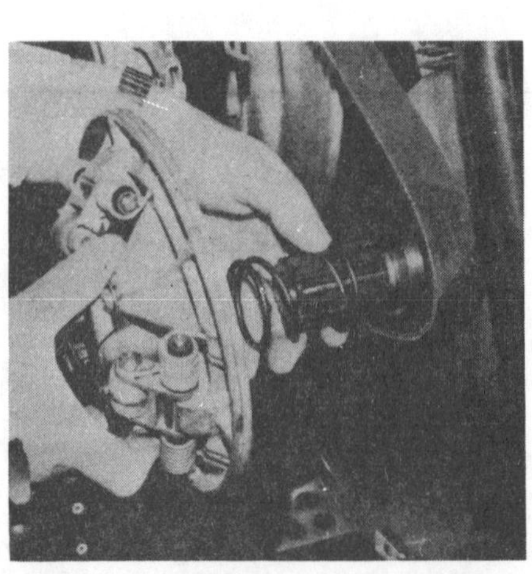

Fig. 14—Removing weight unit and spring of SCORPION clutch.

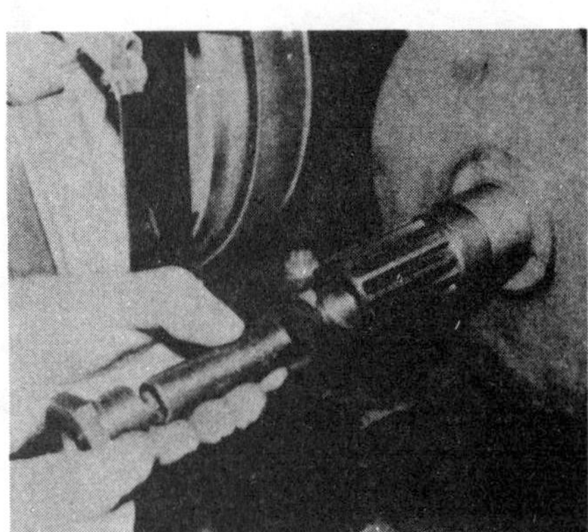

Fig. 15—Use hub stud and correct length spacer plug as a forcing screw to remove clutch hub. Refer to text for details.

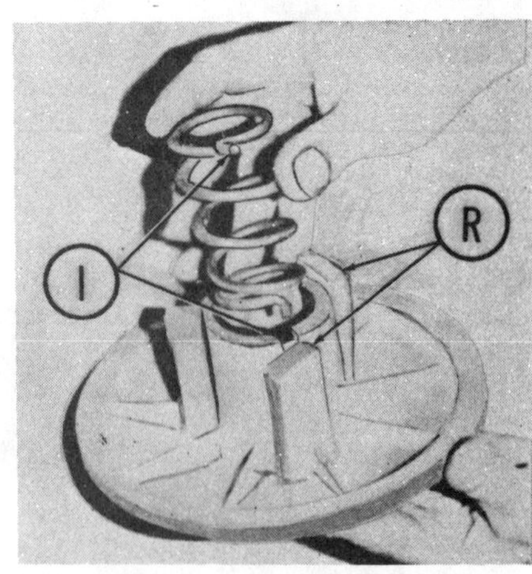

Fig. 16—Spring end indexes in slot as shown at (I), and ramps (R) transmit torque load for more rapid shift control on BRUTANZA clutch.

When assembling BRUT clutch, be sure spring is properly indexed as shown at (I—Figs. 16 and 17) and that spring retainer, nylon bushing and thrust washer are reinstalled on outer end of moveable sheave hub. Use a rubber band (R—Fig. 19) to hold flyweights positioned. Align index marks on stationary sheave, moveable sheave and cover as shown in Fig. 20, reinstall hub stud and tighten securely. When reinstalling clutch, use on 0.010 inch (0.25 mm) shim and tighten retaining cap screw to 75 ft.-lbs. (10.4 kg-m).

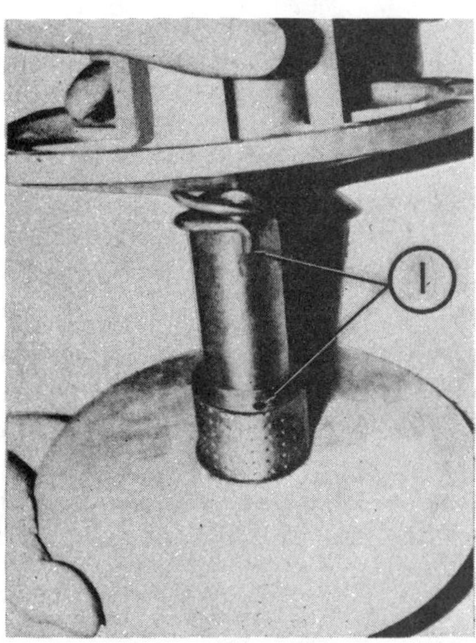

Fig. 17—Inner tang of spring must enter index hole in hub as shown in (I), on BRUTANZA clutch.

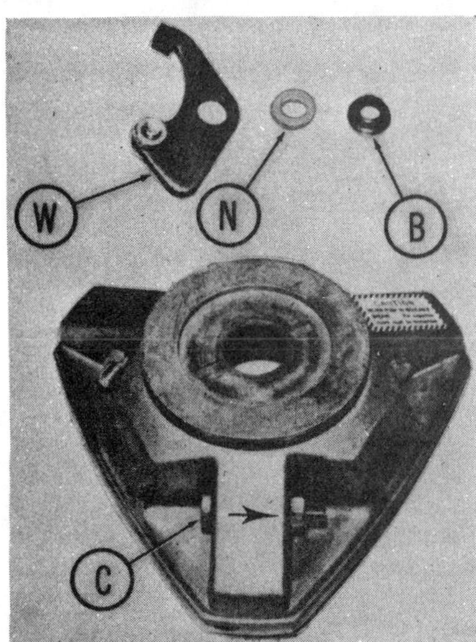

Fig. 18—Partially disassembled view of BRUTANZA clutch cover showing flyweight (W), Nylon washer (N), bushing (B) and retaining cap screw (C). Cap screw must be installed in direction indicated by arrow, with nut on leading edge in normal operation.

On all models except BRUT, check bell housing for cracks near hub area and wear or scoring in weight contact area. The plastic torque hub can be removed from clutch after removing retainer as shown in Fig. 21. Torque plug should have no more than 0.020 inch (0.5 mm) clearance in its bore. To remove or inspect weight units, unhook and remove springs (Fig. 22) then unbolt weight retainers. Weights should be renewed in matched sets. When reinstalling, tighten both the hub stud and retaining cap screw to a torque of 50 ft.-lbs. (6.9 kg-m).

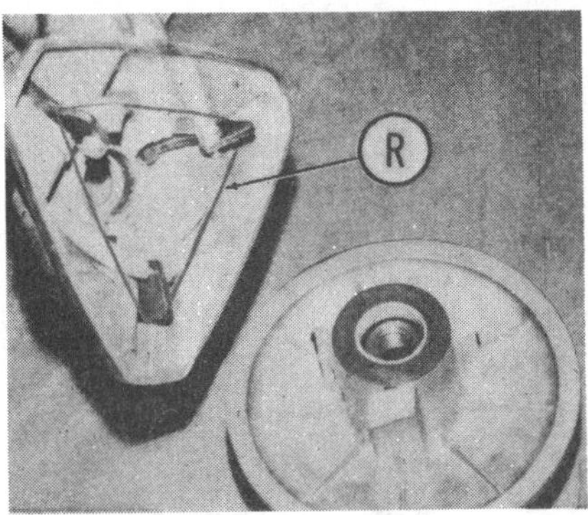

Fig. 19—Use a rubber band (R) to position weights for clutch assembly.

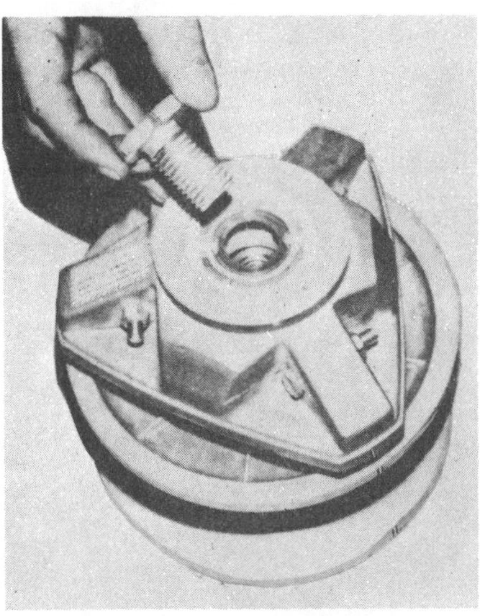

Fig. 20—Align marks and tighten hub stud to a torque of 75 ft.-lbs. (10.4 kgm).

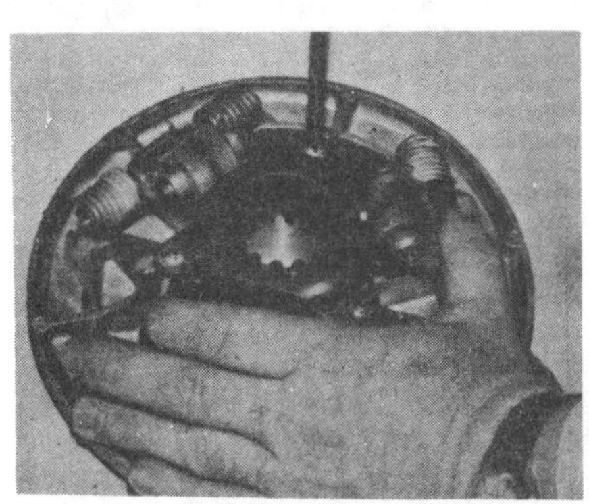

Fig. 21—Removing torque hub retainer on SCORPION clutch.

POWER THRUST II CLUTCH. The Power Thrust II drive clutch is an updated version of the original BRUTANZA clutch, featuring a torque sensing capability which speeds downshift under torque load.

To remove the clutch, first remove the retaining cap screw and hub stud (9—Fig. 25). Both are right hand thread. Reinstall hub stud backed up by a 3¾ inch steel plug as shown in Fig. 15.

With clutch removed, lay aside rope drum (8—Fig. 25) and rethread hub stud about half-way back into stationary hub; then rap clutch sharply on a solid wood block or bench top as shown in Fig. 23, to loosen cover. Lift off clutch cover (Fig. 24). Remove thrust washer (6—Fig. 25), thrust bearing (5) and sliding sheave (3) containing spring retainer (4) and neutral spring (2). Turn spring retainer (4) and withdraw through notches in hub as shown in Fig. 26. Turn sliding sheave over and

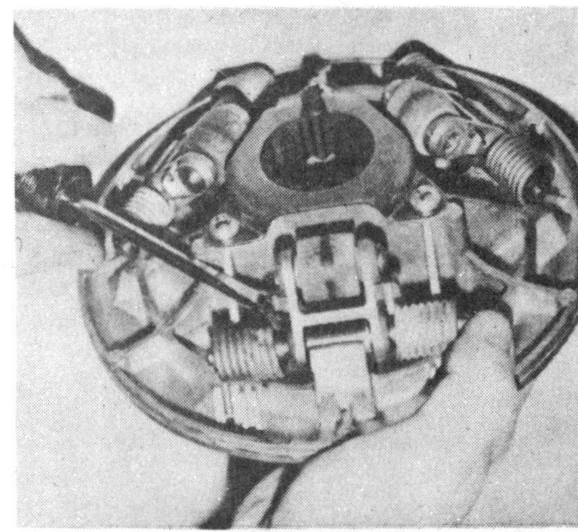

Fig. 22—Weight springs may be removed after unhooking spring ends as shown.

Fig. 23—Clutch nut partially installed to loosen cover. Refer to text for details.

hold securely as shown in Fig. 27, then apply clockwise pressure to neutral spring while withdrawing it from face side of sheave.

Clutch cover contains three wear pads (W—Fig. 28) which can be removed as shown, and three weights arm assemblies (A—Fig. 29) retained by a bushing (7—Fig. 30) and Allen head cap screw (8) in clutch cover. Removing weight arm requires the use of a special tool (T—Fig. 31) and a No. 11 (1/32 inch) nailset (N). Remove the Allen head cap screw and insert tool into side of cover from which cap screw was withdrawn. Be careful that full-sized part of tool does not extend into threaded portion of cover, or threads may be damaged. Tap the nailset into split end of tool expanding the tool, and bushing will be removed by continuing the process. Use care not to damage plastic thrust washers (6—Fig. 30) when weight bushing is reinstalled.

Steel washers (1) control shift response of clutch. Eight washers per weight arm are used on 440cc models, six washers on 400, two washers on 340cc and none on 290cc units.

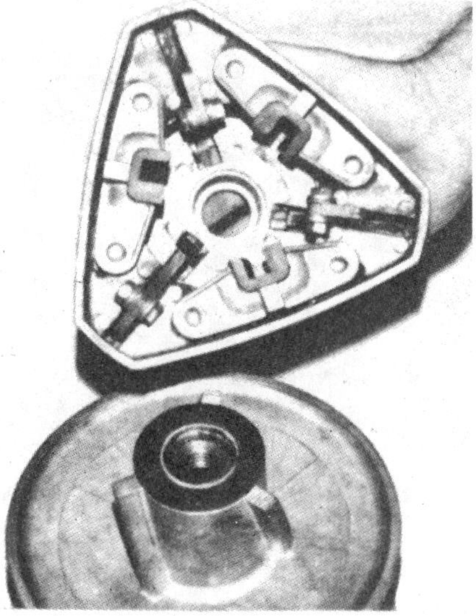

DRIVEN CLUTCH (BRUT). To remove driven clutch unit on BRUT, first remove engine cover, belt guard and drive belt. Remove the cap screw and washer retaining driven clutch hub to cross shaft and pull driven unit outward off of shaft splines.

Place driven clutch spring-end up on a bench, depress cam and remove retainer halves, then lift off cam. Refer to Fig. 32 and note which torque hole is being used as anchor point for torsion spring tang. No. 1 hole is the normal anchor point for 440cc engines; No. 2 hole for 340cc. Moving to a higher numbered hole speeds up downshift time. Pre-load spring one full cam when assembling.

DRIVEN CLUTCH (OTHER MODELS). To remove driven clutch, first remove engine cover, belt guard and drive belt. Drain chaincase and remove chaincase cover. Remove upper sprocket retaining cap screw (1—Fig. 33) and driven shaft locking screw (2); then using a brass drift and hammer, bump driven shaft, bearings and driven clutch inward out of chaincase bore.

Insert chaincase end of shaft through a hole in bench or fixture so cam side of clutch is up. Slightly depress cam

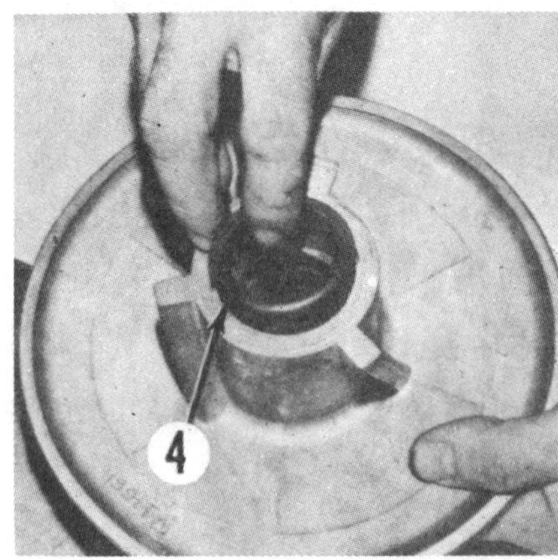

Fig. 26—Use notches in flange to remove spring retainer (4).

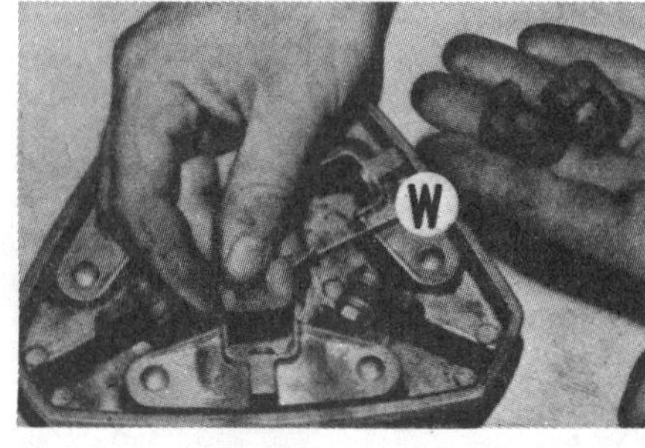

Fig. 28—Installing wear pads (W) in clutch cover.

Fig. 24—Clutch cover removed from Power Thrust II unit.

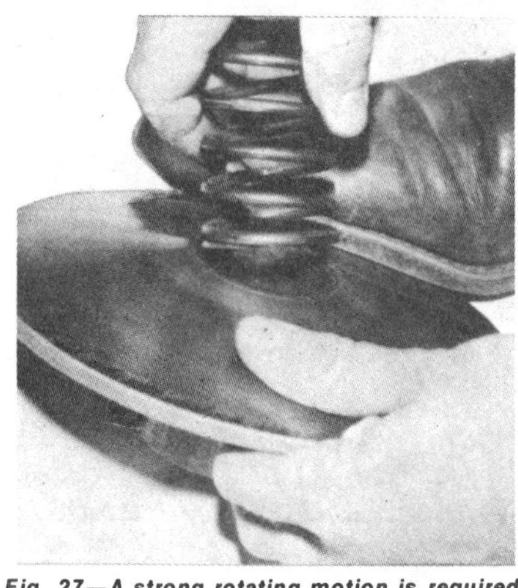

Fig. 27—A strong rotating motion is required to remove neutral spring.

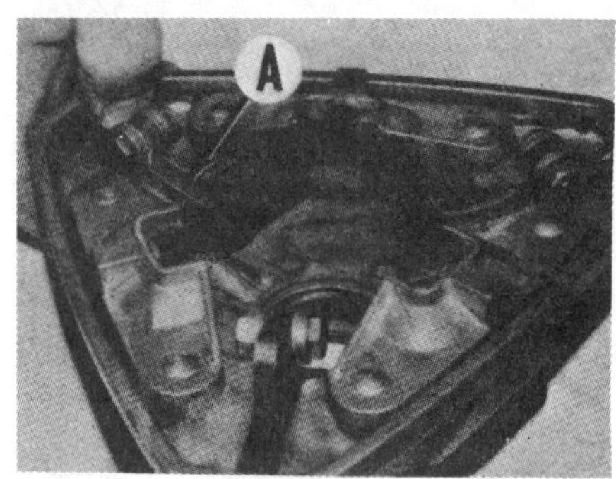

Fig. 29—Installing weight arms (A).

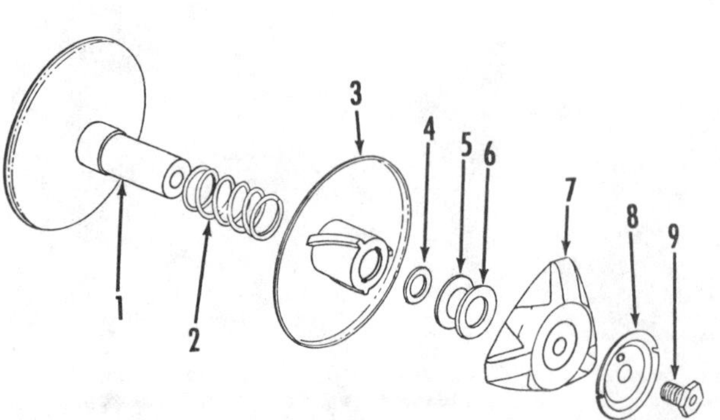

Fig. 25—Exploded view of Power Thrust II clutch showing component parts.

1. Clutch hub
2. Spring
3. Moveable sheave
4. Spring retainer
5. Thrust bearing
6. Thrust washer
7. Clutch cover
8. Rope pulley
9. Clutch nut

Fig. 30—Assembled view of weight arm showing component parts.

1. Washers
2. Bolt
3. Weight arm
4 Shoe
5. Spirol pin
6. Plastic washer
7. Pivot bushing
8. Allen screw

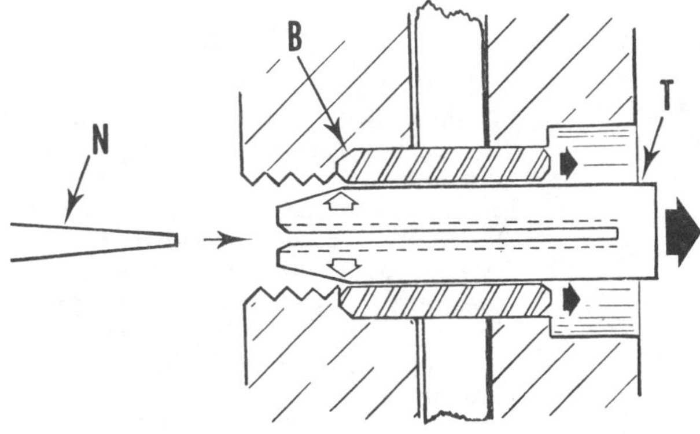

Fig. 31—A 1/32 inch nail set (N) and special tool (T) are required to remove weight arm pivot bushing (B).

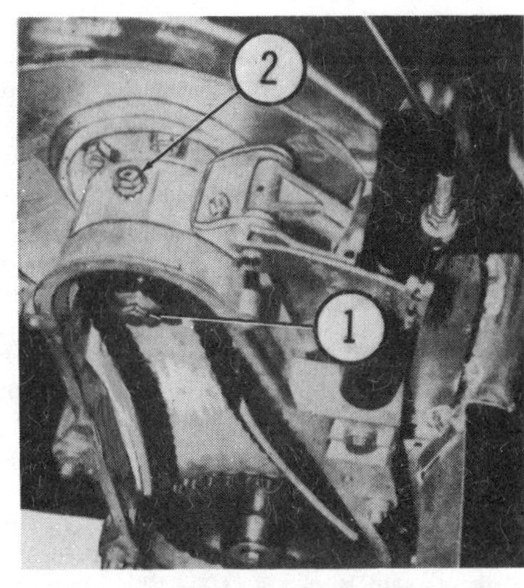

Fig. 33—To remove driven clutch from most units, first remove sprocket retaining cap screw (1) and shaft locking screw (2), then bump shaft, bearings and clutch from housing.

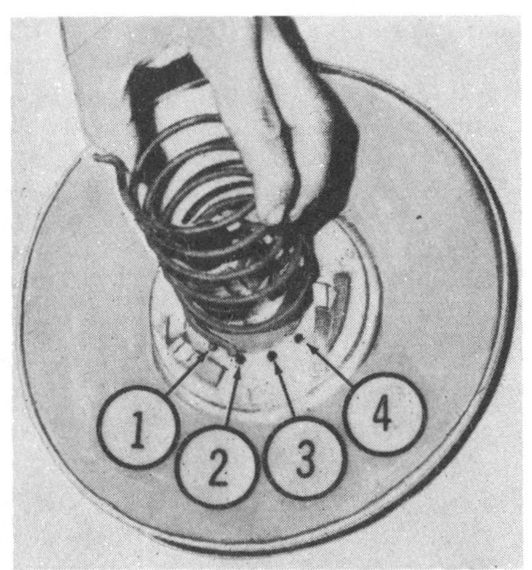

Fig. 32—Four anchor holes allow tailoring of performance of driven clutch by varying torque wrap.

until snap ring is free, then remove snap ring (X—Fig. 34) retaining washer (Y) and cam (Z). Lift off spring and extract Woodruff key. Moveable sheave can now be withdrawn from shaft.

Bronze bushing in moveable sheave hub should be tight in hub and have minimum clearance on shaft, yet still move smoothly without effort. Examine ramp shoes for wear or breakage and renew in sets if damaged. Heat may be used to remove old ramps if necessary.

Pre-load torque spring one ramp (1/3-turn) when reassembling. Examine "O" rings in chaincase bore and cover and renew as required.

Fig. 34—To disassemble removed clutch, slightly depress cam (Z) and remove snap ring (X) then remove retaining washer (Y), cam, spring and Woodruff key.

SEARS

1969-1971

	Engine			Carburetor				Clutch		
Model	Make	Model	Displ.	Make	Model	Sprocket Ratio	Chain Size	Make	Shaft Center	Belt Number
					1969					
Sears 309.....	Kohler	K309-1	309cc	Tillotson	HR31A	13:35	35-2	Salsbury		113532
Hilary 399....	Kohler	K399-2	399cc	Tillotson	HR32A	13:30	35-2	Salsbury		113532
					1970					
Sears 309.....	Kohler	K309-1	309cc	Tillotson	HR31A	13:35	35-2	Salsbury		113532
Hilary 399....	Kohler	K399-2	399cc	Tillotson	HR32A	13:30	35-2	Salsbury		113532
					1971					
Sears 309.....	Kohler	K309-1	309cc	Tillotson	HR31A	13:35	35-2	Salsbury		113532
Hilary 399....	Kohler	K399-2	399cc	Tillotson	HR32A	13:35	35-2	Salsbury		113532

LUBRICATION

The engine is lubricated by oil mixed with the fuel. The manufacturer recommends regular gasoline and SAE 30, 2 Cycle Engine Oil or SAE 30W MS Motor Oil at a ratio of 20:1.

The drive chain runs in an enclosed housing which contains oil to approximately the level of lower inspection cover opening. Approximately 8 ounces of Automatic Transmission Fluid, Type "A" is required.

Lightly coat friction surfaces of drive and driven sheaves with SAE 10 Oil or Lithium Grease every 15-20 hours. Each 25 hours, lubricate ski linkage with SAE 10 Oil, Steering Column Bushing with Lithium Grease, and rear track idler pivot bushings with Sears All-Temp Grease. Lubricate ski legs with Sears All-Temp Grease once each year, or oftener if necessary.

Bogie wheels and track axle bearings are sealed and do not require lubrication.

ADJUSTMENT

STEERING SKIS. Steering skis should be parallel with each other and with vehicle frame when handle bar is in normal straight driving position. To adjust either drag link, it is necessary to disconnect the link at one end.

DRIVE CHAIN. The roller drive chain should have approximately ¼-inch free play measured midway between sprockets or by checking the backlash of driven sheave (S—Fig. 2). To adjust the chain, loosen the three stud nuts (N) which retain intermediate drive shaft bearing housing to chain case. Rotate the housing in the two rear slotted holes until adjustment is correct; then retighten nuts (N).

BRAKE. The caliper type brake uses driven sheave fixed face as a braking surface as shown in Fig. 3. The caliper unit floats in its bracket and is self aligning. Adjustment should normally be made by tightening castellated nut (1) until there is a slight drag on sheave face, backing nut off one castellation and installing cotter pin. Hand lever should be adjusted to fully engage when parking lock can be flipped over as shown in upper view, Fig. 4. Adjust at cable housing anchor (2—Fig. 3).

TRACK. To adjust track tension, raise rear of machine until track is clear of ground, then measure distance (A—Fig. 5) from lower edge of adjusting bracket to lower edge of pivot arm. Distance (A) should be $2\frac{7}{32}$-$2\frac{9}{32}$ inches and equal on both sides of machine. If adjustment is required, loosen clamp bolts (1) and turn adjusting screw (2) until distance is correct.

NOTE: When track tension is adjusted, alignment MUST be checked as outlined in TRACK SERVICE Section of this manual.

Fig. 2—View of intermediate shaft showing secondary sheave (S) and nuts (N) which retain shaft housing to chain case.

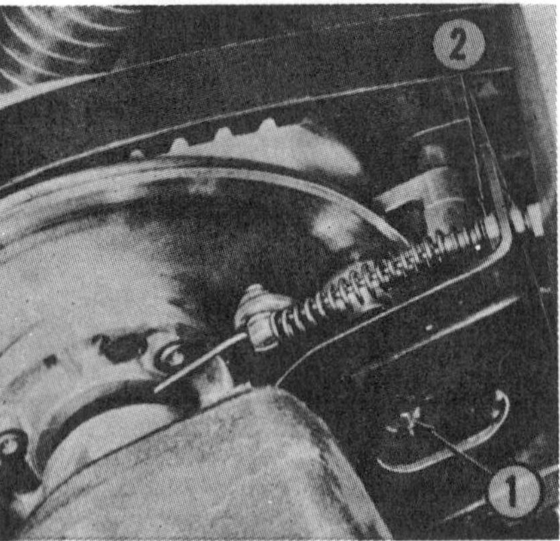

Fig. 3—Normal brake wear adjustment is made by removing cotter pin and turning castellated nut (1). Lever is positioned at cable anchor nuts (2).

OVERHAUL

SKIS AND STEERING. Ski columns (Spindles) are marked "R" and "L" for proper assembly. All other parts are interchangeable from right to left. Steering arms are retained by tapered lock pins which must always be installed with nuts toward center of machine. Upper and lower spindle bushings are renewable, the lower bushing being shouldered to provide a thrust surface.

DRIVE. Salsbury Torque Converters are used.

Track drive and idler sprocket hubs are a shrink fit on shafts and are positioned by a roll pin. New sprockets must be heated to approximately 325° F. in an oven or kiln for installation. Make sure sprockets are in phase when holes are aligned for roll pin installation.

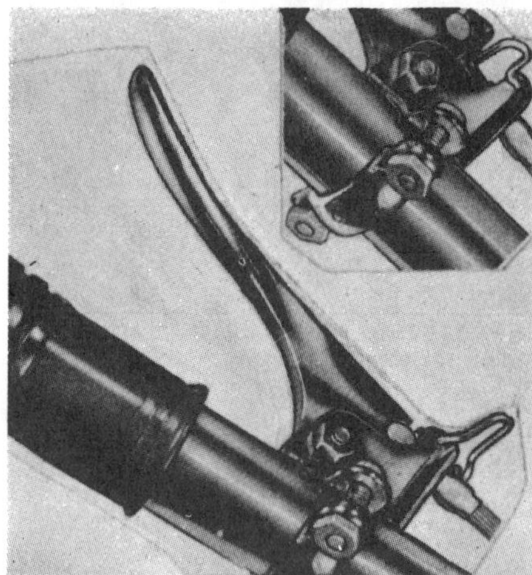

Fig. 4—Views of brake lever showing parking lock.

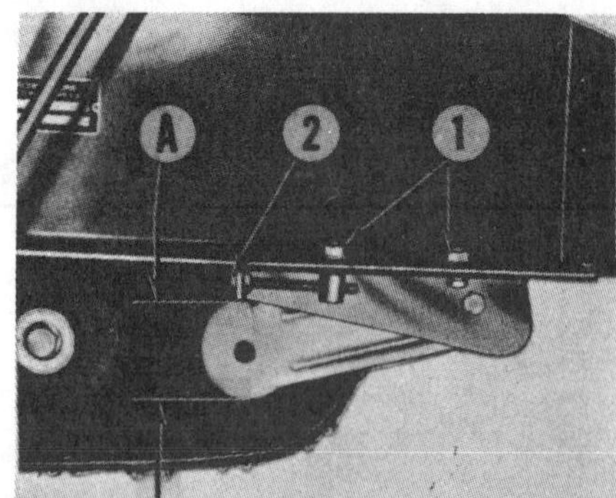

Fig. 5—With rear of machine raised, track tension is correct when distance (A) measures 2¼ inches. Adjust by loosening clamp nuts (1) and turning adjusting screw (2). Refer to text.

SEARS

1972

	Engine			Carburetor				Clutch		
Model	Make	Model	Displ.	Make	Model	Sprocket Ratio	Chain Size	Make	Shaft Center	Belt Number
					1972					
Sportster 244 .	Polaris	EC25P	244cc	Mikuni	VM30	13:35	35-2	Polaris	11.1	3211021
Sportster 335 .	Polaris	EC34P	335cc	Mikuni	VM30(2)	13:39	35-2	Polaris	12.15	3211031
Sportster 450W	Polaris	EC40P	398cc	Mikuni	VM30(2)	13:39	35-2	Polaris	11.1	3211021

LUBRICATION

The engine is lubricated by oil mixed with the fuel. The use of regular gasoline and a recognized (branded) snowmobile oil mixed at the ratio of 20:1 is recommended.

The enclosed chain case should be kept filled to level of check plug (C—Fig. 1) with SAE 10W (non-detergent) motor oil.

Drive train and track are equipped with self-aligning sealed type bearings which do not require lubrication.

ADJUSTMENT

STEERING SKIS. Steering skis should be parallel with each other and with vehicle frame when handlebar is in normal straight driving position. Adjustment is made by turning tie rod after loosening locknuts.

DRIVE CHAIN. To check free play of roller drive chain, refer to Fig. 1 and proceed as follows: With engine not running, rock the torque converter driven sheave and measure backlash (B) at sleeve rim. Slight backlash should exist but total movement should not exceed ½-inch. To adjust the chain, loosen locknut on chain tightener adjusting screw (A), turn screw in until resistance is felt, then back screw out a slight amount until minimum free movement exists at (B).

BRAKE. The hydraulic disc brakes must be bled if necessary to provide solid lever action, and adjusted to provide minimum free clearance for the brake disc. Refer to Fig. 2. Turn adjusting screw (A) in until brake pucks are tight against disc, then back out ¼-turn to provide correct brake clearance. Brake hand lever should not depress more than half way to handlebar grip with brake solidly applied. If lever action is spongy, attach a hose to bleed screw (B) as shown, depress hand lever then open AND close bleed screw to expel the air. Tighten bleed screw before releasing the lever. Repeat the process if necessary until lever has a solid feel. Keep fluid reservoir full (within ⅛-inch of top) while bleeding brake.

TRACK. Raise rear of machine until track is clear. Free play of track measured at middle of slide should be about one inch with a fifteen pound downward pull exerted on track at that point. Adjust by loosening locknuts (A—Fig. 3) and turning adjusting screw (B). A firmer ride can be obtained by moving leading end of suspension spring to one of the upper notches (C). Both sides must be adjusted alike.

NOTE: Whenever track tension has been adjusted, alignment MUST be checked as outlined in TRACK SERVICE Section of this manual.

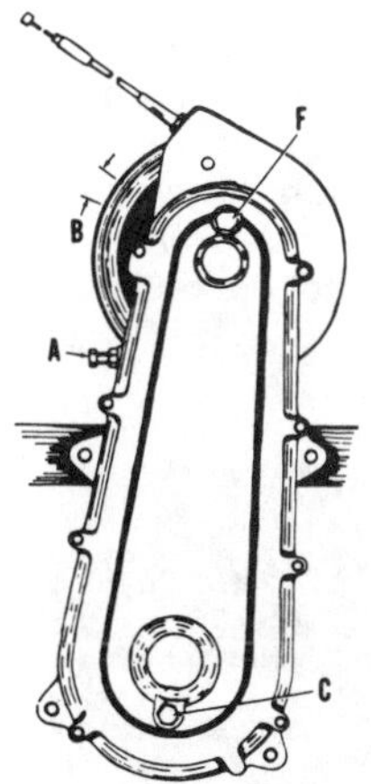

Fig. 1–View of chain case showing adjustment details.

A. Adjusting screw
B. Backlash
C. Check plug
F. Filler plug

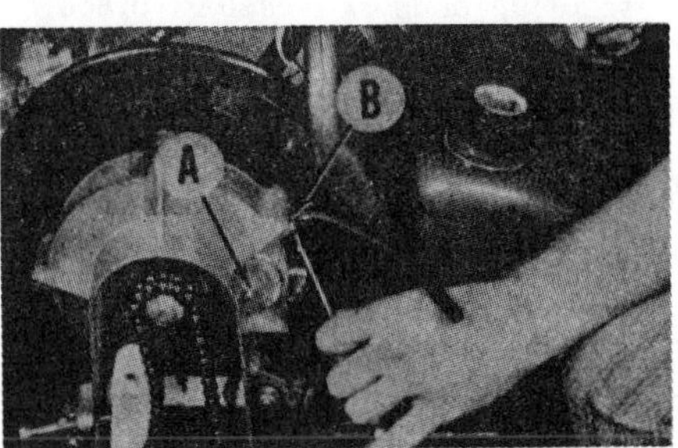

Fig. 2–Bleed hydraulic brakes by opening bleed screw (B) as shown. Wear adjustment for stationary pad is at (A).

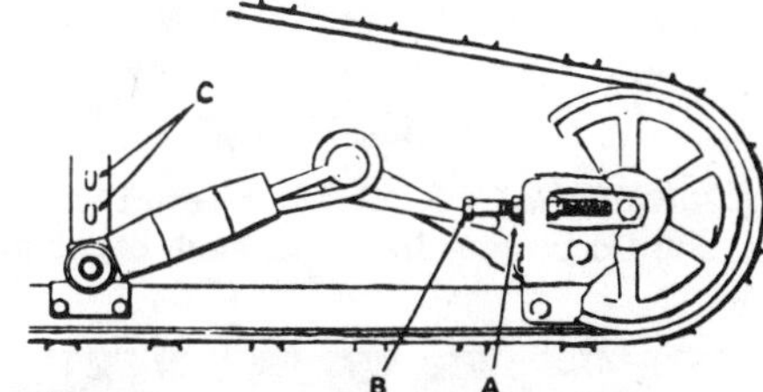

Fig. 3–View of suspension showing points of adjustment.

A. Jam nut
B. Adjusting screw
C. Spring anchors (alternate)

SKI-BEE

1969-1970

	Engine			Carburetor				Clutch		
Model	Make	Model	Displ.	Make	Model	Sprocket Ratio	Chain Size	Make	Shaft Center	Belt Number
					1969					
Scout 130	Sachs	SA280A	277cc	Tillotson	HR8A			Salsbury 770	9.3	702695
Scout 185	Sachs	SA290	297cc	Tillotson	HR8A			Salsbury 770	9.3	702695
Stinger 185 ...	Sachs	SA290	297cc	Tillotson	HR8A			Salsbury 770	9.3	702695
Scout 370	Sachs	SA370	368cc	Tillotson	HD13A			Salsbury 770	10.1	702699
Stinger 370 ...	Sachs	SA370	368cc	Tillotson	HD13A			Salsbury 770	10.1	702699
Stinger 600 ...	Hirth	171R	634cc	Tillotson	HD13A			Salsbury 1190	12½	702874
Commander 285	Sachs	SA290	297cc	Tillotson	HR8A			Salsbury 770	9.3	702695
					1970					
Scout 130	Sachs	SA280	277cc	Tillotson	HR8A			Salsbury 770	9.3	702695
Scout 185	Sachs	SA290	297cc	Tillotson	HR8A			Salsbury 770	9.3	702695
Stinger 185 ...	Sachs	SA290	297cc	Tillotson	HR8A			Salsbury 770	9.3	702695
Scout 370	Sachs	SA370	368cc	Tillotson	HD13A			Salsbury 770	10.1	702699
Stinger 370 ...	Sachs	SA370	368cc	Tillotson	HD13A			Salsbury 770	10.1	702699
Stinger 600 ...	Hirth	171R	634cc	Tillotson	HD13A			Salsbury 1190	12.5	702874
Commander 285	Sachs	SA290	297cc	Tillotson	HR8A			Salsbury 770	9.3	702695

LUBRICATION

The engine is lubricated by oil mixed with the fuel. Recommended fuel-oil ratio is 20:1. Regular gasoline and Air Cooled Two Cycle Motor Oil should be used. Outboard Oil or Automotive Oil is not recommended.

The roller drive chain should be lubriated with SAE 80 EP Gear Oil every ten hours. Oil chain liberally to be sure oil gets inside the rollers.

Lubricate throttle and brake cables every ten hours using SAE 10 oil and handlebar bushings using SAE 140 gear oil.

Grease the bogie wheels and steering king pins every 20 hours with low temperature grease.

ADJUSTMENT

STEERING SKIS. Steering skis should be parallel with each other and with vehicle frame when handlebar is in normal, straight driving position. If adjustment is required, first check to be sure that bolts (B—Fig. 2) securing ski springs to saddle are tight. Slight adjustment can be made by loosening the bolts and repositioning skis on saddle. Adjustment can also be made at tie rods.

DRIVE CHAIN. The roller drive chain should have ¼-¾ inch free play, measured midway between sprockets. To adjust the chain, loosen the three bolts (A—Fig. 3) securing bearing flange to chain case and the two bolts securing ends of jackshaft brace (B—Fig. 4). Slide the jackshaft up until tension is correct and tighten bearing flange bolts evenly. Check to see that torque converter driven sheave is still properly aligned with belt. Alignment is obtained by moving spacer washers from one side of brace (B) to the other. Tighten all nuts securely when proper adjustment is obtained, making sure the three flange bolts (A—Fig. 3) are tightened alternately and evenly.

DRIVE BELT ALIGNMENT. Raise rear of machine until track can turn freely, then start and run engine at a speed which will permit belt to run about half way out in drive sheave. Belt should run straight in both sheaves. Align drive sheave by loosening engine mounting bolts and repositioning engine and/or mounting plate.

Alignment of driven sheave is accomplished in conjunction with drive chain adjustment and as outlined in the preceding DRIVE CHAIN paragraph.

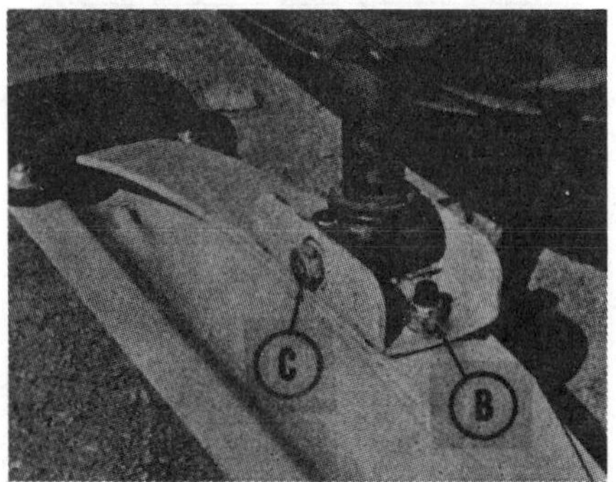

Fig. 2—Minor ski alignment can be made by loosening bolts (B) and shifting ski spring on saddle mounting pads. Cross bolt (C) uses a rubber bushing which assists in positioning the ski.

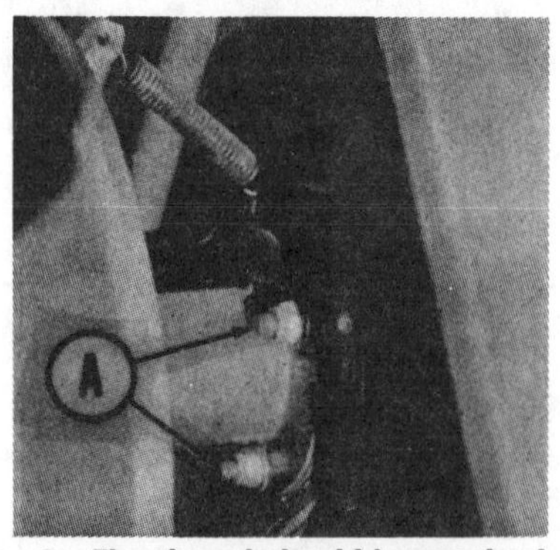

Fig. 3—The three bolts (A) must be loosened to adjust drive chain. Refer also to Fig. 4.

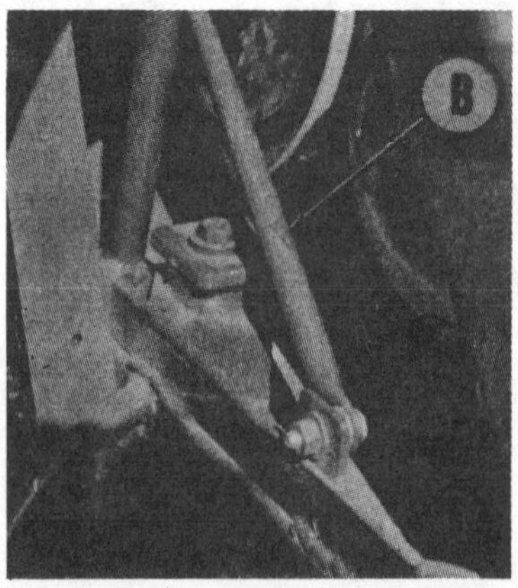

Fig. 4—Jackshaft brace (B) must be loosened and realigned whenever drive chain is adjusted. Refer to Text.

Fig. 5—Measure the distance as shown from center bogie cross tube to inside of track, to adjust track tension. Refer to text for details and adjustment procedure.

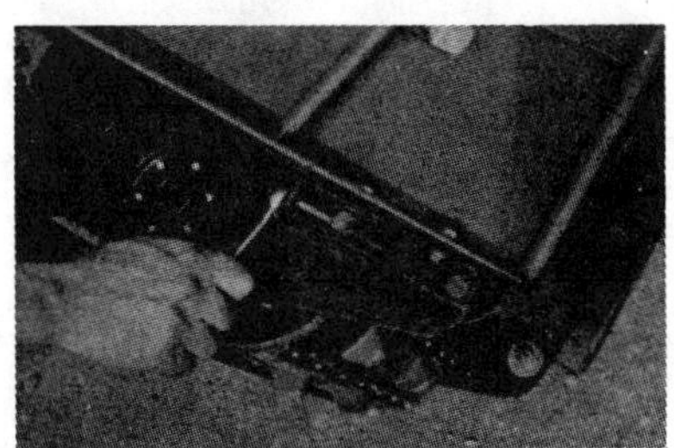

Fig. 6—Adjusting track tension. Refer to Fig. 5 and to text.

BRAKE. Brake shoe should barely clear friction surface of driven sheave when released, and should be firmly applied when hand control is pressed half way to handlebar grip. To adjust the brake, loosen the clamp securing cable housing at brake end, and reposition the housing in clamp.

TRACK. With rear of machine raised until track is clear of ground, measure the distance from center bogie cross tube to inside of track as shown in Fig. 5. The distance should be 4½-5 inches and both sides should measure alike. On Commander Models with four bogie assemblies, measure at second cross tube from rear.

Adjust the track by loosening bracket bolts and turning the adjusting screw as shown in Fig. 6.

NOTE: On all models, when track tension is adjusted, alignment MUST be checked as outlined in TRACK SERVICE Section of this manual.

DRIVE. Refer to the SALSBURY Section for overhaul of torque converter.

TRACK. Track cleats should be renewed if bent, broken or badly worn. When renewing cleats, drill out the rivet from cleat side, then punch out of track. Install using pop rivets.

The manufacturer recommends that the track joint pin be removed and checked at least once each season. If either the pin or lacings are worn to ⅔ their original thickness a new lacing should be installed.

OVERHAUL

SKIS. The longer of the two bolts (B—Fig. 2) in ski saddle should be installed at the front and the shim installed between saddle and spring on the front bolt.

A rubber bushing is installed on the cross bolt (C) which is a friction fit on bolt and in cross hole in ski leg. When installing new bushings, insert the bushings dry, into cross hole of ski leg, then apply brake fluid liberally to inner hole of bushing and to bolt (C). Screw bolt in from the outside. If bushing starts to turn before bolt is fully in place, bolt must be removed and additional brake fluid applied.

SKI-DADDLER

1966-1970

	Engine			Carburetor				Clutch		
Model	Make	Model	Displ.	Make	Model	Sprocket Ratio	Chain Size	Make	Shaft Center	Belt Number
1966										
5810.........	JLO	L22	247cc	Tillotson	HL216A	10:30	40	Salsbury		28726
1967										
5811.........	JLO	L252	247cc	Tillotson (Dual)	HL209A-210A	9:26	40	Salsbury		30226
5812.........	JLO	L292	292cc	Tillotson	HR2A	9:26	40	Salsbury	10¼	30226
5813.........	MAG	2054	540cc	Tillotson	HR3A	11:37	35-2	Salsbury	10	30393
1968										
5811.........	JLO	L252	247cc	Tillotson (Dual)	HL209A-HL210A	9:26	40	Salsbury	10¼	32566
5812.........	JLO	L292	292cc	Tillotson	HR2A	9:26	40	Salsbury	10¼	32566
5813.........	MAG	2054	540cc	Tillotson	HR3A	11:30	35-2	Salsbury	10¾	30393
5814.........	JLO	L297	296cc	Tillotson	HD6B	10:26	40	Salsbury	10¾	30393
5815.........	JLO	L372	372cc	Tillotson	HD6B	18:26	40	Salsbury	10¾	32608
1969										
5811-3000.....	JLO	L292	292cc	Tillotson	HR20A	9:26	40	Salsbury 790	10¾	702695
5811-4000.....	JLO	L227	223cc	Tillotson	HR20A	9:26	40	Salsbury 500	10¼	900392
5813-3100.....	MAG	2054	540cc	Tillotson	HR3B	11:30	35-2	Salsbury	10¾	30393
5814-1000.....	JLO	L297PE	296cc	Tillotson	HD13A	9:34	35-2	Salsbury 790	10¾	702695
5814-1100.....	JLO	L297E	296cc.	Tillotson	HD13A	9:34	35-2	Salsbury 790	10¾	702695
5814-2000.....	JLO	L300E	296cc	Tillotson	HD13A	14:34	35-2	Salsbury 790	10¾	702695
5815-1100.....	JLO	L372	372cc	Tillotson	HD13A	16:35	35-2	Salsbury	10¾	32608
5815-2000.....	JLO	L380	372cc	Tillotson	HD13A	17:35	35-2	Salsbury	10¾	32608
1970										
5811-3000 ...	JLO	L292	292cc	Tillotson	HR20A	9:26	40	Salsbury 790	10¾	702695
5811-4000 ...	JOL	L227	233cc	Tillotson	HR20A	9:26	40	Salsbury 500	10¼	900392
5813-3100 ...	MAG	2054	540cc	Tillotson	HR38	11:30	35-2	Salsbury	10¾	30393
5814-1000 ...	JLO	L297	296cc	Tillotson	HD13A	9:34	35-2	Salsbury 790	10¾	702695
5814-1100 ...	JLO	L297	296cc	Tillotson	HD13A	9:34	35-2	Salsbury 790	10¾	702695
5814-2000 ...	JLO	L300	296cc	Tillotson	HD13A	14:34	35-2	Salsbury 790	10¾	702695
5815-1100 ...	JLO	L372	372cc	Tillotson	HD13A	16:35	35-2	Salsbury 880	10¾	32608
5814-2000 ...	JLO	L380	372cc	Tillotson	HD13A	17:35	35-2	Salsbury 880	10¾	32608

LUBRICATION

The engine is lubricated by oil mixed with the fuel. The vehicle manufacturer's recommended fuel-oil ratio is 20:1 for all engines except Lloyd, which uses a ratio of 40:1. Use regular gasoline and AMF Oil, SAE 30 or 40 non-detergent oil or Outboard Oil.

On Model 5810, sealed bearings are used on bogie wheels and track axles, and final drive chain is open type. Lubricate the chain occasionally with light oil. On other models, lube fittings are used on bogie wheels and ski spindles. The Sno-Scout and Super Scout are equipped with an oil bath final drive chain case and Cruiser 22 with a forward-neutral-reverse chain drive transmission.

On all models, lubricate variable drive sheaves with light engine oil every 25 hours. Lubricate grease fittings every 50 hours with low temperature grease.

On models with closed chain case, oil level in chain housing should be maintained at approximately 2½ inches from bottom of housing; fill through access plug opening at top and measure oil level with a wire, working through access plug opening. Light engine oil is the recommended lubricant.

ADJUSTMENT

STEERING SKIS. With handle bars in normal straight driving position, both skis should point straight ahead and center-to-center distance should be the same at front and rear of skis. To adjust the length of any drag link or tie rod, it is necessary to disconnect the link at one end.

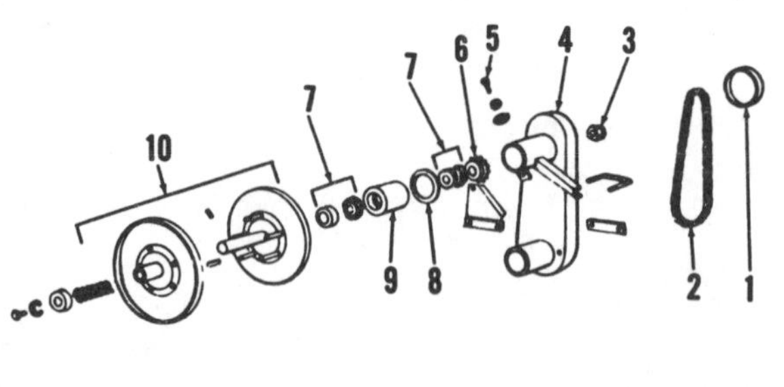

Fig. 2—Exploded view of drive chain housing and intermediate drive shaft which is part of torque converter driven sheave (10).

1. Cover
2. Chain
3. Shaft nut
4. Chain housing
5. Adjusting bolt
6. Drive sprocket
7. Tappered roller bearing
8. Seal ring
9. Eccentric housing
10. Driven sheave

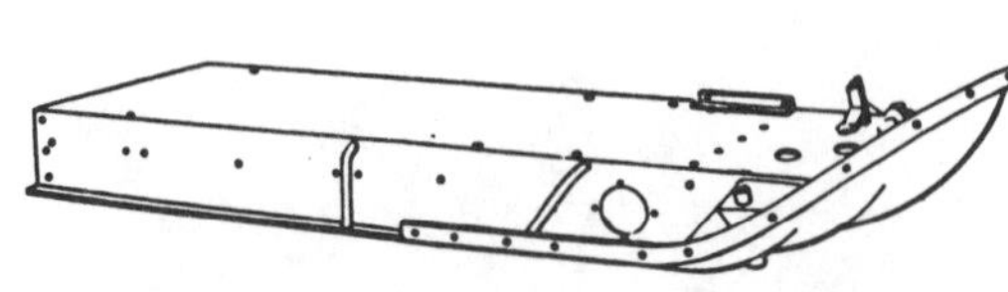

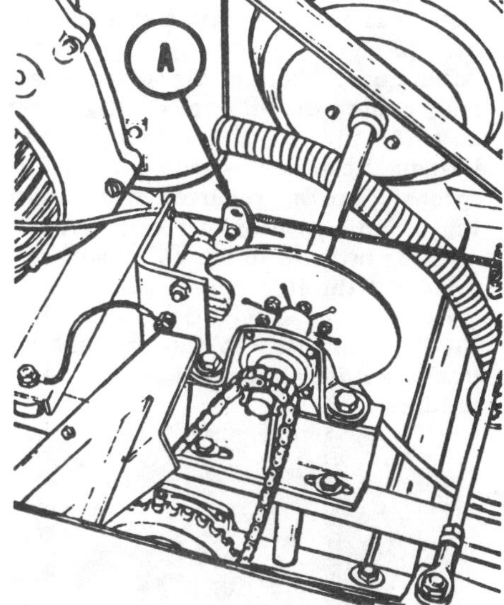

Fig. 3—On Model 5810, adjust brake clearance by tightening castellated nut retaining brake arm (A).

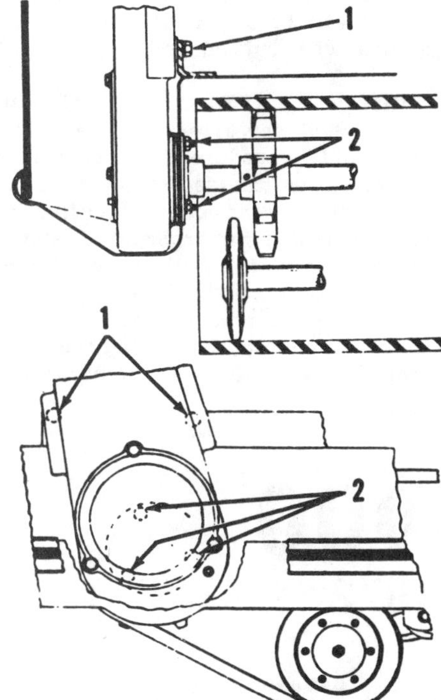

Fig. 5—Cross sectional views of chain case showing attaching points.

1. Bracket bolts
2. Lower mounting bolts

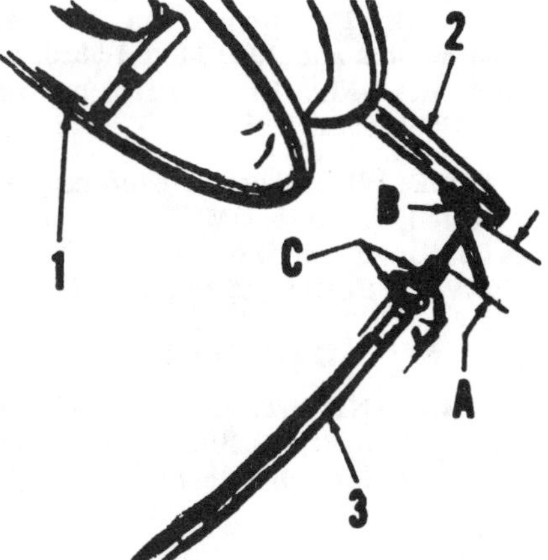

Fig. 6—Some models are equipped with shoe type brake which bears against driven sheave (1). Refer to text for adjustment.

1. Driven sheave
2. Brake arm
3. Brake cable

A. Clearance
B. Cable clamp
C. Housing nuts

DRIVE CHAIN. The roller drive chain is not adjustable on Model 5810 Power Sled nor Cruiser 22 with forward-neutral-reverse transmission. On early Sno-Scout and Super Scout, loosen the locknut and push bolt (5—Fig. 2) down in slot in chain housing (4) until it stops, then back up about $\frac{1}{16}$-inch and tighten locknut.

On late models, the adjustment bolt (Fig. 4) is forward of bearing support as shown, and bolt is pushed UP to tighten chain or DOWN to loosen chain. Chain housing cover is removable for inspecting chain, and about ¼-inch slack is recommended, measured midway between sprockets.

DRIVE BELT. On early models, the drive belt tension can be adjusted by sliding engine in slotted mounting holes. On 1969 models except 5813, loosen the three bolts (A—Fig. 4) and locknut (C); then turn adjusting bolt (D) clockwise to loosen belt. NOTE: DO NOT loosen the two bolts (B). The distance between shaft centers (Measuring Points) should be 10¾ inches. On late Model 5813, refer to Fig. 5. To move the chain housing to tighten or loosen belt, loosen the two bolts (1) and three bolts (2), then manually move the housing until belt tension is correct.

BRAKE. Model 5810 Power Sled and Cruiser 22 are equipped with a caliper type disc brake. Refer to Fig. 3. On models so equipped, remove the cotter pin and turn the castellated nut retaining actuating arm (A) until pucks just clear the brake disc. On models with shoe type brake, loosen the nut (C—Fig. 6) nearest brake arm (2) and tighten the other nut until lining on brake arm (2) barely clears sheave (1). On all models, refer also to BRAKE paragraph in TRACK DRIVE Section of this manual.

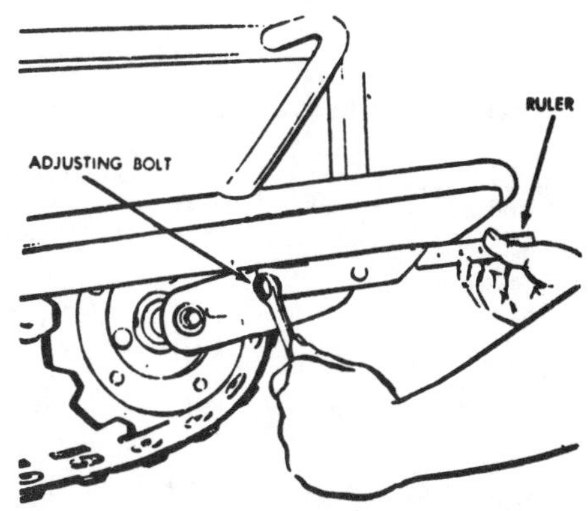

Fig. 7—Adjusting track tension on Model 5810, refer to text.

TRACK. Track tension is adjusted as shown in Fig. 7 or 8. On Model 5810 and all 1969 models except 5813,

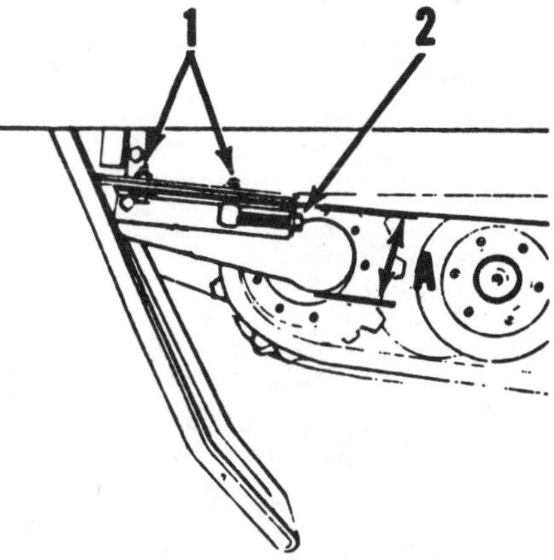

Fig. 8—To adjust track tension on most models, raise machine on kick stand and loosen bolts (1). Turn adjusting screw (2) until distance (A) measures 3¼-3½ inches. Both sides must be adjusted alike.

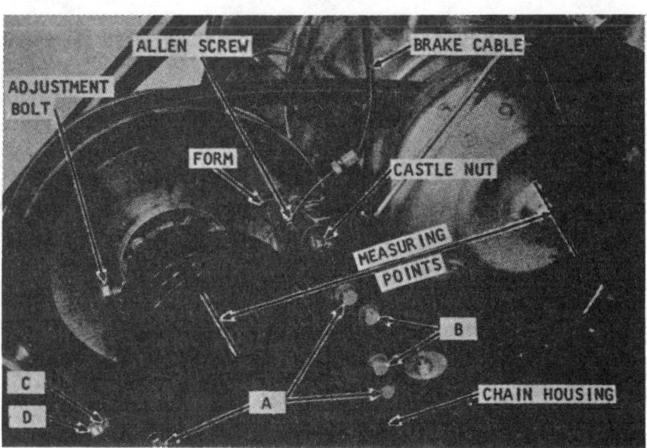

Fig. 4 — Drive train of late models showing points of adjustment.

track should clear center bogie wheels by 1¼ to 1½ inches. On 1967 and 1968 models and 1969 Model 5813, distance (A—Fig. 8) should measure 3¼-3½ inches.

NOTE: When track tension has been adjusted, alignment MUST be checked as outlined in the special TRACK SERVICE Section of this manual.

OVERHAUL

SKIS AND STEERING. Skis, ski legs (spindles), bushings and steering arms are interchangeable from right to left. Skis are equipped with renewable wear bars which must be installed with curved end to rear.

DRIVE TRAIN. On Model 5810 Power Sled, the drive chain is in the open and procedure for renewal is evident after shields are removed.

To remove the chain housing on Sno-Scout and Super Scout, first remove drive belt and disconnect brake cable at brake arm. Remove the securing U-Bolt and one bolt and nut from clamp strap, then swing the strap around out of the way. Remove the housing and torque converter driven sheave as a unit, by using suitable pry bars to slide the housing from frame. After disconnecting the drive chain and removing the chain tightener bolt (5—Fig. 2), the driven sheave, bearing housing, shaft and drive sprocket can be removed from housing as an assembly. Driven sprocket must be brought to top of housing and pried out through upper side opening.

Refer to the special SERVICE SECTIONS elsewhere in this manual for track service information and procedures.

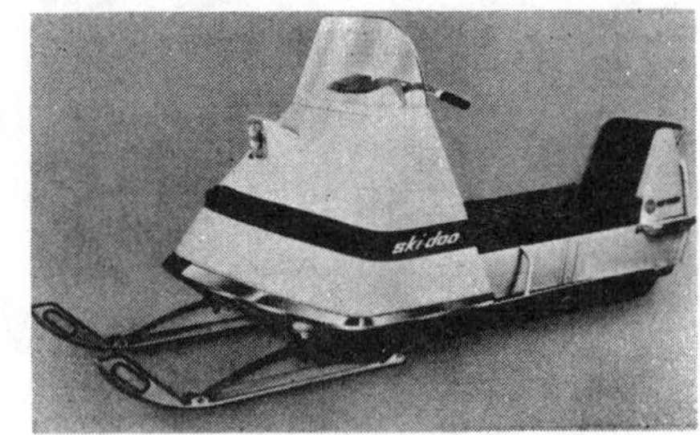

SKI-DOO
1962-1972

Model	Engine Make	Engine Model	Engine Displ.	Carburetor Make	Carburetor Model	Sprocket Ratio	Chain Size	Clutch Make	Clutch Shaft Center	Belt Number
					1962					
Alpine	JLO	L152	148cc	Tillotson	HL233B	9:26		Own		
Alpine	Kohler	K141	16.2ci	Carter	N	9:26		Own		
Alpine	JLO	L197	198cc	Tillotson	HL233B	9:26		Own		
					1963					
R-6	Rotax	165	163cc	Tillotson	HL233B	9:26		Own		
R	Kohler	K141	16.2ci	Carter	N	9:26		Own		
R-8	Rotax	250	247cc	Tillotson	HL233B	9:26		Own		
RD-8	Rotax	250	247cc	Tillotson	HL233B	9:26		Own		
					1964					
AR-6	Rotax	165	163cc	Tillotson	HL233B	9:26		Own		
BR-9	Rotax	250	247cc	Tillotson	HL233B	9:26		Own		
RD-9	Rotax	250	247cc	Tillotson	HL233B	12:39		Own		
					1965					
Chalet	Rotax	165	163cc	Tillotson	HL233B	9:26		Own		
Olympique	Rotax	250	247cc	Tillotson	HL233B	9:26		Own		
Alpine	Rotax	250	247cc	Tillotson	HL233B	12:39		Own		
					1966					
Olympique	Rotax	250	247cc	Tillotson	HL233A	9:26		Own	1⅞*	570-0409
Super Olym.	Rotax	250	247cc	Tillotson (Dual)	HL209A-HL210A	9:26		Own	1⅞*	570-0409
Alpine	Rotax	250	247cc	Tillotson (Dual)	HL209A-HL210A	12:39		Own	1⅞*	570-0409
					1967					
Chalet	Rotax	165	163cc	Tillotson	HL233A	9:26		Own	3¼*	570-0410
Olympique	Rotax	250	247cc	Tillotson	HL233A	9:26		Own	1⅞*	570-0409
Super Olym.	Rotax	300	299cc	Tillotson	HR7A	10:25		Own	1⅞*	570-0409
Alpine	Rotax	300	299cc	Tillotson	HR7A	12:39		Own	1⅞*	570-0409
Super Alpine	Rotax	300	299cc	Tillotson	HD4A	13:39		Own	1⅞*	570-0409
*Pulley Rim, Clearance.										
					1968					
Olympique	Rotax	250	247cc	Tillotson	HL233B	9:26		Own	1⅞*	570-0411
Super Olym	Rotax	300	299cc	Tillotson	HR7A	10:25		Own	1⅞*	570-0411
Super 370	Rotax	370	368cc	Tillotson	HD8A	11:25		Own	1⅞*	570-0411
Alpine	Rotax	300	299cc	Tillotson	HR7A	12:39		Own	1⅞*	570-0411
Super Alpine	Rotax	370	368cc	Tillotson	HD8A	13:39		Own	1⅞*	570-0411
					1969					
Olym. 12/3	Rotax	300	299cc	Tillotson	HR7A	10:25		Own	1⅞*	570-0411
Olym. 12/3SS	Rotax	292	292cc	Tillotson	HD21A	10:25		Own	1⅞*	570-0411
Olympique 320	Rotax	320	318cc	Tillotson	HR17A	11:24		Own	1⅞*	570-0411
Olym. 320SS	Rotax	340	335cc	Tillotson	HD21A	11:25		Own	1⅞*	570-0411
Olympique 370	Rotax	370	368cc	Tillotson	HD8A	16:34		Own	1⅞*	570-0411

*Rim clearance, measured as shown at (B—Fig. 9).

	Engine			Carburetor				Clutch		
Model	Make	Model	Displ.	Make	Model	Sprocket Ratio	Chain Size	Make	Shaft Center	Belt Number
					1969 Cont.					
Nordic 371	Rotax	371	368cc	Tillotson	HR16A	16:34		Own	1 7/8*	570-0411
Alpine 370	Rotax	370	368cc	Tillotson	HD8A	13:39		Own	1 7/8*	570-0411
Alpine 640	Rotax	640	635cc	Tillotson	HD21A	13:29		Own	1 7/8*	570-0414
T'NT 399	Rotax	399	399cc	Tillotson	HD21A	16:34		Own	1 7/8*	570-0411
T'NT 669	Rotax	669	669cc	Tillotson	HD21A	20:34		Own	1 7/8*	570-0414
					1970					
Olym. 12/3 ...	Rotax	300	299cc	Tillotson	HR37A	10:25		Own	1 7/8*	570-0411
Olympique 335	Rotax	335	335cc	Tillotson	HR17C	11:25		Own	1 7/8*	570-0411
Olympique 399	Rotax	401	399cc	Tillotson	HR16B	16:34		Own	1 7/8*	570-0411
Nordic 399	Rotax	401	399cc	Tillotson	HR40A	16:34		Own	1 7/8*	570-0411
Nordic 640	Rotax	640	635cc	Tillotson	HD20A	20:34		Own	1 7/8*	570-0414
Skandic 335 ...	Rotax	335	335cc	Tillotson	HR69A	12:33		Own	1 7/8*	570-0411
T'NT 292	Rotax	292	292cc	Tillotson	HD22A	16:34		Own	1 7/8*	570-0411
T'NT 340	Rotax	340	335cc	Tillotson	HD22A	16:34		Own	1 7/8*	570-0411
T'NT 399	Rotax	400	399cc	Tillotson	HD21A	16:34		Own	1 7/8*	570-0411
T'NT 640	Rotax	641	635cc	Tillotson	HD20A	20:34		Own	1 7/8*	570-0414
Alpine 399R ...	Rotax	401	399cc	Tillotson	HR16B	13:39		Own	Fixed	570-0411
Alpine 399ER .	Rotax	401	399cc	Tillotson	HR16B	13:39		Own	Fixed	570-0411
Invader 640ER.	Rotax	640	635cc	Tillotson	HD20A	13:25		Own	Fixed	570-0414
					1971					
Elan 250	Rotax	247	247cc	Tillotson	HR73A	10:25		Own	1 7/8*	570-0411
Olympique 300	Rotax	302	299cc	Tillotson	HR74A	15:35		Own	1 7/8*	570-0411
Olympique 335	Rotax	337	335cc	Tillotson	HR75A	15:34		Own	1 7/8*	570-0411
Olympique 399	Rotax	401	399cc	Tillotson	HR76A	16:34		Own	1 7/8*	570-0411
Nordic 399	Rotax	401	399cc	Tillotson	HR40A	16:34		Own	1 7/8*	570-0411
Nordic 640E ..	Rotax	640	635cc	Tillotson	HD20B	20:34		Own	1 7/8*	570-0414
Alpine 399R ...	Rotax	401	399cc	Tillotson	HR16B	13:39		Own	Fixed	570-0411
Alpine 540ER .	Rotax	640	635cc	Tillotson	HD20B	13:29		Own	Fixed	570-0414
Valmont 399R .	Rotax	401	399cc	Tillotson	HR40A	13:39		Own	Fixed	570-0411
Valmont 640ER	Rotax	640	635cc	Tillotson	HD66A	13:29		Own	Fixed	570-0414
T'NT 292	Rotax	292	292cc	Tillotson	HD22B	15:34		Own	1 7/8*	570-0411
T'NT 340	Rotax	342	335cc	Tillotson	HD22B	16:34		Own	1 7/8*	570-0411
T'NT 440	Rotax	435	437cc	Tillotson	HD73A	16:34		Own	1 7/8*	570-0411
T'NT 640	Rotax	641	635cc	Tillotson	HD20B	20:34		Own	1 7/8*	570-0414
T'NT 775	Rotax	775	771cc	Tillotson	HD20B	22:34		Own	1 7/8*	570-0414
Skandic	Rotax	337	335cc	Tillotson	HR69A	12:33		Own	1 7/8*	570-0411
					1972					
Elan 250	Rotax	247	247cc	Tillotson	HR73A	10:25		Own	1 7/8*	570-0411
Olympique 300	Rotax	302	299cc	Tillotson	HR74A	15:35		Own	1 7/8*	570-0411
Olympique 335	Rotax	337	335cc	Tillotson	HR75A	15:34		Own	1 7/8*	570-0411
Olympique 399	Rotax	401	399cc	Tillotson	HR76A	16:34		Own	1 7/8*	570-0411
Skandic 335 ...	Rotax	337	335	Tillotson	HR	12:33		Own	1 7/8*	570-0411
Nordic 440	Rotax	434	437cc	Tillotson	HD	16:34		Own	1 7/8*	570-0411
Nordic 640ER .	Rotax	640	635cc	Tillotson	HD	20:34		Own	1 7/8*	570-0414
T'NT 292	Rotax	292	292cc	Tillotson	HD	15:34		Own	1 7/8*	570-0411
T'NT 340	Rotax	343	339cc	Tillotson	HD	16:34		Own	1 5/8*	570-0411
T'NT 400	Rotax	398	399cc	Tillotson	HD104A	18:34		Own	1 5/8*	570-0411
T'NT 440	Rotax	435	437cc	Tillotson	HD	18:34		Own	1 5/8*	570-0411
T'NT 640	Rotax	641	635cc	Tillotson	HD	20:34		Own	1 7/8*	570-0414
T'NT 775	Rotax	775	771cc	Tillotson	HD	22:34		Own	1 7/8*	570-0414
Valmont 440R .	Rotax	434	437cc	Tillotson	HD	13:39		Own	Fixed	570-0414
Valmont 440ER	Rotax	434	437cc	Tillotson	HD	13:39		Own	Fixed	570-0414
Alpine 640ER .	Rotax	640	635cc	Tillotson	HD	13:29		Own	Fixed	570-0414

Rim clearance, measured as shown at (B—Fig. 9).

LUBRICATION

The vehicle manufacturer recommends the use of "SKI-DOO" two-cycle engine oil at the ratio of 20:1.

The drive chain runs in an enclosed chain housing which contains oil to a level approximately even with lower sprocket hub. SAE 80 Hypoid gear lubricant or "SKI-DOO" chain case oil are recommended as the lubricant. Single track models are equipped with a level plug (10—Fig. 7). On Alpine and Invader models, insert a wire through top inspection opening as shown in Fig. 1 and maintain oil level 3 to 4 inches from bottom of case.

The ski-legs (spindles) are equipped with grease fittings at upper end. Lubricate weekly with "SKI-DOO" Grease or an equivalent low-temperature grease.

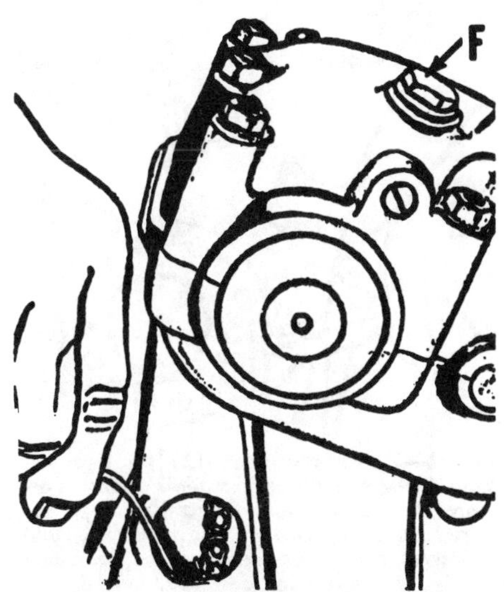

Fig. 1—On late Alpine/Invader Models with Forward-Neutral-Reverse Transmission, lubricant level can be measured with a stiff wire working through inspection hole on left side of case as shown. Fill with Ski-Doo Oil through filler plug (F) to a level of 3-4 inches from bottom of case.

Bogie wheels are equipped with grease fittings. Lubricate weekly, or oftener under adverse conditions or continuous usage, with "SKI-DOO" grease or equivalent. Late models have grease fittings at each end of track idler axle. Lubricate sparingly when bogie wheels are greased.

Lubricate steering linkage and handle bar bushing twice monthly (low temperature grease).

Each week during use season, remove drive belt spread driven sheave and apply a light coating of low temperature grease to shaft. Slide moving pulley back and forth to distribute the grease and wipe off any excess. Each month remove drive pulley centrifugal unit and apply a light coat of low temperature grease to flyweights. On 1971 and later pulley, pack shaft area with grease working through retaining bolt hole. Lubricant is metered to sliding area during operation. On all models use care not to get grease on belt or allow buildup which will be thrown on belt during operation.

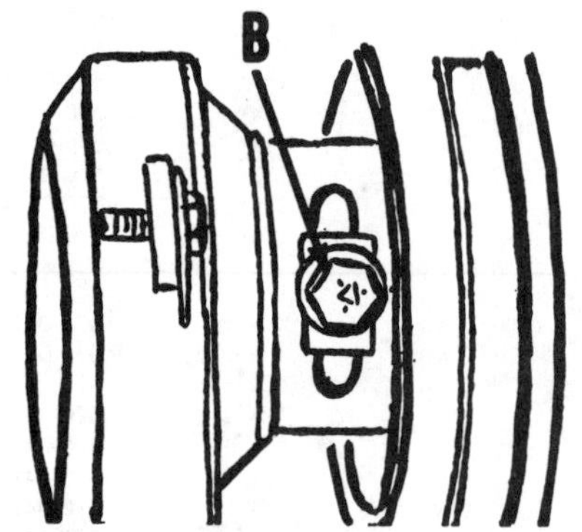

Fig. 2—To adjust chain tension on single track models, loosen adjusting bolt (B) and push down to tighten (or up to loosen) chain. Early Alpine models have two similar tensioners.

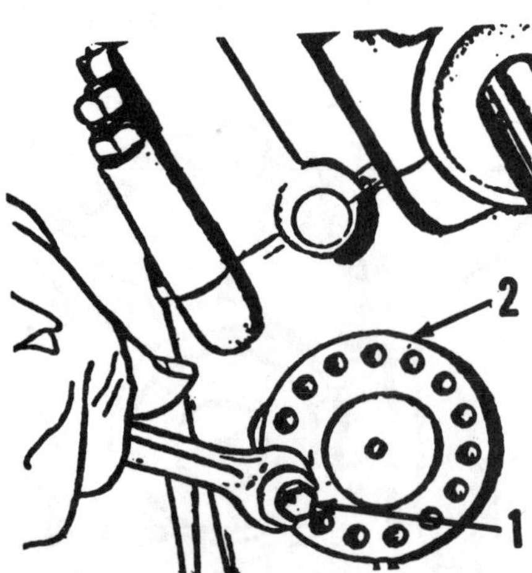

Fig. 3—Chain tensioner (2) on late Alpine/Invader/Valmont models with Forward-Neutral-Reverse transmission is located on right side of chain housing and adjustment can be made after removing adjusting bolt (1).

ADJUSTMENT

STEERING SKIS. To adjust the steering linkage on early models, remove hood and loosen locknuts on each end of tie rod, then turn center tube until distance between skis measures the same front and rear. To adjust handle bar, disconnect drag link at either end.

Late models (Except Elan) use two drag links which should be equally adjusted.

DRIVE CHAIN. The roller drive chain should have approximately ¼-inch of deflection. Direct measurement is not possible on early models with chain case not equipped with inspection cover. The need for adjustment can be determined by carefully rocking the driven pulley and noting the free movement, or backlash.

All 1971 and later models except Alpine and Valmont have an automatic chain tightener and adjustment is not required.

Recommended procedure for all models requiring adjustment is to make 3 checks, turning driven pulley one complete turn between checks. Deflection should not exceed ¼-inch at any time.

Adjustment on early models is by means of the bolt in eccentric bearing housing between driven pulley and upper end of chain case as shown in Fig. 2. Alpine models before 1969 have two eccentric housings as shown in Fig. 8. To adjust the chain, back off the locknut and push down on jam bolt until it stops with moderate pressure applied; then push up approximately $\frac{1}{16}$-inch and tighten the locknut. On Alpine models both bolts (S) must be moved at the same time and same amount.

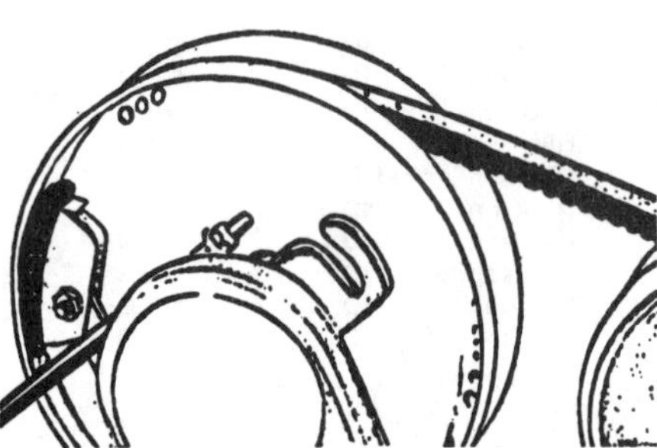

Fig. 4—Some late models have a brake drum built into fixed face of driven sheave as shown.

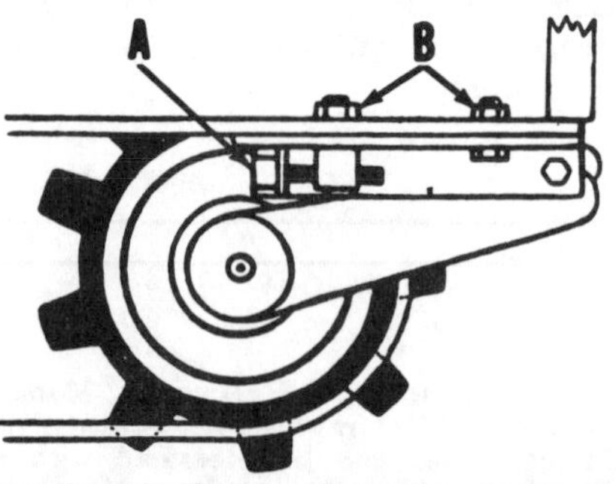

Fig. 5—To adjust track tension, loosen the two clamp bolts (B) and turn adjusting screw (A). Both sides must be adjusted alike. Refer to text.

On 1969-1971 Alpine, Invader and Valmont Series with forward-neutral-reverse transmission, chain adjustment is by means of eccentric tensioner (2—Fig. 3) located on left side of gear box. To adjust the chain, remove locking cap screw (1) and turn tensioner while checking deflection through inspection hole on opposite side of case.

BRAKE. Chalet, Olympique and Super 370 Models before 1969 and some later machines were equipped with a shoe type brake which uses the fixed face of driven sheave as a friction surface. On many late models the brake shoe rides in a drum built into rim of driven sheave as shown in Fig. 4.

All Alpine and Invader Models use H-H Caliper Type Disc Brake which may be adjusted and serviced as outlined in BRAKE paragraph of TRACK DRIVE Section elsewhere in this manual.

Wear adjustment of shoe-type brake is made at brake cable anchor. Adjustment is correct when brake is fully applied with end of lever ¼-inch from handle bar grip.

TRACK. To adjust track tension, raise rear of vehicle until track is clear of ground. Apply down pressure at center of track and measure the distance from track to center bogie

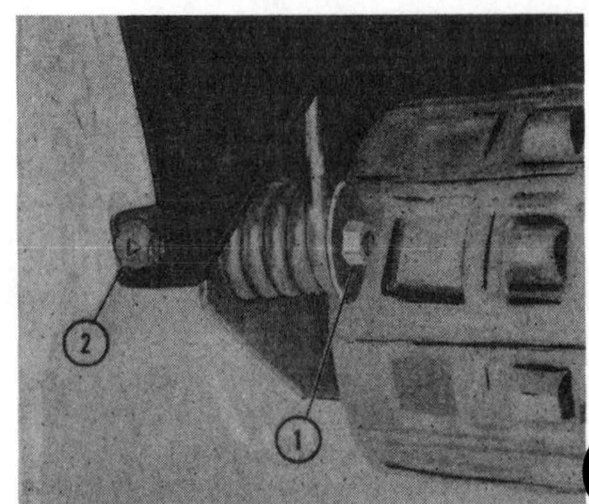

Fig. 6—On 1969-1970 Models Tensioner Clamp Bolt is located in center of suspension spring as shown at (1). Adjusting screw (2) is at rear as shown.

wheels. Distance should be 2½-3 inches and equal on both sides of track (Both sides of BOTH tracks on Alpine and Invader Models).

To adjust track tension on early models, refer to Fig. 5. Loosen clamp bolts (B) and turn adjusting screw (A), making the same adjustment on both sides of single track models or at all four adjusting points on Alpine.

On late models loosen locknuts (1—Fig. 6) in center of suspension springs, then tighten adjusting screws (2) an equal amount. (Four tensioners on Alpine and Invader Models).

NOTE: When track tension has been adjusted, alignment MUST be checked as outlined in TRACK SERVICE section of this manual.

OVERHAUL

SKIS. Skis, ski legs (spindles), springs and steering arms are interchangeable for right or left side of vehicle. Tie rod ends have right hand and left hand threads and are not interchangeable. Skis are equipped with wear bars which are retained by a nut on center stud. Wear bars can be installed either end forward.

CHAIN CASE. On single track models, the chain case serves as the support for driven sheave at upper end and left hand bearing for track drive shaft at lower end. To remove the chain case, first block up rear of vehicle and completely loosen track. Remove hood and torque converter drive belt. On early models, loosen drive chain tension. On 1971 models with self-adjusting drive chain, a tension releaser tool is available from the manufacturer, and is necessary for chain case overhaul. Remove the two clamps (11 & 12—Fig. 7) and suuport rod (3) which hold the chain case to vehicle frame. Work the drive axle seal from lower end of chain case, work the axle from splined lower sprocket and lift off the chain case and driven sheave as an assembly. Be careful not to lose the shims (5) if shims are present. These shims, together with spacer shims located behind torque converter drive sheave, are used for drive belt alignment when vehicle is assembled.

Standard sprocket ratios for most models is given in tables at beginning of this section.

Drive chain (8), upper sprocket (7) or driven sheave can be removed after removing inspection cover (13). Remove the shaft nut and jam bolt (2), then withdraw driven sheave and eccentric bearing housing (1) as an assembly. Driven sprocket (9) can be withdrawn from inspection cover opening after removing upper shaft and sheave assembly. Assemble by reversing the disassembly procedure. Tighten nut (14) to provide a very slight pre-load to shaft bearing.

When reinstalling the chain case, be sure drive axle oil seal is in good condition or a new one installed. Reposition the chain case and install clamps loosely. Reinstall support rod then insert the removed shims (5) in the same position from which they were removed and tighten clamp nuts snugly. Drive sheaves should be properly aligned as shown in Fig. 9. Offset (A) should be ½-inch on all models except 1970 TNT 340, on which an offset of ⅜-inch is recommended. The vehicle manufacturer provides an "Adjusting Bar" (straight-edge), Part

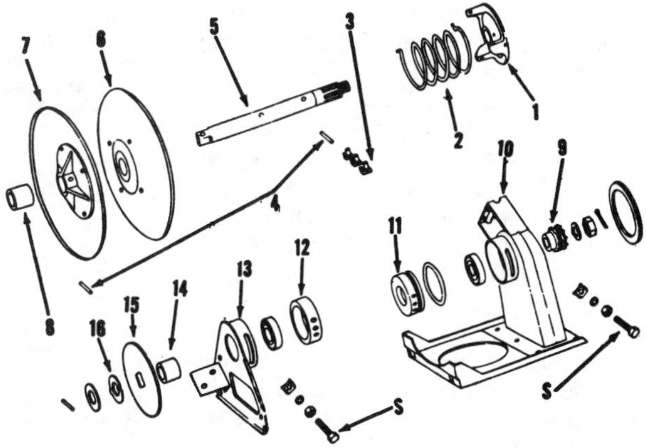

Fig. 8 — Exploded view of driven sheave and associated parts used on early Alpine Models.

S. Adjusting screws
1. Outer cam
2. Spring
3. Cam shoes
4. Spring pin
5. Shaft
6. Moveable face
7. Fixed face
8. Spacer
9. Drive sprocket
10. Chain case
11. Eccentric
12. Eccentric
13. Bracket
14. Spacer
15. Brake disc
16. Wave washer

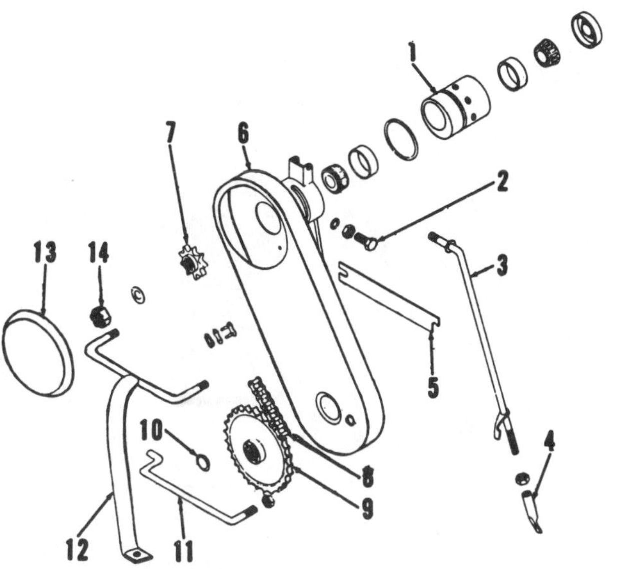

Fig. 7—Exploded view of drive chain housing, supports and associated parts used on early models.

1. Eccentric housing
2. Lock bolt
3. Support rod
4. Socket
5. Shim
6. Chain case
7. Drive sprocket
8. Drive chain
9. Driven sprocket
10. Inspection plug
11. Clamp
12. Support bracket
13. Inspection cover

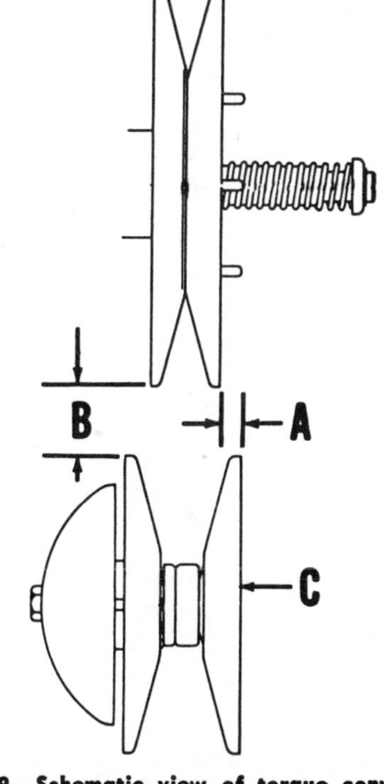

Fig. 9—Schematic view of torque converter showing points of adjustment. Offset (A) is ½-inch on all models except 1970 TNT 340, which should be ⅜-inch. Rim clearance (B) should be 3¼ inches for 1967 Chalet and 1⅞ inches for other models.

A. Offset
B. Rim clearance
C. Adjusting shims

No. SK-1623, which can be used for measuring the offset. Adjust by varying the shim pack (5—Fig. 7) or by removing the drive pulley and adding spacer shims at point shown at (C—Fig. 9). Distance (B) between sheave rims should be 3¼-inches on Chalet Model or 1⅞-inches on Olympique, Super Olympique and Alpine Models. Distance (B) can be varied by shortening or lengthening support rod (3—Fig. 3).

On Alpine models, the chain case (10—Fig. 4) serves as support for driven sheave. The lower half of chain case is built into vehicle frame.

To remove the chain case, loosen both tracks to reduce drive chain tension. Remove belt guard, brake disc and left support bracket (13), then remove drive belt. Remove inspection cover and unhook drive chain; then unbolt and remove chain case.

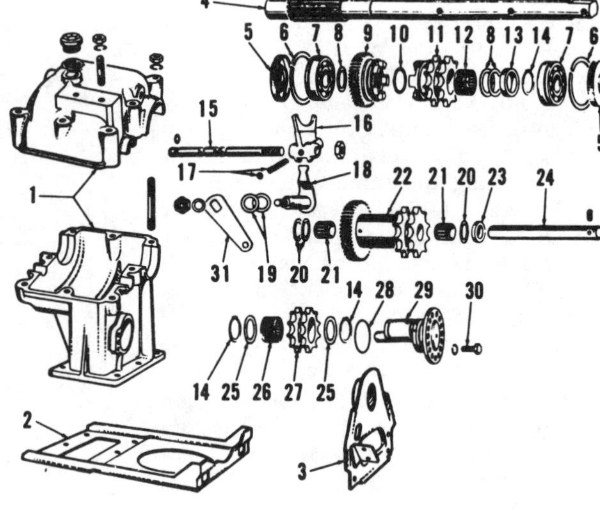

Fig. 10 — Exploded view of Forward-Neutral-Reverse Transmission used on Invader/Alpine/Valmont models so equipped.

1. Housing
2. Bottom plate
3. Support
4. Drive shaft
5. Oil seal
6. Snap ring
7. Bearing
8. Shim (0.5mm)
9. Sliding gear
10. Washer
11. Sprocket
12. Needle bearing
13. Spacer
14. Snap ring
15. Shift rail
16. Shift fork
17. Detent
18. Shift shaft
19. Shims
20. Shims
21. Needle bearing
22. Countershaft gear
23. Spacer
24. Countershaft
25. Washer
26. Needle bearing
27. Idler sprocket
28. O-ring
29. Eccentric housing
30. Lock screw
31. Shift lever

DRIVE. Refer to the appropriate service section elsewhere in this manual for overhaul information on torque converter and associated parts. The vehicle manufacturer recommends the following method to block the piston and keep crankshaft from turning when removing the drive pulley. With spark plug removed from single cylinder engines or pto side spark plug removed from twin, slowly turn crankshaft in normal direction until exhaust port is closed and compression begins. Feed a spare starter rope or similar clean rope into spark plug hole, then turn piston up against rope until crankshaft stops. First remove the centrifugal governor bolt and withdraw governor, moving flange and spring, then insert a punch in cross hole in pulley shaft and turn in normal direction of engine rotation.

SKI-DOO

BOMBARDIER CORPORATION
4505 West Superior Street
Duluth, MN 55806

1973-1982
CONDENSED SERVICE DATA

Model	Make	Engine Model	Engine Displ.	Carburetor Make	Carburetor Model	Sprocket Ratio	Chain Size	Clutch Make	Clutch Shaft Center	Belt Number
1973										
Elan 250	Rotax	247	247cc	Tillotson	HR133A	10:25	½-1	Own	1-⅞*	570-0411
Elan 250T	Rotax	248	247cc	Tillotson	HR136A	14:35	⅜-2	Own	1-⅞*	570-0411
Elan 250SS	Rotax	249	247cc	Tillotson	HR143A(2)	15:35	⅜-2	Own	1¾*	570-0411
Olympique 300	Rotax	302	299cc	Tillotson	HR132A	15:35	⅜-2	Own	1-⅞*	570-0411
Olympique 340	Rotax	338	339cc	Tillotson	HR131A	15:34	⅜-2	Own	1-⅞*	570-0411
Olympique 400	Rotax	401	399cc	Tillotson	HR134A	16:34	⅜-2	Own	1-⅞*	570-0411
Olympique 440	Rotax	434	437cc	Tillotson	HR135A	16:33	⅜-2	Own	1-⅞*	570-0411
T'NT 294	Rotax	294	293cc	Tillotson	HR137A(2)	15:34	⅜-2	Own	1-⅝*	570-0411
T'NT 340	Rotax	343	339cc	Tillotson	HD107A	16:34	⅜-2	Own	1-⅝*	570-0411
T'NT 440	Rotax	435	437cc	Tillotson	HD109A	18:34	⅜-3	Own	1-⅝*	570-0411
T'NT 340FA	Rotax	346	339.2cc	Tillotson	HR149A(2)	15:44	⅜-3	Own	1-⅝*	414-1844
T'NT 400FA	Rotax	396	398.6cc	Tillotson	HD123A(2)	16:44	⅜-3	Own	1-⅝*	414-1884
Nordic 640ER	Rotax	640	635cc	Tillotson	HD110A	19:33	⅜-3	Own	1-⅞*	570-0414
Skandic 335	Rotax	337	335cc	Tillotson	HR75A	12:33	⅜-2	Own	1-⅞*	570-0411
Alpine 440R	Rotax	434	437cc	Tillotson	HD108A	17:46	⅜-3	Own	Fixed	570-0411
Alpine 640ER	Rotax	640	635cc	Tillotson	HD124A	17:38	⅜-3	Own	Fixed	570-0414
Valmont 440R	Rotax	434	437cc	Tillotson	HD108A	17:46	⅜-3	Own	Fixed	570-0411
Elite 440ER	Rotax	434	437cc	Tillotson		17:46	⅜-3	Own	Fixed	570-0411
1974										
Elan 250	Rotax	247	246.8cc	Tillotson	HR133A	10:25	½-1	Own	10½	570-0411
Elan 250T	Rotax	248	247.3cc	Tillotson	HR155A	14:35	⅜-2	Own	10½	570-0411
Elan 250 Deluxe	Rotax	249	247.3cc	Tillotson	HR155A	14:35	⅜-2	Own	10½	570-0411
Elan 294SS	Rotax	294	293.5cc	Tillotson	HR161A	15:34	⅜-2	Own	10½	570-0411
Olympique 300	Rotax	302	299.4cc	Tillotson	HR132A	15:35	⅜-2	Own	10½	570-0411
Olympique 340	Rotax	338	339.2cc	Tillotson	HR131A	15:34	⅜-2	Own	10½	570-0411
Olympique 400	Rotax	401	398.6cc	Tillotson	HR134A	16:34	⅜-2	Own	10½	570-0411
Olympique 440	Rotax	434	436.6cc	Tillotson	HR135A	16:33	⅜-2	Own	10½	570-0411
T'NT 300SM	Rotax	294	293.5cc	Tillotson	HR164A	15:34	⅜-2	Own	10½	570-0411
T'NT 340	Rotax	343	339.2cc	Tillotson	HD134A	16:34	⅜-2	Own	10½	570-0411
T'NT 440	Rotax	440	436.6cc	Tillotson	HD138A	18:34	⅜-3	Own	10½	570-0411
T'NT 340 F/A	Rotax	346	339.2cc	Tillotson	HR149A(2)	15:44	⅜-3	Own	10½	414-1884
T'NT 400 F/A	Rotax	396	398.6cc	Tillotson	HD123A(2)	16:44	⅜-3	Own	10½	414-1884
T'NT Everest	Rotax	440	436.6cc	Tillotson	HD138A	19:38	⅜-3	Own	10½	570-0411
Elite 440ER	Rotax	434	436.6cc	Tillotson	HD140A	17:46	⅜-3	Own	10½	570-0414
Nordic 640ER	Rotax	640	635.1cc	Tillotson	HD133A	19:33	⅜-3	Own	10½	570-0414
1975										
Elan 250	Rotax	247	246.8cc	Tillotson	HR133A	10:25	½-1	Own	10½	570-0411
Elan 250 Deluxe	Rotax	249	247.3cc	Tillotson	HR165A	14:35	⅜-2	Own	10½	570-0411
Elan 300SS	Rotax	294	293.5cc	Tillotson	HR166A	15:34	⅜-2	Own	10½	570-0411
Olympique 300	Rotax	305	295.1cc	Tillotson	HR169A	14:35	⅜-2	Own	10½	570-0411
Olympique 340	Rotax	343	339.2cc	Tillotson	HR170A	15:34	⅜-2	Own	10½	570-0411
T'NT 340	Rotax	343	339.2cc	Tillotson	HD134A	15:34	⅜-2	Own	10½	570-0411
T'NT 440	Rotax	440	436.6cc	Tillotson	HD138A	19:38	⅜-3	Own	10½	570-0411
T'NT Everest	Rotax	440	436.6cc	Tillotson	HD138A	19:38	⅜-3	Own	10½	570-0411
T'NT F/A 440	Rotax	436	436.6cc	Tillotson	HRM5A(2)	16:44	⅜-3	Own	10½	414-1884
T'NT F/A 340	Rotax	346	339.2cc	Tillotson	HR168A(2)	15:44	⅜-3	Own	10½	414-1844
T'NT R/V 245	Rotax	245	247.3cc	Mikuni	VM34(2)	16:40	⅜-2	Own	10½	414-2277
Elite 440	Rotax	434	436.6cc	Tillotson	HD140A	17:46	⅜-3	Own	10½	570-0414
Alpine 640	Rotax	640	635.1cc	Tillotson	HD142A	17:38	⅜-3	Own	10½	570-0414
1976										
Elan 250	Rotax	247	246.8cc	Tillotson	HR173A	10:25	½-1	Own	1-¾*	570-0411
Elan 250 Deluxe	Rotax	248	247.3cc	Tillotson	HR172A	14:35	⅜-2	Own	1-¾*	570-0411
Olympique 300	Rotax	302	299cc	Tillotson	HR174A	15:35	⅜-2	Own	1-⅞*	570-0411
Olympique 300	Rotax	305	295.1cc	Tillotson	HR169A	16:35	⅜-2	Own	1-⅜*	570-0411
Olympique 340	Rotax	343	339.2cc	Tillotson	HR170B	17:34	⅜-2	Own	1-⅜*	570-0411
Olympique Plus	Rotax	434	436.6cc	Tillotson	HR176A	17:34	⅜-2	Own	1-⅜*	570-0411
T'NT 340	Rotax	343	339.2cc	Tillotson	HD148A	16:34	⅜-2	Own	1-⅜*	570-0411
Everest 440	Rotax	440	436.6cc	Tillotson	HD147A	21:38	⅜-3	Own	1-⅜*	570-0414
T'NT R/V 250	Rotax	245	247.3cc	Mikuni	VM34(2)	16:40	⅜-2	Own	1-⅜*	414-2277
T'NT R/V 340	Rotax	345	336.7cc	Mikuni	VM38(2)	18:40	⅜-3	Own	1-⅜*	414-2277
Alpine 640ER	Rotax	640	635.1cc	Tillotson	HRM7A	17:34	⅜-3	Own	1-¾*	414-2277

*Pully rim clearance.

		Engine		Carburetor				Clutch		
Model	Make	Model	Displ.	Make	Model	Sprocket Ratio	Chain Size	Make	Shaft Center	Belt Number
1977										
Elan 250	Rotax	247	246.8cc	Tillotson	HR173A	10:25	½-1	Own	1-¾*	570-0411
Elan 250 Deluxe	Rotax	248	247.3cc	Tillotson	HR172A	14:35	⅜-2	Own	1-¾*	570-0411
Olympique 300	Rotax	302	299cc	Tillotson	HR174A	15:35	⅜-2	Own	1-⅞*	570-0411
Olympique 300	Rotax	305	295.1cc	Mikuni	VM30-90	16:34	⅜-2	Own	1-⅜*	414-2327
Olympique 340	Rotax	343	339.2cc	Mikuni	VM30-91	17:34	⅜-2	Own	1-⅜*	414-2327
T'NT F/A 340	Rotax	346	339.2cc	Mikuni	VM34-118	15:34	⅜-2	Own	1-⅜*	414-2327
T'NT 440 F/A	Rotax	436	436.6cc	Mikuni	VM34-115	18:38	⅜-3	Own	1-⅜*	414-2417
T'NT 440 F/C	Rotax	440	436.6cc	Mikuni	VM34-110	18:38	⅜-3	Own	1-⅜*	414-2417
Everest 340	Rotax	343	339.2cc	Tillotson	HD148B	16:34	⅜-2	Own	1-⅜*	414-2327
Everest 440	Rotax	440	436.6cc	Mikuni	VM34-110	21:38	⅜-3	Own	1-⅜*	414-2417
R/V 340	Rotax	345	336.7cc	Mikuni	VM34-135(2)	18:38	⅜-3	Own	1-⅜*	414-2277
Alpine 640	Rotax	640	635.1cc	Tillotson	HRM7A	17:38	⅜-3	Own	1-¾*	414-2277
1978										
Elan 250	Rotax	247	246.8cc	Tillotson	HR173A	10:25	½-1	Own	10¾	570-0411
Elan 250 Deluxe	Rotax	248	247.3cc	Tillotson	HR172A	14:35	⅜-2	Own	10¾	570-0411
Olympique 300	Rotax	305	295.1cc	Mikuni	VM30-90	16:35	⅜-2	Own	10-9/16	414-2327
Olympique 340	Rotax	343	339.2cc	Mikuni	VM30-91	17:34	⅜-2	Own	10-9/16	414-2327
T'NT 340	Rotax	346	339.2cc	Mikuni	VM34-118	15:34	⅜-2	Own	10-9/16	414-2327
T'NT 440	Rotax	440	436.6cc	Mikuni	VM34-165	18:38	⅜-3	Own	10-9/16	414-2417
Everest 340	Rotax	343	339.2cc	Mikuni	VM30-98	16:34	⅜-2	Own	10-9/16	414-2327
Everest 440	Rotax	440	436.6cc	Mikuni	VM34-165	21:38	⅜-3	Own	10-9/16	414-2417
Everest 444 L/C	Rotax	444	436.3cc	Mikuni	VM34-150	20:34	⅜-3	Own	10-9/16	414-2277
R/V 340	Rotax	345	336.7cc	Mikuni	VM34-135	18:38	⅜-3	Own	10-9/16	414-2277
Blizzard 6500 Plus	Rotax	354	339.2cc	Mikuni	VM34-184	19:38	⅜-3	Own	10-9/16	414-2277
Alpine 640ER	Rotax	640	635.1cc	Tillotson	HRM7A	17:38	⅜-3	Own	10¾	414-2277
Elite	Rotax	444	436.3cc	Mikuni	VM34-177	17:38	⅜-3	Own	10-9/16	414-2277
1979										
Elan 250	Rotax	247	246.8cc	Tillotson	HR173A	10:25	½-1	Own	1-¾ inch*	570-0411
Elan 250 Deluxe	Rotax	248	247.3cc	Tillotson	HR172A	14:35	⅜-2	Own	1-¾ inch*	570-0411
Citation 300	Rotax	294	293.5cc	Mikuni	VM30-104	17:33	⅜-2	Own	1-7/16 inch*	414-2327
Olympique 340	Rotax	343	339.2cc	Mikuni	VM30-91	17:33	⅜-2	Own	1-7/16 inch*	414-2327
Everest 340	Rotax	343	339.2cc	Mikuni	VM30-98	16:34	⅜-2	Own	1-7/16 inch*	414-2327
Everest 440	Rotax	440	436.6cc	Mikuni	VM34-165	21:38	⅜-3	Own	1-7/16 inch*	414-2417
Everest 444 L/C	Rotax	444	436.3cc	Mikuni	VM34-150	20:34	⅜-3	Own	1-7/16 inch*	414-2277
Blizzard 5500	Rotax	503	496.7cc	Mikuni	VM34-203	21:38	⅜-3	Own	1-⅜ inch*	414-2277
Blizzard 7500 Plus	Rotax	354	339.2cc	Mikuni	VM34-184	19:38	⅜-3	Own	1-7/16 inch*	414-2277
Blizzard 9500 Plus	Rotax	454	436.6cc	Mikuni	VM36-78	19:40	⅜-3	Own	1-7/16 inch*	414-3758
Elite 450 L/C	Rotax	444	436.3cc	Mikuni	VM34-201	17:38	⅜-3	Own	1-⅝ inch*	414-2277
Alpine 640 E/R	Rotax	640	635.1cc	Tillotson	HRM-7A	17:38	⅜-3	Own	1-¾ inch*	414-2277
1980										
Elan 250	Rotax	247	250.4cc	Mikuni	VM28-242	10:25	½-1	Own	1-¾ inch*	570-0411-00
Citation 3500	Rotax	277	268.7cc	Mikuni	VM34-228	15:34	⅜-2	Own	Fixed	414-3945-00
Citation 4500	Rotax	377	368.3cc	Mikuni	VM34-229	16:33	⅜-2	Own	Fixed	414-3945-00
Citation SS	Rotax	377	368.3cc	Mikuni	2XVM30-111	18:34	⅜-2	Own	Fixed	414-3945-00
Everest 500	Rotax	503	496.7cc	Mikuni	VM36-83	19:40	⅜-3	Own	1-⅜ inch*	414-3758-00
Everest LC	Rotax	464	462.8cc	Mikuni	VM34-227	17:34	⅜-3	Own	1-⅜ inch*	414-3758-00
Blizzard 5500	Rotax	503	496.7cc	Mikuni	2XVM34-203	21:38	⅜-3	Own	1-⅜ inch*	414-3758-00
Blizzard 7500 Plus	Rotax	354	339.2cc	Mikuni	MAG:VM 34-230 PTO:VM 34-233	17:38	⅜-3	Own	1-⅜ inch*	414-3758-00
Blizzard 9500 Plus	Rotax	454	436.6cc	Mikuni	MAG:VM 36-86 PTO:VM 36-88	19:40	⅜-3	Own	1-⅜ inch*	414-3758-00
Alpine 640	Rotax	640	635.1cc	Mikuni	VM34-215	17:38	⅜-3	Own	1¾ inch*	414-3758-00
Elite 450	Rotax	444	436.3cc	Mikuni	VM34-201	17:38	⅜-3	Own	1-⅝ inch*	414-3758-00
1981										
Elan 250	Rotax	247	250.4cc	Mikuni	VM28-242	10:25	½-1	Own	1-¾ inch*	414-3945-00
Citation 3500	Rotax	277	268.7cc	Mikuni	VM34-255	15:34	⅜-2	Own	Fixed	414-3945-00
Citation 4500	Rotax	377	368.3cc	Mikuni	VM34-256	16:33	⅜-2	Own	Fixed	414-3945-00
Citation SS	Rotax	377	368.3cc	Mikuni	2XVM34-257	18:34	⅜-2	Own	Fixed	414-3945-00
Everest 500	Rotax	503	496.7cc	Mikuni	VM36-104	19:40	⅜-3	Own	1-⅜ inch*	414-3758-00
Everest LC	Rotax	464	462.8cc	Mikuni	VM34-227	17:34	⅜-3	Own	1-⅜ inch*	414-3758-00
Blizzard 5500	Rotax	503	496.7cc	Mikuni	2XVM34-203	21:38	⅜-3	Own	1-⅜ inch*	414-3758-00
Blizzard 7500 Plus	Rotax	354	339.2cc	Mikuni	2XVM34-203	17:38	⅜-3	Own	1-⅜ inch*	414-3758-00

*Pulley rim clearance.

Model	Make	Engine Model	Engine Displ.	Carburetor Make	Carburetor Model	Sprocket Ratio	Chain Size	Clutch Make	Clutch Shaft Center	Clutch Belt Number
Blizzard 9500 Plus	Rotax	454	436.6cc	Mikuni	2XVM34-230	19:40	3/8-3	Own	1-3/8 inch*	414-3758-00
Alpine 640	Rotax	640	635.1cc	Mikuni	VM34-215	17:38	3/8-3	Own	1-¾ inch*	414-3758-00
Elite	Rotax	464	462.8cc	Mikuni	VM34-258	17:34	3/8-3	Own	1-5/8 inch*	414-3758-00
Nordik	Rotax	377	368.3cc	Mikuni	VM34-256	14:35	3/8-2	Own	Fixed	414-3758-00
1982										
Elan 250	Rotax	247	250.4cc	Mikuni	VM28-242	10:25	½-1	Own	1-¾ inch*	570-0411-00
Citation 3500	Rotax	277	268.7cc	Mikuni	VM34-255	15:34	3/8-2	Own	1-5/8 inch*	414-3945-00
Citation 4500	Rotax	377	368.3cc	Mikuni	VM34-276	16:33	3/8-2	Own	1-5/8 inch*	414-3945-00
Citation SS	Rotax	377	368.3cc	Mikuni	2XVM34-277	17:35	3/8-2	Own	1-5/8 inch*	414-3945-00
Everest 500	Rotax	503	496.7cc	Mikuni	VM36-114	19:40	3/8-3	Own	1-3/8 inch*	414-3758-00
Everest LC	Rotax	464	462.8cc	Mikuni	VM34-227	17:34	3/8-3	Own	1-3/8 inch*	414-3758-00
Blizzard 5500MX	Rotax	503	496.7cc	Mikuni	2XVM34-203	19:40	3/8-3	Own	1-3/8 inch*	414-3758-00
Blizzard 9500	Rotax	454	436.6cc	Mikuni	PTO:VM 36-119 MAG:VM 36-118	20:39	3/8-3	Own	1-3/8 inch*	414-3758-00
Alpine	Rotax	640	635.1cc	Mikuni	VM34-215	17:38	3/8-3	Own	1-¾ inch*	414-3758-00
Elite	Rotax	464	462.8cc	Mikuni	VM34-258	17:34	3/8-3	Own	1-¾ inch*	414-3758-00
Nordik	Rotax	377	368.3cc	Mikuni	VM34-276	14:35	3/8-2	Own	1-5/8 inch*	414-3758-00
Skandic	Rotax	377	368.3cc	Mikuni	VM34-276	14:35	3/8-2	Own	1-5/8 inch*	414-3758-00

*Pulley rim clearance.

LUBRICATION

The engine for models without oil injection is lubricated by mixing oil with the fuel. Mix fuel and oil thoroughly in a separate container before pouring mixture into fuel tank. Bombardier concentrated 50:1 oil should be mixed with recommended fuel at a ratio of one pint of oil to six gallons of gasoline. If Bombardier oil is not available, USE ONLY a good quality recognized brand snowmobile oil or two-cycle oil and mix at fuel:oil ratio recommended by oil manufacturer. For cold weather blending, pre-mix the oil with a small amount of gasoline and shake thoroughly until mixture is liquid, then blend with remainder of fuel. Do not use kerosene or fuel oil for pre-mixing.

Normally the engine on models with oil injection will be adequately lubricated by oil delivered and metered by the oil injection pump. In extremely cold weather, the oil injection system may not pump correctly. Below -20 degrees F. (-29 degrees C.), mix one pint of oil with each six gallons of gasoline to supplement oil injection pump to insure proper lubrication.

The enclosed drive chain runs in an oil bath. Bombardier Chaincase oil or a suit-

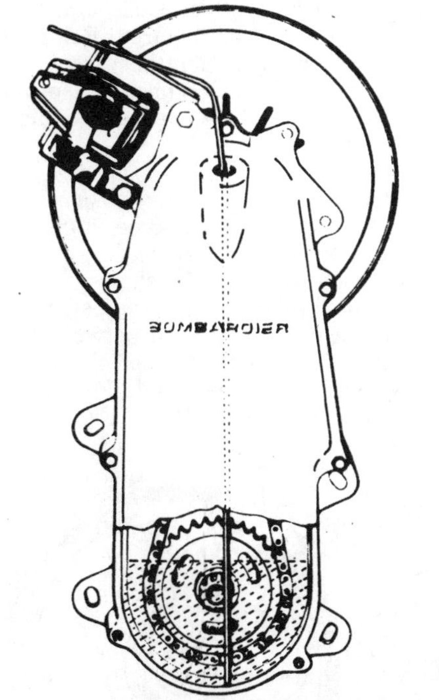

Fig. 1—On early twin track models with center drive, lubricant level can be measured with a stiff wire working through inspection hole as shown. Fill with Bombardier Chaincase oil through filler plug (F) to a level 3-4 inches from bottom of case.

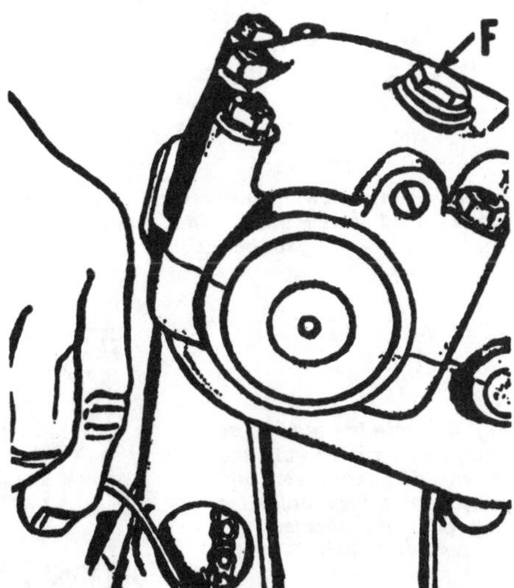

Fig. 1A—On early models with diecast chaincase, use a stiff wire as shown to measure fluid level. Proper level is 3-4 inches from bottom of case.

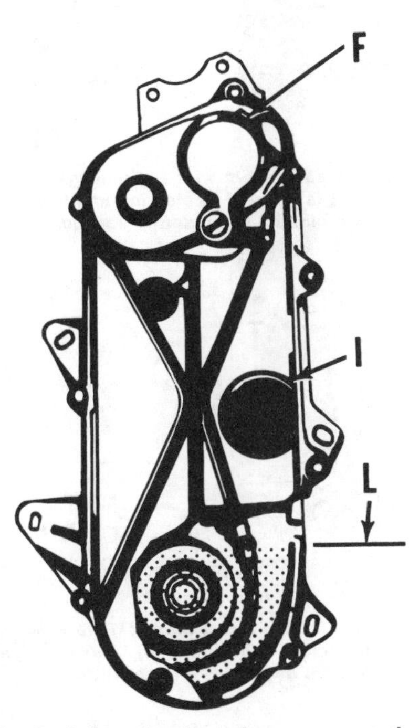

Fig. 2—Schematic view of gearcase used on NORDIC 640ER. Recommended fluid level is shown at (L). Inspection plug is at (I) and fill plug at (F).

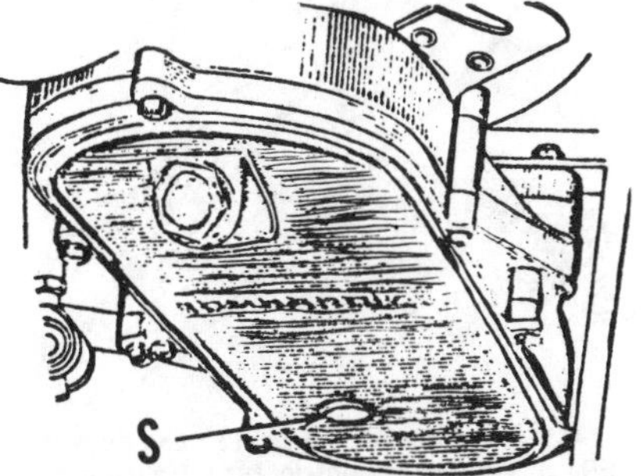

Fig. 3—Some late models have a sight glass or an oil level plug (S) in chaincase cover at recommended fluid level.

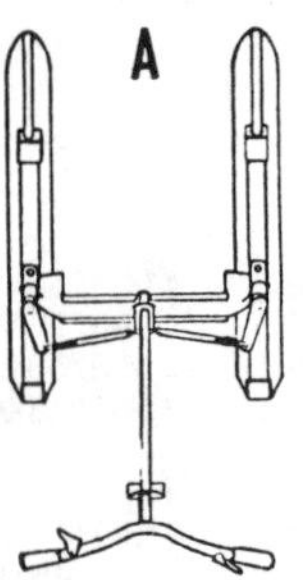
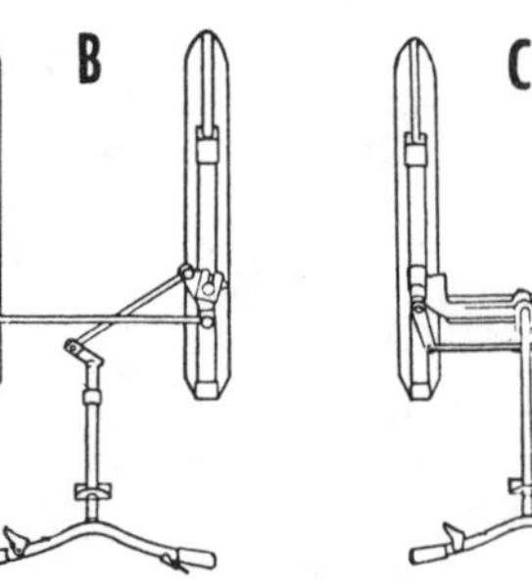

Fig. 4—Schematic view of three steering types used on Ski-Doo units. (A) Separate drag links from handlebar to each ski leg. (B) Tie rod and drag link to front of right steering arm. (C) Tie rod and drag link to rear of right steering arm.

able equivalent is recommended. On early models so equipped lubricant level can be measured through inspection hole using a stiff wire. Refer to Figs. 1, 1A or 2 for view of some early model chaincases. Most later model chaincases have an oil level plug or an oil level sight glass as shown in Fig. 3.

Individual bogie wheels on models so equipped have pressure gun fittings as do drive axle bearing and idler wheels on single sprocket drive models. Idler axle bearings on most units also have pressure gun fittings. Suspension system, drive fittings and ski legs should be lubricated sparingly with low temperature grease in a hand grease gun each 50 hours.

Check drive belt for wear, grease contamination or other damage. Check pulley for wear, missing or damaged cam shoes or other damage and correct any defects before reinstalling drive belt.

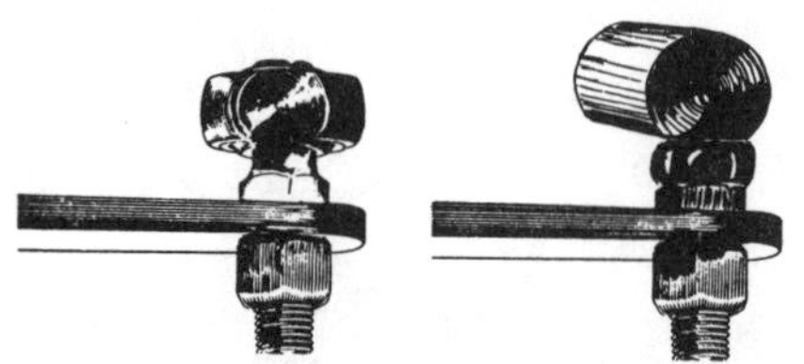

Fig. 5—On all models with ball linkage, make sure socket is parallel to steering arm to eliminate binding when unit is steered.

ADJUSTMENT

STEERING SKIS. Steering skis on single track models should toe-out ⅛-inch (3 mm) when handlebar is in a normal straight ahead driving position. Pull front tips of skis together to remove the slack when measuring toe setting. On models (A–Fig. 5) having two drag links, adjust both links an equal amount to keep handlebar straight. On other models, shorten or lengthen tie rod to adjust toe setting, then adjust drag link as necessary to keep handlebar straight. On models with tie rod ball linkage, align socket parallel with steering arm as shown in Fig. 5 when tightening locknut.

Some models are equipped with adjustable travel stops (T–Fig. 6). Adjust the opposite stop until each ball joint (J) clears bottom of pan by ⅛-inch (3 mm) at extreme turn.

On Alpine models, handlebar must be at right angles to the single ski, and alignment is accomplished during assembly.

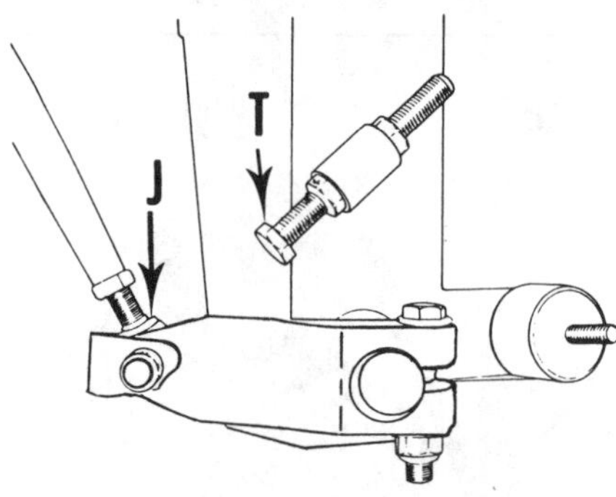

Fig. 6—Adjustable travel stops (T) are used on some models. Ball joint (J) should clear bottom of pan by ⅛ inch (3 mm).

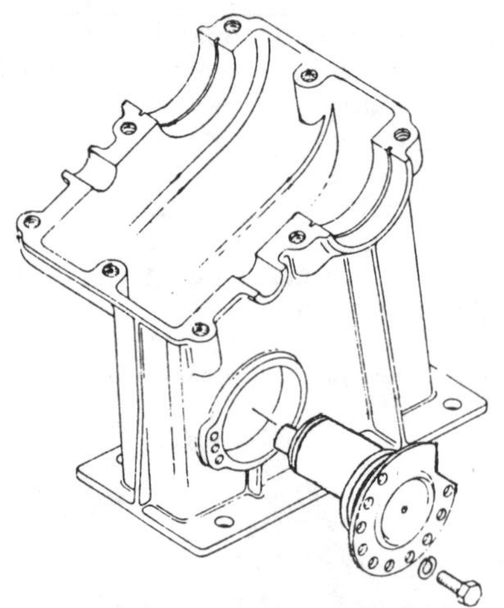

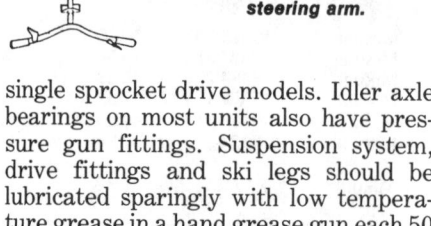

Fig. 7A — View showing drive chain eccentric adjuster used on models with transmission gear box.

DRIVE CHAIN. Models with Forward-Neutral-Reverse or Forward-Reverse transmission have a tightener sprocket mounted on an eccentric as shown in Fig. 7 for early models and Fig. 7A for later gear box models. To adjust the chain, remove locking cap screw and turn the eccentric until chain free play is ¼-inch, measured midway between sprockets. Free play can be estimated by checking backlash at driven pulley rim. Some movement must exist, but backlash should not exceed ½-inch.

On early models with right-hand mounted chaincase and cross shaft, a sprocket idler type chain tensioner is used. Chain tension is correct when backlash (B–Fig. 8) measures ¼-inch (6 mm). Adjust by withdrawing retaining hairpin and turning hex head adjusting bolt (A) in or out as required. Reinstall hairpin when adjustment is correct. On all other models, self-adjusting, spring loaded tighteners are used and adjustment is not required.

BRAKES. Brake may be of pivot lever type, drum or disc type. Figure 9 shows view of early pivot lever type (Elan models) and Fig. 10 shows view of later drum brake model. To adjust, 1/16-inch clearance should exist between lining and friction surface of drum or pulley with brake released. For pivot lever models refer to Inset, Fig. 9 for

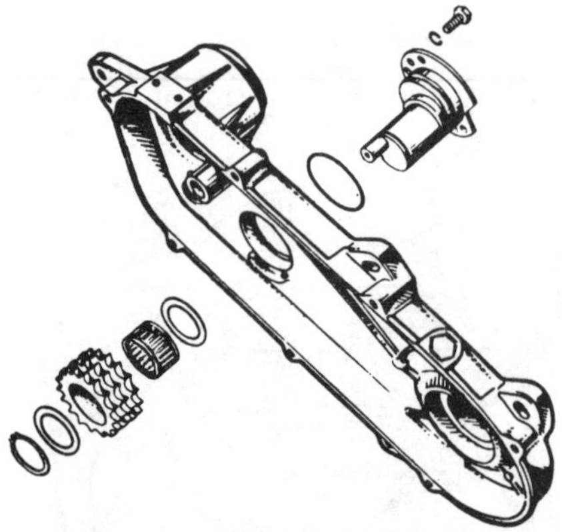

Fig. 7—View of chaincase cover used on Nordic 640ER. A similar eccentric type tightener/idler sprocket is used on other early models with Forward-Neutral-Reverse or Forward-Reverse Transmissions.

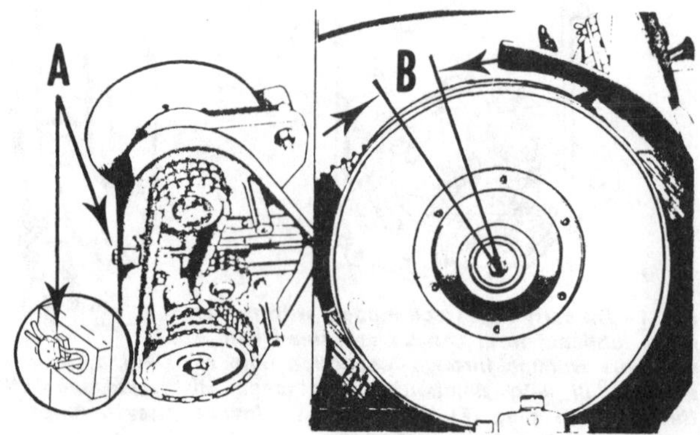

Fig. 8—On early models so equipped with right-hand mounted chaincase, pull hairpin and turn adjusting bolt (A) until backlash (B) measures ¼-inch (6 mm).

proper lacing technique and remove slack from cable working at pivot lever end. On drum type brake, refer to Fig. 10. Adjust by loosening clamp bolt (A), then pulling slack through cable clamp. If equipped with brake light, adjust switch if necessary at nuts (B).

On early models with manual adjusting caliper type disc brake, refer to Fig. 11. Check position of actuating arm to be sure push pins center in valleys of cam. Adjust if necessary at cable housing nuts (C). Brake wear adjustment is made by tightening nut (A) until minimum clearance is obtained without drag. Recheck brake light if so equipped and adjust if necessary by repositioning switch at adjusting nuts (B).

On late models with manual adjusting type disc brake, refer to Fig. 11A. Adjust cable by turning adjuster (1) counter-clockwise until disc pucks are tight against brake disc, then back off adjuster 1½ turns. Brake should fully apply when hand lever is approximately ½-inch from handlebar grip.

On models equipped with self-adjusting brake types, wear adjustment is not required.

RIDE ADJUSTMENT. Models with bogie wheel suspension are equipped with adjustable tensioner for performance modification as shown in Fig. 12. Increasing spring tension (forward notch) increases ski pressure and is recommended for hard-packed snow and (or) heavy loads. Center notch is for normal operation and rear notch is used for trail breaking, traveling in deep fluffy snow or rough terrain. Both sides MUST be adjusted alike.

Models with "Ground Leveler" Slide Suspension have tension adjustments on the four support arm springs as shown in Fig. 12A. The recommended procedure for adjustment is as follows: Raise rear of machine until track is clear and back off all four nuts (A and B on both sides) until spring tension is relaxed but with nuts still touching support boss. Tighten front nuts (B) an equal amount within the limits of ⅛-¼ inch and rear nuts (A) an equal amount within the limits of ¼-½ inch. Rear nuts (A) can be tightened an additional amount for a firmer ride or heavier load if necessary, but front nuts (B) must not be tightened MORE than the specified ¼-inch.

On all models with Torque Reaction Slide Suspension, cams (S–Fig. 12B) provide a ride adjustment for varying load and snow conditions. Front and rear cams may be adjusted independently but right and left cams must be adjusted the same.

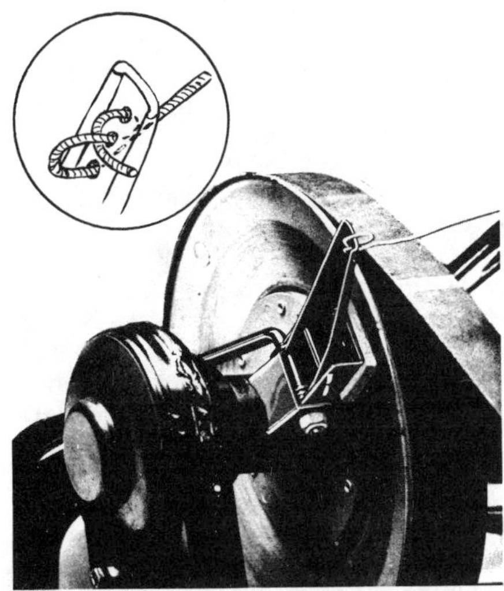

Fig. 9—Installed view of pivot lever type brake used on early Elan models. Inset shows proper lacing technique of actuating cable in lever arm.

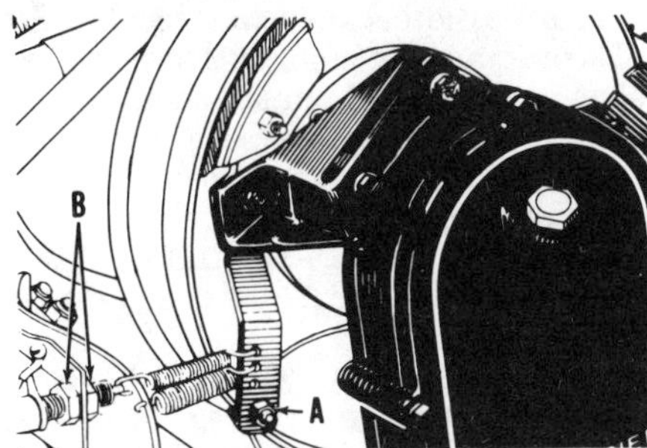

Fig. 10—Installed view of late drum-type brake. Adjust by loosening cable clamp screw (A) and pulling slack from cable until shoe clearance is correct. Adjusting nuts (B) position brake light switch on models so equipped.

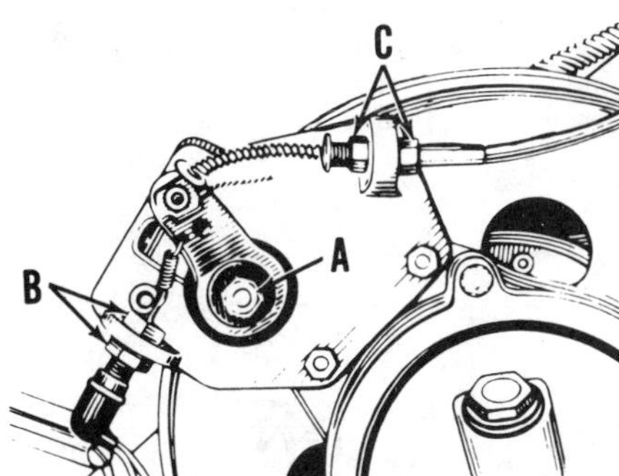

Fig. 11—Installed view of early caliper disc brake. Center cam on push pins by adjusting anchor nuts (C) then adjust brake by turning nut (A). Nuts (B) adjust brake light switch if unit is so equipped.

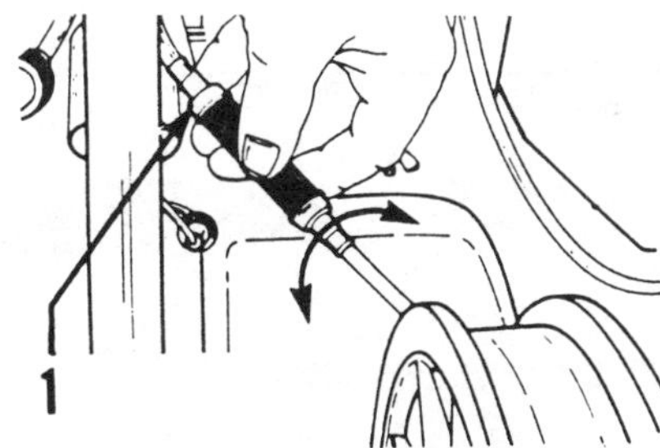

Fig. 11A—View showing brake cable adjuster (1) on late model manual adjusting type disc brake.

Fig. 12—Some models are equipped with an adjustable tensioner at rear of track tunnel for ride adjustment.

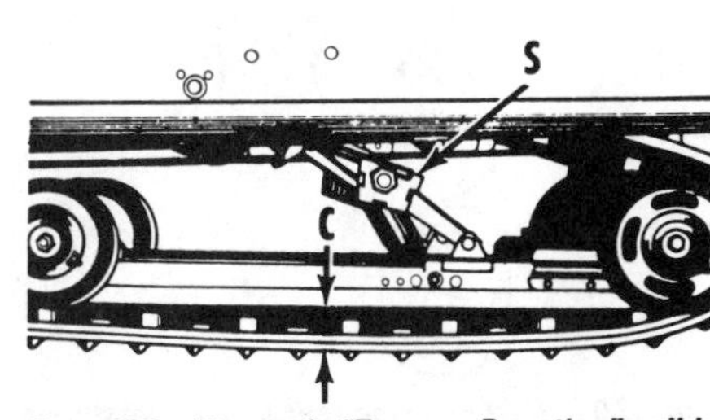

Fig. 12B—View of "Torque Reaction" slide suspension used on some models. Measure clearance at (C). Suspension cams (S) adjust ride.

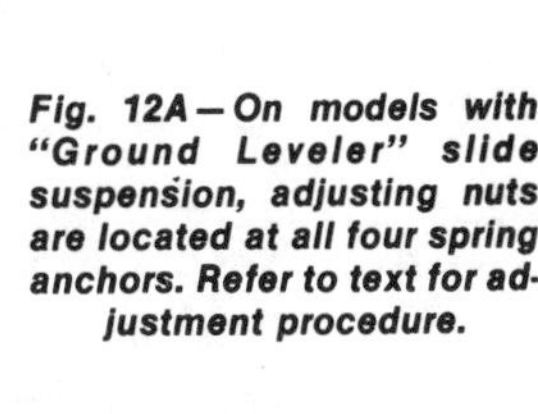

Fig. 12A—On models with "Ground Leveler" slide suspension, adjusting nuts are located at all four spring anchors. Refer to text for adjustment procedure.

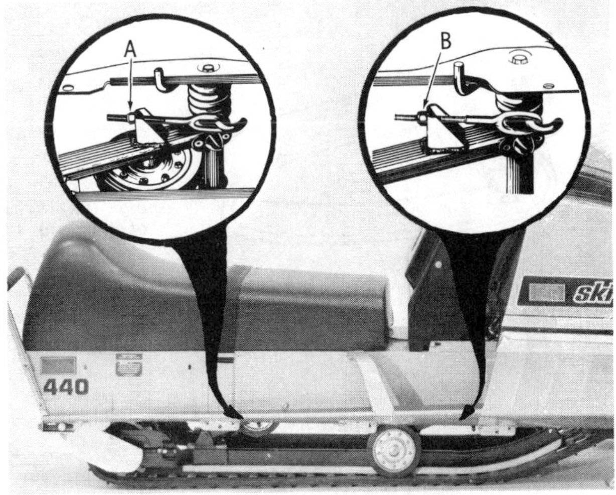

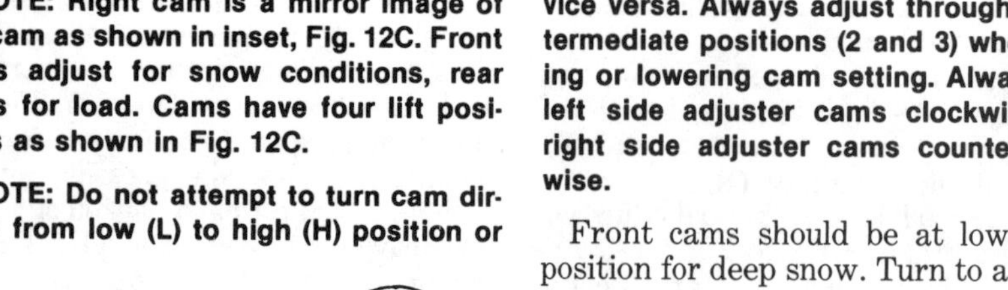

NOTE: Right cam is a mirror image of left cam as shown in inset, Fig. 12C. Front cams adjust for snow conditions, rear cams for load. Cams have four lift positions as shown in Fig. 12C.

NOTE: Do not attempt to turn cam directly from low (L) to high (H) position or vice versa. Always adjust through the intermediate positions (2 and 3) when raising or lowering cam setting. Always turn left side adjuster cams clockwise and right side adjuster cams counter-clockwise.

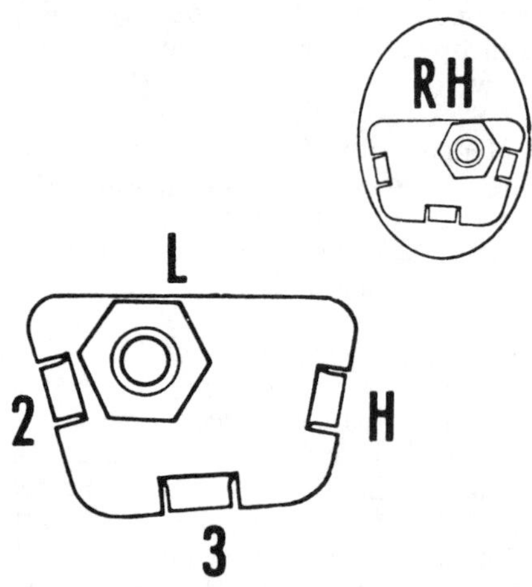

Fig. 12C — View of left-hand adjusting cam showing low (L), high (H) and two intermediate positions (2 and 3). Right hand cam (RH) is a mirror image of left cam as shown.

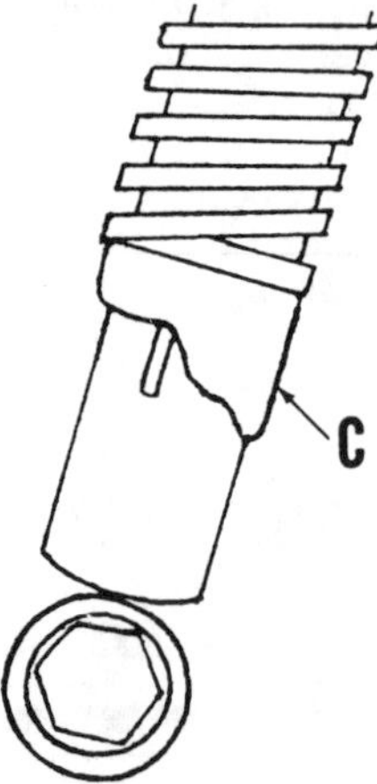

Fig. 12D — View showing rear shock adjustment cam (C) on MX suspension models. Refer to text for adjustment settings.

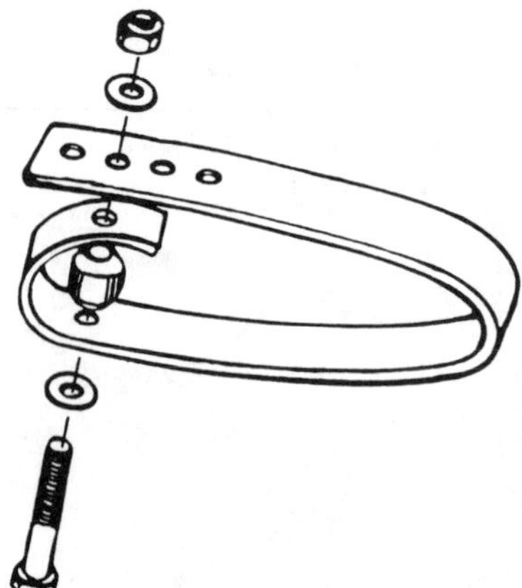

Fig. 12E — Snubber strap used on front slide support is normally adjusted in second hole as shown. Shortening strap limits torque lift of skis during acceleration.

Front cams should be at lowest (L) position for deep snow. Turn to a higher position to increase steering response. Rear cams should be adjusted to provide 4½-5½ inches clearance between rear of footrest and snow surface when carrying normal load. A spark plug wrench fits the adjusting hex on cams.

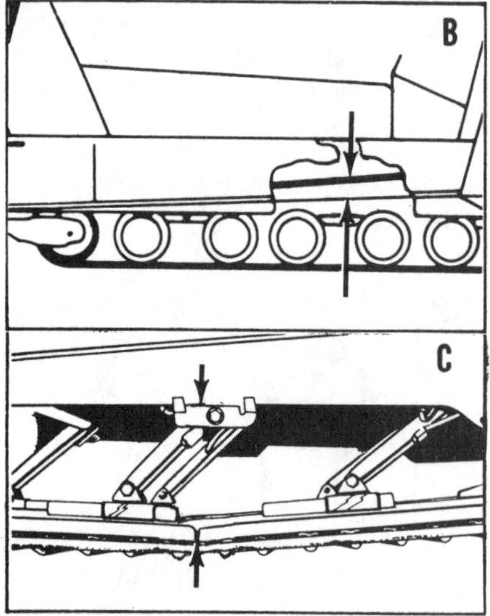

Fig. 13 — Views of suspension systems showing measurements of track tension. Refer to TRACK TENSION paragraph for model identification and procedure.

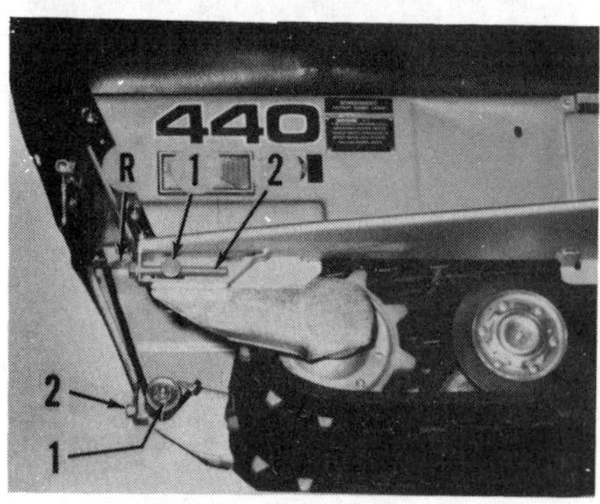

Fig. 14 — To adjust track tension, loosen clamp bolt (1) and turn tensioner adjusting screw (2).

On MX suspension models, front suspension is adjusted by cams as outlined in previous paragraphs. Rear suspension is adjusted by turning cam (C – Fig. 12D) on rear shocks to set desired tension on shock spring. There are three adjustment positions on cam, they are: first position (lowest step) for passenger/driver weight of 0-150 pounds; second position (middle step) for passenger/driver weight of 150-180 pounds and third position (highest step) for passenger/driver weight of 180 pounds and up. Be sure to adjust both sides on same step of cam.

A snubber strap (Fig. 12E) on front slide support limits torque lift of front of machine during acceleration. Normal snubber adjustment is in second hole from outer end as shown. Lengthening snubber strap permits greater acceleration lift while shortening the strap prevents ski lift and provides greater ski control at acceleration.

TRACK TENSION. To adjust track tension on all models, raise rear of machine until track is clear.

On models with bogie wheel suspension, refer to view (B – Fig. 13) and measure distance between top, inside edge of track and bottom of footboard as shown by arrows. Distance should be 1⅜ inches for Elan and 2¼ inches for Alpine and other models so equipped.

Adjust track tension by loosening tensioner clamp bolt (1 – Fig. 14) and turning adjusting screw (2). Both sides must be adjusted alike.

On models with "Ground Leveler" slide suspension, refer to Fig. 14A. Measure the distance between midpoint of slide shoe and inner surface of track as

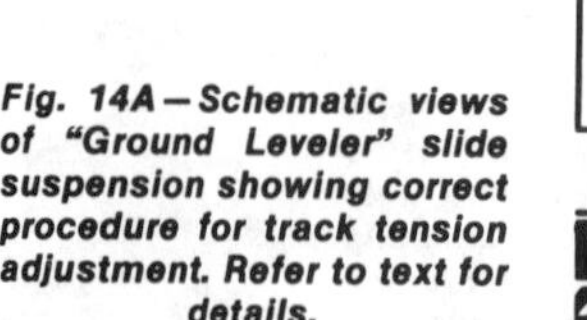

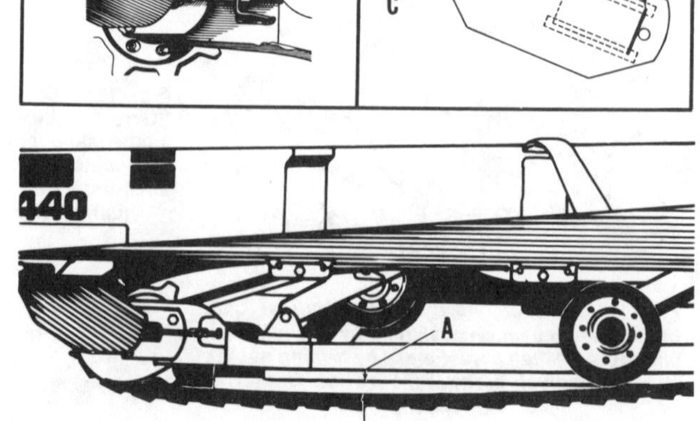

Fig. 14A — Schematic views of "Ground Leveler" slide suspension showing correct procedure for track tension adjustment. Refer to text for details.

shown at (A). Distance should be 5/8-7/8 inch. Adjust by loosening the jam nuts and turning adjusting screw (S) until tension is correct. With track checked and aligned lower machine until it rests on track, then check to see if sliding blocks of rear hub are flush with rear edge of hole in link plate as shown at (B). Adjust by loosening clamp nut and turning link plate adjusting bolt (C).

On all other later models not previously covered clearance should be ½-inch measured between slide rail shoe and bottom inside of track. On all models, adjust by turning adjusting bolts (A–Fig. 14B) at each end of idler axle.

NOTE: When track tension is adjusted, alignment MUST be checked as outlined in TRACK SERVICE Section in this manual.

Fig. 14B – Loosen the locknut and turn adjusting screw (A) on each side of machine to adjust track tension.

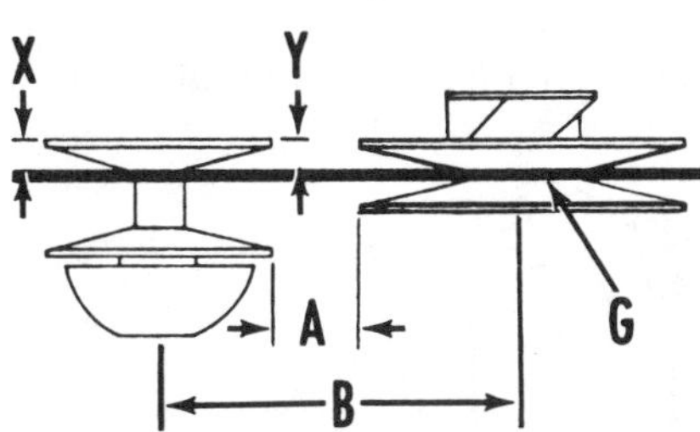

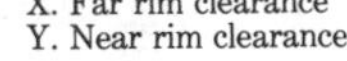

Fig. 14C – Method of checking belt alignment on most models. Refer to text for details.

A. Rim clearance
B. Shaft center
G. Gage bar
X. Far rim clearance
Y. Near rim clearance

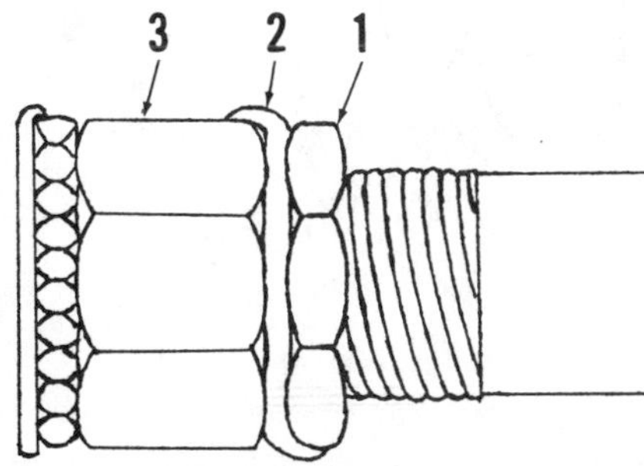

Fig. 14D – View showing thin nut (1), locking tab (2) and adjuster nut (3) used for adjusting driven clutch offset on late Citation, Nordik and Skandic models.

PULLEY OFFSET. To check drive belt alignment on later models, remove belt guard and drive belt and refer to Fig. 14C. Slightly spread rims of driven sheave and insert a 3/8x19 inch gage bar (G) between pulley halves as shown, then measure distance between far edge of gage bar and inner edge of drive sheave rim as shown at (X) and (Y). The two measured distances should be equal except that (X) may exceed (Y) by UP TO 1/16-inch. Distance (Y) MUST NEVER exceed (X). Measured distance on 1979 models should be 1-5/16–1⅜ inches, 1-11/32 inches on 1980 models, 1-5/16 inches on 1981 models except Elan, Nordik and Citation models which should be 1-11/32 inches and 1-11/32 inches on 1982 models except all Blizzard and Everest models which should be 1-9/32 inches.

NOTE: Everest and Blizzard models are equipped with a floating type driven pulley. Pulley must be pushed against bearing flange before measuring distance.

On all models except Citation, Nordik and Skandic models adjust pulley offset as follows: Remove drive pulley and add shims to crankshaft shoulder or remove shims from behind chaincase to DECREASE offset distance; remove shims from crankshaft shoulder or add shims behind chaincase to INCREASE offset distance.

CAUTION: Never use more than five shims on crankshaft shoulder.

On late Citation, Nordik and Skandic models adjust drive pulley by adding or removing shims. To adjust driven pulley offset refer to Fig. 14D. Straighten locking tab ears (2), then loosen thin nut (1). Turn adjuster nut (3) until correct distance is reached. While holding adjuster nut tighten thin nut to 48 ft.-lbs., then bend locking tab ears down.

Drive sheave rim clearance (A–Fig. 14C) or shaft center distance (B) is given in CONDENSED SERVICE DATA tables. Adjust by either loosening engine mounting bolts and sliding the engine, loosening chaincase mounts and repositioning chaincase to correct position or by adding or removing shim between the two driven pulley halves as recommended.

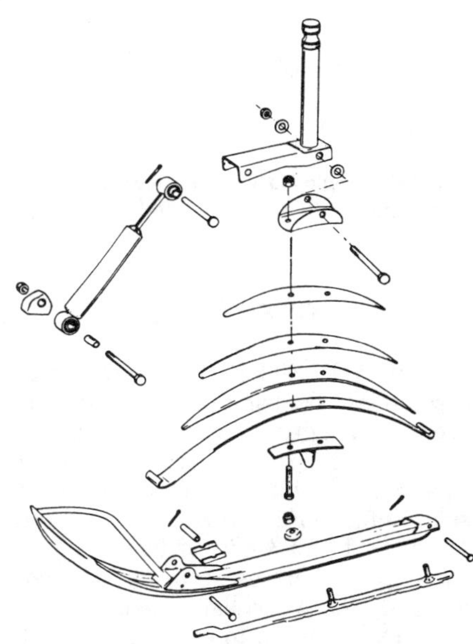

Fig. 14F – Typical view of steering skis and associated parts used on most models except Blizzard 9500 and Everest models.

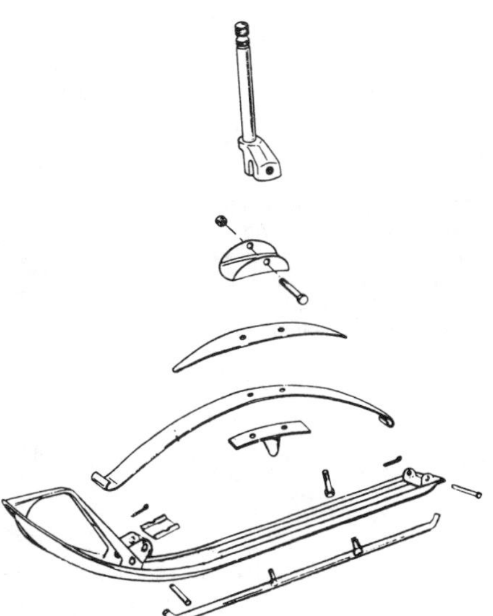

Fig. 14E – Exploded view of steering ski and associated parts used on Elan models. Some models use three springs.

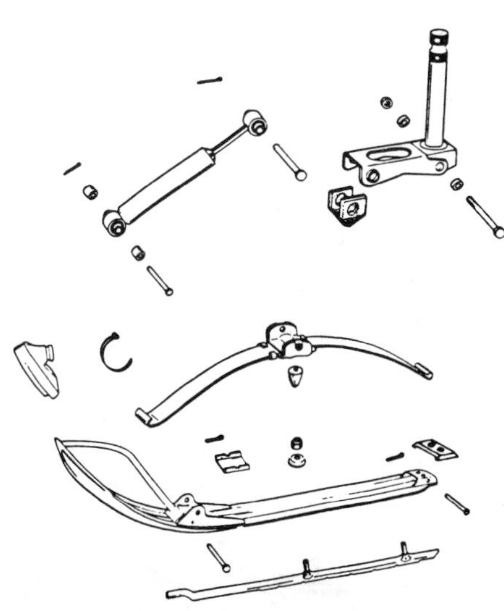

Fig. 14G – Exploded view of steering skis and associated parts used on Blizzard 9500 and Everest models.

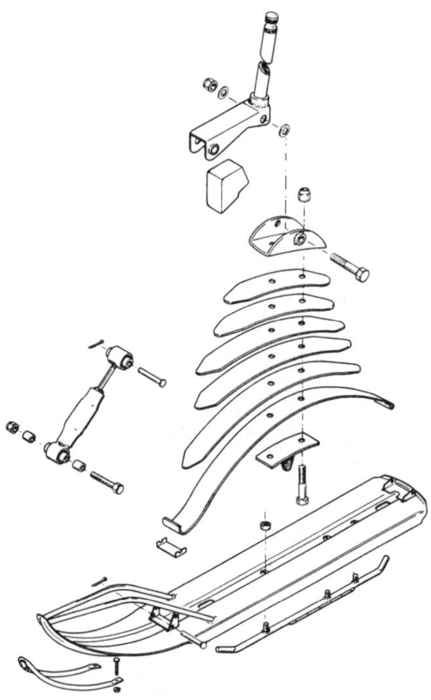

Fig. 14H—Exploded view of steering skis and associated parts used on Alpine models.

OVERHAUL

SKIS AND STEERING. Skis, spring assemblies, ski legs and steering arms are interchangeable from left to right on most models except Blizzard 5500 MX, skis cannot be interchanged from side to side. Refer to Figs. 14E, 14F, 14G, 14H, 14I and 14J for views of front skis and suspension set-ups typical of most models. Ski wear bars should be renewed when worn to one-half or less of their original thickness or if otherwise damaged.

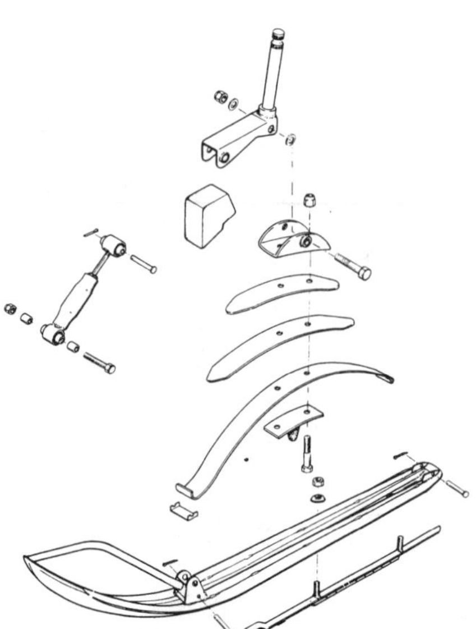

Fig. 14I—Exploded view of steering skis and associated parts used on Elite models.

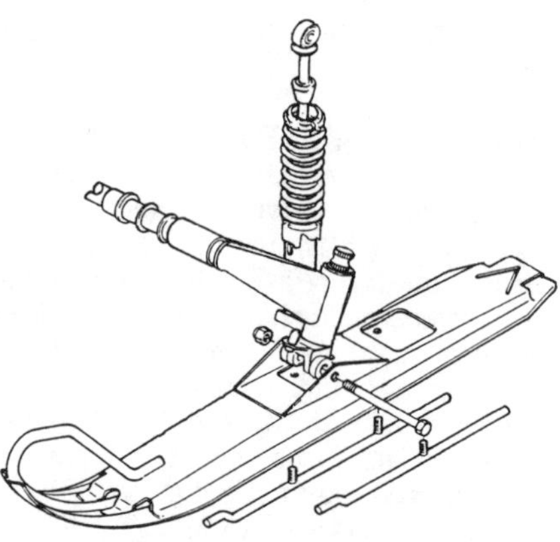

Fig. 14J—View showing MX steering and suspension used on Blizzard 5500 MX.

Tab locks on tie rod and drag link ends should be renewed if machine is so equipped. Use LOCTITE on nuts of tie rod and drag link ends not equipped with tab locks.

CHAINCASE. On single track models, the chaincase serves as support for driven sheave at upper end and bearing for track drive shaft at lower end. Sprocket sizes are given in CONDENSED SERVICE DATA tables.

Release tools (Fig. 16 and T–Fig. 17) should be used as needed on chaincase models to release tension on drive chain for removal of chaincase, chain or sprockets.

On models with welded steel chaincase (Fig. 15), the complete unit should be removed for major service. First drain the case, remove drive belt and disconnect brake. Suitably support the machine and loosen track by unhooking rear suspension springs. Remove lower access plug, cotter pin and lower sprocket spacer. Remove upper plug and insert chain tension release tool as needed. Remove bracket braces and U-bolts securing chaincase to frame, making note of any alignment shims located between chaincase and frame. Using two screwdrivers (Fig. 15A) or similar flat tools as prybars, carefully work the chaincase from frame and track drive axle splines. Remove chain and both sprockets through upper access opening for renewal, service or inspection. Renew all parts as needed. Install and reassemble chaincase by reversing removal procedure. Tighten castellated nut retaining upper sprocket snugly, back off 1/6-turn and install cotter pin,

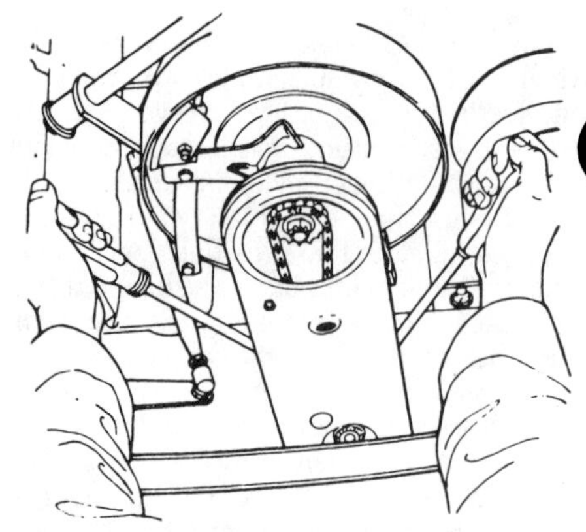

Fig. 15A—Removing chaincase and driven pulley as an assembly.

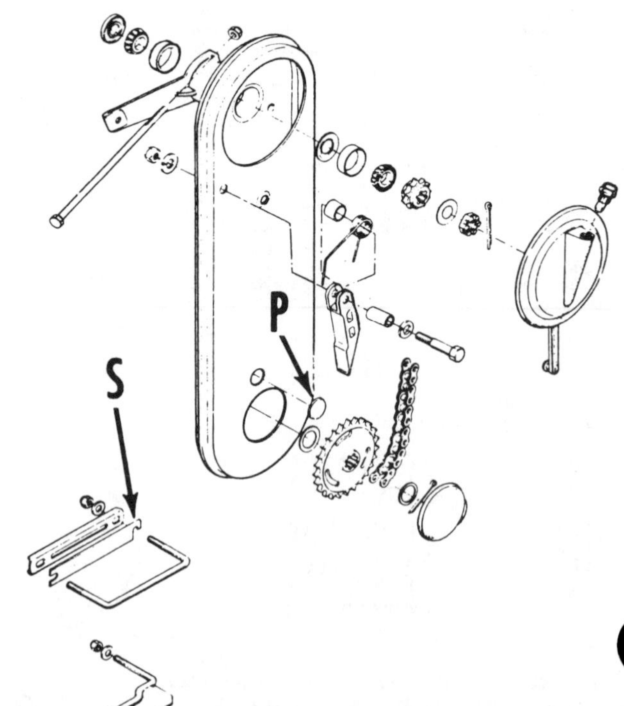

Fig. 15—Welded steel chaincase with automatic tensioner used on some early models and late Elan models. Shims (S) are used in drive belt alignment.

Fig. 16—One type of tensioner release tool provided by manufacturer for chaincase service. Refer also to Fig. 17.

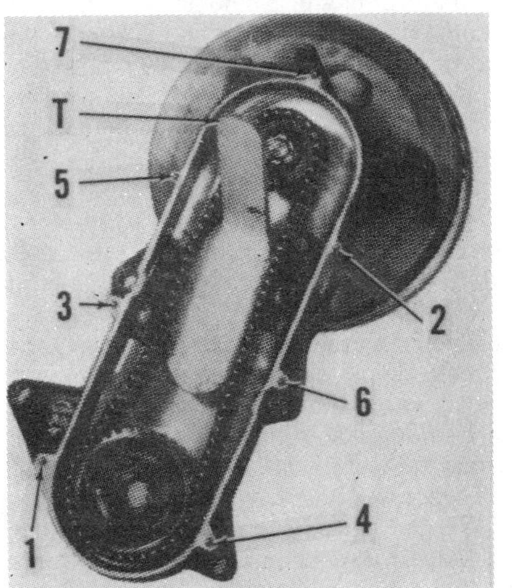

Fig. 17—View of chaincase with cover removed and tensioner release tool (T) installed. Tighten cover retaining screws to 60 inch-pounds in sequence indicated by numbers.

to provide proper adjustment for upper shaft bearings.

Figure 17A shows the diecast aluminum chaincase used on most early models and late Citation models. Chain and sprockets can be renewed after removing chaincase cover and tensioner. To remove the chaincase and driven pulley as a unit; remove pulley guard, drive belt and disconnect brake. Remove chaincase cover, lower sprocket and spacer. Pry oil seal from chaincase, then unbolt and lift off chaincase and driven pulley unit. Save shims (S) for reinstallation if they are present. Shims provide correct belt alignment. If secondary (upper) shaft bearing cup and oil retainer ring is to be removed, heat chaincase to 150 degrees F. Fill chaincase to level of sight glass after reassembly and installation using Bombardier Chaincase Oil.

Figure 17B shows an exploded view of the right-hand mounted chaincase. Most service can be performed after draining lubricant and removing cover. Completely loosen chain idler, then remove both drive sprockets and chain as an

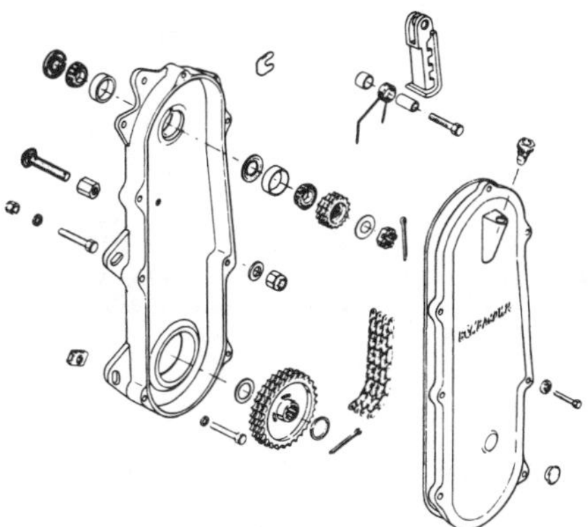

Fig. 17A—Exploded view of diecast aluminum chaincase used on most early models and late Citation models.

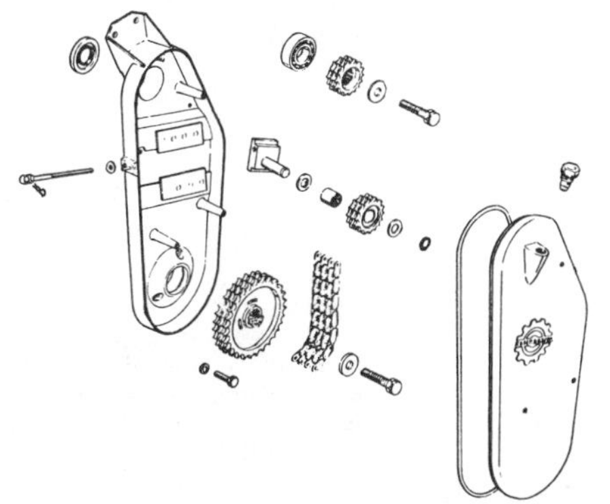

Fig. 17B—Exploded view of early right-hand mounted diecast chaincase with manual chain tension adjustment.

assembly. Upper sprocket is retained by a castellated nut and cotter pin on some models. Idler sprocket and bearing can be withdrawn from stud after removing snap ring. Tightener slide can be removed from rear after removing the chain and tightener adjusting screw. To remove chaincase, remove muffler, starter guide and brake unit. Remove

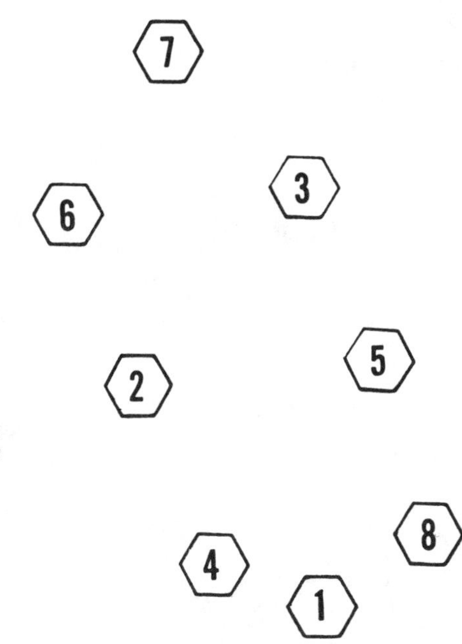

Fig. 19—Schematic view of gearcase cover retaining stud nuts showing tightening sequence.

chaincase cover, chain and sprockets. Raise rear of machine and release track tension. Remove drive axle and seal, then unbolt and remove chaincase. Install by reversing removal procedure and fill chaincase with six ounces of Bombardier Chaincase Oil. Tighten cover retaining cap screw to 60 inch-pounds.

Nordic 640ER uses a gearcase of the type shown in Fig. 18. Remove shift detent plug, spring and ball before attempting to remove housing cover. Complete assembly can be removed following the general procedure outlined for the welded chaincase unit. Main input shaft and countershaft gear should each have an end play of 0.008-0.016 inch in assembled case. End play can be

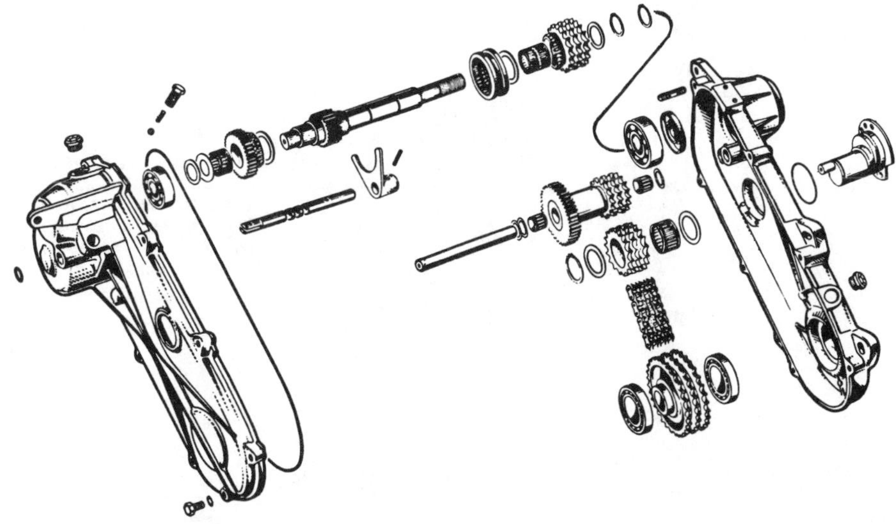

Fig. 18—Exploded view of gearcase and associated parts used on Nordic 640ER.

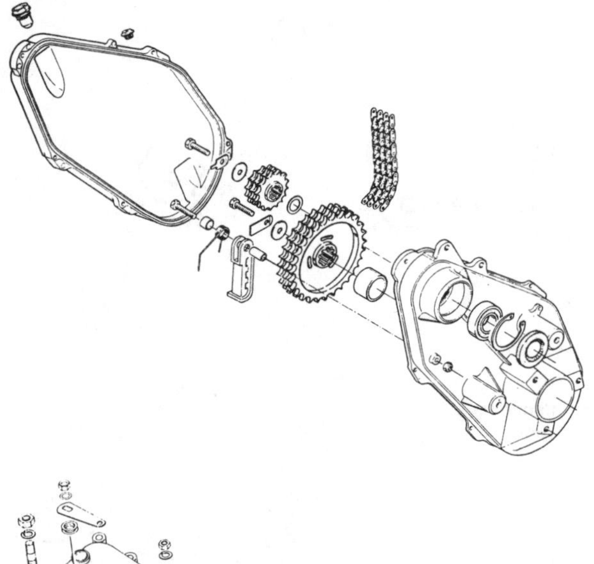

Fig. 19A—Exploded view of chaincase used on late Everest and Blizzard models.

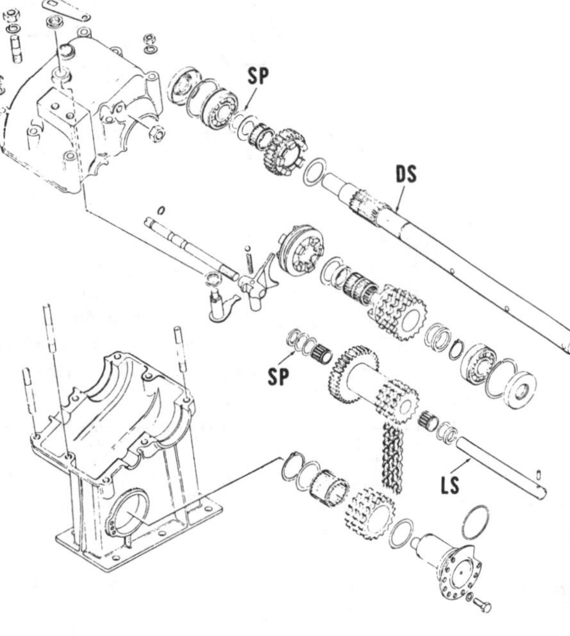

Fig. 20—Exploded view of a typical two speed gear box used on Alpine, Elite and early Valmont models. Shim packs are located at (SP) for drive shaft (DS) and layshaft (LS).

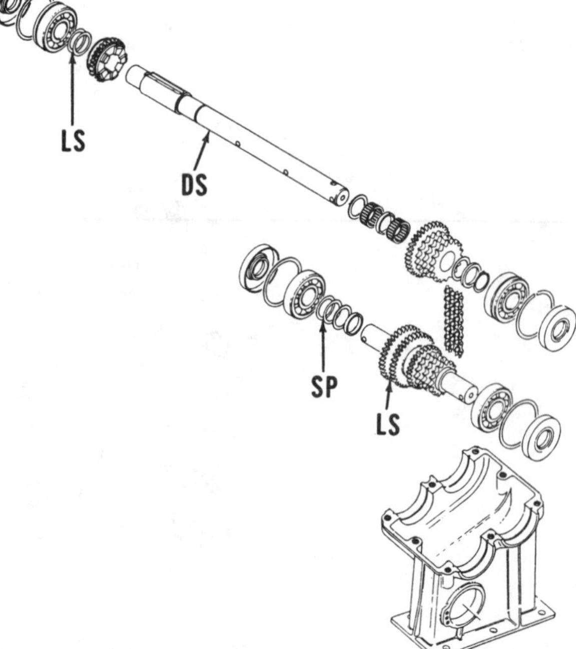

Fig. 20A—View of three speed transmission used on some late models. Refer to Fig. 20 for similarly constructed two speed transmission.

determined by measuring shaft clearance in housing and cover using a depth gage, then measuring assembled thickness of shaft or cluster gear using a micrometer caliper. Adjust if necessary by changing shim pack thickness. Tighten cover retaining nuts to a torque of 15 ft.-lbs. when assembling, using the sequence shown in Fig. 19.

Figure 19A shows chaincase used on late Everest and Blizzard models. To renew chaincase proceed as follows: Remove rear suspension system as outlined in TRACK AND SUSPENSION section. Remove outer chaincase cover and drain oil. Loosen end bearing housing cap screws on drive axle and pry oil seal out of chaincase housing. Bend ears on locking tabs away from sprocket retaining cap screws. Loosen chain tension, then remove retaining cap screws, washers, sprockets and chain. Remove chaincase mounting bolts and nuts, then withdraw chaincase from frame.

Inspect all parts for excessive wear, cracks, roughness or any other damage. Renew oil seals and all other parts as needed. Reinstall and assemble chaincase in reverse order of disassembly. Be sure to bend locking tab ears up against cap screws. Renew locking tabs if ears are damaged. Reinstall chaincase cover and fill chaincase with Bombardier Chaincase Oil.

Figure 20 shows a typical exploded view of the gear box transmission used on Alpine, Elite and early Valmont models. Two speed and three speed gear boxes are similar; but sprockets, drive shaft and other components differ. Late model three speed transmissions use ball bearings on ends of layshaft assembly. Most models are center-mounted and drive a track axle from lower sprocket. Upper housing (shift cover) can be removed for inspection without major disassembly, or chain can be detached and both upper shafts removed without disturbing track axles. Loop a piece of wire through links in each side of master link and secure to housing studs to prevent chain from dropping to bottom of housing. On all models except Elite, if lower sprocket is to be removed, suitably support the machine and completely loosen track tension by unhooking rear suspension springs. Pry center bogies rearward over-center to further relieve spring pressure, then unbolt and remove both drive axle outer bearing housings. Pull drive axles out of lower sprocket splines and lift out sprocket.

To remove gear box from Elite models proceed as follows: Remove pulley guard, drive belt, seat backs, seats and cover plates to allow access to lower engine compartment. Remove engine assembly, brake assembly and detach driven pulley support. Remove shifter

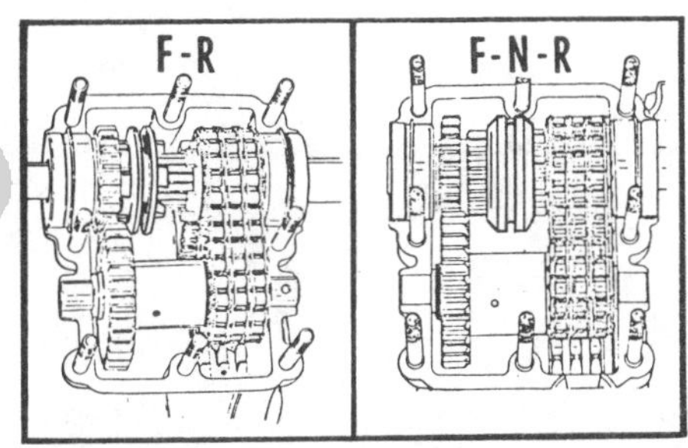

Fig. 21—Center mount gearcase may be Forward-Reverse shift (F-R) as shown on left or Forward-Neutral-Reverse shift (F-N-R) as shown at right. Neutral detent on F-R units is located in shift linkage.

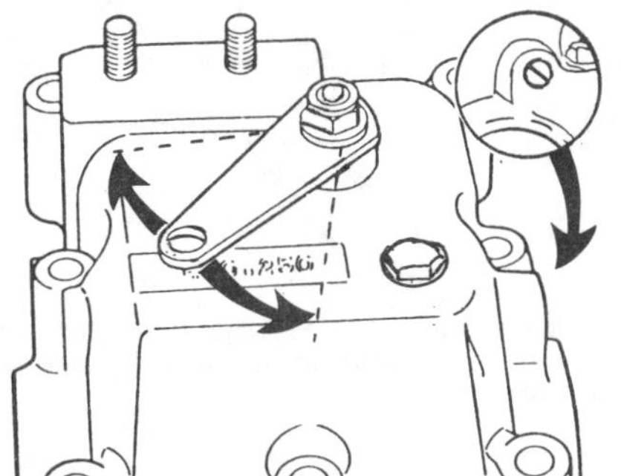

Fig. 22—A screwdriver slot (Inset) in shift rail allows adjustment of detent positions; refer to text.

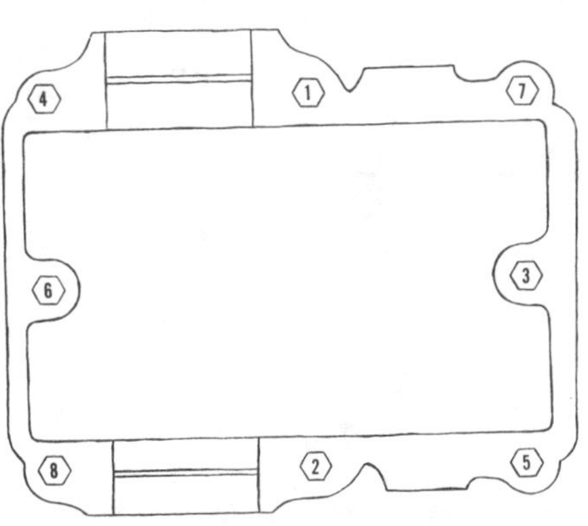

Fig. 23—When installing gearcase cover on early Alpine, Elite or Valmont, tighten retaining cap screws in sequence shown.

components, release track tension and remove suspension system as outlined in TRACK AND SUSPENSION section. Remove end bearing housings, drive axle and then withdraw gear box assembly enough to allow tension on track tunnel chain tensioners to be released. Remove gear box, chain and lower sprocket. Disassemble, inspect and renew all parts that are worn or otherwise damaged.

Two different types of gear box transmissions have been used; the spline-coupled Forward-Neutral-Reverse gear box and the dog-coupled Forward-Reverse unit. Refer to Fig. 21. The shift rail which carries the detent notches threads into upper housing (shift cover)

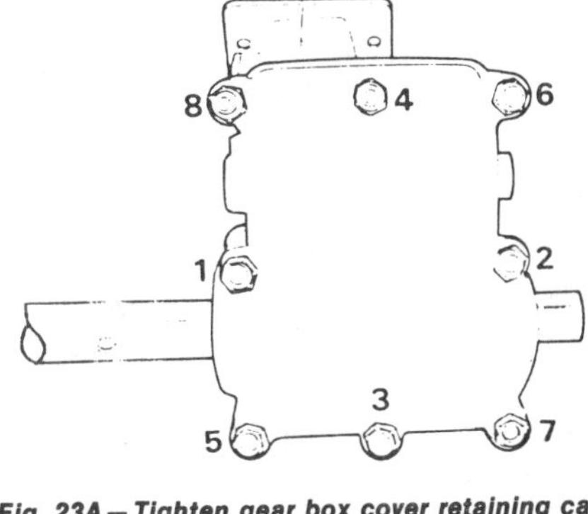

Fig. 23A—Tighten gear box cover retaining cap screws, on late Alpine and Elite models, in sequence shown.

Fig. 23B—Using a screwdriver to keep suspension cross shaft from turning. Refer to text.

and is locked into position by a jam nut. Shifter fork must move fully into forward and reverse detent positions with approximately equal overtravel. On models with neutral detent, coupler must center on shaft spline in neutral detent position, without interference with splines on forward sprockets or reverse gear. Adjust by loosening locknut on drive belt side of shift rail, then turning rail in or out as needed using screwdriver slot (Inset–Fig. 22) in right end of rail. Tighten locknut when adjustment is correct. When transmission is disassembled, the assembled input shaft can be temporarily installed in shift cover while rail is adjusted.

On all models so equipped, eccentric idler sprocket has a drilled oil passage between the teeth on one side. Passage side should be installed on eccentric shaft farthest distance **AWAY** from mounting flange. On two speed models, both drive shaft (DS–Fig. 20) and layshaft (LS) should have end play of 0.006-0.012 inch. On later (3 speed) models, drive shaft (DS–Fig. 20A) and layshaft (LS) should have 0.003-inch end play. Clearance can be mesured with feeler gage after positioning gears, shafts and associated parts in lower case half. Adjust by changing thickness of shim packs (SP–Fig. 20 or Fig. 20A).

Upper housing does not use a gasket but a suitable sealant must be applied. Tighten retaining cap screws to a torque of 21 ft.-lbs. using sequence shown in Fig. 23 for early models and Fig. 23A for later Alpine and Elite models.

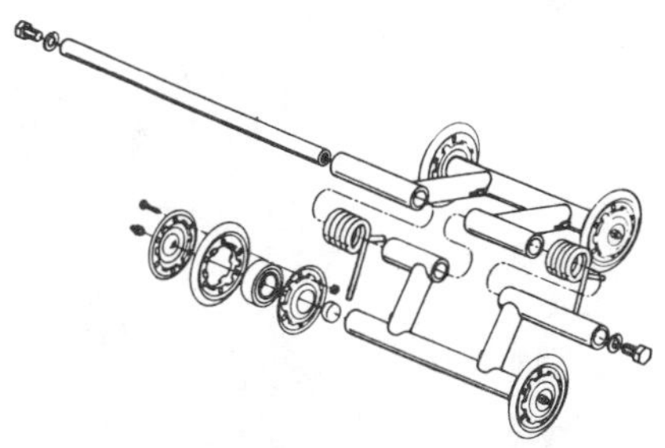

Fig. 23C—Exploded view of bogie wheel suspension using two springs. Some models use a single spring.

TRACK AND SUSPENSION. To remove bogie wheels on models so equipped, raise rear of machine and loosen track tension, then unhook rear suspension springs from track tunnel. Tag bogie wheel units for reinstallation in correct location. Remove center bogie axle first, by removing the two cap screws on outside of track tunnel. If cross shaft turns after one cap screw is removed, wedge with a screwdriver inserted between cross shaft and bogie wheel support as shown in Fig. 23B.

Bogie wheel bearings are a tight press fit on wheel supports. Bogie wheels are factory riveted, but may be disassembled for service by drilling out rivets using a 3/16-inch drill bit. Reassemble using bolts and nuts, tightening in a criss-cross pattern. Bearing should be installed on wheel support shielded side first, until outer edge is flush with end of support.

On some machines, bogie wheel suspension springs are not interchangeable. On models where one set of bogies has heavier springs, the heavy set should be installed at the rear. Clean and lubricate each cross shaft using low temperature grease, then install by reversing removal procedure. Install center set last. Lubricate each bogie wheel until new grease appears, then wipe off excess grease.

Standard slide suspension used on most early models is shown exploded in Fig. 23D and 23E. To remove suspension system, raise rear of machine and release track tension. Loosen spring tension eyebolts and remove the four cap screws securing cross shafts to track tunnel, then remove suspension assembly. If cross shaft turns after one cap screw is removed, wedge a small screwdriver between cross shaft and suspension frame as shown in Fig. 23B. Slide rail wear bars must be renewed if worn to where rivets are flush, or if otherwise damaged. To remove wear bars, drill rivet head using a 3/16-inch drill bit and punch out rivets, using care not to damage rivet holes in metal rail. Remove bolt at front of wear bar and lift off wear bar. When installing new wear

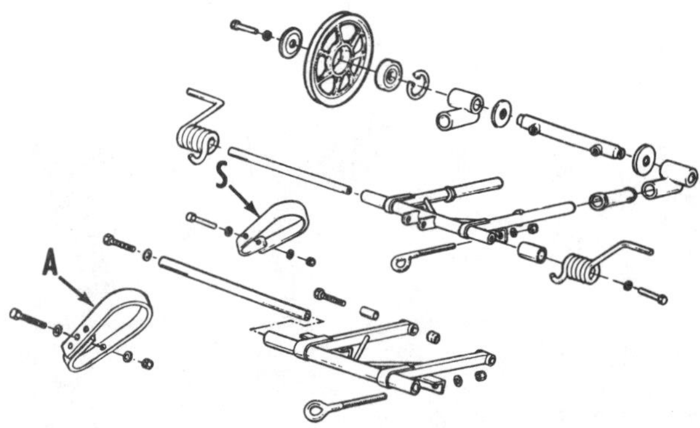

Fig. 23D—Support system of the type used on early models with standard slide suspension. Adjustable snubber strap (A) is installed on front slide support and is normally installed in center hole. Fixed snubber strap (S) is used on rear. See Fig. 23F.

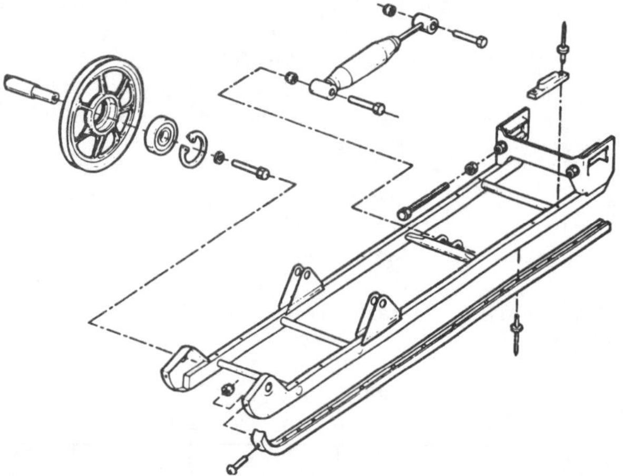

Fig. 23E—Standard slide rail and associated parts used on early models so equipped.

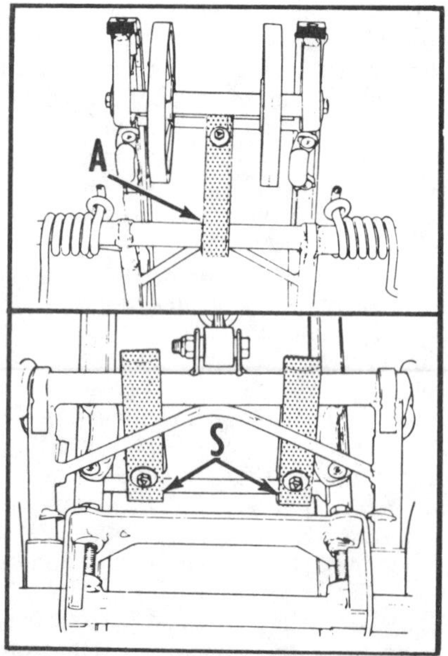

Fig. 23F—Schematic view of standard slide suspension showing front snubber strap (A) and rear snubber straps (S) correctly installed. Shortening front snubber (A) transfers greater share of load to skis for better steering control, while lengthening front snubber transfers more weight to track for improved performance in deep snow.

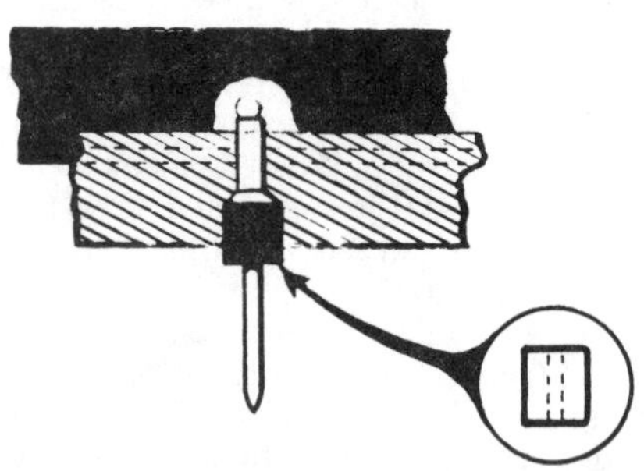

Fig. 23G—A suitable sleeve may be required to apply proper pressure to pop rivet head when installing slider wear bars.

bars, use a spacer sleeve over countersunk rivet stem to properly tighten rivet (Fig. 23G).

On early models so equipped and later models except Blizzard 5500 MX have a torque reaction type slide suspension system similar to that shown exploded in Fig. 23H. To remove the suspension system, first raise rear of machine and release track tension. Turn suspension cams to low (L) position (Fig. 23I). Remove the four cap screws securing suspension cross shafts to track tunnel and lift out the suspension assembly. If cross shaft turns after one bolt is removed, wedge a small screwdriver between cross shaft and suspension frame as shown in Fig. 23B. To renew slide rail wear bar, remove cap screw at front and spirol pin at rear of wear bar and slide wear bar rearward off of runner.

Note that coil diameter of front suspension springs is smaller than rear springs. Front and rear cross shafts differ on some models. Snubber strap (Fig. 23J) on front slide support limits torque lift of front of machine during acceleration. Turning front cams to a higher position increases steering response; to a lower position increases traction in deep snow. Rear cams adjust for load. Recommended adjustment when loaded,

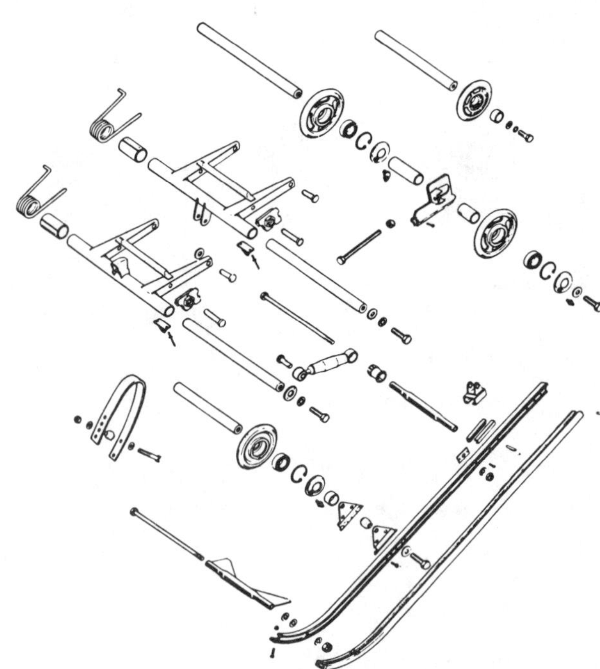

Fig. 23H—Exploded view of a typical "Torque Reaction" slide suspension used on early models so equipped and most late models. Some models differ slightly.

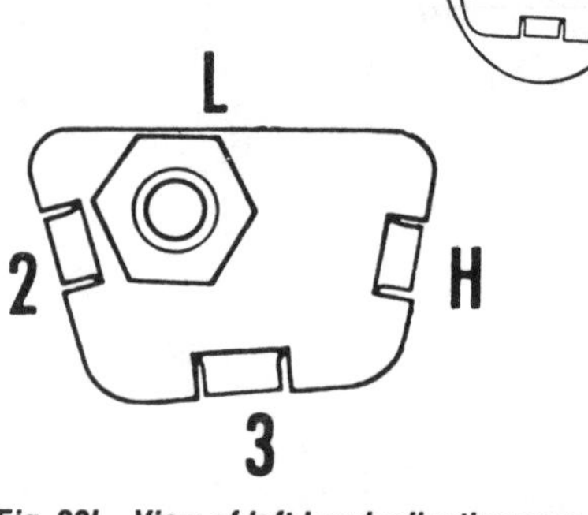

Fig. 23I—View of left hand adjusting cam showing low (L), high (H) and two intermediate positions (2 and 3). Right hand cam (RH) is a mirror image of left cam as shown.

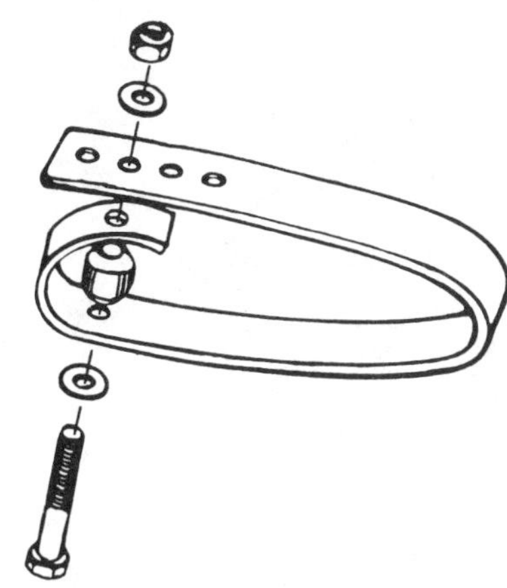

Fig. 23J—Snubber strap used on front slide support is normally adjusted in second hole as shown. Shortening strap limits torque lift of skis during acceleration.

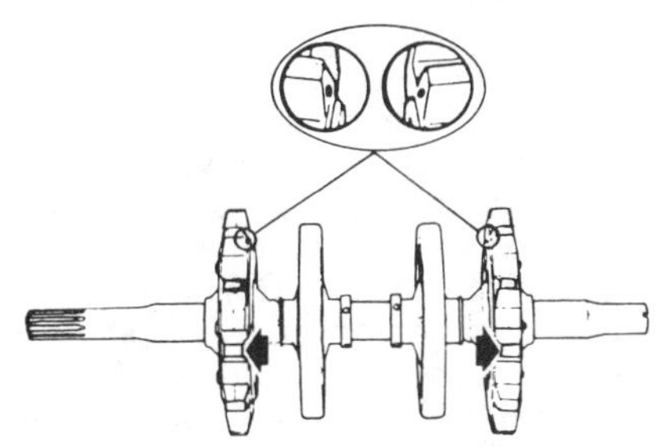

Fig. 23K—Some two-sprocket drive axles must be timed as shown in inset. Sprocket teeth MUST align as shown by arrows.

will provide 4½-5½ inches clearance between rear of footrest and ground. Right and left cams on same support mode must be adjusted alike.

Some two-sprocket drive axles must be timed. Timing marks may be dots or arrows, located on inside of sprocket as shown in Fig. 23K. When installing, align timing marks as shown in inset. Sprocket teeth MUST be in plane as shown by arrows.

Late Blizzard 5500 MX models use a MX suspension system. Suspension system is similar to "Torque Reaction" models except rear shock set-up is as shown in Fig. 23L. To remove the suspension system, first raise rear of machine and release track tension. Turn two front suspension cams to low (L) position (Fig. 23I). Remove two lower shock absorber mounting cap screws. Remove the four cap screws securing suspension cross shafts to track tunnel and lift out suspension assembly. If cross shaft turns after one bolt is removed, wedge a small screwdriver between cross shaft and suspension frame as shown in Fig. 23B. To renew slide rail wear bar, remove cap screw at front and spirol pin at rear of wear bar and slide wear bar rearward off runner.

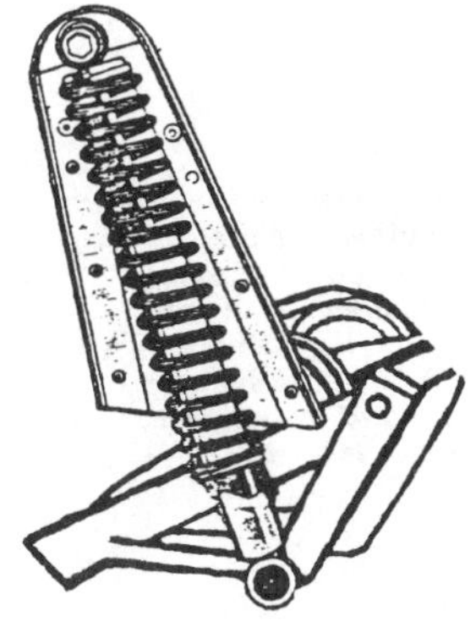

Fig. 23L—View shows rear shock absorber set-up used on MX suspension systems.

Inspect all parts for cracks, breaks or any other damage, check rear shock absorbers for binding, seizing or oil leakage. Renew all parts as needed. Reassemble and install suspension assembly in reverse order of disassembly.

Adjust front cams to a higher position to increase steering response and to a lower position to increase traction in deep snow. Cams on rear shock absorbers adjust for carrying load. Adjusting cam to higher step will increase carrying load. Right and left cams on same support mode must be adjusted alike.

TORQUE CONVERTER. Recommended methods of "locking" crankshaft for drive pulley removal is by either inserting starter rope in engine cylinder or by using a special crankshaft locking tool. To use starter rope proceed as follows:

Remove spark plug on single cylinder engines or drive end spark plug on multi-cylinder units. Turn drive pulley in normal direction until piston is moving upward and exhaust port closes. (Until compression begins against thumb held over spark plug hole). With exhaust port closed, feed a 3/16-inch diameter rope into plug hole as shown in Fig. 24 until cylinder is full, then turn piston up against rope until it stops.

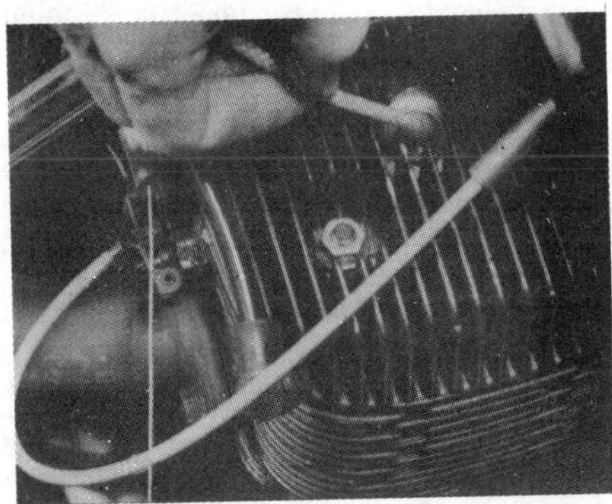

Fig. 24—Approved method of "locking" crankshaft for drive pulley removal is by inserting a 3/16-inch rope in spark plug hole as shown. Refer to TORQUE CONVERTER paragraphs for procedure.

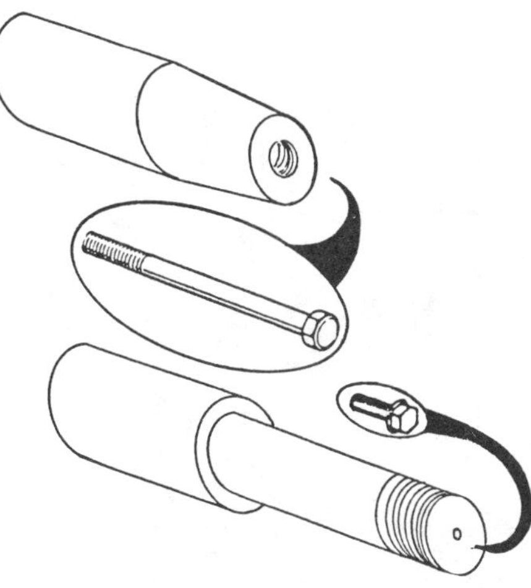

Fig. 25—PTO end of crankshaft may have a 20 degree taper as shown in upper view or be shouldered as shown in lower view. Identify shaft type by size of retaining screw (Insets).

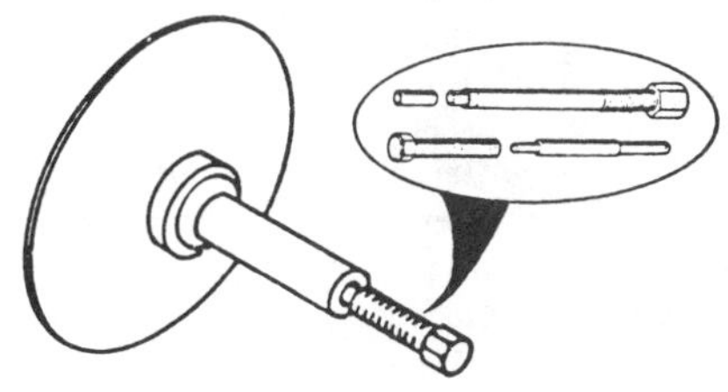

Fig. 26—Puller screws used to remove drive sheave hub from most units with taper shaft are shown in inset.

Engines may be equipped with either; a male threaded, shouldered, straight shaft as shown in lower view (Fig. 25), or a 20 degree tapered shaft as shown in upper view. If type of shaft is not known, refer to drive clutch retaining screw as shown in inset. Taper shaft requires a long screw which threads into crankshaft, while shouldered shaft uses a short screw which threads into clutch hub.

To remove the drive clutch from engines with taper shaft, first remove belt shield and drive belt. Remove retaining cap screw from end of crankshaft, relieving spring pressure if necessary to keep parts from flying. On all except high performance type clutch, remove weight cover, sheave half and spring. Thread the appropriate puller screw (Inset–Fig. 26) into hub of drive pulley and tighten puller screw. Rap head of puller screw lightly if necessary, to loosen pulley hub from tapered shaft. Some models use a high performance drive clutch which does not come apart when retaining cap screw is removed. With the appropriate puller screw, remove the assembled drive clutch as shown in Fig. 27.

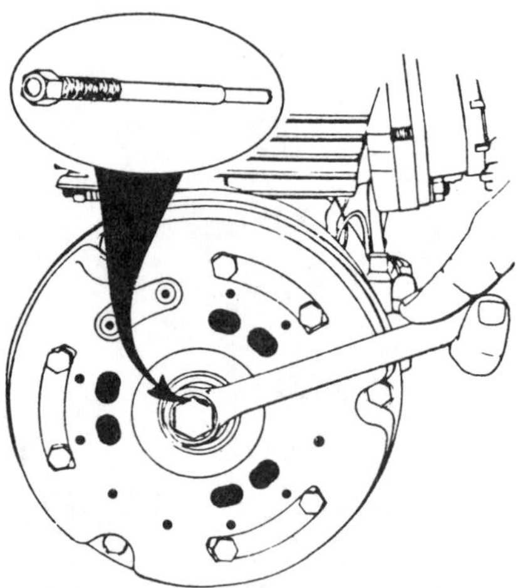

Fig. 27—Removing high performance drive clutch from model with taper shaft.

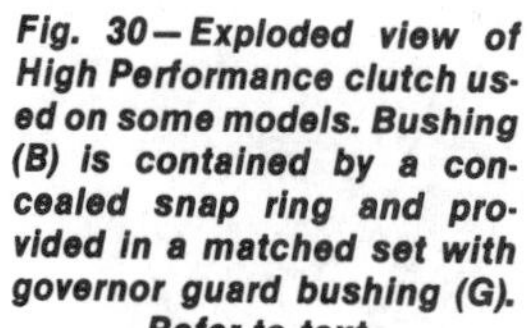

Fig. 30—Exploded view of High Performance clutch used on some models. Bushing (B) is contained by a concealed snap ring and provided in a matched set with governor guard bushing (G). Refer to text.

B. Bushing
G. Bushing
S. Spring
W. Weight

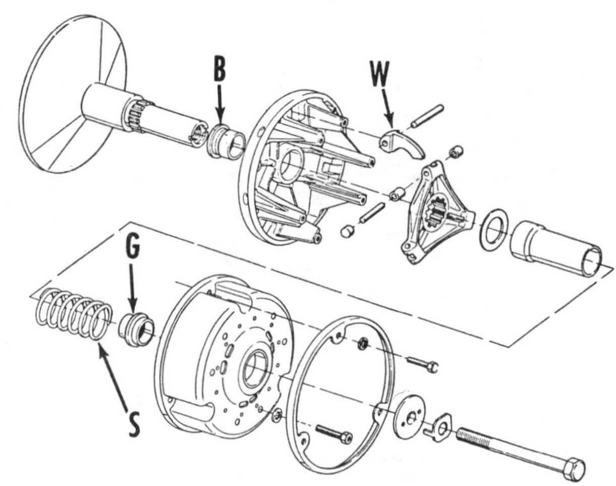

To remove the drive clutch on engines with shouldered shaft, first remove belt guard and belt. Block crankshaft from turning as previously outlined. Remove retaining cap screw, weight cover, sliding sheave and spring. On models with square shaft hub, use a 1⅛-inch open end wrench or large adjustable wrench and unscrew drive pulley fixed face and hub unit from crankshaft. Remove and save the shims found on crankshaft shoulder. Shims are used to align drive sheaves. On round shaft models, slide a length of steel pipe over the hub shaft as shown at (P–Fig. 28) and secure with a 5/16-inch bolt and nut, then unscrew fixed face assembly from crankshaft using a pipe wrench on protected shaft. Check for and save any shims located on shaft shoulder as outlined for square shaft models.

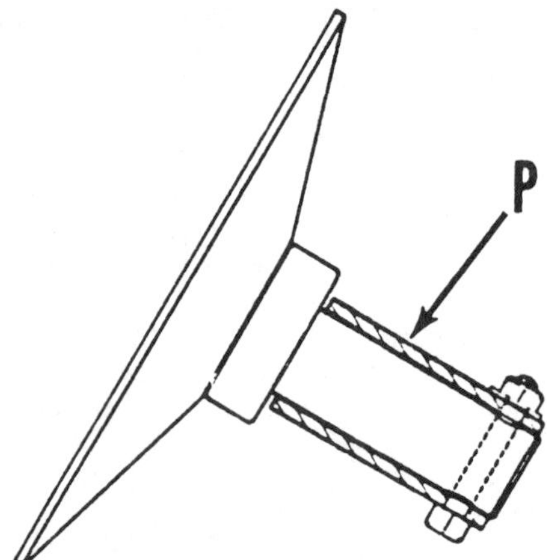

Fig. 28—A pipe spacer/protector (P) may be installed on round shaft model hub, permitting use of a pipe wrench to remove clutch from shouldered shaft.

Most early models use a drive pulley of type shown in Fig. 29. Centrifugal governor unit (7) is available only as an assembly, with weights (12) and associated parts installed. Renew the assembly if excessively worn, bent or otherwise damaged. Spring (5) should have a free length of 2-15/16 inches (74.5 mm) on high performance models and all early Alpine and Valmont models. On all other models so equipped, specified spring free length is 2-13/16 inches (71.4 mm). Renew the spring if cracked, distorted or substantially shortened from specified length.

The 1974 and 1975 T'NT Free Air models use a High Performance drive clutch of type shown exploded in Fig. 30. Bushing (B) is retained in sliding half hub by a concealed snap ring. To remove bushing, make two axial cuts with a hacksaw 180 degrees apart, then extract and discard the snap ring after bushing pieces are out. Inspect hub bore for burrs and smooth only the damaged part without enlarging or distorting bore. Install new snap ring in groove of hub bore and hold ring in place with a pointed tool until retained by bushing edge. Install bushing with a driver of the correct size. Sliding hub bushing (B) is supplied as a matched pair with governor guard bushing (G), and both bushings must be renewed if either is damaged. When assembling, be sure balance marks are aligned as shown by Arrows–Fig. 31.

The 1975 T'NT 245 R/V uses a square shaft drive clutch of the type shown in Fig. 32. Teflon wear pads (P) should be renewed if Teflon coating is worn through to steel backing. Pads can be pried out with a small screwdriver and must be snapped in so that raised center tab on one end of pad interlocks with solid end of adjoining pad as shown in Fig. 33. Counterweight is available only

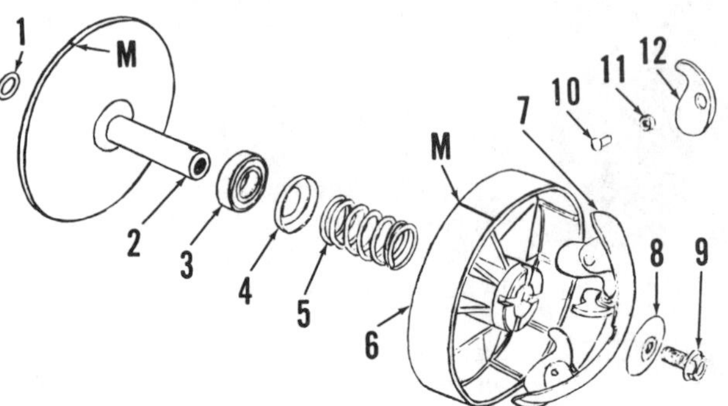

Fig. 29—Exploded view of torque converter drive pulley of the type used on some models. Match marks (M) should be aligned when unit is assembled.

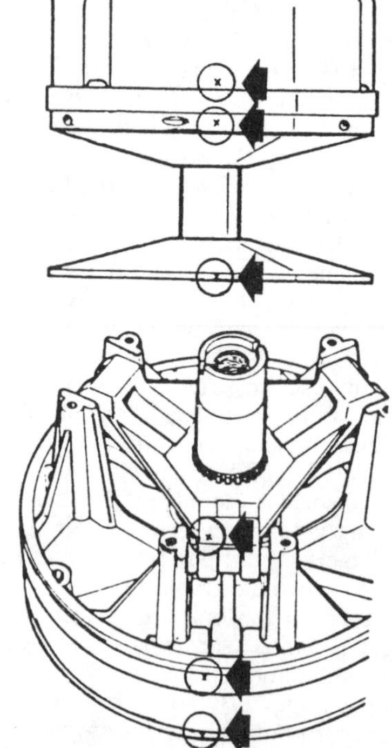

Fig. 31—Match marks (Arrows) must be aligned when clutch is assembled.

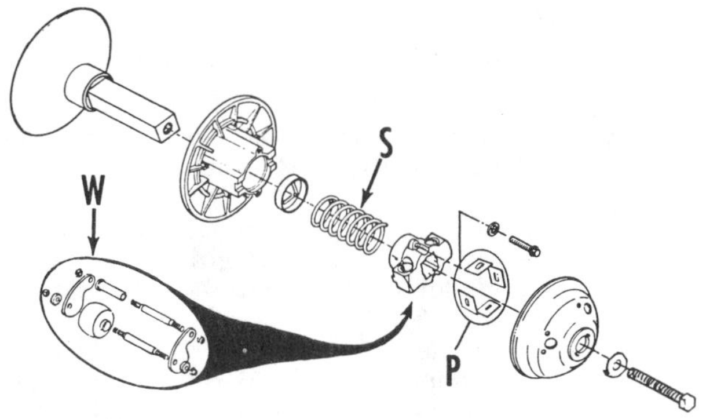

Fig. 32 — Square Shaft clutch with hub plug used on T'NT 245 R/V.

P. Wear pads
S. Spring
W. Counterweight

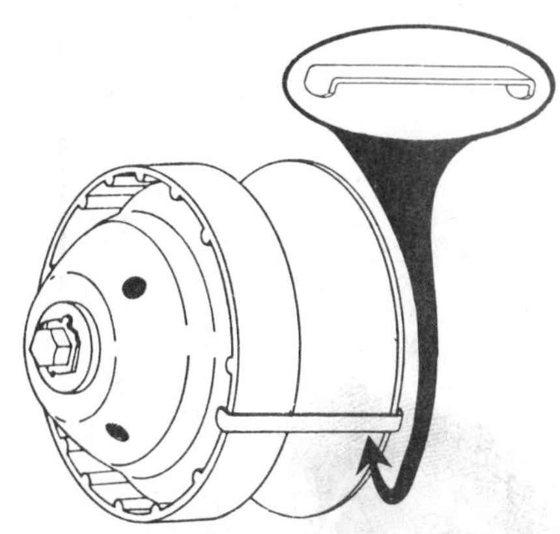

Fig. 37 — A "Drive Pulley Retainer" tool (inset) is required to contain spring pressure for removal and installation on some models.

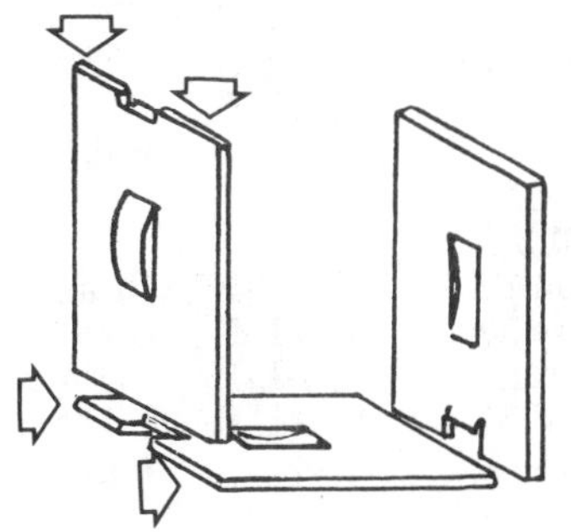

Fig. 33 — Teflon coated wear pads snap into place as shown and are retained by raised center tab on one end which interlocks with opposite end of adjoining pad.

as a complete unit and should not be disassembled unless renewal is planned. Self-locking nuts and shouldered pins are damaged in disassembly and must not be reinstalled.

Figure 34 shows Roller Round Shaft type drive clutch used on **most Elan models and some Olympique models.** Sliding hub and weight unit (H) is available as an assembly or weight units (W) are available separately. Weight unit on early models is identified "D-2" and later models "E-4". Spring (S) is color coded Blue on early models and Bronze on later models. Weight cover retaining cap screw should be torqued to 45 ft.-lbs. on later models. Shims (X), between governor cup and sliding hub, control neutral (disengaged) position of clutch. Spacing is correct when a 0.030-inch (0.8 mm) feeler gage can be inserted on each side of a NEW belt on installed unit as shown in Fig. 35. Correct shim pack can be approximated by pulling a new belt snugly around hub of an assembled but uninstalled clutch. Shim pack (Y – Fig. 34) controls clutch alignment during assembly.

Some later Citation models use a drive pulley that is similar in construction to Roller Round Shaft (Fig. 34). The drive pulley fits onto a tapered crankshaft instead of a shoulder crankshaft.

Some units use a **Roller Square Shaft Drive Clutch** of the type shown in Fig. 36. Condition of wear pads (P) can be checked without disassembly by rocking the sliding half (H) on its hub. If total movement exceeds 1/8-inch, wear pads should be renewed. Strong spring pressure attempts to force clutch apart when retaining bolt is removed. A special "Drive Pulley Retainer" tool (see Fig. 37) can be used during removal and handling to contain spring pressure. To renew wear pads (P – Fig. 36) after clutch is disassembled, pry out old pads using a

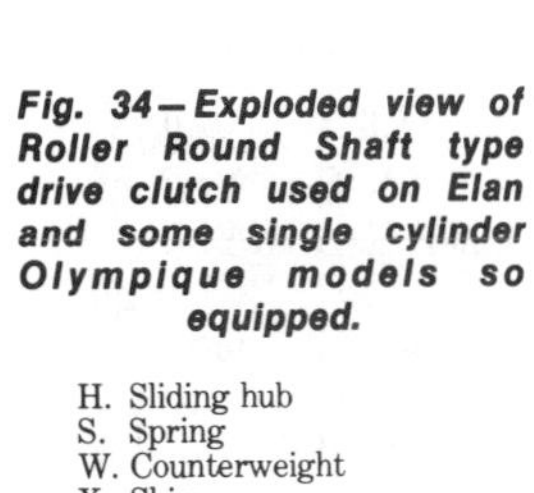

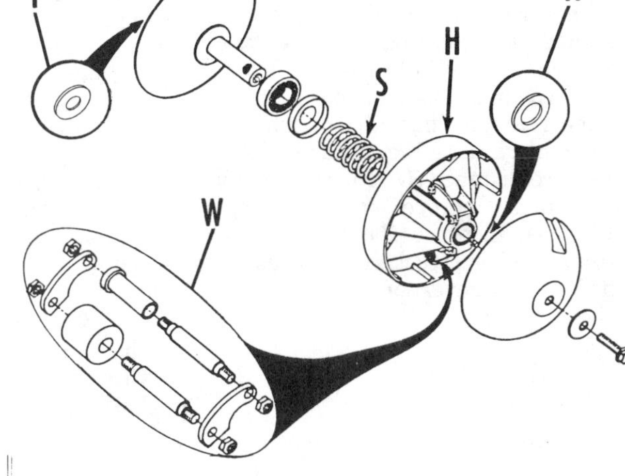

Fig. 34 — Exploded view of Roller Round Shaft type drive clutch used on Elan and some single cylinder Olympique models so equipped.

H. Sliding hub
S. Spring
W. Counterweight
X. Shim
Y. Shim

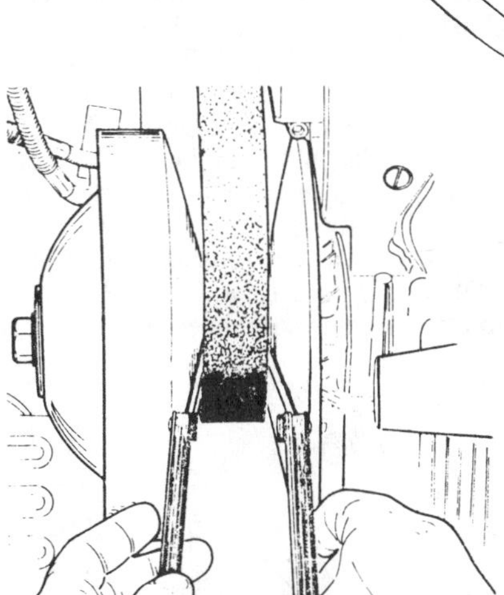

Fig. 35 — On Roller Round Shaft type clutch on Elan, neutral clearance is correct when a 0.030 inch feeler gage can be inserted on both sides of belt with engine not running.

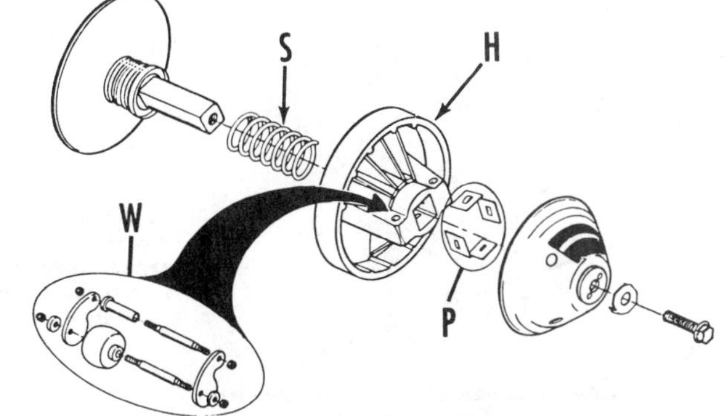

Fig. 36 — Roller Square Shaft clutch with wear pads used on some models.

H. Sliding hub
P. Wear pads
S. Spring
W. Counterweight

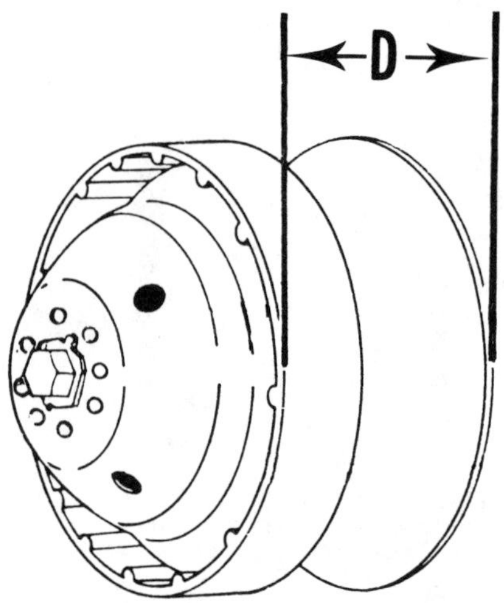

Fig. 38—Distance (D) should measure 3-13/16 inches (97 mm) on clutch of type shown.

small screwdriver. When reinstalling, raised center tab on one end of pad must interlock with solid end of adjoining pad as shown in Fig. 33. When unit is reassembled and before starting engine, measure distance (D–Fig. 38) across installed sheaves. Distance (D) should be 3-13/16 inches (97 mm). If measurement is incorrect, recheck seating of shaft end in governor cup.

CAUTION: Crankshaft can be damaged if unit is improperly assembled.

Figure 39 shows an exploded view of **Hub Type Drive Clutch** with Duralon bushing used on many late models. Some pulleys are match-marked for balance as shown in Fig. 40. If components are not marked, affix suitable marks before disassembly. The

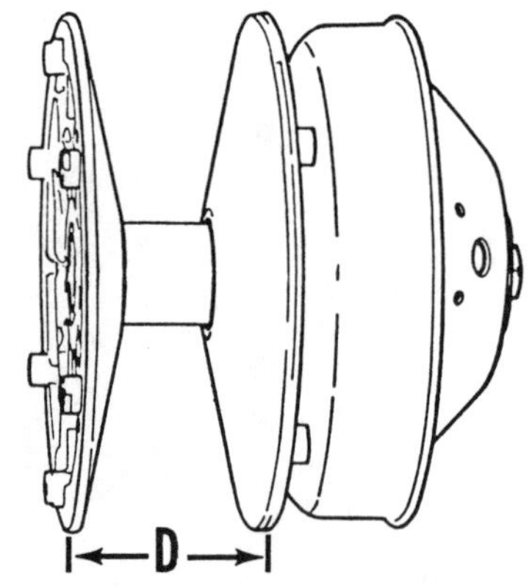
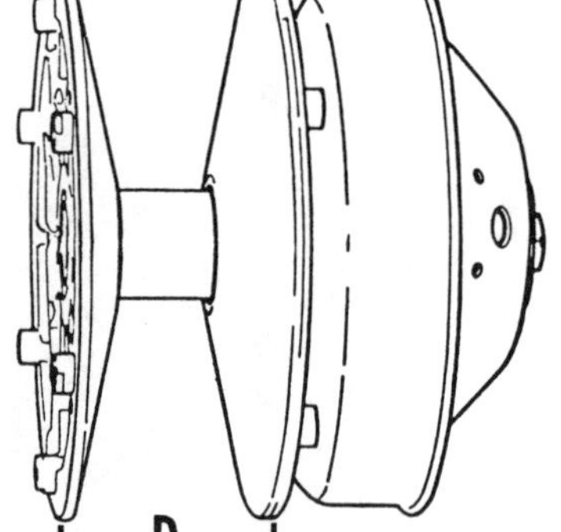

Fig. 41—Distance (D) should measure 3 inches (76 mm) on clutch of type shown.

assembly bolts in drive clutch are installed with LOCTITE and an impact wrench or moderate heat is advised for removal.

The Duralon bushing in hub plug is made of fiberglass with a bearing surface of Teflon impregnated cloth. Bushing should be renewed if bearing surface is badly worn or if fiberglass backing shows through. Remove set screw and use a press to push bushing from the hub. Set screw dimple in bushing is offset toward outer side when reinstalling. Do not remove counterweights unless renewal is indicated. Counterweights are available only as an assembly kit and removed units cannot be reinstalled. When reassembling, always make sure match marks (M–Fig. 40) are realigned. Measure distance (D–Fig. 41) as unit is assembled, before starting engine. Measured distance should be 3 inches (76 mm). If incorrect, recheck seating of shaft end in governor cup.

CAUTION: Crankshaft may be damaged if unit is incorrectly assembled.

Refer to chart shown below for counterweight kit and spring identification on 1979-1982 models.

Model	Counter-weight Kit	Spring
1979		
Citation	A3S	Light Blue
Olympique	C3L	Light Blue
Everest 340	C3L	Light Blue
Everest 440	C4L	Pink
Everest 444 LC	C7L	Yellow
Blizzard 5500	C8M-H	Light Blue
Elite	C8	Light Blue
1980		
Citation SS	A-3-S-H	Orange
Everest 500/E	C-6-L-H	Gold
Everest LC	C-7-L-H	Light Blue
Blizzard 5500	C-6-L-H	Light Blue
Elite 450 LC	C-8	Light Blue
1981		
Citation SS	A-3-S-H	Yellow
Everest 500/E	C-6-L-H	Gold
Everest LC	C-7-L-H	Light Blue
Blizzard MX	C-7-L-H	Light Blue
Blizzard 5500	C-7-L-H	Light Blue
Elite	C-8	Light Blue
1982		
Citation 4500	B-E-K-S-H	Yellow
Nordik	B-3-K-S-H	Yellow
Skandic	B-3-K-S-H	Yellow
Blizzard 5500 MX	C-7-L-H	Orange
Everest 500/E	C-6-L-H	Gold
Everest L/C	C-7-L-H	Light Blue
Elite	C-7-C-H	Light Blue

Figure 42 shows an exploded view of the **Roller Square Shaft Bearing Type Clutch** with Duralon bushing used on late Alpine models. Alpine for 1976 uses a similar clutch with Teflon wear pads (Inset) instead of the Duralon bushing. On both clutches, "Drive Pulley Retainer" (Fig. 37) must be used to contain sliding hub during removal, and installed distance (D–Fig. 38) must be measured after reassembly. Distance (D) should be 3-13/16 inches (97 mm) on both clutches. Recheck installation of

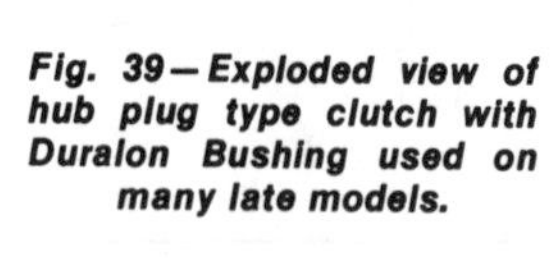

Fig. 39—Exploded view of hub plug type clutch with Duralon Bushing used on many late models.

Fig. 40—Match marks (M) must be aligned when unit is assembled.

Fig. 42—Late Alpine clutch shown exploded. The 1976 Alpine used a similar clutch except wear pads (inset) were used instead of Duralon bushing in late unit.

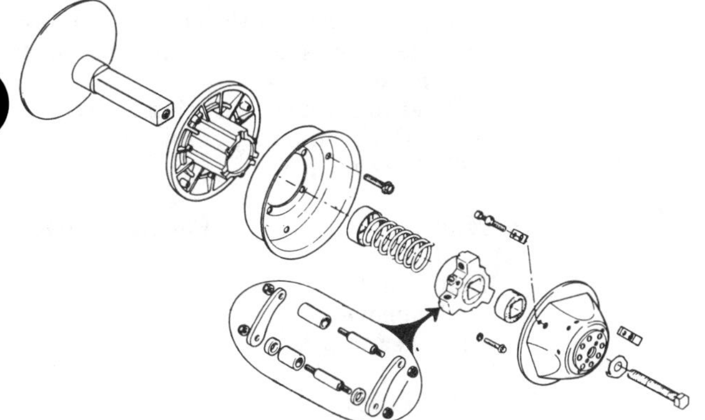

Fig. 42A—Exploded view of a Roller Square Shaft drive pulley with three ramps.

Fig. 49—Exploded view of driven pulley used on late Elan models.

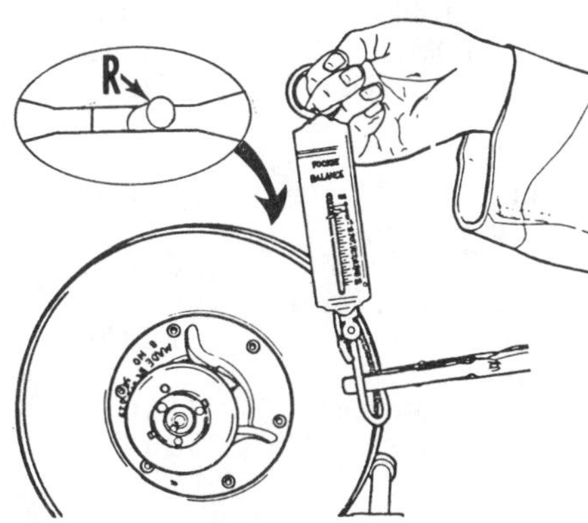

Fig. 43—Using vise grip and spring scale to check torque tension of driven clutch spring. Insert a short piece of ⅛ inch rod (R) between pulley halves to provide rolling friction.

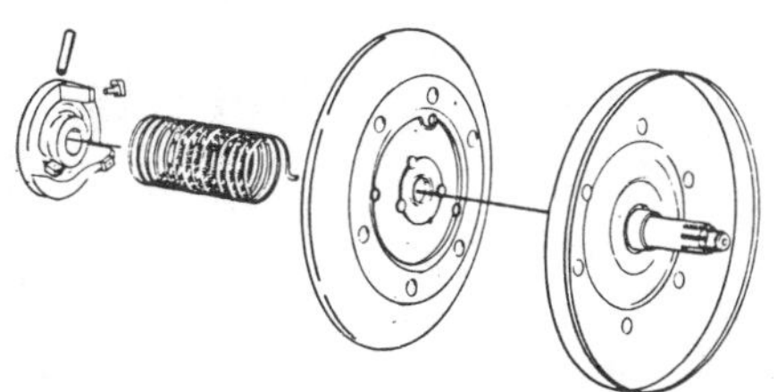

Fig. 44—Exploded view of driven pulley of the type used on early Elan models.

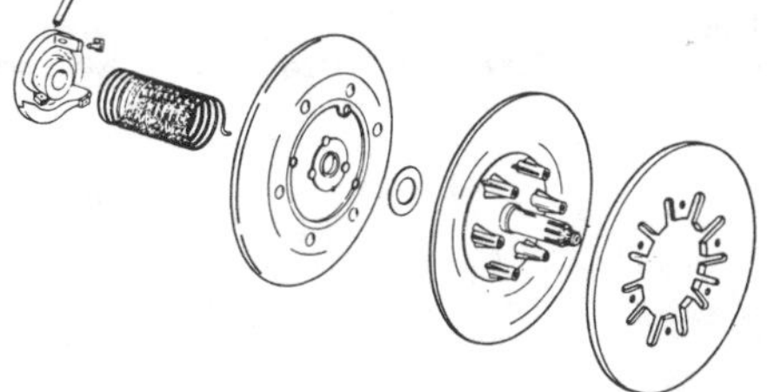

Fig. 45—Exploded view of driven pulley of the types used on early Nordic.

governor cup if measurement is incorrect. On Alpine 1979-1982 models counterweight kit should be C8-Double and spring color should be Pink.

Figure 42A shows exploded view of **Roller Square Shaft with Three Ramps.** Pulley components should be marked for proper assembly. If components are not marked, affix suitable marks before disassembly. To remove, bend tab down from around weight cover retaining cap screw and remove screw. Use caution when removing screw. Remove fixed hub by using a suitable jack screw.

The Duralon bushing in hub is made of fiberglass with a bearing surface of Teflon impregnated cloth. Bushing should be renewed if bearing surface is badly worn or fiberglass backing shows through. Remove set screw and use a suitable pushing tool against bushing, then remove and/or reinstall bushing by using a hammer or press.

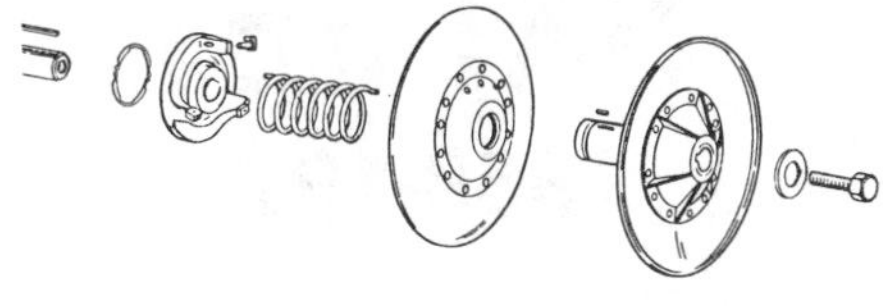

Fig. 47—Exploded view of driven pulley of the type used on early Alpine and Elite.

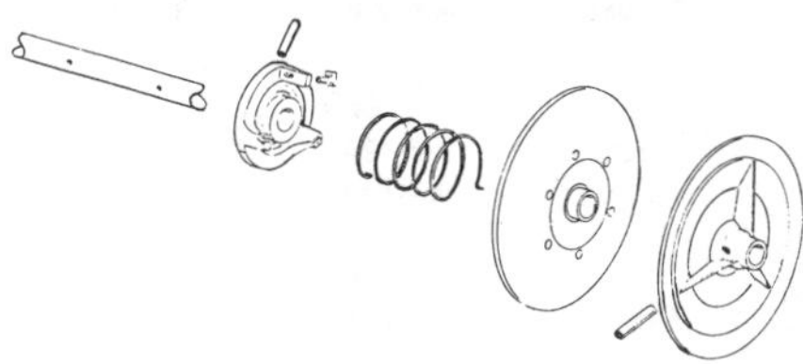

Fig. 48—Exploded view of driven pulley of the type used on late Alpine.

Do not remove counterweights unless necessary. Counterweights are available only as an assembly kit.

Refer to chart shown below for counterweight kit and spring identification on 1979-1982 models.

Model	Counter-weight Kit	Spring
1979		
Blizzard 7500	A3S	Brown
Blizzard Cross Country	A6S	Light Blue
Blizzard 9500	A3S	Violet
1980		
Blizzard 7500	A3S	Purple
Blizzard 9500	A3S	Purple
1981		
Blizzard 7500	A3S	White
Blizzard 9500	A3S	White
1982		
Blizzard 9500	A6S	Brown

To check torque load of driven pulley spring on all models, first slightly spread pulley halves and insert a short piece of ⅛-inch (3 mm) rod (R–Fig. 43) to provide rolling friction to any movement of sliding half. Clamp vise-grip pliers to pulley rim to serve as a pull scale anchor

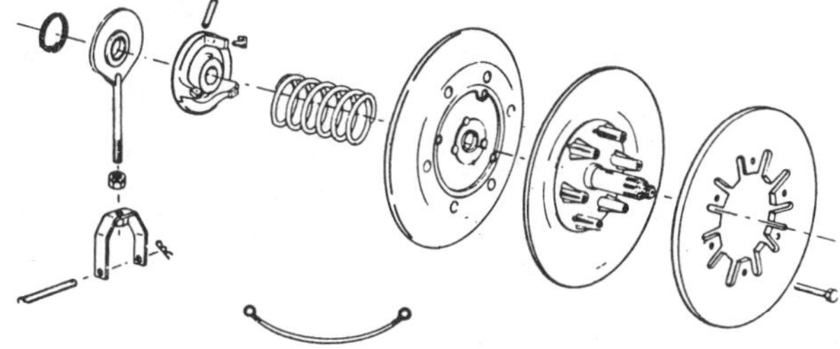

Fig. 46—Exploded view of driven pulley of the type used on early Everest and Olympique models so equipped.

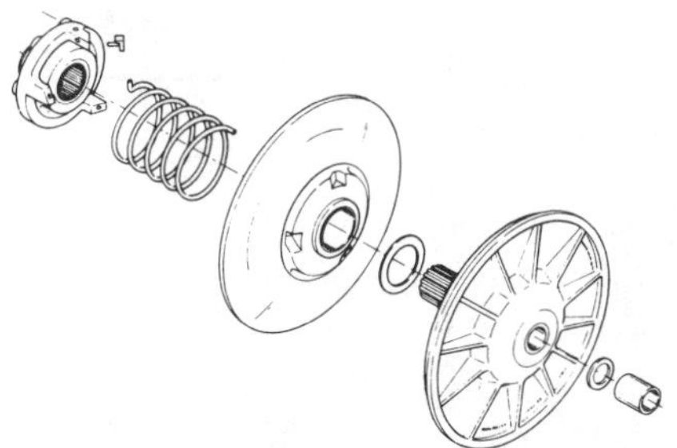

Fig. 50—Exploded view of driven pulley used on Citation, Nordik and Skandic models so equipped.

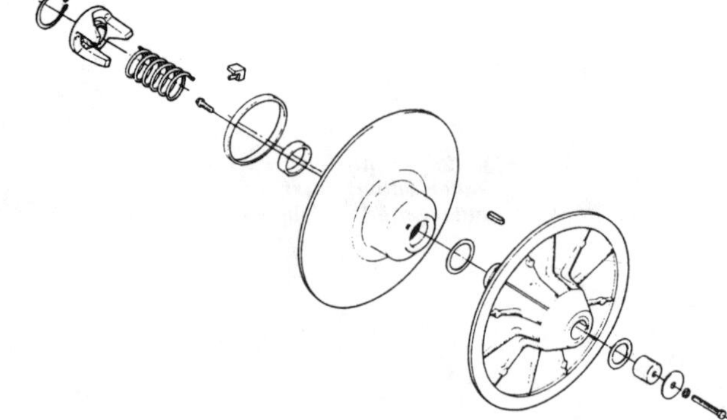

Fig. 51—Exploded view of driven pulley used on Everest and Blizzard models so equipped.

Fig. 52—Exploded view of driven pulley used on late Elite models.

and use a pull scale to measure the force necessary to move friction shoes away from cam. Tension can be modified by relocating spring end in sliding pulley half or by changing torque wrap of cam. Normal torque wrap of most cams is ⅓-turn. Increasing torque load will slow upshift time and increase sensitivity to downshift under varying load.

The nylon ramp shoes can be pulled from drillings in cam, or cut off and the stud punched or drilled out. Renew all ramp shoes if one must be renewed.

Refer to Figs. 44 through Fig. 52 for exploded views of most driven pulley assemblies.

Refer to chart shown below for recommended driven pulley spring tension on 1979-1982 models.

Model	Pounds Tension
1979	
Elan, Citation, Olympique and Everest	8 lbs.
All Other Models	13 lbs.
1980-1981	
Elan, Citation 3500 and Citation 4500	8 lbs.
Nordik (1981)	12 lbs.
All Other Models	13 lbs.
1982	
Elan	7-9 lbs.
Citation (3500, 4500/E and SS)	6-10 lbs.
Citation 4500, Nordik and Skandic	11-13 lbs.
All Blizzard and Everest Models	11-15 lbs.
Elite and Alpine	12-14 lbs.

SKI-JET

1969-1970

	Engine			Carburetor				Clutch		
Model	Make	Model	Displ.	Make	Model	Sprocket Ratio	Chain Size	Make	Shaft Center	Belt Number
					1969					
SJ300	Hirth	191R	300cc	Tillotson	HR19A					702699
SJ300	Sachs	SA290	297cc	Tillotson	HR19A					702699
					1970					
SJ300	Hirth	193R	292cc	Tillotson	HR19A					702699

SKIROULE

1966-1972

	Engine			Carburetor				Clutch		
Model	Make	Model	Displ.	Make	Model	Sprocket Ratio	Chain Size	Make	Shaft Center	Belt Number
					1966					
1966	Hirth	53R	300cc	Tillotson	HR3A		40	Own		SR-414
					1967					
1967	Hirth	53R	300cc	Tillotson	HR3A		40	Own		SR-414
					1968					
300	Sachs	SA290	297cc	Tillotson	HR8A	14:33	35-2	Own		SR-414
300W	Wankel	RC1-18.5	303cc	Tillotson	HL252A	14:33	35-2	Own		SR-414
600T	JLO	L600	592cc	Tillotson	HD13A	17:33	35-2	Own		SR-414S
600T	Hirth	170R	600cc	Tillotson	HD13A	17:33	35-2	Own		SR-414S
					1969					
S300	Sachs	SA290	297cc	Tillotson	HR18A	14:33	35-2	Own	10½	8052-4005
SX300	Sachs	SA290	297cc	Tillotson	HD7AX	14:33	35-2	Own	10½	8052-4005
S370	Sachs	SA370	368cc	Tillotson	HD7AX	16:33	35-2	Own	10½	8052-4005
SX370	Sachs	SA370	368cc	Tillotson	HD7AX	16:33	35-2	Precico	10½	8052-4005
SX740	Sachs	SA2-740	735cc	Tillotson	HD7AX					
SW300	Wankel	RC1-18.5	303cc	Tillotson	HL252A					
					1970					
S225	CCW	225	225cc	Tillotson	HR			Precico	10½	8052-4005
S250	Sachs	SA280A	277cc	Tillotson	HR64A	13:33	35-2	Precico	10½	8052-4005
S300	Sachs	SA290	293cc	Tillotson	HR64A	14:33	35-2	Precico	10½	8052-4005
SX340	Sachs	SA340	335cc	Tillotson	HD28A	16:33	35-2	Precico	10½	8052-4005
SC340T	Hirth	260R	338cc	Tillotson		16:33	35-2	Precico	10½	8052-4005
SRX340	Sachs	SA340SS	335cc	Tillotson	HD28A	15:33	35-2	Precico	10½	2052-4062
SX440	Hirth	211R	439cc	Tillotson	HD28A	17:33	35-2	Precico	10½	8052-4005
SRX440	Sachs	SA2-440	437cc	Tillotson	HD28A(2)	16:33	35-2	Precico	10½	2052-4062
R440	Hirth	211R	439cc	Tillotson	HD28A	17:33	35-2	Precico	10½	8052-4005
RT500	Hirth	220R	493cc	Tillotson	HD28A	17:33	35-2	Precico	10½	8052-4005
RTX640	Hirth	171R	634cc	Tillotson	HD28A(2)	18:33	35-2	Precico	10½	2052-4062
RTX750	Sachs	SA2-740	735cc	Tillotson	HD28A(2)	20:33	35-2	Precico	10½	2052-4062
RTX800	Hirth	230R	793cc	Tillotson	HD28A(3)	20:33	35-2	Precico	10½	2052-4062
					1971					
S-250	Sachs	SA-280	277cc	Tillotson	HR82A	13:33	35-2	Precico	10½	8052-4005
S-300	Sachs	SA-290	293cc	Tillotson	HR82A	14:33	35-2	Precico	10½	8052-4005
SS-300	Sachs	SA-290SS	293cc	Tillotson	HD44A	14:33	35-2	Precico	10½	8052-4005
S-340	CCW	340	339cc	Tillotson	HR90A	15:33	35-2	Precico	10½	8052-4005
S-400	CCW	400	398cc	Tillotson	HR90A	16:33	35-2	Precico	10½	8052-4005
SE-400	CCW	400	398cc	Tillotson	HR90A	16:33	35-2	Precico	10½	8052-4005
SX-440	Sachs	SA2-440	436cc	Tillotson	HD45A	17:33	35-2	Precico	10½	8052-4005
R-400	CCW	400	398cc	Tillotson	HR90A	15:33	35-2	Precico	10½	8052-4005
RE-400	CCW	400	398cc	Tillotson	HR90A	15:33	35-2	Precico	10½	8052-4005
RT-500	Sachs	SA2-440	436cc	Tillotson	HD45A	16:33	35-2	Precico	10½	8052-4005
					1972					
S250	Sachs	SA290	293cc	Tillotson	HR82A	14:33	35-2	Precico	10½	8052-4005
RT300E	Sachs	SA290	293cc	Tillotson	HR82A	14:33	35-2	Precico	10½	8052-4005
RT340	Sachs	SA2-340	338cc	Tillotson	HD	14:33	35-2	Precico	10½	8052-4005
RT440	Sachs	SA2-440	437cc	Tillotson	HD	16:33	35-2	Precico	10½	8052-4005
RTX300	Sachs	SA290SS	293cc	Tillotson	HD	15:33	35-2	Precico	10½	8052-4005
RTX440	Sachs	SA2-440C	437cc	Tillotson	HD	17:33	35-2	Precico	10½	8052-4005
RTX447	Sachs	SA2-440C	437cc	Tillotson	HD	17:33	35-2	Precico	10½	8052-4005

LUBRICATION

The engine is lubricated by oil mixed with the fuel. The vehicle manufacturer recommends a fuel-oil ratio of 20:1 using regular gasoline and Skiroule Mixing Oil or equivalent.

The drive chain should be lubricated periodically with Skiroule X423 Chain Grease or equivalent, by removing the chain case cover.

Lubricate sliding portions of drive pulley about every 10-15 hours with low temperature grease and counterweights of centrifugal governor with a drop of oil.

Grease fittings are located on ski legs, bogie wheels and driven sheave bearings. Lubricate once a week with low temperature grease.

ADJUSTMENT

STEERING SKIS. With handle bars in normal straight driving position, both skis should point straight ahead and center-to-center distance should be the same at front and rear of skis. Each drag link must be adjusted separately after disconnecting either end of link (early models), or turning center section (late units). The splined

Fig. 1—To adjust drive chain, remove cover (2) and loosen adjustment rod (1). Refer to Fig. 2.

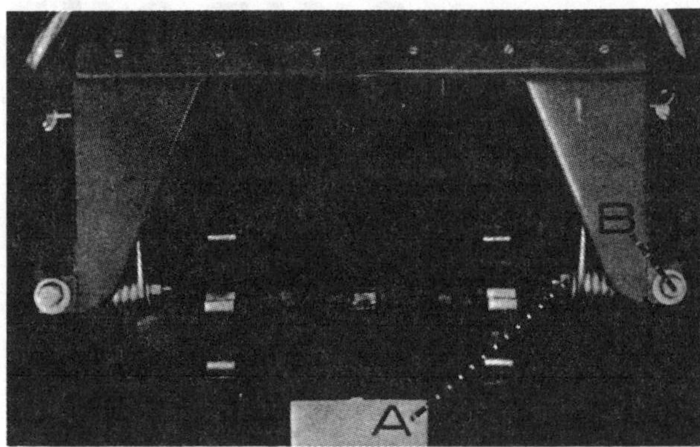

Fig. 4—Loosen pivot bolts (A) and turn adjusting screws (B) to adjust the track.

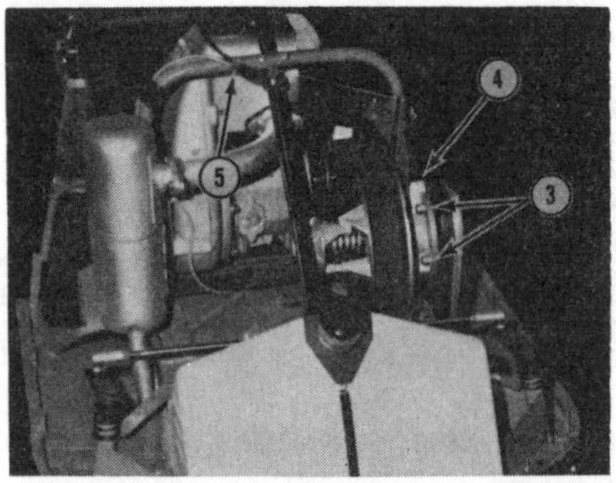

Fig. 2—Loosen flange bolts (3) and turn housing (4) forward to tighten chain or rearward to loosen chain. Loosen cable clamp (5) and reposition housing to adjust the brake.

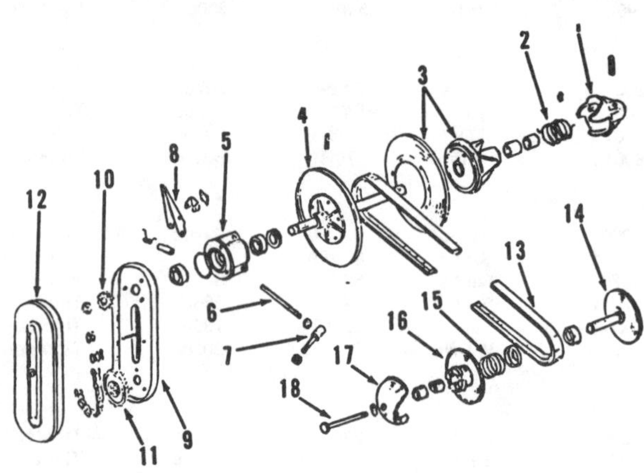

Fig. 5—Exploded view of drive assembly used on 1969 models.

1. Outer cam
2. Spring
3. Moveable face
4. Fixed face
5. Bearing housing
6. Adjustment rod
7. Eyebolt
8. Brake arm
9. Chain case
10. Drive sprocket
11. Driven sprocket
12. Cover

Fig. 3—On 1970 models, turn anchor nuts (A) to adjust brake clearance.

steering arms should point straight to rear parallel with ski.

DRIVE CHAIN. The roller drive chain should have a free play of ⅛-¼ inch. Chain tension can be checked after removing chain housing cover (2—Fig. 1). To adjust chain tension, loosen the three bolts (3—Fig. 2) and adjusting rod (1—Fig. 1); then turn eccentric housing (4—Fig. 2) forward to tighten chain or rearward to loosen chain.

BRAKE. To adjust the shoe-type brake, loosen cable clamp (5—Fig. 2) on early models, and reposition cable housing on frame support. On late units, turn the two adjusting nuts (A—Fig. 3). Move housing toward brake arm to loosen the adjustment or away from brake arm to tighten brake.

TRACK. With rear of machine supported and track free of ground, top of track should sag ½-1 inch when viewed from rear of track tunnel. To adjust the tension, loosen support bolts (A—Fig. 4) and turn adjusting screws (B) clockwise to tighten track or counter-clockwise to loosen.

NOTE: When track tension has been adjusted, alignment MUST be checked as outlined in the special TRACK SERVICE Section of this manual.

OVERHAUL

SKIS AND STEERING. Skis, ski legs (spindles), steering arms and drag links are interchangeable from right to left. Wear bar can be installed either end forward.

All four tie rod ends are right-hand thread and one end of tie rod must be disconnected for adjustment. Steering arms and spindles are splined, and steering arms should be installed pointing straight to rear when skis are straight.

TORQUE CONVERTER. Machines built in the 1969 and later model years use a torque sensing dr' sheave (1 through 4—Fig. 5). Torsion spring (2) should be pre-loaded ⅔ turn (2 cams) when unit is assembled. Renewable bushings are used in sliding members of drive and driven sheaves. Belt (13) should be renewed when less than ⅞ inches wide.

SKIROULE
1973-1977

	Engine			Carburetor				Clutch		
Model	Make	Model	Displ.	Make	Model	Sprocket Ratio	Chain Size	Make	Shaft Center	Belt Number
					1973					
RT300	Sachs	SA290	293cc	Tillotson	HR122A	14:33	35-2	Own	10-7/16	8052-4005
RT300-T	Sachs	SA2-290	291cc	Walbro	WD1	13:33	35-2	Own	10-7/16	8052-4005
RT300-E	Sachs	SA290	293cc	Tillotson	HR122A	14:33	35-2	Own	10-7/16	8052-4005
RT340	Sachs	SA2-340	338cc	Walbro	WD1A	14:33	35-2	Own	10-7/16	8052-4005
RT440	Sachs	SA2-440	437cc	Walbro	WD1A	16:33	35-2	Own	10-7/16	8052-4005
RT440-E	Sachs	SA2-440E	437cc	Walbro	WD1A	16:33	35-2	Own	10-7/16	8052-4005
RTX-300	Sachs	SA290SS	293cc	Walbro	WD5A	15:33	35-2	Own	10-7/16	8052-4005
RTX-340	Sachs	SA2-340C	338cc	Walbro	WD1A	15:33	35-2	Own	10-7/16	8052-4005
RTX-440	Sachs	SA2-440C	437cc	Walbro	WD1A	17:33	35-2	Own	10-7/16	8052-4005
RTX-447	Sachs	SA2-440C	437cc	Walbro	WD1A	17:33	35-2	Own	10-7/16	8052-4005
RTW-300	Wankel	KM-24	294cc	Walbro	WR5	14:33	35-2	Own	10-7/16	8052-4005
					1974					
RT300	Kohler	K295-1	293cc	Walbro	WR	14:33	35-2	Own	10½	8052-4005
RT300T	Kohler	K295-2AX	291cc	Walbro	WD	14:33	35-2	Own	10½	8052-4005
RTX340	Kohler	K340-2AX	338cc	Walbro	WD	15:33	35-3	Own	10½	8052-4005
RTX440B	Kohler	K440-2AX	437cc	Walbro	WDA	17:33	35-3	Own	10½	8052-4005
RTX440	Kohler	K440-2AX	437cc	Walbro	WDA	17:33	35-3	Own	10½	8052-4005
RTX447	Kohler	K440-2AX	437cc	Walbro	WDA	17:32	35-3	Own	10½	8052-4005
RTW300	Wankel	KM24	294cc	Walbro	WR	14:33	35-2	Own	10½	8052-4005
					1975					
300T	Kohler	K295-2AX	291cc	Walbro	WR	14:33	35-2	Own	10½	8052-4005
Sonar 340	Kohler	K340-2AX	338cc	Walbro	WD	15:33	35-3	Own	10½	8052-4005
Sonar 440	Kohler	K440-2AX	437cc	Walbro	WF	17:33	35-3	Own	10½	8052-4005
Skiroule 447	Kohler	K440-2AX	437cc	Walbro	WF	17:32	35-3	Own	10½	8052-4005
					1976					
Sonar 300T	Kohler	K295-2AX	291cc	Walbro	WR	14:33	35-2	Own	10½	8052-4005
Sonar 340	Kohler	K340-2AX	338cc	Walbro	WD	15:33	35-3	Own	10½	8052-4005
Ultra 340	Kohler	K340-2AS	338cc	Walbro	WF	16:33	35-3	Centryx	10½	4052X-4144C
Ultra 440	Kohler	K440-2AS	437cc	Walbro	WF	17:33	35-3	Centryx	10½	4052X-4144C
Ultra 447	Kohler	K440-2AS	437cc	Walbro	WF	17:32	35-3	Centryx	10½	4052X-4144C
Laser 340	Kohler	K340-2AS	338cc	Walbro	WF	16:33	35-3	Centryx	10½	4052X-4144C
Laser 440	Kohler	K440-2AS	437cc	Walbro	WF	17:33	35-3	Centryx	10½	4052X-4144C
Laser 440 Plus	Kohler	K440-2AS	437cc	Walbro	WF	17:33	35-3	Centryx	10½	4052X-4144C
Sprint 340	Kohler	K340-2FA	338cc	Walbro	WF	14:33	35-2	Centryx	10½	4052X-4144C
					1977					
Scamp 300B	Kohler	K295-2AX	291cc	Walbro	WF16	13:33	35-2	Centryx	10½	4052X-4144C
Scamp 300S	Kohler	K295-2AX	291cc	Walbro	WF16	13:33	35-2	Centryx	10½	4052X-4144C
Ultra 340	Kohler	K340-2AS	339cc	Walbro	WF16	16:33	35-3	Centryx	10½	4052X-4144C
Ultra 447	Kohler	K440-2AS	437cc	Walbro	WF16	17:32	35-3	Centryx	10½	4052X-4144C
Laser 340	Kohler	K340-2AS	338cc	Walbro	WF16	16:33	35-3	Centryx	10½	4052X-4144C
Laser 440	Kohler	K440-2AS	437cc	Walbro	WF16	17:33	35-3	Centryx	10½	4052X-4144C
Laser 440 Plus	Kohler	K440-2AS	437cc	Walbro	WF16	17:33	35-3	Centryx	10½	4052X-4144C

LUBRICATION

The engine is lubricated by oil mixed with the fuel. A ratio of 25:1 is recommended for Sachs engines except Wankel. The recommended fuel:oil ratio for Wankel KM24 engine is 50:1. Recommended ratio for Kohler engines is 40:1. A premium quality two-cycle snowmobile oil and regular gasoline are recommended.

The enclosed chaincase should be filled to level of check plug hole using SKIROULE Chaincase Oil or other good low temperature SAE 80 gear (or chain) oil.

NOTE: The rubber plug closing upper inspection opening can be used as a funnel for adding oil as shown in Fig. 1. Chain case capacity is 10 fluid ounces.

Ski leg (spindle) bushings are equipped with pressure gun fittings as is the track drive axle right end bearing. Fittings should be lubricated periodically with low temperature grease, being careful not to overlubricate.

Remove drive belt then spread driven pulley as shown in Fig. 2 and, using low temperature grease and a brush, lightly coat sliding hub as

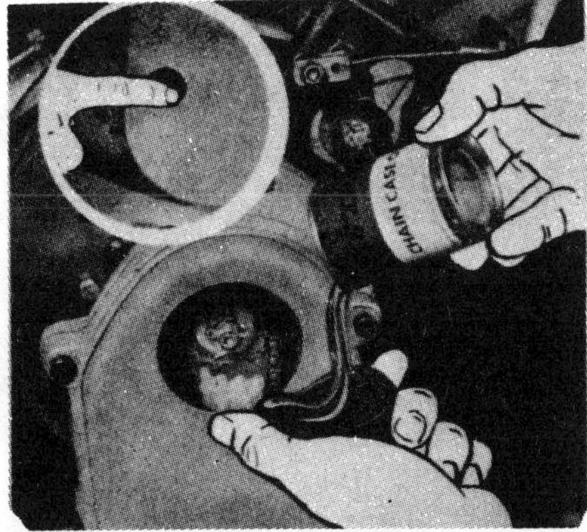

Fig. 1—Chaincase lubricant should be at level of lower check plug opening as shown in inset. Lubricant is added at upper inspection plug opening and plug can be bent to form a trough for pouring lubricant as shown.

shown. Slide pulley back and forth to distribute grease evenly and remove the excess. Remove centrifugal governor, spring and sliding half from drive clutch. Clean and lightly lubricate fixed hub with low temperature grease, lightly oil governor weights and reassemble.

On models with bogie wheel suspension, bogie wheel hubs contain lube fittings. Lubricate with low temperature grease until grease emerges and any water is forced out. Lightly oil remaining friction points and joints as necessary to protect from rust and wear and prevent binding.

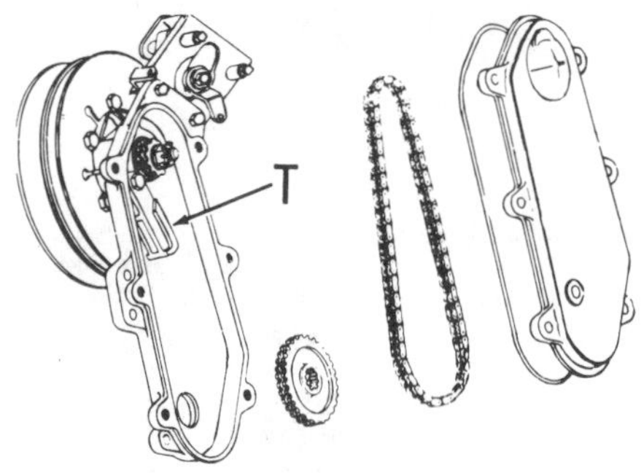

Fig. 3—Rub-block type chain tensioner (T) is spring loaded and adjustment is not required.

Fig. 5—To adjust track tension on models with bogie wheel suspension, loosen clamp nut (1) and turn adjusting screw (2). Both sides must be adjusted alike.

ADJUSTMENT

STEERING SKIS. With handlebars in normal straight driving position, both skis should point straight ahead and center-to-center distance should be equal at front and rear of skis. Tie rod and drag link ends have right-hand and left-hand threads, adjust by turning center section after loosening jam nuts.

DRIVE CHAIN. The roller drive chain is self-adjusting, controlled by a spring-loaded Nylon rub block in chaincase as shown in Fig. 3. Inspect condition of chain, sprockets and rub block by removing upper inspection plug and renew damaged parts, if chain tension is not properly controlled.

BRAKE. All models are equipped with a caliper type disc brake. When brake hand lever is released, push pins should center in valleys of actuating arm cam and brake should fully apply before hand lever travels half the distance to handlebar grip. Reposition actuating arm if required by turning brake cable housing anchor nuts (A—Fig. 4) and adjust free play at actuating arm stud nut (B). Brake light switch (S) should close when brake is applied and open when hand lever is released.

DRIVE BELT. Drive and driven pulley must be parallel and offset should be 9/16-5/8 for all models. Recommended shaft center distance is given in Tables.

Offset and alignment is adjusted by shims located between chain housing and main frame but shaft center distance is fixed.

TRACK. With rear of machine raised until track is clear, center of track should sag ½-1½ inches below center bogie wheels or ½-1 inch below middle of slide shoe.

On models with bogie wheel suspension, refer to Fig. 5. Loosen clamp nut (1) and turn adjusting bolt (2).

On models with slide suspension, refer to Fig. 6. Track tension is adjusted by loosening locknut and turning tension bolts (T). In addition, load distribution (ski pressure) can be modified by changing spring pressure at front of slide at the two screws (L). Increasing spring pressure lightens load on skis and increases percent of load carried at front of track for better traction or acceleration but provides less positive steering control. A softer ride can be obtained by moving upper end of rear shock to rear hole (R1) on track tunnel while passenger weight can be compensated for at shock tube cam adjustment (R2).

NOTE: Whenever track tension has been adjusted, alignment MUST be checked as outlined in TRACK SERVICE Section of this manual.

OVERHAUL

Refer to the appropriate general service sections elsewhere in this manual for basic information on overhaul of machine components.

Fig. 2—Coat sliding hub of driven pulley with low temperature grease using a brush as shown.

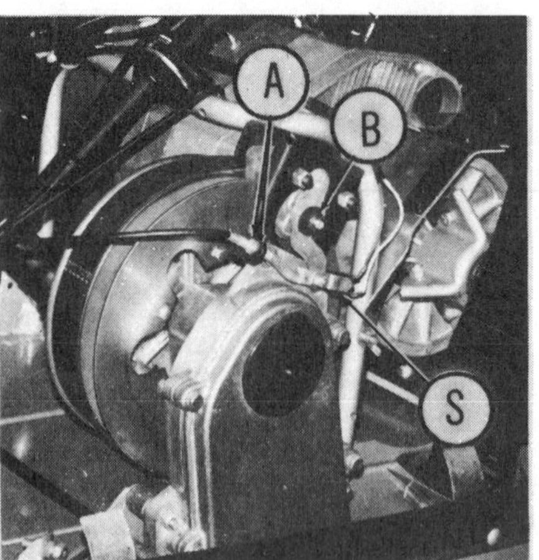

Fig. 4—On RT and RTX models with caliper type disc brake, reposition actuating arm at cable housing anchor nuts (A) and make wear adjustment at stud nut (B). Make sure brake light switch (S) closes when brake is applied and opens when brake hand lever is released.

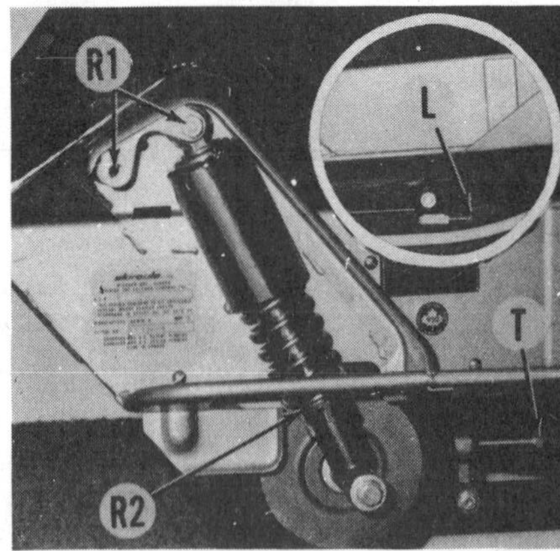

Fig. 6—View of track on models with slide suspension showing points of adjustment. Inset shows front of slide unit.

L. Load adjustment
R1. Shock anchor points
R2. Load adjustment
T. Track tension adjustment

SKI WHIZ

1969-1972

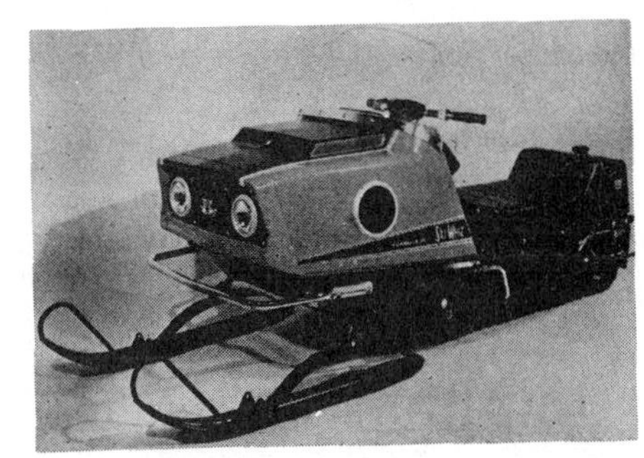

	Engine			Carburetor				Clutch		
Model	Make	Model	Displ.	Make	Model	Sprocket Ratio	Chain Size	Make	Shaft Center	Belt Number
					1969					
297	JLO	L297	296cc	Tillotson	HR33A	15:46	35-2	Salsbury 790		519599
280	JLO	L380	372cc	Tillotson	HD19A	17:46	35-2	Salsbury		520865
					1970					
300S	JLO	L295	292cc	Tillotson	HR33A	19:46	35-2	Drummond	11-9/16	521965
350SS	JLO	L340	336cc	Tillotson	HR33A	19:46	35-2	St. Law.	11-9/16	521965
500SST	JLO	LR 440-2	434cc	Tillotson	HD19A	23:46	35-2	St. Law.	11-9/16	521965
					1971					
300S	JLO	L295	292cc	Tillotson	HR54A	19:46	35-2	Drummond	11-9/16	521695M1
350SS	JLO	L340	336cc	Tillotson	HR56A	19:46	35-2	Drummond	11-9/16	521695M1
400SST	JLO	LR340/2	339cc	Tillotson	HD49A	23:46	35-2	Drummond	11-9/16	521695M1
500SST	JLO	LR399/2	398cc	Tillotson	HD49A	23:46	35-2	Drummond	11-9/16	521695M1
Formula I	JLO	LR399/2	398cc	Tillotson	HD49A	23:46	35-2	Drummond	11-9/16	521695M1
					1972					
300S	JLO	L295	292cc	Tillotson	HR54B	17:38	35-2	Own	11-3/32	521695M1
500SST	JLO	LR399/2	398cc	Tillotson	HD49A	21:38	35-2	Own	11-3/32	521695M1
Formula I	JLO	LR399/2	398cc	Tillotson	HD49A	21:38	35-2	Own	11-3/32	521695M1
Formual III	JLO	LR399/2	398cc	Tillotson	HR123A(2)	21:38	35-2	Own	11-3/32	521695M1
Formula IV ...	JLO	LR440/2	428cc	Tillotson	HR123A(2)	23:38	35-2	Own	11-3/32	521695M1

LUBRICATION

The engine is lubricated by oil mixed with the fuel. The vehicle manufacturer recommends a fuel-oil mixture of 20:1 using regular gasoline and Two Stroke Motor Oil meeting Mil. Spec. 2104-A (Massey Ferguson M-1133 or equivalent).

The enclosed drive chain case should contain approximately ½ cup (4½ fluid oz.) of SAE 80W Gear Oil. Level can be checked and fluid added after removing chain case cover. Case should contain about 1 inch of fluid which will just cover chain at lower part of bottom sprocket.

Lubricate steering tie rod ends, ski spring shackles, steering spindles and steering shaft bearings with light engine oil periodically. Track drive shafts and bogie wheels are equipped with sealed ball bearings and lubrication is not required.

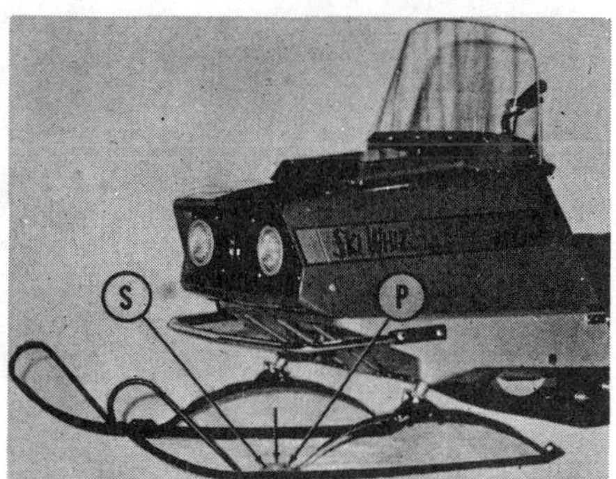

Fig. 1—Skis can be adjusted for snow conditions by moving the front clevis pin in the three holes provided. Use front hole (S) for soft snow and rear hole (P) for packed snow. Center hole is for intermediate conditions. Refer also to Fig. 4.

Fig. 2—View of 1969 chain case with cover removed showing adjustment mechanism.

A. Adjusting screw
B. Rub block
C. Drive chain

ADJUSTMENT

STEERING SKIS AND LINKAGE. Steering skis should be parallel to each other and to vehicle frame when handle bar is in normal straight driving position. Both tie rods should be equal in length. To adjust either tie rod, loosen jam nut and turn rod center section.

WEIGHT DISTRIBUTION. Track suspension and skis can be adjusted to change the handling characteristics for varying snow conditions.

For maximum maneuverability in packed snow, position the front ski clevis pin in rear hole of ski saddle (P—Fig. 1) then back off the rear suspension adjusting bolts (3—Fig. 6, see also Fig. 7).

For maximum flotation on soft snow and improved traction, position ski clevis pins in front holes (S—Fig. 1) and turn rear suspension bolts in.

The middle hole in front ski saddle and intermediate positions of suspension bolts (3—Fig. 6, Fig. 7) are for more normal conditions and individual handling preference.

DRIVE CHAIN. The roller drive chain should have all slack removed but should not be under tension. To adjust the chain, remove chain case cover. On 1969 models refer to Fig. 2, then tighten adjusting screw (A) until tension is correct. On 1970 models, loosen the four bolts (Fig. 3) securing bearing block to chain ease and slide bearing block up until chain is tight. Chain case cover can be removed without loss of lubricant.

On 1970 models check brake caliper alignment after tightening drive chain.

BRAKE. To adjust the caliper type disc brake on 1969 models, refer to Fig. 4 and adjust through-bolt (1) until brake pads (2) clear pulley sheave 0.002-0.010 inch with brake released. Remove slack from brake cable if necessary by loosening clamp screw (3). Pivot bolt (4) should have all slack removed but should not bind.

On 1970 machines, wear adjustment is made by removing the cotter pin and turning adjusting nut (Fig. 5) until brake pads clear pulley sheave 0.002-0.010 inch with brake released. Caliper must be properly aligned with sheave rim and push pins must center valleys in actuating arm when adjustment is made.

TRACK. To adjust track tension, block up rear of machine until track is clear of ground. Track should clear center bogie wheels by 1-2 inches when track is pulled down. Adjust by loosening the two clamp bolts (1—Fig. 6) and turning adjusting screws (2). Both sides must be adjusted alike. Refer also to Fig. 8 for later suspension.

NOTE: Whenever track tension has been adjusted, alignment MUST be checked as outlined in TRACK SERVICE Section of this manual.

OVERHAUL

SKIS. Skis, ski legs (spindles) and drag links are interchangeable from left to right, but steering arms are not. Wear bar can be installed either end forward. Steering arms are keyed to spindles. Both drag links are the same length when properly adjusted.

Fig. 3—Top view of intermediate shaft used on 1970 models. Loosen the four bolts and slide bearing block to adjust drive chain.

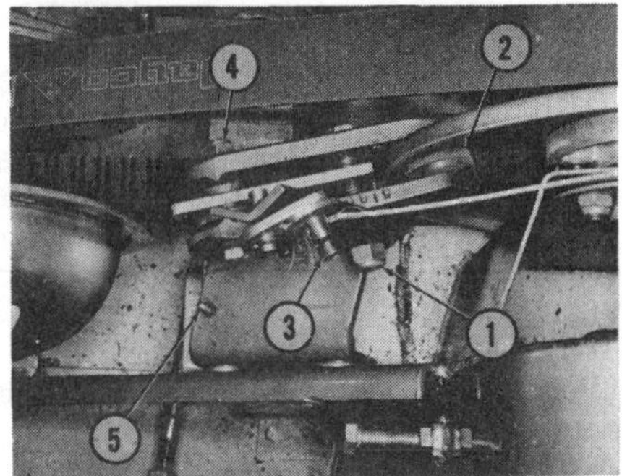

Fig. 4—View of brake and associated parts showing points of adjustment.

1. Through-bolt
2. Brake pads
3. Clamp screw
4. Pivot bolt
5. Mounting bracket

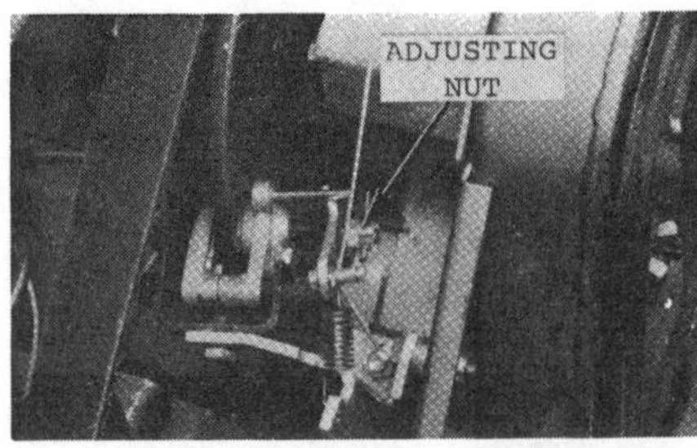

Fig. 5—Brake wear adjustment on 1970 models is made by removing cotter pin and turning adjusting nut. Refer to text.

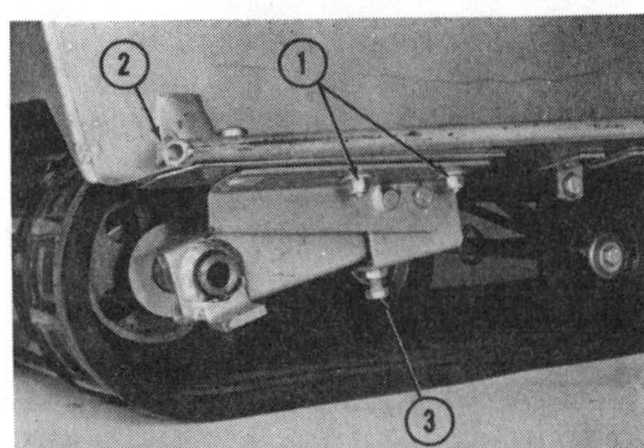

Fig. 6—Rear suspension and associated parts showing means of track adjustment.

1. Clamp screws
2. Adjusting screw
3. Weight adjusting screw

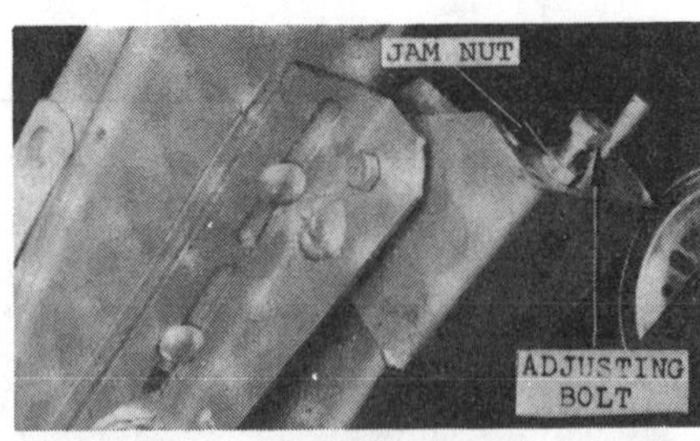

Fig. 7—Rear suspension and associated parts used on 1970 models. Loosen jam nut and turn adjusting bolt for proper ride adjustment.

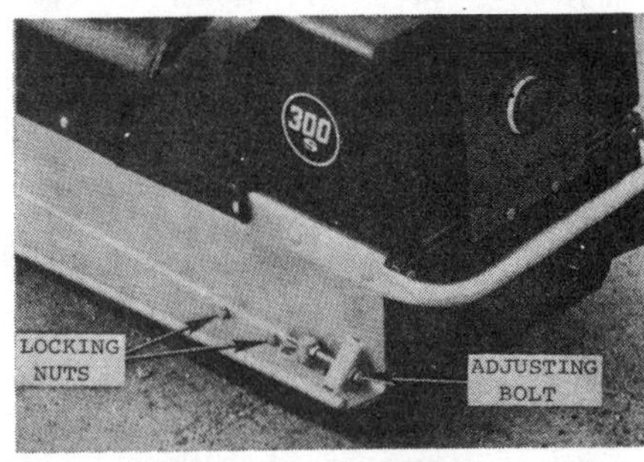

Fig. 8—View of rear suspension used on 1970 models showing points of adjustment.

Fig. 9—Hood removed showing points of carburetor adjustment.

1. Idle mixture screw
2. High speed mixture screw
3. Idle speed screw
F. Fuel line
P. Primer line

Fig. 10—View of engine and drive unit with hood removed.

SKI WHIZ

1973-1977

	Engine			Carburetor				Clutch		
Model	Make	Model	Displ.	Make	Model	Sprocket Ratio	Chain Size	Make	Shaft Center	Belt Number
1973										
300	JLO	L295	292cc	Tillotson	HR54B	19:38	35-2	Own	10-15/16	529-965M1
340T	JLO	LR340/2	339cc	Tillotson	HD49A	19:38	35-2	Own	10-15/16	523-216M1
400T	JLO	LR399/2	398cc	Tillotson	HD49A	19:38	35-2	Own	10-15/16	523-216M1
440T	JLO	LR440/2	428cc	Tillotson	HD49A	19:38	35-2	Own	10-15/16	523-216M1
400WT	JLO	LR399/2	398cc	Tillotson	HD49A	19:38	35-2	Own	10-15/16	523-216M1
440WT	JLO	LR440/2	428cc	Tillotson	HD49A	19:38	35-2	Own	10-15/16	523-216M1
1974										
300S	JLO	L295	292cc	Tillotson	HR146A	19:38	35-2	Own	10-15/16	529-965M1
340T	JLO	LR340/2	339cc	Tillotson	HD120A	19:38	35-2	Own	10-15/16	523-216M1
400T	JLO	LR399/2	398cc	Tillotson	HD120A	19:38	35-2	Own	10-15/16	523-216M1
440T	JLO	LR440/2	428cc	Tillotson	HD120A	19:38	35-2	Own	10-15/16	523-216M1
400WT	JLO	LR399/2	398cc	Tillotson	HD120A	19:38	35-2	Own	10-15/16	523-216M1
440WT	JLO	LR440/2	428cc	Tillotson	HD120A	19:38	35-2	Own	10-15/16	523-216M1
1975										
MF304	JLO	1F-295-7	292cc	Tillotson	HRM1A	17:38	*	Own	10-15/16	529-965M1
MF304T	JLO	2F-295-1	285cc	Tillotson	HRM1A	17:38	*	Own	10-15/16	523-216M1
MF344T	JLO	2F-340-5	339cc	Tillotson	HD136A	17:38	*	Own	10-15/16	523-216M1
MF404T	JLO	2F-400-7	398cc	Tillotson	HD136A	21:38	*	Own	10-15/16	523-216M1
MF444T	JLO	2F-440-7	428cc	Tillotson	HD136A	21:38	*	Own	10-15/16	523-216M1
MF404WT	JLO	2F-400-7	398cc	Tillotson	HD136A	17:38	*	Own	10-15/16	523-216M1
MF444WT	JLO	2F-440-7	428cc	Tillotson	HDB6A	17:38	*	Own	10-15/16	523-216M1
*Silent Chain.										
1976										
Chinook 300	Cuyuna	290	294cc	Walbro	WRA37	14:32	40-1	Scorpion	10½	989900
Whirlwind 340	Cuyuna	340	338cc	Walbro	WF15	18:38	35-2	Scorpion	10½	989910
Whirlwind 440	Cuyuna	440	428cc	Walbro	WF14	19:38	35-2	Scorpion	10½	989910
Cyclone 340	Brooten	LC34	336cc	Mikuni	VM32(2)	17:39	35-2	Brooten	12-3/8	766938
Cyclone 440	Brooten	LC44	439cc	Mikuni	VM34(3)	19:39	35-2	Brooten	12-3/8	766938
1977										
Chinook 300SS PR	Cuyuna	...	294cc	Walbro	WF21	14:32	40-1	Scorpion	10½	989900
Storm 440 PR	Cuyuna	...	428cc	Walbro	WF23	21:38	35-2	Scorpion	10½	989910
Storm 440 PS	Cuyuna	...	428cc	Walbro	WF23	21:38	35-2	Scorpion	10½	989910
Whirlwind 340 PR	Cuyuna	...	339cc	Walbro	WF17	18:38	35-2	Scorpion	10½	989910
Whirlwind 440 PR	Cuyuna	...	428cc	Walbro	WF22	19:38	35-2	Scorpion	10½	989910
Whirlwind 440 PS	Cuyuna	...	428cc	Walbro	WF22	19:38	35-2	Scorpion	10½	989910

NOTE: For specific service information on 1976 and 1977 MASSEY models, refer to SCORPION section.

LUBRICATION

The engine is lubricated by oil mixed with the fuel. The vehicle manufacturer recommends a fuel:oil mixture of 20:1 using regular gasoline and Two-Stroke Motor Oil meeting Mil. Spec. 2104-A (Massey-Ferguson 841-614-MI or equivalent).

The enclosed drive chaincase should contain approximately ½ cup (4½ fluid oz.) of SAE 80W Gear Oil. Level can be checked and fluid added after removing chaincase cover. Case should contain about one inch of fluid which will just cover chain at lower part of bottom sprocket.

Lubricate steering tie rod ends, ski spring shackles, steering spindles and steering shaft bearings with light engine oil periodically. Track drive shafts and bogie wheels are equipped with sealed ball bearings and lubrication is not required.

ADJUSTMENT

STEERING SKIS AND LINKAGE. Steering skis should be parallel to each other and to vehicle frame when handlebar is in normal straight driving position. Both tie rods should be equal in length. To adjust either tie rod, loosen jam nut and turn rod center section.

WEIGHT DISTRIBUTION. Track suspension and skis can be adjusted to change the handling characteristics for varying snow conditions.

For maximum maneuverability in packed snow, position the front ski clevis pin in rear hole of spring bracket (see Fig. 1) then on models so equipped, turn cam adjusting bolts

Fig. 1—Skis can be adjusted for snow conditions by moving the front clevis pin to any of the three holes in front spring bracket. Use front hole for soft snow and rear hole for packed snow. Center hole is for average use. Refer also to Fig. 2.

(A—Fig. 2) forward at top to increase tension on rear suspension springs.

For maximum flotation on soft snow and improved traction, position ski clevis pins in front holes and turn rear cam adjusting bolts rearward at top to soften rear suspension.

The middle hole in front ski saddle and intermediate positions of suspension cams are for more normal conditions and individual handling preference.

DRIVE CHAIN. The roller drive chain used on early models should have all slack removed but should not be under tension. To adjust the chain, remove chaincase cover, loosen the four bolts (Fig. 3) securing bearing block to chaincase and slide bearing block up until chain is tight. Chaincase cover can be removed without loss of lubricant. Check brake caliper alignment after tightening drive chain.

On 1975 models with silent chain, automatic chain tensioners are provided and adjustment is not required.

BRAKE. To adjust the caliper type disc brake, turn adjusting nut (Fig. 4) until brake pads clear pulley sheave 0.002-0.010 inch with brake released. Caliper must be properly aligned with sheave rim and push pins must center in valleys in actuating arm when adjustment is made.

TRACK. To adjust track tension, raise rear of machine until track is clear. About 1-inch clearance should exist between center bogie wheels and bottom of track. Refer to Fig. 2, loosen the two locknuts and adjusting bolt jam nut, and turn adjusting bolt as required until correct clearance is obtained. Both sides must be adjusted alike as indicated by equal protrusion of adjusting bolts.

NOTE: Whenever track tension has been adjusted, alignment MUST be checked as outlined in TRACK SERVICE Section of this manual.

DRIVE BELT. To check the drive pulley alignment remove drive belt, spread driven pulley and insert a suitable straightedge (S—Fig. 5) so that tool contacts hubs of both pulleys as shown. Measured distance (D) from far edge of straightedge to fixed face of drive clutch should be 7/16 inch (11 mm) on single-cylinder models, or ½-inch (12.5 mm) on twin-cylinder units. Misalignment can be corrected by sliding engine; or by adding or removing shims between driven pulley hub and shaft bearing block.

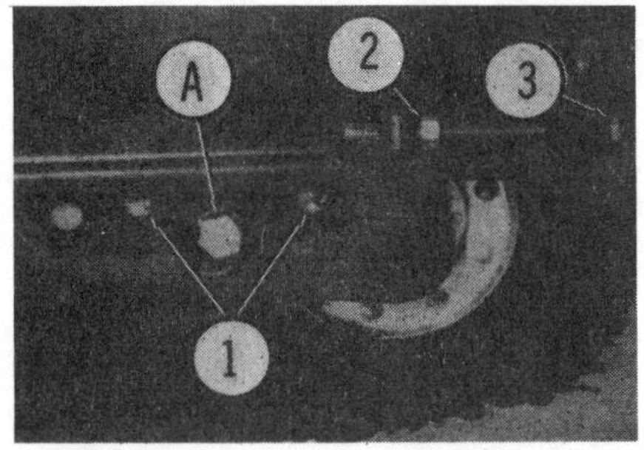

Fig. 2—To adjust track tension, loosen clamp nuts (1 & 2) and turn adjusting screw (3). Cam adjusting bolts (A) control spring tension; see text.

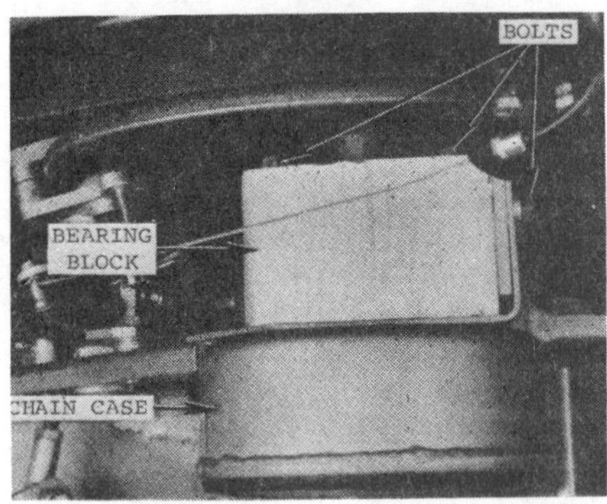

Fig. 3—Top view of intermediate shaft. Loosen the four bolts and slide bearing block to adjust drive chain.

Fig. 4—Brake wear adjustment is made by turning actuating arm adjusting nut indicated above.

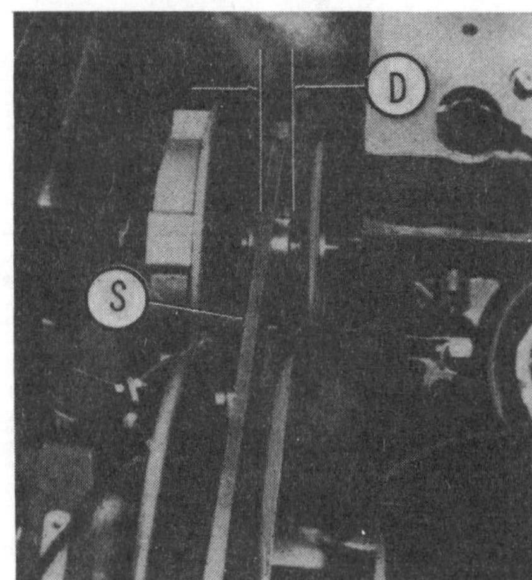

Fig. 5—Correct pulley offset can be checked by inserting a straightedge (S) between faces of driven pulley. Distance (D) should be 7/16 inch for single cylinder models or ½-inch for twins.

SKI ZOOM

1971-1973

	Engine			Carburetor				Clutch		
Model	Make	Model	Displ.	Make	Model	Sprocket Ratio	Chain Size	Make	Shaft Center	Belt Number
					1971					
Fury I	Sachs	SA2-440	437cc				35-2	Eastern Ind.	11 ¼	B2-1220
Fury II	Sachs	SA2-440	437cc				35-2	Eastern	11 ¼	B2-1220
Fury III	Sachs	SA2-440	437cc				35-2	Eastern	11 ¼	B2-1220

	Engine			Carburetor				Clutch		
Model	Make	Model	Displ.	Make	Model	Sprocket Ratio	Chain Size	Make	Shaft Center	Belt Number
					1972					
Rebel	Sachs	SA280	277cc	Tillotson	HR19A		35-2	Eastern	11¼	B2-1220
Rebel I	Sachs	SA290	293cc	Tillotson	HR19A		35-2	Eastern	11¼	B2-1220
Rebel II	Sachs	SA290	293cc	Tillotson	HR19A		35-2	Eastern	11¼	B2-1220
Comet Sport ..	Sachs	SA2-340	338cc				35-2	Precico	11¼	B3-1220
Fury Sport	Sachs	SA2-440	437cc				35-2	Precico	11¼	B3-1220
					1973					
Rebel 280	Sachs	SA280	277cc	Tillotson	HR		35-2	Securistat	11¼	GTS-715
Rebel 290	Sachs	SA290	293cc	Tillotson	HR		35-2	Securistat	11¼	GTS-715
Comet 290SS .	Sachs	SA290C	293cc	Tillotson	HD		35-2	St. Law.	11¼	GTS-715
Comet 340	Sachs	SA2-340	338cc	Walbro	WD6		35-2	St. Law.	11¼	GTS-715
Comet 440	Sachs	SA2-440	437cc	Tillotson	HD		35-2	St. Law.	11¼	GTS-715
Comet 441	Sachs		437cc	Tillotson	HD		35-2	St. Law.	11¼	GTS-715

LUBRICATION

The engine is lubricated by oil mixed with the fuel. Regular or premium gasoline and a good quality branded snowmobile oil should be mixed at a ratio of 25:1.

The enclosed chain case should contain ½ cup of low temperature grease which can be added with a putty knife or similar tool after removing chain case cover. Check grease and chain adjustment about every ten hours. Some models also have a pressure gun fitting located on intermediate shaft bearing. Lubricate lightly each time chain is inspected.

ADJUSTMENT

STEERING SKIS. Steering skis should be parallel with each other and with vehicle frame when handlebar is in normal straight driving position. Adjust both tie rods equally by loosening locknuts and turning center section.

DRIVE CHAIN. The enclosed drive chain should have approximately 3/16-inch free play measured midway between drive sprockets. To adjust the chain, loosen the adjusting bolt located on intermediate shaft bearing housing (A—Fig. 1) and push down in slot to tighten chain or up to loosen chain. (Models with eccentric adjustment). Or loosen the three bearing housing mounting bolts slide housing up (models with sliding adjustment).

Check brake alignment with friction surface of driven sheave after adjusting the chain. Caliper unit must be in perfect alignment with sheave. Align if necessary by loosening bracket mounting bolts, firmly applying the brake then retightening the bolts while brake is applied.

Fig. 1–To adjust the drive chain, loosen adjusting bolt (A) and move in housing slot until adjustment is correct.

BRAKE. The caliper type brake uses fixed face of driven sheave as a friction surface. Brake should fully apply before hand lever contacts handlebar grip and fully release when hand pressure is relaxed.

Before attempting wear adjustment, first check to be sure caliper unit properly aligns with friction surface of sheave. If adjustment is required, loosen the fasteners securing mounting bracket and firmly apply the brake, then tighten fasteners while brake is applied. Check to be sure brake push pins rest in valleys of actuating cam when brake is released; adjust if necessary at brake cable housing anchor nuts. Wear adjustment is made by tightening actuating stud nut (A—Fig. 2) until correct brake pad clearance is obtained.

Fig. 2–Brake wear adjustment is made by turning actuating arm stud nut (A).

TRACK. To adjust track tension, raise rear of machine until track is clear. With firm hand pressure applied, track should clear center bogie wheels by 2½-3 inches and be equal on both sides. Adjust by loosening clamp screw (1—Fig. 3) or jam nut (1—Fig. 4) and turning adjusting screw (2) until adjustment is correct. Both sides must be adjusted alike.

NOTE: Whenever track tension has been adjusted, alignment MUST be checked as outlined in TRACK SERVICE Section of this manual.

RIDE ADJUSTMENT. Some models are equipped with a ride adjustment as shown at (3—Fig. 4). Position upper end of suspension springs in rear notch for soft ride or light loads or forward notch for heavy loads or firm ride. Center notch is intermediate position. Both sides MUST be adjusted alike.

Fig. 3–To adjust track tension, loosen clamp nut (1) and turn adjusting screw (2). Both sides must be adjusted alike.

Fig. 4–On some models, track tension adjusting screw (2) is secured by a jam nut (2) instead of clamp bolt. Suspension spring bracket can be repositioned in any of the three notches for weight and ride control.

SNO CUB
1970-1972

Model	Engine Make	Engine Model	Engine Displ.	Carburetor Make	Carburetor Model 1970-1971-1972	Sprocket Ratio	Chain Size	Clutch Make	Clutch Shaft Center	Belt Number
6300	JLO	L99	100cc	TLT'sn	HL270B	8:1	....	N. American	....	....

LUBRICATION

The engine is lubricated by oil mixed with the fuel. The manufacturer recommends regular gasoline and a branded Snowmobile Oil such as "CASTROL", "WITCO", "Phillips IGLOO" or "OILZUM". Recommended fuel/oil ratio ratio is 20:1.

The upper (primary) drive chain is automatically oiled by a tube (2—Fig. 2) leading from crankcase bleeder valve. Lower (secondary) chain is not automatically oiled. The manufacturer recommends that both chains be greased occasionally with "LUBRIPLATE" or a good grade chassis lube.

Drive train and track are equipped with self-aligning, sealed type bearings and do not require lubrication.

ADJUSTMENT

STEERING SKIS. Steering skis are attached to a double-leaf, transverse spring and controlled by a tiller type steering handle. No adjustment is necessary. If alignment is not correct, check for bent, broken or damaged parts.

DRIVE CHAIN. Upper (primary) drive chain should have a minimum of free play without binding. If adjustment is required, loosen the two upper bolts securing engine (1—Fig. 2) to frame and pivot engine forward on lower mounting bolt until slack is removed. Lower (secondary) chain is equipped with a spring-loaded idler roller (12) and adjustment is not required.

BRAKE. The shoe-type brake (6—Fig. 2) is controlled by hand lever (5) and operates directly on centrifugal clutch drum (4). Adjustment is not required. If lever contacts end of slot in cowl, renew the shoe.

TRACK. To check track tension raise rear of machine until track is clear of ground and measure distance between bottom edge of side plate and farthest part of track as shown in Fig. 3. Distance should be approximately 5¼ inches as shown. To adjust track tension, tighten or loosen rear idler adjusting bolts as shown in Fig. 4. Both sides must be adjusted alike.

NOTE: Whenever track tension is adjusted, alignment MUST be checked as outlined in TRACK SERVICE Section of this manual.

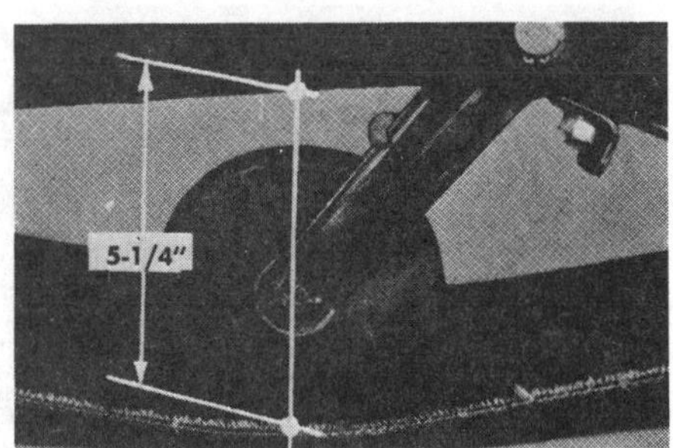

Fig. 3—With rear of machine raised, track should clear side plate by 5¼ inches as shown.

OVERHAUL

Refer to the appropriate paragraphs in the GENERAL SERVICE Sections of this manual for overhaul procedures of vehicle components.

CENTRIFUGAL CLUTCH. A North American, shoe-type centrifugal clutch is used. Clutch is self-energizing when properly assembled but units are built for universal application. Shoes must be installed on clutch hub with drive pins entering notches in trailing edge as shown in Fig. 5.

Fig. 4—Adjust track tension by turning adjusting screws until both sides are equal when measured as shown.

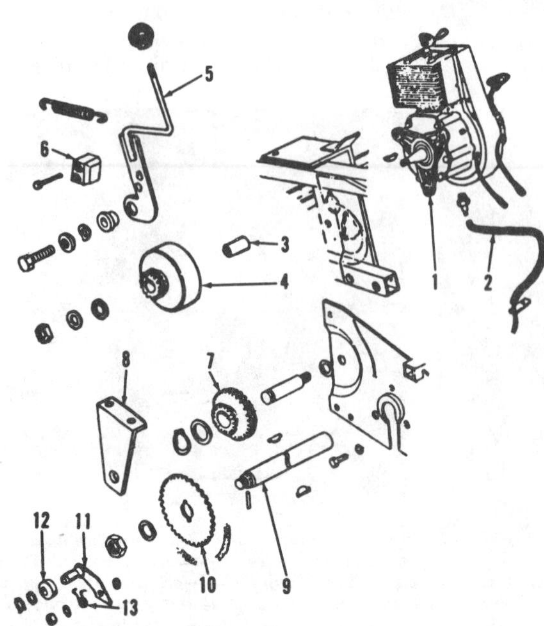

Fig. 2—Exploded view of engine, clutch and dual chain drive used on Sno Cub.

1. Engine
2. Oil bleed line
3. Spacer
4. Centrifugal clutch
5. Brake lever
6. Brake shoe
7. Intermediate sprocket
8. Bracket
9. Drive axle
10. Driven sprocket
11. Idler arm
12. Idler roller
13. Tension spring

Fig. 5—Clutch shoes must be installed with drive pins (P) in trailing edge. Direction of rotation is indicated by arrow.

SNO-FLITE

1968-1969

	Engine			Carburetor				Clutch		
Model	Make	Model	Displ.	Make	Model	Sprocket Ratio	Chain Size	Make	Shaft Center	Belt Number
					1968					
292	JLO	L292	292cc	Tillotson	HR2B	15:33	35-2	Salsbury		702698
297E	JLO	L297	296cc	Tillotson	HR8A	15:33	35-2	Salsbury		702698
298S	Sachs	SA290	297cc	Tillotson	HR8A	15:33	35-2	Salsbury		702698
					1969					
309S	Kohler	K309-1	309cc	Tillotson	HR22A	15:33	35-2	Salsbury 790		K10058
309E	Kohler	K309-1	309cc	Tillotson	HR22A	15:33	35-2	Salsbury 795		K10058
399S	Kohler	K399-2	399cc	Tillotson	HR24A	15:33	35-2	Salsbury 795		K10058
399E	Kohler	K399-2	399cc	Tillotson	HR24A	15:33	35-2	Salsbury 795		K10058
292W	JLO	L292	292cc	Tillotson	HR2B	15:33	35-2	Salsbury 790		K10058

LUBRICATION

The enclosed drive chain housing should be filled to level of check plug with SAE 30 non-detergent engine oil. Spindle shafts are equipped with grease fittings and low-temperature pressure gun grease should be used. Lubricate steering tie rod ends and brake and throttle cables with light machine oil periodically.

Bogie wheels are equipped with sealed ball bearings and lubrication is not required.

ADJUSTMENT

STEERING SKIS AND LINKAGE. Turn handle bar to normal straight driving position and check to see that both skis are parallel with each other and with drive track and vehicle frame. To adjust either tie rod, disconnect the rod at spindle end.

DRIVE CHAIN. The enclosed drive chain should have approximately ¼-inch slack measured midway between sprockets.

Fig. 2—View of drive unit and brake.

A. Brake adjustment nut
B. Bracket bolts
C. Chain case cover

On 1968 models, chain deflection can be measured after removing upper inspection cover (C—Fig. 2). If adjustment is required, slightly loosen the three bolts securing upper drive shaft bearing housing to chain case and move housing upward, being careful not to damage the rubber gasket.

On later models, chain tension is controlled by an idler mounted on adjusting plate (1—Fig. 3). Chain deflection cannot be directly measured. To check the tension, observe the backlash, measured at outer rim of driven sheave. Backlash should be ¼-inch; to adjust, loosen the three clamping stud nuts and turn adjusting plate (1) counter-clockwise until adjustment is correct.

Fig. 3—View of chain case on 1969 model showing idler adjusting plate (1) and oil level plug (2).

Fig. 4—To adjust the track, loosen mounting bolts (A) and turn adjusting screw (B).

BRAKE. The caliper type brake uses the driven sheave fixed face as a braking surface as shown in Fig. 2. The caliper unit floats on its bracket and is self aligning. Bracket can be repositioned if necessary by loosening attaching bolts (B). Adjust the brake by tightening or loosening the castellated nut (A).

TRACK. To adjust track tension, raise rear of vehicle until track is clear of ground. With load removed, there should be some clearance between center bogie wheels and track inner surface. To adjust track tension, loosen the two clamp bolts (A—Fig. 4) on each side of machine and turn adjusting screw (B).

NOTE: When track tension is adjusted, alignment MUST be checked as outlined in TRACK SERVICE Section of this manual.

OVERHAUL

SKIS AND STEERING. Skis, ski legs (spindles), steering arms and tie rod ends are interchangeable from right to left. Skis are fitted with wear bars which can be installed either end forward if renewal is indicated.

Fig.5—View of track and track carriage.

SNO GHIA

1969

Model	Engine Make	Engine Model	Engine Displ.	Carburetor Make	Carburetor Model	Sprocket Ratio	Chain Size	Clutch Make	Clutch Shaft Center	Belt Number
1969										
Sno Ghia	Sachs	SA290	297cc	Tillotson	HR8A	14:45	35-2	Polaris		26063

SNO JET

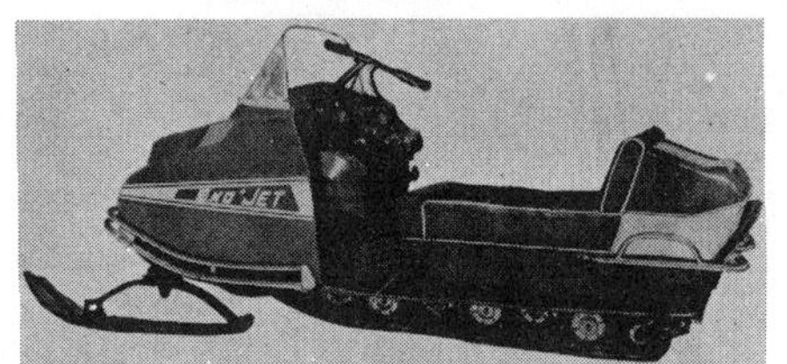

1966-1972

Model	Engine Make	Engine Model	Engine Displ.	Carburetor Make	Carburetor Model	Sprocket Ratio	Chain Size	Clutch Make	Clutch Shaft Center	Belt Number
1966										
Standard	Hirth	54R	300cc	Tillotson	HR3A	11:27	40	Own	10½	050181
1967										
Standard	Hirth	55R	300cc	Tillotson	HR8A	11:27	40	Own	10½	050181
Deluxe	Hirth	55R	300cc	Tillotson	HR8A	11:27	40	Own	10½	050181
1968										
15 Standard	Hirth	55R	300cc	Tillotson	HR8A	11:27	40	Own	10½	050181
17½ Deluxe	Hirth	190R	300cc	Tillotson	HR8A	11:27	40	Own	10½	050181
20 Deluxe	Hirth	160R	372cc	Tillotson	HD7AX	12:27	40	Own	10½	050181
30 Deluxe	Hirth	170R	600cc	Tillotson	HD7AX	13:27	40	Own	10½	050181
1969										
150	Hirth	55R	330cc	Tillotson	HR8A	11:27	40	Own	10½	050181
175	Hirth	191R	300cc	Tillotson	HR8A	11:27	40	Own	10½	050181
190	Hirth	191R	300cc	Tillotson	HR8A	11.27	40	Own	10½	050181
230	Hirth	200R	372cc	Tillotson	HD13A	12:37	40	Own	10½	050181
300	Hirth	170R	600cc	Tillotson	HD13A	13:27	40	Own	10½	050181
350	Hirth	171R	634cc	Tillotson	HD13A	13:27	40	Own	10½	050181
1970										
Jetflite	Hirth	82R	246cc	Tillotson	HR18A	10:27	40	Own	10½	050181
Jetstar	Hirth	193R	292cc	Tillotson	HR18A	11:27	40	Own	10½	050181
Super Sport	Hirth	194R	338cc	Tillotson	HD14A	11:27	40	Own	10½	050181
Super Sport	Sachs	SA340	336cc	Tillotson	HD14A	11:27	40	Own	10½	050181
Super Sport	Yamaha	802	348cc	Tillotson	HR35A	11:27	40	Own	10½	050183
Super Sport	Hirth	220R	493cc	Tillotson	HD14A	17:37	35-2	Own	10½	050180
Super Sport	Hirth	171R	634cc	Tillotson	HD14A	17:35	35-2	Own	10½	050180
Super Jet	Yamaha	808	338cc	Tillotson	HD14A	17:37	35-2	Own	10½	050183
Super Jet	Yamaha	809	396cc	Tillotson	HD78A	17:37	35-2	Own	10½	050183
Super Jet	Hirth	210R	399cc	Tillotson	HD14A	17:37	35-2	Own	10½	050180
Super Jet	Hirth	220R	493cc	Tillotson	HD14A	17:37	35-2	Own	10½	050180
Super Jet	Hirth	171R	634cc	Tillotson	HD14A	15:37	35-2	Own	10½	050180
1971										
62H	Hirth	193R	292cc	Tillotson	HR18A	10:27	40	Own	10½	050181
42Y	Yamaha	SL292	292cc	Tillotson	HR35A	16:37	35-2	Own	10½	050253
46H	Hirth	194R	338cc	Tillotson	HD14A	16:37	35-2	Own	10½	050181
44Y	Yamaha	SL338B	338cc	Tillotson	HD14A	16:37	35-2	Own	10½	050253
68YSS	Yamaha	SS292	292cc	Tillotson	HD14A	16:37	35-2	Own	10½	050253
71YSS	Yamaha	SS433	433cc	Tillotson	HR35A(2)	19:37	35-2	Own	10½	050253
72YSW	Yamaha	SW396	396cc	Tillotson	HD78A	17:37	35-2	Own	10½	050253
54Y	Yamaha	SL396	396cc	Tillotson	HD78A	17:37	35-2	Own	10½	050253
58Y	Yamaha	SW396	396cc	Tillotson	HD78A	17:37	35-2	Own	10½	050253
52H	Hirth	171R	634cc	Tillotson	HD14A	21:37		Own	10½	050180
1972										
Star Jet 292	Hirth	193R	292cc	Tillotson	HR18A	11:27	40	Own	10½	050181
Star Jet 292	Yamaha	Y292	292cc	Tillotson	HR35A	11:27	40	Own	10½	050399
Star Jet +2	Yamaha	Y338	338cc	Tillotson	HD14A	15:37	35-2	Own	10½	050399
SS'T S292	Yamaha	S292	292cc	Tillotson	HD14A	15:37	35	Own	10½	050399
SS'T S338	Yamaha	S338	338cc	Tillotson	HD78A	16:37	35-2	Own	10½	050399
SS'T S433	Yamaha	S433	433cc	Tillotson	HD78A	18:37	35-2	Own	10½	050399
SS'T Y433	Yamaha	Y433	433cc	Tillotson	HD78A	18:37	35-2	Own	10½	050399

LUBRICATION

The engine is lubricated by oil mixed with the fuel. The vehicle manufacturer recommends a ratio of 20:1 for the first one or two fills and 25:1 after engine is broken in. Two cycle motor oil and regular gasoline are recommended. If special oil is used, mix according to oil manufacturer's recommendations.

Front and rear track axles and intermediate drive shaft bearings should be lubricated each 20 hours with SNO JET GREASE or other low temperature grease. Bogie wheels should be lubricated (SNO JET GREASE) each 75 hours.

NOTE. Do not over-lubricate bearings on track and intermediate drive shaft. If bearing seals are damaged, grease will be thrown out on track, drive belt and brake.

Chain case should be filled to proper level with a low temperature, semi-fluid lubricant. On 1969 models, level should be even with lube fitting. Remove fitting to check the level, then fill with pump gun if necessary.

Lightly coat sliding surfaces of torque converter sheaves with Lubriplate or similar grease once a week, being careful lubricant does not get on belt or friction faces of sheaves.

Use light oil on steering linkage, controls and other parts as required for proper operation.

ADJUSTMENT

STEERING SKIS. Steering skis should be parallel with each other and with vehicle frame when handle bar is in normal straight driving position. To adjust either tie rod, back off locknut and turn rod until adjustment is correct.

DRIVE CHAIN. Drive chain deflection should be ¼-inch measured midway between sprockets. To adjust the chain on early models tighten adjusting screw (A—Fig. 1) until resistance is felt; then back off one complete turn.

On 1970 models, chain adjusting screw is at (A—Fig. 2) and chain tension can be checked through inspection plug port (P).

BRAKE. Brake should fully apply before lever contacts handlebar. To adjust the brake on models before 1969, loosen set screw in cable clamp (B—Fig. 1) and reposition cable clamp. 1969 models are equipped with disc brake which uses fixed half of torque converter driven sheave as friction surface. To adjust the brake, remove the cotter pin from brake cam mounting stud and turn the castellated nut until pad clearance is removed, then back off ½ turn. If brake action is still not satisfactory, realign brake unit with friction surface. Refer to BRAKES paragraph of TRACK DRIVE Section of this manual for additional information.

TRACK. To adjust track tension, raise rear of machine until track is clear of ground, then measure distance (A—Fig. 3). Distance (A) should be 2⅞-3⅛ inches and equal on both sides. Adjust by loosening clamp bolts (1) and turning adjusting screw (2).

NOTE: When track tension is adjusted, alignment MUST be checked as outlined in TRACK SERVICE section of this manual.

OVERHAUL

Refer to the appropriate paragraphs in GENERAL SERVICE Sections of this manual for overhaul procedures of vehicle components.

Fig. 1—Adjustment bolt (A) is used to adjust drive chain tension. Reposition cable clamp (B) to adjust the brake.

Fig. 2—View of gearcase and associated parts used on 1970 models. Chain adjusting screw is at (A) and inspection port plug at (P).

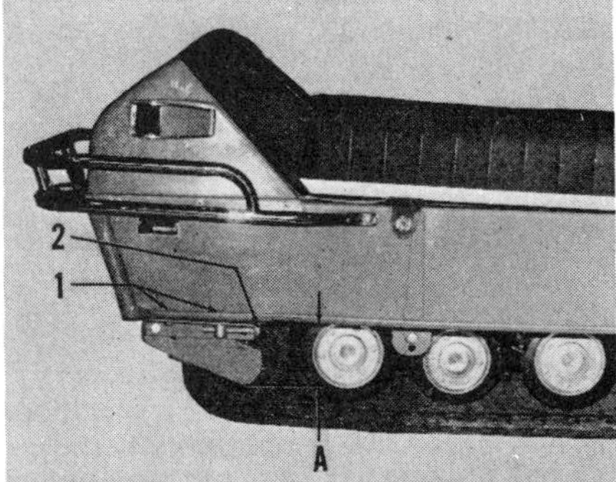

Fig. 3—With track clear of ground, distance (A) should measure 2⅞-3⅛ inches. Adjust by loosening clamp bolts (1) and turning adjusting screw (2).

SNO JET

1973-1976

Model	Engine Make	Engine Model	Engine Displ.	Carburetor Make	Carburetor Model	Sprocket Ratio	Chain Size	Clutch Make	Clutch Shaft Center	Belt Number
1973										
Star Jet 292	Yamaha	Y292	292cc	Tillotson	HR130A	11:27	40	Own	10½	050399
Star Jet 338	Yamaha	Y338	338cc	Tillotson	HD106A	15:37	35-2	Own	10½	050399
Star Jet 433	Yamaha	Y433	433cc	Tillotson	HD106A		35-2	Own	10½	050399
SST 295	Yamaha	S292	292cc	Keihin	CD42	15:37	35-2	Own	10½	050399
SST 340	Yamaha	S338	338cc	Keihin	CD42	16:37	35-2	Own	10½	050399
SST 440	Yamaha	S433	433cc	Keihin	CD42	18:37	35-2	Own	10½	050399
Whisper Jet	Yamaha	Y433	433cc	Bendix	1612	18:36	35-2	Yamaha	10½	050253
1974										
Strato Jet	Hirth	193RO3	295cc	Tillotson	HR153A	11:27	40	Yamaha	10½	050181
Astro Jet 295	Yamaha	Y295	292cc	Tillotson	HR158A	11:27	40	Yamaha	10½	050399
Astro Jet 340	Yamaha	Y340	338cc	Tillotson	HD132A	16:37	35-2	Yamaha	10½	050399
Astro Jet 440	Yamaha	Y440	433cc	Tillotson	HD132A	18:36	35-2	Yamaha	10½	050399
Astro SS 295	Yamaha	Y295	292cc	Tillotson	HR158A	17:37	35-2	Yamaha	10½	050399
Astro SS 340	Yamaha	Y340	338cc	Tillotson	HD132A	18:36	35-2	Yamaha	10½	050399
Astro SS 440	Yamaha	Y440	433cc	Tillotson	HD132A	19:34	35-2	Yamaha	10½	050399
SST 295	Yamaha	S295	292cc	Keihin	CD42	17:37	35-2	Yamaha	10½	050399
SST 340	Yamaha	S340	338cc	Keihin	CD42	18:36	35-2	Yamaha	10½	050399
SST 440	Yamaha	S440	433cc	Keihin	CD42	19:34	35-2	Yamaha	10½	050399
Sabre Jet	Yamaha	S440	433cc	Keihin	SD42	19:36	35-2	Yamaha	10½	050399
Whisper Jet	Yamaha	Y440	433cc	Bendix	1612	18:36	35-2	Yamaha	10½	050399
1975										
Astro Jet	Yamaha	Y295	292cc	Tillotson	HR158A	17:37	35-2	Yamaha	10½	050399
Astro SS	Yamaha	Y340	338cc	Mikuni	VM32	18:37	35-2	Yamaha	10½	050717
SST Fan	Yamaha	S440	433cc	Keihin		19:36	35-2	Yamaha	10½	050717
SST F/A 340	Yamaha	SX340	338cc	Mikuni	VM32	20:36	35-2	Arctic	10½	050655
SST F/A 440	Yamaha	SX440	433cc	Mikuni	VM36	21:34	35-2	Arctic	10½	050655
Whisper Jet	Yamaha	Y440	433cc	Bendix		18:37	35-2	Yamaha	10½	050253
Astro SS	Yamaha	Y440	433cc	Bendix		19:36	35-2	Yamaha	10½	050717
1976										
Astro Jet	Yamaha	Y295	292cc	Tillotson	HR	17:37	35-2	Yamaha	10.3	050399
Astro SS	Yamaha	Y340	338cc	Mikuni	VM34	18:37	35-2	Yamaha	10.5	...
SST F/C	Yamaha	S440	433cc	...	...	...	..	Own	...	...

LUBRICATION

The engine is lubricated by oil mixed with the fuel. Use regular gasoline on Hirth powered machines and premium gasoline on Yamaha powered units. Gasoline should be mixed at a ratio of 20:1 with a recognized Snowmobile Oil or other high quality Air-Cooled Two-Cycle motor oil.

The enclosed chaincase should be filled to oil level plug (L—Fig. 1) with Sno-Jet Chain Lubricant or equivalent. Case may be filled through inspection plug opening (I) if required.

Bogie wheels (when so equipped), rear idler shaft and right-hand bearing of track drive shaft are equipped with pressure gun fittings. Lubricate with two shots of low temperature grease each 25 hours or oftener under wet, sloppy conditions.

Other friction parts should be lubricated with light oil as needed for proper operation or to prevent rust or wear.

ADJUSTMENT

STEERING SKIS. Steering skis should be parallel with each other and with vehicle frame when handlebar is in normal straight driving position. One-half inch toe-in, measured at tips of skis, is recommended. Adjustment of either rod can be made by loosening jam nuts and turning center section.

DRIVE CHAIN. The enclosed drive chain should have ¼-inch deflection measured through inspection plug hole (I—Fig. 1). To adjust the chain, loosen the three cap screws securing bearing housing to chaincase and the jam nut on adjusting screw (A); then turn adjusting screw in or out as required to obtain correct chain tension. Tighten

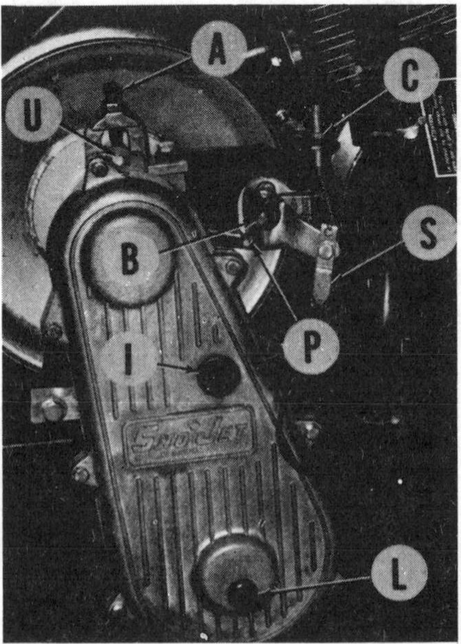

A. Adjusting screw
B. Brake wear adjustment
C. Cable housing anchor nuts
I. Inspection plug
L. Fluid level plug
P. Stop pin
S. Brake light switch
U. Upper housing bolt

Fig. 1—View of chaincase and associated parts showing details of construction and points of adjustment and inspection.

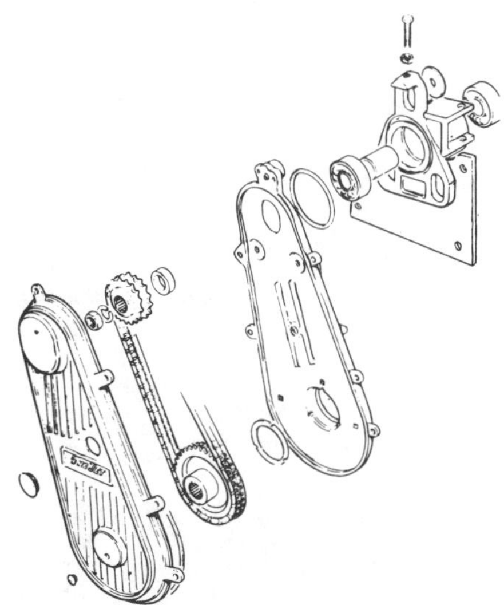

Fig. 2—Exploded view of chaincase showing component parts.

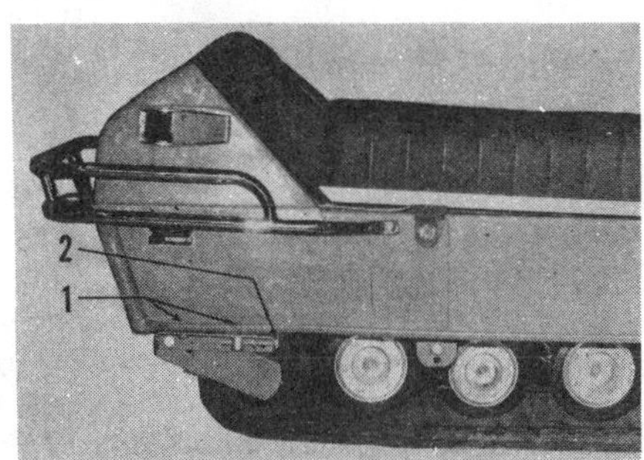

Fig. 3—To adjust track tension, loosen clamp bolts (1) and turn adjusting screw (2). Both sides must be adjusted alike.

upper cap screw (U) first, then the two lower screws, when adjustment is complete.

BRAKE. When hand brake lever is released, actuating cam lever should contact stop pin (P—Fig. 1) and push pins should rest in valleys of actuating cam. Reposition if necessary at brake cable housing anchor nuts (C).

Make wear adjustment by turning actuating lever stud nut (B) until brake fully applies when hand lever has moved through about half its travel. Brake must fully release when lever is released. Caliper unit must correctly align with friction surface of driven sheave. In cases of incorrect alignment, check for a bent pivot bracket or wear in pivot bolt and/or bracket. Some units are equipped with self-adjusting mechanical brakes.

TRACK. To adjust track tension, raise rear of machine until track is clear. Bottom of track at center should sag ¾-1 inch below center bogie wheel. Adjust by loosening clamp bolts (1—Fig. 3) and turning adjusting screw. On models with Arctic Cat slide suspension, refer to ARCTIC CAT Vehicle Section for adjustment procedure.

NOTE: When track tension is adjusted, alignment MUST be checked as outlined in TRACK SERVICE Section of this manual.

OVERHAUL

DRIVE. Drive clutch is Yamaha built but driven pulley unit is manufactured by Sno-Jet Inc. Pre-load the driven pulley cam spring ⅓-turn (one cam) when reassembling.

The asymmetric lugged "Positrac" should be installed with vertical edge toward front of machine as shown in Fig. 5.

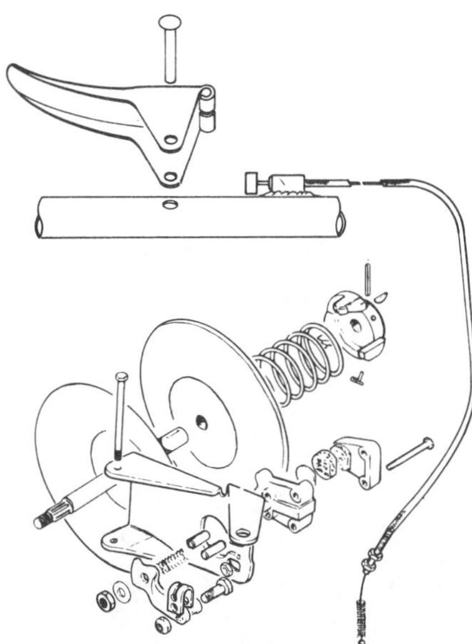

Fig. 4—Exploded view of driven pulley and brake showing component parts.

Fig. 5—On models with "Positrac" tread, vertical edge of cleats should be toward direction of MACHINE travel as shown.

SNO-PAC
1970-1972

Model	Engine Make	Engine Model	Engine Displ.	Carburetor Make	Carburetor Model	Sprocket Ratio	Chain Size	Clutch Make	Clutch Shaft Center	Belt Number
					1970					
S295W	Kohler	K295-1	294cc	Tillotson	HR	10:26	40	Salsbury 780	10½	3045
T399W	Kohler	K399-2	399cc	Tillotson	HR	13:26	40	Salsbury 780	10½	3045
T634W	Hirth	171R	634cc	Tillotson	HD (2)	15:26	40	Salsbury 780	10½	3045
					1971					
SCAT-20	Kohler	K295-1	294cc	Tillotson	HR	10:26	40	Salsbury 780	10½	2050
SCAT-26	Kohler	K399-2	399cc	Tiilotson	HR	13:26	40	Salsbury 780	10½	2050
Pacer-25	Kohler	K340-2	338cc	Walbro	WD	13:26	40	Salsbury 780	10½	2050
Pacer-28	Kohler	K399-2	399cc	Walbro	WD	13:26	40	Salsbury 780	10½	2050
Coyote	Kohler	K440-2	437cc	Walbro	WD	19:35	35-2	Salsbury 780	10½	2050
					1972					
Mavrik	JLO	L230	223cc	Tillotson	HR	11:26	40	Salsbury 780	10½	SV-132
Mavrik	JLO	LR340 2	339cc	Tillotson	HR	13:26	40	Salsbury 780	10½	SV-132
Pacer	JLO	LR340 2	339cc	Walbro	WD	13:26	40	Salsbury 780	10½	2050
Pacer	JLO	LR440 2	428cc	Walbro	WD	19:35	35-2	Salsbury 780	10½	2050
Timberline	JLO	LR340 2	339cc	Walbro	WD	13:26	40	Salsbury 780	10½	2050
Timberline	JLO	LR440 2	428cc	Walbro	WD	19:35	35-2	Salsbury 780	10½	2050
Coyote	JLO	LR440 2	428cc	Walbro	WD	19:35	35-2	Salsbury 780	10½	2050

LUBRICATION

The engine is lubricated by oil mixed with the fuel. Regular gasoline and a good SNOWMOBILE Oil should be used at a ratio of 20:1.

On all models chain case should contain SAE 80 Gear Lube to just cover chain at bottom of case. Lubricant can be checked and fluid added after removing lower chaincase cover.

Drive train and track suspension is equipped with self-aligning, sealed bearings which do not require lubrication.

On all models the intermediate shaft (jackshaft) bearing housing is equipped with a pressure gun fitting. Lubricate every 20 hours with low temperature or general purpose grease.

Fig. 1—View of intermediate shaft and chaincase showing points of adjustment.

A. Lower cover
B. Upper cover
C. Locknut
D. Adjusting bolt

ADJUSTMENT

STEERING SKIS. Steering Skis should be parallel with each other and with vehicle frame when handle bar is in normal straight driving position. Adjust both tie rods equally by loosening locknuts and turning center section.

DRIVE CHAIN. The enclosed drive chain should have approximately ¼-inch free play measured midway between sprockets. To adjust the chain, loosen nut (C—Fig. 1) and move adjusting bolt (D) down to tighten chain or up to loosen chain.

BRAKE. Make minor wear adjustment by turning brake cable housing anchor nuts, or major adjustment by loosening cable end stop clamp screw and moving stop up cable for added braking action.

TRACK. With rear of machine raised so track is clear, track should clear center bogie by ¼ to ½ inch.

To adjust track tension refer to Fig. 3. Loosen clamp screws (B) and turn adjusting screws (C). On all models, adjust both sides alike.

NOTE: Whenever track tension has been adjusted, alignment MUST be checked as outlined in TRACK SERVICE Section of this manual.

OVERHAUL

Refer to the appropriate paragraphs in the GENERAL SERVICE Sections of this manual for overhaul procedures of vehicle components.

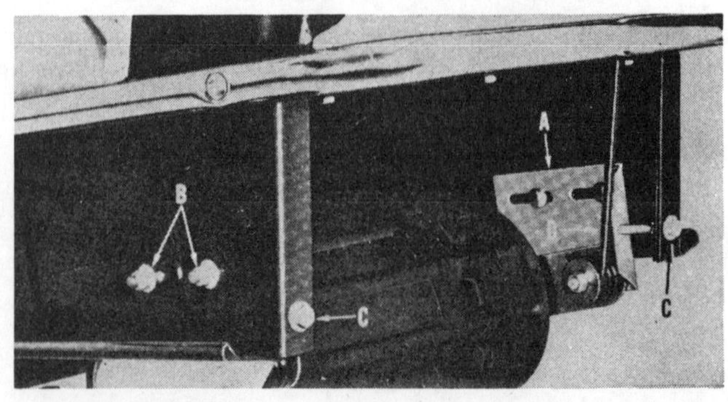

Fig. 3—To adjust track tension on some models, loosen clamp nuts (B) and turn adjusting screws (C). Brackets are shown at (A) and torsion spring at (D).

SNO-PONY

1969-1971

Model	Engine Make	Engine Model	Engine Displ.	Carburetor Make	Carburetor Model	Sprocket Ratio	Chain Size	Clutch Make	Clutch Shaft Center	Belt Number
					1969					
Colt	Chrysler	8200	134cc	Tillotson	HL135	9:36	35-2	Salsbury 500	8½	900391
Pony	Chrysler	8200	134cc	Tillotson	HL135	9:36	35-2	Salsbury 500	8½	900391
Express	Chrysler	8200	134cc	Tillotson	HL135	9:36	35-2	Salsbury 500	8½	900391
Super Express	JLO	L227	223cc	Tillotson	HR19A	9:36	35-2	Salsbury 500	10½	900392
					1970					
Mach I	Chrysler	8200	134cc	Tillotson	HL135	9:36	35-2	Salsbury 500	8½	900391
Mach II	Solo	206	180cc	Tillotson	HR19A	9:36	35-2	Salsbury 500	8½	900391
Mach III	Solo	209	220cc	Tillotson	HR19A	9:36	35-2	Salsbury 500	8½	900391
Super Express	JLO	L230	223cc	Tillotson	HR19A	9:36	35-2	Salsbury 500	8½	900391
Super Express	McCul.	101 (2 eng.)	296cc	McCulloch		12:36	35-2	Salsbury 500	10¼	900392
					1971					
180	Solo	206	180cc	Tillotson	HR19A	9:36	35-2	Salsbury 500	8½	SV-103
220	Solo	209	220cc	Tillotson	HR19A	10:36	35-2	Salsbury 500	8½	SV-103
295R	JLO	L295	292cc	Tillotson	HD13A	16:36	35-2	Salsbury 500	10½	SV-132
340 Twin	JLO	LR340/2	339cc	Tillotson	HD69A	17:36	35-2	Salsbury 500	10½	SV-132

LUBRICATION

The engine is lubricated by oil mixed with the fuel. Use SAE 40 Two Cycle Oil and regular gasoline at a ratio of 25:1.

The enclosed drive chain case should contain approximately 1 cup (8-10 oz.) of low temperature grease. Turn machine on right side and remove chain case cover to check and/or add lubricant.

Drive train and track are equipped with self-aligning sealed type bearings and do not require lubrication.

ADJUSTMENT

STEERING SKIS. Some models are equipped with a center king pin (Fig. 1) and transverse spring (Tension Bar—Fig. 2). Adjust tie rod if necessary until handle bar is properly positioned when skis point straight ahead; then use a carpenters square as shown in Fig. 2 to align the skis as required.

On models with two king pins (ski legs), adjust the two tie rods equally until skis are parallel.

DRIVE CHAIN. The roller drive chain should have a free play of ¼-½ inch measured midway between sprockets. To adjust the chain, loosen the two locking cap screws (1—Fig. 3) in bearing housing and moving bolts forward (direction of arrow) to tighten chain; or rearward to loosen chain.

BRAKE. To adjust the shoe-type brake, loosen the jam nut (1—Fig. 4)

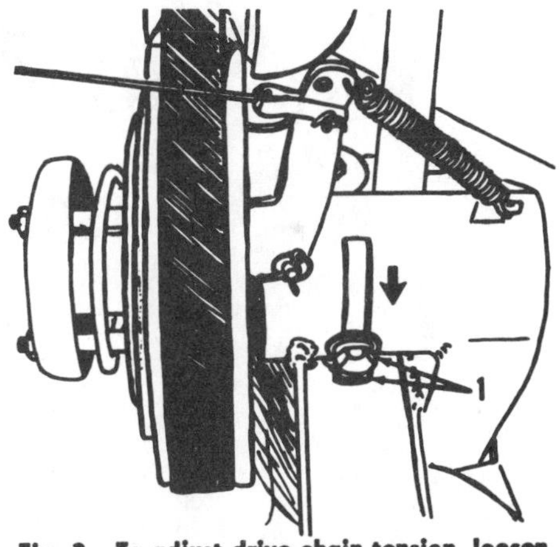

Fig. 3—To adjust drive chain tension, loosen the two locking screws (1). Move in direction of arrow to tighten.

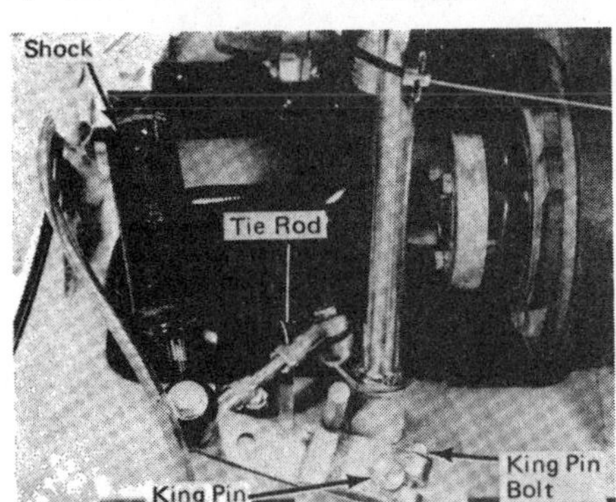

Fig. 1—On models with center king pin, handle bar is centered with skis by adjusting tie rod length.

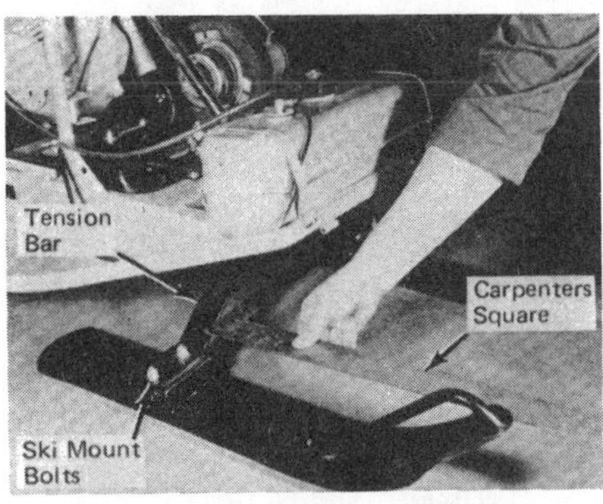

Fig. 2—On models with transverse spring (Tension Bar) use carpenter's square to align skis. Loosen ski mount bolts to adjust.

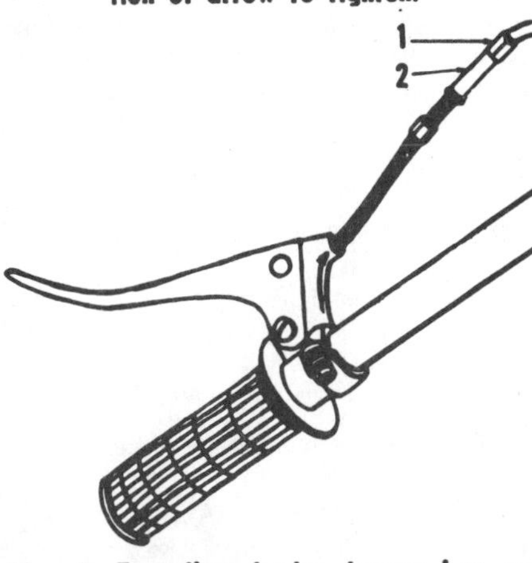

Fig. 4—To adjust brake, loosen jam nut (1) and turn adjusting sleeve (2).

Fig. 5—To adjust track tension, loosen bracket bolts and turn tension adjusting screw. Refer to text.

on control cable housing and turn adjusting sleeve (2) as required until brake is fully applied before lever contacts handle bar grip but does not drag when lever is released.

TRACK. To adjust track tension, raise rear of machine until track is clear of ground. With no weight on track, lower edge should have 2½-3 inches free play. To adjust the tension loosen the two bracket bolts (Fig. 5) on each side of machine and turn tension adjusting screws an equal amount for each bracket.

NOTE: When track tension has been adjusted, alignment MUST be checked as outlined in the TRACK SERVICE Section of this manual.

SNOWMOBILE CONVERSION

To prepare the 220C Convertible model for snowmobile use it is necessary to interchange wheel fork (1—Fig. 6) for king bolt and skis; interchange snowmobile short axle for long axle and wheels (2) and remove delta fenders (3).

To interchange wheel fork and ski king pin, remove hood and refer to Fig. 1. Remove king pin bolt and pry off splined center steering arm, then raise front of machine to interchange fork and king pin. Square the skis if necessary, as outlined in ADJUSTMENT Section.

Block up rear of machine. Remove the four axle bracket bolts & nuts (Fig. 5) and tension adjusting screw,

Fig. 6—Convertible Model equipped with wheels. Refer to text for conversion.

1. Wheel fork
2. Rear wheels
3. Delta fenders

then interchange rear axle assemblies. Readjust track tension and alignment as previously outlined, after parts are interchanged. Delta fenders can be removed or installed by removing (or installing) attaching bolts.

OVERHAUL

Refer to the appropriate paragraphs in the GENERAL SERVICE Sections of this manual for overhaul procedures of vehicle components.

SNO-PRINCE

1968-1973

	Engine			Carburetor				Clutch		
Model	Make	Model	Displ.	Make	Model	Sprocket Ratio	Chain Size	Make	Shaft Center	Belt Number
					1968					
A-16	Hirth	54R	300cc	Tillotson	HR3A		40	St. Law.	10½	D-550
A-17	Hirth	190R	300cc	Tillotson	HR8A		40	St. Law.	10½	A-550
E-17	Hirth	160R	372cc	Tillotson	HD7A		40	St. Law.	10½	A-550
					1969					
A-18	Hirth	191R	300cc	Tillotson	HR8		40	St. Law.	10½	0923303
A-28	Lloyd	LS400	386cc	Tillotson	HR26A		40	St. Law.	10½	0923303
K-28	Hirth	171R	634cc	Tillotson	HD13A			St. Law.	10½	0923303
					1970					
Blizzard	Sachs	SA280A	277cc	Tillotson	HL252A		40	St. Law.	10½	0923303
Tornado I	Lloyd	LS400	386cc	Tillotson	HR26A			St. Law.	10½	0923303
Tornado II	Hirth	191R	300cc	Tillotson	HR8A			St. Law.	10½	0923303
Cyclone I	Lloyd	LS400	386cc	Tillotson	HR47A			St. Law.	10½	0923303
Cyclone II	Sachs	SA370	368cc	Tillotson	HD26A			St. Law.	10½	0923303
Cyclone III	Hirth	200R	372cc	Tillotson	HD26A			St. Law.	10½	0923305
Hurricane I	Hirth	200R	372cc	Tillotson	HD26A			St. Law.	10½	0923305
Hurricane II	Hirth	220R	493cc	Keihin	407			St. Law.	10½	0923304
					1971					
XL-300-S	Sachs	SA280A	277cc	Tillotson	HL252A		35-2	St. Law.	10½	0923303
XL-300-J	JLO	L295	292cc	Tillotson	HR102A		35-2	St. Law.	10½	0923303
XL-340	Hirth	194R	338cc	Tillotson	HD65A		35-2	St. Law.	10½	0923303
XLS-340/2	Lloyd	LS-400	386cc	Tillotson	HR47A		35-2	St. Law.	10½	0923303
XL-400	JLO	LR399/2	398cc	Tillotson	HD65A		35-2	St. Law.	10½	0923307
GTS-340	Hirth	200R2	372cc	Tillotson	HD26A		35-2	St. Law.	10½	0923307
GT-400	JLO	LR399/2	398cc	Tillotson	HD25A		35-2	St. Law.	10½	0923307
GT-500	Hirth	220R4	493cc	Tillotson	HD25A		35-2	St. Law.	10½	0923308
GT-640	Hirth	171R	634cc	Tillotson	HD25A		35-2	St. Law.	10½	0923308

Model	Engine Make	Engine Model	Displ.	Carburetor Make	Carburetor Model	Sprocket Ratio	Chain Size	Clutch Make	Shaft Center	Belt Number
1972										
JR-230	JLO	L230	223cc	Tillotson				St. Law.	10½	0923309
XL-300	JLO	L295	292cc	Tillotson			35-2	St. Law.	10½	0923307
XL-340	Hirth	194R	338cc	Tillotson			35-2	St. Law.	10½	0923308
XL-400	JLO	LR399/2	398cc	Tillotson			35-2	St. Law.	10½	0923308
GT-400	JLO	LR399/2	398cc	Tillotson			35-2	St. Law.	10½	0923308
1973										
XL	Hirth	261R	292cc				35-2	St. Law.	10½	0923307
SST340	Hirth	260R	338cc				35-2	St. Law.	10½	0923303
SST440	Hirth	270R	438cc				35-2	St. Law.	10½	0923307

LUBRICATION

The engine is lubricated by oil mixed with the fuel. The manufacturer recommends a good grade of regular gasoline and a recognized SNOWMOBILE Oil at the ratio of 20:1 for JLO engines, 25:1 for HIRTH & SACHS engines or 40:1 for LLOYD.

The enclosed chain case should contain 19 oz. of fluid grease such as IMPERIAL MARVELUBE EP9F or equivalent.

NOTE: Grease can run out when chaincase cover is removed. Tip machine on right side and remove wingnuts (W–Fig. 1) then lift off cover to check lubricant or chain. Be sure gasket is in good condition and properly positioned when cover is reinstalled.

The tapered roller bearings carrying the driven sheave and drive sprocket should be lubricated with a grease gun and low temperature grease every 25 hours.

Use low temperature grease and grease gun to lubricate front and rear axle bearings every 25 hours and fittings on bogie wheels every 40 hours. Lubricate axle bearings and bogie wheels more often when operating in slush.

Ski legs are equipped with oilite bearings and do not require regular lubrication, however, area between the bearings should be packed with low temperature grease yearly.

Leaf springs, shackle joints and steering mechanism should be lubricated periodically as necessary.

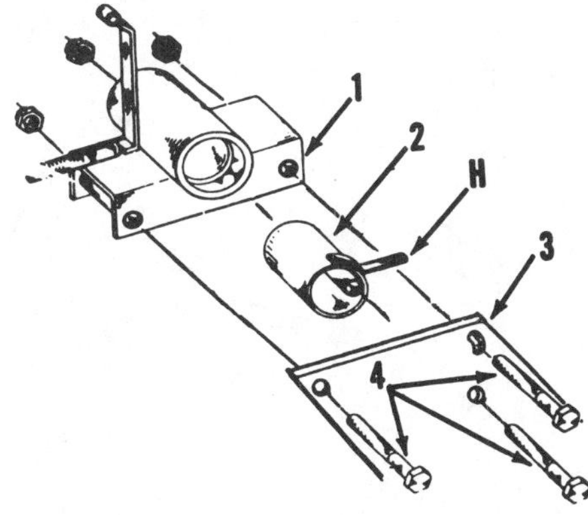

Fig. 2—Exploded view of driven sheave bearing housing showing method of chain adjustment.

H. Adjusting handle
1. Bearing housing
2. Eccentric
3. Main frame
4. Attaching bolts

ADJUSTMENT

STEERING SKIS. Turn handle bar to normal straight driving position and check to see that both skis are parallel with each other and with vehicle frame. Up to ⅛-inch toe-in is permissible. To adjust the skis disconnect tie rod at either end.

DRIVE CHAIN. The drive chain should have ¼-inch free play. If adjustment is required on 1968 models, loosen the three bolts (4–Fig. 2) and push down eccentric handle (H) until adjustment is correct. Tighten bolts securely.

On 1969 models, loosen clamp bolt (A–Fig. 3) and turn chain adjusting screws (C) after loosening the locknuts.

If adjustment is required on 1971 XL or GT models, refer to Fig. 4. Loosen clamp bolt (A) and the two jam nuts (B), and turn the headless adjusting screws

Fig. 4—To adjust chain tension, loosen clamp nut (A) and jam nuts (B), then turn adjusting screws (C) with an Allen wrench as shown.

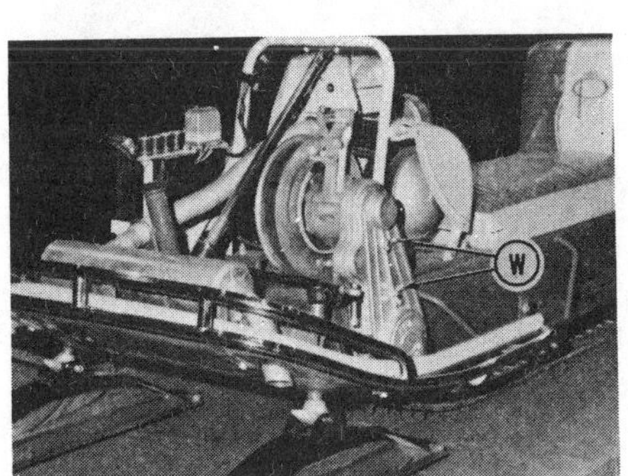

Fig. 1—Chain case cover can be removed after removing wing nuts (W). Tip machine to right to prevent grease loss.

Fig. 3—View of chain case and drive assembly showing points of adjustment.

A. Clamp bolt
B. Brake adjustment
C. Chain adjusting screws
H. Brake housing anchor

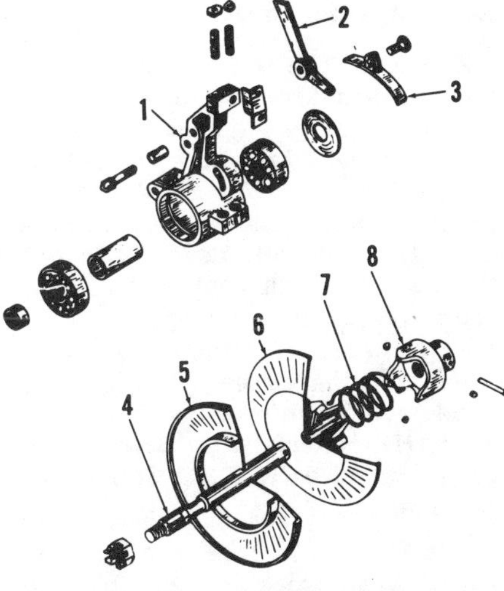

Fig. 5—Intermediate shaft housing and associated parts used on 1971 models and later XL and GT units.

1. Housing
2. Brake arm
3. Brake shoe
4. Shaft
5. Fixed pulley half
6. Sliding half
7. Torque spring
8. Cam

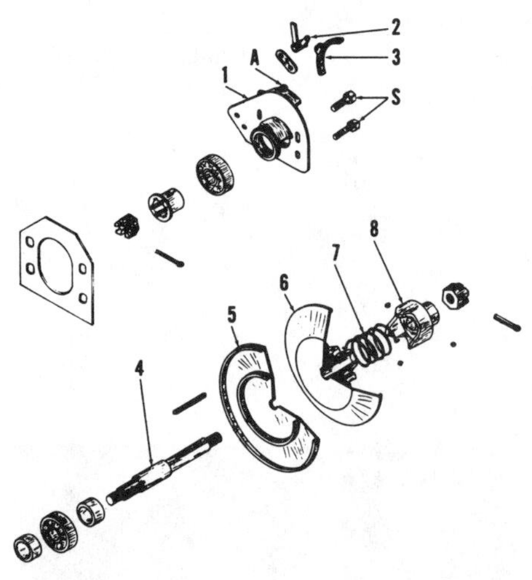

Fig. 6—Exploded view of intermediate shaft and associated parts used on SST. Refer to Fig. 5 for parts identification except for (A) which is chain adjusting screw and (S) which are housing attaching screws.

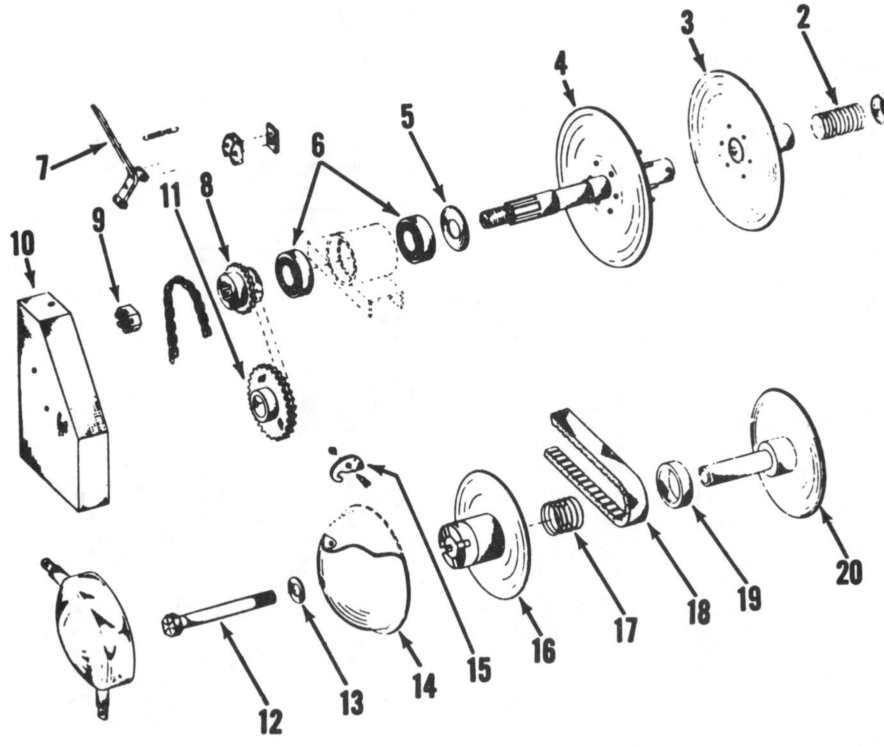

Fig. 7—Exploded view of torque converter and drive assembly showing component parts.

1. Retainer	6. Roller bearings	11. Driven sprocket	16. Moveable face
2. Spring	7. Brake arm	12. Bolt	17. Spring
3. Moveable face	8. Drive sprocket	13. Taper washer	18. Drive belt
4. Fixed face	9. Adjusting nut	14. Governor cover	19. Idler bearing
5. Oil seal	10. Chain guard	15. Governor weight	20. Fixed face

(C) as shown. Cover should be removed to check the adjustment. On SST models, loosen the four bearing housing attaching screws (S–Fig. 6) and turn adjusting screw (A). JR models have an eccentric bearing housing; chain is adjusted by loosening the adjusting screw and rotating housing in its bore.

PULLEY BEARINGS. The tapered roller bearings which carry the torque converter driven pulley should be adjusted to provide a slight rolling torque. To make the adjustment, remove the cotter pin and turn nut (9—Fig. 7) until adjustment is correct, back off to nearest castellation and reinstall cotter pin.

BRAKE. The shoe-type brake on 1968 models uses the fixed flange of torque converter driven sheave as a friction face. Brake shoe should clear sheave by approximately $\frac{1}{16}$-inch. Adjustment is made at cable housing anchor. Later models use a band brake (B–Fig. 8) which contracts against a drum on torque converter driven sheave. Wear adjustment is made at lever adjusting screw (B–Fig. 3) and hand lever positioning at housing anchor (H). Refer also to BRAKE paragraph in TRACK DRIVE Section of this manual.

TRACK. With rear of machine raised until track is clear, bottom of track should sag ¾-1 inch below center bogie wheel. Adjust by loosening clamp bolts (1–Fig. 9) and turning adjusting screw (2). Both sides must be adjusted alike.

NOTE: Whenever track tension has been adjusted, alignment MUST be checked as outlined in TRACK SERVICE Section of this manual.

OVERHAUL

Refer to the appropriate service section elsewhere in this manual for service on track, track drive and associated parts.

Torque converter belt center distance should be 10½ inches and offset distance should be $1\frac{9}{16}$ inches measured from flat side of fixed faces of both sheaves. On 1969 models with torque sensing driven sheave, pre-load the spring ⅓ to ⅔ additional turn for hilly country or to correct for excessive belt slippage. Tension can be lessened if desired, for flatland operation. Adjust by removing the roll pin which secures the stationary cam and turning the cam the required amount.

Fig. 8—Brake band (B) reacts on drum built on driven sheave.

Fig. 9—To adjust track tension, loosen clamp bolts (1) and turn adjusting screw (2). Refer to text for details.

SNOW BIRDIE

1968

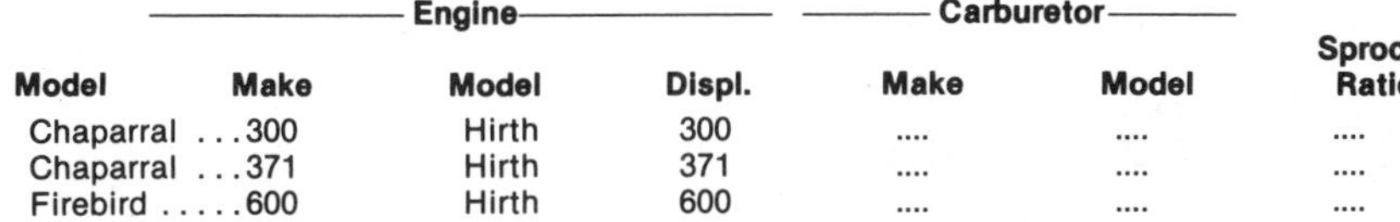

	Engine			Carburetor				Clutch		
Model	Make	Model	Displ.	Make	Model	Sprocket Ratio	Chain Size	Make	Shaft Center	Belt Number
Chaparral	300	Hirth	300	....	....	....	....	....	20¾	....
Chaparral	371	Hirth	371	....	....	....	....	....	10¾	....
Firebird	600	Hirth	600	....	....	....	....	....	10¾	....

LUBRICATION

The engine is lubricated by oil mixed with the fuel. The manufacturer recommends the use of Two Cycle Motor Oil at the ratio of 20:1.

The enclosed chain case should be filled to level of check plug with Automatic Transmission Fluid, Type "A", and should be checked occasionally or when leakage is apparent.

All other parts are self lubricated and require attention only when service is needed.

ADJUSTMENT

STEERING SKIS. With handlebar in normal straight driving position, skis should be parallel with each other and with vehicle frame. Steering arms are splined to spindle and both arms should point straight to rear. Adjust by disconnecting one end of tie rod and turning either end on or off the rod.

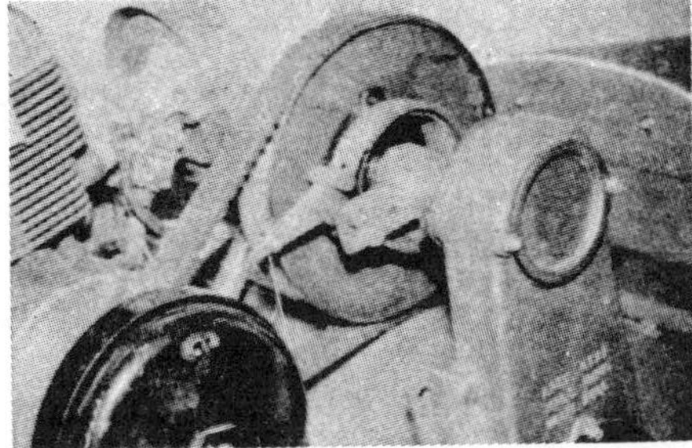

Fig. 2—View of torque converter drive unit, brake & chain case with hood removed.

DRIVE BELT. Correct center distance between torque converter drive and driven sheaves is 10¾ inches. Adjust by sliding engine in mounting plate.

DRIVE CHAIN. Drive chain should have about ½ inch free play. Chain can be inspected by removing chain case inspection cover. Adjust the chain by loosening the stud nuts retaining upper shaft housing to chain case and moving housing in slotted holes.

BRAKE. The band type brake is shown in Fig. 2. Band should just clear drum when brake is released but should fully engage before hand lever contacts handlebar. Adjust by loosening cable clamp at actuating lever and pulling cable through lever.

TRACK. With rear of machine raised so that track is clear of ground, track should have some slack but must not be excessively loose. Adjust by loosening the two screws on each side which secure rear track hanger brackets, then turning adjusting screws until excessive slack is removed. Both sides must be adjusted alike.

NOTE: Whenever track has been adjusted, alignment MUST be checked as outlined in TRACK SERVICE Section of this manual.

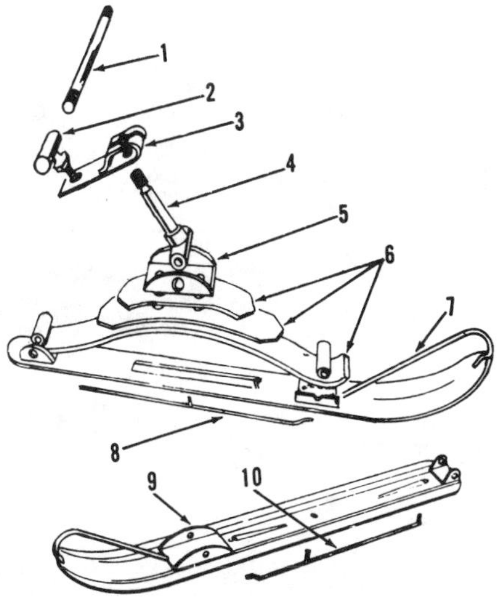

Fig. 3—Exploded view of skis, steering spindle and associated parts. Parts (9 & 10) are special "Rocky Mountain" ski available as an option.

1. Tie rod
2. Tie rod end
3. Steering arm
4. Spindle
5. Hanger
6. Spring
7. Standard ski
8. Standard runner
9. Rocky Mountain ski
10. Ski runner

OVERHAUL

SKIS. Two types of skis are used. The special "Rocky Mountain" ski is wider than the standard ski and the runner is secured by two stud nuts. Refer to Fig. 3. Skis, ski legs and associated parts are interchangeable from right to left.

SNOW BUG

1972-1975

	Engine			Carburetor				Clutch		
Model	Make	Model	Displ.	Make	Model	Sprocket Ratio	Chain Size	Make	Shaft Center	Belt Number
					1972					
Snowbug	Sachs	SA280	277cc	Tillotson				Polaris		1011M
Superbug	Sachs	SA290	293cc	Tillotson	HR18A			Polaris		1011M
Luvbug	Sachs	SA340	338cc	Tillotson	HD14A			Polaris		1011M
					1973					
Snowbug	Sachs	SA280	277cc	Tillotson				Polaris		1011M
Superbug	Sachs	SA290	293cc	Tillotson	HR18A			Polaris		1011M
Luvbug	Sachs	SA340	338cc	Tillotson	HD14A			Polaris		1011M

Model	Engine Make	Engine Model	Engine Displ.	Carburetor Make	Carburetor Model	Sprocket Ratio	Chain Size	Clutch Make	Clutch Shaft Center	Belt Number
					1974					
Snowbug	Sachs	SA290	293cc	Tillotson	HR18A			Polaris	10¾	Dayco
Superbug	Sachs	SA290	293cc	Tillotson	HR18A			Polaris	10¾	Dayco 1268
Luvbug	Sachs	SA2-340	338cc	Tillotson	HD14A			Polaris	10¾	Dayco 1268
					1975					
Snowbug	Sachs	SA290	293cc	Tillotson	HR18A		40	Polaris	10⅞	Dayco 1268
Snowtractor ...	Sachs	SA2-340	338cc	Tillotson	HD14A		50	Comet 100c	10⅞	1974

SNOW CAT

1969

Model	Engine Make	Engine Model	Engine Displ.	Carburetor Make	Carburetor Model	Sprocket Ratio	Chain Size	Clutch Make	Clutch Shaft Center	Belt Number
Mark I	Chrysler	8200	149cc	Tillotson	HL130A	9:36	40	Salsbury	8½	60547
Mark II	Chrysler	8200	149cc	Tillotson	HL130A	9:36	40	Salsbury	8½	60547
Mark II	JLO	L227	223cc	Tillotson		9:36	40	Salsbury	8½	60547

SNOW FLAKE

1970-1973

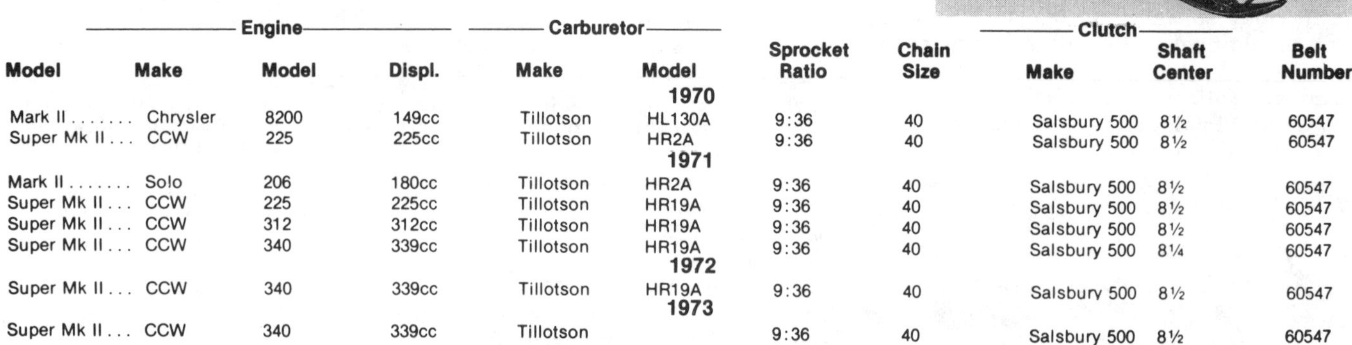

Model	Engine Make	Engine Model	Engine Displ.	Carburetor Make	Carburetor Model	Sprocket Ratio	Chain Size	Clutch Make	Clutch Shaft Center	Belt Number
					1970					
Mark II	Chrysler	8200	149cc	Tillotson	HL130A	9:36	40	Salsbury 500	8½	60547
Super Mk II ...	CCW	225	225cc	Tillotson	HR2A	9:36	40	Salsbury 500	8½	60547
					1971					
Mark II	Solo	206	180cc	Tillotson	HR2A	9:36	40	Salsbury 500	8½	60547
Super Mk II ...	CCW	225	225cc	Tillotson	HR19A	9:36	40	Salsbury 500	8½	60547
Super Mk II ...	CCW	312	312cc	Tillotson	HR19A	9:36	40	Salsbury 500	8½	60547
Super Mk II ...	CCW	340	339cc	Tillotson	HR19A	9:36	40	Salsbury 500	8¼	60547
					1972					
Super Mk II ...	CCW	340	339cc	Tillotson	HR19A	9:36	40	Salsbury 500	8½	60547
					1973					
Super Mk II ...	CCW	340	339cc	Tillotson		9:36	40	Salsbury 500	8½	60547

LUBRICATION

The engine is lubricated by oil mixed with the fuel. The manufacturer recommends regular gasoline and a good motor oil in the ratio of 20:1.

The enclosed drive chain case contains a pressure gun fitting at rear side; lubricate with chassis lube after each 10 hours of operation.

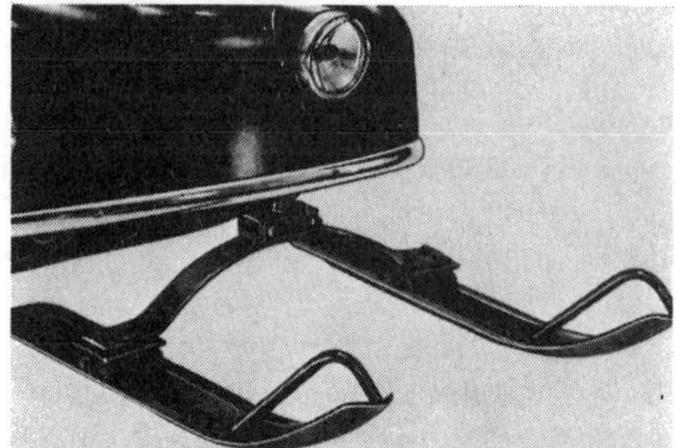

Fig. 2–Mark II models have a single leaf transverse spring as shown.

Drive train and track are equipped with self-aligning, sealed type bearings and do not require lubrication.

ADJUSTMENT

STEERING SKIS. Mark II models have a single leaf, transverse spring which connects the two skis as shown in Fig. 2, and toe-in is fixed. Adjust the drag link until skis are in correct relationship to handlebar in normal driving position.

Super Mark II models are more conventional in construction (Fig. 1). Adjust tie rods until skis are parallel and point straight ahead when handle bar is in normal straight driving position.

DRIVE CHAIN. The roller drive chain should have a free play of 3/16-5/16 inch. Chain tension can be checked after removing cover (1—Fig. 3) by loosening clamp nut on adjusting

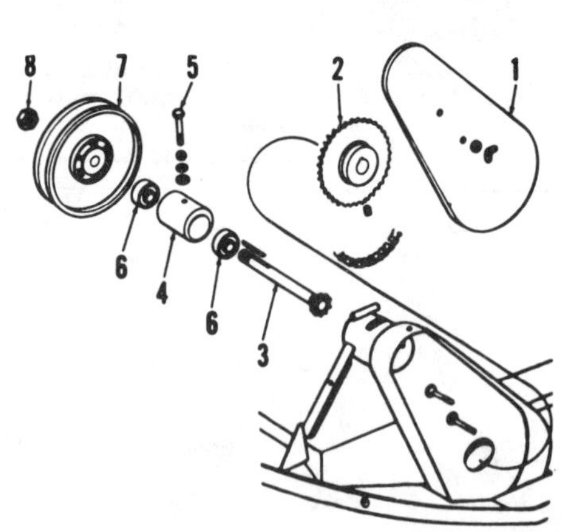

Fig. 3–Exploded view of intermediate shaft, chaincase and associated parts.

1. Cover
2. Driven sprocket
3. Shaft
4. Eccentric housing
5. Adjusting bolt
6. Bearing
7. Driven sheave
8. Nut

bolt (5) and moving bolt in adjusting slot. Move bolt upward to loosen chain or downward to tighten.

BRAKE. To adjust the shoe-type brake, loosen the adjusting nuts and reposition cable housing at mounting bracket on vehicle frame. Brake shoe should clear friction surface of driven sheave when lever is released, but should fully apply before lever contacts handlebar grip.

TRACK. To adjust track tension, raise rear of machine until track is clear of ground. With load removed, there should be some clearance between center bogie wheels and track inner surface. To adjust the tension, loosen the two clamp bolts (A—Fig. 4) on each side of machine and turn adjusting screw (B) an equal amount for each tensioner.

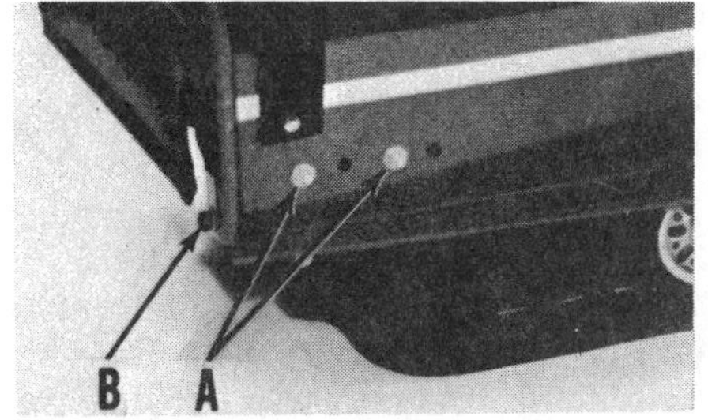

Fig. 4–To adjust track tension, loosen clamp screws (A) and turn adjusting screws (B). Refer to text.

NOTE: When track tension is adjusted, alignment MUST be checked as outlined in TRACK SERVICE Section of this manual.

OVERHAUL

Refer to the appropriate paragraphs in the GENERAL SERVICE Sections of this manual for overhaul procedures of vehicle components.

STARCRAFT
1970-1971

Model	Engine Make	Engine Model	Displ.	Carburetor Make	Carburetor Model	Sprocket Ratio	Chain Size	Clutch Make	Clutch Shaft Center	Belt Number
1970										
Snow Scamp 280	Sachs	SA280	277cc	Tillotson	HR	11:26	40	Featherweight	11.1	76-8
Snow Star 290	Sachs	SA290	293cc	Tillotson	HR	11:26	40	Featherweight	11.1	76-8
Snow Star 400	Kohler	K399-2	399cc	Tillotson	HR	14:27	40	Featherweight	11.1	76-8
Wide Trk 400	Kohler	K399-2	399cc	Tillotson	HR	13:26	40	Featherweight	11.1	76-8
Competition 340	Sachs	SA340	336cc	Tillotson	HD	13:26	40	Featherweight	11.1	76-8
Competition 440	Kohler	K440-2	437cc	Tillotson	HR	14:27	40	Featherweight	11.1	76-8
1971										
Escort 280	Sachs	SA280	277cc	Tillotson	HR52A	11:26	40	Featherweight	11.1	130074
Escort 290	Sachs	SA290	293cc	Tillotson	HR91A	11:26	40	Featherweight	11.1	130074
Escort 340	Kohler	K340-2	338cc	Tillotson	HR79B	13:28	40	Featherweight	11.1	130074
Escort 400	Kohler	K399-2	399cc	Tillotson	HR79B	14:27	40	Featherweight	11.1	130074
Escort 440	Kohler	K440-2	437cc	Tillotson	HR7[illegible]	13:28	40	Featherweight	11.1	130074
Eliminator 290	Sachs	SA290	293cc	Tillotson	HD29A	13:28	40	Featherweight	11.1	130074
Eliminator 340	Sachs	SA340	336cc	Tillotson	HD29A	13:28	40	Featherweight	11.1	130074
Elim. 440	Kohler	K440-2	437cc	Tillotson	HD79B(2)	14:27	40	Featherweight	11.1	130074
Elim. 640	Hirth	171R	634cc	Tillotson	HD48A(2)	14:27	40	Featherweight	11.1	130074
Elim. 740	Sachs	SA2-740	736cc	Tillotson	HD47A(2)	14:27	40	Featherweight	11.1	130074

LUBRICATION

The engine is lubricated by oil mixed with the fuel. Recommended fuel-oil ratio is 25:1 for Sachs or Hirth engines or 20:1 for Kohler. Use regular gasoline and Snowmobile Oil.

The drive chain is enclosed and runs in an oil bath. Tip machine on right side and remove cover (C—Fig. 2). The chain case should contain about ½-pint of SAE 30HD Motor Oil.

Ski legs are equipped with pressure fittings and should be lubricated oc-

Fig. 2—View of converter unit, brake & enclosed chain case showing points of adjustment.

A. Backlash
B. Adjusting bolt
C. Side cover
L. Brake lever
S. Brake shoe

casionally with Low Temperature Grease.

Track drive axles and bogie wheels are equipped with sealed bearings and do not require lubrication.

ADJUSTMENT

STEERING SKIS. Disconnect tie rod from left steering arm and adjust length of rod as necessary until skis are parallel when pointing straight ahead. Steering arms are interchangeable and both have two holes at free (rear) end. Tie rod must be installed in forward hole of both steering arms. Drag link attaches to rear hole of right steering arm. Shorten or lengthen drag link if necessary, until handle bar is in normal straight driving position with both skis pointing straight ahead.

DRIVE CHAIN. The roller drive chain should have a minimum amount of slack but no tension. Adjustment can be measured by checking the backlash (A—Fig. 2) at pulley rim. Adjustment is correct when backlash (A) is approximately ⅜ inch. Adjust by loosening the locknut and turning idler adjusting screw (B) until backlash is correct.

BRAKE. A shoe type brake is used as shown in Figs. 2, 3 and 4. Brake is adjusted at cable housing anchor as shown in Fig. 3 (early Models) or Fig. 4 (late units). Make sure brake does not drag when lever is released but is fully engaged before lever contacts handlebar grip.

TRACK. To adjust track tension, raise rear of machine until track is clear of ground. On early models refer to Fig. 5 and measure distance (A) from lower edge of rear swing arm to edge of frame. Distance should be 3¾ inches and equal on both sides. To adjust the track, loosen the two clamp bolts (1) and turn adjusting screw (2) until tension is correct.

On late models refer to Fig. 6. Loosen pivot bolt nuts (A) if necessary and turn adjusting bolts (B) until top of track sags approximately 1-inch with machine resting on even surface. Both sides must be adjusted alike. Adjuster brackets on frame can be moved rearward for further adjustment.

NOTE: Whenever track tension has been adjusted, alignment MUST be checked as outlined in TRACK SERVICE Section of this manual

Fig. 3—To adjust the brake, loosen locknut (A) and turn connector (B).

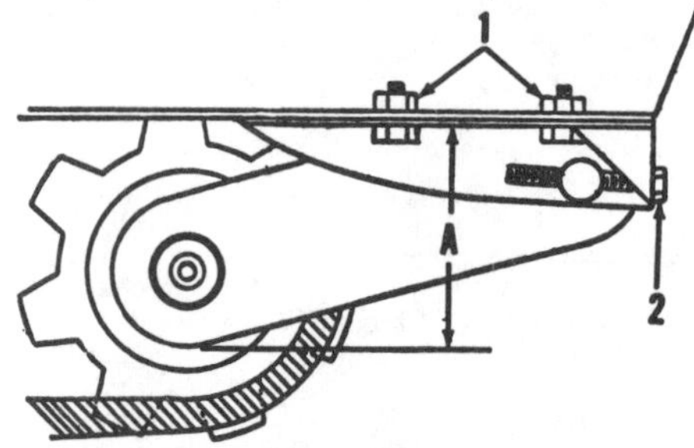

Fig. 5—With rear of vehicle raised, measure distance (A) from lower edge of rear idler bearing housing to edge of frame. Distance should be 3¾ inches and equal on both sides. Adjust by loosening clamp bolts (1) and turning adjusting screw (2).

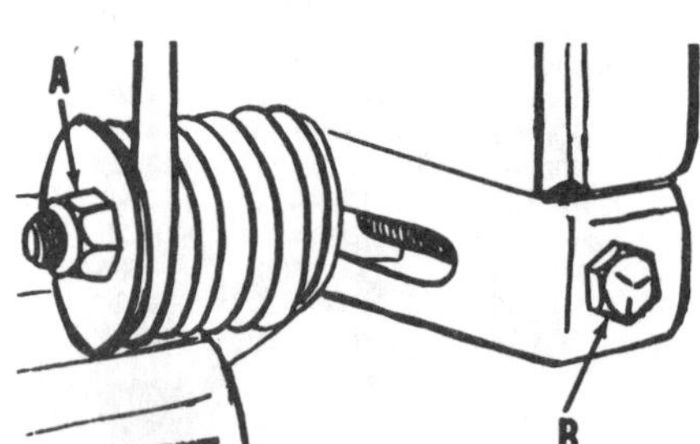

Fig. 6—To adjust track tension on late models, loosen pivot bolt nuts (A) and turn adjusting screws (B) as outlined in text.

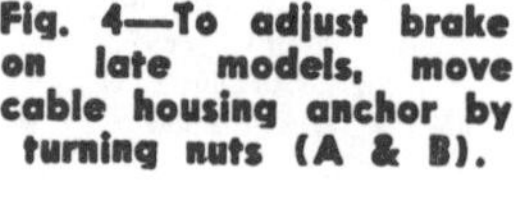

Fig. 4—To adjust brake on late models, move cable housing anchor by turning nuts (A & B).

OVERHAUL

SKIS AND STEERING. Skis, skilegs (spindles), bushings and steering arms are interchangeable from right to left. Steering arms have two holes at rear end. Tie rod attaches to forward hole of both steering arms and drag link to rear hole of right arm. Rear hole of left arm is not used.

ENGINE AND DRIVE. Refer to the appropriate service section elsewhere in this manual for specific data on engines and general service information on remainder of machine.

TORQUE CONVERTER. Refer to Fig. 7 for an exploded view of torque converter drive unit and to Fig. 8 for driven sheave. Torque spring in driven sheave should be pre-loaded ⅓-turn (one cam) when unit is assembled.

Fig. 7—Exploded view of torque converter drive sheave.

Fig. 8—Exploded view of torque sensing driven sheave.

SUZUKI
1971-1972

Model	Engine Make	Engine Model	Engine Displ.	Carburetor Make	Carburetor Model	Sprocket Ratio	Chain Size	Clutch Make	Clutch Shaft Center	Belt Number
					1971					
SM10 Nomad .	Own		359cc	Mikuni	VM26SH	14:34	315-2	Salsbury*	10.2	21711-9705
					1972					
SM10 Nomad .	Own		359cc	Mikuni	VM26SH	15:34	315-2	Salsbury*	10.2	21711-9705
XR400 SM20 . .	Own		395cc	Mikuni	VM26SH(2)	16:32	315-2	Salsbury*	10.2	21711-9705

*Uses Suzuki Driven Pulley.

LUBRICATION

The engine is lubricated by oil mixed with the fuel. The manufacturer recommends Suzuki "CCI" or good quality Snowmobile Oil at a ratio of 20:1 with regular gasoline. On new or rebuilt engines, oil can be increased to 15:1 ratio until new parts are seated.

The chain case uses SAE 10W/30 Motor oil and level should be maintained at level of the center screw (L—Fig. 1) in chain case lower cover. Chain case capacity is approximately 180 cc. (6 fl. oz.). The brake cam (and pins), steering shaft, kingpin bushings and the attaching points of skis should be lubricated at least once a month with chassis grease. The bogie support shafts should be removed and lubricated with chassis grease at least once every three months. Low temperature grease should be used to lubricate brake pivot bolt, speedometer gear box, right axle bearing housing, rear idler wheel and rear suspension arm spacer. The rear idler wheels should be lubricated at least once a month; brake pivot bolt and rear suspension arm spacer should be lubricated at least once every three months.

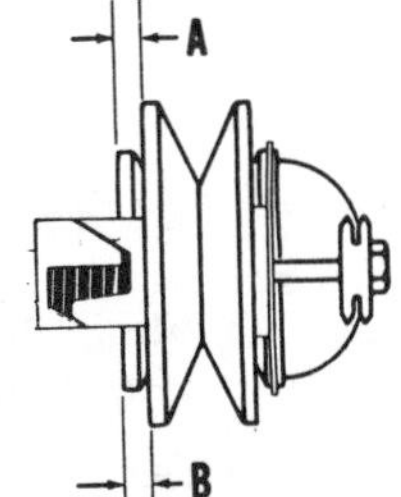

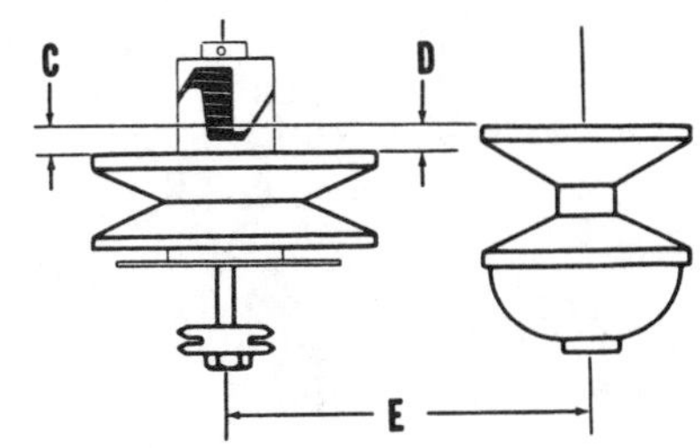

Fig. 2—Faces of pulleys should be parallel vertically (A & B) and horizontally (C & D). Amount of offset (A, B, C D) is listed in text. Belt (pulley) center distance is measured between centers of shafts as shown at (E).

ADJUSTMENT

STEERING SKIS. With handle bars in normal straight driving position, both skis should point straight ahead and center-to-center distance should be the same at front and rear of skis. Adjustment is accomplished by changing length of tie rods. Ends are right and left hand thread and length can be changed by turning center section after loosening lock nuts at ends. Approximate length of each tie rod from centers of ends is 260 mm (10¼-inches).

DRIVE CHAIN. Drive chain should have 5-7 mm (0.20-0.34 in.) deflection measured at lower edge of top hole in chain case as shown at (D—Fig. 1). To adjust, loosen screw (B) and move screw up or down in slotted support, then tighten screw (B). NOTE: Adjusting the drive chain will change the belt (pulley) center adjustment.

DRIVE BELT AND PULLEYS. To check, first remove drive belt. Check to make certain that both pulleys are parallel vertically (A&B—Fig. 2). Shims (A or B—Fig. 3) can be installed to align the pulleys vertically.

Check offset and horizontal alignment of pulley faces as shown at (C & D—Fig. 2). Adjustment is accom-

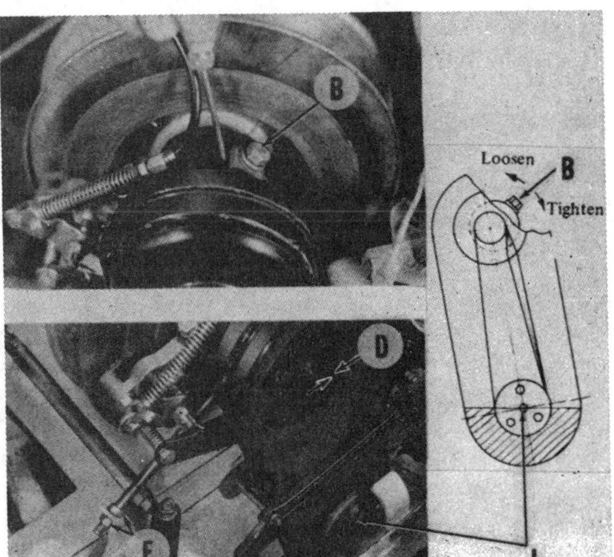

Fig. 1—Oil in chain case should be maintained at level of plug (L) in center of lower cover. Chain tension should be measured at (D). Chain tension lock screw is shown at (B).

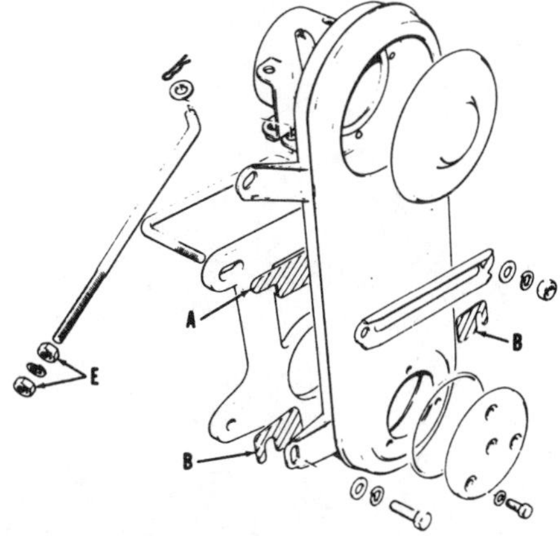

Fig. 3—Exploded view of drive chain housing showing location of shims (A & B). Refer to text for adjustment of vertical alignment.

plished by loosening the engine mounting bracket nuts and moving engine as necessary to obtain offset of 17.65—19.65 mm (0.69-0.77 in.). If offset at (C) is different than at (D) engine can be twisted slightly to correct alignment.

Belt (pulley) center distance can be measured with or without belt installed. Distance (E) between centers of shafts should be within limits of 254-262 mm (10.00-10.31 in.). Drive chain adjustment will affect center distance and should be accomplished as outlined in previous section before changing belt center distance. To change center distance, loosen the four screws attaching chain case to frame and turn nuts (E—Fig. 1 & Fig. 3) as required.

NOTE: Special tool (part number 09920-09710 is available to facilitate checking drive belt and pulley adjustment.

BRAKE. The brake disc is located on the secondary (driven) pulley unit and the caliper unit is attached to the drive chain housing. Total clearance between brake pads and sides of discs should be approximately 1.5 mm (0.059 in.) with brake released. To adjust, remove cotter pin and turn nut (12—Fig. 5) as required. The disc should be centered between the brake pads (17 & 8). Centering is accomplished by turning screw (5) after loosening lock nut (2). Cable adjuster located at lower end of cable housing should be adjusted so that brake is firmly applied when lever has moved ½ of its stroke toward handle bar.

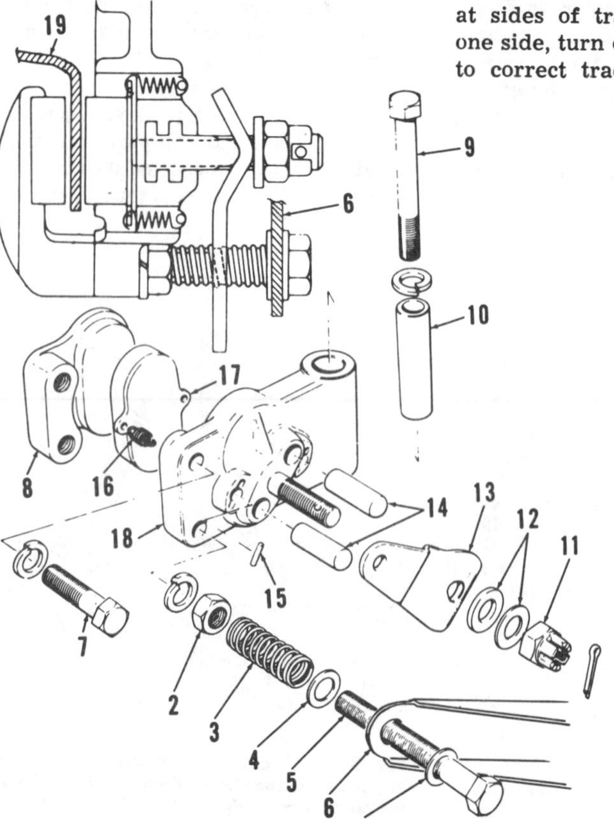

Fig. 5 — Exploded and cross-sectional views of brake assembly. Bracket (6) is part of drive chain housing. Brake disc (19) shown in cross-section is part of driven pulley assembly.

2. Nut
3. Centering spring
4. Washers
5. Adjusting screw
6. Bracket
7. Screw
8. Inner housing and pad
9. Pivot screw
10. Spacer
11. Adjustment nut
12. Washers
13. Cam and lever
14. Operating dowels
15. Spring holder pins
16. Return springs
17. Brake pad
18. Housing
19. Brake disc

TRACK. To adjust track tension, raise rear of vehicle until track is clear of ground. Deflection (D—Fig. 6) should be 30-40 mm (1 3/16-1 9/16-inch) when pressed down with a finger. Adjustment is accomplished by turning adjuster screws (A) after loosening nuts (N). The chassis is marked to assist in making adjustment the same on both sides of track; however, track alignment should be checked as follows: Drive the track at slow speed with vehicle raised off the ground and check clearance (C) at sides of track. If track moves to one side, turn one of the adjusters (A) to correct track alignment.

Fig. 6 — Views showing locations for checking track tension (D) and alignment (C) Nuts (N) must be loosened before turning adjusting screws (A).

OVERHAUL

SKIS & STEERING. Individual parts of skis and springs are interchangeable; however, bracket (10—Fig. 7) must be installed with threaded side for screw (13) toward center of vehicle. On later models, springs are arched higher and spacers (9) are not used. Notch (R) in retainer (5) should be toward rear.

Bushing (4—Fig. 8) should be installed flush with upper (rear) face of support bracket. Bushing can be lubricated with water to facilitate installation. Make certain that bracket (2) is installed straight and clearance (C) should be 0.2-0.5 mm (0.008-0.020 inch). Clearance (C) is changed by adjusting nuts on rod (13). Kingpins (11 & 12) are not interchange-

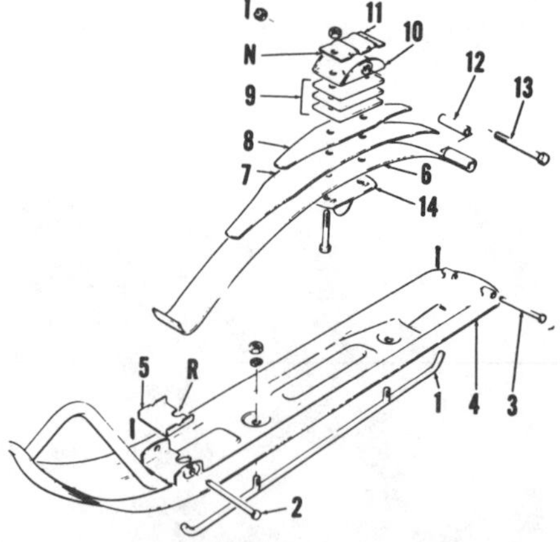

Fig. 7—Exploded view of ski. The same parts are used for both sides; however, threaded side (N) of bracket (10) should be toward inside. Notch (R) in retainer (5) must be toward rear. On later models, springs (6, 7 & 8) are arched higher and spacers (9) are not used.

1. Runner
2. Front pin (73.5 mm)
3. Rear pin (97 mm)
4. Ski
5. Retainer
6. Main spring
7. Center spring
8. Top spring
9. Spacers (three used, early models)
10. Bracket
11. Lock plate
12. Bushing
13. Screw

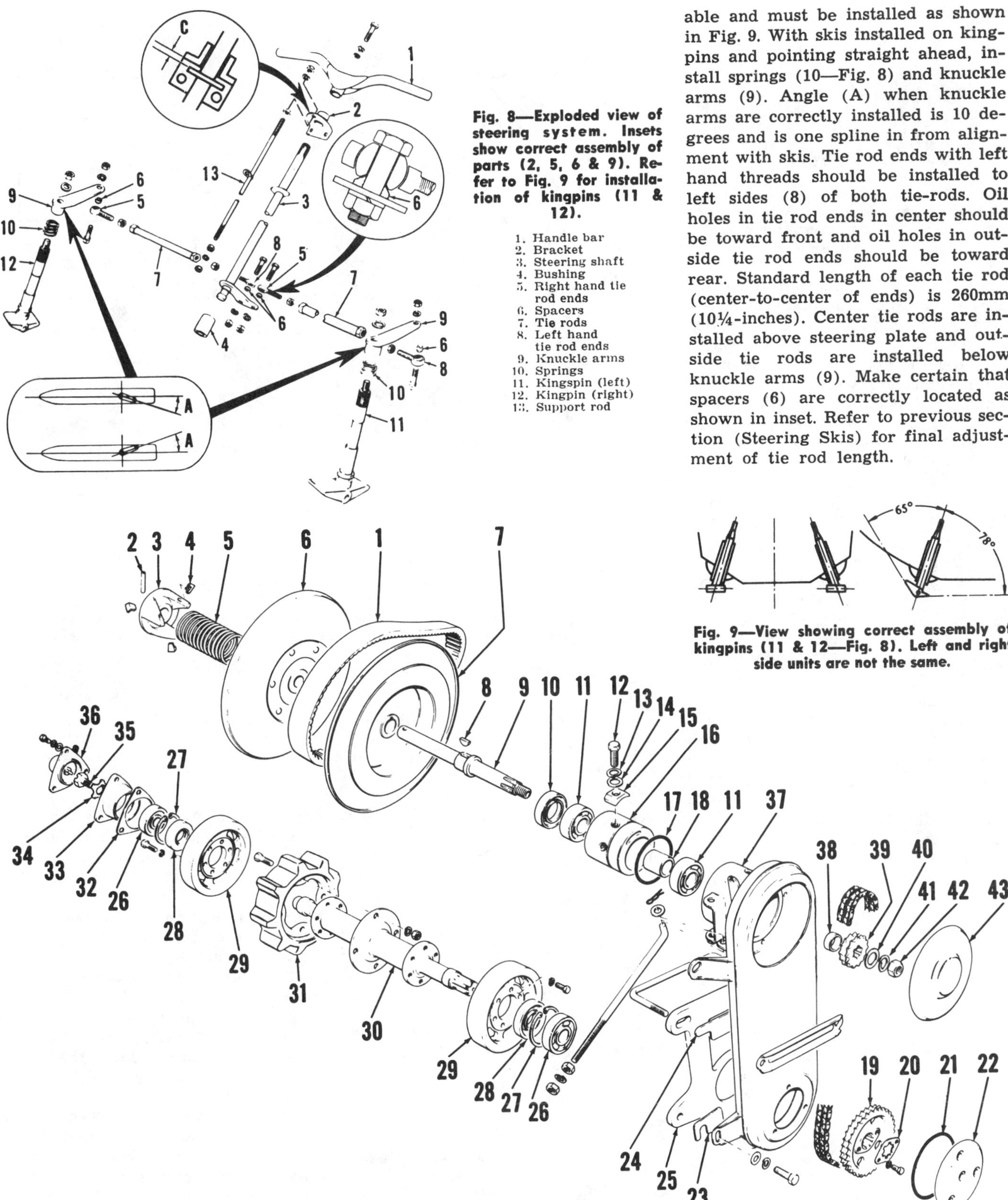

able and must be installed as shown in Fig. 9. With skis installed on kingpins and pointing straight ahead, install springs (10—Fig. 8) and knuckle arms (9). Angle (A) when knuckle arms are correctly installed is 10 degrees and is one spline in from alignment with skis. Tie rod ends with left hand threads should be installed to left sides (8) of both tie-rods. Oil holes in tie rod ends in center should be toward front and oil holes in outside tie rod ends should be toward rear. Standard length of each tie rod (center-to-center of ends) is 260mm (10¼-inches). Center tie rods are installed above steering plate and outside tie rods are installed below knuckle arms (9). Make certain that spacers (6) are correctly located as shown in inset. Refer to previous section (Steering Skis) for final adjustment of tie rod length.

Fig. 8—Exploded view of steering system. Insets show correct assembly of parts (2, 5, 6 & 9). Refer to Fig. 9 for installation of kingpins (11 & 12).

1. Handle bar
2. Bracket
3. Steering shaft
4. Bushing
5. Right hand tie rod ends
6. Spacers
7. Tie rods
8. Left hand tie rod ends
9. Knuckle arms
10. Springs
11. Kingspin (left)
12. Kingpin (right)
13. Support rod

Fig. 9—View showing correct assembly of kingpins (11 & 12—Fig. 8). Left and right side units are not the same.

Fig. 10 – Exploded view of driven sheave, drive chain, front (drive) axle and associated parts. A center bolt is used instead of retainer (20) on later models.

1. Drive belt
2. Pin
3. Cam
4. Cam tips
5. Torque spring
6. Inner pulley half
7. Outer pulley half
8. Key
9. Shaft
10. Seal
11. Bearings
12. Adjusting screw
13. Lock washer
14. Plain washer
15. Plate
16. Eccentric housing
17. O-ring
18. Spacer
19. Lower sprocket
20. Retainer plate
21. O-ring
22. Lower cover
23. Lower shims
24. Upper shims
25. Spacer
26. Bearing
27. Snap ring
28. Seal
29. Idler wheels
30. Front (drive) axle
31. Front sprocket
32. Shim
33. Bearing housing
34. Lock washer
35. Screw
36. Speedometer drive
37. Chain housing
38. Spacer
39. Sprocket
40. Plain washer
41. Lock washer
42. Nut
43. Cover

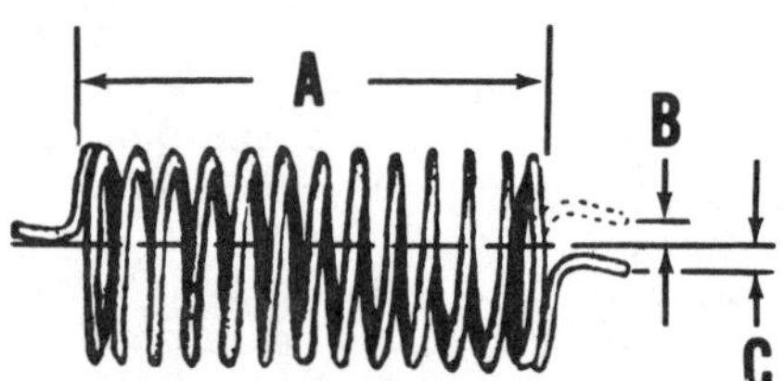

Fig. 11—The torque spring on driven sheave should not be damaged. Standard free length (A), standard offset (C) and limit of offset (B) are listed in text.

DRIVE. The torque converter drive sheave is Salsbury 910 unit. The driven sheave is Suzuki unit; however, service is similar to Salsbury torque sensitive unit. Refer to Fig. 10. The torque spring (5) should be preloaded ⅔ turn when assembling. Standard free length (A–Fig. 11) is 106.5 mm (4.19 inch). Standard offset (C) between ends is 9.5 mm (0.37 inch). Renew spring if offset of ends (B) exceeds 4.5 mm (0.18 inch). Bushing is movable pulley half (6–Fig. 10) should be coated with Molybedenum low temperature grease once each season. Inside diameter of bushing when new is 19.000-19.033 mm (0.748-0.749 inch) and pulley half should be renewed if bushing inside diameter exceeds 19.3 mm (0.76 inch). Diameter of shaft (9) at pulley bushing is 18.939-18.960 mm (0.7456-0.7464 inch) when new. Renew shaft if diameter is less than 18.90 mm (0.744 inch). Both sprockets (19 & 39) and the drive chain are removed through opening for plug (43). Late models use one screw and washer to retain lower sprocket (19) to shaft (3) instead of plate (20) and the two retaining screws. On late models the one retaining screw should be tightened to 37-50 ft.-lbs. torque. On early models, the two screws attaching plate (20) should be tightened to 3-4 ft.-lbs. torque. On all models, nut (42) should be torqued to 84-90 ft.-lbs. Bogie shaft support screws should be tightened to 8-10 ft.-lbs. torque.

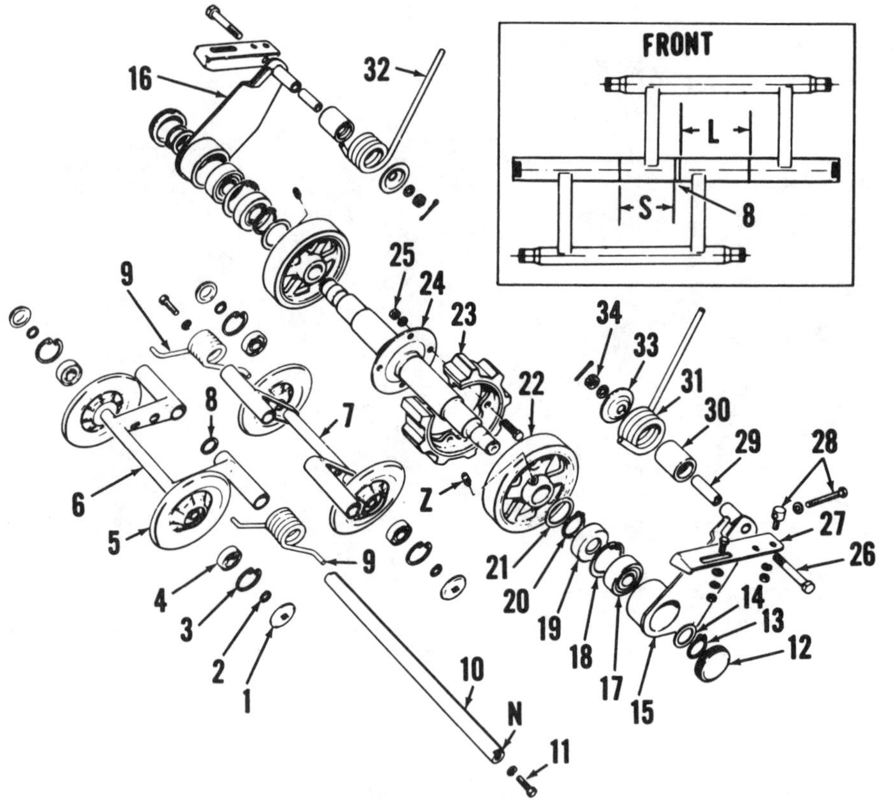

Fig. 13—Exploded view of one set of bogie wheels, rear axle assembly and rear suspension parts. Pipe (S) for front (right) axle is shorter than for rear (left) unit.

1. Cap
2. Snap ring
3. Snap ring
4. Bearing
5. Bogie wheel
6. Front (right) axle
7. Rear (left) axle
8. Thrust washer
9. Springs
10. Bogie shaft
11. Screw
12. Cap
13. Snap ring
14. Thrust washer
15. Left suspension arm
16. Right suspension arm
17. Bearing
18. Snap ring
19. Seal
20. Snap ring
21. Thrust washer
22. Idler wheel
23. Rear-sprocket
24. Rear axle
25. Nut
26. Suspension arm pivot screw
27. Adjuster plate
28. Adjuster
29. Spacer
30. Spring spacer
31. Spring (left)
32. Spring (right)
33. Cap washer
34. Nut

TRACK AND SUSPENSION. When assembling the axles, sprockets and idler wheels refer to Figs. 10, 12 & 13.

On early models, the front drive sprocket (31—Fig. 12) is yellow and rear sprocket (23) is black. Only one side of attaching flange is machined and Suzuki "S" mark and "Made in Japan" is located on side at (M—Inset) indicating side of flange which is machined. The mounting flange of sprockets must be on long side (L) of axles (24 & 30). Sprocket mounting screws should be tightened to 11-18 ft.-lbs. torque. Angle formed by ends of bogie springs (9—Fig. 13) is 164 degrees (standard) and springs should be renewed if angle exceeds 170 degrees. Later springs form 150 degree angle when new.

On late models, both sprockets (23 & 31—Fig. 12) are black. Front sprocket (31) can be identified by "A" mark on side as shown at (I—Inset Fig. 12) and rear sprocket can be identified by "B" marks in same location. Both sides of sprocket flange are machined. Install sprockets with flange on long side (L) of axles (24 & 30). Tighten sprocket mounting screws to 11-18 ft.-lbs. torque. Angle formed by ends of bogie springs (9—Fig. 13) for late models is 150 degrees (standard) and springs should be renewed if angle exceeds 160 degrees.

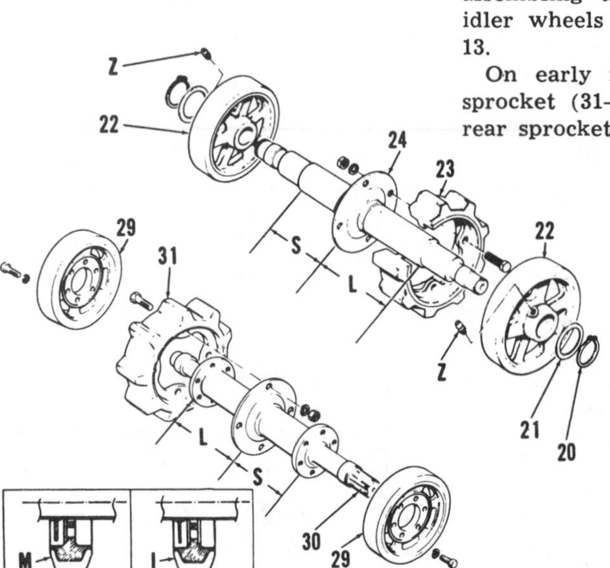

Fig. 12 — View of front axle (30), sprocket (31), idler wheels (29), rear axle (24), sprocket (23), idler wheels (22), washers (21) and snap rings (20). Long sides of axles are indicated by (L) and short side by (S). Refer to text for assembly and identification.

On all models, screws attaching front idler wheels (29—Fig. 12) to flanges of front axle should be tightened to 35-51 inch-pounds torque. Grease fittings (Z) should be toward outside when installing rear idler wheels (22). When assembling bogie assemblies, the front axles (6—Fig. 13) should be offset toward right side as shown. The width of pipe is 3.50 inches (S—Inset Fig. 13) for the front axle and 3.82 inches (L) for the rear axle. Make certain that thrust washer (8) is located in center as shown. Notch (N) in bogie shafts (10) should be toward top and stop against plate on chassis when assembled. Tighten bogie shaft screws (11) to 86-129 inch-pounds torque. Nuts (34) should be tightened to 130-218 inch-pounds torque, then locked in position with cotter pin.

SUZUKI

1973-1975

	Engine			Carburetor				Clutch		
Model	Make	Model	Displ.	Make	Model	Sprocket Ratio	Chain Size	Make	Shaft Center	Belt Number
					1973					
SM30K	Own		292cc	Mikuni	VM32SH	14:34	315-2	Own	10.2	21711-97051
SM11K	Own		336cc	Mikuni	VM26SH	14:32	315-2	Own	10.2	21711-97051
SM21K	Own		395cc	Mikuni	VM26SH(2)	15:31	315-2	Own	10.2	21711-97051
SM40K	Own		432cc	Mikuni	VM30SH(2)	17:29	315-2	Own	10.2	21711-97051
					1974					
292 Nomad	Own	SM30K	292cc	Mikuni	VM32SH	14:34	315-2	Own	10.2	21711-97051
340 Nomad	Own	SM11L	336cc	Mikuni	VM26SH	14:32	315-2	Own	10.2	21711-97051
XR400	Own	SM21L	395cc	Mikuni	VM26SH(2)	15:31	315-2	Own	10.2	21711-97051
Yukon 400	Own	SM21WL	395cc	Mikuni	VM30SH	15:31	315-2	Own	10.2	21711-97051
XR440	Own	SM40L	432cc	Mikuni	VM30SH(2)	18:28	315-2	Own	10.2	21711-97051
					1975					
SM11 Nomad	Own	SM30K	336cc	Mikuni	VM32SH	14:32	315-2	Own	10.2	21711-97051
SM21-XR400	Own	SM21L	395cc	Mikuni	VM26SH(2)	15:31	315-2	Own	10.2	21711-97051
SM21W-Yukon	Own	SM21WL	395cc	Mikuni	VM26SH	15:31	315-2	Own	10.2	21711-97051
SM40-XR440	Own	SM40L	432cc	Mikuni	VM30SH	18:28	315-2	Own	10.2	21711-97051
Fury	Own		432cc	Mikuni	VM	19:35	Silent	Arctic	10.2	0227-007

LUBRICATION

The engine is lubricated by oil mixed with the fuel. The manufacturer recommends Suzuki "CCI" or good quality Snowmobile Oil at a ratio of 20:1 with regular gasoline. On new or rebuilt engines, oil can be increased to 15:1 ratio until new parts are seated.

The chaincase uses SAE 10W/30 Motor oil and level should be maintained at level of the center screw (L—Fig. 1) in chaincase lower cover. Chaincase capacity is approximately 180cc (6 fl. oz.). The brake cam (and pins), steering shaft, kingpin bushings and the attached points of skis should be lubricated at least once a month with chassis grease. The bogie support shafts should be removed and lubricated with chassis grease at least once every three months. Low temperature grease should be used to lubricate brake pivot bolt, speedometer gear box, right axle bearing housing, rear idler wheel and rear suspension arm spacer. The rear idler wheels should be lubricated at least once a month; brake pivot bolt and rear suspension arm spacer should be lubricated at least once every three months.

ADJUSTMENT

STEERING SKIS. With handlebars in normal straight driving position, both skis should point straight ahead and center-to-center distance should be the same at front and rear of skis. Adjustment is accomplished by changing length of tie rods. Ends are right- and left-hand thread and length can be changed by turning center section after loosening locknuts at ends. Approximate length of each tie rod from centers of ends of 260 mm (10¼ inches).

DRIVE CHAIN. Drive chain should have 5-7 mm (0.20-0.34 in.) deflection

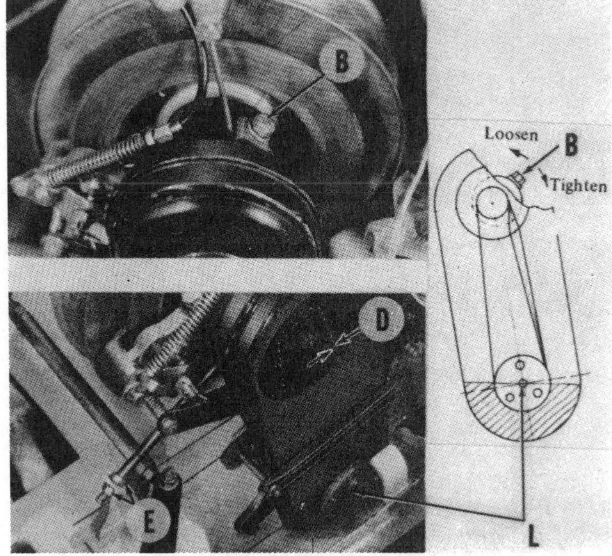

Fig. 1—Oil in chaincase should be maintained at level of plug (L) in center of lower cover. Chain tension should be measured at (D). Chain tension lock screw is shown at (B).

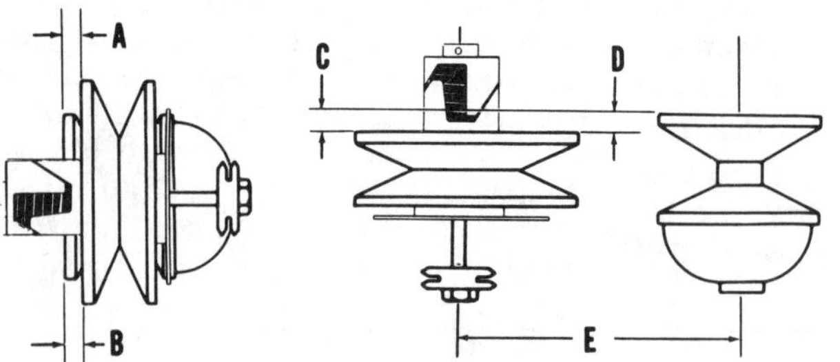

Fig. 2—Faces of pulleys should be parallel vertically (A & B) and horizontally (C & D). Amount of offset (A, B, C, D) is listed in text. Belt (pulley) center distance is measured between centers of shafts as shown at (E).

measured at lower edge of top hole in chaincase as shown at (D—Fig. 1). To adjust, loosen screw (B) and move screw up or down in slotted support, then tighten screw (B).

NOTE: Adjusting the drive chain will change the belt (pulley) center adjustment.

DRIVE BELT AND PULLEYS. To check, first remove drive belt. Check to make certain that both pulleys are parallel vertically (A and B—Fig. 2). Shims (A or B—Fig. 3) can be installed to align the pulleys vertically.

Check offset and horizontal alignment of pulley faces as shown at (C and D—Fig. 2). Adjustment is accomplished by loosening the engine mounting bracket nuts and moving engine as necessary to obtain offset of 17.65-19.65 mm (0.69-0.77 in.). If offset at (C) is different than at (D) engine can be twisted slightly to correct alignment.

Belt (pulley) center distance can be measured with or without belt installed. Distance (E) between centers of shafts should be within limits of 254-262 mm (10.00-10.31 in.). Drive chain adjustment will affect center distance and should be accomplished as outlined in previous section before changing belt center distance. To change center distance, loosen the four screws attaching chaincase to frame and turn nuts (E—Fig. 1 and Fig. 3) as required.

NOTE: Special tool (part number 09920-09710) is available to facilitate checking drive belt and pulley adjustment.

BRAKE. The brake disc is located on the secondary (driven) pulley unit and the caliper unit is attached to the drive chain housing. Total clearance between brake pads and sides of discs should be approximately 1.5 mm (0.059 in.) with brake released. To adjust, remove cotter pin and turn nut (11—Fig. 5) as required. The disc should be centered between the brake pads (17 and 8). Centering is accomplished by turning screw (5) after loosening locknut (2). Cable adjuster located at lower end of cable housing should be adjusted so that brake is firmly applied when lever has moved one-half of its stroke toward handlebar.

TRACK. To adjust track tension, raise rear of vehicle until track is clear of ground. Deflection (D—Fig. 6) should

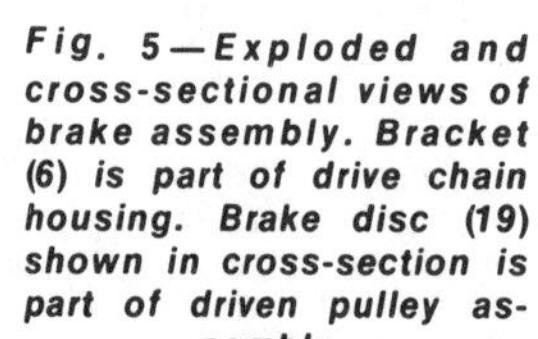

Fig. 5—Exploded and cross-sectional views of brake assembly. Bracket (6) is part of drive chain housing. Brake disc (19) shown in cross-section is part of driven pulley assembly.

2. Nut
3. Centering spring
4. Washers
5. Adjusting screw
6. Bracket
7. Screw
8. Inner housing & pad
9. Pivot screw
10. Spacer
11. Adjustment nut
12. Washers
13. Cam & lever
14. Operating dowels
15. Spring holder pins
16. Return springs
17. Brake pad
18. Housing
19. Brake disc

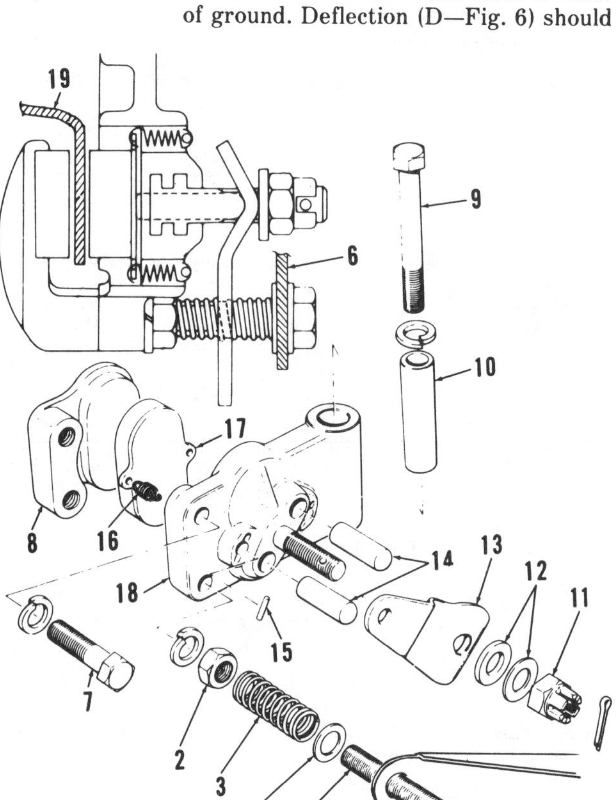

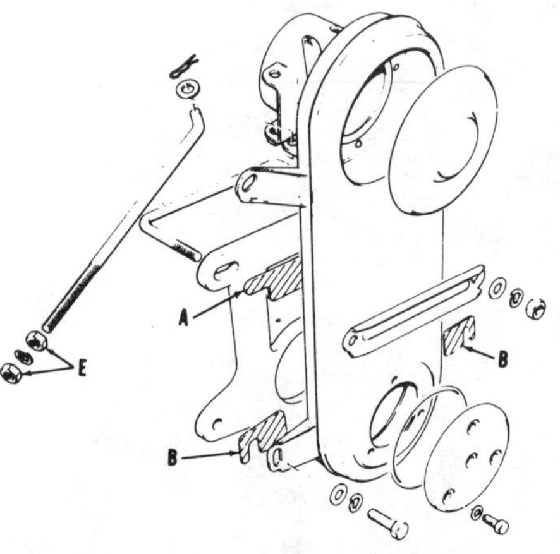

Fig. 3—Exploded view of drive chain housing showing location of shims (A & B). Refer to text for adjustment of vertical alignment.

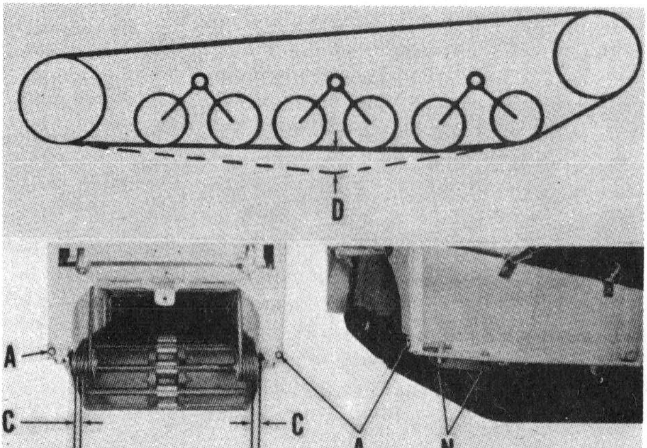

Fig. 6—Views showing locations for checking track tension (D) and alignment (C). Nuts (N) must be loosened before turning adjusting screws (A).

be 30-40 mm (1-3/16 to 1-9/16 inch) when pressed down with a finger. Adjustment is accomplished by turning adjuster screws (A) after loosening nuts (N). The chassis is marked to assist in making adjustment the same on both sides of track; however, track alignment should be checked as follows: Drive the track at slow speed with vehicle raised off the ground and check clearance (C) at sides of track. If track moves to one side, turn one of the adjusters (A) to correct track alignment.

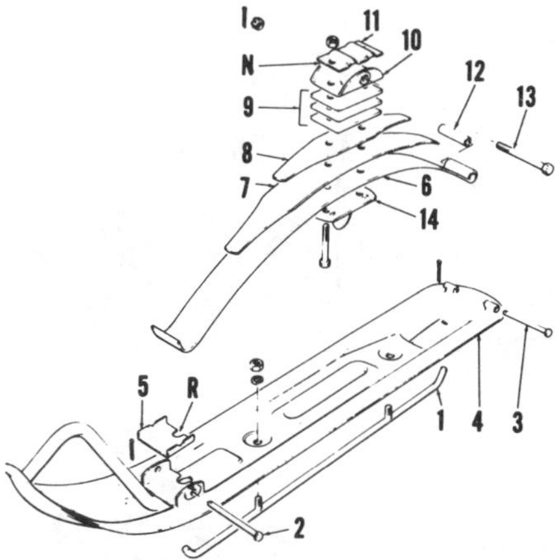

Fig. 7—Exploded view of ski. The same parts are used for both sides; however, threaded side (N) of bracket (10) should be toward inside. Notch (R) in retainer (5) must be toward rear. On later models, springs (6, 7 & 8) are arched higher and spacers (9) are not used.

1. Runner
2. Front pin (73.5 mm)
3. Rear pin (97 mm)
4. Ski
5. Retainer
6. Main spring
7. Center spring
8. Top spring
9. Spacers (3 used, early models)
10. Bracket
11. Lock plate
12. Bushing
13. Screw

OVERHAUL

SKIS AND STEERING. Individual parts of skis and springs are interchangeable; however, bracket (10—Fig. 7) must be installed with threaded side for screw (13) toward center of vehicle. On later models, springs are arched higher and spacers (9) are not used. Notch (R) in retainer (5) should be toward rear.

Bushing (4—Fig. 8) should be installed flush with upper (rear) face of support bracket. Bushing can be lubricated with water to facilitate installation. Make certain that bracket (2) is installed straight and clearance (C) should be 0.2-0.5 mm (0.008-0.020 inch). Clearance (C) is changed by adjusting nuts on rod (13). Kingpins (11 and 12) are not interchangeable and must be installed as shown in Fig. 9. With skis installed on kingpins and pointing straight ahead, install springs (10—Fig. 8) and knuckle arms (9). Angle (A) when knuckle arms are correctly installed is 10 degrees and is one spline in from alignment with skis. Tie rod ends with left-hand threads should be installed to left sides (8) of both tie rods. Oil holes in tie rod ends in center should be toward front and oil holes in outside tie rod ends should be toward rear. Standard length of each tie rod (center-to-center of ends) is 260 mm (10¼ inches). Center tie rods are installed above steering plate and outside tie rods are installed below knuckle arms (9). Make certain that spacers (6) are correctly located as shown in inset. Refer to previous section (Steering Skis) for final adjustment of tie rod length.

DRIVE. The torque converter drive sheave is Salsbury 910 unit. The driven sheave is Suzuki unit; however, service is similar to Salsbury torque sensitive unit. Refer to Fig. 10.

The torque spring (5) should be preloaded ⅔-turn when assembling. Standard free length (A–Fig. 11) is 106.5 mm (4.19 inch). Standard offset (C) between ends is 9.5 mm (0.37 inch). Renew spring if offset of ends (B) exceeds 4.5 mm (0.18 inch). Bushing in movable pulley half (6–Fig. 10) should be coated with Molybdenum low temperature grease once each season. Inside diameter of bushing when new is 19.000-19.033 mm (0.748-0.749 inch) and pulley half should be renewed if bushing inside diameter exceeds 19.3 mm (0.76 inch). Diameter of shaft (9) at pulley bushing is 18.939-18.960 mm (0.7456-0.7464 inch) when new. Renew shaft if diameter is less than 18.90 mm (0.744 inch). Both sprockets (19 and 39) and the drive chain are removed through opening for plug (43). Late models use one screw and washer to retain lower sprocket (19) to shaft (3) instead of plate (20) and the two retaining screws. On late models the one retaining screw should be tightened to 37-50 ft.-lbs. torque. On early models, the two screws attaching plate (20) should be tightened to 3-4 ft.-lbs. torque. On all models, nut (42) should be torqued to 84-90 ft.-lbs. Bogie shaft support screws should be tightened to 8-10 ft.-lbs. torque.

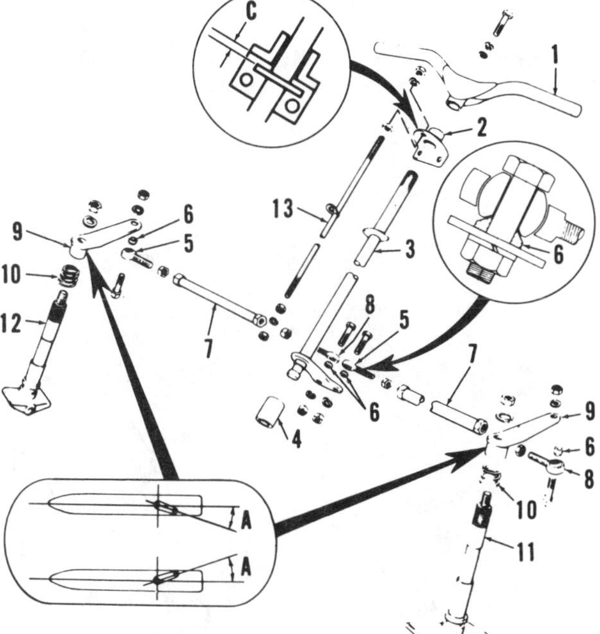

Fig. 8—Exploded view of steering systems. Insets show correct assembly of parts (2, 5, 6 & 9). Refer to Fig. 9 for installation of kingpins (11 & 12).

1. Handle bar
2. Bracket
3. Steering shaft
4. Bushing
5. R.H. tie rod ends
6. Spacers
7. Tie rods
8. L.H. tie rod ends
9. Knuckle arms
10. Springs
11. Kingpin (left)
12. Kingpin (right)
13. Support rod

TRACK AND SUSPENSION. When assembling the axles, sprockets and idler wheels refer to Figs. 10, 12 and 13.

On early models, the front drive sprocket (31—Fig. 12) is yellow and rear sprocket (23) is black. Only one side of attaching flange is machined and Suzuki "S" mark and "Made in Japan" is located on side at (M—Inset) indicating side of flange which is

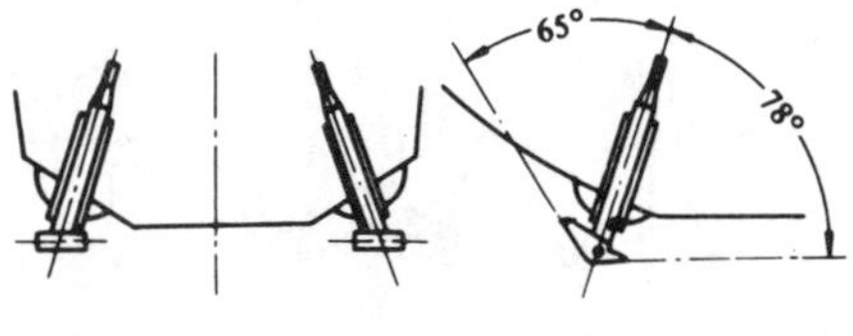

Fig. 9—View showing correct assembly of kingpins (11 & 12—Fig. 8). Left and right side units are not the same.

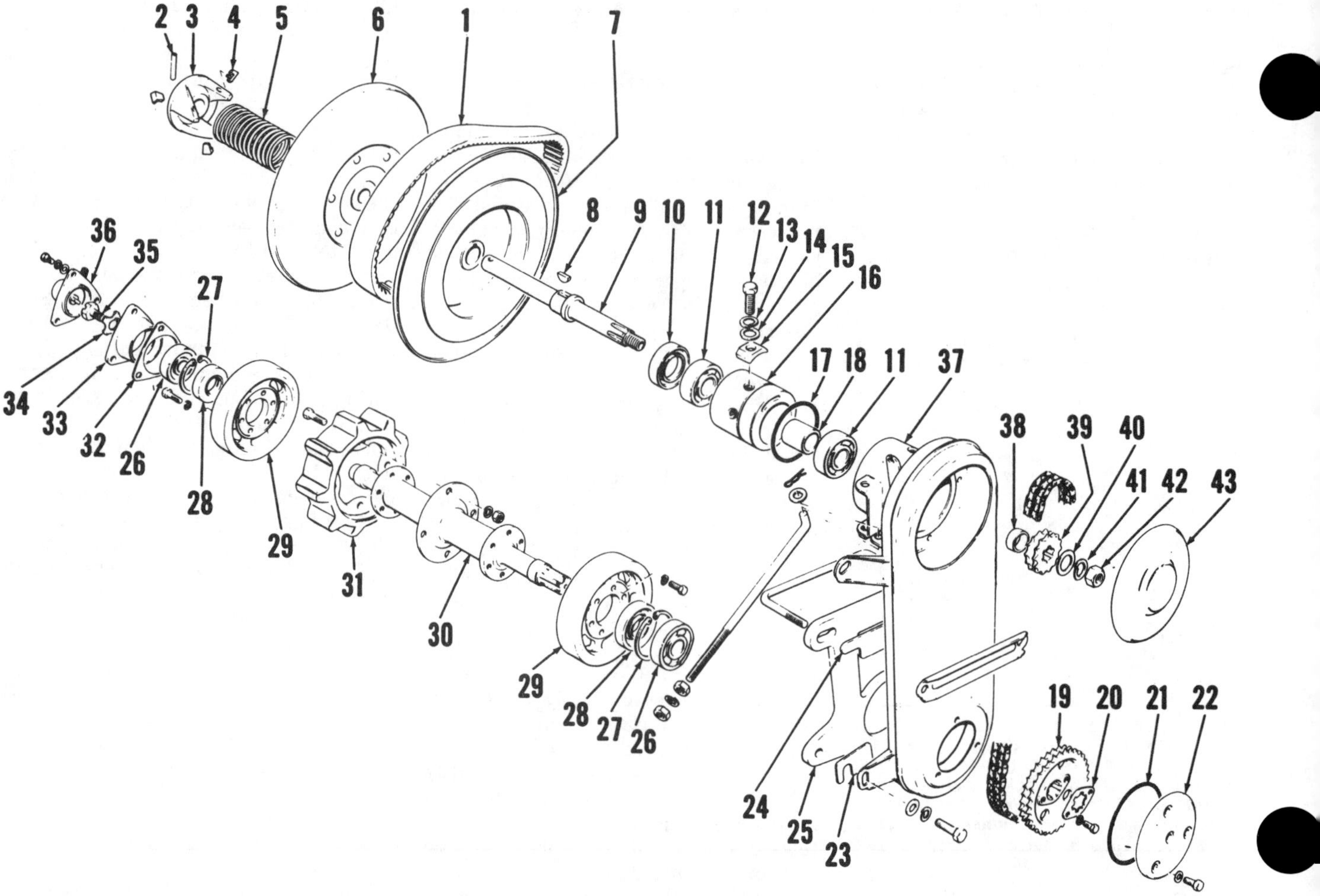

Fig. 10—Exploded view of driven sheave, drive chain, front (drive) axle and associated parts. A center bolt is used instead of retainer (20) on later models.

1. Drive belt
2. Pin
3. Cam
4. Cam tips
5. Torque spring
6. Inner pulley half
7. Outer pulley half
8. Key
9. Shaft
10. Seal
11. Bearings
12. Adjusting screw
13. Lockwasher
14. Plain washer
15. Plate
16. Eccentric housing
17. "O" ring
18. Spacer
19. Lower sprocket
20. Retainer plate
21. "O" ring
22. Lower cover
23. Lower shims
24. Upper shims
25. Spacer
26. Bearing
27. Snap ring
28. Seal
29. Idler wheels
30. Front (drive) axle
31. Front sprocket
32. Shim
33. Bearing housing
34. Lockwasher
35. Screw
36. Speedometer drive
37. Chain housing
38. Spacer
39. Sprocket
40. Plain washer
41. Lockwasher
42. Nut
43. Cover

machined. The mounting flange of sprockets must be on long side (L) of axles (24 and 30). Sprocket mounting screws should be tightened to 11-18 ft.-lbs. torque. Angle formed by ends of bogie springs (9—Fig. 13) is 164 degrees (standard) and springs should be renewed if angle exceeds 170 degrees. Later springs form 150 degree angle when new.

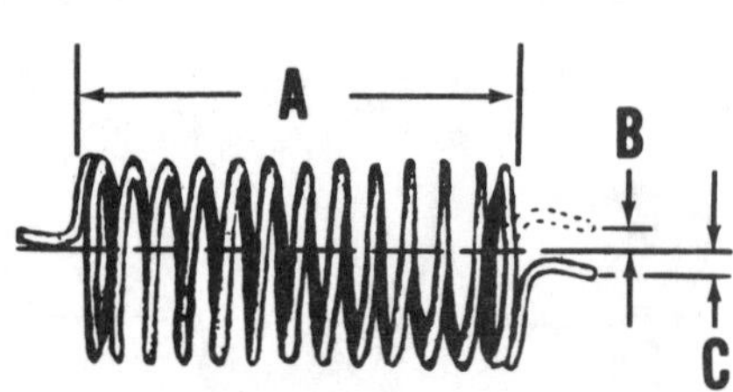

Fig. 11—The torque spring of driven sheave should not be damaged. Standard free length (A), standard offset (C) and limit of offset (B) are listed in text.

On late models, both sprockets (23 and 31—Fig. 12) are black. Front sprocket (31) can be identified by "A" mark on side as shown at (I—Inset Fig.

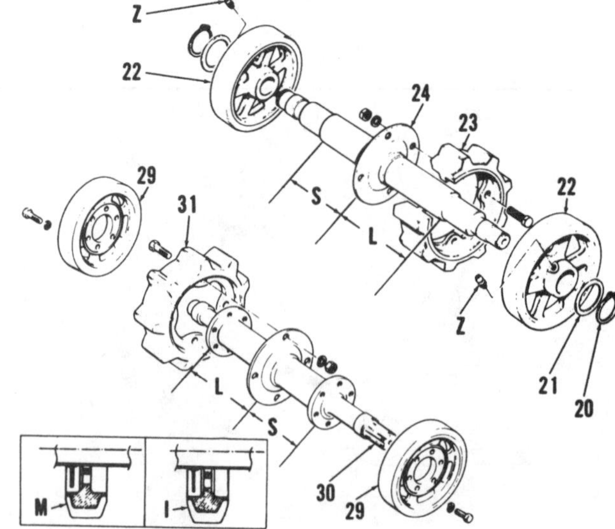

Fig. 12—View of front axle (30), sprocket (31), idler wheels (29), rear axle (24), sprocket (23), idler wheels (22), washers (21) and snap rings (20). Long sides of axles are indicated by (L) and short side by (S). Refer to text for assembly and identification.

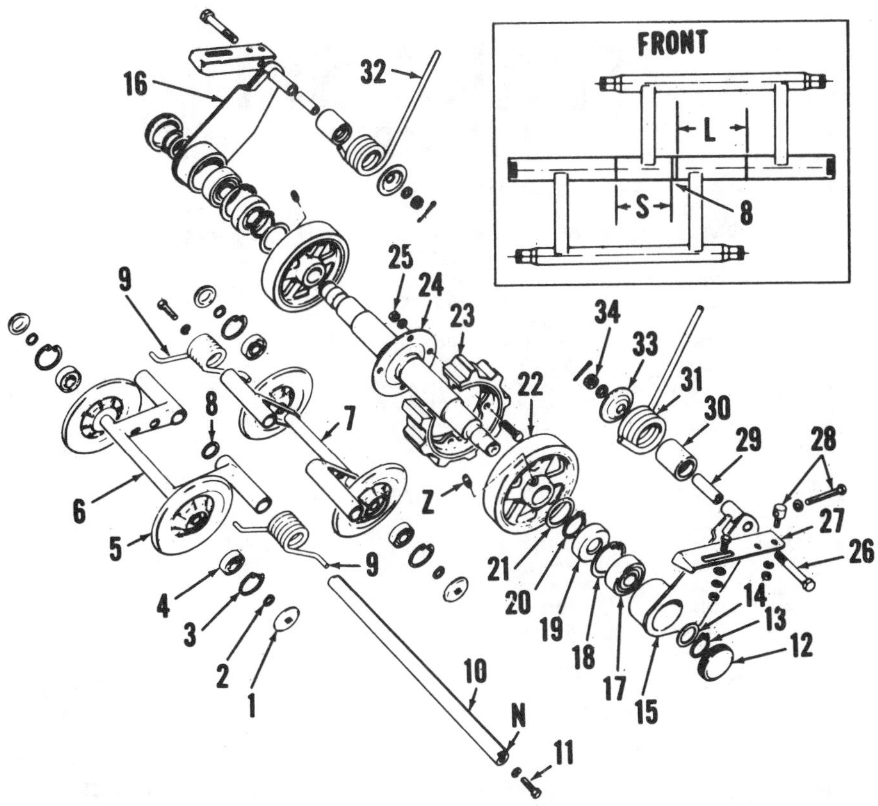

Fig. 13—Exploded view of one set of bogie wheels, rear axle assembly and rear suspension parts. Pipe (S) for front (right) axle is shorter than for rear (left) unit.

1. Cap
2. Snap ring
3. Snap ring
4. Bearing
5. Bogie wheel
6. Front (right) axle
7. Rear (left) axle
8. Thrust washer
9. Springs
10. Bogie shaft
11. Screw
12. Cap
13. Snap ring
14. Thrust washer
15. Left suspension arm
16. Right suspension arm
17. Bearing
18. Snap ring
19. Seal
20. Snap ring
21. Thrust washer
22. Idler wheel
23. Rear sprocket
24. Rear axle
25. Nut
26. Suspension arm pivot screw
27. Adjuster plate
28. Adjuster
29. Spacer
30. Spring spacer
31. Spring (left)
32. Spring (right)
33. Cap washer
34. Nut

12) and rear sprocket can be identified by "B" marks in same location. Both sides of sprocket flange are machined. Install sprockets with flange on long side (L) of axles (24 and 30). Tighten sprocket mounting screws to 11-18 ft.-lbs. torque. Angle formed by ends of bogie springs (9—Fig. 13) for late models is 150 degrees (standard) and srpings should be renewed if angle exceeds 160 degrees.

On all models, screws attaching front idler wheels (29—Fig. 12) to flanges of front axle should be tightened to 35-51 inch-pounds torque. Grease fittings (Z) should be toward outside when installing rear idler wheels (22). When assembling bogie assemblies, the front axles (6—Fig. 13) should be offset toward right side as shown. The width of pipe is 3.50 inches (S—Inset Fig. 13) for the front axle and 3.82 inches (L) for the rear axle. Make certain that thrust washer (8) is located in center as shown. Notch (N) in bogie shafts (10) should be toward top and stop against plate on chassis when assembled. Tighten bogie shaft screws (11) to 86-129 inch-pounds torque. Nuts (34) should be tightened to 130-218 inch-pounds torque, then locked in position with cotter pin.

TRADE WINDS

1967-1968

	Engine			Carburetor				Clutch		
Model	Make	Model	Displ.	Make	Model	Sprocket Ratio	Chain Size	Make	Shaft Center	Belt Number
					1967					
Tiger.........	Hirth	82R	247cc	Tillotson	HR3A		35-2	Salsbury	11½	702413
Super Tiger...	Hirth	54R	300cc	Tillotson	HR3A		35-2	Salsbury	11½	702413
					1968					
Tiger.........	Hirth	82R	247cc	Tillotson	HR3A		35-2	Salsbury	10½	1926V415
Tiger.........	Hirth	54R	300cc	Tillotson	HR8A		35-2	Salsbury	10½	1926V415
Tiger.........	JLO	L297	296cc	Tillotson	HR18A		35-2	Salsbury	10½	1926V415
Tiger.........	JLO	L372	372cc	Tillotson	HD7A		35-2	Salsbury	10½	1926V415
Cheetah......	JLO	LB600	594cc	Tillotson	HD7A					

TRANS-SKI
1971-1972

Model	Engine Make	Engine Model	Engine Displ.	Carburetor Make	Carburetor Model	Sprocket Ratio	Chain Size	Clutch Make	Clutch Shaft Center	Belt Number
1971										
10	CCW	225	225cc	Tillotson	HR71A			St. Law.	10½	SV-135
12	Sachs	280A	277cc	Tillotson	HL242A			St. Law.	10½	SV-135
15SS	Benelli	350-T2	346cc	Tillotson	HR39A			Guidetti	10½	SV-135
20	Guidetti	TT-36	338cc	Tillotson	HR39A			Guidetti	10½	SV-135
20SS	Sachs	340SS	336cc	Tillotson	HR13A			St. Law.	10½	SV-135
20E	CCW	340	339cc	Tillotson	HR27A			St. Law.	10½	SV-135
25	Sachs	SA2-340C	338cc	Tillotson	HR13A			St. Law.	10½	SV-135
30	Sachs	SA2-440	436cc	Tillotson	HD13A			St. law.	10½	SV-211
60	Sachs	SA2-740	735cc	Tillotson	HD13A			St. Law.	10½	SV-211
1972										
C-225-1	CCW	225	225cc	Tillotson				St. Law.	10½	1034M
S-277-1	Sachs	SA280A	277cc	Tillotson				St. Law.	10½	1034M
B-346-1	Benelli	350-T2	356cc	Tillotson				St. Law.	10½	1034M
S-293S-1	Sachs	SA290	293cc	Tillotson				St. Law.	10½	1034M
S-291-2S	Sachs	SA2-290	291cc	Tillotson				St. Law.	10½	1034M
S-336-1	Sachs	SA340	336cc	Tillotson				St. Law.	10½	1034M
S-338-2	Sachs	SA2-340	338cc	Tillotson				St. Law.	10½	1034M
C-339-2S	CCW	340	339cc	Tillotson				St. Law.	10½	1034M
S-436-2S	Sachs	SA2-440	437cc	Tillotson				St. Law.	10½	1034M
S-436-2SC	Sachs	SA2-440C	437cc	Tillotson				St. Law.	10½	1034M
S-735-2S	Sachs	SA2-740C	735cc	Tillotson				St. Law.	10½	1034M
S-630-3S	Sachs	SA3-650-RX	647cc	Tillotson				St. Law.	10½	1034M

LUBRICATION

The engine is lubricated by oil mixed with the fuel. Use a known brand of Snowmobile oil and regular gasoline at a ratio of 20:1.

The enclosed chain case should contain Automatic Transmission Fluid or Engine Oil to a height to just cover the chain where it passes around lower sprocket.

Bogie wheels and axle bearings are equipped with pressure gun fittings and should be lubricated with low temperature grease each 50 hours.

Lubricate steering linkage and handle bar bushings twice a month with low temperature grease.

ADJUSTMENT

STEERING SKIS. Turn handle bar to normal straight driving position and check to see that both skis are parallel with each other and with vehicle track and frame. To adjust either tie rod, loosen jam nut and turn rod center section to lengthen or shorten rod.

DRIVE CHAIN. Drive chain should have approximately ¼-inch free play on that portion of chain which can be observed after removing chaincase cover (2—Fig. 1). To adjust the chain, loosen jam nut on slide adjustment bolt (3) and move bolt downward in slot to tighten chain, or upward to loosen chain.

NOTE: Extensive tightening of drive chain may require realignment of drive sheaves or brake adjustment. Keep this fact in mind when making adjustment.

DRIVE BELT & SHEAVE ALIGNMENT. To check alignment of drive sheaves, first remove belt guard and belt. Slightly spread the driven sheave and insert ¼-inch spacers (S-Fig. 1) 180° apart. between sheave halves. With driven sheave thus separated, right faces of both sheaves should be parallel as indicated at (P).

Specified shaft center distance is 10½ inches which is also 1⅜ inches rim clearance (A).

BRAKE. The shoe type brake uses fixed flange of driven sheave as a friction face. Brake should be free of sheave rim when control lever is released but should fully engage before lever contacts handle bar grip. Adjust by turning cable housing anchor adjusting nuts on steering support.

TRACK. With rear of vehicle raised until track is clear, track sag should be ½-1 inch from center bogie wheels. Adjust by loosening clamp screws (1—Fig. 2) and turning adjusting screws (2). Both sides should be adjusted alike.

NOTE: Whenever track tension has been adjusted, alignment MUST be checked as outlined in TRACK SERVICE Section of this manual.

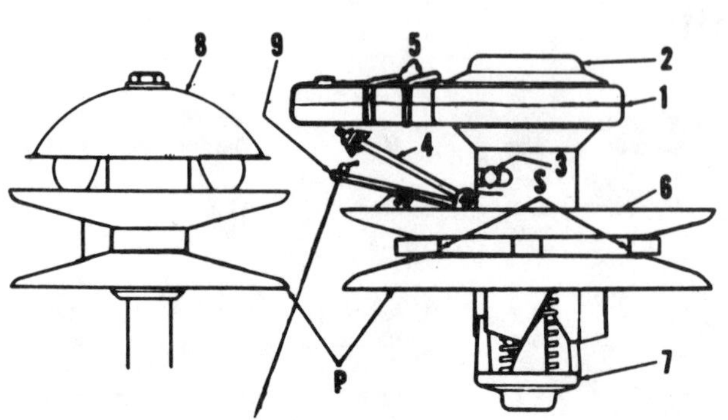

Fig. 1 — Schematic view of drive unit showing component parts. Right edges of torque converter sheaves should be parallel after inserting ¼-inch spacers (S) between sheaves of driven unit.

S. Spacers
P. Parallel edges
1. Chaincase
2. Cover
3. Adjusting bolt
4. Brace rod
5. Clamps
6. Driven sheave
7. Outer cam
8. Drive sheave
9. Brake

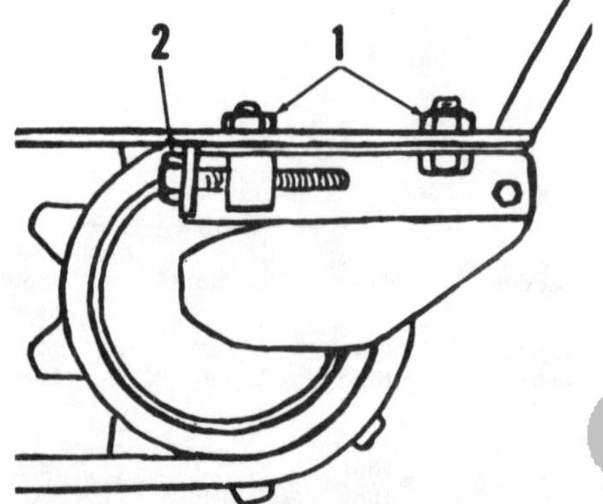

Fig. 2—To adjust track tension, first loosen clamp screws (1) then turn adjusting screw (2). Refer to text for details.

VIKING
1967-1972

	Engine			Carburetor				Clutch		
Model	Make	Model	Displ.	Make	Model	Sprocket Ratio	Chain Size	Make	Shaft Center	Belt Number
					1964					
70999000	Hirth	54R	300cc	Tlt'sn	HR	13:37	....	Polaris	10½"	....
					1968					
8279900	Hirth	190R	300cc	Tlt'sn	HR	13:37	....	Polaris	10½"	....
8277100	Hirth	160R	372cc	Tlt'sn	HD	16:37	....	Polaris	11⅜"	....
8297100	Hirth	160R	372cc	Tlt'sn	HD	16:37	....	Polaris	11⅜"	....
8297101	Hirth	160R	372cc	Tlt'sn	HD	16:37	....	Polaris	11⅜"	....
					1969					
9271900	Hirth	192R	317cc	Tlt'sn	HD	13:37	....	Polaris	10½"	....
9272300	Hirth	200R	372cc	Tlt'sn	HR	16:37	....	Polaris	11⅜"	....
9272700	Hirth	220R	493cc	Tlt'sn	HR	19:33	....	Polaris	11⅜"	....
9271800	Kohler	309-1	309cc	Tlt'sn	HR	13:37	....	Polaris	10½"	....
9272400	Kohler	399-2	399cc	Tlt'sn	HR	16:33	....	Polaris	11⅜"	....
					1970					
0272000	Kohler	309-1	309cc	Tlt'sn	HR	14:37	....	Polaris	11⅜"	....
0272600	Kohler	399-2	399cc	Tlt'sn	HR	16:37	....	Polaris	11⅜"	....
0272800	Kohler	440-2	440cc	Tlt'sn	HR	15:37	....	Salsbury	10-3/16"	....
					1971					
1272000	Kohler	K295-1	294cc	Tlt'sn	HR	14:37	....	Salsbury	11.4"	....
1272500	Kohler	K340-2	338cc	Walbro	WR1	....	....	Salsbury	11.4"	....
1272800	Kohler	K399-2	399cc	Walbro	WR1	....	....	Salsbury	11⅞"	....
1273000	Kohler	K440-2	437cc	Tlt'sn	HR79B	....	....	Salsbury	11⅞"	....
1143000	Kohler	K440-2	437cc	Tlt'sn	HR79B	....	....	Salsbury	11⅞"	....
1145000	Kohler	K440-2	437cc	Tlt'sn	HR79B	....	....	Salsbury	11⅞"	....
1150000	Sachs	SA2-340	338cc	Walbro	WD1	....	....	Salsbury	11⅞"	....
1150000	Sachs	SA2-440	437cc	Walbro	WD1	....	....	Salsbury	11⅞"	....
1150000	Hirth	231R	650cc	Walbro	WD1	....	....	Salsbury	11⅞"	....
					1972					
Vigil.	Kohler	K335-1	335cc	Tlt'sn	HR	....	....	Salsbury	....	....
Vigil. SS	Sachs	SA2-340	338cc	Walbro	....	....	....	Salsbury	11⅞"	....
Vigil. SS	Kohler	K340-2	338cc	Walbro	....	....	....	Salsbury	11⅞"	....
Vagabond	Kohler	K399-2	399cc	Walbro	....	....	....	Salsbury	11⅞"	....
Vanguard	Sachs	SA2-440	437cc	Walbro	....	....	....	Salsbury	11⅞"	....
Vanguard	Kohler	K440-2	437cc	Walbro	....	....	....	Salsbury	11⅞"	....
Vangd. SS	Kohler	K440-2	437cc	Walbro	....	....	....	Salsbury	11⅞"	....
Vanq'her	Hirth	231R	650cc	Walbro	....	....	....	Salsbury	11⅞"	....
Vanq'her	Kohler	K440-2FA	437cc	Walbro	....	....	....	Salsbury	11⅞"	....

LUBRICATION

The enclosed drive chain housing should be filled to level of lower access cover opening with AUTOMATIC TRANSMISSION FLUID, TYPE "A".

Track and drive bearings are sealed type and do not require lubrication. Apply a few drops of oil as required to steering mechanism and to brake and throttle controls.

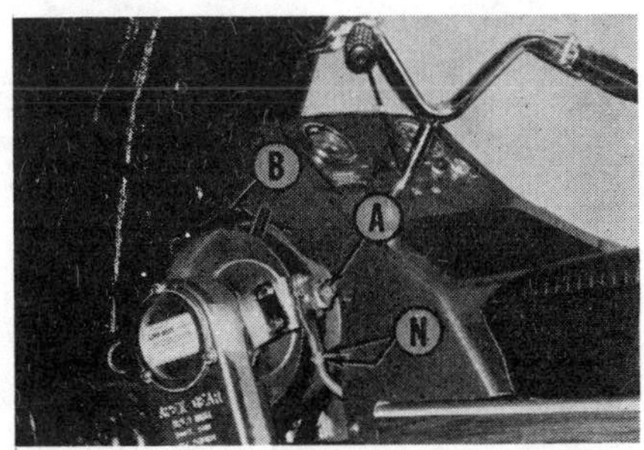

Fig. 1—View of chaincase and drive unit showing points of measurement and adjustment.

A. Brake wear adjustment
B. Backlash
N. Anchor nuts

ADJUSTMENT

STEERING SKIS. Steering skis should be parallel with each other and with vehicle frame when handle bar is in normal straight driving position.

Tie rods must be adjusted individually and can be adjusted after disconnecting either end.

DRIVE CHAIN. The roller drive chain should have some free play which can be measured as backlash at rim of driven sheave. If backlash is excessive, loosen the three stud nuts clamping upper shaft housing to chain case. Pivot housing upward in the two slotted holes until chain is tight, lower housing about ⅛-inch (measured at slotted holes) then tighten stud nuts. Backlash at rim of sheave (B—Fig. 1) should measure approximately ¼-½ inch when adjustment is correct.

BRAKE. Brake band (early models) should barely clear friction surface of driven sheave when released, and should be firmly applied before hand lever touches handle bar grip. Adjust the brake at the two cable housing anchor nuts at brake band end of cable.

Late models use a caliper type disc brake as shown in Fig. 1. Wear adjustment is made by removing cotter pin and turning slotted nut (A) clockwise until snug, then counter-clockwise 1 turn. Push pins must be centered in valleys of actuating arm when adjustment is made. Arm may be repositioned by turning nuts (N) on cable housing anchor.

TRACK. To adjust track tension, raise rear of machine until track is clear of ground.

On early models track should sag about ¼-inch when measured on top section midway between drive and rear idler sprockets.

On 1971 machines, front bogie unit can be installed in two positions. Upper holes raise front of track placing additional weight on skis for better steering control. Lower holes carry more weight on track for improved traction. Track tension is correct when distance from front bogie axle to upper run of track is 4⅞ inches if unit is installed in lower holes or 3¾ inches if installed in upper holes..

Fig. 2 — To adjust track tension, loosen clamp nuts (1) and turn adjusting screws (2). Refer to text for details.

On all models, loosen the two clamp bolts (1—Fig. 2) on each side and turn adjusting screws (2) until adjustment is correct. Both sides must be adjusted alike.

NOTE: Whenever track tension is adjusted, alignment MUST be checked as outlined in TRACK SERVICE Section of this manual.

OVERHAUL

SKIS AND STEERING. Steering skis, spindles, tie rods and associated parts are interchangeabale from right to left. Front spring anchor is equipped with teflon shim and wear pad. Spindle bushings are renewable.

WILDCAT

1970-1971

	Engine			Carburetor				Clutch		
Model	Make	Model	Displ.	Make	Model	Sprocket Ratio	Chain Size	Make	Shaft Center	Belt Number
					1970					
Super	Kohler	K309-1	309cc	Tillotson	HR	14:37	35-2	Polaris	11⅜	109-54
GT	Kohler	K399-2	399cc	Tillotson	HR	16:37	35-2	Polaris	11⅜	109-54
					1971					
Super	Kohler	K309-1	309cc	Tillotson	HR	14:37	35-2	Polaris	11⅜	109-54
GT	Kohler	K399-2	399cc	Tillotson	HR	16:37	35-2	Polaris	11⅜	109-54

YAMAHA

1968-1972

Model	Engine Make	Engine Model	Engine Displ.	Carburetor Make	Carburetor Model	Sprocket Ratio	Chain Size	Clutch Make	Clutch Shaft Center	Belt Number
1968										
SL350........	Own		349cc	Mikuni	VM26X	9:26	35-2	Own	10⅝	80117641
1969										
SL351........	Own		349cc	Mikuni	VM	9:29	35-2	Own	10⅝	80217641
1970										
SL338........	Own		338cc	Keihin	406	12:25	35-2	Own	10⅝	806-17641
SL396........	Own		396cc	Keihin	406	12:25	35-2	Own	10⅝	806-17641
SS338........	Own		338cc	Keihin	406	12:25	35-2	Own	10⅝	806-17641
SS396........	Own		396cc	Keihin	406	13:23	35-2	Own	10⅝	806-17641
1971										
SL292........	Own	Y292	292cc	Mikuni	BN34	13:25	35-2	Own	10⅝	806-17641
SL338B.......	Own	Y338	338cc	Keihin	406	13:25	35-2	Own	10⅝	806-17641
GP396........	Own	Y396	396cc	Keihin	406(2)	13:25	35-2	Own	10⅝	806-17641
SW396.......	Own	Y396	396cc	Mikuni	BN40	13:25	35-2	Own	10⅝	806-17641
SS433........	Own	S433	433cc	Keihin	406(2)	13:2	Own		10⅝	806-17641
SW433E......	Own	Y433	433cc	Mikuni	BN44-40	13:25	35-2	Own	10⅝	806-17641
1972										
SL292B.......	Own		292cc	Mikuni	BN38-34	13:25	40	Own	10⅝	806-17641
GP292........	Own		292cc	Keihin	CD42-38	13:25	40	Own	10⅝	806-17641
SL338C.......	Own		338cc	Keihin	CD42-38	13:25	425-2	Own	10⅝	806-17641
SW433B......	Own		433cc	Keihin	CD42-38	14:25	425-2	Own	10⅝	806-17641
EW433B......	Own		433cc	Keihin	CD42-38	14:25	425-2	Own	10⅝	806-17641
GP433........	Own		433cc	Keihin	CD38-32(2)	13:25	425-2	Own	10⅝	806-17641
GP643........	Own		643cc			13:2	425-2			
EW643.......	Own		643cc			15:21	425-2			

LUBRICATION

On Model SL-350 the engine is lubricated by oil mixed with the fuel. The manufacturer recommends regular gasoline and Two Cycle Snowmobile Oil at a ratio of 20:1.

Later models are equipped with a "Yamalube" automatic metering system which meters the oil into the fuel at mixtures varying from 16:1 at full throttle to 120:1 at idle setting. The oil is contained in a separate tank. The manufacturer recommends YAMALUBE Two Cycle Motor Oil or a known branded Snowmobile Oil.

Chain case uses SAE 10W/30 Motor oil and level should be maintained near top of sight glass located in chain case lower inspection cover. Chain case capacity is 400 cc (about ⅘ pint) on 1968 models, 500 cc (17 oz.) on 1969 models; or 710 cc (1½ pts) on 1970 and 1971 models. The manufacturer recommends a chain case oil change after each 3 months or 100 hours of operation.

Track carriage fittings on SL350 should be lubricated each 40 hours with low temperature grease. Steering spindles (all models) should be lubricated each 40 hours.

ADJUSTMENT

STEERING SKIS. With handle bars in normal straight driving position, both skis should point straight ahead and center-to-center distance should be the same at front and rear of skis.

On SL350, disconnect left end of tie rod and turn end, to adjust. On SL351 the two ends have right hand and left hand threads an adjustment can be made by turning center section. On later models the two drag links should be adjusted alike, by

Fig. 1 — Adjust chain tension on Model SL350 by turning the two draw nuts after loosening housing clamp bolts.

turning center section.

DRIVE CHAIN. Drive chain should have 10 mm (0.4 in.) deflection measured midway between sprockets. Measurement can be taken by removing filler elbow. To adjust the chain on Model SL-350, loosen the three bolts through upper shaft housings and tighten or loosen the two screws (Fig. 1) until deflection is correct. On later models, loosen bolts (See Fig. 2) and rotate housings to adjust the chain. The 1969 and 1970 units have four bolts in housings.

DRIVE BELT. Drive belt (sheave) shaft center distance is 270 mm (10⅝ inches). Adjustment is by sliding engine mounting frame after loosening bolts attaching mount to main frame. Offset is adjusted by loosening bolts attaching engine mount to lower brackets.

Offset of driven sheave is approximately ¼ inch measured at right side of both sheaves as shown in Fig. 2A. Sheave faces must be parallel after adjusting either center distance or offset.

BRAKE. To adjust the caliper type disc brake, refer to Fig. 3 and adjust the stop screw (5—Fig. 11) until a clearance of 1 mm (0.040 in.) exists between outer brake pad and outer face of disc. With outer pad positioned, adjust cable housing anchor (Fig. 4) until inner pad clearance is also 1 mm. Refer to Fig. 11 for exploded view of brake unit.

TRACK. To check track tension, turn machine on its side. Refer to Fig. 5. Track deflection on 15 inch models should be 25 mm (1 inch) at center when tension of 10 kg (22 lbs.) is applied as shown. On 18" models, method of measurement is the same, but deflection should be 15 mm. (19/32").

To adjust track tension, loosen rear carriage pivot bolts as shown in Fig. 6; then turn adjusting screws (Fig. 7) until same scribe mark is aligned on both sides of machine.

NOTE: When track tension has been adjusted, alignment MUST be checked as outlined in TRACK SERVICE Section of this manual.

PERFORMANCE MODIFICATION

On SL351 (1969 Model), modified ski saddles are available as shown in Fig. 8. Both modifications move the ski forward, while M-90 lowers ski 15 mm as shown. Moving skis forward improves handling characteristics under some conditions but may cause oversteer. Lowering the skis usually improves handling on hard-packed snow or ice but may be harmful in deep fluffy snow.

All 1970 machines have a two-position rear suspension spring as shown in Fig. 9. Hooking spring in front position (A) is generally preferred for normal conditions or improved performance on ice or hard-packed snow.

Fig. 2 — On all models except SL350, loosen the clamp bolts and turn housing to adjust chain tension. Measure chain deflection through oil plug hole as shown in lower view. Brake disc has been removed in upper view.

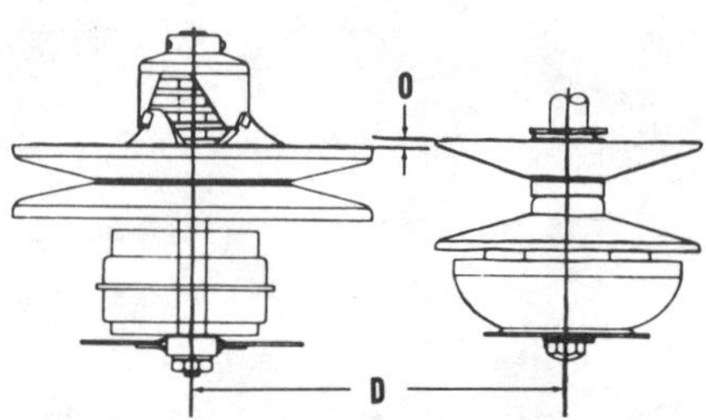

Fig. 2A—Shaft center distance (D) should be approximately 10-5/8 inches when measured as shown. Offset (O) should be ¼-inch.

Fig. 3—Adjusting inner brake pad clearance. Early model is shown.

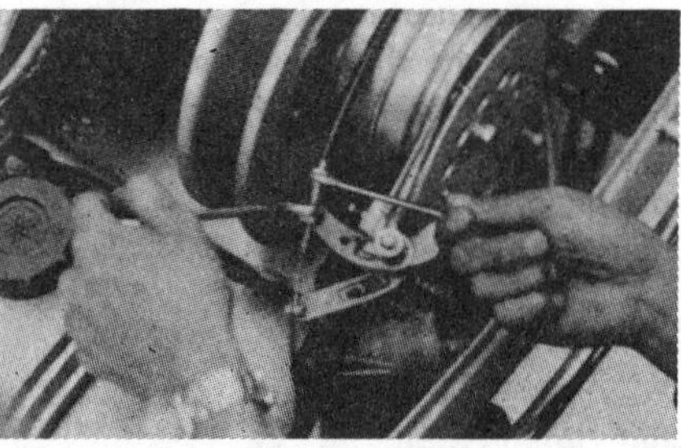

Fig. 4—Adjustment of cable housing anchor completes the brake adjustment. Caliper levers are curved as shown, on late models; and components are not interchangeable.

Fig. 6—To adjust track tension, loosen rear carriage pivot bolts.

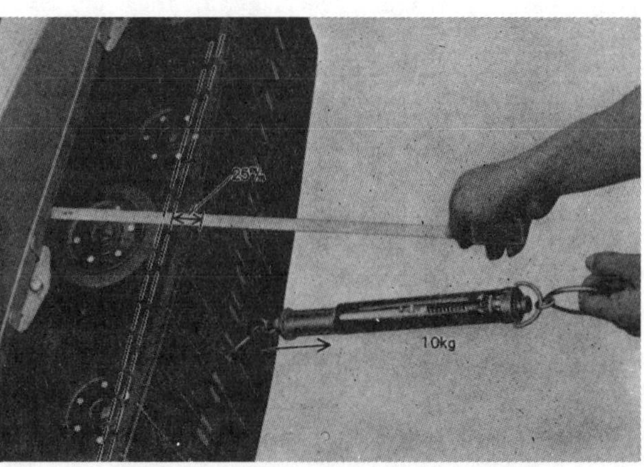

Fig. 5 — With tension of 10 kg (22 lbs.) applied as shown, track deflection should be 25 mm for 15 inch track or 15 mm for 18 inch track.

Rear position (B) lowers rear of machine and takes some weight from skis, which may improve speed under normal conditions or allow greater maneuverabiilty in light fluffy snow.

The torque converter driven sheave can be pre-loaded an additional ⅓ turn if necessary to reduce belt slippage if a GYT (Genuine Yamaha Tuning) Kit is installed; or pre-load reduced or increased as required to compensate for modifications in sprocket ratio. (Minimum pre-load of ⅓ turn MUST be maintained).

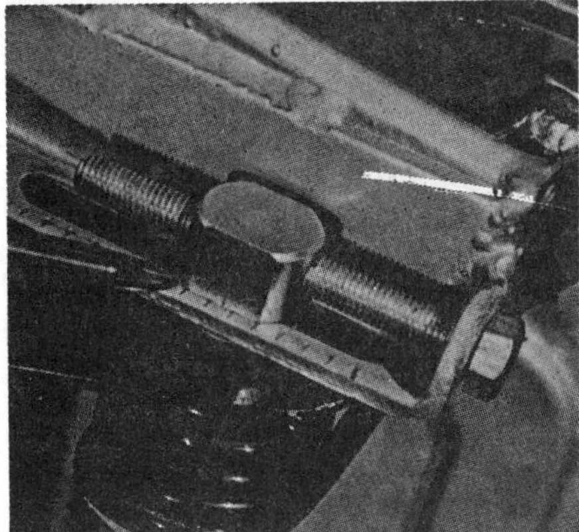

Fig. 7—Scribe lines simplify the problem of equalizing both sides in track adjustment.

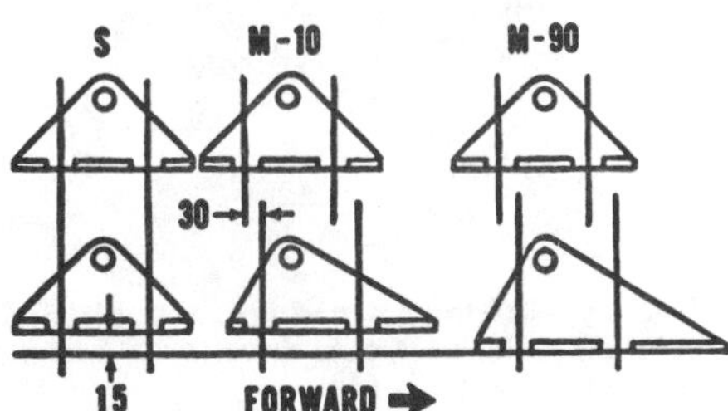

Fig. 8—Modified ski saddles are available for special conditions. Both modifications move ski forward 30mm as shown, while M-90 lowers ski 15mm. Refer to text.

Fig. 9—Late models are equipped with two position spring hooks as shown. Front position (A) puts more weight on skis for easier steering; rear position (B) increases speed under some conditions and permits better traction in deep, fluffy snow.

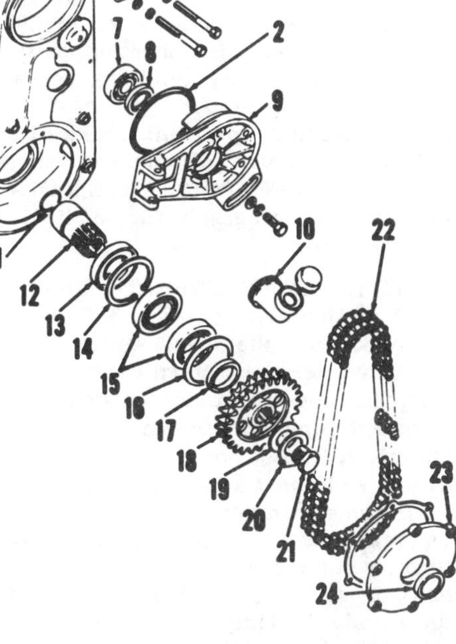

Fig. 10—Exploded view of chaincase and associated parts used on 1969 and 1970 models.

1. Housing
2. O-ring
3. Oil seal
4. Snap ring
5. Bearing
6. Chain case
7. Bearing
8. Oil seal
9. Housing
10. Filler elbow
11. O ring
12. Shaft
13. Oil seal
14. Snap ring
15. Bearing
16. Snap ring
17. Spacer
18. Sprocket
19. Washer
20. Tab washer
21. Cap screw
22. Drive chain
23. Lower cover
24. Sight glass

On all models except SL350, upper (drive) sprocket (3—Fig. 15) is available in 9, 10, 11, 12, 13, 14 and 15 tooth sizes while lower (driven) sprocket (18—Fig. 10) is available in 23, 24, 25, 26 and 29 tooth sizes. Sprockets are interchangeable for all machines, permitting reduction ratios as follows:

Reduction Ratio	Sprocket sizes
3.223:1	9:29*
2.900:1	10:29
2.888:1	9:26
2.778:1	9:25
2.667:1	9:24
2.636:1	11:29
2:600:1	10:26
2.556:1	9:23
2.500:1	10:25
2.417:1	12:29
2.400:1	10:24
2.363:1	11:26
2.300:1	10:23
2.273:1	11:25
2.231:1	13:29
2.182:1	11:24
2.166:1	12:26
2.091:1	11:23
2.083:1	12:25**
2.071:1	14:29
2.000:1	13:26†
2.000:1	12:24
1.939:1	15:29
1.923:1	13:25††
1.917:1	12:23***
1.857:1	14:26
1.846:1	13:24
1.785:1	14:25
1.769:1	13:23
1.733:1	15:26
1.714:1	14:24
1.666:1	15:25
1.643:1	14:23
1.600:1	15:24

* Standard on Model SL-351
** Standard on Models SL-338, SS-338 and SL-396
*** Standard on Model SS-396
† Standard on Model SW 433
†† Standard on most 1971 models.

OVERHAUL

SKIS & STEERING. Skis are interchangeable from right to left; however, ski springs, ski columns (spindles) and steering arms are not. Ski runners are renewable.

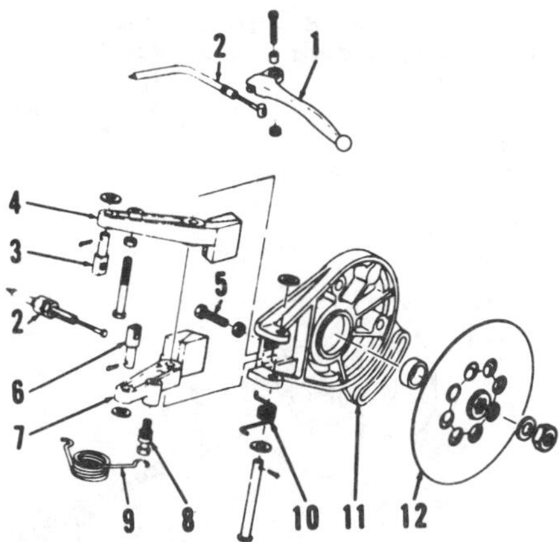

Fig. 11—Exploded view of caliper type disc brake and associated parts used on late models. Early models are similar.

1. Hand lever
2. Cable
3. Threaded pin
4. Outer caliper
5. Adjusting screw
6. Slotted pin
7. Inner caliper
8. Special bolt
9. Spring
10. Spring
11. Housing
12. Disc

DRIVE. All models except the limited production SL-350 are equipped with oil injection, the pump being belt driven from a pulley built on engine side of Torque Converter drive sheave. Be careful of belt when disassembling unit.

Lower drive sprocket can be removed after removing lower cover (23—Fig. 10), then disconnecting drive chain and removing retaining screw (21). To remove upper sprocket, first remove brake caliper unit, brake disc (12—Fig. 11) and left hand housing (11). Refer to PERFORMANCE MODIFICATION paragraph for available sprocket sizes.

TORQUE CONVERTER. The limited production Model SL-350 was equipped with the speed sensing torque converter unit shown exploded in Figs. 12 and 13. Later models use torque sensing unit shown in Figs. 14 and 15. All units have 3.5:1 reduction at low end and 1:1 at high end.

Torque sensing driven sheaves must be pre-loaded during assembly by turning outer cam (10—Fig. 15) after hooking spring ends. Normal preload for standard models is ⅓ turn (one cam); and ⅔ turn (two cams) for high performance models. Refer also to PERFORMANCE MODIFICATION paragraphs immediately preceding. Shim (1) is available in thicknesses of 0.2, 0.3, 0.4, 0.5, 0.6 and 0.7 mm (0.008-0.028 inch) to be used as required to take up sprocket end play.

The primary (drive) sheave must be disassembled during removal. After removing cap screw (1—Fig. 14), weight unit (3) can be withdrawn. Sliding sheave (7) and spring (9) can be withdrawn after removing snap ring (4) and retainer halves (5). A puller is required to break fixed flange (14) from crankshaft taper after removing nut (10), idler bearing (13) and associated parts. Three tapped holes are provided in flange for attaching puller. Remove carefully to prevent damage to Autolube drive belt (B) after sheave is loosened.

New drive belt width is 31 mm 1.22 inch). Renew the belt if worn to 26 mm (1 inch) or if belt is otherwise damaged.

TACHOMETER AND SPEEDOMETER DRIVE. Both the optional tachometer and speedometer drive units are mechanically driven. The tachometer drive units are mechanically driven. The tachometer from the oil injection pump drive shaft as shown in Fig. 16, and the speedometer from track drive axle as shown in Fig. 17.

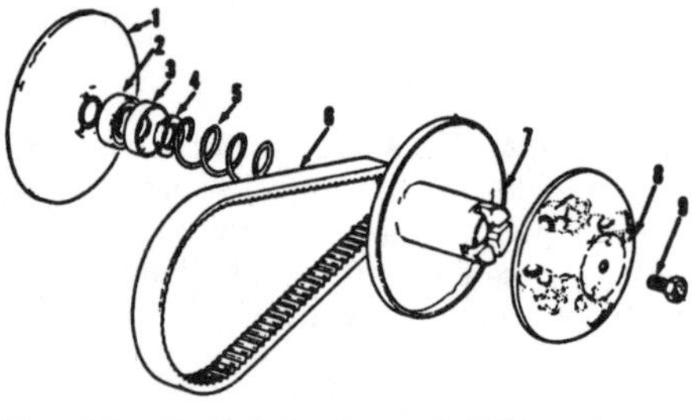

Fig. 12—Exploded view of Drive sheave and associated parts used on Model SL-350.

1. Fixed flange
2. Idler bearing
3. Spring cup
4. Nut
5. Spring
6. Belt
7. Moving flange
8. Governor
9. Cap screw

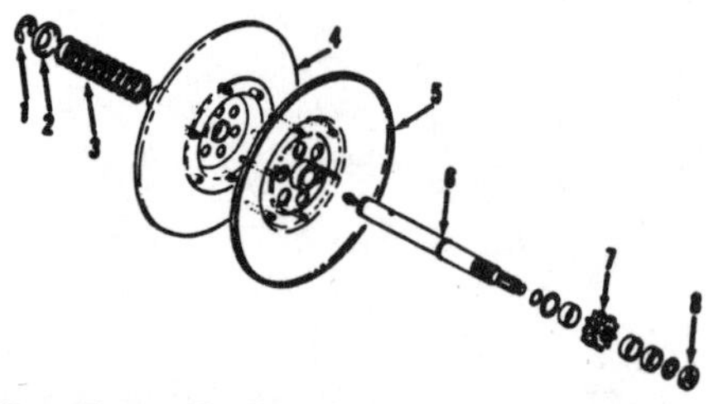

Fig. 13 — Exploded view of Secondary (driven) sheave and associated parts used on Model S1-350.

1. E-ring
2. Spring cup
3. Spring
4. Moving flange
5. Fixed flange
6. Shaft
7. Sprocket
8. Nut

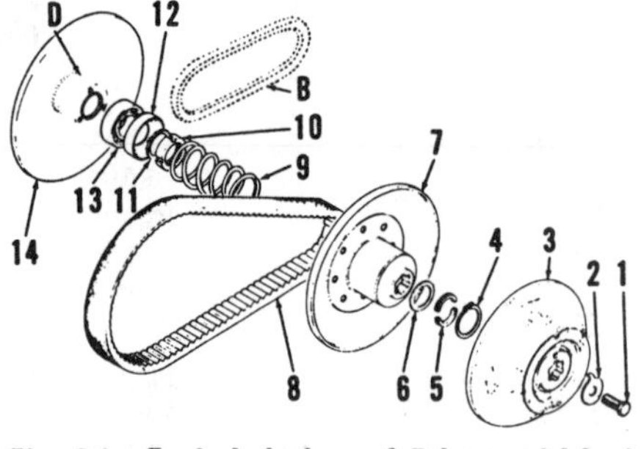

Fig. 14—Exploded view of Primary (drive) sheave used on late models. Autolube drive belt (B) drives from groove (D) on hub of fixed sheave and must not be damaged in removal or installation.

1. Cap screw
2. Tab washer
3. Centrifugal unit
4. Snap ring
5. Split retainer
6. Spacer washer
7. Sliding sheave
8. Drive belt
9. Spring
10. Retaining nut
11. Thrust washer
12. Spring seat
13. Idler bearing
14. Fixed sheave

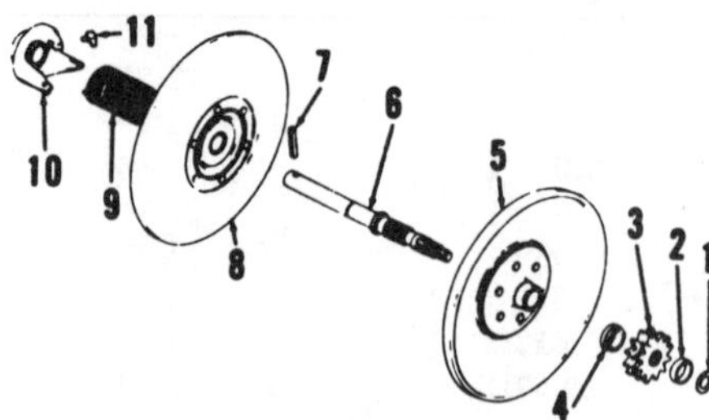

Fig. 15—Exploded view of torque sensing Secondary (driven) unit used on late models.

1. Shim
2. Spacer
3. Sprocket
4. Spacer
5. Fixed sheave
6. Shaft
7. Spring pin
8. Sliding sheave
9. Torque spring
10. Outer cam
11. Cam shoe

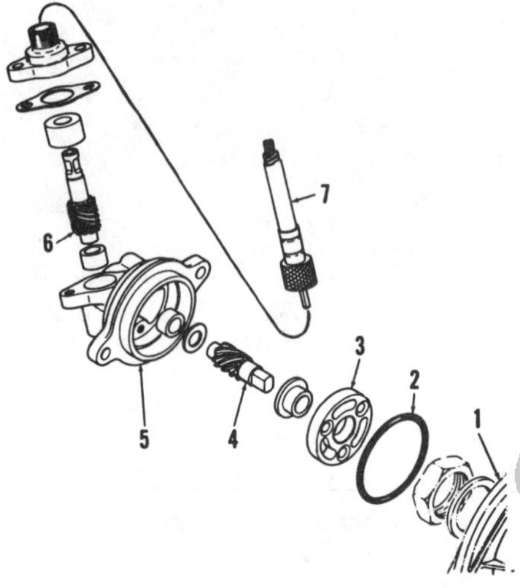

Fig. 16—Speedometer drive unit attaches to right side of track drive axle housing (1).

1. Housing
2. O-ring
3. Bearing
4. Drive-gear
5. Housing
6. Driven gear
7. Speedometer cable

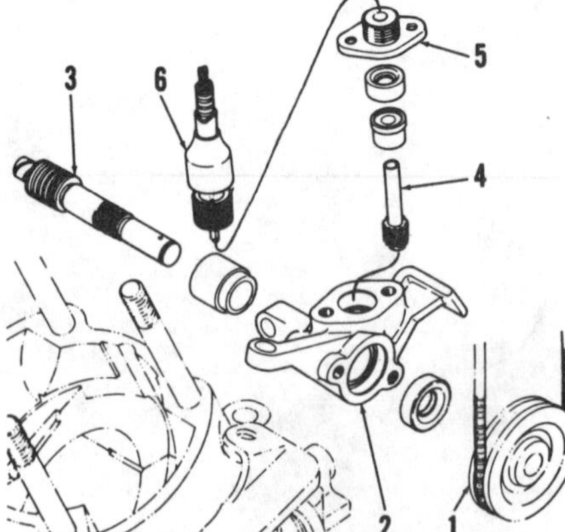

Fig. 17 — Tachometer is mechanically driven from "Yamalube" pump drive worm (3) as shown.

1. Drive pulley
2. Housing
3. Drive worm
4. Driven gear
5. Cap
6. Tacometer cable

YAMAHA

YAMAHA MOTOR COMPANY
6555 Katella Avenue
Cypress, CA 90630

1973-1985

CONDENSED SERVICE DATA

	Engine			Carburetor				Clutch		
Model	Make	Model	Displ.	Make	Model	Sprocket Ratio	Chain Size	Make	Shaft Center	Belt Number
1973										
SL292C	Own	Y292	292cc	Keihin	CD38-32	13:25	40	Own	10⅝	806-17641
SL338D	Own	Y338	338cc	Keihin	CD42-38	13:25	425-2	Own	10⅝	806-17641
SL433B	Own	Y433	433cc	Keihin	CD42-38	14:25	425-2	Own	10⅝	806-17641
EL433B	Own	Y433	433cc	Keihin	CD42-38	14:25	425-2	Own	10⅝	806-17641
SW433C	Own	Y433	433cc	Keihin	CD42-38	14:25	425-2	Own	10⅝	806-17641
EW433C	Own	Y433	433cc	Keihin	CD42-38	14:25	425-2	Own	10⅝	806-17641
EW643B	Own	Y643	643cc	Keihin	CD50-43	15:21	425-2	Hydrokinetic		
GP292B	Own	S292	292cc	Keihin	CD42-38	13:25	425-2	Own	10⅝	806-17641
GP338	Own	S338	338cc	Keihin	CD38-38(2)	13:25	425-2	Own	10⅝	806-17641
GP433B	Own	S433	433cc	Keihin	CD38-32(2)	14:23	425-2	Own	10⅝	806-17641
GP643B	Own	S643	643cc	Keihin	CD42-35(2)	13:21	425-2	Own	10⅝	
1974										
GP246F	Own	S246	246cc	Mikuni	BN38-34SH	11:25	40	Own	10⅝	806-17641
SM292F	Own	Y292	292cc	Keihin	CD34-30	11:25	40	Own	10⅝	806-17641
GP292F	Own	S292	292cc	Mikuni	BN38-34SH	12:23	425-2	Own	10⅝	806-17641
SL338F	Own	Y338	338cc	Keihin	CD42-38	12:23	425-2	Own	10⅝	806-17641
GP338F	Own	S338	338cc	Keihin	CDX42-38	13:23	425-2	Own	10⅝	806-17641
GPX338F	Own	SX338	338cc	Mikuni	BN38-34SH(2)	18:35	35-3	Own	10⅝	806-17641
TL433F	Own	Y433	433cc	Keihin	CD42-38	14:19	425-2	Hydrokinetic		Gilmer
TW433F	Own	Y433	433cc	Keihin	CD42-38	14:18	425-2	Hydrokinetic		Gilmer
SL433F	Own	Y433	433cc	Keihin	CD42-38	12:23	425-2	Own	10⅝	806-17641
GP433F	Own	S433	433cc	Keihin	CDX42-38	13:23	425-2	Own	10⅝	806-17641
GPX433F	Own	SX433	433cc	Keihin	CDX42-38(2)	19:35	35-3	Own	10⅝	806-17641
1975										
SM292F	Own	Y292	292cc	Keihin	CD34-30	11:25	40	Own	10⅝	820-17641
SL338F	Own	Y338	338cc	Keihin	CD42-38	12:23	425-2	Own	10⅝	820-17641
SL433F	Own	Y433	433cc	Keihin	CD42-38	12:23	425-2	Own	10⅝	820-17641
TW433F	Own	Y433	433cc	Keihin	CD42-38	14:18	425-2	Hydrokinetic		Gilmer
TL433F	Own	Y433	433cc	Keihin	CD42-38	14:19	425-2	Hydrokinetic		Gilmer
GP246F	Own	S246	246cc	Mikuni	BN38-34	11:25	40	Own	10⅝	820-17641
GP292F	Own	S292	292cc	Mikuni	BN38-34	12:23	425-2	Own	10⅝	820-17641
GP338F	Own	S338	338cc	Keihin	CD42-38	13:23	425-2	Own	10⅝	820-17641
GP433F	Own	S433	433cc	Keihin	CD42-38	13:23	425-2	Own	10⅝	820-17641
GPX338G	Own	SX338	338cc	Keihin	CDX42-38(2)	18:35	35-3	Own	10⅝	820-17641
GPX433G	Own	SX433	433cc	Keihin	CDX42-38(2)	19:35	35-3	Own	10⅝	820-17641
1976										
GS300	Own	Y292	292cc	Keihin	CD34-30	11:25	40	Own	10⅝	820-17641
GS340	Own	Y338	338cc	Keihin	CDX42-38	12:22	425-2	Own	10⅝	820-17641
GP300	Own	S292	292cc	Mikuni	BN38-34	12:22	425-2	Own	10⅝	820-17641
GP440	Own	S433	433cc	Keihin	CDX42-38	14:23	40-2	Own	10⅝	820-17641
PR440	Own	S433	433cc	Keihin	CDX42-38	15:18	40-2	Own	...	874-17641
EX340	Own	X338	338cc	Keihin	PW42-38	19:33	35-3	Own	10⅝	8A1-17641
EX440	Own	X433	433cc	Keihin	PW42-38	19:33	35-3	Own	10⅝	8A1-17641
SRX340	Own	RX338	338cc	Mikuni	VM36	16:33	35-3	Own	10⅝	8A1-17641
SRX440	Own	RX439	439cc	Mikuni	VM40	18:35	35-3	Own	10⅝	8A1-17641
1977										
ET250A	Own	S246	246cc	Keihin	CDX32	13:22	40	Own	10⅝	820-17641
GS300A	Own	Y292	292cc	Keihin	CD34	11:25	40	Own	10⅝	820-17641
GS340A	Own	Y338	338cc	Keihin	CDX42	12:22	40-2	Own	10⅝	820-17641
GP440A	Own	S433	433cc	Keihin	CDX42	14:23	40-2	Own	10⅝	820-17641
EX340A	Own	SS338	338cc	Keihin	PW42	19:33	35-3	Own	10⅝	8A1-17641
EX440A	Own	SS433	433cc	Keihin	PW42	19:33	35-3	Own	10⅝	8A1-17641
SRX440A	Own	RX439	439cc	Mikuni	VM40SS(2)	...	35-3	Own	10⅝	8A1-17641

Model	Engine			Carburetor		Sprocket Ratio	Chain Size	Clutch		Belt Number
	Make	Model	Displ.	Make	Model			Make	Shaft Center	
1978										
ET250B	Own	S246	246cc	Keihin	CDX32	13:22	40	Own	10⅝	820-17641
ET340B	Own	E338	338cc	Mikuni	B36	13:22	40-2	Own	10½	820-17641
EC340B	Own	SS338	338cc	Keihin	GD-38	19:33	35-3	Own	10⅝	8A1-17641
EX340B	Own	SS433	433cc	Keihin	BD-38	19:33	35-3	Own	10⅝	8A7-17641
SRX440B	Own	RT439	439cc	Mikuni	VM-36	18:29	35-3	Own	10⅝	8A2-17641
SSR440B	Own	RX439	439cc	Mikuni		20:35	35-3	Own	10⅝	8A2-17641
1979										
ET250C	Yamaha	S246	246cc	Keihin	CDX38-32	13:22	40	Own	10½	820-17641
ET300C	Yamaha	E294	294cc	Mikuni	B38-32	13:22	40-2	Own	10½	820-17641
EC340C	Yamaha	E338	338cc	Mikuni	B38-34	13:22	40-2	Own	10½	820-17641
ET340EC	Yamaha	E338	338cc	Mikuni	B38-34	13:22	40-2	Own	10½	820-17641
EX440C	Yamaha	SS433	433cc	Keihin	BD44-38	17:29	35-3	Own	10⅝	8F2-17641
Excel VC	Yamaha	SA535	535cc	Keihin	BD44-38	17:29	35-3	Own	10⅝	8F2-17641
SRX440C	Yamaha	RT439	439cc	Mikuni	VM36	18:29	35-3	Own	10⅝	8F2-17641
1980										
ET250D	Yamaha	S246	246cc	Keihin	CDX38-32	13:22	40	Own	10½	820-17641
ET300D	Yamaha	E294	294cc	Mikuni	B38-32	13:22	40	Own	10½	820-17641
EC340D	Yamaha	E338	338cc	Mikuni	B38-34	13:22	40-2	Own	10½	820-17641
EX440D	Yamaha	SS433	433cc	Keihin	BD44-38	17:29	35-3	Own	10⅝	8F2-17641
Excel VD	Yamaha	SA535	535cc	Keihin	BD44-38	17:29	35-3	Own	10⅝	8F2-17641
SRX440D	Yamaha	RT439	439cc	Mikuni	VM36	18:29	35-3	Own	10⅝	8F2-17641
SS440D	Yamaha	SA437	437cc	Keihin	BD38-34	18:29	35-2	Own	10⅝	8F2-17641
SR540D	Yamaha	SA535	535cc	Keihin	BD44-38	18:29	35-2	Own	10⅝	8F2-17641
1981										
ET250E	Yamaha	S246	246cc	Keihin	CDX38-32	13:22	40	Own	10½	820-17641
ET300E	Yamaha	E294	294cc	Mikuni	B38-32	13:22	40	Own	10½	820-17641
EC340E	Yamaha	E338	338cc	Mikuni	B38-34	13:22	40-2	Own	10½	820-17641
EX440E	Yamaha	SS433	433cc	Keihin	BD44-38	17:29	35-3	Own	10⅝	8F2-17641
SS440E	Yamaha	SA437	437cc	Keihin	BD38-34	18:29	35-2	Own	10⅝	8F2-17641
SS540E	Yamaha	SA535	535cc	Keihin	BD44-38	17:31	35-3	Own	10⅝	8F2-17641
SRX44EC	Yamaha	RT439	439cc	Mikuni	B40-38	17:31	35-3	Own	12	8F2-17641
1982										
BR250F	Yamaha	S246	246cc	Keihin	BD32-28	13:22	40	Own	10½	820-17641
EC340F	Yamaha	E338	338cc	Mikuni	B38-34	13:22	40-2	Own	10½	820-17641
ET340TF	Yamaha	E338	338cc	Mikuni	B38-34	13:22	40-2	Own	10½	820-17641
SS440F	Yamaha	SA437	437cc	Keihin	BD44-38	18:29	35-2	Own	10⅝	8F2-17641
SR540F	Yamaha	SA535	535cc	Keihin	BD44-38	17:31	35-3	Own	10⅝	8F2-17641
SRX500F	Yamaha	SA499	499cc	Mikuni	B44-42	17:31	35-3	Own	10⅝	8F2-17641
1983										
BR250G	Yamaha	R246	246cc	Keihin	BD32-28	13:22	40-1	Own	10½	820-17641
ET300G	Yamaha	E294	294cc	Mikuni	B38-32	13:22	40-2	Own	10½	820-17641
EC340G	Yamaha	E338	338cc	Mikuni	B38-34	13:22	40-2	Own	10½	820-17641
ET340TG	Yamaha	E338	338cc	Mikuni	B38-34	12:23	40-2	Own	10½	820-17641
SS440G	Yamaha	SA437	437cc	Keihin	BD44-38	17:29	35-3	Own	10⅝	8F2-17641
SR540G	Yamaha	SA535	535cc	Keihin	BD44-38	17:31	35-3	Own	10⅝	8F2-17641
VMX540G	Yamaha	8U9	535cc	Mikuni	VM38	18:33	35-3	Own	12	8M6-17641
1984										
BR250H	Yamaha	R246	246cc	Keihin	BD32-28	13:22	40-1	Own	10½	820-17641
ET300H	Yamaha	E294	294cc	Mikuni	B38-32	13:22	40-2	Own	10½	820-17641
EC340H	Yamaha	E338	338cc	Mikuni	B38-34	13:22	40-2	Own	10½	820-17641
ET340H	Yamaha	E338	338cc	Mikuni	B38-34	13:22	40-2	Own	10½	820-17641
ET340TH	Yamaha	E338	338cc	Mikuni	B38-34	12:23	40-2	Own	10½	820-17641
SS440H	Yamaha	SA437	437cc	Keihin	BD44-38	17:29	35-3	Own	10⅝	8F2-17641
PZ480H	Yamaha	8V0	485cc	Mikuni	B38-32	17:29	25-3	Own	10 9/16	8F2-17641
PZ480SEH	Yamaha	8V0	485cc	Mikuni	B38-32	17:29	35-3	Own	10 9/16	8F2-17641
SR540H	Yamaha	SA535	535cc	Keihin	BD44-38	17:31	35-3	Own	10⅝	8F2-17641
VMX540H	Yamaha	8X6	535cc	Mikuni	VM38	18:33	35-3	Own	12	8M6-17641
1985										
BR250J	Yamaha	80F	246cc	Keihin	BD32-28	13:22	40-1	Own	10½	820-17641
EC340J	Yamaha	8Y3	338cc	Mikuni	B38-32	13:22	40-2	Own	10½	820-17641
ET340J	Yamaha	8Y2	338cc	Mikuni	B38-32	13:22	40-2	Own	10½	820-17641
ET340TJ	Yamaha	80E	338cc	Mikuni	B38-32	12:23	40-2	Own	10½	820-17641
SS440J	Yamaha	80R	437cc	Keihin	BD44-38	17:29	35-3	Own	10⅝	8F2-17641
PZ480J	Yamaha	80L	485cc	Mikuni	B38-32	17:29	35-3	Own	10 9/16	8F2-17641-01
PZ480SEJ	Yamaha	80K	485cc	Mikuni	B38-32	17:29	35-3	Own	10 9/16	8F2-17641-01
SR540J	Yamaha	8Y0	535cc	Keihin	BD44-38	17:31	35-3	Own	10⅝	8F2-17641-01
XL540J	Yamaha	8Y7	535cc	Mikuni	B38-32	17:31	35-3	Own	10⅝	8F2-17641-01
VMX540J	Yamaha	80N	535cc	Mikuni	VM38	18:33	35-3	Own	12	8M6-17641

LUBRICATION

All late model vehicles are equipped with an "Autolube" automatic metering system which meters the oil into the fuel at a pre-set amount. Oil to fuel mixture ratio is low at full throttle and large at idle setting. The oil is contained in a separate tank and connected by a hose to Autolube pump. Manufacturer recommends YAMALUBE Two-stroke Motor Oil or a good quality Snowmobile Oil. Refer also to the YAMAHA Engine Section within this manual.

1979

Model	Chaincase Capacity
ET250	449.5 mL (15.2 oz.)
ET300	449.5 mL (15.2 oz.)
ET340	397.4 mL (13.4 oz.)
ET340E	397.4 mL (13.4 oz.)
EX440	319.4 mL (10.8 oz.)
Excel V.	298.7 mL (10.1 oz.)
SRX440	319.4 mL (10.8 oz.)

1980

Model	Chaincase Capacity
ET250	449.5 mL (15.2 oz.)
ET300	449.5 mL (15.2 oz.)
ET340	397.4 mL (13.4 oz.)
EX440	319.4 mL (10.8 oz.)
Excel V	298.7 mL (10.1 oz.)
SRX440	319.4 mL (10.8 oz.)
SS440	251.3 mL (8.5 oz.)
SR540	251.3 mL (8.5 oz.)

1981

Model	Chaincase Capacity
ET250	449.5 mL (15.2 oz.)
ET300	449.5 mL (15.2 oz.)
EC340	397.4 mL (13.4 oz.)
EX440	319.4 mL (10.8 oz.)
SRX440	251.3 mL (8.5 oz.)
SS440	251.3 mL (8.5 oz.)
SR540	251.3 mL (8.5 oz.)

For all early models, chaincase uses SAE 10W/30 Motor Oil and level should be maintained near top of sight glass located in chaincase lower inspection cover. Chaincase capacity is 502.6 mL (1.1 pt.) on all models with left-hand chaincase and 319.4 mL (10.8 oz.) for GPX models with right-hand chaincase.

On 1979-1982 models, manufacturer recommends using SAE 75 or 80 gear oil with an API classification of GL-3. On 1983 and later models, manufacturer recommends a SAE 80W-90 gear oil with an API classification of GL-4. To check chaincase oil level on all models, remove oil level plug at bottom of chaincase cover. Oil level should be even with bottom of level plug opening. Refer to the following table for chaincase oil capacities.

1982

Model	Chaincase Capacity
BR250	198.7 mL (6.7 oz.)
ET340	397.4 mL (13.4 oz.)
ET340T	397.4 mL (13.4 oz.)
SS440	251.3 mL (8.5 oz.)
SR540	251.3 mL (8.5 oz.)
SRX500	251.3 mL (8.5 oz.)

1983

Model	Chaincase Capacity
BR250G	198.7 mL (6.7 oz.)
ET300G	449.5 mL (15.2 oz.)
EC340G	397.4 mL (13.4 oz.)
ET340TG	397.4 mL (13.4 oz.)
SS440G	251.3 mL (8.5 oz.)
SR540G	251.3 mL (8.5 oz.)
VMX540G	251.3 mL (8.5 oz.)

1984

Model	Chaincase Capacity
BR250H	198.7 mL (6.7 oz.)
ET300H	449.5 mL (15.2 oz.)
EC340H	397.4 mL (13.4 oz.)
ET340H	397.4 mL (13.4 oz.)
ET340TH	397.4 mL (13.4 oz.)
SS440H	251.3 mL (8.5 oz.)
PZ480H	251.3 L (8.5 oz.)
PZ480SEH	251.3 mL (8.5 oz.)
SR540H	251.3 mL (8.5 oz.)
VMX540H	251.3 mL (8.5 oz.)

1985

Model	Chaincase Capacity
BR250J	198.7 mL (6.7 oz.)
EC340J	397.4 mL (13.4 oz.)
ET340J	397.4 mL (13.4 oz.)
ET340TJ	397.4 mL (13.4 oz.)
SS440J	251.3 mL (8.5 oz.)
PZ480	251.3 mL (8.5 oz.)
PZ480SEJ	251.3 mL (8.5 oz.)
SR540J	251.3 mL (8.5 oz.)
XL540J	251.3 mL (8.5 oz.)
VMX540J	251.3 mL (8.5 oz.)

For all models, manufacturer recommends changing chaincase oil at least every 40 operational hours or at beginning of each season.

On models with hydrokinetic torque converter, unit should be kept filled to plug level with 1.9 L (20 qt.) of MOBIL ATF220 Automatic Transmission Fluid.

On all models lubricate front steering linkage and pivoting joints with a light multi-purpose grease at least every 40 operational hours or at beginning of each season.

ADJUSTMENT

STEERING SKIS. With handlebars in normal straight driving position, both skis should point straight ahead and center-to-center distance should be the same at front and rear of skis.

To adjust, loosen locknut located at each end of steering relay rod and turn relay rod until correct distance is attained, then retighten locknuts. On models equipped with individual relay rods for each ski, each side should be adjusted equally.

DRIVE CHAIN. On early model vehicles drive chain should have 10 mm (0.4 in.) deflection as shown in Fig. 1 measured midway between sprockets. Measurement can be taken by removing filler elbow. To adjust chain, loosen bolts and rotate housings until correct chain deflection is attained, then retighten bolts.

On all 1979 and later models and some earlier models equipped with drive chain adjustment bolt located in chaincase side housing as shown in Fig. 2 or 3, drive chain deflection should be 8-15 mm (0.32-0.59 in.) measured midway between sprockets. To check chain deflection, remove filler cap from front chaincase cover. Measure chain deflection and adjust as needed. To adjust models with jam nut, loosen jam nut (2 – Fig. 2), then turn adjustment bolt (3) in or out until correct deflection is attained. Retighten jam nut (2). To adjust models with locking clip, remove clip (2 – Fig. 3). Turn adjuster bolt (1) until correct deflection is attained, then reinstall locking clip.

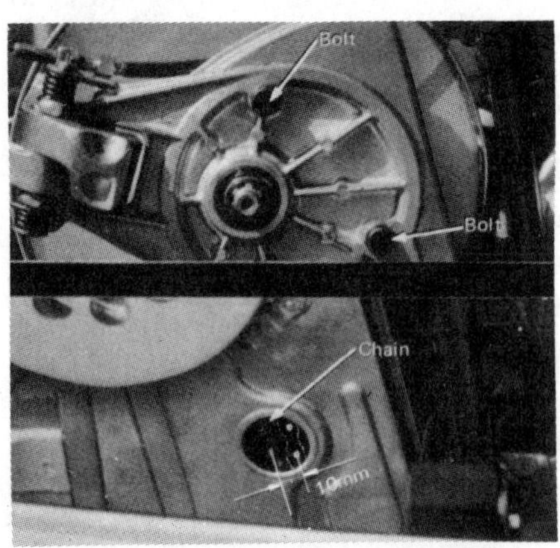

Fig. 1 — On early models loosen the clamp bolts and turn housing to adjust chain tension. Measure chain deflection through oil plug hole as shown in lower view. Brake disc has been removed in upper view.

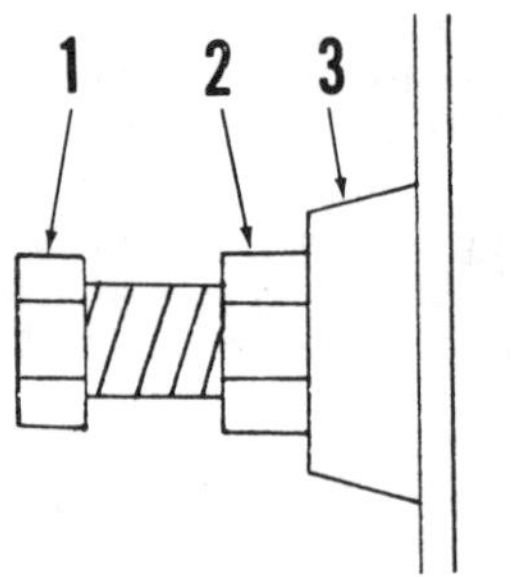

Fig. 2 — View showing drive chain adjustment bolt (1) and jam nut (2) located in chaincase side housing (3) on later model vehicles.

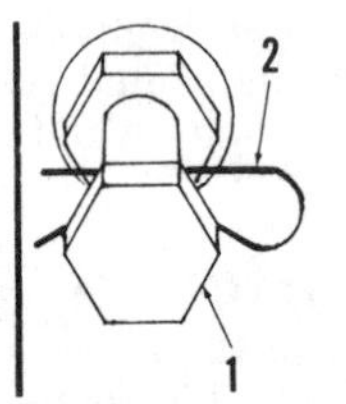

Fig. 3 — View showing drive chain adjustment bolt (1) and locking clip (2).

DRIVE BELT. Drive belt (sheave) shaft center distance is listed in CONDENSED SERVICE DATA table. Adjustment is made by sliding engine mounting frame after loosening bolts attaching mount to main frame. On some models a small adjustment may be made by loosening and tilting chaincase assembly.

Offset of driven sheave on all early models is approximately 6.3 mm (0.25 in.) measured at right side of both sheaves as shown in Fig. 4. Sheave faces must be parallel after adjusting either center distance or offset.

For all later models refer to Table 1. To adjust pulley offset either loosen mounting bolts and slide engine (SE), withdraw driven sheave and change shims (CS) or on Model BR250 no adjustment (NA) is available and replacement of bent or damaged parts is required.

BRAKE. To adjust dual lever type caliper disc brake, refer to Fig. 5 and adjust stop screw (5 – Fig. 23) until clearance between outer brake pad and outer face of disc is 1 mm (0.040 in.). With outer pad positioned, adjust cable housing anchor (Fig. 6) until inner pad clearance is also 1 mm.

Adjustment of disc brake (Fig. 7) is done by first adjusting brake cable (3 – Fig. 8) until distance (D) is 57 mm (2.24 in.). Adjust by loosening locknut (1), then turn adjuster (3) until correct

TABLE 1 — PULLEY OFFSET

Model	Year	Adjustment Procedure	Distance
BR250	82-85	NA	10-12 mm (0.39-0.47 in.)
ET250	77-81	SE	10-12 mm (0.39-0.47 in.)
ET300	79-84	SE	10-12 mm (0.39-0.47 in.)
ET340	81-85	SE	10-12 mm (0.39-0.47 in.)
EC340	78-80, 82-84	SE	10-12 mm (0.39-0.47 in.)
EX340	76-80	SE	5-6 mm (0.197-0.237 in.)
EX440	76-80	CS	5-6 mm (0.197-0.237 in.)
EX440	81	CS	5-6 mm (0.197-0.237 in.)
Excel V	79-80	SE	5-6 mm (0.197-0.237 in.)
SS440	80-85	SE	10.5-11.5 mm (0.413-0.453 in.)
SRX440	79-81	CS	5-6 mm (0.197-0.237 in.)
PZ480	84-85	CS	10.5-11.5 mm (0.413-0.453 in.)
SR540	80-82	CS	10.5-11.5 mm (0.413-0.453 in.)
SR540	83	CS	12.5-13.5 mm (0.49-0.53 in.)
SR540	84-85	CS	10.5-11.5 mm (0.413-0.453 in.)
VMX540	83	CS	10-12 mm (0.39-0.47 in.)
VMX540	84-85	CS	10.5-11.5 mm (0.413-0.453 in.)
XL540	85	CS	10.5-11.5 mm (0.413-0.453 in.)

distance is obtained. Retighten locknut. After setting distance (D) adjust clearance between brake disc and pads. To adjust, loosen locknut (1 – Fig. 7) and turn adjustment bolt (2) until a 0.15 mm (0.006 in.) feeler gage slides between disc and pads with a slight drag as shown. Retighten locknut.

TRACK TENSION. Before checking track tension, ensure track alignment is correct as outlined in TRACK SERVICE section. To check track tension, carefully tilt the vehicle on its side. Attach a suitable spring scale to center of the track as shown in Fig. 9. Apply a 10 kg (22 lbs.) load and measure the deflection (clearance) between the track rail and the track.

Track deflection should be 40-50 mm (1-9/16 to 2 in.) on ET340T models and 20-25 mm (25/32 to 1 in.) on PZ480 models. On all remaining models equipped with a 381 mm (15 in.) wide track, track deflection should be 25-30 mm (1 to 1-3/16 in.) while on models equipped with a 457 mm (18 in.) wide track, track deflection should be 15 mm (19/32 in.).

To adjust track tension on models equipped with bogie wheel type suspension system, loosen rear carriage pivot bolts as shown in Fig. 10. Turn adjusting screw (Fig. 11) until same scribe mark is aligned on both sides of vehicle.

To adjust track tension on BR250, ET300, EC340 and ET340 models and early models equipped with slide rail type suspension system, loosen locknuts securing adjusting screws (T – Fig. 12) on both sides. Rotate adjusting screws equally until correct tension is obtained. Tighten adjusting screw locknut to 35 N·m (25 ft.-lbs.) torque.

On all remaining models equipped with slide rail type suspension system, loosen left and right rear axle locknut (2 – Fig. 13) and turn adjustment nut (3).

Fig. 4 – Distance (D) shows shaft center distance. Distance (O) shows pulley offset.

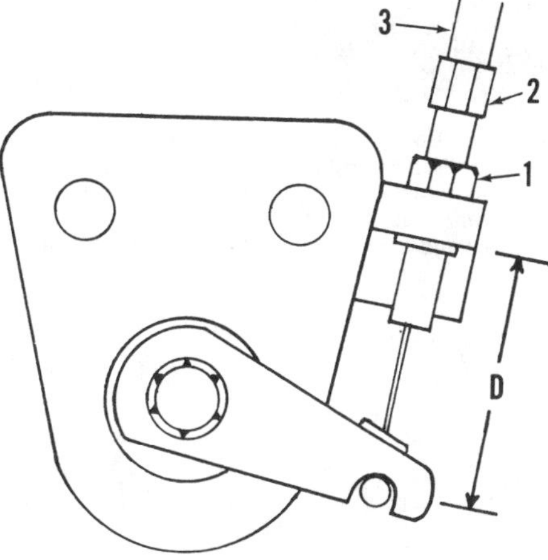

Fig. 8 – View showing caliper assembly and actuating components.

D. Distance
1. Locknut
2. Adjuster
3. Brake cable

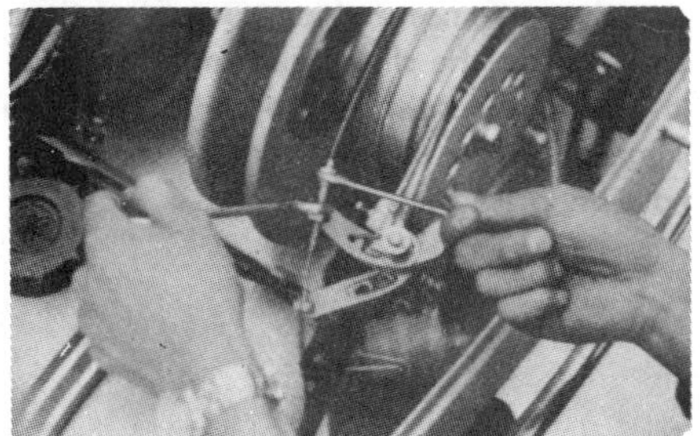

Fig. 5 – Adjusting inner brake pad clearance. Early model is shown.

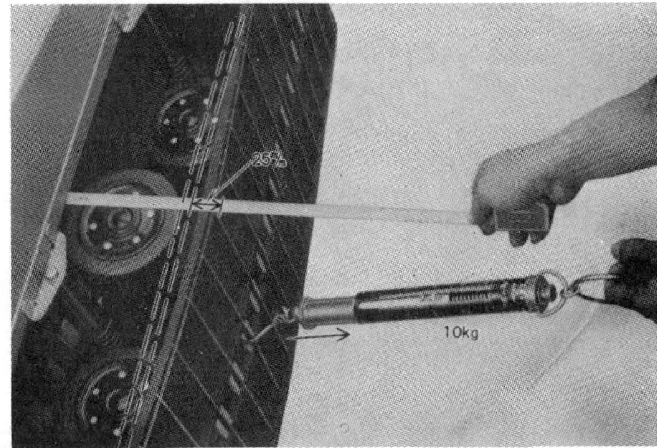

Fig. 9 – With tension of 10 kg (22 lbs.) applied as shown, measure track deflection. Refer to text.

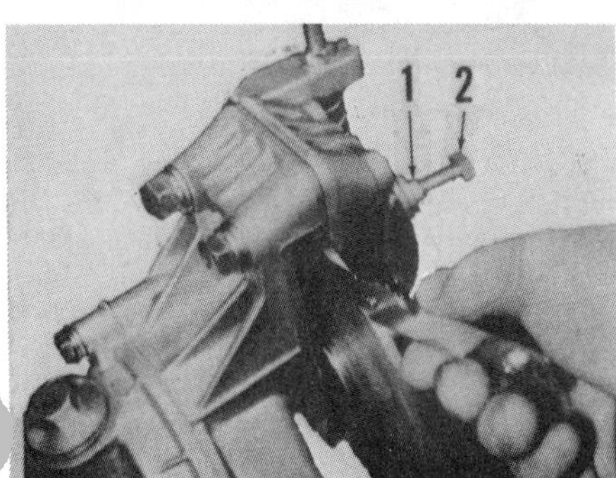

Fig. 6 – Adjustment of cable housing anchor completes the brake adjustment. Caliper levers are curved as shown, on late models; components are not interchangeable.

Fig. 7 – View showing locknut (1) and adjustment bolt (2) used to adjust clearance between brake disc and pads.

Fig. 10 – To adjust track tension, loosen rear carriage pivot bolts.

Fig. 11 – Scribe lines simplify the problem of equalizing both sides in track adjustment.

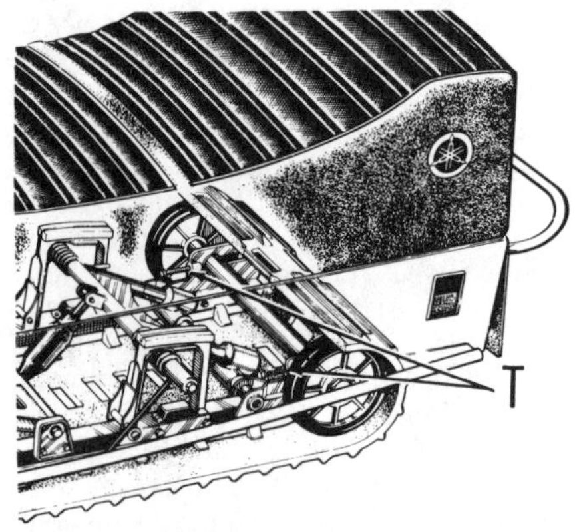

Fig. 12—Adjust track tension on early slide rail models by turning adjusting screws (T). Both sides must be adjusted alike.

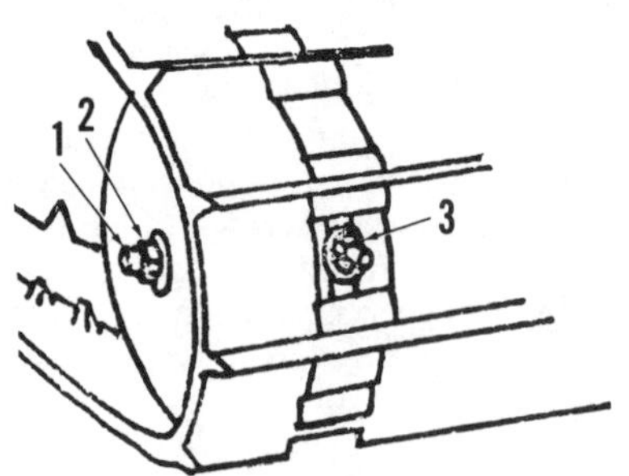

Fig. 13—View showing later model suspension system axle shaft (1), locknut (2) and track tension adjustment nut (3).

Fig. 14—Bogie wheel models are equipped with two position spring hooks as shown. Front position (A) puts more weight on skis for easier steering; rear position (B) increases speed under some conditions and permits better traction in deep, fluffy snow.

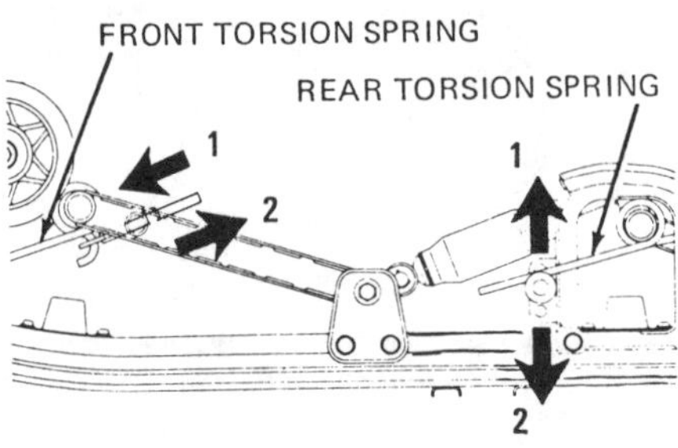

Fig. 15—Adjust torsion spring in direction indicated to (1) improve steering; (2) Improve traction.

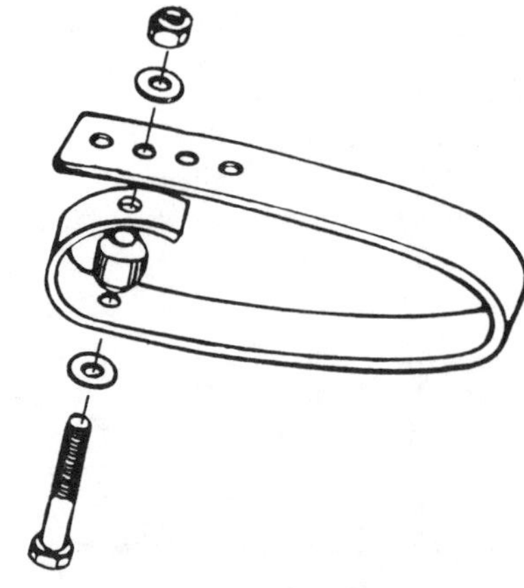

Fig. 16—Snubber strap adjustment will vary from model to model. Refer to text for standard adjustment setting.

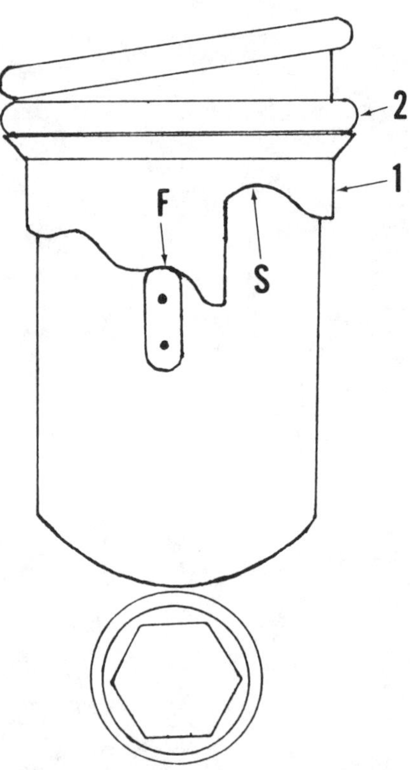

Fig. 17—View showing rear suspension shock absorber used on slide rail models. Turning cam (1) to a high step (F) will increase tension on spring (2). Turning cam to a lower step (S) will decrease spring tension.

Be sure to adjust both sides equally. Recheck track tension and adjust if required.

NOTE: When track tension has been adjusted, alignment MUST be checked as outlined in TRACK SERVICE section of this manual.

REAR SUSPENSION. Models with bogie wheel suspension have a two-position rear suspension spring as shown in Fig. 14. Hooking spring in front position (A) is generally preferred for normal conditions or improved performance on ice or hard-packed snow.

On slide suspension models equipped with individual spring adjustments for front and rear as shown in Fig. 15 adjust as follows: Tighten front torsion springs and/or loosen rear torsion springs to provide increased traction. Loosen front torsion springs and/or tighten rear torsion springs to improve steering. Tighten or loosen both sets of springs individually or together to compensate for heavy or light loads. BOTH SIDES of machine must be adjusted alike.

On slide suspension models equipped with snubber strap (Fig. 16), standard front adjustment will vary from model to model. Refer to following table for standard strap adjustment and vehicle application.

FIRST HOLE FROM BOTTOM
1982-1985 BR250, 1983-1984 ET300, 1978-1980 ET340, 1981 EC340, 1981 SRX440 and 1981-1985 SR540

SECOND HOLE FROM BOTTOM
1983-1985 EC340 and ET340T

FOURTH HOLE FROM BOTTOM
1984-1985 VMX540

FIFTH HOLE FROM BOTTOM
1976-1980 EX340 and EX440

THIRD HOLE FROM BOTTOM
All Other Models

Snubber strap on front slide support limits torque lift of front of machine during acceleration. Lengthening snubber strap permits greater acceleration lift while shortening the strap prevents ski lift and provides greater ski control during acceleration.

Standard adjustment for rear snubber strap is first hole from bottom on PZ480, 1983-1985 SR540, VMX540 and XL540 models, second hole from bottom on BR250 and ET300 models and third hole from bottom on all remaining models. Rear snubber strap does not normally require adjustment.

Adjust models equipped with shock absorber as follows: Turn cam (1–Fig. 17) to increase or decrease tension on spring (2). Turning cam to a higher step (F) will create a firmer ride and a higher load carrying capacity. As cam is turned down towards a lower step (S), the vehicle ride will become softer and the carrying weight should be less.

CHAIN HOUSING. Drive sprocket ratio between upper (drive) sprocket (1–Fig. 18) and lower (driven) sprocket (2) is available in many different combinations. Standard sprocket sizes are given in CONDENSED SERVICE DATA tables. As snow conditions become rougher or more unfavorable, difference in sprocket sizes should be increased. Some top end speed will be lost, but low end power will be increased. If snow conditions become better and/or running conditions become less rough, sprockets with less difference in numbers of teeth may be installed.

DRIVE CLUTCH. Drive clutch may be adjusted to change engagement rpm and/or shifting rpm. This is done by varying number of spring shims, increasing or decreasing spring tension or varying number and/or location of rivets in weight arms.

Shown in Fig. 19 is a typical weight arm. Refer to view showing positioning of rivets in arm for increasing or decreasing shifting rpm.

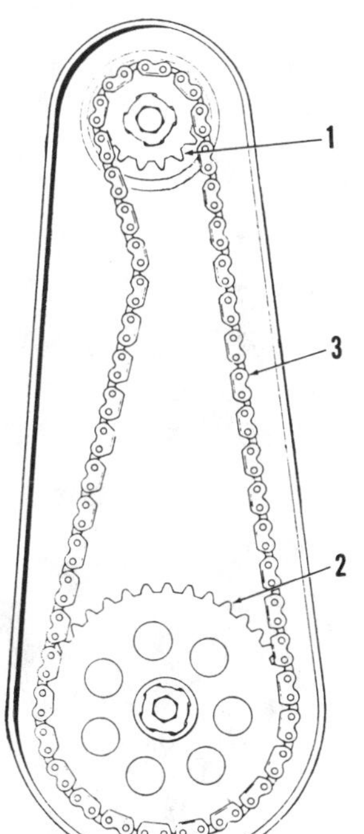

Fig. 18—View showing chain housing upper (drive) sprocket (1), lower (driven) sprocket (2) and drive chain (3).

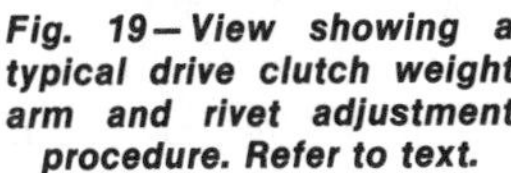

Fig. 19—View showing a typical drive clutch weight arm and rivet adjustment procedure. Refer to text.

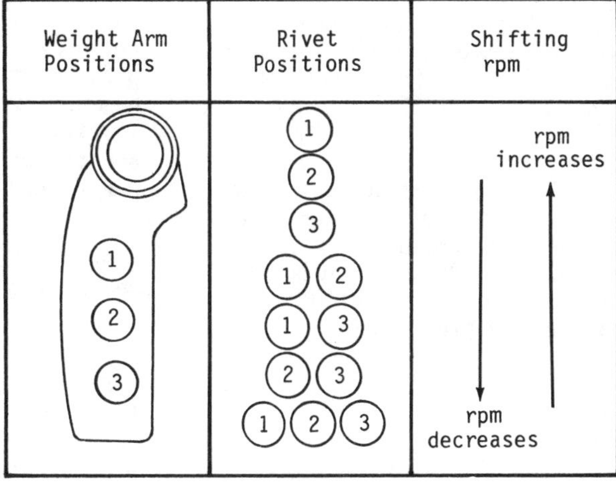

DRIVEN CLUTCH. Spring tension in driven clutch may be adjusted to compensate for snow conditions and/or alterations in drive sprocket ratio. Increasing spring tension will increase the clutch shifting rpm. If snow is wet, then spring tension will need to be greater than on packed snow. If snow conditions are icy, then less spring tension is needed.

On PZ480, VMX540 and XL540 models, secondary spring end may be positioned in one of three holes in the sliding sheave (A, B or C–Fig. 20) and one of four holes in the outer cam (1, 2, 3 or 4–Fig. 21). Standard spring end positions are B and 1 on PZ480 models, C and 2 on VMX540 models and A and 2 on XL540 models. Refer to the following table for spring twist angle possibilities with reference to hole positions.

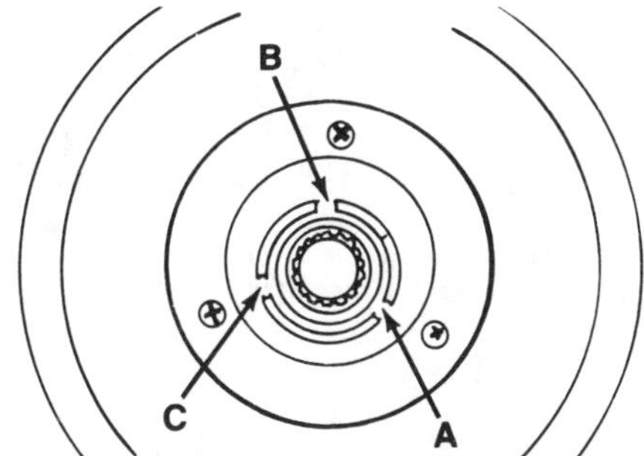

Fig. 20—On P2480, VMX540 and XL540 models, secondary spring can be positioned in one of three holes (A, B or C) in the sliding sheave.

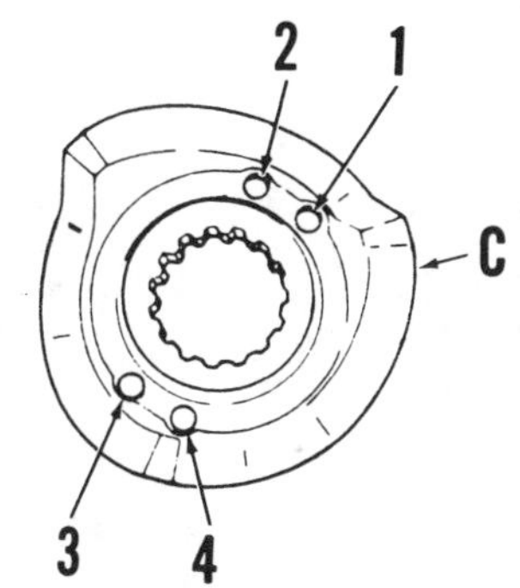

Fig. 21—View showing driven clutch cam (C) and degree positions (1, 2, 3 and 4). Refer to text.

Spring Position	Spring Twist Angle
A and 1	20°
A and 2	50°
A and 3	80°
A and 4	110°
B and 1	30°
B and 2	60°
B and 3	90°
B and 4	120°
C and 1	10°
C and 2	40°
C and 3	70°
C and 4	100°

On all other models, secondary spring end may be positioned in one of four holes in the outer cam (1, 2, 3 or 4–Fig. 21) and outer cam (C) may be turned in ⅓ increments. Refer to the following table for spring twist angle possibilities with reference to hole positions.

Spring Position	Spring Twist Angle
1	30°, 150° and 270°
2	60° and 180°
3	90° and 210°
4	0°, 120° and 240⅞

OVERHAUL

SKIS AND STEERING. Toe-out setting should be absolutely zero on PZ480, SR540 and VMX540 models, 0-15 mm (0 to 19/32 inch) on XL540 models and 0-6 mm (0 to ¼ inch) on all remaining models. Skis are interchangeable from right to left; however, ski springs, ski columns (spindles) and steering arms are not.

Inspect front suspension for bent or worn retaining pins, broken or damaged leaf springs, excessively worn or damaged ski runners and bent or leaking shock absorbers. Renew parts as needed.

Shown in Fig. 22 is an exploded view of a Telescopic Strut (TS) front suspension. Optional coil spring (1) or damper sub assembly (2) may be installed or gas pressure may be increased or decreased to adjust front suspension to operators preference.

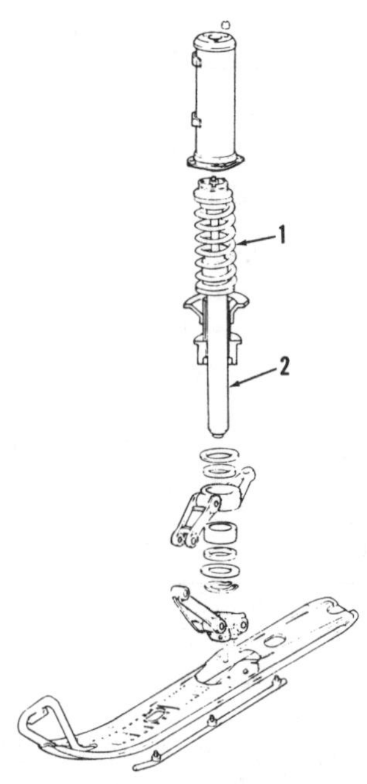

Fig. 22—Exploded view showing Telescopic Strut (TS) front suspension. Refer to text as optional coil spring (1) and damper sub assembly (2) may be used to adjust suspension ride.

NOTE: Special tools must be used to increase or decrease gas pressure. Standard gas pressure setting is 1471 kPa (213 psi) at 20°C (68°F). Pressure should not be less than 1275 kPa (185 psi) nor more than 1961 kPa (284 psi). Use only dry nitrogen to service front suspension. Major damage may result from improper servicing.

ENGINE. Refer to YAMAHA engine section elsewhere in this manual for overhaul data on engines.

CHAIN HOUSING. Shown in Fig. 24 is an exploded view of an early model chaincase. Shown in Figs. 25, 26 and 27 are views of later model chaincases.

On early model chaincase (Fig. 24) lower drive sprocket can be removed after removing lower cover (23), then disconnecting drive chain and removing retaining screw (21). To remove upper sprocket, first remove brake caliper unit, brake disc (12–Fig. 23) and left-hand housing (11).

On later model chaincases (Fig. 25, 26 and 27) loosen chaincase cover cap screws and drain oil. Vehicle may be tilted on its side to expose chaincase on top side.

Caution should be used when tilting vehicle as fuel spillage may occur if fuel level is too high in tank.

Complete removal of cover and inspect sprockets and chain for excessive wear, broken teeth or any other damage. Loosen tension on chain tensioner and remove locknuts and washers retaining drive sprockets, then withdraw drive sprockets and chain. To complete removal of chaincase remove drive belt, brake cable from brake lever and any components that will obstruct removal of chaincase and driven sheave as a complete unit. Remove housing mounting bolts, then withdraw complete unit.

Inspect bearings, oil seals, chain tensioner and all other parts for excessive wear or any other damage. Renew parts as needed.

Reassemble in reverse order of disassembly. Refer to DRIVE CHAIN ADJUSTMENT section for chain tension adjustment procedures and LUBRICATION section for refilling chaincase housing.

REAR SUSPENSION. To remove rear suspension assembly loosen track adjustment screws and on models so equipped unhook rear springs from adjustment slots.

Remove cap screws securing front pivot shaft, then remove cap screws securing rear pivot shaft or shafts on models so equipped. Swing slide rail assembly clear of track tunnel, then withdraw assembly from drive track.

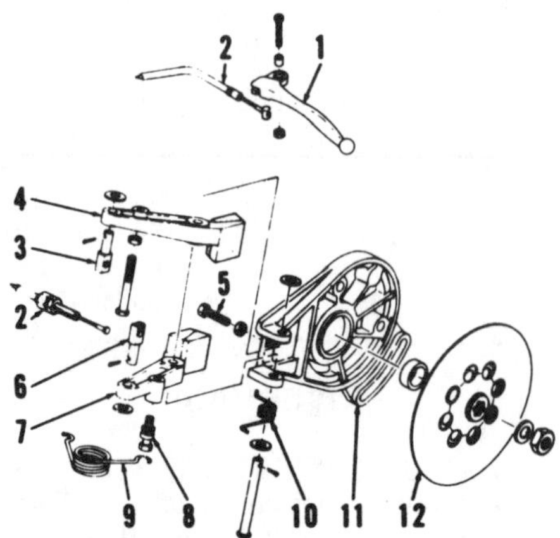

Fig. 23—Exploded view of an early caliper type disc brake and associated parts.

1. Hand lever
2. Cable
3. Threaded pin
4. Outer caliper
5. Adjusting screw
6. Slotted pin
7. Inner caliper
8. Special bolt
9. Spring
10. Spring
11. Housing
12. Disc

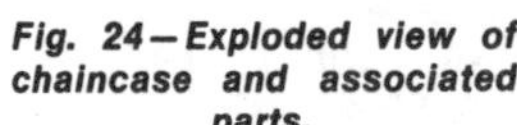

Fig. 24—Exploded view of chaincase and associated parts.

1. Housing
2. "O" ring
3. Oil seal
4. Snap ring
5. Bearing
6. Chaincase
7. Bearing
8. Oil seal
9. Housing
10. Filler elbow
11. "O" ring
12. Shaft
13. Oil seal
14. Snap ring
15. Bearing
16. Snap ring
17. Spacer
18. Sprocket
19. Washer
20. Tab washer
21. Cap screw
22. Drive chain
23. Lower cover
24. Sight glass

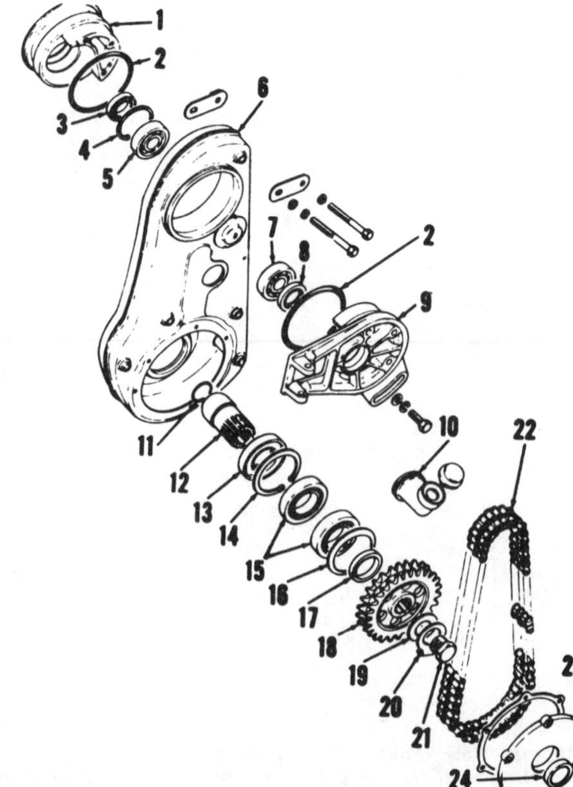

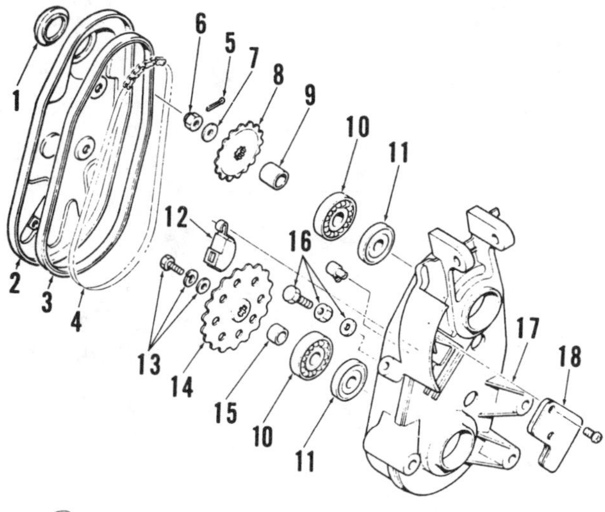

Fig. 25—Exploded view showing a typical late model chaincase.

1. Cover plug
2. Front cover
3. Cover seal
4. Chain
5. Cotter key
6. Locknut
7. Washer
8. Drive sprocket
9. Spacer
10. Bearing
11. Seal
12. Chain tensioner
13. Cap screw, lockwasher & flat washer
14. Driven sprocket
15. Spacer
16. Adjuster bolt, jam nut & flat washer
17. Chain housing
18. Inspection plate

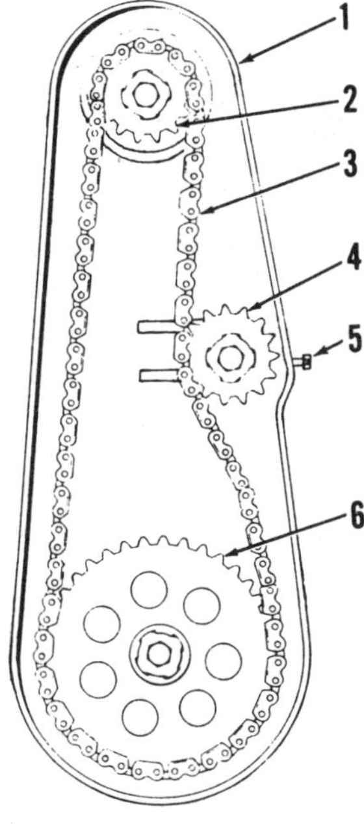

Fig. 27—View showing a late model chaincase.

1. Chain housing
2. Drive gear
3. Chain
4. Chain tensioner assy.
5. Adjuster bolt assy.
6. Driven gear

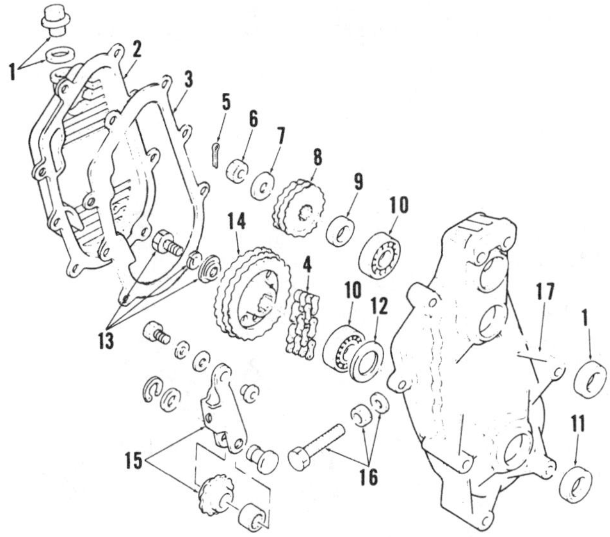

Fig. 26—Exploded view showing a typical late model chaincase.

1. Fill plug & gasket
2. Front cover
3. Gasket
4. Chain
5. Cotter key
6. Locknut
7. Washer
8. Drive gear
9. Spacer
10. Bearing
11. Seal
12. Spacer
13. Cap screw, locknut & washer
14. Driven gear
15. Chain tensioner assy.
16. Adjuster bolt, jam nut & flat washer
17. Chain housing

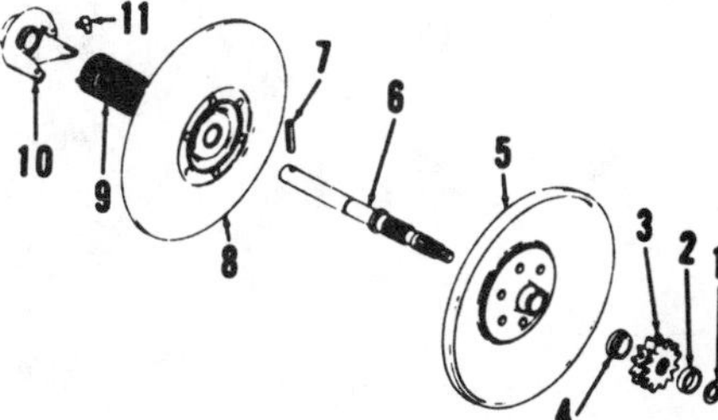

Fig. 28—Exploded view of a typical torque sensing Secondary (driven) unit used on late models.

1. Shim
2. Spacer
3. Sprocket
4. Spacer
5. Fixed sheave
6. Shaft
7. Spring pin
8. Sliding sheave
9. Torque spring
10. Outer cam
11. Cam shoe

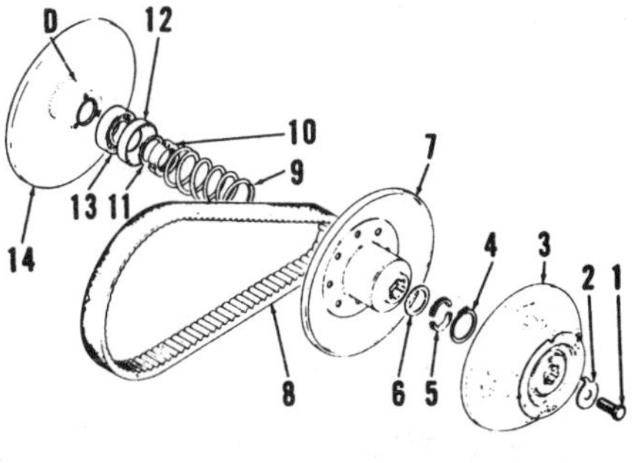

Inspect suspension assembly for bent rails and suspension arms, broken or damaged idler-wheels, springs or shock absorbers. Inspect slide rails for excessive wear and renew parts as needed.

Reassemble in reverse order of disassembly. Refer to TRACK and REAR SUSPENSION sections for adjustment procedures after completing installation.

DRIVEN SHEAVE. Shown in Fig. 28 is torque sensing driven sheave used on late model vehicles. During disassembly inspect ramp shoes (11), sheave faces (5 and 8) and all other parts for excessive wear or any other damage, renew all parts as needed.

Unit must be preloaded during assembly by turning outer cam (10) after hooking spring ends. Refer to DRIVEN CLUTCH ADJUSTMENT section for adjusting spring (9) tension. Shim (1) is available in thicknesses of 0.2, 0.3, 0.4, 0.5, 0.6 and 0.7 mm (0.008-0.028 inch) to be used as required to take up sprocket end play.

DRIVE SHEAVE. Shown in Fig. 29 is an exploded view of an early model drive sheave. Disassembly of drive sheave is done during removal. After removing cap screw (1), weight unit (3) can be withdrawn. Sliding sheave (7) and spring (9) can be withdrawn after removing snap ring (4) and retainer halves (5). A suitable puller is required to break fixed flange (14) from crankshaft taper after removing nut (10), idler bearing (13) and associated parts. Three tapped holes are provided in flange for attaching puller.

Shown in Fig. 30 is an exploded view of a typical later model drive sheave. To remove drive sheave first remove drive belt (2). Remove cap screw (23) retaining sheave assembly, then using a Yamaha special puller or a suitable equivalent withdraw sheave from crankshaft.

To disassemble, loosen outer cover (20) retaining cap screws in small increments until removed. Caution should be used as cover is under spring pressure. With reference to Fig. 30 withdraw all parts from fixed hub (1). Inspect all parts for excessive wear, cracks or any other damage and renew all parts as needed.

Fig. 29—Exploded view of an early primary (drive) sheave.

1. Cap screw
2. Tab washer
3. Centrifugal unit
4. Snap ring
5. Split retainer
6. Spacer washer
7. Sliding sheave
8. Drive belt
9. Spring
10. Retaining nut
11. Thrust washer
12. Spring seat
13. Idler bearing
14. Fixed sheave

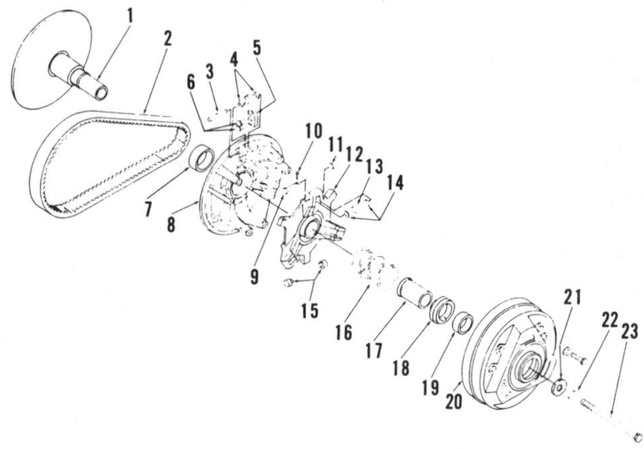

Fig. 30—Exploded view showing a typical drive sheave used on late model vehicles.

1. Fixed hub
2. Drive belt
3. Dowel pin
4. Plate washer
5. Weight arm
6. Rivet
7. Bushing
8. Sliding hub
9. Clevis pin
10. Cotter pin
11. Plate washer
12. Spider assy.
13. Collar
14. Plate washer
15. Spider button
16. Spring
17. Collar
18. Spring cover
19. Bushing
20. Outer cover
21. Spacer
22. Spring washer
23. Cap screw

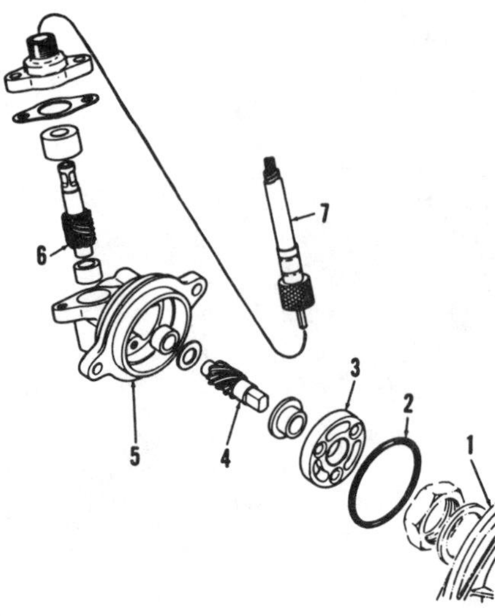

Fig. 32—Speedometer drive unit attaches to right side of track drive axle housing (1).

1. Housing
2. "O" ring
3. Bearing
4. Drive gear
5. Housing
6. Driven gear
7. Speedometer cable

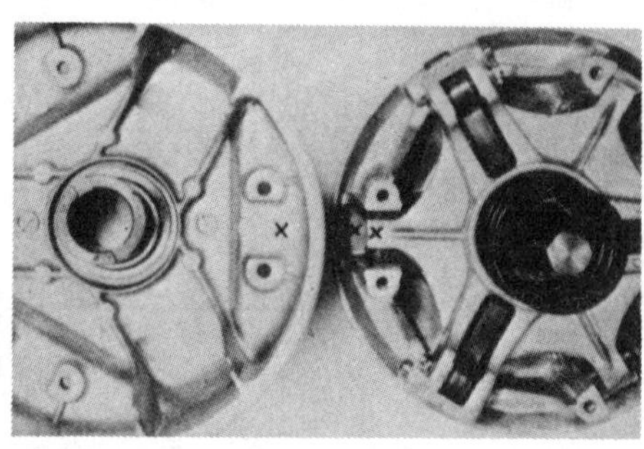

Fig. 31—View showing X-marks used in reassembling late model drive sheave assemblies.

Reassemble in reverse order of disassembly. Clearance between spider buttons (15) and guide in sliding hub (8) should be 0-0.2 mm (0-0.008 in.). Be sure X marks on sliding hub (8), spider assembly (12) and outer cover (20) are aligned as shown in Fig. 31. Refer to DRIVE CLUTCH ADJUSTMENT section for adjusting engagement or shifting rpm. Tighten outer cover retaining cap screws to 10.8 N·m (8 ft.-lbs.) and tighten drive sheave assembly to crankshaft retaining cap screw (23) first to 118 N·m (87 ft.-lbs.), then loosen and retighten to 63.7 N·m (47 ft.-lbs.).

New drive belt width is 31 mm (1.22 inches). Renew belt if worn to 26 mm (1 inch) or if belt is otherwise damaged.

SPEEDOMETER DRIVE AND TACHOMETER. Shown in Figs. 32 and 33 are views of some operational methods used by Yamaha for speedometer drive and tachometer.

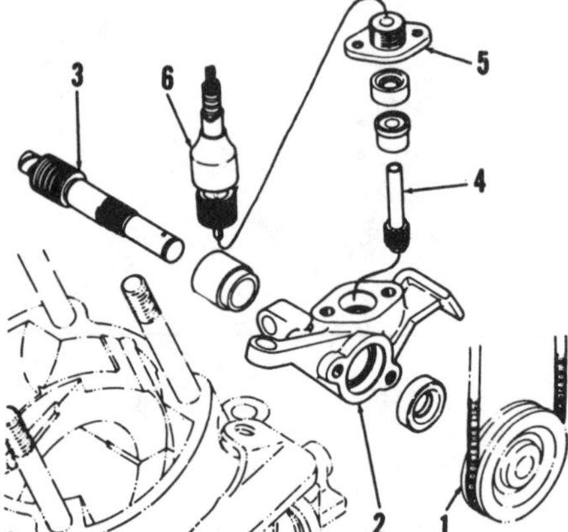

Fig. 33—Tachometer is mechanically driven from "Yamalube" pump drive worm (3) as shown.

1. Drive pulley
2. Housing
3. Drive worm
4. Driven gear
5. Cap
6. Tachometer cable

YUKON KING

1967-1969

Model	Engine Make	Engine Model	Engine Displ.	Carburetor Make	Carburetor Model	Sprocket Ratio	Chain Size	Clutch Make	Clutch Shaft Center	Belt Number
1967										
11	JLO	L252	247cc	Tillotson	HL236A	10:25	40	Own	10⅝	3990012
15.5	JLO	L292	292cc	Tillotson	HR2A	10:25	40	Own	10⅝	3990012
1968										
Husky	JLO	L252	247cc	Tillotson	HL236A	10:26	40	Own	10⅝	3990012
Grizzly	JLO	L292	292cc	Tillotson	HR2A	10:25	40	Own	10⅝	3990012
Grizzly	Lloyd	LS400	386cc	Tillotson	HR8A	10:25	40	Own	10⅝	3990012
Kodiac	JLO	L292	292cc	Tillotson	HR2A	9:25	40	Own	10⅝	3990012
Kodiac	Lloyd	LS400	386cc	Tillotson	HR8A	9:25	40	Own	10⅝	3990012
1969										
Husky	JLO	L252	247cc	Tillotson	HL236A	9:26	40	Own	10⅝	3990012
Grizzly	JLO	L292	292cc	Tillotson	HR2A	10:25	40	Own	10⅝	3990012
Super G	JLO	L297	296cc	Tillotson	HD14A	10:25	40	Own	10⅝	3990012
Kodiac	JLO	L297	296cc	Tillotson	HD14A	10:25	40	Own	10⅝	3990012
Kodiac	Lloyd	LS400	386cc	Tillotson	HR8A	12:25	40	Own	10⅝	3990012

LUBRICATION

The drive chain runs in an enclosed chain case. On early models, the recommended lubricant is SAE 80 Hypoid oil. To check the lubricant, remove rubber access cover (5—Fig. 2) and insert a clean wire to bottom of chain case. Correct oil level is 1-inch from bottom of case. Note: Fuel Tank dipstick can be used to measure oil level, which should be considered satisfactory if dipstick will reach the oil.

On late models the recommended lubricant is SAE 10 Motor Oil and an overflow hole enters case at the proper fluid level (1-inch from bottom). Add oil about once a week until it begins to flow through overflow hole.

Steering spindle housings contain pressure gun fittings which should be lubricated about once a week, using low-temperature type grease. Handle bar base bearing should be lightly oiled at the same time. Also lightly coat driven pulley alignment pins and pulley shaft at outer (spring) end, being careful no oil contacts pulley faces or belt when vehicle is started.

Bogie wheels are equipped with grease fittings which require two or three shots of low-temperature type grease about once a month. Track axles are equipped with self-aligning, sealed type bearings which do not require lubrication.

The manufacturer also recommends that intermediate shaft bearings be lubricated about every 20 operating hours by removing chain adjusting bolt (3—Fig. 2) and pumping low temperature grease into bolt hole until it begins to flow through bearing at sprocket end of shaft.

Fig. 2—Exploded view of chain case and associated parts used on early models. Late models are basically similar except for method of attaching case to vehicle frame.

1. Plug screw
2. Eccentric housing
3. Lock bolt
4. Chain case
5. Inspection cover

ADJUSTMENT

STEERING SKIS & LINKAGE. Steering skis should be parallel with each other and with vehicle frame when handle bar is in normal straight driving position. To adjust tie rod, disconnect either end from spindle arm. To adjust drag link, disconnect inner end from handle bar and turn the end on or off link.

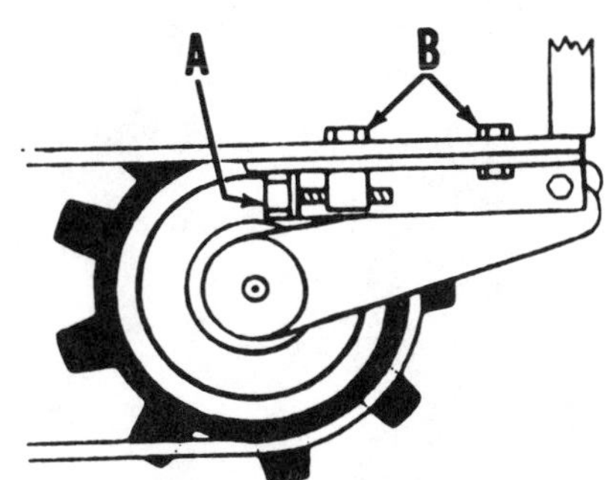

Fig. 3—Adjust track tension by loosening clamp bolts (B) and turning adjusting screw (A). Both sides must be adjusted alike, refer to text.

DRIVE CHAIN. Drive chain deflection should be approximately ¼-inch. The adjustment can be satisfactorily estimated after removing access cover (5—Fig. 2). To make the adjustment, loosen the jam nut and push down on adjusting bolt (3) to rotate eccentric housing (2) in chain housing (4). If adjusting bolt (3) contacts bottom of slot and chain is still not tight, remove Allen head screw (1) from hole which has appeared at top of adjusting slot and exchange with adjusting screw (3).

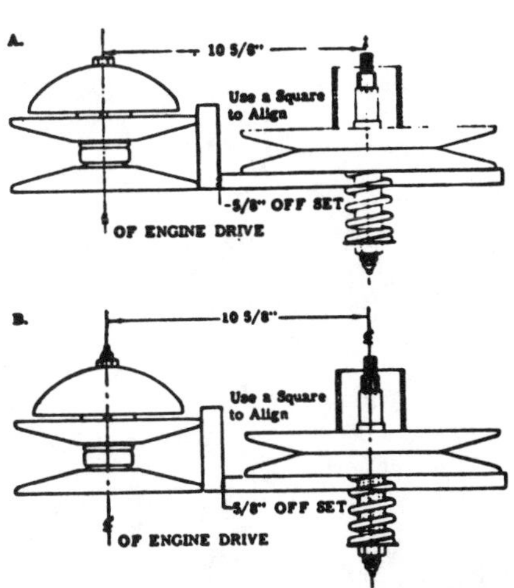

Fig. 4—All converter units have ⅝ inch offset and 10⅝ inch belt center distance as shown.

TRACK. To adjust track tension, raise rear of vehicle on kick stand. With track clear of ground, some clearance should exist between track and center set of bogie wheels.

To make the adjustment, loosen the two clamp nuts (B—Fig. 3) on each side of vehicle and turn adjustment screws (A) equally until adjustment is correct.

NOTE: When track tension has been adjusted, alignment MUST be checked as outlined in the TRACK SERVICE Section of this manual.

ENGINE SERVICE FUNDAMENTALS

CONTENTS

CAUTION: Do not run engines with torque converter drive belt removed unless torque converter drive sheave is also removed from engine output shaft.

TROUBLESHOOTING

Most performance problems such as failure to start, failure to run properly or missing out are caused by malfunction of the ignition system or fuel system. Refer to sequences listed below for assistance in diagnosing and repairing performance problems.

FAILURE TO START

Remove and examine spark plugs. If fuel is reaching the cylinder in proper amount, there should be an odor of gasoline on the plugs if they are cold. Too much fuel or oil can foul the plugs causing engine not to start. Fouled plugs are wet in appearance and easily detected. The presence of fouled plugs is not a sure indication that the trouble has been located, however, the engine might have started before fouling occurred if ignition system had been in good shape.

With spark plug (or plugs) removed, hold wire about 1/8- to 1/4-inch away from an unpainted part of engine and crank engine sharply. Ground one plug wire against engine on two cylinder models. The resulting spark may not be visible in bright daylight but a distinct snap should be heard as the spark jumps the gap.

If carburetor and ignition were both in apparently good condition when checked, examine other elements of engine such as crossed spark plug wires, improper timing, etc. A systematic search will usually pinpoint the cause of trouble with a minimum of delay or confusion.

DIAGNOSIS. If the presence of fuel was not apparent and the spark seemed satisfactory, systematically check the fuel system for the cause of trouble. Possible causes of lack of fuel could be:

1. No fuel in tank
2. Frozen or clogged fuel line or filter
3. Fuel pump impulse line disconnected
4. Damaged or frozen fuel pump diaphragm
5. Carburetor dirty or improperly adjusted
6. Fuel pickup line disconnected or leaking

If no spark occurred during initial check look for the following:

1. Key switch "Off"
2. Emergency kill switch in "Stop" position
3. Shorted stop wire or switch
4. Loose coil connections
5. Open (broken) wire
6. Breaker points improperly adjusted or stuck open
7. Broken or grounded primary wire
8. Faulty coil or condenser

POOR PERFORMANCE

On many two cylinder engines, the ignition system for each cylinder is completely independent, therefore one cylinder can run perfectly while the other will not fire. On some two cylinder engines with Japanese magnetos, a short at one set of points will cause engine not to run. On other models the engine will not fire on either cylinder if one set of points is stuck in the open position.

Complaints of not enough power or speed can usually be traced to improper tuning. Make sure that air filter is clean and in good condition and that exhaust pipe and muffler are open and not clogged or restricted. Ignition timing and carburetor(s) must be correctly adjusted. Both the carburetors and ignition systems must be synchronized on two cylinder models. The proper altitude adjustments must be made for mountain running if the altitude nears or exceeds 5000 ft.

Fig. 1—Normal spark plug. Insulator tip color brown to light tan; electrodes not burned or eroded. Clean, regap and reinstall.

Also check to be sure the engine is actually at fault. Complaints of poor performance can be caused by improper drive sprocket selection, a binding or improperly adjusted track or drive chain, or a torque converter which does not operate properly. Other items to check include:

- Brakes dragging
- Damaged pistons, rings and/or cylinders
- Loose cylinder head nuts or leaking head gasket
- Leaking crankcase seals
- Incorrect fuel/oil mixture
- Incorrect or improperly adjusted spark plugs

ENGINE OVERHEATS. The following lists some possible causes of engine overheating.

1. Dirt, weed seeds or debris accumulation in cooling fins.
2. Incorrect fuel/oil mixture or lean carburetor adjustment.
3. Improper ignition timing.
4. Missing or broken cooling fins or fan blades.
5. Missing or bent shields or fan housing.
6. Cylinder heads improperly installed.

SPARK PLUG DIAGNOSIS

The appearance of the spark plug will change with use and careful examina-

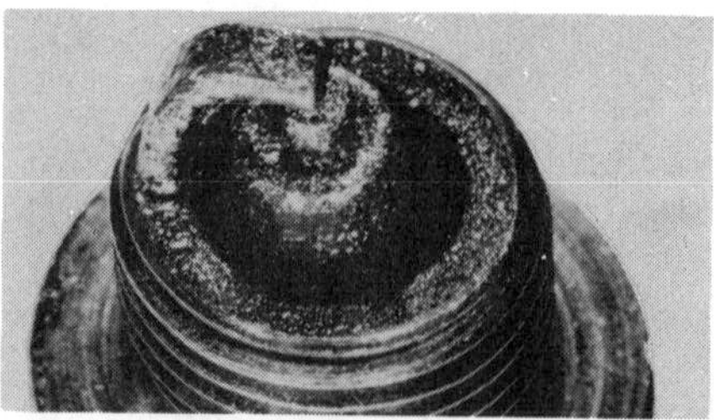

Fig. 2—Wet fouling. Damp oily film over firing end; insulator tip black. Indicates rich fuel mixture, incorrect fuel/oil mix (too much oil); missing (two cylinder engine) or incorrect carburetor mixture setting. If none of the above factors apply, install hotter plug.

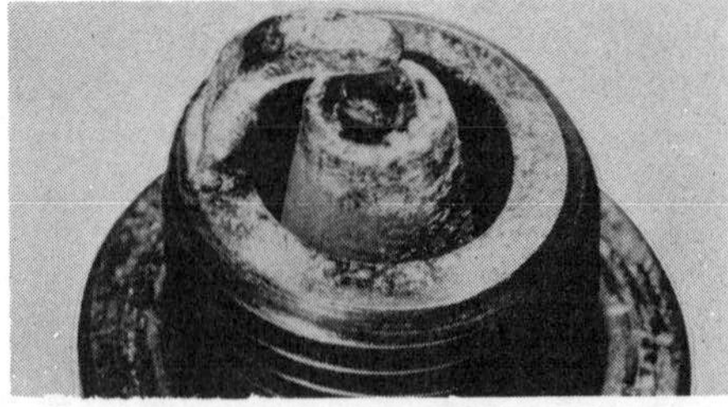

Fig. 3—Too hot. Light tan to white deposits with flaking and blistering. Electrodes eroded and burned. Engine overheating or detonating or plug too hot for operating conditions. Install colder plug and retest. If performance does not improve check for other causes of overheating or detonation.

tion of removed plugs can help in plug selection and in pinpointing other causes of engine malfunction. The accompanying pictures (Fig. 1 through 6) are provided by Champion Spark Plug Company to illustrate typical conditions. Listed also are the probable causes and suggested corrective measures.

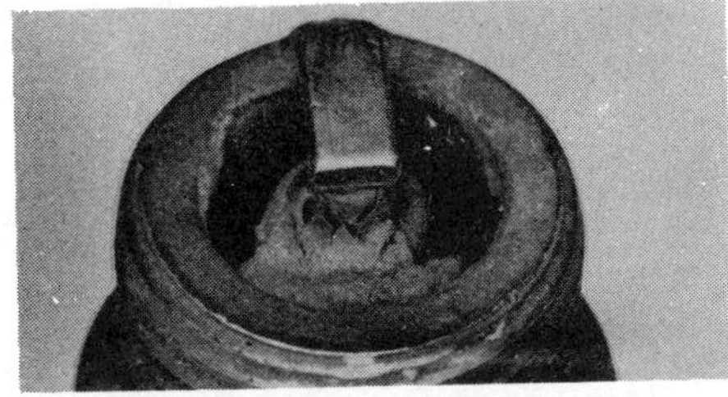

Fig. 4—Core bridging. Caused by excessive carbon deposits in cylinder and/or plugged exhaust system. The deposits break away and fuse on plug during high-speed operation. Check exhaust system, carburetor mixture and fuel/oil mixture. Refer also to Fig. 5.

Fig. 5—Gap bridging. Same causes as Fig. 4. Decarbonizing is recommended in both instances as well as correcting other causes.

Fig. 6—Plug fouled by aluminum deposits. Caused by severe overheating or detonation. Overhaul engine immediately and correct the cause before more serious trouble develops.

Fig. 7—"Gold Palladium" spark plug with center electrode bent in filing. Electrodes are softer than normal and special care must be exercised in handling.

MAINTENANCE

SPARK PLUG

The recommended electrode gap and standard spark plug is listed in the CONDENSED SERVICE DATA Tables for the appropriate engine section. The suggested spark plug or equivalent is usually most suitable for normal or average use. Engine modification or special conditions may call for the installation of a spark plug of a different heat range.

Spark plugs are normally cleaned by abrasive in a compressed air blast. Plugs so cleaned should be thoroughly recleaned and/or flushed to be sure no abrasive material remains in recesses of the plug to later fall and cause engine damage. Rounded or dished electrodes should also be dressed with a point file to return the electrodes as nearly as possible to original shape.

NOTE: Use special caution when filing spark plugs with precious metal electrodes. Fig. 7 shows the center electrode of a CHAMPION "Gold Palladium" spark plug which has been bent in filing. Precious metal electrodes are usually softer than normal and may be easily damaged.

It is often necessary to clean or renew spark plugs shortly after overhaul or after engine has been properly stored. The oil used to coat engine parts may foul plugs quickly.

Each spark plug manufacturer uses a different special code to identify spark plug characteristics. It has been found impossible to provide a plug cross reference chart which is accepted by all manufacturers, however the following code identification for some spark plugs may be helpful in selecting the correct plug. Although not universally true, it can be generally assumed that two plugs of different manufacture falling within similar portions of the heat range scale will interchange. In some cases it may be necessary to move up or down the scale one or two steps for best performance.

AC SPARK PLUGS

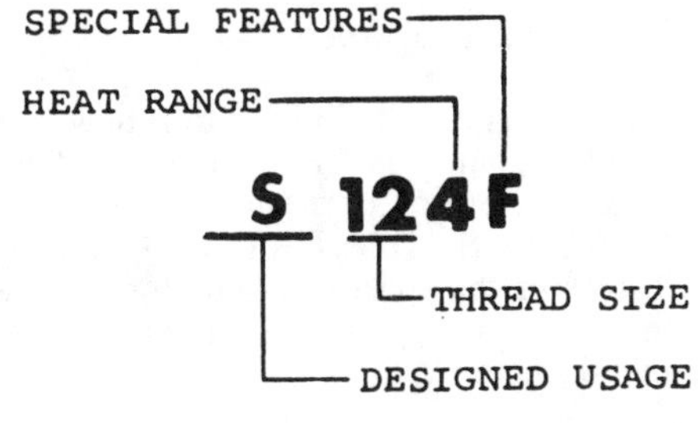

Thread Size—the first digit or digits of the number code indicates thread size. The pictured sample indicates a 12 mm plug.

Heat Range—the last digit of number code indicates heat range. Plugs may be numbered from "0" to "9", the lower number indicating the colder plug. The pictured example "4" falls approximately in mid-range.

Suffix Letters—a letter (or letters) after the number indicates special features. The "F" in pictured example indicates that plug is "Special Reach for Foreign Applications".

Prefix Letters—letter (or letters) before number code indicates designed usage. In the case of snowmobiles, the prefix of S is added only when a special plug or modification is required.

BOSCH SPARK PLUGS

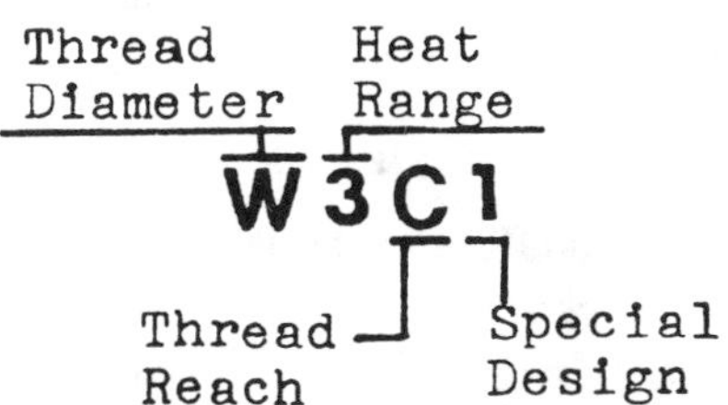

Thread Diameter—the first letter of the identification code indicates thread diameter. The pictured sample indicates a 14 mm plug.

Heat Range—the first digit or digits following the thread diameter indicates heat range. Numbers range from zero to twelve. The middle numbers are medium range, the lower numbers are cold range and the upper numbers are hot range. The pictured sample indicates a cold range plug.

Thread Reach—the letter following the heat range digit or digits indicates thread reach. The pictured sample indicates a ¾-inch thread reach with a regular electrode.

Special Design—the last digit or letter indicates if plug has a special design feature.

CHAMPION SPARK PLUGS

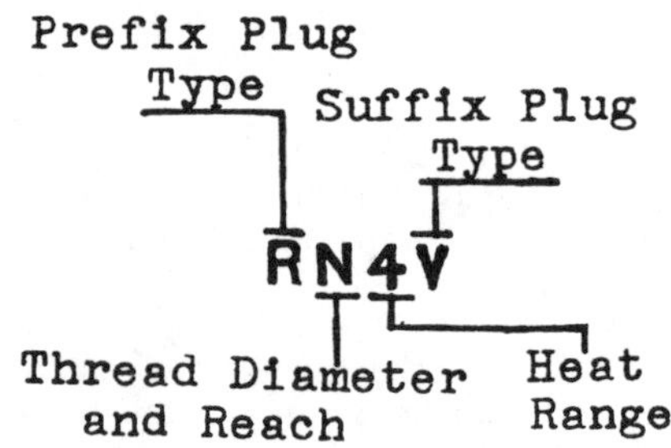

Prefix Plug Type—the first letter of the identification code indicates whether the plug is a resistor or has an auxillary gap. The pictured sample indicates a resistor type plug.

Thread Diameter And Reach—the letter following the prefix plug type indicates thread diameter and reach. The pictured sample indicates a 14 mm plug with a ¾-inch thread reach.

Heat Range—the first digit or digits indicates heat range. The higher number (within type range) indicates hotter plug. The pictured sample indicates a cold range plug.

Suffix Plug Type—the last letter indicates if the plug has a special feature or application. The pictured sample indicates a surface gap type plug.

NGK SPARK PLUGS

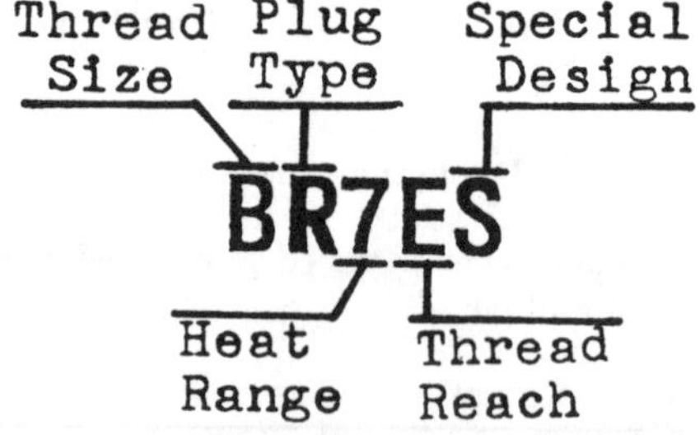

Thread Size—the first letter of the identification code indicates thread size. The pictured sample indicates a 14 mm plug.

Spark Plug Type—the second letter indicates plug type. The pictured sample indicates a resistor type plug.

Heat Range—the first digit or digits indicates heat range. Numbers range from two to ten. Lower numbers indicate hotter plugs, higher numbers indicate colder plugs. The pictured sample indicates a medium range plug.

Thread Reach—the letter following the heat range digit indicates thread reach. The pictured sample indicates a ¾-inch thread reach.

Special Design—the last letter indicates special design feature or application. The pictured sample indicates having a standard copper core center electrode.

PRESTOLITE SPARK PLUGS

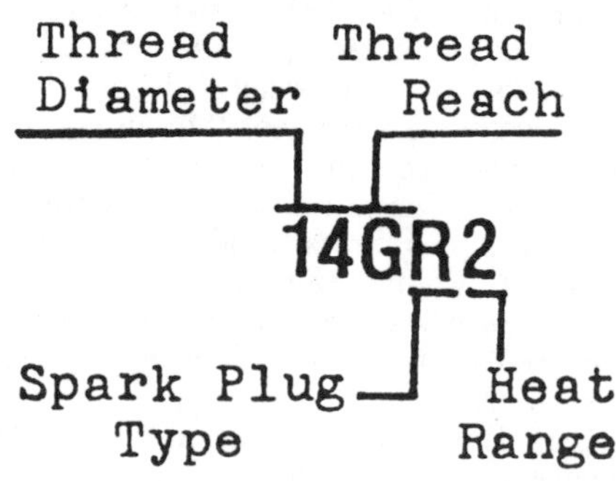

Thread Diameter—the first digit or digits of the number code indicates thread diameter. The pictured sample indicates a 14 mm plug.

Thread Reach—the first letter following the thread diameter indicates thread reach. The pictured sample indicates a ¾-inch thread reach.

Spark Plug Type—the second letter indicates spark plug type. The pictured sample indicates a resistor type plug.

Heat Range—the last digit or digits of the number code indicates heat range. Numbers range from zero to eleven. The middle numbers are medium range, the lower numbers are cold range and the upper numbers are hot range. The pictured sample indicates a cold range plug.

CARBURETOR

Refer to **CARBURETOR REPAIR** section for data on specific carburetor types.

IGNITION AND ELECTRICAL

Flywheel Magneto

Repair is usually limited to renewal of breaker points and/or condenser and adjustment of ignition timing. Refer to CONDENSED SERVICE DATA Tables of the specific engine for recommended point gap and timing recommendations.

BREAKER POINTS. On some units, breaker points can be inspected and adjusted through a flywheel window as shown in Fig. 8 but, although an inspection window is present on most models, accurate adjustment is not always possible. Flywheel must usually be removed for renewal of parts.

NOTE: On some engines, a special puller is required for flywheel removal. Check engine sections for procedure.

On most models with automatic timing advance, the breaker cam can be quickly removed from flywheel and temporarily installed on crankshaft for point adjustment as shown in Fig. 9. Use a clean greaseless feeler gage for checking the gap and be sure points are not pitted. Contact surfaces must seat squarely and properly align when points are closed. Loosen retaining screw (R–Fig. 8) and insert a blade screwdriver in notches (N) to make the adjustment. Recheck gap after retaining screw (R) is tightened.

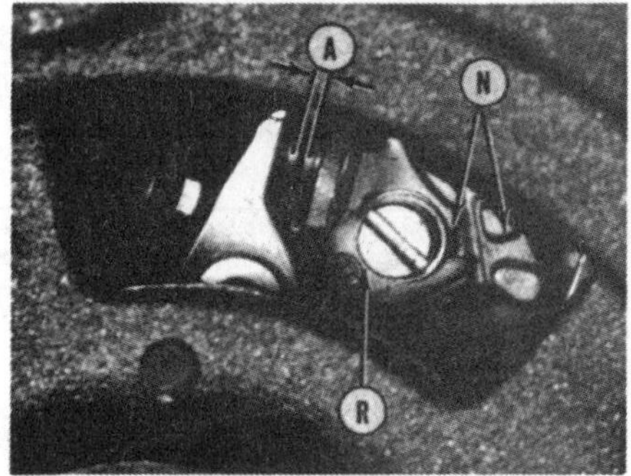

Fig. 8—Ignition points viewed through flywheel opening

A. Point gap
N. Adjusting notches
R. Retaining screw

Fig. 9—On some engines, breaker cam can be removed from flywheel and positioned over crankshaft for point adjustment.

CONDENSER. A defective condenser can cause point failure or complete failure of engine to start and run. On many units, condenser is pressed into armature plate and leads are soldered. Use an iron and a minimum amount of heat when making the connections. Condenser should not be removed unless renewal is indicated. If condenser is to be renewed, armature plate must be removed and condenser pressed out from bottom. Condenser is swaged or staked in place (S – Fig. 10) when installed. If burrs remain from previous staking, remove with a scraper or file. Press in new condenser working from top (flywheel) side of plate. If condenser is not tight after installation, stake in three or four places. Use care not to crush the case when condenser is installed.

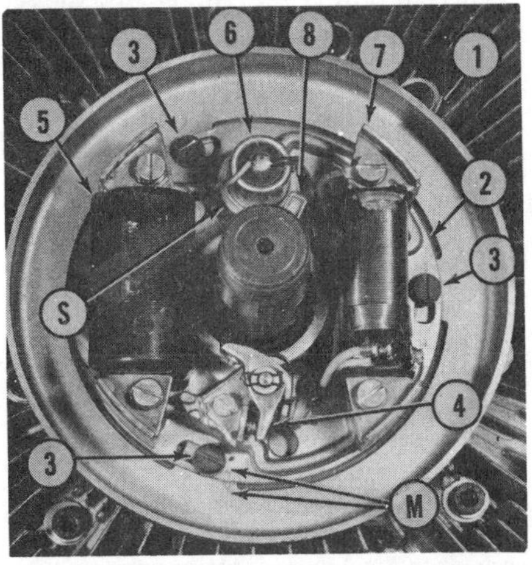

Fig. 10 — Assembled view of high tension magneto unit with flywheel removed.

M. Timing marks
S. Swaging
1. Mounting plate
2. Armature plate
3. Mounting screws
4. Breaker points
5. Ignition coil
6. Condenser
7. Lighting coil
8. Oiler wick

Fig. 11 — Installed view of energy transfer magneto plate with flywheel removed, showing component parts. Refer to Fig. 10 for parts identification.

IGNITION COIL. On models with a conventional flywheel magneto system the ignition coil (5 – Fig. 10) is mounted on the armature plate. On models with an energy transfer system, the armature plate contains only an ignition generating coil (5 – Fig. 11) and the ignition coil (or coils) is externally mounted. Plug-in connectors are used; refer to fundamentals section for typical wiring diagrams. If testing equipment is not available, output can be checked by holding spark plug wire about ¼-inch away from block while turning engine with a starter. If no spark occurs or if spark is weak or yellow, renewal of ignition coil may be indicated.

IGNITION TIMING. Ignition timing is usually specified in degrees of crankshaft rotation before piston reaches Top Dead Center, or by measuring piston travel before TDC with a dial indicator as shown in Fig. 12. If the spark plug hole is angled, special dial indicators are available as shown in Fig. 13.

Timing should be checked using a light or buzzer connected to the blue primary lead or black kill lead. If advance timing is being checked on models with automatic timing advance, cam may be blocked in the fully advanced position as shown in Fig. 15. Manufacturer's timing recommendations are given in the individual ENGINE SERVICE Sections. Increasing the breaker point gap will advance the timing.

Fig. 12 — To measure piston travel, install a dial indicator (such as Central Tool Co. indicator shown) in spark plug hole. Find TDC, then move piston by rotating crankshaft until ignition timing is correct. Refer to Fig. 13 if spark plug hole is not parallel to cylinder bore centerline.

Fig. 13-Special dial indicators are available as shown for measuring piston travel in angled spark plug holes.

MAGNETO EDGE GAP. For maximum strength of the ignition spark, the breaker points should just start to open when the flywheel magnets are at the specified position relative to the ignition coil pole shoe. This distance is variously known as Edge Gap, Break-Away Gap, Pole Shoe Break or Straight Gap. Sometimes the edge-gap is not adjustable and will be maintained at the proper dimension if the breaker points are correctly adjusted and the correct breaker cam installed. Magneto Edge Gap can change (and spark intensity reduced) due to the following.

1. Improper adjustment.
2. Flywheel key sheared.
3. Flywheel key or key seat worn (flywheel loose).
4. Excessive breaker cam wear.

Fig. 14 — Breaker cam in retard (starting) position, with advance weight resting against stop pin (S). Refer also to Fig. 15.

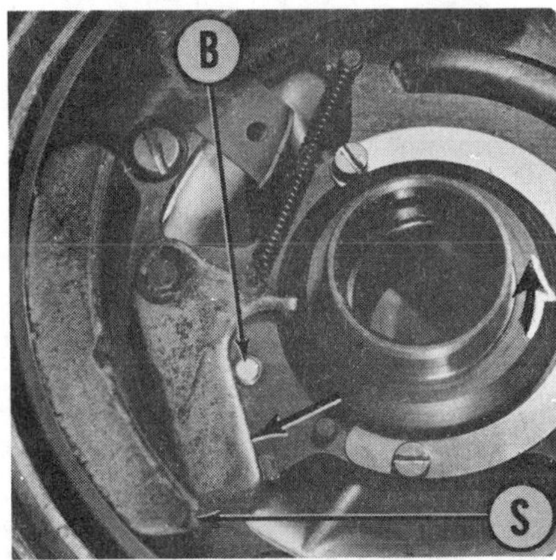

Fig. 15 — Breaker cam is fully advanced when advance weight is in contact with flywheel magnet (S). On some engines, a bolt (B) can be dropped in hole provided to block the cam in advanced position for engine timing as shown.

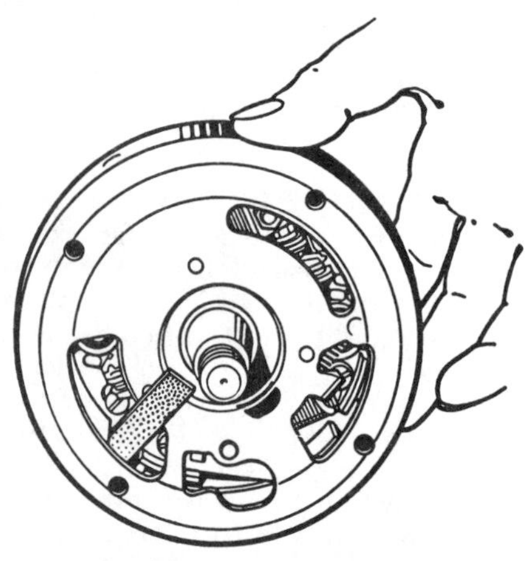

Fig. 16—A cardboard strip of suitable width can be used to measure edge gap.

Magneto Edge Gap can be adjusted on those models where breaker cam can be moved independently of flywheel or breaker pivot can be moved independently of armature plate. Edge gap can be measured using a strip of cardboard the correct width and working through flywheel opening as shown in Fig. 16.

Energy Transfer System

An energy transfer ignition system operates very much like the previously described flywheel magneto system except that the components are not in one area on the engine. Single cylinder models present no particular problems in understanding or in service.

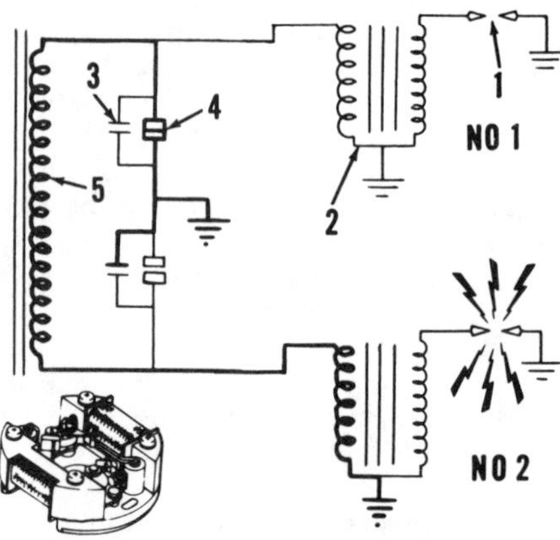

Fig. 18—Schematic wiring diagram of SAWAFUJI two cylinder ET magneto used on CCW 340S engine. Ignition systems for the two cylinders are interconnected through the single ignition generating coil (5). Ignition generating circuit is complete only when both breaker points (4) are closed and pulse of current flows to one ignition coil primary when one set of points open as shown. Refer to Fig. 17 for parts identification.

Basic differences exist in construction and in the service of some twin units, however, and these differences must be understood to avoid confusion. Fig. 17 is wiring diagram of a Kokusan magneto used by Canadian Curtiss Wright on some engines and also typical of Bosch used on European engines. Low Tension generating coils for both cylinders are piggy-backed as shown in inset, and magneto consists essentially of two timed single-cylinder magnetos.

Fig. 18 is a wiring diagram for the Sawafuji magneto used on CCW 340S (manual start) engine. A single low tension coil is used for both cylinders and the closed set of points provides part of the primary circuit as shown. One set of points which fail to make contact will therefore cause engine to stop, rather than miss out. A shorted set of points will permit the opposite cylinder to fire.

It should be mentioned that an ET magneto differs from a conventional magneto in that the secondary current (spark) is induced by a primary voltage rise, rather than by primary circuit interruption in a battery ignition system or conventional magneto. Refer again to Fig. 17. Note that with points closed (Cyl. No. 1) the ignition generating current (heavy lines) flows through the points and generating coil, with no current to ground or ignition coil. When points open (Cyl. No. 2) the normal path of current flow is interrupted and the remaining current path is through ground and ignition coil primary. The resulting voltage rise in ignition primary induces the secondary current which fires the spark plug.

With these differences in mind ET magneto service is identical to that given for Flywheel Magneto.

Capacitor Discharge System

Because of differences in CD ignition construction, it is impractical to outline a general procedure for CD ignition service. Refer to the specific engine section for testing, overhaul notes and timing of capacitor discharge ignition systems.

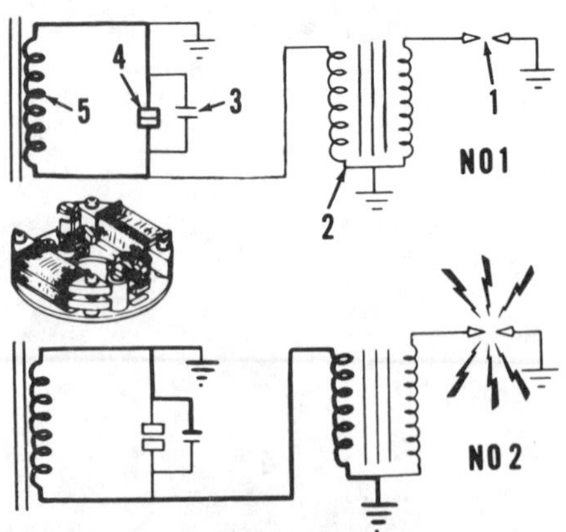

Fig. 17—Schematic wiring diagram of KOKUSAN two cylinder ET magneto used on some CCW engines. Ignition generating coils (5) are "Piggy Backed" and ignition systems for each cylinder are independent. Ignition generating current circuit for No. 1 cylinder is completed through points (4) as indicated by heavy lines. On No. 2 cylinder points have opened breaking the circuit and a rising voltage pulse passes through primary windings of ignition coil (2) initiating the spark at No. 2 plug (1) as shown.

1. Spark plug
2. Ignition coil
3. Condenser
4. Breaker points
5. Generating coil

REPAIRS

Because of the close tolerance of the internal parts, cleanliness is of utmost importance. It is suggested that the exterior of the engine and all nearby areas be absolutely clean before any repair is started. The manufacturer's recommended torque values for tightening screw fasteners should be followed closely. The soft threads in aluminum castings are often damaged by carelessness in overtightening fasteners or in attempting to loosen or remove seized parts.

PISTON, PIN, RINGS AND CYLINDER

Two cycle engines do not have a complex valve mechanism and the piston rings have no oil control function. On the other hand, carbon build-up is more likely to occur, and where oil consumption is the most common service problem on four cycle engines, carbonization is the two-cycle counterpart.

The simple construction of two stroke engines and the benefits to be gained from periodic carbon removal make decarbonization a part of the recommended maintenance procedure of most two cycle experts. Because the piston rings have no oil control function, ring renewal is not required at carbon removal except to correct for wear or other damage.

Excessive carbon build-up can be harmful in two ways. First, it insulates to keep the heat from escaping normally. Second, it raises the compression ratio to create more heat. This places an additional heat load on that portion of the cylinder which is scraped clean of carbon by the piston rings.

The need for carbon removal is often first indicated by inability to properly adjust the carburetor. If performance is erratic and improper carburetion is indicated, but attempts to adjust the carburetor fail, check first for excessive carbon build up. No cleaning or adjustment of the carburetor can materially improve performance if exhaust passages are partially carbon blocked.

No problems will be encountered in removing cylinder head and/or cylinder for carbon removal provided normal standards of care and cleanliness are observed.

Examine the parts as engine is disassembled for clues to engine condition, to correct possible future trouble, or identify the cause of existing trouble. As an example, refer to Fig. 19. On this particular piston, the skirt is not scored and the first glance will show melted aluminum which has covered the ring on one side. The melted spot (D) on top and below piston crown is conclusive proof of detonation damage and the cause must be corrected during overhaul or the same failure can be expected to reoccur.

Fig. 19—Top and bottom view of piston severely damaged by detonation. Spot (D) on top and bottom of crown show where metal has started to melt. Absence of scoring on skirt rules out seizure, over-heating or lack of lubrication as a contributing cause.

If pistons are scuffed or scored, look for metal transfer to cylinder walls. Metal transfer and score marks must be removed from cylinder walls with a hone. Chrome plated cylinder bores should not be honed.

Full strength muriatic acid can be used to remove aluminum deposits from a cast iron cylinder bore. Muriatic acid can be purchased in a drug store. It is also used as a soldering acid, although the supply kept in most radiator shops has usually been cut (diluted) with zinc. Use acid carefully, it can cause painful burns if spilled on the skin and the fumes are toxic. It is most easily used by carefully transferring a small amount to a plastic squeeze bottle, or to another small container and applying with a cotton swab. DO NOT allow the acid to spill or run onto aluminum portions of the cylinder, it will rapidly attack and dissolve the metal. Do not use the acid on a chrome bore. When applied to aluminum deposits, the acid will immediately start to boil and foam. When the action stops the aluminum has been dissolved or the acid is diluted; wipe the area with an old rag or towel which can be discarded. If deposits remain, repeat the process. Flush the area with water when aluminum is removed. Water will dilute the acid and can be used to stop the action if desired, or if acid runs off onto aluminum portion of cylinder, is accidentally spilled, etc. Immediately coat treated portion of cylinder with oil, as the acid makes the cast iron especially susceptible to rust.

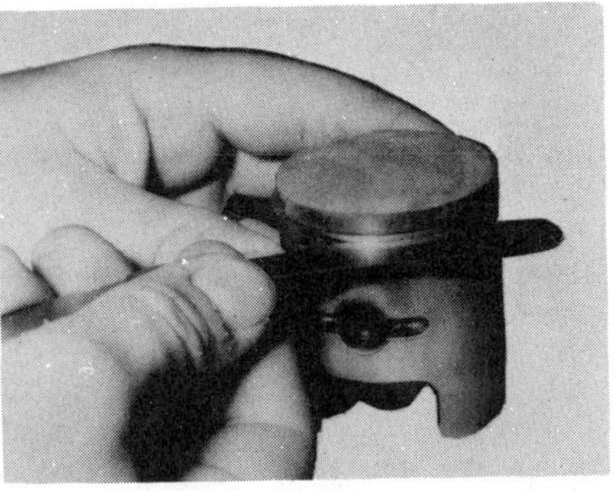

Fig. 21—Ring side clearance in groove should be measured with feeler gage as shown. Clearance should be within recommended limits and the same all the way around piston.

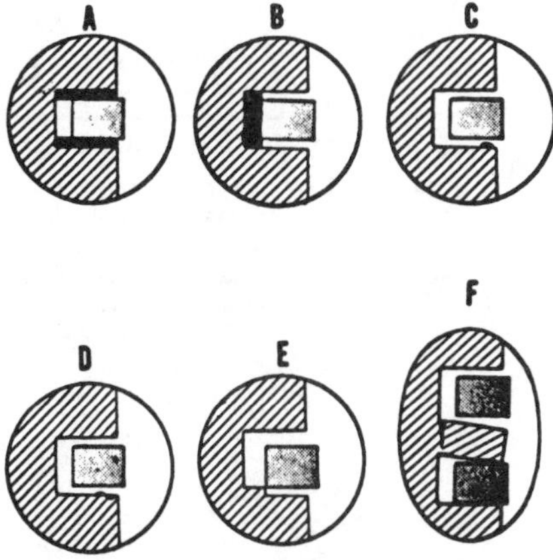

Fig. 22—Examine piston for damage before removing old rings. Shown are some common faults.

A. Carbon buildup, sides of groove
B. Carbon buildup behind ring
C. Incomplete carbon removal, loose carbon
D. Nicks in groove
E. Stepped wear
F. Broken or bent land

Fig. 20—Example of severe case of port carbon. Carbon must be removed to restore performance.

A rule of thumb says scuffing or scoring of piston above the piston pin is due to overheating. Damage below the pin is more likely due to insufficient lubrication or improper fit. Overheating may be caused by a lean mixture, overloading, a damaged cooling fan or fins, air leaks in carburetor mounting gasket or manifold, blow-by (stuck or broken rings) as well as carbon build-up.

The greatest cylinder wear of a two-stroke engine generally occurs in port area of cylinder wall instead of at top of ring travel. Cast iron or aluminum bores should be measured using ring gap as an indicator or an inside micrometer. Check for spots on chromed bores which are different in appearance. Spots may be metal deposits from overheated pistons or may be where the thin chrome plating is worn through. Deposited metal can be scraped or carefully hand sanded from the chrome. If plating is worn through, cylinder must be renewed. Aluminum will be easily scratched by a sharp object but chrome will not.

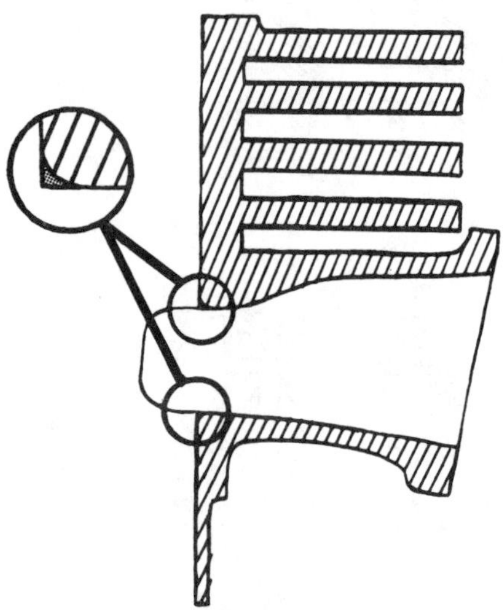

Fig. 23 — Some manufacturers recommend that edges of ports be chamfered as shown in insert, after reboring.

On models with cast iron cylinder, the bore should be honed when engine is overhauled, to true the bore, remove the glaze and remove the ridge at top and bottom of ring travel area. If ridge is not removed, new unworn rings may strike the ridge and bend ring lands in piston as shown at (F – Fig. 22). The finished cylinder should have a light cross-hatch pattern. After honing, wash cylinder assembly with soap and water, then swab with new oil on a clean rag until all tendency of rag to discolor is gone. Washing in solvent will not remove the abrasive from finished cylinder walls.

Some manufacturers have oversize piston and ring sets available. If care and approved procedures are used, installation of oversize units should result in a highly satisfactory overhaul.

The cylinder bore may be over-sized by using either a boring bar or hone; however, if a boring bar is used, finish sizing should be done with a hone. Before attempting to rebore, first check to be sure that new standard units cannot be fitted within the recommended clearances and that the correct oversize is available.

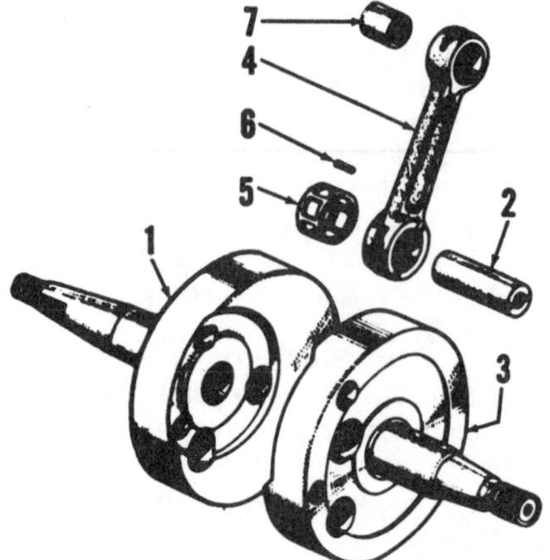

Fig. 24 — Exploded view of typical built-up crankshaft.

1. Counterweight
2. Crankpin
3. Counterweight
4. Connecting rod
5. Bearing cage
6. Needle roller
7. Bushing or bearing

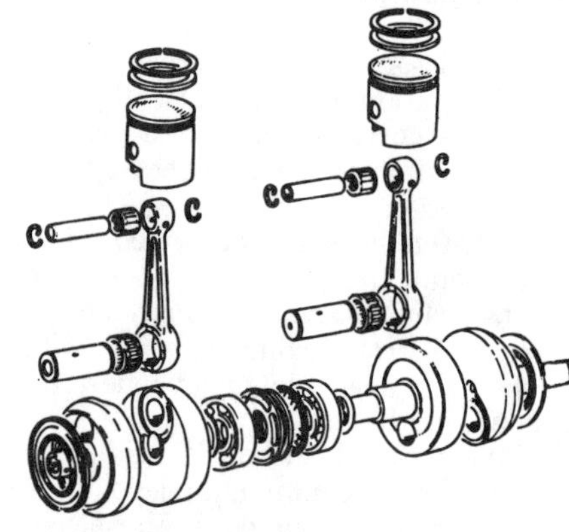

Fig. 25 — Exploded view of built-up crankshaft and associated parts used on some two cylinder engines.

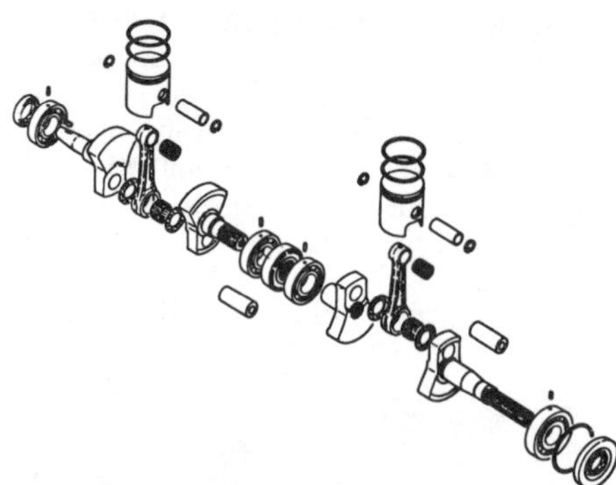

Fig. 26 — Another type of built-up crankshaft assembly used on two cylinder models.

Some manufacturers recommend that after boring a cylinder to an oversize, the top and bottom edges of cylinder wall ports be rounded to prevent rings from catching. Fig. 23 shows typical port cross section with area to be removed indicated in the inset.

When assembling piston to connecting rod, observe special precautions outlined in the individual repair sections. The pistons in some engines may have the pin offset, rings pinned or other design features which prevent piston from being safely installed backward. Check for assembly marks or other indicators on the piston and in the individual repair sections.

Fig. 27 — View showing mesurement of runout using vee blocks.

Lubricate piston pin bearing (or bushing), piston, rings and cylinder as engine is assembled. Run engine with slightly rich carburetor setting during break-in period and do not overload, to prevent overheating until the parts wear in. It is sometimes advisable to install a hotter heat range spark plug in an attempt to prevent oil fouling in a newly started engine. Plug fouling during this period is not uncommon and it is advisable to have spare plugs along when running in a newly overhauled engine.

CONNECTING ROD, CRANKSHAFT AND BEARINGS

Before detaching connecting rods from crankshaft, mark rods and caps for correct assembly to each other and to proper cylinder. Most damage to ball and roller bearings is evident after visual inspection and turning the assembled bearing by hand. If bearing shows evidence of overheating, renew the complete assembly. On models with plain (bushing) bearings, check the crankpin and main bearing journals for wear with a micrometer. Crankshaft journals will usually wear out-of-round with most wear on side that takes the force of power stroke (strokes). If main bearing clearances are excessive, new crankcase seals may not be able to prevent pressure from blowing fuel and oil around crankshaft. All crankcase seals should be renewed when crankshaft, connecting rods and bearings are serviced.

Built-up crankshafts should be checked for runout when removed. Typical built-up crankshafts are shown in Figs. 24, 25, and 26. Check for runout using either vee blocks (Fig. 27) or lathe centers (Fig. 28). Should the shaft not meet specifications, then it should be taken to a machine shop, motorcycle rebuilder or a shop experienced in straightening built-up shafts.

Fig. 28 — View showing measurement of runout using lathe centers.

CARBURETOR SERVICE

CONTENTS

OPERATION

Function of the carburetor is to atomize and mix fuel in proper proportions with air flowing into the engine intake port or intake manifold. Fuel mixture must be rich when engine is cold and leaned out as engine warms up.

In order to maintain correct mixture, the amount of fuel must be decreased as altitude or weather temperature increases and increased as altitude or weather temperature decreases. Use a smaller carburetor main jet to decrease flow of fuel and a larger main jet to increase flow of fuel. Be especially cautious when operating at a lower altitude, because too lean of fuel mixture will cause extreme localized overheating in engine cylinders which will cause damage to engine.

To check for correct fuel mixture, first: Remove engine spark plug(s) and clean, regap and reinstall. Start engine and bring up to normal operating temperature. Run snowmobile a short distance, turn engine off and remove spark plug(s). Inspect spark plug(s) for color and condition. Spark plug electrode and insulator should be brown to light tan in color and burning clean. If electrode and insulator is black in color and wet, then fuel mixture is too rich. If electrode and insulator is light tan to white in color with evidence of flaking or blistering, then fuel mixture is too lean. Change carburetor main jet as needed to correct condition and to insure top performance of engine. Thereafter, periodically inspect spark plug(s) condition.

BENDIX

A BENDIX float type carburetor was used on some OMC snowmobile engines.

ADJUSTMENT

Refer to Fig. 1 for location of points of adjustment. Initial setting for High Speed Needle Valve and Low Speed Needle Valve should be approximately 1¼-1½ turns open from closed position. Re-adjust for best performance under operating conditions. NOTE: High speed needle valve should never be closed to less than one turn open.

Idle Adjustment Screw (Speed Adjustment) should be set to maintain the recommended idle speed of 800-900 rpm. Carburetor is equipped with an inlet screen which should be washed in gasoline for cleaning. Do not oil screen when reinstalling.

OVERHAUL

Refer to Fig. 1 for exploded view of carburetor assembly. Float bowl (10) can be removed by unscrewing main jet (11). Fuel bowl is removed to drain carburetor.

Disassembly of choke and throttle valves and shafts is recommended only if carburetor is to be immersed in carburetor cleaner. Choke and throttle valve attaching screws are staked after assembly to prevent loosening; file off the staking before attempting to remove the screws. Re-install using LOCTITE or equivalent to prevent loosening. Float lever setting should be ⅛ inch measured from gasket surface to nearest edge of float opposite pivot as shown in Fig. 3.

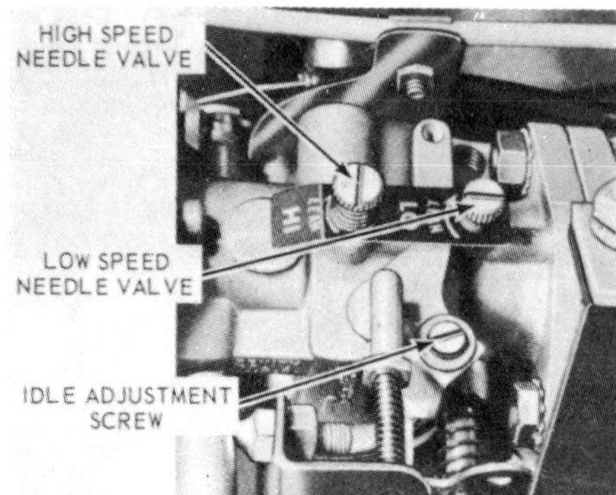

Fig. 1–Installed view of BENDIX carburetor showing points of adjustment.

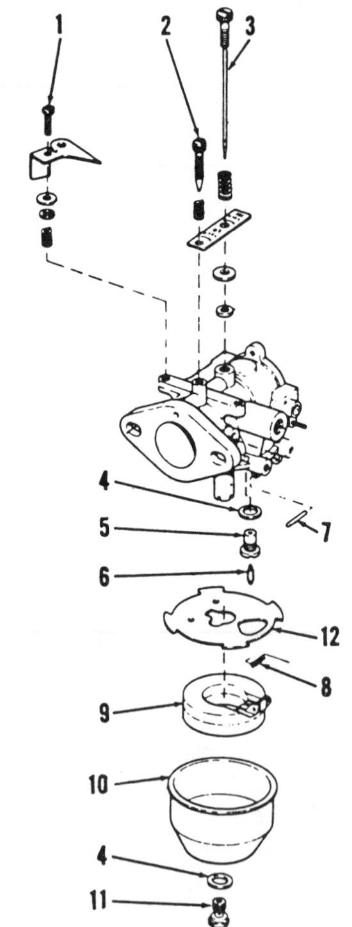

Fig. 2–Exploded view of Bendix carburetor used on OMC snowmobile engine.

1. Idle speed screw
2. Low speed mixture screw
3. High speed mixture screw
4. Gasket
5. Inlet valve seat
6. Inlet valve
7. Float pin
8. Float spring
9. Float
10. Fuel bowl
11. Main jet
12. Fuel bowl gasket

CARTER

TYPE N CARBURETOR

This model float type carburetor is no longer produced by the Carter Carburetor Company. Manufacturing rights have been obtained by the Kohler Company, Kohler, Wisconsin 53044. Parts may be obtained from the Kohler Company.

TROUBLE SHOOTING. If fuel starvation is suspected, all filters in carburetor, fuel pump, and/or tank should be inspected. Improper handling of fuel may result in foreign matter in the fuel causing a fuel stoppage or reduced flow. Filters should not be removed as blockage will result in the carburetor and cleaning will be more frequent and difficult.

Carburetor flooding may also occur. Wear of the fuel inlet needle, needle seat, or the float linkage can result in flooding. Other possible causes are a loose fuel valve seat, loose nozzle, cracked carburetor body, or binding float.

One of the common causes of carburetor malfunctioning is the formation of gum and varnish. During disassembly this condition should be noted and all parts cleaned in a suitable solvent. New parts may be needed if small passages are blocked and cannot be cleaned. Fuel systems along with the carburetor should be drained when not in use to prevent a buildup of gum as a result of the gasoline decomposing.

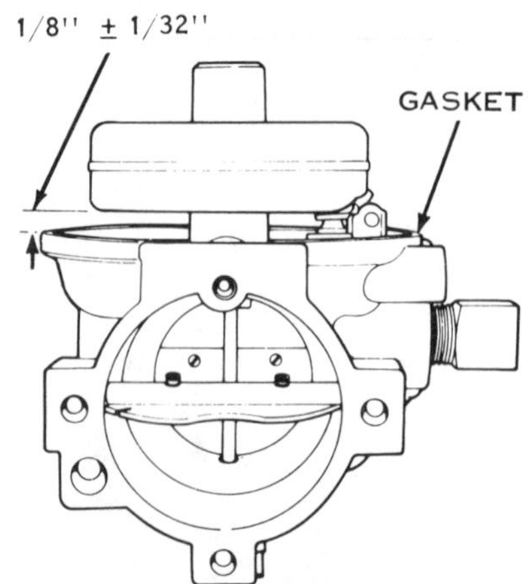

Fig. 3–Float height should be ⅛-inch measured from gasket surface as shown.

Carburetor malfunctioning can also be caused by worn parts. Needle valve and seat should be checked and replaced as a unit if necessary. Needle valves should be checked for grooves caused by overtightening. Seats will usually be damaged if this is the case. Needle valve adjusting should be done lightly to prevent needle and seat damage.

DISASSEMBLY. Refer to Fig. 4. Remove retaining screw (15) and fuel bowl (13). Knock out float pin and remove float. Check float for dents, leaks and wear on float lip or in float pin holes. Remove inlet needle (9) and seat (8). Remove idle mixture needle (21), main fuel needle (1) and springs. Note condition of choke and throttle shafts and plates. If wear exists, carburetor body assembly must be renewed.

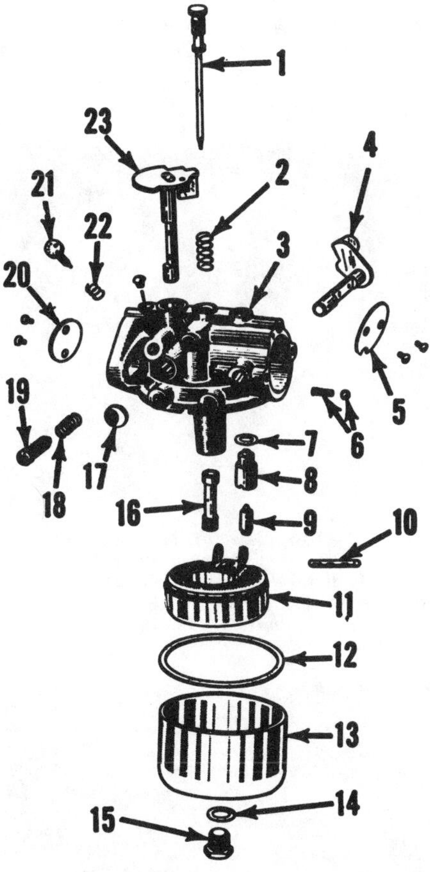

ASSEMBLY. Install inlet seat and needle. Install float and float pin. Set float level by inverting carburetor with float resting lightly on inlet needle. Measure between body gasket flange and float at the point opposite the needle valve. The measurement should be 11/64-inch. Float adjustment is made by bending tang contacting needle valve. Install new fuel bowl gasket, fuel bowl, retaining screw gasket (if needed), and retaining screw. Install main fuel needle. Install idle mixture needle. Do not overtighten needles in seats. Make running adjustments.

Fig. 4—Exploded view of typical Carter Model "N" carburetor.

1. Main fuel needle
2. Spring
3. Carburetor body
4. Choke shaft
5. Choke disc
6. Choke detent
7. Sealing washer
8. Inlet valve seat
9. Inlet valve
10. Float pin
11. Float
12. Gasket
13. Float bowl
14. Sealing washer
15. Retainer
16. Main jet
17. Plug
18. Spring
19. Idle stop screw
20. Throttle disc
21. Idle fuel needle
22. Spring
23. Throttle shaft

KEIHIN DIAPHRAGM CARBURETOR

KEIHIN diaphragm type carburetors are designed for snowmobile use and, prior to 1972 production, were available in two series; 406 which is roughly equivalent in size and application to Tillotson HR; and 407, equivalent to Tillotson HD.

Starting with the 1972 model year, a new method of identification was used. Model number of all carburetors begins with prefix letters "CD," followed by a number such as "33-28." First part of number indicates throttle bore (in millimeters) and second part of number indicates venturi diameter.

OPERATION

Fuel level (Main) diaphragm (7—Fig. 5) is below fuel pump diaphragm (2). A choke shutter closes the carburetor air horn to initiate the starting mode.

Slow speed operation is controlled by setting of idle adjustment needle (I) and by a series of drilled discharge ports (See Fig. 6) located below the edge of closed throttle shutter. Drilled ports (three or four) are uncovered sequentially as throttle shutter is moved from idle position, thus supplying additional fuel for correct mixture as air flow increases. At high speed, the primary venturi and main fuel discharge nozzle are brought into operation, supplementing the fuel which continues to flow through the idle discharge ports. In this manner, fuel and air are balanced throughout the operating range.

ADJUSTMENT

Carburetors are divided into early and late types as outlined in introduc

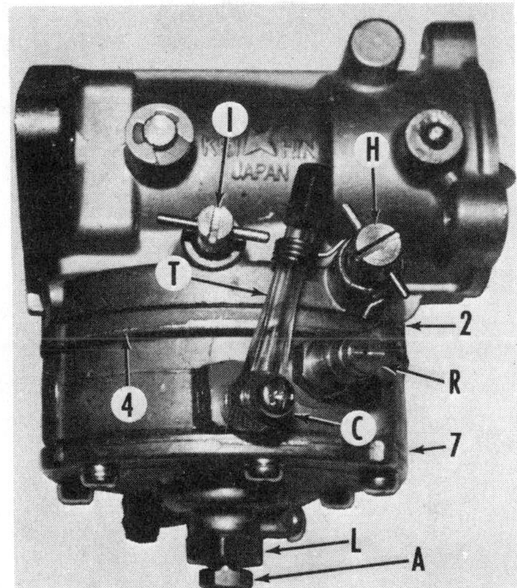

Fig. 5—View of Keihin Diaphragm Carburetor showing points of adjustment.

A. Adjusting stud
C. Check plug
H. High speed needle
I. Idle needle
L. Locknut
R. Return fitting
T. Sight tube
2. Fuel pump diaphragm
4. Lower gasket surface
7. Operating diaphragm

Fig. 6—View of lower surface of carburetor body showing idle bypass cover removed.

1. Gasket
I. Idle bypass cover
P. Pulse passage
X. Fuel ports

Fig. 7—View of lower surface of carburetor body with idle bypass cover (I) and expansion plug (M) installed. Refer also to Fig. 6.

tory paragraphs. Principles of adjustment are similar for all models but the procedure differs on early units which have not been updated. The CD units are shown in Fig. 5. On early unmodified units, check plug (C) was to the right of return fitting (R), or bleed plug if return fitting was not installed. Most early carburetors have been modified by installing late fuel pump body, in which case carburetor will be adjusted as a late unit.

FUEL LEVEL. Fuel level must be checked with engine running. Install sight tube (T—Fig. 5) as shown, then start and run engine at approximately 1500 rpm. Fuel level should rise in plastic sight tube to lower gasket surface of upper fuel pump cover (4). On models with early fuel pump body make sure sight tube is installed in RIGHT port opening and adjust fuel level to upper gasket surface of upper cover.

If fuel level is incorrect, loosen locknut (L) and turn adjusting stud (A) IN to RAISE fuel level or OUT to LOWER fuel level.

NOTE: Some early models may use a lock screw (19—Fig. 12) to secure adjusting stud (A—Fig. 5) instead of locknut (L).

With fuel level correctly adjusted at idle speed, raise rear of machine and run engine at 3000 rpm; fuel level should not change. If fuel level varies or correct adjustment cannot be obtained, overhaul carburetor as outlined in appropriate following paragraphs.

MIXTURE ADJUSTMENT. Normal intitial settings are 1¼-turns open for idle mixture adjustment screw (I—Fig. 5) and one-turn open for high speed mixture screw (H). Final adjustments must be made for best performance with engine at operating temperature and fuel level properly adjusted. High speed mixture must be rechecked whenever idle mixture has been readjusted.

OVERHAUL

To disassemble the Keihin diaphragm carburetor, remove the six Phillips head through-bolts and carefully separate the units. Check throttle shaft and bores for wear and throttle shutter for damage and renew the carburetor if damage is found. Choke components are available and may be renewed, however, new screws must be used and staked or installed with "Loctite." Remove high speed adjusting screw (H—Fig. 5) and idle adjusting screw (I), and examine tapered ends for damage. Renew screws if tapered ends are visibly ringed or if otherwise damaged. Renew carburetor if adjusting screw seats are damaged.

Remove idle bypass cover (I—Fig. 6) and its gasket and examine idle well and port drillings for dirt or gum. Soak in solvent and blow out with compressed air if deposits are found. Do not use a drill or wire probe in an attempt to clean ports. Reinstall idle bypass cover (I) as shown in Fig. 7, tightening retaining screws securely. Check main nozzle expansion plug (M) to be sure it is tight and correctly installed. Do not attempt to remove expansion plug or main nozzle.

When reassembling carburetor, fuel main and idle supply passage (X) must remain open. Install gasket (1) and pump diaphragm (2—Fig. 8) making sure holes for fuel passages align. Install the large "O" ring (3) and the two small "O" rings (in fuel ports "X") in fuel pump upper cover (4) and position cover over the dowels in throttle body.

Install check valve (5—Fig. 9) making sure the three middle flaps are centered over inlet ports (IP) in upper cover (4) and that fuel ports (X) align. The six check flaps MUST be in good condition.

If inlet needle valve seat is to be renewed, remove Phillips head screw (S—Fig. 10) and retainer (R). Invert pump body and remove valve lever, spring and needle valve; then using a

Fig. 8—Fuel pump diaphragm (2) installed on carburetor body. Install large "O" ring (3) and small "O" ring on fuel ports (X) of fuel pump upper cover (4).

Fig. 9—Fuel pump upper cover (4) installed on carburetor body. Position check valve (5) over upper cover with the three center flaps centered over inlet ports (IP) and fuel passages (X) open.

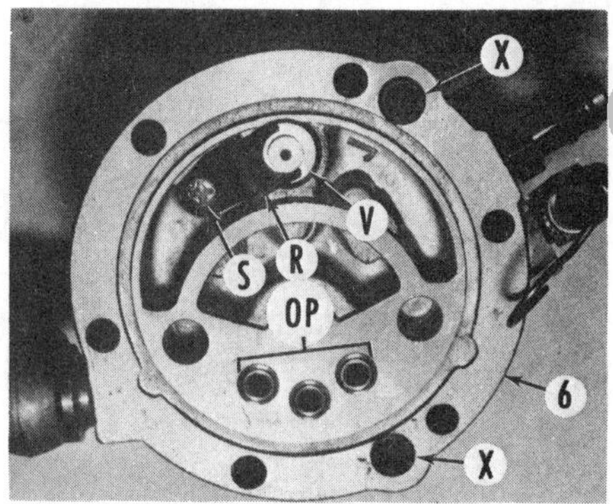

Fig. 10—Top view of fuel pump lower body (6) showing outlet ports (OP) and top side of inlet valve seat (V). Seat is secured by retainer (R) and screw (S). Fuel passage ports are at (X).

Fig. 11—Inlet valve lever button (B) should be flush with floor on bottom side of valve body (6). Inlet valve seat is at (V) and inlet needle at (N).

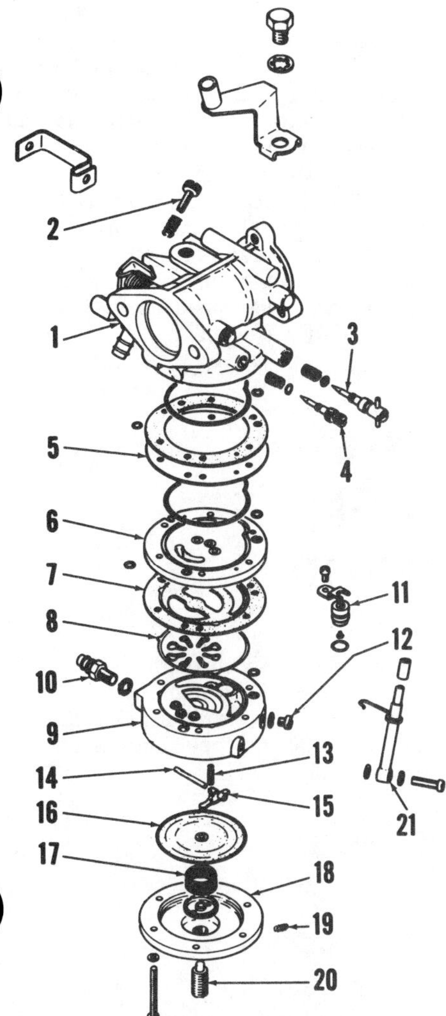

Fig. 12—Exploded view of KEIHIN diaphragm type carburetor showing component parts. Sight tube (21) is used to set fuel level and is not a part of the carburetor.

1. Throttle body
2. Low speed screw
3. High speed needle
4. Low speed needle
5. Pump diaphragm
6. Pump upper cover
7. Gasket
8. Pump check valves
9. Pump (regulating) body
10. Inlet fitting
11. Inlet needle & seat
12. Bleed plug
13. Spring
14. Pivot shaft
15. Valve lever
16. Regulating diaphragm
17. Spring
18. Regulator cover
19. Lock screw
20. Adjusting screw
21. Sight tube

Fig. 13—Operating diaphragm (7) and associated parts installed on lower side of valve body.

7. Operating diaphragm
8. Spring
9. Spring seat
F. Inlet fuel fitting
P. Pulse fitting
R. Return fitting
X. Fuel passages

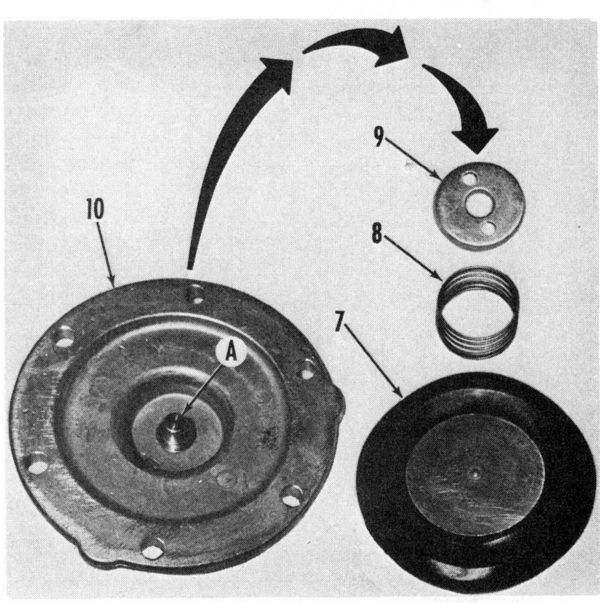

Fig. 14—Exploded view of operating diaphragm (7), spring (8), spring seat (9) and regulator cover (10). Upper end of adjusting stud is shown at (A).

good pin punch of appropriate size, drive valve seat (V) upward out of valve body. Valve seats are available in standard size and OD oversizes of 0.01 mm and 0.002 mm. Oversize valves are identified by one or two annular grooves around outside of body while standard body is smooth. Reinstall retainer (R—Fig. 10), needle valve and lever, then check height of actuating button (B—Fig. 11) which should be flush with valve body floor. Adjust if necessary by bending tang which contacts valve needle (N).

Fig. 13 shows operating diaphragm (7), spring (8) and spring seat (9) correctly positioned. Parts are shown exploded in proper order in Fig. 14. An initial starting point for adjusting stud (A) in regulator cover (10) is with two threads showing when viewed from inside as shown. Adjust the assembled carburetor after installation as previously outlined.

KEIHIN TYPE FLOAT CARBURETOR WITH BUTTERFLY THROTTLE

Carburetors are identified by a model number which consists of a letter prefix "BD" followed by a set of numbers such as "44-38". First part of number indicates throttle bore (in millimeters) and second part of number indicates venturi diameter.

ADJUSTMENT

FLOAT LEVEL. Float is adjusted by bending metal tang between float body (16–Fig. 14A) and float pin (17). As shown in Fig. 14B, distance (D) should be 0.48-0.67 inch when carburetor is tilted at a 20-30 degree angle.

IDLE SPEED. Idle speed is adjusted by turning screw (8–Fig. 14A). Idle speeds vary from model to model, consult respective manufacturer specification for recommended speed setting.

IDLE MIXTURE. Idle mixture adjustment is done by turning screw (6–Fig. 14A). Start engine and bring up to normal operating temperature. Turn screw either in (lean) or out (rich) to obtain an even engine idle. Readjust idle speed to recommended setting after idle mixture is set.

MAIN JET. To insure top performance of engine, main jet (13–Fig. 14A) may need to be changed if there is a 2000 feet change in altitude or an 18 degree F change in temperature. When altitude or weather temperature increases a lower number of jet should be used. Whenever altitude or weather temperature decreases a larger number of jet should be used. Caution should be taken especially when operating at a lower altitude, too lean of fuel mixture could shorten engine life.

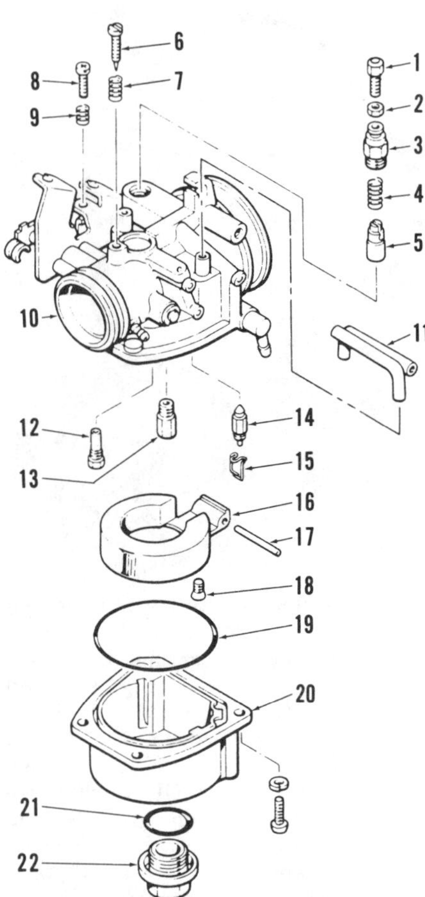

Fig. 14A—Exploded view showing Keihin Float Type Carburetor with Butterfly Throttle.

1. Cable adjuster
2. Jam nut
3. Starter plunger cap
4. Spring
5. Starter plunger
6. Pilot screw
7. Spring
8. Throttle stop screw
9. Spring
10. Main body
11. Hose
12. Slow jet
13. Main jet
14. Needle and seat assy.
15. Needle clip
16. Float
17. Pin
18. Flathead screw
19. "O"ring
20. Float bowl
21. Gasket
22. Plug

Periodic inspection of spark plug tip will indicate how engine is performing. Normal insulator tip color is brown to light tan. If tip color is black, then either oil mixture is too high or carburetor is running too rich. If tip color is light tan to white with flaking and blistering deposits, then combustion chamber is running too hot and engine damage could occur. A larger size main jet may need to be installed.

Fig. 14B—View showing procedure for setting float level. Distance (D) should be 0.48-0.67 inch.

OVERHAUL

Remove carburetor from engine. Refer to Fig. 14A for reference in disassembling carburetor. Check all parts for cracks, distortions or any other damage and renew as needed. Remove all gaskets and "O" rings, then clean all parts with an approved cleaner. Rinse thoroughly with solvent and blow all parts and passages clean with compressed air. Caution should be taken in not using paper towels or rags to dry parts, lint from material could plug jets or fuel passages. Reassemble carburetor in reverse order of disassembly. Install new gaskets and "O" rings. Adjust carburetor float setting as outlined in FLOAT LEVEL ADJUSTMENT section. Reinstall carburetor on engine, then start engine and bring up to normal operating temperature. Readjust idle mixture and idle speed as outlined in ADJUSTMENT section.

MIKUNI DIAPHRAGM CARBURETOR

Mikuni diaphragm carburetors are identified by a model number composed of the prefix letters "BN" followed by a number identification which indicates throttle bore in millimeters. Refer to Fig. 15 for cross-sectional view of carburetor and to Fig. 16 for exploded view and parts identification.

ADJUSTMENT

Initial setting for high speed adjusting screw (2–Fig. 16) is 1¼-1½ turns open from closed position. Initial setting for idle mixture adjusting screw (4) is approximately 1¼-turns. Final adjustments must be made under operating conditions at operating temperature. Clockwise rotation of either needle leans the mixture.

OVERHAUL

Refer to Fig. 16 for exploded view of carburetor. Fuel pump unit and main diaphragm (8) can be removed after removing the six-through bolts. Note that alignment tabs manufactured into each piece fit into a relief in carburetor body to assist in proper alignment during assembly.

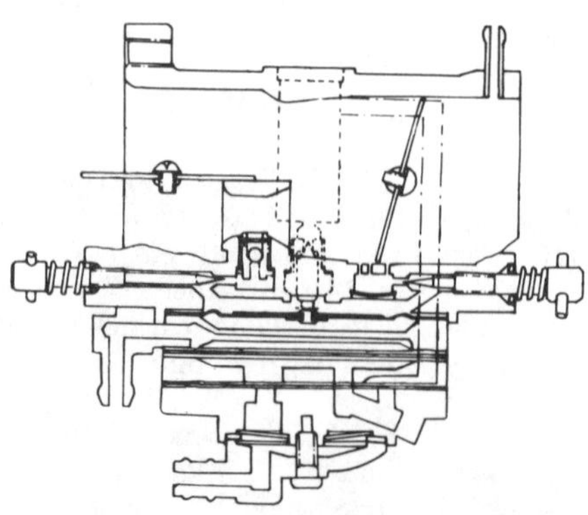

Fig. 15—Cross-sectional view of MIKUNI diaphragm carburetor. Refer to Fig. 16 for exploded view.

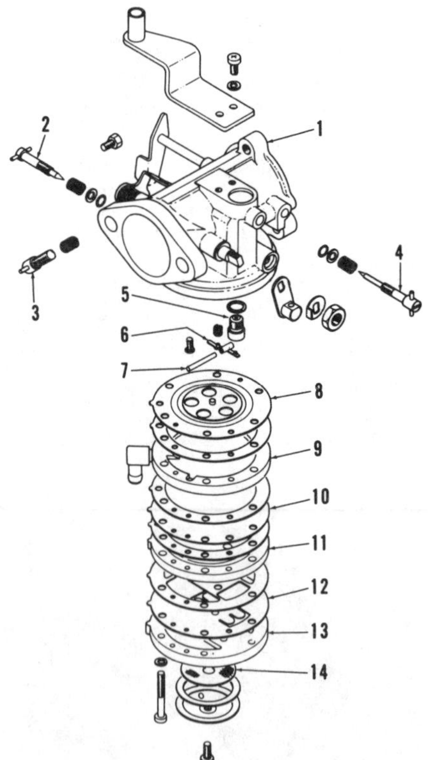

Fig. 16—Exploded view of MIKUNI diaphragm carburetor showing component parts.

1. Throttle body
2. High speed adjusting screw
3. Idle speed adjusting screw
4. Idle mixture adjusting screw
5. Inlet needle & seat
6. Valve lever
7. Pivot shaft
8. Regulating diaphragm
9. Diaphragm cover
10. Pump diaphragm
11. Pump body
12. Check valve diaphragm
13. Inlet body
14. Inlet screen

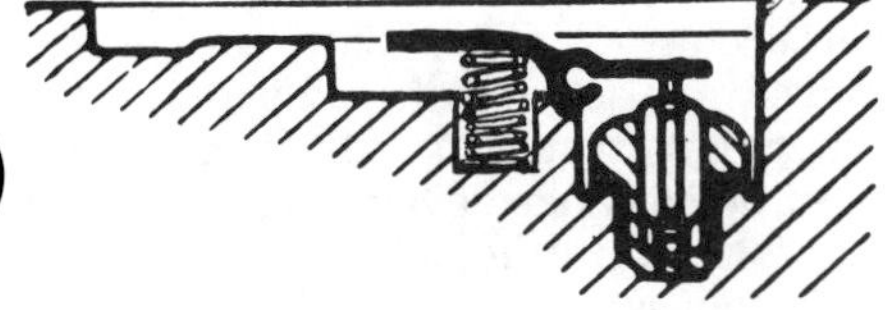

Fig. 17—Inlet needle valve lever should be flush with floor of housing recess as shown.

Do not remove choke or throttle valves or shafts unless necessary, plate retaining screws are staked to prevent loosening. Also a spring loaded friction detent is contained in choke shaft bore; be careful not to lose the parts if choke is disassembled. Inlet needle valve lever should be flush with floor of housing recess when needle valve is seated. Refer to Fig. 17. If lever must be adjusted, push down on lever immediately above spring to collapse the spring; then bend the end which contacts needle valve.

Expansion plug on top (outside) of throttle body (1–Fig. 16) closes the "starting well" and is under pressure. A loose expansion plug in this location will cause fuel pressure leak when engine is operating. Loose expansion plugs below main nozzle idle ports will cause erratic operation. Main nozzle contains a loose check ball which prevents air entry into diaphragm chamber during idle.

MIKUNI FLOAT TYPE CARBURETOR WITH SLIDE THROTTLE

MIKUNI float type variable venturi (slide) type carburetors are identified by a model number which consists of a letter prefix "VM" followed by a number identification which indicates throttle bore size in millimeters. Adjustment specifications are given in the respective ENGINE SERVICE Sections. The following gives basic adjustment information and general overhaul procedures.

ADJUSTMENT

FLOAT LEVEL. To check float level, invert carburetor so that float arm contacts the needle valve, but do not compress spring-loaded plunger in the needle. Float arm should be parallel to carburetor base (Fig. 18A). To adjust, carefully bend tang that contacts the needle valve until arm is parallel.

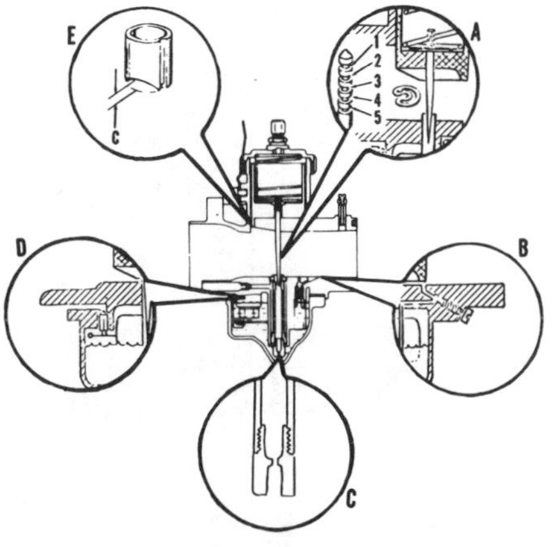

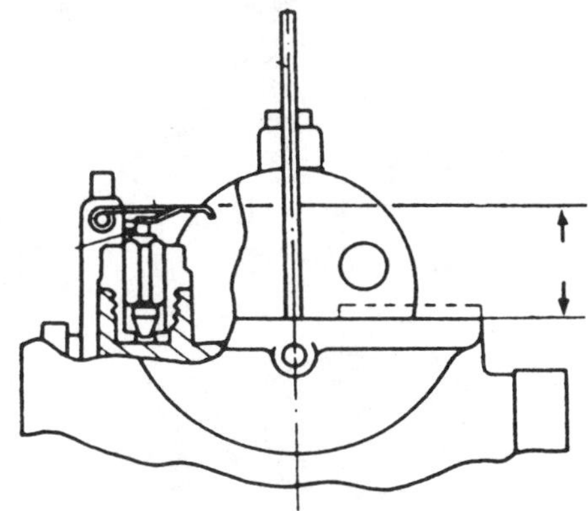

Fig. 18A—With carburetor inverted, float arm should be parallel to carburetor base.

MIXTURE ADJUSTMENTS. Basic settings, jet sizes, throttle slide cutaway, etc. are given in engine sections. Following is a more detailed description of specific adjustments to correct operating problems.

SLOW IDLE. Slow idle mixture is adjusted by the pilot screw (B—Fig. 18). Clockwise rotation of pilot-air screw richens the mixture. Slow idle speed is adjusted by changing closed height of throttle slide, using idle speed screw (10—Fig. 19). Pilot jet size controls fuel flow and jets are stamped with a number which indicates gravity flow in cc per minute.

SLOW SPEED. With throttle 1/8 to 1/2 open, mixture is controlled by throttle cutaway (E—Fig. 18) as well as by pilot screw. Throttle slides are available with cutaway from 1.5 mm to 3.5 mm in increments of 0.5 mm. A larger cutaway leans the mixture.

Fig. 18—Cross-sectional view of slide type carburetor showing points of adjustment.

A. Valve needle setting used to modify engine performance at intermediate speeds.
B. Idle mixture screw used to modify slow idle performance.
C. Main jet size determines full speed mixture.
D. Float level affects overall carburetor operation.
E. Throttle cutaway (C) may be larger or smaller to modify performance at half or below. Adjustment is made by changing throttle slides.

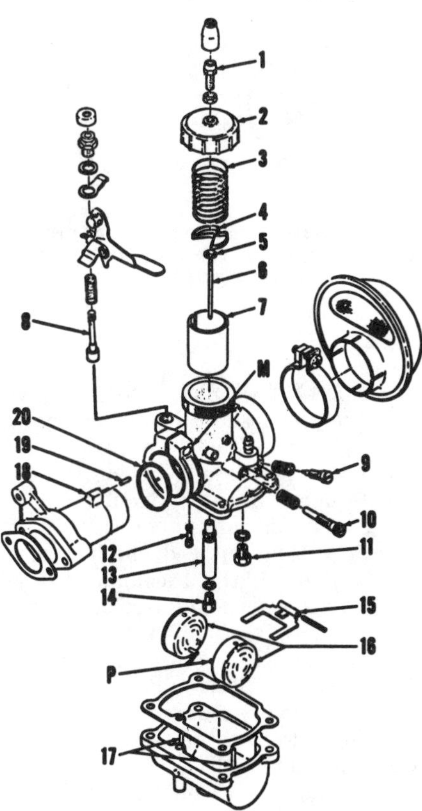

Fig. 19—Exploded view of Mikuni carburetor used on early 1969 Yamaha models. Other models are similar.

1. Cable adj. screw
2. Cap
3. Slide spring
4. Retainer
5. Clip
6. Jet needle
7. Throttle slide
8. Starter plunger
9. Idle mixture needle
10. Idle speed screw
11. Float valve
12. Pilot jet
13. Needle jet
14. Main jet
15. Float lever
16. Floats
17. Guide rods
18. Inlet elbows
19. Dowel pin
20. "O" ring
M. Marking (late models)
P. Actuating pins

INTERMEDIATE SPEED. With throttle 1/4 to 3/4 open, fuel air mixture is principally controlled by jet needle setting (A—Fig. 18. Adjustment is made by raising or lowering needle position in throttle slide. Needle contains a series of notches which are arbitrarily numbered from top to bottom. Needles can also be obtained with a different taper which will provide further modification. Needle is retained by a clip which is installed in one of the notches. Moving clip to a higher notch in needle lowers the needle in slide and provides a leaner intermediate mixture. Installing clip in a lower notch raises needle and richens mixture.

FULL SPEED. Full speed mixture is determined by the size of main jet (C–Fig. 18). The jet is stamped with a number which indicates gravity fuel flow in cc per min. The point at which jet needle height ceases to control the mixture and jet size assumes control depends on needle setting and jet size, but will usually be somewhere between 3/4 to 7/8 full throttle setting.

1. Throttle slide
2. Retainer
3. Clip

Fig. 20—Retainer must be positioned over clip as shown or throttle cable will not fit throttle slide correctly.

ADJUSTMENT SEQUENCE. It will be noted that each adjustment has an overlapping effect on other adjustments, therefore following the correct sequence can save trouble in providing good full range operation. If carburetor is being serviced, check main jet size and install the recommended jet unless machine is being used at extreme high altitudes (above 5000 ft.), in which case use a jet with a guide number about 20-30 smaller. Check and/or adjust float level as recommended. Install correct throttle slide with jet needle clip in recommended notch.

Adjust pilot air screw for best idle. If air screw must be opened more than 2½ turns, install a smaller pilot jet (12–Fig. 19). If air screw is within ½-turn or less of closed position, install a larger pilot jet. Pilot jets are manufactured in increments of #5 and a smaller number indicates a smaller jet.

Test engine at full throttle. If a supply of main jets is on hand, install a jet the next size larger and recheck. If an improvement in performance is noted, install the next larger size. If no improvement was noticed, install the next smaller size and retest. A main jet one size larger than the largest size which shows an improvement in engine speed is desired. Main jets are calibrated in increments of #5 up to size 200, and increments of #10 above size 200.

If a supply of main jets is not available, check engine operation at ⅞ throttle. Stop the engine and move jet needle clip one notch up toward top of needle; then recheck at ⅞ throttle. If performance improves, obtain and install a main jet one size smaller. If no improvement is noted, move needle jet clip to first notch below original setting. If improvement is now observed, install larger main jet.

With main jet selected, test machine at ¼, ½ to ¾ throttle. Raise jet needle to richen the mixture or lower jet needle to lean the mixture. After setting jet needle, slowly open the throttle from idle position, looking for rough operation between full idle and ¼ throttle. If rough operation is detected, hold the setting and turn pilot air screw. If turning needle out improves performance, install throttle slide with next higher cutaway number. If turning needle into body improves performance, install slide with smaller cutaway.

Some carburetors are equipped with a lever or cable operated starting valve. With valve raised and throttle slide closed, fuel is drawn through a starting jet and mixed with the correct amount of air for starting. Wear or malfunction of starter plunger may cause rich mixture at slower idle speeds.

OVERHAUL

Refer to Fig. 19 for exploded view of carburetor. Throttle slide can be removed or jet needle adjusted after unscrewing cap nut (2). Retainer (4) must be positioned over clip as shown in Fig. 20, or throttle cable will not correctly fit the slide.

Floats (16–Fig. 19) slide on guide rods (17) in float bowl. Actuating pins (P) on floats must be installed down and toward each other as shown. Both arms of lever (15) should have the same angle and measure alike. Unless arms require straightening, adjustment should be made by bending the tang which contacts valve needle.

MIKUNI FLOAT TYPE CARBURETOR WITH BUTTERFLY THROTTLE

Carburetors are identified by a model number which consists of a letter prefix "B" followed by a number identification which indicates throttle bore size in millimeters.

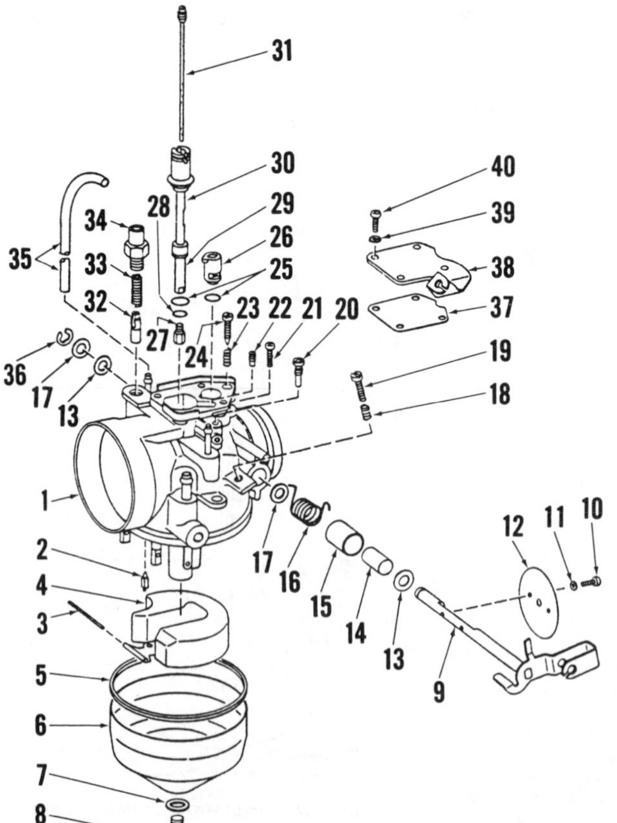

Fig. 20A—Exploded view of butterfly type Mikuni float carburetor.

1. Main body
2. Inlet needle valve
3. Float pin
4. Float
5. Gasket
6. Float bowl
7. Washer
8. Bolt
9. Throttle shaft
10. Machine screw (2 used)
11. Lockwasher (2 used)
12. Butterfly throttle plate
13. Seal
14. Ring
15. Hose
16. Spring
17. Gasket
18. Spring
19. Idle screw
20. Pilot jet
21. Machine screw
22. Air jet
23. Spring
24. Idle mixture screw
25. "O"ring
26. Pilot by-pass
27. Main jet
28. "O" ring
29. Holder
30. Nozzle
31. Main air jet
32. Starter valve
33. Spring
34. Cap
35. Fuel line (2 used)
36. E-clip
37. Gasket
38. Bracket
39. Lockwasher (4 used)
40. Machine screw (4 used)

ADJUSTMENT

FLOAT LEVEL. Float is adjusted by bending metal tang between float body (4–Fig. 20A) and float pin (3). Float body should be parallel with edge of carburetor main body (Fig. 20B) when metal tang is in contact with needle valve and valve is seated.

IDLE SPEED. Idle speed is adjusted by turning screw (19–Fig. 20A). Idle speeds vary from model to model, consult respective manufacturer specification for recommended speed.

IDLE MIXTURE. Idle mixture adjustment is done by turning screw (24–Fig. 20A). Start engine and bring up to normal operating temperature. Turn screw either in (lean) or out (rich) to obtain an even engine idle. Readjust idle speed to recommended setting after idle mixture is set.

MAIN JET. To insure top performance of engine, main jet (27–Fig. 20A) may need to be changed if there is a 3000 feet change in altitude or a 30 degree F change in temperature. When altitude or weather temperature increases a lower number of jet should be used. Whenever altitude or weather temperature decreases a larger number of jet should be used. Caution should be taken especially when operating at a lower altitude, too lean of fuel mixture could shorten engine life.

OVERHAUL

Remove carburetor from engine. Refer to Fig. 20A for assistance in disassembling carburetor. Check all parts for cracks, distortions, or any other damage and renew as needed. Remove all gaskets and "O" rings, then clean all parts with approved cleaner. Rinse thoroughly with solvent and blow all parts and passages clean with compressed air. Caution should be taken in not using paper towels or rags to dry parts, lint from material could plug jets or fuel passages. Reassemble carburetor in reverse order of disassembly. Install new gaskets and "O" rings. Adjust carburetor float setting as outlined in **FLOAT LEVEL ADJUSTMENT** section. Reinstall carburetor on engine, then start engine and bring up to normal operating temperature. Readjust idle mixture and idle speed as outlined in **ADJUSTMENT** section.

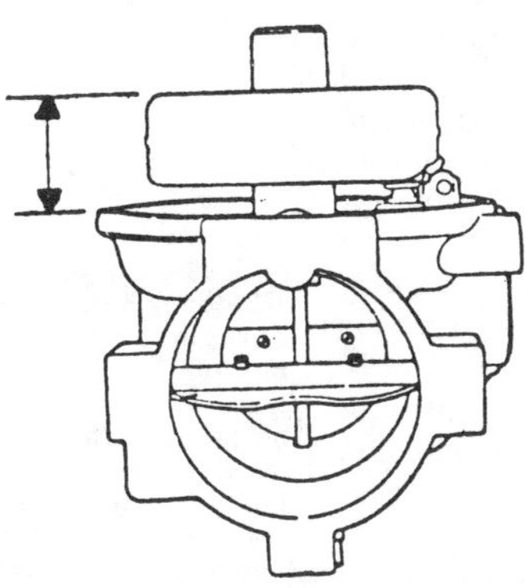

Fig. 20B – Float setting for butterfly type Mikuni carburetor.

TILLOTSON HD, HL & HR DIAPHRAGM CARBURETORS

Of the Tillotson carburetors used in snowmobiles, the HD, HL, and HR series are the most common. All are diaphragm carburetors utilizing the same basic design.

ADJUSTMENT

Initial adjustment is given in the specific engine sections of this manual. Final adjustment must be made for best performance under operating conditions.

TROUBLESHOOTING

The Tillotson diaphragm carburetor is designed to operate under slight pressure. Carburetor can be checked before and after overhaul by connecting a 3 psi supply of filtered air to fuel inlet passage. Refer to Figs. 26 and 27. Immerse carburetor in liquid; air bubbles will indicate leaking pump diaphragm, passage plugs or inlet needle valve, but cannot indicate plugged passages, malfunctioning meter-

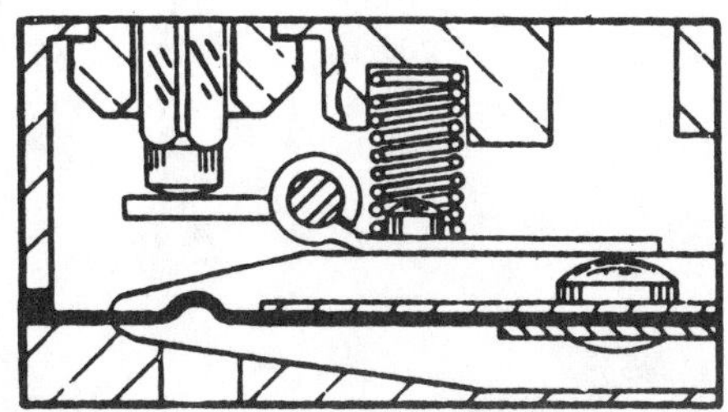

Fig. 21 – Diaphragm end of fuel inlet lever must be flush with diaphragm chamber floor as shown. Adjust by bending lever.

Fig. 21A – Installed view of Tillotson Diaphragm carubretor showing points of adjustment. Vapor return fitting (R) is plugged in illustration, but is connected to fuel tank return line in most late installations.

H. High speed needle
L. Low speed needle
S. Low speed stop screw

ing diaphragm or maladjustment. When overhauling carburetor, diaphragm end of inlet control lever (14—Fig. 22) should be flush with diaphragm chamber floor as shown in Fig. 21. Refer to the following partial list of causes for carburetor malfunction:

IDLE SYSTEM. If idle mixture is too lean and cannot be properly adjusted, consider the possibility of plugged idle fuel passages, expansion plug for main fuel check valve (11—Fig. 22) loose or missing, main fuel check valve (11) not seating, improperly adjusted inlet control lever, leaking metering diaphragm or malfunctioning fuel pump.

If idle mixture is too rich, check idle mixture screw (L—Fig. 21A) and its seat in carburetor body for damage. Refer also to causes for carburetor flooding.

HIGH SPEED SYSTEM. If high speed mixture is too lean and cannot be properly adjusted, check for dirt or plugging in main fuel passages, improperly adjusted inlet control lever (14—Fig. 22), malfunctioning diaphragm or main fuel check valve (11). Also check for damaged or missing packing for high speed mixture screw (H—Fig. 21A) and for malfunctioning fuel pump.

If high speed mixture is too rich, check high speed mixture screw (H) and its seat for damage. Refer also to causes for carburetor flooding.

CARBURETOR FLOODING. The main causes of carburetor flooding are improper seating of inlet needle valve (12—Fig. 22), loose needle valve seat or missing gasket. Check also for improperly adjusted inlet control lever (14), damaged inlet control lever or pivot pin (15) or loose or improperly installed

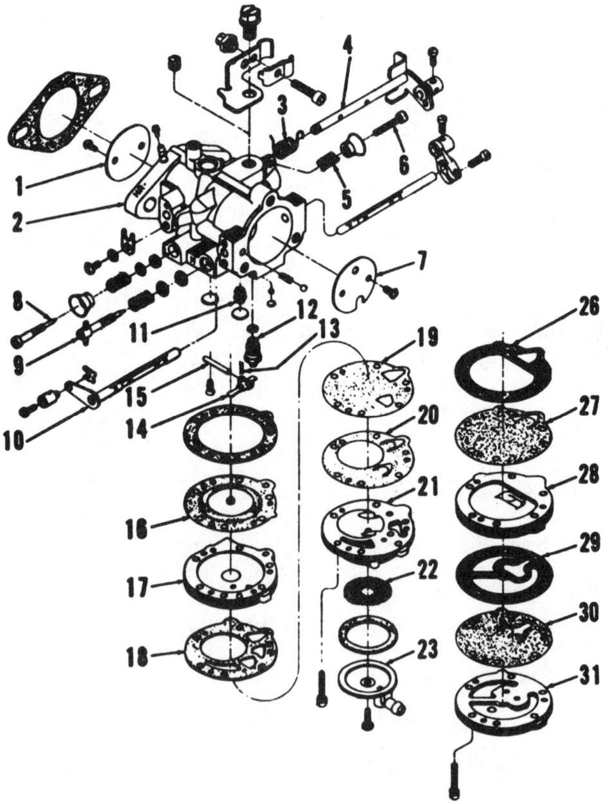

Fig. 22—Exploded view of Tillotson Model HR diaphragm carburetor with built-in fuel pump of the type used on most engines. On some HR carburetors, fuel pump components (26 through 31) are used in place of components (18 through 21).

1. Throttle plate
2. Body
3. Throttle spring
4. Throttle shaft
5. Spring
6. Idle speed screw
7. Choke plate
8. Idle mixture screw
9. High speed mixture screw
10. Choke shaft
11. Main fuel check valve
12. Inlet needle & seat
13. Spring
14. Inlet control lever
15. Pivot shaft
16. Metering diaphragm
17. Diaphragm cover
18. Gasket
19. Pump diaphragm
20. Valve diaphragm
21. Pump body
22. Inlet screen
23. Inlet body
24. Main fuel jet
25. Gland nut
26. Gasket
27. Pump diaphragm
28. Pump body
29. Gasket
30. Inlet valve diaphragm
31. Inlet valve body

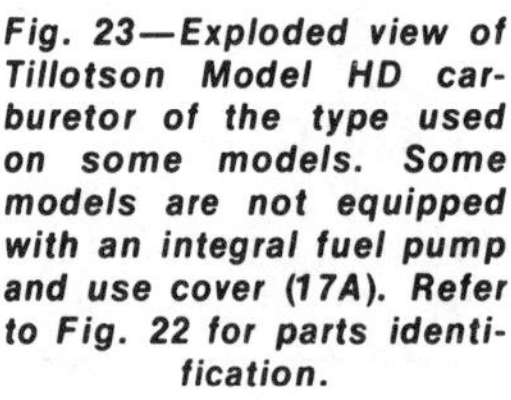

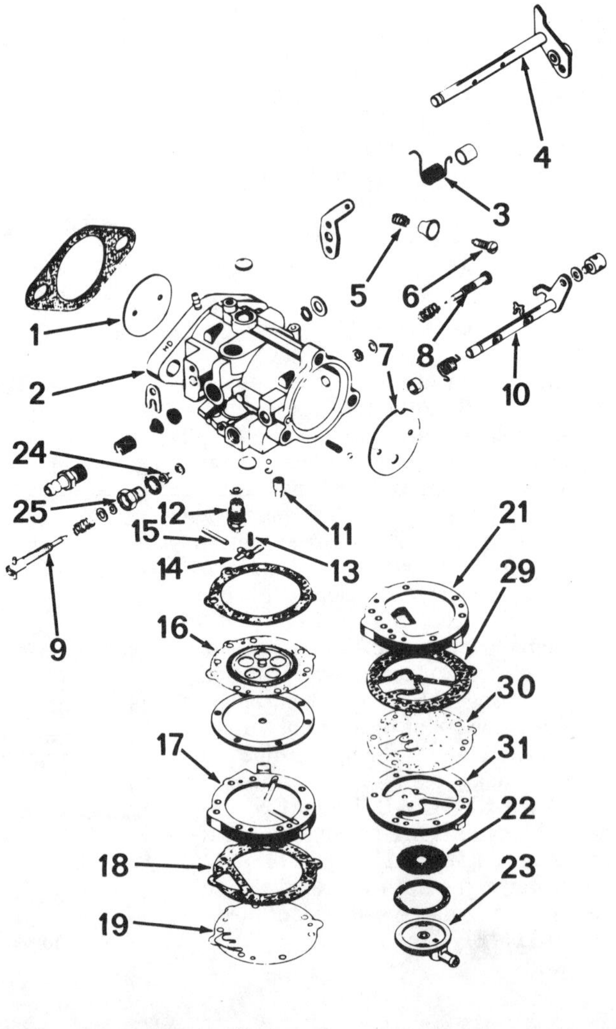

Fig. 23—Exploded view of Tillotson Model HD carburetor of the type used on some models. Some models are not equipped with an integral fuel pump and use cover (17A). Refer to Fig. 22 for parts identification.

Fig. 21B—Throttle cable linkage may be adjusted at operating lever clamp (C) or cable housing anchor clamp (A).

inlet control lever and pivot pin assembly.

Other possible malfunctions can be found in Fig. 25 and should be considered during disassembly.

OVERHAUL

Inasmuch as the HR model is the most frequently used Tillotson carburetor, it will be covered in this section. However, the following procedure for overhaul is applicable to both the HD and HL series Tillotson carburetors. These carburetors should be cleaned and inspected at regular intervals, depending on the type of service.

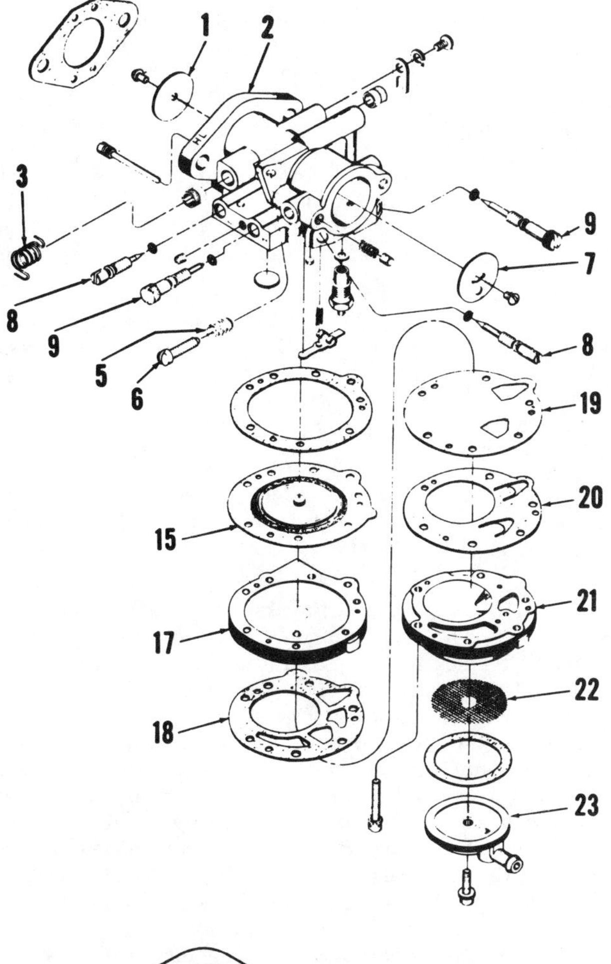

Fig. 24—Exploded view of Tillotson Model HL carburetor. Refer to Fig. 22 for parts identification.

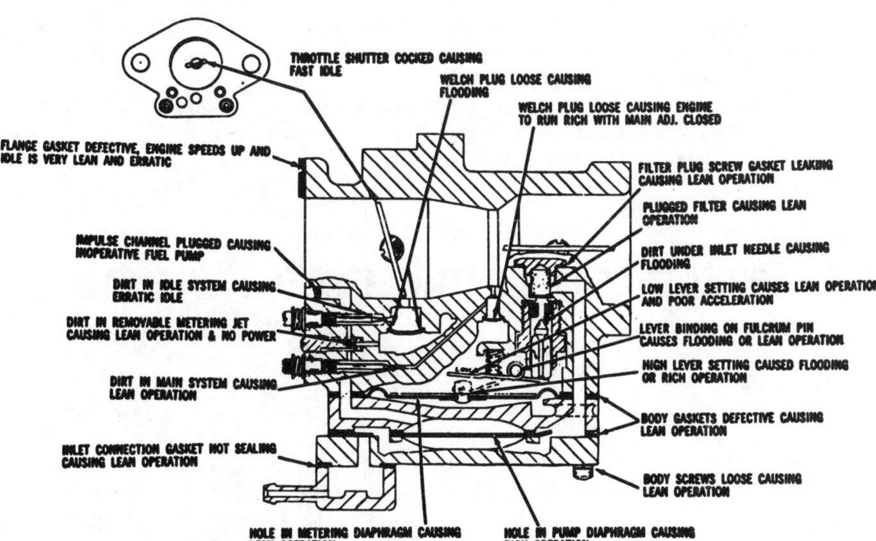

Fig. 25—Schematic cross-sectional view of a diaphragm type carburetor illustrating possible causes of malfunction. Refer to appropriate engine repair section for adjustment information.

DISASSEMBLY. Remove idle speed screw. Inspect idle speed screw, washer, and tension spring. Inspect threads in casting for damage. Should damage be present, repair using an 8-32 Heli-Coil 3/16-inch long.

Remove the filter cover, cover gasket, and filter screen. Clean filter screen by flushing with solvent and dry with compressed air. The cover gasket should be renewed whenever filter screen is serviced. Clean all dirt from plastic cover before assembly.

Remove the six body screws, fuel pump cover casting, fuel pump diaphragm and gasket. Diaphragm should be flat and free from holes. The gasket should be renewed if there are holes or creases in the sealing surface.

Remove the diaphragm cover casting, metering diaphragm and diaphragm gasket. Inspect the diaphragm for holes, tears and other imperfections.

Remove the fulcrum pin retaining screw, fulcrum pin, inlet control lever and inlet tension spring. Care must be used while removing parts due to spring pressure on inlet control lever. The spring must be handled carefully to prevent stretching or compressing. Any alteration to the spring will cause improper carburetor operation. If in doubt as to its condition, renew it.

Remove inlet needle. Remove inlet seat assembly using a 5/16 inch thin wall socket. Remove the inlet seat gasket.

The inlet seat assembly consists of a brass cage and a rubber insert for the inlet needle seat. The insert goes into the cage only one correct way. Looking at the insert, one side is flat and smooth; the other side has a ridge or rim molded around the outside edge. This ridge is to be assembled away from the inlet needle point.

Some models of the HR carburetor are equipped with a rubber tipped needle, a brass inlet seat and a copper gasket. The installation instructions below are applicable to both types of inlet seats.

Inlet needles and seats are in matched sets and should not be interchanged. Needle and seat assembly must be clean for proper performance. Use a new gasket when installing the insert cage. Do not force cage as threads may be stripped or the cage distorted. Use a torque wrench and tighten cage to 25-30 inch-pounds torque.

Remove both high speed and idle mixture screws and inspect points. Notice the idle mixture screw point has the step design to minimize point and casting damage. The mixture screws may be damaged from being forced into the casting seat or possibly broken off in the casting. They may be bent. If damage is present be sure to inspect the condition of the casting. If the adjustment seats are damaged, a new body casting is required.

Welch plugs seal the idle bypass ports and main nozzle ball check valve from the metering chamber. Removal of these plugs is seldom necessary because of lack of wear in these sections and any dirt that may accumulate can usually be blown out with compressed air through the mixture screw holes. If removal of the welch plugs is necessary, drill through the welch plug using a 1/8 inch drill. Allow the drill to just break through the welch plug. If the drill travels too deep into the cavity, the casting may be ruined. Pry the welch plug out of its seat using a small punch.

Inspect the idle bypass holes to insure they are not plugged. Do not push drills or wires into the metering holes. This may damage the flow characteristics of the holes and damage carburetor performance. Blow out plugged holes with compressed air. Remove main nozzle ball check assembly with a screwdriver of correct blade width. If ball check is defective, engine idling will be hampered unless high speed mixture screw is shut off or there will be poor high speed performance with the high speed mixture screw adjusted at 1¼-turns open. Replace the ball check if defective.

Removing choke and throttle plates before cleaning the body is not necessary if there is no evidence of wear. Indication of wear will require the removal of plates to check the casting. To remove the plates, first mark the position of plates on their respective shafts to assure correct reassembly. The plates are tapered for exact fit in the carburetor bore. Remove two screws and pull the plate out of the carburetor body. Remove the throttle shaft clip and pull the shaft out of the casting. Examine both the shaft and body bearing areas for wear. Should either part show wear then either the shaft or the body or both will have to be replaced. Remove the choke shaft from the body carefully so that the friction ball and spring will not fly out of the casting. Inspect the shaft and bushings for wear.

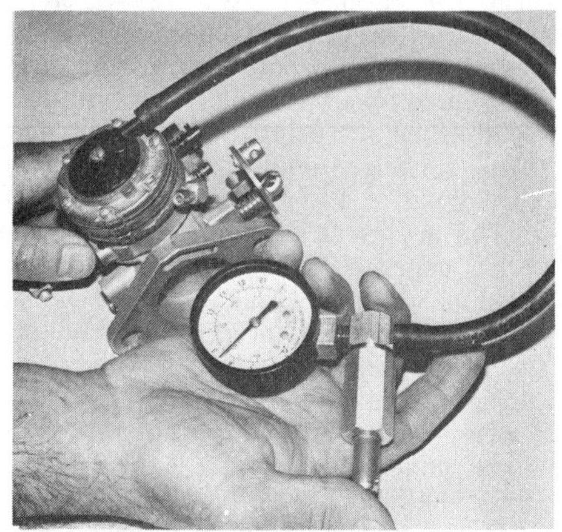

Fig. 26—Checking fuel passage using the Tillotson Leak Detector. Refer to text for details.

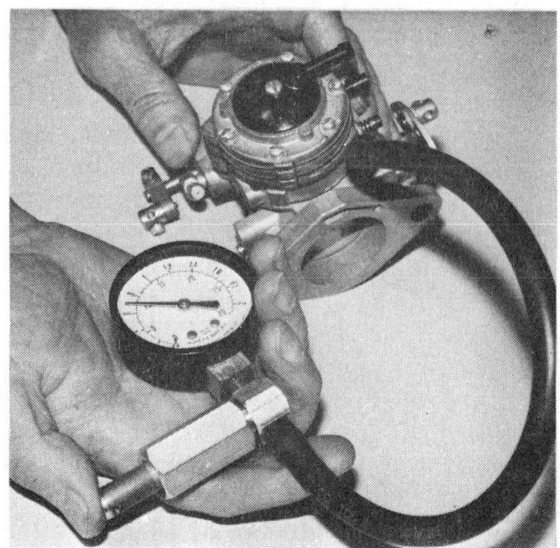

Fig. 27—Checking fuel pump pulse passage using the Tillotson Leak Detector.

ASSEMBLY. Install the main nozzle ball check valve if this part was found to be defective. Do not overtighten as distortion will result. Install new welch plugs if they were removed. Place the new welch plug into the casting counter bore convex side up and flatten it to a tight fit using a 5/16-inch flat end punch. If the installed welch plug is concave, it may be loose and cause an uncontrolled fuel leak. The correctly installed welch plug is flat.

Install inlet seat and tighten to 25-30 inch-pounds torque. Install inlet needle. Install inlet tension spring, inlet control lever, fulcrum pin and fulcrum pin retaining screw. The inlet control lever must rotate freely on the fulcrum pin. Adjust inlet control lever so that the center of the lever that contacts the metering diaphragm is flush to the metering chamber wall as shown in Fig. 21.

Place metering diaphragm gasket on the body casting. Install metering diaphragm next to gasket. Reinstall diaphragm cover casting over metering diaphragm and gasket. Install pump gasket on diaphragm cover first, then the fuel pump diaphragm should be assembled next to the gasket and the flap valve member next to the fuel pump diaphragm so that the flap valves will seat against the fuel pump cover. Reinstall fuel pump cover and attach with six body screws. The above parts must be assembled in the proper order or the carburetor will not function properly.

Install filter screen on fuel pump cover. Install gasket on filter screen and replace filter cover over filter screen and gasket and attach with center screw.

Install high speed and idle mixture screws in their respective holes being careful not to damage the points. The idle speed mixture screw has the step design point.

Check the assembled carburetor using the Tillotson Leak Detector as shown in Figs. 26 and 27. Block return bleed fitting when checking fuel passage as shown in Fig. 26. Fuel system pressure should build up to 10-12 psi and hold steady. At some point above 12 psi, inlet needle will be forced off its seat and pressure will drop rapidly. A slow pressure drop in fuel passage will indicate a leak at gaskets, diaphragms or inlet needle. Leak can sometimes be isolated by submerging carburetor in liquid and watching for air bubbles. A pressure drop in pulse passage (Fig. 27) will indicate a leak in pump diaphragm or gaskets. Pump check valves cannot be tested with the Leak Detector.

TILLOTSON HRM DIAPHRAGM CARBURETOR

Model HRM is a "Works In A Drawer" modular carburetor with most critical metering parts housed in a relatively inexpensive "Adjustment Module" (M—Fig. 28).

The plastic venturi (V—Fig. 29) slides into inlet end of carburetor throat and is retained by threading the brass nozzle (N) into carburetor body. Refer also to Fig. 30. Pulse passage fitting (P—Fig. 31) provides external connection to operate fuel pump, or internal passage (D) may be drilled from carburetor flange.

ADJUSTMENT

Initial adjustment for both the high speed mixture needle (H—Fig. 32) and idle speed mixture needle (L) is one (1) turn open from the seated position. Final adjustment must be made for best performance under operating conditions.

TROUBLESHOOTING

The Tillotson diaphragm carburetor is designed to operate under slight pressure. Carburetor can be checked before and after overhaul using the Tillotson Leak Detector as shown in Figs. 26 and 27. When checking fuel system pressure hold thumb over bleed return fitting (B—Fig. 33) as shown in Fig. 26 and actuate pump plunger while watching gage reading. Pressure should hold steady at about 10 psi with bleed fitting orifice blocked. A slow pressure drop will indicate a leak at gaskets, diaphragm or inlet needle. If pressure is pumped up to 12-15 psi, inlet needle will move off its seat, resulting in rapid pressure drop.

Check pulse passage by connecting leak detector as shown in Fig. 27. Pressurize pump diaphragm area to about 10 psi and watch gage reading which should hold steady. A pressure drop in pulse passage will indicate a leak in pump diaphragm or gaskets.

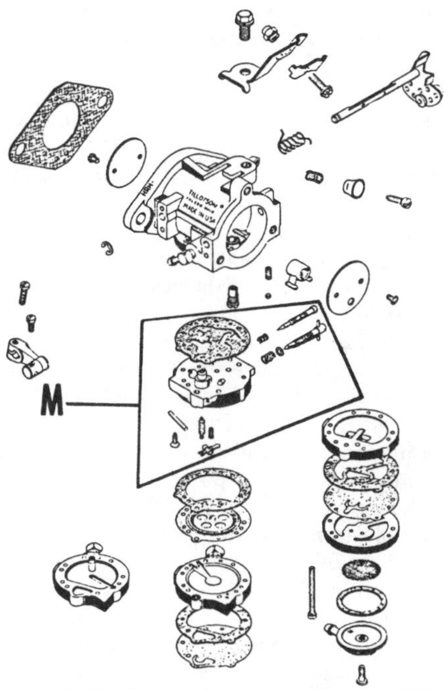

Fig. 28—Exploded view of Tillotson HRM carburetor. Adjustment module is at (M).

NOTE: If internal pump passage drilling (D—Fig. 31) is open and fitting (P) is not installed, condition of pump area cannot be checked. A slow leak in either fuel or pulse passage can sometimes be isolated by immersing the pressurized carburetor in liquid and watching for air bubbles.

Refer also to the following partial list of causes for carburetor malfunction.

IDLE SYSTEM. If idle mixture is too lean and cannot be properly adjusted, check for plugged idle fuel passages, air leaks in idle system, improperly adjusted inlet control lever, leaking metering diaphragm or malfunctioning fuel pump.

If idle mixture is too rich and cannot be adjusted, check idle mixture screw (L—Fig. 32) and its seat in adjustment module for damage. Refer also to causes of carburetor flooding.

HIGH SPEED SYSTEM. If high speed mixture is too lean and cannot be adjusted, check for dirt or plugging in main fuel passages, improperly adjusted inlet lever, malfunctioning diaphragm, broken or dislocated venturi or malfunctioning fuel pump.

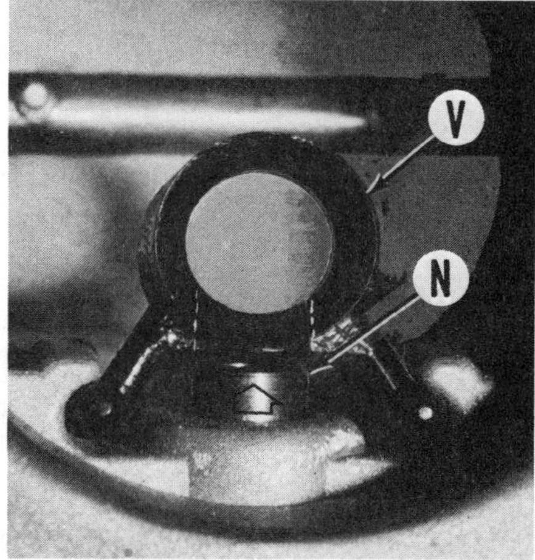

Fig. 30—Partially installed view of primary venturi (V). Main nozzle (N) must enter hole provided in venturi when correctly installed.

Fig. 31—Pressure/vacuum pulsations to operate the fuel pump enter the carburetor through pulse fitting (P). An internal pulse passage from mounting flange may be drilled at (D).

Fig. 29—On Tillotson HRM carburetor, the plastic primary venturi (V) slides out of carburetor from inlet side after removing choke assembly and main nozzle (N).

Fig. 32—View of Tillotson HRM carburetor showing location of high speed mixture needle (H) and low speed mixture needle (L).

If high speed mixture is too rich, check high speed mixture screw (H—Fig. 32) and its seat in adjustment module for damage. Refer also to causes for carburetor flooding.

CARBURETOR FLOODING. The main cause of carburetor flooding is improper seating of inlet needle valve. Check also for improperly adjusted inlet control lever (See Fig. 35), damaged inlet control lever or loose or improperly installed inlet control lever and pivot pin.

OVERHAUL

DISASSEMBLY. Note alignment lugs (X—Fig. 33) then remove the six through-bolts which hold carburetor together. Lift off fuel pump components and adjustment module containing mixture screws and inlet needle valve and lever.

Remove the two screws retaining choke plate and lift out the plate, then withdraw choke shaft, catching choke detent ball and spring which will jump out through bolt hole (D—Fig. 34). Use a heavy blade screwdriver and remove main nozzle then slip venturi from lugs in carburetor body.

INSPECTION. Place venturi end of main nozzle (N—Fig. 29) in mouth and alternately draw and blow air through the nozzle. Air should draw freely when suction is applied but check valve should close with outward air movement. Nozzle is provided as a part of Repair Kit.

Examine inlet needle valve and needle seating surface in adjustment module. Inlet needle is available separately but adjustment body must be renewed if inlet needle seat or mixture needle seats are damaged. Examine high speed and idle mixture needles for bent points or step wear which might interfere with accurate adjustment.

Check the four idle drillings in carburetor body and carefully clean. Do not remove throttle plate and lever unless renewal is indicated.

ASSEMBLY. If throttle plate and lever were removed, reinstall the parts noting that throttle edges are slightly angled to match throttle bore. Location mark must face outward when throttle is closed. Use LOCTITE on screw threads when installing.

Position venturi in body, largest diameter forward, and secure by threading nozzle into carburetor body. Be sure nozzle properly enters hole in venturi.

With venturi in position, choke can be installed. Drop detent spring and ball in through-bolt hole (D—Fig. 34) and depress the ball with a small punch while starting choke shaft. Use LOCTITE on choke plate screw threads and install choke plate with hole down (over venturi) and location mark facing outward.

Position body gasket as shown in Fig. 34. Be sure inlet needle control lever (L—Fig. 35) is flush with floor of adjustment module as shown in inset. Position the module over body gasket and install metering diaphragm as shown in Fig. 36. Top view of diaphragm is shown in inset.

Position diaphragm cover as shown in Fig. 37. Top views of alternate covers are shown in Fig. 28. Install gasket as shown in Fig. 37, then place fuel pump diaphragm over gasket as shown in Fig. 38. Fig. 39 shows fuel

Fig. 33—Assembled view of carburetor showing proper alignment of lugs (X), and location of return (bleed) fitting (B).

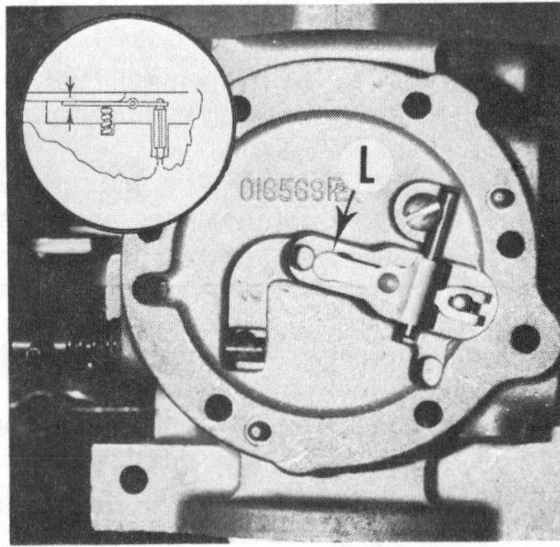

Fig. 35—Inlet needle control lever (L) should be flush with floor of adjustment module as shown in inset.

Fig. 34—Choke detent ball and spring are installed through bolt hole (D) before installing choke shaft.

Fig. 36—Metering diaphragm correctly installed. Top view of diaphragm is shown in inset.

Fig. 37—Diaphragm cover and gasket correctly installed. Fuel pump diaphragm is installed on top of gasket as shown in Fig. 38.

Fig. 38—Fuel pump diaphragm correctly installed.

Fig. 39—Fuel pump body and gasket properly installed. Inlet valve diaphragm is installed on top of gasket as shown in Fig. 40.

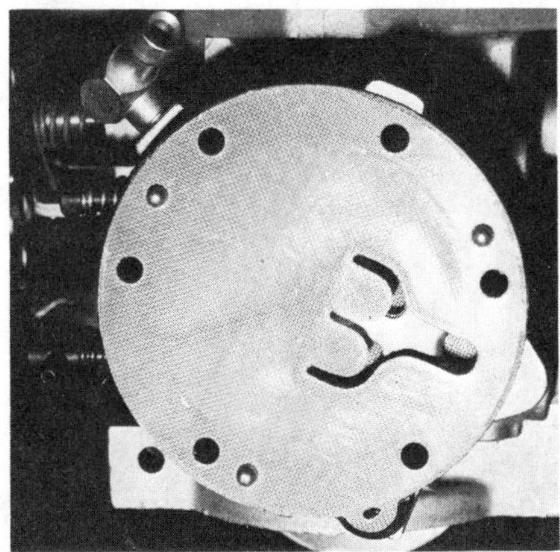
Fig. 40—Inlet diaphragm correctly installed over fuel pump body gasket.

Fig. 41—Inlet valve body and through-bolts installed.

pump body and gasket installed. Inlet valve diaphragm is placed on top of gasket as shown in Fig. 40. Inlet valve body and through-bolts are shown installed. Inlet cover and strainer screen are retained by one center bolt and inlet fitting in cover can be turned in any direction.

Tighten through-bolts alternately and evenly a little at a time, then check assembly with leak detector as outlined in TROUBLESHOOTING Section.

WALBRO BDC CARBURETORS

The Walbro BDC carburetor is a diaphragm type with built in fuel pump. Refer to Fig. 42 for exploded view.

OVERHAUL

To disassemble, remove bottom cover (15—Fig. 42), fuel pump diaphragm (14), diaphragm spring (13), diaphragm

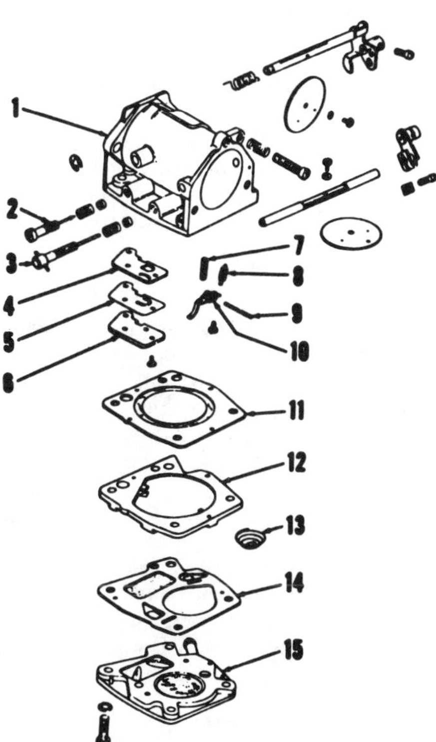

Fig. 42—Exploded view of Walbro BDC carburetor.

1. Body
2. Idle speed mixture needle
3. Main fuel mixture needle
4. Gasket
5. Circuit plate diaphragm
6. Circuit plate
7. Spring
8. Inlet fuel needle
9. Pin
10. Lever
11. Metering diaphragm
12. Diaphragm plate
13. Spring
14. Fuel pump diaphragm
15. Cover

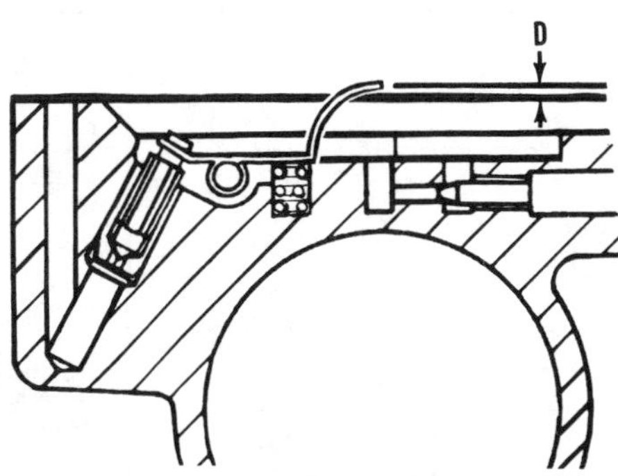

Fig. 43—Adjust metering diaphragm lever to extend 0.005-0.020 inch above surface of body as shown at (D).

plate (12) and metering diaphragm (11). Remove lever pin (9), control lever (10), spring (7) and inlet fuel needle valve (8). Remove circuit plate (6), diaphragm (5) and gasket (4). Remove idle speed mixture needle (2) and main fuel mixture needle (3). Choke and throttle plates may be removed if necessary.

Clean components in a suitable solvent. Inspect diaphragms for holes, tears or other imperfections. Inspect mixture needles for wear. Inspect fuel inlet needle and seat for wear. Do not attempt to clean fuel orifices with wire or drill tips as carburetor performance will be affected. To reassemble, reverse disassembly procedure. Adjust metering diaphragm lever so that it is 0.005-0.020 in. above level of body as shown in Fig. 43. Initial adjustment should be ¾-turns open for idle speed mixture needle and 1-turn open for main fuel mixture needle.

WALBRO WD, WDA AND WR CARBURETORS

OPERATION

Walbro WD, WDA and WR carburetors are diaphragm type equipped with integral pulse operated fuel pumps. All are equipped with vapor return pump and lines which evacuate trapped air and vaporized fuel back to fuel tank. Refer to Figs. 44 and 45 for operating principles.

Units are equipped for external or internal pulse passages (P—Fig. 44). Fuel inlet fitting (F) and vapor return fitting (R) are identical in appearance and both located on pump cover. Model WDA uses a primary power venturi in a cylindrical throttle bore as shown in

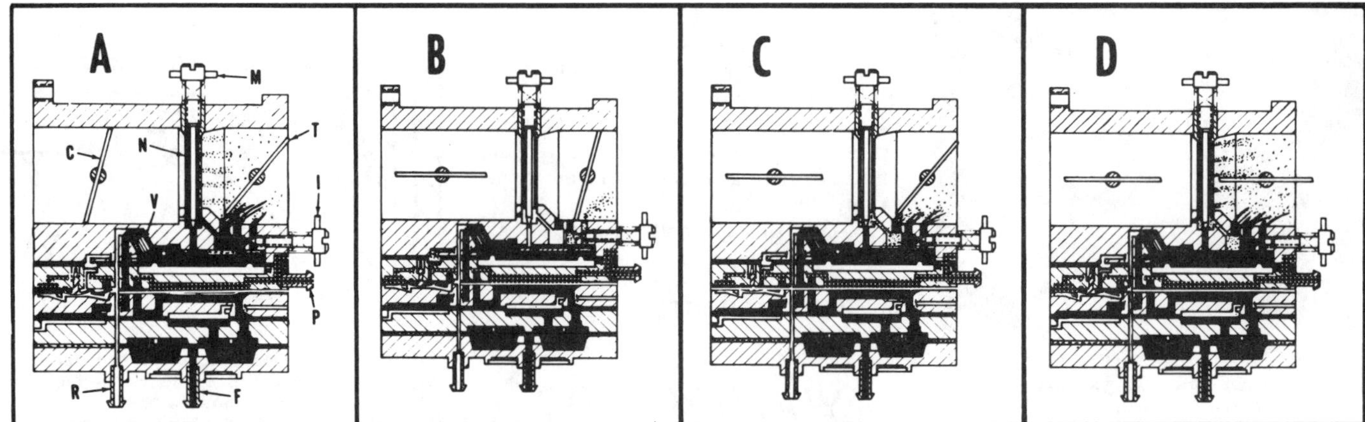

Fig. 44—Cross-sectional views of Walbro WD carburetor; WR is similar. View A shows starting position, with choke plate closed and throttle slightly open. View B shows slow idle position; note that only the first idle port is controlled by the idle mixture needle. View C shows part throttle operation, with all part throttle ports uncovered by the throttle plate. View D shows full throttle operation. Part throttle ports are still operating but the greatest fuel flow is from main nozzle located in venturi at point of greatest pressure drop.

C. Choke plate
F. Fuel inlet
I. Idle mixture needle
M. Main fuel needle
N. Main nozzle
P. Pulse passage
R. Vapor return
T. Throttle plate
V. Inlet needle valve

Fig. 45. Models WR and WD have a vertical main fuel nozzle passing through the circumferential venturi as shown in at D—Fig. 44. Sequential idle ports open with throttle plate movement to provide a progressively greater fuel flow through partial throttle positions and continue to function as fuel supply ports at full throttle position. Only the slow-idle port is regulated by idle mixture needle (I). Secondary idle ports are unregulated and accelerating ports are controlled by main fuel needle setting.

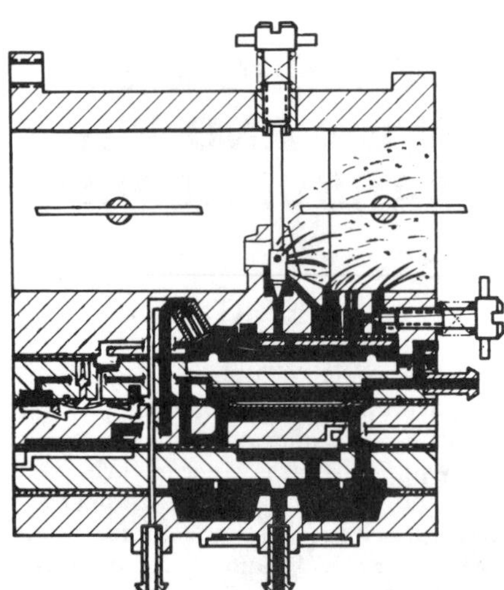

Fig. 45—Cross-sectional view of WDA carburetor showing high speed fuel flow. Fuel induction occurs through primary power venturi and that portion of carburetor throat lying below the opened throttle valve plate. Upper portion of throttle bore is relatively unrestricted permitting greater air flow at high engine speeds.

ADJUSTMENT

Initial adjustment is 1¼-turns open for idle mixture needle (L—Fig. 46) and main adjustment needle (H). Final adjustment must be made for best performance under operating conditions.

TROUBLESHOOTING

Before removing or attempting to overhaul the carburetor first check for leaks or plugging in fuel lines and filters. Check to see that all carburetor screws including mounting screws are tight.

In the event of lean operation that cannot be corrected by adjustment, check for plugged or partially plugged inlet line, pulse line or internal carburetor passages. Check pulse line for collapse, leaks or softening which might dampen pressure and vacuum impulses and retard fuel flow. Upon carburetor disassembly, check for low metering lever setting, leaky diaphragm (or diaphragms) or dirty inlet screen.

In cases of flooding, check for high diaphragm lever setting, dirty or damaged inlet needle valve, dirty check valve or leaking fuel pump diaphragm.

OVERHAUL

Refer to Fig. 47 for an exploded view of carburetor unit. Make sure fuel pump diaphragm (18), check valve diaphragm (21) and the diaphragm in circuit plate assembly (8) are all installed BELOW their respective gaskets, with check valve tabs properly closing fuel passages in plates. Make sure the three springs (16) are positioned in recesses in plate (12) and contact the two fuel check valve tabs and vapor return tab on diaphragm (18). Metering lever (10) should extend 0.005-0.020 inch above surface of inverted valve body (2) as shown in Inset—Fig. 48. Adjustment is correct when bumper end of lever slightly interferes with a straightedge passed across gasket surface of valve body. If adjustment is required, hold down bumper end of lever and bend needle end. Do not press down on needle. Renew gasket/diaphragm kit whenever carburetor is disassembled.

Fig. 46—View of Model WDA carburetor showing low speed mixture needle (L) and high speed mixture needle (H). High speed needle may be located at port (0) on some models.

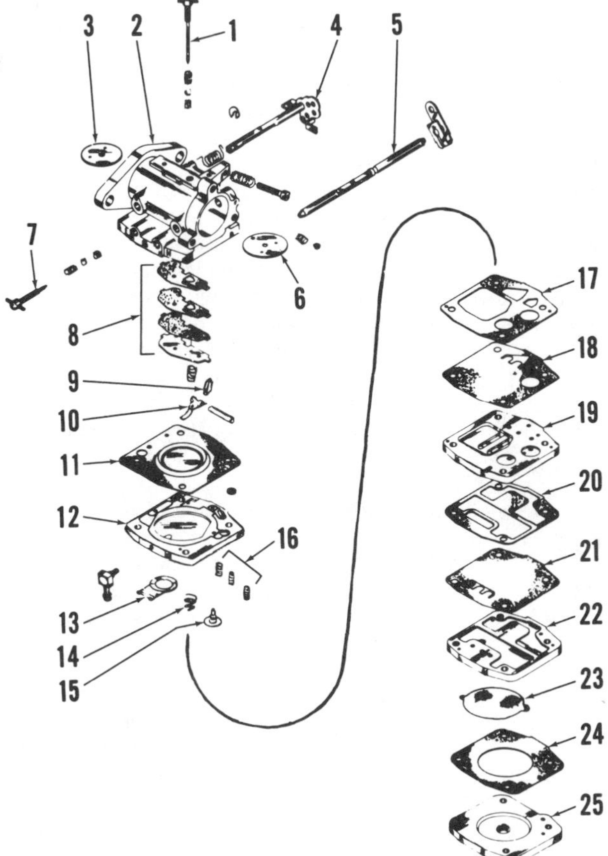

Fig. 47—Exploded view of Walbro diaphragm type carburetor showing component parts.

1. Main fuel needle
2. Carburetor body
3. Throttle valve plate
4. Throttle shaft
5. Choke shaft
6. Choke plate
7. Idle mixture needle
8. Circuit plate assy.
9. Inlet needle
10. Metering lever
11. Metering diaphragm
12. Metering plate
13. Leaf spring
14. Diaphragm spring
15. Return check valve
16. Check valve springs
17. Gasket
18. Pump diaphragm
19. Diaphragm plate
20. Gasket
21. Check valve diaphragm
22. Diaphragm plate
23. Filter screen
24. Gasket
25. Inlet plate

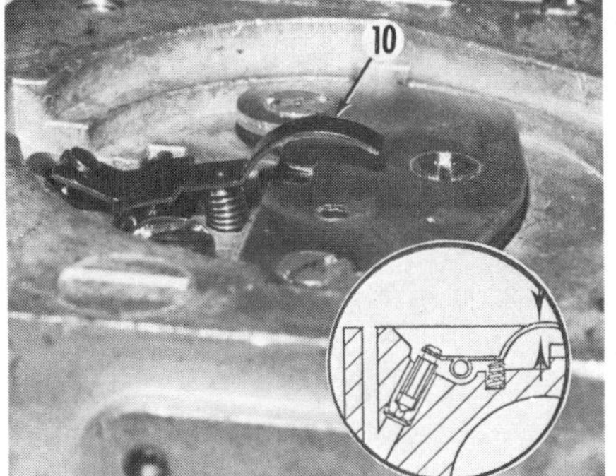

Fig. 48—Metering lever (10) should extend 0.005-0.020 inch above gasket surface of body as shown in inset.

WALBRO WF CARBURETOR

The Walbro WF carburetor is a "Pumper/Floater" type, designed specifically for snowmobiles and similar recreational vehicles. The carburetor is equipped with a built-in pulse type fuel pump and float controlled fuel level.

OPERATION

A ported rotary enrichment valve (A—Fig. 50) is used instead of a choke for starting enrichment as shown. When starting engine, throttle plate (B) must be closed. Enrichment valve lever is pulled, opening passage (F) as shown. Vacuum caused by the closed throttle plate draws fuel up the idle feed tube where it mixes with air entering through air bleeds (E, J, K and L) and flows out as a fuel mist through enrichment port (F) and idle port (H). Starting enrichment valve is

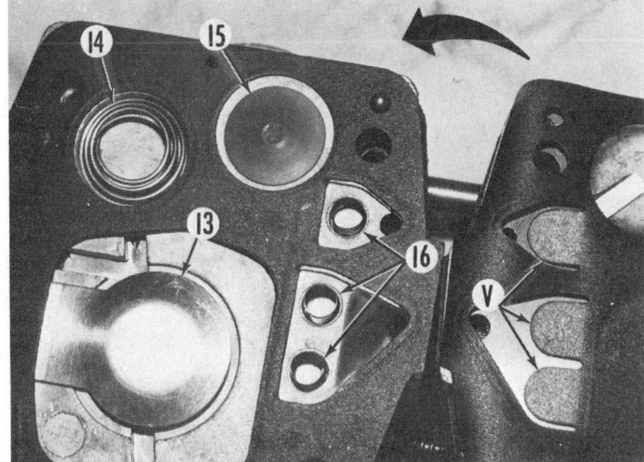

Fig. 49—View of metering plate and associated parts before installation of pump diaphragm. Valve tabs (V) must lay on top of springs (16) when diaphragm is installed. Refer to Fig. 47 for parts identification.

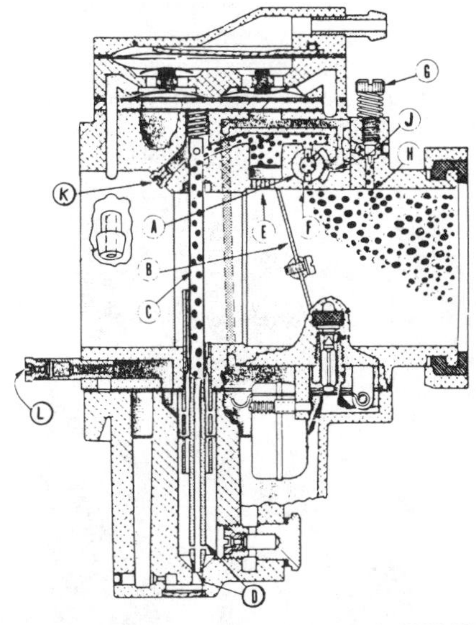

Fig. 50—Cross-sectional view of WALBRO WF carburetor in starting mode.

A. Enrichment valve
B. Throttle plate
C. Feed tube
D. Feed ports
E. Air bleeds
F. Starting feed port
G. Idle mixture needle
H. Idle feed port
K. Air bleed jet
L. Air bleed jet

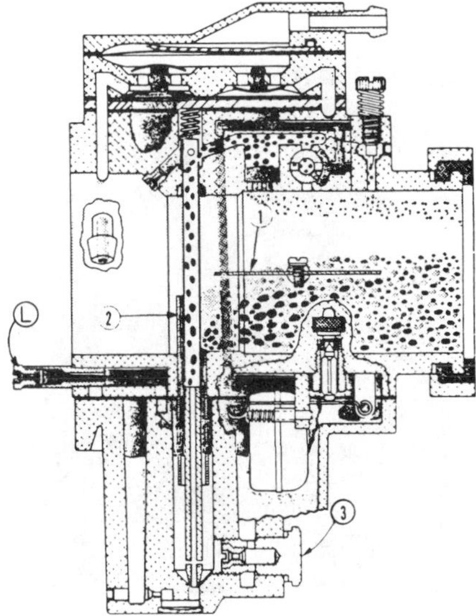

Fig. 51—Cross-sectional view of WF carburetor at full throttle operation. Some fuel still enters air stream through part throttle and idle ports but main fuel flow is through shielded main nozzle (2).

1. Throttle plate
2. Main nozzle
3. Bowl plug (main jet)
L. Air bleed jet

detented in open and closed positions and may be left fully or partially open until engine warms up. Refer also to Fig. 52.

Idle mixture is controlled by the low speed mixture needle (G—Fig. 50) and (on some early carburetors only) by the air bleed screw (B—Fig. 53). Backing out the low speed mixture needle richens the mixture while backing out the air bleed screw leans the mixture.

Fuel flow through idle feed port (H—Fig. 50) is relatively constant throughout the operating range. Additional fuel for part throttle operation is provided by the three drillings (E) which become fuel feed ports as they are uncovered by the opening throttle plate (B). The air required to burn the added fuel enters around the partially opened throttle plate.

A cross-sectional view of full throttle operation is shown in Fig. 51. Idle feed port and part throttle drillings continue to spill fuel into the throttle bore, however the quantity is small when compared to the much greater volume of air entering past the wide-open throttle plate. Vacuum created by the air passing through the venturi draws fuel up the shielded main nozzle (2) where it spills into the air stream as shown. Total fuel flow is limited and controlled by the fixed jet contained in bowl plug (3). Refer also to Fig. 54.

Fig. 52—Enrichment lever (E) opens a port from idle fuel supply to throttle bore as shown in inset. Broken lines indicate running position of lever.

Fig. 54—Fixed main fuel jet (arrow) is located in bowl plug as shown.

ADJUSTMENT

Initial adjustment of the low speed mixture needle (L—Fig. 53) is 1-1¼ turns open from the seated position. Final adjustment must be made for best performance under operating conditions. Turning low speed mixture needle clockwise LEANS the mixture. Air bleed screw (B) was only used on some early carburetors and Model WF-6 Service Carburetor is the recommended replacement if required service is extensive. If bleed screw (B) is present, open 1/8 to ¼ turn initially, then adjust if necessary after engine is warm and low speed needle (L) has been adjusted for smoothest obtainable idle. Turning needle clockwise richens the mixture. Adjust idle speed screw (I) for desired idle speed after idle adjustment needle has been set.

High speed jet is fixed on most models as shown by arrow—Fig. 54. Retainer plug may be in front or rear of fuel bowl and an adjustable needle may be substituted on some units. If an adjustable high speed needle is used, initial setting is 1¼-turns open from

Fig. 53—View of WF carburetor showing points of adjustment. An early model is shown; the solid mounting flange and air bleed (B) are not found on most units.

B. Air bleed screw
E. Enrichment lever
I. Idle speed screw
L. Low speed mixture needle

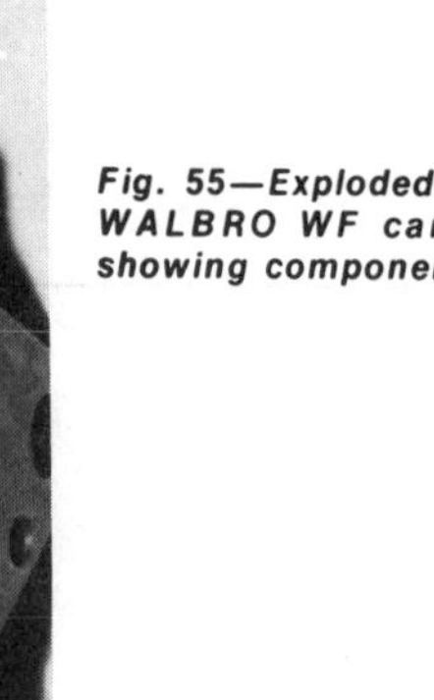

Fig. 55—Exploded view of WALBRO WF carburetor showing component parts.

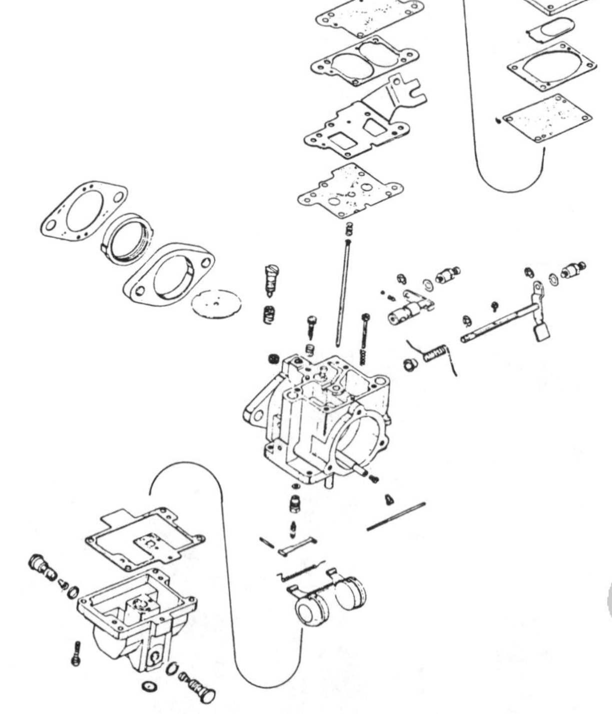

Fig. 56—Inverted view of fuel level control mechanism. Correct installation of balance spring is shown in inset.

B. Float balance spring
F. Float
L. Float lever
V. Inlet needle valve

closed position with final adjustment made with engine warm and running. On models with fixed jet, part number suffix denotes jet drilling size in thousandths of an inch (114-**0760** equals 0.076-inch diameter jet). The size is also stamped on top of jet. Jet size may need to be increased for operation in extreme cold; or decreased for altitudes above 3000 feet. DO NOT operate the engine with too small a carburetor main jet.

OVERHAUL

To disassemble the removed carburetor, evenly loosen the four mounting screws retaining fuel pump components to top of carburetor body and lift off the parts. Remove fuel bowl if necessary and push out idle feed tube and spring.

Needle valve and seat can be removed by swinging float and actuating lever back out of the way. Refer to Fig. 56. Float can be removed by pushing out pivot shaft. When float is reinstalled, float balance spring (B) should be pre-loaded 1¼ turns in direction to CLOSE valve (V). When unit is reassembled, float height distance (D—Fig. 58) should be 1 to 1-1/16 inch above gasket surface of carburetor body. Float height is adjusted by bending float lever (L—Fig. 56).

Fuel pump uses two mushroom type neoprene check valves as shown in Fig. 60. Renew valves by pushing stem out from back side of plate. Use Fig. 55 as a guide when assembling pump parts and note that idle feed tube spring will hold pump parts away from body until mounting screws are tightened. See Fig. 61.

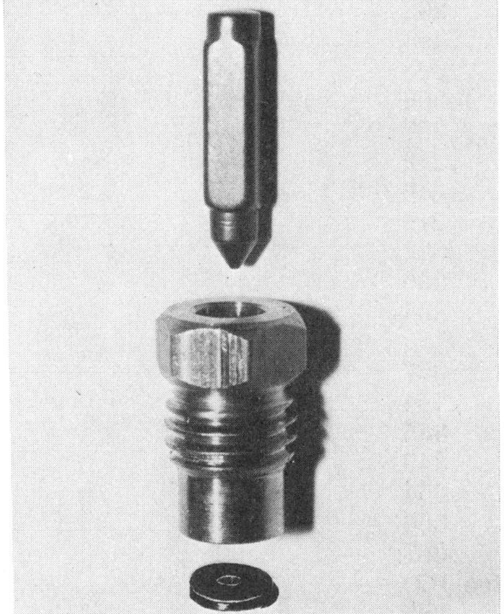

Fig. 57—Exploded view of inlet needle valve, needle and seat.

Fig. 59—Idle feed tube and spring partially removed from carburetor body. Inset shows complete tube and spring assembly removed.

Fig. 61—When fuel pump screws are loose, idle feed tube spring holds parts away from carburetor as shown.

Fig. 58—Float mechanism is correctly adjusted when distance (D) from gasket surface to farthest edge of float is 1 to 1-1/16 inches.

Fig. 60—Fuel pump body removed from top of carburetor. Top side of body is shown in inset. The two mushroom type neoprene check valves (C) are interchangeable.

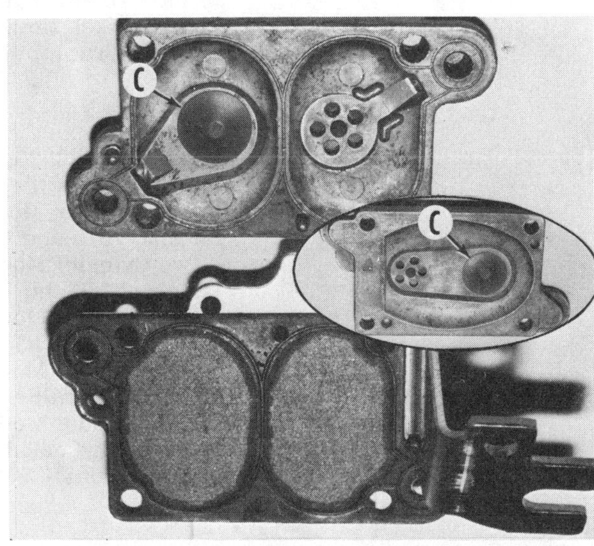

ENGINE SERVICE

CONTENTS

B.S.E.

CONDENSED SERVICE DATA

ENGINE MODEL	250	340	440
Bore—mm	72.5	60	60
Inches	2.855	2.362	2.362
Stroke—mm	60	60	68
Inches	2.362	2.362	2.677
No. of Cylinders	1	2	2
Displacement—cc	247.7	336	435.8
Cubic Inches	15.1	20.5	26.5
Horsepower—rpm	16	27	33
Cooling Type	Fan	Axial Fan	Axial Fan
Carburetor Make		Tillotson	
Model	HR117A	HR118A	HD86A
Number Used	1	1	1

ENGINE MODEL	250	340	440
Ignition Type		E. T. Magneto	
Make	Nippondenso	Nippondenso	Kokusan
Point Gap—mm		0.3-0.4	
Inch		0.012-0.016	
Timing Advance?	Yes	Yes	Yes
Timing (Deg. BTDC)			
Retarded		9°-11°	
Advanced		24°-26°	
Spark Plug:			
NGK		7HS	
Electrode Gap			
MM		0.6	
Inch		0.024	
Fuel:Oil Ratio		20:1	

MAINTENANCE

CARBURETOR. Refer to TILLOTSON Carburetor Section for operational and overhaul data. Normal initial setting for idle speed mixture needle is one (1) turn open from the closed position; high speed mixture needle setting should be 1¼-turns open. Slow idle speed should be 1800-2000 rpm but must be below clutch engagement speed. Both needles must be adjusted for smoothest operation under actual conditons with engine warm.

SPARK PLUG. NGK 7HS spark plugs are standard equipment. A different heat range plug may improve performance under some conditions. Refer to Spark Plug Selection paragraphs of ENGINE SERVICE FUNDAMENTALS for interchange and selection information.

IGNITION AND TIMING. Breaker point gap should be 0.3-0.4 mm (0.012-

Fig. 1—Exploded view of cooling fan housing and associated parts used on single cylinder engine. Other models are similar. Shims (S) are removed from between pulley halves to tighten drive belt.

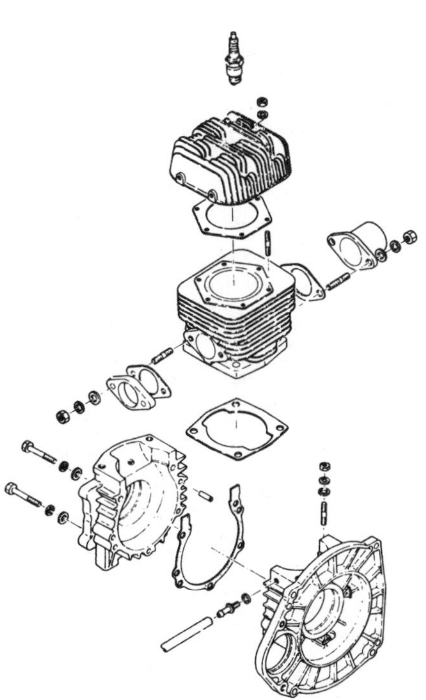

Fig. 2—Exploded view of single cylinder engine housings showing component parts.

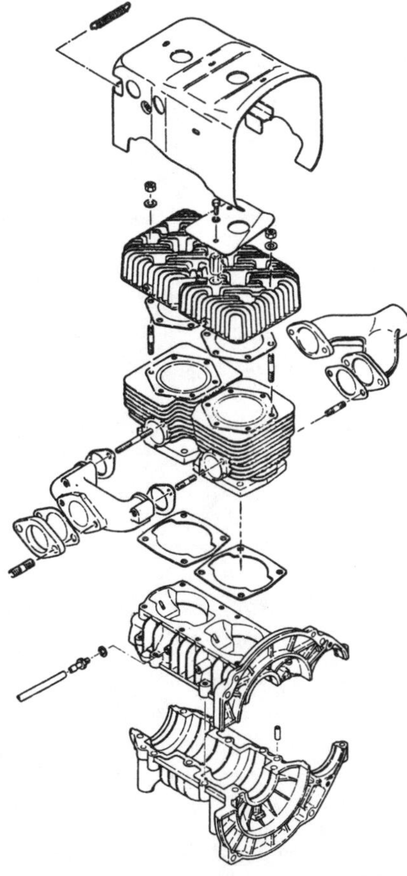

Fig. 3—Exploded view of twin cylinder engine housings showing component parts.

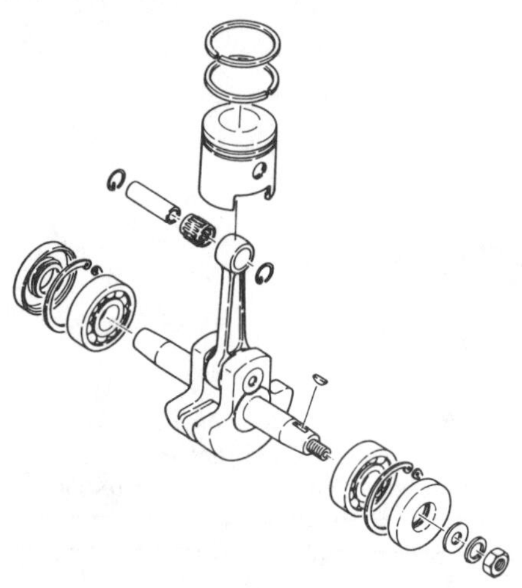

Fig. 4—Crankshaft, piston and associated parts used on single cylinder engines.

0.016 inch) on all models. Points can be adjusted after removing recoil starter, starter pulley and flywheel cover. All models are equipped with a centrifugal timing advance which provides retarded timing for starting only.

On all models, both cylinders must be timed as nearly as possible alike. It is suggested that point gap and timing be checked on one cylinder; then timing synchronized by varying the point gap on other cylinder if necessary.

LUBRICATION. The engine is lubricated by oil mixed with the fuel. The manufacturer recommends a known brand of regular gasoline and Moto-Ski Motor Oil or equivalent branded snowmobile oil mixed at a ratio of 20:1. (Use 16:1 for first ten hours on new or overhauled engine). Refer also to vehicle manufacturer's recommendation.

COOLING FAN AND BELT. Cooling fan belt should have approximately ¼-inch deflection midway between pulleys. Refer to Fig. 1. To adjust the belt, remove fan guard and shaft nut and transfer one or more shims (S) from between pulley halves to outside, behind shaft nut. Be sure not to pinch belt when reinstalling shaft nut. Tighten nut to a torque of approximately 30 ft.-lbs.

REPAIRS

Refer to Figs. 2 through 6 for exploded views of engines. Fig. 1 shows exploded view of cooling fan and housing used on single cylinder engines. Components for twin are similar except for conformation of main fan case.

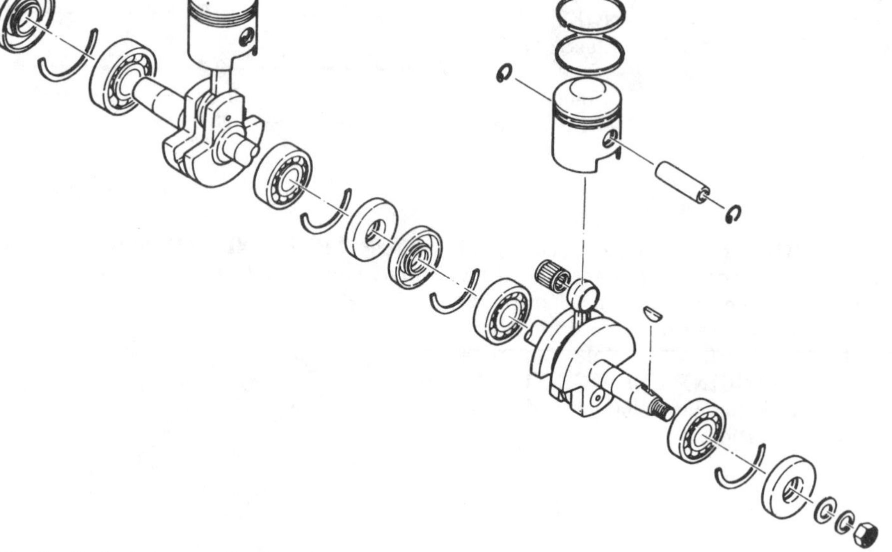

Fig. 5—Exploded view of crankshaft, pistons and associated parts used on twin cylinder engines.

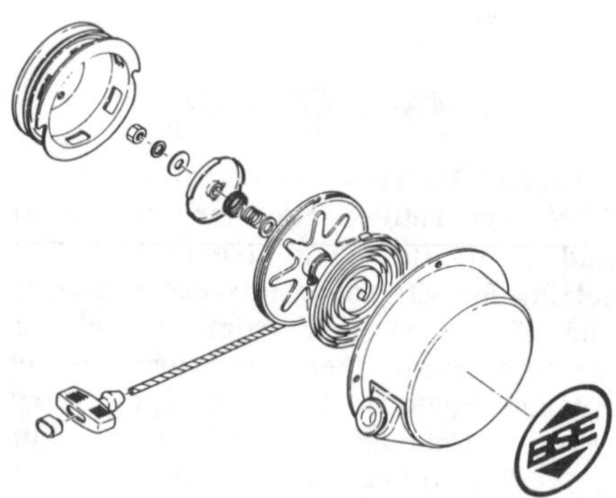

Fig. 6—Exploded view of recoil starter and associated parts used on all models.

BOLENS

CONDENSED SERVICE DATA

Year Made	1970	1971	1971	1971	1971	1971
ENGINE MODEL	T2-2Z15	2Z15.70	2Z300	2Z340	3Z400	3Z440
Bore—(mm)	60	60	58	62	55	58
Inches	2.362	2.362	2.283	2.441	2.165	2.283
Stroke—(mm)	55	55	55	55	55	55
Inches	2.165	2.165	2.165	2.165	2.165	2.165
No. of Cylinders	2	2	2	2	3	3
Displacement (cc)	310	310	291	332	393	432
Cubic Inches	18.9	18.9	17.8	20.3	24.0	26.4
Horsepower @ RPM	21@5700	17@6000	22@6000	24@6000	28@6000	32@6000
Cooling Type	Centrifugal Fan					
Carburetor Model	HL279A	HL279A	HR89A	HR89A	HR89A	HR89A
Number Used	2	1	1	1	1	1
Ignition						
Type	BOSCH Energy Transfer Magneto					
Point Gap (mm)	0.35-0.45					
Inch	0.014-0.018					
Timing Advance?	No	No	Yes	Yes	No	No
Timing BTDC (mm)	2.2	2.2	2.35	2.25	2.2	2.2
Inch	0.087	0.087	0.093	0.093	0.087	0.087
Measured At	....	....	Advance	Advance	....	....
Sprak Plug:						
Bosch	W260T1	W260T1	W260T1	W260T1	W260T1	W260T1
KLG	FF100	FF100	FF100	FF100	FF100	FF100
Champion	L5	L5	L5	L5	L5	L5
Electrode Gap (mm)	0.6	0.6	0.6	0.6	0.6	0.6
Inch	0.024	0.024	0.024	0.024	0.024	0.024
Fuel/Oil Ratio	20:1	20:1	20:1	20:1	20:1	20:1

Fig. 1–On SPRINT, TW-315, an Adjustment Plate is attached to carburetor baffle. Check to see that plate is in place and that main jet for No. 2 carburetor is ¼-turn rich as shown.

MAINTENANCE

CARBURETOR. On 1970 model TW-315, twin carburetors are used. Adjustment instructions are carried on an instruction plate attached to carburetor deflector as shown in Fig. 1. Recommended adjustment specifies that high speed jet for left hand cylinder be ¼ turn farther open than right hand setting. Normal adjustment range is 1-1½ turns open from closed position for right hand (No. 1) carburetor. Refer to appropriate Carburetor paragraphs in FUNDAMENTALS Section for additional adjustment and overhaul information.

IGNITION AND TIMING. Breaker points for No. 1 (flywheel end) cylinder

Fig. 2–Breaker plate with flywheel removed. Wires leading to ignition coils are identical and continuity should be checked to make sure correct wire leads to No. 1 coil.

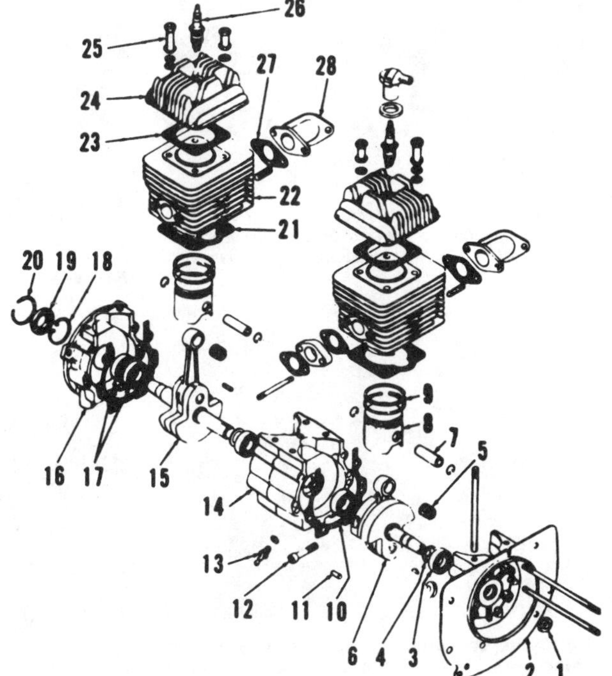

Fig. 3–Exploded view of 2Z15 engine.

1. Oil seal
2. Front crankcase
3. Bearing
4. Shim
5. Pin bearing
6. Front crankshaft
7. Piston pin
8. Piston
9. Piston rings
10. Gasket
11. Dowel
12. Crankshaft lock screw
13. Pulse fitting
14. Center crankcase
15. Rear crankshaft
16. Rear crankcase
17. Rear bearings
18. Snap ring
19. Oil seal
20. Snap ring
21. Gasket
22. Cylinder
23. Gasket
24. Cylinder head
25. Special nut
26. Spark plug
27. Gasket
28. Exhaust pipe

are to the right when looking at magneto plate with flywheel removed. Refer to Fig. 2. To adjust and synchronize ignition timing first adjust No. 1 set of points to recommended gap, then adjust timing for No. 1 cylinder using a timing gage and suitable continuity tester; and moving breaker plate as required until timing is correct. With No. 1 piston properly timed, move timing gage to No. 2 cylinder and synchronize the timing by adjusting gap at No. 2 points. Timing must be synchronized as nearly alike as possible.

LUBRICATION. The engine is lubricated by mixing oil with the fuel. Air Cooled Two Cycle Engine Oil and Regular Gasoline mixed at the ratio of 20:1 are recommended.

Mix fuel and oil thoroughly using a separate container before pouring mixture into fuel tank. For cold weather blending, pre-mix the oil with a small amount of gasoline and shake thoroughly until mixture is liquid, then blend with remainder of fuel. Do not use kerosene or fuel oil for premixing.

REPAIRS

TIGHTENING TORQUES. Recommended tightening torques are as follows: Values are given in ft.-lbs.

Cylinder head nuts	20
Crankcase nuts	10
Crankshaft clamp screw	30
Flywheel nut	80

Fig. 4–Lock screw (12–Fig. 3) clamps crankshafts together by means of split weight and countersunk hole indicated by arrows.

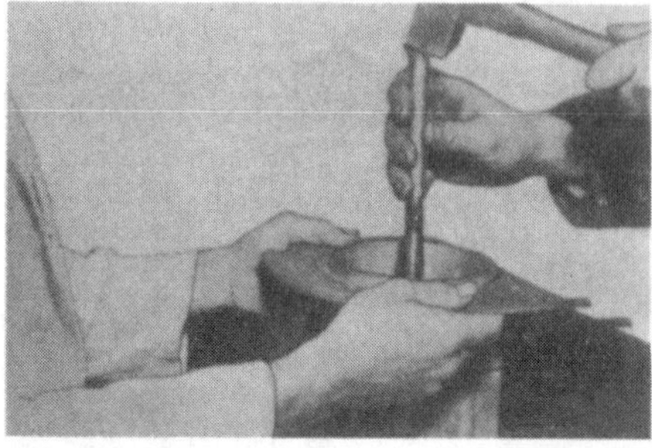

Fig. 5–Use soft drift and hammer to separate crankcases after removing stud nuts and clamp screw.

DISASSEMBLY AND REASSEMBLY. Refer to Fig. 3 for exploded view of engine. When service is required, first remove engine, then remove carburetors, cooling shrouds, ignition block, recoil starter, flywheel and magneto.

Remove cylinder heads. Heads are interchangeable, but No. 1 (magneto side) head is installed with fins running parallel with crankshaft while No. 2 (output side) head is installed with cooling fins crosswise.

Remove cylinders, piston pins and pistons. Pins are full floating and can usually be pushed out after removing retaining rings. Heat pistons slightly using mild heat, if necessary. Crankshaft units are keyed together and retained by a clamp screw (12) and split counterweight. Refer to Fig. 4. Loosen the screw and remove nuts from crankcase through-studs; then tap on crankshaft (Fig. 5) to separate the doweled housings.

The five crankshaft bearings are a tight press fit in housings at room temperature but can be easily removed after heating housings with an electric heat gun or other form of mild heat. If bearings are renewed, measure depth of each housing half (Fig. 6); add the two measurements and subtract the distance between crankshaft shoulders (Fig. 7); then add shims (4—Fig. 3) as necessary so end clearance in each crankshaft half is 0.008-0.012 (inch), measured without gasket (10). Shims (4) are available in thicknesses of 0.1, 0.2 and 0.3 mm (0.004, 0.008 and 0.012 in.).

Fig. 6–Measuring crankcase depth to determine thickness of crankshaft shims.

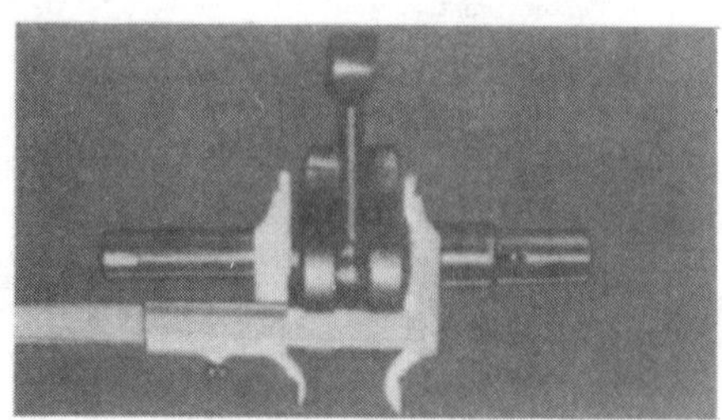

Fig. 7–Measuring crankshaft length to determine shim pack thickness.

Arrow on piston crown must be installed toward exhaust port side of cylinder block. Refer to the appropriate following paragraphs for inspection and overhaul notes.

PISTON RINGS AND CYLINDER. Cast iron cylinder can be rebored, and pistons and rings are available in oversizes of 0.010 and 0.020 as well as standard. Arrow on top of piston crown must be installed toward exhaust port.

Cylinder head is symmetrical and interchangeable. Cooling fins must be installed as shown in Fig. 8 on two cylinder models and as shown in Fig. 9 on three cylinder engines.

CRANKSHAFT AND CONNECTING ROD. The crankshaft and connecting rod for one cylinder is only available as an assembled unit. Wear of parts at rod big end can be tested by rocking small end of rod. Play should not exceed 1/16 inch.

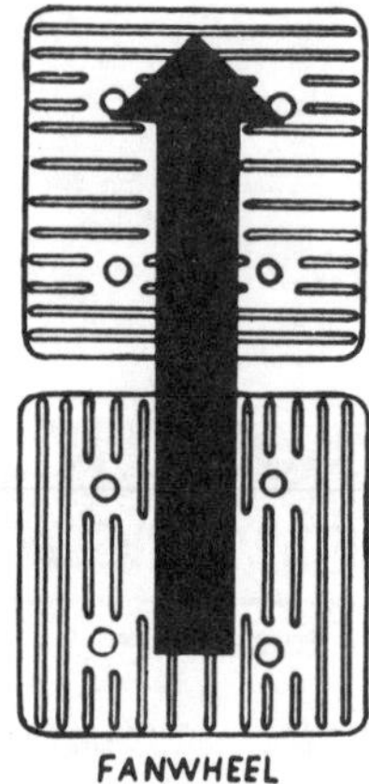

Fig. 8–On BOLENS Twins, No. 2 cylinder head is installed with fins crosswise as shown. Refer also to cylinder heads in Fig. 3.

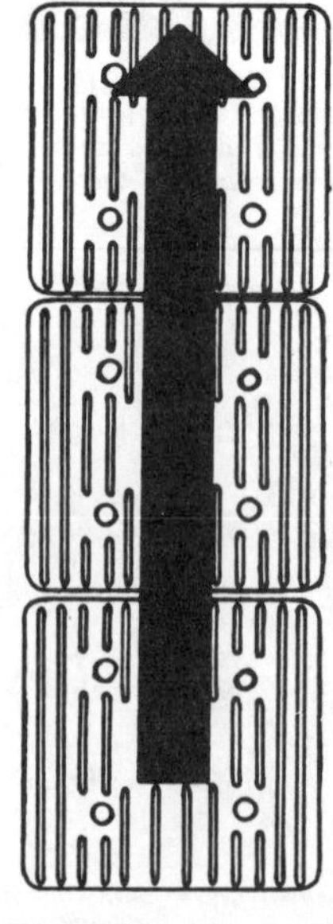

Fig. 9–On Three Cylinder Engines, cylinder head fins run parallel to crankshaft as shown.

CCW

ONE CYLINDER MODELS CONDENSED SERVICE DATA

ENGINE MODEL	CCW225	CCW248	CCW312	CCW335	CCW375	CCW390
Bore—(mm)	68	71.5	77	80	80	82
Inches	2.57	2.8	3.031	3.149	3.15	3.23
Stroke—(mm)	62	62	67	67	74	74
Inches	2.44	2.44	2.638	2.638	2.91	2.91
No. of Cylinders	1	1	1	1	1	1
Displacement—(cc)	225	248.8	311.8	336.6	371.8	390.6
Cubic Inches	13.7	15.1	19.02	20.54	22.7	23.8
Horsepower @ RPM	12.5@5500	17.5@6000	19.5@5000	21@5000	23.5@5000	24.5@5000
Cooling Type	Centrifugal Fan					
Carburetor Model	Tlt'sn HR	Tlt'sn HR	Tlt'sn HD (HR)	Tlt'sn HD (HR)	Tlt'sn HD	Tlt'sn HD
Number Used	1	1	1	1	1	1
Ignition:						
Type	Flywheel Magneto					
Point Gap—(mm)	0.3-0.5	0.35	0.35	0.35	0.35	0.35
Inch	0.012-0.016	0.014	0.014	0.014	0.014	0.014
Edge Gap (mm)	0.5	0.5	0.7	0.7	0.5	0.5
Inch	0.020	0.020	0.028	0.028	0.028	0.028
Timing Advance?	No	No	Yes	Yes	Yes	Yes
Timing BTDC—Degrees	25°	25°	12°	5°	8°	8°
MM	3.91	3.91	0.915	0.015	0.411	0.411
Inch	0.154	0.154	0.036	0.0006	0.162	0.162
Measured at	....	....	Retard	Retard	Retard	Retard
Spark Plug:						
NGK	A7C	A7C	A7,A7C	A7C	A7,A7C	A7C
Electrode Gap (mm)	0.7	0.7	0.7	0.7	0.7	0.7
Inch	0.027	0.027	0.027	0.027	0.027	0.027
Fuel/Oil Ratio	20:1	20:1	20:1	20:1	20:1	20:1

MAINTENANCE

CARBURETOR. Refer to TILLOTSON Carburetor Section for operation and overhaul data. Normal initial setting for both needles is one turn open from closed position. Both needles must be adjusted for smoothest engine operation under actual conditions with engine warm.

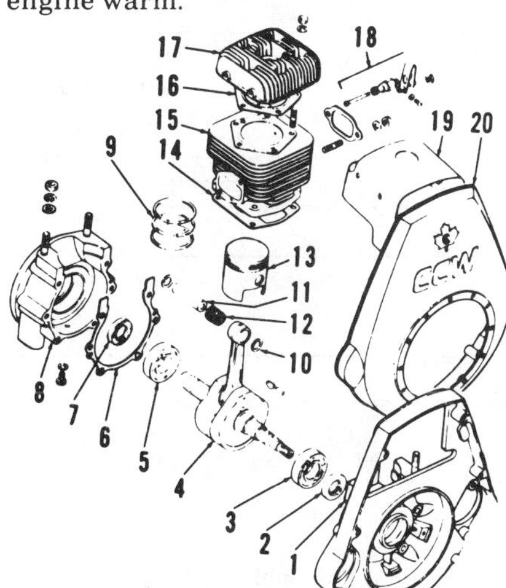

Fig. 1–Exploded view of CCW 225 engine showing component parts.

1. Front crankcase
2. Oil seal
3. Bearing
4. Crankshaft
5. Bearing
6. Gasket
7. Oil seal
8. Rear crankcase
9. Piston rings
10. Retaining ring
11. Piston pin
12. Pin bearing
13. Piston
14. Gasket
15. Cylinder
16. Gasket
17. Cylinder head
18. Decompresser
19. Shroud
20. Shroud

SPARK PLUG. NGK Spark Plugs are standard equipment. The recommendations given in CONDENSED SERVICE DATA Tables are for normal operation. A different heat range may give more satisfactory performance under some conditions. Refer to Spark Plug Selection paragraphs of FUNDAMENTALS Section for information.

IGNITION AND TIMING. Breaker point gap should be 0.3-0.4 mm (0.12-0.016 inch) on all models. Except for Model 225 and 248, engines are equipped with a centrifugal timing advance which provides retarded timing for starting only.

Points can be adjusted after removing recoil starter, starting pulley and flywheel window plates.

LUBRICATION. The engine is lubricated by oil mixed with the fuel. The manufacturer recommends Air Cooled, Two Stroke Engine Oil, SAE 30 and Regular gasoline at a ratio of 20:1. Refer also to vehicle manufacturer's recommendation.

REPAIRS

TIGHTENING TORQUES. Refer to following table for correct tightening torques. Measurements are given in ft.-lbs.

Cylinder head	15-18
Crankcase	15-18
Flywheel	75

Remainder of bolts should be tightened to standard torque.

ASSEMBLY AND DISASSEMBLY. Refer to Fig. 1 for an exploded view of 225 engine and Fig. 2 for view of engine typical of other models.

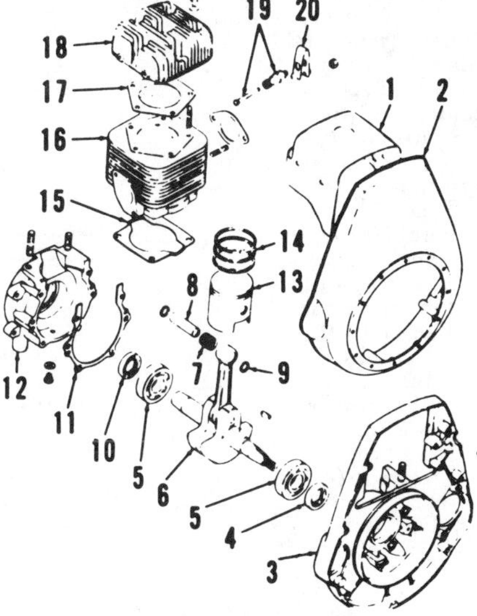

Fig. 2–Exploded view of CCW 312 engine. Other single ciylinder models are similar.

1. Shroud
2. Shroud
3. Front crankcase
4. Oil seal
5. Bearing
6. Crankshaft
7. Pin bearing
8. Piston pin
9. Retainer
10. Oil seal
11. Gasket
12. Rear crankcase
13. Piston
14. Piston rings
15. Gasket
16. Cylinder
17. Gasket
18. Cylinder head
19. Decompresser
20. Lever

CCW
TWO CYLINDER MODELS CONDENSED SERVICE DATA

ENGINE MODEL	CCW290/1	CCW290/2	CCW340 /(1&2)	CCW340/3	CCW340/4	CCW400 /(1&2)	CCW400/3
Bore—(mm)	58.5	58.5	60	60	60	65	65
Inches	2.30	2.30	2.36	2.36	2.36	2.56	2.56
Stroke—(mm)	54	54	60	60	60	60	60
Inches	2.13	2.13	2.36	2.36	2.36	2.36	2.36
No. of Cylinders	2	2	2	2	2	2	2
Displacement—(cc)	290.1	290.1	339	339	339	398	398
Cubic Inches	17.7	17.7	20.7	20.7	20.7	24.3	24.3
Horsepower @ RPM	20@6000	23@6500	25@5800	28@6500	32@6500	30@5800	33@6500
Max Torque @ RPM	17.2@6000	18.2@6000	23@5250	22.4@6000	26@6500	27.3@5500	26.7@6000
Cooling Type				Axial Fan			
Induction Type				Third Port			
Carburetor Model	Tlt'sn HR	Tlt'sn HR	Tlt'sn HR	Tlt'sn HR	Tlt'sn HR	Tlt'sn HR	Tlt'sn HD
Number Used	1	1	1	1	1	1	1
Ignition:							
Type				Energy Transfer Magneto			
Point Gap—(mm)				0.3-0.4			
Inch				0.012-0.016			
Edge Gap—(mm)	....	....	....	....	....	....	....
Timing Advance?				Yes			
Timing BTDC—							
Degrees	10°	10°	8°	10°	10°	8°	10°
Inch	0.020	0.020	0.015	0.023	0.023	0.015	0.023
Measured at				Retard			
Spark Plug:							
NGK	....	....	B8H	B8H	B9HS	B8H	B8H
Electrode Gap (mm)	0.6-0.7	0.6-0.7	0.5-0.6	0.5-0.6	0.5-0.6	0.5-0.6	0.5-0.6
Inch	0.024-0.028	0.024-0.028	0.020-0.024	0.020-0.024	0.020-0.024	0.020-0.024	0.020-0.024
Fuel/Oil Ratio				20:1			

ENGINE MODEL	CCW400/4	CCW400/21	CCW440/1	CCW440/2&3	CCW440/4	CCW440/21
Bore—(mm)	65	63	68	68	68	66
Inches	2.56	2.48	2.68	2.68	2.68	2.6
Stroke—(mm)	60	64	60	60	60	64
Inches	2.36	2.52	2.36	2.36	2.36	2.52
No. of Cylinders	2	2	2	2	2	2
Displacement—(cc)	398	398.8	436	436	436	437.7
Cubic Inches	24.3	24.3	26.6	26.6	26.6	26.7
Horsepower @ RPM	36@6500	39@6500	33@6000	37@6500	40@6500	43@6500
Max Torque @ RPM	28.7@6500	31@6000	30.5@6000	29.6@5750	30@6500	34.7@6000
Cooling Type			Axial Fan			
Induction Type	Third Port	Reed Valve	Third Port	Third Port	Third Port	Reed Valve
Carburetor Model	Tlt'sn HD	Tlt'sn HD	Tlt'sn HR	Tlt'sn HD	Tlt'sn HD	Tlt'sn HD
Number Used	1	1	1	1	1	1
Ignition:						
Type			Energy Transfer Magneto			
Point Gap—(mm)			0.3-0.4			
Inch			0.012-0.016			
Edge Gap—(mm)	....	....	....	....	....	....
Timing Advance?			Yes			
Timing BTDC—						
Degrees	10°	5°	8°	8°	10°	10°
Inch	0.023	0.006	0.015	0.015	0.023	0.024
Measured at			Retard			
Spark Plug:						
NGK	B8HS	B8HS	B8H	B8H	B8HS	B8HS
Electrode Gap (mm)	0.5-0.6	0.6-0.7	0.5-0.6	0.5-0.6	0.5-0.6	0.6-0.7
Inch	0.020-0.024	0.024-0.028	0.020-0.024	0.020-0.024	0.020-0.024	0.024-0.028
Fuel/Oil Ratio			20:1			

MAINTENANCE

CARBURETOR. Tillotson or Walbro carburetors are used. Refer to the appropriate CARBURETOR SERVICE Sections elsewhere in this manual for service specifications.

SPARK PLUG. NGK Spark Plugs are standard equipment. The recommendations given in CONDENSED SERVICE DATA Tables are for normal operation. A different heat range plug may improve performance under some conditions. Refer to Spark Plug Selection paragraphs of SERVICE FUNDAMENTALS Section for additional information on spark plug selection.

IGNITION AND TIMING. Breaker point gap should be 0.3-0.4 mm (0.012-0.016 inch) on all models. Points can be adjusted after removing recoil starter, starting pulley and fan drive sheave. All models are equipped with a centrifugal timing advance which provides retarded timing for starting only.

On all models, both cylinders must be timed as nearly as possible alike. It is suggested that point gap and timing be checked on one cylinder; then timing synchronized by varying the point gap on other cylinder if necessary.

LUBRICATION. The engine is lubricated by oil mixed with the fuel. The manufacturer recommends regular gasoline and Special Air Cooled, Two Stroke engine oil mixed at a ratio of 20:1. Refer also to vehicle manufacturer's recommendations.

COOLING FAN AND BELT. There should be sufficient belt tension at all times to prevent belt from touching housing when deflected with the fingers with engine stopped (approximately ¼-inch deflection measured midway between pulleys). Refer to Figs. 3 or 11. To adjust the belt, transfer shims (6) from between sheave halves (5) to the front of front half. Tighten fan shaft nut to a torque of 30 ft.-lbs.

Fig. 1–View of CCW twin engine with third port induction. Normal finger pressure midway between pulleys should not deflect belt into fan housing.

Fig. 2–View of CCW twin engine with reed valve induction system. Engine is similar in general appearance to third port engine shown in Fig. 1 except for low positioning of carburetor and intake manifold. Most late engines have the completely enclosed cooling fan and belt shown in Fig. 2.

REPAIRS

TIGHTENING TORQUES. Tightening torques are as follows. Measurements are given in ft.-lbs.

Cylinder to crankcase	
Third Port Models	15-18
Reed Valve Models	See Cyl. Head
Cylinder head	
Third Port Models	15-18
Reed Valve Models	
Long stud nuts	12-15
Short stud nuts	5-7
Crankcase	
Third Port Models	12-15
Reed Valve Models	13-18
Flywheel	45-50
Fan shaft	28-31
Intake manifold	
Reed Valve Models	5-7

Remainder of bolts should be tightened to standard torque.

DISASSEMBLY AND REASSEMBLY. Although similar in appearance, disassembly procedures differ between the Third Port engines shown in Fig. 1 and Reed Valve models shown in Fig. 2. Refer to the appropriate following paragraphs for procedures.

THIRD PORT ENGINES. Refer to Fig. 3 for an exploded view of cooling fan and associated parts and to Figs. 4 & 5 for engine parts.

To disassemble the removed engine, first remove spark plugs and cylinder shroud (15—Fig. 3), then remove inlet and exhaust manifolds leaving carburetor attached to inlet manifold. Cylinder heads and cylinders can now be removed for top-end work. Crankcase disassembly will require removal of fan housing, flywheel and housing plate.

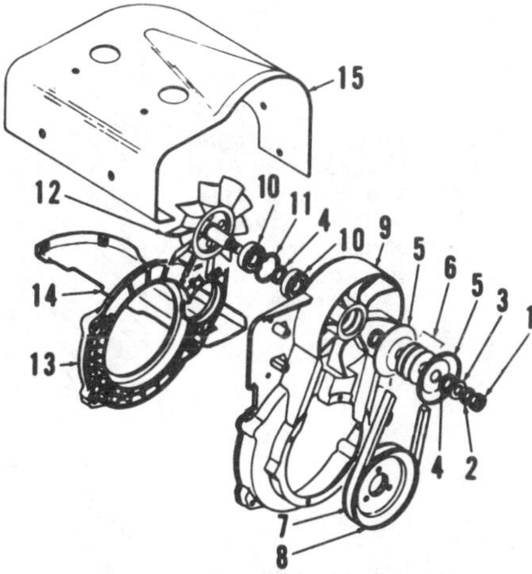

Fig. 3–Exploded view of axial cooling fan, fan housing and associated parts used on early models.

1. Shaft nut
2. Lockwasher
3. Washer
4. Spacer
5. Sheave half
6. Spacer shims
7. Belt
8. Drive pulley
9. Housing
10. Bearings
11. Snap ring
12. Fan
13. Housing plate
14. Cover
15. Cylinder shroud

Use a heat gun or other suitable means to thoroughly warm the piston before removing piston pin. Be sure that bearing retaining half-washers are properly installed in crankcase lower half. Lubricate crankshaft components thoroughly. Coat sealing surface of both crankcase halves with a good non-hardening sealant. Note that center bearing left-hand spacer on CCW290 engine has a drain groove as shown in Fig. 6. Drain groove must be installed at bottom of crankcase. Fit upper crankcase, install the four center topside bolts (1, 8, 9 and 10—Fig. 7) and tighten the four bolts evenly with fingers until crankcase halves meet. Install remainder of bolts using Fig. 7 as a guide and tighten evenly in se-

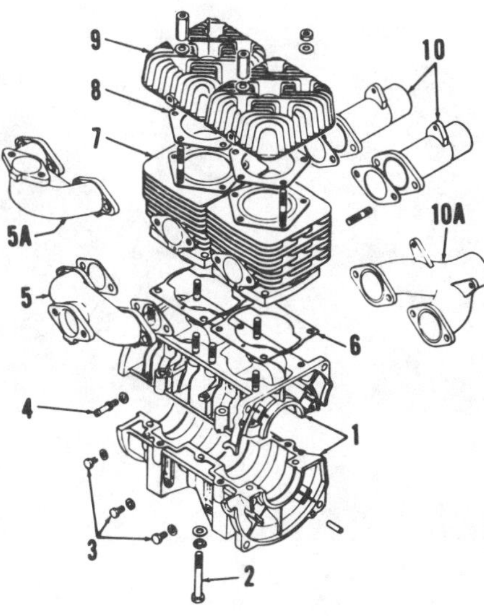

Fig. 4–Exploded view of crankcase housing and associated parts used on two cylinder models. Cylinder heads can only be installed in one position. When assembling engine, fasten cylinders lightly to crankcase, then install and tighten manifolds to ensure proper alignment. Optional manifolds are shown at (5A and 10A).

1. Crankcase
2. Crankcase screw
3. Port plugs
4. Impulse nipple
5. & 5A. Intake manifold
6. Gasket
7. Cylinder
8. Gasket
9. Cylinder head
10. & 10A. Exhaust manifolds

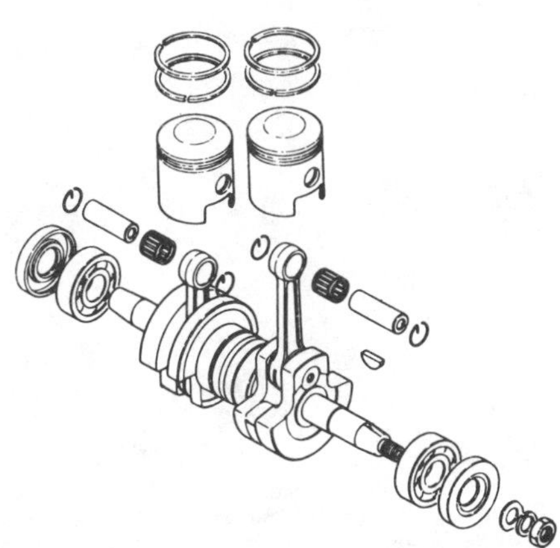

Fig. 5–Exploded view of crankshaft, pistons and associated parts. Refer to Fig. 4 for housings.

quence shown to the recommended torque of 12-15 ft.-lbs.

Use a heat gun to warm pistons and install pin, with arrow on top of piston pointing toward exhaust ports. Chrome plated piston ring is installed in top groove. Cylinders are not interchangeable and are marked "L" (left) and "R" (right) by stamping on cylinder flange. Install cylinders using a suitable ring compresser, wooden blocks to hold piston steady, and new base gaskets. Tighten cylinder stud nuts just past finger tight, then install and tighten intake manifold to properly align the cylinders. Tighten cylinder nuts in a criss-cross pattern as shown in Fig. 8.

Cylinder heads are not interchangeable and should be installed with machined sides together. The long standoff nuts which retain cylinder shroud should be installed at (3—Fig. 9) on CCW290 engine or (5—Fig. 10) on other models. Tighten cylinder head stud nuts to a torque of 15-18 ft.-lbs. in the sequence shown in Fig. 9 for CCW 290 engine or Fig. 10 for other models.

REED VALVE ENGINES. Refer to Figs. 11, 12 and 13 for exploded views. Cooling fan differs from third port engines in that impeller assembly is outboard of drive pulley. Cooling shroud attaches to standoff nuts and cylinder heads at the four points indicated by arrows, Fig. 12. Cylinders, cylinder heads and pistons are not interchangeable for left and right cylinders. Cylinders are retained to crankcase by four through-studs which extend through cylinders and cylinder heads, forming four of the eight cylinder head studs.

To disassemble the removed engine, first remove spark plugs and cylinder shroud, then remove inlet and exhaust manifolds and reed valve plates. Cylinder heads and cylinders can now be removed for top end overhaul. Crankcase disassembly will require removal of fan housing, flywheel and magneto plate.

Use a heat gun or other suitable means to thoroughly warm the piston

Fig. 6–On CCW 290, drain groove in center bearing spacer should be located at the bottom when crankshaft is installed.

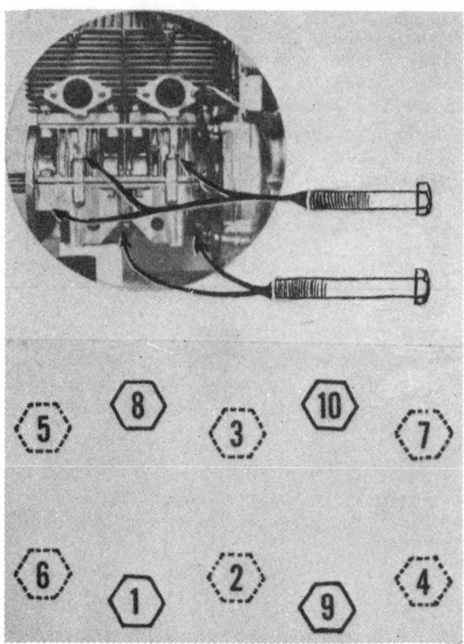

Fig. 7–Tighten crankcase screws in sequence shown. Upper view indicates proper location for short and long screws. Broken lines indicate heads are located on bottom of crankcase.

Fig. 8–Tighten cylinder stud nuts in criss-cross pattern as shown. Intake manifold should be installed and tightened before cylinder nuts are torqued to align manifold flanges.

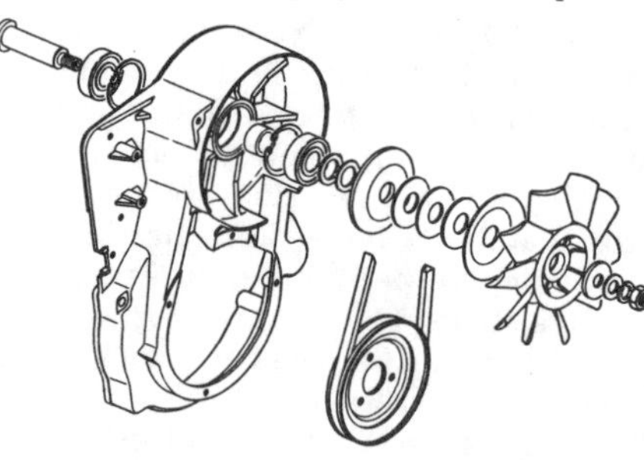

Fig. 11–Exploded view of cooling fan, fan housing and associated parts used on reed valve induction engines. Refer to Fig. 3 for parts identification.

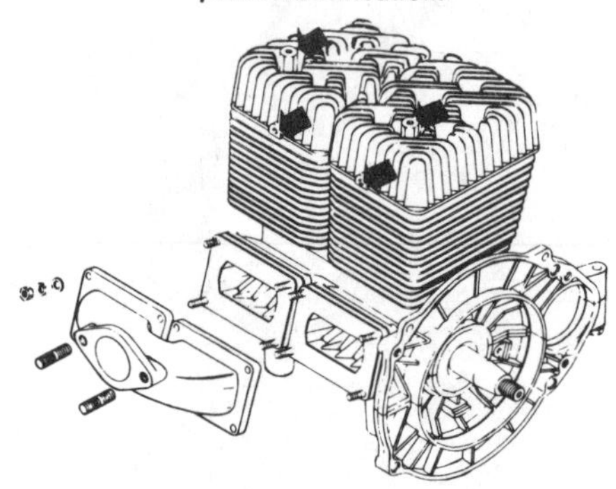

Fig. 12–Partially exploded view of reed valve induction engine. Cooling shroud is attached at points indicated by black arrows.

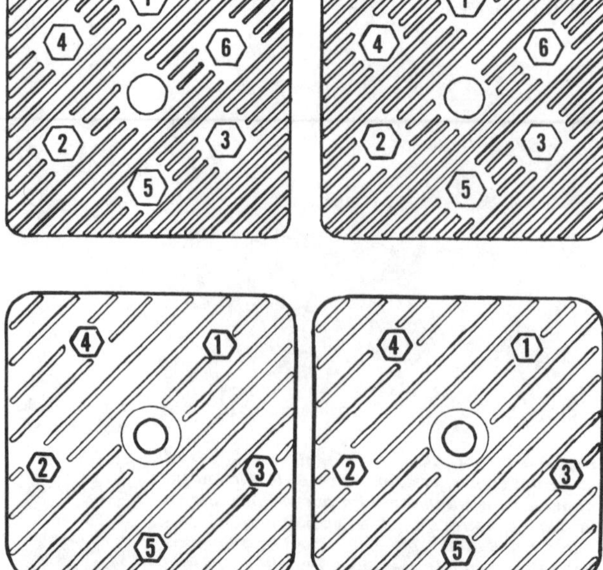

Fig. 9–Cylinder head tightening sequence to be used on CCW290 engine. Standoff nuts which support cooling shroud are to be installed in No. 3 position on both heads.

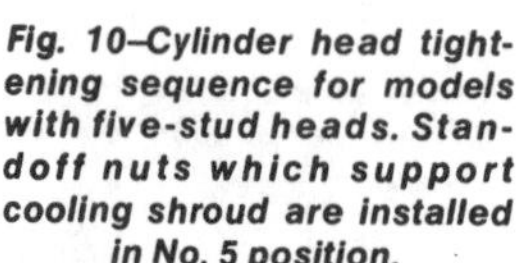

Fig. 10–Cylinder head tightening sequence for models with five-stud heads. Standoff nuts which support cooling shroud are installed in No. 5 position.

before removing piston pin. Note that exhaust port locating arrows on tops of pistons angle outward toward ends of shaft.

To assemble the engine, suitably support upper half of crankcase on cylinder studs and position bearing retaining half-washers in their grooves. Lubricate components thoroughly and coat both crankcase flanges with a suitable non-hardening sealant. Reposition crankshaft assembly and install crankcase lower half, being sure locating dowels seat properly. Tighten retaining cap screw and stud nuts evenly to a torque of 13-18 ft.-lbs. in the sequence shown in Fig. 14.

With crankcase assembled, reposition with cylinder studs uppermost. Warm the pistons and reinstall with exhaust valve locating arrows angling outward and away from reed valve opening side of crankcase. Chrome plated piston rings are installed in top grooves. Cylinders are not interchangeable and are stamped "L" (left) and "R" (right) on cylinder flange. Install cylinders using a suitable ring compresser, wooden blocks to hold piston steady, and new base gaskets. Exhaust port side of cylinders must be on opposite side of engine from reed valve openings in crankcase. Using new head gaskets, install cylinder heads with shroud retaining bosses (Arrows—Fig. 12) on reed plate side of engine. Install cylinder head nuts, flat washers and lockwashers finger tight. Long standoff nuts which secure cylinder shroud are installed at (2—Fig. 15) as shown by black arrows, Fig. 12. Install and tighten exhaust manifold to assure cylinder alignment. Tighten cylinder head stud nuts in the sequence shown in Fig. 15, the large nuts (Nos. 1 through 4) being tightened to full torque before tightening the small nuts (5 through 8).

Complete the assembly by reversing the disassembly procedure, adjusting fan belt, ignition points and timing as previously outlined.

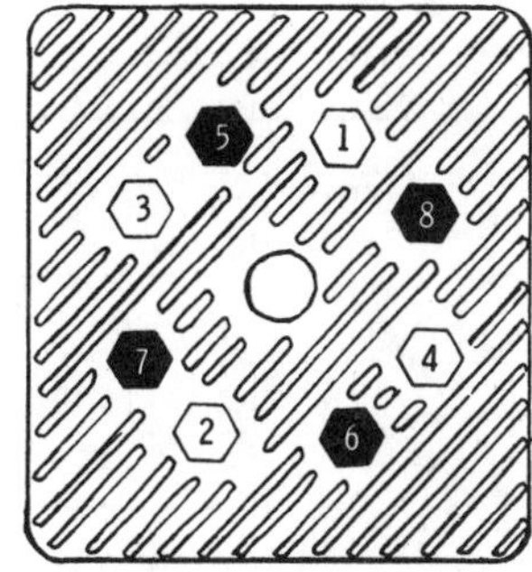

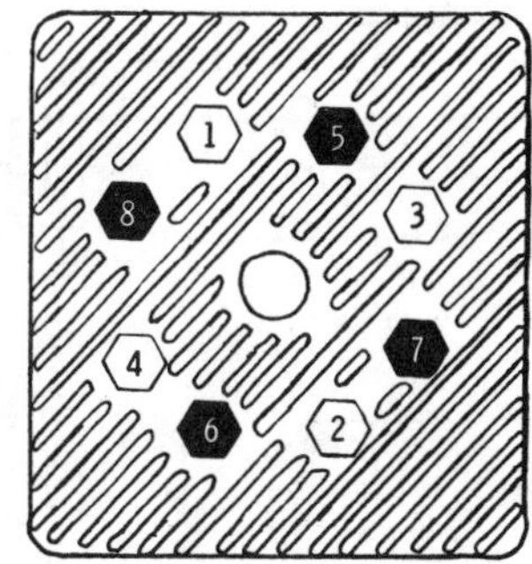

Fig. 15–When installing cylinders and cylinder heads first tighten through-studs (1 through 4) to indicated torque, then short studs (5 through 8). Recommended sequence is as shown.

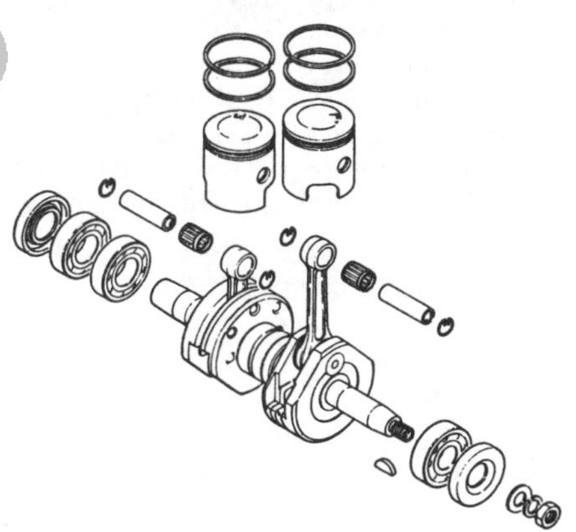

Fig. 13–Crankshaft, pistons and associated parts used in reed valve engines. Note angled exhaust arrows and ported areas of piston skirt.

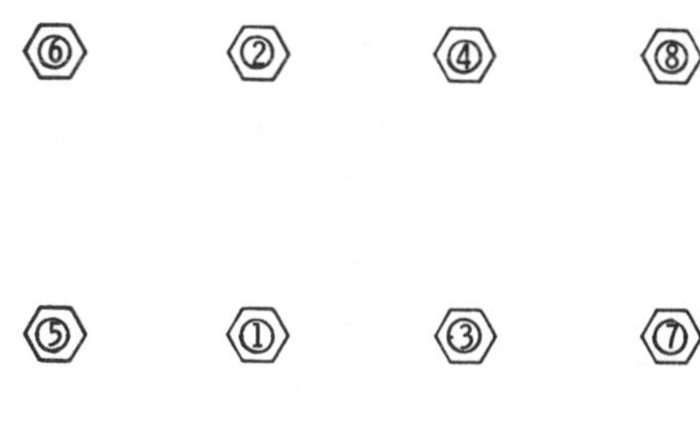

Fig. 14–Tighten crankcase retaining stud nuts and cap screw in sequence indicated, viewed from bottom.

PISTONS, PINS, RINGS AND CYLINDERS. Piston pin should be a tight fit in piston bore at room temperature and needle bearing should not have perceptible clearance between piston pin and connecting rod bore.

The two piston rings are pinned in place. Recommended side clearance is 0.0025-0.004 for upper ring and 0.0014-0.003 for lower ring. Recommended end gap is 0.004-0.012 for either ring. Recommended piston clearance in cylinder is 0.011-0.012 at top land and 0.004-0.005 at skirt.

CONNECTING RODS, CRANKSHAFT AND BEARINGS. The crankshaft and connecting rods, including center main bearings and seals, is only available as an assembly. Disassembly is not recommended in the average shop. Measure side shake of connecting rod at piston end after removing cylinders and pistons. If shake exceeds 3.0 mm (0.118 inch), install a new or rebuilt assembly. Outer (end) bearings can be renewed if care is used in removal and installation to keep from damaging shaft in any of its built-up joints. Support shaft on vee-blocks on installed outer bearings and measure runout at ends of shafts using a dial indicator. If runout exceeds 0.1 mm (0.004 inch) renew or straighten shaft.

REED VALVE UNITS. Refer to Fig. 16 for an exploded view of reed valve unit used on models so equipped. Valve leaf (3) is of stainless spring steel and seating surface of reed plate (5) has a bonded plastic coating. One shim (4) must be installed underneath valve reed to properly position the reed. Reed stop (2) is carefully arched for best performance and should not be reformed. Do not attempt to straighten a bent or damaged reed or to reform reed or stop in an attempt to alter performance. Renew reed or reed stop if damaged in any way and reed plate if coating is damaged at reed seating area. Tighten reed plate retaining screws evenly and securely to slightly compress plastic coating beneath the shim.

MAGNETO. Two different types of Energy Transfer Magneto have been used. Most models use two "piggy-backed" ignition generating coils as shown in Fig. 17, but early 340 models with manual start used a Sawafuji magneto with a single generating coil as shown in Fig. 18. Note that on Sawafuji unit, low tension coil is insulated from armature plate and circuit is completed through both sets of points. On all other models, one end of each coil winding is grounded to the armature plate.

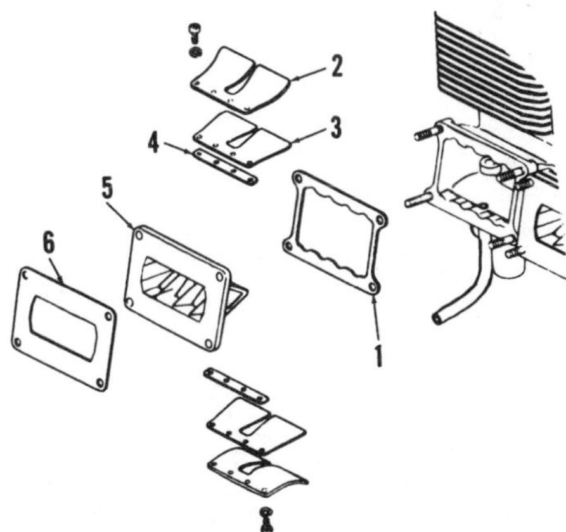

Fig. 16–Exploded view of reed valve plate and associated parts used on models so equipped.

1. Gasket
2. Reed stop
3. Valve leaf
4. Shim
5. Reed plate
6. Gasket

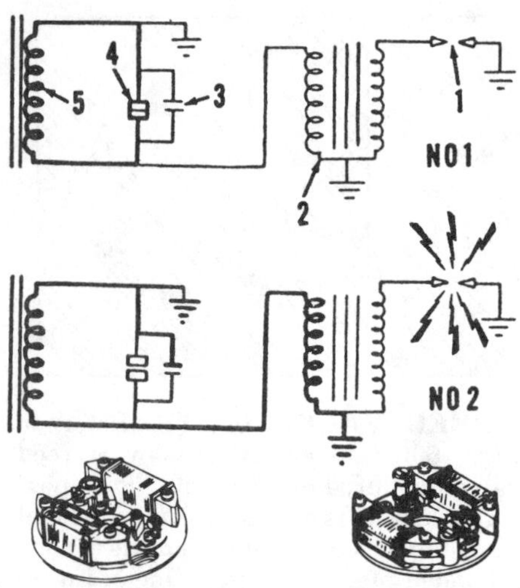

Fig. 17–Wiring diagram of independent ignition system used on most models. Note the "piggy-backed" low tension ignition coils.

1. Spark plug
2. Ignition coil
3. Condenser
4. Breaker points
5. Low tension (generating) coil

On condensers with soldered connections, an iron and low heat should be used to prevent service damage.

	Primary	Secondary
Sawafuji	0.37 Ohms	8,350 Ohms
Denso	0.37 Ohms	8,350 Ohms
Kokusan	1.65 Ohms	5,200 Ohms

Preferred method of timing is by piston position BTDC using a timing indicator in spark plug hole. The vertical spark plug location permits direct reading on all models. Static timing is as follows:

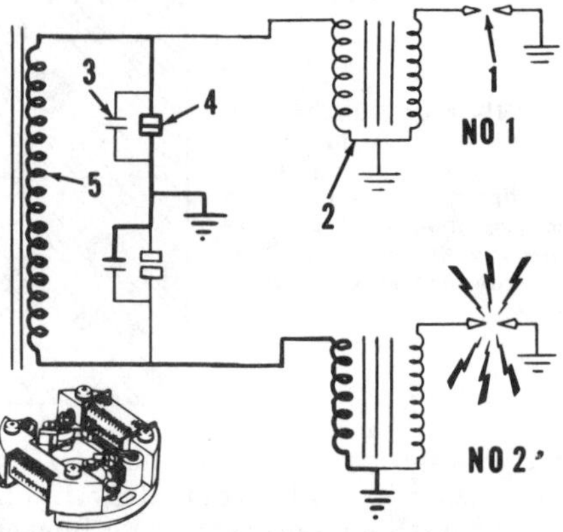

Fig. 18–On Sawafuji magneto, both systems share the common low tension coil (5), which is insulated from breaker plate. Refer to Fig. 17 for parts identification.

	Piston Position Inch BTDC	Crankshaft Degrees BTDC
CCW 290 (all)	0.020	10°
CCW340/1 & 2	0.015	8°
CCW340/3 & 4	0.023	10°
CCW400/1 & 2	0.015	8°
CCW400/3 & 4	0.023	10°
CCW400/21	0.006	5°
CCW440/1, 2 & 3	0.015	8°
CCW440/4 & 21	0.023	10°

Both cylinders must be timed as nearly as possible alike and adjustment is by varying point opening for timing the second cylinder. Armature plate may be moved for major adjustment by loosening retaining screws, which requires flywheel removal.

RECOIL STARTER. Refer to Fig. 19 for exploded view. Starter must be disassembled to renew rope or recoil spring.

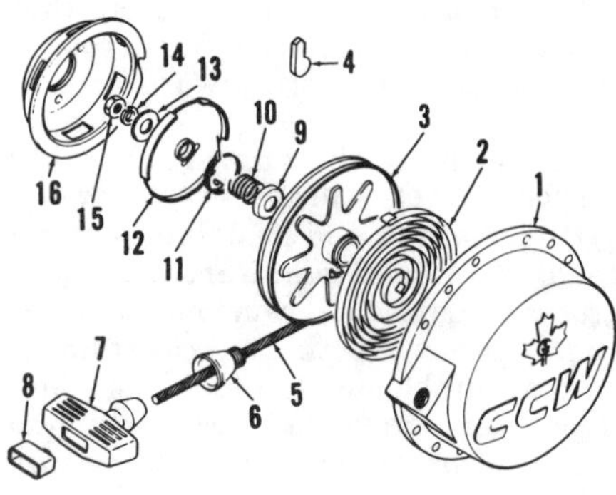

Fig. 19–Exploded view of recoil starter of the type used on all models.

1. Housing
2. Recoil spring
3. Pulley
4. Pawl
5. Rope
6. Guide
7. Grip
8. Retainer
9. Spring seat
10. Friction spring
11. Return spring
12. Friction plate
13. Washer
14. Lockwasher
15. Nut
16. Starter cup

Return spring (11) enters a hole in rope pulley (3) and a notch in friction plate (12) and turns the plate at recoil to retract pawls (4). Wind return spring in housing counter-clockwise starting at oustide. Wind rope on pulley and fit outer end in notch in pulley rim. Install pulley and engage recoil spring inner end; then turn pulley three turns counter-clockwise to preload recoil spring. Feed free end of rope out through hole in housing and rope guide (6) and tie a loose slip knot in free end while installing grip (7). Complete the assembly by reversing the disassembly procedure.

CHRYSLER

CONDENSED SERVICE DATA

Engine Model .... 82001,'002,'003 '004,'005,'006,'007 '008,'010,'012,&'015
Bore—Inches 2 17/32
Stroke—Inches 1⅝
No. of Cylinders 1
Displacement—(cc) 134
Cubic Inches 8.2
Horsepower @ RPM .... 10 @ 6000
Carburetor Model .... HL
Number Used 1
Ignition:
Type .... Wico
Point Gap—(mm) ....
Inch 0.015
Edge Gap .... Fixed
Timing Advance? .... No
Timing BTDC (mm) ...... See Text
Inch ....
Degrees ....
Measured at ....
Spark Plug:
Champion L4
AC AC42FF
Electrode Gap (mm) ....
Inch 0.030
Fuel/Oil Ratio 16:1

MAINTENANCE

CARBURETOR. All models are equipped with a Tillotson series HL carburetor. Refer to Tillotson Carburetor Section for operation and overhaul.

Clockwise rotation of both the idle and high speed fuel needles leans the mixture. For initial adjustment, open both needles approximately 1¾ turns. Make final adjustment with engine running at operating temperature. Adjust idle needle for smoothest operation at idle speed, then check acceleration from idle speed to approximately 6000 RPM. Readjust idle fuel needle if engine does not accelerate properly; then, adjust high speed needle with engine under load and at operating speed. Turn the high speed needle clockwise until engine just stops four-cycling (starts to fire on every power stroke). CAUTION: Do not attempt to operate engine with a too lean fuel mixture; improper lubrication and engine seizure may result.

FUEL PUMP. An externally attached impulse line connects diaphragm cover to engine crankcase and pressure and vacuum pulsations in crankcase actuate the pump. Be sure that the gasket, pump diaphragm and valve diaphragm are installed in the order removed, that all passages are open and that vacuum or pressure leaks are eliminated.

GOVERNOR. All models except model 82012 are non-governed. Maximum governed speed on model 82012 should not exceed 7000 RPM. An air vane type governor is used.

MAGNETO AND TIMING. A Wico flywheel type magneto is used on all models. Refer to Fig. 1.

Fig. 1–View of magneto stator plate assembly removed from engine.

1. Breaker cover spring
2. Armature core
3. Ignition coil
4. Breaker point gap adjusting screw
5. Breaker cam
6. Condenser

To inspect or service magneto, proceed as follows: Unbolt and remove fan housing and recoil starter assembly as a unit. On engines with model number ending in zero or even number (such as model 82002), turn flywheel retaining nut clockwise to remove; on engines with model number ending in an uneven number, turn nut counter-clockwise to remove. After removing flywheel retaining nut, remove flywheel using special knockoff nut.

Breaker contact points are accessible after removing flywheel and dust cover from stator plate. Adjust breaker point gap to 0.015 on all models. Condenser capacity is 0.16-0.20 mfd. Timing specifications are as follows:

TIMING CHART

MODEL NUMBER	Stator Position*	Degrees BTDC	Inches BTDC
82001	MR	26°	0.102
82002	MR	26°	0.102
82003	MR-FA	28°	0.118
82004	FR	22°	0.070
82005	FR	22°	0.070
82006	FR	22°	0.070
82007	MR-FA	28°	0.118
82008	MR	26°	0.102
82010	FR-MR	24°	0.090
82012	FR	22°	0.070
82015	FR	22°	0.070

*MR=Mid-Range, FR=Full Retard and FA=Full Advance. Mid-range setting of timing is when stator mounting screws are tightened in center of slotted stator mounting holes. Full retard is when magneto stator is moved all the way to end of slots in direction of flywheel rotation. Full advance is when magneto stator is moved all the way to end of slots in direction opposite flywheel rotation. The specifications FR-MR or MR-FA indicates a stator setting midway between the two positions.

REPAIRS

TIGHTENING TORQUES. Refer to following table for correct tightening torques. All values are in inch-pounds.

Connecting rod 80-90
Cylinder head:
All 820 models
except 82012 85-90
82012 120-130

Flywheel 420
Spark Plug—Finger tight plus ½ to ⅝-turn

Standard screws:
No. 10-24 thread 30
No. 10-32 thread 35
No. 12-24 thread 45
¼-in., 20 thread 70
5/16-in., 18 thread 160
⅜-in., 16 thread 270

CYLINDER HEAD. Cylinder head is removable on all models and is retained to cylinder with socket head cap screws and plain washers. The cylinder head gasket is available in various thicknesses and care should be taken to select the correct thickness gasket for the engine being serviced. Refer to following table.

HEAD GASKET THICKNESS CHART

ENGINE MODEL NO.	Gasket Thickness
82001 & '02	0.032
82003	0.094
82004, '05 & '06	0.125
82007	0.094
82008 & '10	0.125
82012	0.062
82015	0.125

When reinstalling cylinder head, be sure that gasket, cylinder head and cylinder surfaces are clean and smooth. Install the socket head cap screws with plain washers and tighten screws to the correct torque as given in preceding paragraph.

CONNECTING ROD. Piston and connecting rod assembly can be removed after removing cylinder head, crankcase cover and rod cap. Be careful not to lose any of the 28 loose needle rollers when removing connecting rod cap.

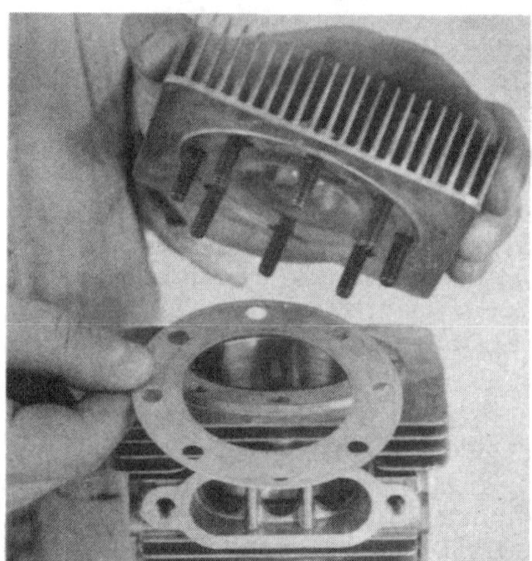

Fig. 2–Cylinder head gasket is available in various thicknesses and care should be taken to select correct thickness for engine being serviced. Refer to text.

The caged needle roller bearing in pin end of connecting rod is not renewable. Renew the connecting rod assembly if any roller in pin end bearing is rough or flat, if pin end rollers can be separated with width of one roller or if crankpin bearing surface is rough or shows signs of wear.

Match marks on connecting rod and cap (See Fig. 3) and piston ring anchor pin should be towards tapered (flywheel) end of crankshaft. When assembling connecting rod to crankshaft, coat crankpin with a light grease such as Lubriplate and use tweezers to place 14 of the rollers between rod and crankpin (Fig. 4); then, stick remaining 14 rollers to crankpin and carefully reinstall rod cap with match marks on rod and cap aligned as shown in Fig. 3. The parting surfaces of rod and cap are fractured and if cap is correctly installed, the parting line will be almost invisible and cannot be felt with fingernail. Tighten connecting rod cap screws to a torque of 80-90 inch-pounds.

PISTON, PIN AND RINGS. Piston is equipped with two pinned compression rings. Piston and rings are available in standard size only. Renew piston if scored, ring side clearance is excessive or pin is loose in piston bosses.

The floating type piston pin is retained by a snap ring at each end of pin in piston bosses. Install flat snap rings with square-cut edge away from pin. Chrysler advises to heat the piston on a light bulb prior to removing or installing piston pin; otherwise, pin bosses in piston may be damaged. Install closed end of piston pin towards side of piston with piston ring anchor pin. Piston pin is available in standard size only.

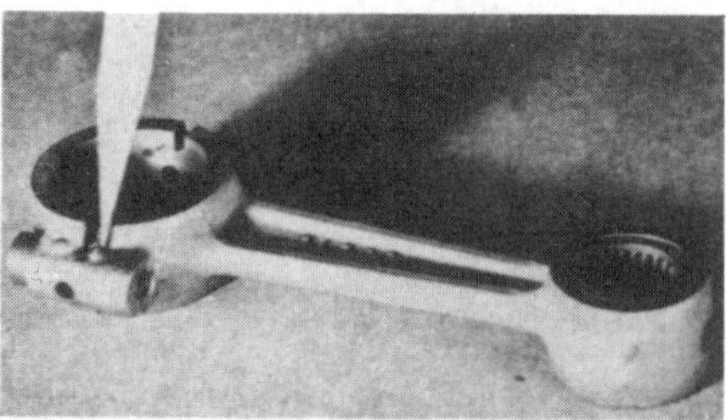

Fig. 3–Be sure to align match marks when reassembling cap to connecting rod. Match marks on rod assembly and anchor pin for piston rings should be towards flywheel end of crankshaft.

Fig. 4–Installing crankpin needle rollers. Coating crankpin with Lubriplate will hold needle rollers in place. Refer to text.

Be sure that piston ring end gaps are aligned with anchor pin in ring grooves. Rings are available in standard size only. Install beveled edge of rings towards top of piston. Rings can be compressed with fingers when installing the piston and connecting rod assembly.

CRANKCASE, CRANKSHAFT, BEARINGS AND SEALS. The crankcase and cylinder are an integral unit of die-cast aluminum with either a cast-in iron cylinder liner or chrome plated cylinder bore. Renew crankcase and cylinder if chrome plating has worn through or if cast iron cylinder bore is worn or out-of-round 0.002 or more.

Crankshaft is supported in two ball bearings. Bearings should be a light press fit on crankshaft and in crankcase and support plate. However, a slip fit in crankcase or support plate is permissible if there is no end play of bearings. Crankshaft must be supported on flat surface inside crankpin throw when pressing bearings onto shaft.

As with all two-cycle engines, sealing of crankcase is very important. Renew crankshaft seals using a driver that will contact outer edge of seal only. Install seals in crankcase and bearing support plate with lip of seal to inside. Do not scrape gasket material from crankcase or support plate as this may damage the sealing surfaces; soak old gasket material loose with solvent.

REED INLET VALVE. Reeds must

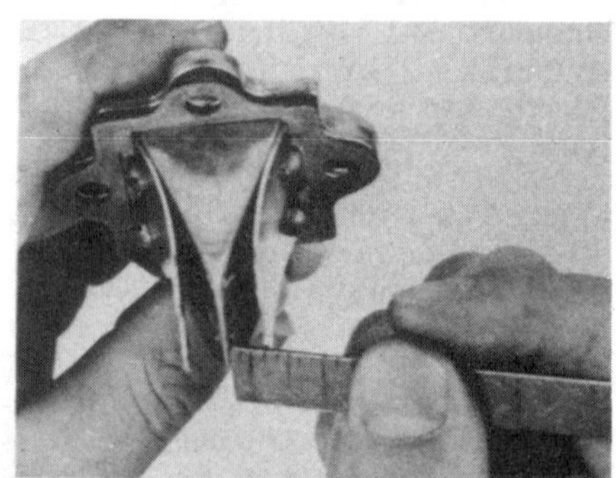

Fig. 5–Reed stop spacing should be ¼-inch when measured as shown.

seat lightly against reed plate along full length of reed and reed must entirely cover hole in reed plate. Renew reeds if rusted, cracked, broken or warped. Renew the complete reed valve unit if reed plate seats are rough, pitted or worn. Dimension measured from reed plate to reed stop as shown in Fig. 5 should be ¼-inch.

CUYUNA

CONDENSED SERVICE DATA

ENGINE MODEL	295	340	400	440
Bore—mm	55.5	60	65	67.5
Inches	2.185	2.362	2.559	2.658
Stroke—mm	60	60	60	60
Inches	2.362	2.362	2.362	2.362
No. of Cylinders	2	2	2	2
Displacement—cc	290.3	339.3	398.2	429.4
Cubic Inches	17.7	20.7	24.3	26.2
Horsepower—rpm	29/6500	32/6500	38/6500	40/6500
Cooling Type	Axial Fan	Axial Fan	Axial Fan	Axial Fan
Carburetor Model	Walbro WF	Walbro WF	Walbro WF	Walbro WF
Number Used	1	1	1	1
Ignition:				
Type	ET	ET	ET	ET
Point Gap—mm	0.4	0.4	0.4	0.4
Inch	0.016	0.016	0.016	0.016
Edge Gap—mm	.....	.....	.....	.....
Inch	.....	.....	.....	.....
Timing Advance?	Yes	Yes	Yes	Yes
Timing—Degrees BTDC	.....	.....	.....	.....
MM	2.6-2.8	2.6.-2.8	2.6-2.8	2.6-2.8
Inch	0.102-0.112	0.102-0.112	0.102-0.112	0.102-0.112
Measured at	Adv.	Adv.	Adv.	Adv.
Spark Plug:				
Bosch	W260T2	W260T2	W260T2	W260T2
Champion	N3	N3	N3	N3
Electrode Gap—mm	0.45	0.45	0.45	0.45
Inch	0.018	0.018	0.018	0.018
Fuel:Oil Ratio	40:1	40:1	40:1	40:1

MAINTENANCE

SPARK PLUG. The recommended spark plug is BOSCH W260T2 or CHAMPION N3. Hotter or colder plugs may be required for particular applications. Recommended spark plug gap is 0.018 inch (0.45 mm) and recommended tightening torque is 25 ft.-lbs.

CARBURETOR. Walbro WF carburetors are used on most engines. Refer to the Walbro carburetor section for operation and overhaul procedure.

IGNITION AND TIMING. Recommended ignition timing is 0.102-0.112 inch (2.6-2.8 mm) BTDC with timing fully advanced. Use a dial indicator in spark plug hole as shown in Fig. 1, plus an ohmmeter (shown) or buzzer to determine when points open. Use a screwdriver or similar tool to block advance weights in advanced positions as shown in Fig. 2. Time one cylinder by adjusting to 0.016 inch (4 mm) point gap then rotating armature plate as required. Time the second cylinder by adjusting point gap only. Point gap of the second cylinder must be within the limits of 0.014-0.018 inch (3.5-4.5 mm); if it is not, adjust to the appropriate point within those limits, then readjust the first set of points.

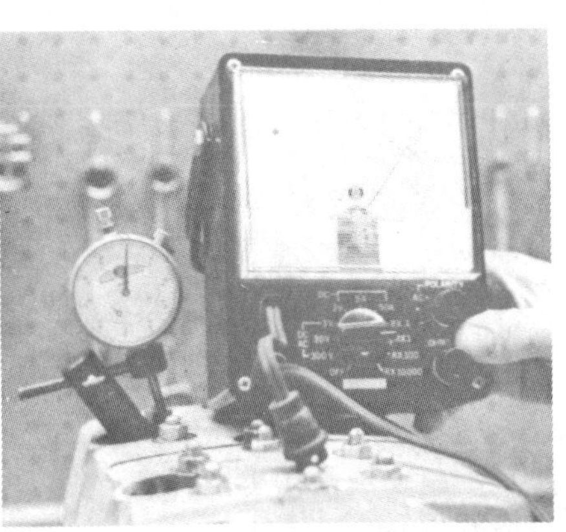

Fig. 1—Using a piston timing gage and ohmmeter to check ignition timing.

LUBRICATION. The engine is lubricated by oil mixed with the fuel. The manufacturer recommends a good grade of premium gasoline and special two-cycle oil mixed at the ratio of 40:1.

COOLING FAN AND BELT. The cooling fan drive belt should have approximately ¼-inch (6 mm) free play measured midway between pulleys. Free play is adjusted by adding or removing shims (10—Fig. 3) between halves of driven pulley. To remove shaft nut (7) insert a small punch through locking hole (L) in fan housing and (F) in fan hub to lock the shaft from turning, as shown in Fig. 4. Four shims are normally installed in original assembly and removing shims tightens the belt. Turn the pulley as nut is tightened to keep from pinching belt.

REPAIRS

TIGHTENING TORQUES. Recommended tightening torques are as follows:

	Ft.-Lbs.	Kg-m
Cylinder base (crankcase) nuts	16-18	2.2-2.5
Cylinder head nuts:		
290-340	28-32	2.9-4.4
400-440	16-18	2.2-2.5
Fan housing	16-18	2.2-2.5
Flywheel	20-24	2.8-3.3
Flywheel	44-50	6.1-6.9
Ring gear (6 mm)	6-7	0.8-1.1
8 mm	10-12	1.4-1.7

DISASSEMBLY AND REASSEMBLY. Only the cylinder heads, cylinders, pistons, rings and piston pins differ between the four engine models. All other parts (more than 90% of the total) interchange. The two halves of the crankcase are secured only by the four long studs (eight total) which secure each cylinder unit.

IMPORTANT: If only the cylinders and pistons are to be serviced, proceed as follows to avoid crankcase separation: Remove manifolds, spark plugs and both cylinder heads, then unbolt and remove PTO side cylinder without disturbing cylinder on magneto side. Drop two hex head bolts with flat washers in mounting stud holes next to installed cylinder as shown in Fig. 5. Snug up nuts on the two installed bolts to hold crankcase in position, then unbolt and remove the other cylinder.

Install pistons with arrow on piston crown pointing toward exhaust side of engine. Rings are marked for correct installation. It may be necessary to slightly heat the piston for easy installation of piston pin. Pin retainers should be installed with gap down, surrounding the opening in retaining ring groove. Install base gaskets on cylinder studs and use a ring compressor to install the cylinders. Install cylinder stud nuts finger tight then install intake manifold, tightening manifold stud nuts securely to align cylinders. Tighten cylinder stud (crankcase) nuts to 16-18 ft.-lbs. (2.2-2.5 kg-m) using the sequence shown in Fig. 6. With cylinders installed, turn each piston in turn to TDC position and measure piston height relative to top of cylinder. Use a straightedge and feeler gage. If piston protrudes more than 0.008 inch (0.2 mm) above top surface of block, a thicker base gasket must be used.

Install cylinder head gasket with wide side of inner metal flange facing up toward cylinder head. Tighten retaining cap screws in a criss-cross

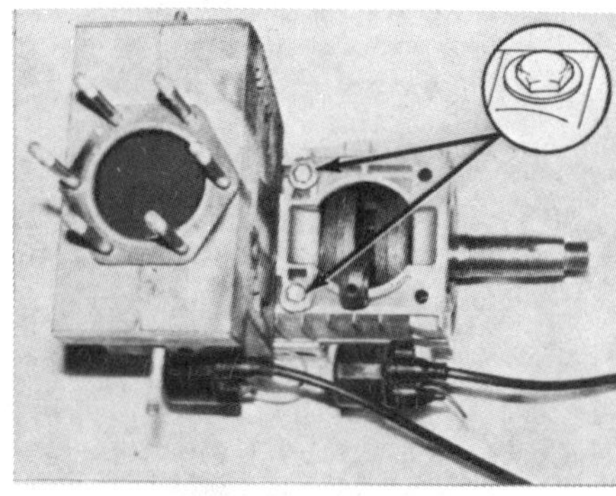

Fig. 5—To hold crankcase from separating during top end repair, install long bolts in two center cylinder stud holes as shown.

Fig. 2—When checking timing, advance weights must be held in advance position as shown.

Fig. 4—Insert a small pin punch through locking holes in housing and fan to hold shaft from turning during disassembly.

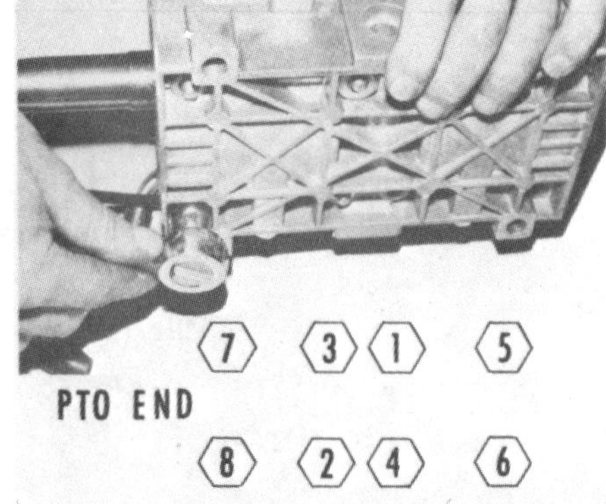

Fig. 6—Tighten cylinder base nuts to 16-18 ft.-lbs. (2.2-2.5 kg-m) using sequence shown.

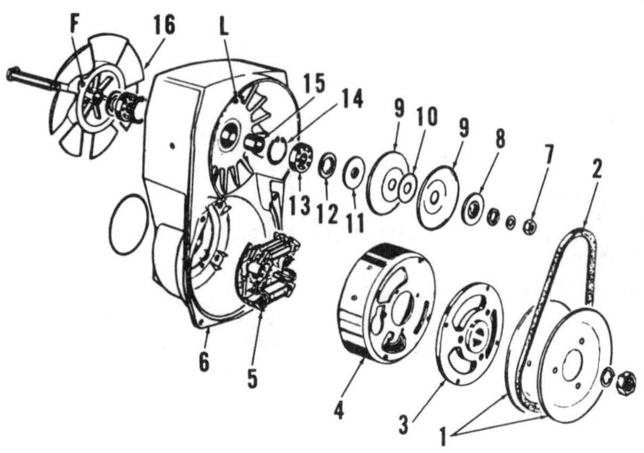

Fig. 3—View of fan housing and associated parts shown exploded.

1. Pulley half
2. Drive belt
3. Flywheel hub
4. Magneto ring
5. Magneto plate
6. Fan housing
7. Fan shaft nut
8. Tapered spacer
9. Pulley half
10. Adjusting shims
11. Tapered spacer
12. Nilos ring
13. Bearing
14. Snap ring
15. Spacer
16. Fan wheel

F. Locking hole (fan)
L. Locking hole (hsg)

Fig. 7—Using puller (444-31-843-2) to remove flywheel.

pattern to the torque given in TIGHTENING TORQUES paragraph.

To remove the fan housing, first remove recoil starter, starter cup and lower fan pulley. Remove flywheel using puller 444-31-843-2 as shown in Fig. 7.

CAUTION: Lift off flywheel carefully to be sure key does not hang in crankshaft slot and damage advance mechanism. An icepick or small screwdriver may be used to dislodge the key if desired. Use an impact driver to loosen the four screws retaining fan housing to crankcase as shown in Fig. 8. Lift off fan housing, fan, magneto armature and wiring as a unit from crankcase. Install by reversing removal procedure, tightening the four fan housing screws to 16-18 ft.-lbs. (2.2-2.5 kg-m).

To separate the crankcase, it is first necessary to remove the fan housing, then unbolt and lift off both cylinder units. Before reassembling, thoroughly clean all old sealant from sealing surfaces and dress down any burrs or roughness. Use a light coating of suitable sealant when reassembling. Refer to the following paragraphs for further disassembly and inspection procedure.

PISTONS, RINGS AND CYLINDERS. Piston pin is a floating fit in piston at operating temperature. Connecting rod small end bearing is a caged needle roller as shown in Fig. 9. The two piston rings are pinned in place. Pistons and rings are provided in standard size only.

The aluminum cylinders have cast iron cylinder sleeves and shrouding is cast into cylinder and cylinder head, providing additional surface for heat dissipation.

CRANKSHAFT AND CONNECTING RODS. The crankshaft and connecting rod assembly is available only as a complete unit and should not be disassembled. End bearings, however, can be renewed if proper care is exercised. Use bearing puller 444-31-870-0 as shown in Fig. 11 to remove the bearings. Open (unshielded) side of bearings should face outward when bearings are reinstalled. Heat new bearings in oil to 180 degrees F. and they should slide into position on shaft.

Check for wear at connecting rod big end by measuring the play (rock) at connecting rod small end. Rock should not exceed 0.080 inch (2.0 mm). Check crankshaft runout just before installation by supporting the shaft end bearings on "V" blocks and using a dial indicator at center bearings and shaft ends. Runout should not exceed 0.004 inch (0.1 mm).

FAN HOUSING. To remove the fan, first remove fan housing as outlined in disassembly paragraphs. Insert a small punch through index hole in housing and impeller as shown in Fig. 12 and remove shaft nut, pulley halves, and spacer washers. Note assembly order of sheave halves and spacer washers, spacers control tension on fan drive belt.

With driven pulley removed, tap threaded end of shaft with a soft hammer and remove shaft and impeller. Either shaft bearing can be tapped out by reaching through near bearing with a small punch and catching inner race of fan bearing. Bearings seat against snap rings in housing bore, a spacer filling the space between the bearings.

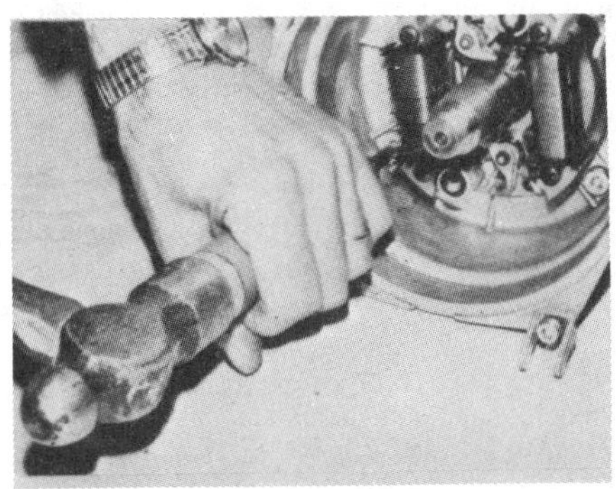

Fig. 8—An impact driver is required to loosen fan housing screws.

Fig. 10—Piston may need to be warmed for pin to be pushed in by hand.

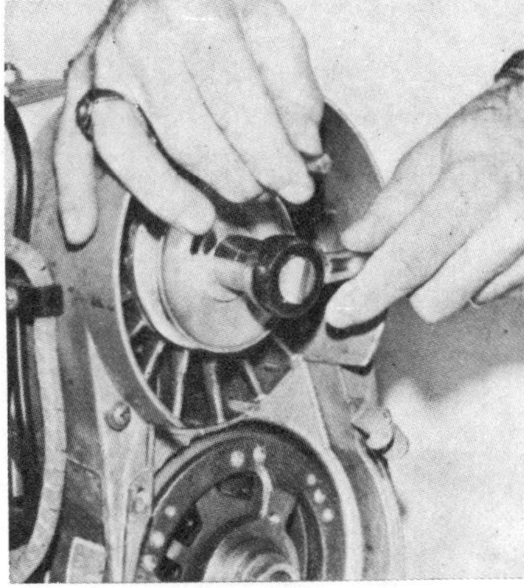

Fig. 12—Use a pin punch in locking holes to disassemble fan.

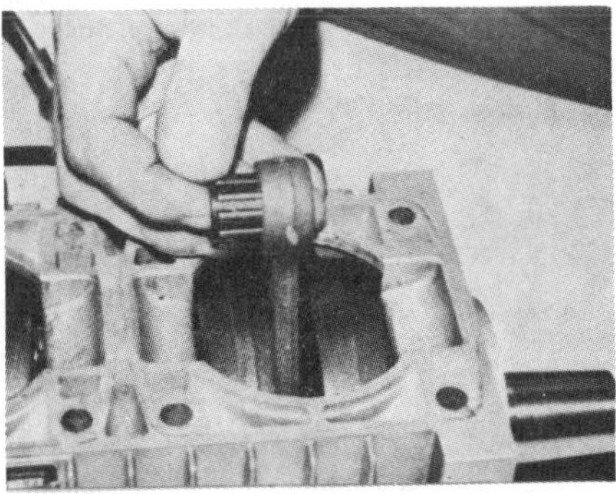

Fig. 9—A caged needle roller bearing is used at connecting rod small end.

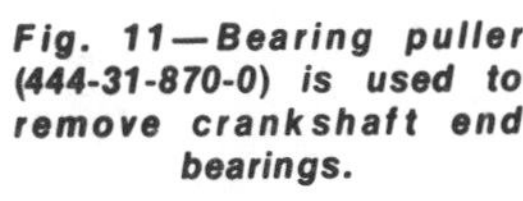

Fig. 11—Bearing puller (444-31-870-0) is used to remove crankshaft end bearings.

Refer to Fig. 13 for a disassembled view of bearing arrangement.

Magneto stator and wiring can be removed after housing is off. Use a sharp chisel and index stator setting before removal, to assist in timing at reassembly.

RECOIL STARTER. Refer to Fig. 14 for an exploded view of recoil starter assembly. Internal parts except rope should be cleaned in solvent and lightly coated with Lubriplate during assembly. Fig. 15 shows an installed view of starter.

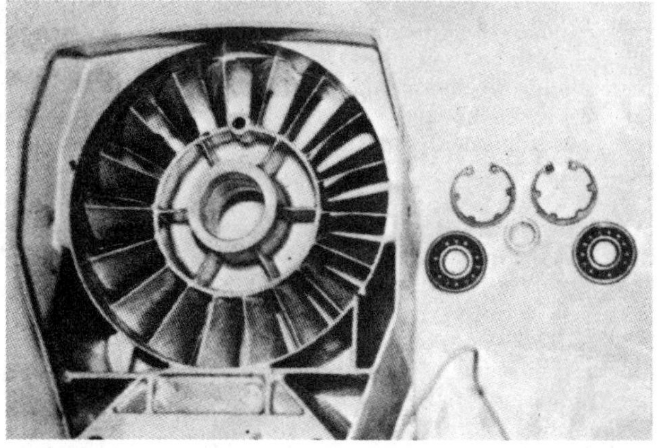

Fig. 13—View of fan housing showing fanshaft bearings removed.

Fig. 14—Exploded view of recoil starter assembly.

Fig. 15—Installed view of starter.

JOHN DEERE

DEERE & COMPANY
400 North Vine
Horicon, WI 53032

CONDENSED SERVICE DATA

ENGINE MODEL	TA340A*	TB340A*	TA440A*	TA440B*	TC440A*
Bore–(mm)	60	60	68	68	68
Inches	2.362	2.362	2.67	2.67	2.67
Stroke–(mm)	60	60	60	60	60
Inches	2.362	2.362	2.362	2.362	2.362
No. of Cylinders	2	2	2	2	2
Displacement–(cc)	339	339	436	436	436
Cubic Inches	20.6	20.6	26.6	26.6	26.6
Cooling Type	Axial Fan	Free Air	Axial Fan	Axial Fan	Liquid
Carburetor Model	VM	B	VM	VM	VM
Number Used	1	1	1	1	2
Ignition Type	CDI	CDI	CDI	CDI	CDI
Timing BTDC	22°	22°	22°	18°	16°
Measured at	6500 rpm	6500 rpm	6000 rpm	6500 rpm	6500 rpm
Spark Plug:					
Champion	QN-3	ON-3	QN-3	QN-2 or N-2	N-2
Electrode Gap–(mm)	0.635	0.635	0.635	0.635	0.635
Inch	0.025	0.025	0.025	0.025	0.025
Fuel/Oil Ratio	50:1	50:1	50:1	50:1	50:1

*Engines manufactured for John Deere by Kawasaki Heavy Industries, Japan.

MAINTENANCE

SPARK PLUG. The recommended plug for normal service is given in **CONDENSED SERVICE DATA** table. A different heat range or type of plug may be needed for a particular application. Refer to **ENGINE SERVICE FUNDAMENTALS** section when selecting a spark plug for other than normal usage.

CARBURETOR. Mikuni type VM or B carburetors are used. Refer to the appropriate **CARBURETOR SERVICE** section for overhaul data. An external impulse line from engine crankcase is used to operate fuel pump. Be sure there are no vacuum or pressure leaks.

IGNITION SYSTEM. Timing specifications for individual engines are given in **CONDENSED SERVICE DATA** tables. All models are equipped with Capacitor Discharge Ignition System. Because timing is electronic, it should not change once properly adjusted. The first step in adjustment, therefore, would be to check for loose flywheel nut, sheared flywheel key, or loose mounting screws on stator base plate. On Models TA340A, TA440A, TA440B and TC440A ignition timing is set by aligning mark on stator plate (1–Fig. JD1) with top of crankcase ridge (2). For Model TB340A align longest mark (1–Fig. JD2) with top of crankcase ridge (2). To adjust remove recoil starter. On some models timing can be adjusted by reaching through inspection holes in flywheel. If these are not provided, then remove starter pulley

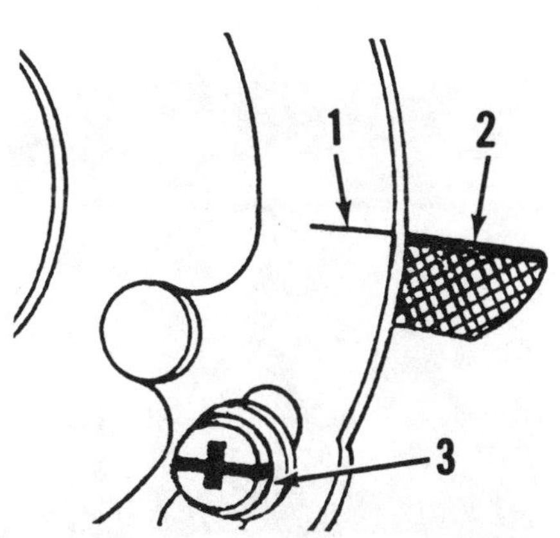

Fig. JD1–Set ignition timing by aligning mark on stator plate (1) with crankcase ridge (2) and adjust by loosening screw (3), then rotating stator plate for Models TA340A, TA440A, TA440B and TC440A.

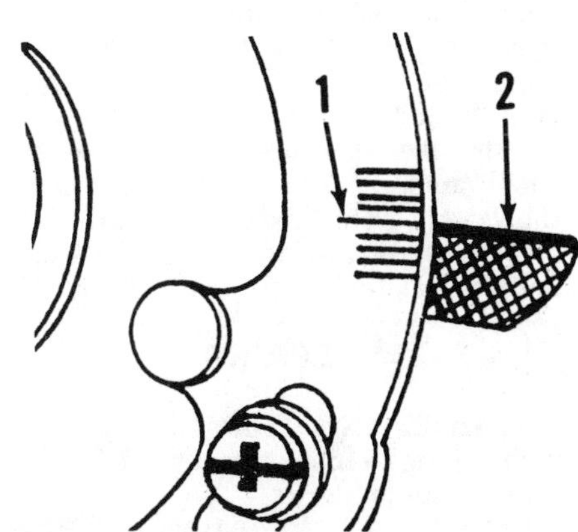

Fig. JD2–Align longest mark on stator plate (1) with top of crankcase ridge (2) to set timing on Model TB340A.

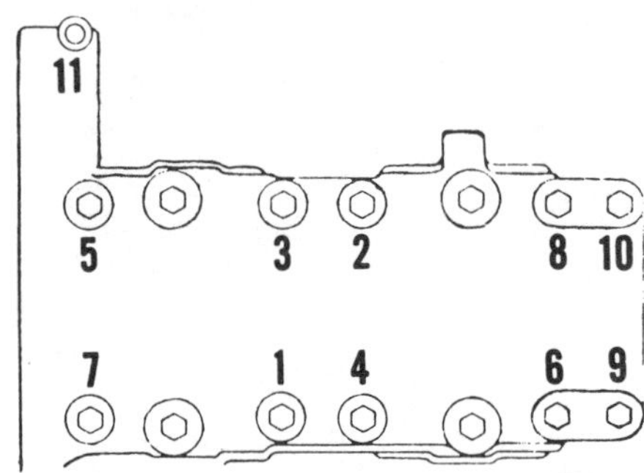

Fig. JD3—Crankcase cap screw tightening sequence for Models TA340A, TB340A and TA440A.

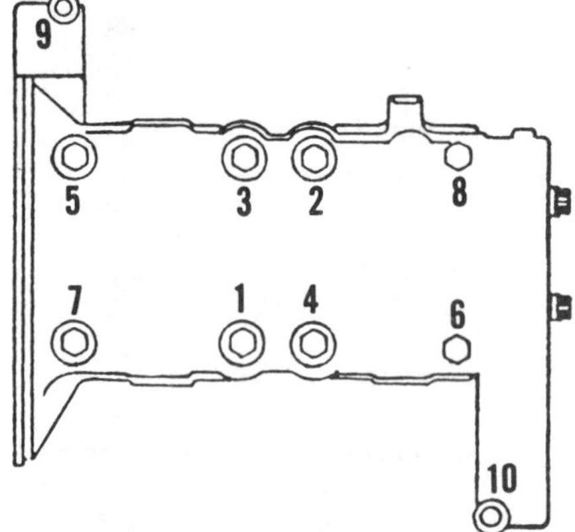

Fig. JD4—Crankcase cap screw tightening sequence for Model TC440A.

and flywheel retaining nut and lockwasher. Use a suitable puller and withdraw flywheel from crankshaft. Be sure not to lose key in crankshaft keyway. Adjust timing by loosening screws (3–Fig. JD1) and turning stator plate. Reassemble in reverse order of disassembly.

LUBRICATION. The engine is lubricated by mixing oil with fuel. Use John Deere 2-cycle oil or a suitable equivalent. Recommended fuel/oil ratio for all engines is 50:1. For models without oil injection pumps mix fuel and oil thoroughly in a separate container before pouring mixture into fuel tank. For cold weather blending, pre-mix the oil with a small amount of gasoline and shake thoroughly until mixture is liquid, then blend with remainder of fuel. Do not use kerosene or fuel oil for pre-mixing.

REPAIRS

TIGHTENING TORQUES. Recommended tightening torques are as follows for all models:

Crankcase . . . . 16 ft.-lbs. (22 N•m)
Cylinder-to-crankcase . . . . 16 ft.-lbs. (22 N•m)
Cylinder head . . . . . . 16 ft.-lbs. (22 N•m)

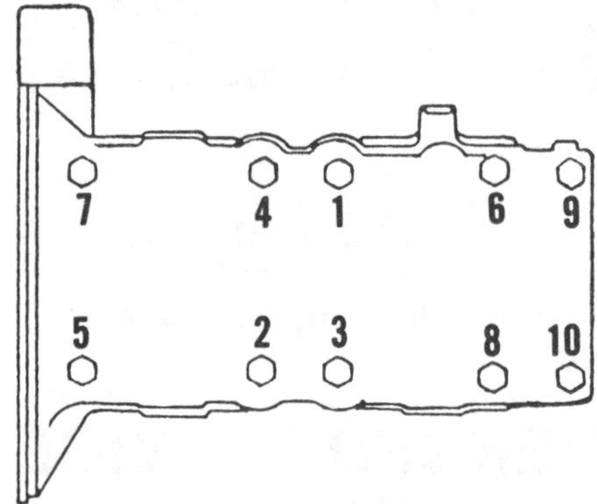

Fig. JD5—Crankcase cap screw tightening sequence for Model TA440B.

Flywheel nut . . . . 60 ft.-lbs. (81 N•m)
Spark plug . . . . 20 ft.-lbs. (27 N•m)
Recoil starter mounting bolts . . . . . 5 ft.-lbs. (7 N•m)

DISASSEMBLY AND REASSEMBLY. Remove carburetor, intake manifold, muffler, exhaust manifold, drive sheave and recoil starter. On models with axial fans, remove cooling shrouds, fan belt and fan assembly. On liquid cooled Model TC440A remove necessary coolant hoses and related parts. Remove starter cup and flywheel. Remove spark plug leads and ignition coil. Remove engine wiring as needed, mark location for reassembly. Remove stator plate retaining screws and withdraw plate with leads and grommet from mounting base. Remove and identify cylinder heads, cylinders and pistons, so that parts can be reinstalled in original positions. Remove crankcase securing capscrews and separate crankcase halves. Refer to appropriate section to service components.

To reassemble, reverse disassembly procedure. Refer to **TIGHTENING TORQUE** section for torque specifications. Refer to **IGNITION SYSTEM** section for setting ignition timing. Refer to Fig. JD3 for crankcase tightening sequence for Models TA340A, TA440A and TB340A, Fig. JD4 for Model TC440A and Fig. JD5 for Model TA440B.

LOCATING MARK TOWARD OUTPUT SHAFT

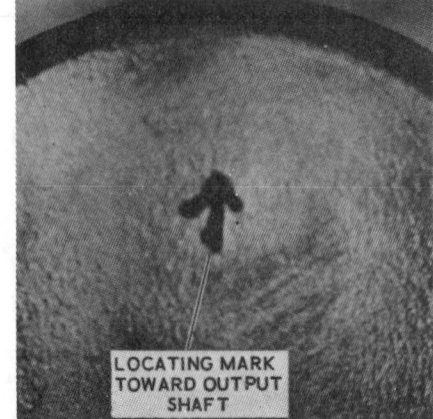

Fig. JD6—Install piston so that arrow on piston crown points towards exhaust port.

PISTON, RINGS & CYLINDER. Piston crown is marked with an arrow as shown in Fig. JD6 to indicate piston position in cylinder. Arrow must point towards exhaust port. Cylinder assembly has a chrome-plated bore and must be renewed if out of specification or damaged. Small deposits of aluminum from piston on cylinder wall may be removed by very careful sanding. Cylinder should be inspected for cracking, flaking or any other deterioration of the chrome lining. Also check for appearance of underlying base metal through chrome which indicates excessive wear. Inspect piston for excessive wear or damage.

Piston pins are full floating with retaining rings on each end. Piston rings are pinned in place as shown in Fig. JD7. Widest part of ring gap must be facing up when ring is installed as shown in Fig. JD7. Piston ring end gap for Model TA340A should be 0.006-0.014 inch, 0.011-0.019 inch for Model TB340A and 0.008-0.016 inch for Models TA440A, TA440B and TC440A. Cylinder bore diameter should be no more than 2.3669 inches for Model TA340A, 2.3675 inches for Model TB340A, 2.6818 inches for Models TA440A and TA440B and 2.6811 inches for Model TC440A. If cylinder bore diameter exceeds specification, cylinder assembly must be renewed. Piston diameter measured at skirt should be no less than 2.3554 inches for Model TA340A, 2.3551 inches for Model TB340A, 2.6703 inches for Model TA440A, 2.6693 inches for Model TA440B and 2.6701 inches for Model TC440A. If piston diameter is less than specification, then piston will need to be renewed.

CRANKSHAFT AND CONNECTING ROD ASSEMBLY. The crankshaft and connecting rods are available only as an assembled unit and should not be disassembled. Crankshaft main bearings

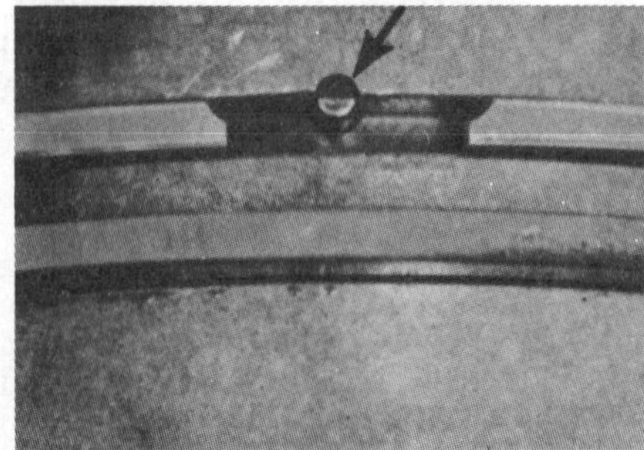

Fig. JD7—Piston rings are pinned as shown (arrow). Note that upper ring is installed so that notches in ring ends are up.

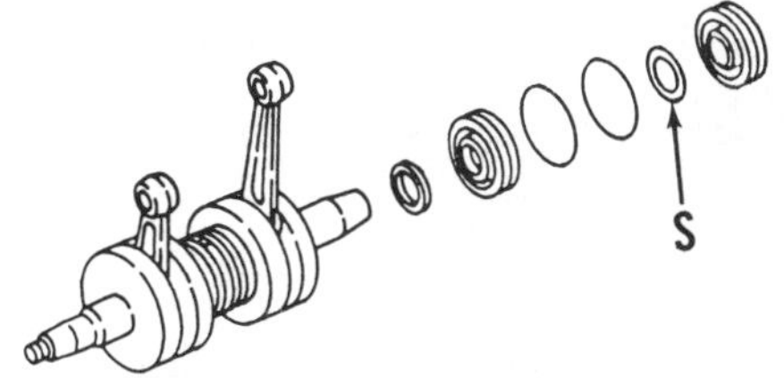

Fig. JD8 — End play adjustment shim for Models TA340A, TB340A, TA440A and TA440B.

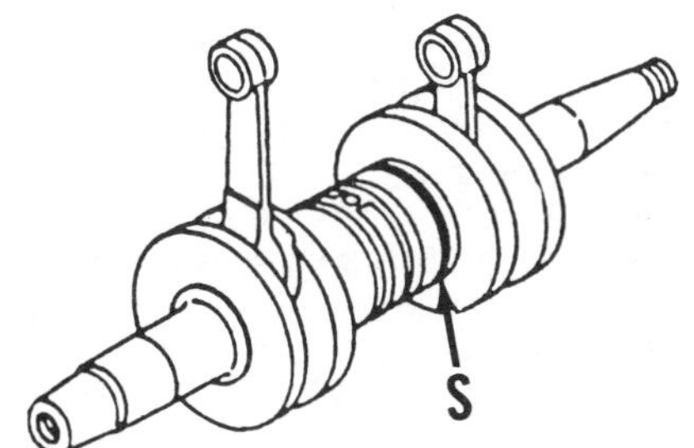

Fig. JD9 — End play adjustment shim for Model TC440A.

are a press fit on crankshaft. Rotate all bearings and renew those that are rough or frozen. Outside bearings may be renewed, but inner bearings are available only with crankshaft assembly. Special tools must be used to remove and renew outside bearings in order to prevent damaging crankshaft and components. Be sure to identify shims and washers as they are removed, so as to reinstall in same position as removed.

If crankshaft, bearings or crankcase are renewed, crankshaft must be centered in crankcase by measuring end play. Crankshaft end play should not exceed 0.030-inch on Models TA340A, TB340A and TA440A, 0.040-inch on Model TA440B and 0.015-inch on Model TC440A. If end play is out of specification, then shim (S – Fig. JD8) will need to be changed for all models except TC440A. For Model TC440A shim (S – Fig. JD9) will need to be changed.

Check crankshaft runout with a dial indicator after reassembly in crankcase. Runout should not exceed 0.002 inch on all models. If runout exceeds specifications, replace crankshaft assembly.

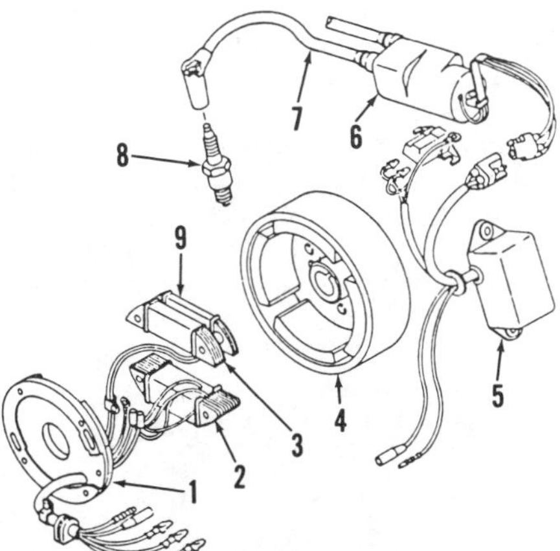

Fig. JD10 — View of a typical Capacitor Discharge Ignition system.

1. Stator plate
2. Lighting coil
3. Exciter coil
4. Flywheel
5. CDI unit
6. Ignition coil
7. Spark plug wire
8. Spark plug
9. Pulser coil

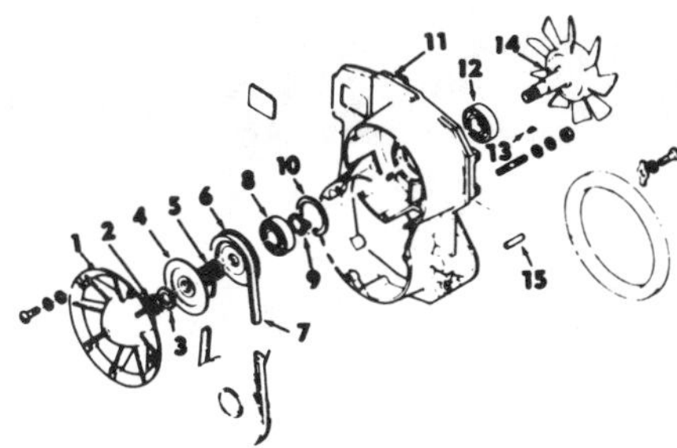

Fig. JD11 — Exploded view of cooling fan and housing unit.

1. Cover
2. Nut
3. Lockwasher
4. Pulley half
5. Shims
6. Pulley half
7. Belt
8. Bearing
9. Shim
10. Snap ring
11. Housing
12. Bearing
13. Key
14. Fan

ELECTRICAL SYSTEM. Refer to Fig. JD10 for view of a typical CDI unit. The Capacitor Discharge Ignition (CDI) system uses a permanent magnet flywheel (4) to induce voltage into exciter coil (3). The exciter coil then sends current to CDI unit (5) where a diode allows only DC current to flow into a capacitor. When gate control switch in CDI unit receives the small current signal from pulser coil (9), it closes and allows the capacitor to discharge its stored voltage into the ignition coil (6). The coil then "steps up" voltage enough to fire both spark plugs simultaneously.

If an engine problem is experienced check fuel system, electrical connections, wiring and spark plugs. To test CDI ignition system a special tester or ohmmeter must be used. **DO NOT** use a 12 volt test light as it may damage the CDI system.

COOLING FAN AND BELT. Belt tension should be adjusted to allow no more than 3/8-inch deflection midway between pulleys when depressed with finger. Belt can be adjusted by adding or removing shims (5 – Fig. JD11) from between fan pulley halves. Removing shims will tighten belt by allowing pulley rims to move closer together. Turn pulley slowly when assembling to keep from pinching belt in pulley. Removed shims can be stored outside of outer pulley half for re-use when a new belt is installed.

To renew belt, remove recoil starter, fan protector cover and air intake duct. Remove fan pulley outer half, then withdraw belt and slip it off lower drive pulley. Install new belt and adjust as outlined in previous paragraph. Reinstall parts removed during disassembly.

RECOIL STARTER. Refer to exploded view of a typical starter in Fig. JD12. Caution should be taken when disassembling starter, parts are under spring pressure.

To disassemble starter, remove starter from engine. Remove nut (1), lockwasher (2) and flat washer (3), then withdraw retaining plate (4). Remove center spring (5), return spring (6), pawls (13) and pawl springs (12). Remove bushing (7), thrust washer (8) and plates (9 and 10) on so equipped models. Rotate reel (11) to release spring (14) and lift reel (11) out of cover assembly (17). Unknot rope (16) to remove from reel (11). **DO NOT** remove spring (14) unless replacement is needed, as spring will rewind during removal.

Inspect and renew all parts that are damaged. Reassemble starter in reverse order of disassembly. Be sure springs hook in notches during assembly to insure proper operation of starter.

Fig. JD12 — View of a typical recoil starter assembly.

1. Nut
2. Lockwasher
3. Flat washer
4. Plate
5. Center spring
6. Return spring
7. Bushing
8. Thrust washer
9. Plate
10. Plate
11. Reel
12. Spring
13. Pawl
14. Spring
15. Handle
16. Rope
17. Cover

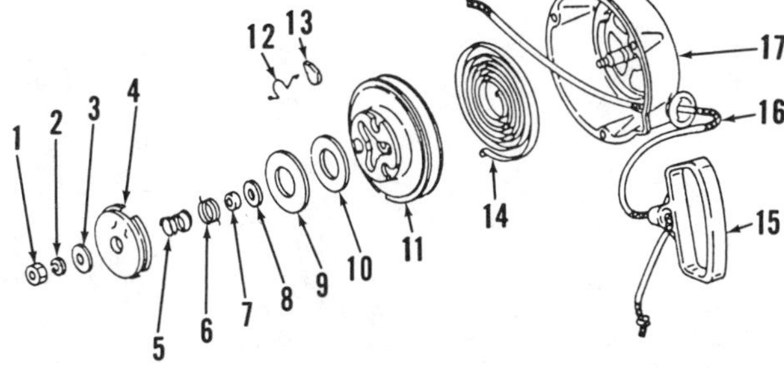

HARLEY-DAVIDSON

CONDENSED SERVICE DATA

ENGINE MODEL	Y-398	Y-440
Bore—(mm)	65.2	68
Inches	2.567	2.677
Stroke—(mm)	59.6	59.6
Inches	2.346	2.346
No. of Cylinders	2	2
Displacement—(cc)	398	433
Cubic Inches	24.3	26.4
Horsepower at RPM	34.5 at 6800	37.5 at 6800
Cooling Type	Centrifugal Fan	
Induction Type	Third Port	
Carburetor Make	Tillotson	Tillotson
Model	HD	HD
Number Used	1	1
Ignition Type	CD	CD
Timing Advance	Electronic	Electronic
Timing BTDC (Static)	To Dot	To Dot
(Running)	To Line	To Line
Spark Plug Make	Harley-Davidson	
Model	SD-20	SD-20
Electrode Gap	Fixed	Fixed
Fuel/Oil Ratio	50:1	50:1

MAINTENANCE

SPARK PLUG. Spark plugs are surface gap type. Gap is fixed and plug operates satisfactorily over a wide heat range. Look for serious erosion of center electrode or physical damage and renew plugs as indicated. Spark plug tightening torque is 28 ft.-lbs. (4 kg/m).

CARBURETOR. A single Tillotson HD carburetor is used on all models. Initial setting for idle mixture needle on all 1973 and earlier models is 7/8-turns open from closed position. Initial idle mixture setting for 1974 and later Y-398 engine is 3/4-turn open; for 1974 and later Y-440, 1-turn. Initial mixture setting for high speed mixture needle is 3/4-turn for 1973 and earlier Y-398 models; 7/8-turn for later Y-398 and all Y-440 units. Adjust slow idle speed to approximately 1200 rpm with engine at operating temperature and idle mixture needle adjusted for best performance.

Refer to TILLOTSON Section in CARBURETOR SERVICE for carburetor overhaul data and procedures.

LUBRICATION. The engine is lubricated by oil mixed with the fuel. The manufacturer recommends that only high octane (Premium) leaded gasoline and Harley-Davidson 50/1 Sno-Oil be mixed at a ratio of 50:1. This is equivalent to one 16 oz. can to 6 US Gallons of fuel.

Do not use unleaded or low lead gasoline which contains phosphorus. A good grade air-cooled, two-cycle engine oil can be substituted for Sno-Oil in case of emergency.

IGNITION AND ELECTRICAL SYSTEM. A breakerless CD ignition system is combined with the flywheel alternator. Timing is fixed and not adjustable, and can only be checked with a power timing light at running speed. Primary charging coils, capacitor, and associated parts are common for both cylinders; while trigger windings, SCR's and pulse transformers (ignition coils) are individually provided for each cylinder.

Failure to start or failure to run where the ignition system is the cause would probably indicate a fault in the common ignition components which include cranking winding (in stator), running winding (in stator), ignition module, key switch, emergency stop switch or wiring.

Missing on one cylinder from ignition cause would probably indicate a fault in trigger winding (in stator), pulse transformer (ignition coil), spark plug or wiring. Components and connectors are mounted on front side of console underneath the hood.

If the battery fails to charge on electric start models or lights fail to light on manual start, temporarily disconnect regulator at plug connector. If lights now light or generator charges, regulator is at fault. Remaining components can be individually checked using an ohmmeter or battery powered continuity light of 12 volts or less.

Refer to Fig. 2 for an underhood (front) view of console showing location of connector plugs and electrical system components. Disconnect battery

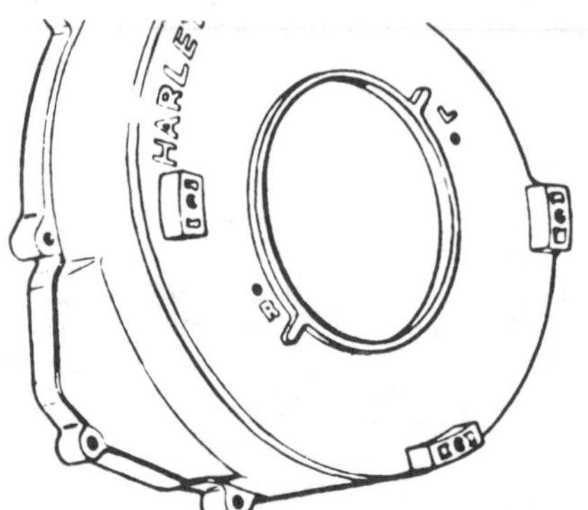

Fig. 1—Fan shroud carries retard (dot) and running (bar) timing marks for right and left cylinder as shown. Timing can only be checked with a power timing light at running speed.

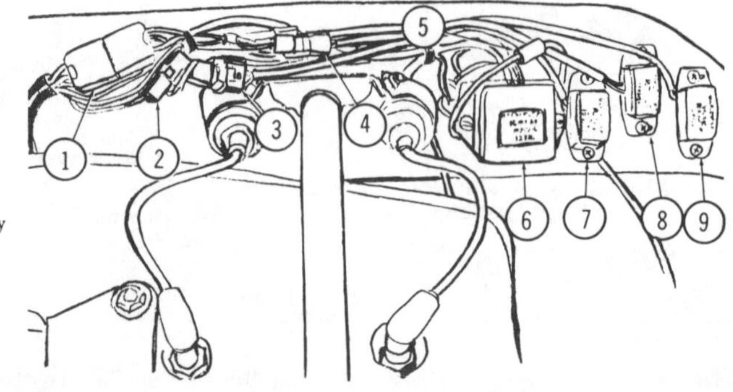

Fig. 2—Front view of console showing electrical system components and wiring.

1. Ignition Module Connector
2. Voltage Regulator Connector
3. Isolation Diode Connector
4. Rectifier Connector
5. Isolation Diode Wire to Battery
6. Ignition Module
7. Isolation Diode
8. Rectifier
9. Voltage Regulator

ground strap (if so equipped) and plugs (1, 2, 3, 4 and 5) before attempting to make any tests. Refer to Fig. 3.

Ignition module connector (1) joins the ignition module (6) to the ignition units of stator, located underneath engine flywheel. The connector unites six wires with functions and color codes as follows:

BROWN—Cranking impulse coil; which provides current to capacitor at cranking speed. The other end of cranking coil is grounded to stator frame.

LIGHT GREEN—Running impulse coil; which provides current to capacitor at running speed. The other end of running coil is grounded to stator frame.

GRAY—Ground lead; which provides a common ground for stator frame.

DARK GREEN—Common return lead for both trigger coils. Trigger coils are insulated from stator frame and from output coils of alternator.

YELLOW—Right trigger coil lead. The other end of coil is connected to Dark Green lead. The right trigger coil turns on the SCR which sends the capacitor charge to the ignition coil firing the right spark plug.

BLUE—Left trigger coil lead. The other end of coil is connected to Dark Green lead. The left trigger coil turns on the SCR which sends the capacitor charge to the ignition coil firing the left spark plug.

The voltage regulator connector (2) joins the RED regulating coil wire in stator and also connects the BLACK loop lead from isolation diode connector (3) to zener diode in regulator. Regulating coil windings in stator are wound continuously around all of the twelve pole shoe legs, but in the opposite direction to the two charging coils. When battery voltage increases to more than 14 volts, current passes the zener diode and turns on the SCR in regulator to complete the circuit to regulating coil. Output voltage is thus stopped or reduced to prevent battery overcharge or system damage.

Isolation diode connector (3) carries the DC output current from the WHITE center tapping of the two phase alternator windings through an isolation diode to the positive battery terminal (if so equipped), or to light switch on manual start models. The BLACK wire loop leads to voltage regulator connector to provide control current for the regulator.

The rectifier connector (4) connects both end windings of the two phase alternator coil to a common ground within the rectifier body. Both leads are black but one is identified by a flag (L-1) attached to stator lead wire adjacent to the female plug. This winding is farthest from the red lead running from regulator winding. The two diodes in rectifier body are identical in capacity and bias. Diodes provide alternate half-wave rectification to the two phases, resulting in the equivalent of full wave rectification on a single phase alternating current. Connector is installed with male plug on rectifier module and female plug on stator cable to prevent accidental interconnecting of the two units during installation or service. Refer to Fig. 3 for an exploded view of electrical system components and wiring.

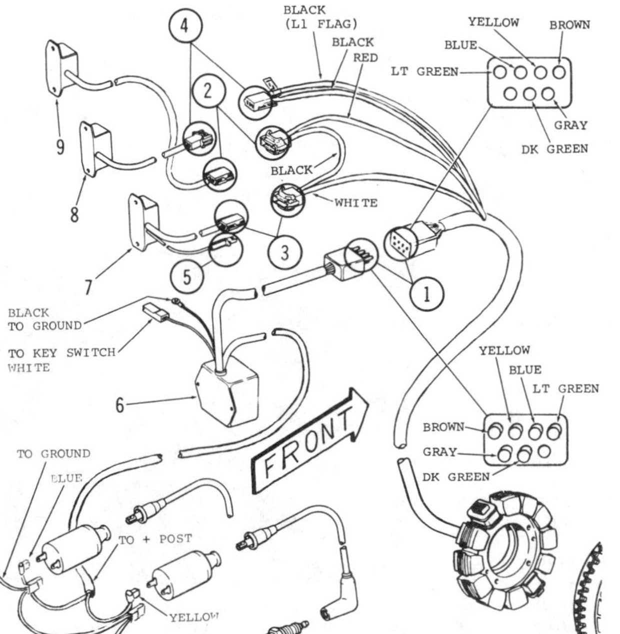

Fig. 3—Schematic exploded view of wiring harness and components showing color coding. Refer to Fig. 2 for number designations.

STATOR TEST. Stator windings can be checked for shorts, grounds and continuity without removing stator from engine. First disconnect ground wire from battery (if so equipped) and all connectors (1, 2, 3, 4, & 5—Fig. 3). Check alternator windings for grounds to stator frame by touching ohmmeter probes to GRAY terminal of ignition module female plug (1) and WHITE terminal of isolation diode male plug (3). There should be NO CONTINUITY. Check regulator and output windings for shorts and opens by touching ohmmeter probes to FLAGGED BLACK LEAD of rectifier female plug (4) and RED terminal of regulator male plug (2). This checks current flow through regulator windings and both output windings; ohmmeter reading should be 3.0-3.5 on accurate low meter scale. A lower reading would indicate a short within the windings, while an extremely high or infinity reading would indicate an open.

Ignition generating windings are grounded to stator frame but trigger windings are not. Check trigger windings for grounds by touching ohmmeter probes to DARK GREEN and GRAY terminals of ignition module female plug (1). There should be NO CONTINUITY. Touch ohmmeter probes to GRAY and BROWN terminals of ignition module female plug; ohmmeter reading should be 2300-2500 ohms measured on high reading scale of ohmmeter. Touch ohmmeter probes to GRAY and LIGHT GREEN terminals of ignition module female plug (1); ohmmeter reading should be 85-95 ohms. Trigger windings can be checked for continuity and shorts using the ohmmeter. Check between DARK GREEN and BLUE leads of ignition module female plug for LEFT trigger coil; and DARK GREEN and YELLOW leads for RIGHT trigger coil. Reading should be 1.3-1.7 ohms for either coil. Plug terminals can be renewed if damaged, or damaged stator leads can be repaired. If stator windings are damaged, renew the unit.

System modules can be checked using an ohmmeter or battery powered continuity light of 12 volts or less.

IGNITION MODULE. The ignition module has ten terminals; six in the male plug (1—Fig. 3) leading to stator, two in the twin lead to pulse transformer (ignition coil) plus terminals, and the two single leads to module ground and key switch.

There should be continuity in either direction between BLACK (module ground) lead and GRAY (stator ground) terminal in multiple plug (1). There should be continuity in either direction between BROWN terminal in multiple plug and either of the ground terminals. There should be continuity in either direction between DARK GREEN terminal in multiple plug and WHITE terminal leading to key switch.

There should be continuity in ONE DIRECTION ONLY when checking between DARK GREEN terminal and BROWN terminal in multiple plug. There should be continuity in one direction only when checking between DARK GREEN terminal in multiple plug and either of the ground leads. There should be continuity in one direction only when checking between WHITE (key switch) lead and BROWN terminal in multiple plug or either of the ground leads. There should be continuity in one direction only when checking between BLUE or YELLOW terminal in multiple plug and either of the grounded leads.

There should be NO CONTINUITY IN EITHER DIRECTION when checking between YELLOW or BLUE flag leads leading to pulse transformers and ANY OTHER TERMINAL. There should be no continuity in either direction between LIGHT GREEN terminal in multiple plug and ANY OTHER TERMINAL.

If module fails to test as indicated, renew the unit.

ISOLATION DIODE. The isolation diode (7—Fig. 3) permits charging current to enter battery circuit but prevents reverse flow from battery. Touch ohmmeter or test light probes to the two terminals of female plug (3). There should be continuity in one direction but no continuity when probes are reversed. Battery positive lead (5) is connected to BLACK lead of connector plug. If module fails to test as indicated, renew the unit.

RECTIFIER. The rectifier module (8—Fig. 3) contains two diodes of identical bias, grounded to module base and connected to the two leads of male plug (4). Touch one ohmmeter probe to module base and the other probe to each plug terminal in turn; then reverse the probes and repeat the test. There should be continuity in one direction but no continuity in the other, and both terminals should test the same. If rectifier fails to pass the test, renew the unit.

VOLTAGE REGULATOR. The voltage regulator (9—Fig. 3) contains a zener diode and SCR, both of which ground to regulator base. There is no suitable test of regulator. There should be continuity in one direction only between the BLACK terminal of female plug (2) and module base. There should be no continuity in either direction between the two plug terminals, or between RED plug terminal and module base. If alternator fails to charge, the most effective test is to temporarily disconnect regulator plug (2) and restart engine. If unit charges with regulator disconnected, renew the regulator. In the event of chronic overcharge, renew the regulator.

REPAIRS

ENGINE REMOVAL AND INSTALLATION. On 1973 and earlier models, remove engine from rear after removing seat cushion, battery box and drive belt. Remove the bolts securing handlebar support tube and control panel to frame and using a suitable overhead support, tie handlebar and control panel up out of the way. Disconnect fuel lines, exhaust pipe, wiring and controls.

On 1974 and later models, remove engine from front after removing fuel tank, battery, fan housing head shield, muffler and drive belt. Remove the socket head pipe plug from lower end of steering column and pull column upward out of steering arm and lower support. Disconnect throttle and brake control cables at handlebar ends. Unmount cutout switch and dimmer switch from handlebar, then withdraw handlebar and steering column upward out of machine.

On all models, mark position of engine mounting braces on two diagonally opposite frame cross braces so engine can be reinstalled without major belt realignment. Remove the four cap screws securing engine mounting braces to frame.

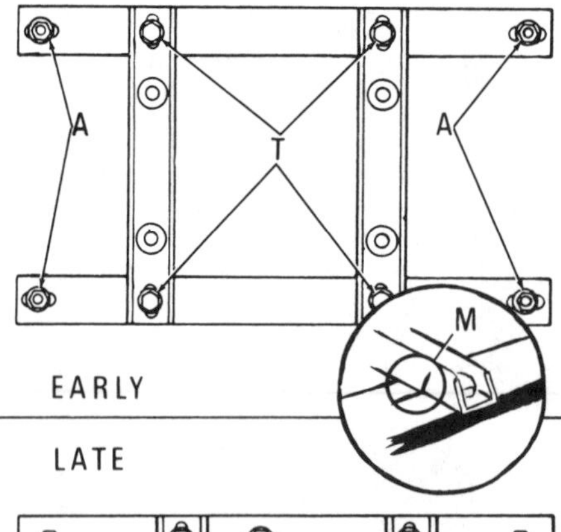

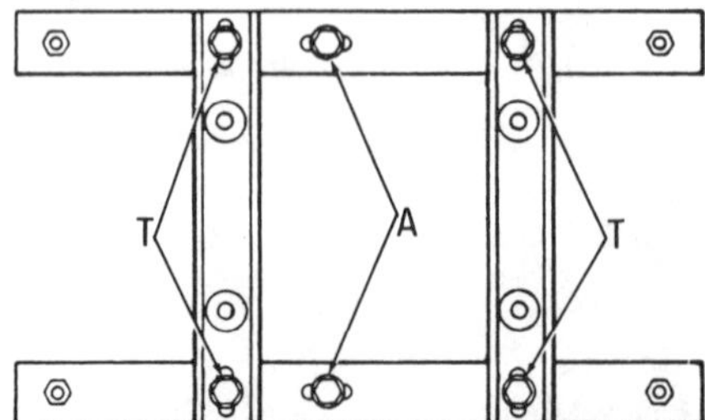

Fig. 4—Schematic view of early and late type engine mounts showing adjustments (A) for drive belt alignment; and (T) for tightening drive belt. Scribed installation marks (M) will assist in engine removal and installation.

On 1973 and earlier models, move engine to rear, passing under control panel; then lift engine out. On 1974 and later models, lift engine slightly and turn counter-clockwise until engine shroud will clear driven pulley. Slide engine forward and lift from machine.

On all models, install by reversing removal procedure, aligning scribe marks as mounting bolts are tightened. Check belt alignment after installation. Tighten mounting bolts to a torque of 35 ft.-lbs. (4.8 kg-m).

TIGHTENING TORQUES. Harley-Davidson engine tightening torques are as follows:

Crankcase flange bolts
(6 mm) . . . . 72 in.-lbs. (83 kg-cm)
Crankcase bolts
(8 mm) . . . . 15 ft.-lbs. (2 kg-m)
Cylinder head
nuts . . . . 10 ft.-lbs. (1.4 kg-m)
Engine to mounting
brace . . . . 80 ft.-lbs. (11 kg-m)
Exhaust pipe to
cylinder . . . . 12 ft.-lbs. (1.7 kg-m)
Fan housing to
crankcase . . . . 6 ft.-lbs. (0.8 kg-m)
Muffler to cylinder
head . . . . 20 ft.-lbs. (2.8 kg-m)
Mounting bolts to cross-
brace . . . . 35 ft.-lbs. (4.8 kg-m)

DISASSEMBLY AND REASSEMBLY. It is recommended that engine be removed for most engine service. Remove primary drive clutch as outlined in VEHICLE SECTION. Remove cylinder air shroud and outer & inner fan shrouds. Remove fan wheel nut, then remove fan wheel using the special puller (Part. No. 97293-71) as shown in Fig. 5.

Cylinders and/or cylinder heads can be removed without removing fan wheel or fan shrouds. Cylinders, cylinder heads, pistons and rings are interchangeable between right and left sides, and should be appropriately marked during removal if they are to be reinstalled. When reassembling, note that exhaust port side of cylinder goes to mounting base side of crankcase and that arrow on top of piston

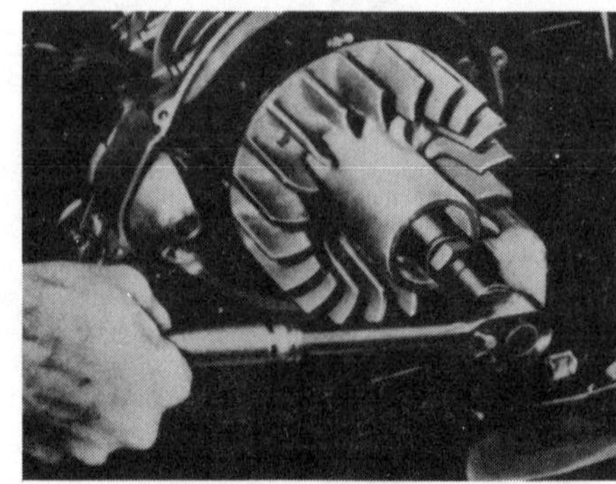

Fig. 5—A wood block wedged in fanwheel fins will assist in holding for flywheel nut removal.

crown points toward exhaust port side of cylinder. Edges of cylinder head fins align on exhaust port side.

Crankcase can be separated after removing drive clutch, shrouds, fan wheel, cylinder heads, cylinders and pistons. Stator is secured to fan wheel end of crankcase by four slotted head screws and two dowels, and can be installed 180 degrees off. Mark stator for correct reassembly, then remove stator. Drive the drive-end locating dowel downward out of crankcase flange as shown in Fig. 6.

Bend down corners of lockplates then remove engine mounting bolts, mounting braces and spacers, noting that longest bolts and spacers are installed to rear, engine mounted. If crankshaft is not to be disassembled or crankcase renewed, measure crankshaft end play using a dial indicator as shown in Fig. 7 End play should be 0.006-0.008 inch (0.15-0.2 mm), and is controlled by shims installed on both ends of crankshaft at reassembly. Remove flange cap screws, then tap crankcase apart using a plastic hammer. Lift out crankshaft and main bearings as an assembly. Handle crankshaft carefully while removed; crankshaft is pressed together and misalignment is possible if roughly handled. Refer to the appropriate following paragraphs for service on shaft and main bearings.

When reassembling, thoroughly clean mating flanges of crankcase halves of old cement and examine for nicks and burrs. When positioning crankshaft assembly in lower crankcase half, note that main bearing components are positioned by locating dowels; make sure dowels enter dowel hole in bearing shells. Apply a thin coating of LOCTITE Plastic Gasket (HD Part No. 99622-65) or PERMATEX No. 2 to mating surfaces of crankcase halves. Tighten cap screws evenly to 72 in.-lbs. (83 kg-cm) for flange screws and 15 ft.-lbs. (2 kg-m) for 8 mm screws, then reinstall aligning dowel. Complete the assembly by reversing disassembly procedure.

PISTONS, PINS, RINGS AND CYLINDERS. Mark the cylinders, pistons, rings and piston pin bearings as they are removed, for correct reassembly to each other and in the original location (flywheel or output shaft end of engine). Used parts MUST NOT be interchanged between the cylinders when reassembling. Be careful to prevent anything from falling into crankcase. Also use care to prevent distortion or damage to connecting rods.

Most 1972 Y398 engines were equipped with a cast iron cylinder. On these engines, pistons and rings are available in oversizes of 0.2, 0.4, 0.6 and 0.8 mm (0.008, 0.016, 0.024 and 0.315 inch) as well as standard. On later Y398 and all Y440 engines use a chrome plated aluminum cylinder, and cylinder and piston are only available as a matched set.

Piston to cylinder clearance, measured at right angles to piston pin, 3/4-inch from bottom of skirt, should be 0.003-0.004 inch (0.08-0.1 mm) for models with cast iron cylinder, or 0.001-0.0025 inch (0.025-0.06 mm) for models with chrome cylinder. Piston ring end gap should be 0.010-0.016 inch (0.25-0.4 mm). On engines with cast iron cylinder, piston ring side clearance should be 0.004-0.006 inch (0.1-0.15 mm) for both rings; on later engines, top ring side clearance should be 0.006-0.008 inch (0.15-0.2 mm) and lower ring side clearance should be 0.003-0.005 inch (0.07-0.13 mm). Piston pin should have a slight interference fit in piston bosses at room temperature, but should be a light push fit when piston is heated. Piston rings are pinned to prevent rotation of ring ends. Top of piston crown is marked with the stamped letters "SC" and an arrow. Arrow should point toward exhaust port location when piston is installed.

CONNECTING RODS, CRANKSHAFT AND BEARINGS. The crankshaft assembly consists of three machined counterweight and main bearing sections which press onto the two crankpins; see Figs. 10 and 11. The center main journal contains two split, caged needle bearings and a split pressure seal as shown in Fig. 9. End main journals are each supported in a

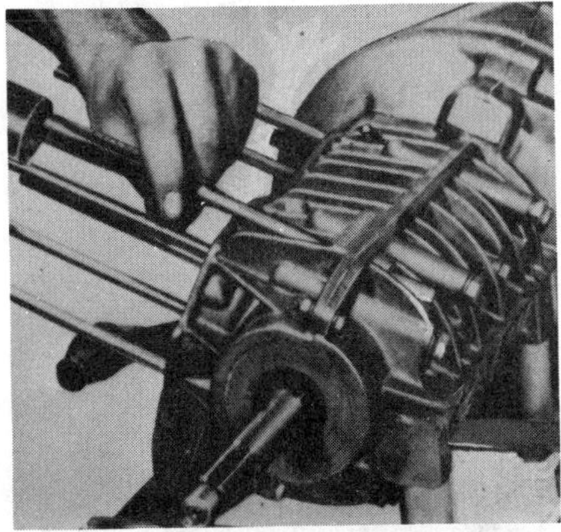

Fig. 6—Drive out front crankcase aligning dowel as shown, for easier disassembly.

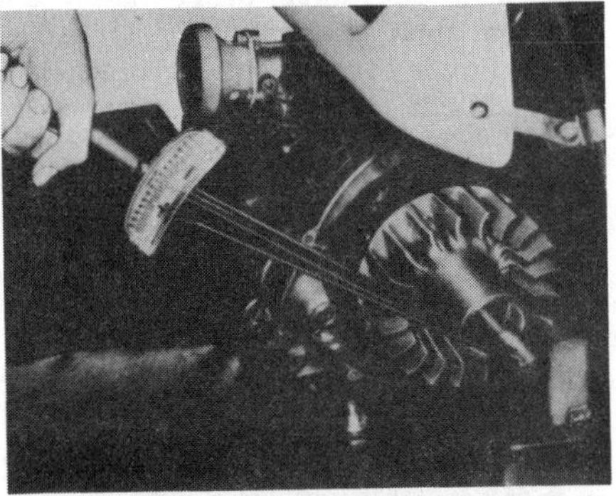

Fig. 8—Tighten flywheel nut to 80 ft.-lbs. (11.0 kg-m) using a torque wrench.

Fig. 7—Measure crankshaft end play using a dial indicator to determine shims required in assembly.

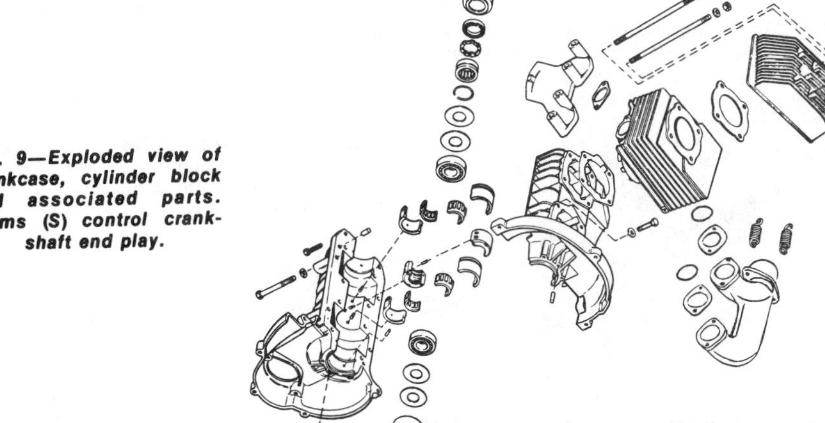

Fig. 9—Exploded view of crankcase, cylinder block and associated parts. Shims (S) control crankshaft end play.

ball-type main bearing and a caged needle bearing housing which also contains the outer crankshaft seal. Center main bearing outer races are machined in one piece and precision ground, then "fractured" for perfect realignment when installed. Parts MUST NOT be intermixed or turned end-for-end when unit is assembled. If in doubt, fit the two empty halves together before installing and check the parting line; when correctly assembled, the two edges can hardly be seen and cannot be felt with fingernail.

To disassemble the outer main bearing housing, pry out the outer retaining ring with a small screwdriver as shown in Fig. 12. Press out the caged needle bearing, spacer and seal at the same time, using a suitable arbor. Leave inner retaining ring installed in housing bore. Assemble by reversing disassembly procedure.

Crankshaft and connecting rods are available as an assembly which includes all of the parts shown in Fig. 11. Individual crank units are also available separately except that crankpin, connecting rod and caged needle roller are furnished as a matched set. Do not attempt to disassemble the crankshaft unit unless proper equipment and training is available to correctly reassemble the unit. End play of connecting rod in the assembled unit should be 0.012-0.016 inch (0.3-0.4 mm) for 1973 and earlier models; or 0.016-0.020 inch (0.4-0.5 mm) for later engines. Crankshaft runout should not exceed 0.001 inch (0.025 mm) measured at center journal or flywheel end journal; or 0.002 inch (0.05 mm) measured at drive end journal.

Crankshaft end play should be 0.006-0.008 inch (0.15-0.2 mm) and is controlled by shims (S—Fig. 9). Make a trial assembly if adjustment is required, and measure end play with a dial indicator. Divide shims equally at each end of housing. Shims (S) are available in thicknesses of 0.4, 0.6 and 0.8 mm (0.016, 0.024 and 0.315 inch).

RECOIL STARTER (EARLY MODELS). Some early models use the Fairbanks-Morse type friction starter shown in Fig. 13. Most starter trouble is likely to occur in one of three major areas: failure to engage, broken starter cable, or damaged or broken recoil spring.

If handle pulls out and recoils properly but starter fails to engage or hold on flywheel, trouble is probably in friction shoe assembly (F). With starter removed, examine assembly for damage and adequate lubrication. The friction shoe assembly (Inset) can be turned over to reverse the rotation. Be sure shoe is installed with sharp edges trailing as shown. Edges may be resharpened if desired, providing original contour is not changed. Refer to Fig. 14 when reassembling friction shoe unit. Lubricate center shaft with General Electric Versilube G-322-L or equivalent when friction shoe is reassembled.

If it becomes necessary to unload the recoil spring for pulley removal, pull a little slack into cable and turn pulley until cable notch in pulley rim aligns with cable hole in housing as shown in Fig. 15. Pull a section of cable out between pulley rim and housing using a

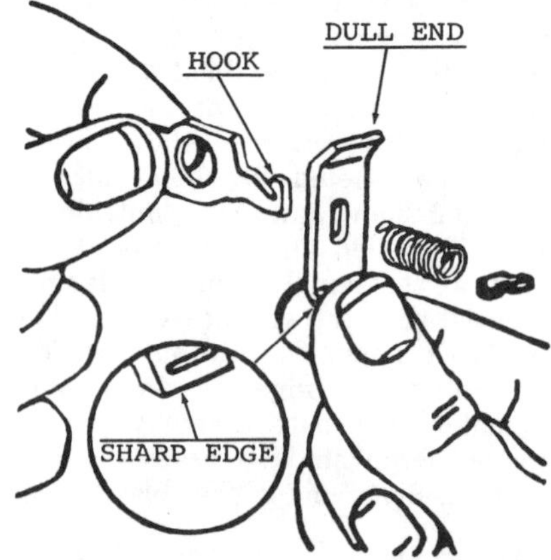

Fig. 14—Correct method of assembling friction shoe assembly.

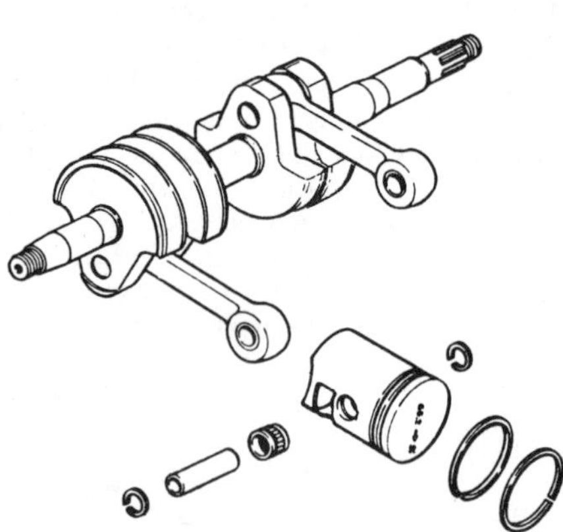
Fig. 10—Assembled view of crankshaft and connecting rod unit with piston assembly exploded.

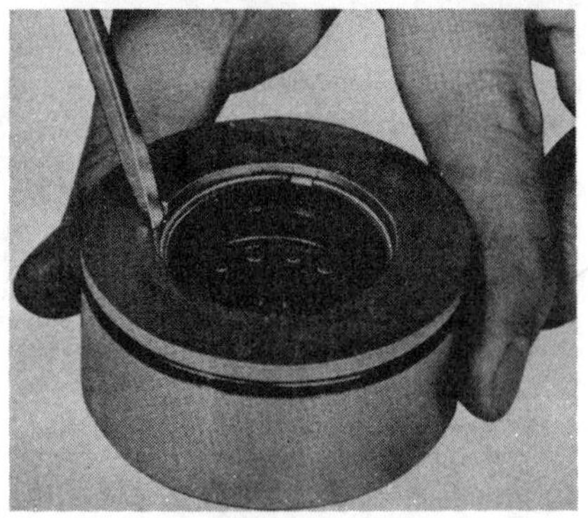
Fig. 12—Disassembling outer main bearing housing.

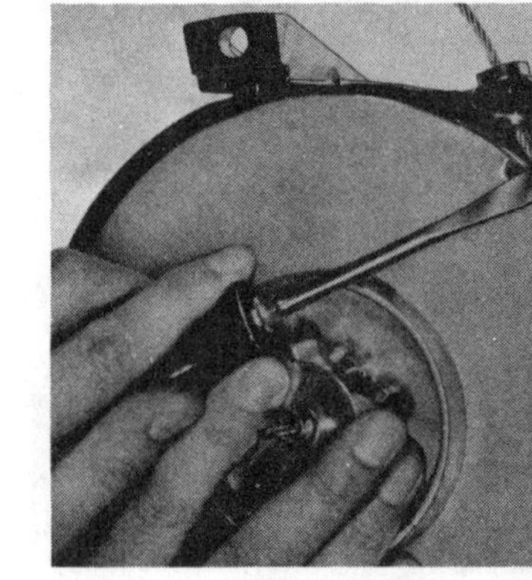
Fig. 15—To remove pulley or recoil spring, first pick up recoil cable using a hooked tool or screwdriver as shown.

Fig. 11—Exploded view of crankshaft and connecting rod unit. Refer to Fig. 10 for assembled view.

Fig. 13—Exploded view of Fairbanks Morse type recoil starter used on some early models.

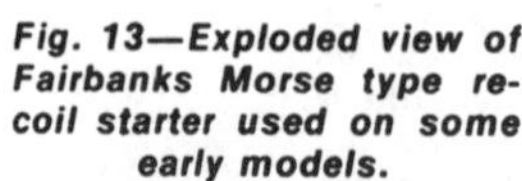
C. Cable
F. Friction shoe assy.
P. Centering pin
R. Recoil spring

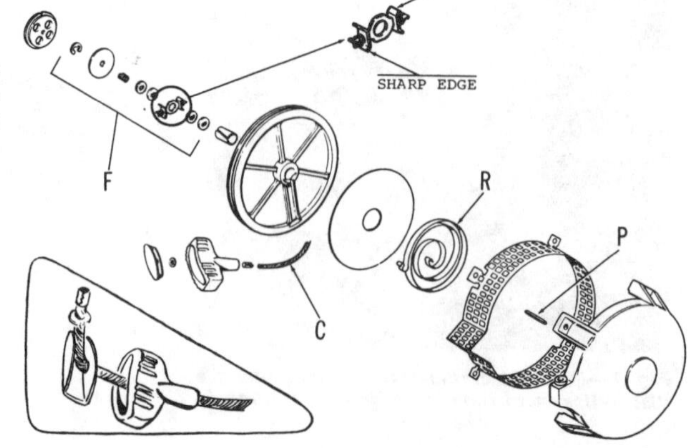

screwdriver or hooked wire; draw cable into unloading notch and hold in place while spring unwinds. Remove friction shoe assembly, then carefully lift pulley out of housing well, making sure inner end of spring unhooks from lug on back face of pulley. Recoil spring can be installed for clockwise or counter-clockwise rotation. Spring must be installed as shown in Fig. 13. Install spring in recess in housing, making sure hooked outer end engages anchor pin. Make sure inner hook engages tab in pulley hub as pulley is installed, and that cable is pulled up into unloading notch in pulley rim. Turn pulley counter-clockwise until spring is fully wound; allow pulley to unwind until cable notch aligns with cable hole in housing. Pull all slack to outside, then allow spring to recoil; cable handle should pull up against housing.

To install a new cable, remove pulley as previously outlined, then remove old cable. Thread new cable through hole in housing. Pry metal keeper out of rubber handle and remove old cable, saving handle, keeper and metal washer. Thread new cable through handle and keeper as shown in inset. Install the old washer, then install the new cable clip at extreme outer end of cable, crimping the clip with pliers until points are imbedded in cable strands. Solder clip into position and work clip back into position in keeper. Pull rubber handle back over keeper. Anchor opposite end of cable into pulley and complete the installation as previously outlined for spring renewal.

RECOIL STARTER (LATE MODELS). Refer to Fig. 16 for exploded view of recoil starter of the type used on late models. Pawls (P) are retracted by spring action and extended by friction of actuating cam (A) when rope is pulled. Pawl action can be observed by pulling rope slowly with starter removed, and serviced by removing the retaining cap screw (S).

A new starter cord (C) can be installed without removing pulley, if old cord can be withdrawn. Turn pulley counter-clockwise until spring is fully wound, then allow spring to unwind until rope anchor hole in pulley aligns with rope bushing in housing. Tie a knot in end of new rope and thread the rope in through anchor hole in pulley and out through rope bushing. Tie a slip knot in free end of rope and allow pulley to retract until stopped by the temporary knot. Reinstall handle and allow rope to retract.

To remove the pulley, pry retainer out of rubber handle and untie or cut retaining knot; then allow pulley to turn until spring is unwound. Remove retaining cap screw (S) and lift off pulley, making sure inner end of spring unhooks from notch on under side of pulley hub. When reassembling, make sure spring winds counter-clockwise from anchor post in housing and that inner end engages anchor notch in pulley hub. Unwind rope from pulley groove and pull rope into notch in pulley rim. After reinstalling retaining cap screw (S), wind pulley counter-clockwise until spring is fully wound. Allow spring to retract until pulley notch aligns with rope bushing hole in housing, feed rope out through bushing and install the handle. Allow rope to slowly retract into housing.

ELECTRIC STARTER. Refer to Fig. 17 for an exploded view. Starter has a no-load speed of 4500 rpm at 11.0 volts and 60 amperes.

Armature shaft end play should be 0.002-0.014 inch (0.05-0.35 mm) and is controlled by thickness of shim washers (W) located at drive end of armature shaft. Washers (W) are available in thicknesses of 0.004 and 0.012 inch (0.1-0.3 mm). Also a 0.040 inch (1.0 mm) shim (S) is provided to space starter away from flywheel if it meshes too deep.

Starter drive clutch is positioned on shaft by a stop collar (C—Fig. 18) and snap ring (R) which fits in a deep groove (G) in shaft and shallow groove in collar. To remove drive clutch, bump collar toward drive pinion using an appropriate size pipe spacer, extract snap ring (R), then slip collar and drive from the shaft. When reassembling, suitably support the shaft and pry collar down over snap ring until it snaps in place. Maximum permissible shaft side play in any bushing is 0.008 inch (0.2 mm). Maximum permissible commutator runout is 0.016 inch (0.4 mm). Undercut mica to a depth of 0.025 inch (0.635 mm) whenever commutator is turned.

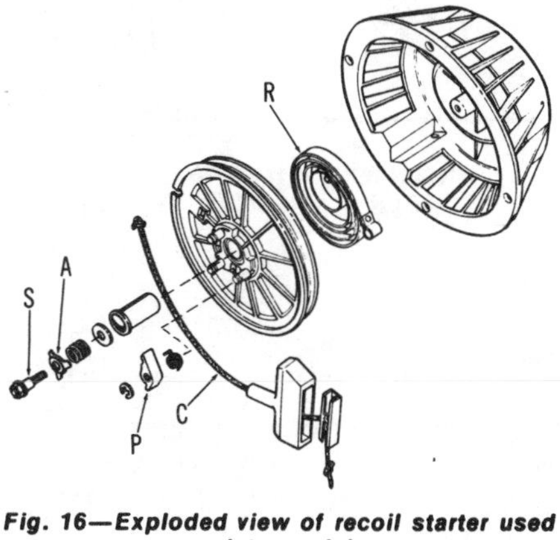

Fig. 16—Exploded view of recoil starter used on late models.

A. Actuating cam
C. Starter cord
P. Pawl (3 used)
R. Recoil spring
S. Cap screw

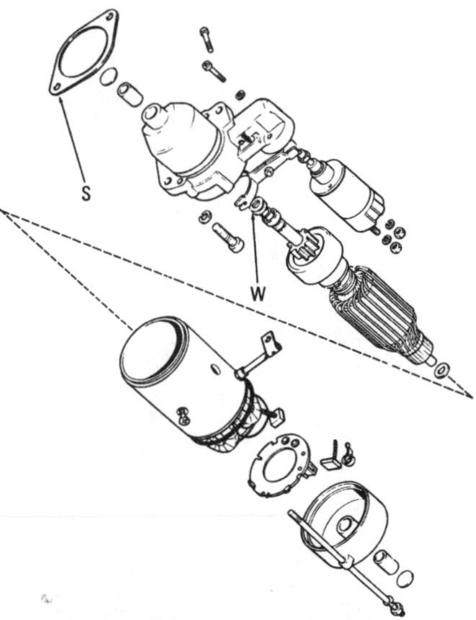

Fig. 17—Exploded view of electric starter of type used on models so equipped.

S. Spacer shim
W. Shim washer

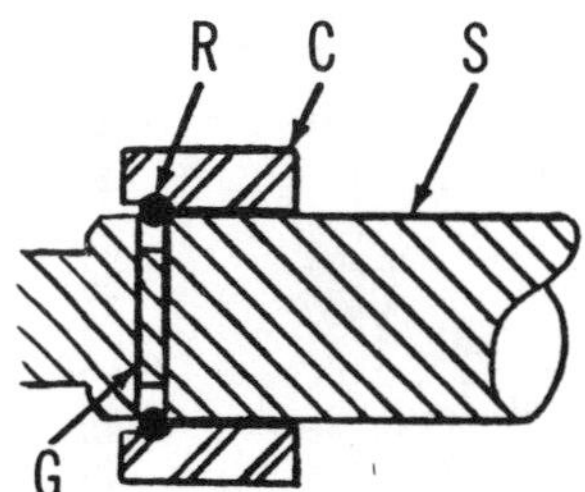

Fig. 18—Cross sectional view of armature shaft showing details of drive clutch stop collar. Refer to text for details of removal and installation.

C. Stop collar
G. Shaft groove
R. Snap ring
S. Armature shaft

HIRTH SINGLE CYLINDER

CONDENSED SERVICE DATA

Years Made	1965-66	1966-70	1969-70
ENGINE MODEL	81R	82R	56R
Bore—(mm)	70	70	74
Inches	2.756	2.756	2.913
Stroke—(mm)	64	64	68
Inches	2.520	2.520	2.677
No. of Cylinders	1	1	1
Displacement—(cc)	246	246	292
Cubic Inches	15.0	15.0	17.8
Horsepower @ RPM	10 @ 5000	12 @ 5000	15 @ 5000
Cooling Type		Centrifugal Fan	
Carburetor Model	HL	HR	....
Number Used	1	1	1
Ignition:			
Type		BOSCH Magneto	
Point Gap—(mm)	0.4	0.4	0.4
Inch	0.016	0.016	0.016
Timing Advance?	No	No	Yes
Timing BTDC (mm)	2.6	2.6	0.3
Inch	0.102	0.102	0.013
Degrees	21°	21°	7°
Measured	....	....	Retard
Spark Plug:			
Bosch	M225T1	M225T1	M225T1
Electrode Gap (mm)	0.5	0.5	0.5
Inch	0.020	0.020	0.020
Fuel/Oil Ratio	25:1	25:1	25:1

Years Made	1966-67	1967-68	1967-68
ENGINE MODEL	54R	55R	190R
Bore—(mm)	75	75	75
Inches	2.953	2.953	2.953
Stroke—(mm)	68	68	68
Inches	2.677	2.677	2.677
No. of Cylinders	1	1	1
Displacement—(cc)	300	300	300
Cubic Inches	18.3	18.3	18.3
Horsepower @ RPM	15 @ 5000	15 @ 5000	19 @ 5000
Cooling Type		Centrifugal Fan	
Carburetor Model	HR	HR	HR
Number Used	1	1	1
Ignition			
Type		BOSCH Magneto	
Point Gap—(mm)	0.4	0.4	0.4
Inch	0.016	0.016	0.016
Timing Advance?	Yes	Yes	Yes
Timing BTDC (mm)	0.32	0.32	0.32
Inch	0.0126	0.0126	0.0126
Degrees	7°	7°	7°
Measured at	Retard	Retard	Retard
Spark Plug:			
Bosch	M225T1	M225T1	M225T1
Electrode Gap (mm)	0.5	0.5	0.5
Inch	0.020	0.020	0.020
Fuel/Oil Ratio	25:1	25:1	25:1

Years Made	1969-70	1964-65	1965-66
ENGINE MODEL	193R	52R	53R
Bore—(mm)	74	75	75
Inches	2.913	2.953	2.953
Stroke—(mm)	68	68	68
Inches	2.677	2.677	2.677
No. of Cylinders	1	1	1
Displacement—(cc)	292	300	300
Cubic Inches	17.8	18.3	18.3
Horsepower @ RPM	19 @ 5500	12.5 @ 5000	13 @ 5000
Cooling Type		Centrifugal Fan	
Carburetor Model	HD	HL	HL
Number Used	1	1	1
Ignition:			
Type		BOSCH Magneto	
Point Gap—(mm)	0.4	0.4	0.4
Inch	0.016	0.016	0.016
Timing Advance?	Yes	No	No
Timing BTDC (mm)	0.3	2.1	2.1
Inch	0.013	0.083	0.083
Degrees	7°	18°	18°
Measured at	Retard	....	....
Spark Plug:			
Bosch	M225T1	M225T1	M225T1
Electrode Gap (mm)	0.5	0.5	0.5
Inch	0.020	0.020	0.020
Fuel/Oil Ratio	25:1	25:1	25:1

Years Made	1968-69	1968-70	1969-70
ENGINE MODEL	191R	192R	194R
Bore—(mm)	75	77	79.5
Inches	2.953	3.032	3.129
Stroke—(mm)	68	68	68
Inches	2.677	2.677	2.677
No. of Cylinders	1	1	1
Displacement—(cc)	300	317	338
Cubic Inches	18.3	19.3	20.6
Horsepower @ RPM	19 @ 5500	20.5 @ 5750	28 @ 6500
Cooling Type		Centrifugal Fan	
Carburetor Model	HR	HR	HD
Number Used	1	1	1
Ignition:			
Type		BOSCH Magneto	
Point Gap—(mm)	0.4	0.4	0.4
Inch	0.016	0.016	0.016
Timing Advance?	Yes	Yes	Yes
Timing BTDC (mm)	0.32	0.32	0.32
Inch	0.0126	0.0126	0.0126
Degrees	7°	7°	7°
Measured at	Retard	Retard	Retard
Spark Plug:			
Bosch	M225T1	M225T1	M225T1
Electrode Gap (mm)	0.5	0.5	0.5
Inch	0.020	0.020	0.020
Fuel/Oil Ratio	25:1	25:1	25:1

Years Made	1967-68	1968-69
ENGINE MODEL	160R	200R
Bore—(mm)	80.5	80.5
Inches	3.169	3.169
Stroke—(mm)	73	73
Inches	2.874	2.874
No. of Cylinders	1	1
Displacement—(cc)	372	372
Cubic Inches	22.7	22.7
Horsepower @ RPM	20 @ 5000	23 @ 5250
Cooling Type	Centrifugal Fan	
Carburetor Model	HD	HD
Number Used	1	1
Ignition:		
Type	BOSCH Magneto	
Point Gap—(mm)	0.4	0.4
Inch	0.016	0.016
Timing Advance?	Yes	Yes
Inch	0.0134	0.0134
Degrees	7°	7°
Measured at	Retard	Retard
Spark Plug:		
Bosch	M225T1	M225T1
Electrode Gap (mm)	0.5	0.5
Inch	0.020	0.020
Fuel/Oil Ratio	25:1	25:1

MAINTENANCE

CARBURETOR. Tillotson diaphragm type carburetors are used. Refer to TILLOTSON Carburetor section for operation and overhaul information. An external impulse line is used on most models to connect fuel pump diaphragm cover to engine crankcase. Be sure that all passages are open and that vacuum and pressure leaks are eliminated.

IGNITION AND TIMING. Breaker point gap should be approximately 0.4 mm (0.016 in.). Points can be adjusted after removing the recoil starter, starter cup and flywheel cover plate. Most engines are equipped with a centrifugal timing advance which provides retarded spark timing for starting only. When points are serviced, check to see that advance mechanism moves freely without binding. If binding occurs, disassemble and clean the advance mechanism and/or renew the parts concerned. Models 52R, 53R, 81R & 82R use a fixed cam (C—Fig. 1) which keys to crankshaft.

The fan wheel (flywheel) contains a mark and the letters "OT" on outer rim and a similar mark appears on fan housing. Piston is at top dead center when the two marks are aligned. Static timing position may not be marked. Timing position (Piston crown BTDC) is given in specification data for use if timing marks cannot be located. Advance timing is 25° BTDC for all models equipped with timing advance.

Refer to MAGNETO Section of SERVICE FUNDAMENTALS for overhaul data and service procedures.

LUBRICATION. The engine is lubricated by mixing oil with the fuel. A suitable two-cycle air cooled engine oil is recommended. Standard grade SAE 30 automotive motor oil may be used if two-cycle oil is not available.

Recommended fuel-oil mixture is 25:1. Mix fuel and oil thoroughly using a separate container before pouring mixture into fuel tank. For cold weather blending, pre-mix the oil with a small amount of gasoline and shake thoroughly until mixture is liquid, then blend with remainder of fuel. Do not use kerosene or fuel oil for premixing.

REPAIRS

TIGHTENING TORQUES. Recommended tightening torques are as follows:

	Foot-Lbs.	Kilogram-Meters
Flywheel nut	70	10
Cylinder head nuts	18	2.5
Crankcase nuts	8	1

DISASSEMBLY AND REASSEMBLY. Refer to Figs. 1, 2 and 3 for exploded views of engines. With engine removed from machine, remove carburetor(s), drive sheave, starter, air shroud and flywheel.

Special assembly tools are available from engine distributor and metric wrenches are required.

On all models the ball-type main bearings are a press fit in crankcase halves and on crankshafts, and crankcase must be heated for disassembly

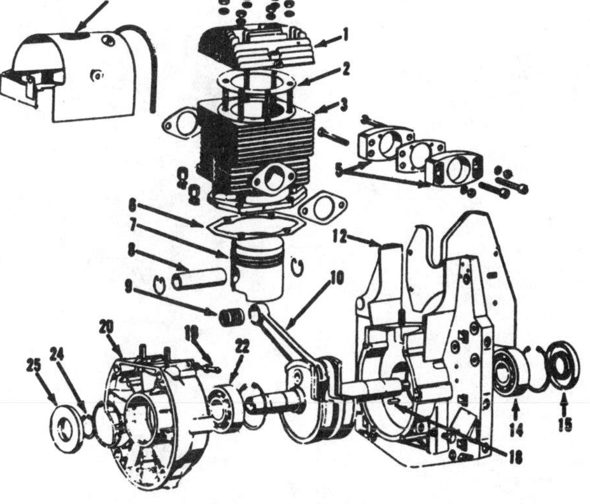

Fig. 2–Exploded view of Model 160R engine. Refer to Fig. 3 for parts identification.

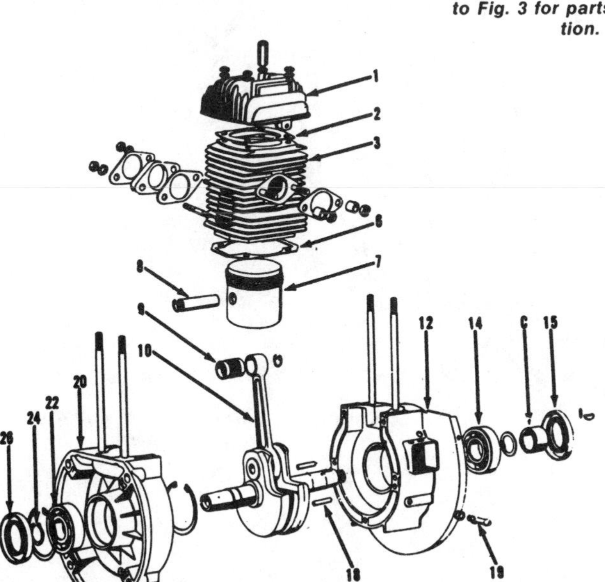

Fig. 1–Exploded view of 246cc engine. Ignition cam (C) is fixed on this model. Refer to Fig. 3 for parts identification.

and reassembly. The use of special tools or extreme care is recommended in reassembly to prevent misalignment of the built-up crankshaft unit.

PISTON, RINGS & CYLINDER. Piston pin is a floating fit in piston and connecting rod. Piston rings are pinned in place. On early engines, the three piston rings were 2.5 mm (0.098 in.) thick; on late engines 2.0 mm (0.079 in.) rings are used. Early rings are still available for service, but if piston must be renewed, the late piston and rings are used. The piston and both the early and late type rings are available in standard size and oversizes of 0.5 mm (0.020 in.) and 1.0 mm (0.039 in.) for engines with cast iron cylinders. Arrow on top of piston crown must be installed toward exhaust port side of cylinder.

Late engines use a chrome plated aluminum cylinder which is available in standard size only, and which must not be honed or rebored.

CRANKSHAFT AND CONNECTING ROD ASSEMBLY. The crankshaft and connecting rod is available only as an assembled unit and disassembly is not recommended. Bearings are a tight press fit on shaft and in crankcase bores at room temperature. PTO and flywheel shafts are provided with lathe centers for all models except those where the pto shaft is drilled and tapped for a center bolt. To check crankshaft alignment, mount crankshaft in a lathe and measure runout with a dial indicator at bearing area of shafts (as close as possible to crankshaft webs). Allowable runout is 0.001 (inch).

RECOIL STARTER. The recoil starter unit may be of the type shown in Fig. 6 or 12. To disassemble the unit shown in Fig. 6, proceed as follows:

With starter removed from fan housing, unseat and remove snap ring (19) and withdraw sprag cage (15) and associated parts. Turn spring cover (11) slightly clockwise to unhook the notches from roll pins (7) in housing, lift cover to clear the pins, then allow recoil spring to unwind. Working through slots in housing as shown in Fig. 7, disengage inner end of spring from pulley (8—Fig. 6), then lift out spring cover (11), spring (10) and pad (12) as a unit. With spring removed, grasp handle (2) and pull starter cable (5) out of housing (6).

Turn pulley until the three evenly spaced cutout notches in pulley rim align with the roll pins (7) protruding

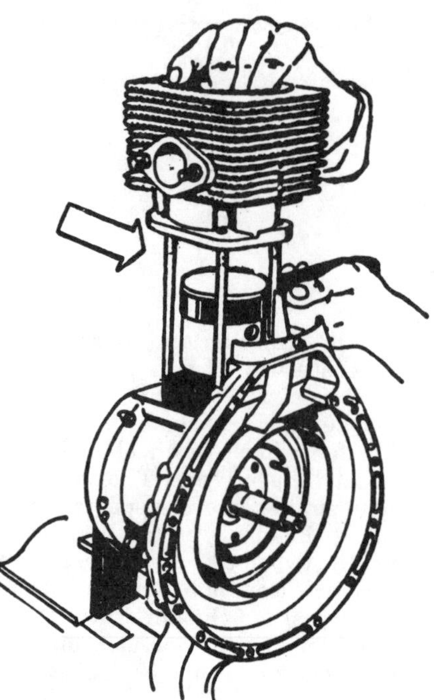

Fig. 4–Installing cylinder.

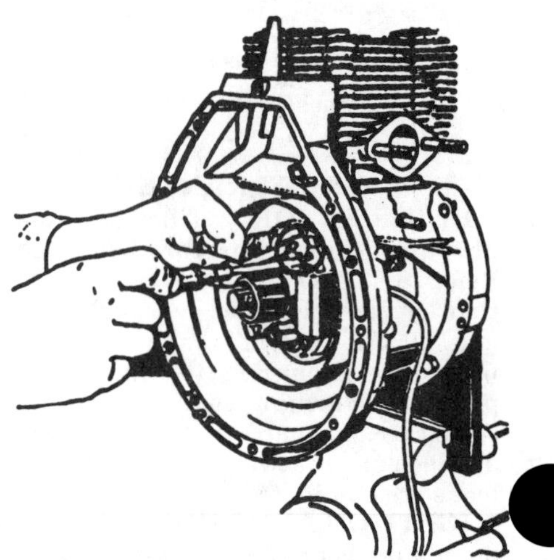

Fig. 5–Breaker point setting collar permits magneto adjustment with flywheel removed.

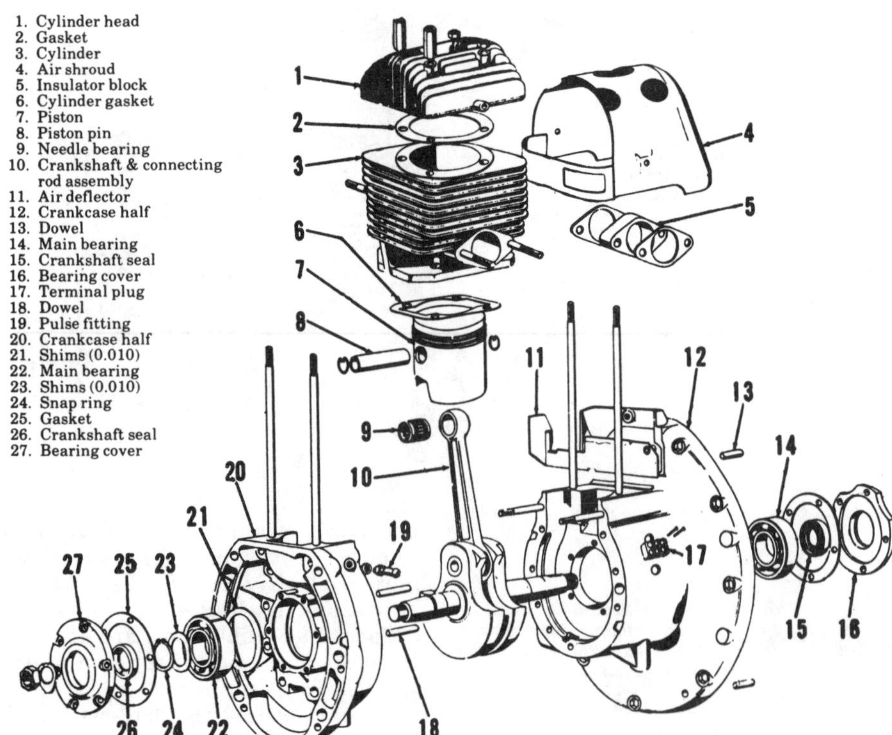

1. Cylinder head
2. Gasket
3. Cylinder
4. Air shroud
5. Insulator block
6. Cylinder gasket
7. Piston
8. Piston pin
9. Needle bearing
10. Crankshaft & connecting rod assembly
11. Air deflector
12. Crankcase half
13. Dowel
14. Main bearing
15. Crankshaft seal
16. Bearing cover
17. Terminal plug
18. Dowel
19. Pulse fitting
20. Crankcase half
21. Shims (0.010)
22. Main bearing
23. Shims (0.010)
24. Snap ring
25. Gasket
26. Crankshaft seal
27. Bearing cover

Fig. 3–Exploded view of crankcase, crankshaft assembly and cylinder assembly used on early 300cc engines.

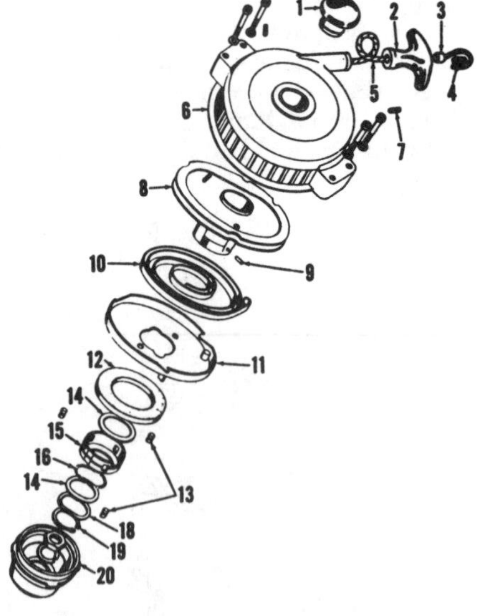

Fig. 6–Exploded view of recoil starter showing component parts.

1. Plug
2. Handle grip
3. Clamp ring
4. Tapered cone
5. Starter cable
6. Housing
7. Roll pin
8. Pulley
9. Roll pin
10. Recoil spring
11. Spring cover
12. Sealing ring
13. Sprag roller
14. Washer
15. Sprag cage
16. Garter spring
18. Wave washer
19. Snap ring
20. Starter cup

through housing inner wall, then lift out the pulley.

Fig. 8 shows method of attaching the steel starter cable to pulley. Outer end is attached to rope handle (2—Fig. 6) by doubling around tapered cone (4), then pulling tight into handle grip. The plastic guide bushing where rope emerges from housing (6) can be turned in housing to provide a new wear surface if bushing is grooved. If bushing must be renewed and difficulty is encountered in removal, heat bushing to soften then pry from housing bore.

The standard starter cable is 1920 mm (75.5 in.) long. Special lengths are available for some applications where handle grip location is remote from the engine. It should be noted that starter cable is not fully anchored in pulley and that recoil spring serves as pulley stop. If starter is only partially disassembled therefore, it is of particular importance that spring adjustment procedure given at end of assembly instruction be carefully followed.

When assembling starter unit, thread rope through guide bushing in housing and insert inner end about ½-inch under retaining lug in pulley in the direction shown in Fig. 8. Double cable back as shown be dotted lines and take about three wraps around pulley to prevent accidental removal. Align the three evenly spaced cutouts in pulley rim with roll pins in housing, with the cable resting in fourth cut-out next to cable guide. Pull out the slack in cable as pulley is installed.

If rubber seal ring (12—Fig. 6) is damaged or missing, cement a new ring to spring cover (11). If recoil spring has been removed, coil the spring into cover in a clockwise direction as shown in Fig. 9, being sure loop in outer end of spring is placed over pin in cover. Install cover and spring, checking through cut-outs in bores of cover, to make sure hooked inner end of spring properly engages pulley. Seat inner end of spring in pulley lugs using a screwdriver and working through cut-outs in cover.

NOTE: The recoil spring serves as the pulley stop and cable can be pulled out if spring is not properly tensioned as follows:

On models where starter handle (grip) retracts to starter housing, wind pulley clockwise until handle stop contacts the housing and cable is fully wound on pulley.

On models where starter handle retracts to a stop located on instrument panel (or elsewhere), carefully measure the distance from remote stop to starter housing; then lightly install a clamp or vise grips on cable with the proper amount of cable exposed. Wind pulley clockwise until the installed stop contacts starter housing and cable is fully wound on pulley.

On all models, tension the recoil spring by turning the spring cage (11—Fig. 6) clockwise 10 notches (3⅓ turns). With recoil spring properly tensioned, pull out on cable until it stops; then measure the distance between handle stop (or vise grips) and housing as shown in Fig. 10. The distance should be approximately 50½ inches. Readjust, if necessary, by repositioning the spring cover. NOTE: One notch will change cable length about 4 inches.

With recoil spring properly tensioned, install and adjust the sprag cage and snap ring as follows: Coat washers (14—Fig. 6) with "LUBRIPLATE" or similar grease. Sprag cage (15) has two notches on outer rim and corresponding arrows on flat lower surface as shown in Fig. 11, place the notch corresponding to direction of engine rotation over pin (9—Fig. 6) in pulley hub and install sprag cage. Install the other thrust washer (14), wave washer (18) and snap ring (19), then check the installation by pulling the starter rope. The sprag cage (15) should not move with pulley until roll pin (9) contacts forward edge of notch in cage; if sprag cage moves, remove snap ring (19) and install a second wave washer (18) to apply more tension to cage. With cage properly adjusted, reinstall the three sprags (13) and garter spring (16), coat sprags with low temperature grease and reinstall the starter unit.

To overhaul the recoil starter of the type shown in Fig. 12, first remove screw (2) and cover plate (7). Pull starter cable into notch in pulley as shown in Fig. 13 and allow recoil spring to completely unwind.

Remove snap ring (16—Fig. 12), cage (13) and associated parts. Insert a

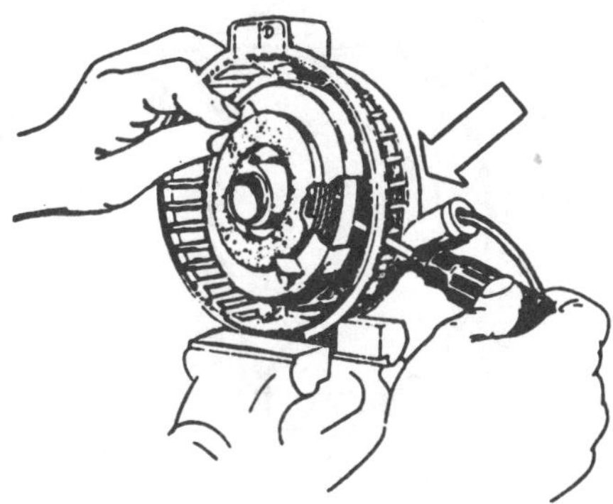

Fig. 7–Seat inner end of spring with a screwdriver as cover and spring assembly is installed.

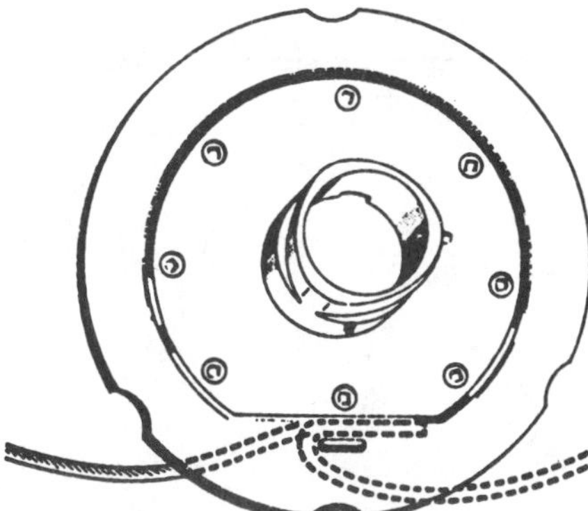

Fig. 8–Double cable under pulley lug as shown. Cable is not anchored.

Fig. 9–Winding the recoil spring into cover.

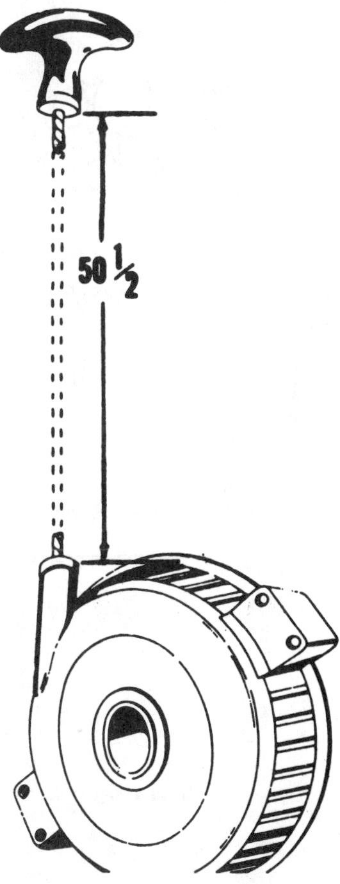

Fig. 10–Wind the recoil spring unitl extended portion of rope measures 50½ inches as shown. Recoil spring functions as pulley stop.

screwdriver or similar tool through sight hole in cable pulley as shown in Fig. 14 and disengage inner end of recoil spring; then lift off cable pulley, cable and recoil spring as a unit. Make sure recoil spring remains in its cage on top face of pulley. Fig. 15 shows the proper direction for coiling spring in pulley if spring is removed.

Fig. 16 shows proper method of attaching starter cable to pulley. Cable is not anchored and recoil spring serves as pulley stop. If starter is only partially disassembled therefore, it is important that spring be properly adjusted to keep cable from being pulled out.

When assembling the starter, insert about ½-inch of cable under pulley retaining lug as shown in Fig. 16 then bend cable back sharply and wind all but about 4-6 inches of cable on pulley. Insert small pins or nails through the holes (D) close to pulley hub and place inner coil of spring inside the pins. Install the assembled unit in starter housing and turn clockwise until inner end of spring snaps into place in anchor slot in starter housing. Engagement can be verified through sight hole (S). When inner end of spring is properly hooked, wind the spring two full turns counter-clockwise while holding free end of cable in notch in pulley rim. With spring pre-stressed, reinstall cover plate (7—Fig. 12). Starter should contact stop (spring fully wound) when cable is pulled out 65-70 inches.

Install sprag cage and associated parts as previously outlined for the other starter.

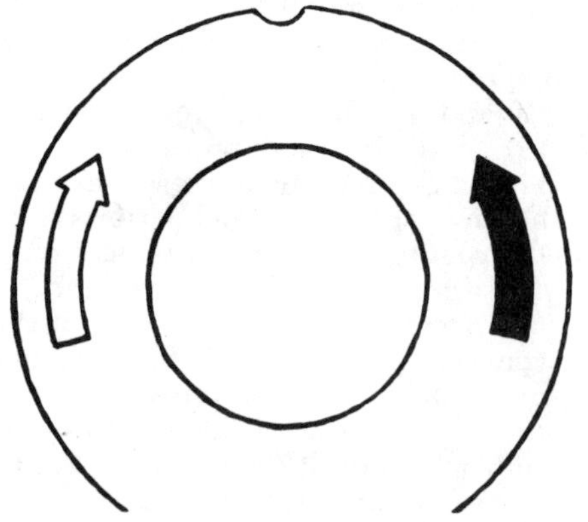

Fig. 11–Arrows on underneath side of sprag cage correspond to notches of pulley pin and indicate direction of sprag engagement. Refer to text for proper method of assembly.

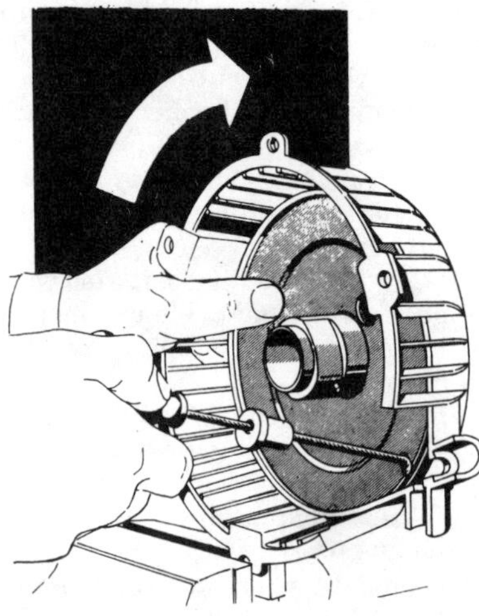

Fig. 13–Pull starter cable into notch as shown to allow recoil spring to unwind.

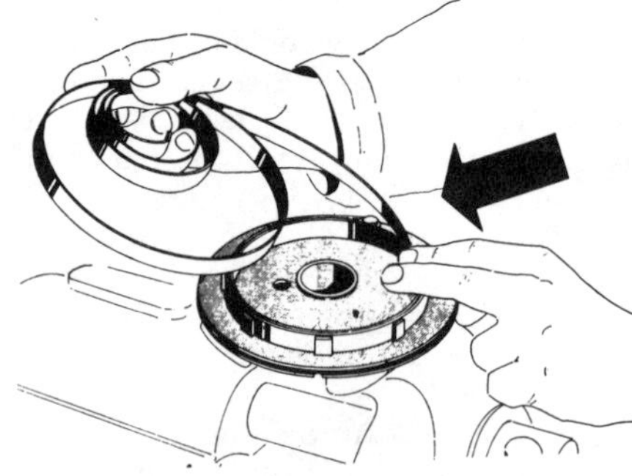

Fig. 15–Coiling recoil spring into cage on outer face of pulley.

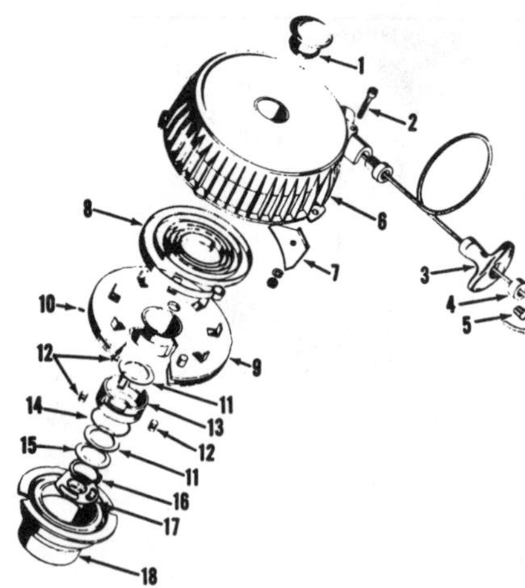

Fig. 12–Exploded view of recoil starter of the type used on larger engines.

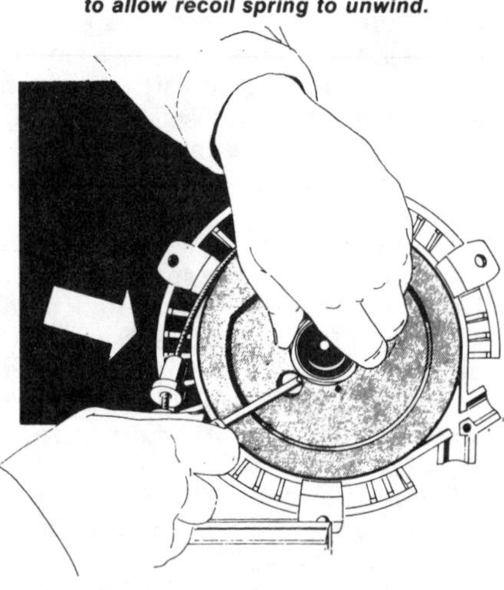

Fig. 14–Reach through sight hole as shown to disengage inner end of spring.

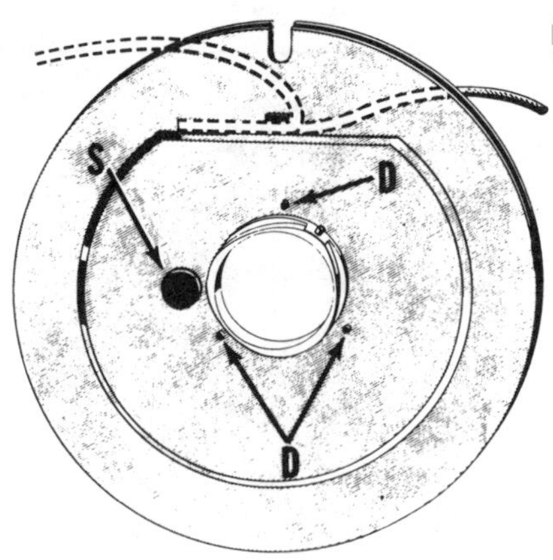

Fig. 16–Double cable under pulley lug as shown. Cable is not anchored.

D. Drilled holes
S. Sight hole

HIRTH TWO & THREE CYLINDER

CONDENSED SERVICE DATA

Years Made	1968-70	1969-70	1967-69	1968-70
ENGINE MODEL	210R	211R	180R	220R
Bore—(mm)	63	66	70	70
Inches	2.480	2.598	2.756	2.756
Stroke—(mm)	64	64	64	64
Inches	2.520	2.520	2.520	2.520
No. of Cylinders	2	2	2 (Opposed)	2 (In Line)
Displacement—(cc)	399	438	493	493
Cubic Inches	23.8	26.7	30.1	30.1
Horsepower @ RPM	21.5@5500	24@5500	24@5000	27@5500
Cooling Type	Centrifugal Fan			
Carburetor Model	HD	HD	HR	HD
Number Used	1	1	2	1
Ignition				
Type	BOSCH E. T. Magneto			
Point Gap—(mm)	0.4	0.4	0.4	0.4
Inch	0.016	0.016	0.016	0.016
Timing Advance?	Yes	Yes	Yes	Yes
Timing BTDC (mm)	0.3	0.3	0.3	0.3
Inch	0.012	0.012	0.012	0.012
Degrees	7°	7°	7°	7°
Measured at	Retard	Retard	Retard	Retard
Spark Plug:				
Bosch	M240T1	M240T1	M240T1	M240T1
Electrode Gap (mm)	0.5	0.5	0.5	0.5
Inch	0.020	0.020	0.020	0.020
Fuel/Oil Ratio	25:1	25:1	25:1	25:1

Years Made	1967-68	1968-70	1970-	1968-70
ENGINE MODEL	170R	171R	172R	230R
Bore—(mm)	75	77	78	72.5
Inches	2.953	3.032	3.071	2.854
Stroke—(mm)	68	68	68	64
Inches	2.677	2.677	2.677	2.520
No. of Cylinders	2	2	2	3
Displacement—(cc)	600	634	650	793
Cubic Inches	36.6	38.5	39.7	42.3
Horsepower @ RPM	30@5000	36@5500	59@6500	80@6500
Cooling Type	Centrifugal Fan	Centrifugal Fan	Centrifugal Fan	Free Air
Carburetor Model	HR	HD	....	HD
Number Used	2	1	....	3
Ignition:				
Type:	BOSCH E. T. Magneto			
Point Gap—(mm)	0.4	0.4	0.4	0.4
Inch	0.016	0.016	0.016	0.016
Timing Advance?	Yes	Yes	Yes	No
Timing BTDC (mm)	0.32	0.32	0.32	3.75
Inch	0.0126	0.0126	0.0126	0.148
Degrees	7°	7°	7°	25°
Measured at	Retard	Retard	Retard	....
Spark Plug:				
Bosch	M240T1	M240T1	M260T2	W340T16
Electrode Gap (mm)	0.5	0.5	0.5	0.5
Inch	0.020	0.020	0.020	0.020
Fuel/Oil Ratio	25:1	25:1	25:1	25:1

YEARS MADE	1970-	1970-	1970-
ENGINE MODEL	231R	260R	261R
Bore—(mm)	65.5	62	57.5
Inches	2.579	2.441	2.264
Stroke—(mm)	64	56	56
Inches	2.520	2.205	2.205
No. of Cylinders	3	2	2
Displacement—(cc)	647	338	291
Cubic Inches	39.5	20.6	17.8
Horsepower @ RPM	65 @ 6500	28 @ 6500	25 @ 6500
Cooling Type	Free Air	Axial Fan	Axial Fan
Carburetor Model	HD	....	....
Number Used	3	1	1

YEARS MADE	1970-	1970-	1970-
ENGINE MODEL	231R	260R	261R
Ignition:			
Type	Bosch E. T. Magneto		
Point Gap—(mm)	0.4	0.4	0.4
Inch	0.016	0.016	0.016
Timing Advance?	No	Yes	Yes
Timing BTDC (mm)	3.75	0.1	0.1
Inch	0.148	0.004	0.004
Degrees	25°	4°	4°
Measured at	....	Retard	Retard
Spark Plug:			
Bosch	W340T16	W260T1	W260T1
Electrode Gap (mm)	0.5	0.5	0.5
Inch	0.020	0.020	0.020
Fuel/Oil Ratio	25:1	25:1	25:1

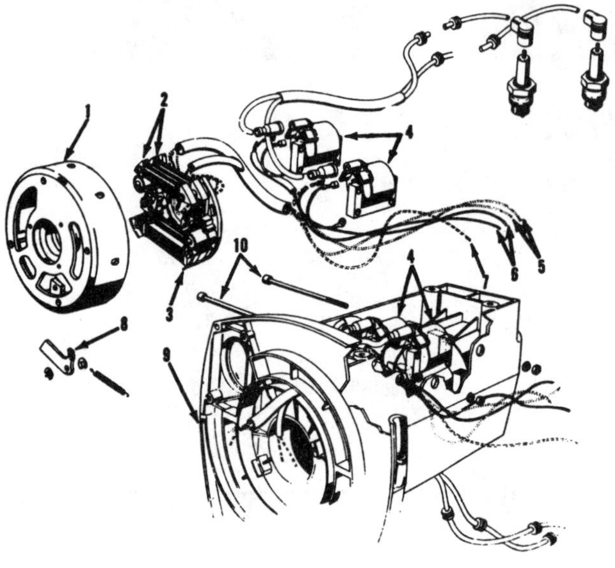

Fig. 1–Exploded view of magneto, high tension coils and associated parts used on In-Line Twin.

1. Flywheel
2. Generating coils
3. Lighting coil
4. High-tension coils
5. Lighting wires (yellow)
6. Ground cables (black)
7. Stop cable (brown)
8. Advance weight
9. Crankcase
10. Through bolts

MAINTENANCE

CARBURETOR. Tillotson diaphragm type carburetors are used.

Refer to TILLOTSON Carburetor section for operation and overhaul information. An external impulse line is used on most models to connect fuel pump diaphragm cover to engine crankcase. Be sure that all passages are open and that vacuum and pressure leaks are eliminated.

IGNITION AND TIMING. Breaker point gap should be approximately 0.4 mm (0.016 in.). Points can be adjusted after removing the recoil starter, starter cup and flywheel cover plate. Most engines are equipped with a centrifugal timing advance which provides retarded spark timing for starting only. When points are serviced, check to see that advance mechanism moves freely without binding. If binding occurs, disassemble and clean the advance mechanism and/or renew the parts concerned.

The fan wheel (flywheel) contains a mark and the letters "OT" on outer rim and a similar mark appears on fan housing. Piston is at top dead center when the two marks are aligned. Static timing position may not be marked. Timing position (Piston crown BTDC) is given in specification data for use if timing marks cannot be located.

On alternate firing twins, points must be set to open exactly 180° apart. Twin cylinder engines use energy transfer type ignition system, with a low tension (generating) ignition coil located underneath the flywheel. On alternate firing twin the generating coils are "Piggy-Backed" or stacked as shown at (2—Fig. 1) and high tension coils (4) are concealed underneath the crankcase and secured by through-bolts (10).

On opposed twin, only one generating coil is required and high tension coils are connected in series as shown in Fig. 2. Coils are located in fan housing and bolted to crankcase casting.

Refer to MAGNETO Section of SERVICE FUNDAMENTALS for overhaul procedures.

LUBRICATION. The engine is lubricated by mixing oil with the fuel. A suitable two-cycle air cooled engine oil is recommended. Standard grade SAE 30 automotive motor oil may be used if two-cycle oil is not available.

Recommended fuel-oil mixture is 25:1. Mix fuel and oil thoroughly using a separate container before pouring mixture into fuel tank. For cold weather blending, pre-mix the oil with a small amount of gasoline and shake thoroughly until mixture is liquid, then blend the remainder of fuel. Do not use kerosene or fuel oil for pre-mixing.

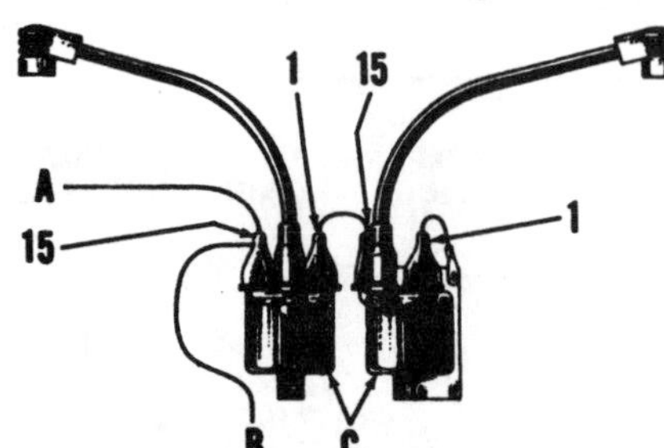

Fig. 2–High-tension coils on Opposed Twin, properly wired. Numbers (1 & 15) appear on coils.

A. Shorting cable
B. Generator coil wire (Blue)
C. High tension coils

REPAIRS

TIGHTENING TORQUES. Recommended tightening torques are as follows. Data is given in ft.-lbs.

Cylinder Head

Models 170R, 180R	20
Model 171R (Studs)	20
Model 171R (Bolts)	6½
Models 210R, 211R, 220R	6½
Model 230R	17

Crankcase

Model 180R	6½
All Other Models	17

Cylinder Base

Models 210R, 211R, 220R, 230R	17

Intake Manifold

Models 210R, 211R, 220R	17
Model 230R	6½

Exhaust Manifold

Model 230R	6½
All Other Models	17

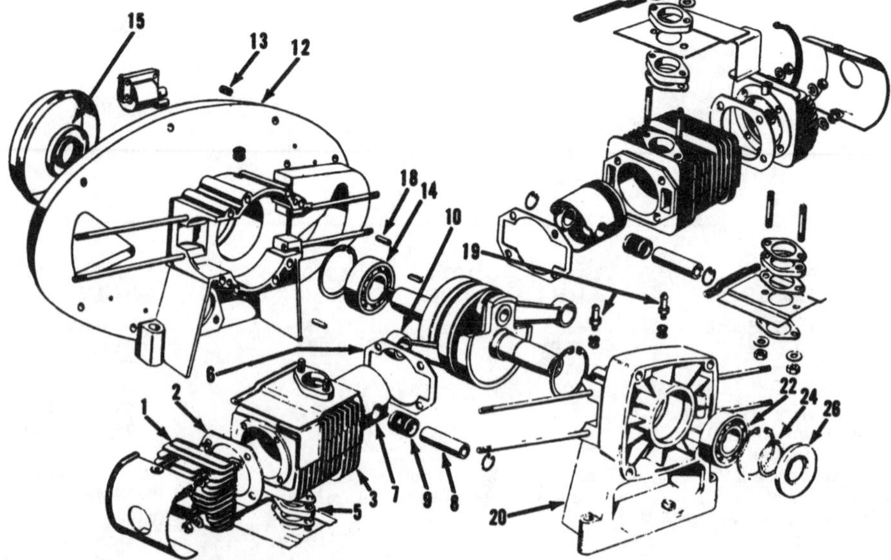

Fig. 3–Exploded view of Opposed Twin. Refer to Fig. 4 for parts identification.

DISASSEMBLY AND REASSEMBLY. Refer to Figs. 3 and 4 for exploded views of engines. With engine removed from machine, remove carburetor(s), drive sheave, starter, air shroud and flywheel.

Special assembly tools are available from engine distributor and metric wrenches are required.

On opposed twin, the ball-type main bearings are a press fit in crankcase halves and on crankshafts, and crankcase must be heated for disassembly and reassembly. The use of special tools and extreme care is recommended in reassembly to prevent misalignment of the built-up crankshaft unit.

PISTON, RINGS & CYLINDER. Piston pin is a floating fit in piston and connecting rod. Piston rings are pinned in place. On early engines, the three piston rings were 2.5 mm (0.098 in.) thick; on late engines 2.0 mm (0.079 in.) rings are used. Early rings are still available for service, but if piston must be renewed, the late piston and rings are used. The piston and both the early and late type rings are available in standard size and oversizes of 0.5 mm (0.020 in.) and 1.0 mm (0.039 in.) for engines with cast iron cylinders. Arrow on top of piston crown must be installed toward exhaust port side of cylinder.

Late engines used a chrome plated aluminum cylinder which is available in standard size only, and which must not be honed or rebored.

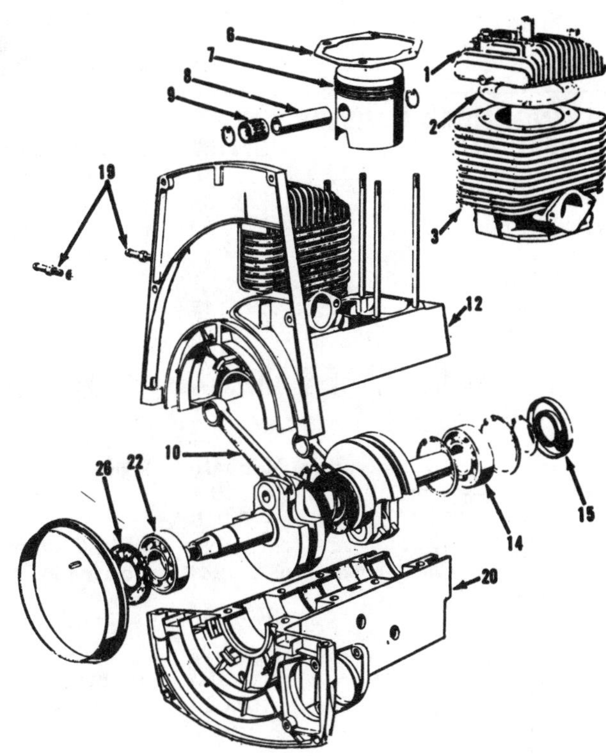

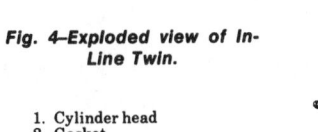

Fig. 4–Exploded view of In-Line Twin.

1. Cylinder head
2. Gasket
3. Cylinder
5. Insulator block
6. Cylinder gasket
7. Piston
8. Piston pin
9. Needle bearing
10. Crankshaft & connecting rod assembly
12. Crankcase half
13. Dowel
14. Main bearing
15. Crankshaft seal
18. Dowel
19. Pulse fitting
20. Crankcase half
22. Main bearing
24. Snap ring
26. Crankshaft seal

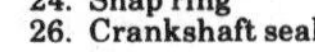

CRANKSHAFT AND CONNECTING ROD ASSEMBLY. The crankshaft and connecting rod is available only as an assembled unit and disassembly is not recommended. Bearings are a tight press fit on shaft and in crankcase bores at room temperature. PTO and flywheel shafts are provided with lathe centers for all models except those where the PTO shaft is drilled and tapped for a center bolt. To check crankshaft alignment, mount crankshaft in a lathe and measure runout with a dial indicator at bearing area of shafts (as close as possible to crankshaft webs). Allowable runout is 0.001 (inch).

HUSQVARNA

CONDENSED SERVICE DATA

ENGINE MODEL	SM150
Bore—(mm)	60
Inches	2.362
Stroke—(mm)	52
Inches	2.047
No. of Cylinders	1
Displacement—(cc)	147
Cubic Inches	8.9
Horsepower @ RPM	10 @ 6500
Carburetor Model	HL230A
Number Used	1
Ignition:	
Type	Flywheel Magneto
Point Gap—(mm)	0.4
Inch	0.016
Timing Advance?	No
Timing BTDC—Degrees	24°
Spark Plug:	
Bosch	W225T1
Champion	L78
Electrode Gap (mm)	0.5
Inch	0.020
Fuel/Oil Ratio	25:1

MAINTENANCE

CARBURETOR. A Tillotson, Model HL, diaphragm type carburetor is used on snowmobile engines. Refer to TILLOTSON Carburetor Section for overhaul information.

LUBRICATION. The engine in lubricated by oil mixed with the fuel. The engine manufacturer recommends the use of Regular gasoline and a reliable, known brand two-stroke oil at a ratio of 25:1.

Mix fuel and oil thoroughly using a separate container, before pouring mixture into fuel tank. For cold weather blending, pre-mix the oil with a small amount of gasoline and shake thoroughly until mixture is liquid, then blend with remainder of fuel. Do not use kerosene or fuel oil for premixing.

IGNITION AND TIMING. The breaker cam is machined on crankshaft. Blower housing and flywheel must be removed for service on ignition system.

NOTE: Flywheel nut is left-hand thread.

A special tool, Husqvarna Part No. 17 10 199-04 is necessary for easy and accurate ignition timing, because flywheel must be removed for access to points and piston position cannot be measured. If the special tool is not available, carefully mark the armature plate position before removal and adjust point gap with extreme care. The adjusting tool is shown in Fig. 2 and its use is demonstrated in Fig. 3; proceed as follows:

Fig. 2–A special timing tool, Husqvarna Part Number 17 10 199-04 is needed for accurate timing. Refer to text.

First examine and renew parts as required. Install the timing tool as shown and turn crankshaft until long leg of tool aligns with threaded hole in cylinder as shown. Loosen the mounting screws if necessary, and turn armature plate until edge of ignition coil (2) aligns with short pointer of tool shown at (3). Retighten armature plate retaining screws and using a buzzer (6) or continuity meter, adjust the breaker points until they just begin to open.

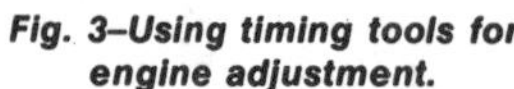

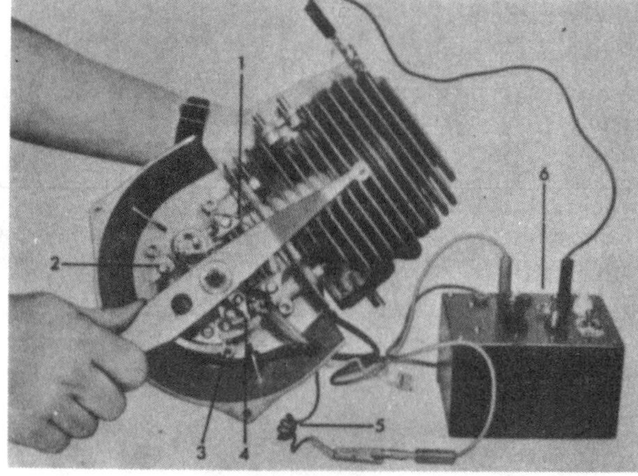

Fig. 3–Using timing tools for engine adjustment.

1. Lighting coil
2. Ignition coil
3. Align pole shoe
4. Breaker points
5. Stop cable
6. Timing buzzer

If the flywheel has two keyways marked "A" and "B", use keyway marked "B" if engine is equipped with lighting coil. Tighten flywheel retaining nut to a torque of 30 ft.-lbs.

REPAIRS

DISASSEMBLY AND REASSEMBLY. To disassemble the removed engine, first remove muffler, decompression valve, spark plug, air cleaner and carburetor. Blower housing and recoil starter assembly can be removed as a unit after removing the three slotted head retaining screws.

Ball type main bearings are a tight fit on crankshaft, and in the aluminum crankcase at room temperature. Heat the crankcase assembly to approximately 275° F. in an oven or kiln after removing cylinder, piston, magneto assembly and Allen head crankcase screws; then bump housings from crankcase using a plastic hammer as shown in Fig. 4.

The cylinder is available only in an assembly which includes the piston, but pistons are available separately as are the piston rings. Cylinders are classed as to size and coded "A" to "E". Be sure to state size code when ordering piston only.

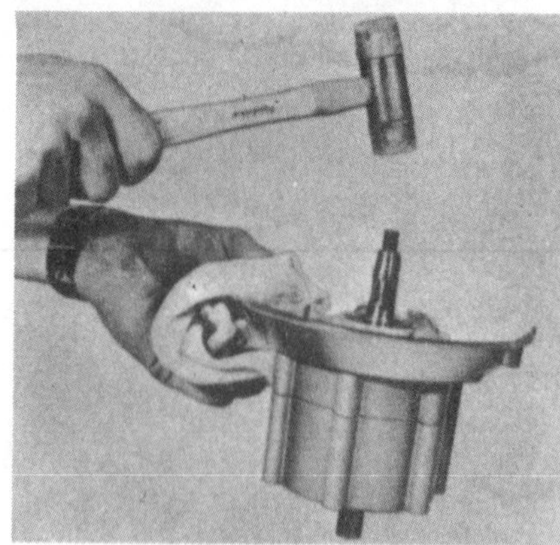

Fig. 4–Heat crankcase to 275° F. for crankshaft removal. Refer to text.

JLO

ONE CYLINDER MODELS
CONDENSED SERVICE DATA

ENGINE MODEL	L99	L152	L197	L227, L230	L230	L252	L292
Bore—(mm)	55	59	66	70	70	69	75
Inches	2.165	2.323	2.60	2.756	2.756	2.716	2.953
Stroke—(mm)	42	54	58	58	58	66	66
Inches	1.653	2.126	2.28	2.283	2.283	2.598	2.598
No. of Cylinders	1	1	1	1	1	1	1
Displacement—(cc)	100	148	198	223	223	247	292
Cubic Inches	6.1	9	12.08	13.6	13.6	15.07	17.8
Horsepower @ RPM	4.75@5500	5.7@4500	7.3@4500	12.5@5500	14.0@6000	9.1@4250	14.6@4500
Cooling type	Centrifugal Fan						
Carburetor Model	HL	HL	HL	HR	HD	HL, HR	HR or HD
Number Used	1	1	1	1	1	1	1
Ignition:							
Type	E120	RB1 6V/17W	RB1 6V/17W	RB1 6V/17W	RCP1V 12V /40W	SB1 6V/16 (36)W	SB1 6V/16W
Point Gap—(mm)	0.3-0.5	0.35-0.45	0.35-0.45	0.35-0.45	0.35-0.45	0.35-0.45	0.35-0.45
Inch	0.015	0.016	0.016	0.016	0.016	0.016	0.016
Edge Gap—(mm)	8.5-12.5	14-18	11-14	14-18	14-18	15-19	15-19
Inch	0.334-0.492	0.551-0.709	0.433-0.551	0.471-0.708	0.471-0.708	0.59-0.75	0.590-0.748
Timing Advance?	No	No	No	No	No	No	No
Timing BTDC (mm)	2.1-2.5	2.3-2.8	2.3-2.8	2.75	2.8-3.2	2.8-3.2	3.5-3.8
Inch	0.082-0.098	0.091-0.110	0.091-0.110	0.108	0.091-0.126	0.110-0.126	0.138-0.150
Degrees	....	....	....	....	....	....	....
Measured at	....	....	....	....	....	....	....
Spark Plug:							
Bosch	M240T1	M225T1	M225T1	M225T1	M240T1	M225T1	M225T1
Champion	....	UK10	UK10	UK10	K57R	UK10	K9
Electrode Gap (mm)	0.4-0.5	0.4-0.5	0.4-0.5	0.4-0.5	0.4-0.5	0.4-0.5	0.4-0.5
Inch	0.018	0.018	0.018	0.018	0.018	0.018	0.018
Fuel/Oil Ratio	20:1	25:1	25:1	20:1	20:1	25:1	20:1

ENGINE MODEL	L295	L297	L300	L340	L372	L380	L395
Bore—(mm)	74.5	75	75	80	80	80	82.5
Inches	2.933	2.953	2.953	3.149	3.150	3.150	3.248
Stroke—(mm)	67	67	67	67	74	74	74
Inches	2.638	2.638	2.638	2.638	2.913	2.913	2.913
No. of Cylinders	1	1	1	1	1	1	1
Displacement—(cc)	292	296	296	336	372	372	396
Cubic Inches	17.8	18.1	18.1	20.5	22.7	22.7	24.16
Horsepower @ RPM	18.5@5500	17.5@5000	19.5@5500	22.0@5500	21@5000	23.5@5000	24.5@5000
Cooling Type	Centrifugal Fan						
Carburetor Model	HR, HD	HR, HD	HR, HD	HD	HD	HR, HD	HD
Number Used	1	1	1	1	1	1	1
Ignition:							
Type	SCP1V 12V /75W	SC1V 12V /40W	SC1 12V /40W	RCP1V 12V /75W	SC1V 12V /40W	SC1V or CP1V	RCP1V 12V /75W
Point Gap—(mm)	0.35-0.45	0.35-0.45	0.35-0.45	0.35-0.45	0.35-0.45	0.35-0.45	0.35-0.45
Inch	0.016	0.016	0.016	0.016	0.016	0.016	0.016
Edge Gap—(mm)	17.5-22.5	17.5-22.5	17.5-22.5	17.5-22.0	18-23	18-23	....
Inch	0.689-0.88	0.869-0.886	0.689-0.886	0.689-0.886	0.709-0.906	0.709-0.906	....
Timing Advance?	Yes	Yes	Yes	Yes	Yes	Yes	Yes
Timing BTDC (mm)	3.0-3.5	3.0-3.5	3.0-3.5	3.0-3.5	3.1-3.6	3.1-3.6	3.1-3.6
Inch	0.118-0.138	0.118-0.138	0.118-0.138	0.118-0.138	0.122-0.142	0.122-0.142	0.122-0.142
Degrees	....	21.7-23.5	21.7-23.5	....	21.1-22.8	21.1-22.8	....
Measured at	Advanced Cam						
Spark Plug:							
Bosch	M240T1	M225T1	M225T1	M240T1	M225T1	M225T1	M240T1
Champion	K57R	UK10	K185	K57R	K9	K9	K57R
Electrode Gap (mm)	0.4-0.5	0.4-0.5	0.4-0.5	0.4-0.5	0.4-0.5	0.4-0.5	0.4-0.5
Inch	0.018	0.018	0.018	0.018	0.018	0.018	0.018
Fuel/Oil Ratio	20:1	20:1	20:1	20:1	20:1	20:1	20:1

MAINTENANCE

SPARK PLUG. The recommended plug for normal service is given in CONDENSED SERVICE DATA Tables. Hotter or colder plugs may be required for particular applications. CHAMPION Gold Palladium plugs are gapped at 0.015 which is the correct setting for this plug. Recommended spark plug tightening torque is 25 ft.-lbs.

CARBURETOR. Tillotson diaphragm type carburetors are used on all snowmobile engines. Most engines are equipped with an integral, pulse-type fuel pump built into carburetor, but some models may be equipped with a carburetor without fuel pump. See Tillotson carburetor section for operation and overhaul procedure.

Refer also to Figs. 1 through 4 for views of pulse passages and induction ports. Internal pulse passage (1—Fig. 1 and P—Fig. 3 & 4) is not present in all engines. The tapped hole for plug (2—Fig. 1 or 3—Fig. 2 & 3) is always present. If internal pulse passage (P) is present and used, hole in gaskets, cylinder shield, adapter flange and carburetor must be open and aligned and plug (2—Fig. 1) must be installed.

On HL carburetors, initial adjustment is ¾ turn open for idle adjustment screw and 1¼ turn open for main adjustment screw. On HR or HD series carburetors, initial adjustment is one turn open for both needles. Both needles must be readjusted for smoothest engine operation after unit reaches proper operating temperature. Refer to CARBURETOR SERVICE SECTION for overhaul and additional service information.

IGNITION AND TIMING. Timing specifications for individual engines are given in CONDENSED SERVICE DATA TABLES. Timing can be checked on models with fixed timing using a light or buzzer, by connecting the tester to kill switch wire or external coil wire and a suitable ground, then measuring piston position through spark plug hole. Flywheel must be removed to adjust points or timing.

On models L227, L230, L295, L297, L300 and L340, recoil starter must be removed separately from fan cover as shown in Figs. 5 through 7. On all models, the special puller (7—Fig. 9) is essential for flywheel removal.

On models with automatic timing advance, a hole is provided in fanwheel which can be used to block the weight in advance position for timing adjustment.

On some models with fixed timing, the breaker cam can be installed for clockwise or counter-clockwise crankshaft rotation. The cam may be marked

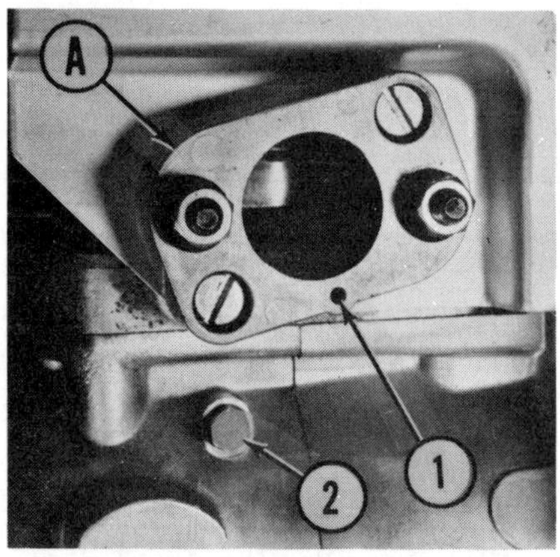

Fig. 1–Carburetor adapter flange of the type equipped with internal pulse passage for fuel pump operation. External passage port must be plugged as shown.

A. Adapter flange
1. Pulse passage
2. External port plug

Fig. 2–Carburetor adapter flange (B) is type not equipped with internal pulse passage. Fitting (3) in external passage port operates fuel pump. Refer also to Figs. 1 and 3.

Fig. 3–Intake port of cylinder with adapter flange removed, showing the drilled pulse passage (P). Refer to Figs. 1 & 2 for assembled options.

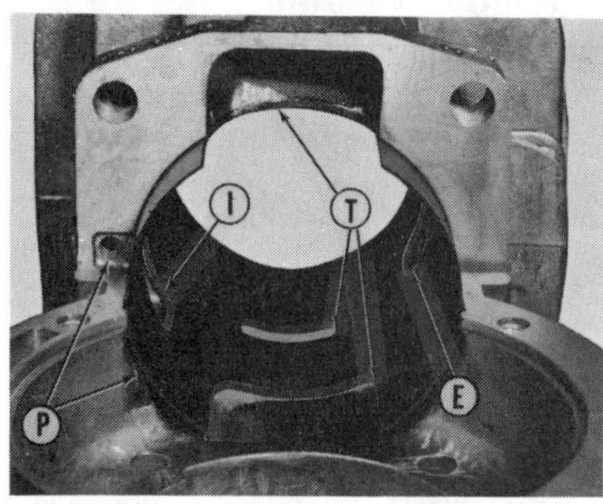

Fig. 4–Cylinder installed on crankcase half showing relative location of cylinder ports.

E. Exhaust port
I. Intake port
P. Pulse passages
T. Transfer ports

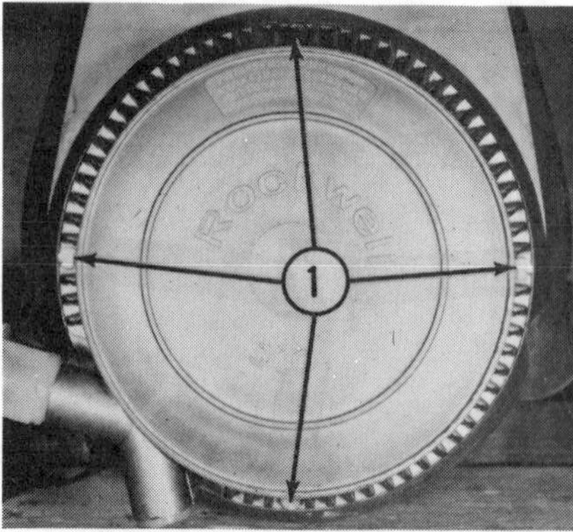

Fig. 5–Recoil starter is retained by four slotted screws (1). On some models, starter must be removed separately for access to flywheel.

Fig. 6–With starter removed as shown in Fig. 5, remove the three screws (2) and lift off starter hub (3) and rope pulley (4). Fan cover (5) can now be unbolted and removed.

Fig. 7–View of fan cover with rope pulley removed, showing details of construction.

Fig. 8–Remove flywheel nut (6).

Fig. 9–The special puller (7) is a practical necessity for flywheel removal.

Fig. 10–Cutaway of JLO engine.

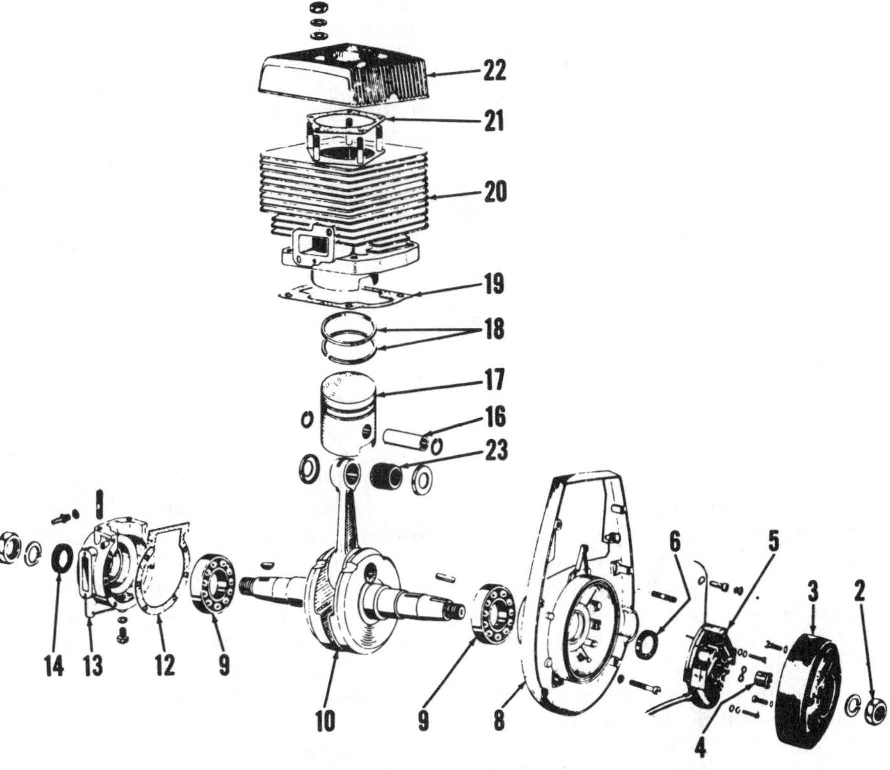

Fig. 12–Exploded view of JLO L297 engine. All engines except L252 and L152 are similar. For parts identification use Fig. 11 except for: 23. Needle roller bearing.

with the letters "R" and "L" which refers to direction of rotation when viewed from drive end; or by arrows which point to direction of rotation. Flywheel key must be installed in notch marked "L" for normal rotation on cams marked with the letters.

LUBRICATION. The engine is lubricated by mixing oil with the fuel. A suitable two-cycle, air cooled engine oil is recommended. Standard grade SAE 30 Automotive Motor Oil may be used if two-cycle oil is not available.

Recommended fuel/oil mixture ratio for each engine model is given in CONDENSED SERVICE DATA Tables at the beginning of this section. Mix fuel and oil thoroughly in a separate container before pouring mixture into fuel tank. For cold weather blending, pre-mix the oil with a small amount of gasoline and shake thoroughly until the mixture is liquid, then blend with remainder of fuel. Do not use kerosene or fuel oil for pre-mixing.

1. Fanwheel
2. Flywheel nut
3. Flywheel
4. Breaker cam
5. Armature plate
6. Crankshaft seal
7. Fan housing
8. Crankcase half
9. Main bearing
10. Crankshaft assembly
11. Spacer (governor gear)
12. Gasket
13. Crankcase half
14. Crankshaft seal
15. Bushing
16. Piston pin
17. Piston
18. Ring set
19. Cylinder gasket
20. Cylinder
21. Head gasket
22. Cylinder head

REPAIRS

TIGHTENING TORQUES. Recommended tightening torques are as follows:

Flywheel Nut
- Model L99 . . . . 29-32 ft.-lbs.
- Model L152 . . . . 20-25 ft.-lbs.
- Model L197, L227, L230 32-36 ft.-lbs.
- Model L252, L292 . . . . . 43-50 ft.-lbs.
- Models L295, L297, L300, L340, L372, L380, L395 . . . 79-86 ft.-lbs.

Standard Nuts
- 6mm . . . . 80-85 in.-lbs.
- 8mm . . . . 16-18 ft.-lbs.
- 10mm . . . . 31-33 ft.-lbs.

DISASSEMBLY AND REASSEMBLY. Refer to Figs. 11 and 12 for exploded views of engines. When service is required, first remove engine as

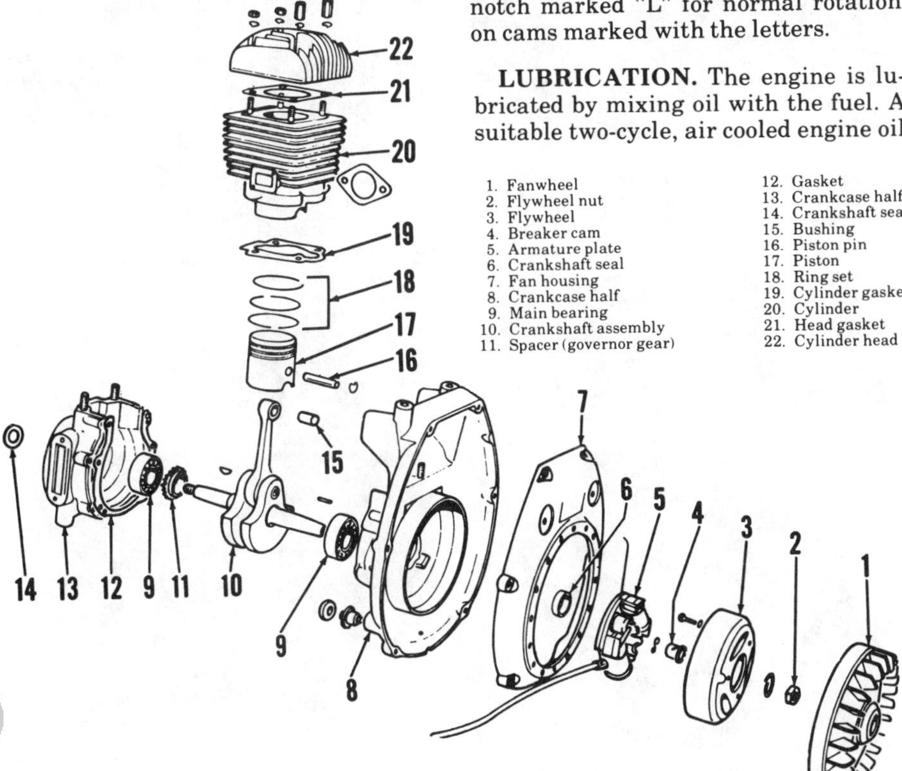

Fig. 11–Exploded view of JLO L252 engine. L152 is similar.

outlined in vehicle section of this manual and remove carburetor, drive sheave, recoil starter and muffler. NOTE: Some engines installed on BOLENS HUS-SKI are counter-rotating (clockwise, viewed from drive end). All other engines are normal (counter-clockwise) rotation.

Cylinder and/or cylinder head can be removed without further disassembly of engine. Crankshaft main bearings (9) are a tight press fit on crankshaft and in crankcase at room temperature. Bearing area of crankcase should be heated for disassembly. Some engines use the governor drive gear (11) as a spacer when engine is assembled. Crankshaft and connecting rod are available only as an assembled unit.

When assembling the crankcase, heat main bearings (9) in oil to approximately 160°-200° F. and install on shaft, supporting shaft underneath the counterweight to prevent misalignment. Heat bearing area of crankcase halves, being careful not to damage oil seals. Assemble by reversing the disassembly procedure. Refer to the appropriate following paragraphs for further disassembly and inspection procedure.

PISTON, RINGS & CYLINDER. Piston pin is a floating fit in piston and connecting rod. Piston rings are pinned in place as shown in Fig. 13. Three ring pistons or pistons with one ring are sometimes used.

Pistons are marked for size (S—Fig. 14) and for proper installation, the letter "V" and Arrow pointing toward exhaust port (E). Pins in ring grooves (P—Fig. 13) are installed toward flywheel end of crankshaft.

The cylinder head on some models contains a "Squish Area" (Fig. 15). The position of correct head installation is not marked, but flat area should go toward exhaust port as shown.

On snowmobile engines except earlier Model L372, the cylinder, gaskets and carburetor adapter flange are drilled to provide a pulse passage for operation of the diaphragm type fuel pump built into the carburetor. Be sure drilled passages are open and aligned when parts are installed.

Upper connecting rod bearing is bushing type on Models L152 and L252 and a needle roller bearing on other models.

CRANKSHAFT & CONNECTING ROD ASSEMBLY. The crankshaft and connecting rod unit is available only as an assembled unit and disassembly is not recommended. Bearings are a tight press fit on shaft and in crankcase bores at room temperature. Heat bearings in oil to a temperature of 160°-200° F. and support crankshaft between counterweights before installing bearings on shaft. On some engines, governor drive gear (11—Fig. 11) is used as a spacer for pto side bearing.

Figs. 17 & 18 show details of the "Piston Guided" rod used on many late models. The rod is positioned by piston bosses rather than by big end, and critical centering of crankshaft in crankcase is not necessary.

RECOIL STARTER. The basic recoil starters can be assembled for clockwise or counter-clockwise engine rotation, although some of the parts may not be machined for counter-rotation. Fig. 19 shows a removed starter correctly assembled for normal rotation (counter-clockwise viewed from drive end).

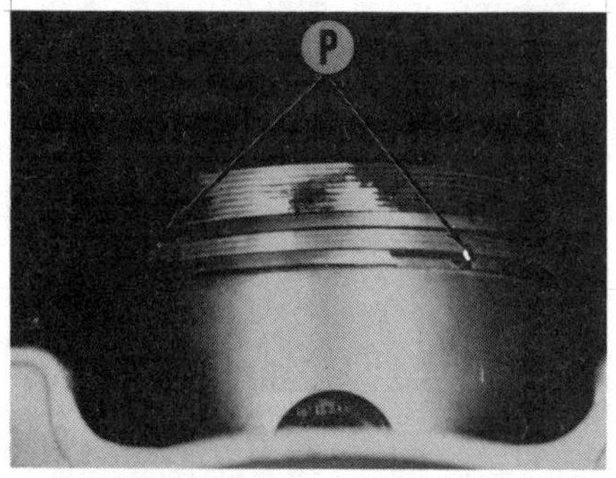

Fig. 13–Pins (P) in ring grooves prevent rotation of ring ends into cylinder ports and consequent ring breakage. Piston is installed with pins (P) toward flywheel end of crankshaft.

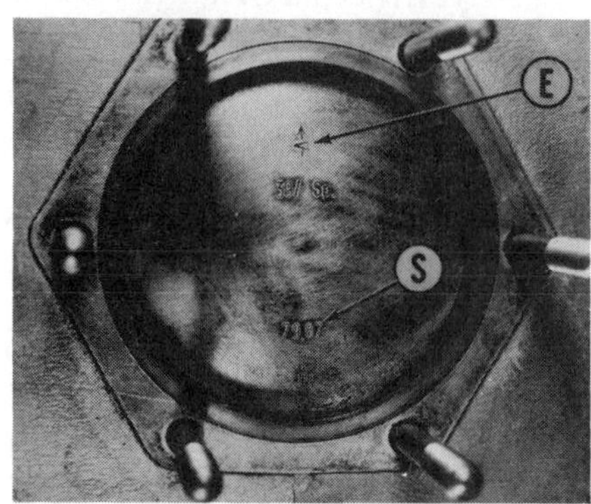

Fig. 14–Top of piston showing size marking (S) which gives exact diameter of piston at skirt; and letter & arrow marking (E) which must be installed toward exhaust side of cylinder. Other markings shown have no service significance.

Fig. 15–On models with squish area built into combustion chamber, flat portion should be installed toward exhaust ports as shown.

Fig. 16–Crankshaft and piston unit used on L340 engine. Other models with full circle crank are similar.

Fig. 17–Crankshaft end of "Piston Guided" connecting rod. Refer also to Fig. 18.

Fig. 18–"Piston Guided" connecting rod pushed forward to expose bearing rollers. Lower end of rod is centered on crankshaft by the piston.

To disassemble the removed starter unit, remove the four screws and lift off cover plate (1—Fig. 20). Items (2, 3 & 4) comprise an engaging brake which overcomes tension of return spring (6—Fig. 21) and causes pawl engagement when starter rope is pulled. Be careful not to lose these parts when cover plate is removed. Unhook springs (6) at pulley end, then lift off pawls, engaging brake and inner cover (7).

If rope is intact, remove handle grip and wind rope end into housing. Working through pulley anchor hole (C—Fig. 24) disengage inner end of spring from pulley and carefully lift off pulley. Spring (9—Fig. 23) will remain in recess of housing as shown if inner end is properly disengaged.

When assembling, unseat inner rope anchor from hole (R—Fig. 24) in pulley and withdraw the rope. Make sure spring is installed as shown in Fig. 23. Working through anchor hole (C) with a suitable punch to make sure spring is anchored in pulley, reinstall the pulley without the rope. Insert a punch (P—Fig. 25) part way into pulley and completely wind the spring. Allow spring to uncoil until anchor hole (R) is aligned with outlet hole (X—Fig. 24), then block pulley from further rotation by wedging punch (P) against spring anchor pin (A—Fig. 23). With pulley correctly positioned, install rope from inside as shown in Fig. 24 and 25. Complete the assembly by reversing the disassembly procedure.

Fig. 19–Recoil starter of the type used on most models.

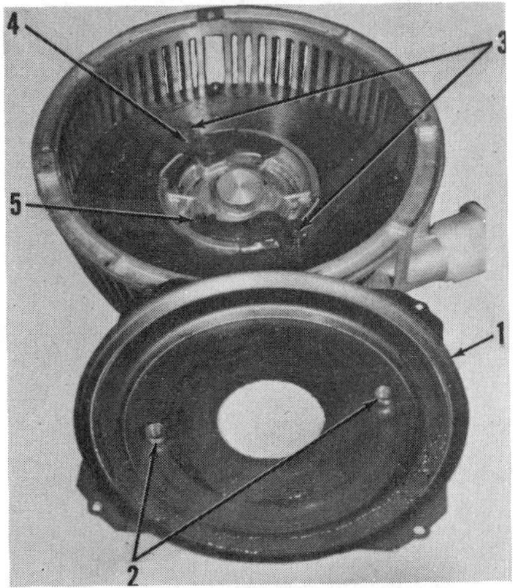

Fig. 20–To disassemble the starter, remove the retaining screws and lift off cover plate (1). Engaging brake units consist of friction cups (2 & 4) and spring (3) which fit holes in pawls and may fall out when cover (1) is removed.

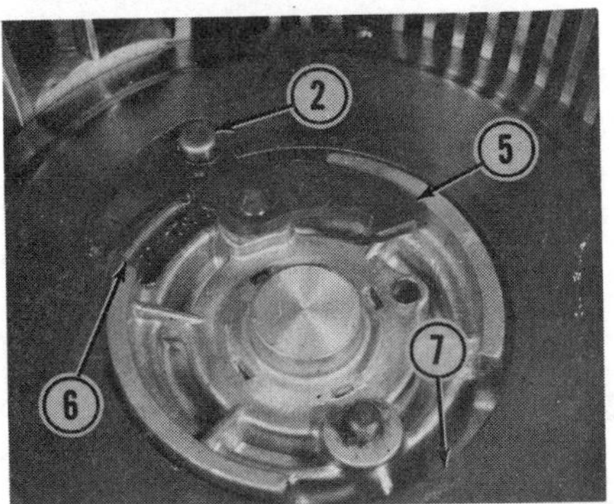

Fig. 21–Springs (6) return pawls (5) to running (disengaged) position. Pawls may be lifted off after removing cover plate (1-Fig. 20) and unhooking springs (6). Inner cover (7) can be lifted off after pawls are removed.

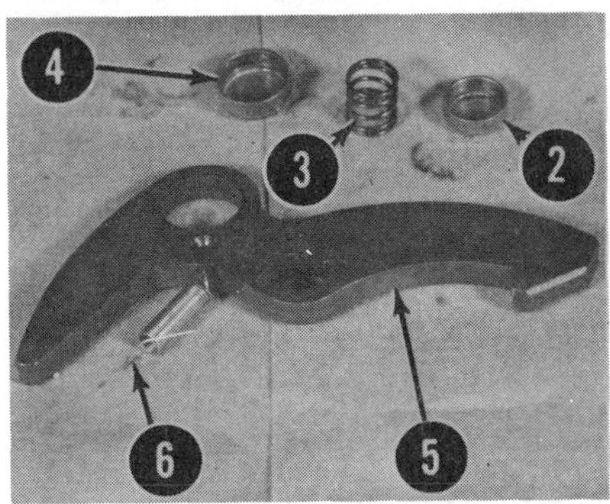

Fig. 22–Disassembled view of pawl (5), engaging brake (2, 3 & 4) and return spring (6). Refer to Fig. 20 or 21 for correct installed position.

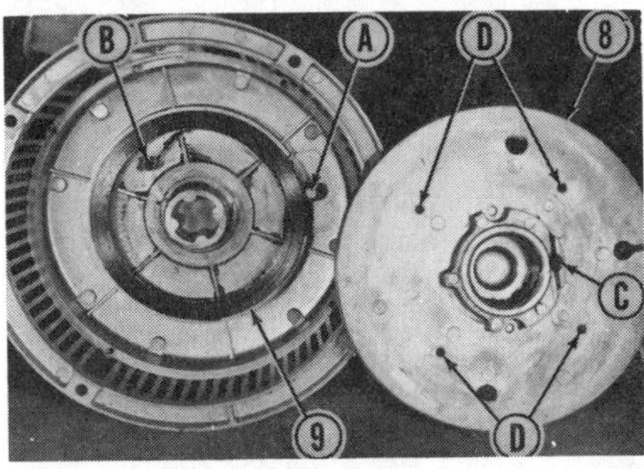

Fig. 23–View of starter housing with pulley removed, showing proper installation of recoil spring. Loop (B) in inner end anchors in hole (C) in pulley. Outer end is installed over anchor pin (A).

8. Pulley
9. Spring
A. Anchor pin
B. Inner loop
C. Anchor hole
D. Installation tool holes

Fig. 24–Opposite side of spring anchor hole (C) (See Fig. 23) permits insertion of punch for aligning spring end. Insert punch (P) and wind recoil spring completely; then back off until rope anchor hole (R) aligns with outlet hole (X) in housing. Insert rope cable from inside as shown.

Fig. 25–Rope anchor (R) properly seated in pulley. Install starter grip, then allow spring to slowly recoil.

JLO

TWO CYLINDER MODELS CONDENSED SERVICE DATA

ENGINE MODEL	LR340/2	LR399/2	LR440/2	LR600/2	LR760/2
Bore—(mm)	60	65	69	75	80
Inches	2.362	2.559	2.716	2.953	3.149
Stroke—(mm)	60	60	58	74	74
Inches	2.362	2.362	2.283	2.913	2.913
No. of Cylinders	2	2	2	2	2
Displacement—(cc)	339	398	433.8	592	744
Cubic Inches	20.68	24.28	26.46	36.2	45.38
Horsepower @ RPM	24 @ 6000	28 @ 6000	26.0 @ 6000	32.5 @ 5000	45.0 @ 5500
Cooling Type	Axial Fan	Axial Fan	Axial Fan	Centrif. Fan	Centrif. Fan
Carburetor Model	HD	HD	HR	HD	HD
Number Used	1	1	2	2	2
Ignition:					
Type	SCP2V 12V/75W	SCP2V 12V/75W	RPC1V 12V/75W	SCP 1x2V 12V/40W	RCP1V 12V/75W
Point Gap—(mm)	0.35-0.45	0.35-0.45	0.35-0.45	0.35-0.45	0.35-0.45
Inch	0.016	0.016	0.016	0.016	0.016
Edge Gap—(mm)	....	....	....	17.5-22.5	....
Inch	....	....	....	0.689-0.886	....
Timing Advance?	Yes	Yes	Yes	Yes	Yes
Timing BTDC (mm)	(A)	(A)	2.1-2.6	3.0-3.5	3.0-3.5
Inch	(A)	(A)	0.083-0.102	0.118-0.138	0.118-0.138
Degrees	....	....	....	....	....
Measured at	Adv. Cam	Adv. Cam	Adv. Cam	Adv. Cam	Adv. Cam
Spark Plug:					
Bosch	W240T2	W240T2	M240T1	M225T1	M240T1
Champion	N3	N3	K57R	UK10	K57R
Electrode Gap (mm)	0.4-0.5	0.4-0.5	0.4-0.5	0.4-0.5	0.4-0.5
Inch	0.018	0.018	0.018	0.018	0.018
Fuel/Oil Ratio	20:1	20:1	20:1	20:1	20:1

(A) Advance timing is 0.104-0.124 (Inch BTDC) for LR340/2 before Serial No. 14851 or LR399/2 before Serial No. 30298. On later models, correct advance timing is 0.083-0.102 Inch BTDC.

MAINTENANCE

SPARK PLUG. The recommended plug for normal service is given in CONDENSED SERVICE DATA Tables. Hotter or colder plugs may be required for particular applications. Recommended spark plug tightening torque is 25 ft.-lbs.

CARBURETOR. Tillotson or Walbro diaphragm type carburetors are used on most snowmobile engines. Most engines are equipped with an integral, pulse-type fuel pump built into carburetor, but some models may be equipped with a carburetor without fuel pump. See Tillotson carburetor section for operation and overhaul procedure. All models use either HR or HD carburetors which should have idle and high speed mixture needles open one turn for initial adjustment.

External pulse passages are used and cylinder blocks and manifolds do not contain pulse passage drillings.

IGNITION AND TIMING. Timing specifications for individual engines are given in CONDENSED SERVICE DATA Tables. All models have a centrifugal advance mechanism which provides retarded ignition timing for starting only. The mechanism should be blocked in advance position for timing. Axial fan twins have two timing marks cast into fan housing and two marks machined into flywheel as shown in Fig. 1. Advance timing for either cylinder can be checked with a power timing light using the left mark on fan housing. Static (retarded) timing can be checked using the right cast mark. Correct the timing for one cylinder by first adjusting to correct point gap, then rotating armature plate as required. Time the second cylinder by adjusting point gap only.

Correct breaker point gap is 0.014-0.018 (inch) for all models and correct piston timing is given in CONDENSED SERVICE DATA Tables.

LUBRICATION. The engine is lubricated by oil mixed with the fuel. The engine manufacturer recommends a good brand of premium gasoline and special 2-cycle engine oil mixed at a ratio of 20:1. Refer also to vehicle manufacturer's recommendations.

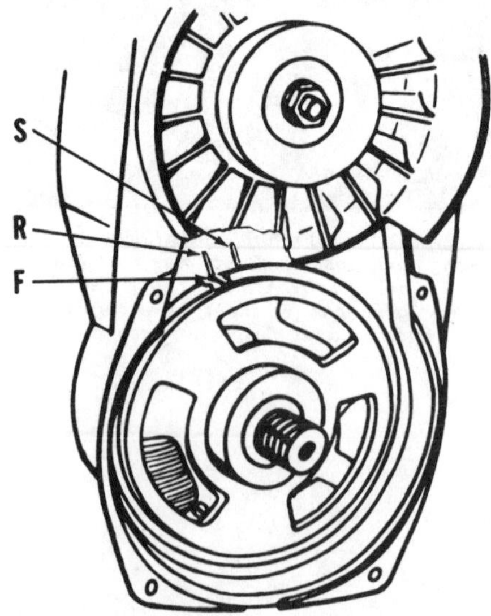

Fig. 1–View of flywheel and fan housing showing timing marks.

F. Flywheel Mark
R. Running timing
S. Static timing

COOLING FAN AND BELT. The cooling fan drive belt should have approximately ¼-inch free play measured midway between pulleys. Free play is adjusted by adding or removing shims (10—Fig. 4) between halves (9) of driven pulley. To remove shaft nut (7) insert a suitable small punch through locking hole (L) in fan housing and (F) in fan to lock the shaft as shown in Fig. 3. Four shims are normally installed in original assembly and removing shims tightens the belt. Turn the pulley as nut is tightened to keep from pinching belt.

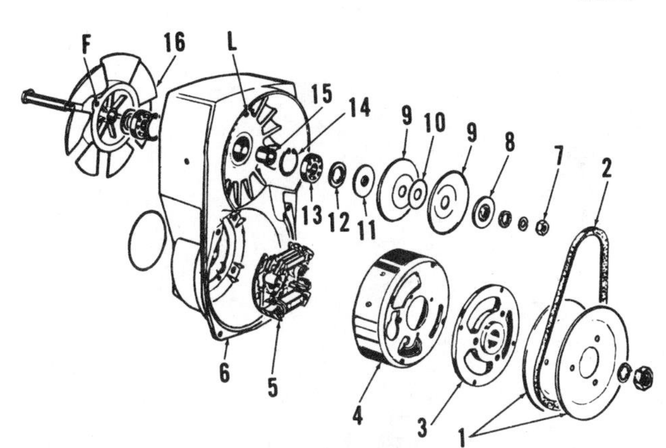

Fig. 4–View of fan housing and associated parts showing component parts.

1. Pulley half
2. Drive belt
3. Flywheel hub
4. Magneto ring
5. Magneto plate
6. Fan housing
7. Fan shaft nut
8. Tapered spacer
9. Pulley half
10. Adjusting shims
11. Tapered spacer
12. Nilos ring
13. Bearing
14. Snap ring
15. Spacer
16. Fan wheel
F. Locking hole (fan)
L. Locking hole (hsg)

REPAIRS

TIGHTENING TORQUES. Recommended tightening torques are as follows. Measurements are given in ft.-lbs.

Crankcase screws 16-18
Cylinder
  Model LB600/2 28-32
  All Other Models 16-18
Cylinder Head
  Model LB600/2 16-18
  All Other Models 28-32
Intake manifold
  Model LB600/2 (Adapter) 5-7
  All Other Models 10
Flywheel nut
  Model LB600/2 80-85
  All Other Models 45-50

Fig. 2–View of engine with recoil starter removed.

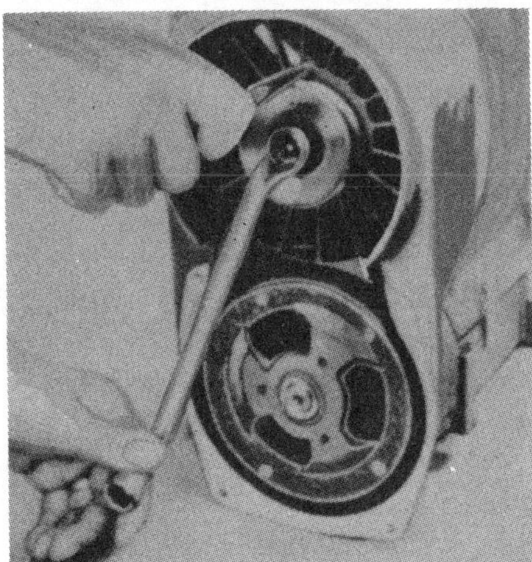

Fig. 3–Use a punch in locking holes to hold fan for disassembly.

Fig. 5–Carefully lower crankshaft assembly into lower crankcase half.

DISASSEMBLY AND REASSEMBLY. Engines consist of two types; the axial fan, inline twin and the simultaneous firing opposed twin. A third type listed in CONDENSED SERVICE DATA Tables is the centrifugal fan, in-line type LR760/2. This engine was of limited production and is not covered specifically in this paragraph. With cooling shrouds removed, service on this engine is similar to basic engine components of axial fan twins.

AXIAL FAN TWINS. Fan housing can be removed as a unit after removing recoil starter, starter drive

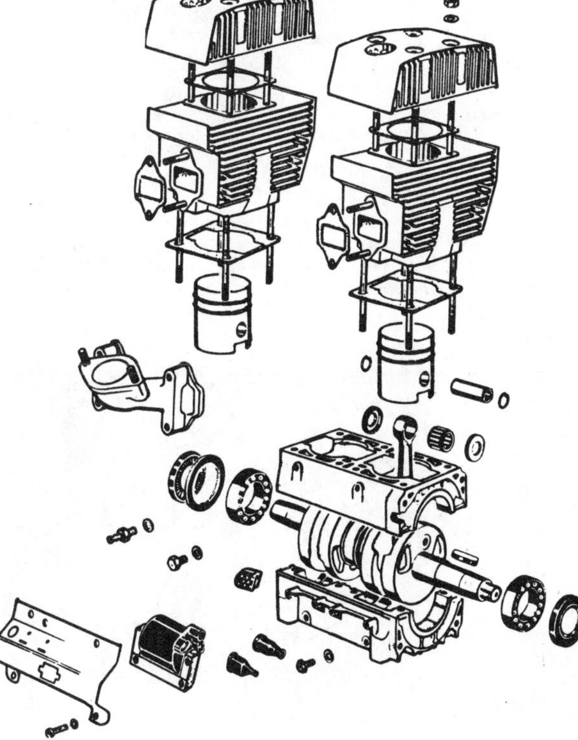

Fig. 6–Exploded view of axial twin engine showing component parts.

Fig. 7–Use a notched two by four to support piston while installing the cylinder.

hub, flywheel and the four retaining cap screws. Magneto armature plate is attached to fan housing and can be removed with housing or separately.

Cylinder heads and cylinders can be removed from crankcase after fan housing is removed or with fan housing in place if upper end service only is contemplated. Because crankcase through-studs retain the cylinders, it is suggested that cylinders be removed one at a time and reinstalled unless complete disassembly is planned, to prevent the possibility of crankcase and cylinder misalignment. If both cylinders and fan housing are removed, crankcase may be separated by breaking the sealant grip and lifting off upper crankcase half. Refer to the appropriate following paragraphs for service details on crankshaft, cylinders and associated parts.

When reassembling, thoroughly clean mating surfaces of crankcase halves and examine for burrs or other damage. Lightly coat lower crankcase flange and bearing surfaces with a suitable sealant. Carefully lower crankshaft assembly into position, aligning spacers with machined grooves. Install oil seal on PTO end, flush with outside of housing, then turn crankshaft by hand to check freedom of movement. Bump upper crankcase half lightly to seat the bearings.

Install pistons with "V" mark and arrow pointing toward exhaust side of engine then support piston on a notched two by four board as shown in Fig. 7. Use a suitable ring compresser and install cylinders. Temporarily install intake manifold to assure perfect cylinder alignment. Tighten cylinder base nuts alternately and evenly to recommended torque of 16-18 ft.-lbs. Install cylinder head gasket with wide metal band toward the head. Install cylinder heads with spark plug holes toward carburetor side.

When installing cooling fan pulley halves on flywheel, rotate crankshaft as retaining screws are tightened to permit belt to move outward and prevent damage to pulley halves or fan belt.

On electric starting models, starting gear attaches to output end of crankshaft as shown in Fig. 9. Gear is an easy slip fit on shaft and is retained by two wedge rings as shown in inset. Lightly lubricate shaft and hub and install gear until it bottoms on bearing. Proper positioning of wedge rings is shown in inset.

OPPOSED CYLINDER TWIN. Any disassembly of engine with the exception of carburetors requires prior removal of recoil starter, fan housing cover and flywheel. Refer to Figs. 11 and 12. Fan housing rear cover may be removed after removing flywheel, without removing magneto plate assembly. Remove cylinder heads, cylinders and pistons. Heat must be applied to crankcase to expand bearing bores before crankcase can be separated.

Install pistons with "V" mark and arrow pointing toward exhaust side of engine. Support piston on crankcase using a slotted two by four board as shown in Fig. 7, and install cylinder using a suitable ring compresser. Install cylinder head gasket with wide side of metal band toward cylinder

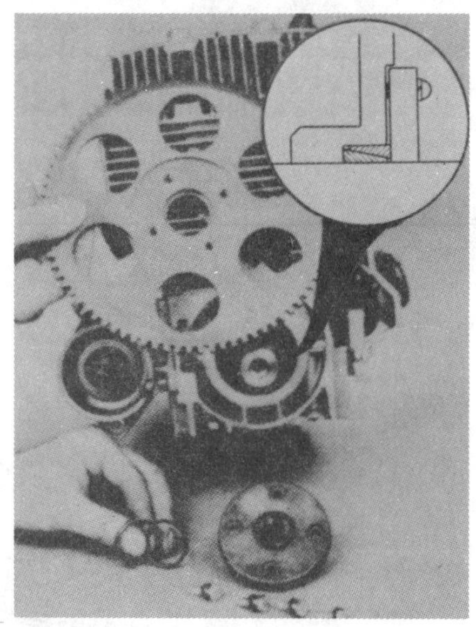

Fig. 9–Starter ring gear attaches to output end of crankshaft using two wedge rings as shown in inset. Disassembly is accomplished by sharply bumping the gear after removing pressure flange.

Fig. 10–Installed view of Opposed Cylinder Twin engine.

Fig. 11–View of engine with cooling shroud and starter hub removed, showing flywheel nut (F).

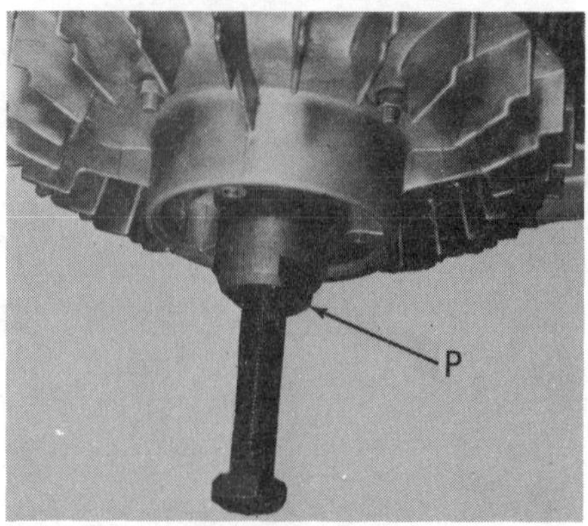

Fig. 12–Flywheel removal requires the use of a special puller (P).

Fig. 8–Installing lower fan pulley and starter drive hub.

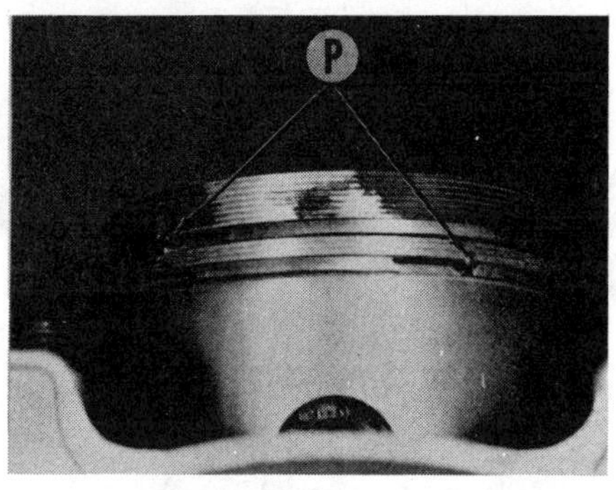

Fig. 13–Pins (P) in ring grooves prevent rotation of ring ends into cylinder ports and consequent ring breakage.

head. The five stud head can only be installed in one position. Recommended tightening torques are given in a previous paragraph.

PISTONS, RINGS AND CYLINDERS. Piston pin is a floating fit in piston and connecting rod. Connecting rod upper bearing is caged needle roller type which uses machined surfaces of pin and rod as bearing races. The two piston rings are pinned in place as shown in Fig. 13. Pistons and rings are available in standard size only.

The aluminum cylinders have cast iron cylinder sleeves. On axial fan twins, shrouding is cast into cylinder and head providing additional surface for heat dissipation. Free air versions of the axial fan twins are available for high performance applications.

CRANKSHAFT AND CONNECTING ROD ASSEMBLY. The crankshaft and connecting rod assembly is available only as a complete unit and should not be disassembled. End bearings, however, can be renewed if proper care is exercised. Use a knife-edged puller which applies pressure to bearing race and shaft end for removal, and support the shaft underneath the counterweight for installation. Refer to Fig. 14.

Check for wear at connecting rod big end by measuring the play (rock) at connecting rod small end. Check crankshaft for runout just before installation by supporting the shaft on end bearings and using a dial indicator at shaft ends and center bearings. Runout should not exceed 0.1 mm (0.004 inch). If runout is excessive, it is suggested that correction be made by a shop experienced and equipped for this work.

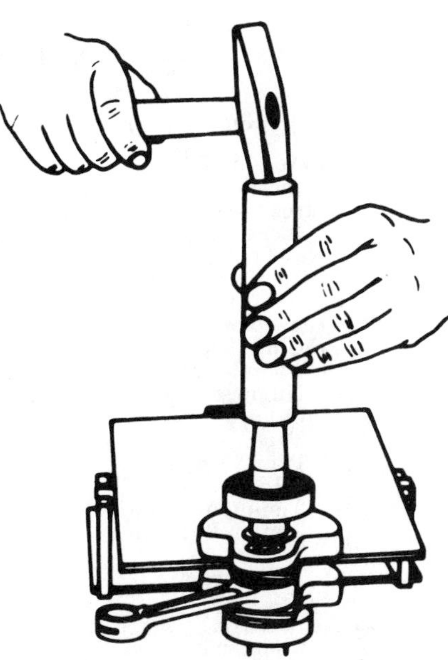

Fig. 14–Support end crankshaft under counterweight as shown, for bearing installation.

KAWASAKI

ONE CYLINDER MODELS

CONDENSED SERVICE DATA

ENGINE MODEL	KT-150A	KT-150B	KT-150C	T4B292
Bore—(mm)	74	74	79	74
Inches	2.913	2.913	3.110	2.913
Stroke—(mm)	68	68	68	68
Inches	2.677	2.677	2.677	2.677
No. of Cylinders	1	1	1	1
Displacement—(cc)	292	292	333	292
Cubic Inches	17.8	17.8	20.3	17.8
Horsepower @ RPM	20@5500	22@6000	24@6000	....
Cooling Type	Centrifugal Fan			
Carburetor Model	HR	HR	HD	WRD2
Number Used	1	1	1	1
Ignition:				
Type	Flywheel Magneto			
Point Gap—(mm)	0.3-0.4	0.3-0.4	0.3-0.4	0.3-0.4
Inch	0.012-0.016	0.012-0.016	0.012-0.016	0.012-0.016
Timing Advance?	Yes	Yes	Yes	Yes
Timing BTDC (mm)	0.65	0.65	0.65	0.14
Inch	0.0256	0.0256	0.0256	0.005
Measured At	Retard	Retard	Retard	Retard
Spark Plug:				
Bosch	M280T31	M280T31	....	....
Champion	K9	K9	....	....
NGK	....	....	B9ES	B9ES
Electrode Gap (mm)	0.5-0.6	0.5-0.6	0.5-0.6	0.5
Inch	0.020-0.024	0.020-0.024	0.020-0.024	0.020
Fuel/Oil Ratio	20:1	20:1	20:1	20:1

MAINTENANCE

SPARK PLUG. The recommended plug for normal service is given in CONDENSED SERVICE DATA Table. A different heat range or type of plug may be needed for particular applications. Refer to ENGINE SERVICE FUNDAMENTALS Section when selecting a spark plug for other than normal usage.

CARBURETOR. A Tillotson diaphragm carburetor is used on all models. Refer to Tillotson section to overhaul and service carburetors. An external impulse line is used to operate fuel pump. Be sure that vacuum and pressure leaks are eliminated.

IGNITION SYSTEM. Timing specifications for individual engines are given in CONDENSED SERVICE DATA Tables. Breaker point gap may be adjusted after removing recoil starter, starter pulley and inspection cover. To renew breaker points, the flywheel must be removed.

Timing can be checked using a light or buzzer connected to black wire coming from engine with other connector of timing light or buzzer being grounded to engine. Remove recoil starter and note timing holes in flywheel plate as shown in Fig. 1. Use right hole to check ignition timing. Stationary timing mark is found on a raised portion of crankcase at base of cylinder. Right hole indicates 10° BTDC when aligned with crankcase timing mark. Left hole indicates TDC when aligned with crankcase timing mark. Flywheel must be removed to adjust timing. Loosen screws (1 & 2—Fig. 2) and move base plate to adjust timing.

LUBRICATION. The engine is lubricated by mixing oil with fuel. A good quality two-cycle oil designed for air-cooled engines is recommended. Recommended fuel-oil ratio for all engines is 20:1. Mix fuel and oil thoroughly in a separate container before pouring mixture into fuel tank. For cold weather blending, pre-mix the oil with a small amount of gasoline and shake thoroughly until the mixture is liquid, then blend with remainder of fuel. Do not use kerosene or fuel oil for pre-mixing.

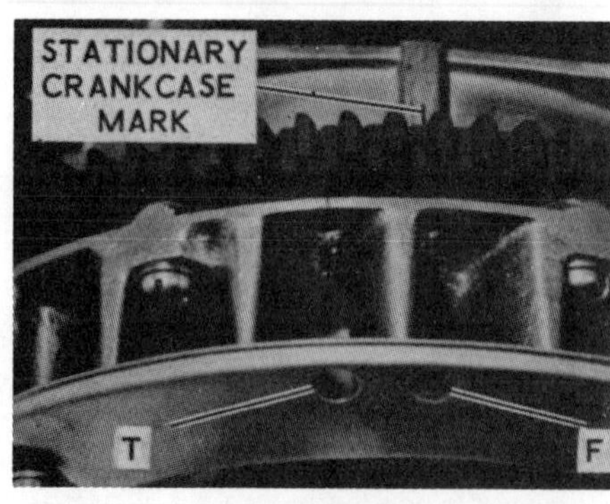

Fig. 1–View showing timing holes in flywheel plate. Hole (F) indicates 10 BTDC and hole (T) indicates TDC when aligned with crankcase mark.

REPAIRS

TIGHTENING TORQUES. Recommended tightening torques are as follows:

- Cylinder head .... 16 ft.-lbs.
- Crankcase bolts .... 13 ft.-lbs.
- Flywheel nut .... 56 ft.-lbs.
- Recoil starter mounting bolts .... 13 ft.-lbs.
- Spark plug .... 25 ft.-lbs.

DISASSEMBLY AND REASSEMBLY. Refer to Fig. 4 for exploded

Fig. 2–To adjust ignition timing, loosen screws (1 and 2) and move base plate.

view of engine. To disassemble engine, remove carburetor, muffler, drive sheave and recoil starter. Remove cooling shroud to remove cylinder head and cylinder. To disassemble crankcase, remove starter cup and flywheel. Mark position of magneto base assembly and remove. Remove timing advance mechanism. Remove cylinder head, cylinder and piston. Remove crankcase bolts and separate crankcase halves. Note that two of the crankcase bolts are longer than the other four bolts and their location should be marked in reassembly. Refer to CRANKSHAFT section to service crankshaft assembly.

To reassemble, reverse disassembly procedure. It may be necessary to heat bearing area of crankcase halves when installing crankshaft assembly. Do not damage oil seals when applying heat. Be sure to install correct length crankcase bolts in crankcase. Tighten crankcase bolts to a torque of 13 ft.-lbs. by tightening in a crisscross pattern.

PISTON, RINGS & CYLINDER. Piston pin is fully floating in piston and connecting rod. Piston rings are pinned in place as shown in Fig. 5. Top ring is identified by "1 NPR" stamped on upper surface of ring and must be installed with notch in ring end on upper surface as shown in Fig. 5. Bottom ring is stamped "2 NPR". Piston ring end gap should be 0.006-0.014 in. (0.15-0.35 mm). Piston pin and connecting rod small end bearing are available only as a matched pair and must be renewed as a set. It may be necessary to heat piston to install piston pin.

Piston crown is marked with an arrow to indicate piston location in cylinder. Arrow must point towards output end of crankshaft. Piston skirt to cylinder wall clearance should be 0.0035-0.005 in. Cylinder is constructed of aluminum alloy with a cast iron sleeve on models KT-150A and KT-150B. Sleeve may be honed slightly to remove imperfections. Model KT-150C is equipped with a chrome lined cylinder. Check for cracking, flaking or other imperfections in chrome lining. Small deposits of aluminum from piston on chrome bore may be removed with very careful sanding. When reinstalling cylinder head, be sure cooling fins are parallel with crankshaft.

CRANKSHAFT & CONNECTING ROD ASSEMBLY. The crankshaft and connecting rod are available only as an assembled unit and should not be disassembled. Crankshaft main bearings are a press fit on crankshaft. Support crankshaft between counterweights as shown in Fig. 7 when pressing bearings on shaft. Crankshaft runout should not exceed 0.0012 in. (0.03mm). Radial play of connecting rod big end should not exceed 0.0009 in. (0.023mm). Crankshaft end play should be 0.002-0.013 in. (0.05-0.335mm). Shims (10—Fig. 4) are available from manufacturer.

RECOIL STARTER. Refer to exploded view of starter in Fig. 8. To disassemble starter, remove starter from engine and remove waterproofing plate (1). Pull rope out until it is possible to position rope in notch of rope

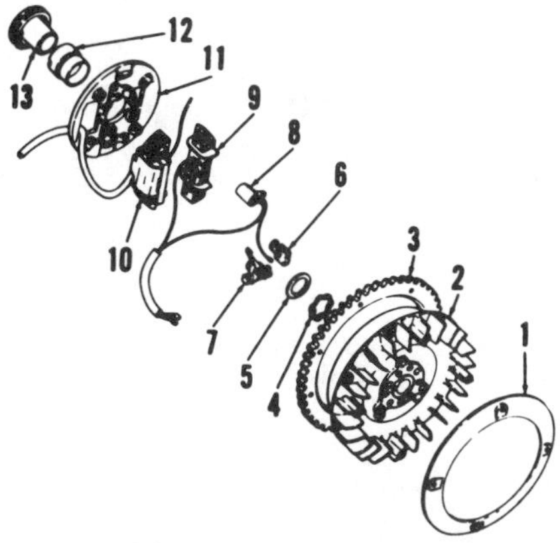

Fig. 3–Exploded view of flywheel magneto assembly.

1. Plate
2. Flywheel
3. Ring gear
4. Spring washer
5. Lock plate
6. Wiper felt
7. Breaker points
8. Condenser
9. Lighting coil
10. Ignition coil
11. Base plate
12. Cam
13. Advance mechanism

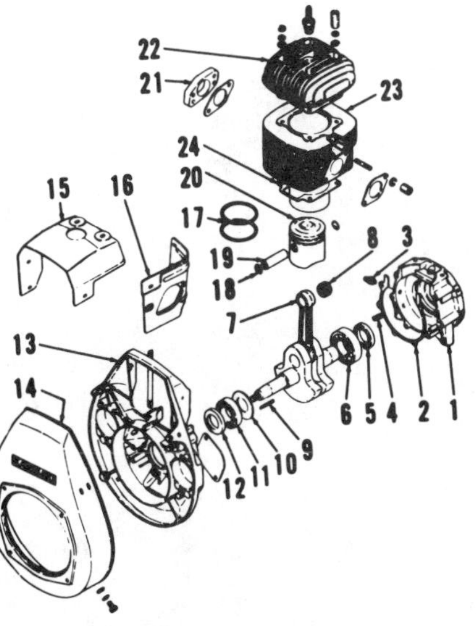

Fig. 4–Exploded view of single cylinder models.

1. Crankcase half
2. Gasket
3. Pulse fitting
4. Drain plug
5. Oil seal
6. Bearing
7. Crankshaft assy.
8. Needle bearing
9. Key
10. Shim
11. Bearing
12. Oil seal
13. Crankcase half
14. Cover
15. Upper cooling shroud
16. Side cooling shroud
17. Piston rings
18. Snap ring
19. Piston pin
20. Piston
21. Carburetor insulator
22. Cylinder head
23. Cylinder
24. Gasket

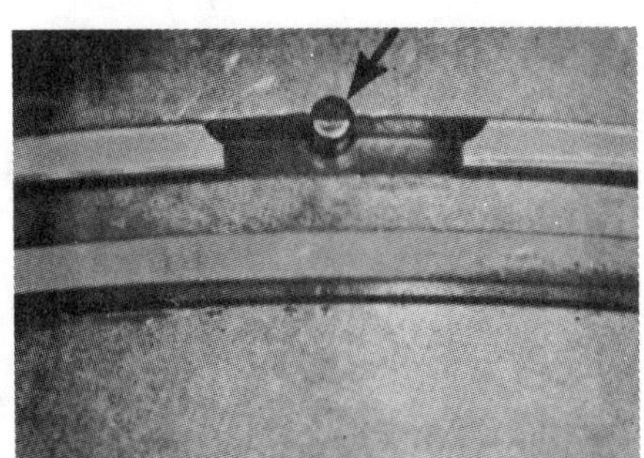

Fig. 5–Piston rings are pinned as shown (arrow). Note that upper ring is installed so that notches in ring ends are up.

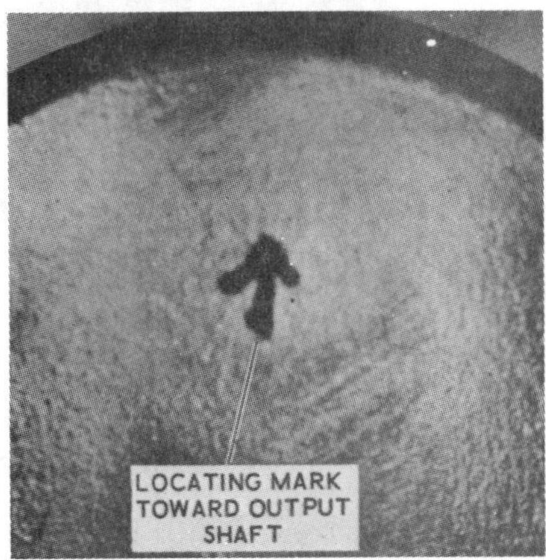

Fig. 6–Install piston so that arrow on piston crown points towards output end of crankshaft.

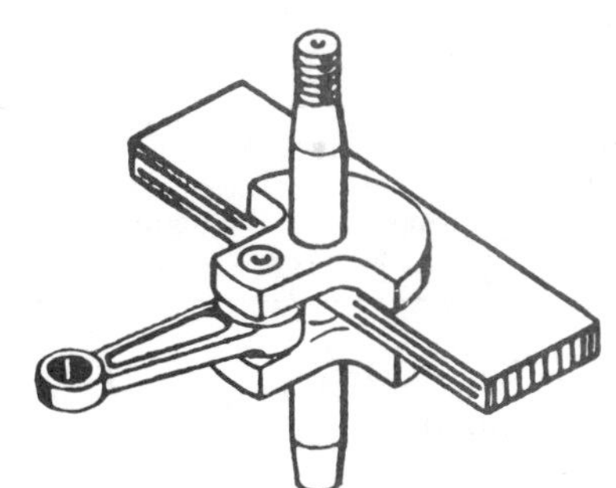

Fig. 7–Be sure to place a support between counterweights of crankshaft when pressing bearings.

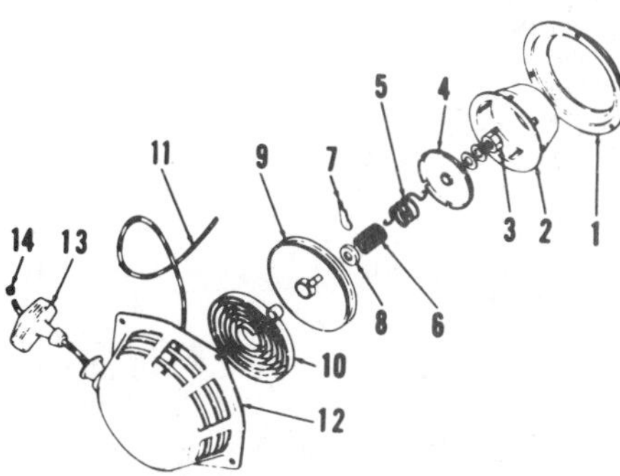

Fig. 8–Exploded view of recoil starter.

1. Waterproofing plate
2. Starter cup
3. Nut
4. Retainer
5. Return spring
6. Spring
7. Pawls
8. Washer
9. Rope pulley
10. Recoil spring
11. Rope
12. Cover
13. Handle
14. Retainer

pulley. Release rope and allow recoil spring to unwind. Remove retaining nut (3) and components (6 thru 8). Carefully remove rope pulley so that recoil spring remains in cover. If necessary to remove recoil spring, guard against uncontrolled uncoiling of spring which may cause personal injury.

To assemble starter, install recoil spring in cover so that spring is wound in counterclockwise direction and outer hook of spring contacts lug of cover. Install rope pulley and rope so that lug of pulley engages with inner hook of recoil spring. Install washer (8), pawls (7), spring (6) and pawl return spring (5). Install retainer cover (4) so that end of return spring (5) protrudes through retainer cover (4) and turn retainer cover one-third turn clockwise to pre-load spring. Install washers and retaining nut. If rope handle was not removed during disassembly, position rope in notch of rope pulley and turn pulley two turns counter-clockwise to pre-load recoil spring. If handle was removed, turn rope pulley counter-clockwise two or three turns and insert end of rope through rope outlet in cover. Tension on rope should be apparent. Tie a temporary knot to hold rope and install rope handle.

KAWASAKI TWO CYLINDER

CONDENSED SERVICE DATA

ENGINE MODEL	T1A340F1	T1A340S1	T1A400F1	T1A400S1	*T1A440F2	T1A440S1
Bore—(mm)	60	60	65	65	68	68
Inches	2.362	2.362	2.559	2.559	2.677	2.677
Stroke—(mm)	60	60	60	60	60	60
Inches	2.362	2.362	2.362	2.362	2.362	2.362
No. of Cylinders	2	2	2	2	2	2
Displacement—(cc)	339	339	398	398	436	436
Cubic Inches	20.7	20.7	24.3	24.3	26.6	26.6
Horsepower @ RPM	35 @ 7500	27.5 @ 6500	40 @ 7500	32 @ 6500	45 @ 7500	35 @ 6500
Cooling Type	Free Air	Axial Fan	Free Air	Axial Fan	Free Air	Axial Fan
Carburetor Model	HR	HD	HD	HD	HD	HD
Number Used	2	1	2	1	2	1
Ignition:						
Type	Energy Transfer					
Point Gap—(mm)	0.3-0.4	0.3-0.4	0.3-0.4	0.3-0.4	0.3-0.4	0.3-0.4
Inch	0.012-0.016	0.012-0.016	0.012-0.016	0.012-0.016	0.012-0.016	0.012-0.016
Timing Advance?	Yes	Yes	Yes	Yes	Yes	Yes
Timing BTDC (mm)	0.37	0.37	0.37	0.37	0.37	0.37
Inch	0.015	0.015	0.015	0.015	0.015	0.015
Measured at	Retard	Retard	Retard	Retard	Retard	Retard
Spark Plug:						
NGK	B10E	B9ES	B10E	B9ES	B10E	B9ES
Electrode Gap (mm)	0.5-0.6	0.5-0.6	0.5-0.6	0.5-0.6	0.5-0.6	0.5-0.6
Inch	0.020-0.024	0.020-0.024	0.020-0.024	0.020-0.024	0.020-0.024	0.020-0.024
Fuel/Oil Ratio	20:1	20:1	20:1	20:1	20:1	20:1

*May be equipped with Capacitor Discharge Ignition; all data is for Energy Transfer models.

ENGINE MODEL	T1B340S1	T1B400S1	T1B440S1	T1C340S2A	T1C440S2A	T1D250F1
Bore—(mm)	60	65	68	60	68	51
Inches	2.362	2.559	2.667	2.362	2.677	2.001
Stroke—(mm)	60	60	60	60	60	60
Inches	2.362	2.362	2.362	2.362	2.362	2.362
No. of Cylinders	2	2	2	2	2	2
Displacement—(cc)	339	398	436	339	436	245
Cubic Inches	20.7	24.3	26.6	20.7	26.6	14.9
Horsepower RPM	....	....	....	....	....	....
Cooling Type	Axial Fan	Axial Fan	Axial Fan	Axial Fan	Axial Fan	Free Air
Carburetor Model	WDA	WDA	WDA	WF1A	WF1A	VM
Number Used	1	1	1	1	1	1
Ignition:						
Type	Energy Transfer			CDI	CDI	ET
Point Gap—(mm)	0.3-0.4	0.3-0.4	0.3-0.4	....	....	0.3-0.4
Inch	0.012-0.016	0.012-0.016	0.012-0.016	....	....	0.012-0.016
Timing Advance?	Yes	Yes	Yes	Electronic	Electronic	Yes
Timing BTDC	0.14 mm	0.14 mm	0.14 mm	25°	25°	5°
	0.005 In.	0.005 In.	0.005 In.	....	....	....
Measured at	Retard	Retard	Retard	6000 rpm	6000 rpm	Retard
Spark Plug:						
NGK	B9ES	B9ES	B9ES	B8ESA	B8ESA	BR8ESA
Electrode Gap—(mm)	0.5	0.5	0.5	0.75	0.75	0.5
Inch	0.020	0.020	0.020	0.030	0.030	0.020
Fuel/Oil Ratio	20:1	20:1	20:1	20:1	20:1	20:1

CONDENSED SERVICE DATA CONT.

ENGINE MODEL	T1D340F1	T1D340A2A	T1D440A2A	T7C340FR1	T7C440FR1
Bore—(mm)	60	60	68	60	68
Inches	2.362	2.362	2.677	2.362	2.677
Stroke—(mm)	60	60	60	60	60
Inches	2.362	2.362	2.362	2.362	2.362
No. of Cylinders	2	2	2	2	2
Displacement—(cc)	339	339	436	339	436
Cubic Inches	20.7	20.7	26.6	20.7	26.6
Horsepower RPM	....	....	....	....	....
Cooling Type	Free Air	Axial Fan	Axial Fan	Free Air	Free Air
Carburetor Model	VM	WF7	WF7	VM	VM
Number Used	1	1	1	2	2
Ignition:					
Type	ET	CDI	CDI	Dual CDI	Dual CDI
Point Gap—(mm)	0.3-0.4	....	....	....	....
Inch	0.012-0.016	....	....	....	....
Timing Advance?	Yes	....	....	....	....
Timing BTDC	5°	25°	25°	14°	17°
Measured at	Retard	6000 rpm	6000 rpm	6000 rpm	6000 rpm
Spark Plug:					
NGK	BR8ESA	B8ESA	B8ESA	BR9EVA	BR9EVA
Electrode Gap—(mm)	0.5	0.75	0.75	0.75	0.75
Inch	0.020	0.030	0.030	0.030	0.030
Fuel/Oil Ratio	20:1	20:1	20:1	20:1	20:1

MAINTENANCE

SPARK PLUG. The recommended plug for normal service is given in CONDENSED SERVICE DATA Table. A different heat range or type of plug may be needed for a particular application. Refer to ENGINE SERVICE FUNDAMENTALS Section when selecting a spark plug for other than normal usage.

Some engines use a heat indicator thermo couple instead of a spark plug gasket. REMOVE GASKET if thermo couple is used. Thermo couple sensor (lead terminal) must be installed DOWNWIND from cooling air blast when spark plug is tightened; directly to rear on free air models or at 7-o'clock position on axial fan units.

CARBURETOR. Mikuni, Tillotson or Walbro carburetors are used. Refer to the appropriate CARBURETOR SERVICE Section for overhaul data. An external impulse line from engine crankcase is used to operate fuel pump. Be sure there are no vacuum or pressure leaks.

IGNITION SYSTEM. Timing specifications for individual engines are given in CONDENSED SERVICE DATA Tables. Breaker point gap may be adjusted after removing recoil starter, starter pulley and inspection cover. To renew breaker points, the flywheel must be removed.

On models having an energy transfer type ignition system, timing marks are found on fan cover and flywheel. Flywheel has two "F" marks which are 180° apart. To check timing, connect one lead of a light or buzzer to the black wire coming from either cylinder of the engine and ground the other lead on the engine. Timing is correct if points separate when one of the "F" marks is aligned with the stationary mark on the fan cover. Check timing of other cylinder using corresponding black wire and second "F" mark on flywheel.

On models with capacitor discharge system, ignition timing is checked using an automobile type timing light with engine running. To check the timing, remove recoil starter and install a suitable power timing light. Solidly support rear of machine with a hoist so track can turn freely without danger of accident. Start and run engine at 6000 rpm. With timing light directed at flywheel rim the scribed "T" mark on flywheel should align with cast timing boss on fan housing. If "T" mark is clockwise from stationary mark, timing is retarded; if counter-clockwise, timing is advanced.

Because timing is electronic, it should not change once properly adjusted. The first step in adjustment, therefore, would be to check for loose flywheel nut, sheared flywheel key, or loose mounting screws on stator base plate. To adjust the timing, stop engine and remove the three screws retaining emergency starter pulley and belt pulley. Remove the pulleys and, working through holes in flywheel, loosen the two stator base plate mounting screws. Move stator plate clockwise to retard the timing or counter-clockwise to advance the timing. Tighten screws securely then recheck running timing.

LUBRICATION. The engine is lubricated by mixing oil with fuel. A good quality two-cycle oil designed for air-cooled engines is recommended. Recommended fuel-oil ratio for all engines is 20:1. Mix fuel and oil thoroughly in a separate container before pouring mixture into fuel tank. For cold weather blending, pre-mix the oil with a small amount of gasoline and shake thoroughly until the mixture is liquid, then blend with remainder of fuel. Do not use kerosene or fuel oil for pre-mixing.

REPAIRS

TIGHTENING TORQUES. Recommended tightening torques are as follows:

Cylinder head	16 ft.-lbs. (2.2 kg-m)
Crankcase nuts	16 ft.-lbs. (2.2 kg-m)
Crankcase bolts	5 ft.-lbs. (0.7 kg-m)
Flywheel nut	60 ft.-lbs. (8.3 kg-m)
Recoil starter mounting bolts	5 ft.-lbs. (0.7 kg-m)
Spark plug	20 ft.-lbs. (2.8 kg-m)

DISASSEMBLY AND REASSEMBLY. Remove carburetor, muffler, drive sheave and recoil starter. On models with axial fans, remove fan belt and fan assembly. Remove cooling shrouds. Remove starter cup, flywheel and ignition coils. Mark position of magneto base assembly and remove the two retaining screws from slotted holes; wiring loom fits in a grommet in crankcase parting line and magneto assembly cannot be lifted out until crankcase is split. Remove cylinder heads, cylinders and pistons and mark so that they will be installed in their original positions. Remove ten nuts and one bolt and separate crankcase halves. Refer to appropriate section to service components.

To reassemble, reverse disassembly procedure. Tighten crankcase nuts to 16 ft.-lbs. and crankcase bolt to 5 ft.-lbs. Refer to Fig. 1 for tightening sequence.

PISTON, RINGS & CYLINDER. Piston pins are fully floating. Piston rings are pinned in place as shown in Fig. 2. Bottom ring is equipped with an expander. Top ring is identified by "1 NPR" stamped on upper surface of ring. Bottom ring is stamped "2 NPR". Notches of ring ends must be up when ring is installed as shown in Fig. 2. Piston ring end gap for 250 and 340 cc models should be 0.006-0.014 inch (0.15-0.35 mm). Piston ring end gap for 440 cc models should be 0.008-0.016 inch (0.2-0.4 mm). Top ring side clearance should be 0.004-0.006 inch (0.1-0.15 mm) and lower ring side clearance should be 0.002-0.004 inch (0.05-0.1 mm) for all models. Piston pin and piston pin bearing are available only as a matched pair and must be renewed as a set. It may be necessary to heat piston to install piston pin.

Piston crown is marked with an arrow as shown in Fig. 3 to indicate piston position in cylinder. Arrow must point towards exhaust port. Piston skirt to cylinder wall clearance should be 0.0008-0.002 inch (0.02-0.05 mm) for all engines. Cylinder has a chrome bore. Small deposits of aluminum from piston on cylinder wall may be removed by very careful sanding. Cylinder should be inspected for cracking, flaking or other deterioration of the chrome lining. Also check for appearance of underlying base metal through chrome which indicates excessive wear.

CRANKSHAFT & CONNECTING ROD ASSEMBLY. The crankshaft and connecting rod are available only as an assembled unit and should not be disassembled. Crankshaft main bearings are a press fit on crankshaft. Support crankshaft between counterweights as shown in Fig. 4 when pressing bearings on shaft. Crankshaft runout should not exceed 0.0012 in. (0.03mm). Radial play of connecting rod big end should not exceed 0.0009 in. (0.023mm). Crankshaft end play should not exceed 0.030 in. (0.77mm).

If crankshaft, bearings or crankcase are renewed, crankshaft must be centered in crankcase by measuring the clearance between counterweight and crankcase wall at each end; then varying the thickness of selective washers (S—Fig. 5). It is suggested, therefore, that if shaft bearings are removed the washers be properly identified and reinstalled on correct end of shaft. If crankcase is the item renewed, make a trial installation in the new crankcase before bearings are removed; then install thicker or thinner washers as required to center the shaft. Factory recommended method of centering is to use dummy bearings which are the same dimensions as regular bearings but a slip fit on shaft journals. Washers (S) are available in thicknesses of 0.004, 0.008, 0.012, 0.016, 0.020 and 0.024 inch (0.1, 0.2, 0.3, 0.4, 0.5 and 0.6 mm).

ELECTRICAL SYSTEM. Fig. 7 shows an exploded view of flywheel magneto and CD ignition system used on most models. Ignition timing should be correct when timing scribe line (T) aligns with timing boss on crankcase. Timing can only be checked with a power timing light as outlined in MAINTENANCE Section, but can be adjusted without major disassembly by reaching through holes in flywheel (1), loosening the two slotted head screws retaining base plate (5) to crankcase, and moving base plate in slotted holes.

The condition of coils (2, 3 and 4) can be checked with an ohmmeter without removal of flywheel or major disassembly. Disconnect the two individual plugs and multi-plug leading to wire loom (8). Check the pulser coil (2) by connecting the two ohmmeter leads to the individually connected (RED) and (WHITE) leads; reading should be 23.5 ohms. Check the exciter coil (3) by connecting ohmmeter leads to the individual (RED) lead and a suitable engine ground; reading should be 195

Fig. 1—Follow the above tightening sequence when installing crankcase nuts and bolt. Refer to text for tightening torque.

Fig. 2—Piston rings are pinned as shown (arrow). Note that upper ring is installed so that notches in ring ends are up.

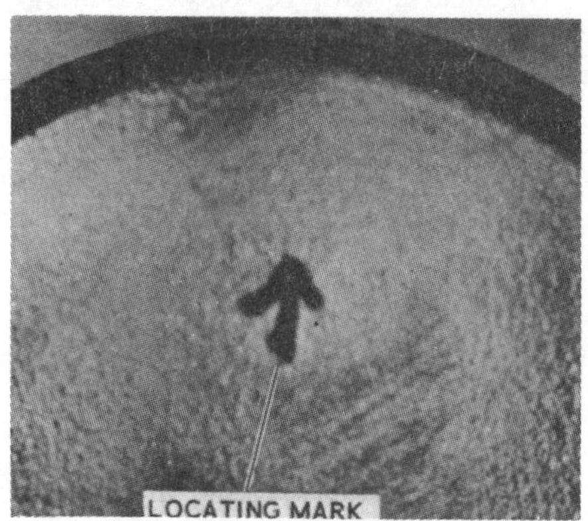

Fig. 3—Install piston so that arrow on piston crown points towards exhaust port.

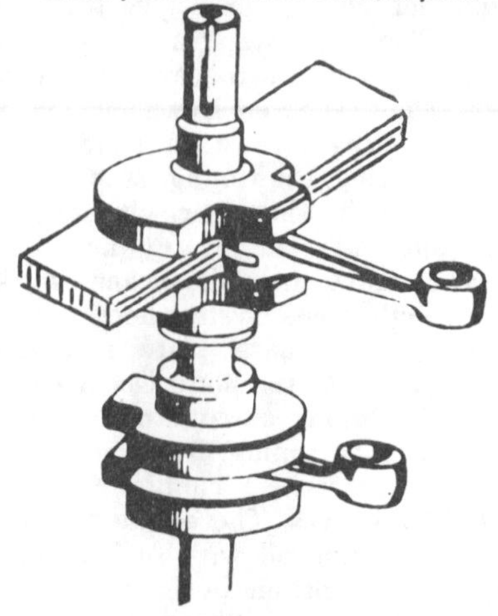

Fig. 4—A support should be placed between crankshaft counterweights when pressing bearings on shaft.

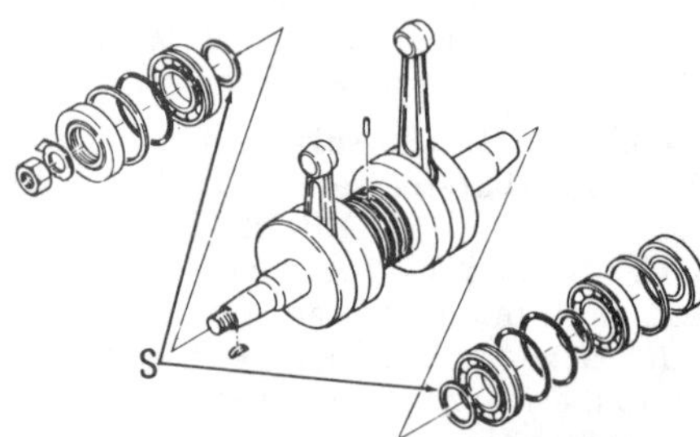

Fig. 5—View of engine crankshaft with end bearings exploded. Shims (S) control end play and center shaft in crankcase.

Fig. 6—Crankshaft unit installed in crankcase upper half. Counterweights must center in crankcase within 0.005 inch (0.13 mm). Refer to Fig. 5.

ohms. Check the lighting coil (4) by connecting ohmmeter probes to the TWO YELLOW leads in multi-plug; reading should be 0.18 ohms.

Some models are equipped with a temperature indicator light which connects to a thermal switch threaded into right cylinder head. Heat indicator light should test 4 ohms when checked between the terminals on back of light bulb. Heat indicator thermal switch which is threaded into cylinder head should test at infinity when test probes are connected to terminal wire and threaded end and unit is at normal room temperature. When unit is heated to 500 degrees F. and retested, resistance should be at zero ohms.

Some models are equipped with individual temperature gages which operate from thermocouples which substitute for the regular spark plug gasket for each cylinder. The gage is calibrated to register from COLD at a sensor temperature of 250 degrees F. or below, to HOT at a temperature of 475 degrees F. or above; with intermediate readings between the two extremes. Gage unit can be considered satisfactory if it registers "COLD" when engine is first started; and "HOT" when a jumper wire is touched to sensor wire and a suitable ground.

Sensor units are affected by cooling air blast and should be installed "downwind" from the direction of cooling air flow; directly to the rear (six-o'clock) on free air models or at seven-o'clock on axial fan units. Sensor unit should register 11,000 ohms at 60-70 degrees F. and resistance should lower as temperature rises. Resistance should be approximately 16 ohms at 455 degrees F.

RECOIL STARTER. Refer to exploded view of starter in Fig. 8. To disassemble starter, remove starter from engine and remove waterproofing plate. Pull rope out until it is possible to position rope in notch of rope pulley. Release rope and allow recoil spring to unwind. Remove retaining nut (3) and components (6 thru 8). Carefully remove rope pulley so that recoil spring remains in cover. If necessary to remove recoil spring, guard against uncontrolled uncoiling of spring which may cause personal injury.

To assemble starter, install recoil spring in cover so that spring is wound in counterclockwise direction and outer hook of spring contacts lug of cover. Install rope pulley and rope so that lug of pulley engages with inner hook of recoil spring. Install washer (8), pawls (7), spring (6) and pawl return spring (5). Install retainer cover (4) so that end of return spring (5) protrudes through retainer cover (4) and turn retainer cover one-third turn clockwise to pre-load spring. Install washers and retaining nut. If rope handle was not removed during disassembly, position rope in notch of rope pulley and turn pulley two turns counterclockwise to pre-load recoil spring. If handle was removed, turn rope pulley counterclockwise two or three turns and insert end of rope through rope outlet in cover. Tension on rope should be apparent. Tie a temporary knot to hold tope and install rope handle.

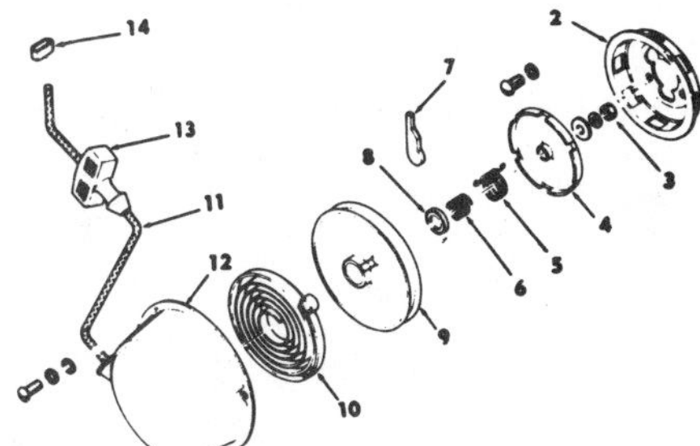

Fig. 8—Exploded view of recoil starter.

2. Starter cup
3. Nut
4. Retainer
5. Return spring
6. Spring
7. Pawls
8. Washer
9. Rope pulley
10. Recoil spring
11. Rope
12. Cover
13. Handle
14. Retainer

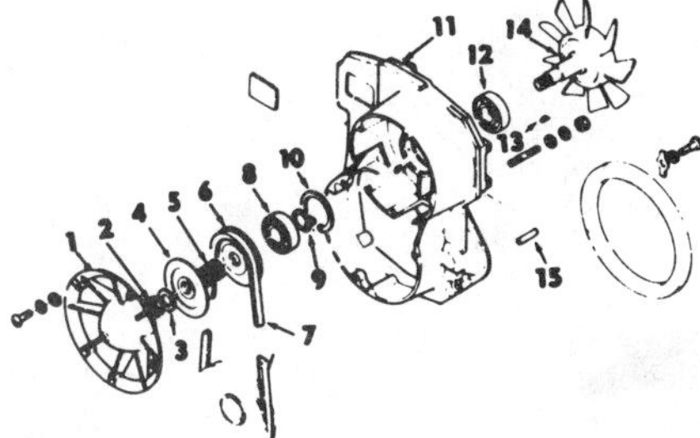

Fig. 9—Exploded view of cooling fan and housing unit.

1. Cover
2. Nut
3. Lockwasher
4. Pulley half
5. Shims
6. Pulley half
7. Belt
8. Bearing
9. Shim
10. Snap ring
11. Housing
12. Bearing
13. Key
14. Fan

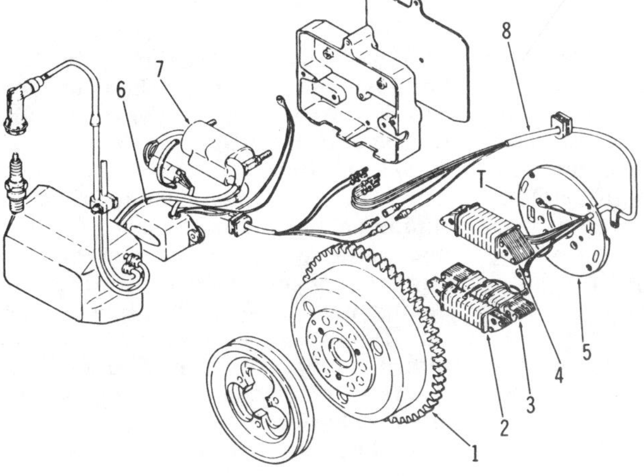

Fig. 7—Exploded view of typical engine electrical system used on models with CD ignition system.

1. Flywheel
2. Pulser coil
3. Exciter coil
4. Lighting coil
5. Base plate
6. CD unit
7. Ignition coil
8. Wiring harness
T. Timing mark

KIEKHAEFER AEROMARINE

CONDENSED SERVICE DATA

Engine Model	440	440S
Bore—(mm)	63.5	63.5
Inches	2.5	2.5
Stroke—(mm)	68.5	68.5
Inches	2.69	2.69
No. of Cylinders	2	2
Displacement—(cc)	433	433
Inches	26.4	26.4
Horsepower @ RPM	38@6500	41@6500
Cooling Type	Axial Fan	

Engine Model	440	440S
Carburetor Type	HD	HR
Number Used	1	2
Ignition:		
Type	CD	
Timing Advance?	Electronic	
Timing BTDC—Degrees	12°	
Measured at	Advance	
Spark Plug	18 mm Surface Gap	
Fuel/Oil Ratio	20:1	20:1

MAINTENANCE

CARBURETOR. Refer to TILLOTSON carburetor section for operation and overhaul data. Normal initial settings are one turn open for both needles. Set idle speed screw to obtain an engine speed of approximately 2000 rpm. On models with dual carburetors, both units must be set as nearly as possible alike. Carburetors must be readjusted for smoothest engine operation under actual conditions of temperature and load.

SPARK PLUG. An 18mm surface gap spark plug, Champion D77V or equivalent must be used. Spark plug gap is fixed and not adjustable and selection for heat range is not required.

IGNITION AND TIMING. The Capacitor Discharge ignition system is powered by a flywheel mounted generating coil and operated by a trigger coil attached to flywheel housing. Timing is accomplished by two small magnets (M—Fig. 2) on flywheel rim which generate a simultaneous spark at both plugs each time they pass the trigger coil.

Adjustments are provided for trigger coil air gap and ignition timing. To adjust air gap, remove recoil starter and trigger coil cover. Turn flywheel until trigger magnet aligns with coil as shown in Fig. 2 and check air gap (G) which should be 0.030-0.040. Adjust if required by loosening the two clamp screws (1) and sliding trigger coil adjusting plate in or out as required. Clearance at both magnets must be within 0.030-0.040 range. NOTE: Make sure adjustment is even at both ends; do not attempt to adjust by moving only one end of adjusting plate.

Timing must be checked with a power timing light with engine running AT LEAST 2000 rpm, to be sure electronic advance is operating. Refer to Fig. 3. Remove the plug in carburetor side of flywheel housing and attach timing light to either spark plug wire as shown. With engine running at 2000 rpm, timing punch mark on magneto ring of flywheel should center in timing hole as shown in inset. If it does not, remove trigger coil cover and slightly loosen the two timing adjusting nuts (2—Fig. 2). Slide trigger coil UP to advance timing or DOWN to retard timing as shown. Tighten nuts securely when correct timing adjustment is obtained.

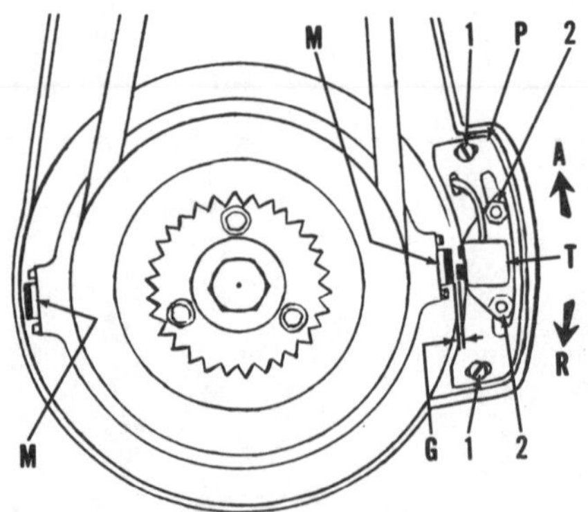

Fig. 2–Schematic view of flywheel and trigger coil showing major components and points of adjustment.

A. Advance
G. Clearance gap
M. Trigger magnets
P. Adjusting plate
R. Retard
T. Trigger coil
1. Clearance adjusting screws
2. Timing Adjusting screws

NOTE: Advance (running) timing

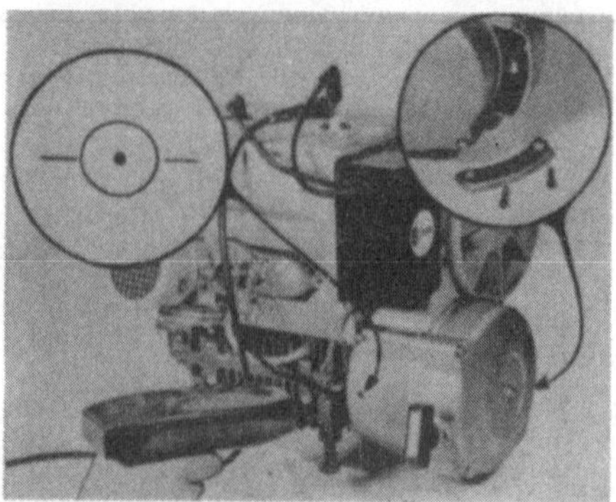

Fig. 3–Timing must be checked with a power timing light, engine running 2000 rpm. Timing punch mark on pulley rim should center timing hole when viewed with timing light. To adjust the timing remove access plate shown in inset and refer to Fig. 2.

occurs when flywheel speed enables the short, leading leg of trigger coil to induce the spark. The lower trigger voltage available at starting speeds operates through the longer trailing leg of coil to induce the retarded ignition spark required for starting.

LUBRICATION. The engine is lubricated by oil mixed with the fuel. The manufacturer recommends a top quality two-stroke or snowmobile oil and Regular gasoline, 92 octane or higher. Refer also to vehicle manufacturer's recommendations and to Lubrication paragraphs or FUNDAMENTALS Section.

COOLING FAN AND BELT. Belt tension should be adjusted to allow ¼ inch deflection midway between pulleys when depressed with finger. The belt can be adjusted by adding or removing shims from between fan pulley halves. Removing shims will tighten belt by allowing pulley rims to move closer together. Turn pulley slowly when assembling to keep from pinching belt in pulley. Removed shims can be stored outside of outer pulley half for re-use when a new belt is installed.

To renew the belt, remove recoil starter, fan protector cover and starter hub (drive pulley). Be sure to check and/or readjust belt tension if necessary.

Fan shaft threads into housing hub. When unscrewing the shaft to remove fan assembly, MAKE SURE fan blade clears cover attaching boss in housing shown in Fig. 4. Fan damage can result if blades are incorrectly turned during removal. Shaft and bearings can be withdrawn from fan hub after unit is removed from housing and pulley assembly is removed from fan. Bearings are installed on shaft with fiber-sealed side outward and spacer positioned between bearings as shown in inset. Shaft is prevented from loosening by the external nut retaining fan cover.

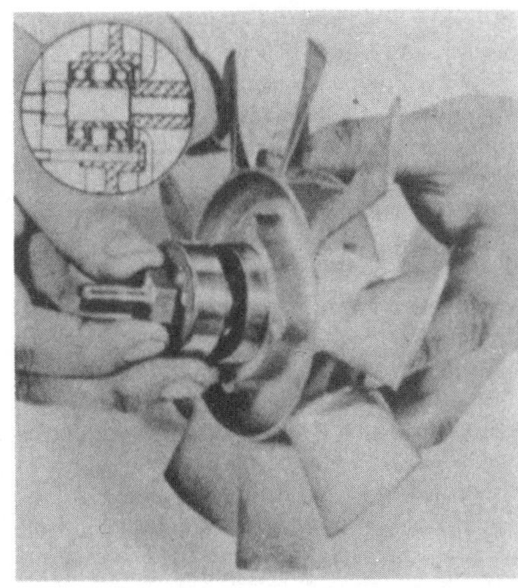

Fig. 5–Fan bearings are separated by a spacer and installed with fiber shields to outside.

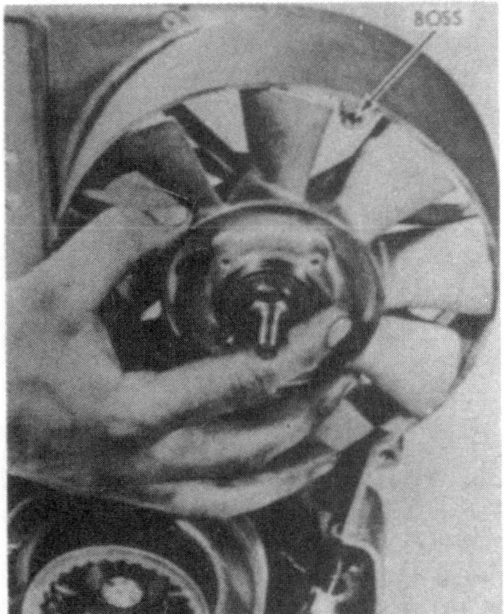

Fig. 4–Make sure fan blades clear boss in housing when center bolt is unscrewed.

REPAIRS

NOTE: U. S. Standard measurements, dimensions and screw-threads are used throughout in the manufacture of all KIEKHAEFER snowmobile engines.

TIGHTENING TORQUES. Recommended tightening torques are as follows:

Crankcase flange bolts 180 inch-lbs.
Cylinder through-bolts 225 inch-lbs.
Flywheel bolt . . . . 45-50 ft.-lbs.

DISASSEMBLY AND REASSEMBLY. Refer to Fig. 6 for exploded view of major components. Cylinders and cylinder heads are retained to crankcase by through-bolts which also serve as main bearing support bolts, although crankcase halves are also sealed by short flange bolts.

To remove cylinder heads or cylinders, it is first necessary to remove carburetor (9), exhaust manifold (4) and cylinder shrouds (1). Manifold is retained by two stud nuts at ends which are visible and two center stud

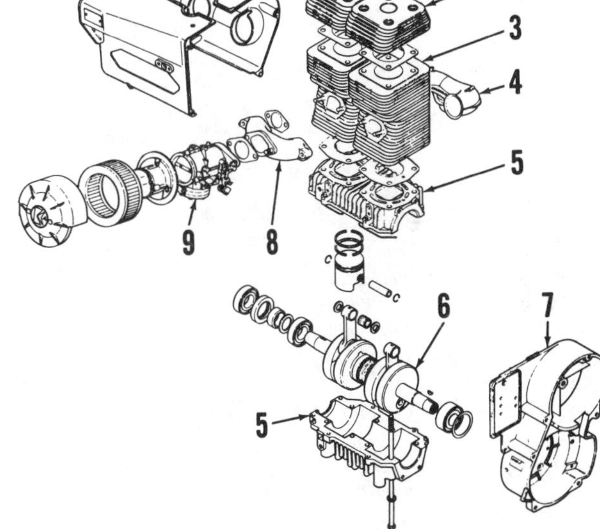

Fig. 6–Exploded view of engine showing major components.

1. Shrouds
2. Cylinder heads
3. Cylinders
4. Exhaust manifold
5. Crankcase
6. Crankshaft assy
7. Fan housing
8. Intake manifold
9. Carburetor

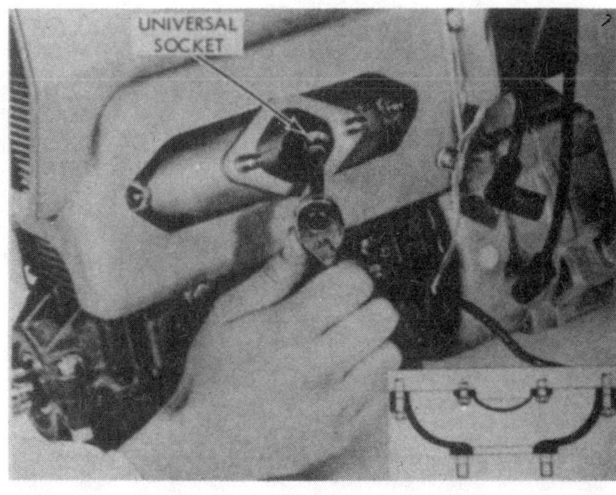

Fig. 7–Two manifold studs are concealed inside manifold and must be removed with a universal socket as shown.

nuts which are inside manifold passage and accessible only through carburetor opening as shown in Fig. 7. Before removing inner manifold nuts, turn crankshaft until both pistons block intake ports as shown in Fig. 8, to prevent the nuts from dropping into crankcase before they can be retrieved.

With manifolds removed, through-bolts, cylinder heads and cylinders can be removed for service on pistons, rings, cylinders and associated parts. Through-bolts are interchangeable but the four long standoff nuts which serve as supports for shroud must be installed in the proper location. Cylinder heads are interchangeable and may be installed in either of two positions. Cylinders are not interchangeable and correct positioning can be determined by intake manifold studs, the two shorter ones being positioned together as shown in Inset—Fig. 7.

Fan housing (7—Fig. 6) must be removed to separate the crankcase. First remove recoil starter, fan drive pulley, flywheel and magneto plate; then remove the four socket head cap screws and lift off fan housing, being careful not to lose main bearing shims which are free to drop when end housing is removed. Shims control crankshaft end play and must be reinstalled when unit is reassembled. Remove the six flange bolts and separate crankcase halves by bumping lightly with a soft hammer if necessary.

When assembling, make sure both surfaces of crankcase flange are perfectly clean and free of old sealer as well as nicks or burrs which might interfere with a perfect seal. Lay new rubber sealing strips in grooves at drive end and press strips into place, allowing excess to extend from chamfered end of grooves at magneto end. Apply a thin, even coat of suitable sealant and rejoin crankcase. Tighten crankcase flange bolts evenly to a torque of 180 inch-lbs. and cut sealing strips off even with edge of housing.

NOTE: If crankshaft end play must be checked and/or adjusted, refer to following crankshaft repair paragraph for procedure.

Be sure piston rings are properly positioned over locating pins and install cylinders using new gaskets and an approved ring compressor (Manufacturer's Part No. 81-100316-142) as shown in Fig. 9. Long intake manifold studs (L—Fig. 11) should be to outside as shown, separated by short studs (S). Intake manifold must be installed and tightened before through-bolts are tightened. The long standoff nuts (N) which support shroud should be installed at the four locations marked (X). Tighten through-bolt nuts to a torque of 225 inch-lbs.

Reinstall fan housing using the removed (or predetermined) shim pack. Magneto end plate does not require timing. Tighten flywheel retaining cap screw to a torque of 45-55 ft.-lbs. Adjust fan belt if necessary as outlined in MAINTENANCE Section.

PISTONS, RINGS & CYLINDERS. Piston pin is a tight fit in piston bosses and rides in loose needle rollers in connecting rod. Piston and pin are available only as a matched assembly. Pistons are not marked, but piston ring locating pins should be positioned on exhaust side of cylinder when unit is installed.

Two identical piston rings are used on each piston. Rings are not marked and may be installed either side up, making sure however, that end gap is positioned over locating pins positioned about 90° apart on exhaust side of piston. Ring end gap should be 0.010-0.023 and piston skirt clearance should be 0.004-0.007. Rings and pistons are

Fig. 8–When removing nuts from intake manifold studs, make sure crankshaft is turned so pistons block ports as shown.

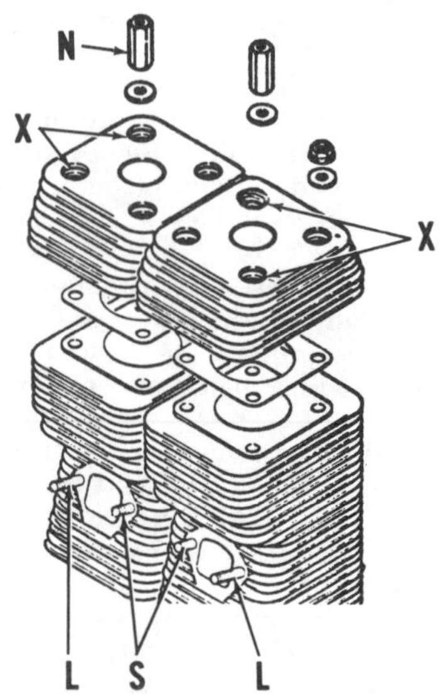

Fig. 11–Cylinders are installed with long studs (L) to outside, short studs (S) together. Shroud retaining (standoff) nuts (N) are installed at the four locations marked (X).

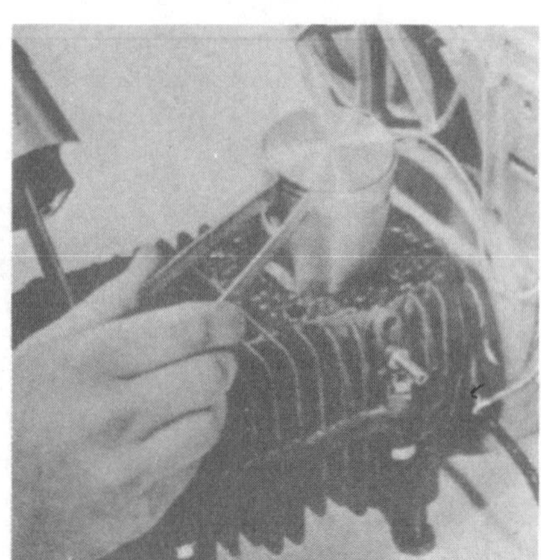

Fig. 9–Use the correct ring compressor when installing cylinders.

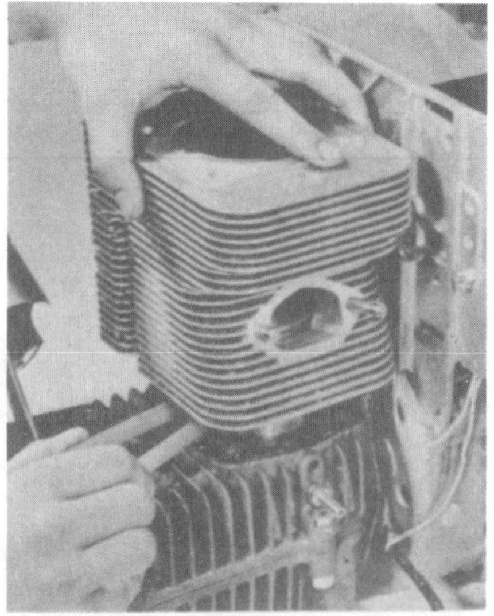

Fig. 10–Intake manifold ports must be on same side as impulse fitting when installing cylinders.

Fig. 12–Shims at flywheel end bearing control crankshaft end play.

Fig. 13–Procedure for measuring shim pack thickness for correct crankshaft end play. Refer to text.

available in 0.015 oversize as well as standard.

CRANKSHAFT AND CONNECTING ROD ASSEMBLY. Crankshaft and connecting rods are available only in an assembled unit which contains all main bearings. Because of lack of parts availability, shop disassembly of crankshaft unit is not recommended.

Crankshaft end play is controlled by shims (See Fig. 12) located between magneto end bearing and fan housing. Recommended end play is 0.005-0.015 and shims are available in thicknesses of 0.005, 0.010, 0.015 and 0.020. To determine shim pack thickness refer to Fig. 13 and proceed as follows: Place crankshaft unit in crankcase lower half, then install fan housing omitting all shims, shaft seal and housing O-ring. Install the two socket head retaining screws and tighten snugly. Bump drive end of crankshaft to seat magneto end bearing, then measure clearance between drive end outer bearing and shoulder in crankcase bearing bore using a feeler gage as shown. Select a shim (or shims) which will reduce the measured clearance to the recommended 0.005-0.015 and lay aside for use in final assembly.

RECOIL STARTER. Refer to Fig. 14 for exploded view of starter unit. To disassemble the starter, allow recoil spring to unwind by removing handle grip (or other means). Remove center screw (10), retracting cam (9) and associated parts, then carefully lift out pulley (6).

Outer loop of recoil spring (4) fits over an anchor pin in housing (1), while inner hook must engage notch in pulley hub. Protect hands and face from unwinding spring (4) when removing pulley and/or spring.

When reassembling starter, lubricate spring with low temperature grease or graphite and install spring and pulley. Lubricate dogs (12) and make sure they move freely and are retracted by springs (11). Fit cam (9) between dogs and install screw (10), then check to be sure cam extends dogs when pulley is rotated in cranking direction.

Wind pulley all the way (counterclockwise with housing (1) lying on bench, pulley up); then back off until square window (W) in pulley aligns with rope hole in housing. While holding pulley in this position, thread rope through housing hole and window (W) and knot inner end of pulley. Reinstall pull handle (2) and reinforcement (3) and allow pulley to slowly unwind. Pull starter rope a few times to make sure starter works correctly, then reinstall on engine leaving mounting bolts loose. Pull rope until dogs engage and one piston comes up on compression, thus centering starter; then tighten mounting screws.

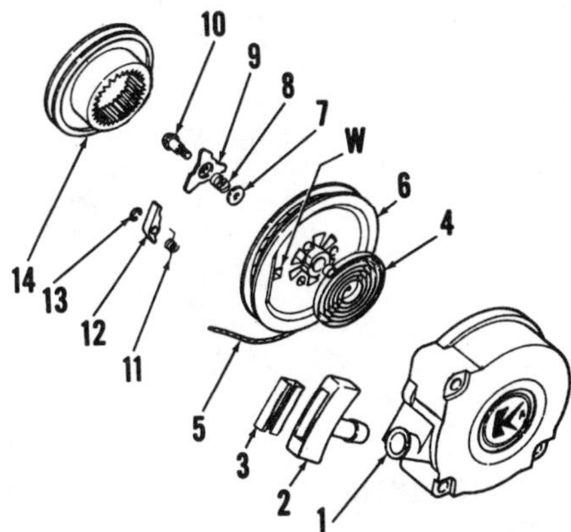

Fig. 14–Exploded view of recoil starter showing component parts.

1. Housing
2. Handle
3. Reinforcement
4. Recoil spring
5. Rope
6. Pulley
7. Washer
8. Spring
9. Cam
10. Cap screw
11. Spring
12. Pawl
13. Retainer
14. Hub (on flywheel)

KIORITZ

CONDENSED SERVICE DATA

ENGINE MODEL	KEC295RS/2	KEC340RS/2	KEC340/5	KEC340/22 KEC340/22A	KEC340/22B	KEC340/23LC
Bore—mm	56	60	60	60	58	58
Inches	2.205	2.362	2.362	2.362	2.283	2.283
Stroke—mm	60	60	60	60	64	64
Inches	2.362	2.362	2.362	2.362	2.520	2.520
No. of Cylinders	2	2	2	2	2	2
Displacement—cc	295.6	339.3	339.3	339.3	338.2	338.2
Cubic Inches	18.03	20.7	20.7	20.7	20.6	20.6
Cooling Type	Axial Fan	Axial Fan	Axial Fan	Axial Fan	Axial Fan	Liquid
Induction Type	Third Port	Third Port	Third Port	Reed Valve	Reed Valve	Reed Valve
Carburetor Model	Mikuni	Mikuni	Bendix	Walbro	Mikuni	Mikuni
Number Used	2	2	1	1	1	2
Ignition:						
Type	CD	CD	ET	ET	CD	CD
Point Gap—mm	.....	.....	0.3-0.4	0.3-0.4	.....	.....
Inch	.....	.....	0.014	0.014	.....	.....
Edge Gap—mm	.....	.....	.....	.....	.....	.....
Timing Advance?	Yes	Yes	Yes	Yes	Yes	Yes
Timing BTDC—Degrees	20	20	10	5	20	20
Inch	0.096	0.096	0.023	0.006	0.096	0.096
Measured at	Adv.	Adv.	Retard	Retard	Adv.	Adv.
Spark Plug:						
Champion	QN1	QN1	RN2	RN2	QN1	QN1
Electrode Gap—mm	(1)	(1)	0.5	0.5	(1)	(1)
Inch	(1)	(1)	0.020	0.020	(1)	(1)
Fuel:Oil Ratio	20:1	20:1	50:1	50:1	50:1	50:1

(1) Spark plug is factory gapped at 0.028 inch. Renew plug when gap reaches 0.060.

ENGINE MODEL	KEC400/22	KEC440/5	KEC440/22 KEC440/22A	KEC440/22B	KEC440/23LC
Bore—mm	63	68	66	66	66
Inches	2.480	2.677	2.598	2.598	2.598
Stroke—mm	64	60	64	64	64
Inches	2.520	2.362	2.520	2.520	2.520
No. of Cylinders	2	2	2	2	2
Displacement—cc	399	435.8	437.9	437.9	437.9
Cubic Inches	24.34	26.58	26.71	26.71	26.71
Cooling Type	Axial Fan	Axial Fan	Axial Fan	Axial Fan	Liquid
Induction Type	Reed Valve	Third Port	Reed Valve	Reed Valve	Reed Valve
Carburetor Model	Walbro	Bendix	Mikuni	Mikuni	Mikuni
Number Used	1	1	1	1	2
Ignition:					
Type	ET	ET	ET	CD	CD
Point Gap—mm	0.3-0.4	0.3-0.4	0.3-0.4	.....	.....
Inch	0.014	0.014	0.014	.....	.....
Edge Gap—mm	.....	.....	.....	.....	.....
Timing Advance?	Yes	Yes	Yes	Yes	Yes
Timing BTDC—Degrees	5	10	10	20	20
Inch	0.006	0.023	0.024	0.096	0.096
Measured at	Retard	Retard	Retard	Adv.	Adv.
Spark Plug:					
Champion	RN2	RN2	RN2	QN1	QN1
Electrode Gap—mm	0.5	0.5	0.5	(1)	(1)
Inch	0.020	0.020	0.020	(1)	(1)
Fuel:Oil Ratio	20:1	20:1	20:1	50:1	50:1

(1) Spark plug is factory gapped at 0.028 inch. Renew plug when gap reaches 0.060.

MAINTENANCE

CARBURETOR. Bendix, Mikuni or Walbro carburetors are used. Refer to appropriate paragraphs of CARBURETOR SERVICE Section for overhaul details.

SPARK PLUG. CHAMPION RN2 spark plugs are used in engines with Energy Transfer ignition systems. Recommended spark plug gap is 0.020 inch (0.5 mm).

Models with Capacitor Discharge ignition use a QN1 Surface Gap resistor plug. Built-in plug gap is 0.028 inch; renew plug when gap widens to 0.060 inch.

The recommendations given in CONDENSED SERVICE DATA tables are for normal operation. A different heat range plug may improve performance under some conditions. Refer to Spark Plug Selection paragraphs of SERVICE FUNDAMENTALS Section for additional information on spark plug selection.

IGNITION AND TIMING. Breaker point gap on ET models should be 0.3-0.4 mm (0.012-0.016 inch). Points can be adjusted after removing recoil starter, starting pulley and fan drive sheave. All models are equipped with a centrifugal timing advance which provides retarded timing for starting only. Both cylinders must be timed as nearly as possible alike. It is suggested that point gap and timing be checked on one cylinder; then timing synchronized by varying the point gap on the other cylinder, making sure point gap on both cylinders remains within the setting range provided.

Fig. 1—A homemade wire timing pointer and timing marks painted on drive sheave are used to time CD ignition system.

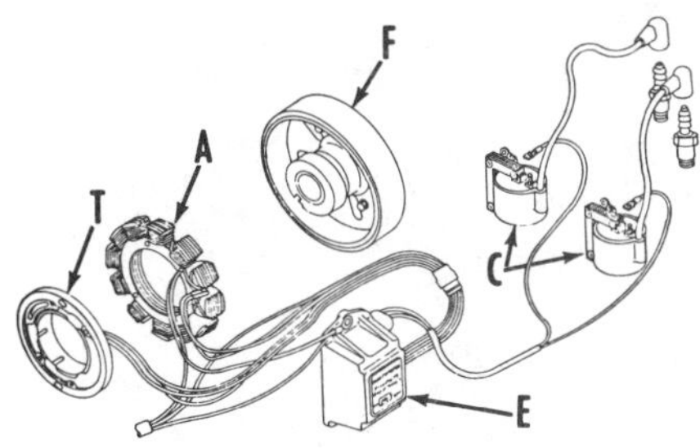

Fig. 2—Schematic view of CD ignition system.

A. Alternator stator
C. Ignition coils
E. Electronic pack
F. Flywheel
T. Timing ring

On models with CD ignition, both cylinders fire simultaneously. Running advance is electronic and occurs at an engine speed of 2500-2800 rpm. Timing is done with a timing light at operating speed after first painting timing marks on fixed face of drive sheave and fashioning a timing pointer as shown in Fig. 1. JOHN DEERE provides a temporary timing decal as shown. To time the engine, remove drive belt and either spark plug. Install a dial indicator in spark plug hole then find and mark TDC on sheave face. Turn sheave clockwise about 1/8 turn; then counterclockwise until piston is 0.096 inch (2.438 mm) below TDC position. Mark the second 20° BTDC line at this point, aligning with the installed timing pointer. Remove dial indicator and reinstall spark plug. Connect the power timing light to either spark plug, then start and run engine at 3000 rpm or faster. Spark should occur when 20° BTDC mark aligns with timing pointer. If timing is incorrect, remove starter, flywheel housing, flywheel and alternator stator. Loosen the four screws securing timing ring (T—Fig. 2) to crankcase and move timing ring counter-clockwise to advance the timing or clockwise to retard timing. Because both spark plugs fire at the same time, timing needs to be checked for only one cylinder.

Fig. 3—Checking coolant fan belt tension on air cooled models.

LUBRICATION. The engine is lubricated by oil mixed with the fuel. The manufacturer recommends Regular or Premium gasoline and a good ashless Two-Cycle Oil which meets BIA Specification TC-W. Do not use no-lead gasoline. Refer also to Vehicle Manufacturers recommendations and to Two-Cycle Lubrication in ENGINE DESIGN FUNDAMENTALS Section of this manual.

COOLING FAN AND BELT. Fan belt tension is correct when deflection is approximately 9 mm (3/8 inch) on Reed Valve Engines or 6 mm (¼ inch) on Piston Ported Engines; measured

Fig. 4—Checking coolant pump drive belt tension on liquid cooled units.

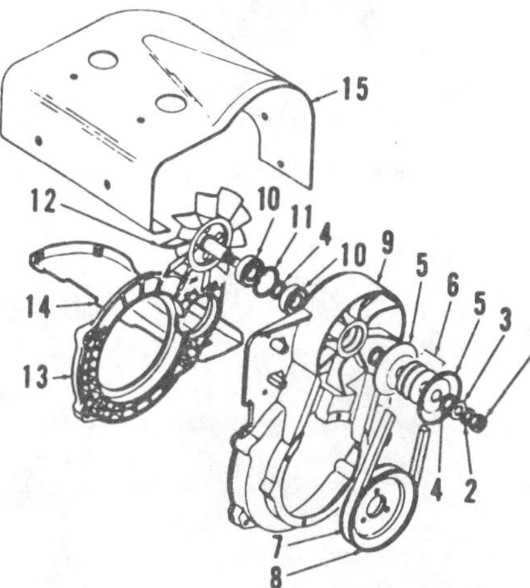

Fig. 5—Exploded view of coolant fan, fan housing and associated parts used on piston ported models.

1. Shaft nut
2. Lockwasher
3. Washer
4. Spacer
5. Sheave half
6. Spacer shims
7. Belt
8. Drive pulley
9. Housing
10. Bearings
11. Snap ring
12. Fan
13. Housing plate
14. Cover
15. Cylinder shroud

midway between pulleys as shown in Fig. 3. To tighten the cooling fan belt, transfer shims (6—Fig. 5) from between sheave halves (5) to front of front half, increasing effective diameter of driven sheave. Refer also to Fig. 6. Tighten fan shaft nut to a torque of 30 ft.-lbs.

COOLANT PUMP AND BELT. On liquid cooled models, coolant pump belt should have approximately 9 mm (3/8 inch) deflection measured midway between pulleys as shown in Fig. 4. Adjust belt tension by loosening pump mounting bolts and moving pump up or down as required.

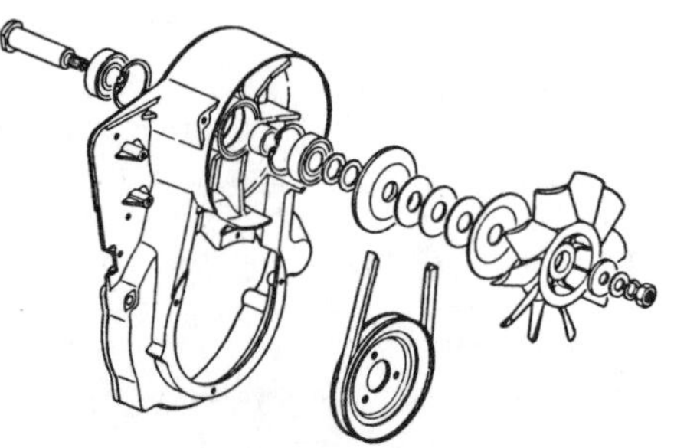

Fig. 6—Cooling fan, fan housing and associated parts used on reed valve induction engines.

Fig. 7—View of Kioritz engine with third port induction.

Fig. 8—View of Kioritz engine with reed valve induction system. Engine is similar in appearance to third port engine except for low positioning of carburetor and intake manifold.

REPAIRS

Air-Cooled Models

TIGHTENING TORQUES. Tightening torques are as follows:

	Ft.-Lbs.	Kg-m
Cylinder to crankcase:		
Third port models	15-18	2.1-2.5
Reed valve models (See Cylinder Head)		
Cylinder head:		
Third Port Models	15-18	2.1-2.5
Reed valve models.		
Long stud nuts	12-15	1.7-2.1
Short stud nuts	5-7	0.7-1.0
Crankcase:		
Third port models	12-15	1.7-2.1
Reed valve models	13-18	1.8-2.5
Flywheel	45-50	6.2-6.9
Fan shaft	28-31	3.9-4.3
Intake manifold,		
Reed valve models	5-7	0.7-1.0

DISASSEMBLY AND REASSEMBLY. Although similar in appearance, disassembly procedures differ between the Third Port Engines shown in Fig. 7 and Reed Valve Models shown in Fig. 8. Refer to the appropriate following paragraphs for procedures.

THIRD PORT ENGINES. Refer to Fig. 5 for cooling fan and associated parts and to Fig. 9 for main engine components.

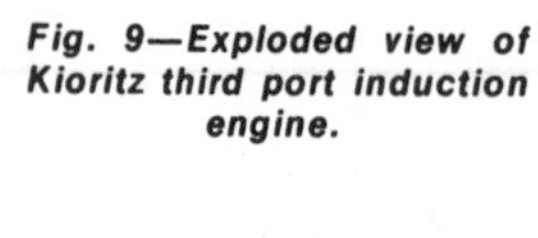

Fig. 9—Exploded view of Kioritz third port induction engine.

To disassemble the removed engine, first remove spark plugs and cylinder shroud, then remove inlet and exhaust manifolds leaving carburetor attached to inlet manifold. Cylinder heads and cylinders can now be removed for top end work. Crankcase disassembly will require removal of fan housing, flywheel and housing plate.

Identify pistons for reinstallation and note that arrows on piston crown point to exhaust side. Use a suitable piston pin tool for pin removal or heat the piston.

To separate the crankcase, remove retaining bolts and break sealant grip by tapping upper crankcase half lightly with a soft hammer as shown in Fig. 10. DO NOT attempt to pry crankcase halves apart with a screwdriver or similar tool. Prying can damage mating surfaces.

When reassembling crankcase, lubricate crankshaft components thoroughly

Fig. 10—Break sealant grip on crankcase halves by tapping with a small hammer.

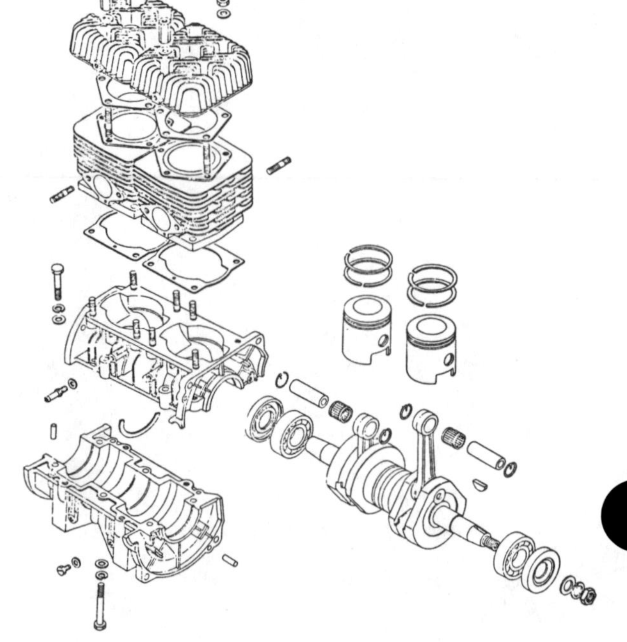

and install oil seals on each end of crankshaft, lips inward. Be sure retaining half-washers (Arrows—Fig. 11) are installed in their grooves in lower crankcase half then position shaft assembly on crankcase lower half. Make sure sealing surfaces are clean and smooth and coat both sealing surfaces with a good non-hardening sealant. Fit upper crankcase half and install the four center topside bolts (1, 8, 9 and 10—Fig. 12) and tighten the four bolts evenly until crankcase halves meet. Install remainder of bolts and tighten evenly in sequence shown to the recommended torque of 12-15 ft.-lbs. (1.7-2.1 kg-m).

Fig. 11—Retaining half-washers (Arrows) must be in position in bottom crankcase half before positioning crankshaft.

5

Fig. 12—Tighten crankcase screws in sequence shown. Broken lines indicate heads are located on bottom of crankcase.

Fig. 13—Cylinders are marked "R" (right) and "L" (left) on cylinder flange as shown by arrow.

Use a heat gun or oven to warm pistons and install pin, with arrow on top of piston pointing toward exhaust port side. Cylinders are not interchangeable, and are marked "L" (left) and "R" (right) (Arrow—Fig. 13) by stamping on cylinder flange. Install cylinders using a suitable ring compressor, wooden blocks to hold piston steady, and new base gaskets. Tighten cylinder base nuts just past finger tight, then install and tighten intake manifold to properly align cylinders. Tighten cylinder base nuts in a criss-cross pattern to a torque of 15-18 ft.-lbs. (2.1-2.5 kg-m).

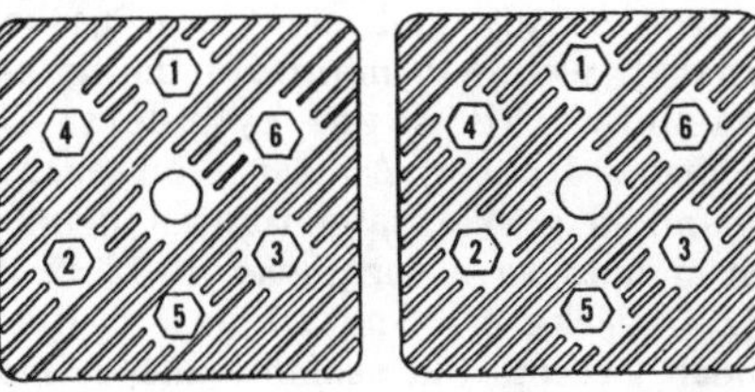

Fig. 14—Cylinder head tightening sequence to be used on six-stud cylinder heads.

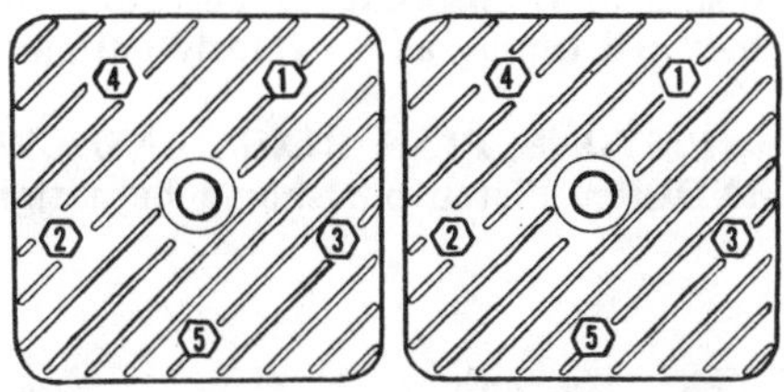

Fig. 15—Cylinder head tightening sequence to be used on models with five-stud cylinder head.

Cylinder heads are not interchangeable and should be installed with machined sides together. Cylinder head gaskets are marked "TOP" for correct assembly. Cylinder head gaskets should be installed dry. The long standoff nuts which support shroud should be installed at (3—Fig. 14) on KEC 295 engine or (5—Fig. 15) on other models. Tighten cylinder head stud nuts to a torque of 15-18 ft.-lbs. (2.1-2.5 kg-m) in the sequence shown in Fig. 14 for KEC 295 engine or Fig. 15 for other models.

REED VALVE ENGINES. Refer to Figs. 6 and 16 for exploded views. Cooling fan differs from third port engine in that impeller assembly is outboard of drive pulley. Cooling shroud attaches to cylinder head bosses and standoff nuts located as shown by arrows, Fig. 17. Cylinders, cylinder heads and pistons are not interchangeable for left and right side. Cylinders are retained to crankcase by four studs which extend through cylinders and become four of the eight cylinder head studs for each cylinder unit.

To disassemble the removed engine, first remove spark plugs and cylinder shroud, then remove inlet and exhaust manifolds and reed valve plates. Cylinder heads and cylinders can now be removed for top end overhaul. Crankcase disassembly will require removal of fan housing, flywheel, alternator stator and timing ring. Punch mark

Fig. 16—Exploded view of reed valve type induction engine.

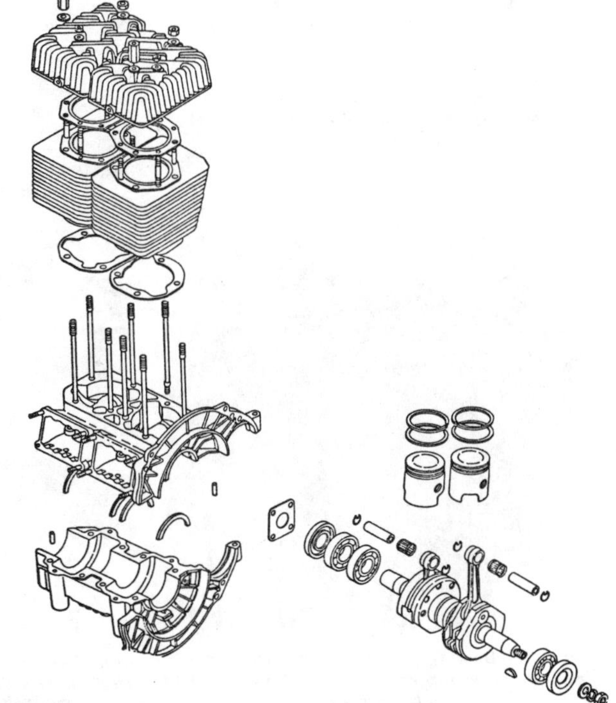

installed position of timing ring before loosening retaining screws to avoid retiming problems on assembly.

Use a heat gun or other suitable means to thoroughly warm the piston before removing piston pin. Note that exhaust port locating arrows on tops of pistons angle outward toward ends of shaft.

To assemble the engine, suitably support upper half of crankcase on cylinder studs and position bearing retaining half-washers in their grooves as shown by arrows, Fig. 18. Lubricate components thoroughly and coat both crankcase flanges with a suitable non-hardening sealant. Reposition crankshaft assembly and install crankcase lower half, being sure locating dowels seat properly. Tighten retaining cap screw and stud nuts evenly to a torque of 13-18 ft.-lbs. (1.8-2.5 kg-m) in the sequence shown in Fig. 19.

When installing timing ring (B—Fig. 20) align the previously made punch marks. If timing position is not marked, center mounting screw holes in adjusting slots then check timing after engine is running. Install alternator stator (A) and flywheel by reversing removal procedure. Some engines have a pto end seal guard (Arrow—Fig. 21) which prevents a broken drive belt from damaging crankshaft seal. Center hole in guard over shaft when installing, to prevent guard from touching shaft.

With crankcase assembled, reposition with cylinder studs uppermost. Warm the pistons and reinstall the exhaust port locating arrows angling outward and away from reed valve opening side of crankcase. Cylinders are not interchangeable and are stamped "L" (left) and "R" (right) on cylinder flange. Install cylinders using a suitable ring compressor, wooden blocks to hold piston steady and new base gaskets. Install exhaust manifold using new gaskets; this aligns cylinders. Use Silicone Rubber Adhesive on exhaust manifold gaskets and tighten manifold stud nuts to a torque of 10-12 ft.-lbs. (1.4-1.7 kg-m). Install new cylinder head gaskets (no sealant) and cylinder heads. Tighten long stud nuts (1 through 4—Fig. 22) to full torque of 12-15 ft.-lbs. (1.7-2.1 kg-m) before tightening small nuts (5 through 8).

Complete the assembly by reversing disassembly procedure, adjusting fan belt and timing as previously outlined.

PISTONS, PINS, RINGS AND CYLINDERS. Piston pin should be a tight fit in piston bore at room temperature and needle bearing should not have perceptible clearance between piston pin and connecting rod bore.

Piston rings are pinned in place. Top rings on most 1977 and later engines are Semi-Keystone type. On other rings recommended side clearance is 0.0012-0.0028 inch (0.03-0.07 mm). Recommended piston clearance in cylinder is 0.0055-0.007, with a wear limit of 0.008.

CONNECTING RODS, CRANKSHAFT AND BEARINGS. The crankshaft and connecting rods, including center main bearings and seals, are only available as an assembly. Measure side shake of connecting rod at small end after removing cylinders and pistons. If shake exceeds 3.0 mm (1/8 inch) install a new or rebuilt crankshaft assembly. Outer end bearings can be renewed if care is used in removal and installation to keep from damaging shaft in any of its built-up joints. Support shaft on V-blocks on installed outer bearings and measure runout at ends of shaft using a dial indicator. If runout exceeds 0.002 inch (0.5 mm), renew or straighten shaft.

REED VALVE UNITS. Refer to Fig. 23 for an exploded reed valve unit. Valve leaf (3) is of stainless spring steel and seating surface of reed plate (5)

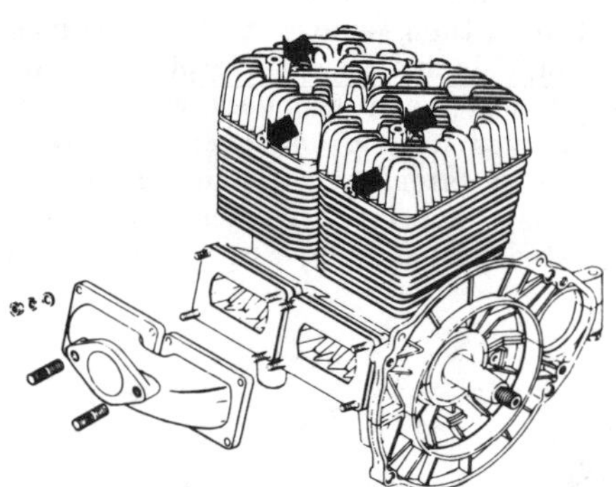

Fig. 17—Partially exploded view of engine. Cooling shroud attaches to points indicated by arrows.

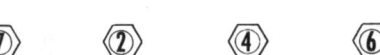

9

Fig. 19—Tighten crankcase retaining stud nuts and cap screw in sequence indicated when viewed from bottom.

Fig. 21—Some engines have a pto-end seal guard as shown by arrow.

Fig. 18—Bearing retaining half-washers are positioned in top crankcase half as indicated by arrows.

Fig. 20—When installing timing ring (B) align previous marks if present, or center mounting studs in slotted holes.

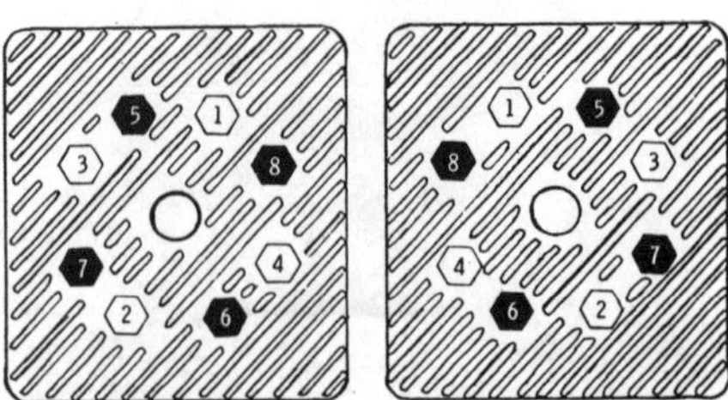

Fig. 22—When installing cylinder heads, first tighten through-stud nuts (1 through 4) to indicated torque, then short studs (5 through 8). Recommended sequence is shown.

has a bonded plastic coating. One shim (4) must be installed underneath valve reed to properly position the reed. Reed stop (2) is carefully arched for best performance and should not be reformed. Do not attempt to straighten a bent or damaged reed or reform reed stop in an attempt to alter performance. Renew reed or reed stop if damaged in any way and reed plate if coating is damaged at reed seating area. Tighten reed plate retaining screws evenly and securely to slightly compress plastic coating beneath the shim.

Liquid Cooled Models

TIGHTENING TORQUES. Tightening torques are as follows:

	Ft.-Lbs.	Kg-m
Crankcase	15-18	2.1-2.5
Cylinder to crankcase	15-18	2.1-2.5
Cylinder Head:		
Crankcase stud nuts	21-23	2.9-3.2
Capscrews to cylinder block	14-16	1.9-2.2
Top tank to head	13-14	1.8-1.9
Flywheel	55-60	7.6-8.3
Manifold stud nuts	10-12	1.4-1.7

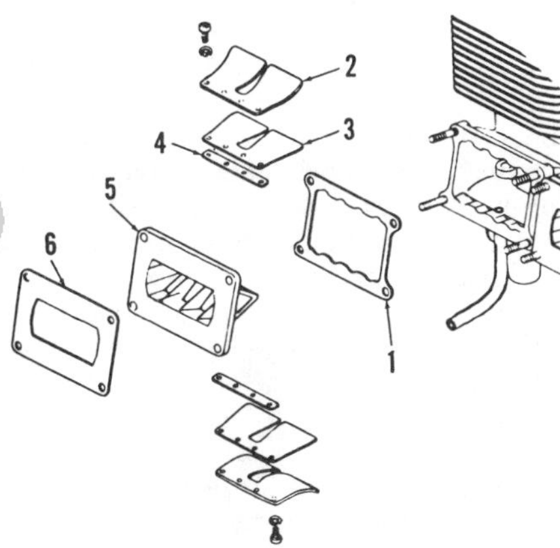

Fig. 23—Exploded view of reed valve plate and associated parts.

1. Gasket
2. Reed stop
3. Valve leaf
4. Shim
5. Reed plate
6. Gasket

DISASSEMBLY AND REASSEMBLY. To disassemble the removed engine, first remove coil cover, coils, electronic pack and spark plugs. Remove intake and exhaust manifolds leaving fuel pump attached to manifold.

Remove coolant pump cover, recoil starter, starter cup and coolant pump drive pulley. Remove coolant pump and flywheel housing.

Cylinder head and cylinders can now be removed for service on pistons, rings and cylinders. Crankcase disassembly will require removal of fan housing, flywheel, alternator stator and ignition timing ring. Before removing timing ring, punch-mark the installed position to aid in timing during assembly.

Identify pistons for reinstallation and note that arrows on piston crown point to exhaust side and angle outward toward end of crankcase as shown in Fig. 28. Use a suitable piston pin removal tool or heat pistons to expand pin bosses for removal.

Fig. 25—Arrows on piston crowns point to exhaust side and slant outward towards end of engine.

To separate the crankcase, remove retaining bolts and break sealant grip by tapping upper crankcase half lightly with a soft hammer. DO NOT attempt to pry crankcase halves apart with a screwdriver or similar tool. Some engines have a pto-end seal guard which must be removed before crankcase halves can be separated.

When assembling crankcase, lubricate crankshaft components thoroughly and install on each end of crankshaft, lips inward. Be sure retaining half-washers (Arrows—Fig. 26) are installed in their grooves in upper crankcase half. Coat both crankcase flanges with a suitable non-hardening sealant. Reposition crankshaft assembly and install crankcase lower half, being sure locating dowels seat properly. Tighten retaining cap screw and stud nuts evenly to a torque of 15-18 ft.-lbs. (2.1-2.5 kg-m) in the sequence shown in Fig. 27.

When installing timing ring, align the previously made punch marks. If timing position is not marked, center mounting screw holes in adjusting slots and install the screws, then check timing after engine is running. Install alternator stator and flywheel. If engine is equipped with pto-end oil seal guard,

Fig. 27—Tighten crankcase stud nuts in sequence shown.

Fig. 24—View of Kioritz Liquid Cooled engine as used by John Deere.

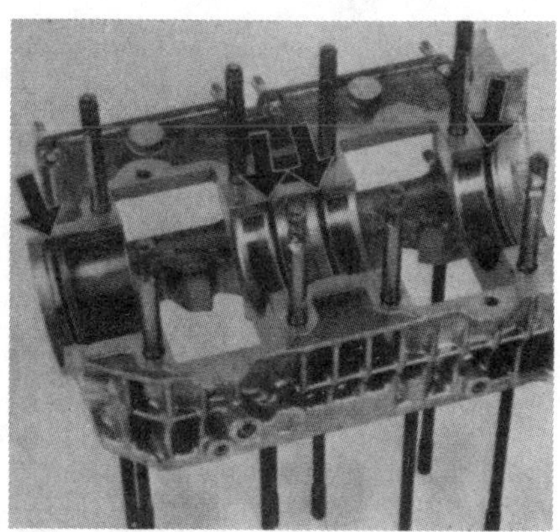

Fig. 26—Bearing retaining half-washers are located in top crankcase half as indicated by arrows.

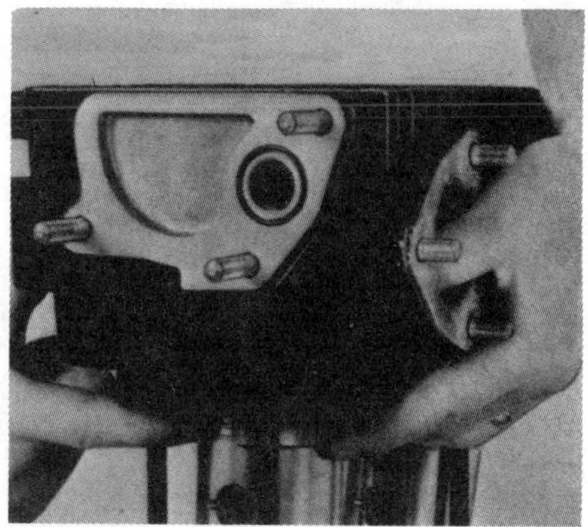

Fig. 28—Compress piston rings with fingers and gently lower cylinder head over both pistons as shown.

center hole in guard over shaft to prevent contact.

With crankcase assembled, reposition with cylinder studs uppermost. Warm the pistons and reinstall with exhaust port locating arrows angling outward and away from reed valve opening. Install new base gasket and with cylinders and pistons well lubricated, compress rings with fingers as shown in Fig. 28 and install cylinder over both pistons as shown. Install cylinder head gasket dry, then install cylinder head, thermostat, top cover gasket and top cover. Tighten cylinder head stud nuts and cap screws in sequence shown in Fig. 29 and to the following torques: Stud nuts (1 through 8) 21-23 ft.-lbs. (2.9-3.2 kg-m); capscrews to cylinder block (9 through 15) 14-16 ft.-lbs. (1.9-2.2 kg-m); top tank to cylinder head (16 through 19) 13-14 ft.-lbs. (1.8-1.9 kg-m).

Use new gaskets and install reed valve assembly. Install flywheel housing (F—Fig. 30) and starter cup (A) along with coolant pump lower pulley.

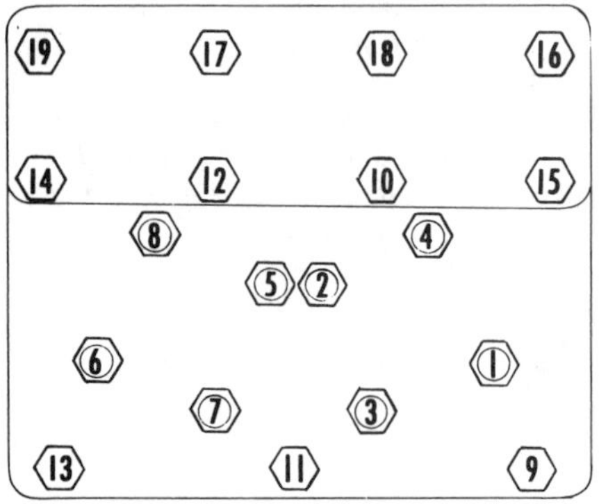

Fig. 29—Cylinder head tightening sequence. Tighten crankcase stud nuts (1 through 8) to 21-23 ft.-lbs. (2.9-3.2 kg-m); head cap screws (9 through 15) to 14-16 ft.-lbs., (1.9-2.2 kg-m) and top tank to head nuts (16 through 19) to 13-14 ft.-lbs. (1.8-1.9 kg-m).

Fig. 30—View of partially assembled engine.

A. Starter cup
B. Pump pulley
C. Bleed hose
D. Coolant pump
E. Coolant hose
F. Flywheel housing

Be sure "O" ring is in place, then install coolant pump (D) leaving mounting screws loose. Install coolant pump belt and pump pulley (B), tightening pulley mounting screws securely. Install bleed hose (C) and pump to cylinder hose (E). Adjust coolant pump belt tension by moving pump upward in slotted holes until deflection is 3/8 inch (9 mm) when measured midway between pulleys as shown in Fig. 31. Complete the assembly by reversing disassembly procedure.

PISTONS, PINS, RINGS AND CYLINDERS. Piston pin should be a tight fit in piston bore at room temperature and needle bearing should not have perceptible clearance between piston pin and connecting rod bore.

Fig. 31—Coolant pump belt should have 3/8 inch (9 mm) deflection midway between pulleys as shown.

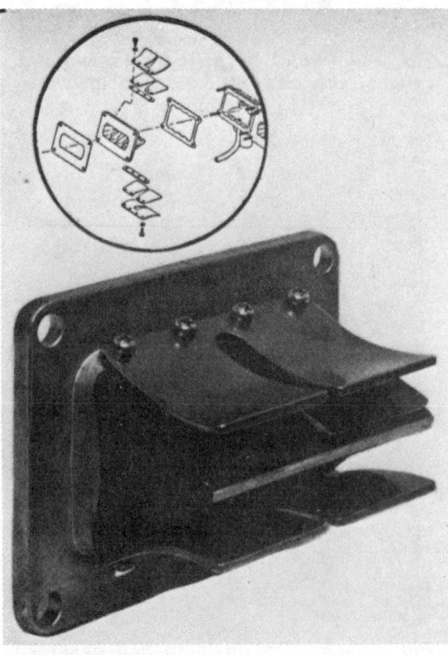

Fig. 32—Removed view of reed valve assembly. Exploded view is shown in inset.

Piston rings are pinned in place. Top rings are semi-keystone type. Recommended piston ring end gap is 0.012-0.016 inch (0.3-0.4 mm). Recommended piston clearance in cylinder is 0.0056-0.007, with a wear limit of 0.008.

CONNECTING RODS, CRANKSHAFT AND BEARINGS. The crankshaft and connecting rods, including center main bearings and seals, are only available as an assembly. Measure side shake of connecting rod at small end after removing cylinders and pistons. If side shake exceeds 3.0 mm (1/8 inch) install a new or rebuilt crankshaft assembly. Outer end bearings can be renewed if care is used in removal and installation to keep from damaging shaft in any of its built-up joints. Support shaft on "V" blocks at outer bearings, and measure runout at ends of shaft using a dial indicator. If runout exceeds 0.002 inch (0.05 mm), renew or straighten shaft.

REED VALVE UNITS. Refer to Fig. 32 for a removed view of reed valve unit. Inset shows an exploded view. Valve leaf is of stainless spring steel and seating surface of reed plate has a bonded plastic coating. One shim must be installed underneath valve leaf to properly position the leaf. Reed stop is carefully arched for best performance and should not be reformed. Do not attempt to straighten a bent or damaged reed or bend the stop in an attempt to alter performance. Renew reed or reed stop if damaged in any way and reed plate if seating surface coating is damaged. Tighten reed plate retaining screws evenly and securely to

Fig. 33—Installed view of engine. Cooling system filler cap is shown at (F). Bleed plug (B) should be temporarily removed for filling or draining the system. Drain plug is at front lower corner of block on pto side as shown at (D).

slightly compress plastic coating beneath the shim.

COOLING SYSTEM. The liquid cooling system is pressurized to 15 psi and thermostatically controlled at 144°F (61°C). The centrifugal coolant pump delivers 12 gpm at 7200 rpm engine speed.

Coolant reservoir is carried on cylinder head and the pressure filling cap is at (F—Fig. 33). A cylinder head bleed screw is at (B) and a cylinder block drain plug is located on lower front corner of cylinder block on drive side as shown at (D). The cylinder head bleed screw should be removed whenever filling or draining cooling system. When filling the system use a 50/50 mixture ethylene glycol anti-freeze and water. Pour the solution slowly into filler cap until it flows out bleed plug port. Reinstall bleed plug and continue filling reservoir.

KOHLER TWO-CYCLE

ONE CYLINDER MODELS

KOHLER COMPANY
Kohler, Wisc. 53044

CONDENSED SERVICE DATA

Engine Model	K-295-1	K295-1T	K309-1	K335-1
Bore—(mm)	75	75	75	75
Inches	2.95	2.95	2.95	2.95
Stroke—(mm)	66.5	66.5	70	76
Inches	2.62	2.62	2.75	2.99
No. of Cylinders	1	1	1	1
Displacement—(cc)	294	294	309	335
Cubic Inches	18.0	18.0	18.9	20.5
Horsepower @ RPM	18 @ 5500	20 @ 6000	20 @ 5500	23 @ 5500
Cooling Type	Centrifugal Fan			
Carburetor Model	HR	HR or WR	HR	BDC
Number Used	1	1	1	1
Ignition:				
Type	BOSCH Magneto			
Point Gap—(mm)	....	....	....	....
Inch	0.014-0.018			
Timing Advance?	yes			
Timing BTDC (mm)	2.4-2.6	2.4-2.6	3.0	2.4-2.6
Inch	0.095-0.100	0.095-0.100	0.118	0.095-0.100
Degrees	Timing Marks			
Measured at	Advanced cam			
Spark Plug:				
Bosch	M225T1	M225T1	M225T1	M225T1
Champion	K7	K7	K7	K7
Electrode Gap (mm)	0.5	0.5	0.5	0.5
Inch	0.020	0.020	0.020	0.020
Fuel/Oil Ratio	20:1	20:1	20:1	20:1

MAINTENANCE

CARBURETOR. TILLOTSON diaphragm type carburetors are used on most models. Refer to Tillotson Carburetor Section for operation and overhaul information. An external impulse line is used to operate the fuel pump. Be sure all passages are open and that vacuum and pressure leaks are eliminated. Walbro BDC diaphragm type carburetors are used on some later engines.

NOTE: On some K335-1 models equipped with Walbro carburetors, a plastic insulator was used between carburetor and manifold which may melt when subjected to high temperatures. Remove insulator and install later insulator with part no. 37 168 01 and gasket no. 37 055 02. Both insulators are white but heat sensitive insulator has a metal plug as shown in Fig. 1.

IGNITION AND TIMING. Breaker point gap should be 0.016 in. Engines are equipped with a centrifugal timing advance which provides retarded timing for starting only. Advance timing position is marked by a chipped fan blade and an aligment mark on fan housing. Hold flyweight in advanced position as shown in Fig. 2, when checking ignition timing.

Refer to MAGNETO SERVICE Section of ENGINE SERVICE FUNDAMENTALS for overhaul data and service procedures.

LUBRICATION. The engine is lubricated by mixing oil with the fuel. The manufacturer recommends the use of Regular or Premium gasoline (92 octane) and SAE 40 (Diluted) 2-cycle (air cooled) engine oil mixed at a ratio of 20:1.

Mix fuel and oil thoroughly using a separate container before pouring mixture into fuel tank. For cold weather blending, pre-mix the oil with a small amount of gasoline and shake thoroughly until mixture is liquid, then blend with remainder of fuel. Do not use kerosene or fuel oil for premixing.

REPAIRS

TIGHTENING TORQUES. Recommended tightening torques are as follows: (All values are given in ft.-lbs.).

Cylinder head bolts	32
Crankcase screws (nuts), 8mm	18
Crankcase screws (nuts) 10 mm	32
Intake manifold	18
Cylinder nuts	32
Flywheel	90
Spark plug	25

NOTE: To determine type of threads used on engine, refer to engine specification number. If number has six digits, threads are U.S. standard. If specification number has seven digits, refer to suffix of two numbers. Numbers from 01 to 05 indicate metric threads while numbers from 06 to 20 indicate U.S. standard threads.

DISASSEMBLY AND REASSEMBLY. Refer to Figs. 3 and 4 for

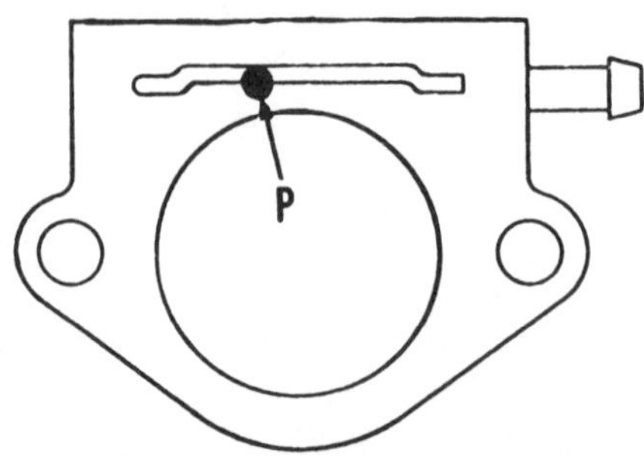

Fig. 1–Heat sensitive insulator is identified by presence of metal plug (P) which is absent and hole is filled on later insulators.

Fig. 2–Breaker cam must be held in advanced position when checking timing.

exploded views of engines. With engine removed from machine, remove carburetor, manifolds, drive sheave, starter, air shroud and flywheel.

Mark cylinder heads with relation to cylinders and note that intake manifold ports in cylinder blocks are on same side of engine as pulse passage fitting in crankcase.

When reassembling engines, crankshaft end play should be 0.006-0.012 (in.). End play is controlled by thrust washers (8—Fig. 4). Thrust washers are all 0.006 in. thickness. Refer to Fig. 8 for tightening sequence of crankcase screws.

PISTONS, RINGS AND CYLINDERS. Cylinder heads can be installed in any position. Head should be marked before removal and when reinstalling, note that fins run in direction of air flow on single cylinder models. Refer to Fig. 5. Piston pin is a floating fit in piston bosses and retained by snap rings.

Top piston ring is Moly-Coated and darker in appearance than bottom ring. Piston ring end gap should be 0.012-0.016 (in.). Piston ring side clearance should be 0.0035-0.0048 in. for top ring and 0.003-0.004 in. for bottom ring. Piston rings are pinned in place in piston grooves. Pistons are marked "EHC" on top of piston crown. Marking must be installed toward exhaust port side of cylinder. Pistons and rings are available in oversizes of 0.010, 0.020 and 0.040 (in.).

CRANKSHAFT AND CONNECTING ROD ASSEMBLY. The crankshaft and connecting rod are available only as a complete unit and should not be disassembled.

Check for wear of the connecting rod big end by measuring the play at the connecting rod small end. Move the small end laterally as shown in Fig. 7. Small end play should be 0.006-0.016 in. Renew crankshaft assembly if play is excessive.

Bearings (9—Fig. 4) are a press fit on their shafts and will not normally need to be removed unless renewal is indicated. If bearings must be removed, support the shaft behind counterweight as shown in Fig. 6 when reinstalling.

Whenever crankshaft assembly has been removed, check for runout before installation. Runout should not exceed

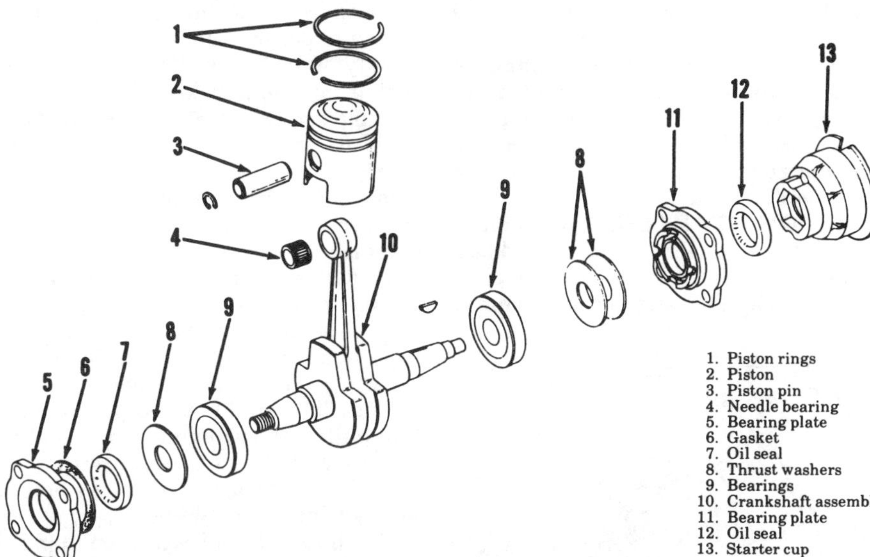

Fig. 4–Exploded view of crankshaft, piston and associated parts used on single cylinder models.

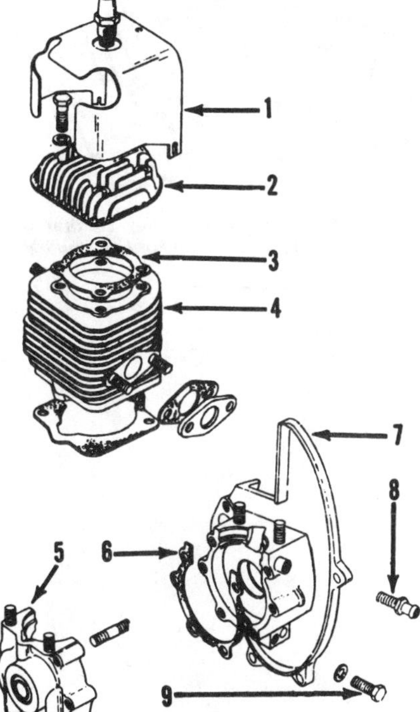

Fig. 3–Exploded view of crankcase, cylinder and associated parts on single cylinder models.

1. Shroud
2. Cylinder head
3. Gasket
4. Cylinder
5. Crankcase half
6. Gasket
7. Crankcase half
8. Pulse passage fitting
9. Plug

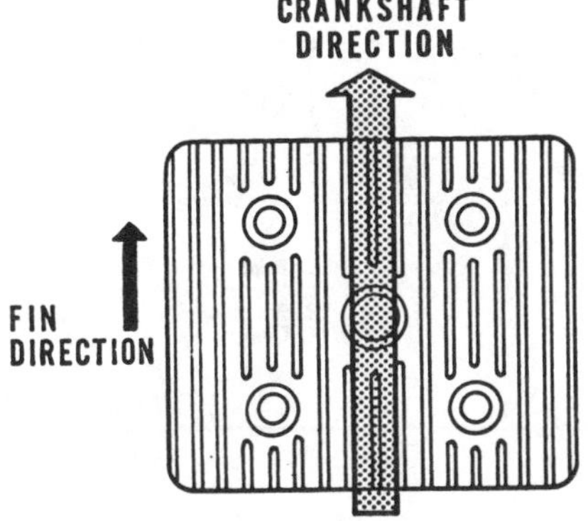

Fig. 5–Cylinder head fins are installed parallel with crankshaft on single cylinder models.

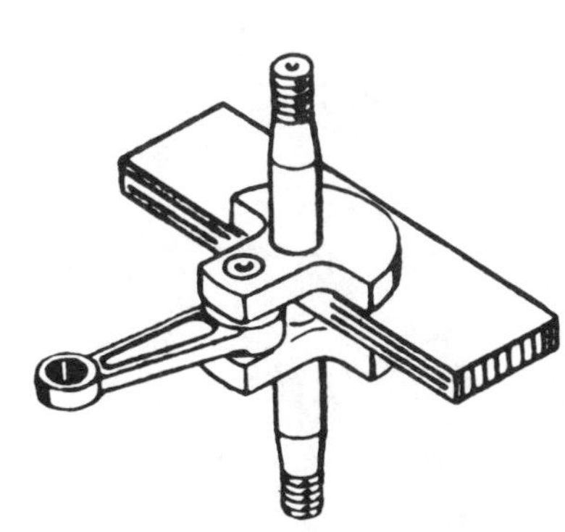

Fig. 6–Support crankshaft behind counterweight when pressing on bearings.

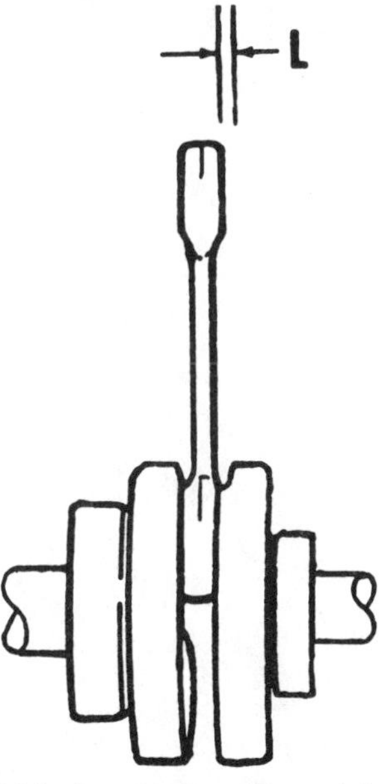

Fig. 7–Axial play of connecting rod is determined by moving connecting rod small end laterally. Axial play (L) should be 0.006-0.016 in.

0.001 (in.). If runout is excessive and remainder of unit is reusable, the unit may be straightened by a machine shop, motorcycle engine rebuilder or others experienced with this type of construction. If bearings, shafts or connecting rods are unserviceable, renew the complete unit.

RECOIL STARTER. Refer to Fig. 9 for exploded view of starter. To disassemble starter, remove from engine. Pull rope handle and tie a temporary knot in rope. Remove rope handle, untie temporary knot and allow rope to slowly wind on pulley until recoil spring tension is released. Remove retaining screw (1) and components (2 thru 8). Remove pulley (9) being careful to disengage recoil spring (13) before withdrawing pulley. If necessary to remove spring (13), remove carefully to prevent personal injury.

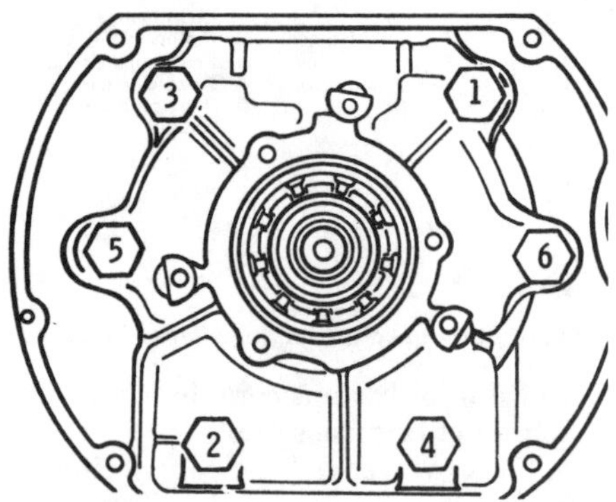

Fig. 8–View of tightening sequence for crankcase screws. Tighten to 16 ft-lbs.

To assemble starter, insert recoil spring on lug (L—Fig. 10) of cover and wind in a counterclockwise direction. If rope was removed from pulley, install rope on pulley so that washer (W—Fig. 11) fits between knot and pulley. Position pulley on spring and cover so that knotted end of rope is up. Insert a piece of stiff wire or a nail through hole in pulley to guide inner end of spring onto pulley hub so pulley will drop in place. Install remainder of components. Tighten retaining screw to 50 in.-lbs. This will create a slight drag causing dogs to move readily into engaged position. If retaining screw is loose, dogs may not fully engage resulting in damage to teeth in starting cup.

If rope has a tendency to come off pulley during operation, Kohler Starter Repair Kit No. 33 757 01 is available which includes a flange attached to starter cover that guides rope into pulley.

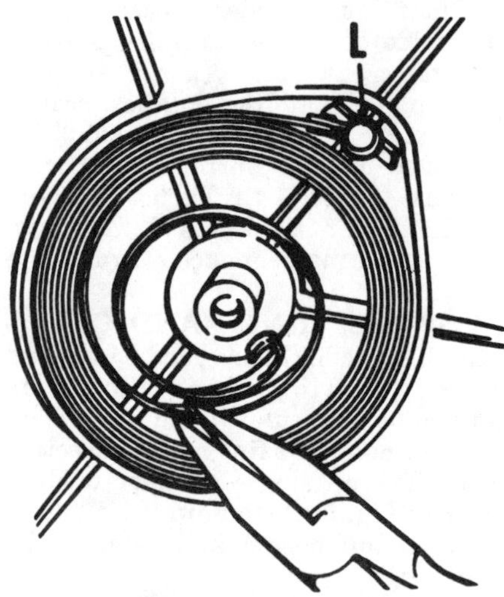

Fig. 10–Install recoil spring in outer cover so that outer end of spring is around lug (L) of cover. Wind spring in counterclockwise direction.

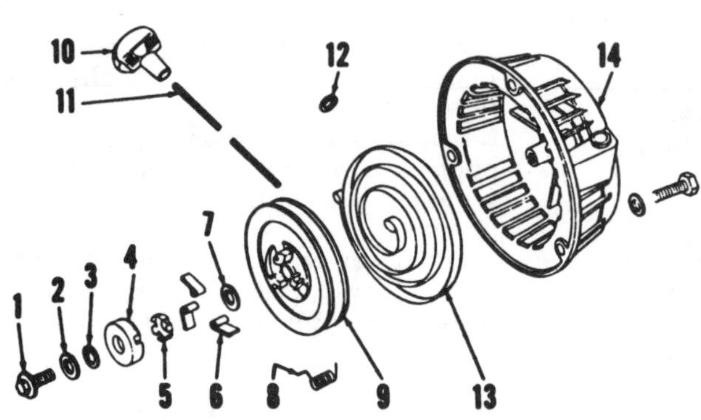

Fig. 9–Exploded view of recoil starter used on Kohler two cycle engines.

1. Retaining screw
2. Washers
3. Washers
4. Retainer
5. Brake spring
6. Dogs
7. Washer
8. Dog spring
9. Pulley
10. Handle
11. Rope
12. Washer
13. Recoil spring
14. Cover

Fig. 11–Install rope on pulley so that washer (W) is between rope knot and pulley.

KOHLER TWO-CYCLE

TWO AND THREE CYLINDER MODELS CONDENSED SERVICE DATA

ENGINE MODEL	K295-2T	K295-2AX	K340-2T	K340-2AX	SK340-2AS	K-340-2FA	K399-2T	K399-2AX
Bore–(mm)	57.5	57.5	62	62	60	62	65	65
Inches	2.26	2.26	2.44	2.44	2.362	2.44	2.56	2.56
Stroke–(mm)	56	56	56	56	60	56	60	60
Inches	2.2	2.2	2.2	2.2	2.362	2.2	2.36	2.36
No. of Cylinders	2	2	2	2	2	2	2	2
Displacement–(cc)	292	292	338	338	339	338	398	398
Cubic Inches	17.8	17.8	20.6	20.6	20.7	20.6	24.3	24.3
Horsepower @RPM	....	24@6500	24@5500	28@6500	....	....	28@6000	32@6500
Cooling Type	Cent. Fan	Axial Fan	Cent. Fan	Axial Fan	Axial Fan	Free Air	Cent. Fan	Axial Fan
Carburetor Model	HR-WR	HR-WR	HR-WR	HR-WR	HR-WR	VM or B	HR-WR	HR-WR
Number Used	1	1	1	1	1	1	1	1
Ignition:								
Type	ET	ET	ET	ET	CD	CD	ET	ET
Point Gap–(mm)	0.4	0.4	0.4	0.4	....	....	0.4	0.4
Inch	0.016	0.016	0.016	0.016	....	....	0.016	0.016
Timing Advance?	Yes	Yes	Yes	Yes	Yes	Yes	Yes	Yes
Timing BTDC (mm)	2.3	2.3	2.3	2.3	....	2.12	2.3	2.3
Inch	0.090	0.090	0.090	0.090	....	0.085	0.090	0.090
Degrees	....	....	....	....	....	....	....	....
Measured at	Adv.	Adv.	Adv.	Adv.	....	6000	Adv.	Adv.
Spark Plug:								
Bosch	W260T2	W260T2	W260T1	W260T2	....	....	M240T1	W260T2
Champion	N2	N2	L78	N2	N19V	QN-3	K8	N2
Electrode Gap–(mm)	0.5	0.5	0.5	0.5	....	0.635	0.5	0.5
Inch	0.020	0.020	0.020	0.020	....	0.025	0.020	0.020
Fuel/Oil Ratio	20:1	20:1	20:1	20:1	20:1	50:1	20:1	20:1

ENGINE MODEL	K440-2T	K440-2AX	K440-2SS	K440-2AS	K618-2	K645-3SS
Bore–(mm)	68	68	67.5	68	75	67.5
Inches	2.68	2.68	2.66	2.677	2.95	2.66
Stroke–(mm)	60	60	60	60	70	60
Inches	2.36	2.36	2.36	2.362	2.75	2.36
No. of Cylinders	2	2	2	2	2	3
Displacement–(cc)	436	436	430	436	618	644
Cubic Inches	26.7	26.7	26.0	26.7	37.7	39.2
Horsepower @ RPM	30@6000	37@6500	....	....	33@5000	....
Cooling Type	Cent. Fan	Axial Fan	Free Air	Axial Fan	Cent. Fan	Free Air
Carburetor Model	HR-WR	HR-WR	HD-WD	HD-WD	HR	HD-WD
Number Used	1	1	2	2	1	3
Ignition:						
Type	ET	ET	ET	CD	ET	ET
Point Gap–(mm)	0.4	0.4	0.4	...	0.4	0.4
Inch	0.016	0.016	0.016	....	0.016	0.016
Timing Advance?	Yes	Yes	Yes	Yes	Yes	Yes
Timing BTDC (mm)	2.3	2.3	2.3	....	3.0	2.3
Inch	0.090	0.090	0.090	....	0.118	0.090
Degrees	....	....	....	....	....	....
Measured	Adv.	Adv.	Adv.	....	Adv.	Adv.
Spark Plug:						
Bosch	M240T1	W260T2	....	....	M225T1	....
Champion	K8	N2	....	N19V	K7	....
Electrode Gap–(mm)	0.5	0.5	0.5	....	0.5	0.5
Inch	0.020	0.020	0.020	....	0.020	0.020
Fuel/Oil Ratio	20:1	20:1	20:1	....	20:1	20:1

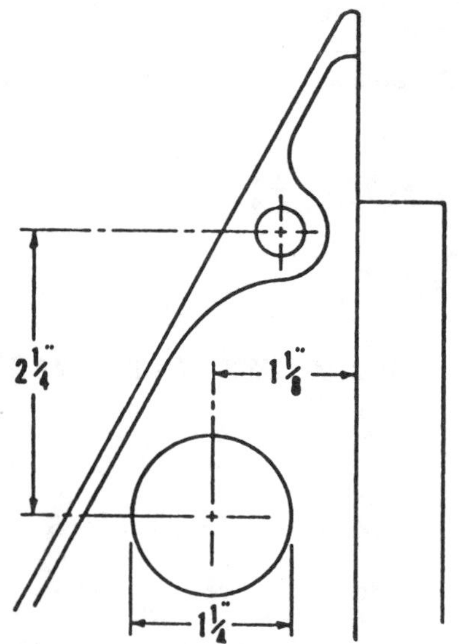

Fig. 1 — To cure vapor lock on models K399-2 and K440-2, cut hole in end plate to dimensions shown above as outlined in text.

MAINTENANCE

CARBURETOR. Tillotson, Walbro or Mikuni carburetors are used. Refer to appropriate Carburetor Section for specific overhaul information. An external impulse line is used to operate the fuel pump. Be sure all passages are open and that vacuum and pressure leaks are eliminated.

NOTE: On models K399-2 and K440-2 encountering vapor lock, a 1¼ in. hole cut in end plate adjacent to carburetors will allow air to be blown across carburetors. Cut hole using dimensions in Fig. 1. Access to end plate is possible by removing starter and blower housing, or by removing intake manifold assembly. Stuff rags in intake ports if hole is cut from carburetor side.

IGNITION AND TIMING. On models equipped with breaker points, point gap should be 0.016 in. Both sets of points must be adjusted to open exactly 180° apart. Engines are equipped with a centrifugal timing advance which provides retarded timing for starting only. Advance timing position is marked by a chipped fan blade and an alignment mark on fan housing. Hold flyweight in advanced position as shown in Fig. 2, when checking ignition timing.

The Capacitor Discharge Ignition (CDI) system uses a permanent magnet flywheel to induce voltage into exciter coil. The exciter coil then sends current to CDI unit where a diode allows only DC current to flow into a capacitor. When gate control switch in CDI unit receives the small current signal from the pulser coil, it closes and allows the capacitor to discharge its stored voltage into the ignition coil. The coil then "steps up" voltage enough to fire both spark plugs simultaneously.

If an engine problem is experienced check fuel system, electrical connections, wiring and spark plugs. To test CDI ignition system a special tester or ohmmeter must be used. **DO NOT** use a 12 volt test light as it may damage the CDI system.

Timing is electronic and should not change once properly adjusted. Check timing with an electronic timing light. If timing has changed, check for a loose flywheel nut, sheared flywheel key, or loose mounting screws on stator base plate. To check ignition timing, first remove drive belt. Connect a timing light to No. 1 spark plug wire and a tachometer to No. 2 plug wire. Start engine and run at 6000 rpm. Aim timing light at hole in flywheel housing and check to see if mark on flywheel lines up with mark on flywheel housing. If timing is incorrect, adjust timing stator plate and recheck timing marks for correct alignment. Reinstall drive belt.

LUBRICATION. Engine is lubricated by mixing oil with the fuel. The recommended ratio is 20:1 for all models except K-340-2FA. Use Regular or Premium gasoline and SAE 40 (Diluted) two-cycle (air-cooled) engine oil.

For Model K-340-2FA manufacturer recommends a gasoline with an octane rating of 88 or higher, mixed with a two-cycle BIA certified oil or suitable equivalent at a ratio of 50:1.

Mix fuel and oil thoroughly using a separate container before pouring mixture into fuel tank. For cold weather blending, pre-mix the oil with a small amount of gasoline and shake thoroughly until mixture is liquid, then blend with remainder of fuel. Do not use kerosene or fuel oil for premixing.

COOLING FAN AND BELT. The cooling fan drive belt should have approximately ⅜-inch deflection measured midway between pulleys as shown by arrows, Fig. 3. To adjust the belt, use a suitable pin-type spanner (W) to hold the upper pulley and remove fan shaft nut. Transfer shims from between pulley halves to front of pulley to tighten belt or add shims to loosen belt. Tighten fan shaft nut to a torque of 35 ft.-lbs. When a new belt is installed, tension should be checked after the first 2 or 3 hours of operation.

Fig. 2 — Breaker cam must be held in advanced position when checking timing.

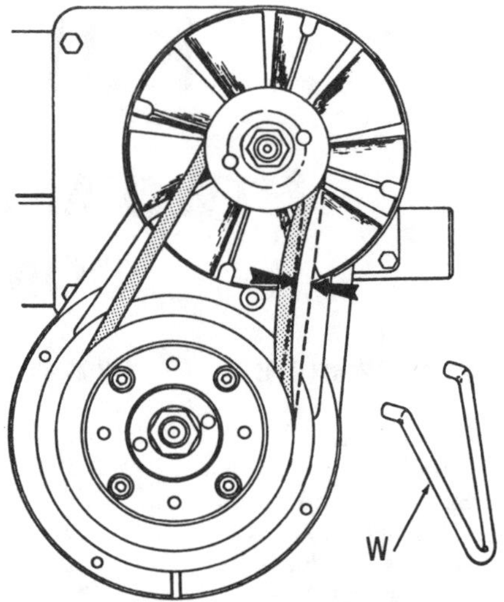

Fig. 3 — On axial fan models, cooling fan drive belt should have approximately ⅜-inch deflection when finger pressure is applied at point shown by arrows. A pin-type spanner wrench (W) is used to hold fan pulley to remove shaft nut.

REPAIRS

TIGHTENING TORQUES. Recommended tightening torques are as follows: (All values are given in ft.-lbs.).

CENTRIFUGAL FAN MODELS
Bearing Plates
K618-2 16
All Other Models 13
Crankcase and Cylinder Nuts
K618-2 32
All Other Models 18
Crankcase Flange Bolts (K618-2) 17
Cylinder Head Bolts
K295-2T 18
K618-2 32
Other Models 22
Flywheel 100
Intake Manifold 13
Spark Plug
K295-2T-K340-2T 14
Other Models 18

NOTE: To determine type of threads used on engine, refer to engine specification number. If number has six digits, threads are U.S. standard. If specification number has seven digits, refer to suffix of two numbers. Numbers from 01 to 05 indicate metric threads while numbers from 06 to 20 indicate U.S. standard threads.

AXIAL FAN MODELS

Crankcase and Cylinder Nuts	16
Crankcase Flange Bolts	13
Cylinder Head	18
Drain Plug	8
Fan Shaft Nut	40
Flywheel	95
Manifold Halves	8
Spark Plug	14

MODEL K-340-2FA

Crankcase Halves	9
Crankcase to Cylinder	18
Cylinder Head	18
Intake Manifold	18
Exhaust Manifold	18
Flywheel	90
Spark Plug	20

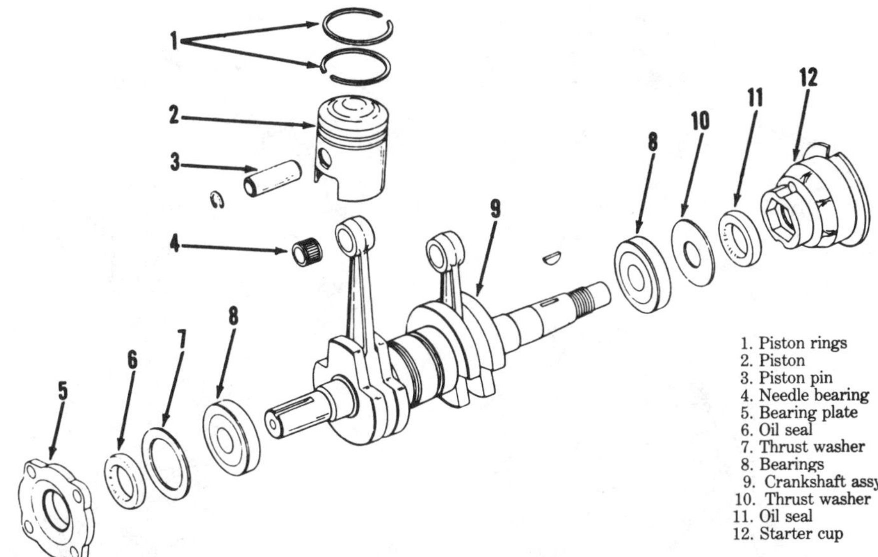

Fig. 5—Exploded view of crankshaft, pistons and associated parts used on centrifugal fan engines.

DISASSEMBLY AND REASSEMBLY. Repair sections are divided into three types; axial fan twin, centrifugal fan twin and late K-340-2FA model. K-440-2SS and K-645-3SS models are listed in CONDENSED SERVICE DATA Tables but specific overhaul data is not given. Repair procedures differ on engine models, refer to the appropriate following paragraphs for suggested procedures.

CENTRIFUGAL FAN MODELS. Refer to Figs. 4 and 5 for exploded views of engine. If the Engine Specification number has seven digits and the last two are 05 or lower, the engine has metric threads. All other engines have U.S. Standard threads. As an example, metric threads will be found on K399-2 and K618-2 engines.

To disassemble the removed engine, first remove carburetor, manifolds, drive clutch, starter, air shroud and flywheel. Cooling fins on early models were cast square with heads as shown in upper view, Fig. 6. Late models have oblique fins as shown in lower view. Cylinder heads or shrouds are not interchangeable between the two types. On all models, carefully note or mark positioning of heads so they can be installed in correct position.

When removing drive-end bearing plate (5–Fig. 5) note number of shims (7) on shaft. Keep shims with bearing plate for reassembly. Scratch-mark magneto plate to assist in timing during reassembly, then remove magneto plate, flywheel end plate and shims (10). Note number of shims (10) and keep with end plate for reassembly.

Scratch-mark cylinders and crankcase for identification and remove cylinders and pistons, keeping No. 1 and No. 2 assemblies separate and identified. Remove the retaining stud nuts and, supporting upper crankcase half, bump crankshaft gently with a soft hammer to break the sealant and separate the halves; then lift off upper crankshaft half and lift out crankshaft.

When reassembling the engine, make sure all parts are clean. Insert crankcase through-bolts in lower crankcase half and attach to a suitable engine stand, then lower crankshaft into position in crankcase half. Install both crankcase end plates and removed shim packs on

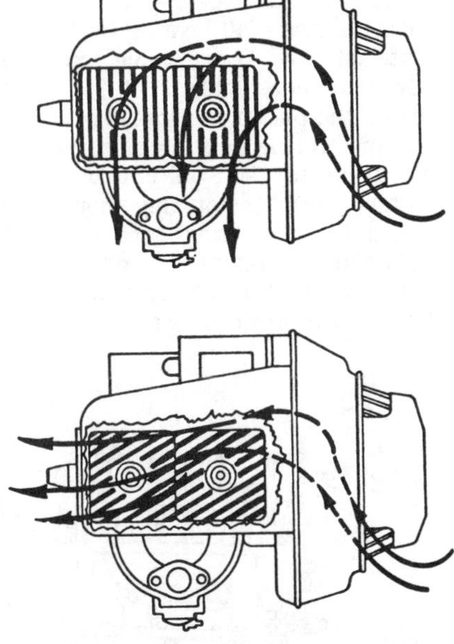

Fig. 6—On early models, cooling air outlet was located on carburetor side of engine and cylinder head cooling fins run crosswise as shown in upper view. On later engines, cooling air outlet is located at drive end of engine and oblique cooling fins are used (lower view).

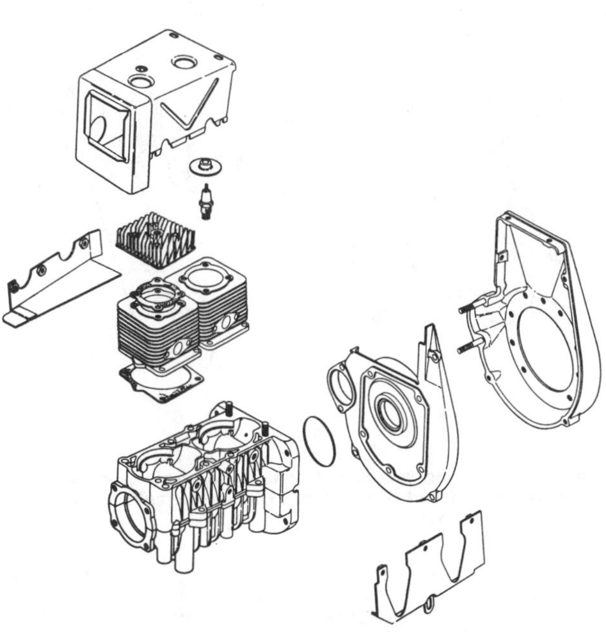

Fig. 4—Exploded view of major housing components used on centrifugal fan models.

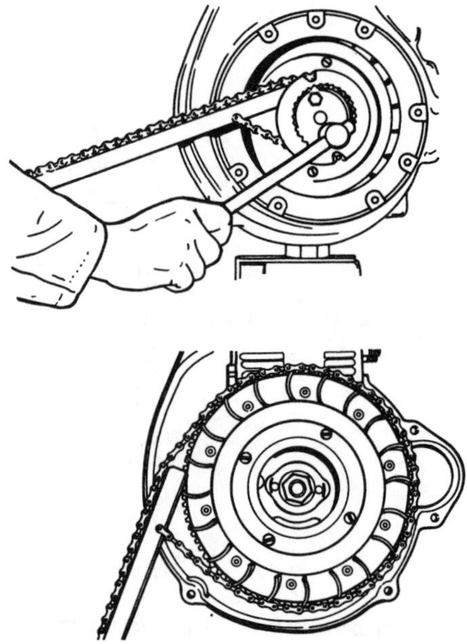

Fig. 7—A Chain Clamp Tool is available from the engine manufacturer which can be used for a number of holding operations.

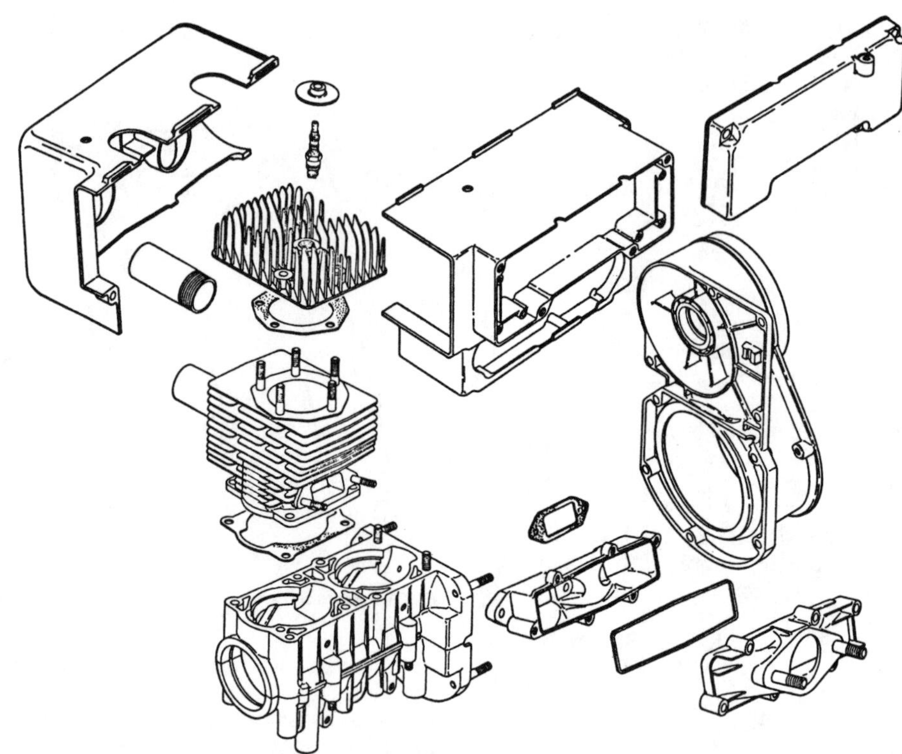

Fig. 9—Exploded view of major housing components used on axial fan models. Note split cylinder shroud and two-piece intake manifold. Minor differences exist between large and small engines; refer also to Fig. 11.

lower crankcase half and snug up retaining cap screws. Slide crankshaft solidly toward flywheel end of housing as shown in Fig. 8 and measure end clearance between crankshaft bearing and drive end housing using a feeler gage as shown. Clearance should be 0.006-0.012; if it is not, vary the thickness of either shim pack (7 or 10–Fig. 5) as required. Shims are available in thicknesses of 0.006 and 0.012. Remove both bearing plates leaving shim pack in position on crankshafts. Coat flange areas of both crankcase halves evenly and lightly with KOHLER Crankcase Sealer (or equivalent). Lubricate all bearings with clean, light oil and reassemble crankcase halves and end plates.

Heat the piston and install piston pin, with piston ring locating pins positioned on carburetor side of crankcase. The lighter colored piston ring should be installed in lower ring groove and the darker (moly coated) ring in top groove. Make sure both rings are properly positioned over locating pins, then install cylinders using new base gaskets and a suitable ring compresser. Install and tighten intake manifold to align the cylinders, then tighten all crankcase through-bolts. Complete the assembly by reversing the disassembly procedure.

AXIAL FAN MODELS. Refer to Figs. 9, 10 and 11 for exploded views. All engines are equipped with U. S. Standard threads.

To disassemble the removed engine, first remove drive clutch, starter, air

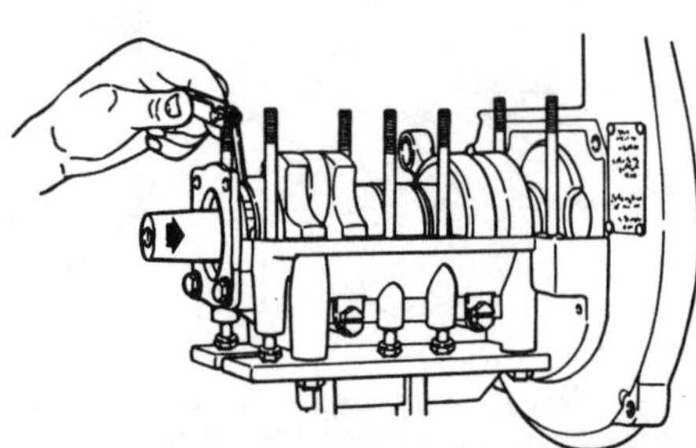

Fig. 8—Push crankshaft of partially assembled engine to flywheel side and measure end play with a feeler gage as shown.

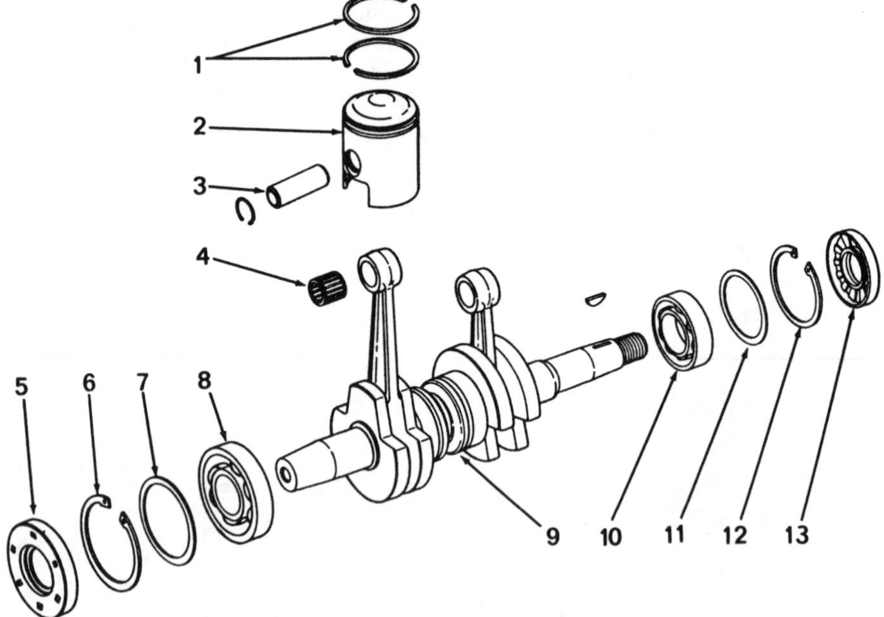

Fig. 10—Exploded view of crankshaft, pistons and associated parts used on big block axial fan models. Small block engines are similar except end plates (Fig. 11) control crankshaft end play instead of snap rings (6 & 12).

1. Piston rings
2. Piston
3. Piston pin
4. Needle bearing
5. Oil seal
6. Snap ring
7. Shim pack
8. Bearing
9. Crankshaft assy.
10. Bearing
11. Shim pack
12. Snap ring
13. Oil seal

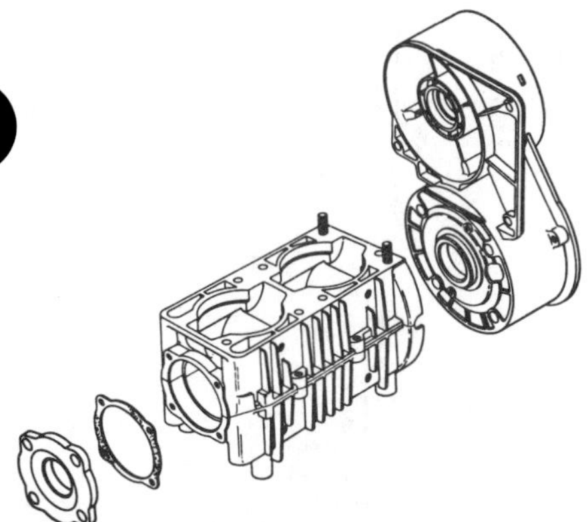

Fig. 11—On small block engines, end plates control crankshaft end play instead of snap rings shown in Fig. 10.

shrouds and flywheel. Intake manifold carburetor side may be removed along with carburetor; removal is necessary for access to the two center manifold stud nuts. Do not attempt to remove threaded exhaust tubes unless renewal is indicated. Tubes are installed with a special hardening sealer, and removal is difficult and unnecessary for normal service.

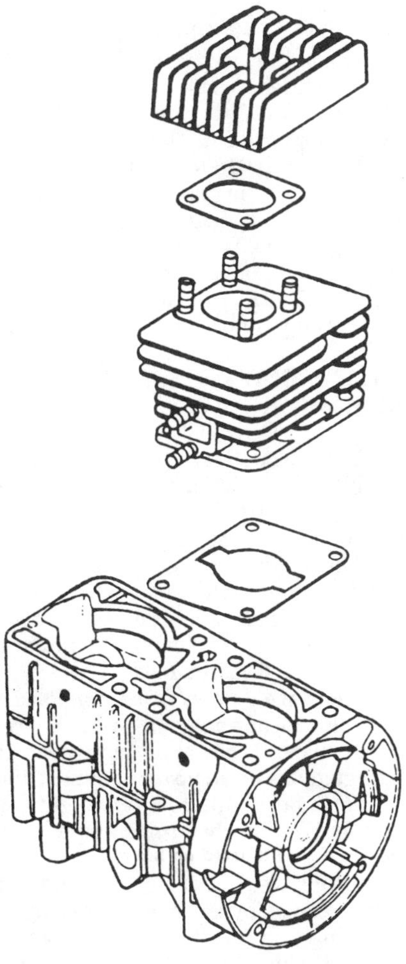

Fig. 11A—Exploded view of crankcase and cylinder assembly for Model K-340-2FA.

Scratch-mark cylinder heads, cylinders and crankcase for identification, then remove cylinder heads, cylinders and pistons. Keep No. 1 and No. 2 assemblies separate and identified. Scratch-mark armature plate to assist in timing at reassembly and remove armature plate and fan housing. On model K295-2AX and K340-2AX, remove drive-end bearing plate. Remove flange bolts or stud nuts. Support upper crankcase half and bump crankshaft gently with a soft-faced hammer to break the sealant grip, then separate crankcase halves and remove crankshaft unit.

When reassembling the engine, make sure all parts are clean. Install crankcase through-bolts in lower crankcase half and attach crankcase half to a suitable engine stand, then lower crankshaft in position. On large block engines, install the removed shim packs (7 & 11–Fig. 10) and fit snap rings (6 & 12) in crankcase bore grooves. On small block models, install removed shim packs and end plates (Fig. 11). On all models, slide crankshaft toward flywheel end and measure crankshaft end clearance using a feeler gage as shown in Fig. 8. Clearance should be 0.006-0.012; if it is not, vary the thickness of either shim pack (7 or 11–Fig. 10). Shims are available in thicknesses of 0.006 and 0.012. On engines so equipped, remove end plates leaving shim packs in place; on other models, position oil seals (5 & 13–Fig. 10) on shaft in lower crankcase half. Lubricate all bearings using light oil and coat both crankcase mating flanges with KOHLER Crankcase Sealer or equivalent. Reinstall crankcase upper half and on models so equipped, install bearing end plates.

Heat the piston and install piston pin, with piston ring locating pins positioned on carburetor side of crankcase. A square-section ring is used in lower ring groove, an L-ring in upper groove. Make sure rings are properly positioned over locating pins, then install cylinders using new base gaskets and a suitable ring compresser. Install and tighten intake manifold base half to align the cylinders, then tighten all crankcase through-bolts. Complete the assembly by reversing the disassembly procedure.

MODEL K-340-2FA. Refer to Fig. 11A and 11B for exploded views of engine assembly.

To disassemble the removed engine, first remove drive clutch, engine base, intake and exhaust manifolds, spark plugs and recoil starter. Remove flywheel retaining nut and locking plate, then using a suitable puller withdraw flywheel from crankshaft. Remove flywheel housing with CDI unit and coil attached to housing, then remove stator assembly. Remove cylinder heads and cylinders. Remove piston pin retaining rings, then push piston pins out and remove pistons. Remove crankcase retaining cap screws and split case in half. Lift crankshaft assembly out of housing.

Inspect crankcase halves for pitting, scoring or any other damage. Inspect cylinder heads and cylinders for excessive distortion. Cylinder head or cylin-

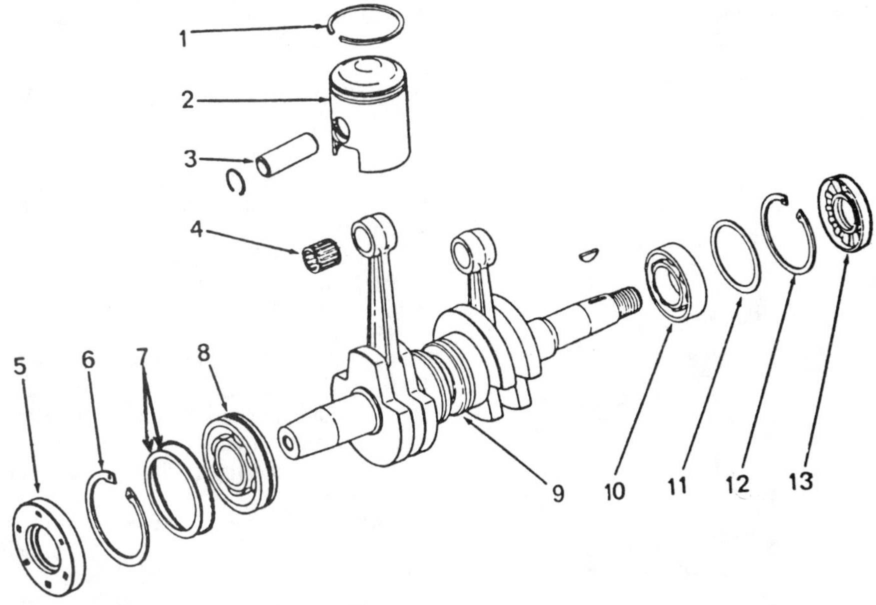

Fig. 11B—Exploded view of crankshaft assembly and associated parts for Model K-340-2FA.

1. Piston ring
2. Piston
3. Piston pin and circlip
4. Needle bearing
5. Oil seal
6. Snap ring
7. Shim pack and "O" ring
8. Roller bearing
9. Crankshaft assembly
10. Roller bearing
11. Shim pack
12. Snap ring
13. Oil seal

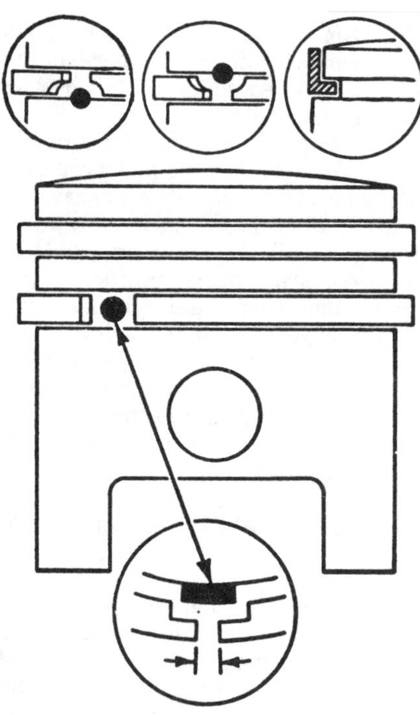

Fig. 12 – Various locations of piston ring positioning pin have been used as shown. L-ring (upper right) is used in top groove on K295-2T and all axial fan models.

der should be renewed if distortion is more than 0.002-inch. Measure cylinder bore for out-of-roundness or excessive taper. Accepted allowable wear tolerance is 0.002-inch. Cylinder assembly must be renewed if beyond specification. Cylinder bore is chrome-plated and cannot be honed or rebored. Check pistons for pitting, scoring, corrosion or any other damage. Measure piston pin bore, pin diameter and piston skirt diameter. Specifications are as follows: piston skirt, 2.4364-2.4370 inches; piston pin diameter, 0.6297-0.6301 inch; piston pin bore, 0.6298-0.6302 inch. Inspect crankshaft for excessive wear, damaged roller bearings or any other damage. Connecting rod side clearance should be 0.006-0.016 inch. Crankshaft runout should not be more than 0.002-inch. Renew all parts as needed. Crankshaft outer bearings may be renewed using a suitable puller and installation tool.

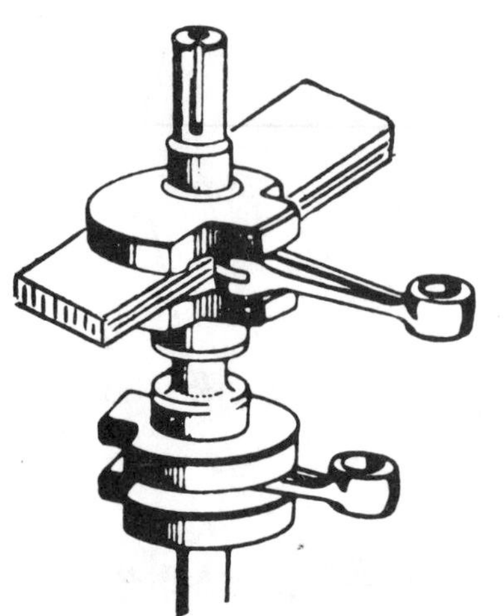

Fig. 13 – Support crankshaft behind counterweights when pressing bearings.

During reassembly all "O" rings, gaskets and seals should be renewed. Correct crankshaft end play is 0.006-0.012 inch. Add or remove shims from between end bearings and retaining rings until correct distance is obtained.

Reassemble engine in reverse order of disassembly. Listed below are some items to follow during reassembly:

1. Install piston on connecting rods with arrows pointing toward exhaust side.
2. Piston ring end gap measured one-inch down from top of cylinder should be 0.010-0.015 inch. If necessary, file ring end until correct measured gap is obtained.
3. Install new cylinder-to-crankcase gaskets with tabs toward exhaust port side.
4. During installation of cylinder assemblies, install intake manifold to cylinders before tightening cylinder retaining nuts as to insure alignment of cylinders.

Refer to TIGHTENING TORQUE section for torque specifications. Tighten cylinder head retaining nuts in a criss-cross sequence.

PISTONS, RINGS AND CYLINDERS. Engine Models K-440-2SS and K-645-3SS are listed in CONDENSED SERVICE DATA Tables but specific repair data is not given. For Model K-340-2FA refer to DISASSEMBLY AND REASSEMBLY section for repair procedures. For all other engine models refer to the following paragraphs for service data.

On some engines, cylinder head can be installed in more than one position and should be marked before removal. Renew any head with broken or missing fins, damaged spark plug threads or other damage.

Maximum cylinder taper or out-of-round is 0.006. Cylinders can be honed or rebored, and pistons and rings are available in oversizes of 0.010, 0.020 and 0.040.

Piston ring locating pins may be installed at top, bottom or center of ring groove as shown in Fig. 12, and the correct ring must be installed. On axial fan engines and K295-2T an L-ring is used in top ring groove. Other engines used a dark colored (moly coated) top ring. Recommended piston ring end is 0.012-0.018 for model K618-2, 0.008-0.014 for K295-2T and all axial fan models; and 0.010-0.016 for all other models. Piston ring side clearance using new rings should not exceed 0.005 for top ring or 0.004 for bottom ring on model K618-2, 0.003 for bottom ring on models K295-2T or axial fan engines; or 0.004 for any other ring on any model.

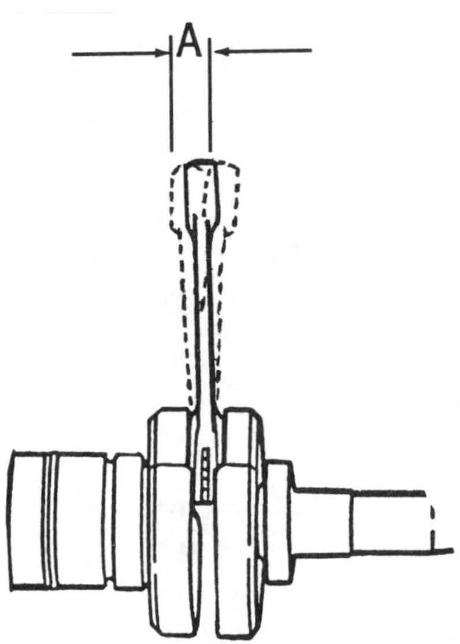

Fig. 14 – Wear of connecting rod big-end bearing and crankpin can be checked by determining the axial "rock" or "Side Shake" of rod at small end as shown at (A). Wear may be considered excessive if side shake exceeds 0.080 in. (2.0 mm).

CRANKSHAFT ASSEMBLY. Engine Models K-440-2SS and K-645-3SS are listed in CONDENSED SERVICE DATA Tables but specific repair data is not given. For Model K-340-2FA refer to DISASSEMBLY AND REASSEMBLY section for repair procedures. For all other engine models refer to the following paragraphs for service data.

The crankshaft and connecting rods are available only as a complete unit and should not be disassembled.

Bearings are a press fit on crankshaft and will not normally need to be removed unless renewal is indicated. If bearings must be removed, support the crankshaft below the counterweights as shown in Fig. 13 when reinstalling bearings.

Check for wear of the connecting rod big end bearing by measuring the play at connecting rod small end as shown in Fig. 14. If side shake (A) exceeds 0.080 inch (2.0 mm), unit is excessively worn and crankshaft assembly should be renewed. Also check for damage or roughness of crankshaft bearing by turning the rod around crankpin.

Check for runout before installation by mounting the shaft between lathe centers as shown in Fig. 15. Runout should not exceed 0.0015. If runout is excessive and remainder of unit is reusable, the unit may be straightened by a machine shop or engine rebuilder experienced with this type of construction. If bearings, shafts or connecting rods are unserviceable, renew the crankshaft unit.

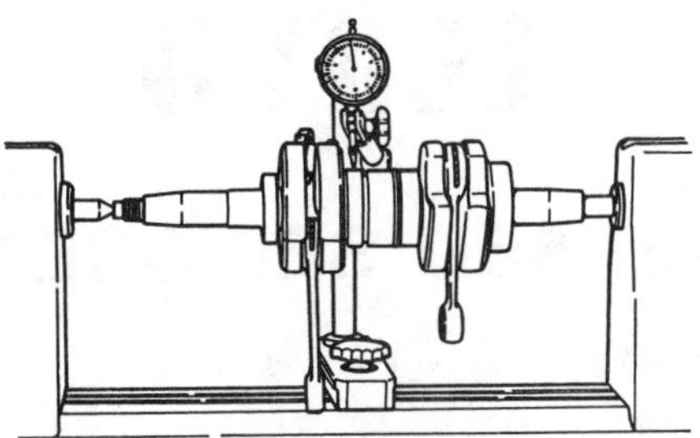

Fig. 15—Crankshaft runout should be checked before installation by mounting the unit in lathe centers as shown and measuring runout with a dial indicator.

LLOYD

CONDENSED SERVICE DATA

Engine Model	LS400/18	LS400/20
Bore—(mm)	62	62
Inches	2.44	2.44
Stroke—(mm)	64	64
Inches	2.52	2.52
No. of Cylinders	2	2
Displacement—(cc)	386	386
Cubic Inches	23.75	23.75
Horsepower @ RPM	18 @ 4200	20 @ 4200
Carburetor Model	HR	HD
Number Used	1	1
Ignition:		
Type	Energy Transfer	
Point Gap—(mm)	0.35-0.45	0.35-0.45
Inch	0.014-0.018	0.014-0.018
Edge Gap—(mm)	8-12	8-12
Inch	0.315-0.473	0.315-0.473
Timing Advance?	No	No
Timing BTDC (mm)	3.1-3.3	3.1-3.3
Inch	0.126-0.130	0.126-0.130
Degrees	22-24	22-24
Spark Plug:		
Bosch	W240T1	W240T1
Champion	L81	L81
Electrode Gap (mm)	0.5	0.5
Inch	0.020	0.020
Fuel/Oil Ratio	40:1	40:1

MAINTENANCE

CARBURETOR. Tillotson diaphragm carburetors are used on both engines. The LS 400/18 uses an HR 8 A Tillotson and the LS 400/20 uses an HD 7 A or HD 3559. Refer to Tillotson carburetor section for operation and overhaul.

Normal initial setting of low speed mixture needle is from ½ to ¾ turns open on all carburetors. Settings for the high speed mixture needles are: at least one turn open for the HR 8 A and HD 3559, and at least ½ turn open for HD 7 A. These are only beginning settings and will vary according to operating conditions.

FUEL PUMP. The fuel pump is pulse actuated from engine crankcase. Check pulse passage in crankcase, pulse nipple and hose for plugging, collapse or leakage. The fuel pump is a part of the lower part of the carburetor. Check pulse diaphragm and valve diaphragm for deterioration or damage. Check fuel lines and filters to be sure they are open and clean.

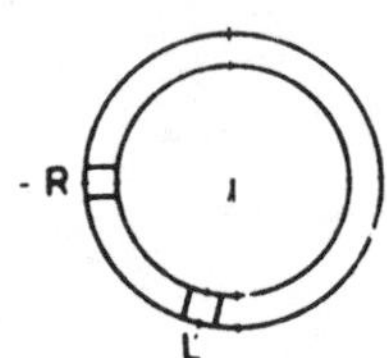

Fig. 3–View of magneto breaker cam. Left keyway (L) should be on key.

LUBRICATION. The engine is lubricated by mixing oil with the fuel. A suitable two-cycle air cooled engine oil is recommended. Standard grade SAE 30 automotive motor oil may be used if two-cycle oil is not available.

Recommended fuel-oil mixture is 40:1. Mix fuel and oil thoroughly using a separate container before pouring mixture into fuel tank. For cold weather blending, pre-mix the oil with a small amount of gasoline and shake thoroughly until mixture is liquid, then blend the remainder of fuel. Do not use kerosene or fuel oil for premixing.

IGNITION AND TIMING. Breaker point gap should be 0.35-0.45mm (0.014-0.018 in.) on both models. Timing is possible by removing starter, front cover, and cover plates. Breaker point edge gap is 8-12mm (0.315-0.473

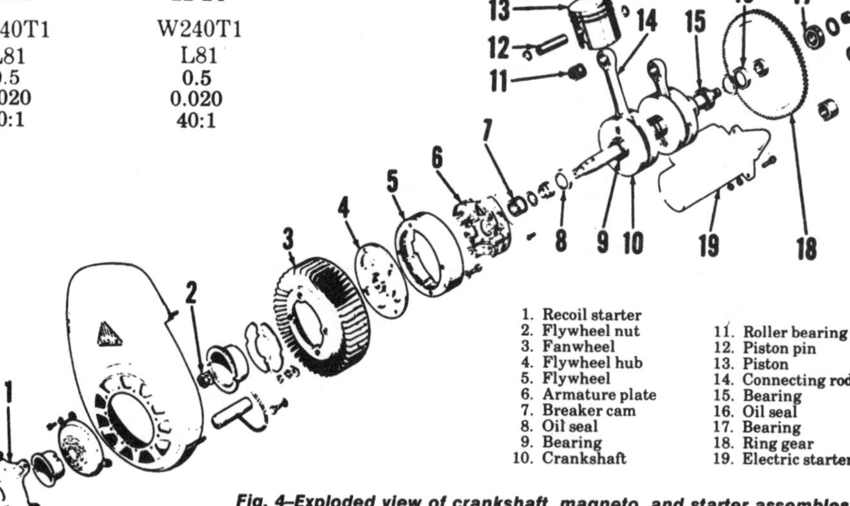

1. Recoil starter
2. Flywheel nut
3. Fanwheel
4. Flywheel hub
5. Flywheel
6. Armature plate
7. Breaker cam
8. Oil seal
9. Bearing
10. Crankshaft
11. Roller bearing
12. Piston pin
13. Piston
14. Connecting rod
15. Bearing
16. Oil seal
17. Bearing
18. Ring gear
19. Electric starter

Fig. 4–Exploded view of crankshaft, magneto, and starter assemblies.

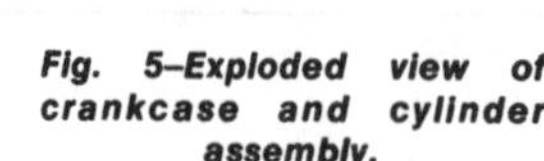

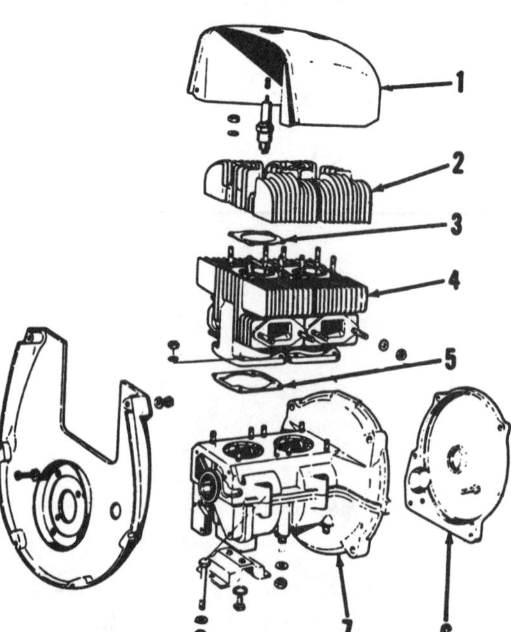

Fig. 5–Exploded view of crankcase and cylinder assembly.

1. Cylinder hood
2. Cylinder head
3. Head gasket
4. Cylinder
5. Cylinder gasket
6. Ring gear cover
7. Crankcase

in.) The flywheel must be removed to change edge gap.

Adjust No. 1 cylinder points so they open when piston is at 3.1-3.3mm (0.126-0.130 in.) BTDC. Adjust cylinder No. 2 as done on cylinder 1 and check for point opening. If points do not open then repeat procedure for No. 1 cylinder.

Note position of breaker cam. Left keyway should be on key. See Fig. 3.

The ignition system is a Bosch energy transfer system. The high tension ignition coils are mounted outside the engine. Terminal #1 of high tension coils is grounded; terminal 15 connected to magneto wire.

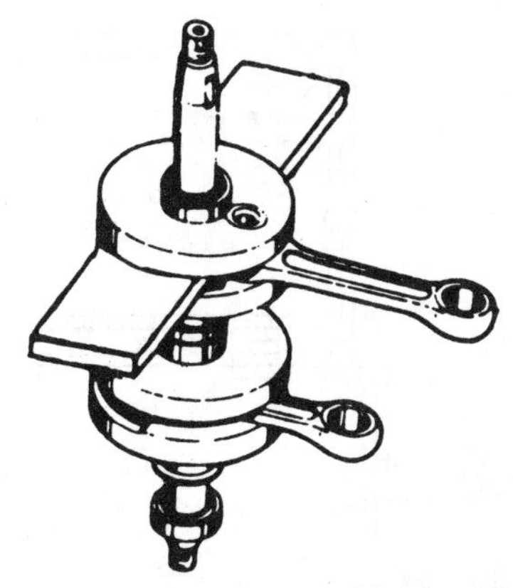

Fig. 6–Support crankshaft behind counterweight when pressing on bearings.

REPAIRS

TIGHTENING TORQUES. Recommended tightening torques are as follows:

Flywheel nut	50-58 ft.-lbs.
Cylinder head	20 ft.-lbs.
Cylinder nuts	20 ft.-lbs.

DISASSEMBLY AND REASSEMBLY. Refer to Figs. 4 and 5. When service is required, first remove engine then remove carburetor and intake manifold, cylinder hood, recoil starter, front cover, and flywheel magneto assembly.

Remove cylinder heads. Cylinder head No. 1 has tapped hole for cylinder hood screw. Bring piston to bottom of cylinder and remove cylinder. Piston and cylinders should be marked for match up when assembling. Remove piston pin and piston. Note arrow on piston points to exhaust port. Remove bearings and end covers. Separate crankcase. When assembling, ring gear cover must be heated to 100° C. and shrunk on bearing.

Refer to the appropriate following paragraphs for inspection and overhaul notes. Assemble by reversing the disassembly procedure.

PISTONS, RINGS, AND CYLINDERS. Pistons are marked with arrow pointed towards exhaust port. No. 1 cylinder head has hole tapped for cylinder hood screw.

Pistons may be renewed with pistons of same size. Due to chromed cylinders, pistons and cylinders must be renewed in sets. Piston tolerance is 0.05mm (0.00197 in.). Piston size is stamped on piston head.

CRANKSHAFT AND CONNECTING ROD ASSEMBLY. The crankshaft and connecting rod assembly is available only as a complete unit and should not be disassembled. Bearings (9 & 15—Fig. 4) are a press fit on their respective shafts and will not normally need to be removed unless renewal is indicated. If bearings must be removed, support the shaft behind counterweight as shown in Fig. 6.

Whenever crankshaft assembly has been removed, check for runout before installation by placing outer bearings on suitable blocks and measuring runout on center bearings. See Service Fundamentals Section for procedure. Runout should not exceed 0.001 inch. If runout is excessive and remainder of unit seems to be reusable, the assembly may be straightened by a machine shop, motorcycle engine rebuilder or others experienced with this type of construction. If bearings, shafts or connecting rods are unserviceable, renew the complete unit.

MERCURY

CONDENSED SERVICE DATA

Engine Model	220	250
Bore—(mm)	....	....
Inches	....	....
Stroke—(mm)	....	....
Inches	....	....
No. of Cylinders	2	2
Displacement—(cc)	399	439
Cubic Inches	24.3	26.8
Horsepower @ RPM	22 @ 5000	25 @ 5000
Carburetor Model	MD	MD
Number Used	1	1
Ignition:		
Type	CD	CD
Point Gap—(mm)	....	....
Inch	....	....
Edge Gap—(mm)	....	....
Inch	....	....
Timing Advance?	Yes	No
Timing BTDC (mm)	....	....
Inch	....	....
Degrees	14°	14°
Measured at	See Text	
Spark Plug:		
AC	V40FF	V40FF
Champion	L19V	L19V
Electrode Gap (mm)	Surface Gap	
Inch	....	....
Fuel/Oil Ratio	20:1	20:1

MAINTENANCE

SPARK PLUG. The surface gap spark plugs (See Fig. 1) should be renewed only if center electrode is eroded away 1/32-inch or more below plug surface, if porcelain is cracked or if plug is otherwise physically damaged. A badly fouled spark plug will ordinarily fire if ignition system is in satisfactory condition.

CARBURETOR. A TILLOTSON Model MD float type carburetor is used. Clockwise rotation of low speed mixture needle leans the mixture.

Fig. 1–Surface gap spark plugs should be renewed if center electrode is more than 1/32 inch below plug surface when measured as shown.

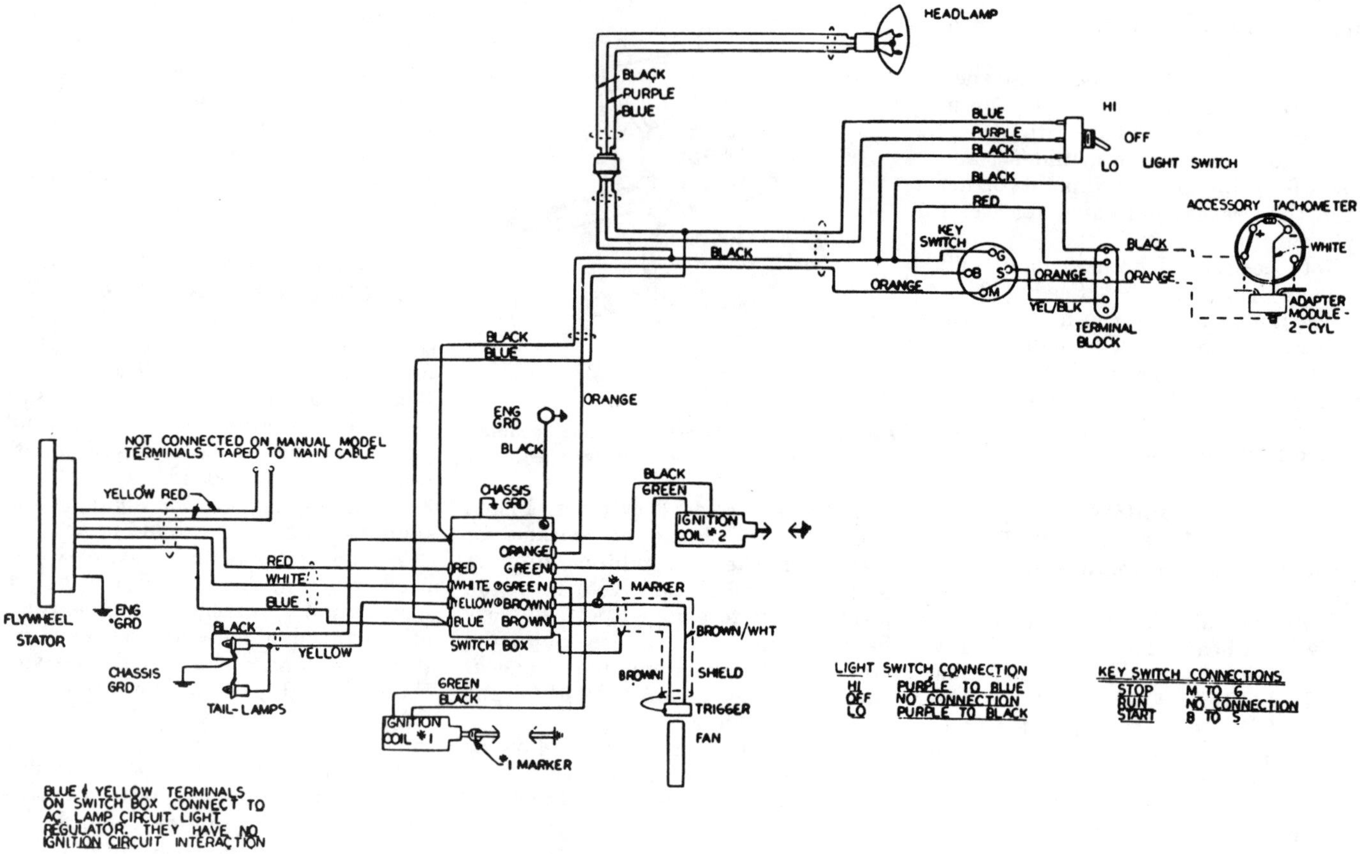
HEADLAMP
BLACK
PURPLE
BLUE
HI
OFF
LO
LIGHT SWITCH
RED
KEY SWITCH
ACCESSORY TACHOMETER
WHITE
ORANGE
YEL/BLK
TERMINAL BLOCK
ADAPTER MODULE - 2-CYL
ENG GRD
NOT CONNECTED ON MANUAL MODEL TERMINALS TAPED TO MAIN CABLE
YELLOW RED
CHASSIS GRD
GREEN
IGNITION COIL #2
WHITE
YELLOW
BROWN
SWITCH BOX
#1 MARKER
BROWN/WHT
SHIELD
TRIGGER
FAN
FLYWHEEL STATOR
TAIL-LAMPS
IGNITION COIL #1
LIGHT SWITCH CONNECTION
HI PURPLE TO BLUE
OFF NO CONNECTION
LO PURPLE TO BLACK
KEY SWITCH CONNECTIONS
STOP M TO G
RUN NO CONNECTION
START B TO S
BLUE & YELLOW TERMINALS ON SWITCH BOX CONNECT TO AC LAMP CIRCUIT LIGHT REGULATOR. THEY HAVE NO IGNITION CIRCUIT INTERACTION

Fig. 2–Wiring diagram for use on models with manual start.

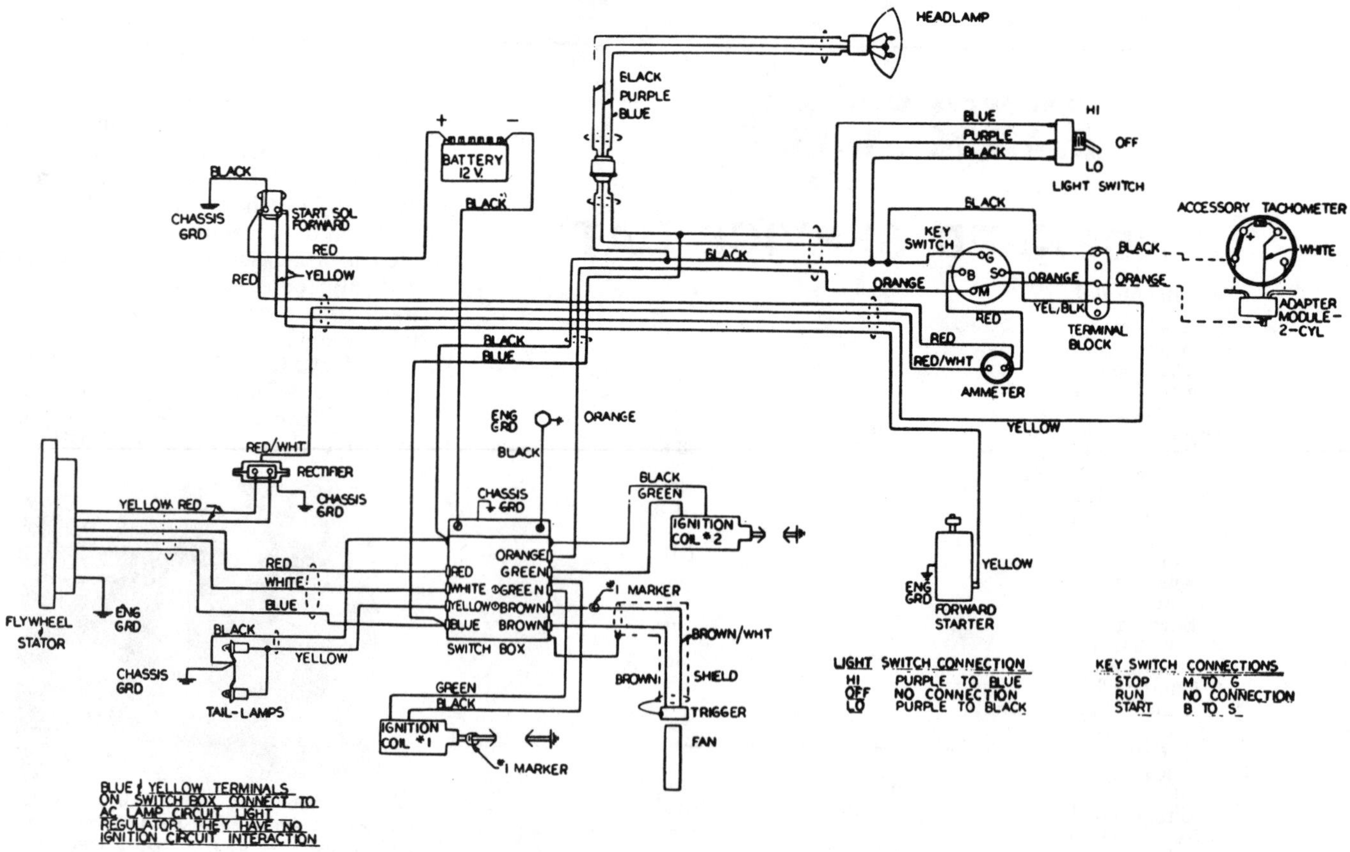
HEADLAMP
BLACK
PURPLE
BLUE
BATTERY 12 V.
CHASSIS GRD
START SOL FORWARD
RED
YELLOW
HI
OFF
LO
LIGHT SWITCH
KEY SWITCH
ACCESSORY TACHOMETER
WHITE
ORANGE
YEL/BLK
TERMINAL BLOCK
ADAPTER MODULE - 2-CYL
RED/WHT
AMMETER
ENG GRD
RED/WHT
RECTIFIER
YELLOW RED
GREEN
IGNITION COIL #2
SWITCH BOX
#1 MARKER
BROWN/WHT
BROWN
SHIELD
TRIGGER
FAN
FORWARD STARTER
FLYWHEEL & STATOR
TAIL-LAMPS
IGNITION COIL #1
LIGHT SWITCH CONNECTION
HI PURPLE TO BLUE
OFF NO CONNECTION
LO PURPLE TO BLACK
KEY SWITCH CONNECTIONS
STOP M TO G
RUN NO CONNECTION
START B TO S
BLUE & YELLOW TERMINALS ON SWITCH BOX CONNECT TO AC LAMP CIRCUIT LIGHT REGULATOR. THEY HAVE NO IGNITION CIRCUIT INTERACTION

Fig. 3–Wiring diagram for electric starting models without direct reverse.

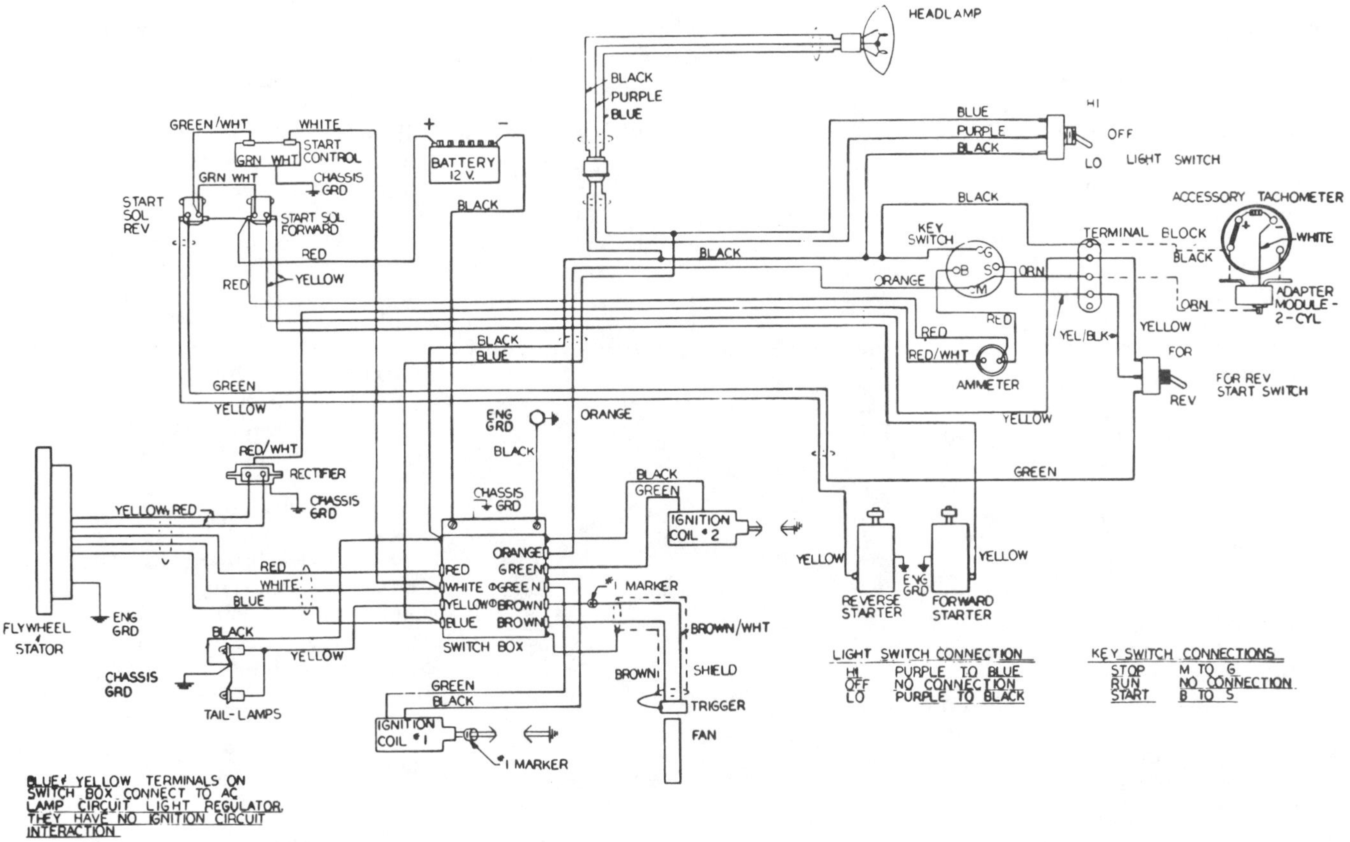

LIGHT SWITCH CONNECTION

HI	PURPLE TO BLUE
OFF	NO CONNECTION
LO	PURPLE TO BLACK

KEY SWITCH CONNECTIONS

STOP	M TO G
RUN	NO CONNECTION
START	B TO S

BLUE & YELLOW TERMINALS ON SWITCH BOX CONNECT TO AC LAMP CIRCUIT LIGHT REGULATOR. THEY HAVE NO IGNITION CIRCUIT INTERACTION

Fig. 4–Wiring diagram for electric starting model equipped with direct reverse.

High speed system uses a fixed main jet.

Initial setting of low speed mixture needle is ¾ to 1 turn open from closed position. Standard main jet (0.067) is generally satisfactory for operation at elevations from sea level to 4000 ft. A smaller jet may be required for high altitude operation. Available jets with Tillotson parts numbers are as follows:

Main jet 0.069	012515
Main jet 0.067	011397
Main jet 0.065	011252
Main jet 0.063	011385

CAUTION: A main jet smaller than the one required may result in under-lubrication and overheating as well as loss of power and MUST not be used. If a small jet is installed for high altitude operation and vehicle is removed to a lower altitude, the larger jet must be reinstalled.

With fuel bowl removed and inverted, lowest portion of float should project approximately 1/64 inch below gasket surface of bowl. Adjust by bending the tang which contacts needle valve.

REED VALVES. Twin pyramidal type reed valves are located on crankcase side of intake manifold. Reed valves can be inspected or renewed after manifold is removed.

Valve reeds should seat lightly throughout their entire length. Renew reed cluster if any leaf is broken, bent or otherwise damaged. DO NOT attempt to bend or straighten a reed in order to improve or restore performance.

IGNITION SYSTEM. Breakerless, capacitance discharge "THUNDERBOLT" ignition systems are used. Refer to Figs. 2, 3 and 4 for wiring diagrams. Note that one wire leading from trigger coil carries a No. 1 Marker. This lead attaches to the second Brown terminal on switch box and adjacent Green terminal connects to Ignition coil for No. 1 Cylinder.

Air gap between blower fan magnet and trigger coil pole shoe must be 0.020-0.040 inch. Refer to Fig. 5. Air gap is adjusted by shims added or removed behind trigger coil mounting plate. Do not attempt to test for spark by pulling high tension lead from spark plug. A suitable tester can be made by removing the ground electrode from a discarded conventional spark plug, connecting the plug to high tension wire, grounding the plug and turning engine with starter. DO NOT attempt to hold the test plug in contact with ground. Spark should jump from plug center terminal to shell.

If engine misses on one cylinder or one wire fails to spark when checked with tester, first check wiring and connections for shorts and continuity. If trouble is not corrected, disconnect the three trigger coil leads from switch box and using RXI scale of ohmmeter, test trigger coil as follows:

Between Brown/White & Shielded Leads	115-135 Ohms
Between Brown & Shielded Leads	76-94 Ohms

If trigger coil tests are satisfactory, disconnect ignition coil primary leads from switch box and secondary lead from spark plug; then using an ohmmeter, check ignition coil as follows; Connect ohmmeter leads to the two primary leads and using RX1 scale check resistance which should be zero.

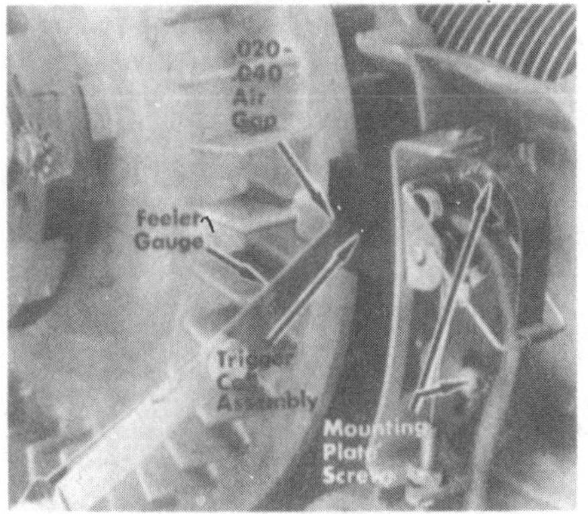

Fig. 5–First step in THUNDERBOLT ignition service is adjusting air gap as shown.

Connect ohmmeter leads to either primary lead and the secondary lead. Using RX100 scale, a reading of 3.0-3.6 should be obtained. There should be no continuity between any of the leads and mounting bracket; test using RX100 scale of ohmmeter.

If ignition coil tests are satisfactory, renew the switch box.

NOTE: Resistance tests of neither the trigger coil nor ignition coil are conclusive. If switch box fails to correct the trouble, renew trigger coil and/or ignition coil in that order.

If engine will not start and there is no spark at either spark plug lead, check continuity of ignition switch. Magneto (M) terminal should only make contact with Ground (G) terminal, and only in "OFF" position. Battery (B) terminal should only make contact with Starter (S) terminal, and only in "START" position.

If ignition switch tests are satisfactory, disconnect Red and White magneto leads and, using an ohmmeter check ignition windings in stator as follows: Connect ohmmeter leads to low speed (Red) wire and a suitable ground and using RX100 scale, check reading which should be 24-26. Connect ohmmeter leads between high speed (White) wire and a suitable ground and using RX1 scale, check reading which should be 100-125.

If stator winding tests are satisfactory, test trigger coil with ohmmeter as previously outlined and, if trouble is not located, renew the switch box.

IGNITION TIMING. To adjust (or check) the static timing, first turn crankshaft until timing marks are aligned as shown in Fig. 6. Remove trigger inspection plate and plastic plugs from right lower corner of blower housing and check the distance between leading edge of blower magnet to leading edge of trigger coil pole (Fig. 7). Distance should be 5/16 inch as shown. On Model 220, trigger coil must be in fully retarded position. If adjustment is not correct, loosen mounting plate screws and shift plate AND coil until distance is correct.

Running timing can be checked with a power timing light (Use separate battery on manual units). Connect pickup lead to No. 1 (blower side) spark plug wire and, with rear of machine raised on kick stand, start and run engine at 2000 rpm. Timing marks should align as shown in Fig. 6.

NOTE: Some Model 220 units were timed on No. 2 cylinder. If timing mark on flywheel rim is not visible, recheck with pickup lead attached to No. 2 (flywheel side) spark plug wire.

If engine does not start or misses at slow speeds, check for open or short between RED alternator lead and ground. If engine runs satisfactorily at slow speed but misfires or dies at high speed, check for open or short between WHITE alternator lead and ground. Blue and yellow leads from alternator provide lighting and charging current and have no bearing on ignition system.

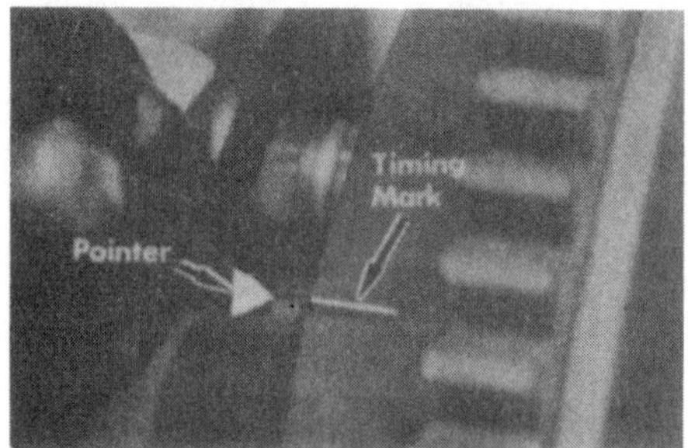

Fig. 6–Running timing marks can be checked with a power timing light. Model 250 has electronic advance.

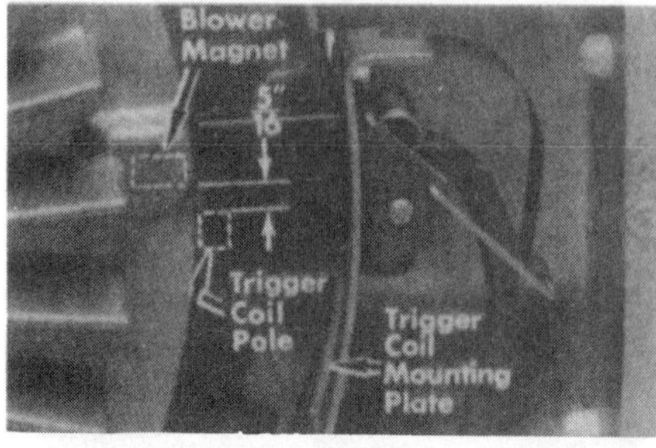

Fig. 7–With timing marks aligned as shown in Fig. 6, blower magnet should lead trigger coil pole by 5/16 inch. Model 220 must be in retard position.

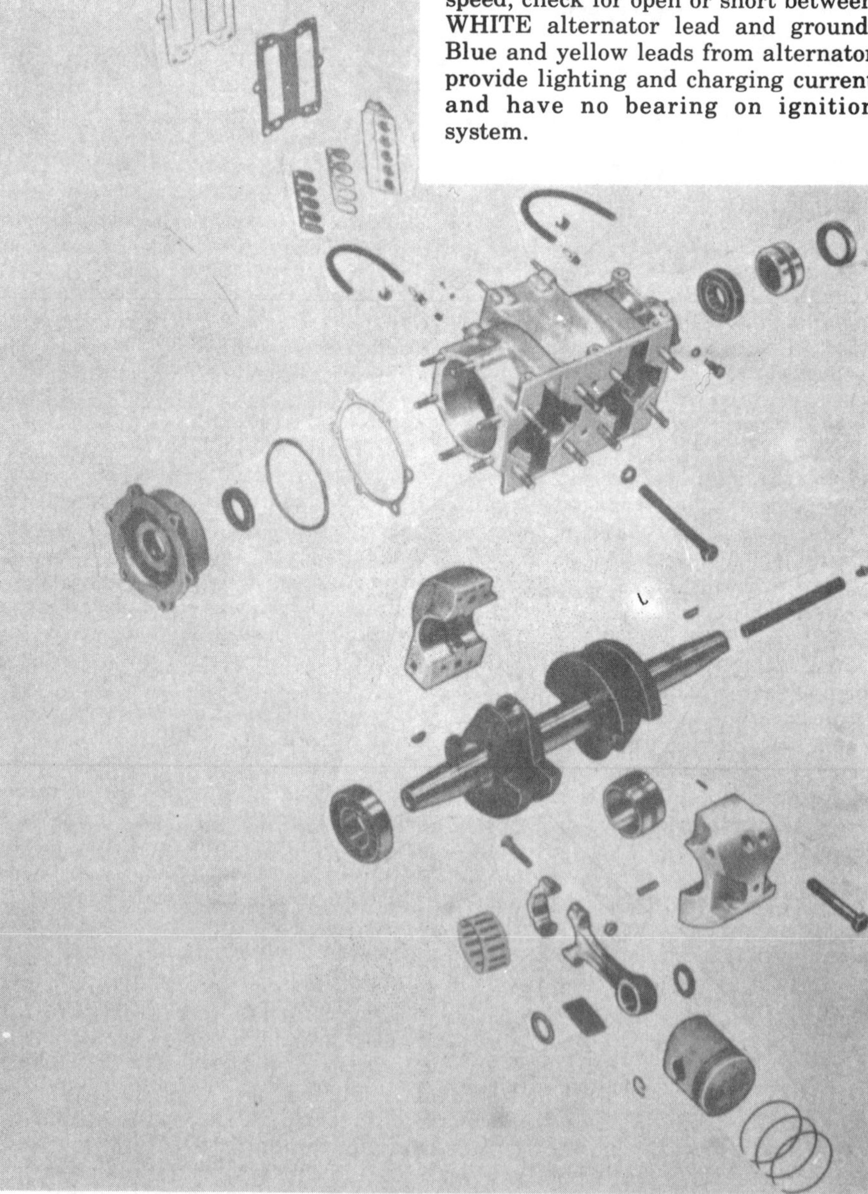

Fig. 8–Exploded view of engine showing component parts.

OVERHAUL

Refer to Fig. 8 for exploded view of crankshaft, crankcase and associated parts. Cylinder is closed end type, install with exhaust ports to bottom. Crankshaft and center main bearing housing are removed from fanwheel end of crankcase after removing fanwheel & housing, cylinders, rod & piston units, flywheel, and the two center main bearing through-bolts.

TIGHTENING TORQUES. Recommended tightening torques are as follows:

Fanwheel Cap Screw .... 40-45 ft.-lbs.
Flywheel Nut .... 60-65 ft.-lbs.
Spark Plug .... 20-ft.-lbs.
Backplate Nuts .... 200 in.-lbs.
Blower Housing .... 130 in.-lbs.
Carburetor Mtg. Nuts .... 130 in.-lbs.
Center Main Allen Screw .. 25 in.-lbs.
Center Main Phillips Screw .... 60 in.-lbs.
Center Main Retaining Bolt .... 110 in.-lbs.
Cylinder to Crankcase Nuts .... 350 in.-lbs.
Connecting Rod Nuts ..... 180 in.-lbs.
Manifold Nuts .... 75 in.-lbs.
Mounting Plate Bolt PTO Side .... 200 in.-lbs.
Reed Stop Screws .... 20 in.-lbs.
Trigger Mtg. Plate Screws . 75 in.-lbs.

O.M.C. OPPOSED TWIN

CONDENSED SERVICE DATA

Bore—Inches	2.5	2.625	2.75
Stroke—Inches	2.25	2.25	2.25
No. of Cylinders	2 Opposed	2 Opposed	2 Opposed
Displacement—(cc)	362	399	437
Cubic Inches	22	24.35	26.7
Horsepower @ RPM	16 @ 4800	21 @ 6000	25 @ 4500
Carburetor Model	Carter or Bendix	OMC	HD
Number Used	1	1	1

Ignition:			
Type	Energy Transfer*		
Point Gap—Inch	0.020-0.022	0.020-0.022	0.020-0.022
Edge Gap	Fixed	Fixed	Fixed
Timing Advance?	Yes	Yes	Yes
Timing BTDC (mm)	See Text	See Text	See Text
Spark Plug:			
Champion	J8J	J7J	J6J*
Electrode Gap—Inch	0.028-0.030	0.028-0.033	0.028-0.030
Fuel/Oil Ratio	See Text	See Text	See Text

*1974 models use CD system and champion UL-77V surface gap plug which has no gap adjustment.

MAINTENANCE

CARBURETOR. A Carter Model N carburetor was used on models prior to 1968. Late 16 horsepower models use the Bendix carburetor. Twenty-five horsepower units use a Tillotson HD carburetor, refer to overhaul section under SERVICE FUNDAMENTALS for overhaul data. Carburetors are similar in configuration and in adjustment except for idle speed stop adjustment. Refer to Fig. 1. Clockwise rotation of either adjustment screw will lean the mixture. Initial adjustment of high speed mixture screw (1—Fig. 1) or low speed mixture screw (2) is 1¼ turns open from the closed position. High speed mixture needle (1) must be open at least 1 1/6 turns to assure adequate lubrication. Recommended slow idle speed of 1500 rpm is adjusted by idle speed stop screw.

With carburetor inverted and fuel bowl removed, float should be parallel with gasket surface of carburetor body. Adjust by bending tab on float which contacts needle valve. Refer also to CARTER portion of SERVICE FUNDAMENTALS section of this manual.

REED VALVES. Reed valves (Fig. 3) used on 16 hp models can be removed for service or inspection when carburetor is off by removing primer line from fitting (1) and unbolting and removing intake manifold (2).

Examine the six valve reeds (4) visually. Do not attempt to straighten a bent reed or to bend reeds by hand to change performance. Renew reeds or reed body (3) if any damage is apparent.

On 25 Hp models, twin vee valve bodies are used as shown in Fig. 3A. Leaf unit, leaf stop and valve body is only available as an assembly and the entire unit should be renewed if any part is worn or damaged.

FUEL PUMP. The diaphragm type fuel pump (Fig. 4) attaches to intake manifold (2—Fig. 3) and is actuated by pressure and vacuum pulsations in the crankcase. The fuel pump (2—Fig. 4) is available only as a complete assembly, however, filter unit (3 through 7) can be removed for cleaning or parts renewal. NOTE: Parts can be assembled with gasket (3) reversed, but pump will not work. Be sure gasket is properly installed.

FUEL PRIMER. All models are equipped with a plunger type fuel primer pump (Fig. 5). Inlet fuel line (1) tees into main fuel line beneath fuel tank. Outlet line (2) connects to fitting (1—Fig. 3) located in inlet manifold, by-passing the regular fuel pump and carburetor.

To check the operation of primer pump, disconnect outlet hose (2—Fig. 5) at manifold. Depress plunger rod (6); if a spurt of fuel is not ejected through outlet hose, check inlet line, outlet line and check valve (3) for plugging and, if trouble is not corrected, remove, disassemble and inspect the pump unit using Fig. 5 as a guide.

MAGNETO AND TIMING. The magneto on all early models is the energy transfer type, with low tension magneto driver coils beneath the flywheel generating the primary current, and individual automotive type ignition coils connected in series to provide the secondary current. Timing is controlled by a single set of points located on magneto stator plate and a centrifugal advance breaker cam mounted on inner side of flywheel provides a retarded spark for starting only.

On 1974 models, CD ignition systems are used. System is similar to that described in Engine Sections for Rotary Combustion and Alternate Firing Twin engines, and those sections can be used for service procedures. On all models, both spark plugs fire together.

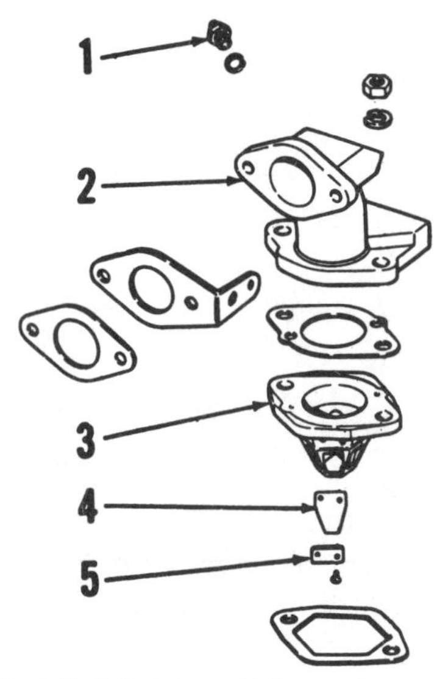

Fig. 3–Exploded view of inlet manifold and reed valves.

1. Primer fitting
2. Manifold
3. Reed plate
4. Valve reed
5. Retainer

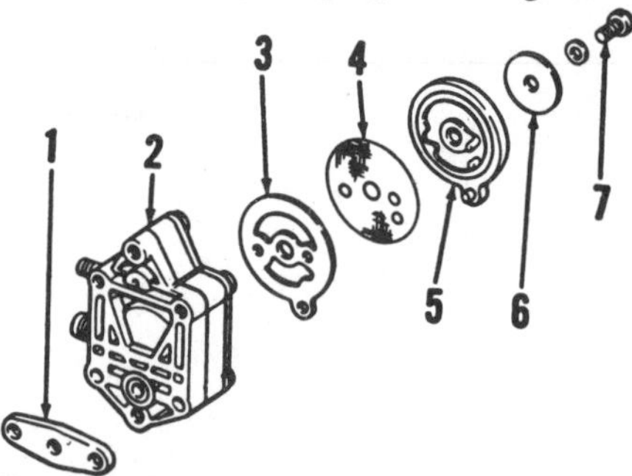

Fig. 4–Diaphragm type fuel pump (2) is available as an assembly only, but filter unit is serviced.

1. Gasket
2. Fuel pump
3. Gasket
4. Screen
5. Cap
6. Washer
7. Screw

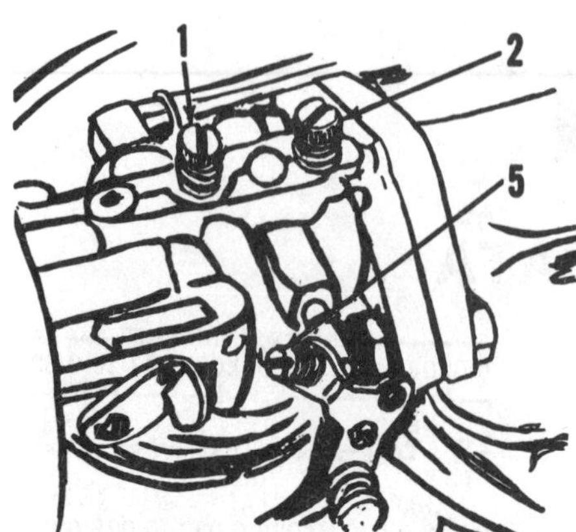

Fig. 1–Assembled view of early carburetor showing points of adjustment. Late models are similar except for idle speed adjustment screw (5).

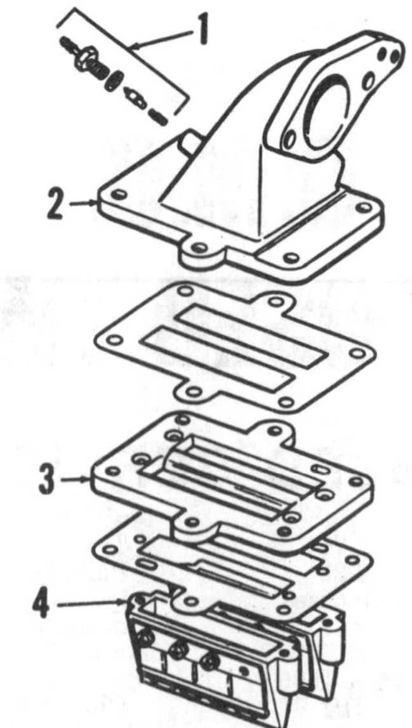

Fig. 3A–Exploded view of intake manifold and twin vee leaf valve unit used on 25 horsepower models.

1. Check valve
2. Manifold
3. Leaf plate
4. Leaf assembly

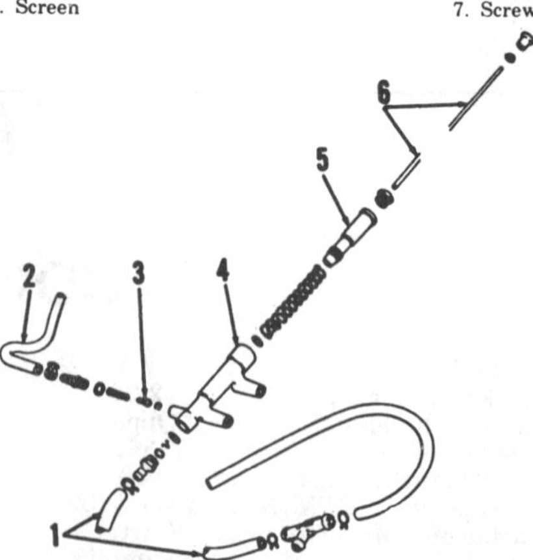

Fig. 5–Exploded view of primer pump which bypasses carburetor for cold starting.

1. Fuel line
2. Primer line
3. Outlet valve
4. Pump body
5. Pump plunger
6. Primer rod

Timing is not adjustable except that, on models with points, minor adjustment can be made by varying the point gap. The fixed breaker contact point is insulated and movable point is grounded. To adjust or renew the breaker points, first remove flywheel using a suitable puller. Refer to Figs. 6 and 7. To adjust the point gap, remove retaining clamp and withdraw breaker cam (1—Fig. 6) from flywheel and temporarily install cam over end of crankshaft. Turn cam to widest point opening and adjust gap to 0.020-0.022. Reinstall breaker cam in flywheel, making sure teeth of advance weight and cam are fully meshed as shown in Fig. 6. Turn crankshaft until flywheel key is pointing directly away from breaker point mounting post, then reinstall flywheel assembly. When flywheel is properly seated, outer edge will be approximately 1/32-inch above crankshaft shoulder. If difficulty is encountered in installing flywheel, do not use force. Breaker cam may be catching on breaker point rub block or oiler wick; recheck crankshaft position and cam installation and eliminate the trouble before proceeding further. Tighten flywheel nut (5) to a torque of 40-45 ft.-lbs.

Timing may be checked with a timing light with engine at slow idle speed (1500 rpm). One cooling fin on flywheel (4) contains a raised boss and paint mark. The marked fin should be visible through timing hole (Fig. 8) using a timing light, when timing is correct.

Magneto drive coil resistance is 0.8 ohm; ignition coil primary resistance is 1.5 ohms.

LUBRICATION. Engine is lubricated by oil mixed with the fuel. Johnson or Evinrude Snowmobile Oil or standard grade, SAE 30 automotive motor oil should be used. Do not use inferior grade automotive oils or multi-viscosity oil. Outboard motor oil is not recommended. Use only good grade regular gasoline.

Recommended fuel/oil ratio was 16:1 in 1965 and 1966; and 24:1 in 1967 through 1972. In 1973 a 50:1 fuel/oil ratio is recommended ONLY if JOHNSON or EVINRUDE 50:1 Snowmobile Oil is used. If other oils are used, mix at standard 24:1 ratio. Mix fuel and oil together in a separate container before pouring mixture into fuel tank. For cold weather blending, pre-mix the oil with gasoline and shake thoroughly until the mixture is liquid; then blend in remainder of fuel. Do not use kerosene or fuel oil for pre-mixing.

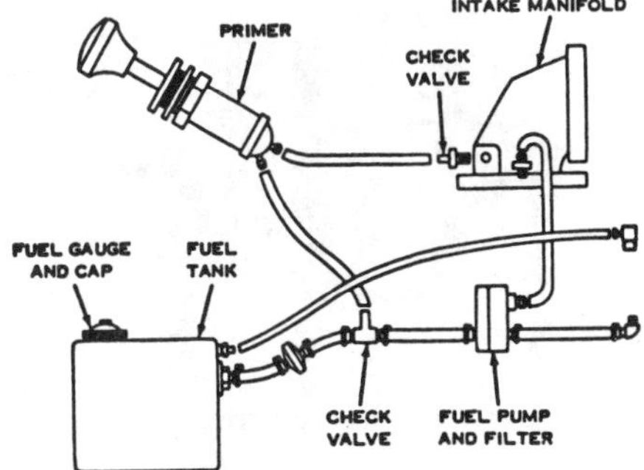

Fig. 5A–Schematic view of fuel primer assembly used on late models.

REPAIRS

TIGHTENING TORQUES. Recommended tightening torques are as follows:

Flywheel nut . . . . 40- 45 ft.-lbs.
Connecting rod screws . . . . 29- 31 ft.-lbs.
Cylinder head . . . . . 100-120 in.-lbs.
Crankcase screws . . . 60- 80 in.-lbs.
Spark plugs . . . . 20 ft.-lbs.

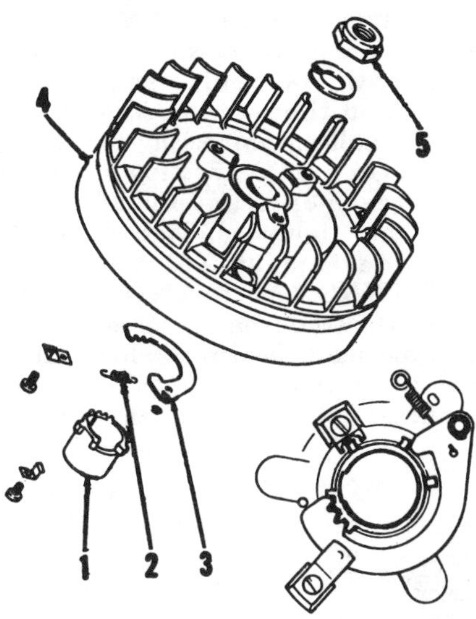

Fig. 6–Exploded view of flywheel assembly showing timing advance cam and associated parts. Bottom view is shown in inset.

1. Breaker cam
2. Spring
3. Advance weight
4. Flywheel
5. Flywheel nut

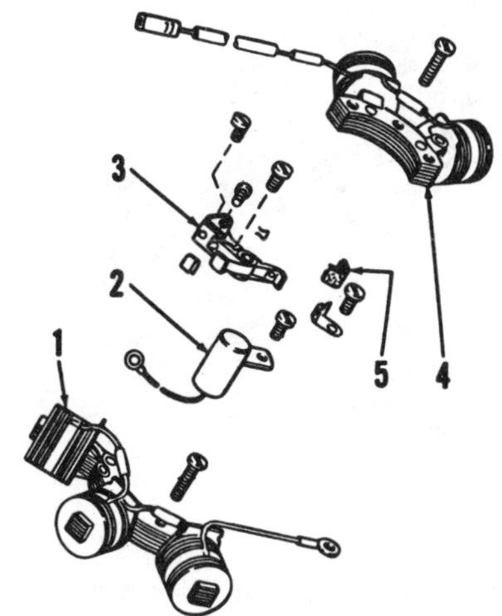

Fig. 7–Exploded view of low tension magneto.

1. Ignition primary coils
2. Condenser
3. Point set
4. Lighting coils
5. Oiler wick

DISASSEMBLY AND REASSEMBLY. Refer to Fig. 9 for an exploded view of engine. When service is required, first remove engine as outlined in vehicle section of this manual and remove carburetor, drive sheave, starter and flywheel.

Remove exhaust manifold (1), rear fan housing and cylinder shrouds; cylinders (2), intake manifold (16) and reed valve (15). Drive out the three tapered alignment pins (18) toward flywheel side of crankcase, remove crankcase screws and separate the crankcase halves, using a rawhide mallet if necessary to break gasket seal. If crankcase halves cannot now be separated, heat bearing area with a heat gun or other means, until crankcase halves can be removed.

When reassembling, remove dried cement and old gasket material from joint faces, using a suitable solvent if necessary. Mating surfaces of crankcase and gasket surfaces of cylinders must be absolutely flat and free from nicks and burrs. Surfaces may be lapped if necessary, to remove minor surface imperfections. Use new gaskets, seals and a suitable sealant when parts are reassembled. Crankcase halves should be heated to approximately 350° F. to allow easy entry of main bearings into crankcase bores. Tighten crankcase screws finger tight, then install the three tapered pins from flywheel side to assure perfect alignment of crankcase halves. With tapered pins installed, tighten crankcase retaining screws to recommended torque.

Crankshaft end play should not exceed 0.025 inch. If end play is excessive install shims on drive side of crankshaft between bearing and thrust face of shaft.

Use a suitable hinge-type ring compressor when installing cylinders.

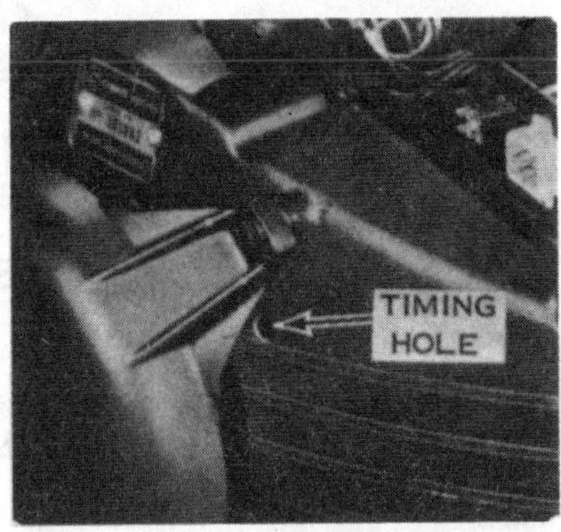

Fig. 8–View of engine showing location of timing hole.

Tighten cylinder retaining stud nuts alternately in a criss-cross fashion to the recommended torque of 100-120 inch-pounds. Complete the assembly by reversing the disassembly procedure.

PISTONS, RINGS AND CYLINDERS. Pistons, rings and connecting rods may be installed either side up when new. Used assemblies should be marked before disassembly and reassembled in the same relative position. Piston skirt should be round at room temperature, and should be rounded if distorted, before piston to cylinder clearance is measured. Measure clearance at right angles to piston pin at bottom of cylinder. On engines used in 1972 and later models, piston rings are positively positioned in ring grooves by locating pins. On earlier engines, rings are not pinned and ring end gaps should be staggered during piston installation. Check the components against the values which follow:

Piston ring end gap 0.010-0.013
Piston ring
side clearance 0.001-0.002
Piston skirt clearance . . 0.009-0.012

COMPRESSION RELIEF. Beginning in 1969, engines are equipped with a compression relief valve which is installed in one cylinder only. When knob is pulled (for starting) part of the compression escapes into the exhaust port. Be sure to push knob in after engine starts and make sure some clearance exists at valve-end of cable with knob pushed in. Adjust at cable housing anchor.

PISTON PIN. Piston pin is a press fit in piston boss bores at room temperature, and is retained in piston by snap rings. Piston pin needle bearing uses connecting rod bore and piston pin for bearing races. Check piston pin for heat discoloration, ridging, scoring or wear in needle bearing area. Install retaining snap rings with marked (lettered) side to outside.

CONNECTING ROD. A 5/16-inch, 12 point deep socket is required to remove the connecting rod cap screws. Rod and cap are marked for correct assembly as are the needle bearing cage halves. Use special OMC Needle Bearing Grease (Part No. 378642) or a non-fibrous, low melting point grease to position the loose needle rollers when installing connecting rod. Bearings, cages, and connecting rod must turn freely on crankpin after cap screws are tightened. Tighten screws evenly to a torque of 29-31 ft.-lbs.

CRANKSHAFT AND BEARINGS. The crankshaft is carried in two ball-type main bearings which are a press fit on crankshaft and a tight fit in crankcase halves at room temperature. When installing bearings on shaft, support the shaft under the counterweight next to bearing.

MANUAL STARTER. The manual starter can be removed for inspection or repair by removing the four retaining cap screws and lifting off the starter unit.

To disassemble the removed starter unit, refer to Fig. 10. Pry anchor (11) from handle grip (12) and remove the anchor; then allow starter rope (13) to retract into handle and housing until recoil spring (10) is completely unwound. Remove the spindle retaining nut, washers and through-bolt, then lift out spindle, pulley and associated parts, allowing recoil spring (10) to remain in housing (14) if possible.

Starter rope (13) is 7/32-inch nylon rope 72¾-inch in length. Fuse both cut ends with an open flame to prevent unraveling. Inner end is retained in pulley (9) by a single knot while outer end is secured by anchor (11). A new rope can be installed without disassembling the starter if pieces can be removed. Tie a knot in one end of rope

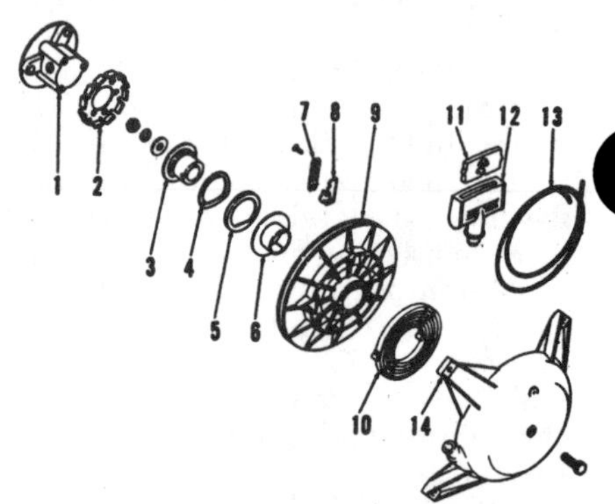

Fig. 10–Exploded view of recoil starter showing component parts.

1. Ratchet mount
2. Ratchet
3. Spindle
4. Spring washer
5. Friction ring
6. Spindle bushing
7. Retainer
8. Pawl
9. Pulley
10. Recoil spring
11. Anchor
12. Handle
13. Rope
14. Housing

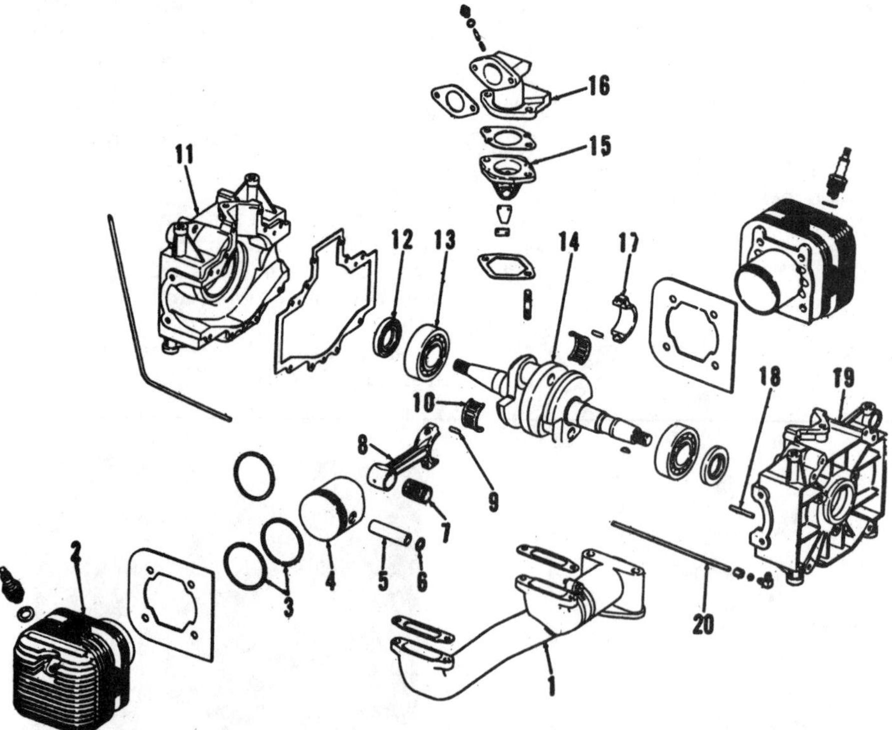

Fig. 9–Exploded view of 362 cc engine showing component parts. Larger engine is similar.

1. Exhaust manifold
2. Cylinder
3. Piston rings
4. Piston
5. Piston pin
6. Retainer
7. Needle bearing
8. Connecting rod
9. Needle roller
10. Bearing cage
11. Crankcase half
12. Crankshaft seal
13. Main bearing
14. Crankshaft
15. Reed plate
16. Intake manifold
17. Rod cap
18. Dowel pin
19. Crankcase half
20. Chain oiler line

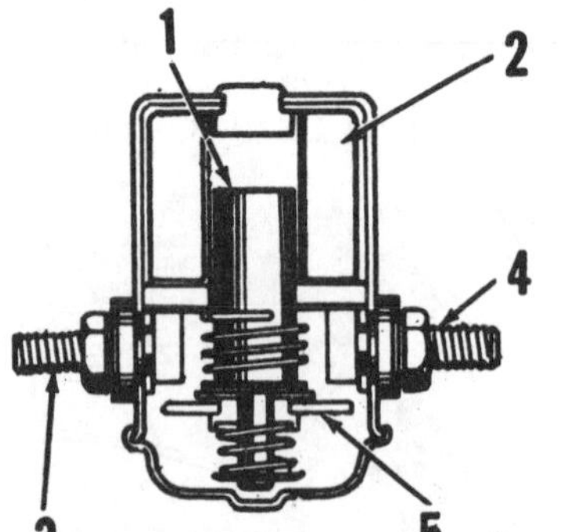

Fig. 11–OMC electric starter solenoid.

1. Plunger
2. Windings
3. Motor terminal
4. Battery terminal
5. Contact disc

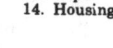

and place starter engine-side up on a bench or in a vise. Turn pulley (9) counter-clockwise until spring (10) is completely wound; then let pulley unwind approximately one turn until rope hole in pulley aligns with exit hole in housing (14). Tie a slip knot in free end of rope to prevent spring from completely unwinding, while handle grip (12) and anchor (11) are installed.

ELECTRIC STARTER. The electric starter system consists of the starter, solenoid and circuitry. The solenoid, as shown in Fig. 11, opens and closes the circuit between the battery and starter motor. The solenoid winding, when energized, causes the contact disc to move against the terminal contacts by magnetic pull on the solenoid plunger. The starter motor drive pulley engages the starter motor drive belt by rotation of the motor armature. When the engine is running the pulley sheave is driven faster than the armature and becomes disengaged.

BELT TENSION. Belt tension must be correct. Refer to Fig. 13. A loose belt will slip and a tight belt will ruin the starter through overspeeding. With the belt between the pulleys, turn the movable pulley counter-clockwise to drive position. Move starter upward to tighten belt. Pulley halves should be closed and in drive position for this adjustment. Belt must be free when pulley is in fully clock-wise or running position.

STARTER TEST DATA. Test data to determine starter condition are as follows:

Volts 12
Rotation .... CW
Brush spring tension (oz.) 35-90

No-Load Test
Volts 6
Amperes 60
RPM 4200

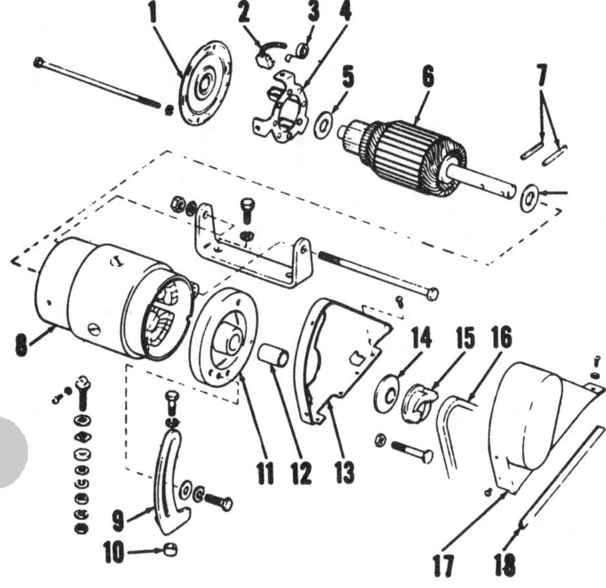

Fig. 12–Exploded view of electric starter motor assembly.

1. Commutator end head
2. Brush
3. Brush spring
4. Brush plate
5. Thrust washer
6. Armature
7. Spirol pins
8. Field coil assy.
9. Adjusting bracket
10. Adjusting spacer
11. Drive end head
12. Drive end bearing
13. Rear belt housing
14. Stationary pulley
15. Movable pulley
16. Belt
17. Front belt housing
18. Housing seal

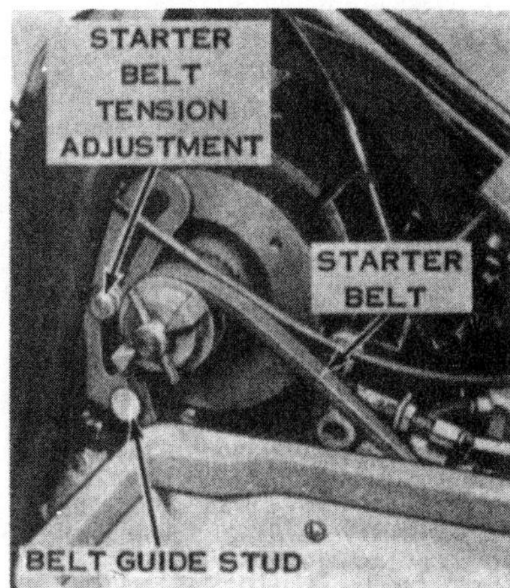

Fig. 13–View of starter belt adjustment.

O.M.C.

ROTARY COMBUSTION

CONDENSED SERVICE DATA

Displacement .... 528 cc
32.3 cu. in.
Horsepower at RPM .... 35 at 5500
or 45 at 6500
Carburetor Make .... Own
Spark Plug Make &
Model .... CHAMPION UP-77V
Ignition Type .... CD
Ignition Timing .... Fixed

MAINTENANCE

SPARK PLUG. A CHAMPION UP-77V surface gap spark plug is used. It is essential that ONLY the specified spark plug be used and that spark plug be correctly torqued in clean threads. Be sure gasket is in place, end of spark plug is swept by rotor apex seal and plug MUST NOT protrude into rotor housing.

CARBURETOR. The OMC float-type carburetor has a fixed main jet and adjustable idle mixture screw. Initial setting of idle mixture needle is 1½ turns open and needle must be readjusted with engine at operating temperature. Reset engine idle speed to 800-1200 rpm after mixture is adjusted. If engine falters on acceleration or a flat spot develops, back out idle mixture screw about 1/8 turn and recheck.

Carburetor float should be parallel to gasket surface of valve body with body inverted as shown in Fig. 14, and distance (H) should measure approximately 1/16 inch (1.6 mm). Float arm can be bent to conform, if necessary, using needle nose pliers.

The high performance throttle link (Fig. 15) must rest in lower end of throttle lever slot at slow idle position and must begin to move high performance throttle valve when carburetor throttle has moved approximately 15 degrees as shown in inset. Link may be bent if necessary, until action is as specified.

FUEL PUMP. The pulse type fuel pump is operated by pressure and vacuum pulsations in the intake cham-

Fig. 14—Carburetor float height (H) should be 1/16 inch (1.6 mm) measured from nearest edge of float to gasket surface of valve body.

ber of rotor housing which pass through a small drilling in housing outer wall as shown in Fig. 16.

The fuel pump is available as an assembly only, however inlet filter unit can be removed for cleaning or parts renewal as shown in Fig. 17. Fuel line connections are secured with plastic "Tie Straps" as shown in Fig. 18. The tie will be destroyed in removal and must be renewed. Install with serrated edge to inside and tighten as shown in Fig. 18.

Fig. 15—High performance throttle link should rest in bottom of slot at slow idle position, and must begin to move high performance throttle valve when carburetor throttle shaft has moved approximately 15 degrees (Arrows—Inset). Bend link (L) if necessary to adjust.

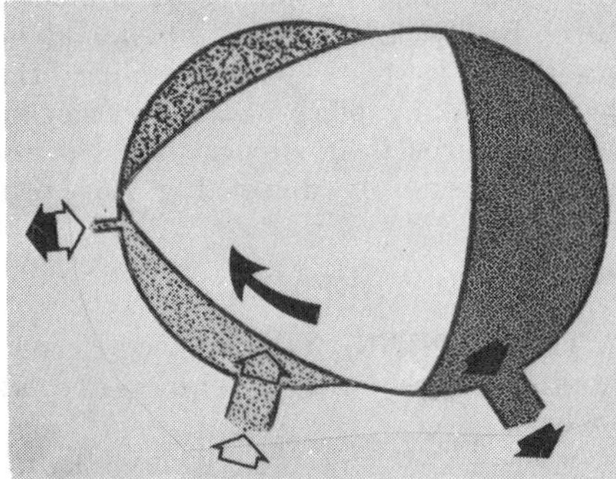

Fig. 16—Pulse type fuel pump is operated by a pulse drilling located in intake side of rotor housing as shown. Black arrows indicate pressure, white arrows vacuum.

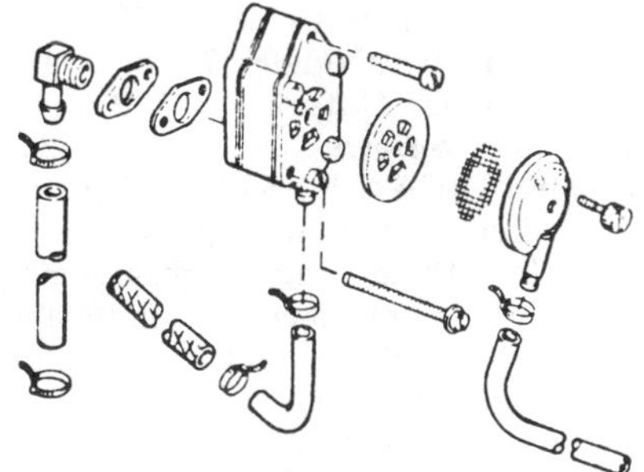

Fig. 17—Pulse type fuel pump is available as an assembly only, but inlet filter unit can be disassembled, cleaned and renewed as shown.

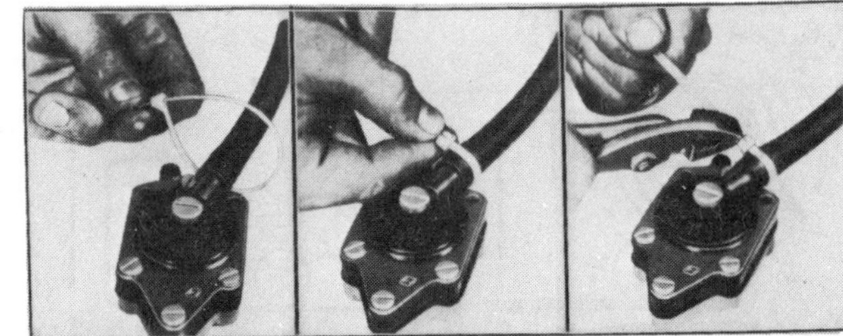

Fig. 18—Plastic "Tie Straps" on fuel lines are installed as shown. Twist locking head with pliers to remove, destroying the tie.

FUEL PRIMER. The diaphragm type fuel primer pump is shown in cross section in Fig. 19 and exploded in Fig. 20. All parts are available individually. Primer cable must be adjusted to provide ¼-inch stroke of plunger when primer knob is fully depressed. Failure within the primer pump is likely to result from damaged pump diaphragm or sticking plunger. Check also for damaged or collapsed fuel lines or damaged pickup valve.

IGNITION SYSTEM. The Capacitor Discharge ignition system is mounted underneath the engine flywheel (PTO end) and uses magneto generator coils as the power source.

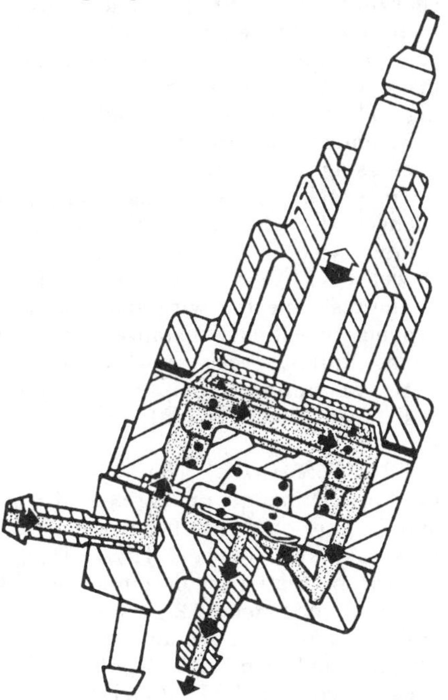

Fig. 19—Cross sectional view of diaphragm type fuel primer pump. Arrows indicate direction of fuel flow.

Refer to Fig. 21 for a schematic view. Maintenance service consists of checking the system main components and renewal of system main assemblies which consist of the following:

(1). Ignition Coil
(2). Ignition Switch
(3). Power Pack
(4). Charging Coils
(5). Trigger (Sensor) Coil
(6). Overspeed Sensor Coil

IGNITION COIL. Output should be a MINIMUM of 18 kilovolts using a suitable spark meter and turning engine with electric or recoil starter. This is the equivalent to the ability to jump a 7/16 inch (11 mm) atmospheric gap. Failure to perform as outlined can be caused by a component other than the ignition coil.

The disconnected or removed coil should have a primary resistance of 1.2 Ohms and a secondary resistance of 3000 Ohms.

IGNITION SWITCH. The key switch is a grounding switch where the ignition system is concerned. There should be NO continuity in RUN position, and perfect continuity (O—Ohms) between Magneto and ground terminals in OFF position. Refer to Fig. 22 for terminal identification and existing continuity in all switching positions.

If engine stops and fails to start, disconnect ignition switch (Orange & Black) wire from #5 terminal of power pack and again attempt to start engine. If engine now starts and runs, key switch, safety start switch or wiring is

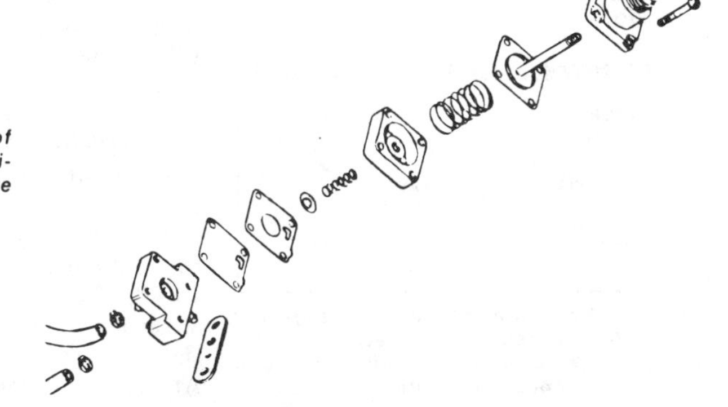

Fig. 20—Exploded view of diaphragm type fuel primer pump. All parts are available individually.

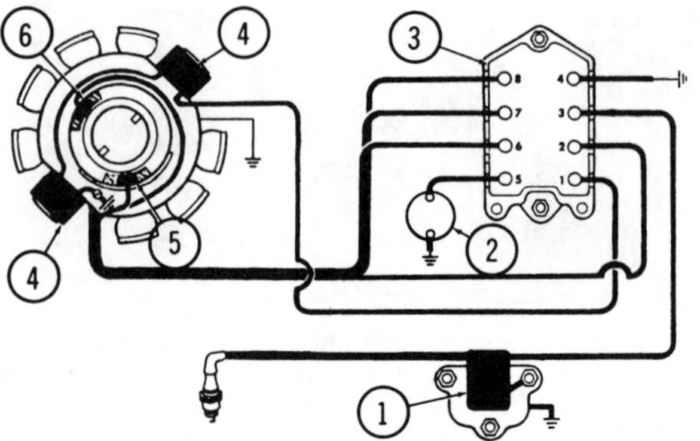

Fig. 21—Schematic diagram of electronic Capacitor Discharge ignition system showing component parts and wiring.

1. Ignition Coil
2. Ignition Switch
3. Power Pack
4. Charging Coils
5. Trigger Coil
6. Overspeed sensor

shorted or grounded.

If engine fails to stop when key switch is turned to OFF position, switch is defective or wiring is open or disconnected.

In the event of failure from any cause, isolate the cause by separate checks of each component involved.

POWER PACK. The Power Pack (3—Fig. 21) is serviced only as a unit. Power pack contains the electronic components (Capacitor, SCR's, Diodes and Resistors) of the ignition system. In the event of ignition failure, check other ignition components using outlined procedures and available equipment which should include an Ohmmeter; and if all other units check satisfactory, renew the Power Pack.

Fig. 22—Backside of Ignition/Lighting Switch showing terminal connections. Lower schematic views show continuity existing in various key positions.

NOTE: Power Pack output can be checked using a CD comparator tester such as Merc-O-Tronic M-80, Stevens S-80 or ESI Model 1 or 2.

CHARGING COILS. The ignition charging coils (4—Fig. 21) are located underneath the engine flywheel (drive clutch) and energized by permanent magnets cast into flywheel rim. Charging coils can be tested for output using CD comparator testers, or for resistance using an ohmmeter.

To check the charging coils, disconnect the charging coil (Brown & White) wire from No. 1 terminal of Power Pack, then connect meter leads to the disconnected wire and a suitable ground. Specified resistance is 860-880 Ohms. Infinite resistance would indicate an open circuit while lower resistance would indicate a short or ground.

TRIGGER COIL. The trigger coil (5—Fig. 21) mounts on engine end plate and is energized by permanent magnets cast into flywheel HUB. Trigger coil can be tested for output using ESI Model 1 or Model 2 tester or for resistance using a suitable Ohmmeter. Trigger coil can also be tested by substituting an ESI Model 20 Pulse Simulator or using a Merc-O-Tronic M-80 or Stevens S-80 as a pulse simulator for trigger coil; then testing remainder of system.

To test the trigger coil, disconnect the White & Green wire from No. 6 terminal of Power Pack and Black & White wire from terminal 7. Resistance should be 27-29 Ohms when a meter is connected between the two wires.

OVERSPEED SENSOR COIL. The overspeed sensor coil (6—Fig. 21) grounds out the ignition system at approximately 6500 crankshaft rpm, thus eliminating the danger of overspeed. The overspeed circuit consists of a second SCR and resistor built into the capacitor circuit of the power pack. At the governed speed, the sensor impulse becomes strong enough to close the SCR gate and the ignition charging current is directed back to ground instead of charging the capacitor, inactivating the ignition system until engine slows.

To test the overspeed sensor coil, disconnect the Orange & White wire from No. 2 terminal of Power pack and the Orange & Black wire from No. 8 terminal. Resistance should be 22-24 Ohms when a meter is connected between the two wires.

TEST PRECAUTIONS. Make sure key switch is properly connected and always turn key switch to OFF position after completing EACH test. This will discharge the capacitor if charged, thus preventing painful shock.

DO NOT attempt to crank engine with any of the wires disconnected, except as indicated for system tests. Make sure wires are properly connected to correct terminals. Electronic components may be damaged if excess current enters the wrong circuits of Power Pack.

LUBRICATION. Engine is lubricated by oil mixed with the fuel. The recommended lubricant is OMC Rotary Combustion Oil mixed at the ratio of 50:1 with a good grade of Regular Gasoline.

Mix fuel and oil thoroughly before pouring mixture into fuel tank. Mixing should take place at temperatures above 32°F. whenever possible. Whenever fuel must be mixed at temperatures below 32°F., lubricant should be pre-mixed 1 to 1 with gasoline, the pre-mix taking place at above freezing temperatures if at all possible. Do not use kerosene or diesel fuel for premixing.

REPAIRS

TIGHTENING TORQUES. Recommended tightening torques are as follows:

	ft.-lbs.	kg-m
Engine Mtg. Bolts	18-20	2.63
Flywheel Nut	35-45	5.53
Spark Plug	12-15	1.86
	in.-lbs.	kg-cm
Carburetor Mtg. Nuts	75-85	92
Engine Thru-bolt Nuts	75-85	92
Exhaust Flange Nuts	110-120	132
Sensor Mtg. Screws	10-12	12.5

ELECTRICAL SYSTEM. Ignition coil, switch and power pack can be renewed without engine disassembly after testing as outlined in maintenance section. Drive clutch and flywheel can be removed for access to trigger coil, overspeed sensor coil and charging coils without removal of engine from sled if desired.

Remove belt guard and neutral control arm; then remove drive belt. Remove drive clutch lock plate (Fig.

23). Use a spanner type flywheel holding tool as shown in Fig. 24, slightly compress clutch spring and install a retaining clamp as shown, then remove end cap bolt, end cap, garter spring, sliding sheave and primary spring from mainshaft, being careful to save the two neutral lockout balls as sliding sheave is removed.

Fig. 23—Drive clutch must be disassembled for access to magneto components located beneath flywheel.

Fig. 24—Flywheel holding tool and clutch retaining clamp installed for clutch disassembly.

Fig. 25—Splined mainshaft holding tool and flywheel nut adapter being used for flywheel nut removal.

Slip off spring cup and belt idler bearing. Use flywheel holding tool (Fig. 24), splined mainshaft holding tool (Fig. 25) or equivalent to hold the shaft and OMC Wrench Adapter 318541 (Fig. 25) or suitable open or box-end wrench to remove shaft nut. NOTE: LOCTITE is used for nut installation. Use suitable pulling equipment to remove flywheel.

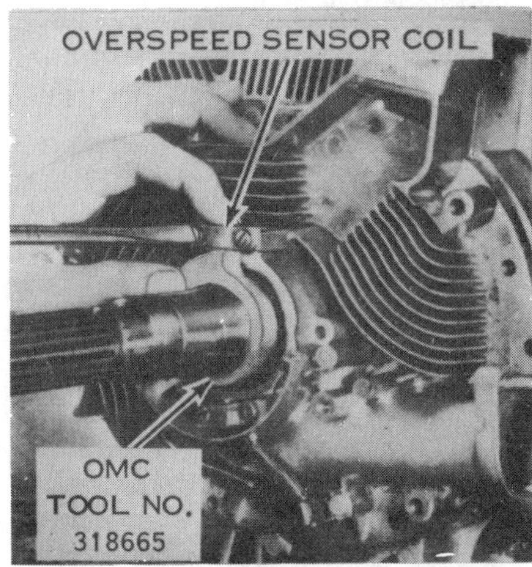

Fig. 26—A special gage is essential for properly positioning trigger sensor and overspeed sensor.

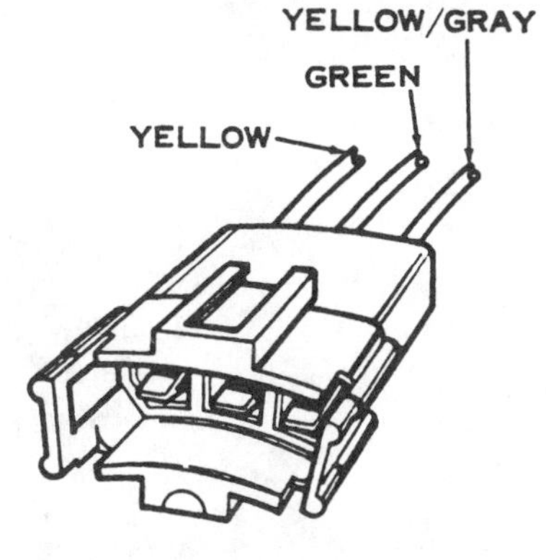

Fig. 27—Female magneto connector showing wires properly connected.

Ignition charging coils and alternator coils are only available in an assembly which also contains mounting frame. Coil assembly can be removed and renewed after flywheel is off. Overspeed sensor coil and trigger coil are available individually with mounting shield and wiring, and either unit can be renewed after removing alternator coil assembly. Overspeed sensor coil and trigger coil must be properly positioned relative to flywheel hub and a positioning gage (OMC 318665) is available (See Fig. 26). When installing alternator coil assembly, make sure coil laminations are flush with machined bosses on end housing.

Ignition coil specifications are given in MAINTENANCE Section. Alternator specifications can be checked before or after assembly removal. Disconnect curved plug from behind belt guard, then check at female connector (Fig. 27) as follows:

Using Ohmmeter low (Rx1) scale, check resistance between the two end (Yellow & Yellow/Gray) terminals. Resistance should be 0.82-1.0 ohm.

Using Ohmmeter low (Rx1) scale, check resistance between Yellow/Gray and Green terminals. Resistance should be 0.34-0.42 ohms.

Set ohmmeter on highest scale and check resistance between any lead and a suitable ground. Reading should be infinity. A lower reading would indicate grounded windings.

ROTOR DISASSEMBLY. To disassemble the engine (rotor) assembly, remove engine from frame and remove clutch, flywheel and armature windings as previously outlined. Remove recoil starter, air duct, outer fan housing, cooling fans and counterweight. Remove carburetor, high performance throttle link, carburetor insulating

Fig. 28—Rotary Combustion Engine removed for service.

block and electric starter.

Remove rotor housing cover shield and the through-bolts retaining inner fan housing and flywheel housing cover. Remove mainshaft fan end seal by collapsing outer wall as shown in Fig. 31, then prying out the seal. Remove mainshaft bearing external retaining ring as shown in Fig. 32. Loosen the remaining through-bolts (Fig. 33) and remove all except the two minor axis bolts. Remove engine mounting frame then position rotor assembly on a bench or fixture, drive end down, as shown in Fig. 34.

Remove the two remaining through-bolts, then pry fan-end housing off of locating ring dowels using screwdrivers in slots provided as shown in Fig. 35.

CAUTION: Side seals or button seals may adhere to end plate as it is removed. Be careful not to lose, intermix or damage any seals as end housing is removed.

SEAL REMOVAL AND IDENTIFICATION. Rotor seals consist of:

6—Side Seals (Three on each side)
6—Side Seal Springs
6—Button Seals
6—Button Seal Springs
3—Apex Seals
3—Corner Seals
3—Apex Seal Springs

Side seals are hand fit to length when they are installed, by filing seal ends. Apex and corner seals establish directional wear patterns. If seals may be re-used when engine is disassembled, they should be identified and reinstalled in the same place and position in rotor.

To identify the parts, the manufacturer recommends that a marked holding fixture be made of scrap lumber as shown in Figs. 36, 38 and 40, and that flanks of rotor be scribe-marked for reassembly as shown in Fig. 39. If the same end of each seal is always inserted in retaining holes,

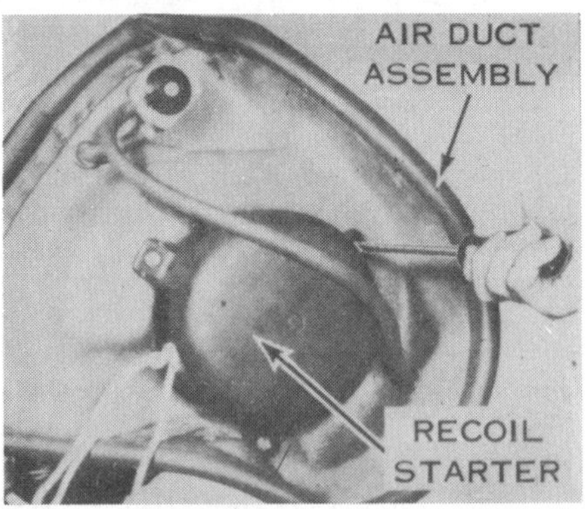

Fig. 29—Recoil starter and fuel pump are located in cooling air intake duct as shown.

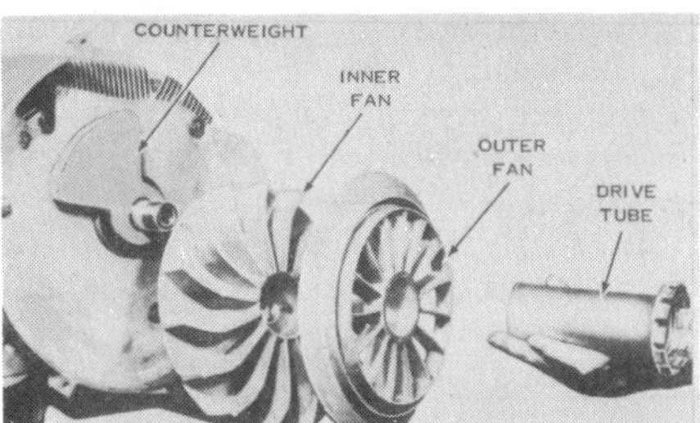

Fig. 30—Counterweight and cooling fan partially disassembled.

Fig. 31—Fan end shaft seal can be removed by collapsing seal as shown. Seal must be removed for access to bearing retaining snap ring (Fig. 32).

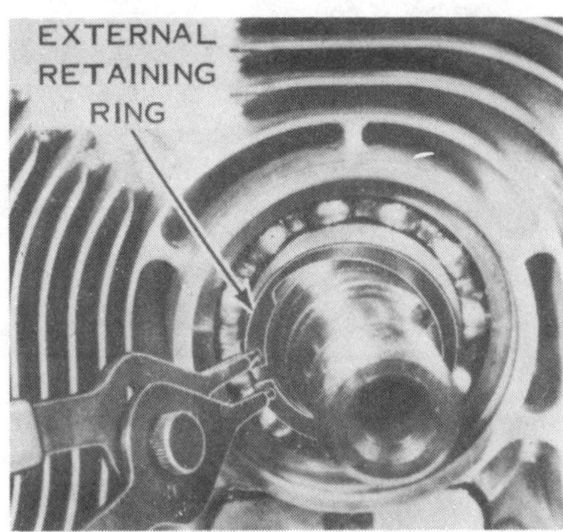

Fig. 32—Removing bearing retaining snap ring from fan end housing.

Fig. 33—Loosen minor axis through-bolt nuts and remove remaining through-bolts as next step in rotor disassembly.

Fig. 34—Position rotor drive-end down through hole in bench or holding fixture as shown.

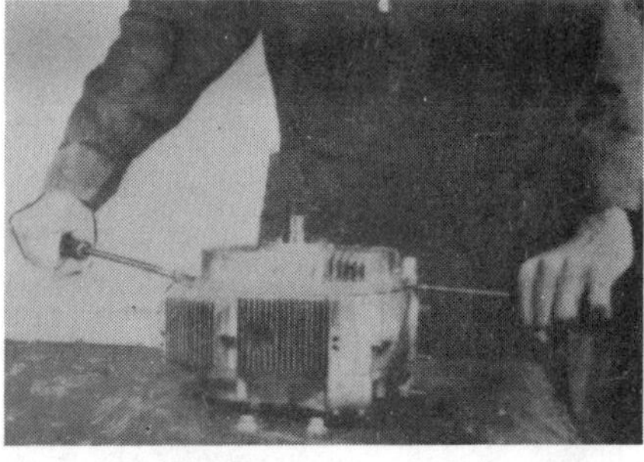
Fig. 35—Remove minor axis through-bolts and pry off fan-end housing using screwdriver slots as shown.

Fig. 36—Side seals and button seals may remain with rotor or adhere to end housing as shown. Keep all seals in order by using a holding block as shown in Fig. 38.

Fig. 37—Prying off rotor housing.

parts can be easily reassembled in proper order.

OVERHAUL. Clean seal grooves in rotor (Figs. 42 and 43), using sharpened discarded seals or similar tool. Clean rotor flanks using a power wire brush, being careful to stay clear of rotor sides and apex seal area. Check seal grooves and side edges for burrs. Remove any burrs with corner of a fine sharpening stone.

Clean apex seals (6—Fig. 39) with a suitable solvent and brass wire brush. Measure apex seal height about 1/2 inch from each end. If any measurement is less than 0.265 inch (6.73 mm) or if any seal is otherwise damaged, ALL apex seals should be renewed.

Clean side seals (2) with a suitable solvent and brass wire brush. Measure side seal height. If any seal is less than 0.070 inch (1.78 mm) in height or otherwise damaged, ALL side seals must be renewed.

Clean button seals (4) and check for damage at points of side seal contact. Renew all button seals if damage exists or if measured height of any button seal is less than 0.200 inch (5.1 mm).

Temporarily install each apex seal in its groove in rotor and check the fit. Seal should fit closely but freely, with no excess clearance at top of groove. Apex seal grooves tend to wear tapered and if clearance is excessive at top of groove, rotor should be renewed.

Install each side seal in turn in its groove and check the fit which should be close without binding. Install button seal at each end of side seal, then measure end clearance of side seal which should be 0.003-0.006 inch (0.08-0.15 mm). If new side seals are being installed, seals must be file-fit to the dimension given; then installed in seal holder until engine is assembled.

Inspect rotor housing for deep scratches, surface flaking or thermal stress cracks on trochoid surface. Check spark plug threads for damage and high performance throttle plate for proper fit. Examine cooling fins for damage and rotor housing side surface for indications of combustion pressure leakage.

Inspect side housing wear surfaces for scratches, wear or scuffing. Inspect fixed timing gear teeth for damage.

Check mainshaft bearing and seal surfaces for wear, scoring or other

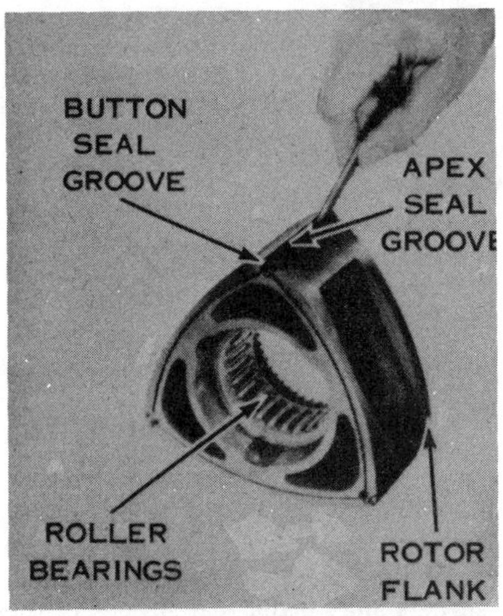

Fig. 42—View of rotor showing use of discarded seal to clean carbon from grooves.

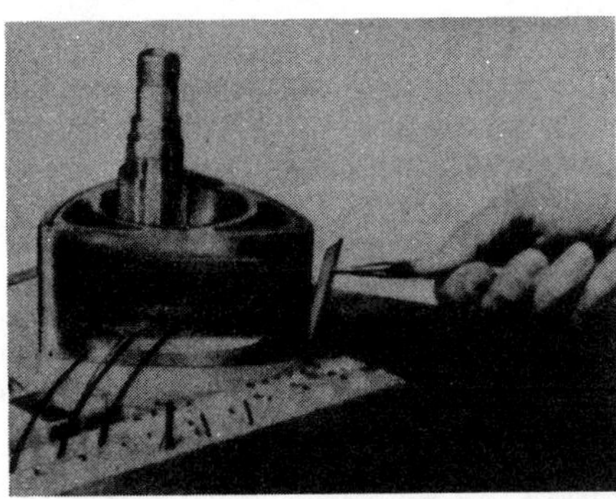
Fig. 40—Keep rotor seals in proper order when they are removed.

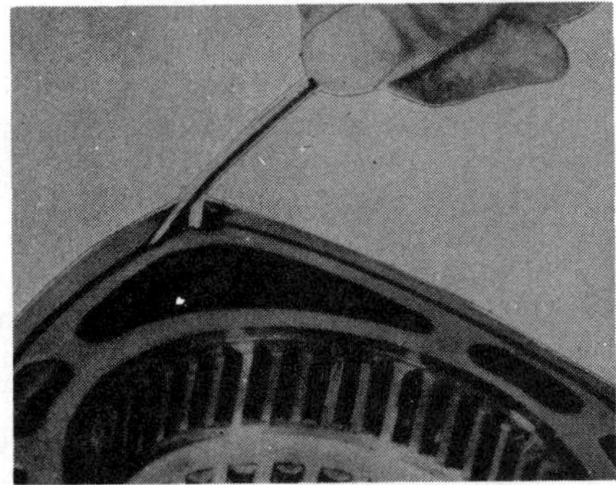
Fig. 43—Cleaning carbon from side seal grooves.

Fig. 38—Drilled holes in a block of wood provide a holder to keep rotor seals in correct order for reassembly. Refer to text and to Figs. 36 and 40.

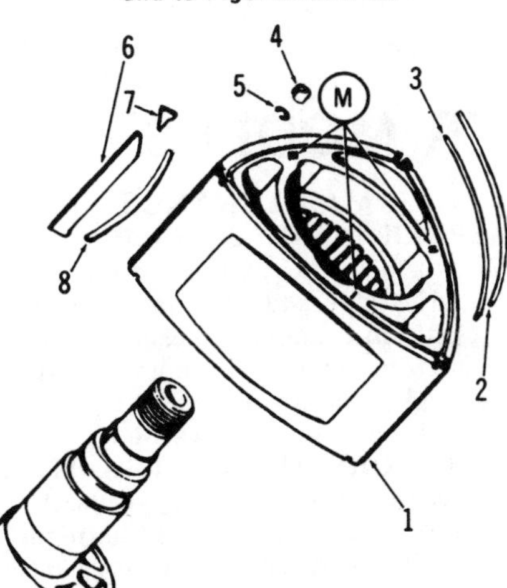

Fig. 39—Exploded view of rotor and seals. Identifying scribe marks (M) can be ink-marked on machined surfaces or scribe-marked on unfinished areas of rotor flank.

1. Rotor
2. Side seals
3. Leaf spring
4. Button seals
5. Seal springs
6. Apex seals
7. Corner seals
8. Seal springs

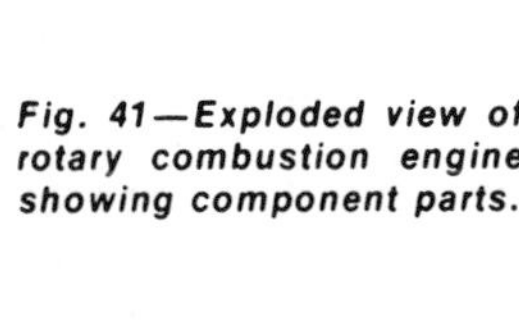
Fig. 41—Exploded view of rotary combustion engine showing component parts.

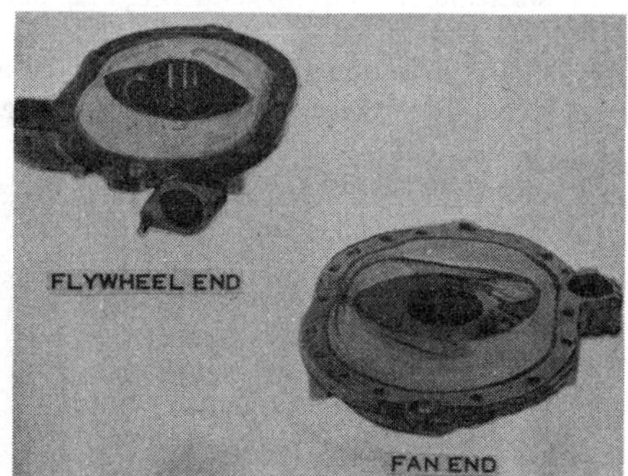

Fig. 44—View of end housings showing identifying features.

damage. Also inspect splines, threads, keyways and flywheel taper.

ASSEMBLY. Lubricate bearing in flywheel end housing and place housing inner side up over assembly hole in bench or fixture.

Place rotor gear side up on clean working surface. Position side seal springs and button seal springs in their proper positions in gear side of rotor, then put a small amount of high temperature grease in side seal grooves and button seal bores to retain the seals during assembly. Avoid smearing grease on sides of rotor and make sure open ends of button seal springs align with apex seal slots.

New side seals and button seals can be installed either side up. If side seals and button seals are re-used, bright side should be out. Position seals in rotor, then invert rotor into position on flywheel end housing. When positioning rotor, align one apex point with either minor axis bolt hole as shown in Fig. 45; then push timing gears into mesh as shown. Entire bulk of rotor must occupy wear area on end housing.

Lubricate mainshaft and slide flywheel (splined) end of mainshaft down through rotor and end housing. NOTE: DO NOT ALLOW rotor to separate from end housing once it is installed, or side seals are apt to drop from their grooves making it necessary to disassemble and start again from beginning.

Recheck slots in installed button seals and springs to make sure they are perfectly aligned so that apex seals can be slid into position without difficulty. Apply slight pressure to top side of rotor and check to see that seal springs compress and rotor moves down into close contact with housing. If binding or clearance exists, correct the cause before proceeding.

Position rotor housing over end housing and rotor, making sure finned quadrant of rotor housing is on opposite side from carburetor mounting flange of end housing and that housing cover attaching bosses align. (See Fig. 37). Press rotor housing down until the two end ring dowels fully seat.

Insert square end of each apex seal into correct slot in rotor and push seals down until they bottom. If beveled end of seal protrudes, seal is not properly entering lower button seal. If alignment cannot be accomplished with a suitable probe working from the top, rotor housing must be pried off (Fig. 37) and the trouble corrected. Insert apex seal spring behind the seals.

Lubricate side seal grooves, button seal bores, rotor and rotor housing lightly with engine oil, then install side seal springs, side seals, button seal springs, button seals and corner seals

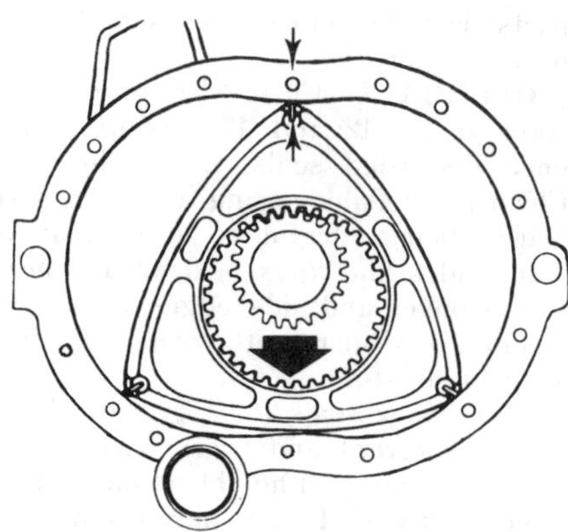

Fig. 45—To install and time the rotor, position rotor on drive end housing with one (any) apex point aligned with minor axis bolt hole (small arrows), then push in direction of large arrow until gears mesh. DO NOT lift rotor from housing or side seals will fall out of position. Refer to text.

in their proper positions. Check all seals to be sure they are free in grooves.

Lubricate rotor contact surface of fan end housing and install the housing. Install bolts through the two major diameter bolt holes containing the ring dowels and tighten alternately and evenly until ring dowels seat. Check shaft rotation at this point to make sure it turns freely, correcting the cause if trouble exists. Install mainshaft external retaining ring (Fig. 32) and fan end housing seal.

Install remaining through-bolts and tighten all through-bolts to 50 in.-lbs. (58 kg-cm) beginning with the two bolts containing ring dowels. Retighten all nuts to a torque of 80 in.-lbs. (92 kg-cm). Complete the assembly by reversing disassembly procedure, using tightening torques previously given where applicable.

O.M.C.

ALTERNATE FIRING TWO CYLINDER MODELS

CONDENSED SERVICE DATA

Model	M242 M247	M243 M248	M244 M249
Bore—(mm)	69.85	73.0	82.55
Inches	2.750	2.875	3.250
Stroke—(mm)	52	52	60.3
Inches	2.05	2.05	2.375
No. of Cylinders	2	2	2
Displacement—(cc)	399	436	646
Cubic Inches	24.4	26.6	39.4
Horsepower at RPM	35 at 6750	40 at 6750	50 at 6750
Cooling Type		Axial Fan	
Carburetor Make & Model		Tillotson HD	
Ignition:			
Type	CD	CD	CD
Timing Advance		Electronic	
Timing BTDC		See Text	
Spark Plug:			
Champion	UL-77V	UL-77V	UL-77V
Electrode Gap	Fixed	Fixed	Fixed
Fuel/Oil Ratio	50:1	50:1	50:1

MAINTENANCE

SPARK PLUG. A CHAMPION UL-77V surface gap plug is used. Gap is not adjustable and plug should normally run until engine overhaul without attention. The recommended spark plug tightening torque of 20 ft.-lbs. (2.8 kg-m) should not be exceeded.

CARBURETOR. The TILLOTSON HD carburetor is equipped with an accelerator pump. Initial adjustment of slow idle mixture needle is 7/8-turn open for 399 cc models and one turn open for other models. Initial adjustment of high speed mixture needle is one turn open for all models. Clockwise adjustment of either needle leans the mixture. Adjust idle speed stop screw for a slow idle speed of 1200-1400 rpm with engine warm and mixture needles properly adjusted. Accelerator pump lever is fixed on throttle shaft and pump stroke is not adjustable.

Fuel inlet diaphragm lever should be parallel and flush with diaphragm chamber floor as shown in Fig. 50. Bend diaphragm lever to align. Some carburetors use a rubber tipped inlet needle and realigning of lever is best performed by applying finger or tool pressure to both ends of lever. Refer also to TILLOTSON Section of CARBURETOR SERVICE portion of this manual.

REED VALVES. The Vee type reed valve units are shown exploded from intake manifold in Fig. 51. Leaf valves, stops and base unit are only available as an assembly for one cylinder. Renew the assembly if valve leaves fail to seat properly, are bent, broken or otherwise damaged.

FUEL PUMP. The pulse type fuel pump is operated by pressure and vacuum pulsations in crankcase on right side of engine. Impulses are directed through drilled passages in intake manifold and fuel pump mounting base.

Fuel pump is available as an assembly only, however inlet filter unit can be removed for cleaning or parts renewal as shown in Fig. 51. Fuel line connections are secured with plastic "Tie Straps" as shown in Fig. 52. The tie will be destroyed in removal and must be renewed. Install with serrated edge to inside and tighten as shown in Fig. 52.

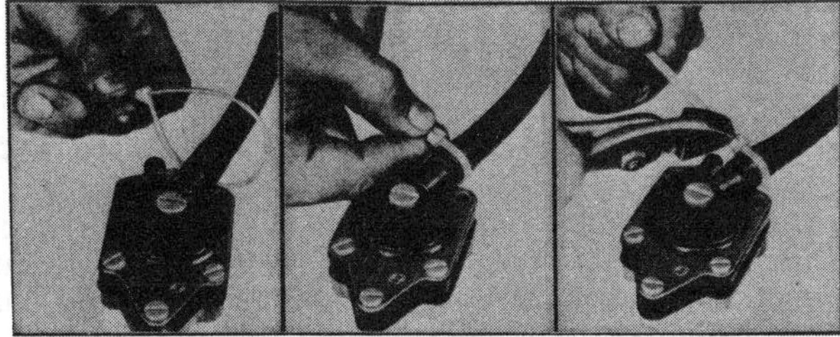

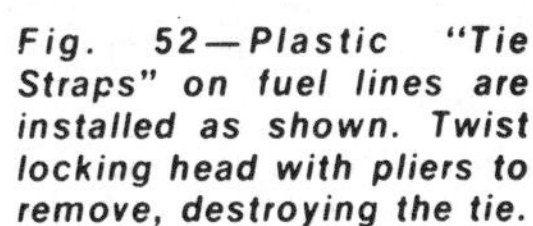

Fig. 52—Plastic "Tie Straps" on fuel lines are installed as shown. Twist locking head with pliers to remove, destroying the tie.

FUEL PRIMER. The diaphragm type fuel primer pump is shown in cross section in Fig. 53 and exploded in Fig. 54. All parts are available individually. Failure within the primer pump is likely to result from damaged pump diaphragm or sticking plunger. Check also for damaged or collapsed fuel lines or damaged pickup valve.

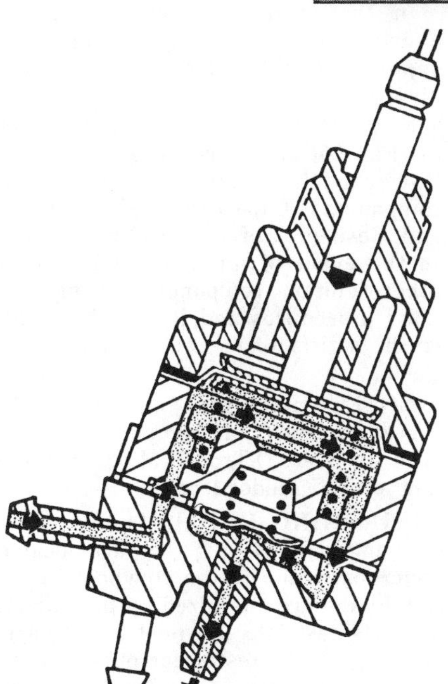

Fig. 53—Cross sectional view of diaphragm type fuel primer pump. Arrows indicate direction of fuel flow.

IGNITION SYSTEM. The Capacitor Discharge ignition system is mounted underneath the engine flywheel (PTO end) and uses magneto coils as the power source.

Refer to Fig. 55 for a schematic view. Maintenance service consists of checking system main components and renewal of main assemblies which consist of the following:

(1). Ignition Coils
(2). Ignition Switch
(3). Power Pack
(4). Charging Coils

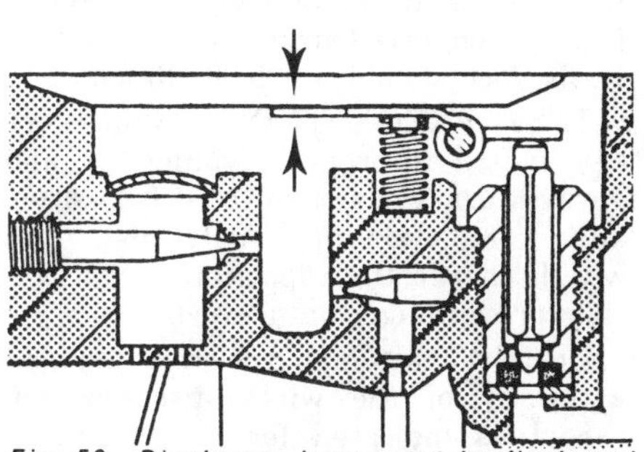

Fig. 50—Diaphragm lever must be flush and parallel with chamber floor as shown by arrows.

Fig. 54—Exploded view of diaphragm type fuel primer pump. All parts are available individually.

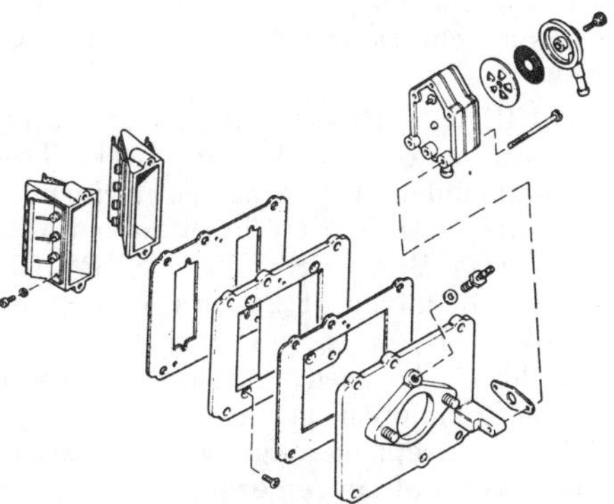

Fig. 51—Exploded view of intake manifold, reed plates and associated parts of the type used on all models. Fuel pump mounts on intake manifold boss and pulse passages are internally drilled.

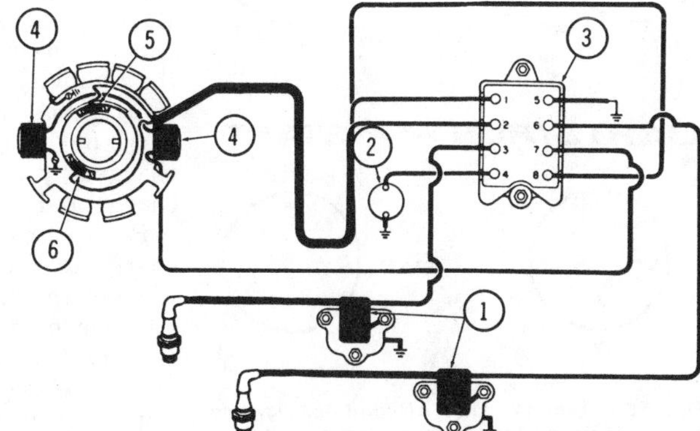

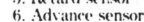

Fig. 55—Schematic drawing of electronic capacitor discharge ignition system showing component parts and wiring.

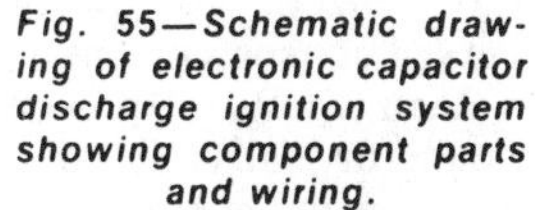

1. Ignition coils
2. Ignition switch
3. Power pack
4. Charging coils
5. Retard sensor
6. Advance sensor

(5). Retard Sensor (Trigger)
(6). Advance Sensor

IGNITION COILS. Output should be a MINIMUM of 18 Kilovolts using a suitable spark meter and turning engine with electric or recoil starter. This is the equivalent to the ability to jump a 7/16 inch (11 mm) atmospheric gap. Failure to perform as outlined can be caused by a component other than the ignition coil. In the event of weak or erratic spark from one coil lead only, switch primary leads on terminals "3" and "6" on power pack and recheck. If the same coil shows weak, renew the coil; if the other coil now appears weak, renew the power pack.

IGNITION SWITCH. The key switch is a grounding switch where the ignition system is concerned. There should be NO continuity in RUN position and perfect continuity (0-Ohms) between Magneto and Ground terminals in OFF position. Refer to Fig. 56 for terminal identification and existing continuity in all switching positions.

If engine stops and fails to start, disconnect magneto (Orange & Black) wire from #4 terminal of power pack and again attempt to start engine. If engine now starts and runs, key switch, safety start switch or wiring is shorted or grounded.

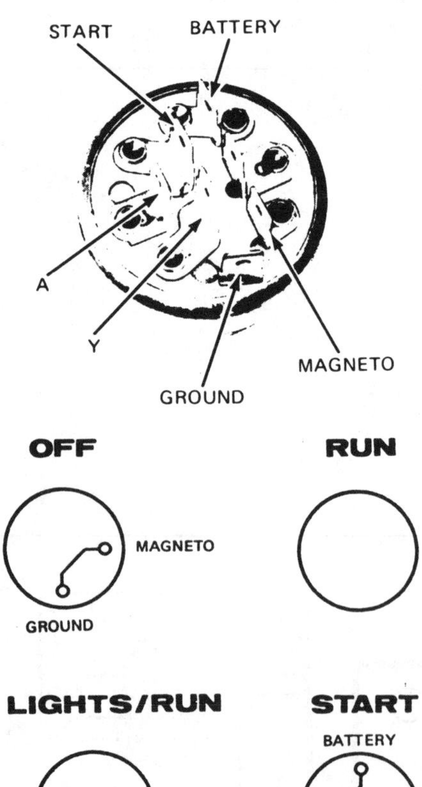

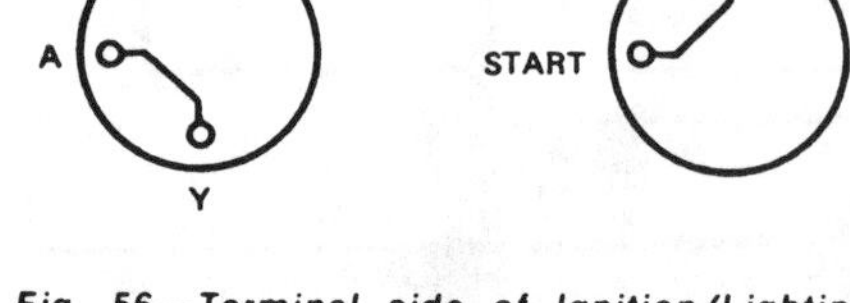

Fig. 56—Terminal side of Ignition/Lighting switch showing terminal connections. Lower schematic views show continuity in various key positions.

If engine fails to stop when key switch is turned to OFF position, switch is defective or wiring is open or disconnected.

In the event of failure from any cause, isolate the faulty unit by separate checks of each component involved.

POWER PACK. The Power Pack (3—Fig. 55) is serviced only as a unit. Power pack contains the electronic components (Capacitors, SCRs, Diodes and Resistors) of the ignition system. In the event of ignition failure, check other ignition components using outlined procedures and if all other units check satisfactory, renew the Power Pack.

NOTE: Power pack output can be checked using a CD comparator tester such as Merc-O-Tronic M-80, Stevens S-80 or ESI Model 1 or 2.

CHARGING COILS. The ignition charging coils (4—Fig. 55) are located underneath the engine flywheel (drive clutch) and are energized by permanent magnets cast into flywheel rim. Charging coils can be tested for output using a CD comparator tester, or for resistance using an ohmmeter.

To check the charging coils, disconnect the Brown/White lead from No. 7 terminal of power pack and connect ohmmeter leads to the disconnected wire and a suitable ground. Specified resistance is 550-650 Ohms. Infinite resistance would indicate an open circuit and lower resistance would indicate a short or ground.

SENSOR (TRIGGER) COILS. The Retard and Advance Sensor Coils (5 & 6—Fig. 55) mount on engine crankcase and are energized by permanent magnets built into flywheel hub. The two sensors are similar except advance sensor contains fewer windings, therefore produces less current and will not trigger the spark at starting speeds. When engine speed increases above starting range, the less powerful advance sensor is energized, advancing the timing. The retard sensor continues to trigger the retard SCR in power pack but the capacitor, already discharged by advance sensor, contains no charge and no spark occurs.

Both sensors produce a positive charge to fire one plug and a negative charge to fire the other plug. The advance or retard spark occurs when flywheel timing mark aligns with "Advance" or "Retard" timing mark even though sensors are physically located almost 180 degrees apart. This is accomplished by reversing the polarity in one of the sensor coils relative to the other, and equipping flywheel hub with North/South and South/North magnets located 180 degrees apart.

If retard sensor coil is inoperative, engine will not start, or will start with extreme difficulty if enough cranking speed can be obtained. If advance sensor is inoperative, engine will start satisfactorily but will be extremely sluggish. Sensor coils can be checked by connecting a power timing light to the No. 1 spark plug wire, turning ignition switch to START or RUN position and turning engine over with starter. Cylinders are marked on cooling shroud near spark plugs. If light flashes and timing marks do not align, check for sheared flywheel key or similar damage. If light does not flash, fault may lie with any system component.

To check sensor coils using an ohmmeter, disconnect White/Black wire from No. 1 terminal of power pack, White/Green lead from No. 2 terminal and Black/White lead from No. 8 terminal. Check advance sensor by connecting ohmmeter leads to White/Black lead disconnected from No. 1 terminal and Black/White lead disconnect from No. 8 terminal. Resistance should be 17-19 Ohms. Check retard sensor by connecting ohmmeter leads to White/Green lead disconnected from No. 2 terminal and Black/White lead disconnected from No. 8 terminal. Resistance should be 28-30 Ohms.

TEST PRECAUTIONS. Make sure key switch is properly connected and always turn key switch to OFF position after completion of EACH test. This will discharge the capacitor if charged, thus preventing painful shock.

DO NOT attempt to crank engine with any of the wires disconnected, except as indicated for system tests. Make sure wires are properly connected to correct terminals. Electronic components may be damaged if excess current enters the wrong circuits of power pack.

LUBRICATION. Engine is lubricated by oil mixed with the fuel. The recommended lubricant is Evinrude, Johnson or OMC 2 Cycle Oil mixed at a 50:1 ratio. BIA CERTIFIED SERVICE TC-W Oil mixed at 24:1 ratio may be used. OMC Rotary Combustion Oil should not be used. Automotive Motor Oil or commercial pre-mixes should not be used except on a temporary basis in the event of an emergency. Regular gasoline is the specified fuel. Premium gasoline is satisfactory but seldom necessary. No-Lead or low lead fuels containing phosphorus additives should not be used.

Mix fuel and oil thoroughly before pouring mixture into fuel tank. Mixing should be done at temperatures above 32°F. whenever possible. Whenever fuel must be mixed at temperatures below 32°F., lubricant should be premixed 1 to 1 with gasoline, the pre-mix taking place at above freezing temperatures where possible. Do not use kerosene or diesel fuel for pre-mixing.

REPAIRS

TIGHTENING TORQUES. Recommended tightening torques are as follows:

	ft.-lbs.	kg-m
Connecting Rod Cap Screw	29-31	4.01-4.08
Crankcase Screws 3/8-16	18-20	2.49-2.76
Crankcase Screws 5/16-24	10-12	1.38-1.66
Cylinder to Crankcase	18-20	2.49-2.76
Engine to Main Frame	18-20	2.49-2.76
Exh. Manifold to Cylinder	10-12	1.38-1.66
Flywheel	145-150	20.05-20.74
Primary Clutch End Cap	90-100	12.44-13.82
Spark Plug	18-20	2.49-2.76
	in.-lbs.	kg-cm
Crankcase Drain Plug	25-30	28.8-34.6
Cylinder Head	175-180	201.6-207.4
Power Pack Cover	40-50	46.1-57.6

Fig. 57—Withdraw lynch pins (L) to lift off belt guard.

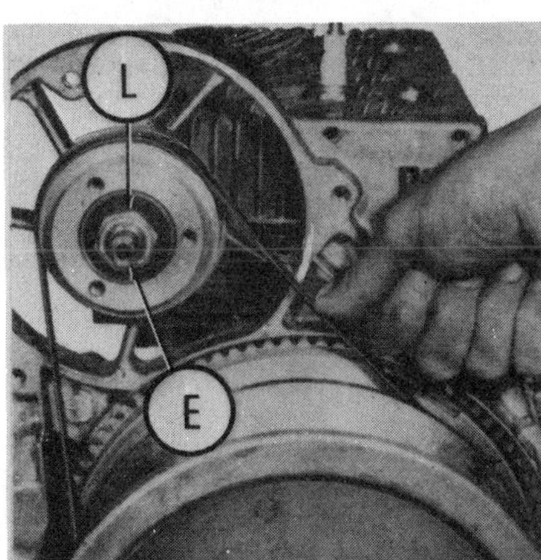

Fig. 58—To adjust fan belt or loosen belt for removal, loosen locknut (L) and turn eccentric shaft (E). When properly adjusted, belt should deflect 1/16-inch with thumb pressure midway between pulleys as shown.

ELECTRICAL SYSTEM. Ignition coil, switch and power pack can be renewed without engine disassembly after testing as outlined in maintenance section. Drive clutch and flywheel can be removed for access to sensor coils and charging coils without removal of engine from sled if desired.

Fig. 59—Flywheel holder (114594) and primary drive clamp (114584) installed for clutch disassembly.

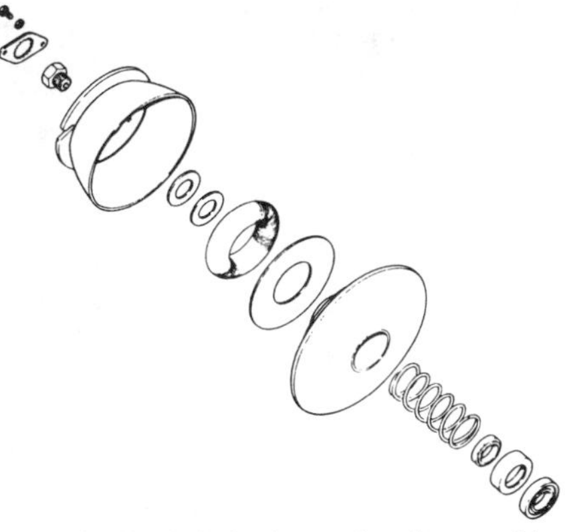
Fig. 60—Exploded view of primary drive clutch showing component parts.

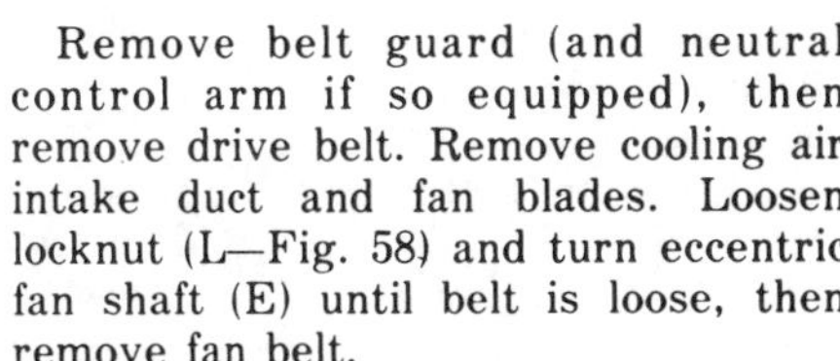

Remove belt guard (and neutral control arm if so equipped), then remove drive belt. Remove cooling air intake duct and fan blades. Loosen locknut (L—Fig. 58) and turn eccentric fan shaft (E) until belt is loose, then remove fan belt.

Remove manual or electric starter. Refer to Fig. 59. Install flywheel holder (OMC Tool No. 114594) on starter mounting bolt holes to keep flywheel from turning, install primary drive clamp (OMC Tool No. 114584), then remove clutch cover retaining cap screw. Release primary drive clamp and lift off clutch parts shown in Fig. 60. Remove flywheel nut, then remove flywheel using a suitable puller.

Electrical system components are removable in two pieces as shown in Fig. 61, ignition charge coils and alternator coils being available only as a stator unit which includes frame and wiring. Ignition charge coil specifications are given in MAINTENANCE Section. Alternator specifications can be checked before or after removal. Alternator is composed of a three-leg stator unit which is grounded to frame and provides current for lights, plus a separate two-coil winding which is isolated from frame and rectified to provide direct current for battery charging. Battery charging coils and wires to terminal are provided with manual start models. To check the lighting coils, touch ohmmeter leads to No. 8 (Yellow Wire) terminal of terminal block and to a suitable ground if stator is installed; or to yellow lead and brown/yellow stator ground lead if stator is removed. Resistance should be 1.0-1.6 Ohms.

To check the charging coils, disconnect Green/White stator lead from #1 terminal of terminal block and Green terminal lead from terminal #2. Touch ohmmeter leads to the two disconnected stator leads; reading should be 4.25 Ohms. There should be infinite resistance between either lead and a suitable ground when both leads are disconnected. Charging coils provide

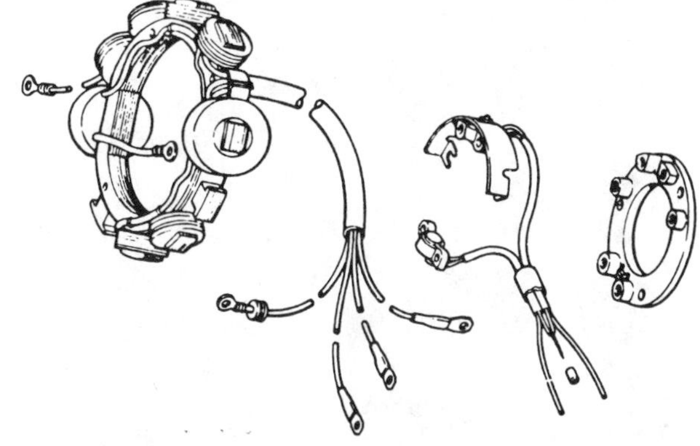
Fig. 61—Electrical system components are removable in two components, charging and lighting coils being a component part of the large stator housing and both sensor coils being attached to a smaller mounting base.

current for brake light on all models including those without battery and rectifier.

Alternator stator can be removed after removing flywheel and disconnecting wiring harness. Alternator stator must be removed before sensor coils can be removed. Sensors are available individually or as an assembly including mounting base plate. Sensor common (Black/White) leads must be separated at splice and rejoined if an individual sensor is renewed. If sensors are removed from base plate, install retaining screws with OMC NUT LOCK (Part No. 384849) or equivalent, and make sure sensors contact locating stops as shown in Fig. 63.

Route wiring leads where they will not touch flywheel (Fig. 64), pull tight and cement to housing using General Electric RTV 102 cement as shown in Fig. 65. Fig. 66 shows wiring connections to power pack and terminal block. Color codes and terminal identification numbers appear on covers to aid in correct installation.

DISASSEMBLY AND REASSEMBLY. Refer to Fig. 67 for an exploded view of engine castings and sheet metal, and to Fig. 68 for crankshaft, bearings, pistons and associated parts.

When service is required, first remove engine as outlined in vehicle section of this manual. Remove drive clutch, flywheel and magneto. Disconnect spark plug wires and remove ignition coils, power pack and mounting bracket as a unit. Remove carburetor,

Fig. 62—Magneto stator housing must be removed for engine disassembly or access to sensor coils and wiring.

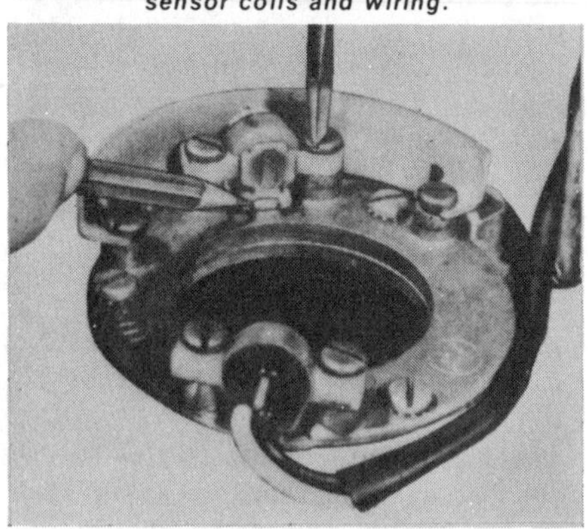

Fig. 63—Sensor base must contact locating stop on mounting base as indicated by pencil pointer.

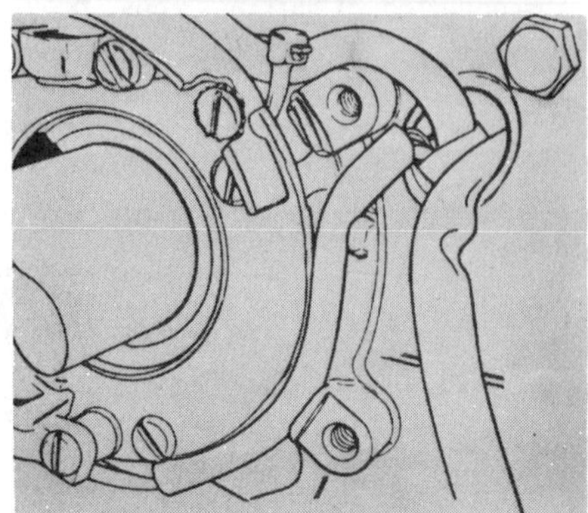

Fig. 64—Route wiring where it will not touch flywheel, pull tight and cement in place. Refer to text and Fig. 65.

Fig. 65—Use GE RTV-102 cement to seal and secure wiring.

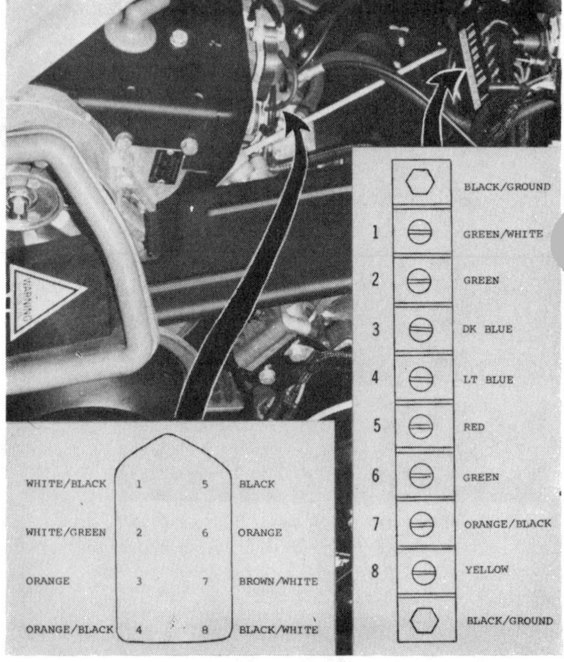

Fig. 66—Terminal block and power pack both are color coded to aid in attaching wiring harness.

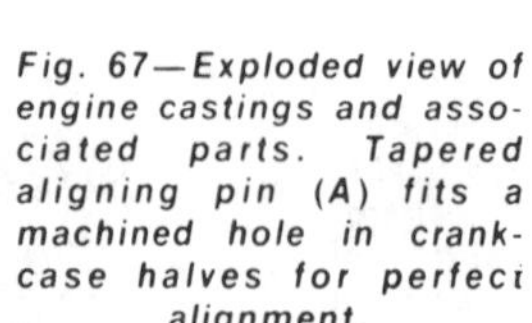

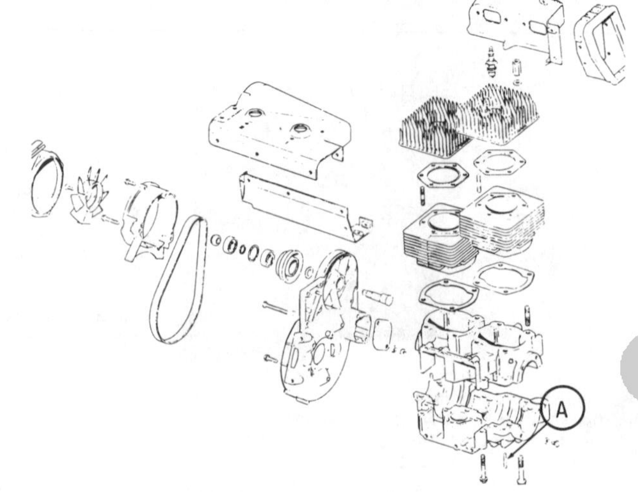

Fig. 67—Exploded view of engine castings and associated parts. Tapered aligning pin (A) fits a machined hole in crankcase halves for perfect alignment.

intake manifold and exhaust manifold. Unbolt and remove cooling shrouds. Remove the three cap screws securing fan end housing to crankcase (Fig. 70), and lift off fan end housing. Using a felt-tip pen or other means, mark cylinder numbers on cylinders and heads. The correct cylinder number is stamped on top cooling shroud adjacent to spark plug hole.

Remove cylinder heads and mark crown of pistons with cylinder numbers. Invert engine and remove mounting frame. Using a punch and working from cylinder side, drive out the tapered aligning dowel (A—Fig. 67) at carburetor side of engine opposite flywheel end. Remove crankcase retaining cap screws and pry crankcase halves apart using pry slots provided.

Mark connecting rod caps with cylinder number, then remove connecting rod caps and bearings. Connecting rod bearing consists of a split bearing cage and 16 loose needle rollers for each rod. Do not lose any of the rollers at disassembly and do not intermix. Push piston and connecting rod unit out top of cylinder.

Crankshaft and main bearings can now be lifted out of upper crankcase half. Center main bearing consists of a split outer race and a split bearing cage containing trapped rollers. Center main bearing and flywheel end bearing are positively located in upper crankcase half by a dowel which fits a hole in bearing outer race.

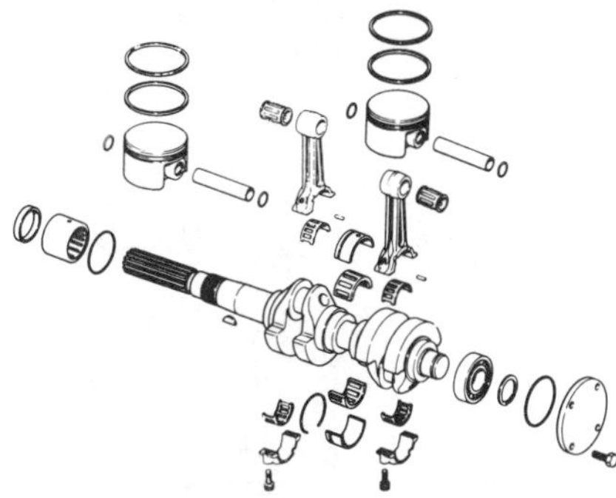

Fig. 68—Exploded view of crankshaft, bearings, connecting rods, pistons and associated parts similar to that used on all engines.

Fig. 69—Removing air shrouds for top end inspection.

When reassembling, make sure all parts are clean, that mating surfaces are not nicked, burred or warped, and that moving parts are lightly lubricated with clean oil. Coat both sides of cylinder base gaskets with OMC Gasket Sealing Compound (Part No. 317201) and install cylinders to upper crankcase half with exhaust port flanges opposite intake manifold mounting flange in crankcase half. If new cylinders are used, they are interchangeable. If cylinders are reused, they should be installed in same location from which removed. Use exhaust manifold or a suitable straightedge to carefully align exhaust port flanges before tightening cylinder stud nuts. Recommended tightening torque is 18-20 ft.-lbs. (2.49-2.76 kg-m).

Center main bearing should be assembled with retaining ring toward flywheel end of crankshaft. Make sure both main bearing locating holes align over dowels when crankshaft is installed. Lubricate and install piston, ring and connecting rod assemblies in their proper cylinders, positioning dot on piston crown on exhaust side of cylinder. Install cylinder head gaskets dry with tab toward exhaust side, then install the correct (marked) cylinder heads with spark plug holes offset toward intake side. The three standoff nuts which serve as mounting points for air shroud are installed on intake side nearest spark plug (Position 1—Fig. 71) on both heads and at position 2 on No. 1 head only. Snug nuts up evenly, then tighten to 175-180 inch pounds (201-207 kg-cm) using tightening sequence shown in Fig. 71. Use OMC Needle Bearing Grease (Part No. 387642) or equivalent to retain connecting rod bearing needle rollers during assembly. Install rod caps with identification dots aligned. Install retaining screws loosely and make sure irregular (fractured) parting surfaces of rod and cap align, then tighten cap screws to 29-31 ft.-lbs. (4 kg-m).

Fig. 70—Fan end housing is retained to crankcase by three cap screws as shown.

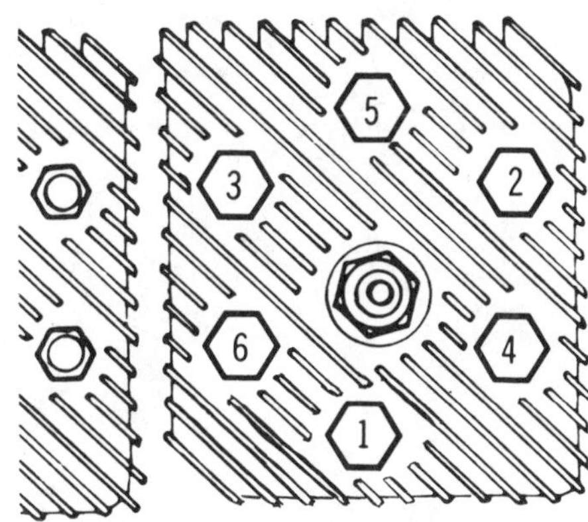

Fig. 71—Tighten cylinder head stud nuts evenly to 175-180 inch pounds (201-207 kg-cm) using sequence shown.

Seat crankshaft ball bearing against shoulder in upper crankcase half using a hammer and punch as shown in Fig. 72. Apply a continuous thin bead of

Fig. 72—Seat ball-type main crankshaft bearing against crankcase bore shoulder using a hammer and punch as shown.

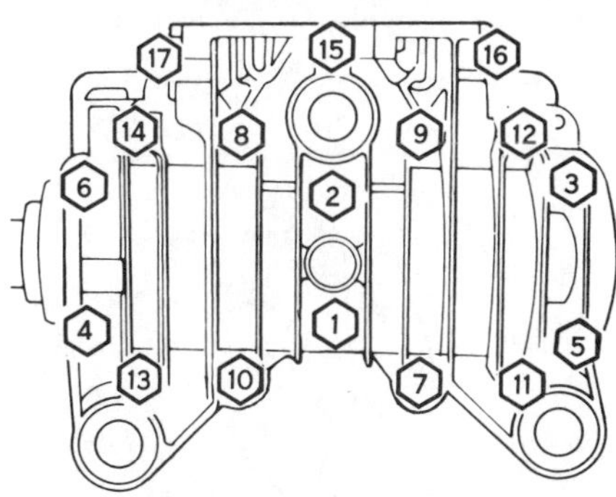

Fig. 73—Recommended tightening sequence for crankcase screws. Check text for procedure. The 3/8-inch diameter main bearing cap screws (1 through 6) are final tightened to torque of 220-240 inch pounds (2.5 kg-m) while remaining screws are tightened to 120-140 inch pounds (150 kg-cm).

OMC Adhesive M (Part No. 318535) to crankcase flange and immediately install lower half. Install all crankcase screws finger tight, then install tapered aligning pin (A—Fig. 67) from the bottom using a punch and hammer. NOTE: Do not install rubber engine mounts at this time nor the engine mount retainers located on cap screws (11, 13 and 15—Fig. 73); these must be installed after crankcase is properly torqued. Tighten all cap screws to 100 inch-pounds (115 kg-cm) using the sequence shown in Fig. 73; retightening cap screws (1 through 6) to 220-240 inch-pounds (2.5 kg-m) and cap screws (7 through 17) to a torque of 120-140 inch-pounds (150 kg-cm).

Remove the three crankcase cap screws (11, 13 and 15). Install rubber engine mounts, positioning the harder, green colored mount nearest flywheel (adjacent to cap screw hole 13) and black mounts in the other two holes. Install mount retainers on the three removed cap screws, reinstall the screws and re-torque to 130 inch-pounds (150 kg-cm). Complete the assembly by reversing disassembly procedure.

PISTONS, PINS, RINGS AND CYLINDERS. Pistons are equipped with two identical rings which are pinned in place and should be installed with dot on piston crown toward exhaust port side of cylinder. Piston ring end gap should be 0.007-0.017 inch (0.18-0.43 mm). Piston pin is a light push fit in piston bosses and rides on a caged needle bearing in connecting rod. Pistons and rings are available in standard size only.

CRANKSHAFT AND BEARINGS. The one-piece cast crankshaft uses split crankpin bearings and center main bearing which are fit around the shaft and secured by bearing caps (Connecting rods) or housing bore. Bearing outer races are separated by "fracturing" to provide a perfect fit when carefully reassembled. Shaft journals serve as needle bearing inner races.

Examine shaft journals for scoring, ridging or heat discoloration and renew the bearings if shaft must be renewed. Shaft cannot be re-ground.

COOLING FAN AND DRIVE. Refer to Fig. 74 for an exploded view. The cooling fan is driven by a flat belt which drives from a slight recess machined into flywheel rim. Blades can be removed after raising hood and removing intake duct. To remove fan belt, it is first necessary to remove fan blades, fan guard (G—Fig. 74) and snowmobile drive belt. Belt tension (1/16-inch deflection) is adjusted by loosening locknut (L—Fig. 58) and turning eccentric shaft (E).

MANUAL STARTER. Refer to Fig. 75 for an exploded view. To remove the starter, first remove handle grip and tie a knot in pull rope. Remove the two retaining cap screws and lift off starter unit.

To remove the rope, remove the two bolts holding housing together and lift off spring housing and pulley unit. Cut new starter rope to a length of 73¾ inches. Wrap around pulley in clockwise direction while holding spring housing. Pre-load spring 2-2½ turns then reassemble by reversing disassembly procedure.

To renew the spring, remove "C" ring on outer end of pulley shaft and withdraw pulley, being careful spring does not fly out and cause injury. Hook inner spring eye of new spring in spring pin near pulley hub and feed flat spring coil out slot in rim of housing. Reinstall pulley and "C" ring, then turn pulley until spring is fully wound in pulley recess. Allow spring to relax then install pull rope. Renew other parts as required while starter is disassembled. Lubricate spring, pulley hub, bushings and other moving parts with a light coating of Lubriplate when reassembling.

ELECTRIC STARTER. Refer to Fig. 76 for an exploded view. Starter drive gear and helix should be cleaned and regreased using LUBRIPLATE 777 on both sides of gear each 50 hours.

If starter will turn engine at normal cranking speed with available voltage of 9.5-10.5, motor should be considered satisfactory. Starter no-load rpm should be 5750-8000 rpm with a current draw of 32 Amperes maximum. Brushes seat against END of commutator and seating surface can be turned in a lathe if required. Undercut mica to a depth of approximately 1/32-inch after resurfacing.

New brush length is 3/8-inch and brushes should be renewed in sets when any brush is worn to 1/8-inch. New springs are provided in brush kit and should be installed when brushes are renewed.

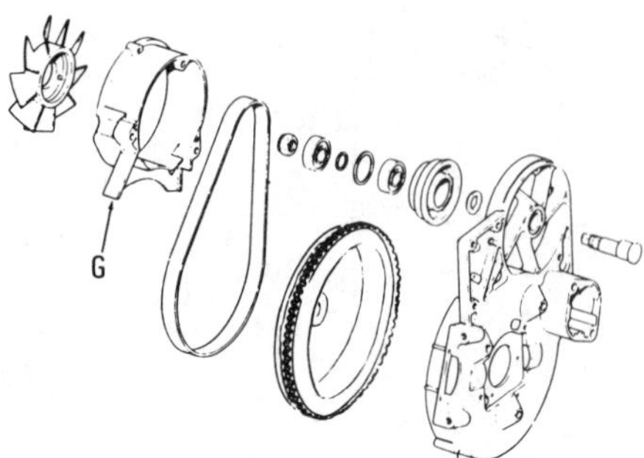

Fig. 74—Exploded view of cooling fan, housings and drive assembly. Fan blades, fan guard (G) and main drive belt must be removed for service on cooling fan belt.

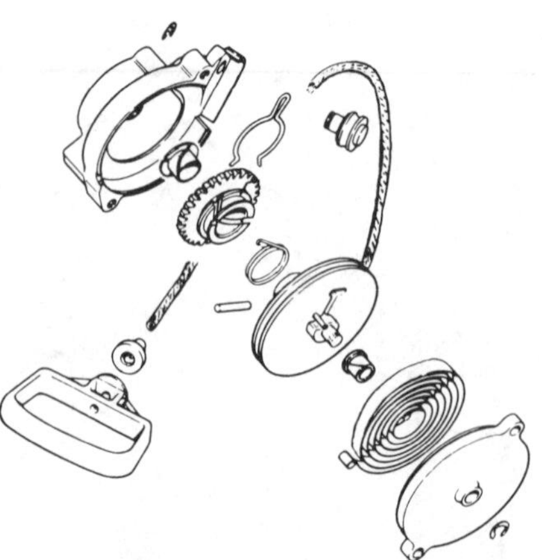

Fig. 75—Exploded view of manual starter showing component parts.

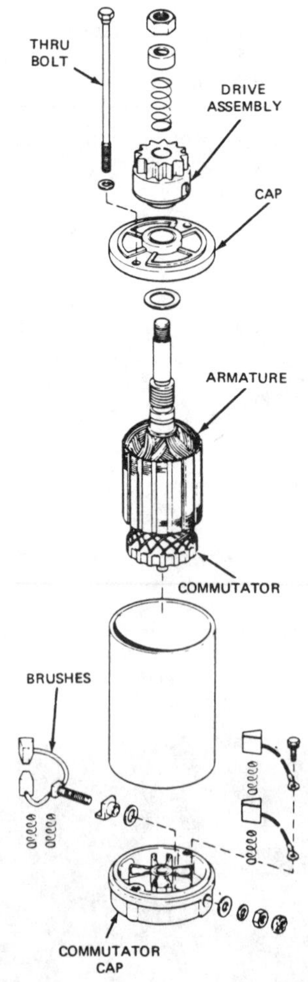

Fig. 76—Exploded view of electric starter showing component parts.

POLARIS

POLARIS INDUSTRIES INC.
1225 N. County Road 18
Minneapolis, MN 55441

The engine identification decal (Fig. 1) is attached to the engine crankcase. A six- or seven-digit code is used to identify the engine model. Subsequent numbers or letters may follow to distinguish engine variations. In the following CONDENSED SERVICE DATA tables, the engines are identified by the base designation when specifications are the same. The engine will be identified by the complete designation code when service specifications differ.

CONDENSED SERVICE DATA

ENGINE MODEL	EC17PM	EC25PC	EC25PM	EC25PS	EC25PS-05/06	EC25PT
Bore–mm	62	53.5	52.9	72	72	53.5
Inches	2.441	2.106	2.083	2.835	2.835	2.106
Stroke–mm	58	55.6	55.6	60	60	55.6
Inches	2.283	2.189	2.189	2.362	2.362	2.189
No. of Cylinders	1	2	2	1	1	2
Displacement–cc	175	250	244	244	244	250
Cubic Inches	10.7	15.2	14.9	14.9	14.9	15.2
Cooling Type	Cent. Fan	Free Air	Cent. Fan	Cent. Fan	Cent. Fan	Free Air
Ignition:						
Type	Magneto	Magneto	ET	Magneto	CD	CD
Point Gap–mm	0.28-0.43	0.28-0.43	0.35	0.35	.....	.....
Inch	0.011-0.017	0.011-0.017	0.014	0.014	.....	.....
Timing Advance?	No	Yes	Yes	Yes	Yes	Yes
Timing BTDC–						
mm	2.5	0.048	0.048	0.36	4.19	2.26
Inch	0.100	0.002	0.002	0.014	0.165	0.089
Degrees	.....	.....	3°	8°	27.5°	.....
Measured at	.....	Retard	Retard	Retard	See Text	Adv.
Spark Plug:						
AC	42XL	41XL	R42XL	R42XL	R42XL	41XL
Champion	N3	N2	RN3C	RN3C	RN3C	N2
NGK	B7ES	B9ES	BR8ES	BR8ES	BR8ES	B8ES
Electrode Gap–						
mm	0.38	0.5	0.5	0.5	0.5	0.5
Inch	0.015	0.020	0.020	0.020	0.020	0.020
Fuel:Oil Ratio	40:1	40:1	40:1	40:1	40:1	40:1
Fuel Grade	Reg.	Reg.	Reg.	Reg.	Reg.	Reg.

ENGINE MODEL	EC25PT-05/06	EC25PT-07	EC29PF	EC34PC	EC34PL-01	EC34PL-02/05
Bore–mm	53.4	53.4	58	62	61.8	61.8
Inches	2.101	2.101	2.283	2.441	2.433	2.433
Stroke–mm	55.6	55.6	55.6	55.6	55.6	55.6
Inches	2.189	2.189	2.189	2.189	2.189	2.189
No. of Cylinders	2	2	2	2	2	2
Displacement–cc	249	249	294	336	333	333
Cubic Inches	15.1	15.1	17.9	20.5	20.3	20.3
Cooling Type	Free Air	Free Air	Free Air	Free Air	Liquid	Liquid
Ignition:						
Type	CD	CD	ET	ET	CD	CD
Point Gap–mm	.....	.....	0.28-0.43	0.28-0.43	.....	.....
Inch	.....	.....	0.011-0.017	0.011-0.017	.....	.....
Timing Advance?	Yes	Yes	Yes	Yes	Yes	Yes

CONDENSED SERVICE DATA (Cont.)

ENGINE MODEL	EC25PT-05/06	EC25PT-07	EC29PF	EC34PC	EC34PL-01	EC34PL-02/05
Timing BTDC–						
mm	1.35	4.305	0.41	0.127	1.70	5.05
Inch	0.053	0.169	0.016	0.005	0.067	0.198
Degrees	.....	29°	8°	.....	.....	31.5°
Measured at	Adv.	See Text	Retard	Retard	Adv.	See Text
Spark Plug:						
AC	41XL	S41XLR	43XL	41XL	41XL	S41XLR
Champion	N2	RN2C	N3	N2	N2	RN2C
NGK	B9ES	BR9ES	B7ES	B8ES	B9ES	BR9ES
Electrode Gap–						
mm	0.5	0.5	0.45-0.50	0.5	0.5	0.5
Inch	0.020	0.020	0.017-0.020	0.020	0.020	0.020
Fuel:Oil Ratio	40:1	40:1	40:1	40:1	40:1	40:1
Fuel Grade	Reg.	Reg.	Reg.	Reg.	Reg.	Reg.

ENGINE MODEL	EC34PM	EC34PQ	EC34PS	EC34PT	EC34-2PM-01/02	EC40PL-02
Bore–mm	61.8	60	62	62	62	65
Inches	2.433	2.362	2.441	2.441	2.441	2.559
Stroke–mm	55.6	60	55.5	55.6	55.6	60
Inches	2.189	2.362	2.185	2.189	2.189	2.362
No. of Cylinders	2	2	2	2	2	2
Displacement–cc	333	339	335	336	336	398
Cubic Inches	20.3	20.7	20.4	20.5	20.5	24.3
Cooling Type	Cent. Fan	Cent. Fan	Free Air	Free Air	Cent. Fan	Liquid
Ignition:						
Type	ET	CD	CD	CD	CD	CD
Point Gap–mm	0.35	.....	.....	.....	.....	.....
Inch	0.014	.....	.....	.....	.....	.....
Timing Advance?	Yes	Yes	Yes	Yes	Yes	Yes
Timing BTDC–						
mm	0.048	2.25	3.04	1.35**	3.41	5.19
Inch	0.002	0.089	0.120	0.053**	0.134	0.204
Degrees	3°	.....	Marks	.....**	25.5°	30.5°
Measured at	Retard	Adv.	Adv.	Adv.**	See Text	See Text
Spark Plug:						
AC	42XL*	S42XL	41XL	S41XLR	S41XLR	S41XLR
Champion	N3*	N3	N2	RN2C	RN2C	RN2C
NGK	BR8ES*	B7ES	B8ES	BR9ES	BR9ES	BR9ES
Electrode Gap–						
mm	0.5	0.5	0.45-0.50	0.5	0.5	0.5
Inch	0.020	0.020	0.017-0.020	0.020	0.020	0.020
Fuel:Oil Ratio	40:1	20:1	20:1	40:1	40:1	40:1
Fuel Grade	Reg.	Prem.	Prem.	Prem.	Reg.	Reg.

*Applies to EC34PM-03 prior to 1981; 1981 Model EC34PM-03 should use Champion N2 or NGK BR9ES. All EC34PM-04 models should use Champion N2 or NGK BR9ES.

**Dynamic ignition timing for 1978, 1979 and 1980 models should be 4.29 mm (0.169 in.) at 3000 rpm.

ENGINE MODEL	EC40PM	EC44PM-01/02	EC44-2PM	EC44PQ	EC44PT	EC44PT-05
Bore–mm	65	67.72	67.72	67.75	67.75	67.75
Inches	2.559	2.656	2.656	2.667	2.667	2.667
Stroke–mm	60	60	60	60	60	60
Inches	2.362	2.362	2.362	2.362	2.362	2.362
No. of Cylinders	2	2	2	2	2	2
Displacement–cc	398	432	432	433	433	433
Cubic Inches	24.3	26.4	26.4	26.4	26.4	26.4
Cooling Type	Cent. Fan	Cent. Fan	Cent. Fan	Cent. Fan	Free Air	Free Air
Ignition:						
Type	ET	ET	CD	CD	CD	CD
Point Gap–mm	0.28-0.43	0.35	.....	.....	.....	.....
Inch	0.011-0.017	0.14	.....	.....	.....	.....
Timing Advance?	Yes	Yes	Yes	Yes	Yes	Yes

CONDENSED SERVICE DATA (Cont.)

ENGINE MODEL	EC40PM	EC44PM-01/02	EC44-2PM	EC44PQ	EC44PT	EC44PT-05
Timing BTDC–						
mm	0.47	0.05	3.93†	2.23	2.25	4.192
Inch	0.018	0.002	0.155†	0.088	0.089	0.164
Degrees	.....	3°	26.5°†	.....	.....	27.5°
Measured at	Retard	Retard	See Text	Adv.	Adv.	See Text
Spark Plug:						
AC	42XL	42XL	S41XLR	42XL	S40XL	41XL
Champion	N3	N3	RN2C	N3	N57	N2
NGK	B7ES	BR8ES	BR9ES	B7ES	B10E	BR9ES
Electrode Gap–						
mm	0.45-0.50	0.5	0.5	0.5	0.5	0.5
Inch	0.017-0.020	0.020	0.020	0.020	0.020	0.020
Fuel:Oil Ratio	40:1	40:1	40:1	40:1	20:1	40:1
Fuel Grade	Reg.	Reg.	Reg.	Reg.	Prem.	Reg.

†Ignition timing for Model EC44-2PM-5100 should be 3.40 mm (0.134 in.) or 24½° at 3000 rpm.

ENGINE MODEL	EC44PT-06	EC50PM	EC51PL	EC51PT	EC60PL
Bore–mm	67.75	72	61.78	62	65
Inches	2.667	2.835	2.432	2.441	2.559
Stroke–mm	60	60	55.6	55.5	60
Inches	2.362	2.362	2.189	2.185	2.362
No. of Cylinders	2	2	3	3	3
Displacement–cc	433	488	500	502.6	597
Cubic Inches	26.4	29.7	30.5	30.6	36
Cooling Type	Free Air	Cent. Fan	Liquid	Free Air	Liquid
Ignition:					
Type	CD	CD	CD	CD	CD
Point Gap–mm	.....	.....	.....	.....	.....
Inch	.....	.....	.....	.....	.....
Timing Advance?	Yes	Yes	Yes	Yes	Yes
Timing BTDC–					
mm	1.45	3.26	3.748	2.05	4.10
Inch	0.057	0.128	0.147	0.081	0.162
Degrees	.....	24.0°	27.0°	.....	27°
Measured at	Adv.	See Text	See Text	Adv.	See Text
Spark Plug:					
AC	41XL	S41XLR	41XLR	S41XL	S41XLR
Champion	N2	RN2C	N2	N2	RN2C
NGK	B9ES	BR9ES	BR9ES	B8ES	BR9ES
Electrode Gap–					
mm	0.5	0.5	0.5	0.5	0.5
Inch	0.020	0.020	0.020	0.020	0.020
Fuel:Oil Ratio	40:1	40:1	40:1	20:1	40:1
Fuel Grade	Reg.	Reg.	Reg.	Prem.	Reg.

MAINTENANCE

All Models

SPARK PLUG. Recommended spark plugs are given in CONDENSED SERVICE DATA tables. Refer also to spark plug data in SERVICE FUNDAMENTALS section of this manual.

CARBURETOR. Mikuni slide type carburetors are used on most models. Refer to CARBURETOR SERVICE section of this manual for general overhaul data.

Fuel level is adjusted by bending tang (A–Fig. 2) on float lever after removing fuel bowl and inverting carburetor body. Float arms (C) must be parallel with gasket surface of carburetor body and equal in height.

Normal jetting, needle clip position and throttle cutaway are given in TABLE I.

Main jet size recommendations are for 1000 ft. altitude and 0°F (–17°C). Decrease jet size 10 for each 3000 ft. increase in altitude or for each 20° increase in ambient temperature. Increase jet size 10 for each 20° drop in temperature below 0°F (–17°C).

All carburetors on one engine must be very carefully adjusted to provide equal fuel mixture and volume throughout the operating range. DO NOT use too small a jet for existing temperature and altitude conditions.

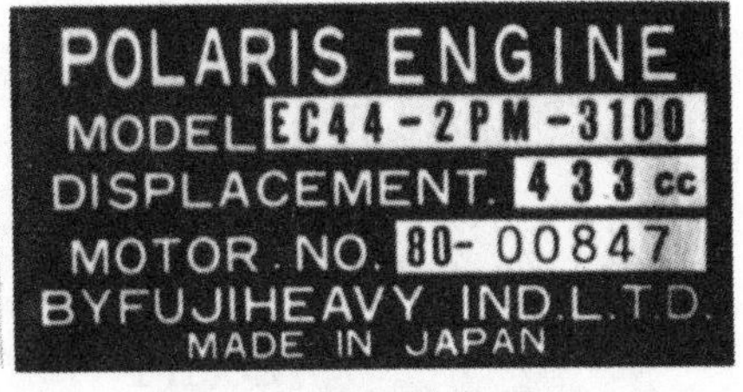

Fig. 1–Typical engine identification decal located on engine crankcase.

TABLE 1—CARBURETOR SETTINGS

Engine Model	Year	Carburetor No. & Model	Jet Size Main	Jet Size Pilot	Clip Position	Throttle Cut-away
EC17PM	1974-1976	1-VM24SH	102.5	35	3	2.0
EC25PC	1972	2-VM26SS	110	35	3	3.0
EC25PC	1975	2-VM26SS	105	35	3	3.0
EC25PC	1976-1978	2-VM26SS	112.5	35	3	3.0
EC25PM-01	1977	2-VM26SS	130	35	2	2.5
EC25PM-01	1979-1980	2-VM26SS	120	35	2	2.5
EC25PS	1974-1976	1-VM30SH	125	35	4	3.0
EC25PS	1977-1979	1-VM30SH	117.5	35	4	3.0
EC25PS	1980-1981	1-VM30SS	120	60	2	3.0
EC25PS	1983	1-VM30SS	130	60	3	3.0
E25PS-05/06	1984-1986	1-VM30SS	130	60	3	3.0
EC25PT	1974	2-VM30SS	125	35	3	3.0
EC25PT	1975	2-VM30SS	120	35	3	3.0
EC25PT-05	1976	2-VM32SS	230	35	3	2.0
EC25PT-06	1976	2-VM32SS	260	30	3	2.0
EC25PT-07	1977-1979	2-VM30SS	220	35	3	2.5
EC29PF	1974	2-VM26SH	115	35	3	3.0
EC34PC	1974	2-VM26SH	125	35	3	3.0
EC34PC	1975	2-VM26SS	112.5	35	3	3.0
EC34PC	1976	2-VM26SS	107.5	35	3*	3.0
EC34PL-01	1977	2-VM38SS	340	45	3	2.5
EC34PL-02	1978	2-VM38SS	310	45	3	2.5
EC34PL-02/05	1979-1982	2-VM38SS	260	45	3	2.5
EC34PL-05	1983	2-VM38SS	260	40	3	2.5
EC34PM-03	1977	2-VM26SS	150	35	2	2.5
EC34PM-03	1979-1980	2-VM26SS	130	35	2	2.5
EC34PM-03	1981	2-VM26SS	130	30	3	2.5
EC34PM-04/04N	1978	2-VM26SS	130	35	3	3.0
EC34PM-04	1979	2-VM26SS	130	35	2	3.0
EC34PM-04	1980	2-VM26SS	110	35	2	3.0
EC34PQ	1974	1-VM32SS	125	40	4	2.0
EC34PQ	1975-1977	2-VM30SS	122.5	30	4	2.0
EC34PS	1974	2-VM30SS	127.5	35	3	3.0
EC34PT-05	1976	2-VM32SS	270	30	3	2.0
EC34PT-05	1977-1978	2-VM32SS	280	30	3	2.0
EC34PT-05	1979	2-VM32SS	290	30	2	2.0
EC34PT-06	1976	2-VM34SS	270	30	3	1.5
EC34PT-07	1980	2-VM32SS	280	30	2	2.0
EC34-2PM-01/02	1986	2-VM30SS	145	35	3	3.0
EC40PL-02	1985	2-VM34SS	220	35	2	3.0
EC40PL-02	1986	2-VM34SS	220	30	2	2.0
EC40PM	1974	2-VM30SH	120	40	3	3.0
EC44PM-01/02	1978-1981	2-VM34SS	200	35	3	2.5
EC44-2PM-1100	1981-1982	2-VM34SS	270	35	3	3.5
EC44-2PM-2100	1984-1985	2-VM34SS	230	35	2	3.0
EC44-2PM-3100*	1981-1982	1-VM38SS	290	40	3	2.0
EC44-2PM-3100*	1982-1986	1-VM34SS	280	40	3	2.5
EC44-2PM-3300	1981	1-VM38SS	290	40	3	2.0
EC44-2PM-5000	1983	1-VM30SS	190	35	3	2.5
EC44-2PM-5000	1984-1985	1-VM30SS	200	30	3	2.5
EC44-2PM-5100	1983	1-VM30SS	190	35	3	2.5
EC44-2PM-5100	1986	1-VM30SS	200	30	3	2.5
EC44PQ	1974	1-VM38SS	135	40	3	3.0
EC44PQ	1975-1976	2-VM30SS	125	25	3	3.0
EC44PQ	1977	2-VM30SS	115	25	3	3.0
EC44PT	1974	2-VM38SS	135	35	4	1.5
EC44PT	1975	2-VM38SS	140	40	4	1.5
EC44PT-05	1976-1977	2-VM34SS	320	35	3	2.5
EC44PT-05	1978	2-VM34SS	370	45	3	2.5
EC44PT-05	1979-1980	2-VM34SS	320	30	2	2.5
EC44PT-06	1977	2-VM34SS	320	35	3	2.5
EC50PM-01	1986	2-VM34SS	210	30	2	3.0
EC51PL-01/02	1979-1982	3-VM34SS	220	35	2	3.0
EC51PT	1974	3-VM32SS	117.5	35	4	2.5
EC51PT	1975	3-VM32SS	120	40	5	2.5
EC60PL-01/02	1983-1984	3-VM38SS	250	40	3	3.5
EC60PL-02	1985-1986	3-VM38SS	260	35	3	3.0

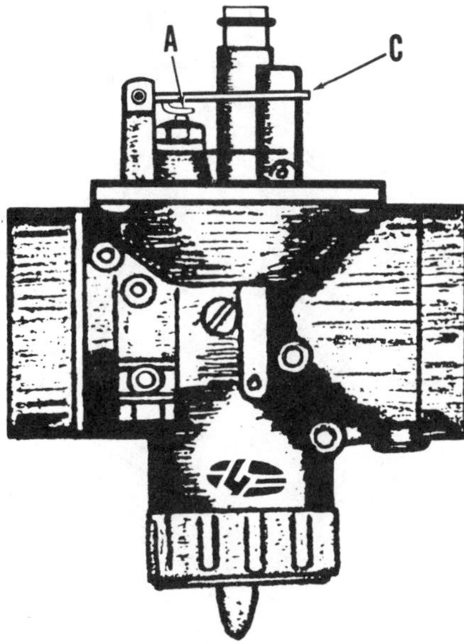

Fig. 2—With carburetor throttle body inverted and inlet needle valve closed, bend tab (A) if necessary until float arms (C) are parallel with gasket surface of body as shown.

Fig. 4—Install dial indicator in spark plug hole and zero the dial when piston is at top dead center. Connect timing light or buzzer to correct coil lead and to a suitable ground as shown in lower view.

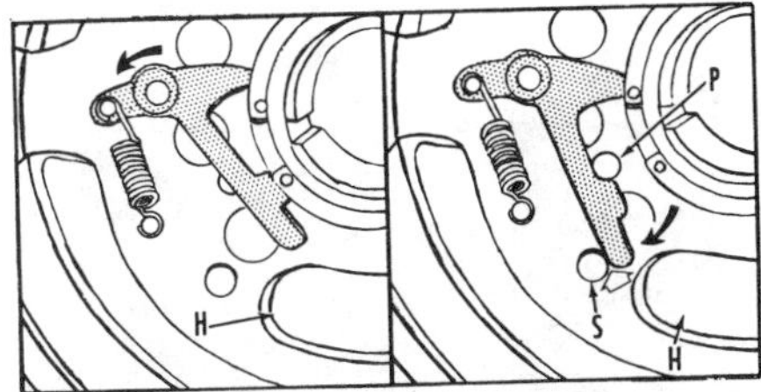

Fig. 5—Inside view of flywheel showing centrifugal weights in retarded position (left-hand view) and advance position (right-hand view). Note that weight contacts stop pin (S) at full advance. Starting pulley bolt hole (P) can be used to block weight in advanced position as outlined in text.

Fig. 6—Arrow shows timing marks etched on fan housing of some units with CD ignition.

IGNITION AND TIMING. Breaker point gap and timing specifications are given in CONDENSED SERVICE DATA tables. Recommended timing procedure is by using a dial indicator and timing light or buzzer as shown in Fig. 3. To time the engine, remove both spark plugs, recoil starter and primary wire connections from coil(s). Set breaker point gap for single cylinder engine or number 2 cylinder breaker points (identified by WHITE lead wires on points and condenser) on twin cylinder engines, to 0.014 inch (0.35 mm).

Install dial indicator and, with piston at top dead center, zero indicator dial as shown in Top View—Fig. 4. On two cylinder models, number 2 cylinder (clutch side of engine) should be timed first.

Attach one lead of the timing light or buzzer to a suitable ground on engine or magneto backing plate. Attach the other lead to RED coil lead on single cylinder engine; or WHITE lead on twin cylinder engine. (Red lead on twin cylinder engine goes to number 1 cylinder ignition coil). Working from magneto end, turn crankshaft counterclockwise beyond the point of correct timing, then clockwise slowly until light dims or buzzer changes tone. Note dial indicator reading at this time. Dial indicator will show fixed timing on 175cc single or static (retarded) timing on other models, as determined by piston position. Retarded timing is shown in CONDENSED SERVICE DATA tables.

Fig. 3—Use a dial indicator and timing light of buzzer to find piston position when breaker points open and spark occurs.

Advanced (or running) timing can be checked by blocking governor weights in running position as follows: Reach through timing window (H—Fig. 5) with finger and move governor weight outward until it contacts stop pin (S) as shown in right-hand view. Thread a suitable cap screw into rope starting pulley hole (P) to block governor weight and cam in advanced (running) position, then time as previously outlined, using the following advanced timing settings.

EC25PS	0.115 inch	2.96 mm
EC25PC	0.067 inch	1.69 mm
EC25PM	0.067 inch	1.69 mm
EC29PF	0.135 inch	3.37 mm
EC34PC	0.082 inch	2.10 mm
EC34PM	0.067 inch	1.69 mm
EC40PM	0.142 inch	3.60 mm
EC44PM	0.072 inch	1.83 mm

To adjust the timing, loosen the two screws in slotted holes securing stator plate (1—Fig. 16) to cylinder block and move the plate counterclockwise to ADVANCE the timing or clockwise to RETARD the timing. With timing adjusted for number 2 cylinder (twin cylinder engines), vary the point gap on number 1 cylinder until timing is EXACTLY the same for both cylinders. Point gap on number 1 cylinder when adjustment is completed, should be within the limits of 0.011-0.017 inch (0.3-0.4 mm). If gap is not within specified limits, reset within limits, then readjust breaker plate to correct timing position. Finally, reset

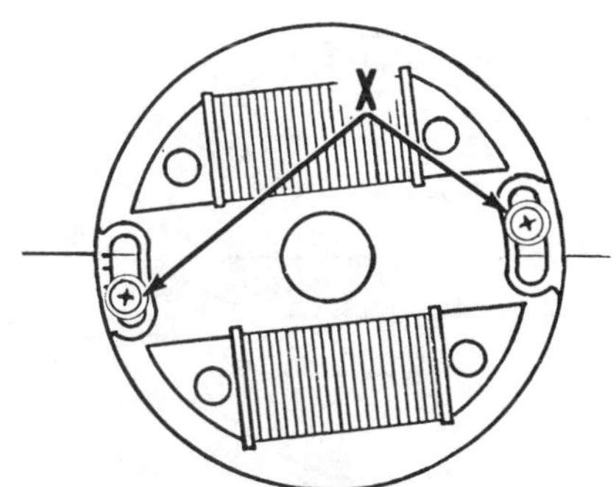

Fig. 7—Timing is adjusted on CD ignition models by loosening stator screws (X) and turning stator plate.

Fig. 8—Liquid-cooled Model EC34PL, timing is checked by removing coolant pump housing and checking from exhaust side using a power timing light.

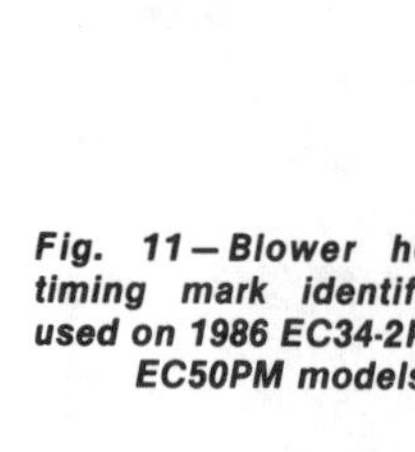

Fig. 11—Blower housing timing mark identification used on 1986 EC34-2PM and EC50PM models.

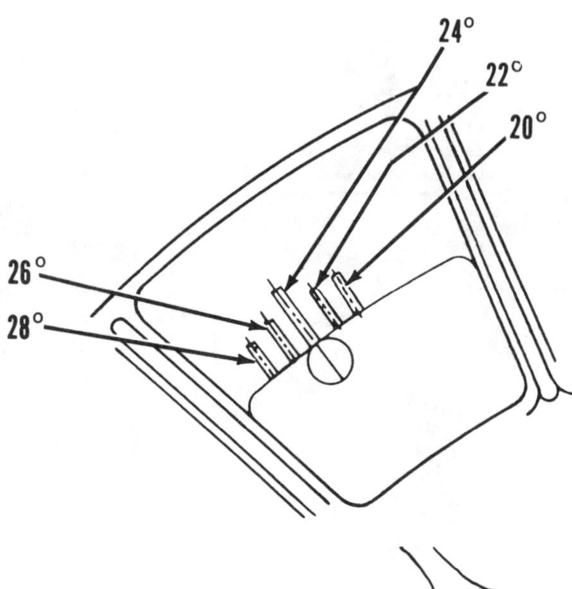

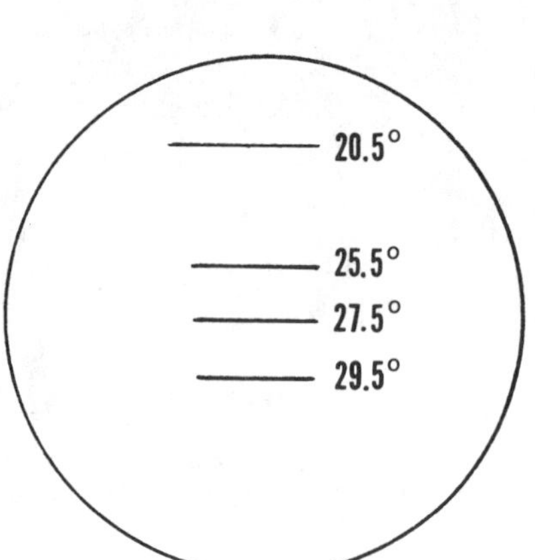

Fig. 9—Flywheel timing mark identification used on single-cylinder models equipped with CD ignition system.

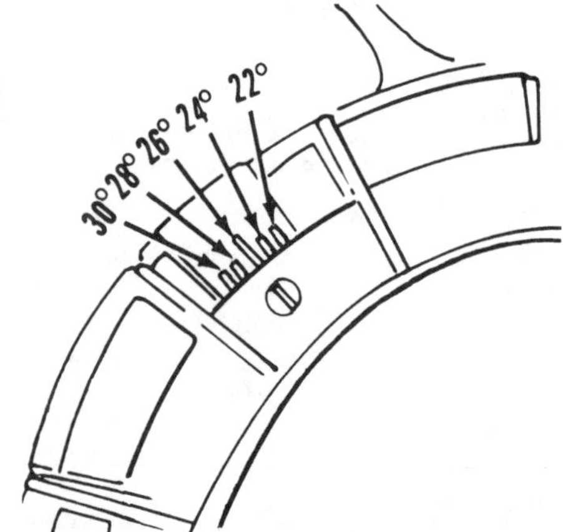

Fig. 13—Blower housing timing mark identification used on 1981 and later EC44-2PM models.

points for number 2 cylinder until timing is correct and equal, and gap range is within specifications for both cylinders.

On models with CD ignition systems, (Figs. 17, 18 and 19), spark plugs fire simultaneously. Two cylinder models fire twice each crankshaft revolution and three cylinder models fire three times. Spark advance is electronic, with no mechanical governor. CD timing is checked with a power timing light at running speed. On all models before 1978, paint timing marks on flywheel and housing (or use previous marks) using a dial indicator to find piston position as shown in Fig. 3. Timing specifications are given in CONDENSED SERVICE DATA tables. Remove belt and drive clutch, attach power timing light, then increase engine speed to 5000 rpm momentarily to check timing mark alignment. Timing light may be attached to either spark plug lead and only one cylinder need be checked.

To adjust the timing, remove starter cup and, working through timing windows, loosen the two screws (X–Fig. 7) which secure stator plate to crankcase. Turn stator plate counterclockwise to advance the timing or clockwise to retard timing. Timing given in CONDENSED SERVICE DATA tables is the maximum recommended, but timing may vary 0.020 inch (0.51 mm) toward retard.

All 1978 and later models with CD ignition have degree timing marks scribed on outer rim of flywheel. A timing port is located on carburetor side of magneto housing on all models except liquid cooled EC34PL-02 and 05. On EC34PL-02 and 05, timing is checked from exhaust side after removing water pump cover, using machined top surface of magneto housing as a timing pointer as shown in Fig. 8. Refer to CONDENSED SERVICE DATA section for timing specifications and to the appropriate illustrated view (Figs. 9 through 14) for timing mark identification. On all 1978 and later models with

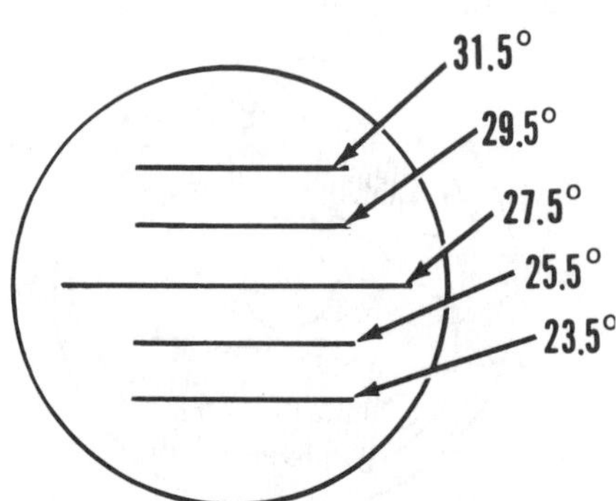

Fig. 10—Flywheel timing mark identification used on 1978 and later EC25PT, EC34PT and EC44PT models.

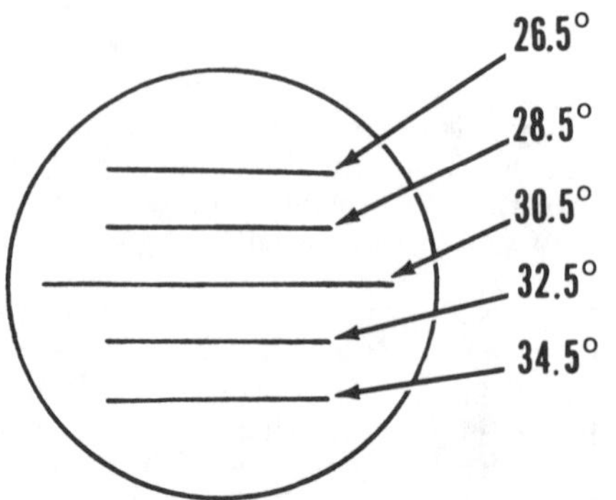

Fig. 12—Flywheel timing mark identification used on 1985 and later EC40PL models.

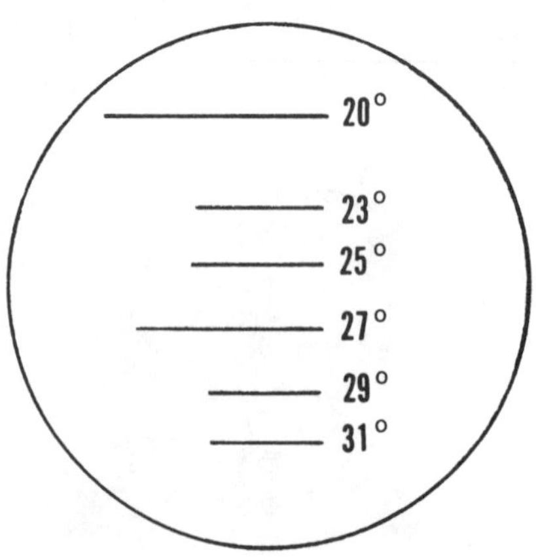

Fig. 14—Flywheel timing mark identification used on EC51PL and EC60PL models.

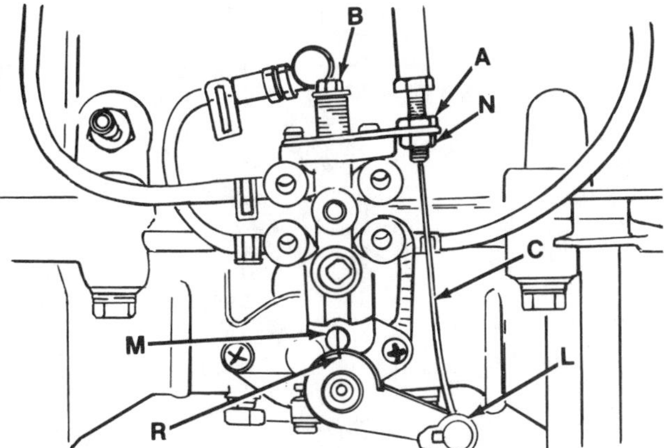

Fig. 15—View of oil injection pump showing adjustment and bleed screw locations.

A. Adjusting nut
B. Bleed screw
C. Cable
L. Control lever
M. Stationary mark
N. Locknut
R. Reference mark

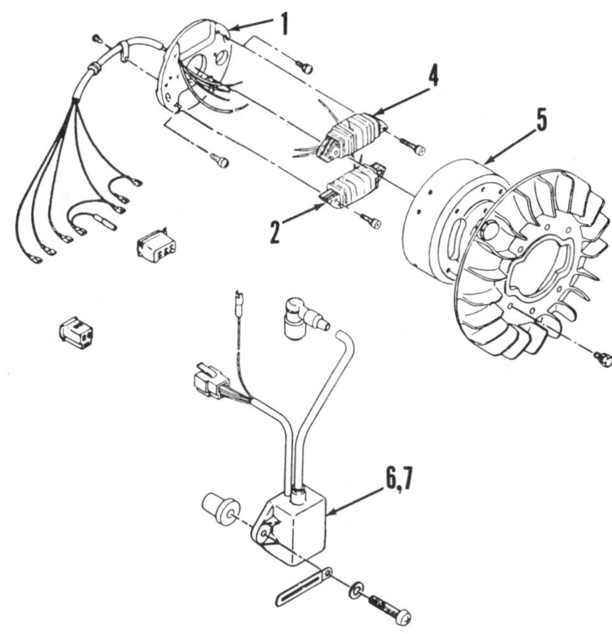

Fig. 17—Exploded view of CD ignition system used on EC25PS-05 and EC25PS-06 models. Refer to Fig. 19 for parts identification.

CD ignition, timing is checked with the engine running at 3000 rpm.

On EC34-2PM models, the stator plate has been omitted and ignition timing is fixed and not adjustable. If timing is not within the limits of 22°-28° BTDC then CDI module, excitor coil and flywheel should be inspected and renewed if defective. On all remaining models, adjust the timing by removing recoil starter and starter cup, then loosening stator mounting screws (X–Fig. 7) and turning stator plate as required. Stator mounting slot on carburetor side of 1978 and later models has three timing scribe marks as shown. The upper scribe mark aligns with crankcase parting line as shown to static time engine Models EC34PL-02 and 05. Center scribe mark is factory setting for EC25PT-07 and EC34PT-05 and 07, while lower line is factory setting for EC44PT-05.

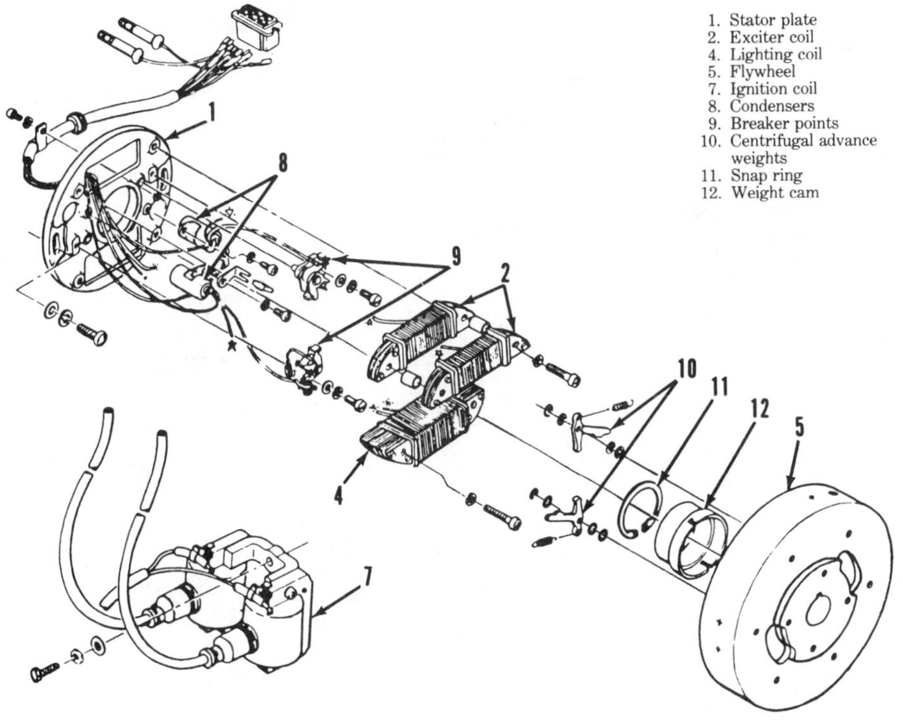

On all models, recheck timing after adjustment then securely tighten stator attaching screws. Reassemble removed components by reversing removal procedure.

LUBRICATION. Polaris snowmobile engines are lubricated by either an injection pump or a fuel premixture of oil and gasoline. Recommended oils are Polaris Injection Oil on oil injected models and Polaris Snowmobile Oil on premixture models. Recommended fuel grade is regular leaded or premium unleaded gasoline.

New or overhauled engines require additional lubrication during break-in. On oil injected models, the first tank of fuel must contain a 40:1 fuel:oil premixture in conjunction with oil injection to ensure adequate lubrication. On premixture models, increase fuel:oil ratio to 20:1 for the first tank of fuel. After break-in, recommended fuel:oil ratio for normal operation is 40:1 on all premixture models.

Mix fuel and oil thoroughly in a separate container before pouring the mixture into fuel tank. Fuel should preferably be mixed at normal room temperature; for outdoor mixing at cold temperatures, mix the oil with a small amount of gasoline until oil is fluid, then add remainder of fuel and remix. **DO** NOT use kerosene or diesel fuel as a blending agent.

On models equipped with oil injection system, a separate oil tank and metering system is used. The system delivers varying amounts of oil depending upon engine rpm and throttle setting (load).

1. Stator plate
2. Exciter coil
4. Lighting coil
5. Flywheel
7. Ignition coil
8. Condensers
9. Breaker points
10. Centrifugal advance weights
11. Snap ring
12. Weight cam

Fig. 16—Exploded view of twin-cylinder magneto ignition system. Energy transfer (ET) ignition system is similar.

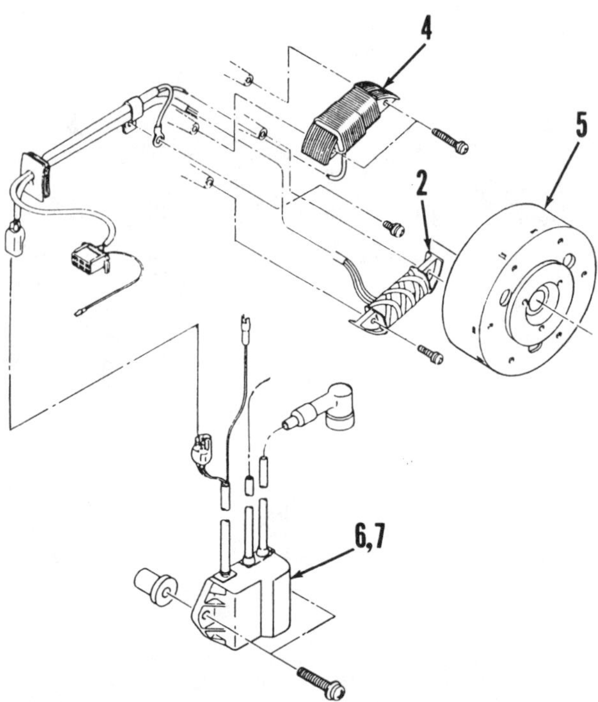

Fig. 18—Exploded view of CD ignition system used on EC34-2PM-02 and EC-34-2PM-02 models. Refer to Fig. 19 for parts identification.

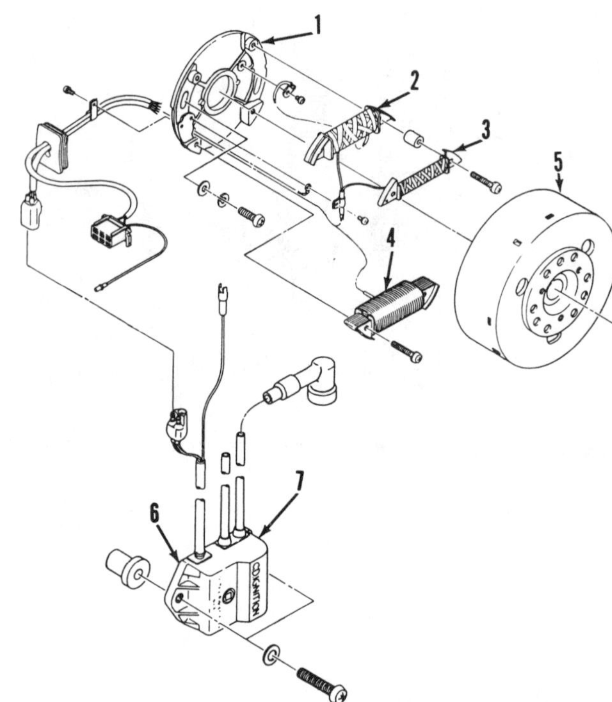

Fig. 20—Exploded view of CD ignition system used on EC40PL models. Ignition used on EC34-2PM, EC44-2PM and EC50PM models is similar. Refer to Fig. 19 for parts identification.

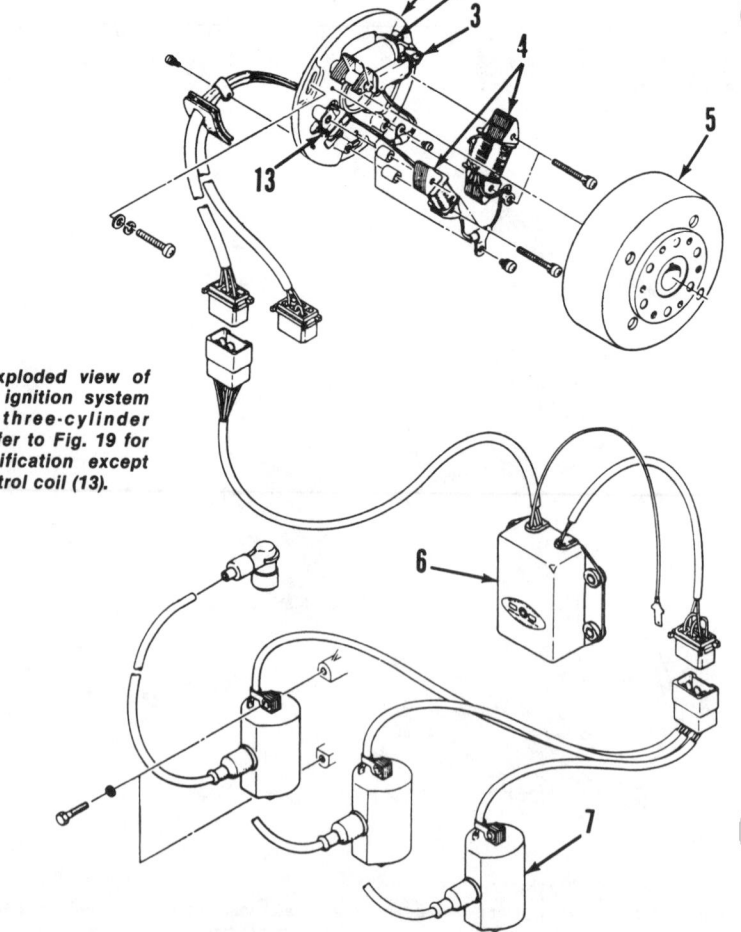

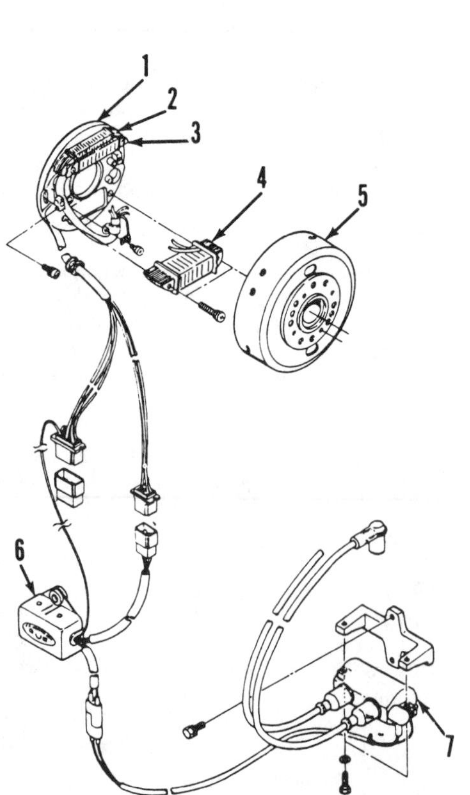

Fig. 19—Exploded view of typical CD ignition system used on twin-cylinder engines except for models shown in Fig. 20.

1. Stator plate
2. Excitor coil
3. Pulser coil
4. Lighting coil
5. Flywheel
6. CDI module
7. Ignition coil

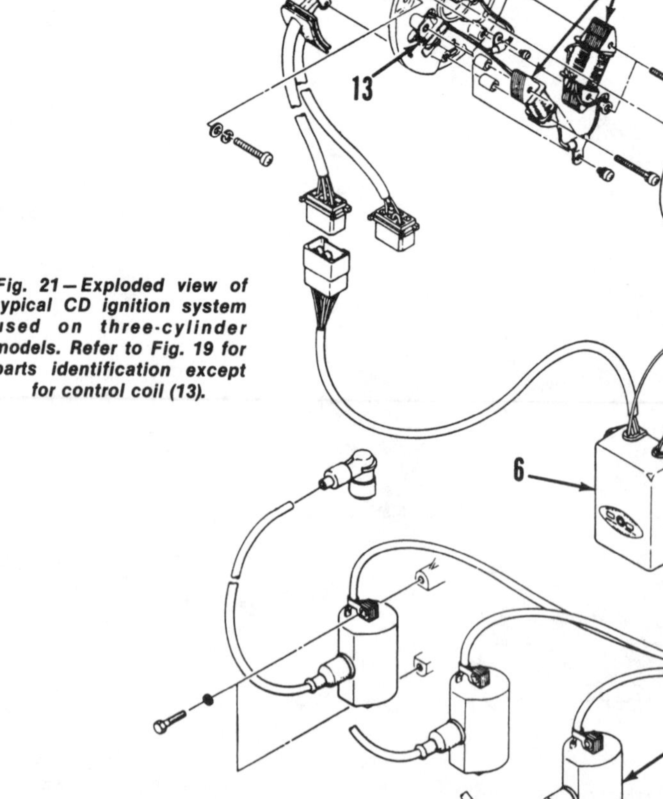

Fig. 21—Exploded view of typical CD ignition system used on three-cylinder models. Refer to Fig. 19 for parts identification except for control coil (13).

Oil delivery is controlled by cable (C–Fig. 15) attached to pump control lever (L) at one end and carburetor throttle lever at other end. Oil injection pump should be adjusted after all carburetor adjustments are complete. With the throttle at idle, reference mark (R) on pump lever should align with stationary mark (M). To adjust pump, loosen locknut (N) and turn adjuster nut (A).

Any operation that required draining or repair of oil injection components will make it necessary to fill and bleed system. Check oil reservoir fluid level before proceeding and fill with Polaris injector oil or a manufacturer approved equivalent.

Bleed air from injection pump before running engine. To bleed injection pump, loosen bleeder screw (B–Fig. 15) until air-free oil flows from around screw then retighten screw. Disconnect oil supply hoses at the carburetor or manifold being careful not to lose washers. Reinstall banjo bolts without the hoses but do not tighten bolts. Ensure oil hoses are positioned away from clutch area. Start engine and run at idle speed only. Rotate oil pump lever counterclockwise to maximum output position and observe oil discharge rate. After 1-2 minutes of operation, a consistent drop of oil every few seconds should drip from each hose. If an oil injection malfunction occurs, carefully inspect check valves in banjo fittings, hoses and inline filter and renew defective components. Renew the complete oil injection pump assembly if required.

FUEL PUMP. The pulse type diaphragm fuel pump is actuated by pressure and vacuum pulsations in crankcase. Air should flow freely in normal direction of fuel flow but pump should hold 11 psi (76 kPa) when fuel flow is reversed. All parts are available individually.

REPAIRS

Air-Cooled Models

TIGHTENING TORQUES. Recommended tightening torques are as follows:

	Ft.-Lbs.	N·m
Crankcase:		
EC17P	12	16.2
EC25P	20	27.1
All Other Models–		
8 mm screws	18	24.4
10 mm screws	25	33.8
Cylinder Head:		
All Models	18	24.5
Flywheel:		
All Models	65	88.1

ENERGY TRANSFER IGNITION SYSTEM. Point gap can be adjusted working through flywheel. To renew points, condensers or magneto coils, flywheel must be removed. Refer to Fig. 16

TABLE 2–CD IGNITION COIL TEST SPECIFICATIONS (Air-Cooled)

	EXCITER COIL		PULSER COIL	
ONE-CYLINDER MODELS	Check Position	Resistance Reading	Check Position	Resistance Reading
1984-1986 Star and Star LT	Brown/White to Black/Red	123 Ohms	.....	.....
TWO-CYLINDER MODELS				
1986 Sprint	Brown/White to Black/Red	225 Ohms	.....	.....
1986 Indy Trail	Brown/White to White	164 Ohms	Brown/White to Black/Red	17 Ohms
1983-1986 Long Track 1983-1985 Indy Trail 1983 Sport 1982-1986 SS 1981-1982 Cutlass SS 1981 Galaxy	Brown/White to Black/Red	164 Ohms	Brown/White to Black/Red	45 Ohms
1979-1980 TX-C 1978-1980 TX	Brown/White to White	114 Ohms	Brown/White to Black	63 Ohms
1977 TX-L 1976 Starfire 1975-1977 TX	Black to White	246 Ohms	Brown/White to Black	61 Ohms
1972-1977, except models listed above	Black to White	192 Ohms	Brown/White to Black	24 Ohms
THREE-CYLINDER MODELS				
1974-1975 TX	Red to Ground	275 Ohms	White to Red	42 Ohms

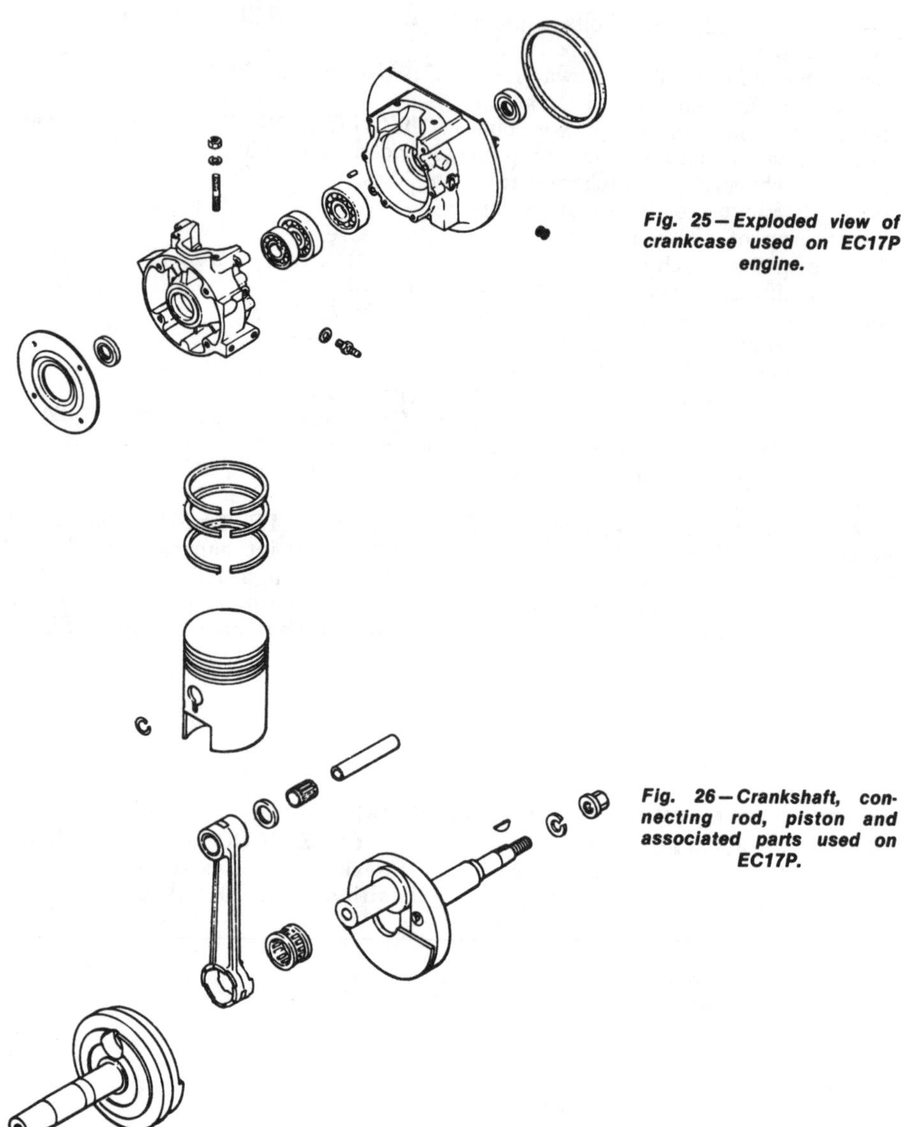

Fig. 25—Exploded view of crankcase used on EC17P engine.

Fig. 26—Crankshaft, connecting rod, piston and associated parts used on EC17P.

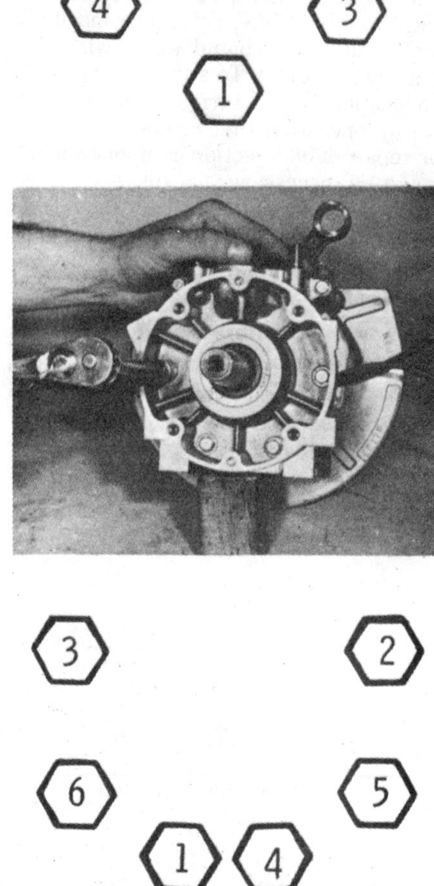

Fig. 28—Crankcase tightening sequence for single cylinder engines. Tighten the six cap screws on E17P engine to 12 ft.-lbs. using sequence shown in lower view. On EC25P engine tighten the five cap screws to 20 ft.-lbs. as in upper view.

for an exploded view of ET ignition system. On two-cylinder models, ignition components for each cylinder are entirely independent from the other cylinder and each must be timed separately to fire 180 degrees apart.

CAPACITOR DISCHARGE IGNITION SYSTEM. Refer to Figs. 17, 18, 19, 20 and 21 for an exploded view of CD ignition systems used on models so equipped. On all models except EC25PS-05, EC25PS-06, EC34-2PM-01 and EC34-2PM-02 engines used in Star, Star LT and Sprint models, ignition exciter and pulser coils are mounted together and are similar in appearance to ignition generating coils of ET system. On Star, Star LT and Sprint models, the pulser coil is integrated with the exciter coil (2–Fig. 17 or 18).

The exciter coil and pulser coil may be tested without removal from engine using a suitable ohmmeter. Separate wiring from exciter and pulser coils to CDI module at connector. Refer to TABLE 2 for vehicle application, check position and resistance reading specifications. If ohm reading is not within 10 percent of test specification, coil may be considered defective and should be renewed.

The CD ignition system used on 1973-1975 TX models also has a control coil. An ohmmeter should indicate 18 ohms when connected to coil leads.

ENGINE R&R. Standard engine removal procedures apply. When installing, make sure pulley shaft centers are properly adjusted and sheaves are cor-

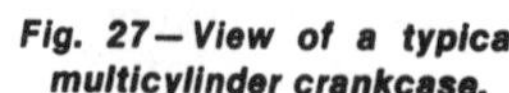

Fig. 27—View of a typical multicylinder crankcase.

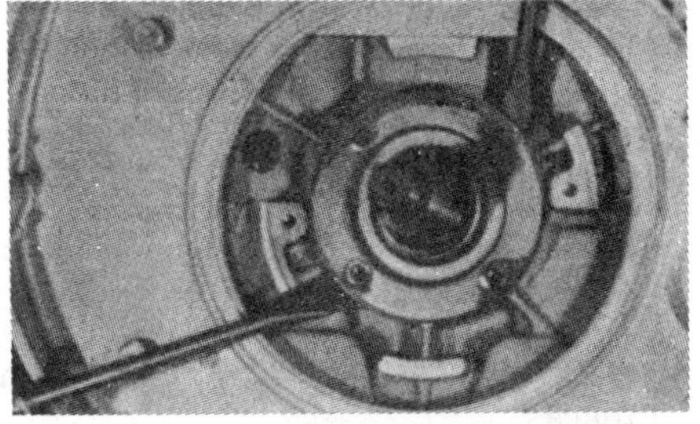

Fig. 29—Two screwdrivers can be used as shown to work out flywheel end seal housing.

rectly aligned as outlined in VEHICLE section. Tighten motor mount nuts to 55 ft.-lbs. (74.5 N·m) torque.

DISASSEMBLY AND REASSEMBLY. Recoil starter and fan housing can be removed as an assembly during engine service. The factory recommended flywheel puller is secured to the threaded holes for manual starter cup. Exploded views of typical single-cylinder engine are shown in Figs. 25 and 26. View of a typical multi-cylinder crankcase is shown in Fig. 27. Conventional disassembly and assembly methods are used.

Stator plate piston should be marked prior to removal to aid in reassembly. On two- and three-cylinder models, remove the four stud nuts and use two screwdrivers to pry off flywheel side oil seal housing using fan housing as a fulcrum as shown in Fig. 29. Turn drive end seal housing by tapping corners with

Fig. 30—Tap lightly on ears of drive end seal housing to loosen gasket. Housing can be lifted off after crankcase is separated.

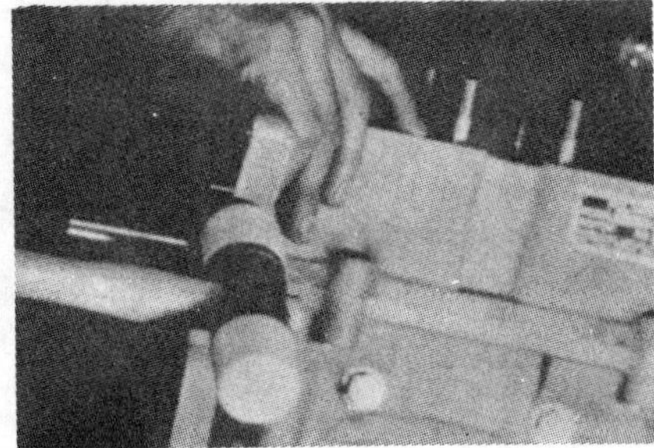

Fig. 31—Tap on fan housing bosses as shown to loosen crankcase bond.

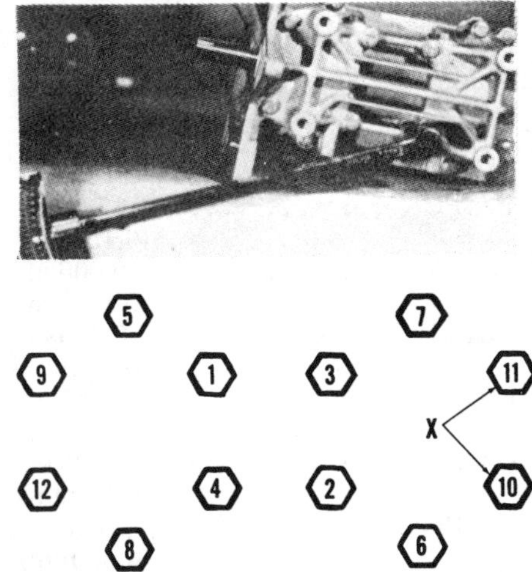

Fig. 32—On two-cylinder engines, tighten crankcase screws in sequence shown. The two drive end screws (X) are 10 mm, remainder are 8 mm screws.

a hammer as shown in Fig. 30, to loosen gasket.

On models equipped with oil-injection, detach oil lines at intake manifold. Be careful not to lose washers on either side of banjo fittings. Disconnect oil pump control cable at pump and oil line from pump to crankcase at crankcase. Plug all openings in oil-injection system to prevent the entrance of dirt or other foreign material. Unbolt and withdraw pump from crankcase.

New pistons, cylinders and cylinder heads are interchangeable on all engines except EC44-2PM engines. On EC44-2PM engines, new pistons and cylinder heads are interchangeable but the cylinders are directionally marked and should not be interchanged. The base flange of each cylinder is marked with either a number 1 or a number 2. The

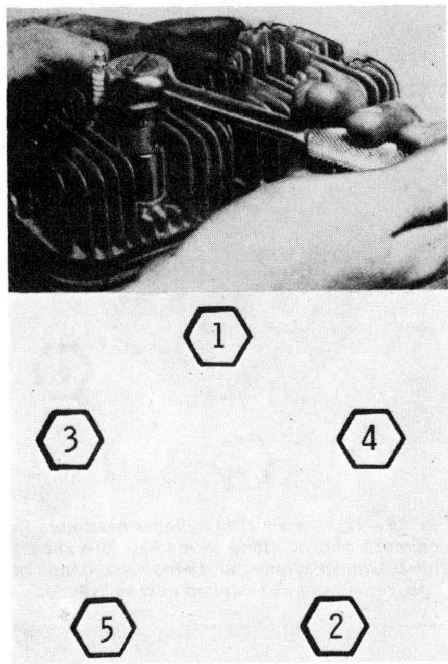

Fig. 34—On five-stud cylinder head, tighten stud nuts in sequence shown. Refer also to Fig. 21 for proper positioning of head gasket.

number 1 marked cylinder is installed towards flywheel end of crankshaft while number 2 marked cylinder is installed towards drive end of crankshaft. On all models, used parts should not be intermixed.

Remove fan housing and crankcase screws, then break sealant bond by tapping fan housing bosses with a plastic hammer as shown in Fig. 31.

When reassembling, coat labyrinth seal between crankshaft center bearings with nonfibrous grease. Coat both crankcase flanges with a good non-hardening sealer and join the halves.

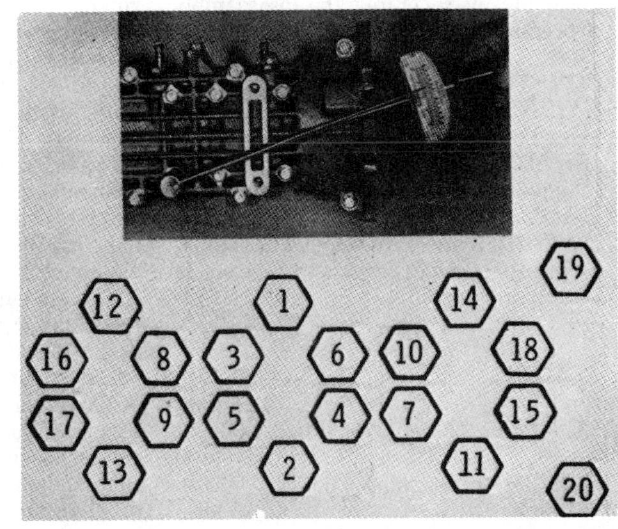

Fig. 33—On air-cooled, three-cylinder engines, tighten crankcase screws in sequence shown.

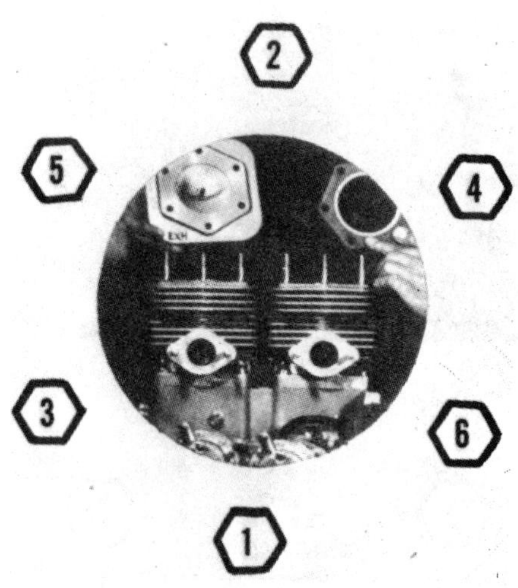

Fig. 35 – Tighten six-stud cylinder head nuts in sequence shown. Head is marked for exhaust side as shown in inset, and wide metal flange of gasket should be installed next to cylinder.

Tighten cap screws finger tight then tap firmly on pto end of crankshaft to move all slack toward fanwheel end of crankcase. Tighten crankcase screws in the sequence shown in Fig. 32 or 33, the two 10 mm screws (X) being tightened to 25 ft.-lbs. (33.8 N·m) and remainder to 18 ft.-lbs. (24.5 N·m). The "F" or arrow mark on piston crown must be installed toward fan side of crankcase. Install cylinders using new gaskets, being sure exhaust ports are to front (opposite fuel pump boss). Tighten stud nuts finger tight, then install and tighten exhaust manifold to align the cylinders before tightening cylinder stud nuts. Install cylinder heads and tighten stud nuts in two stages using the sequence shown in Fig. 34 or 35. Note that wide metal flange of head gasket is installed down, and that exhaust port side of head is marked "EXH" on cooling fin. Standoff nuts which support cooling shroud are installed on right, front stud marked "4" in tightening sequence. Complete the assembly by reversing the disassembly procedure.

PISTONS, PINS, RINGS AND CYLINDERS. Piston skirt clearance should not exceed the maximum given in the following table. Minimum recommended clearance is 0.004 inch (0.1 mm) less than that listed. Engines used on Starfire, TX and TX-C models are equipped with chrome bores and resizing is not recommended.

Model	Clearance
EC17PM	0.007 in. (0.18 mm)
EC25PC	0.006 in. (0.15 mm)
EC25PM	0.005 in. (0.13 mm)
EC25PS	0.006 in. (0.15 mm)
EC25PT	0.005 in. (0.13 mm)
EC29PF	0.005 in. (0.13 mm)
EC34PC	0.006 in. (0.15 mm)
EC34PM	0.006 in. (0.15 mm)
EC34-2PM	0.005 in. (0.13 mm)
EC34PQ	0.0065 in. (0.165 mm)
EC34PS	0.006 in. (0.15 mm)
EC40PM	0.008 in. (0.20 mm)
EC44PM	0.008 in. (0.20 mm)
EC44-2PM	0.006 in. (0.15 mm)
EC44PQ	0.008 in. (0.20 mm)
EC50PM	0.0055 in. (0.14 mm)
EC54PM	0.008 in. (0.20 mm)

Piston ring end gap is 0.005-0.008 in. (0.13-0.20 mm) on 1976 and earlier models, 0.006-0.012 in. (0.15-0.30 mm) on 1977-1983 models and 0.006-0.016 in. (0.15-0.040 mm) on 1984-1986 models. Piston rings are pinned in place and ring ends fall on each side of exhaust port. The "F" mark on piston crown should be installed towards flywheel end of crankshaft.

Piston pin is caged needle roller type which uses machined surfaces of rod bore and piston pin as bearing races. Check these areas for ridging or "washboarding" and bearing for worn, broken or missing needle rollers.

CONNECTING RODS, CRANKSHAFT AND BEARINGS. Connecting rod big end bearing can be checked after removing cylinder and piston. Measure connecting rod side shake at piston pin end of rod. If shake exceeds 1/8 in. (3.0 mm), install a new or rebuilt crankshaft assembly.

Crankshaft, connecting rods and all bearings are available only as a complete assembly, however front and rear bearings are available individually. Renew old bearing carefully, supporting crankshaft by nearest counterweight to keep from damaging the builtup crankshaft unit. Check the shaft for runout after bearings are installed by supporting outer bearings on "V" blocks then measuring runout with a dial indicator at center bearings and machine surfaces of each end shaft. If runout exceeds 0.006 in. (0.15 mm) renew the shaft.

REPAIRS

Liquid-Cooled Models

TIGHTENING TORQUES. Recommended tightening torques are as follows:

	Ft.-Lbs.	N·m
Crankcase:		
All Models –		
8 mm Screws	18	24.5
10 mm Screws	25	33.8
Cylinder Head:		
All Models –		
8 mm	17.5	23.7
10 mm	25	33.8
Flywheel:		
All models	65	88.1

CAPACITOR DISCHARGE IGNITION SYSTEM. Refer to Figs. 19, 20 and 21 for exploded views of CD ignition systems used on liquid-cooled models. The exciter coil, pulser coil and, on three-cylinder models, control coil may be tested without removal from engine using a suitable ohmmeter. Separate wiring from CDI module to stator plate at connector. Refer to TABLE 3 for vehicle application, check position and resistance reading specification. Control coil (13 – Fig. 21) used on three-cylinder models, has a green to blue check position and a 29.4 ohm test specification. On all models, if ohm reading is not within 10 percent of test specification, coil may be considered defective and should be renewed.

The CD ignition system used on three-cylinder models also has a control coil. An ohmmeter should indicate 29.4 ohms when connected to coil leads.

Fig. 36 – Lower side of running board showing heat exchanger used on liquid-cooled models. Drain plug is at (D).

TABLE 3—CDI COIL TEST SPECIFICATIONS (Liquid-Cooled)

	EXCITER COIL		PULSER COIL	
	Check Position	Resistance Reading	Check Position	Resistance Reading
TWO-CYLINDER MODELS				
1985-1986 Indy 400	Brown/White to White	164 Ohms	Brown/White to Black/Red	45 Ohms
1983 Indy Cross Country 1980-1982 TX-L Indy 1978-1982 TX-L	Brown/White to White	114 Ohms	Brown/White to Black	63 Ohms
THREE-CYLINDER MODELS				
1986 Indy 600 LE 1980-1986 Indy 600 1985 Indy 600 SE 1981-1982 Centurion Indy 1979-1980 Centurion	Black to White	261 Ohms	Red to White	20 Ohms

COOLING SYSTEM. The coolant liquid is thermostatically temperature controlled and positively circulated by an engine driven centrifugal coolant pump. On EC34PL engines, coolant passing through two series-connected aluminum heat exchangers dissipate heat generated by the engine. The heat exchangers are located underneath each running board as shown in Fig. 36. Three series-connected aluminum heat exchangers are used on remaining liquid-cooled engines.

Recommended coolant liquid is ethylene glycol and water mixed at a 50:50 ratio which protects system to a temperature of minus 36°F (−18°C). Do not exceed a ratio of 60 parts ethylene glycol to 40 parts water. System capacity is 1 gallon (3.7 L) and thermostatic temperature control is at 126°F (108°C).

Schematic views of cooling systems are shown in Figs. 37, 38 and 39 indicating major components and coolant flow. To drain the cooling system, remove filler cap (F−Fig. 40) and drain plugs (D−Fig. 36) at rear of both heat exchangers. Remove coolant drain plug from engine cylinder block.

To fill the cooling system on EC34PL engines, remove bleed plug (B−Fig. 40) and filler cap (F). Add coolant through filler plug opening until coolant emerges from bleeder vent, then install bleeder plug. Continue filling until coolant level reaches filler neck. Start and idle engine until thermostat opens then add coolant if fluid level drops.

To fill the cooling system on remaining liquid engines, raise and suitably support the front of the vehicle approximately 10 inches (254 mm). Loosen bleeder plug (Fig. 41) on top of the water pump. Add coolant through filler opening until air-free coolant flows from bleeder plug opening. Close bleeder plug and continue filling until coolant level reaches filler neck. On models with positive bleed recovery system (Fig. 38),

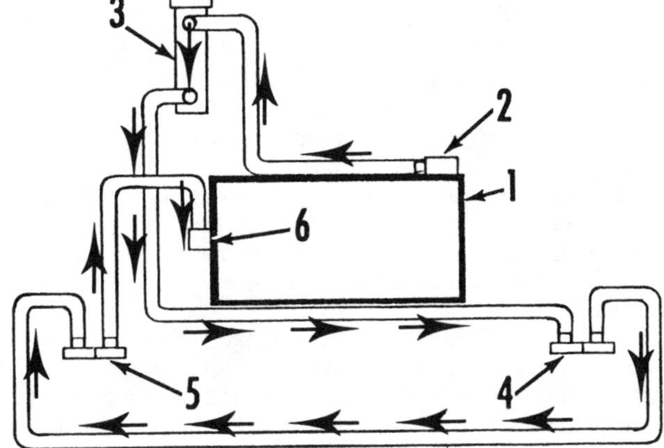

Fig. 37—Schematic view of liquid-cooling system used on EC34PL models. Arrows indicate direction of coolant flow.

1. Engine
2. Thermostat housing
3. Surge tank
4. Left heat exchanger
5. Right heat exchanger
6. Water pump

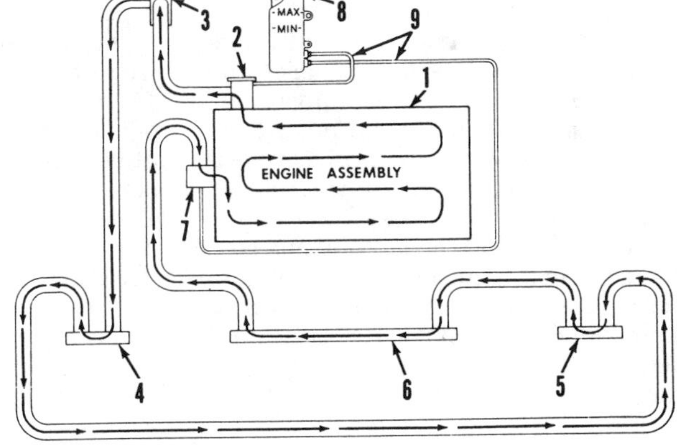

Fig. 38—Schematic view of positive bleed recovery cooling system used on EC40PL and some EC60PL models. Liquid-cooling system used on other EC60PL models is similar.

1. Engine
2. Filler opening
3. Brake cooler
4. Right heat exchanger
5. Left heat exchanger
6. Center heat exchanger
7. Water pump
8. Expansion reservoir
9. Overflow hoses

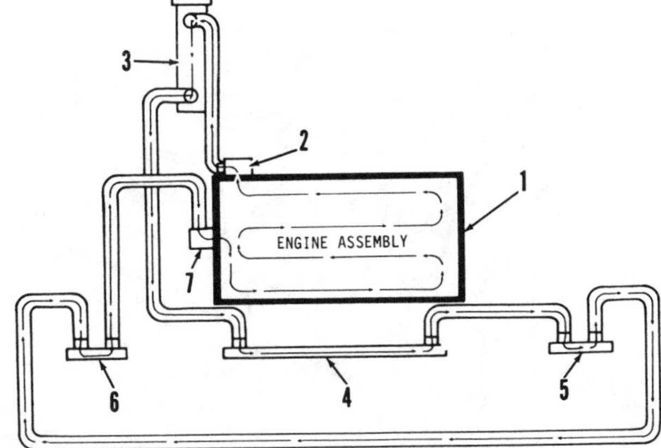

Fig. 39—Schematic view of typical three-cylinder liquid-cooling system.

1. Engine
2. Thermostat housing
3. Surge tank
4. Center heat exchanger
5. Left heat exchanger
6. Right heat exchanger
7. Water pump

Fig. 40—Installed view of EC34PL liquid-cooled engine showing block bleeder plug (B) and system filler cap (F).

Fig. 42—View of engine with coolant pump removed. Outlet nipple is "O" ring sealed and serves as pivot for belt tightener.

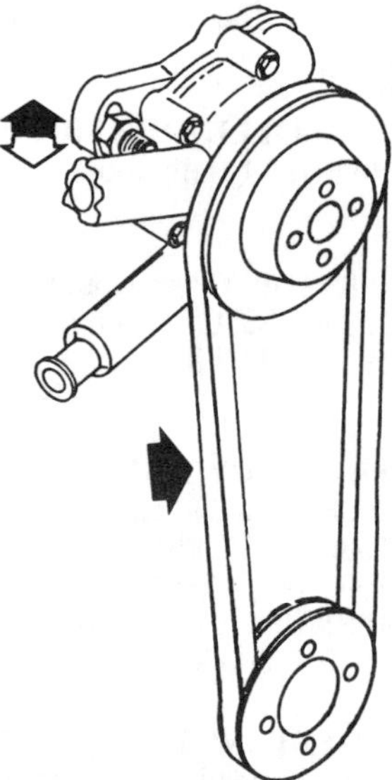

Fig. 43—Belt deflection should be ¼-inch (6 mm) measured midway between pulleys as shown by arrow. Loosen mounting nuts and rotate pump to adjust belt tension.

add coolant to expansion reservoir if required, to maximum level mark on reservoir. Install the pressure cap but do not engage lever lock on cap. Run the engine at fast idle for approximately 3 minutes to remove any air remaining in cooling system. Engage lever lock on pressure cap and refill expansion reservoir if required.

COOLANT PUMP. The centrifugal cooling system pump mounts on magneto end of cylinder block and is belt driven from a pulley bolted to flywheel. The pump pivots on an "O" ring sealed outlet nipple as shown in Fig. 42 and is retained by two 8 mm stud nuts.

To remove the pump, drain cooling system and disconnect pump inlet and bypass hoses. Remove pump housing and the two retaining stud nuts. Rock coolant pump downward until drive belt can be removed, then lift pump away from engine.

When installing coolant pump, coat "O" ring and outlet nipple with lithium base grease. Install retaining stud nuts loosely then rotate pump clockwise until belt deflection is ¼ inch (6 mm) measured midway between pulleys as shown by Arrow—Fig. 43. Tighten stud nuts to 15 ft.-lbs. (20.4 N·m) and install coolant pump housing.

THERMOSTAT. On EC34PL engines, the coolant thermostat is located beneath the outlet elbow on left rear corner of cylinder head as shown in Fig. 44. To remove the thermostat, drain down the coolant and remove the three cap screws retaining coolant outlet housing to cylinder head. Lift off housing and gasket, then lift thermostat from well in cylinder head. Thermostat should begin to open at 126°F (52°C) and should fully close at room temperature. Discard any thermostat which does not open or close properly. Use a new gasket when installing thermostat and tighten retaining cap screws to 15 ft.-lbs. (20.4 N·m) torque.

Model EC51PL-02 is equipped with a thermostat located in end of water outlet manifold. Check thermostat operation if coolant temperature is incorrect.

ENGINE R&R. To remove the engine, first drain cooling system as previously outlined. Remove clutch guard and drive belt. Remove exhaust manifold nuts and muffler clamp and lift off exhaust manifold and muffler as an assembly. Disconnect coolant hoses, temperature indicator switch wire and spark plug wires.

Unbolt recoil starter from engine and lay it aside in engine compartment without removing starter grip. Disconnect wiring harness and disconnect and plug fuel line. Disconnect throttle and choke

Fig. 44—View of cylinder head with thermostat removed.

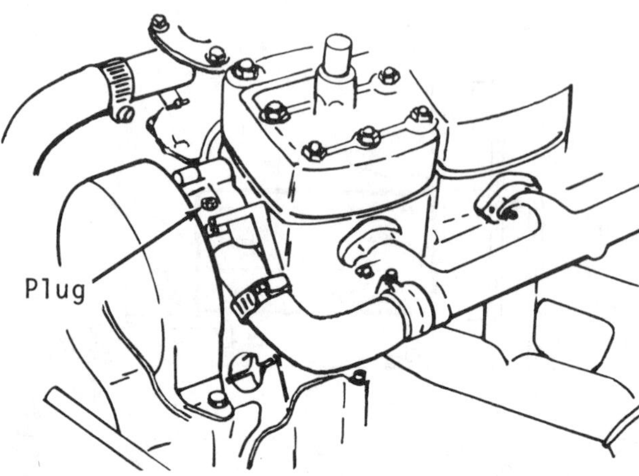

Fig. 41—Cooling system bleeder plug is located on water pump housing as shown on all liquid-cooled models except EC34PL models. Refer to text for filling and bleeding procedure.

Fig. 46—Liquid-cooled, two-cylinder engine removed.

Fig. 47—Partially disassembled view of two-cylinder engine showing starter cup, coolant pump drive sheave and coolant pump belt removed from flywheel.

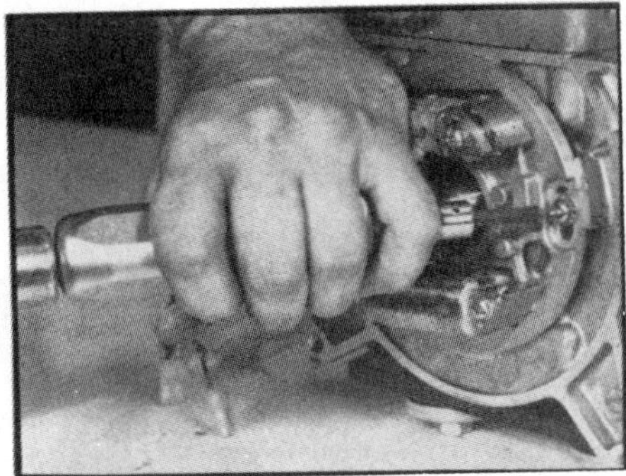

Fig. 51—Use an impact screwdriver to loosen stator screws.

linkage. Remove engine mounting plate bolts and lift engine and mounting plate from position in engine compartment. Disconnect wires from headlights and pull wires from between engine and mounting plate, then lift engine from machine. Install by reversing the removal procedure.

DISASSEMBLY AND REASSEMBLY. With engine removed as previously outlined, remove carburetors and water pump housing, then unbolt and remove water pump.

On two-cylinder models, remove magneto housing, starter cup water pump drive pulley and water pump drive belt (Fig. 47). Use Polaris strap wrench 2870336 or equivalent to hold flywheel and remove flywheel nut. With flywheel secured with strap wrench, use Polaris puller 2870384 or equivalent to remove flywheel as shown in Fig. 48.

On three-cylinder models, remove starter cup and flywheel nut. Install Polaris flywheel puller 2870384. Wrap a chain wrench around puller yoke to secure the assembly (Fig. 49) and remove the flywheel.

On all models, use a hammer and sharp chisel to scribe alignment marks on magneto stator plate and crankcase as shown in Fig. 50. Use an impact screwdriver to remove stator plate retaining screws (Fig. 51) and withdraw stator plate.

On two-cylinder models, remove cylinder head and gasket. On three-

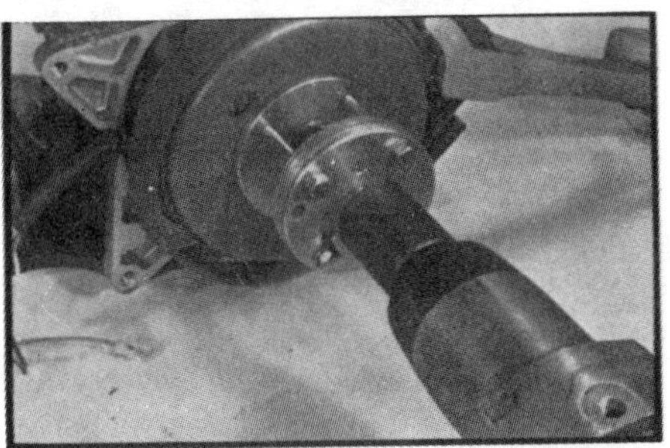

Fig. 48—Using strap wrench and puller to remove flywheel on two-cylinder models.

Fig. 49—On three-cylinder models, a chain wrench wrapped around puller yoke is used to prevent crankshaft rotation during flywheel removal.

Fig. 50—Using a sharp chisel and hammer to scribe assembly marks on ignition stator and crankcase.

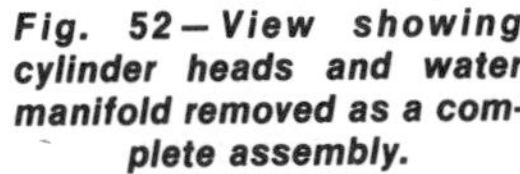

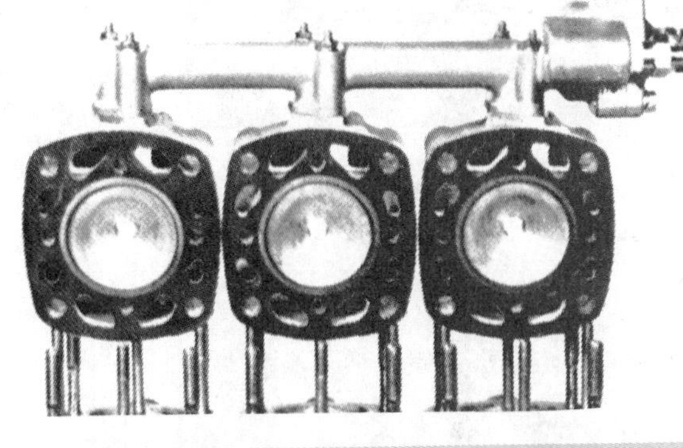

Fig. 52—View showing cylinder heads and water manifold removed as a complete assembly.

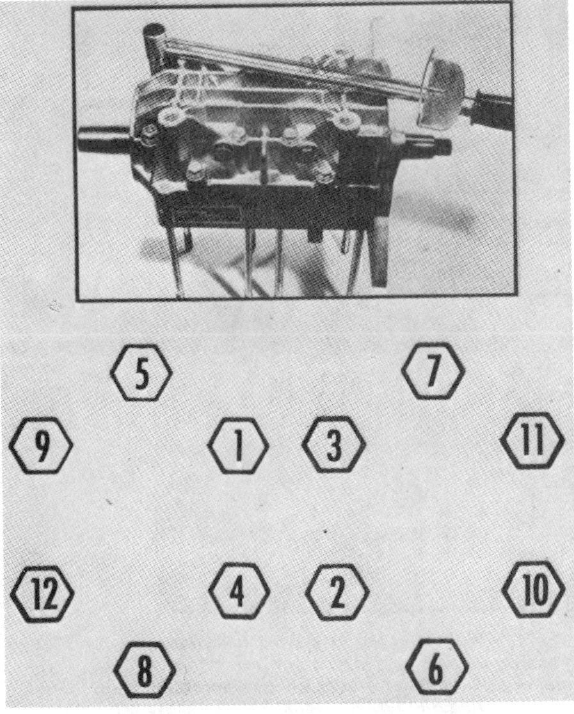

Fig. 53—Tighten crankcase screws in sequence shown.

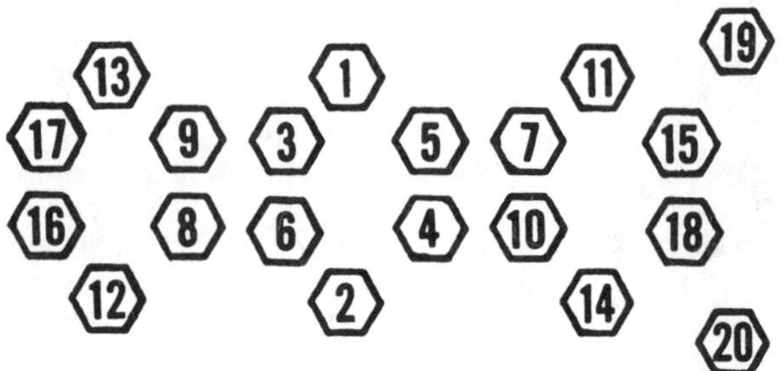

Fig. 54—On three-cylinder, liquid-cooled engines, tighten crankcase screws in sequence shown.

1 7 4

5 6

3 8 2

Fig. 60—On three-cylinder, liquid-cooled engines, tighten cylinder head nuts in sequence shown.

cylinder models, cylinder heads can be removed with water manifold as a complete assembly as shown in Fig. 52. Match mark both pistons and cylinders to ensure components are reinstalled in original positions. Lift cylinder assembly on two-cylinder models or individual cylinders on three-cylinder models, from crankcase. Remove spiral lock piston pin retainers and use Polaris piston pin puller 2870386 to remove piston pins. Withdraw the pistons. Remove crankcase screws, then break sealant bond by tapping crankcase halves with a soft hammer. New pistons, pins and rings are interchangeable but used parts should not be lubricated.

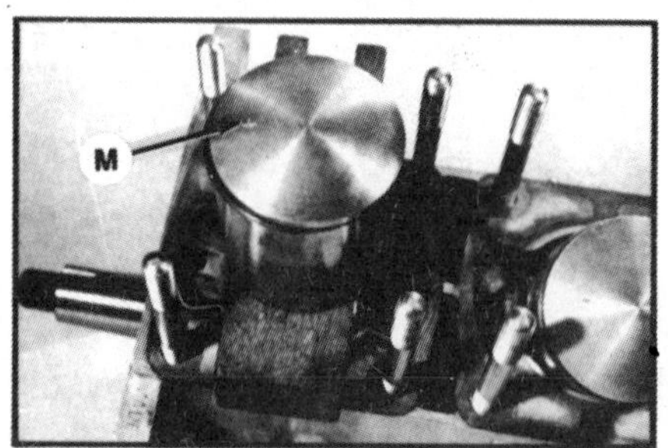

Fig. 55—Pistons are installed with "arrow" or "F" mark (M) toward flywheel end of engine.

When reassembling, coat labyrinth seal between crankshaft center bearing with nonfibrous grease. Coat both crankcase flanges with a good nonhardening sealer and join the halves. Be sure bearing locating dowels in bearing outer races properly enter drillings in crankcase lower half. Tighten cap screws finger tight, then tap firmly on pto end of crankshaft to move all slack toward flywheel end of crankcase. Tighten crankcase screws in sequence shown in Fig. 53 for two-cylinder models. The two 10 mm screws should be tightened to 25 ft.-lbs. (33.9 N·m) and the 8 mm screws to 18 ft.-lbs. (24.4 N·m). Tighten crankcase screws in sequence shown in Fig. 54 for three-cylinder models.

The arrow or "F" mark on top of piston crown (M–Fig. 55) must be towards flywheel end of crankshaft when installing pistons on connecting rods. The keystone piston rings must be installed with inner bevel towards top of piston. Piston rings are pinned to prevent rotation. Install the cylinder base gaskets and lubricate the pistons and cylinder bores with clean oil. Cut a slot in a short piece of 2x4 inch board for use as a piston support as shown in Fig. 56.

On two-cylinder models, place the support under either piston. Compress the piston ring on supported piston making sure ends of ring correctly engage pin in ring groove, then install the cylinder (Fig. 56). With one piston started in cylinder transfer the support block to a position beneath cylinder flange as shown in Fig. 57. Compress the remaining piston ring as previously described and guide piston into cylinder by turning crankshaft.

On three-cylinder models, place the piston support under number one piston. Compress the piston ring on supported piston making sure ends of ring correctly engage pin in ring groove, then install

Fig. 56—On two-cylinder models, support one piston and guide cylinder over one ring, then refer to Fig. 57.

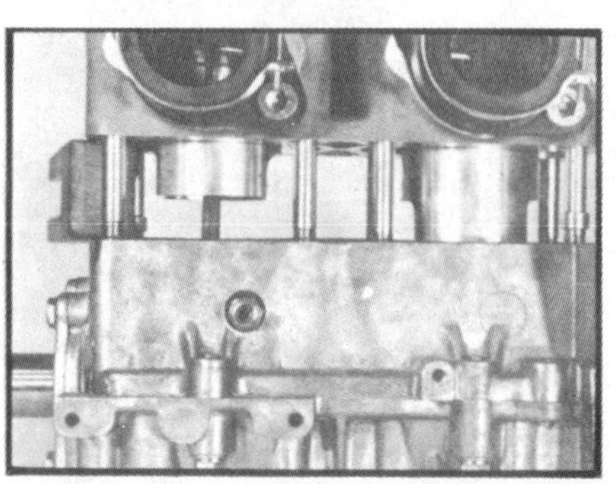

Fig. 57—With one piston started in cylinder, transfer support to cylinder and guide the remaining piston into cylinder while compressing ring and turning crankshaft.

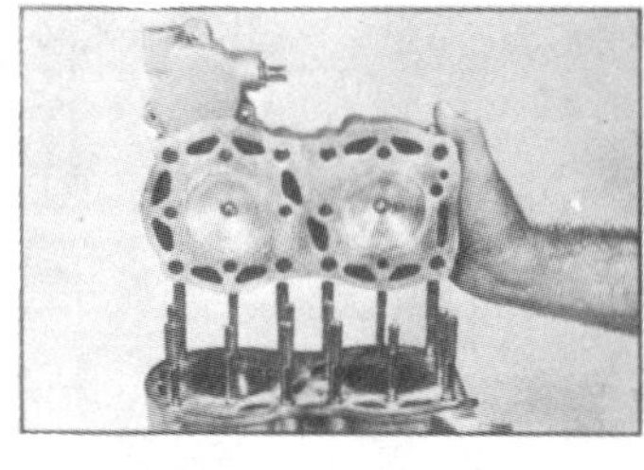

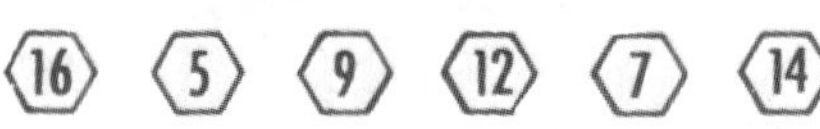

3 1 2 4

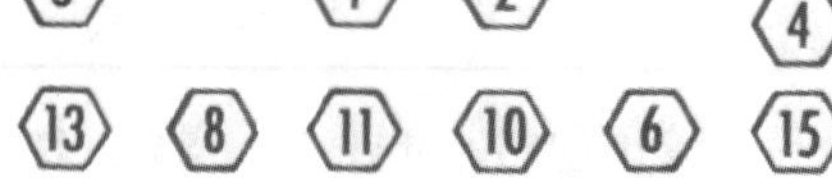

Fig. 58—On EC34PL models, tighten cylinder head stud nuts in sequence shown.

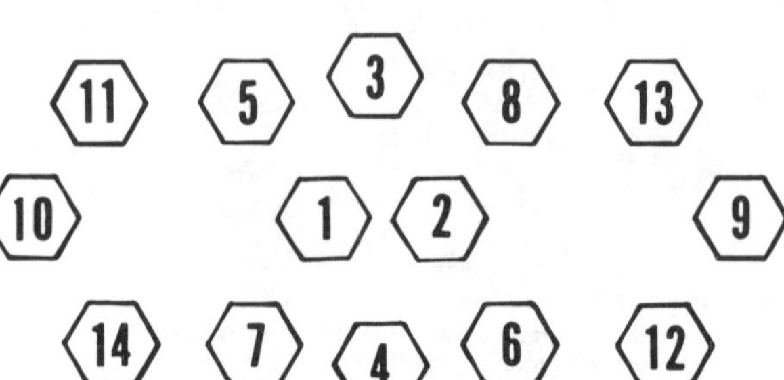

Fig. 59—On EC40PL models, tighten cylinder head nuts in sequence shown.

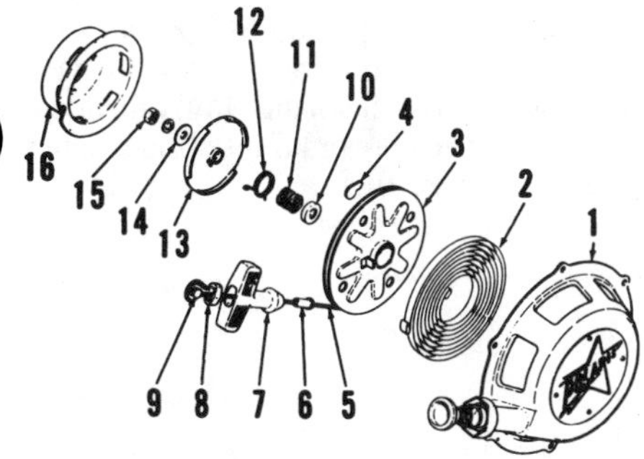

Fig. 61—Exploded view of recoil starter of the type used on early models.

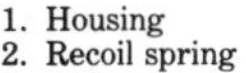

1. Housing
2. Recoil spring
3. Pulley
4. Pawl
5. Cable
6. Guide
7. Handle
8. Retainer
9. Retainer
10. Retainer
11. Friction spring
12. Retracting spring
13. Retracting plate
14. Washer
15. Nut
16. Starter cup

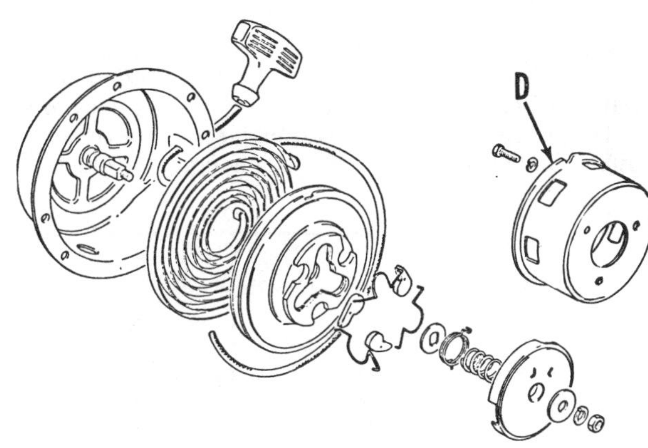

Fig. 62—Exploded view of recoil starter used on most late models. Drive cup (D) is bolted to engine flywheel and is not part of removed assembly.

the corresponding cylinder. Repeat the procedure for the remaining cylinders.

Install cylinder head gasket(s) and cylinder head(s). On two-cylinder models gasket will fit in only one position. On three-cylinder models, install gaskets with small discharge hole toward the intake side of motor. Cylinder head nut tightening sequence is shown in Fig. 58 for EC34PL models, Fig. 59 for EC40PL models and Fig. 60 for all three-cylinder models. On all models, tighten the 8 mm nuts to 17 ft.-lbs. (23 N•m) and the 10 mm nuts to 29 ft.-lbs. (39.3 N•m). Retighten 8 mm nuts after 10 mm nuts are tightened. Complete the assembly by reversing the disassembly procedure. If a new stator plate or crankcase is to be installed, note position of chisel mark on faulty part and chisel an alignment mark on new part.

PISTONS, PINS, RINGS AND CYLINDERS. On EC34PL and EC51PL models, piston skirt clearance should be 0.003-0.007 in. (0.08-0.18 mm). On EC40PL and EC60PL models, piston skirt clearance should be 0.0045-0.0075 inch (0.11-0.19 mm). On all models, pistons and rings are available in 0.020 inch (0.5 mm) oversize as well as standard, and resizing is recommended if a new piston exceeds clearance specifications in a used cylinder. Oversized pistons and rings are available for cast-iron lined cylinders only.

Piston rings are semi-keystone, with tapered side going toward top of piston.

Piston pin is caged needle roller type which uses machined surfaces of rod bore and piston pin as bearing races. Check these areas for ridging or "washboarding," and bearings for worn, broken or missing needle rollers.

CONNECTING RODS, CRANKSHAFT AND BEARINGS. Connecting rod big end bearing can be checked after removing cylinder assembly and piston. Measure side shake of rod at piston pin end. If shake exceeds 1/8 inch (3.0 mm) install a new or rebuilt crankshaft assembly.

Crankshaft, connecting rods and all bearings are available only as a complete assembly. Check the shaft for runout by supporting outer bearings on "V" blocks then measuring runout with a dial indicator. If runout exceeds 0.006 inch (0.15 mm), renew the shaft unit.

RECOIL STARTER. Refer to Fig. 61 for exploded view of recoil starter of the type used on early models. Pulley must be removed to renew cable (5) or recoil spring (2).

To disassemble the starter, pry out retainer (9) and remove handle (7), and allow cable to recoil into housing. Remove nut (15) and flat washer (14). Unhook eye end of retracting spring (12) from slot in plate (13) and remove plate, retracting spring (12), friction spring (11), retainer (10) and pawls (4). Carefully lift out pulley (3) while unhooking inner end of recoil spring (2).

To reassemble, hook outer end or recoil spring (2) and coil the spring into housing well in a counterclockwise direction. Fully wind the cable into pulley (3), pulling free outer end into notch provided in pulley rim. Turn pulley counterclockwise until inner end of spring hooks tab of pulley, then turn pulley three more turns. Thread the cable through hole in housing, pull out sufficient cable and reinstall handle. Hook straight end of retracting spring (12) in hole in pulley. Reinstall pawls (4), retainer (10) and friction spring (11); then install retracting plate (13), hooking eye of spring (12) through slot of plate. After nut (15) is installed, pull starter handle and check to see that plate (13) moves to open the slots for pawls (4). Complete the assembly by reversing the disassembly procedure.

Fig. 62 shows an exploded view of the recoil starter of the general type used on most late models. To disassemble the starter, apply slight pressure to the drive plate and remove nut, lockwasher and flat washer from center stud. Lift off the drive plate, compression spring, return spring and compression spring seat. Remove the three pawl springs and pawls.

Carefully lift the rope pulley from housing, turning pulley clockwise as it is lifted, to unhook inner end of recoil spring from lug on pulley. Recoil spring should remain in starter housing well when pulley is removed.

Recoil spring and rope can be renewed at this time. To install a new spring, hook outer end of spring on lug in starter housing and wrap spring in a counterclockwise direction in spring well. Lubricate the spring and spring well with lithium base grease.

Thread a new rope through hole in bottom of rope slot in pulley. Tie a knot in end of rope and pull tight; then while facing pawl side of pulley, wind the rope into pulley in a counterclockwise direction. Lubricate pulley hub with lithium base grease and install pulley, aligning inner hook of recoil spring with spring notch in pulley hub.

Install pawls and pawl springs as shown in Fig. 63. Install spring seat and compression spring. Install return spring with straight end down, then install drive plate making sure hooked upper end of return spring engages chev-

Fig. 63—Partially assembled view of starter showing pawls and springs installed.

ron slot in drive plate. Secure with flat washer, lockwasher and nut, tightening nut to 15 ft.-lbs. (20.3 N·m).

Thread outer end of rope through rope guide in housing and pull out enough rope to reach through cowl, then tie a temporary slip knot in rope. Turn rope pulley until notch in pulley rim aligns with rope guide in housing and using a hooked wire, pull a loop of rope outside of pulley rim. Continue to turn pulley in same direction for four to six turns to preload the recoil spring. Pull on rope to check the tension and if insufficient, preload one more turn.

ROTAX

ONE CYLINDER MODELS (Prior to 1983)

BOMBARDIER CORPORATION
4505 West Superior Street
Duluth, MN 55806

CONDENSED SERVICE DATA

ENGINE MODEL	165	250,247	290,292	277	300,302	320	335,337 340,342
Bore–mm	62	69	75	72	76.0	76.0	78.0
Inches	2.441	2.717	2.952	2.835	2.992	2.992	3.070
Stroke–mm	54	66	66	66	66	70	70
Inches	2.126	2.598	2.598	2.6	2.598	2.756	2.756
No. of Cylinders	1	1	1	1	1	1	1
Displacement–cc	163	247	291.6	268.7	299.4	318	334.5
Cubic Inches	9.94	15.0	17.8	16.4	18.2	19.4	20.4
Horsepower at Rpm	7 at...	12 at...	22 at...	....	12-15 at...	18 at...	18-20-26 at...
Carburetor Model	HL	HR,VM	HD	VM	HR	HR	HR**
Number Used	1	1	1	1	1	1	1
Ignition:	Flywheel Magneto	Flywheel Magneto	Flywheel Magneto	Flywheel Magneto*	Flywheel Magneto	Flywheel Magneto	Flywheel Magneto
Type							
Point Gap–mm	0.35-0.45	0.35-0.45	0.35-0.45	0.35-0.45	0.35-0.45	0.35-0.45	0.35-0.45
Inch	0.014-0.018	0.014-0.018	0.014-0.018	0.014-0.018	0.014-0.018	0.014-0.018	0.014-0.018
Edge Gap–mm	....	5-8	6.4-22.2	8-12	5-8	8-12	6.4-22.2
Inch	....	0.200-0.320	0.250-0.875	0.315-0.472	0.200-0.315	0.315-0.472	0.250-0.875
Timing Advance?	No	Yes	Yes	Yes	Yes	Yes	Yes
Timing BTDC–mm	3-3.5	4-4.5	3.7-4.2	2.35-2.85	4-4.5	4.5 Max.	4.1-4.4
Inch	0.118-0.138	0.150-0.170	0.145-0.165	0.092-0.112	0.150-0.170	0.170 Max.	0.160-0.170
Measured at	....	Advanced Cam	Advanced Cam	....	Advanced Cam	Advanced Cam	Advanced Cam
Spark Plug:							
Bosch	M175T1	M240T1	M280T31	W275T2*	M240T1	M240T1	M240T1**
Electrode Gap–mm	0.5	0.5	0.5	0.5	0.5	0.5	0.5
Inch	0.020	0.020	0.020	0.020	0.020	0.020	0.020
Fuel: Oil Ratio	See Text	See Text	See Text	See Text	See Text	See Text	See Text

*1982 models are equipped with CD ignition and recommended spark plug is NGK BR-8ES with 0.016-inch electrode gap.
**Engines used in T'NT models are equipped with HD carburetors and use M280T31 spark plug.

MAINTENANCE

CARBURETOR. Tillotson diaphragm and Mikuni Model VM carburetors are used.

For Tillotson normal initial setting of low speed mixture needle is ¾-turn open from closed position. Normal initial setting of high speed mixture needle is 1¼-turns open. Both needles must be readjusted with engine at operating temperature. Idle speed should be 1200-1500 rpm.

For Mikuni normal initial setting of pilot air jet is 1½-turns out from closed position. Idle speed should be 1100-1300 rpm.

Refer to **TILLOTSON or MIKUNI** Service section in **CARBURETOR** Service Fundamentals for complete procedure on carburetor fine tuning and overhaul.

IGNITION AND TIMING. Breaker point gap should be 0.014-0.018 inch (0.35-0.45 mm) on all models. Points can be adjusted after removing recoil starter unit and starter cup.

Ignition timing is fixed on 165 model engine. Other models have a centrifugal timing advance which provides a retarded spark for starting only.

On all models before 1968, set the ignition timing with breaker point cam in full advanced position. Breaker points should just open when piston is in BTDC position indicated in the Condensed Service Data table. Check the magneto edge gap (with breaker cam fully advanced) after setting point gap and timing. Edge gap should be within limits in **CONDENSED SERVICE DATA** and should be correct with point gap and timing correctly adjusted.

Beginning in 1968, ignition timing should be checked in starting (retarded) position using the timing marks visible after removing recoil starter. Breaker point gap should be within limits of 0.014-0.018 inch and points should just open as the timing marks (Fig. 1) align. It is important that breaker point cam is in retarded position when checking ignition timing. Edge gap should be within limits in **CONDENSED SERVICE DATA** when checked with breaker point cam in fully advanced position. Edge gap should be correct if breaker point gap and ignition timing are correctly set.

When checking and adjusting ignition on all models with centrifugal advance,

Fig. 1—Flywheel housing with recoil starter removed showing retarded (starting) timing marks used on late models.

Fig. 3—Position crankshaft with Woodruff key (K) straight up, locate the cam slot (S) at 8 o'clock position, then install flywheel. Check to make certain that lug on weight engages the cam slot by moving cam through holes in flywheel. Keyway is shown at (W).

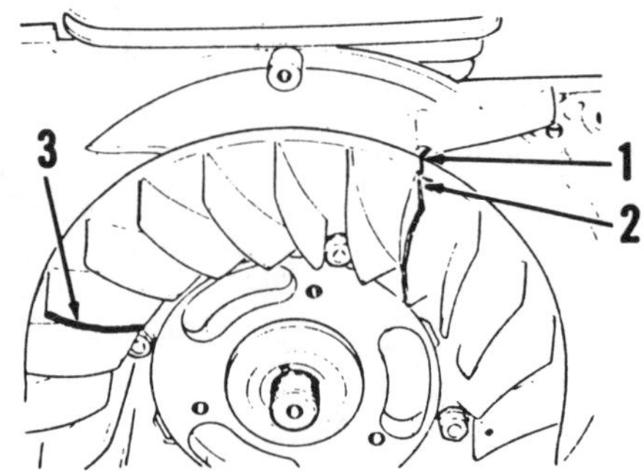

Fig. 3A—View showing timing marks for models equipped with CD ignition.

1. Crankcase mark
2. Fan mark
3. Fan pawl (Yellow Mark)

check to be sure that advance mechanism moves freely and does not bind. If binding occurs, remove the flywheel, then disassemble and clean the advance mechanism and/or renew parts as required. Refill the lubricant groove in breaker cam bore with a cold resistant and water repellent grease whenever flywheel is removed. When reinstalling flywheel, make sure lobe of centrifugal weight properly engages breaker cam. Refer to Fig. 3. Tighten flywheel nut to a torque of approximately 32 ft.-lbs. on Model 165 engines or 50 ft.-lbs. on other models.

Fig. 2 shows an assembled view of the magneto armature plate.

To check ignition timing on models with CD ignition remove fan cover, spark plug and then install TDC gage in cylinder head. Set gage to zero, then rotate crankshaft counter-clockwise until reading of 2.85 mm (0.112-inch) BTDC is obtained. Crankcase mark (1–Fig. 3A) and fan mark (2) must be aligned. If marks do not align, then reinstall fan cover and check to see if yellow pawl mark (3) aligns with cover mark. If marks align, then remove cover and make a new mark on outer circumference of fan in line with crankcase mark. If yellow pawl mark and cover mark do not align, then make a new mark on fan cover in line with yellow pawl mark.

Using a timing light with a separate battery source run engine at 6000 rpm and check timing mark alignment. If marks do no align, then stator plate will need to be adjusted. Remove recoil starter assembly and starter pulley. Turn stator plate clockwise to retard timing and counter-clockwise to advance timing. Reinstall removed components, then recheck engine timing.

NOTE: Ignition timing should be checked with engine cold. Temperature variations may affect components.

LUBRICATION. 1981-1982 engine Model 277 is equipped with automatic oil injection, all other engines are lubricated by mixing oil with the fuel. Bombardier concentrated 50:1 oil should be mixed with regular gasoline at a ratio of one pint of oil to six gallons of gasoline. If Bombardier oil is not available, USE ONLY a good quality recognized brand snowmobile oil or two-cycle oil and mix at fuel:oil ratio recommended by oil manufacturer.

Normally the engine on models with oil injection will be adequately lubricated by oil delivered and metered by the oil injection pump. In extremely cold weather, the oil injection system may not pump correctly. Below -20 degrees F. (-29 degrees C.), mix one pint of oil with each six gallons of gasoline to supplement oil injection pump and insure proper lubrication.

DECOMPRESSOR VALVE. On models with decompressor valve, clearance (A–Fig. 4) should be 1/16-inch between end of cable housing (3) and lever. Adjustment is accomplished by turning the spring screw (S) in detent housing (D). Valve may be damaged if not fully sealed. When cylinder is removed for service, remove valve (2) and clean passages (1 and 4). Renew valve assembly if damaged.

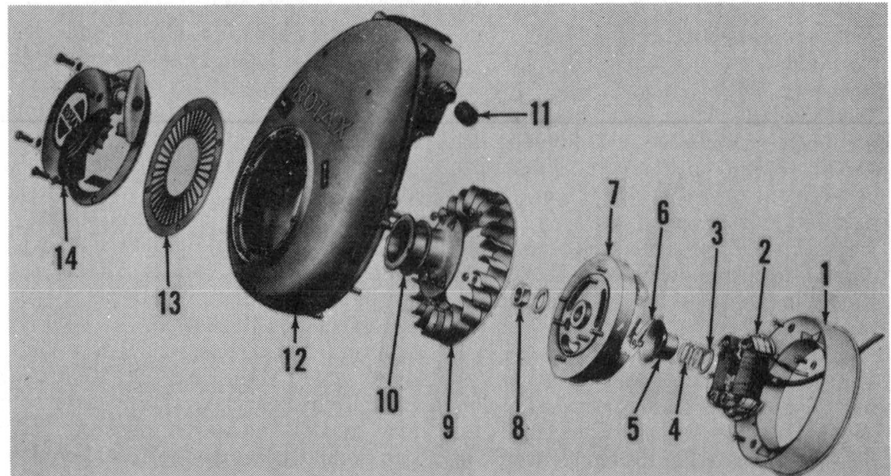

Fig. 2—Exploded view of magneto, flywheel, fan housing, starter and associated parts.

1. Labyrinth ring
2. Armature plate
3. Washer
4. Spring
5. Breaker cam
6. Advance weight
7. Flywheel
8. Nut
9. Fanwheel
10. Starter cup
11. Insulator
12. Fan housing
13. Shield
14. Recoil starter

REPAIRS

TIGHTENING TORQUES. Recommended tightening torques are as follows:

Flywheel nut:
- Model 165 . . . . 32 ft.-lbs.
- Model 247 and 277 . . . . 63 ft.-lbs.
- Other models . . . . 50 ft.-lbs.

Cylinder Head:
- Model 250 (screws) . . . . 32 ft.-lbs.
- Other models (nuts) . . . . 16 ft-lbs.

Crankcase:
- Model 165 (screws) . . . . 84 in.-lbs.
- Other models (nuts . . . . 16 ft.-lbs.

Decompressor valve:
- Models so equipped . . . . 10 ft.-lbs.

Fig. 4—Drawing showing decompressor used on some models. Clearance (A) should be 1/16 inch and is adjusted by turning spring screw(s).

A. Clearance
D. Detent housing
S. Spring screw
1. Passage to cylinder
2. Decompressor valve
3. Cable housing
4. Passage to exhaust
5. Exhaust port

Engine mounts:

Model 247 . . . . 28 ft.-lbs.
Model 277 . . . . 16 ft.-lbs.
Other models . . . . 33 ft.-lbs.

DISASSEMBLY AND REASSEMBLY. Refer to Fig. 5 for exploded view of typical single cylinder engines. When service is required, first remove engine as outlined in vehicle section of this manual and remove carburetor, drive sheave, recoil starter and muffler. Remove fan cover, flywheel, armature plate, cylinder head and cylinder.

On 165 model, outer race of crankshaft bearings remain in crankcase while remainder of bearing is removed with shaft. On this engine, crankcase can be separated by tapping gently with soft hammer after removing the crankcase screws.

On 247, 277 and 302 models, remove the seal housing (9–Fig. 5), then remove snap ring (6L and 6S). On all models, remove the stud nuts attaching crankcase halves together. Heat crankcase around main bearings and carefully separate crankcase halves.

CAUTION: Crankshaft and/or crankcase may be damaged if crankcase is not heated to allow easy withdrawal of main bearings.

On 247, 277, 290, 300, 302, 335 and 340 models, crankshaft end play should be carefully adjusted by varying the thickness of shims (13–Fig. 5). Selection of shim thickness can be accomplished by measuring the length of crankshaft and depth of crankcase before assembling. Shim will usually not need to be changed unless crankshaft or crankcase is renewed. Install the correct amount of shims to limit end play between 0.006-0.016 inch.

Crankshaft end play on 292, 337 and 342 models is limited by output end main bearing and is not adjusted. If end play is excessive, renew main bearing.

The "AUS" mark and arrow on top of piston should be toward exhaust port. Heat piston to 140-150 degrees F before installing piston pin. The cylinder head should be tightened evenly to 10 ft.-lbs. before tightening to the final torque of 16 ft.-lbs. Tighten crankcase and cylinder head retaining nuts in diagonal pattern.

PISTON, PIN, RINGS AND CYLINDER. The piston can be removed after removing muffler, carburetor, cylinder head and cylinder. Piston and rings are available in standard size and oversizes. Arrow and "AUS" mark on piston crown must be toward exhaust port in cylinder when engine is assembled. Piston pin is full floating type but is a tight fit in piston bores at room temperature. Heat piston to 140-150 degrees F. for easy assembly. The piston pin retaining rings should be installed so that open section is toward top of piston. On all models, rebore or renew cylinder if out of round more than 0.002 inch, if tapered more than 0.003 inch or if wear exceeds 0.004 inch. Piston to cylinder clearance should be measured 5/16-inch above lower edge of piston skirt. Piston to cylinder clearance should be 0.0026-0.008 inch for 247 models; 0.0024-0.008 inch for 277 models; 0.0035-0.004 inch for 300, 302, 335 and 337 models; 0.004-0.005 inch for 290, 292, 340 and 342 models. Ring side clearance in groove should be 0.002-0.008 inch, for all models. Ring end gap should be 0.008-0.014 inch for 247 and 277 models; 0.012-0.063 inch for all other models.

On 1968 and later 300cc models, 2 mm piston rings are used instead of 2.5 mm rings previously used, to reduce wall friction. 1968 pistons are grooved for the thinner rings. The new style pistons and rings can be installed in sets in older models.

CRANKSHAFT AND CONNECTING ROD ASSEMBLY. The crankshaft

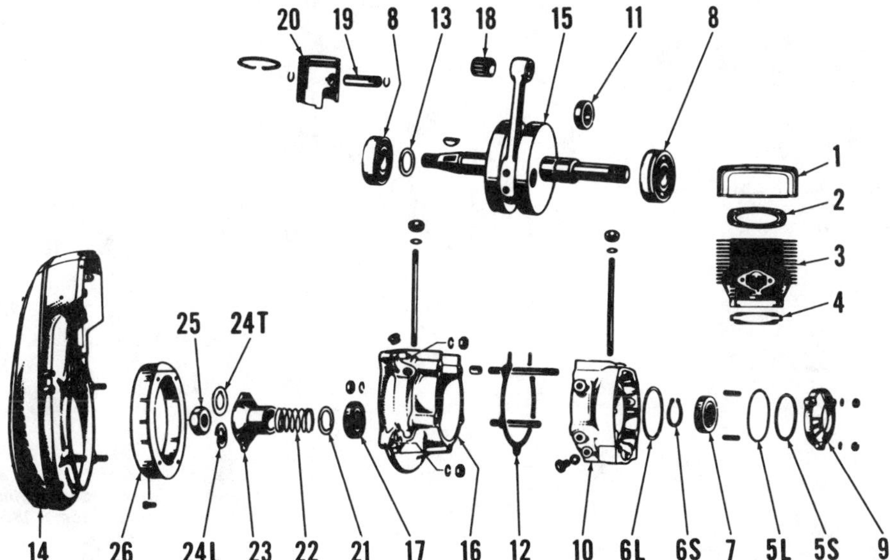

Fig. 5—Exploded view of a typical single cylinder engine. On some models parts (5L, 5S, 6L, 6S, and 9) are not used.

1. Cylinder head
2. Head gasket
3. Cylinder
4. Base gasket
5L. Large "O"ring
5S. Small "O" ring
6L. Bearing locating ring
6S. Bearing snap ring
7. Seal
8. Main bearing
9. Retainer plate
10. Crankcase pto half
11. Spacer
12. Gasket
13. Shim
14. Fan housing
15. Crankshaft
16. Crankcase magneto half
17. Seal
18. Piston pin bearing
19. Piston pin
20. Piston
21. Washer
22. Spring
23. Ignition cam
24L. Spring lockwasher
24T. Tab lock
25. Flywheel retaining nut
26. Labyrinth ring

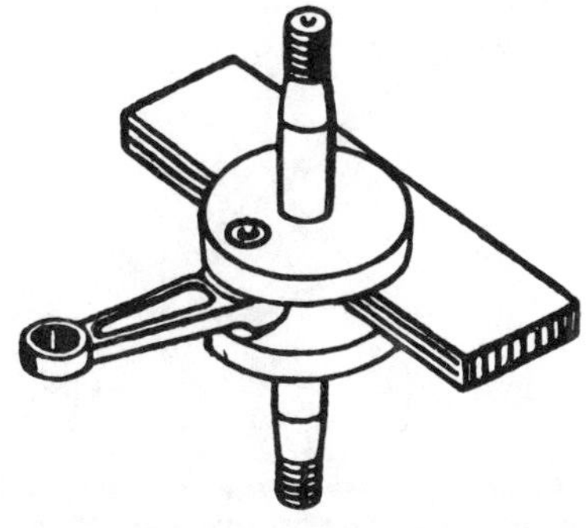

Fig. 7—When installing bearings, support crankshaft behind counterweight as shown.

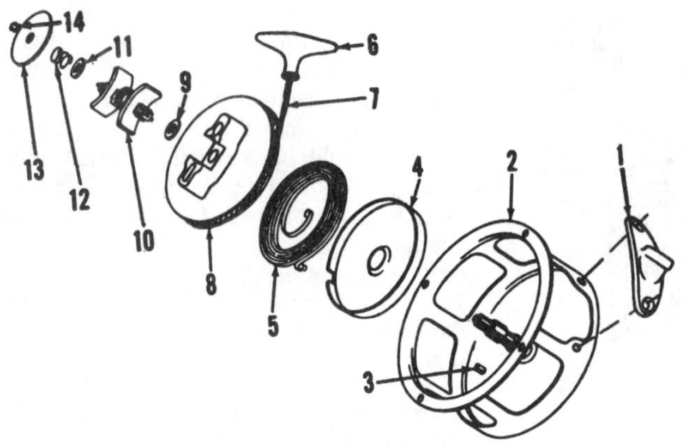

Fig. 8—Exploded view of early recoil starter.

1. Rope guide
2. Housing
3. Pin
4. Spring guide
5. Recoil spring
6. Handle
7. Rope
8. Pulley
9. "D" washer
10. Pivot arm
11. Friction washer
12. Spring
13. Washer
14. Snap ring

and connecting rod assembly is available only as a complete unit and should not be disassembled. Bearings are a press fit on shafts and shaft must be properly supported when installing bearings as shown in Fig. 7. To check the removed crankshaft and connecting rod assembly, mount the unit between lathe centers and check shafts for runout as near as possible to crankshaft webs. Runout should not exceed 0.004 inch. Side clearance between connecting rods and crankshaft webs should be 0.008-0.039 inch for 247 and 277 models and 0.020 inch for all other models. Renew crankshaft and connecting rod assembly if wear is excessive or there is any other damage.

RECOIL STARTER. Early recoil starter assembly is shown exploded in Fig. 8. To disassemble early starter unit, proceed as follows:

Remove the two screws securing rope guide (1) to housing (2), pass the guide through hole in housing and allow the recoil spring to unwind. Remove snap ring (14) and disassemble the starter, allowing spring (5) to remain nested in spring guide (4). To remove the starter rope, insert a punch through hole indicated by arrow, Fig. 9, push rope end (7) out of pulley (8) and withdraw the locking pin (bolt) (B). Unit can now be disassembled.

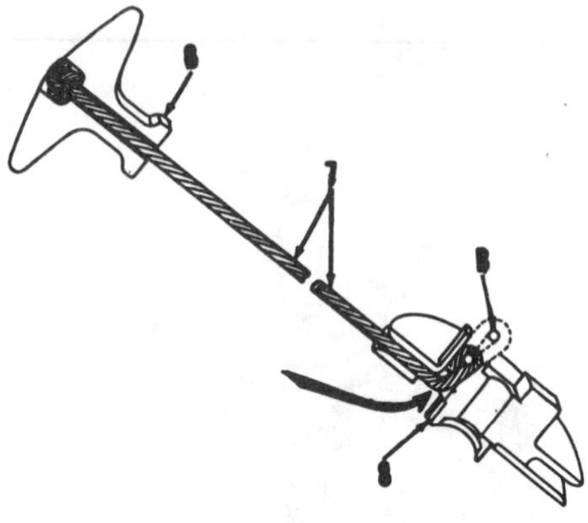

Assemble by reversing the disassembly procedure. Make sure serrations of pivot arm (10–Fig. 8) and friction washer (11) are together and lightly oiled. Also make sure that rope (7) and spring (5) are installed as shown. Outer end of spring (5) must hook over pin (3) and inner end of spring must engage slot in pulley (8). Wind rope pulley three or four turns to achieve proper recoil tension, pass rope guide (1) up through proper slot in housing (2) and secure with screws. Check the operation of starter before reinstalling on engine.

The recoil starter used on many models before 1981 is shown in Fig. 10. To overhaul starter, proceed as follows: Remove rope handle and allow rope to rewind into starter housing. Remove pawl guide (1), snap ring (2) and disassemble starter while allowing spring (14) to remain in spring guide (13).

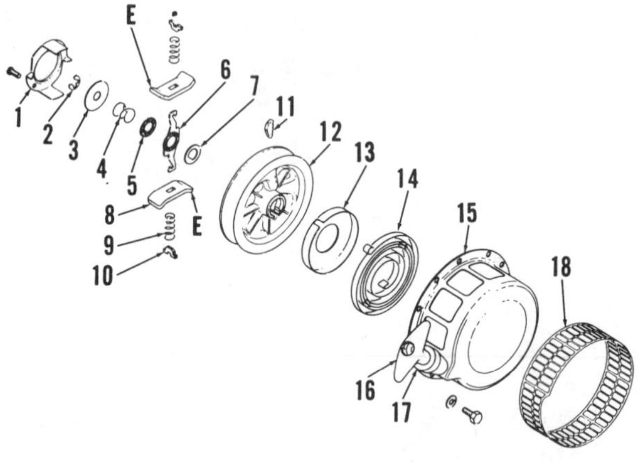

Assemble by reversing disassembly procedure. Rewind spring (14) is wrapped in spring guide (13) in clockwise direction from outer end of spring. Rope is secured in pulley by a serrated key (11). Rope is wound around pulley in counterclockwise direction as viewed with pulley in housing. Rotate pulley (12) six turns counterclockwise before passing rope through starter housing so rewind spring is preloaded. Make sure serrations of pivot arm (6) and friction washer (5) are together and lightly oiled. Note locations of sharp edges (E) on pawls (8).

The recoil starter used on many 1980 and later models is shown in Fig. 11. To overhaul starter, proceed as follows: Remove snap ring (1), lock spring (2), "E" clip (3), pawl lock (4) and pawl (5). Pull rope (6) out of pulley (8) until rope is fully extended. Disengage key (7) and pull rope completely out of pulley. Withdraw pulley (8), spring guide (9) and spring (10). Inspect all parts for damage and renew as needed.

Assemble in reverse of disassembly. Rope is wound around pulley in counterclockwise direction as viewed with pulley in housing. Rotate pulley (8) six turns counter-clockwise before passing rope through starter housing so rewind spring is preloaded, then complete reassembly.

Fig. 10—Exploded view of rewind starter used up to and on some 1980 models.

1. Pawl guide
2. Snap ring
3. Washer
4. Spring
5. Friction washer
6. Pivot arm
7. "D" washer
8. Pawl
9. Spring
10. Spring keeper
11. Serrated key
12. Rope pulley
13. Spring guide
14. Rewind spring
15. Starter housing
16. Rope handle
17. Rope guide
18. Shield

Fig. 9—Cross-sectional view of early starter pulley and rope showing approved method of securing rope. Refer to Fig. 8 for parts identification except for bolt (B).

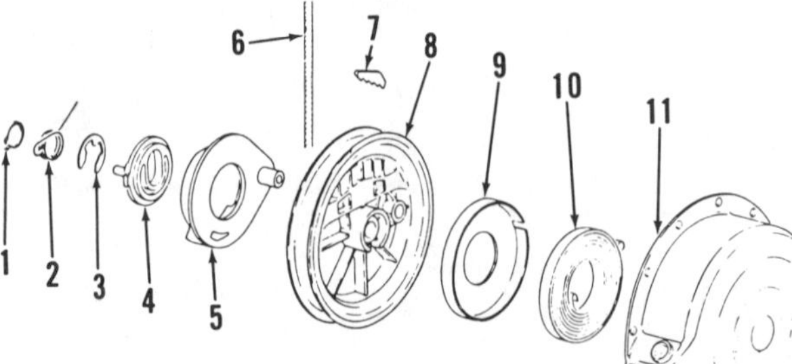

Fig. 11—Exploded view of rewind starter used during 1981-82 and on some 1980 models.

1. Snap ring
2. Lock spring
3. "E" clip
4. Pawl lock
5. Pawl
6. Rope
7. Key
8. Rope pulley
9. Spring guide
10. Rewind spring
11. Starter housing

ROTAX

TWO CYLINDER MODELS
(Prior to 1983)

CONDENSED SERVICE DATA

ENGINE MODEL	245	248, 249	294	305
Bore – mm	54	54	57	55.5
Inches	2.124	2.124	2.242	2.185
Stroke – mm	54	54	57.5	61
Inches	2.124	2.124	2.262	2.402
Displacement – cc	247.3	247.3	293.5	295.1
Cubic Inches	15.1	15.1	17.9	18.0
Cooling Type	Free Air	Axial Fan	Axial Fan	Axial Fan
Carburetor Model	VM	HR	HR	HR, VM
Ignition:				
Type	CD	ET	ET	ET
Point Gap – mm	....	0.35-0.45	0.35-0.45	0.35-0.45
Inch	....	0.014-0.018	0.014-0.018	0.014-0.018
Timing Advance?	Yes	Yes	Yes	Yes
Timing BTDC – mm	0.95-1.4	2.0-2.5	2.2-2.6	2.8-3.3*
Inch	0.037-0.055	0.079-0.098	0.087-0.102	0.110-0.130
Measured at	Adv.	Adv.	Adv.	Adv.
Spark Plug:				
Type	Bosch	Bosch	Bosch	Bosch
Number	W280MZ2	W240T1	W260T1	W240T1
Electrode Gap – mm	0.5	0.5	0.5	0.5
Inch	0.020	0.020	0.020	0.020
Fuel:Oil Ratio	See Text			

*Ignition timing is 2.1 mm (0.083) BTDC on Model 305 after Serial No. 2852345

ENGINE MODEL	338, 343	345	346 (Prior to 1977)	346 (1977)
Bore – mm	59.5	63	59.5	59.5
Inches	2.343	2.480	2.343	2.343
Stroke – mm	61	54	61	61
Inches	2.402	2.124	2.402	2.402
Displacement – cc	339	336.7	339.2	339.2
Cubic Inches	20.6	20.5	20.6	20.6
Cooling Type	Axial Fan	Free Air	Free Air	Free Air
Carburetor Model	HD, VM	VM	HR	VM
Ignition:				
Type	ET	CD	CD	ET
Point Gap – mm	0.35-0.45	....	....	0.35-0.45
Inch	0.014-0.018	....	....	0.014-0.018
Timing Advance?	Yes	Yes	Yes	Yes
Timing BTDC – mm	2.8-3.3*	0.75-1.25	1.8-2.3	2.3-2.7
Inch	0.110-0.130	0.030-0.061	0.071-0.090	0.071-0.090
Measured at	Adv.	Adv.	Adv.	Adv.
Spark Plug:				
Type	Bosch	Bosch	Bosch	Bosch
Number	W260T1	W280MZ2	W280M2	W260MZ2
Electrode Gap – mm	0.5	0.5	0.5	0.5
Inch	0.020	0.020	0.020	0.020
Fuel:Oil Ratio	See Text			

*Ignition timing is 2.1 mm (0.083) BTDC on Model 343 after Serial No. 2930684

CONDENSED SERVICE DATA Continued

ENGINE MODEL	354 (Prior to 1981)	354 (1981)	370, 371	377 (Prior to 1982)
Bore – mm	59.50	59.50	62	62
Inches	2.3425	2.3425	2.441	2.4409
Stroke – mm	61	61	61	60
Inches	2.402	2.402	2.402	2.39
Displacement – cc	339.2	339.2	368	368.3
Cubic Inches	20.6	20.6	22.5	22.4
Cooling Type	Liquid	Liquid	Axial Fan	Axial Fan
Carburetor Model	VM	VM	HR	VM
Ignition:				
Type	CD	CD	ET	ET
Point Gap – mm	....	....	0.35-0.45	0.30-0.40
Inch	....	....	0.014-0.018	0.012-0.016
Timing Advance?	Yes	Yes	Yes	Yes
Timing BTDC – mm	1.14-1.64	2.27-2.77	3.5-4.0	1.82-2.32
Inch	0.045-0.065	0.089-0.109	0.140-0.160	0.071-0.091
Measured at	6000 rpm	6000 rpm	Adv.	Adv.
Spark Plug:				
Type	Bosch	Bosch	Bosch	Bosch
Number	W300T2	W300T2	W240T1	W275T2
Electrode Gap – mm	0.5	0.5	0.5	0.4
Inch	0.020	0.020	0.020	0.016
Fuel:Oil Ratio	See Text			

ENGINE MODEL	377 (1982)	396	400, 401	402
Bore – mm	62	64.5	64.5	64.5
Inches	2.4409	2.539	2.539	2.539
Stroke – mm	60	61	61	61
Inches	2.39	2.402	2.402	2.402
Displacement – cc	368.3	398.6	398.6	398.6
Cubic Inches	22.4	24.3	24.3	24.3
Cooling Type	Axial Fan	Free Air	Axial Fan	Axial Fan
Carburetor Model	VM	HD	HR, HD	VM
Ignition:				
Type	CD	CD	ET	ET
Point Gap – mm	....	....	0.35-0.45	0.30-0.40
Inch	....	....	0.014-0.018	0.012-0.016
Timing Advance?	Yes	Yes	Yes	Yes
Timing BTDC – mm	2.06-2.56	2.8-3.3	2.8-3.3	2.21-2.71
Inch	0.081-0.101	0.110-0.130	0.110-0.130	0.087-0.107
Measured at	6000 rpm	Adv.	Adv.	Adv.
Spark Plug:				
Type	NGK	Bosch	**	Bosch
Number	BR8ES	W280M2		W280MZ1
Electrode Gap – mm	0.4	0.5	0.5	0.5
Inch	0.016	0.020	0.020	0.020
Fuel:Oil Ratio	See Text			

**Recommended spark plug for Model 400 is Bosch W260T1; for Model 401 recommended spark plug is W240T1 for models using 14 mm plugs or M240T1 for models with 18 mm plugs.

CONDENSED SERVICE DATA Continued

ENGINE MODEL	434	435	436 (Prior to 1977)	436 (1977-1979)
Bore–mm	67.5	67.5	67.5	67.5
Inches	2.657	2.657	2.657	2.657
Stroke–mm	61	61	61	61
Inches	2.402	2.402	2.402	2.402
Displacement–cc	437	437	436.6	436.6
Cubic Inches	26.7	26.7	26.6	26.6
Cooling Type	Axial Fan	Axial Fan	Free Air	Free Air
Carburetor Model	HD	HD	HRM	VM
Ignition:				
Type	ET	ET	CD	ET
Point Gap–mm	0.35-0.45	0.35-0.45	....	0.35-0.45
Inch	0.014-0.018	0.014-0.018	....	0.014-0.018
Timing Advance?	Yes	Yes	Yes	Yes
Timing BTDC–mm	2.8-3.3	2.8-3.3	1.8-2.3	2.3-2.7
Inch	0.110-0.130	0.110-0.130	0.071-0.090	0.090-0.106
Measured at	Adv.	Adv.	Adv.	Adv.
Spark Plug:				
Type	Bosch	Bosch	Bosch	Bosch
Number	M240T1	M280T1	W280M2	W260MZ2
Electrode Gap–mm	0.5	0.5	0.5	0.5
Inch	0.020	0.020	0.020	0.020
Fuel:Oil Ratio	See Text			

ENGINE MODEL	440	444	454 (Prior to 1981)	454 (1981-1982)
Bore–mm	67.5	69.50	67.5	67.5
Inches	2.657	2.7362	2.6575	2.6575
Stroke–mm	61	56.75	60	60
Inches	2.402	2.27	2.4	2.4
Displacement–cc	436.6	438.8	436.6	436.6
Cubic Inches	26.6	26.77	26.64	26.64
Cooling Type	Axial Fan	Liquid	Liquid	Liquid
Carburetor Model	HD, VM	VM	VM	VM
Ignition:				
Type	ET	ET	CD	CD
Point Gap–mm	0.35-0.45	0.30-0.40	....	....
Inch	0.014-0.018	0.012-0.016	....	....
Timing Advance?	Yes	Yes	Yes	Yes
Timing BTDC–mm	2.8-3.3	2.10-2.60	1.14-1.64	2.27-2.77
Inch	0.110-0.130	0.082-0.102	0.045-0.065	0.089-0.109
Measured at	Adv.	Adv.	6000 rpm	6000 rpm
Spark Plug:				
Type	NGK	Bosch	Bosch	Bosch
Number	A-8	W275T2	W300T2	W300T2
Electrode Gap–mm	0.5	0.4	0.4	0.4
Inch	0.020	0.016	0.016	0.016
Fuel:Oil Ratio	See Text			

CONDENSED SERVICE DATA Continued

ENGINE MODEL	464 (1980)	464 (1981-1982)	503 (Prior to 1982)	503 (1982)
Bore–mm	69.50	69.50	72	72
Inches	2.7362	2.7362	2.8346	2.8346
Stroke–mm	60	60	60	60
Inches	2.4	2.4	2.4	2.4
Displacement–cc	462.8	462.8	496.7	496.7
Cubic Inches	28.24	28.24	30.31	30.31
Cooling Type	Liquid	Liquid	Axial Fan	Axial Fan
Carburetor Model	VM	VM	VM	VM
Ignition:				
Type	ET	CD	ET	CD
Point Gap–mm	0.30-0.40	....	0.30-0.40	....
Inch	0.012-0.016	....	0.012-0.016	....
Timing Advance?	Yes	Yes	Yes	Yes
Timing BTDC–mm	1.82-2.32	2.27-2.77	1.82-2.32	2.04-2.54
Inch	0.071-0.091	0.089-0.109	0.071-0.091	0.080-0.100
Measured at	Adv.	6000 rpm	Adv.	6000 rpm
Spark Plug:				
Type	Bosch	NGK	Bosch	NGK
Number	W275T2	BR8ES	W275T2	BR7ES
Electrode Gap–mm	0.4	0.4	0.4	0.4
Inch	0.016	0.016	0.016	0.016
Fuel:Oil Ratio	See Text			

ENGINE MODEL	640, 641	771	775
Bore–mm	76	82	82
Inches	2.992	3.228	3.228
Stroke–mm	70	72	73
Inches	2.756	2.834	2.874
Displacement–cc	635	771	771
Cubic Inches	38.7	47.0	47.0
Cooling Type	Axial Fan	Axial Fan	Axial Fan
Carburetor Model	HD, HRM	HD	HD
Ignition:			
Type	ET	ET	ET
Point Gap–mm	0.35-0.45	0.35-0.45	0.35-0.45
Inch	0.014-0.018	0.014-0.018	0.014-0.018
Timing Advance?	Yes	Yes	Yes
Timing BTDC–mm	4.2	4.5	4.5
Inch	0.167	0.177	0.177
Measured at	Adv.	Adv.	Adv.
Spark Plug:			
Type	Bosch	Bosch	Bosch
Number	M280T31	M310T31	M310T31
Electrode Gap–mm	0.5	0.5	0.5
Inch	0.020	0.020	0.020
Fuel:Oil Ratio	See Text		

MAINTENANCE

SPARK PLUGS. The recommended spark plug for normal service is given in **CONDENSED SERVICE DATA** table. A different heat range or type of plug may be needed for a particular application. Refer to **ENGINE SERVICE FUNDAMENTALS** section when selecting a spark plug for other than normal usage.

CARBURETOR. Mikuni Model VM and Tillotson diaphragm carburetors are used.

For Mikuni normal initial setting of pilot air jet is 1½-turns out from closed position. Idle speed should be 1800-2000 rpm.

In order to maintain correct mixture, the amount of fuel must be decreased as altitude or weather temperature increases and increased as altitude or weather temperature decreases. Use a smaller carburetor main jet to decrease flow of fuel and a larger main jet to increase flow of fuel. Be especially cautious when operating at a lower altitude, because too lean of fuel mixture will cause extreme localized overheating in engine cylinders which will cause damage to engine. Check spark plug tip color periodically in order to maintain correct jetting.

Float level is determined by height of float arm. Invert carburetor and measure distance from gasket surface to float arm. Distance should be 0.93-inch (23.6 mm) on VM 30, 32 and 34 carburetors and 0.070-inch (17.8 mm) on VM 36 and 38 carburetors.

An external impulse line from engine crankcase is used to operate fuel pump. Be sure there are no vacuum or pressure leaks.

For Tillotson diaphragm carburetors high speed mixture screw initial setting is 1⅛ turns open on 346 engine models prior to 1977, ⅝ turn open on 396 engine models, 1¼ turns open on 436 engine models and 1-turn open on all other models. Initial idle mixture screw setting is ¾-1 turn open.

Refer to TILLOTSON or MIKUNI Service section in **CARBURETOR** Service section for complete procedure on carburetor fine tuning and overhaul.

IGNITION SYSTEM. Capacitor Discharge Ignition (CDI) and Energy Transfer (ET) ignition systems have been used. Note type of system in **CONDENSED SERVICE DATA.**

Capacitor Discharge system is breakerless and advances ignition electronically. Ignition timing can be checked only with engine running at 6000 rpm. Using a power timing light connected to magneto side spark plug wire, view timing mark on flywheel through crankcase timing hole shown in Fig. 1. If marks do not align, loosen stator plate retaining screws and rotate stator plate clockwise to retard ignition timing or counterclockwise to advance ignition timing. Connect timing light to magneto side spark plug wire and repeat procedure.

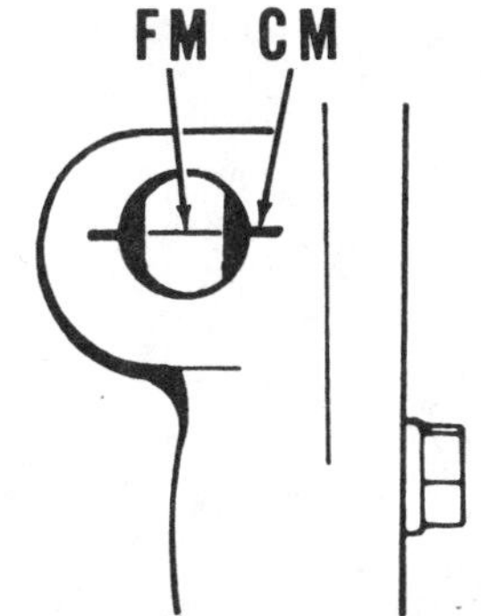

Fig. 1—Flywheel mark (FM) should align with crankcase mark (CM) with engine running at 6000 rpm on CD equipped models.

NOTE: On manual start models a separate battery source must be used to supply timing light.

Ignition timing marks may be checked using a dial indicator and specifications in **CONDENSED SERVICE DATA.**

Models with Energy Transfer ignition system have timing marks on flywheel and fan housing as shown in Fig. 1A. Timing is correct when breaker points just open when timing marks align with advance mechanism in retard (static) position; or with piston at BTDC position given in **CONDENSED SERVICE DATA** Tables and advance mechanism held in advance position. Timing may be adjusted by varying the point gap within the limits of 0.014-0.018 on early models and 0.012-0.016 on later models or by loosening the armature (stator) mounting screw and moving stator. Magneto edge gap is fixed and will be correct when breaker point gap is properly adjusted and advance mechanism operates properly.

On 370 (opposed two cylinder) models, refer to Fig. 2. Ignition occurs for both cylinders at the same time. Blue low tension wire leads to terminal (15) of first high tension coil and coils are wired in series as shown.

Fig. 1A—Breaker points should just open when timing marks (TM) align. Marks are for retarded ignition timing.

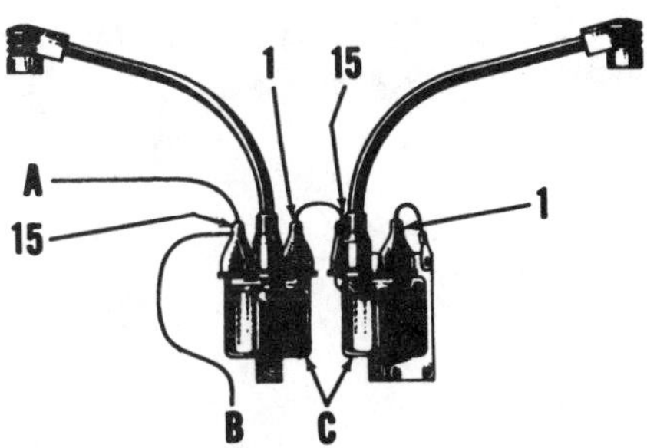

Fig. 2—View of high tension coil wiring for Model 370. Alternate firing models are NOT connected together.

A. Shorting cable
B. Generator coil wire (Blue)
C. High tension coil

On all other models equipped with Energy Transfer ignition, the top breaker points are for cylinder closest to magneto and the lower breaker points are for cylinder closest to output end of crankshaft. The flywheel is marked at two locations and ignition timing must be adjusted for each cylinder. The recoil starter and drive pulley (for the axial fan) must be removed before changing breaker point gap. The flywheel must be removed to relocate stator plate or remove breaker points.

When checking and adjusting ignition on models equipped with Energy Transfer ignition, check to make certain that advance mechanism moves freely and does not bind. If binding occurs, remove flywheel, then disassemble and clean advance mechanism and/or renew parts as required. Refill the lubricant groove in breaker point cam bore with a cold resistant and water repellent grease whenever flywheel is removed. When reinstalling flywheel, make sure lobe of centrifugal weight properly engages breaker cam. Installation of

Fig. 3—Position crankshaft with Woodruff key straight up, locate cam slot between 7 and 8 o'clock, then install flywheel. Check to make certain that lug on weight engages the cam slot by moving cam through the holes in flywheel.

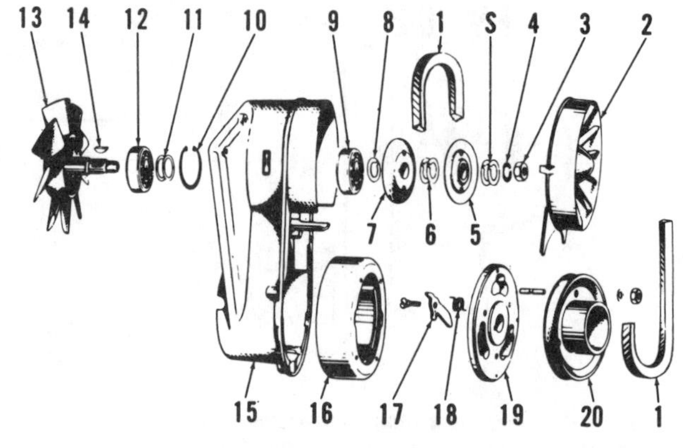

Fig. 4—Exploded view of internal type cooling fan. Refer to text for assembly notes.

1. Belt
2. Fan protector
3. Nut
4. Lockwasher
5. Outer pulley half
6. Adjusting washer
7. Inner pulley half
8. Washer
9. Bearing
10. Snap ring
11. Shims
12. Bearing
13. Fan & shaft
14. Woodruff key
15. Fan housing
16. Flywheel magnets
17. Advance weight
18. Spring
19. Flywheel hub
20. Cooling fan pulley

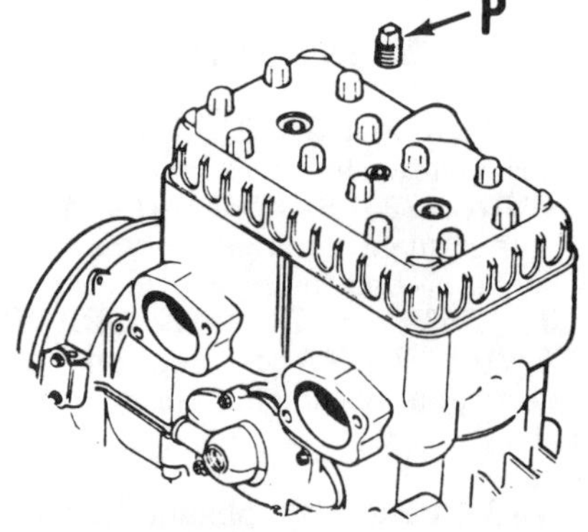

Fig. 5A—View of bleed plug in cylinder head used on liquid-cooled models to remove air pockets from cooling system during refilling.

flywheel is easier if crankshaft is turned until Woodruff key is straight up (12 o'clock) and cam slot is located between 7 and 8 o'clock positions. Refer to Fig. 3. Tighten flywheel nut to 50 ft.-lbs. torque. Refer to **SERVICE FUNDAMENTALS** for overhaul data and service procedures.

LUBRICATION. The engine for models without oil injection is lubricated by mixing oil with the fuel. Mix fuel and oil thoroughly in a separate container before pouring mixture into fuel tank. Bombardier concentrated 50:1 oil should be mixed with recommended fuel at a ratio of one pint of oil to six gallons of gasoline. If Bombardier oil is not available, USE ONLY a good quality recognized brand snowmobile oil or two-cycle oil and mix at fuel:oil ratio recommended by oil manufacturer. For cold weather blending, pre-mix the oil with a small amount of gasoline and shake thoroughly until mixture is liquid, then blend with remainder of fuel. Do not use kerosene or fuel oil for pre-mixing.

Normally the engine on models with oil injection will be adequately lubricated by oil delivered and metered by the oil injection pump. In extremely cold weather, the oil injection system may not pump correctly. Below −20 degrees F. (−29 degrees C.), mix one pint of oil with each six gallons of gasoline to supplement oil injection pump to insure proper lubrication.

COOLING FAN AND BELT (All Except 370). Cooling fan may be located internally as shown in Fig. 4 or externally as shown in Fig. 5. Belt tension should be adjusted to allow 6 mm (¼-inch) deflection midway between pulleys when pressed with finger. Belt can be tightened by removing shims (6–Fig. 4 or 5) from between pulley halves (5 and 7). On some external fan models, fan is outboard pulley half. Shims removed from between pulley halves should be relocated outside of outer pulley half (or fan) as shown at (S). Four shims are originally installed. Do not pinch belt in bottom of pulley groove when tightening nut (3). Recommended torque is 46 ft.-lbs.

Refer to Figs. 4 and 5 for assistance in disassembling and inspection of unit. Fan housing should be heated to assist in removal of bearings. Note snap ring (10) located between bearings. Install bearings with open sides facing snap ring (10). Two washers (11) should be installed between bearings. Newer style pulley halves (5 and 7) do not have a shoulder on pulley hub and a 6 mm spacer must be installed on concave side of pulley half.

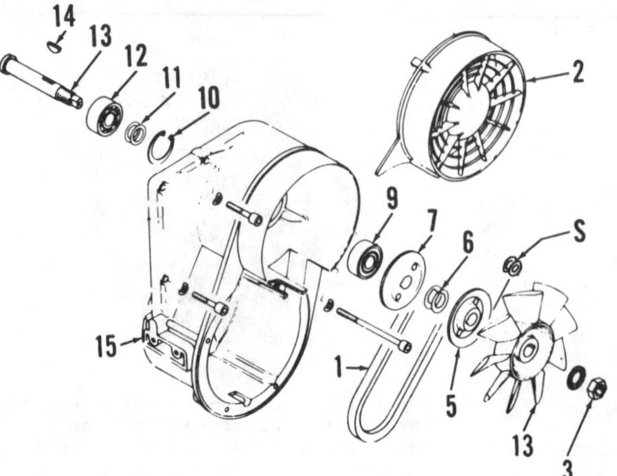

Fig. 5—Exploded view of external fan type cooling system. Pulley half (5) and fan are integral on some models. Refer to Fig. 4 for parts identification.

LIQUID COOLING SYSTEM. The coolant liquid is thermostatically temperature controlled and positively circulated by an engine driven centrifugal coolant pump. Cooling is by either two series-connected aluminum heat exchangers located underneath each running board or by a radiator. Recommended coolant liquid is ethylene glycol and water mixed at a 50:50 ratio which protects system to a temperature of 36 degrees below zero, F. Do not exceed a ratio of 55 parts ethylene glycol to 45 parts water. Engines are equipped with either a 110 degree F. or 126 degree F. thermostat. Thermostat should be fully open at 110 or 126 degrees F. and should fully close at room temperature. Discard any thermostat which does not open or close properly.

To drain the system, remove filler cap and open petcock on bottom of coolant pump housing for Models 354 and 454; open petcock on bottom of radiator for Model 444 and some 464 models; use a primer pump and withdraw coolant from system on 464 models without petcocks.

To fill the cooling system, remove bleed plug (P–Fig. 5A) and filler cap. Add coolant through filler plug opening until it emerges from bleeder vent, then install bleeder plug. Continue filling until coolant level reaches filler neck. Start and idle engine until thermostat opens then add coolant if fluid level drops.

REPAIRS

TIGHTENING TORQUES. Recommended tightening torques are as follows:

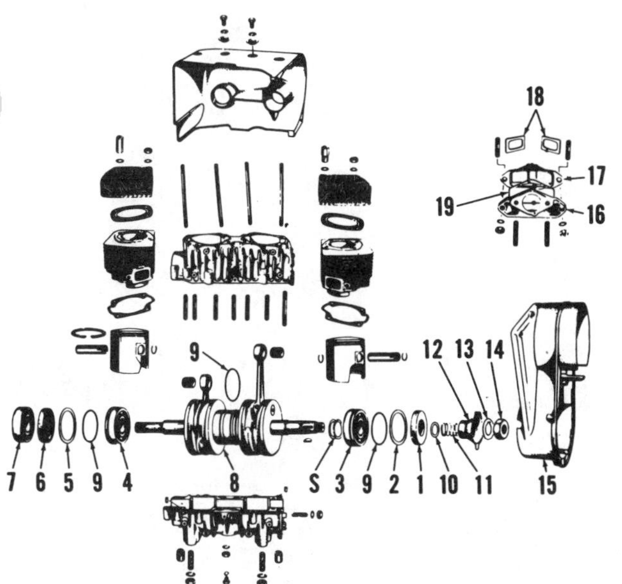

Fig. 6 – Exploded view of alternate firing (in-line) twin. Model 641 is shown; but others are similar.

1. Seal
2. Retainer ring
3. Bearing
4. Bearing
5. Retainer ring
6. Seal
7. Bearing
8. Crankshaft
9. "O" ring
10. Washer
11. Spring
12. Ignition cam
13. Tab washer
14. Flywheel nut
15. Fan housing
16. Inlet manifold cover
17. "V" block
18. Gaskets
19. Seal ring

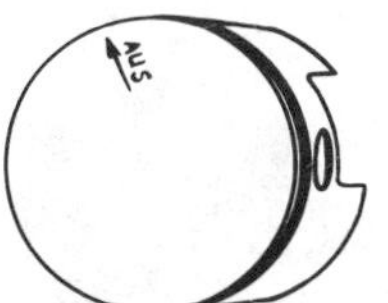

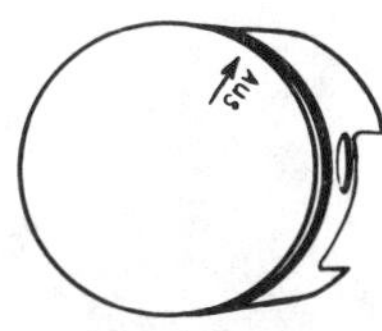

Fig. 7 – Pistons are not interchangeable between cylinders of alternate firing, in-line twins. Arrows and "AUS" marks should be angled apart as shown and on exhaust side of engine.

Crankcase Nuts* . . . . 16 ft.-lbs.
Cylinder Head Nuts** . . . . . 16 ft.-lbs.
Engine to Mounting Bracket –
8 mm nuts . . . . 75-100 in.-lbs.
10 mm nuts . . . . 150-200 in.-lbs.
12 mm nuts . . . . 175-225 in.-lbs.
Engine Mounting to Vehicle . . . . 28 ft.-lbs.
Fan Shaft Nut . . . . 46 ft.-lbs.
Flywheel Nut . . . . 63-70 ft.-lbs.

*Crankcase stud nuts for models except 370 should be tightened in sequence working from center fasteners to each end of crankcase, first to torque of 10 ft.-lbs., then to final torque of 16 ft.-lbs.

**Tighten cylinder head stud nuts diagonally to 10 ft.-lbs., then to final torque of 16 ft.-lbs.

ENGINE R&R. Standard engine removal procedures apply. When installing, make certain that centers of pulley grooves are aligned before tightening engine mounting nuts. Pulley offset should be as follows:

SKI-DOO

Model Year	Pulley Offset
1970	
T'NT 340	3/8 inch
All Others	1/2 inch
1971	1/2 inch
1972	
T'NT 340 and 440	7/16 inch
All Others	1/2 inch
1973	
T'NT 294, 340 and 440	7/16 inch
All Others	1/2 inch
1974	
Elan 294SS and 300SS	1/2 inch
Everest 440	1/2 inch
Nordic 640ER	1/2 inch
T'NT F/C 300, 340 and 440	1/2 inch
T'NT F/A 340, 400 and 440	Self-adjusting
All Others	9/16 inch
1975	
Alpine 640ER	9/16 inch
Elan 250, 250E, 250T, and 250 Deluxe	9/16 inch
Elite 440ER	9/16 inch
T'NT F/A 340, 400 and 440	Self-adjusting
All Others	1/2 inch
1976	1-5/16 inch
1977	1-11/32 inch
1978	1-11/32 inch
1979	1-11/32 inch
1980	1-11/32 inch
1981	
Everest 500, Everest LC, Blizzard 5500, Blizzard 7500 and Blizzard 9500	1-5/16 inch
All Others	1-11/32 inch
1982	
Everest 500, Everest LC, Blizzard 5500 and Blizzard 9500	1-9/32 inch
All Others	1-11/32 inch

MOTO-SKI

Model Year	Pulley Offset
1975	
Futura 340 and 440	1-3/16 inch
Nuvik 300 and 340	1/2 inch
TS-400	1-3/16 inch
1976	1-5/16 inch
1977	1-11/32 inch
1978	1-11/32 inch
1979	1-11/32 inch
1980	1-11/32 inch
1981	
Futura 500, Futura LC, Grand Prix Special, Super Sonic and Ultra Sonic	1-5/16 inch
All Others	1-11/32 inch
1982	
Sonic, Ultra Sonic, Futura 500 and Futura LC	1-9/32 inch
All Others	1-11/32 inch

Pulley faces for all models must be parallel. Engine mounting nuts should be tightened to 32 ft.-lbs.

DISASSEMBLY AND REASSEMBLY (All Except 370). Normal disassembly procedures should be used. When assembling, observe the following: Clean all old sealer from mating surfaces of crankcase halves and make certain that surfaces are not distorted or nicked. Invert the upper crankcase half and make certain that "O" rings (9 – Fig. 6) are in good condition. Position crankshaft in upper crankcase half making certain that tapered end of crankshaft is extending through magneto end of crankcase. Be sure to correctly seat the retaining washers in grooves of crankcase half. Coat mating surface of crankcase half with "Loctite" sealer or equivalent and install the lower half of crankcase. Install pistons so that arrows and "AUS" mark are angled apart and toward exhaust side of engine as shown in Fig. 7. Cylinders are not interchangeable and cylinder to crankcase gaskets must not block the pulse passage for fuel pump. Cylinder heads are not interchangeable and must be installed as shown in Fig. 8 and Fig. 9.

NOTE: Before tightening cylinder and head retaining nuts, the cylinders must be correctly aligned by installing the complete inlet manifold assembly. Make certain that all inlet manifold gaskets are installed and do not leak after tightening the cylinder and head retaining nuts to the recommended torque. On all models except 245 and 345, gaskets (18 – Fig. 6) between "V" block (17) and cylinder are not

Fig. 8 – The side of cylinder head indicated by pointer must be installed toward exhaust port side of engine.

Fig. 9—Installed view of cylinder heads with slanted fins.

interchangeable on some models. Make certain that gaskets are installed correctly and do not block pulse passage for fuel pump.

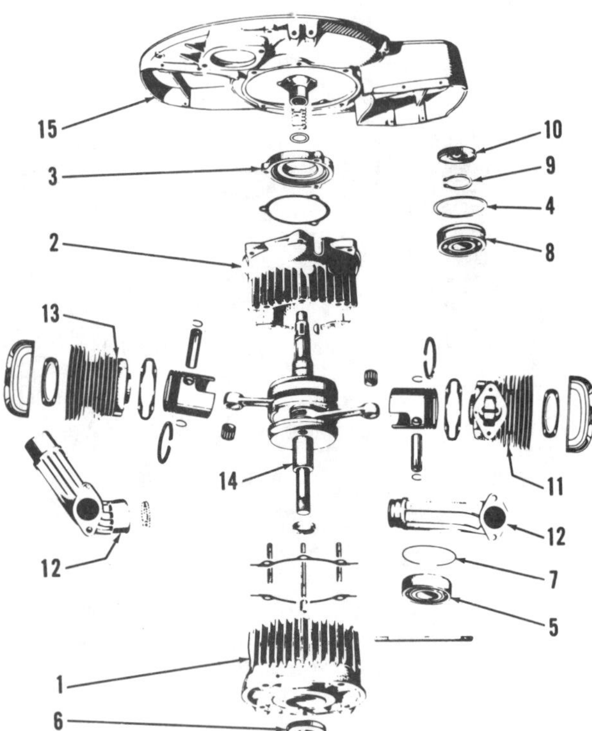

Fig. 11—Exploded view of Model 370 opposed cylinder engine.

1. Crankcase (pto) half
2. Crankcase (magneto) half
3. Bearing plate
4. Snap ring
5. Roller bearing
6. Seal
7. Snap ring
8. Ball bearing
9. Snap ring
10. Seal
11. Cylinder (carburetor mounting)
12. Exhaust manifold
13. Cylinder
14. Crankshaft
15. Fan cowl

Model 370. To disassemble, remove recoil starter, carburetor, ignition coils, electric starter (if so equipped), exhaust manifold, fan cover, flywheel, magneto and fan cowl. Remove both cylinder heads, cylinders and pistons. Remove bearing plate (3–Fig. 10) and screws attaching crankcase halves together; then bump output end of crankshaft to separate crankcase halves. Crankshaft can be removed from magneto side crankcase half after removing snap rings (4 and 9). Crankcase halves should be heated to approximately 170°-180° F. to facilitate withdrawing main bearing (8) and outer race of roller bearing (5). Snap ring (7) must be removed before outer race (5) can be removed. Arrow and "AUS" mark on pistons should be toward exhaust side. Cylinder head should be installed with "Squish Area" shown in Fig. 8 down toward exhaust side of cylinders.

PISTONS, RINGS AND CYLINDER. The piston pin should be an easy fit in piston boss when piston is heated to 140-150 degrees F. Pin is retained in piston by snap rings. The arrow and "AUS" stamped on top of piston must be installed toward exhaust port side of cylinder when unit is reassembled. Refer to Fig. 7 for alternate firing, in-line twins.

Renew or rebore cylinder if out-of-round exceeds 0.002 inch, taper exceeds 0.003 inch or if wear exceeds 0.004 inch. Piston skirt to cylinder clearance should be as follows:

Engine Model (Prior to 1982)	Piston Clearance
245	0.0028-0.0041 inch
248 and 294	0.002-0.0055 inch
249, 305 and 345	0.002-0.0033 inch
338, 401 and 434	0.0031-0.0045 inch
343 and 354	0.0031-0.0079 inch
377 and 464	0.0028-0.008 inch
402, 440, 444 and 640	0.0028-0.0071 inch
346, 396, 400, 435, 436, 641 and 775	0.004-0.005 inch
454	0.0035-0.0087 inch
503	0.0024-0.0063 inch
(1982)	
377, 464, 503 and 640	0.003-0.004 inch
454	0.004-0.005 inch

Measure piston diameter 5/16-inch above edge of skirt at right angles to piston pin. Ring side clearance in

Fig. 10—Assembled view of opposed twin (Model 370) crankcase and crankshaft assembly.

1. Crankcase (pto side)
2. Crankcase (magneto side)
3. Bearing plate
4. Snap ring
5. Roller bearing
6. Oil seal
7. Snap ring
8. Ball bearing
9. Snap ring

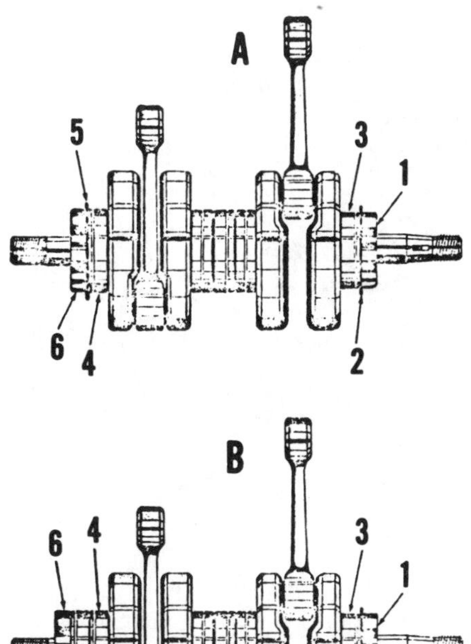

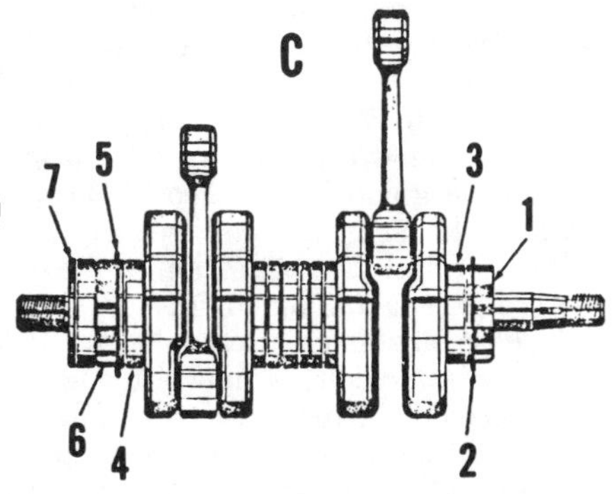

Fig. 12 — Views showing correct bearing and seal installation. See text.

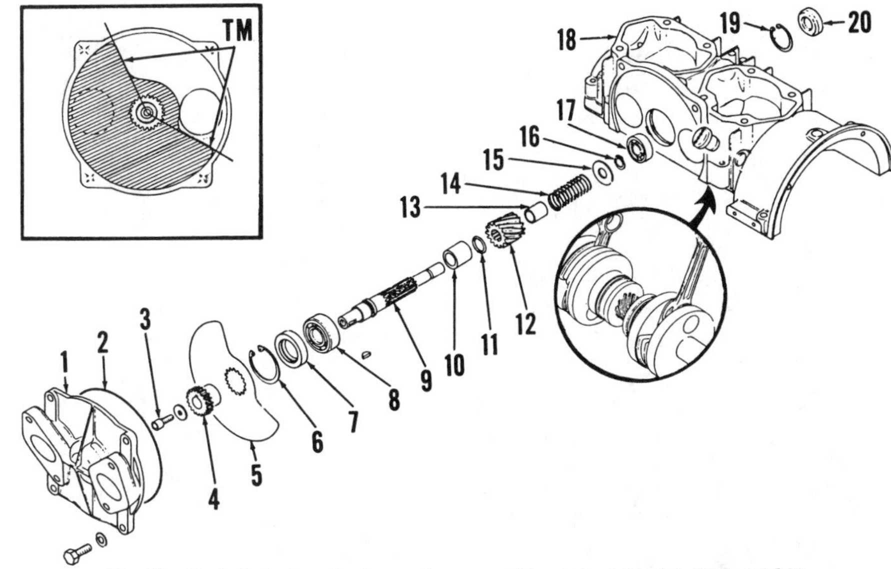

Fig. 13 — Exploded view of rotary valve assembly used on Models 245 and 345.

1. Cover
2. "O" ring
3. Screw
4. Gear
5. Rotary valve
6. Snap ring
7. Seal
8. Bearing
9. Shaft
10. Spacer
11. "O" ring
12. Gear
13. Sleeve
14. Spring
15. Washer
16. Snap ring
17. Bearing
18. Crankcase
29. Snap ring
20. Plug

grooves should be 0.002-0.008 inch and ring end gaps in cylinder should be 0.010-0.063 inch.

CRANKSHAFT AND CONNECTING RODS. Connecting rods and crankshaft are available only as an assembly. End main bearings and seals are available separately. Fig. 12A shows a bearing puller used to remove end main bearings. Refer to Fig. 12 for correct assembly of bearing and seals for alternate firing twins. View "A" applies to 305, 338, 343, 400, 401, 434, 440, 640 and early 248 models; view "B" applies to 245, 294, 345, 346, 396, 435, 436 and later 305 and 343 models; view "C" applies to Models 641 and 775. Model 440 is similar to View "A" but two bearings are used on magneto end of crankshaft. Runout when supported between lathe centers and measured at main bearings, must not exceed 0.003 inch. Side clearance of rods between crankshaft webs should not exceed 0.020 inch. If crankshaft runout or side clearance is not within specifications, crankshaft assembly must be renewed. Crankshaft end play on some early model engines and on most later model engines is limited by ball type main bearings. Crankshaft end play of 248, 294, 305, 338, 343, 400, 401, 640, 641, 775 and 1977 440 models should be 0.004-0.016 inch. End play is adjusted by adding shims (S – Fig. 6), between main bearings (3 and 4) and crankshaft. The same thickness of shims should be installed behind bearings (3 and 4) to center the crankshaft.

ROTARY VALVE (Air-Cooled Models). Models 245 and 345 are equipped with a rotary valve. Refer to Fig. 13 for an exploded view of rotary valve assembly. Rotary valve shaft is driven by gear (12) which mates with a gear at center of crankshaft.

To remove rotary valve assembly, remove cover (1), unscrew retaining screw (3) and remove rotary valve (5), gear (4) and snap ring (6). Using a suitable puller, extract rotary valve shaft assembly from crankcase. To install rotary valve assembly, reverse disassembly procedure. Be sure sharp edge of snap ring (16) is towards near end of shaft. Apply sealant to mating surfaces of bearing (8) and gear (4). Install rotary valve (5) so edges of valve

Fig. 13A — Exploded view of a typical rotary valve and coolant pump assembly. Some models use three number 17 seals.

1. Rotary valve cover
2. "O" ring
3. Rotary valve
4. Snap ring
5. Rotary valve shaft
6. Seal
7. Ball bearing
8. Shim (0.5 mm)
9. Spacer sleeve (24.5 mm)
10. Shim (0.5 mm)
11. "O" ring
12. Gear
13. Spring
14. Spring seat
15. Snap ring
16. Ball bearing
17. Seal
18. Spacer ring
19. Washer (8.4 mm)
20. Pump impeller
21. Gasket
22. Pump housing

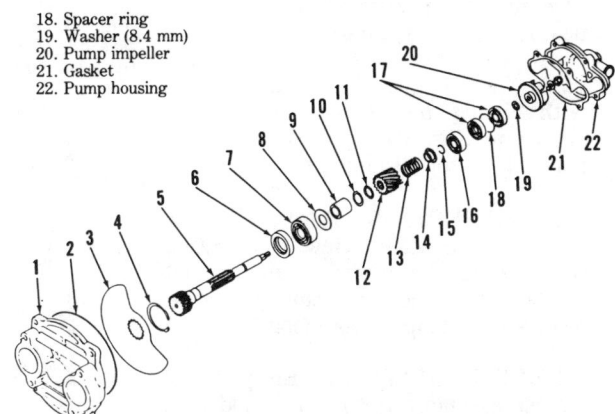

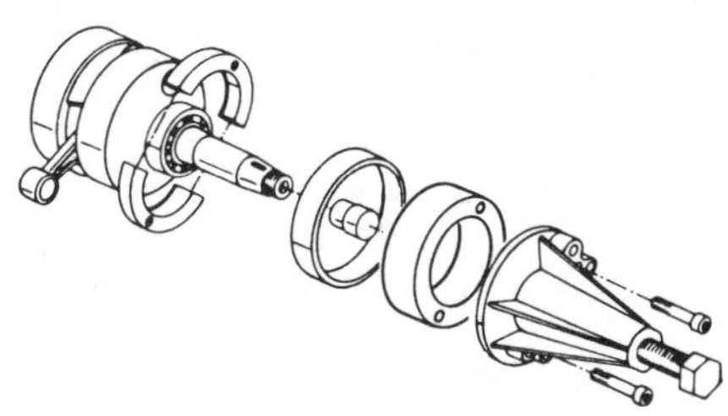

Fig. 12A — View of a end main bearing puller.

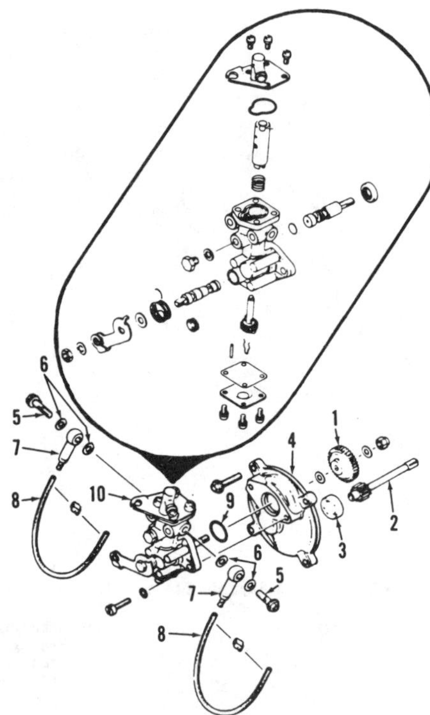

Fig. 14—Exploded view of oil injection pump and related parts.

1. Pump drive gear
2. Gear and shaft
3. Ball bearing
4. Pump mounting flange
5. Banjo bolt
6. Washers
7. Banjo fitting
8. Oil line
9. "O" ring
10. Pump assy.

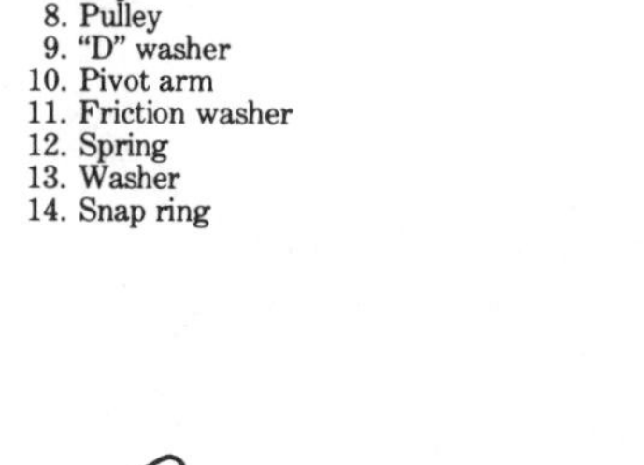

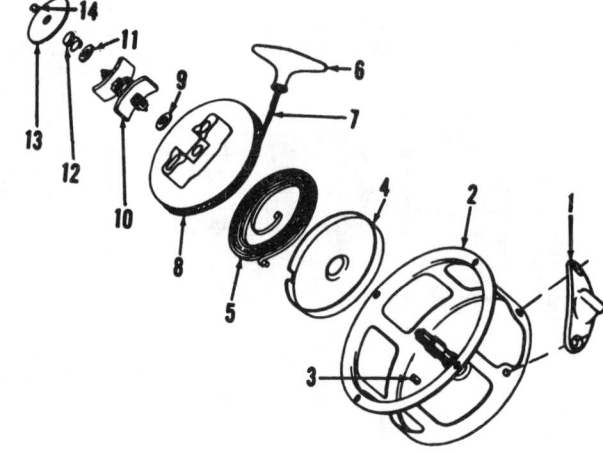

Fig. 15—Exploded view of recoil starter.

1. Rope guide
2. Housing
3. Pin
4. Spring guide
5. Recoil spring
6. Handle
7. Rope
8. Pulley
9. "D" washer
10. Pivot arm
11. Friction washer
12. Spring
13. Washer
14. Snap ring

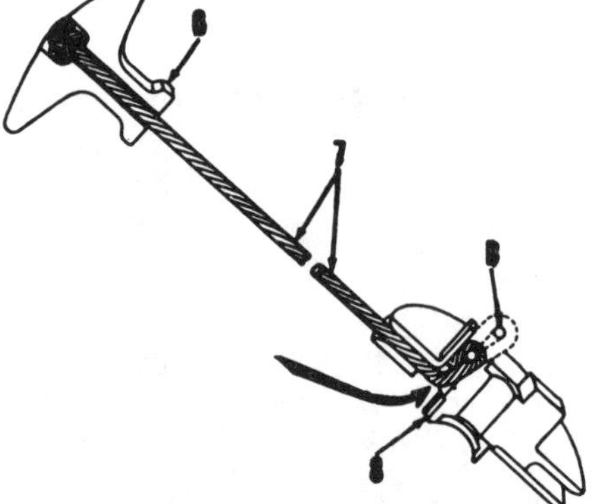

Fig. 16—Cross-sectional view of starter pulley and rope showing approved method of securing rope. Refer to Fig. 15 for parts identification except for bolt (B).

are aligned with timing marks on crankcase as shown in Fig. 13 when magneto side piston is at top dead center.

(Liquid-Cooled Models). Refer to Fig. 13A for an exploded view of rotary valve and coolant pump assembly. Rotary valve shaft is driven by gear (12) which mates with a gear at center of crankshaft. To remove rotary valve assembly, remove coolant pump cover (22), impeller (20), rotary valve cover (1), rotary valve (3) and snap ring (4). Using a suitable driver and hammer, tap rotary valve shaft out of crankcase. To install rotary valve assembly, reverse disassembly procedure. During reassembly make sure snap ring (18) is positioned so opening is in line with crankcase drain hole. Install rotary valve (3) so edges of valve are aligned with timing marks on crankcase as shown in Fig. 13 when magneto side piston is at top dead center.

OIL INJECTION PUMP. Refer to Fig. 14 for exploded view of operating components. Pump components are not available as single parts, unit must be renewed as a complete assembly.

RECOIL STARTER. Early recoil starter assembly is shown exploded in Fig. 15. To disassemble the early starter unit, proceed as follows:

Remove the two screws securing rope guide (1) to housing (2), pass the guide through hole in housing and allow the recoil spring to unwind. Remove snap ring (14) and disassemble the starter, allowing spring (5) to remain nested in spring guide (4). To remove the starter rope, insert a punch through hole indicated by arrow, Fig. 16, push rope end (7) out of pulley (8) and withdraw the locking pin (bolt) (B). Unit can now be disassembled.

Assemble by reversing the disassembly procedure. Make sure serrations of pivot arm (10–Fig. 15) and friction washer (11) are together and lightly oiled. Also make sure that rope (7) and spring (5) are installed as shown. Outer end of spring (5) must hook over pin (3) and inner end of spring must engage slot in pulley (8). Wind rope pulley 3 or 4 turns to achieve proper recoil tension, pass rope guide (1) up through proper slot in housing (2) and secure with screws. Check the operation of starter before reinstalling on engine.

The recoil starter, used on some 1980 and earlier models, is shown in Fig. 17. To overhaul starter, proceed as follows: Remove rope handle and allow rope to rewind into starter housing. Remove pawl guide (1), snap ring (2) and disassemble starter while allowing spring (14) to remain in spring guide (13).

Assemble by reversing disassembly procedure. Rewind spring (14) is wrapped in spring guide (13) in clockwise direction from outer end of spring. Rope is secured in pulley by a

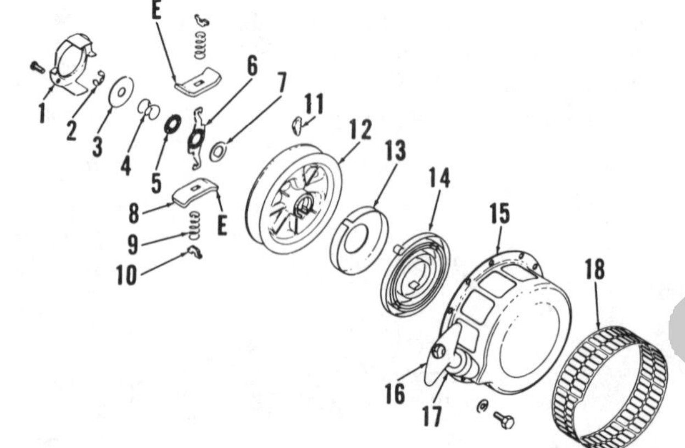

Fig. 17—Exploded view of rewind starter used up to and on some 1980 models.

1. Pawl guide
2. Snap ring
3. Washer
4. Spring
5. Friction washer
6. Pivot arm
7. "D" washer
8. Pawl
9. Spring
10. Spring keeper
11. Serrated key
12. Rope pulley
13. Spring guide
14. Rewind spring
15. Starter housing
16. Rope handle
17. Rope guide
18. Shield

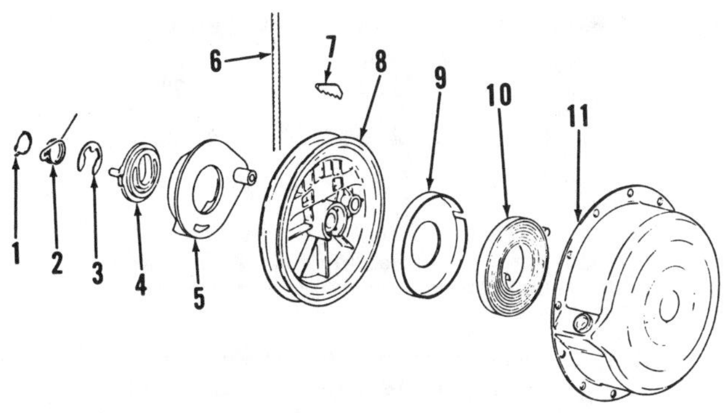

Fig. 18—Exploded view of rewind starter used during 1981-82 and on some 1980 models.

1. Snap ring
2. Lock spring
3. "E" clip
4. Pawl lock
5. Pawl
6. Rope
7. Key
8. Rope pulley
9. Spring guide
10. Rewind spring
11. Starter housing

serrated key (11). Rope is wound around pulley in counter-clockwise direction as viewed with pulley in housing. Rotate pulley (12) six turns counter-clockwise before passing rope through starter housing so rewind spring is preloaded. Make sure serrations of pivot arm (6) and friction washer (5) are together and lightly oiled. Note locations of sharp edges (E) on pawls (8).

The recoil starter used on 1981-82 and some 1980 models is shown in Fig. 18. To overhaul starter, proceed as follows: Remove snap ring (1), lock spring (2), "E" clip (3), pawl lock (4) and pawl (5). Pull rope (6) out of pulley (8) until rope is fully extended. Disengage key (7) and pull rope completely out of pulley. Withdraw pulley (8), spring guide (9) and spring (10). Inspect all parts for damage and renew as needed.

Assemble in reverse of disassembly. Rope is wound around pulley in counter-clockwise direction as viewed with pulley in housing. Rotate pulley (8) six turns counter-clockwise before passing rope through starter housing so rewind spring is preloaded, then complete reassembly.

RUPP

CONDENSED SERVICE DATA

<table>
<tr><th>Engine Model</th><th>TR-295</th><th>TR-295S</th><th>TR-340</th><th>TR-340S</th><th>TR-400S-2</th></tr>
<tr><td>Bore—(mm)</td><td>57</td><td>57</td><td>61</td><td>61</td><td>63</td></tr>
<tr><td>Inches</td><td>2.244</td><td>2.244</td><td>2.402</td><td>2.402</td><td>2.480</td></tr>
<tr><td>Stroke—(mm)</td><td>57.5</td><td>57.5</td><td>57.5</td><td>57.5</td><td>64</td></tr>
<tr><td>Inches</td><td>2.268</td><td>2.268</td><td>2:268</td><td>2.268</td><td>2.520</td></tr>
<tr><td>No. of Cylinders</td><td>2</td><td>2</td><td>2</td><td>2</td><td>2</td></tr>
<tr><td>Displacement—(cc)</td><td>294</td><td>294</td><td>336</td><td>336</td><td>399</td></tr>
<tr><td>Cubic Inches</td><td>17.9</td><td>17.9</td><td>20.5</td><td>20.5</td><td>24.3</td></tr>
<tr><td>Horsepower @ rpm</td><td>19@</td><td>....</td><td>24@</td><td>....</td><td>....</td></tr>
<tr><td>Cooling Type</td><td>Axial Fan</td><td>Axial Fan</td><td>Axial Fan</td><td>Axial Fan</td><td>....</td></tr>
<tr><td>Carburetor Model</td><td colspan="5">Keihin Diaphragm</td></tr>
<tr><td>Number Used</td><td>1</td><td>1</td><td>1</td><td>1</td><td>1</td></tr>
<tr><td>Ignition:</td><td></td><td></td><td></td><td></td><td></td></tr>
<tr><td>Type</td><td colspan="5">E. T. Magneto*</td></tr>
<tr><td>Point Gap—(Inch)</td><td>0.014</td><td>0.014</td><td>0.014</td><td>0.014</td><td>0.012-0.014</td></tr>
<tr><td>Timing (Degrees BTDC)—</td><td></td><td></td><td></td><td></td><td></td></tr>
<tr><td>Retarded**</td><td>7-10</td><td>7-10</td><td>7-10</td><td>7-10</td><td>7-10</td></tr>
<tr><td>Advanced**</td><td>22-25</td><td>22-25</td><td>22-25</td><td>22-25</td><td>22-25</td></tr>
<tr><td>Spark Plug:</td><td></td><td></td><td></td><td></td><td></td></tr>
<tr><td>Champion</td><td>L-78</td><td>L-77J</td><td>L-78</td><td>L-77J</td><td>L-77J</td></tr>
<tr><td>Electrode Gap (Inch)</td><td>0.028</td><td>0.028</td><td>0.028</td><td>0.028</td><td>0.028</td></tr>
<tr><td>Fuel/Oil Ratio</td><td>20:1</td><td>20:1</td><td>20:1</td><td>20:1</td><td>20:1</td></tr>
</table>

*CD Ignition Unit on some models.
**Refer to text for piston position BTDC

Engine Model	TR-440	TR-440-2	TR-440S-2	TR-650	TR-650S
Bore—(mm)	66	66	66	76	76
Inches	2.600	2.600	2.600	2.992	2.992
Stroke—(mm)	64	64	64	71	71
Inches	2.520	2.520	2.520	2.795	2.795
No. of Cylinders	2	2	2	2	2
Displacement—(cc)	438	438	438	644	644
Cubic Inches	26.7	26.7	26.7	39.3	39.3
Horsepower @ rpm	35@6250	....	....	40@	....
Cooling Type	Axial Fan	Axial Fan	Axial Fan	Axial Fan	Axial Fan
Carburetor Model	Keihin Diaphragm				
Number Used	1	1	1	1	1
Ignition:					
Type	E. T. Magneto*				
Point Gap—(Inch)	0.012-0.014	0.014	0.014	0.014-0.016	0.014-0.016
Timing (Degrees BTDC)—					
Retarded**	10-13	10-13	7-10	....	....
Advanced**	25-28	22-25	22-25	....	....
Spark Plug:					
Champion	L81	L-77J	L-77J	....	....
Electrode Gap (Inch)	0.030	0.028	0.028	0.028	0.028
Fuel/Oil Ratio	20:1	20:1	20:1	20:1	20:1

*CD Ignition Unit on some models.
**Refer to text for piston position BTDC.

MAINTENANCE

SPARK PLUGS. The recommended Champion spark plug for normal service is listed in the CONDENSED SERVICE DATA tables. Spark plugs should be tightened to 180 inch-pounds torque.

CARBURETOR. Keihin diaphragm carburetors are used on all models. Refer to Keihin Carburetor Section for operation and overhaul information. Initial setting of idle mixture needle (needle closest to inlet manifold) is 2¼ turns open. Initial setting of high speed mixture needle is 1⅝ turns open from seated position. High speed mixture should be set while operating under normal load.

IGNITION SYSTEM. An energy transfer (E.T.) magneto is used. The auxiliary lighting coil is installed on magneto stator plate and utilizes the flywheel magnets as a power source.

Breaker point gap is listed in CONDENSED SERVICE DATA tables. Use a dial indicator (1—Fig. 1) in spark plug holes to correctly position the crankshaft and continuity meter or light (2) to indicate breaker points opening. Timing should be set with the ignition cam in full advanced position (advance weights pulled out). Piston position Before Top Dead Center is as follows: TR-295, TR-295S, TR-340, TR-340S

Full advance
22°-25° .... 0.102-0.131 inch
TR-400S-2
Full advance
22°-25° .... 1.114-1.147 inch
TR-440
Full advance
25°-28° .... 0.149-0.189 inch
TR-440-2, TR-440S-2
Full advance
22°-25° .... 0.114-0.147 inch

If timing is incorrect, loosen the two stator plate retaining screws (5) and move stator plate as required to provide correct timing. Ignition timing for the second cylinder can be synchronized to the first cylinder by varying the breaker point gap slightly. Flywheel and fan housing on some models are equipped with ignition timing marks.

Fig. 1–Dial indicator (1) should be used to locate piston at correct timing position and continuity light (2) is used to show when breaker points open. Weights (3) can be pulled out to move the ignition cam to full advance, by working through holes in flywheel as shown at (4). Stator plate retaining screws (5) are accessible through holes in flywheel. Lighting coil is shown at (6) and low tension ignition coils at (7). Breaker points (M) are for cylinder closest to magneto end and breaker points (D) are for cylinder near drive end.

LUBRICATION. The engine is lubricated by mixing oil with the fuel. A suitable two-stroke air cooled engine oil is recommended. Recommended ratio is 20:1. Fuel and oil must be mixed thoroughly before filling vehicle tank.

COOLING FAN AND BELT. Belt tension should be adjusted to allow slight deflection between pulleys, when pressed with thumb. Tightening is accomplished by removing shims (4—Fig. 2) from between pulley halves (3 & 6). Shims removed from between pulley halves should be relocated behind inner pulley (at 4S) to prevent loss. Seven shims 4 and 4S are originally installed. Do not pinch belt in bottom of pulley groove when tightening nut.

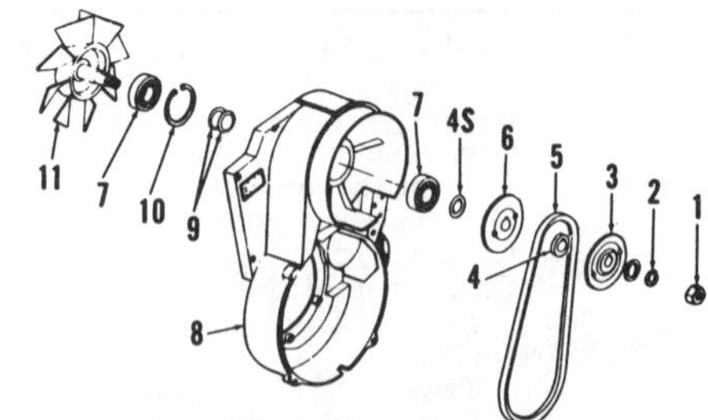

Fig. 2–Exploded view of the axial flow fan and drive assembly. Shims (4) which are not used between pulley halves to adjust belt tension should be stored at (4S).

1. Nut
2. Lock washer
3. Pulley half
4. Shims
5. Belt
6. Pulley half
7. Bearings
8. Fan housing
9. Shims
10. Snap ring
11. Fan and shaft

To renew belt, remove recoil starter, nut, outside pulley half and adjusting shims. Install new belt and adjust as outlined in preceding paragraph.

Fan and shaft (11—Fig. 2) can be renewed after removing flywheel and fan housing. To remove bearings (7), heat fan housing and bump housing against wooden block. NOTE: Snap ring (10) is located between bearings. Do not lose washers (9) located between bearings. Bearings should be packed with high temperature bearing grease. Install bearings with open sides together toward snap ring (10) and washers (9).

REPAIRS

TIGHTENING TORQUES. Recommended tightening torques are as follows:

Air Shroud—	
Cap screws	190 in.-lbs.
Phillips head screws	50 in.-lbs.
Carburetor Nuts	120 in.-lbs.
Crankcase Screws	190 in.-lbs.
Cylinder Head Nuts	190 in.-lbs.
Exhaust Pipe	22 ft.-lbs.
Fan Case to Crankcase screws	120 in.-lbs.
Fan Screws	50 in.-lbs.
Flywheel Nut (left hand thread)	50 ft.-lbs.
Ignition Coil Screws	50 in.-lbs.
Inlet Manifold Nuts	150 in.-lbs.
Spark Plugs	180 in.-lbs.
Long Stud (through air shroud)	17 in.-lbs.

ENGINE R & R. Standard engine removal procedures apply. When installing, make certain that centers of pulley grooves are aligned before tightening engine mount screws. Pulley faces must be exactly parallel and offset should be approximately 15/32-inch.

DISASSEMBLY AND REASSEMBLY. Normal disassembly procedures should be used. When assembling, observe the following: Clean all old sealer from mating surfaces of crankcase halves and make certain that surfaces are not distorted or nicked. Invert the upper crankcase half and make certain that the four crankcase locating dowels (9—Fig. 6) and the two center seal locating dowels (7) are correctly located. Pack both seals (2 & 6) with silicone low temperature grease, then position gaskets (4 or 5), retainers (3) if so equipped and seals (2 & 6) over ends of crankshaft. Make certain that "O" rings (15) are in good condition, then position crankshaft in the upper crankcase half with external threaded end toward magneto end of crankcase. Carefully make certain that gaskets (4 & 5) enter grooves in crankcase correctly and that the two dowels (7) enter holes in center seals (14) correctly. Coat mating surface of crankcase half with "3M Scotch Sealant #1814" or equivalent and install lower half of crankcase. NOTE: On TR-400S-2 and all 440 models, the two longer crankcase screws should be located next to magneto end. Install pistons so that arrows are angled apart and toward exhaust side of engine. Refer to Fig. 4. Install piston rings with manufacturers mark "N" toward top. Cylinders are not interchangeable and cylinder to crankcase gasket must not block the pulse passage for fuel pump. Install head gaskets with "H" side toward top. NOTE: The two cylinder head gaskets are not interchangeable on some models. Make certain that gasket is aligned before installing cylinder head. Cylinder heads are not interchangeable and must be installed with flat sides with square corners together (toward center). Make certain that the large cylinder and head retaining nuts are correctly positioned for assembly of cooling shroud. NOTE: Before tightening cylinder and head nuts to the recommended torque, the cylinders must be correctly aligned by installing the complete inlet manifold **without** gaskets. Inlet manifold screws must be tightened to provide correct

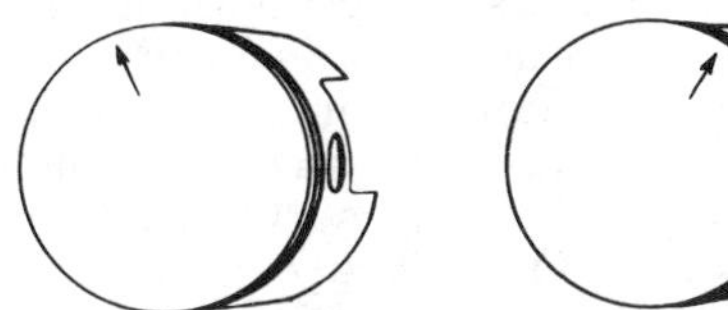

Fig. 4–Arrows on pistons must be angled apart as shown and arrows must be toward exhaust side of engine. Pistons are not interchangeable between the two cylinders.

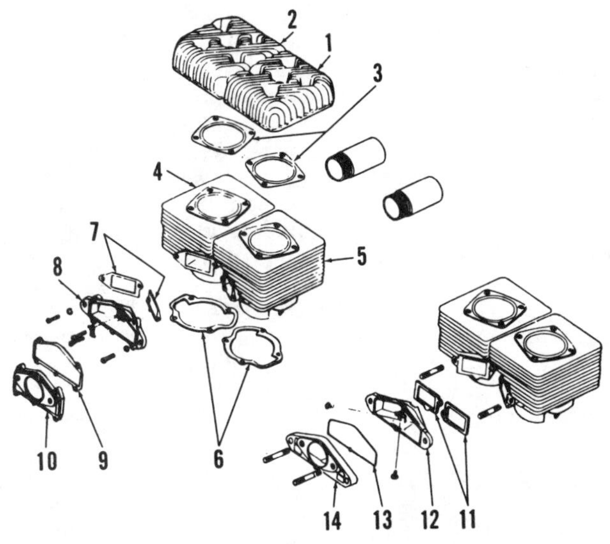

Fig. 5–View of two typical cylinder and inlet manifold assemblies. Most parts are not interchangeable between the two cylinders, including cylinder head gaskets (3), base gaskets (6) and inlet manifold gaskets (7).

1. Cylinder head (magneto side)
2. Cylinder head drive side)
3. Head gaskets
4. Cylinder (drive side)
5. Cylinder (magneto side)
6. Base gaskets
7. Gaskets (295 & 340 cc)
8. Manifold "V" block (295 & 340 cc)
9. Gasket (295 & 340 cc)
10. Carburetor adapter (295 & 340 cc)
11. Gaskets (400 & 440 cc)
12. Manifold "V" block (400 & 440 cc)
13. Gasket (400 & 440 cc)
14. Carburetor adapter (400 & 440 cc)

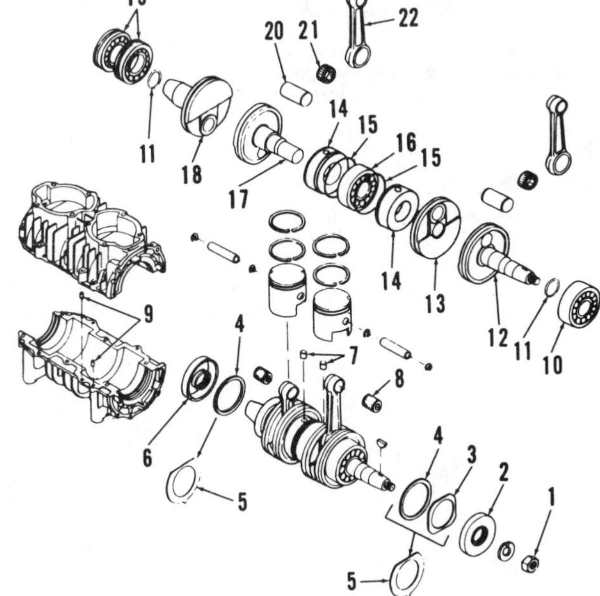

Fig. 6–Exploded view of engine crankshaft and crankcase. Parts (3 & 4) are used on 400 and 440 cc models; parts (5) are used on 295 and 340 cc models.

1. Nut
2. Seal
3. Oil seal retainer
4. Gaskets for bearings
5. Gaskets for bearings
6. Seal
7. Center seal dowels
8. Piston pin bearings
9. Crankcase align-dowels (4 used)
10. Magneto end bearing
11. Shims
12. Crankshaft (magneto end)
13. Counterweight (magneto side)
14. Center seals
15. "O" rings
16. Center main bearing
17. Counterweight and center journal
18. Crankshaft (drive end)
19. Drive end main bearings
20. Crankpin
21. Rod bearing
22. Connecting rod

alignment as the cylinder and head retaining nuts are tightened, then remove inlet manifold and install using the correct gaskets. Make certain that all inlet manifold gaskets are installed correctly to prevent blockage of pulse passage for fuel pump. The two gaskets (7 or 11—Fig. 5) between "V" block (9 or 12) and the cylinders are different and must not be interchanged.

IGNITION AND ELECTRICAL. Ignition high tension coils can be checked on a standard coil tester available from several sources, including the following:

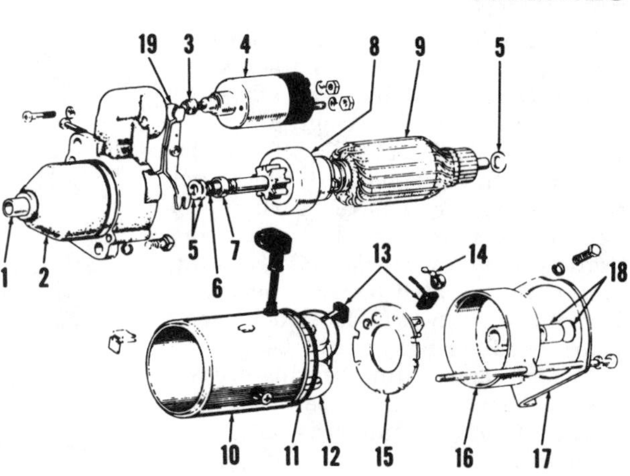

Fig. 10–Exploded view of the electric starter. Shims (5) are available in thickness of 0.004 and 0.012 inch.

1. Bushing
2. Drive housing
3. Solenoid adjusting nut
4. Solenoid
5. Shims
6. Retaining ring
7. Stop collar
8. Clutch and pinion
9. Armature
10. Housing
11. Seal ring
12. Field windings
13. Brushes
14. Brush spring
15. Brush holder
16. End cover
17. Mounting plate
18. Bushing and plug

Fig. 7–Side shake of connecting rod small (piston pin) end is used to check clearance of connecting rod crankpin bearing. The measured side shake should not include the normal side clearance of rod between crankshaft counterweights.

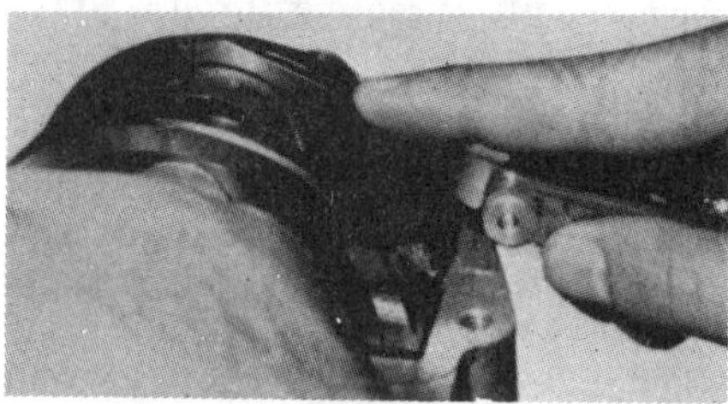

Fig. 8–Side clearance of connecting rods between crankshaft counterweights should be carefully checked.

Graham-Lee Electronics, Inc.
4220 Central Avenue, N.E.
Minneapolis, Minn. 55421

Resistance of the primary winding of high tension coil should be 1.2-1.4 ohms and resistance of secondary windings should be 5,500-6,000 ohms. Ignition low tension coil for cylinder closest to magneto end is located next to stator plate and has a yellow wire. Breaker points for the magneto end cylinder are located at (M—Fig. 1). Refer to Ignition System paragraphs in MAINTENANCE Section for setting the ignition timing.

PISTONS, PINS, RINGS AND CYLINDERS. Inspect all parts and renew any which are questionable.

TR-440
Standard Cylinder
Bore Diameter .... 2.5984-2.5992 in.
Piston Skirt Diameter—
Right Angles to Pin .... 2.5925-2.5937 in.
Parallel with Pin Bore .... 2.5898-2.5909 in.
Piston Skirt to Cylinder Bore Clearance—
Right Angles to Pin (Desired) .... 0.0047-0.0066 in.
Maximum Allowable ... 0.012 in.
Piston Pin Standard Diameter .... 0.669 in.
Piston Pin Clearance in Piston Bore—
Wear Limit .... 0.003 in.
Ring End Gap .... 0.014-0.022 in.
Ring Side Clearance in Groove—
Top Ring (Desired) 0.0040-0.0055 in.
Second Ring (Desired) .... 0.0015-0.0030 in.

When installing pistons, arrows (Fig. 4) should be angled apart as shown and should point toward exhaust side of engine. Install rings on pistons with manufacturers mark toward top. Refer to DISASSEMBLY AND REASSEMBLY paragraphs for remainder of assembly and alignment notes.

CRANKCASE AND CRANKSHAFT. The connecting rods, crankshaft, center main bearing and center seals are available only as an assembled unit. Condition of connecting rod crankpin bearing should be checked by measuring side shake of small end as shown in Fig. 7. Normal clearance is indicated by side shake of 0.0146-0.0264 inch and wear limit is 0.0709 inch. Normal side clearance of connecting rod between crankshaft counterweights is 0.0118-0.0185 inch and is measured as shown in Fig. 8. NOTE: Do not include the side clearance when measuring connecting rod shake. Main bearings at ends of crankshaft can be renewed separately. Main bearings should be renewed if axial clearance exceeds 0.0157 inch, if side play exceeds 0.00197 inch or if bearing is rough when rolled by hand. When installing main bearings at ends of crankshaft, add shims (11—Fig. 6) as required to obtain a crankshaft length between outer edges of main bearings of 8.0295-8.0335 inches. The crankshaft is a pressed together unit and improper handling can easily cause distortion (misalignment). Alignment should be checked at ends of crankshaft with crankshaft supported by main bearings and on the center main bearing outer race with crankshaft supported by end main bearings. If distortion exceeds 0.002 inch, repair or renewal is necessary.

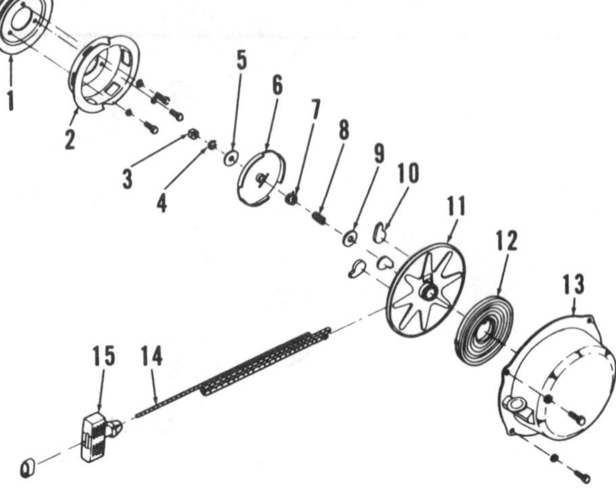

Fig. 9–Exploded view of recoil starter. Rewind spring (12) should be wound into housing (13), beginning at outside in counter-clockwise direction.

1. Drive pulley for fan
2. Starter cup
3. Nut
4. Lock washer
5. Thrust washer
6. Drive plate
7. Return spring
8. Drive spring plate
9. Thrust washer
10. Pawls
11. Starter pulley
12. Rewind spring
13. Housing
14. Rope
15. Handle

RECOIL STARTER. Refer to Fig. 9. The starter must be removed and disassembled to renew rope and/or rewind spring. The rewind spring (12) should be wound into housing (13), beginning at outside and in counterclockwise direction. Preload the rewind spring enough to make certain that handle is pulled against housing when released.

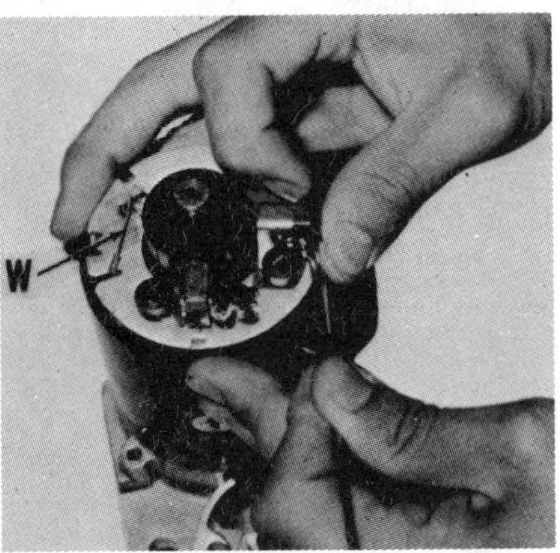

Fig. 11–Wire (W) should be detached before removing the brush holder. Be sure to reattach when assembling.

ELECTRIC STARTER. Refer to Fig. 10. Length of brushes (13) is 0.55 inch when new. Renew brushes if less than 0.35 inch long. Brush spring tension should be 30-40 ounces with new brushes installed. Renew bushings (1 & 18) if shaft to bushing clearance exceeds 0.008 inch. Check commutator for mica depth and out-of-round. If commutator is out-of-round more than 0.016 inch, the commutator should be turned. Mica should be undercut 0.008 inch. End play of armature shaft should be 0.002-0.014 inch and is adjusted by adding shims (5) at ends of armature shaft. Shims are available in thicknesses of 0.004 and 0.012 inch. When disassembling, be sure to note wire (W—Fig. 11) which should be unsoldered before removing brush holder. The special tool (Fig. 12) can be manufactured to drive the stop collar (7—Fig. 10) down so that snap ring (6) can be removed.

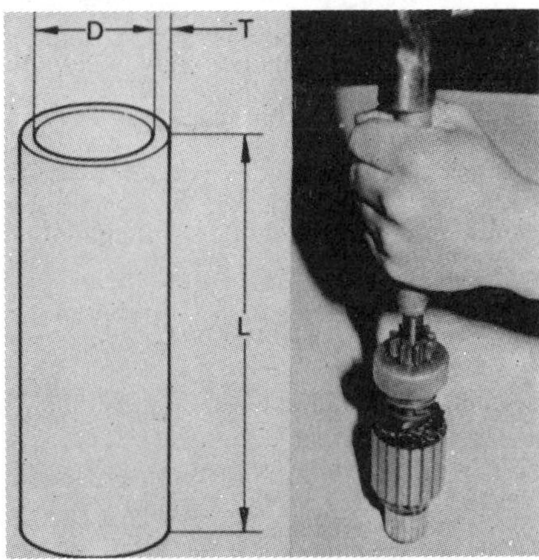

Fig. 12–Drawing at left shows special tool used for disassembling the starter. View at right shows method of use. Inside diameter (D) should be 0.65 inch, thickness (T) should be 0.07 inch and length (L) should be more than 1 inch.

SACHS

ONE CYLINDER MODELS

CONDENSED SERVICE DATA

Years Made Engine Model	1966 SA280	1967-70 SA280	1971-72 SA280	1967-70 SA280A	1971-72 SA280A
Bore—(mm)	71	71	71	71	71
Inches	2.795	2.795	2.795	2.795	2.795
Stroke—(mm)	70	70	70	70	70
Inches	2.756	2.756	2.756	2.756	2.756
No. of Cylinders	1	1	1	1	1
Displacement—(cc)	277	277	277	277	277
Cubic Inches	16.9	16.9	16.9	16.9	16.9
Horsepower @ RPM	16@5500	16@5500	16@5500	14@4800	14@4800
Cooling Type	Cent. Fan	Cent. Fan	Cent. Fan	Cent. Fan	Cent. Fan
Carburetor Model	HR	HR	HR	HL	HL
Number Used	1	1	1	1	1
Ignition:					
Type	BOSCH Magneto				
Point Gap—(mm)	0.35-0.45	0.35-0.45	0.35-0.45	0.35-0.45	0.35-0.45
Inch	0.014-0.018	0.014-0.018	0.014-0.018	0.014-0.018	0.014-0.018
Edge Gap—(mm)	15-19	15-19	14-18*	15-19	14-18
Inch	0.591-0.748	0.591-0.748	0.551-0.708*	0.591-0.748	0.551-0.708
Timing Advance?	No	Yes	Yes**	Yes	Yes**
Timing BTDC—(mm)	4.0-4.5	4.0-4.5	4.0-4.5	4.0-4.5	4.0-4.5
Inch	0.157-0.177	0.157-0.177	0.157-0.177	0.157-0.177	0.157-0.177
Measured at	....	Adv. Cam	Adv. Cam**	Adv. Cam	Adv. Cam**
Spark Plug:					
Bosch	M240T1	M240T1	M240T1	M240T1	M240T1
Electrode Gap—(mm)	0.4-0.5	0.4-0.5	0.4-0.5	0.4-0.5	0.4-0.5
Inch	0.016-0.020	0.016-0.020	0.016-0.020	0.016-0.020	0.016-0.020
Fuel/Oil Ratio	25:1	25:1	25:1	25:1	25:1

*Edge gap should be 7-11 mm (0.276-0.433 inch) for models with 12 volt 75 watt electrical system.
**Timing does not advance on models with 6 volt 36 watt electrical system.

Years Made	1967-69	1969-70	1971-73	1971-73	1971
Engine Model	SA290	SA290	SA290	SA290SS	SA290R
Bore—(mm)	73.5	73	73	73	73
Inches	2.894	2.874	2.874	2.874	2.874
Stroke—(mm)	70	70	70	70	70
Inches	2.756	2.756	2.756	2.756	2.756
No. of Cylinders	1	1	1	1	1
Displacement—(cc)	297	293	293	293	293
Cubic Inches	18.1	17.9	17.9	17.9	17.9
Horsepower @ RPM	20@5500	19.5@5500	19.5@5500	25@6000	N/A
Cooling Type	Cent. Fan	Cent. Fan	Cent. Fan	Cent. Fan	Free Air
Carburetor Model	HR	HR	HR	HD	HD
Number Used	1	1	1	1	1
Ignition:					
Type	BOSCH Magneto				
Point Gap—(mm)	0.35-0.45	0.35-0.45	0.35-0.45	0.35-0.45	0.35-0.45
Inch	0.014-0.018	0.014-0.018	0.014-0.018	0.014-0.018	0.014-0.018
Edge Gap—(mm)	16-19	16-19	14-18*	14-18*	14-18
Inch	0.630-0.748	0.630-0.748	0.551-0.708*	0.552-0.708*	0.552-0.708
Timing Advance?	Yes	Yes	Yes**	Yes	Yes
Timing BTDC—(mm)	4.0-4.5	4.0-4.5	4.0-4.5	4.0-4.5	4.0-4.5
Inch	0.157-0.177	0.157-0.177	0.157-0.177	0.157-0.177	0.157-0.177
Measured at	Adv. Cam	Adv. Cam	Adv. Cam**	Adv. Cam	Adv. Cam
Spark Plug:					
Bosch	M240T1	M240T1	M240T1	W290T16	W290T16
Electrode Gap—(mm)	0.4-0.5	0.5-0.5	0.4-0.5	0.35	0.35
Inch	0.016-0.020	0.016-0.020	0.016-0.020	0.014	0.014
Fuel/Oil Ratio	25:1	25:1	25:1	25:1	25:1

*Edge gap should be 7-11 mm (0.276-0.433 inch) for models with 12 volt 75 watt electrical system.

**Timing does not advance on models with 6 volt 36 watt electrical system.

Years Made	1969-70	1969-70	1971-72	1971	1971	1967-71
Engine Model	SA340	SA340SS	SA340SS	SA340C	SA340R	SA370
Bore—(mm)	75.5	75.5	75.5	78	78	79
Inches	2.972	2.972	2.972	3.07	3.07	3.11
Stroke—(mm)	75	75	75	70	70	75
Inches	2.953	2.953	2.953	2.756	2.756	2.953
No. of Cylinders	1	1	1	1	1	1
Displacement—(cc)	336	336	336	334	334	368
Cubic Inches	20.5	20.5	20.5	20.4	20.4	22.4
Horsepower @ RPM	22@5200	26@6000	26@6000	29@6500	N/A	24@5300
Cooling Type	Cent. Fan	Cent. Fan	Cent. Fan	Cent. Fan	Free Air	Cent. Fan
Carburetor Model	HD	HD	HD	HD	HD	HR-HD
Number Used	1	1	1	1	1	1
Ignition:						
Type	BOSCH Magneto					
Point Gap—(mm)	0.35-0.45	0.35-0.45	0.35-0.45	0.35-0.45	0.35-0.45	0.35-0.45
Inch	0.014-0.018	0.014-0.018	0.014-0.018	0.014-0.018	0.014-0.018	0.014-0.018
Edge Gap—(mm)	16-19	16-19	14-18*	14-18*	14-18	16-19
Inch	0.630-0.748	0.630-0.748	0.552-0.708*	0.552-0.708*	0.552-0.708	0.630-0.748
Timing Advance?	Yes	Yes	Yes	Yes	Yes	Yes
Timing BTDC—(mm)	4.0-4.5	4.0-4.5	4.0-4.5	4.0-4.5	4.0-4.5	4.0-4.5
Inch	0.157-0.177	0.157-0.177	0.157-0.177	0.157-0.177	0.157-0.177	0.157-0.177
Measured at	Adv. Cam	Adv. Cam	Adv. Cam	Adv. Cam	Adv. Cam	Adv. Cam
Spark Plug:						
Bosch	M240T1	M260T1	M260T1	W290T16	W290T16	M260T1
Electrode Gap—(mm)	0.4-0.5	0.4-0.5	0.4-0.5	0.35	0.35	0.4-0.5
Inch	0.016-0.020	0.016-0.020	0.016-0.020	0.014	0.014	0.016-0.020
Fuel/Oil Ratio	25:1	25:1	25:1	25:1	25:1	25:1

* Edge gap should be 7-11 mm (0.276-0.433 inch) for models with 12 volt 75 watt electrical system.

MAINTENANCE

SPARK PLUG. The recommended Bosch spark plug for normal service is listed in the CONDENSED SERVICE DATA tables. The 14 mm (Bosch series W) spark plugs should be torqued to 20 ft.-lbs. and 18 mm (Bosch series M) plugs should be torqued to 25 ft.-lbs.

CARBURETOR. Tillotson diaphragm type carburetors are used. Refer to Tillotson Carburetor Section for operation and overhaul information. An external impulse line is used to operate fuel pump on some models. Be sure that all passages are open and that vacuum and pressure leaks are eliminated.

The HL carburetor used on most SA280 engines is equipped with a fixed main jet. Initial setting for idle mixture needle is 1¼ turns open.

On HR and HD carburetors, initial setting for idle mixture needle is 1 turn open and 1-1¼ turns open for high speed mixture needle. The idle mixture needle should be set rich enough to provide smooth acceleration from idle to fast speed. The high speed mixture should be set while operating under normal load.

IGNITION SYSTEM. A Bosch, flywheel type magneto is used on all models. All models are also equipped with an auxiliary lighting coil which is installed on the magneto armature plate and utilizes the permanent flywheel magnets as a power source.

Breaker point gap and timing specifications for individual engines are given in CONDENSED SERVICE DATA tables. Most engines are provided with ignition timing mark (M—Fig. 2) on flywheel and line (L) on crankcase which should align just as the breaker points open. If the flywheel

Fig. 1–Cut away view of SA290 engine typical of all one cylinder models.

is not marked, the piston position listed in the table can be used to correctly locate crankshaft for marking the flywheel. Clearance between ignition and lighting coil shoes and the flywheel magneto should be 0.25-0.35 mm (0.0098-0.0138 in.). Refer to MAGNETO paragraphs in the Service Fundamentals section for servicing procedures. The ignition systems used on 75 watt electrical systems use an externally mounted high tension coil with ignition generating coil mounted on magneto plate.

LUBRICATION. The engine is lubricated by mixing oil with the fuel. A suitable two-cycle air cooled engine oil is recommended. Standard grade SAE 30 automotive motor oil may be used if two-cycle oil is not available. Recommended fuel-oil mixture is 25:1. Mix fuel and oil thoroughly using a separate container before pouring mixture into fuel tank. For cold weather blending, pre-mix the oil with a small amount of gasoline and shake thoroughly until mixture is liquid, then blend with remainder of fuel. Do not use kerosene or fuel oil for pre-mixing.

Fig. 2–View of Top Dead Center mark (O) aligned with line (L) on crankcase. Flywheel mark (M) should be used for setting ignition timing.

REPAIRS

TIGHTENING TORQUES. Recommended tightening torques are as follows:

	kgm	ft.-lb.
Breaker cam (non-advancing ignition)	0.6-0.8	4.3-5.8
Crankcase halves	2.2-2.4	15.9-17.4

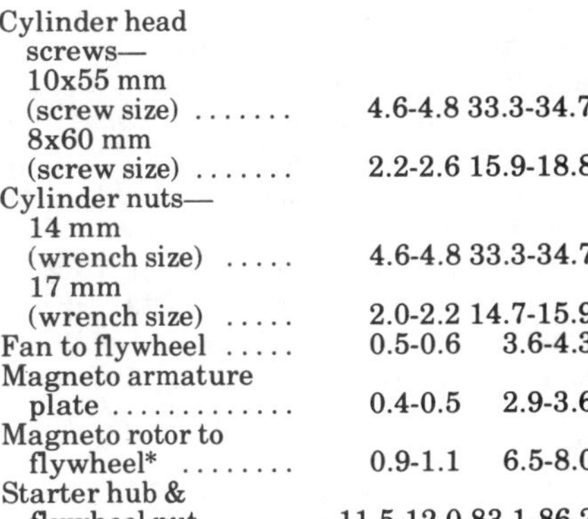

	kgm	ft.-lb.
Cylinder head screws— 10x55 mm (screw size)	4.6-4.8	33.3-34.7
8x60 mm (screw size)	2.2-2.6	15.9-18.8
Cylinder nuts— 14 mm (wrench size)	4.6-4.8	33.3-34.7
17 mm (wrench size)	2.0-2.2	14.7-15.9
Fan to flywheel	0.5-0.6	3.6-4.3
Magneto armature plate	0.4-0.5	2.9-3.6
Magneto rotor to flywheel*	0.9-1.1	6.5-8.0
Starter hub & flywheel nut	11.5-12.0	83.1-86.2

*These screws should be coated with "Loctite" before installing.

DISASSEMBLY AND REASSEMBLY. The cylinder head, cylinder, piston, rings and piston pin bushing can be serviced without removal of flywheel or disassembling crankcase. CAUTION: Be especially careful to prevent anything from falling into crankcase, if crankcase halves are not to be separated.

The connecting rod, crankpin, bearing and crankshaft are available only as an assembled unit and disassembly is not recommended. The crankshaft main bearings (2 & 9—Fig. 4) may be cylindrical roller type at both ends or one may be a ball bearing and the other a roller bearing. Spacers may be shaped different than the one shown at (3), more than one spacer may be used and spacers may be located differently than shown. NOTE: Be sure to note location of spacers before removing from crankshaft.

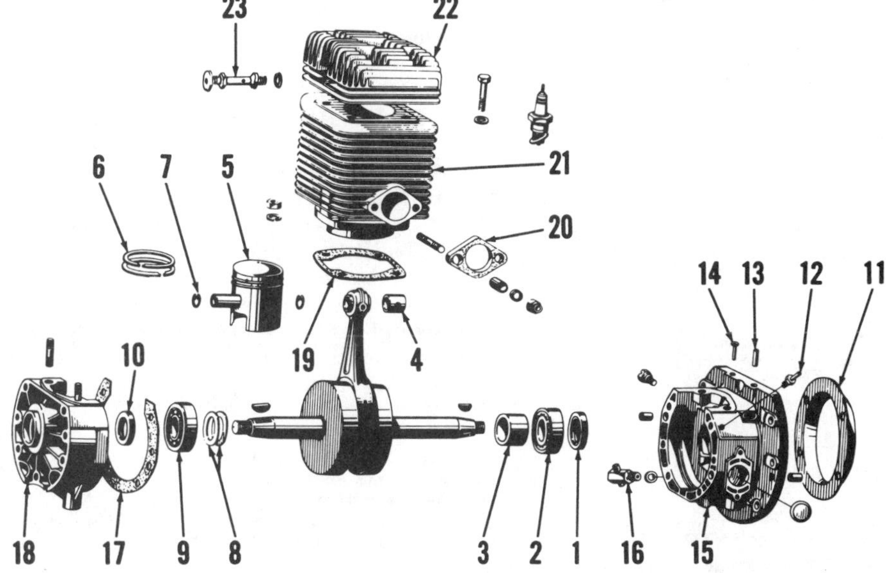

Fig. 4–Exploded view of engine typical of all models. Differences in crankshaft spacers should be noted upon disassembly.

1. Seal
2. Bearing
3. Spacer
4. Pin bushing
5. Piston
6. Piston rings
7. Piston pin
8. Shims
9. Bearing
10. Seal
11. Labyrinth ring
12. Impulse fitting
13. Insulator tube
14. Plug
15. Crankcase half
16. Bleeder valve
17. Gasket
18. Crankcase half
19. Gasket
20. Insulator block
21. Cylinder
22. Cylinder head
23. Decompressor valve

On models with a ball type main bearing, the crankcase around bearing must be heated before crankshaft (and ball bearing) can be withdrawn from crankcase. On all models, the specified crankshaft end play of 0.1-0.2 mm (0.004-0.008 in.) is controlled by adding or removing shims (8) behind pto end bearing (9) before it is installed on shaft. Shims (8) are available in thicknesses of 0.2, 0.3, 0.4 and 0.5 mm (0.008, 0.012, 0.016 and 0.020 in.). Shim pack thickness is determined by measuring depth of both crankcase halves (as shown in Fig. 5) then measuring length of crankshaft at shoulder or spacers that contact bearing inner races (A—Fig. 6).

Heat bearing bores of crankcase halves to approximately 200°-300° F. to remove or install bearing outer races. Install inner races on crankshaft with a suitable press, supporting the shaft between crank webs to prevent distorting crankshaft alignment or crushing rod between crank webs. On models which use a ball type main bearing, install bearing on shaft and heat crankcase half before assembling to allow bearing outer race to properly enter housing bore. Crankshaft seals should be installed with lip toward inside, after crankshaft and crankcase are assembled.

Fig. 5–Use gage as shown to measure depth of both crankcase halves. Gasket should be positioned on one of the halves when measuring.

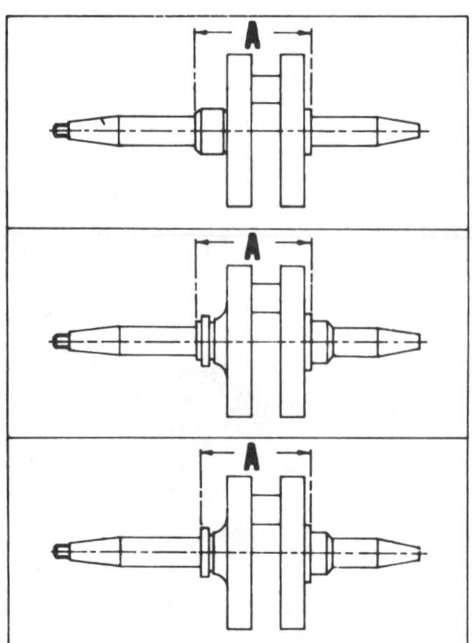

Fig. 6–Length of crankshaft should be measured at (A). Make certain that all spacers are installed correctly.

PISTON, PIN, RINGS & CYLINDER. The piston can be removed after removing muffler, carburetor, cylinder head and cylinder. Except for engine with chrome cylinder bores, piston and rings are available in standard size and oversizes of 0.5, 1.0 and 1.5 mm (0.020, 0.039 and 0.059 in.). Models with chrome cylinder bores should not be honed or rebored. Piston rings are interchangeable and are pinned in place. Arrow in piston crown must point toward exhaust port in cylinder when engine is assembled. Piston pin is full floating type but is a tight fit in piston bores at room temperature. Heat piston to 160°-175° F. for easy assembly.

Install cylinder gasket with graphited side facing crankcase, lightly oil cylinder, and tighten cylinder flange nuts in diagonally opposite pairs. Install cylinder head with decompressor on pto side of engine if so equipped. If fins on cylinder head are shorter on one end, the end with lower fins should be toward fan. On all models, tighten cylinder head cap screws in diagonally opposite pairs. Tightening torques are given at beginning of REPAIRS section.

CRANKCASE AND CRANKSHAFT ASSEMBLY. Both ends of crankshaft have lathe centers. Place the assembly in a lathe and check the runout with a dial indicator at bearing area as near as possible to crankshaft webs. Runout should not exceed 0.001 in. If runout is excessive, the entire unit must be renewed or shaft may be straightened by a shop equipped and experienced in rebuilding the built-up shafts.

The only part of crankshaft assembly available separately is the piston pin bushing. Bushing must be align reamed after installation to an inside diameter of 18.03-18.05 mm (0.7099-0.7101 in.) to provide a close slip fit for piston pin. Be sure oil holes in rod and bushing are aligned when a new bushing is installed.

Spacers on crankshaft main journals may be shaped different than the one shown at (3—Fig. 4), more than one spacer may be used and spacers may be used at both ends of crankshaft. Be sure to note location of spacers before removing from crankshaft. Regardless of location, bevel in spacer should be toward crankshaft web.

Refer to DISASSEMBLY AND REASSEMBLY paragraphs and to Figs. 5 & 6 for determining thickness of shims (8—Fig. 4) to be installed. Crankshaft seals should be installed with lip toward inside, after crankshaft and crankcase is assembled.

RECOIL STARTER. Three types of recoil starters have been used. Refer to the appropriate following paragraphs for service.

Type shown in Fig. 9. To overhaul starter with unit removed, first remove snap ring (9), disc (10), spring (11) and fiber washer (12) from end of spindle; then carefully lift off pulley (14), making sure recoil spring (19) remains in housing (20) as shown in Fig. 10.

When assembling, wind spring into housing in correct direction (refer to Fig. 10). Attach inner end of rope to

Fig. 10–Starter housing with recoil spring installed for counter-clockwise (normal) engine rotation.

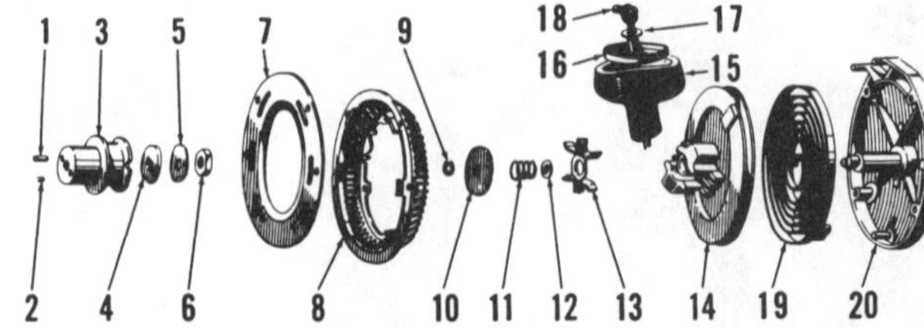

Fig. 9–Exploded view of Fairbanks starter. Unit can be assembled for either clockwise or counter-clockwise rotation.

1. Pin
2. Roller
3. Starter cup
4. Washer
5. Lock washer
6. Nut
7. Cover
8. Screen
9. Snap ring
10. Disc
11. Brake spring
12. Fiber washer
13. Friction shoe assembly
14. Pulley
15. Handle
16. Insert
17. Rivet
18. Rope
19. Recoil spring
20. Cover

pulley as shown in Fig. 11. Position pulley over spindle shaft and make certain that inner and outer ends of spring are correctly hooked on cover and center of pulley. Pre-load the rewind spring between 1 and 2 turns before placing rope in guide slot with rope fully wound on pulley to assure full recoil. Check sharp end of friction shoes (13—Fig. 9) and sharpen if necessary. Install friction shoe assembly, fiber washer (12), brake spring (11), disc (10) and snap ring (9). If friction shoe assembly (13) is properly installed, sharp ends will extend when rope is pulled.

Type shown in Fig. 12. Starter actuating parts (7 through 12) can be serviced without cutting cable. If recoil spring (14) is broken or detached at ends, the cable must be cut to properly assemble and pre-load the recoil spring. If cable is to be reused, cut as close as possible to the grip and allow pulley to turn slowly until spring is completely unwound.

Remove cover (5) and snap ring (6); then, lift off actuating parts (7 through 12). Remove pulley (13), leaving spring (14) in housing. Protect hands if spring is to be removed, and lift out carefully to prevent personal injury.

When assembling, install spring in housing, beginning at outside anchor. Spring should be wound in direction shown in Fig. 10 for normal (counter-clockwise) engine rotation. Supporting ring (16—Fig. 12) has a section removed to provide clearance for inner spring loop and a relieved outer edge to provide clearance for spring rivets. Be sure supporting ring is installed to correctly engage inner end of spring. New cable (24) is 70⅞ inches long with inner nipple attached. Wind cable completely around pulley and install pulley with tab engaging the inner loop of spring. Wind pulley three turns before passing cable through hole in housing. Reinstall handle to prevent re-entry of cable. A new retaining ferrule (25) will be needed.

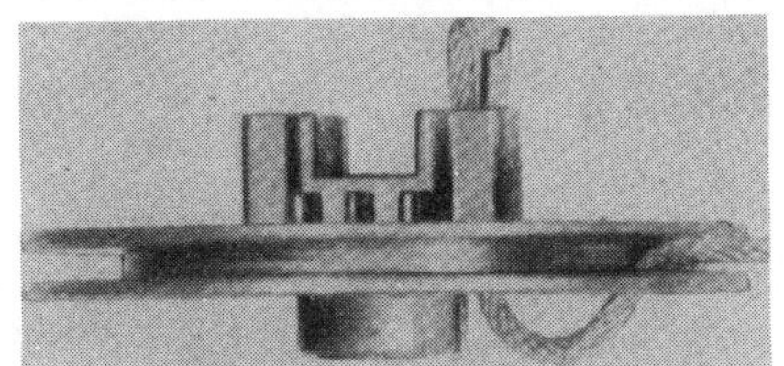

Fig. 11–Inner end of rope should be attached and routed through pulley as shown.

Fig. 14–Exploded view of starter used on some models. Unit can be assembled for either clockwise or counter-clockwise rotation.

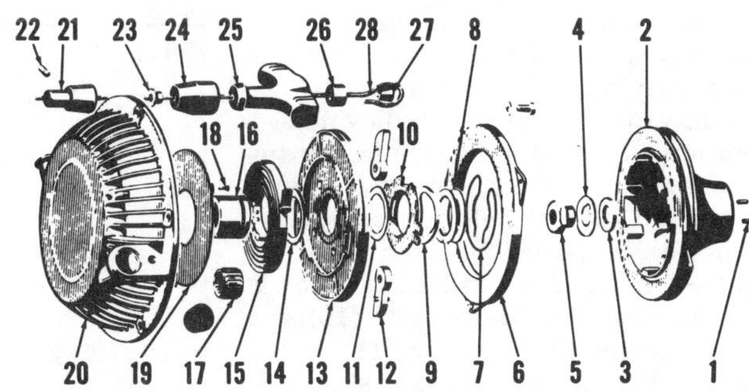

1. Pin
2. Starter drum
3. Washer
4. Lock washer
5. Nut
6. Cover
7. Brake spring
8. Shims
9. Wave washer
10. Brake plate
11. Washer—0.1 mm (0.004 inch) thick
12. Pawls
13. Pulley
14. Washer—0.8 mm (0.032 inch) thick
15. Recoil spring
16. Bushing
17. Tolerance ring
18. Rivets (3 used)
19. Check plate
20. Housing
21. Cable guide
22. Set screw
23. Bushing
24. Bumper
25. Handle
26. Clamp ring
27. Clamp cone
28. Cable

Shims (12) next to pulley have a larger inside diameter than shims (7). Shims (12) are available in thicknesses of 0.15, 0.3, 0.5 and 0.8 mm (0.006, 0.012, 0.020 and 0.032 inch), and shim pack should be correct thickness to permit top hub flange of plate (11) to ride 0.1-0.2 mm (0.004-0.008 inch) below end of bushing (18). Install levers (10), friction washer (9), wave washer (8) and shims (7). Enough shims (7) should be installed to compress wave washer (8) slightly when snap ring (6) is installed. Shims (7) are available in thicknesses of 0.3 and 0.5 mm (0.012 & 0.020 inch).

NOTE: The purpose of the wave washer and adjustment is to create a light drag on friction washer (9) and cause levers to swing out (engage) when cable is pulled. If not enough shims (7) are installed, levers (10) may not engage cup (2). If too many shims (7) are installed, the starter cable may not rewind properly.

Type shown in Fig. 14. To disassemble the removed starter, remove brake spring (7), shims (8), wave washer (9), brake plate (10), washer (11) and pawls (12). Remove cover (6), pull cable out enough to remove handle (25) and allow recoil spring (15) to unwind and draw cable into housing. A wire retaining tool can be made to hold pulley as shown in Fig. 15 while removing handle. Be careful to prevent recoil spring and pulley from coming out of housing as spring unwinds. Spring should remain in pulley. A puller can be used to remove bushing (16—Fig. 14) if renewal is necessary.

Spring should be installed in pulley as shown in Fig. 16. Use a small amount of grease to hold washer (14) in position while assembling. Washer should be 0.8 mm (0.032 in.) thick. Insert pulley into recess in housing, making certain that loop at inner end

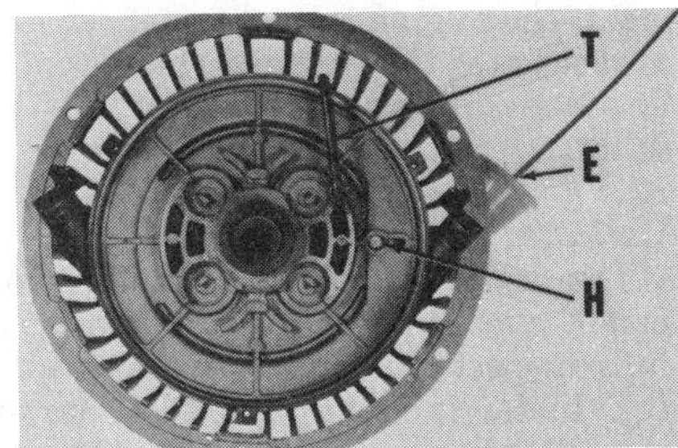

Fig. 15–A piece of heavy wire can be bent and used as shown at (T) to prevent pulley from turning while removing or attaching handle.

Fig. 16–Spring should be installed in direction shown.

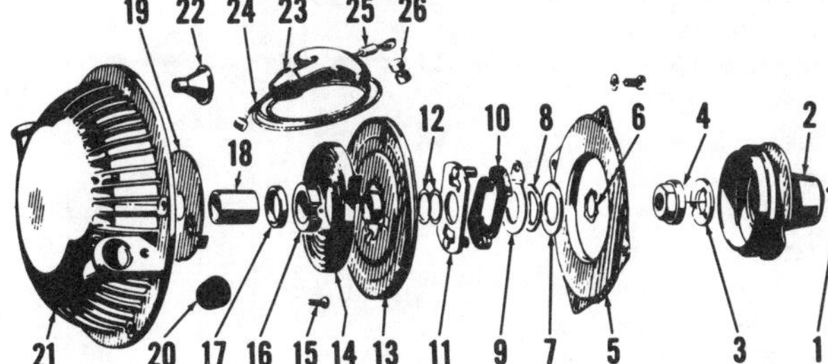

Fig. 12–Exploded view of the recoil starter used on some models. Levers (10) are different on clockwise rotation starters than on counter-clockwise.

1. Pins
2. Cup
3. Washer
4. Nut
5. Cover
6. Snap ring
7. Shim—22.2 mm (⅞ inch) I.D.
8. Wave washer
9. Friction washer
10. Starter levers
11. Lever support plate
12. Shims—25.3 mm (1 inch) I.D.
13. Pulley
14. Recoil spring
15. Rivet
16. Supporting ring
17. Spacer
18. Bushing
19. Check washer
20. Plug
21. Housing
22. Cable guide
23. Handle
24. Cable
25. Ferrule
26. Pin

of recoil spring engages lug in housing. Turn pulley until the recoil spring is completely wound and pulley will not turn any more, then back pulley up ½-1 turn until hole (H—Fig. 15) for cord is near exit (E). Insert cord through pulley and out exit hole, attach handle, then release pulley to wind cord. Install cover (6—Fig. 14). Install pawls (12), washer (11), brake plate (10) and wave washer (9). Washer (11) is 0.1 mm (0.0039 in.) thick. Install shims (8) and brake spring (7). Shims (8) should be selected to provide 0.1-0.2 mm (0.0039-0.0079 in.) play at brake plate when wave washer is flattened. When correctly assembled, pawls (12) will extend as handle is pulled.

NOTE: Shims (8) and washers (11 & 14) are identical except for thickness used. Shims (8) are available in thicknesses of 0.1, 0.3 and 0.8 mm (0.0039, 0.012 & 0.032 in.) and should be selected to provide correct adjustment of wave washer (9) and brake plate (10). Washer (14) should be 0.8 mm (0.032 in.) thick and washer (11) should be 0.1 mm (0.0039 in.) thick.

SPEED TUNING

NOTE: Specifications in the following paragraphs are suggested by the manufacturer for increased performance. Any change from the original configuration will probably decrease the service life of an engine and if changes are carelessly done, may decrease power and cause extensive damage. Normal tuning such as ignition timing, point gap, fuel mixture, lubrication, etc. will become more critical if the engine is modified. It should also be noted that gearing changes may be necessary in order to make the fullest use of the modified engine.

Cylinder Modifications

The cylinder head, cylinder and piston should be removed, then carefully inspect condition of cylinder bore. If cylinder is to be rebored to larger size, it should be done before any port modification.

Before any grinding is done, carefully examine original ports and note location, size and shape. Location and shape of ports can be transferred to a paper positioned in cylinder bore and gently pressed against all of the port openings and top and bottom edges of cylinder bore. If carefully done, the removed paper should be marked similar to Fig. ST1. All suggested radii are difficult (or impossible) to draw in the cylinder and if first drawn on the paper pattern can be more easily transferred to the cylinder.

Changes in port sizes and shapes should be drawn on inside of cylinder bore before grinding. Coat the area of cylinder where changes are to be made with machinist dye or similar material, then scratch lightly through the coating to show material to be removed. In many cases, a pattern of the modified port will facilitate marking.

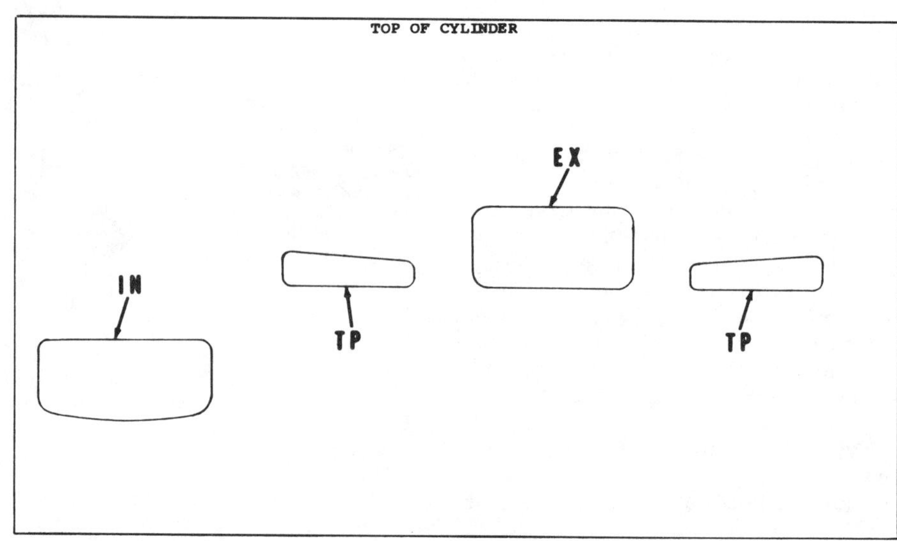

Fig. ST1–Drawing typical of cylinder ports. Raising exhaust port (EX) and transfer ports (TP) causes them to open sooner and remain open longer. Inlet port (IN) timing is usually changed by removing part of piston skirt. Changes to side of all ports only increase size.

Work carefully and slowly when grinding out ports and passages. Use as fine a stone as practical. A stone which is too coarse will have a tendency to work into one area; will be difficult to use and will result in rough, irregular shapes.

SA290 (CAST IRON CYLINDER). Refer to Fig. ST2 for drawings of typical inlet port. Radius of inlet port lower edge should remain the same (110 mm.); however, port width should be increased from 45 mm. (N1) to 50 mm. (N2). The corners should have approximately 3-4 mm. radius as shown at (C). The top and bottom edges should remain the same distance from lower edge of cylinder. Advanced inlet timing and increased inlet duration will be accomplished by removing material from piston skirt. Round off lower edge of inlet port to a radius of approximately 2 mm. as shown at (NR) to prevent piston skirt from catching on edge. Inlet passage diameter at carburetor flange should be increased from 34 mm. to 36 mm. and passage should be smoothed into the cylinder modifications.

Refer to Fig. ST3 for drawing of typical exhaust port. Width of exhaust port should be increased from 42 mm. (E1) to 47 mm. (E2) at center. Top edge of exhaust port should be raised 1 mm. Originally top edge of port was 91.5 mm. from bottom of cylinder (H1). The sides of port should be changed from vertical to rounded. Radius (S) should be 15 mm. to all four corners (C) which are 4 mm. radius. Round the top flat

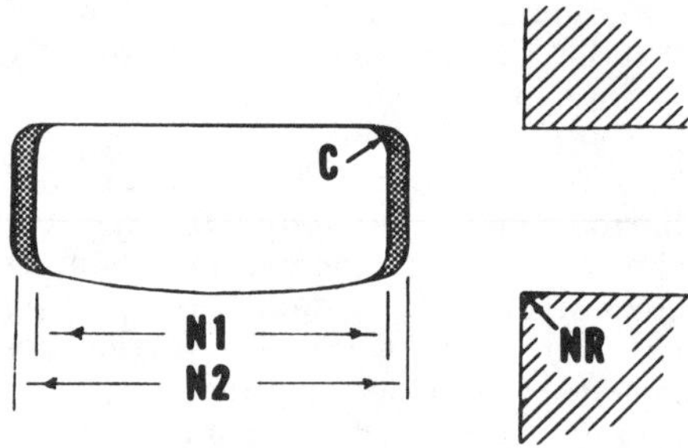

Fig. ST2–Drawing of typical inlet port. Refer to text for suggested changes.

C. Radius of corners
F. Carburetor flange opening diameter
N1. Original width
N2. Modified width
NR. Radius of lower edge

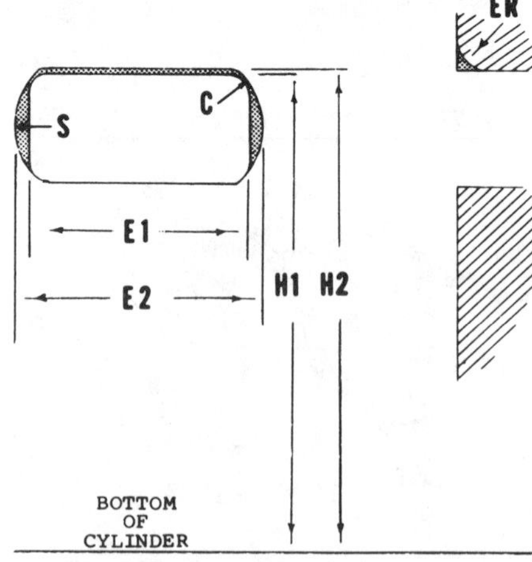

Fig. ST3–Drawing of typical exhaust port. Refer to text for suggested changes.

C. Radius of corners
E1. Original width
E2. Modified width
ER. Radius of top edge
H1. Original height
H2. Modified height
S. Radius of sides

(center) edge of port to approximately 6 mm. radius (ER), gradually blending in at ends of port. The radius (ER) in addition to radii (S&C) should prevent piston rings from catching in exhaust port.

Refer to Fig. ST4 for drawings of typical transfer port. When modifying transfer ports make certain that both ports and both passages are **EXACTLY** the same and to correct specifications. The transfer ports are more difficult to modify than inlet and exhaust ports. The top edge of transfer ports should be raised 2 mm. and angle (TA) of 4° 30' should be maintained. The uppermost edge of transfer ports originally is 79.5 mm. (T1) from lower edge of cylinder. The angle of entry into cylinder (A) should be increased from 10° to 18°. If angle is too large, fuel will be wasted and cylinder will not be correctly cleared of old gases.

SA290SS (CAST IRON SLEEVE, ALUMINUM CYLINDER). In original condition, the cylinder is designed for reasonably high output and only minor changes are suggested. Width of inlet port (Fig. ST2) should be increased from 47 mm. (N1) to 50 mm. (N2). Original radii should be continued. Lower edge (NR) should be rounded to a radius of 3 mm. to prevent piston from catching on edge. Inlet timing and duration is changed by removing material from lower edge of piston skirt.

Width of exhaust port (E2—Fig. ST3) should be increased to 46 mm. Shape of sides should remain as original. Do not raise exhaust port. Round the top flat (center) edge of port to approximately 5 mm. radius (ER), gradually blending in at ends of port. The radius (ER) in addition to radii (S&C) of sides should prevent rings from catching in exhaust port.

The width of transfer ports (W—Fig. ST4) should be increased from 40 mm. to 44 mm. Smooth the transfer passage into the wider port.

Piston

On SA290 models with cast iron cylinder, it is recommended that piston (part 1414 003 210) using one "L" ring (part 1415 010 000) be used in place of original piston. The piston skirt should be shortened 2 mm. on inlet side as shown in Fig. ST6. Removing material from piston skirt will advance inlet timing and increase duration of inlet port opening.

NOTE: Do not remove material from piston skirt in front of exhaust port. The arrow on top of piston points toward exhaust. Piston skirt to cylinder clearance should be 0.099-0.131 mm. (0.0039-0.0052 inch) and ring end gap should be 0.2-0.35 mm. (0.008-0.014 inch).

On SA290SS models with aluminum cylinder and iron sleeve, the piston skirt should be shortened 2 mm. on inlet side as shown in Fig. ST6 to advance inlet timing and increase duration of inlet port opening. The width (W) of the openings in piston skirt should be increased to 44 mm. (from 34 mm.) and matched to the transfer port openings. Piston skirt to cylinder clearance should be 0.144-0.183 mm. (0.0057-0.0068 inch) and ring end gap should be 0.3-0.45 mm. (0.012-0.018 inch).

Cylinder Head

On SA290 models with cast iron cylinder, the compression ratio should be raised by milling the lower surface of cylinder head. Original depth (D—Fig. ST7) at center is 23 mm. and modified depth should be 20.5 mm. After milling the cylinder head lower surface, it is necessary to reshape the tapered area (T) around circumference of combustion chamber to provide sufficient clearance for the domed piston. Clearance between the tapered area of cylinder head and top of piston (at TDC) should be 1.5 mm. The spark plug is located on center line of combustion chamber and taper (T) can be cut on a lathe. Angle of taper should follow original and should provide necessary clearance (1.5 mm) between cylinder head and piston.

Carburetor

Tillotson HD13A is suggested for all models. Initial setting for main fuel needle is 1¼ turns open and 1 turn open for idle mixture needle. Intermediate flange (part number 1467 015 000), insulating flange (part number 1450 007 006) and intake silencer (part number 1483 012 100) are recommended for use on SA 290 Cast Iron cylinder models.

Exhaust Pipe and Muffler

On models with cast iron cylinder, exhaust pipe should be 45 mm. diameter and 380 mm. long. Models with sleeve in aluminum cylinder should use 45 mm. diameter exhaust pipe 400 mm. long. Muffler suggested by engine manufacturer for all models is part number 1473 026 000.

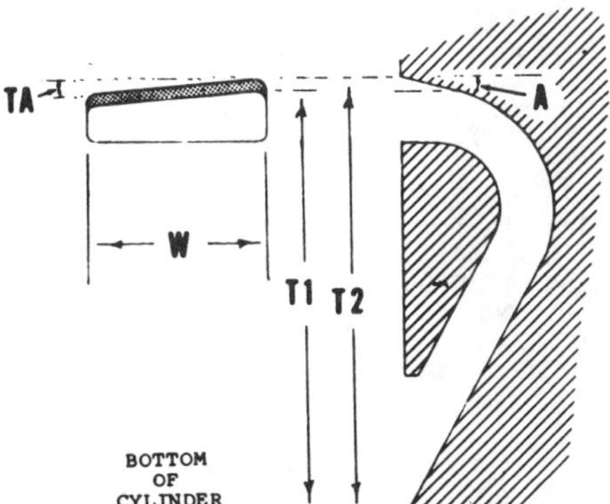

Fig. ST4–Drawings of typical transfer port. Two ports and passages are used. Refer to text for suggested changes.

A. Angle of top of passage
T1. Original height
T2. Modified height
TA. Angle at top edge
W. Port width

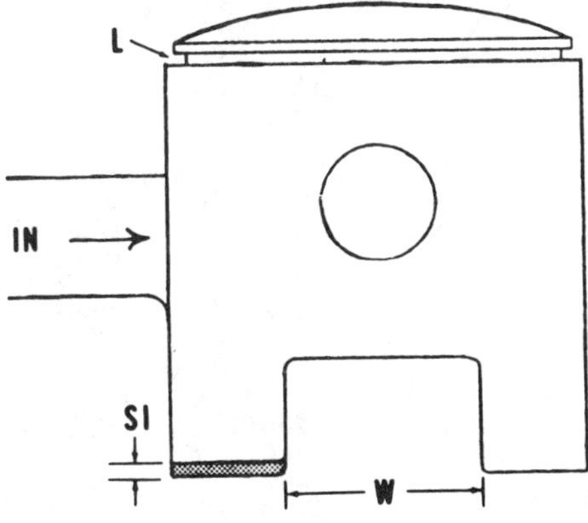

Fig. ST6–Drawing of piston showing location of piston skirt cut-outs. Refer to text for suggested changes.

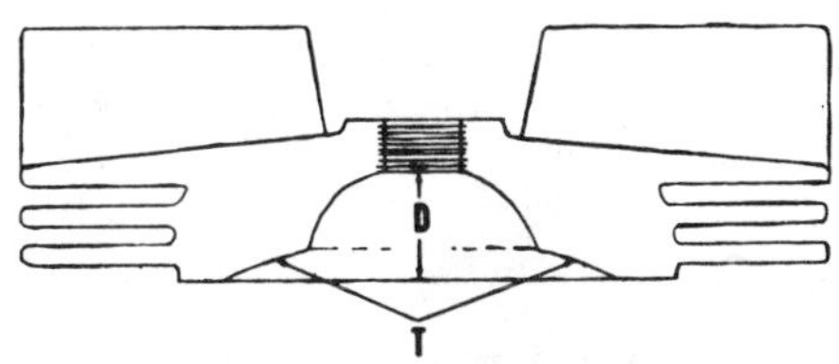

Fig. ST7–Drawing of cylinder head. Taper (T) should provide 1.5 mm clearance for piston.

SACHS

TWO AND THREE CYLINDER MODELS

CONDENSED SERVICE DATA

Year Made Engine Model	1971-73 SA2-290	1971-73 SA2-340	1970-72 SA2-440	1971-73 SA2-440C	1971 SA2-440R	1969-71 SA2-740C
Bore—(mm)	57.5	62	67.5	67.5	67.5	79
Inches	2.26	2.44	2.66	2.66	2.66	3.11
Stroke—(mm)	56	56	61	61	61	75
Inches	2.2	2.2	2.40	2.40	2.40	2.95
No. of Cylinders	2	2	2	2	2	2
Displacement—(cc)	291	338	437	437	437	735
Cubic Inches	17.75	20.63	26.64	26.64	26.64	44.8
Horsepower @ RPM	24@7200	28@7200	35@6500	40@7000	45@7500	60@6000
Cooling Type	Axial Fan	Axial Fan	Axial Fan	Free Air	Free Air	Free Air
Carburetor Model	HR	HD	HD	HD	HR	HD
Number Used	1	1	1	1	2	2
Ignition:						
Type	BOSCH Energy Transfer Magneto					
Point Gap—(mm)	0.35-0.45	0.35-0.45	0.35-0.45	0.35-0.45	0.35-0.45	0.35-0.45
Inch	0.014-0.018	0.014-0.018	0.014-0.018	0.014-0.018	0.014-0.018	0.014-0.018
Edge Gap—(mm)	7-11	7-11	7-11	7-11	7-11	7-11
Inch	0.276-0.433	0.276-0.433	0.276-0.433	0.276-0.433	0.276-0.433	0.276-0.433
Timing Advance?	Yes	Yes	Yes	Yes	Yes	Yes
Timing BTDC—(mm)	3.2-3.6	3.2-3.6	3.5-4.0*	3.2-3.6*	3.5-4.0*	4.3-4.7*
Inch	0.126-0.142	0.126-0.142	0.138-0.1575*	0.126-0.142*	0.138-0.1575*	0.169-0.185*
Measured at	Adv. Cam	Adv. Cam	Adv. Cam	Adv. Cam	Adv. Cam	Adv. Cam
Spark Plug:						
Bosch	W260T2	W260T2	See Text	W260T2	See Text	M260T1
Electrode Gap—(mm)	0.5	0.5	0.5	0.5	0.5	0.5
Inch	0.020	0.020	0.020	0.020	0.020	0.020
Fuel/Oil Ratio	25:1	25:1	25:1	25:1	25:1	25:1

*Actual piston position Before Top Dead Center.

Year Made Engine Model	1973 SA2-441	1973 SA2-340C	1973 SA2-340RX	1973 SA2-440RX	1973 SA3-650RX
Bore—(mm)	67.5	59.5	62	70	70
Inches	2.66	2.34	2.44	2.76	2.76
Stroke—(mm)	61	61	56	56	56
Inches	2.40	2.40	2.2	2.2	2.2
No. of Cylinders	2	2	2	2	3
Displacement—(cc)	437	339	338	431	647
Cubic Inches	26.64	20.67	20.63	26.3	39.5
Horsepower @ RPM	38@7000	33@7000	-@9000	-@9000	-@9000
Cooling Type	Axial Fan	Axial Fan	Free Air	Free Air	Free Air
Carburetor Model	HD	HD	HD	HD	HD
Number Used	1	1	2	2	3
Ignition:					
Type	BOSCH Energy Transfer Magneto				
Point Gap—(mm)	0.35-0.45	0.35-0.45	0.35-0.45	0.35-0.45	0.35-0.45
Inch	0.014-0.018	0.014-0.018	0.014-0.018	0.014-0.018	0.014-0.018
Timing Advance?	Yes	Yes	No	No	No
Timing BTDC—(mm)	3.2-3.6	2.3-2.7	3.2-3.4	3.2-3.4	3.2-3.4
Inch	0.126-0.142	0.091-0.106	0.126-0.134	0.126-0.134	0.126-0.134
Measured at	Adv.	Adv.	....	....	....
Spark Plug:					
Bosch	W260T2	W260T2	W260T2	W260T2	W260T2
Electrode Gap—(mm)	0.5	0.5	0.5	0.5	0.5
Inch	0.020	0.020	0.020	0.020	0.020
Fuel/Oil Ratio	25:1	25:1	16:1	16:1	16:1

MAINTENANCE

SPARK PLUGS. On all models except SA2-440 and SA2-440R, refer to CONDENSED SERVICE DATA table for recommended Bosch spark plugs. On all models, 14 mm (Bosch series W) spark plugs should be torqued to 21 ft.-lbs. and 18 mm (Bosch series N) plugs should be torqued to 25 ft.-lbs.

Because of differences in cylinder heads, length of spark plug threads should be checked before installing spark plugs in SA2-440 and SA2-440R engines. If thread length in head is approximately 13 mm (½ inch) install Bosch W240T1 or equivalent spark plug. If thread length in head is approximately 17 mm (21/32 inch), install Bosch W260T2 or equivalent spark plug. CAUTION: If incorrect spark plug is installed cylinder head may be damaged.

CARBURETOR: Tillotson diaphragm carburetors are used on all models. Racing models SA2-440R, SA2-440RX and model SA2-740C are equipped with two carburetors racing model SA3-650RX with three. Refer to the Tillotson carburetor section for operation and overhaul information. An external impulse line is used to operate fuel pump. Be sure that all passages are open and vacuum and pressure leaks are eliminated.

On all models, initial setting for idle mixture needle is 1 turn open and high speed mixture needle 1¼ turns open. The idle mixture needle should be set rich enough to provide smooth acceler-

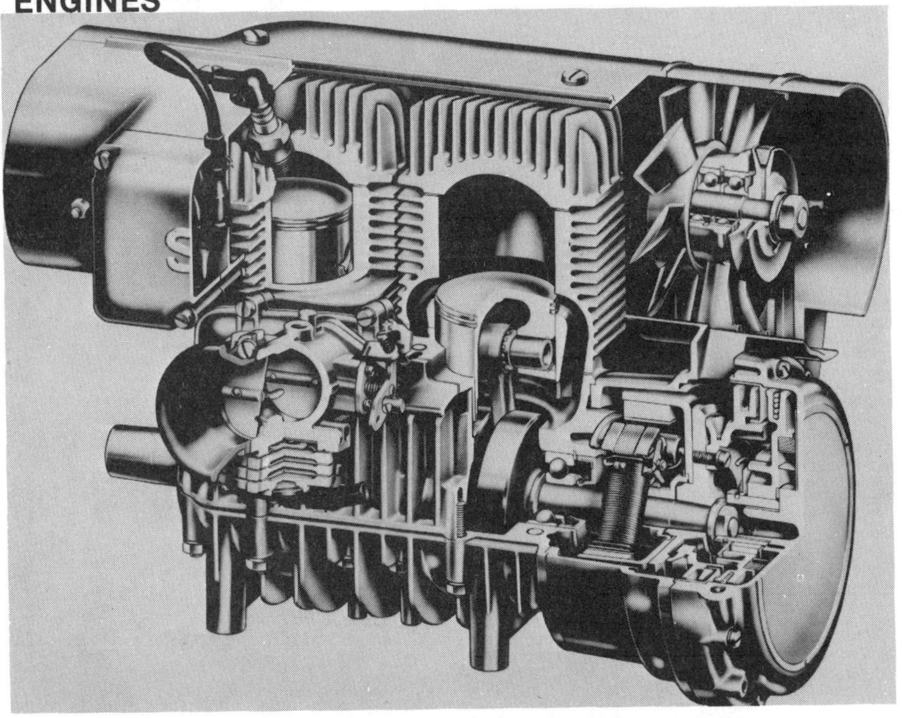

Fig. 1–Cut-away view of SA2-440 engine.

ation from idle to fast speed. The high speed mixture should be set while operating under normal load.

IGNITION SYSTEM. Breaker point gap should be set at 0.35-0.45 mm. (0.014-0.018 inch) for all models. Timing specifications for individual engines are given in CONDENSED SERVICE DATA table; however, piston position can not be directly measured through an angled spark plug hole without correct timing gage; refer to ENGINE SERVICE FUNDAMENTALS for details.

Fig. 2–Timing marks "O-1-M" on flywheel are for cylinder at output end. Marks "O-M" are for cylinder at flywheel end.

Fig. 5–View of magneto armature (stator) assembly. Breaker points (1), condenser (2) and ignition generating coil (3) are for cylinder at output end. Lighting coil is shown at (7). Make certain that wires (8) are correctly routed through relief and do not pinch wires when mounting fan housing.

Most engines are provided with ignition advance timing marks (1 M&M—Fig. 2) on flywheel and line (L) on fan housing. Mark (1M) should be used for cylinder at output end and mark (M) should be used for cylinder at flywheel end. Timing pin (P—Fig. 3) should be used to hold advance weight in advanced position while checking ignition timing. The top breaker points (1—Fig. 5), condenser (2) and inside ignition generating coil (3) are for cylinder at output end. Other breaker points (4), condenser (5) and outside ignition generator coil (6) are for cylinder at flywheel end. Ignition timing will usually be correct if stamped marks (M) are aligned and breaker point gaps are correctly set. Service ignition stator plate should be stamped as shown at (M) after being correctly installed and timed. Clearance between shoes of ignition generating coils (3 & 6), lighting coil (7) and the flywheel magnets should be 0.25-0.35 mm. (0.0098-0.0138 inch).

LUBRICATION. The engine is lubricated by mixing oil with the fuel. A suitable two-cycle air cooled engine oil is recommended. Standard grade SAE 30 automotive oil may be used if two-cycle oil is not available.

Recommended fuel-oil mixture is 25:1 for most commercial engines and 16:1 for some racing models. Do not use substitute oils in racing engines. Mix fuel and oil thoroughly using a separate container before pouring mixture into fuel tank. For cold weather blending, pre-mix the oil with a small amount of gasoline and shake thoroughly until mixture is liquid, then blend with remainder of fuel. Do not use kerosene or fuel oil for pre-mixing.

COOLING FAN AND BELT. Belt tension should be adjusted to provide approximately 1.5 centimeters (⅝-inch) deflection between the pulleys,

Fig. 3–Pin (P) should be used to hold ignition advance weight in the full advanced position when checking timing.

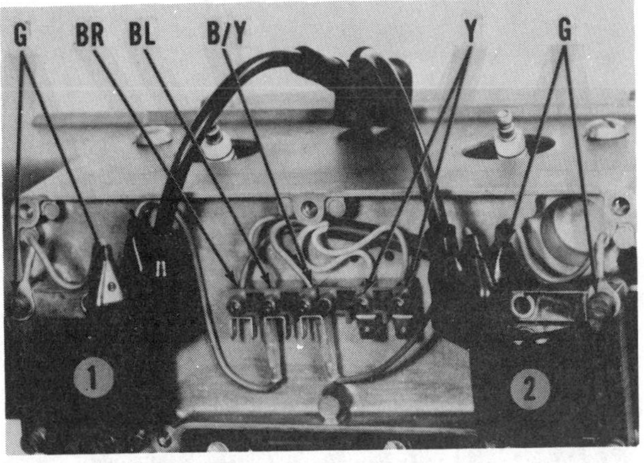

Fig. 5A–View of terminal block and coils showing correct installation of wires. Coil ground wires are shown at (G) and the two yellow lighting wires at (Y). The blue with yellow striped wire (B/Y) should be attached to coil (2) for cylinder at flywheel end. Blue wire (BL) is attached to coil (1) for cylinder at output shaft end. The brown (BR) grounding wire should be attached to end terminal as shown.

when pressed with thumb. Tightening is accomplished by removing shims (12—Fig. 7) from between pulley halves (11 & 14). A pulley holding tool (T—Fig. 6) can be made by bending rod. Shims removed from between pulley halves can be relocated between washer and outside pulley half to prevent loss. Nut (N) should be tightened to 4.0-4.5 kgm (28.9-32.5 ft.-lbs.) torque. Do not pinch belt in bottom of pulley groove when tightening nut.

To renew belt, remove recoil starter, nut (N), outside pulley half and adjusting shims, then remove starter cup from flywheel. After installing new belt, recheck belt deflection after about 20 hours of operation.

Fan and shaft (19—Fig. 7) can be renewed after removing flywheel, magneto and fan housing. To remove bearings (15 & 18), heat fan housing (212-302° F.) and bump fan housing against a wooden block. NOTE: Snap ring (16) is located between bearings. Do not lose washer (17). Bearings should be packed with high temperature bearing grease. Install bearing with open sides together toward snap ring (16) and 2 mm washer (17). Bump bearings into bores only on outside races.

Fig. 6–Special tool (T) can be made to hold pulley when removing or installing nut (N).

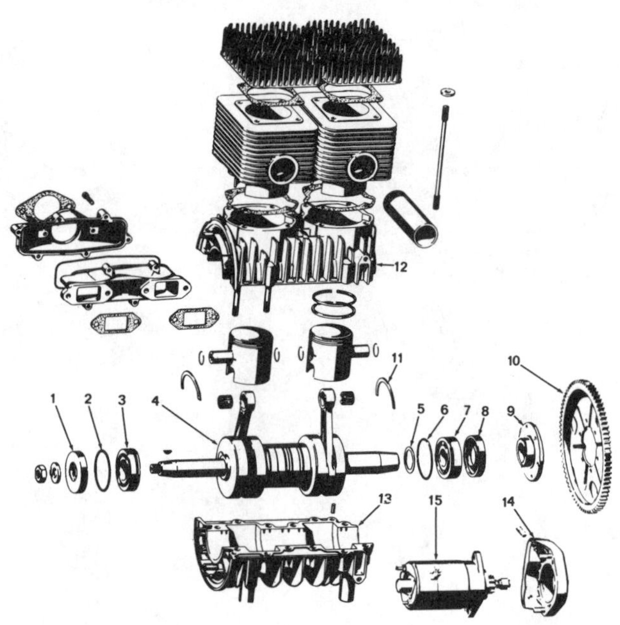

Fig. 10–Exploded view of SA2-440 engine assembly. Refer to Fig. 7 for fan and magneto assembly.

1. Front seal
2. "O" ring
3. Ball bearing
4. Crankshaft
5. Shims
6. "O" ring
7. Roller bearing
8. Rear seal
9. Starter gear hub
10. Starter gear
11. Bearing locking discs
12. Crankcase top half
13. Crankcase lower half
14. Starter adaptor
15. Starter

REPAIRS

TIGHTENING TORQUES. Recommended tightening torques are as follows:

	Kgm	Ft.-Lbs.
Carburetor nuts	0.8- 1.1	5.8- 8.0
Crankcase halves	2.3- 2.8	16.6-20.3
Cylinder cover & fan housing (fan cooled models)—25 and 75 mm. long screws	1.5- 2.0	10.8-14.4
30 mm long screws	0.5- 0.6	3.6- 4.3
Cylinder and Cylinder heads	2.8- 3.0	20.3-21.7
Fan shaft nut	4.0- 4.5	28.9-32.5
Flywheel hub nut	11.0-12.0	79.6-86.8
Flywheel to hub screws*	0.9- 1.1	6.5- 8.0
Magneto armature plate	0.4- 0.5	2.9- 3.6
Starter cup and fan drive pulley	0.8- 1.1	5.8- 8.0

*Screws should be coated with Loctite.

DISASSEMBLY AND REASSEMBLY. Cylinders, pistons, rings, piston pins and piston pin bearings MUST NOT be interchanged when reassembling. Mark these parts as they are removed for correct assembly in original location. Cylinder heads, cylinders, pistons, rings and piston pin bearings can be serviced without disassembling crankcase. Refer to PISTONS, PINS, RINGS AND CYLINDER paragraphs for disassembly and reassembly notes. CAUTION: Be careful to prevent anything from falling into crankcase.

Crankcase halves must be separated to remove crankshaft assembly. The connecting rods, crankshaft and center main bearings are available only as an assembled unit and disassembly is NOT recommended. Refer to CRANKCASE AND CRANKSHAFT paragraphs for disassembly and reassembly notes. CAUTION: Be very careful to prevent damage to the crankshaft assembly.

PISTONS, PINS, RINGS AND CYLINDERS. Mark the cylinders, pistons, rings and piston pin bearings as they are removed for correct assembly to each other and in the original location (flywheel or output shaft end of engine). Parts must NOT be interchanged between the two cylinders when reassembling. CAUTION: Be careful to prevent anything from falling into crankcase. Also, use care to prevent distortion or nicking connecting rods.

Oversize parts (for models with chrome aluminum cylinder bores) are not available; however, parts are marked and originally assembled according to manufactured tolerance group. (A, B, etc.). Recommended piston skirt to cylinder clearance is obtained by matching piston to cylinder with same mark (A to A, B to B, etc.). Recommended ring end gap is 0.30-0.45 mm. (0012-0.018 inch).

When installing pistons, arrow (Fig.

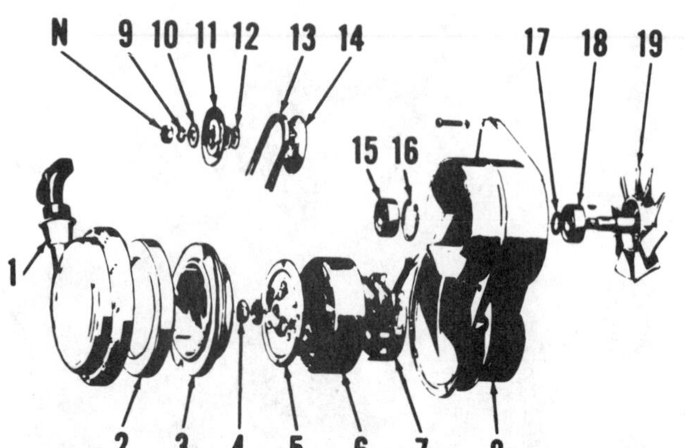

1. Recoil starter
2. Spacer
3. Starter cup
4. Flywheel nut
5. Flywheel hub
6. Flywheel
7. Magneto
8. Fan housing
9. Lock washer
10. Flat washer
11. Outside pulley half
12. Shims
13. Belt
14. Inside pulley half
15. Bearing
16. Snap ring
17. Washer (2 mm thick)
18. Bearing
19. Fan and shaft

Fig. 7–Exploded view of cooling fan and drive. Some models are cooled by free air instead of axial fan (19).

11) should be toward exhaust side of engine. Assemble both pistons and cylinders, then install inlet manifold inner half (IN—Fig. 12) and exhaust manifold (M—Fig. 13) to align cylinders. Install head gaskets with small sheet metal rim toward cylinder head. Install cylinder heads with spark plug holes toward inlet side of engine. Tighten retaining nuts for each cylinder head diagonally to torque recommended in TIGHTENING TORQUES section. After heads are correctly tightened, remove exhaust manifold to allow installation of cooling shroud. Sealing ring must be correctly positioned between inlet manifold halves to prevent air leak which will cause lean fuel-air mixture.

CRANKCASE AND CRANKSHAFT. The connecting rods, crankshaft and center main bearings are available only as an assembled unit.

To remove the crankshaft assembly, remove magneto, fan housing, cylinders and pistons. Refer to the appropriate sections for precautions regarding removal and installation of these units.

Invert crankcase assembly and remove stud nuts evenly to prevent distorting crankcase halves. Carefully bump crankcase halves apart. NOTE: Crankcase and/or crankshaft can easily be damaged by careless handling. Refer to Fig. 14.

The ball type main bearing at flywheel end and roller bearing at output end can be renewed separately. Special removal and installation tools are available from the manufacturer which will not distort crankshaft (alignment). Before installing main bearings at ends of crankshaft, determine the thickness of shims (5—Fig. 10) that should be installed to provide crankshaft end play within limits of 0.3-0.6 mm. (0.0118-0.0236 inch).

Insert locking disc halves (11—Fig. 15) into grooves in upper half of crankcase and measure distance (A) between insides of locking discs. Record this measurement. Measure thickness of both end main bearings (inner race next to crankshaft shoulder to outside of outer race), then measure distance (C—Fig. 16) between shoulder on crankshaft. Record these measurements. The combined thicknesses of bearings and crankshaft should then be subtracted from distance between insides of bearing locking discs. The resulting difference would be the amount of end play if no shims were installed. Subtract the desired end play (0.3-0.6 mm.—0.0118-0.0236 inch permissible) to determine the thickness of shims (5—Fig. 10) that should be installed between roller bearing inner race and crankshaft shoulder. An example follows:

Thickness of main bearings:

Ball bearing . . .	17.0 mm.	0.6693 in.
Roller bearing . . . +	16.0 mm.	+0.6299 in.
Distance (C—Fig. 16)	+175.5 mm.	+6.9095 in.
=Combined length	208.5 mm.	8.2087 in.
Distance (A—Fig. 15) .	209.4 mm.	8.2441 in.
Combined length	208.5 mm.	8.2087 in.
	0.9 mm.	0.0354 in.
Desired end play	0.5 mm.	0.0197 in.
Shims (5—Fig. 10) =	0.4 mm.	0.0157 in.

The ball bearing at flywheel end should be installed with "O" ring groove toward crankshaft web. Heat ball bearing and roller bearing inner race in oil to 70-80° C. (158-176° F.) before installing on crankshaft journals. When bearings are heated, they should slide into position without much difficulty. NOTE: Be sure that correct thickness of shims (5—Fig. 10) are in position before installing roller bearing inner race. "O" rings should be coated lightly with oil before installing in

Fig. 11–When installing pistons, arrow on crown should point toward exhaust side of engine.

Fig. 12–Inlet manifold inner half (IN) is secured to cylinders with four stud nuts. Nuts inside manifold are prevented from coming loose by lock plates (LP). End nuts use standard lock washers.

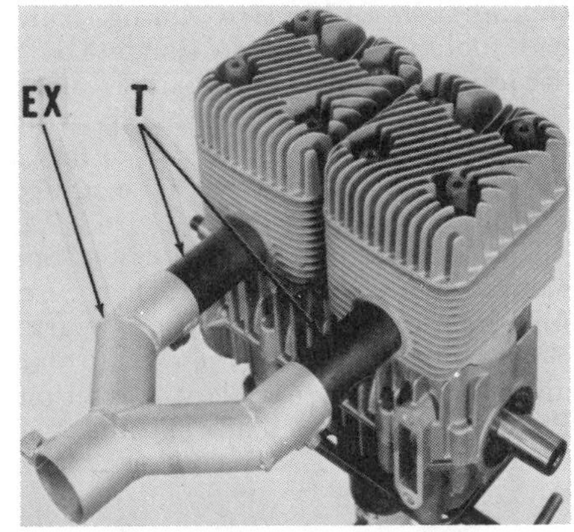

Fig. 13–Exhaust manifold (EX) is clamped to exhaust tubes (T). Tubes are screwed into cylinder ports.

Fig. 14–View of upper (cylinder) half of crankcase with crankshaft in position. Seals (F & R) should be flush with outside faces of crankcase. Dowel pins are shown at (D).

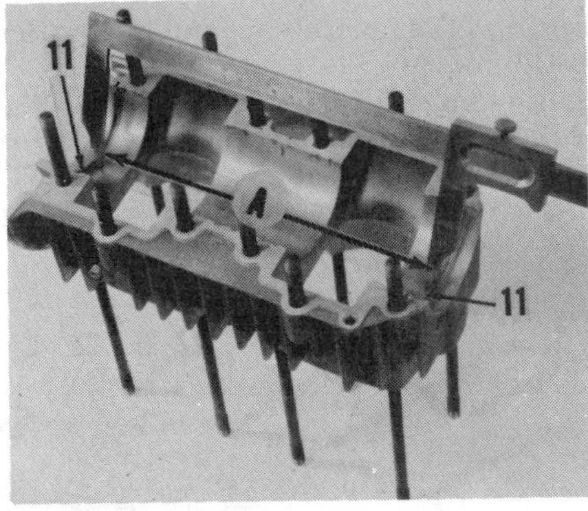

Fig. 15–View showing measurement (A) used for checking crankshaft end play. Bearing locking discs are shown at (11). Refer to text.

Fig. 16–View showing measurement (C) used for checking crankshaft end play. Crankshaft front and rear bearing thickness must also be measured.

main bearing outer race grooves. The grooved inner surface of seals (F & R—Fig. 14) should be packed with high temperature grease and positioned in bores with outside (flat) surface flush with outer edge of crankcase. Coat sealing surface of upper crankcase half with sealer and install lower crankcase half. Tighten crankcase stud nuts to torque recommended in TIGHTENING TORQUES section, starting in the center and working diagonally outward toward ends.

RECOIL STARTER. To disassemble the removed starter, remove brake spring (7—Fig. 20), shims (8), wave washer (9), brake plate (10), washer (11) and pawls (12). Remove cover (6), pull cable out enough to remove handle (25) and allow recoil spring (15) to unwind and draw cable into housing. A wire retaining tool can be made to hold pulley as shown in Fig. 21 while removing handle. Be careful to prevent recoil spring and pulley from coming out of housing as spring unwinds. Spring should remain in pulley. A puller can be used to remove bushing (16—Fig. 20) if renewal is necessary.

Spring should be installed in pulley as shown in Fig. 22. Use a small amount of grease to hold washer (14—Fig. 20) in position while assembling. Washer (14) should be 0.8 mm. (0.032 inch) thick. Insert pulley into recess in housing making certain that loop at inner end of recoil spring engages lug in housing. Turn pulley until recoil spring is completely wound and pulley will not turn any more, then back pulley up ½-1 turn until hole (H—Fig. 21) for cable is near exit (E). Insert cable through pulley and out exit hole, attach handle then release pulley to wind cable. Install cover (6—Fig. 20). Install pawls (12), washer (11), brake plate (10) and wave washer (9). Washer (11) is 0.1 mm. (0.0039 inch) thick. Install shims (8) and brake spring (7). Shims (8) should be selected to provide 0.1-0.2 mm. (0.0039-0.0079 inch) play at brake plate when wave washer is flattened. When correctly assembled, pawls (12) will extend when handle is pulled.

NOTE: Shims (8) and washers (11 & 14) are identical except for thicknesses used. Shims (8) are available in thicknesses of 0.1, 0.3 and 0.8 mm. (0.0039, 0.012 & 0.032 inch) and should be selected to provide correct adjustment of wave washer (9) and brake (10). Washer (14) should be 0.8 mm. (0.032 inch) thick and washer (11) should be 0.1 mm. (0.0039 inch) thick.

SPEED TUNING

NOTE: Specifications in the following paragraphs are suggested by the manufacturer for increasing performance of standard engines. Any change from the original configuration will probably decrease the service life of an engine and if changes are carelessly done, may decrease power and cause extensive damage. Normal tuning such as ignition timing, point gap, fuel mixture, lubrication, etc. will become more critical if engine is modified. It should be noted that gearing changes may be necessary in order to make the fullest use of the modified engine.

The cylinder heads, cylinders and pistons should be removed, then carefully inspect condition of original parts. Before modification, make certain that all parts are in excellent condition. Pistons and cylinders are marked A, B or C, indicating manufacturing tolerance. Parts marked "A" have the smallest diameter (bore) and "C" the largest. In order to obtain the required clearance, piston marked "A" should be installed in cylinder marked "B" or piston marked "B" should be installed in cylinder marked "C". Although not normally recommended, piston "A" may be installed in cylinder marked "C". Piston skirt clearance should be 0.098-0.128 mm. (0.0039-0.0050 inch) and recommended ring end gap is 0.030-0.045 mm. (0.012-0.018 inch).

In original condition, the cylinder is designed for reasonably high output and only minor changes are suggested. The exhaust port upper edge should be raised 4.2 mm. The radius of corners should be increased from 5 mm. to 10 mm. When enlarging, be especially careful not to damage the chrome cylinder bore plating. All port passages should be smoothed.

Engines are originally equipped with one Tillotson HD carburetor. Two Tillotson HR carburetors such as HR 18A should be installed on modified engine. Initial setting for two HR 18A carburetors is high speed mixture needle 1¼ turns open, idle mixture needle 1 turn open.

Individual exhaust pipes and mufflers should be used for each cylinder. Exhaust manifold (EX—Fig. 13) should not be used.

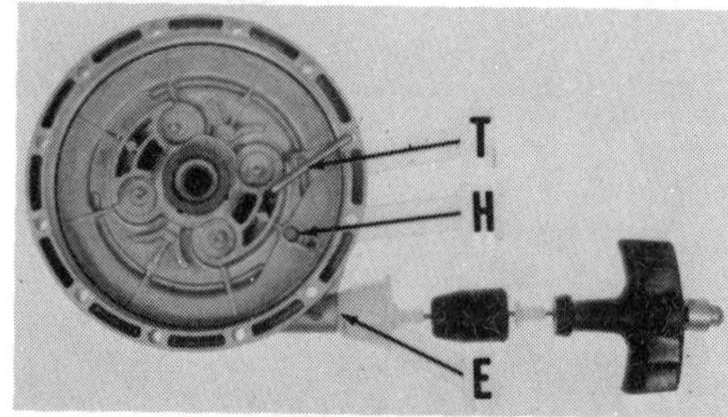

Fig. 21–A piece of heavy wire can be bent and used as shown at (T) to prevent pulley from turning while removing or attaching handle.

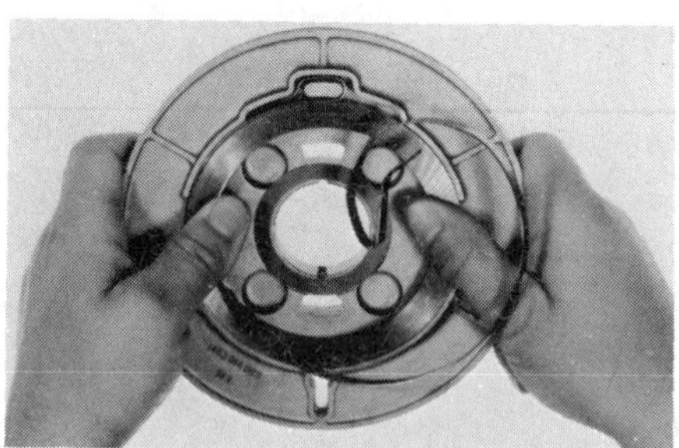

Fig. 22–Spring should be installed in direction shown.

Fig. 20–Exploded view of starter of the type used.

1. Pin
2. Starter cup
3. Washer
4. Lock washer
5. Nut
6. Cover
7. Brake spring
8. Shims
9. Wave washer
10. Brake plate
11. Washer (0.1 mm thick)
12. Pawls
13. Pulley
14. Washer (0.8 mm thick)
15. Recoil spring
16. Bushing
17. Tolerance ring
18. Rivets (3 used)
19. Check plate
20. Housing
21. Cable guide
22. Set screw
23. Bushing
24. Bumper
25. Handle
26. Clamp ring
27. Clamp cone
28. Cable

SACHS WANKEL

MODELS

CONDENSED SERVICE DATA

Model	RC 1-18.5*	KM914B	KM24
Displacement	303 cc 18.5 cu. in.	303 cc 18.5 cu. in.	294 cc 17.9 cu. in.
Horsepower @ RPM	19 @ 5500	19 @ 5500	23 @ 6000
Carburetor Model	HL	HL	HR
Spark Plug			
Bosch	W150M11S	W150M11S	W260T1
Champion	L86	L85	K7
Spark Plug Gap	0.019-0.020	0.018-0.020	0.020
Point Gap	0.014-0.018	0.014-0.018	0.014-0.018
Ignition Timing	10°-14° BTDC	10°-12° BTDC	20° BTDC
Fuel/Oil Mixture	40:1	50:1	50:1

*Previous Curtiss Wright Model

MAINTENANCE

Models RC 1-18.5 & KM914B

SPARK PLUG. A Bosch W 150 M 11 S spark plug is used. The Champion equivalent is L86 or L90. Recommended spark plug gap is 0.019-0.020 in.

CARBURETOR. Tillotson Diaphragm Type carburetors are used. Model HL 242A used on some engines is equipped with a fixed main jet. Model HL 252A which is alternately used has a main adjustment needle. Refer to TILLOTSON Carburetor Section in SERVICE FUNDAMENTALS for operation and overhaul.

On Model H 242A, initial setting for idle mixture adjusting screw is 1½ turns open. On Model HL 252A, set idle mixture adjusting screw at ¾ turn and main adjusting needle at 1½ turns open. Adjustments must be checked under operating conditions of temperature and load. On Model HL 252A adjust main needle so engine will accelerate over full operating range without hesitation and run smoothly without excessive smoking. Readjustment of idle mixture needle and idle speed needle may also be necessary.

On Model HL 242A, a 0.041 main jet is recommended for altitudes up to 4000 ft. and a 0.039 main jet for higher altitudes.

FUEL PUMP. The fuel pump is operated by a pulse passage (P—Fig. 19) which enters the rotor housing midway between intake and compression areas. An external line connects the diaphragm type fuel pump to engine pulse passage. The line must be kept open and must not leak.

LUBRICATION. The engine is lubricated by oil mixed with the fuel. Recommended fuel/oil ratio is given in CONDENSED SERVICE DATA Tables. Fuel should be good quality regular gasoline.

IGNITION TIMING. A Bosch flywheel magneto is used. Magneto contains an auxiliary lighting coil which utilizes the permanent magnets as the power source. Power output is 40 watts at 12 volts.

Recommended ignition point gap is 0.014-0.018 in. Ignition timing is 12 degrees BTDC and magneto edge gap is 0.590-0.748 in.

When the "O" timing mark on flywheel aligns with reference mark on fan housing, rotor is at Top Dead Center (TDC). See Fig. 1. The "M" mark designates 12 degrees BTDC when aligned with reference mark. Points should begin to open and magneto edge gap should be 0.590-0.748 in. when "M" mark is aligned.

Magneto cam can be installed for either clockwise or counter-clockwise rotation when viewed from Power Take-Off End of crankshaft. On the Wankel engine, cam MUST be installed with "L" mark aligned with reference mark on flywheel as shown in Fig. 2.

Assembly marks are generally used with all components for correct timing. Fig. 3 shows alignment marks for ar-

Fig. 1–View of Wankel engine with recoil starter removed, showing timing scribe line (Arrow) on blower housing. "M" mark on magneto housing indicates firing point, "O" mark TDC.

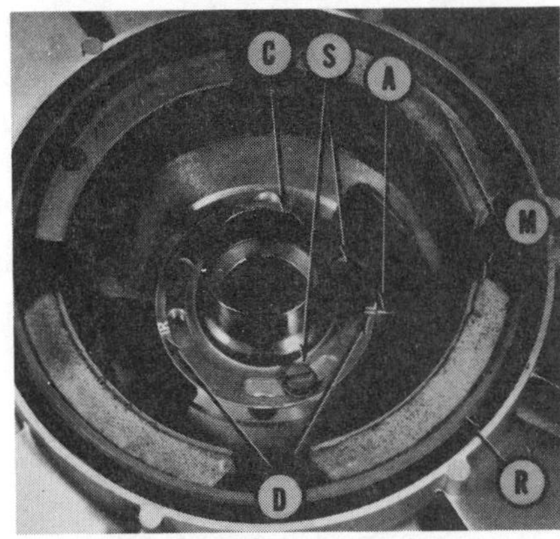

Fig. 2–Inside view of flywheel showing magnets and breaker cam. Refer to text for details.

A. Assembly mark
C. Breaker cam
D. Direction marks
M. Magnets
R. Magneto housing
S. Retaining Screws

Fig. 3–Chisel marks (Arrow) indicating proper location for armature plate installation can be viewed through flywheel as shown. Refer to text.

mature plate positioning. Replacement parts may not be marked, however, and the complete procedure for correct timing is as follows:

Temporarily position the flywheel and turn crankshaft until "M" timing mark on magneto housing aligns with scribe mark on crankcase as shown in Fig. 1. Measure the edge gap (A—Fig. 4) working through opening in magneto housing. Edge gap should be 0.590-0.748 in.; if it is not, lift off the flywheel and loosen the three screws (Fig. 5) securing armature plate to crankcase. Reposition the plate and recheck by installing flywheel. When edge gap is correctly adjusted, set breaker point gap to recommended opening (0.4 mm or 0.016 in.) and turn crankshaft until "M" timing mark on flywheel is again aligned. Breaker points should be just starting to open; if they are not, remove flywheel and loosen the four screws (S—Fig. 2) securing breaker cam (C) to flywheel. Reposition the cam and recheck, then tighten screws securely when cam is properly positioned.

Refer to Fig. 6 for an exploded view of armature plate showing component parts. Refer also to MAGNETO SERVICE Section in ENGINE SERVICE FUNDAMENTALS.

REPAIRS

Models RC 1-18.5 & KM914B

TIGHTENING TORQUES. Recommended tightening torques are as follows:

Flywheel Nut	55 ft.-lbs.
Rotor Housing End Plate Screws	55-70 in.-lbs.
Counterweight Screw	15 ft.-lbs.
Retaining Flange Screws—PTO End	55-70 in.-lbs.
Fan Housing Nuts	15 ft.-lbs.

DISASSEMBLY. Screws and nuts are metric. Metric wrenches should be used, however, 1 7/16-inch and 7/16-inch sockets will fit the nuts. Metric Allen wrenches MUST be used on socket head screws.

Disassembly should begin at starter end. Remove starter and cooling fan housing (Fig. 7). Remove mainshaft nuts, washer and starter cup, being careful not to lose the dowel pins (5—Fig. 11). Remove flywheel assembly using a suitable puller attached to

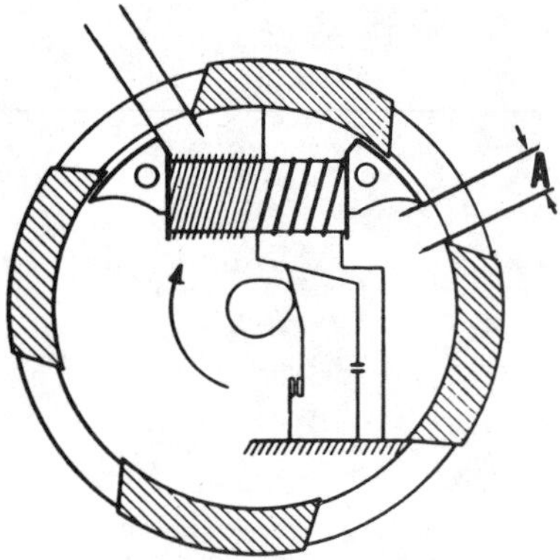

Fig. 4–With "M" timing mark aligned, edge gap (A) should measure 15-19 mm (0.590-0.748 inch).

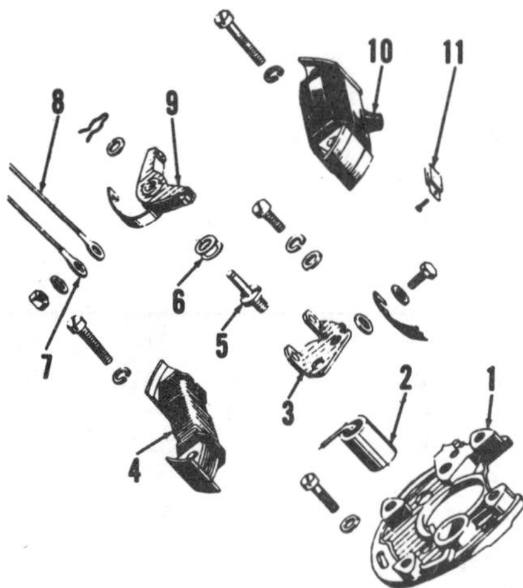

Fig. 6–Exploded view of magneto armature plate showing component parts.

1. Plate
2. Condenser
3. Stationary point
4. Lighting coil
5. Pivot shaft
6. Shims
7. Kill wire
8. Condenser wire
9. Breaker arm
10. Ignition coil
11. Oiler wick

Fig. 5–View of engine with flywheel removed, showing armature plate attaching screws (Arrows).

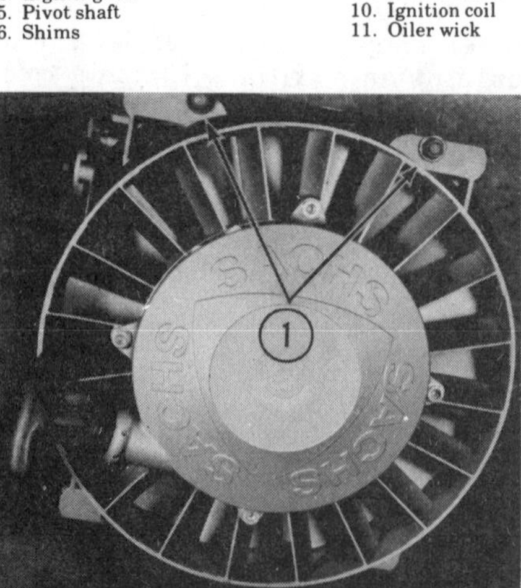

Fig. 7–Remove the six stud nuts (1) and lift off blower housing. Starter may first be removed if desired.

Fig. 8–Remove flywheel nut (2) using a 36 mm socket. A 1-7/16-inch socket will work.

Fig. 9–Remove washer (3).

Fig. 10–Lift off starter cup (4).

Fig. 11–Be careful not to lose the two small (loose) dowels (5). Lift out the dowels and remove flywheel by attaching a puller to threaded holes (P). Holes are M18 (metric) threads.

threaded holes (P). Remove ignition plate assembly and magneto mounting plate as shown in Figs. 12 & 13; remove the circle of socket head cap screws (8) and lift off ignition side end plate.

Rotor removal should be done carefully to prevent damage to rotor, housing or seals. Seals may stick to end plates when engine is disassembled. Protect inside and end surfaces of rotor housing against damage and be careful not to dislodge or damage the hollow locating dowels (Fig. 14).

Remove counterweight (A—Fig. 15), Woodruff key and retaining flange (B) from drive end of mainshaft. O-ring seal around retaining flange hub should be renewed. Remove snap ring (1—Fig. 16), shims (2) and thrust washer (3); then withdraw mainshaft from drive end plate.

INSPECTION. Note condition of rotor seals (Fig. 17). Side seal (wave) springs (1) are installed with tips of spring pointing down in groove. Apex seal pin springs (5) should be mated as shown in Fig. 18. Carbon should be carefully removed from seal grooves. Seal side clearance should not exceed 0.004 in. Renew rotor and bearing assembly if clearance is excessive.

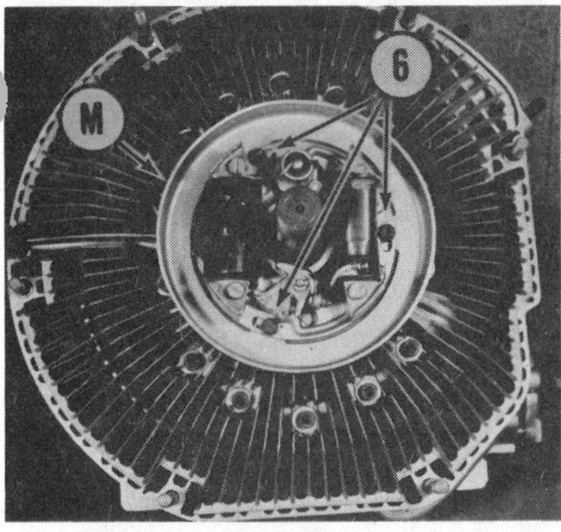

Fig. 12–Remove the three screws (6) and lift armature out of mounting plate (M).

Fig. 13–Remove the four screws (7) and lift off armature and mounting plate as a unit.

Inspect rotor roller needle bearing. Bearing is retained in rotor bore by snap rings. Rotor and bearing are only available in an assembly which also includes the complete rotor seal kit.

Inspect mainshaft surfaces and end plate bearings for wear. Drive side roller bearing and inner race must be renewed as an assembly. Inner race must be pressed from mainshaft. Heat the new inner race to approximately 300° F. and press into position on shaft until it seats on shaft shoulder. Either end plate must be heated to approximately 300° F. to remove and install the shaft bearings. Mainshaft eccentric, bearing and seal surfaces should be checked for wear or damage and shaft renewed if its condition is questionable.

Check rotor gear teeth and pinion gear in magneto end plate. If stationary (pinion) gear is damaged, it can be renewed by first heating magneto end plate to 300° F., then pressing out the pinion and bearing. The stationary gear flange must be carefully installed with the four magneto mounting bolt holes aligned. Install as follows:

Heat new stationary gear to 300° F. and install the old or new bearing, then allow gear to cool. Two metric (M6) alignment studs are required. Studs can be made by removing the heads from M6 cap screws at least 2 inches long. Heat end plate to 300° F. and install the studs in holes 180 degrees apart; then press pinion and bearing into plate until squarely seated on machined surface of plate.

End plates (side plates) may be re-

Fig. 14–View of rotor and rotor housing with ignition end plate removed. Be careful not to lose ring dowels (1) when engine is disassembled.

1. Ring dowel
2. Pulse passage
3. Intake port
4. Exhaust port
5. Seal pin
6. Apex seal
7. Side seal

Fig. 15–Working from pto side of engine, remove counterweight (A) and retaining flange (B). Metric size Allen wrenches are required.

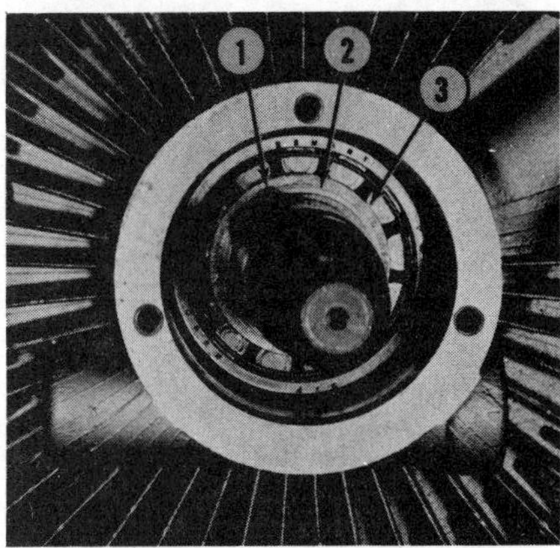

Fig. 16–Mainshaft can be removed after removing snap ring (1), spacer shims (2) and thrust washer (3).

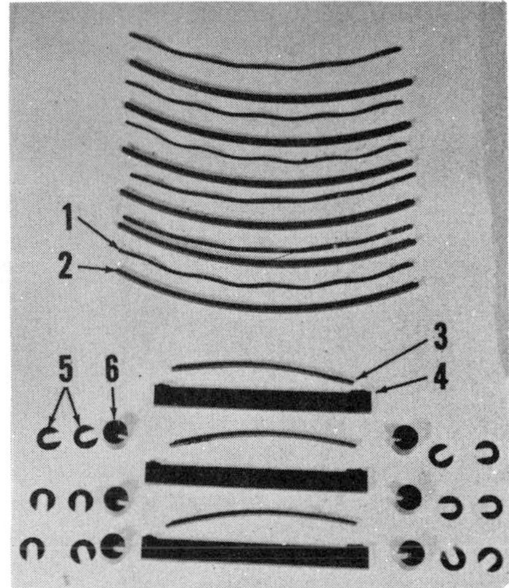

Fig. 17–Exploded view of rotor seals which take the place of piston rings in piston engine.

1. Wave springs
2. Side seals
3. Apex seal springs
4. Apex seals
5. Pin springs
6. Apex seal pins

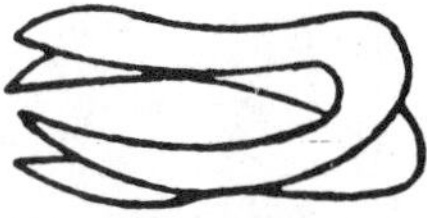

Fig. 18–Apex seal pin springs must be installed with convex sides together as shown.

machined approximately 0.035 inch provided minimum plate thicknesses shown in Fig. 20A are not exceeded. Magneto end plate is measured adjacent to center hole after removing stationary gear. Drive end plate is measured through mounting pad hole as shown.

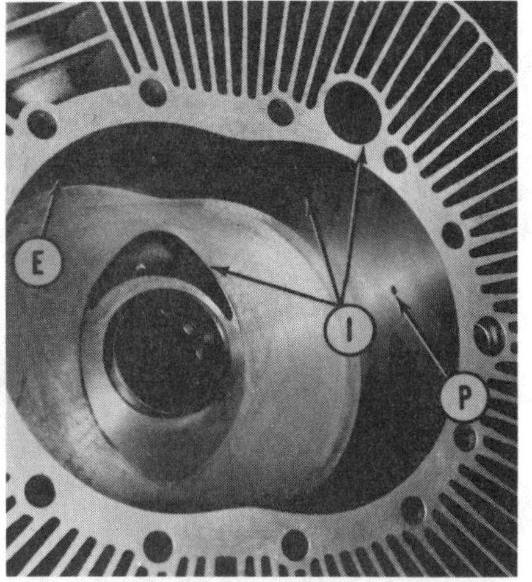

Fig. 19–Rotor housing and drive end plate with rotor and shaft removed. Inlet fuel charge passes through both end plates, rotor and rotor housing to provide lubricant to the moving parts.

E. Exhaust port
I. Intake ports
P. Pulse passage port

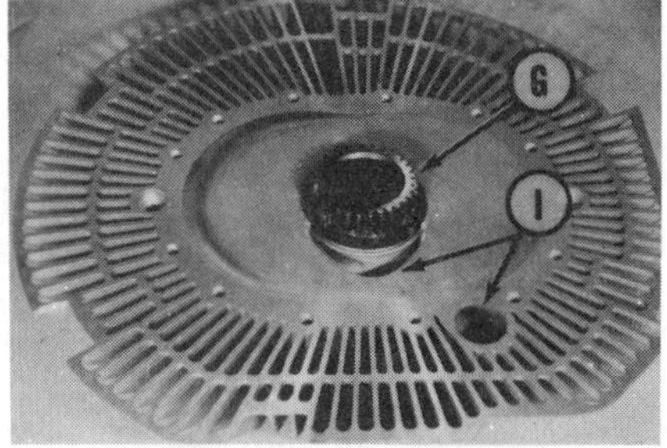

Fig. 20–Inside view of ignition side end plate showing stationary gear (G) and intake ports (1). Refer also to Fig. 19.

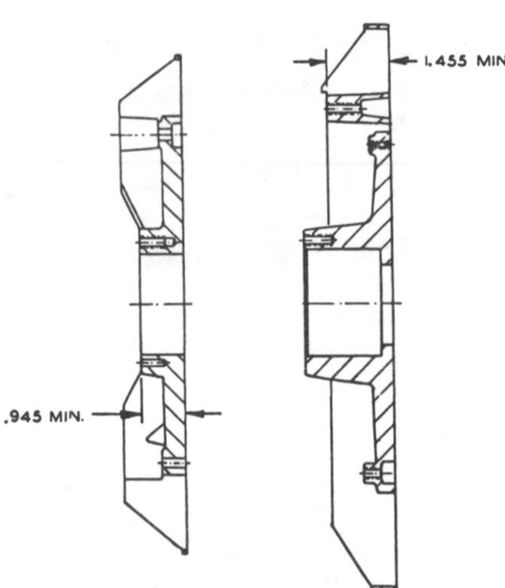

Fig. 20A–Rotor side plates may be re-machined (about 0.035 inch) provided the minimum thicknesses shown are maintained. Magneto end plate is on left, drive end plate on right.

Positioning arbors are required when refinishing end plates. Arbors must be locally made, using the dimensions and materials shown in Fig. 28 for magneto end plate arbor and Fig. 29 for drive end plate tool. Fig. 30 shows set-up procedure for using the tools.

The manufacturer recommends using a sharp carbide bit positioned to permit a shave cut. Use a machine feed of not more than 0.0025 inch per spindle revolution and machine from center outward. Start at center with a spindle speed of approximately 330 rpm, decrease speed to approximately 200 rpm at a 3½ inch radius and to 100 rpm at 5 inch radius.

Hand lap using 320 grit emery paper and finish lap with crocus cloth.

ASSEMBLY. All bearings, seals and moving surfaces should be lubricated as engine is assembled. Install mainshaft in drive side end plate being careful not to damage bearing. Install thrust washer (3—Fig. 16) on drive end of mainshaft and install as many shims (2) as possible and still permit installation of snap ring (1). Shims (2) are 0.1 mm (0.004 in.) thick. Install snap ring (1), then check main shaft for ease of rotation. Lubricate O-ring and place in groove on hub of retaining flange. Also lubricate oil seal in bore of flange. Use a protecting sleeve to prevent damage to oil seal lip and install the flange, tightening retaining screws to 55-70 in.-lbs. torque. Install Woodruff key and counterweight and torque retaining cap screw to 15 ft.-lbs.

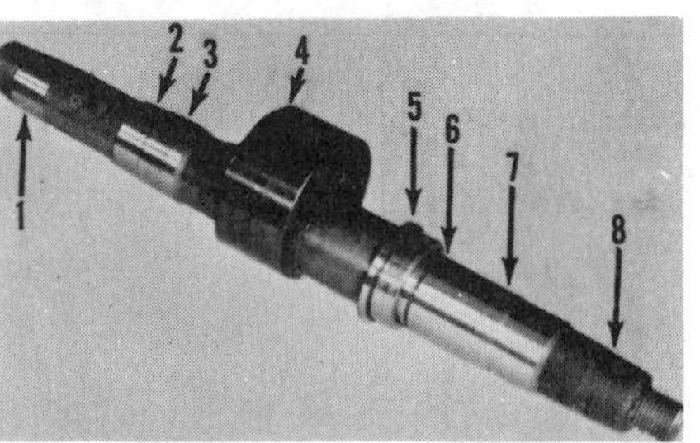

Fig. 21–Engine mainshaft showing points of inspection.

1. Flywheel end
2. Seal seat
3. Bearing race
4. Actuating cam
5. Bearing race
6. Snap ring groove
7. Seal surface
8. Drive end

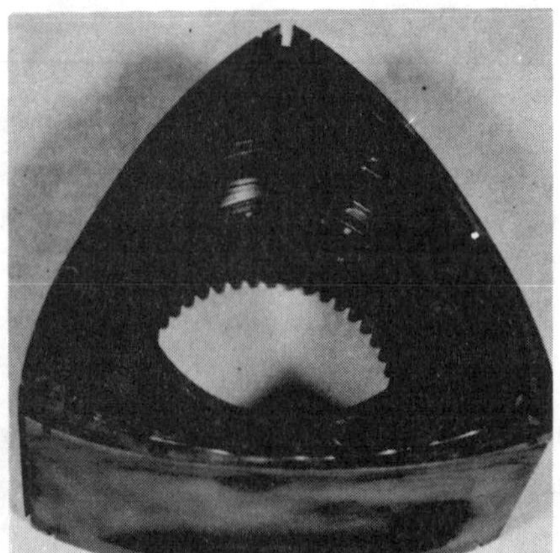

Fig. 22–Inspect roller bearing and seal surfaces of rotor. Carbon should be carefully removed from seal grooves.

Install two locating ring dowels in drive side end plate and install rotor housing. Install apex seal pin, spring pins, side seal wave spring and side seals in drive side of rotor (opposite side from gear). Place rotor housing and drive end plate on its side with spark plug hole up as shown in Fig. 24. Counterweight and mainshaft eccentric should point downward. Install the three apex springs and seals in slots and, holding seals firmly in place install the rotor as shown. One point of rotor must point up toward spark plug port. Care should be taken not to damage edge of apex seals as rotor is

Fig. 23–Magneto end of partially assembled engine.

1. Ignition side end plate
2. Stationary gear flange
3. Threaded holes
4. End plate screws

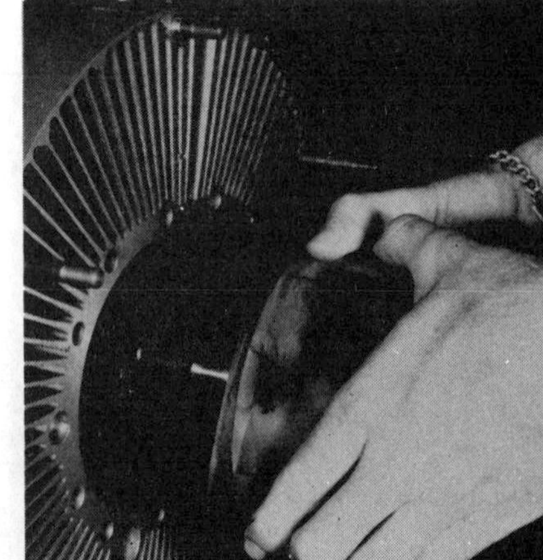

Fig. 24–Reinstalling rotor assembly. Refer to text for details.

installed. Also use extreme care not to lose side seals. Rotor should not be permitted to move from contact with drive end plate once it is installed, or side seals may adhere to plate and be withdrawn from their grooves.

Oil and install the remaining side seals, springs and pins on ignition side of rotor. Install ring dowels and ignition side end plate. It may be necessary to rock the crankshaft back and forth until gears mesh. Install end plate screws and torque to 55-70 in.-lbs. Rotate mainshaft and check for freedom of movement.

Fig. 25–Removed view of recoil starter assembly.

1. Snap ring
2. Spacer shims

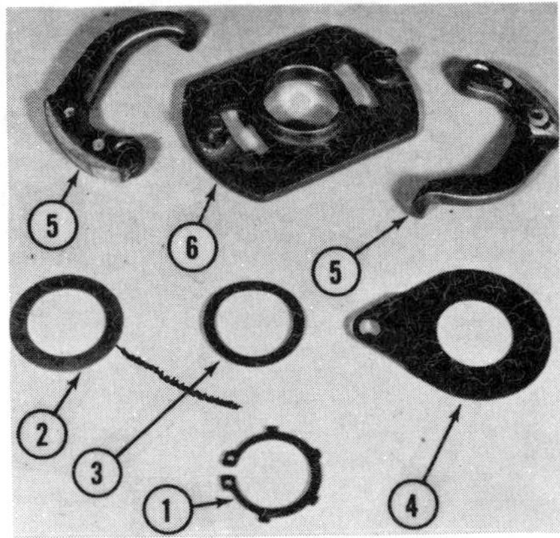

Fig. 26–Disassembled view of starter actuating mechanism.

1. Snap ring
2. Spacer shims
3. Wave washer
4. Brake disc
5. Actuating levers
6. Lever plate

Fig. 27–Cable pulley removed showing return spring correctly installed.

7. Cable pulley
8. Cable
9. Recoil spring
10. Guide ring
11. Housing
12. Sleeve
L. Loop
T. Tab

Place lubricated O-ring seal around stationary pinion flange and install magneto/generator mounting plate and armature plate. Plate must be installed with large hole for wires pointing toward spark plug port. Install Woodruff key, flywheel, starter cup, dowels and washer. Install and tighten flywheel nut to a torque of 55 ft.-lbs. Reinstall cooling fan housing and starter and tighten retaining stud nuts to 13-16 ft.-lbs.

RECOIL STARTER. To disassemble starter, cut cable as close as possible to grip and allow pulley to turn slowly until spring is completely unwound. Remove snap ring (1—Fig. 25) and washers (2), then lift off the actuating assembly. Remove pulley (7—Fig. 27), leaving spring (9) in housing. Protect hands if spring is to be removed, and lift out carefully to prevent personal injury.

When assembling the starter, use Fig. 27 as a guide. With inner side of housing facing upward as shown, install spring so it coils counter-clockwise beginning with outside anchor, securing loop over pin (P). Spring guide ring (10) has a section removed to provide clearance for inner spring loop (L) and a relieved outer end to provide clearance for spring rivets. Be sure guide is installed right side up as shown. Wind cable completely around pulley in the direction shown and install pulley with tab (T) engaging inner spring loop (L). Wind pulley three turns counter-clockwise before passing cable through housing hole. Reinstall handle grip to prevent re-entry of

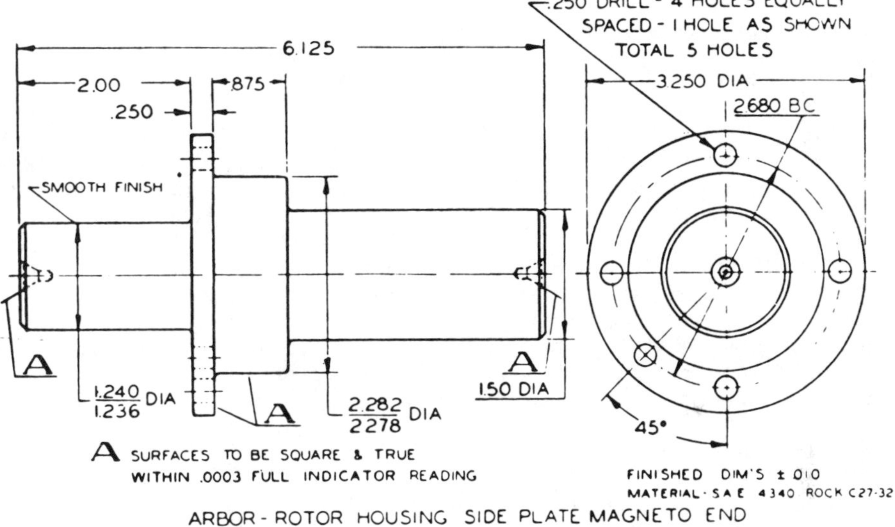

Fig. 28–Machining diagram for local fabrication of magneto end plate arbor.

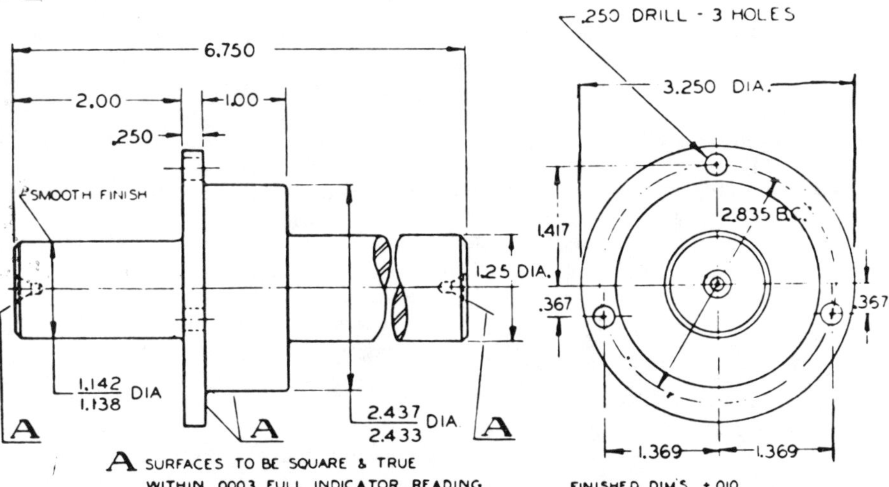

Fig. 29–Machining diagram for local fabrication of drive end plate arbor.

cable. A new retaining ferrule will be needed.

Shims (2—Fig. 26) are in two sizes, the larger (1-inch ID) being placed on top of pulley (7—Fig. 27) and underneath lever plate (6—Fig. 26). These shims are available in thicknesses of 0.15, 0.3, 0.5 and 0.8 mm (0.006, 0.012, 0.020 and 0.032 inch), and shim pack should be of correct thickness to permit top hub flange of carrier (6) to ride 0.1-0.2 mm (0.004-0.008 inch) below shoulder of sleeve (12—Fig. 27). Install lever plate (6—Fig. 26), levers (5) and brake disc (4). Install wave washer (3) and smaller shims (2). These shims are ⅞-inch ID and 0.3 or 0.5 mm (0.012 or 0.020 inch) in thickness. Enough shims should be used to permit wave washer to compress but not to flatten when snap ring (1) is installed.

NOTE: The purpose of the wave washer and adjustment is to create a light drag on brake disc (4) and cause levers to swing out (engage) when cable is pulled. If too many shims are used, starter may not properly re-wind.

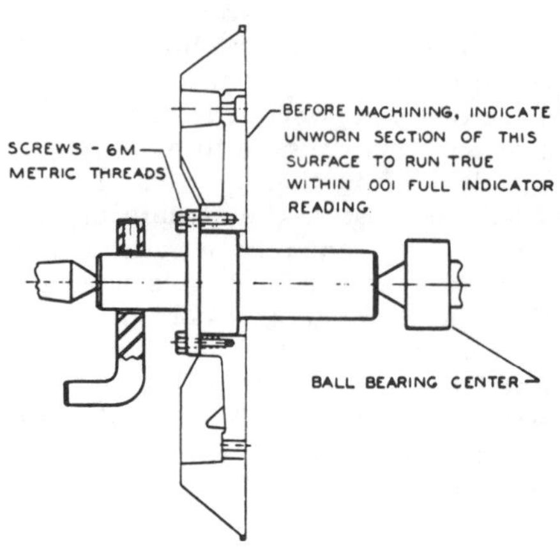

Fig. 30–Set up procedure for re-machining rotor housing side plates. Refer to Figs. 20A, 28 and 29, and to text.

MAINTENANCE

Model KM24

SPARK PLUG. A BOSCH W240T1 or Champion K7 plug having a half-inch reach is used on engines before Serial Number 7565102. Later engines use a ¾ inch reach plug (BOSCH W240T2). PLUGS CANNOT BE INTERCHANGED.

Adjust air gap to 0.5 mm (0.020 inch) and tighten plug to a torque of 2.2-2.5 kg-m (16-18 ft.-lbs.).

CARBURETOR. A Walbro WR or Tillotson HR carburetor is used. A separate, plunger type, diaphragm fuel pump is used and carburetor is not equipped with pulse pump. Fuel pump pressure should be about 3.5 psi at all engine speeds and service consists of renewing the pump.

LUBRICATION. Engine is lubricated by oil mixed with the fuel. Use Regular gasoline and a good two stroke or rotary engine motor oil mixed at the rate of 25:1. Approved oils are Arctic Cat Rotolube; Shell Rotella SAE 30HD, Mobilmix TT, Essolube HD30 or Fina Poly 8.

IGNITION TIMING. Ignition points should just begin to open when scribe mark on rope pulley inner sheave aligns with "M" mark on fan housing. Timing is adjusted by regapping ignition points or loosening the three screws retaining magneto base plate to mounting plate and repositioning base plate in the slotted holes. Specified point gap is 0.014-0.018 inch (0.35-0.45 mm).

REPAIRS

Model KM24

TIGHTENING TORQUES. Recommended tightening torques are as follows:

	ft.-lbs.	kg-m
Counterweight clamp bolt	20-22	3
End covers	5-8	0.6-1.1
Engine plate	30	4
Fan housing	5.5	0.75
Fuel pump drive (adapter nut)	55-60	8
Manifolds	10	1.4
Stationary gear	6	0.8

DISASSEMBLY. Remove carburetor and inlet manifold elbow as a unit. Remove muffler. Disconnect wires and remove ignition coil. Remove recoil starter assembly and fan housing. Clamp PTO end counterweight in a vise to hold shaft, then remove fuel pump drive adapter nut.

Remove fan and flywheel using a suitable puller, protecting threaded end of mainshaft from forcing screw. Remove magneto and mounting plate as a unit by removing the retaining throughbolts.

Heat counterweights in area of retaining set screws to break the LOCTITE seal, then remove set screws and counterweights. Remove throughbolts, noting that a flat washer is positioned under bolt head and nut.

Carefully work PTO end cover from its doweled position on rotor housing and lift off the cover, checking to see that side seals, sealing pins, springs and ring dowels do not adhere to cover and become lost as cover is removed.

Remove rotor and rotor housing, making sure none of the sealing components are accidentally lost or damaged. Rotor seals to be accounted for are as follows:

Side seals	6
Side seal springs	6
Sealing pins	6
Sealing pin springs	12
Long apex seals	3
Short apex seals	3
Apex seal springs	3

There are also two ring dowels between each end cover and rotor housing, four in all. These ring dowels may remain with cover or housing, or may fall out as parts are handled.

Punch a hole in magneto end cover seal. Thread a self-tapping screw into the hole and pull the seal by prying on the screw. With seal removed, unseat the exposed snap ring and withdraw mainshaft from magneto end cover.

NOTE: Spacer shims may be located beneath the snap ring. Also two spacer thrust rings are used on every mainshaft. These parts provide the correct mainshaft end play and must be saved for reinstallation.

INSPECTION. Inspect end covers for scratches, scoring or cracks. Visible wear pattern is normal. End covers cannot be re-machined, renew covers if damaged.

Examine stationary gear teeth and mating gear in rotor. If either is damaged, both must be renewed.

Inspect running surface of rotor housing for scoring or other damage. Rotor housing cannot be re-machined. If rotor housing is renewed, new apex seals must also be installed.

Examine apex seal grooves in rotor for pitting or pounding. Insert apex seal in groove and attempt to slide a 0.010 inch feeler gage into groove beside the seal. If feeler gage will start, renew rotor.

Measure depth of cleaned apex seal at middle and near each end. If measurement is less than 0.280 inch (7.0 mm) or varies more than 0.008 inch (0.2 mm) at either end, all three seals must be renewed. Measure thickness of apex seal, which should not be less than 0.1173 inch (2.97 mm).

Measure length of sealing pins, which should not be less than 0.2086 inch (5.3 mm). If measurement is less or if pins vary in length more than 0.002 inch (0.05 mm), renew all three pins on that side.

Measure depth of side seals, which should not be less than 0.0865 inch (2.2 mm). If thickness is less, or if end of any seal measures 0.004 inch (0.1 mm) less than at center, all side seals must be renewed.

ASSEMBLY. Thoroughly clean and decarbonize all parts. Lubricate magneto end cover bearing with engine oil and slide mainshaft through bearing. Heat the two thrust rings in hot oil and press into position until they bottom on shaft shoulder. Install any removed shims and the retaining snap ring. Grease sealing lip of oil seal with high temperature grease. Lightly coat outside edge of seal with LOCTITE and install seal with lip to outside.

Invert magneto end cover, rotor contact side up on a bench. Install ring dowels and rotor housing. Lubricate working surfaces of rotor housing and end cover. Turn mainshaft until high portion of cam points directly toward narrow part of rotor housing. Place rotor gear-side up on a clean rag and install sealing pins, side seals and their springs in gear side of rotor, using high temperature grease to hold them in place. Turn rotor until one point is aligned with high point of cam, then carefully upend rotor over shaft with flat of rotor aligned with high point of cam. Gently slide gears into mesh. DO NOT lift rotor again at this point or side seals will fall out. Carefully push down on rotor. If it cannot be pushed flush with top of rotor housing it is likely seals have fallen out; remove rotor and try again.

Install remaining seal pins and springs. Position short apex seal in one seal pin. Place end of apex seal spring against step of short seal, put long apex seal in place and push the entire assembly in its groove until it bottoms. Install the remaining apex and side seals, then install PTO end cover and ring dowels using a suitable seal protector. Install through-bolts and tighten alternately and evenly to recommended torque. Complete the assembly by reversing the disassembly procedure using LOCTITE on counterweight set screws and fuel pump drive adapter nut.

SCORPION BRUT

CONDENSED SERVICE DATA

ENGINE MODEL	LC34	LC44
Bore—(mm)	62	58
Inches	2.441	2.283
Stroke—(mm)	55.6	55.5
Inches	2.189	2.185
No. of Cylinders	2	3
Displacement—(cc)	335.7	439.9
Cubic Inches	20.4	26.8
Horsepower at RPM		
Standard		
Stock Tuned		
Cooling Type	Liquid Cooled	Liquid Cooled
Carburetor Make	Mikuni	Mikuni
Model	VM32	VM34
Number Used	2	3
Ignition Type	ET	CD
Make	Kokusan Denk.	Kokusan
Point Gap—(mm)	0.4	....
Inch	0.015	....
Timing Advance?	Yes	Yes
Timing checked at	Adv.	Adv.
Setting	20°-30°	20°-30°
Spark Plug:		
NGK	B8ES	B8ES
Electrode Gap—(mm)	0.45	0.45
Inch	0.018	0.018
Fuel/Oil Ratio	20:1	20:1

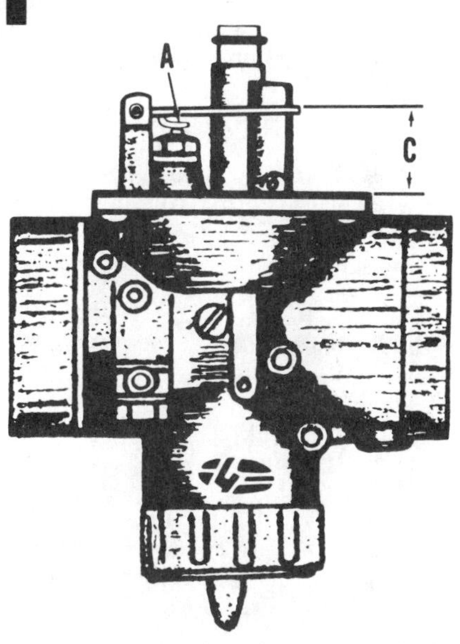

Fig. 1—Carburetor float level is correct when distance (C) from gasket surface of carburetor body to end of float arm measures 22-24 mm (0.85-0.95 inch). Adjust by bending tab (A) which contacts valve.

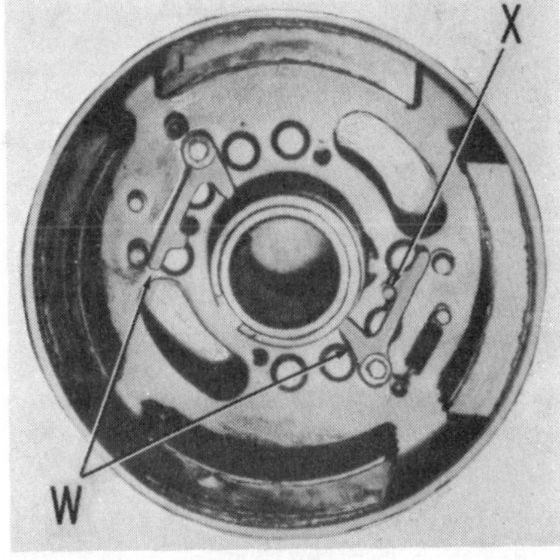

Fig. 2—On LC34, ignition cam advance weights (W) can be moved to advance position as shown by reaching through flywheel timing windows. Hold in advance position by threading bolt (X) into coolant pulley hole. Refer also to Fig. 3.

MAINTENANCE

SPARK PLUG. The recommended spark plug is NGK B8ES for all models. Recommended electrode gap is 0.018 inch (0.45 mm).

CARBURETOR. MIKUNI VM Type carburetors are used, with one carburetor individually connected to each intake elbow. It is of utmost importance that all carburetors on an engine be jetted and adjusted alike.

Float level should be maintained at 22-24 mm (0.85-0.95 inch) measured from end of float arm to gasket surface of carburetor body as shown at (C—Fig. 1). Adjust by bending the short valve contact lever (A). Standard main jet size is 220 for carburetors on LC34 and 340 for carburetors on LC44.

IGNITION AND TIMING. On the CD ignition systems of LC44, timing is fixed and not adjustable. On LC34, each set of points must be individually adjusted to open when piston is 3.5 mm (0.1365 inch) before top dead center with cam in ADVANCED position; or 0.6 mm (0.024 inch) BTDC with cam in retard position. Cam may be locked in advance position for static testing by reaching through flywheel window and pulling advance weight against stop (Fig. 2) and installing a bolt or pin into coolant pulley bolt hole as shown in Fig. 3. When new points are installed, widen point gap until timing advances to 3.8 mm (0.150 inch), to allow for cam block wear as points seat in. Red/white coil lead attaches to right (flywheel side) cylinder coil; white lead is for drive end (left) cylinder.

LUBRICATION. Engine is lubricated by oil mixed with the fuel. Use a good grade of Premium gasoline and an approved branded snowmobile oil mixed at a ratio of 20:1. Refer also to SCORPION Vehicle Section and to TWO CYCLE LUBRICATION in ENGINE FUNDAMENTALS Section of this manual.

COOLING SYSTEM. The cooling system reservoir should be filled to within 1½ inches (35 mm) of top with a 50/50 mixture of approved Ethylene Glycol (Permanent) Anti Freeze and water. More anti-freeze should be added if temperatures lower than -40 degrees are expected. Coolant pump belt should have approximately 10 mm (½-inch) deflection, measured midway between pulleys.

REPAIRS

TIGHTENING TORQUES. Recommended tightening torques are as follows:

	ft.-lbs.	kg-m
Crankcase (8 mm)	20	2.8
Crankcase (10 mm)	25	3.4
Cylinder base nuts	25	3.4
Cylinder head nuts	20	2.8
Flywheel nut	50	6.9
Manifold (Coolant)	15	2.1
Manifold (Exhaust)	20	2.8
Manifold (Intake)	20	2.8

Cylinder head stud nuts should be tightened in the sequence shown in Fig. 4, crankcase screw tightening sequence is shown in Fig. 5.

DISASSEMBLY AND REASSEMBLY. To remove the engine, first remove hood and main drive belt, then remove drive clutch as outlined in SCORPION Vehicle Section paragraphs. Disconnect tie rods from steering frog, then unbolt and move steering post out of the way. Separate carburetors from inlet elbows at rubber mounting clamps, disconnect fuel lines and move carburetors rearward. Disconnect electrical system wires. Disconnect coolant hoses from manifolds and plug the openings to prevent coolant loss. Unbolt front motor mounts from chassis and rear motor mounts from cylinder heads. If recoil starter is not to be disassembled, unbolt starter from engine. Lift engine from chassis and drain coolant through manifold hose openings.

Remove intake elbows and exhaust manifold. Disconnect coolant bypass hose and remove coolant manifolds. Remove water pump and front motor mounts. Remove cylinder heads and cylinders after first marking the parts so they can be reinstalled in the same relative position. Remove piston pin, piston and pin bearing; keeping the parts in their proper order for correct reinstallation.

Remove coolant pump drive pulley and flywheel (rotor) nut, then remove flywheel or rotor using a suitable puller. Unbolt and remove magneto or alternator/CD stator. Remove seal housing from both ends of crankcase. Remove crankcase screws and separate crankcase halves by holding bottom half and tapping top half with a plastic hammer.

When reassembling, make sure mating surfaces of crankcase halves are absolutely clean and free from nicks, burrs, old sealant or other defects which might interfere with an air-tight seal. Place the cleaned lower crankcase half right-side up on a clean work area; the cleaned upper crankcase half upside down. Lightly oil crankshaft main bearings and apply a light coat of non-fibrous grease to labyrinth seal area between center bearings. On LC44, install rotor key in shaft. On all models, position crankshaft on lower crankshaft half. Coat mating flange of lower crankcase half with a thin coat of a suitable sealant, then install upper crankshaft half. Install and tighten crankcase retaining screws using recommended torque and tightening sequence shown in Fig. 5.

With crankcase joined and using a suitable depth micrometer, measure the distance from drive end seal housing flange (F—Fig. 6) without the gasket, to nearest face of ball bearing outer race; then use this measurement to select required thickness of gasket (G). If measured distance was less than 0.080 inch (2.0 mm), use 0.020 inch (0.5 mm) gasket. If measured distance was 0.081-0.091 inch (2.05-2.3 mm), use 0.012 inch (0.3 mm) thick gasket. If measured distance was 0.091 inch (2.3 mm) or over, use 0.008 inch (0.2 mm) thick gasket.

Fig. 3—A suitable bolt (X) threaded into coolant pulley hole can be used to hold magneto cam in advanced position for engine timing. Refer also to Fig. 2.

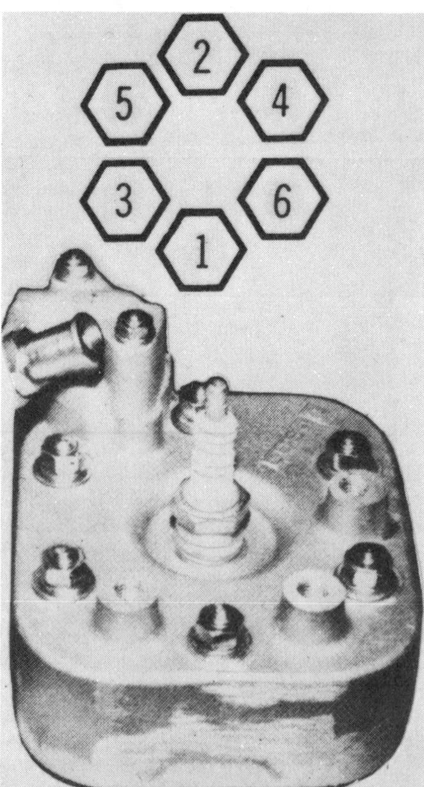

Fig. 4—Use the indicated sequence when tightening cylinder head stud nuts. Recommended tightening torque is 20 ft.-lbs. (2.8 kg-m).

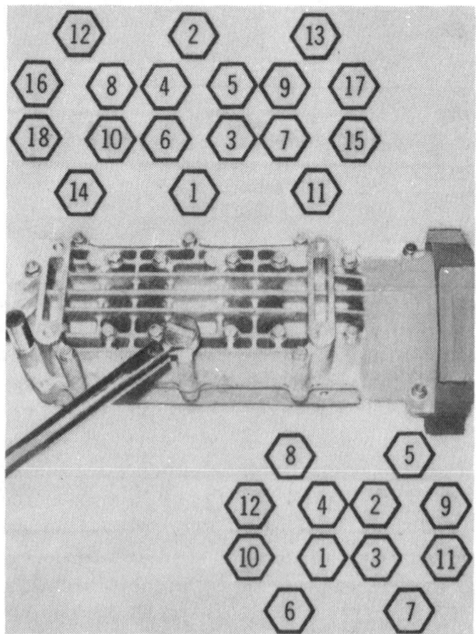

Fig. 5—Recommended tightening sequence for crankcase screws. LC44 is shown at top, LC34 below. Recommended tightening torque is 25 ft.-lbs. (3.4 kg-m) for the two 10 mm screws, 20 ft.-lbs. (2.8 kg-m) for remainder.

Install piston with top ring locator pin toward carburetor side of crankcase (side with impulse fittings), then install cylinders using a suitable piston support and ring compresser. Install and tighten coolant inlet manifold before tightening cylinder stud nuts. Complete the assembly by reversing disassembly procedure, using recommended tightening torques and cylinder head torqueing sequence shown in Fig. 4.

PISTONS, PINS, RINGS AND CYLINDERS. Use care when cleaning ring grooves. All carbon must be removed, but gouges or deep scratches on lands (especially at bottom) can result in pressure leakage. Oil based mineral solvents can assist in loosening some hard carbon, but dègreasing solvents can remove absorbed oil and harden the deposit.

Fig. 6—Drive end seal housing gasket (G) is available in selective thicknesses of 0.2, 0.3 and 0.5 mm (0.008, 0.012 and 0.020 inch) to establish correct crankshaft end play. Gasket thickness is determined by measuring distance from housing flange (F) to outer bearing race.

Pin should fit snugly in piston bore so that it drags when turned. If pin is loose, parts must be renewed. If pin has step-wear at center, renew pin and needle bearing.

CONNECTING RODS, CRANKSHAFT AND BEARINGS. Connecting rod big end bearing can be checked after removing cylinder and piston. Measure side shake of rod at piston pin end. If side shake exceeds 3.0 mm (1/8-inch) install a new or rebuilt crankshaft assembly.

Crankshaft, connecting rods and bearings are a built-up unit and should not be disassembled. Careless or rough handling of the assembly can cause misalignment which must be corrected before unit is reinstalled. Runout should not exceed 0.1 mm (0.004 inch).

SOLO

CONDENSED SERVICE DATA

ENGINE MODEL	206	209
Bore—(mm)	65	71
Inches	2.56	2.8
Stroke—(mm)	54	54
Inches	2.13	2.13
No. of Cylinders	1	1
Displacement—(cc)	180	220
Cubic Inches	10.9	13.4
Horsepower @ RPM	15.5@6500	16.5@6600
Cooling Type	Centrifugal Fan	
Carburetor Model	Tillotson HR	
Number Used	1	1
Ignition:		
Type	Bosch 12V/19 or 40W	
Point Gap—(mm)	0.3-0.4	0.3-0.4
Inch	0.015-0.018	0.014-0.018
Edge Gap—(mm)	7-10	7-10
Inch	0.3-0.4	0.3-0.4
Timing Advance?	No	No
Timing BTDC—(mm)	....	....
Inch	0.118	0.118
Spark Plug:		
Bosch	W175T1	W175T1
Electrode Gap—(mm)	0.45-0.5	0.45-0.5
Inch	0.018-0.020	0.018-0.020
Fuel/Oil Ratio	25:1	25:1

MAINTENANCE

CARBURETOR. A Tillotson HR 19A carburetor is normally used; however, some motors may be equipped with Tillotson HL278A carburetor. Initial setting is one turn open for the idle mixture needle; 1¼ turns open for the main (high speed) mixture needle. Refer to Tillotson Carburetor Section for operation and overhaul information. An external impulse line is used to operate fuel pump. Be sure that all passages are open and that vacuum and pressure leaks are eliminated.

IGNITION SYSTEM. A Bosch, flywheel type magneto is used on all models. The auxiliary lighting coil used on some models is 19 watt while others are equipped with 40 watt lighting coil. Refer to the CONDENSED SERVICE DATA table for timing and adjustment specifications. Refer to MAGNETO SERVICE FUNDAMENTALS for overhaul data. Breaker point gap can be checked or adjusted after removing the recoil starter (fan cover), cooling fan and felt ring. Cooling fan should be installed with arrow (A—Fig. 1) toward top of cylinder when piston is at TDC.

On some models, the ignition (stop) switch grounds the ignition through the lights to stop engine. The engine will not stop if lights are burned out, removed etc.

LUBRICATION. The engine is lubricated by mixing oil with the fuel. A suitable two-cycle, SAE 30, air cooled engine oil is recommended. Fuel and oil should be mixed in ratio of 25:1. Mix fuel and oil thoroughly in separate container before pouring mixture into fuel tank. For cold weather blending, pre-mix the oil with a small amount of gasoline and shake thoroughly until mixture is liquid, then blend with remainder of fuel. Do not use kerosene or fuel oil for pre-mixing.

REPAIRS

DISASSEMBLY AND REASSEMBLY. Refer to Fig. 3 for typical exploded view. Cylinder head, cylinder, piston and rings can be removed without removal of flywheel or disassembly of crankcase. A drop of sealer should be applied to crankcase joints before installing gasket (27G) and cylinder.

To remove the crankshaft and main bearings, it is necessary to separate the crankcase halves. After removing the cylinder, piston and magneto assembly, remove screws attaching halves together, heat side of crankcase around bearing area to approximately 350-400° F. and carefully remove the crank-

Fig. 1–Arrow (A) on fan should point toward top of cylinder when piston is at Top Dead Center.

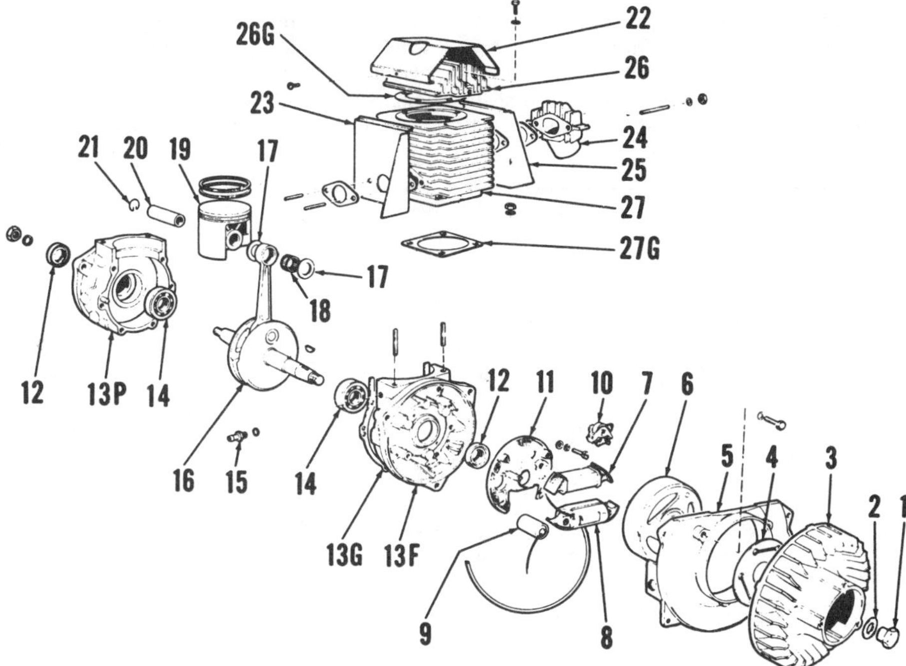

Fig. 3–Exploded view typical of 206 and 209 engines. Seals (12) and main bearings (14) are identical at both ends of crankshaft.

1. Flywheel nut
2. Washer
3. Cooling fan
4. Felt ring
5. Fan cover
6. Flywheel
7. Lighting coil
8. Ignition coil
9. Condenser
10. Breaker points
11. Stator plate
12. Crankcase seals
13F. Crankcase half (flywheel side)
13G. Gasket
13P. Crankcase half (output side)
14. Main bearing
15. Crankcase pulse fitting
16. Crankshaft assembly
17. Side washers
18. Piston pin bearing
19. Piston
20. Piston pin
21. Retaining ring (2 used)
22. Top air shroud
23. Air shroud (inlet side)
24. Exhaust manifold
25. Air shroud (exhaust side)
26. Cylinder head
26G. Gasket
27. Cylinder
27G. Gasket

case half. The crankshaft and connecting rod are available only as an assembled unit and disassembly is not recommended. Use a suitable puller to remove main bearing (14) from crankshaft using extreme care not to distort the crankshaft. Main bearings should be a tight fit on crankshaft journals. Bearings should be heated to approximately 300° F. before installing. Allow bearings to cool completely before assembling into heated crankcase halves. Always renew gaskets and seals. Lips of seals (12) should be toward inside and outside edge of seal should be flush with crankcase flange.

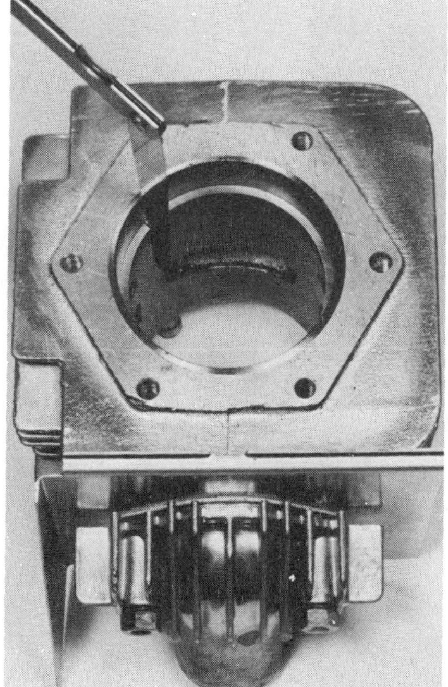

Fig. 4–Piston ring end gap should be within specified limits. Refer to text.

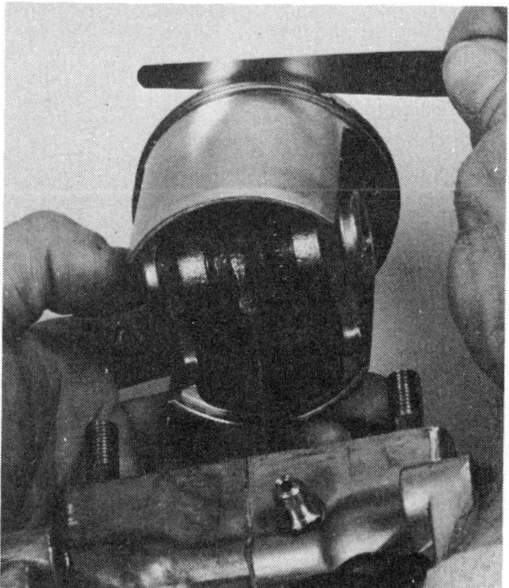

Fig. 5–Refer to text for recommended ring side clearance in groove.

PISTON, PIN, RINGS & CYLINDER. The piston and rings are available in standard size only. Arrow on top of piston must point toward exhaust side of cylinder. Ring end gap (Fig. 4) should be 0.012-0.015 inch. Ring side clearance in groove (Fig. 5) should be 0.002-0.003 inch. Piston skirt to cylinder minimum clearance should be 0.006 inch. Grooves in piston are equipped with pins and rings must be correctly installed to engage the pins.

CRANKCASE AND CRANKSHAFT. The crankcase should be heated before removing (or installing) main bearing from crankcase bores. The main bearings should be heated to approximately 300° F. before installing on crankshaft journals. Refer to DISASSEMBLY and REASSEMBLY paragraphs.

Seals (12—Fig. 3) may be removed and renewed without separating crankcase halves. Lips of seals should be toward inside of crankcase and seals should be installed flush with crankcase flange.

The crankshaft is a built-up unit and should be carefully handled to prevent distortion. Crankshaft alignment can be checked using "V" blocks at main bearing journals and dial indicator at both ends of crankshaft and both crankshaft webs (counter weights). Any crankshaft distortion may cause main bearings to be damaged.

RECOIL STARTER. Refer to Fig. 7. Remove pin (1), spring washer (2) and thrust washer (3). Remove snap rings (4) and lift pawls (5) off. Remove thrust washer (6), then remove anchor (9) and handle (10). Allow rope (11) to rewind into housing, remove snap ring (7) and washer (8); then, lift pulley (12) out.

When assembling, install washer

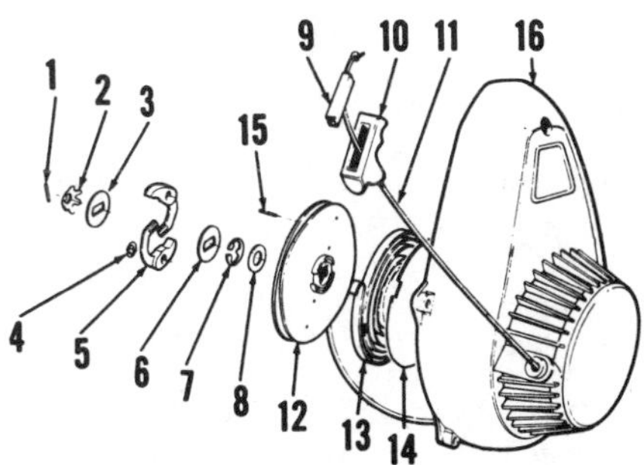

Fig. 7–Exploded view of the recoil starter assembly. Washers (3 & 6) are identical.

1. Pin
2. Spring washer
3. Thrust washer
4. Snap rings (2 used)
5. Pawls
6. Thrust washer
7. Snap ring
8. Washer
9. Anchor
10. Handle
11. Rope
12. Pulley
13. Recoil spring
14. Washer
15. Pin
16. Housing

(14), spring (13) and pulley (12) in housing (16). Turn pulley counter-clockwise (as viewed from engine side) approximately 5 turns and insert rope through pulley and exit hole in housing. Rope (11) should be approximately 43-inches long. Press knot (at pulley end of rope) into recess in pulley until knot is flush with face of pulley. Install handle (10), anchor (9), washer (8) and snap ring (7). Assemble thrust washer (6), pawls (5) and snap rings (4). Install thrust washer (3), spring washer (2) and pin (1). Check operation before installing starter on engine.

SPIRIT

(Prior to 1985)

CONDENSED SERVICE DATA

ENGINE MODEL	AB25F1	AA28F	AA34F	AF34A	AC44A
Bore–mm	70	54	60	60	65
Inch	2.756	2.126	2.362	2.362	2.559
Stroke–mm	65	60	60	60	65
Inches	2.559	2.362	2.362	2.362	2.559
No. of Cylinders	1	2	2	2	2
Displacement–cc	250	274.8	339.3	339.3	431.4
Cubic Inches	15.25	16.76	20.70	20.70	26.31
Cooling Type	F/A	F/A	F/A	Fan	Fan
Carburetor Model	VM-30*	VM-30*	VM-30*	B-34	VM-34
Number Used	1	1	1	1	1
Ignition Type	Mag	CDI	CDI	CDI	CDI
Point Gap–mm	0.3-0.4	.....	.....	.....	.....
Inch	0.012-0.016	.....	.....	.....	.....
Timing BTDC–mm	3	1.86	1.44	1.86	2.02
Inch	0.118	0.073	0.056	0.073	0.080
Degrees	22	18	16	18	18
Spark Plug:					
NGK	BR9ES	BR8ES	BR8ES	BR8ES	BR8ES
Gap–mm	0.5	0.5	0.5	0.5	0.5
Inch	0.020	0.020	0.020	0.020	0.020
Fuel:Oil Ratio–					
W/Spirit Oil	50:1	50:1	50:1	Oil Injection	50:1
Other Oil	20:1	20:1	20:1	.....	20:1

*Some models are equipped with a Mikuni B-34 carburetor.

ENGINE MODEL	AF44LI	AG44A	AD50F	AE50A	AH50L	AL50A
Bore–mm	68	65	70	70	70	70
Inch	2.677	2.559	2.756	2.756	2.756	2.756
Stroke–mm	60	65	65	65	65	65
Inches	2.362	2.559	2.559	2.559	2.559	2.559
No. of Cylinders	2	2	2	2	2	2
Displacement–cc	435.8	431.4	500.3	500.3	500.3	500.3
Cubic Inches	26.58	26.31	30.52	30.52	30.52	30.52
Cooling Type	Liquid	Fan	F/A	F/C	Liquid	Liquid
Carburetor Model	VM-34	VM34*	VM-32	VM-34	VM-38	VM-34*
Number Used	2	1	2	1	2	2
Ignition Type	CDI	CDI	CDI	CDI	CDI	CDI
Point Gap–mm	.....	.....	.....	.....	.....	.....
Inch	.....	.....	.....	.....	.....	.....
Timing BTDC–mm	3	2.02	2.02	2.49	3.85	2.02
Inch	0.118	0.080	0.080	0.098	0.151	0.080
Degrees	22	18	18	20	25	18
Spark Plug:						
NGK	BR9ES	BR9ES	BR9ES	BR9ES	BR10EV	BR9ES
Gap–mm	0.5	0.5*	0.5	0.5	0.5	0.5
Inch	0.020	0.020*	0.020	0.020	0.020	0.020
Fuel:Oil Ratio–						
W/Spirit Oil	20:1	Oil Injection	50:1	50:1	Oil Injection	Oil Injection
Other Oil	20:1	.....	20:1	20:1	.....	.....

*Some models are equipped with a Mikuni B-40 carburetor.

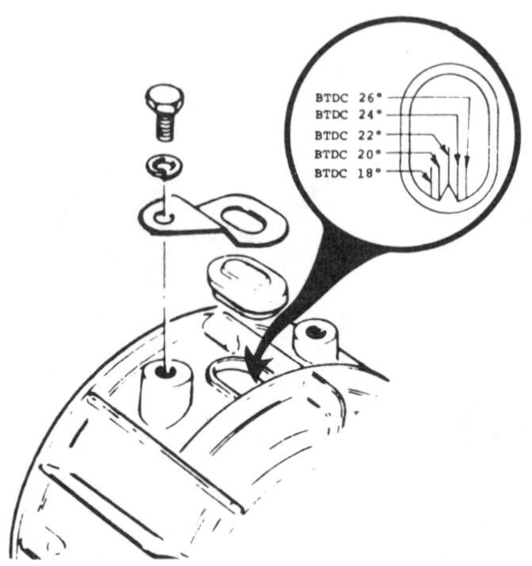

Fig. 1 — View of magneto case on single cylinder engine showing timing marks aligned.

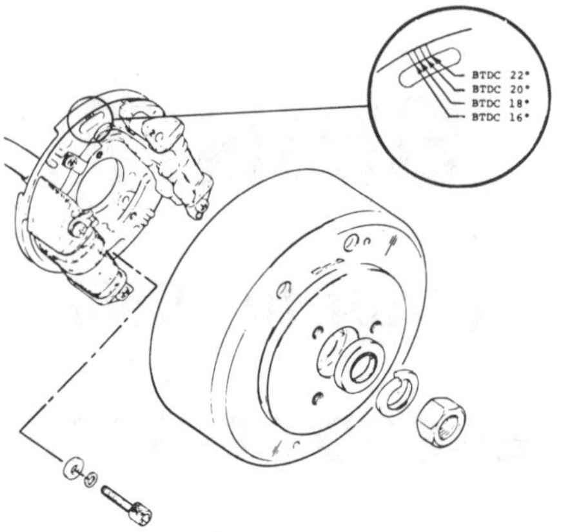

Fig. 3 — View of stator timing marks on most twin cylinder models. Refer to text for timing procedure.

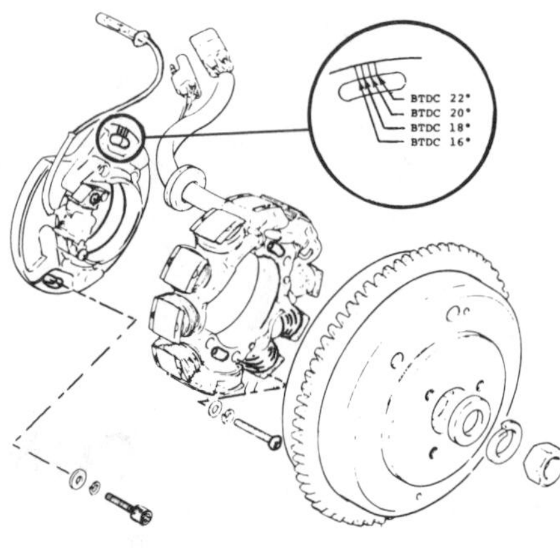

Fig. 4 — View of ignition stator timing marks on twin cylinder models with 150W lighting system. Flywheel and lighting stator will need to be removed to check or adjust stator timing.

MAINTENANCE

SPARK PLUG. The recommended NGK spark plug for normal service is listed in CONDENSED SERVICE DATA tables. Spark plugs should be tightened to 18-20 ft.-lbs. (24.4-27.1 N·m).

CARBURETOR. All models use a Mikuni Model VM carburetor with a separate impulse type fuel pump located in engine compartment.

Normal initial setting of the pilot air screw from a lightly seated position is 3/4 to 1½ turns on 1981 and earlier models and 1¼ to 1¾ turns on 1984 and later models. Refer to MIKUNI service section in CARBURETOR SERVICE FUNDAMENTALS section for complete procedure on carburetor fine tuning and carburetor overhaul.

IGNITION SYSTEM. An energy transfer magneto ignition system with breaker points is used on the single cylinder AB25F1 engine. All other models use a Nippon Denso or Kokusan breakerless capacitor discharge ignition system. The ignition manufacturer may be identified by examining the CD unit mounted on top of the magneto case on free air and liquid cooled models or rear side of fan housing on fan cooled models.

Fig. 2 — To check the timing on twin cylinder models, install a temporary timing pointer as shown in inset and check at high idle (6000 rpm) using a timing light. Timing pointer must be as close to drive pulley rim as possible without touching. Refer to text for procedure.

Breaker Point Ignition. On single cylinder AB25F1 engine, breaker point gap should be 0.012-0.016 inch (0.3-0.4 mm) and timing should be 22° BTDC. Timing can be checked by removing the timing cap on top side of magneto case and viewing the scribed timing marks on magneto rotor (flywheel) as shown in Fig. 1. The long single mark indicates TDC position when aligned with timing pointer, and correct (22° BTDC) timing mark is the center mark of the group of five, counterclockwise from the single TDC mark. Timing is correct when points open at the moment indicated (22° BTDC). Point opening can be best determined using a buzzer equipped ignition tester, a change in sound indicating the moment the points break. Flywheel must be removed to renew breaker points or adjust timing by moving breaker plate.

Breakerless Ignition. On twin cylinder models a CDI Tester and Trigger Pulse Simulator (such as the Model IL, available from Electro-Specialties, Inc., 11225 W. Bluebound Road, Wauwatosa, WI 53225) is recommended for complete system testing. If suitable testing equipment is not available, parts may be removed and taken to a tester equipped shop for component testing, or trial and error parts replacement process must be followed. Timing seldom changes on a CDI system unless parts loosen. The only practical way to check the timing on a Spirit CD system is with a timing light at 6000 engine rpm.

On early models, affix a short piece of malleable wire to cylinder block base as shown in Inset, Fig. 2. Use a flexible, heat-proof adhesive such as RTV silicone seal to hold the wire. Bend free end of wire as close as possible to outer rim of drive sheave inner half as shown, making sure clearance exists at all speeds. Remove number 2 (pto end) spark plug, install a dial indicator and note correct BTDC timing position as listed in CONDENSED SERVICE DATA tables. With crankshaft positioned, mark the pulley half in direct line with timing pointer as shown. Reinstall spark plug and attach timing light, then check timing at 6000 rpm using the temporary timing pointer and mark.

On later models, a timing pointer is affixed to the magneto case and timing marks are present on the flywheel. Timing marks on fan cooled models are visible after removing the fan cover or fan belt cover. Timing marks on liquid-cooled models are visible after removing the cover plate adjacent to the CDI module. A typical set of timing marks is shown in Fig. 1. Each mark indicates an increment of 2°. The center mark indicates 22° BTDC on Models AA28F, AB25F and AD50F, 27° BTDC on Model AH50L and 18° BTDC on all other models. If accuracy of timing marks is doubted, verify timing marks using static timing procedure. Refer to CONDENSED SERVICE DATA for ignition timing specifications. Dynamic timing is performed with engine running at 6000 rpm.

On all models, adjust ignition timing by rotating the stator plate. The stator plate is accessible after removing manual starter and flywheel. On models equipped with 150 watt alternator, remove alternator stator. The stator plate on most models has timing marks located as shown in Figs. 3 and 4 to

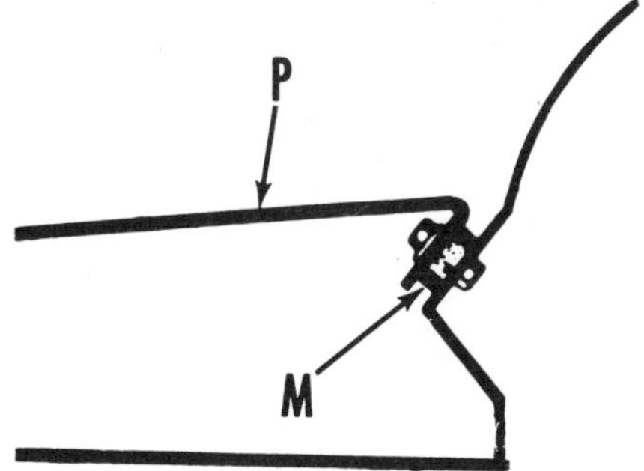

Fig. 5—On some models, rear engine mounts (M) are only accessible from below. Mounting plate (P) must be removed with the engine.

serve as a reference when assembling engine. The stator plate should be marked before disassembly so original timing can be obtained when engine is reassembled.

LUBRICATION. Arctic Cat snowmobile engines are lubricated by either an oil injection pump or a fuel mixture of oil and gasoline. Recommended oils are Arctco Injection Oil on oil injected models and Spirit Synthetic Oil on fuel:oil mix models. Recommended fuel grade is regular leaded with a minimum octane rating of 88.

Most new or overhauled engines require additional lubrication during break-in. On oil injected models, the first tank of fuel must contain a 50:1 fuel:oil mixture in conjunction with oil injection to ensure adequate lubrication. On fuel:oil mix models having a 50:1 fuel:oil ratio for normal operation, increase fuel:oil ratio to 25:1 for the first tank of fuel. On models having a 20:1 fuel:oil ratio for normal operation, additional lubrication during break-in is not required. A ratio of 20:1 should be used for all fuel:oil mix models if other two-stroke oil is substituted for Spirit Synthetic Oil.

Mix fuel and oil thoroughly in a separate container before pouring mixture into fuel tank. For cold weather blending, premix the oil with a small amount of gasoline and shake thoroughly until mixture is liquid, then blend with remainder of fuel. Do not use kerosene or fuel oil for premixing.

On models equipped with oil injection system, a separate oil tank and metering system is used. The system delivers varying amounts of oil depending upon engine rpm and throttle setting (load).

Oil delivery is controlled by a cable attached to pump control lever at one end and throttle control lever at other end. Oil injection pump should be adjusted after all carburetor adjustments are completed. With the throttle lever held in wide open position, mark on oil pump control lever should align with stationary mark on pump housing. To adjust oil pump, loosen cable adjuster locknut at the oil pump and reposition the adjuster as required.

Any operation that required draining or repair of oil injection components will make it necessary to fill and bleed system. During bleeding procedure, the fuel tank must contain a 50:1 fuel:oil mixture to prevent severe engine damage due to loss of engine lubrication. Check oil reservoir fluid level and fill with Arctco Injection Oil or a manufacturer approved equivalent. Bleed air from injection pump before running engine. To bleed injection pump, remove bleeder screw on pump until air-free oil flows from screw opening then reinstall screw. Start engine and run at idle speed only. Rotate oil pump control lever to maximum output position until air-free oil is observed passing through the clear oil delivery hoses to engine. If an oil injection malfunction occurs, carefully inspect check valves in banjo fittings, hoses and oil tank filter and oil tank filter and renew defective or questionable components. Renew the complete oil injection pump assembly if required.

REPAIRS

TIGHTENING TORQUES. Recommended tightening torques are as follows:

Cylinder head nuts:
- Six-stud heads* . . . . 14-18 ft.-lbs. (19.0-24.4 N·m)
- Four-stud heads . . . . 13-16 ft.-lbs. (17.6-21.7 N·m)

Cylinder base nuts:
- 8 mm . . . . 13-16 ft.-lbs. (17.6-21.7 N·m)
- 10 mm . . . . 22-29 ft.-lbs. (29.8-39.3 N·m)

Crankcase bolts:
- 6 mm . . . . 6-7 ft.-lbs. (8.1-9.5 N·m)
- 8 mm . . . . 13-16 ft.-lbs. (17.6-21.7 N·m)
- 10 mm . . . . 15-22 ft.-lbs. (20.3-29.8 N·m)

Flywheel nut . . . . 49-63 ft.-lbs. (66.4-85.4 N·m)

Manifolds . . . . 11-14 ft.-lbs. (15-19 N·m)

Engine mounting bolts . . . . 50-55 ft.-lbs. (67.8-74.5 N·m)

Spark plugs . . . . 18-22 ft.-lbs. (24.4-29.8 N·m)

*Six-stud head on liquid-cooled engine should be tightened to 22-29 ft.-lbs. (29.8-39.3 N·m) torque.

ENGINE REMOVAL. On all models open or remove hood then remove drive belt shield, drive belt and muffler. Unbolt recoil starter and lay it out of the way. Remove air intake silencers, loosen spigot clamps and slide carburetor(s) out of mounting flange without disconnecting fuel lines or linkage.

On oil injection engines, detach oil pump control cable and oil supply hose at injection pump. Plug openings in hose and pump to prevent oil loss and the entrance of dirt.

On liquid-cooled engines, disconnect the hose from water manifold and use a suitable container to catch the coolant. Disconnect coolant hose from thermostat housing and heat exchanger end cap. Carefully remove temperature gage sending unit from thermostat housing. Make certain sending unit does not rotate with retaining nut during removal as permanent damage to temperature gage will result.

On all models, disconnect wiring and fuel pump impulse hose. Engine is removed along with mounting plate. On some units rear mounts are only accessible from below as shown in Fig. 5. On these units tip snowmobile on right side and remove rear nuts, then tip machine upright and remove engine and mounting plate. On other models all mounting nuts are accessible from above and engine and plate assembly can be lifted off after nuts are removed. Check for and save any shims used on left rear engine mount. These shims help align drive sheaves and may be needed when engine is reinstalled.

Install engine by reversing removal procedure. Refer to vehicle section for pulley alignment procedure. Tighten engine mounts to a torque of 23 ft.-lbs. (31.3 N·m). When reinstalling starter, install mounting cap screws loosely and pull starter rope until pawls engage to properly align the units, then tighten screws to 7 ft.-lbs. (9.5 N·m).

DISASSEMBLY AND REASSEMBLY. On all models, remove engine

Fig. 6—Method of constructing a manual pressure tester for checking crankshaft seals. Never exceed 15 psi when checking the seals.

Fig. 7—Lifting off the cylinder block on single cylinder engine.

mounting plate and torque converter drive. Suggested procedures include pressure testing crankcase for leaks which requires removal of flywheel (plus magneto if engine is to be submerged) for observation of magneto end seal.

Construct a manual pressure tester consisting of a hand pump, piping, a shut-off valve, pressure gage and connections as shown in Fig. 6. Also prepare suitable sealing plates and gaskets for intake and exhaust port flanges in cylinders. Pressurize the crankcase to 12 psi (NEVER EXCEED 15 psi or seals may be damaged). Close shut-off valve and record pressure drop which should not exceed 1 pound per minute, or 2 pounds for a two cylinder engine. If pressure drop exceeds the accepted rate, check for leaks with soapy water and a brush. Engine may be submerged if preferred, but all electrical components must be stripped off before submersion.

Fig. 8—Use a rubber band as shown to protect engine parts from damage when cylinder and piston are off. Refer to text.

Fig. 9—An impact screwdriver is required to loosen or tighten magneto housing screws.

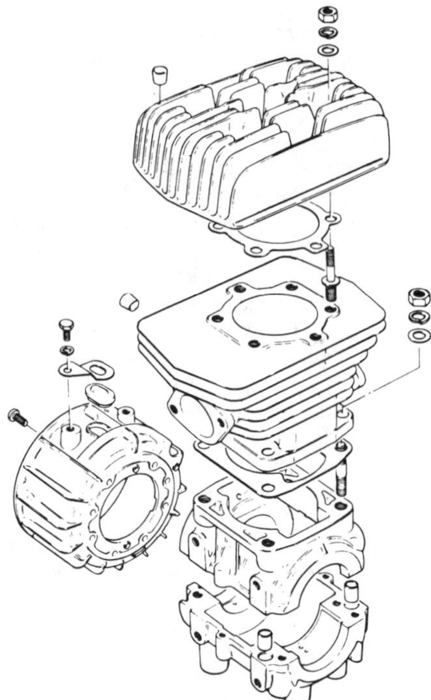

Fig. 10—Exploded view of housing components and associated parts used in single cylinder engine.

Disassembly sequence for the different engine types is outlined in the appropriate following paragraphs.

SINGLE CYLINDER ENGINE. With engine removed as previously outlined, remove cylinder head nuts, cylinder head and gasket. Unbolt and remove cylinder by lifting it straight up, catching piston as cylinder is lifted off. Remove piston pin retainers and push out the pin using a suitable removing tool. Use a rubber band to center rod as shown in Fig. 8, thus avoiding damage to parts if crankshaft should be accidentally turned.

Remove flywheel using a suitable puller if not previously removed. DO NOT hammer on end of crankshaft in an effort to loosen flywheel. Scribe mark on magneto baseplate to aid in reassembly, remove the two retaining screws and lay baseplate aside as shown in Fig. 9. Do not attempt to remove at this time. Use an impact driver to loosen magneto case retainng cap screws as shown, and lift off case and magneto baseplate as an assembly. Use a soft mallet to loosen magneto case if it sticks.

Remove the eight cap screws securing crankcase halves and separate the halves by tapping sides with a soft mallet. Do not use a pry in separating crankcase. Lift out crankshaft assembly and slide off end seals.

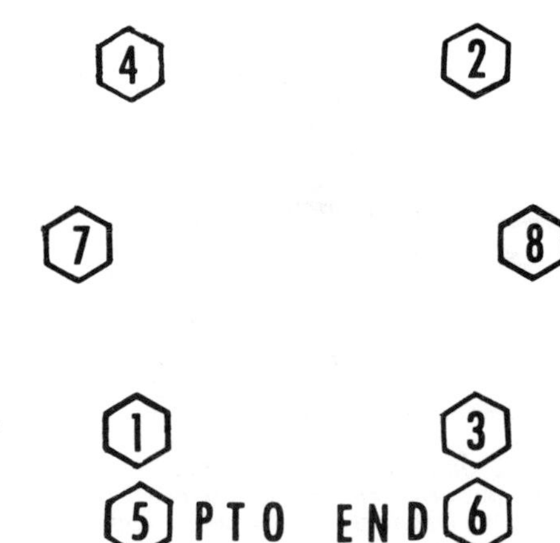

Fig. 11—Tighten crankcase retaining cap screws in the sequence shown. Refer to text for tightening torques of the various sized screws.

Refer to the appropriate service sections which follow to service engine components.

Assemble by reversing the disassembly procedure. Apply a liberal amount of grease between double lips of crankshaft seals and slip on shaft with spring side of seal toward bearing. Also make sure alignment hole in outer race of each crankshaft bearing fits over dowel in bearing bore.

Apply a thin coat of sealer such as RTV silicone seal to cleaned mating surfaces of each crankcase half and install top half. Install the various sized crankcase cap screws finger tight. Make sure correct size and length is installed in each hole, that heads seat and that crankcase parting line closes along its entire length; then tighten cap screws in small increments using the sequence shown in Fig. 12. Tightening torques are as follows:

Screws	Ft.-Lbs.	N·m
6mm	6-7	8.2-9.5
8 mm	13-16	17.7-21.7
10 mm	15-22	20.4-29.9

Fig. 12—Use a block of wood or plastic to support piston while installing cylinder assembly.

Fig. 13—Installing the cylinder using an approved ring compressor.

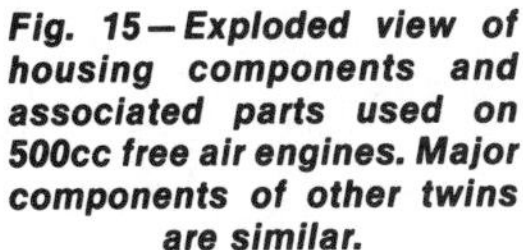

Fig. 15—Exploded view of housing components and associated parts used on 500cc free air engines. Major components of other twins are similar.

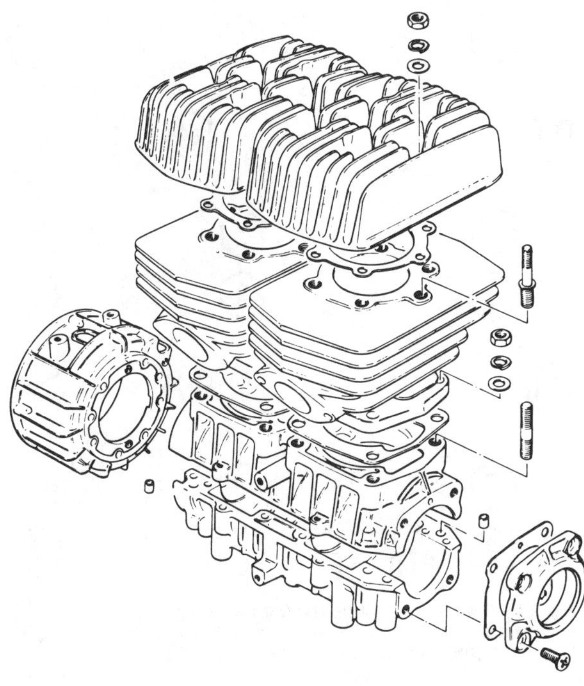

Install piston with arrow on piston crown pointing toward exhaust side of engine, insert piston pin and secure with retaining rings, making sure rings fully seat in their grooves. Coat cylinder base gasket on both sides with a light coating of RTV silicone sealer and install the gasket. Insert a small piece of wood underneath piston skirt as shown in Fig. 12, then using a ring compressor as shown in Fig. 13, slide cylinder down over piston making sure inlet port flange is on same side as pulse passage fitting. Tighten cylinder base nuts to 22-29 ft.-lbs. (30-39 N·m) using a crisscross pattern.

Install cylinder head gasket and cylinder head, tightening stud nuts to 13-16 ft.-lbs. (17.7-21.7 N·m) using a crisscross pattern, then pressure test crankcase for air leaks as previously outlined.

Install magneto case to crankcase using Loctite on attaching screws and installing with an impact driver. Align scribe marks and reinstall magneto base plate, install flywheel and tighten retaining nut to 50-63 ft.-lbs. (66.4-85.4 N·m).

FREE AIR TWIN ENGINES. With engine removed as previously outlined, remove cylinder heat nuts, cylinder heads and gaskets. Identify pistons and cylinders for reassembly. Remove exhaust manifold and if so equipped, the intake manifold. Unbolt and remove cylinders by lifting them straight up, holding pistons as cylinders are removed, to prevent damage. Remove piston pin retainers and push out the pins using a suitable removing tool. Use rubber bands to center rods and prevent damage if crankshaft is accidentally turned. (Fig. 8).

Fig. 14—Some twin cylinder models have a seal retainer on pto end of housing as shown.

Remove flywheel using a suitable screw type puller if not previously removed. Scribe a mark on magneto baseplate so it can be reinstalled in the same position. Remove the two retaining screws and lay baseplate aside. Use an impact driver to loosen magneto case retaining screws. Loosen magneto case if necessary, using a soft mallet, and lift off the case and magneto baseplate as an assembly.

Some models have a seal retainer on pto end of crankcase as shown in Fig. 14. Use an impact driver to loosen the screws, then unbolt and remove the plate. On all models remove the cap screws securing the crankcase halves and separate the crankcase by tapping sides with a soft mallet. Do not pry when separating the crankcase. Check dowels in bearing bores and "C" ring in center bearing bore of lower crankcase half when crankshaft is lifted out, to prevent loss. Refer to the appropriate following service sections to service engine components.

Assemble by reversing the disassembly procedure. Apply a liberal amount of grease between double lips of crankshaft seals and slip on shaft with spring side of seal toward bearing. Also make sure alignment holes of bearing races fit on dowels in bearing bores and that alignment "C" ring in center bore is properly positioned.

Apply a thin coat of RTV silicone seal to cleaned mating surfaces of each crankcase half, then lay a piece of #50 cotton thread just to the inside of bolt holes on lower crankcase half as shown at T–Fig. 16. Carefully insert rods up through cylinder mounting holes and install crankcase top half. Tip crankcase on its side and install the various sized crankcase cap screws finger tight. Make sure correct size and length is installed in each hole, that heads seat and that crankcase parting line closes along its entire length; then tighten cap screws in small increments using the sequence

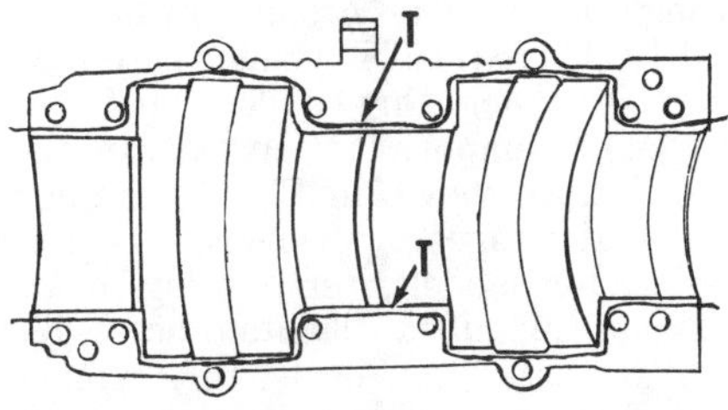

Fig. 16—After applying sealant to crankcase lower half, lay a cotton thread at inside of bolt holes as shown at (T).

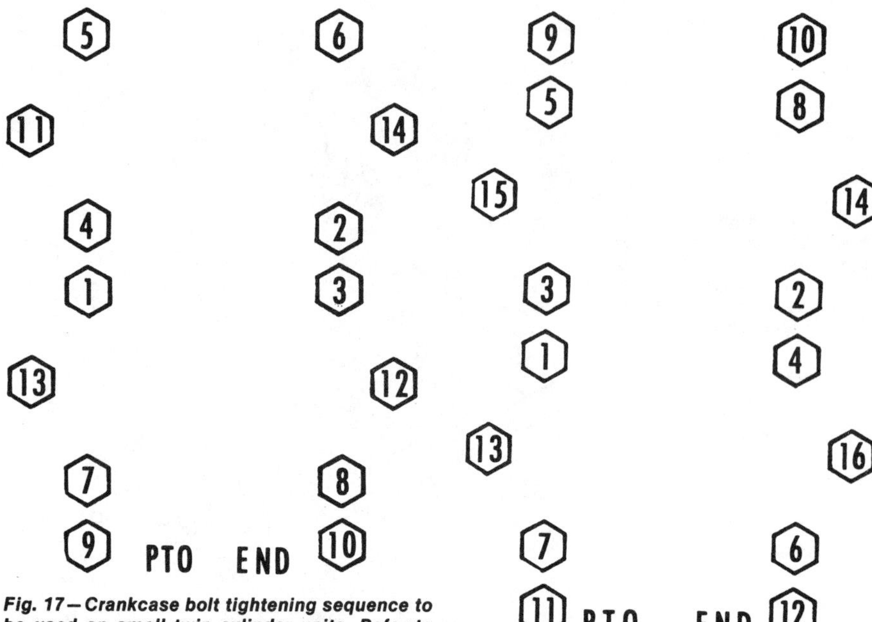

Fig. 17—Crankcase bolt tightening sequence to be used on small twin cylinder units. Refer to text for tightening torques of the various bolt sizes.

Fig. 18—Crankcase bolt tightening sequence for big twin cylinder motors except 1984-1985 Panther and 1985-1986 Jag models. Refer to text for tightening torques.

shown in Fig. 17 or Fig. 18. Tightening torques are as follows:

Screws	Ft.-Lbs.	N·m
6 mm	6-7	8.2-9.5
8 mm	13-16	17.7-21.7
10 mm	15-22	20.4-29.9

On models so equipped, install crankshaft seal end plate (Fig. 14). Use RTV silicone seal on gasket surface, Loctite on screw threads and tighten screws using an impact driver.

Thoroughly lubricate crankshaft and rod bearings then install pistons with arrow on piston crowns pointing toward exhaust side of engine. Insert piston pins and secure with retaining rings, making sure rings fully seat in their grooves. Coat cylinder base gaskets on both sides with a light coating of RTV sealer and install gaskets. Insert a small piece of wood underneath skirt of piston (Fig. 12) then using a ring compressor, slide cylinder down over piston making sure inlet port flange of cylinder is on same side as pulse passage fitting in crankcase. Install the other cylinder using the same procedure. Install but DO NOT TIGHTEN cylinder base nuts at this time. On single carburetor models, temporarily install intake manifold as shown in Fig. 19 to align manifold flanges of cylinders. On dual carburetor models, temporarily install exhaust manifold. Tighten accessible cylinder base nuts firmly, then remove installed manifold and tighten all cylinder base nuts to 22-29 ft.-lbs. (30-39 N·m) using a crisscross pattern.

Coat both sides of cylinder head gaskets with RTV sealer and install cylinder heads, noting that heads reverse for opposite cylinders as shown in Fig. 20. Tighten nuts on four-stud cylinder heads to a torque of 22-29 ft.-lbs. (30-39 N·m) and nuts on six-stud heads to 13-16 ft.-lbs. (17.7-21.7 N·m). Use a crisscross tightening pattern. With crankcase and cylinders assembled, pressure test for air leaks as previously outlined.

Install magneto case on crankcase using Loctite on attaching screws and installing with an impact driver. Align scribe marks and reinstall magneto base plate. Install flywheel and tighten retaining nut to 50-63 ft.-lbs. (66.4-85.4 N·m).

FAN COOLED TWINS. With engine removed as previously outlined, remove the three cap screws and lockwashers securing the starter pulley then remove starter pulley and fan drive pulley. Unbolt and remove upper cowling, exhaust gaskets, front cowling, intake manifold and rear cowling. Unbolt and remove fan housing as an assembly.

Remove flywheel using a suitable puller. It may be necessary to reinstall starter/fan pulley in order to use the flywheel holding tool. Unbolt and lay aside the alternator stator without withdrawing wiring from housing. Scribe reassembly lines on ignition stator and magneto case or note and record positioning of timing marks. Unbolt ignition

Fig. 19—Install intake or exhaust manifold to align cylinders before tightening cylinder mounting stud nuts.

stator and move it aside, then remove screws securing magneto case to crankcase using an impact driver. Loosen magneto case if necessary using a soft mallet, then lift off case and stators as an assembly.

Unbolt and remove cylinder heads noting that long, stand-off nuts go on outer studs at magneto and pto end. Identify pistons and cylinders for proper reassembly, then unbolt and remove cylinders by lifting them straight up, holding pistons to prevent damage. Remove piston pin retainers and push out the pins using a suitable removing tool. Use rubber bands to center rods and prevent damage if crankshaft is accidentally turned.

Some models have a seal retainer on pto end of crankcase as shown in Fig. 14. Use an impact driver to loosen the screws, then unbolt and remove the plate. On all models, remove the cap screws securing the crankcase halves and separate the crankcase by tapping sides with a soft mallet. Do not pry when separating the crankcase. Check dowels in bearing bores and "C" ring in center bearing bore of lower crankcase half when crankshaft is lifted out. Refer to the appropriate service sections which follow, to service engine components.

Assemble by reversing the disassembly procedure. Apply a liberal amount of grease between double lips of crankcase seals and slip on shaft with spring side of

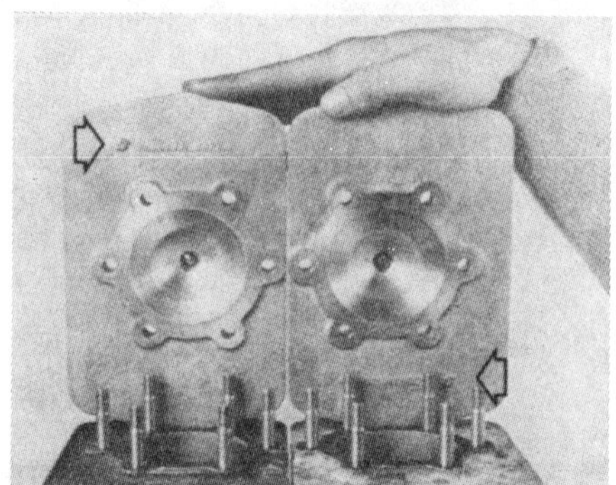

Fig. 20—Cylinder heads are identical but reversed on twin cylinder free engines.

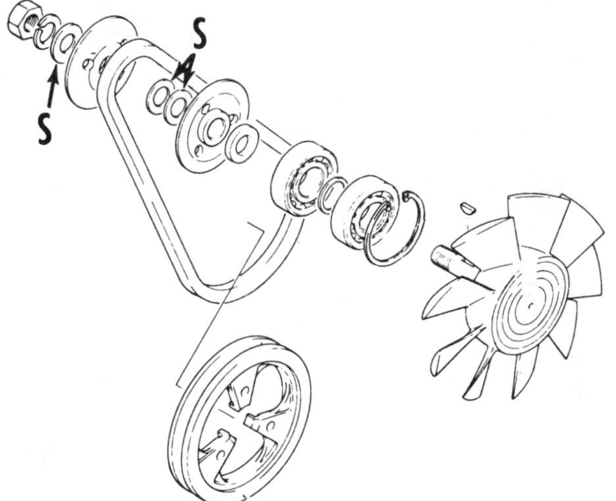

Fig. 21—Cooling fan drive belt is adjusted by moving shims (S) on fanshaft sheave. Refer to text for details.

seal toward bearing. Also make sure alignment holes of bearing races fit on dowels in bearing bores and that alignment "C" ring in center bore is properly positioned.

Apply a thin coat of RTV sealer to cleaned mating surfaces of each crankcase half, then lay a pice of #50 cotton thread just to the inside of bolt holes on lower crankcase half as shown at T–Fig. 16. Carefully insert rods through cylinder mounting holes and install crankcase top half. Tip crankcase on its side and install the various sized crankcase cap screws finger tight. Make sure correct size is installed in each hole, that heads seat and that crankcase parting line closes along its entire length; then tighten cap screws in small increments using the sequence shown in Fig. 17. Tightening torques are as follows:

Screws	Ft.-Lbs.	N•m
6 mm	6-7	8.2-9.5
8 mm	13-16	17.7-21.7
10 mm	15-22	20.4-29.9

On models so equipped, install crankshaft seal end plate (Fig. 14). Use RTV silicone seal on gasket surface and Loctite on screw threads, and tighten screws using an impact driver.

Thoroughly lubricate crankshaft and rod bearings then install pistons with arrow on piston crowns pointing toward exahust side of engine. Insert piston pins and secure with retaining rings, making sure rings fully seat in their grooves. Coat cylinder base gaskets on both sides with a light coating of RTV sealer and install gaskets. Insert a small piece of wood underneath skirt of piston (Fig. 12) then using a ring compressor, slide cylinder down over piston making sure inlet port flange of cylinder is on same side as pulse passage fitting in crankcase. Install the other cylinder using the same procedure.

On models equipped with six-stud cylinder heads, install but DO NOT TIGHTEN cylinder base nuts. Temporarily install intake manifold to align manifold flanges of cylinders. Tighten front cylinder base nuts firmly to maintain alignment of cylinders, then remove intake manifold. Install the remaining cylinder base nuts and tighten all nuts to 22-29 ft.-lbs. (30-39 N•m) using a crisscross pattern.

On models equipped with four-stud cylinder heads, install intake manifold and tighten to 6-7 ft.-lbs. (8.2-9.5 N•m) to align cylinders.

On all models, install cylinder head gaskets and cylinder heads. Note that standoff (long) stud nuts go on end studs to support shroud. Using a crisscross tightening pattern, tighten six-stud cylinder head nuts to 14-18 ft.-lbs. (19.0-24.4 N•m) and four-stud cylinder head nuts to 13-16 ft.-lbs. (17.7-21.7 N•m). With crankcase and cylinders assembled, pressure test for air leaks as previously outlined.

Install magneto case on crankcase using Loctite on attaching screws and install with an impact driver. Align scribe marks and reinstall ignition base plate. Reinstall alternator stator and flywheel. Refer to TIGHTENING TORQUES section and tighten flywheel retaining nut to specified torque.

Complete assembly by reversing disassembly procedure. Cooling fan belt tension should be adjusted to allow 1/4 inch belt deflection midway between pulleys when depressed with finger. Belt tension is adjusted by adding or removing spacer shims (S–Fig. 21) between pulley halves on fan shift. (IF shims are removed, store spare shims on outside of sheave half behind shaft nut). Turn pulleys slowly while assembling, to keep from pinching belt.

LIQUID-COOLED ENGINE. With engine removed as previously outlined, remove the screws retaining the outside magneto cover and lift off cover as shown in Fig. 22. Using a holding spanner as shown in Fig. 3, loosen flywheel nut, then remove the three cap screws securing starter pulley and water pump drive pulley to flywheel. Remove pulleys and belt, then remove flywheel using a suitable screw puller as in Fig. 24.

Loosen the screw securing magneto wiring harness clamp. Scribe mark on magneto backing plate timing position to help in reassembly, then unbolt and lay magneto aside. Disconnect coolant bypass hose from cylinder head. Use an impact driver to loosen the magneto housing retaining screws and remove the screws. Use a rubber mallet to loosen magneto housing from crankcase, the remove magneto housing, water pump and magneto plate as an assembly as shown in Fig. 25.

Remove the cap screws, lockwashers and flat washers securing cylinder head, loosen cylinder head uisng a soft mallet as shown in Fig. 26, then lift off the head. Remove head gaskets. Unbolt and remove the water intake manifold. (Fig. 27).

Remove cylinder base nuts, lockwashers and flat washers. Use a soft

Fig. 22—Removing magneto housing cover on liquid-cooled engines.

Fig. 23—A spanner wrench is available for use in loosening flywheel nut and starter pulley retaining cap screws.

Fig. 24—Use a suitable screw puller to remove the flywheel.

mallet to tap cylinders free of crankcase, then lift cylinders straight up over piston assemblies. Mark the cylinders and pistons so they can be reinstalled in same location.

NOTE: Use care when handling cylinder units to prevent head surface from becoming scratched or reed stops from becoming bent.

Remove piston pin retainers and push out the pins using a suitable removing tool. Use rubber bands to center rods and prevent damage if crankshaft is accidentally turned.

Lay crankcase on its side and remove the 16 bolts and washers securing the crankcase halves. Separate the crankcase by tapping sides with a soft mallet. Do not use a pry in separating the crankcase. Check dowel in bearing bore and "C" ring at center bearing of lower

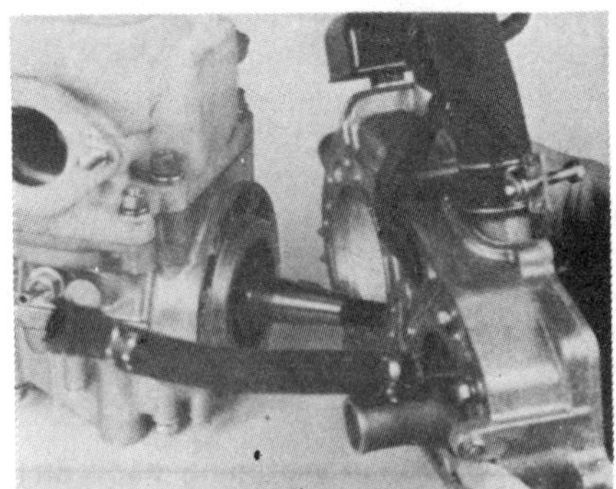

Fig. 25—Removing magneto housing on liquid-cooled engine.

Fig. 26—Removing cylinder head on liquid-cooled engine.

Fig. 27—Removing water manifold.

crankcase half when crankshaft is lifted out. Refer to the appropriate service sections which follow to service engine components.

Assemble by reversing the disassembly procedure. Apply a liberal amount of grease between double lips of crankcase seals and slip on shaft with spring side of seal toward bearing. Also make sure alignment holes of bearing races fit on dowels in bearing bores and that alignment "C" ring in center bore is properly positioned.

Apply a thin coat of RTV sealer to cleaned mating surfaces of each crankshaft half, then lay a piece of #50 cotton thread just to the inside of bolt holes on lower crankcase half as shown at T–Fig. 28. Carefully insert rods through cylinder mounting holes and install crankcase top half. Tip crankcase on its side and install the various sized crankcase cap screws finger tight. Make sure correct size and length is installed in each hole, that head seat and crankcase parting line closes along its entire length; then tighten cap screws in small increments using the sequence shown in Fig. 29. Tightening torques are as follows:

Screws	Ft.-Lbs.	N•m
6 mm	6-7	8.2-9.5
8 mm	13-16	17.7-21.7
10 mm	15-22	20.4-29.9

Thoroughly lubricate crankshaft and rod bearings then install pistons with ar-

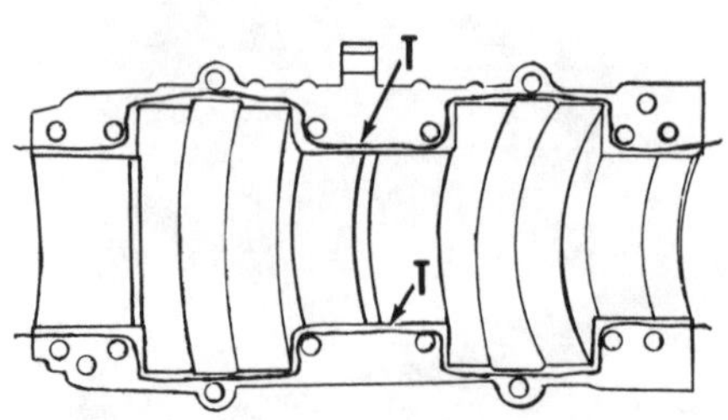

Fig. 28—After applying sealant to crankcase lower half, lay a cotton thread (T) inside bolt holes as shown.

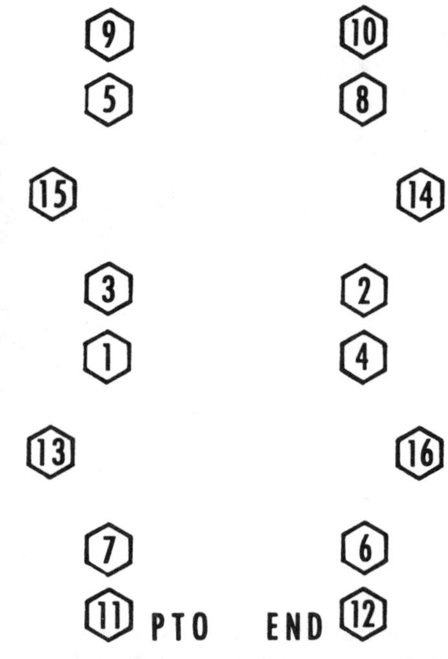

Fig. 29—Crankcase bolt tightening sequence to be used for liquid-cooled engines. Refer to text for tightening torques.

row on piston crowns pointing toward exhaust side of engine. Insert piston pins and secure with retaining rings, making sure rings fully seat in their grooves. Coat cylinder base gaskets on both sides with a light coating of RTV sealer and install gaskets. Insert a small piece of wood underneath skirt of piston as shown in Fig. 30, then using a ring compressor, slide cylinder down over piston. Install the other cylinder using the same procedure. Install but do not tighten cylinder base nuts at this time. Coat water manifold gaskets lightly with RTV sealer and install water manifold, tightening retaining cap screws to 5-7 ft.-lbs. (6.8-9.5 N•m). Installation of water manifold aligns cylinder flanges. Tighten all six stud nuts on each cylinder firmly, then torque the four 8 mm nuts to 13-16 ft.-lbs. (17.7-21.7 N•m) using a crisscross pattern. With large stud nuts torqued, tighten the 6 mm nuts to a torque of 6-7

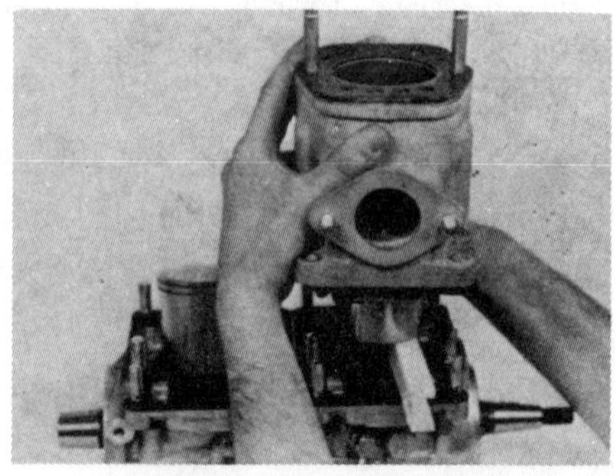

Fig. 30—Use a suitable ring compressor to install cylinders.

ft.-lbs. (8.2-9.5). Use a very thin coat of RTV Sealer on head gaskets then position over cylinders, making sure large water passage holes are toward INTAKE side of cylinders. Position cylinder head and install the twelve cap screws, lockwashers and flat washers which secure the head. Snug up the cylinder head cap screws then torque to 22-29 ft.-lbs. (30-39 N·m) using the tightening sequence shown in Fig. 33. With crankcase and cylinder assembled, pressure test for air leaks as previously outlined.

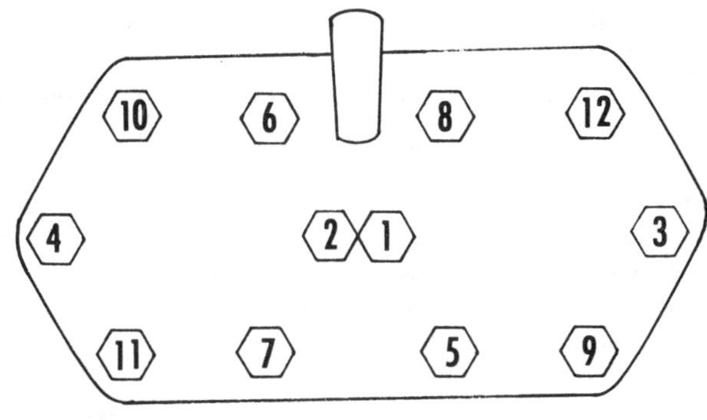

Fig. 33—Cylinder head tightening torque for liquid-cooled six studs per cylinder engine. Recommended tightening torque is 22-29 ft.-lbs. (3.0-4.0 kg-m).

Install thermostat as shown in Fig. 34, gasket and outlet elbow as in Fig. 35. Install thermostat housing retaining screws using Loctite and tighten using an impact driver.

Install magneto case on crankcase using Loctite on attaching screws and tightening with an impact driver. Align scribe marks and reinstall magneto base plate. Reinstall flywheel, tightening retainer nut to a torque of 50-63 ft.-lbs. (66.4-85.4 N·m). Reinstall coolant pump belt and pulley, starter pulley and pulley retaining screws. Check coolant pump belt tension, which should allow ¼-inch deflection midway between pulley sheaves. Adjust belt tension if necessary by slackening the three water pump mounting cap screws and turning belt adjusting screw (S–Fig. 36) either way as required.

PISTONS, RINGS AND CYLINDERS. Piston pins are fully floating. Piston rings are pinned in place and should be installed with identifying letter up. Piston ring end gap should not exceed 0.033 inch (0.84 mm) for 70 mm piston or 0.031 inch (0.79 mm) for other sizes. Disassembly notches (N–Fig. 37) in pin bosses may be located at top or sides. Gap of pin retaining circlip should be located at bottom of pin boss when disassembly notch is at the top, and at top or bottom when disassembly notch is at sides.

Most pistons are marked with an arrow (A) on top of piston crown. Arrow should point toward exhaust side of engine when reassembling. If piston is not marked, ring locating pins (P) should be on intake side of the assembly. Piston to cylinder wall clearance should be 0.002-0.0025 inch (0.05-0.06 mm) with a

Fig. 31—Water manifold can be used to align cylinders before tightening stud nuts.

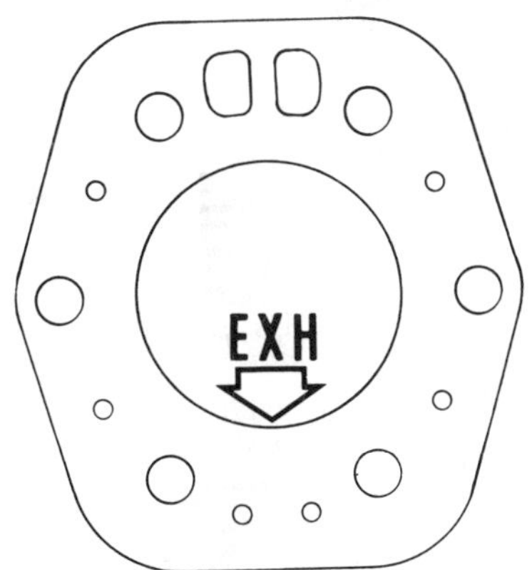

Fig. 32—Large water passage holes in cylinder head gasket must be installed toward intake port side of engine.

Fig. 34—Installing thermostat in liquid cooled engine.

Fig. 35—Installing outlet elbow.

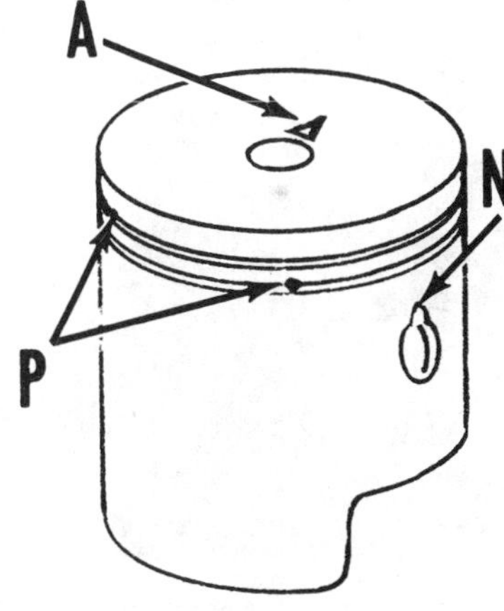

Fig. 37—View of typical Spirit piston. Arrow (A) on piston crown points to exhaust side of engine. Ring locating pins (P) are on intake side. Disassembly notches for piston pin retainers may be on top or sides of pin bore.

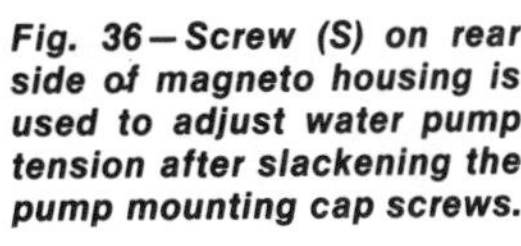

Fig. 36—Screw (S) on rear side of magneto housing is used to adjust water pump tension after slackening the pump mounting cap screws.

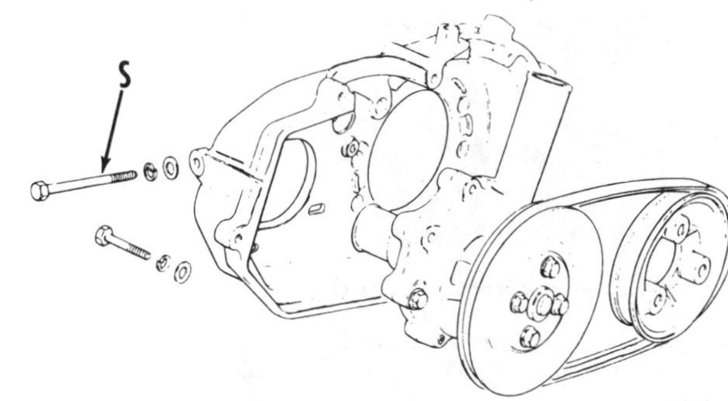

wear limit of 0.006 inch (0.15 mm) for all models.

Maximum allowable out-of-round, taper or barreling is 0.002 inch (0.05 mm). Minor imperfections in the cylinder can be removed with a 500 grit cylinder hone. Inspect threaded areas for damaged or stripped threads and gasket surfaces for warped areas or scratches. Check pistons for cracks in skirt areas or piston pin bosses. Use a piece of broken ring and carefully remove carbon from piston ring grooves. Because all engines use keystone rings, a conventional ring groove tool cannot be used. Pistons and rings are available in standard size only.

CRANKSHAFT AND CONNECTING ROD ASSEMBLIES. Thoroughly wash crankshaft assembly in a mineral base solvent and inspect for external wear, scoring or scuffing. Rotate the bearings by hand to be sure they turn freely without binding or roughness.

Mount crankshaft assembly on "V" blocks and check runout at seal area as shown in Fig. 38. Runout should not exceed 0.002 inch (0.05 mm). Check radial clearance of connecting rod bearing using a dial indicator as shown in Fig. 39. Radial clearance should be within the limits of 0.0008-0.0012 inch (0.02-0.03 mm). If end play is excessive, if bearing is rough, or if other defects exist, affected parts should be renewed.

Fig. 38—Crankshaft runout should not exceed 0.002 inch (0.05 mm) when measured as shown.

Fig. 39—Radial clearance of assembled connecting rod bearing should not exceed 0.0008-0.0012 inch (0.02-0.03 mm). Method of measurement is shown.

All crankshaft parts are available individually but shaft overhaul should not be attempted without proper equipment and a certain amount of experience.

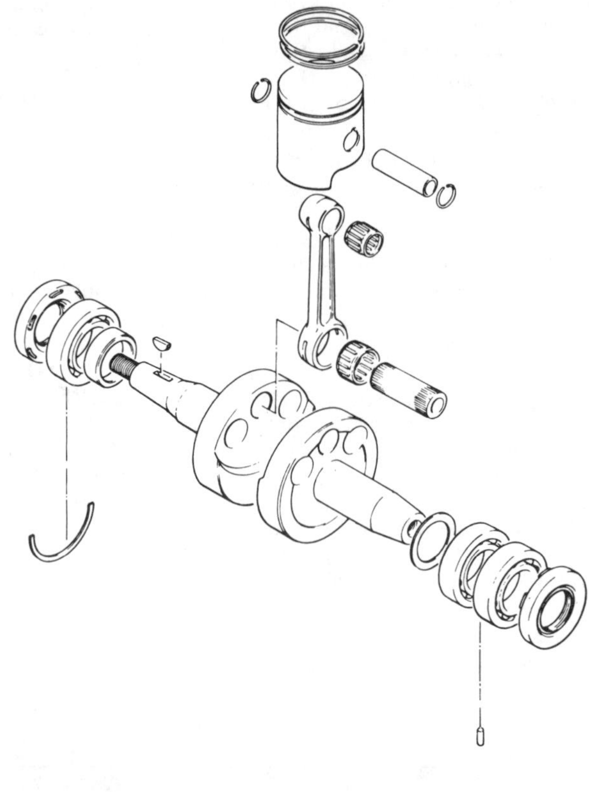

Fig. 40—Exploded view of crankshaft, connecting rod and associated parts used on single cylinder engine.

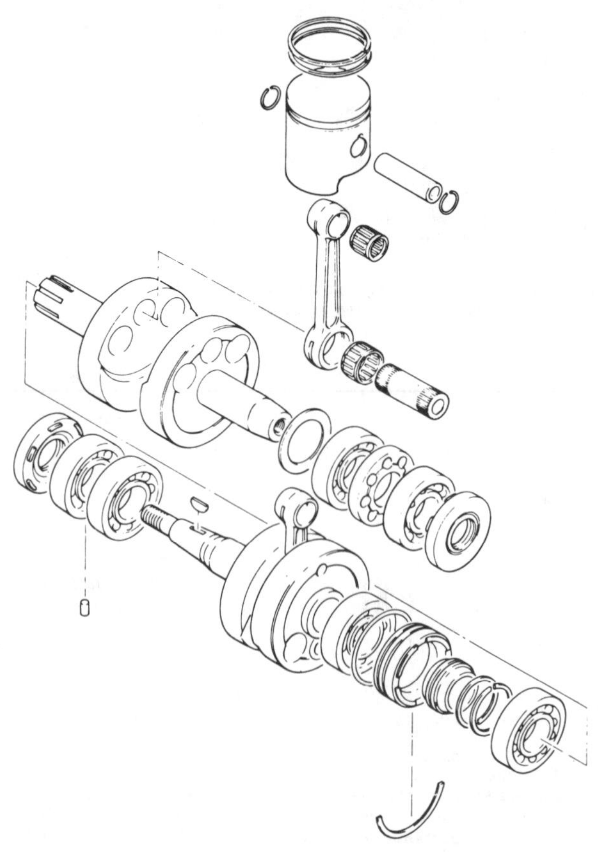

Fig. 41—Exploded view of crankshaft, connecting rod and associated parts used on twin cylinder engine.

REED INLET VALVE. Liquid-cooled engines are equipped with a two-reed induction plate instead of piston porting. Reed block assembly fastens to

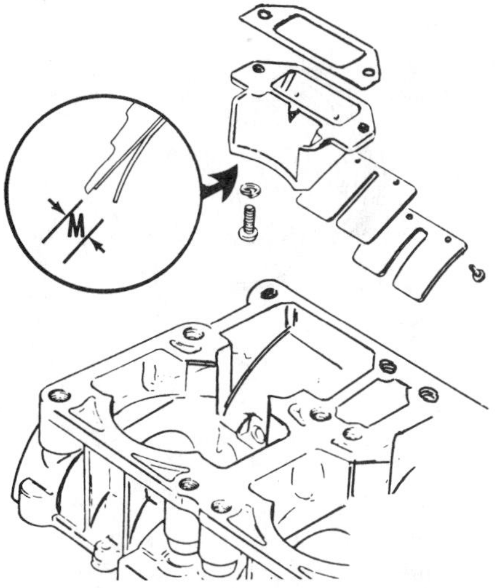

Fig. 42—Exploded view of intake reed valve and associated parts used on liquid-cooled engines. Measured height (M) of reed stop should be 0.362 inch (9.2 mm).

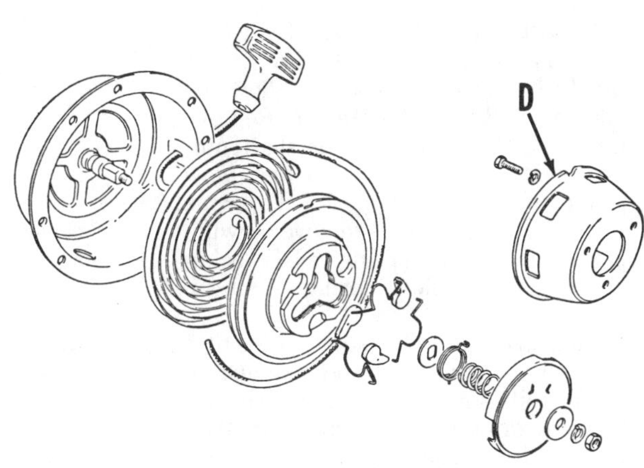

Fig. 44—Exploded view of recoil starter showing comnent parts. Drive (D) is bolted to engine flywheel and is not a part of removed assembly.

bottom of each cylinder block and can be removed after cylinder is off.

Reed leaves should lie flat against rubber seating surface of reed block throughout their entire length. Do not attempt to straighten a bent reed or bend a reed to modify performance. Rubber seating surface of reed block must not be excessively worn, cracked, flaked or chipped.

Reed stop must be uniform and properly arched. A bent or malformed stop can cause reed damage and improper engine operation. Measure the distance between outside edge of stop and seating surface of reed block as shown at (M–Fig. 42). Distance should measure 0.362 inch (9.2 mm). If measurement is incorrect, renew the reed stop.

When assembling reed valve unit, put beveled corner of reed to lower right as shown in Fig. 43. Install reed retaining screws and block retaining screws with Loctite and tighten securely.

RECOIL STARTER. 1981 Tiger Cat And All Other Models Prior to 1981. If stator is being removed for service, first raise the hood. Pull a small amount of slack into recoil rope and untie the knot securing pull handle; then allow rope to slowly retract into starter housing. Remove the four mounting cap screws and lift off starter unit.

To disassemble the removed starter, apply slight pressure to the drive plate and remove nut, lockwasher and flat washer from center stud. Lift off the drive plate, compression spring, return spring and compression spring seat. Remove the three pawl springs and pawls.

Carefully lift the rope pulley from housing, turning pulley clockwise as it is lifted, to unhook inner end of recoil spring from lug on pulley. Recoil spring should remain in starter housing well, when pulley is removed.

Recoil spring and rope can be renewed at this time. To install a new spring, refer to Fig. 44. Hook outer end of spring on lug in starter housing and wrap spring in a counterclockwise direction in spring well. Lubricate the spring and spring well with Lithium base grease.

Thread a new rope through hole in bottom of rope slot in pulley. Tie a knot in end of rope and pull tight; then while facing pawl side of pulley, wind the rope into pulley in a counterclockwise direction. Lubricate pulley hub with Lithium base grease and install pulley, aligning inner hook of recoil spring with spring notch in pulley hub.

Install pawls and pawl springs as shown in Fig. 45. Install spring seat and compression spring. Install return spring with straight end down, then install drive plate making sure hooked upper end of return spring engages chevron slot in drive plate. Secure with flat washer, lockwasher and nut, tightening nut to 15 ft.-lbs. (20.4 N•m).

Thread outer end of rope through rope guide in housing and pull out approximately 50 cm (20 inch) of rope to reach through cowl then tie a temporary slip knot in rope. Turn rope pulley until notch in pulley rim aligns with rope guide in housing and, using a hooked wire, pull a loop of rope outside pulley rim. Continue to turn pulley in same direction for three more turns to preload the recoil spring. Pull on rope to check recoil tension and if insufficient, preload one more turn.

When installing starter, install the four mounting cap screws loosely, then pull on starter rope until starter pawls engage, then tighten mounting cap screws. Pull starter rope end through rope guide in cowl and install handle, then untie the temporary slip knot in rope.

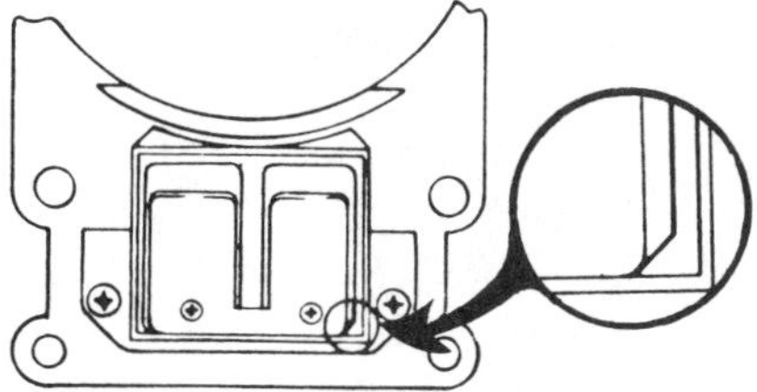

Fig. 43—Beveled locating corner of reed valve components should be installed at lower right as shown.

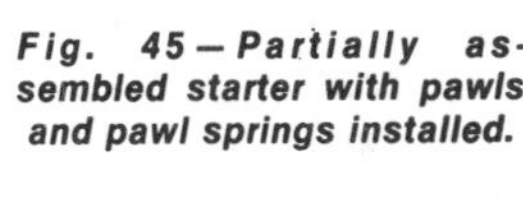

Fig. 45—Partially assembled starter with pawls and pawl springs installed.

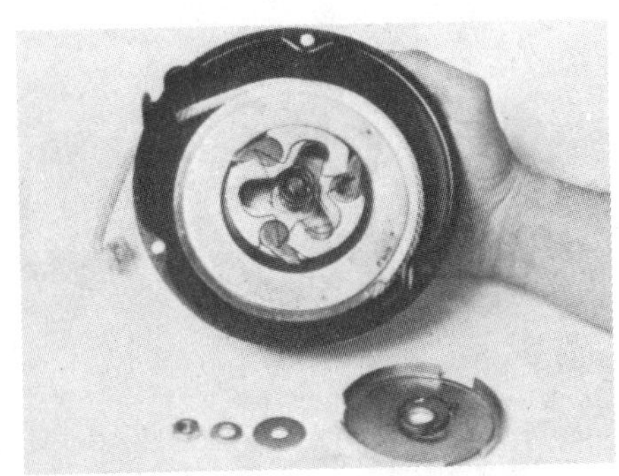

1981-1984 Models Except Trail Cat. To disassemble the starter (Fig. 46), detach the starter handle and allow the rope to wind into the starter. Remove starter. Remove the starter shaft nut, drive plate, wire clip, pawl and pawl spring. Carefully remove the rope pulley. If necessary, remove rewind spring cover and spring while being careful not to allow spring to uncoil uncontrolled.

When assembling the starter note that the rewind spring must be installed so spring coils are wound in a counterclockwise direction from outer end. If so equipped, install decompression mechanism with springs in proper location. Wrap the starter rope around the rope pulley in a counterclockwise direction as viewed from pawl side of pulley. Leave approximately 50 cm (20 inch) of rope unwrapped. Install rope pulley, pass rope end through rope outlet and install rope handle. Install the pawl spring and pawl with the long end of the spring inserted into the rope pulley and the short end against the backside of the pawl. Install pawl so narrow end points in a clockwise direction. Install wire clip, drive plate and nut; closed end of wire clip must be adjacent to wide end of pawl. Pull rope into notch in pulley and rotate pulley four turns clockwise to preload rewind spring. Check starter operation then install starter on engine.

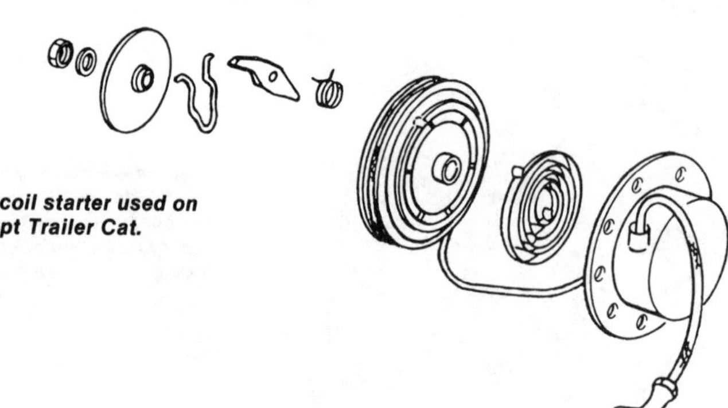

Fig. 46 — Exploded view of recoil starter used on 1981-1984 models except Trailer Cat.

SUZUKI

CONDENSED SERVICE DATA

Model	SM10 & SM10D†	SM11 & SM11D †	SM20	SM21	SM30	SM40
Bore–(mm)	61	59	64	64	73	65
Inches	2.40	2.32	2.52	2.52	2.87	2.56
Stroke–(mm)	61.5	61.5	61.5	61.5	70	65
Inches	2.42	2.42	2.42	2.42	2.76	2.56
No. of Cylinders	2	2	2	2	1	2
Displacement–(cc)	359	336	395	395	292	432
Cubic Inches	21.9	20.5	24.1	24.1	17.8	26.4
Horsepower @ RPM	28 @ 6500	26 @ 5500	35 @ 6000	33 @ 6000	20 @ 6000	36 @ 6000
Cooling Type	Cent. Fan.	....	Cent. Fan.	....	....	....
Carburetor Type (Mikuni)	VM26	VM26SH	VM26	VM26SH	VM32SH	VM30SH
Number Used	1	1	2	2	1	2
Ignition:						
Type–Manual Start	E.T. Mag.	E.T. Mag.	E.T. Mag.	E.T. Mag.	E.T. Mag.	P.E.I.
Type–Electric Start	Batt. Ign.	Batt. Ign.	Batt. Ign.	....	....	....
Point Gap–(mm)	0.3-0.4	0.3-0.4	0.3-0.4	0.3-0.4	0.3-0.4	....
Inch	0.012-0.016	0.012-0.016	0.012-0.016	0.012-0.016	0.012-0.016	....
Timing Advance	No	No	No	No	Yes	Yes
Timing BTDC-Deg.	22	22	22	22	22 @ 2000	22 @ 3000
Piston Position (mm) BTDC	2.84	2.84	2.84	2.84	3.45	3.00
Inch	0.112	0.112	0.112	0.112	0.136	0.118
Spark Plug:						
Electrode Gap (mm)	0.6-0.7	0.6-0.7	0.6-0.7	0.6-0.7	0.6-0.7	0.6-0.7
Inch	0.024-0.028*	0.024-0.028	0.024-0.028*	0.024-0.028	0.024-0.028	0.024-0.028
Type–NGK	B7-HS	B7-HS	B7-HS	B7-HS	B7-HS	B7-HS
Champion	L81 (L3G)	....	L81 (L3G)	....	....	....
Fuel/Oil Ratio	20:1	20:1	20:1	20:1	20:1	20:1

† Electric Start models.
*Electrode gap for Champion L-3G should be 0.015 inch.

MAINTENANCE

SPARK PLUGS. Selection of spark plugs will depend upon type of service and ambient temperature. NGK type B7-HS, Champion L-81 (L-36) or equivalent spark plugs are recommended for normal use. Excessively cold weather and/or light load conditions may require spark plugs of warmer heat range. Hard usage, heavy loads and/or warm weather may require spark plugs for colder heat range. Electrode gap should be 0.6-0.7 mm (0.024-0.028 inch) for standard plugs, 0.015 inch for "Gold Palladium L-3G Champion" spark plugs.

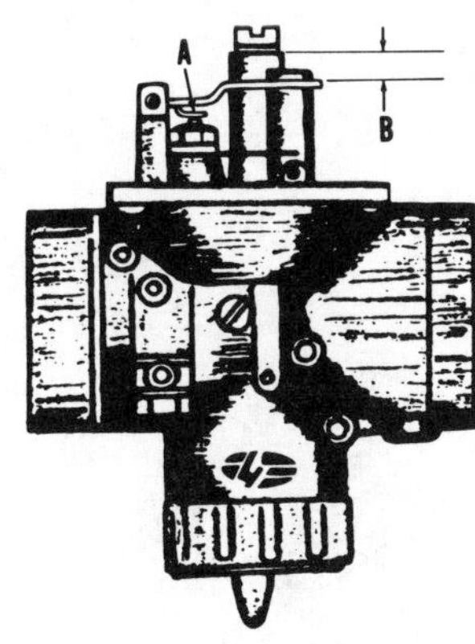

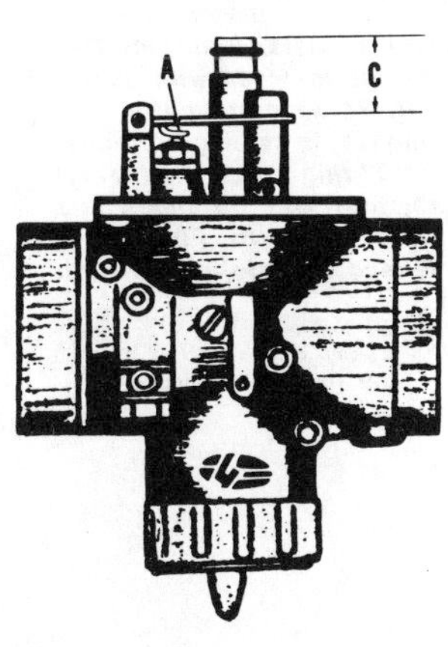

Fig. 1 — View of fuel level adjustment. Early carburetor is shown on left and later carburetor is at right. Carefully measure distance (B or C) before and after bending the adjusting tang (A).

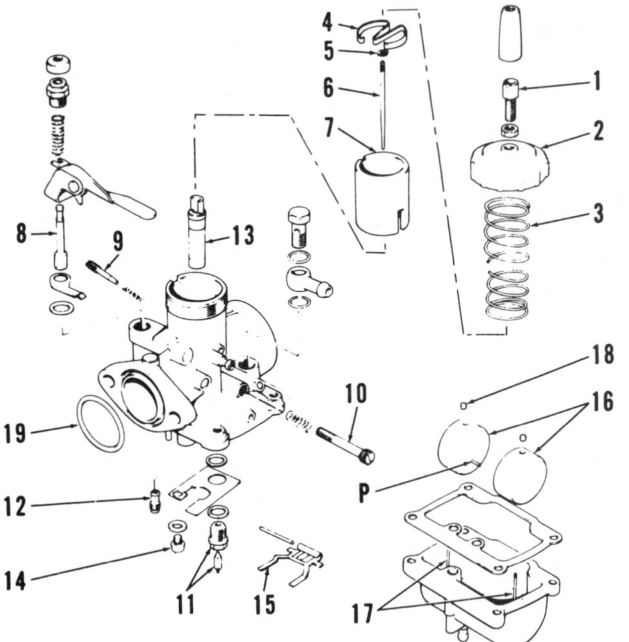

Fig. 2—Exploded view of carburetor used on early Nomad models. Float bowl must be removed before removing main jet (14). Refer to Fig. 3 for late carburetor.

1. Cable adjuster
2. Cap
3. Throttle spring
4. Retainer
5. Clip
6. Jet needle
7. Throttle slide
8. Starting mixture plunger
9. Idle mixture needle
10. Idle speed stop screw
11. Fuel inlet valve
12. Pilot jet
13. Needle jet
14. Main jet
15. Float lever
16. Floats
17. Guide rods
18. Clips
19. "O" ring

CARBURETORS. Early (1970-1971) SM10 models are equipped with carburetor shown in Fig. 2. Later SM10 models and all other models are equipped with carburetor (Fig. 3) which has main jet holder (20).

On early (1970-1971) SM10 models, fuel level is measured as shown at (B–Fig. 1) and should be 8 mm (5/16-inch). Later SM10 models and SM20 models can be identified by main jet holder (20–Fig. 3). The fuel level on these later models should be measured as shown at (C–Fig. 1) and should be 14.0 mm (9/16-inch). Models SM11, SM21, SM30 and SM40 have an external main jet holder as shown at (20–Fig. 3), but fuel level should be measured between arm of float lever (15) and shoulder of needle jet retainer (22). Correct float level distance is 5.9-7.9 mm (0.232-0.311 inch) for SM11 and SM21 models, 9.1-11.1 mm (0.358-0.437 inch) for SM30 models, 12.7-14.7 mm (0.500-0.579 inch) for SM40 models.

On all models, the measured float level should be exactly the same for both arms of float lever. Change float level by bending tang (A–Fig. 1). Refer to appropriate Fig. 2 or Fig. 3 and the following standard specifications.

Early SM10
Refer to Fig. 2
Clip (5) position in needle (6)-
from top . . . . 4th groove
Main jet (14) standard . . . . #125
Pilot jet (12) . . . . #30
Jet Needle (6) 4DH5
Throttle valve (7) cut-away . . . . . 2.5 mm
Pilot air screw (9)
standard setting . . . . 1 turn open

Late SM10
Refer to Fig. 3
Clip (5) position in needle (6)-
from top . . . . 3rd groove
Main jet (14) standard . . . . #145
Pilot jet (12) . . . . #40
Needle jet (13) 0-6
Jet needle (6) 4F10
Throttle valve (7) cut-away . . . . . 2.5 mm
Pilot air screw (9)
standard setting . . . . . . 1½ turns open

SM11
Refer to Fig. 3
Clip (5) position in needle (6)-
from top . . . . 4th groove
Main jet (14) standard . . . . #140
Pilot jet (12) . . . . #25
Needle jet (13) P-4
Jet needle (6) 5DH17
Throttle valve (7) cut-away . . . . . 2.5 mm
Pilot air screw (9)
standard setting . . . . . . 1½ turns open

SM20
Refer to Fig. 3
Clip (5) position in needle (6)-
from top . . . . 3rd groove
Main jet (14) standard . . . . #135
Pilot jet (12) . . . . #35
Needle jet (13) P-2
Jet needle (6) 5DO17
Throttle valve (7) cut-away . . . . . 2.0 mm
Pilot air screw (9)
standard setting . . . . . . 1½ turns open

SM21
Refer to Fig. 3
Clip (5) position in needle (6)-
from top . . . . 4th groove
Main jet (14) standard . . . . #120
Pilot jet (12) . . . . #25
Needle jet (13) P-2
Jet needle (6) 5DH17
Throttle valve (7) cut-away . . . . . 2.5 mm
Pilot air screw (9)
standard setting . . . . . . 1½ turns open

SM30
Refer to Fig. 3
Clip (5) position in needle (6)-
from top . . . . 3rd groove
Main jet (14) standard . . . . #140
Pilot jet (12) . . . . #30
Needle jet (13) Q-6
Jet needle (6) 6DP5
Throttle valve (7) cut-away . . . . . 2.0 mm
Pilot air screw (9)
standard setting . . . . . . 1½ turns open

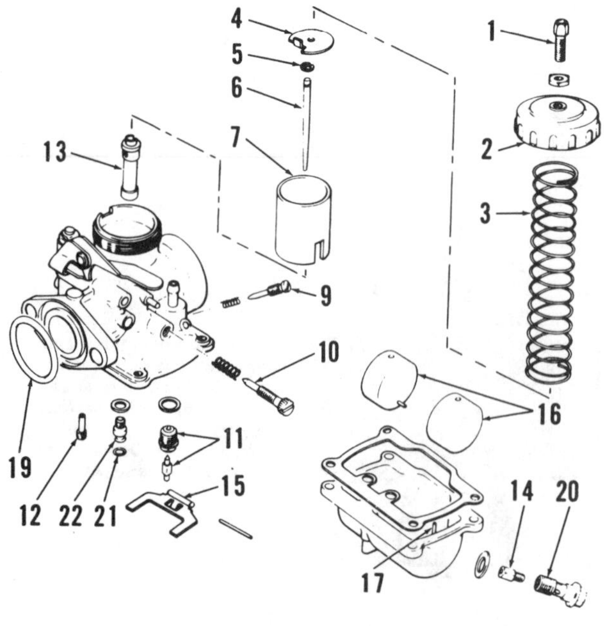

Fig. 3—Exploded view typical of carburetor used on late models. Main jet (14) can be removed with holder (20). Make certain that "O" ring (21) is sealing correctly. If "O" ring leaks, the fuel-air mixture will be much too rich. Refer to Fig. 2 for legend except the following.

20. Holder
21. "O" ring
22. Needle jet retainer

SM40
Refer to Fig. 3
Clip (5) position in needle (6)-
from top . . . . 3rd groove
Main jet (14) standard . . . . #120
Pilot jet (12) . . . . #35
Needle jet (13). P-8
Jet needle (6) 5EI16
Throttle valve (7) cut-away . . . . . 2.5 mm
Pilot air screw (9)
standard setting . . . . . . 1½ turns open

REED VALVES. Reed valves are located between manifold and crankcase of all except SM30 and SM40 models which are piston ported. On models so equipped, examine valve reeds, reed stops and valve body visually. Individual parts are not available. Do not attempt to straighten a bent reed or to bend reeds or reed stops to change performance. Renew reed assembly if any damage is apparent. When assembling, tighten manifold retaining stud nuts to 70-86 inch-pounds torque in sequence shown in Fig. 4.

FUEL PUMP. The diaphragm type fuel pump is actuated by pressure and vacuum pulsations in left cylinder crankcase. Fuel pump is available only as an assembly. The fuel filter located in tank should be removed, cleaned and inspected at least once each season. If fuel pump does not deliver 800 cc (or more) of fuel per minute at engine speed of 6000 rpm, check condition of fuel filter, fuel lines, pressure-vacuum line and fuel pump. Fuel pump mounting screws should be tightened to 35-51 inch-pounds torque.

IGNITION AND TIMING. Electric starting SM10D, SM11D and SM20 models are equipped with battery ignition and SM40 models are equipped with PEI (Pointless Electronic Ignition). All other models are equipped with energy transfer magneto ignition.

On all models except SM40, breaker point gap at maximum opening should be 0.3-0.4 mm (0.012-0.016 inch). Ignition timing on some models automatically advances as engine speed increases. On all models, ignition should occur at 22 degrees BTDC with ignition fully advanced. Refer to CONDENSED SERVICE DATA for piston position at 22 degrees BTDC. All models are equipped with timing marks similar to those shown in Fig. 6. Ignition should occur when timing mark (B) is aligned with pointer (A). The second mark "T" indicates TDC and should not be used for ignition timing. Small changes in ignition timing can be accomplished, on models so equipped, by varying breaker point gap within limits of 0.3-0.4 mm (0.012-0.016 inch). Initial ignition timing must be accomplished by correctly locating the stator plate. Breaker point gap can be changed through holes in flywheel, after removing recoil starter assembly. To renew breaker points or change ignition timing by moving stator plate, the flywheel must be removed. Flywheel retaining nut should be tightened to 37-50 ft.-lbs. torque. Timing marks (A & B – Fig. 6) are aligned when crankshaft is 22 degrees BTDC and piston is located 2.84 mm (0.112 inch) before top of stroke.

On SM40 models, ignition timing should be checked with power timing light and engine operating above 3000 rpm. Ignition should occur at 22 degrees BTDC above 3000 rpm and marks (A & B – Fig. 6) should be aligned as shown. Position of the small signal coil on the stator plate is pre-set and sealed by ignition manufacturer and should not be changed. Index mark is located on the stator and should be aligned at center of stator attaching screw. Mounting holes in stator are slotted for precise timing adjustment, but large changes should not be necessary. Some components can be checked with an ohmmeter as follows:

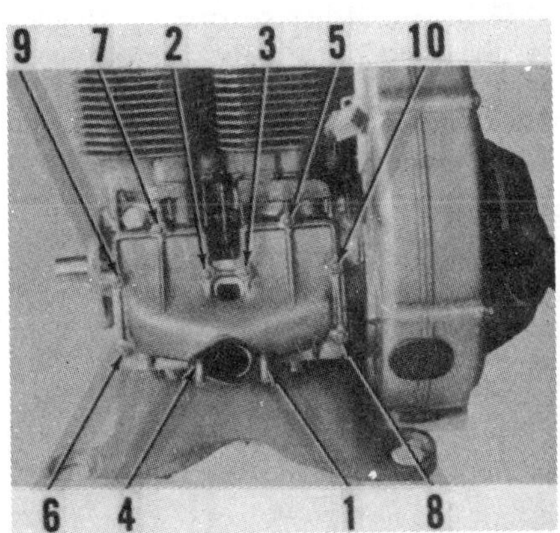

Fig. 4 – Reed valve and inlet manifold screws should be tightened in sequence shown. Make certain that gaskets are correctly positioned to prevent crankcase leaks. To prevent distortion, loosen screws in reverse of the order shown.

Fig. 6 – Ignition timing marks (A&B) can be viewed after removing plug from fan housing. Ignition stator can be moved after loosening the three attaching screws. On manual start models, coils (1 & 2) are ignition coils and (3) is lighting coil. On electric starting models all three coils are for charging battery and are identical.

Stator Coils
Slow Speed Charge Coil –
Black/White to Black/Red
wires . . . . 400 ohms
Black/White to Black
wires . . . . 400 ohms
High Speed Charge Coil –
Black/Red to Black
wires . . . . 0.5-1.5 ohms
Green to Black wires . . . . 1.5-3.0 ohms
Signal Coil –
Red/White to Black
wires . . . . 4.0-5.0 ohms

P.E.I. Unit

Set ohmmeter to "RX100" position for the following tests. Attach positive ohmmeter lead to Black/White wire and negative lead to White/Blue wire. Ohmmeter needle should move once, then return which indicates capacitor charges. To discharge capacitor, touch Black/White wire to White/Blue wire for approximately ½ minute. Attach ohmmeter leads to opposite wires (negative to Black/White and positive to White/Blue) and recheck. Ohmmeter needle should move once, charging capacitor, then return. Be sure to discharge capacitor by touching Black/White wire to White/Blue wire after checking.

Attach positive ohmmeter lead to Black/Red wire and negative lead to Black/White wire. Ohmmeter should indicate no continuity (infinite resistance). Connect positive test lead to Red/White wire and negative lead to Black wire. Ohmmeter should indicate continuity.

Attach positive ohmmeter lead to the Black wire and negative test lead to Black/White wire. The needle of ohmmeter should move once, then return after charging capacitor. Discharge capacitor after checking by touching Black wire to Black/White wire for ½ minute.

Attach positive ohmmeter lead to Black wire and negative test lead to Red/White wire. Ohmmeter should indicate 50-150 ohms resistance.

Attach positive ohmmeter lead to Black wire and negative test lead to White/Blue wire. Ohmmeter should indicate continuity. Reverse test leads, positive to White/Blue wire and negative to Black wire and recheck. The ohmmeter should indicate infinite resistance (no continuity).

Attach positive ohmmeter lead to Black/Yellow wire and negative test lead to the Black/Red wire. Ohmmeter should indicate continuity.

LUBRICATION. The engine is lubricated by mixing oil with the fuel.

A suitable two-stroke air cooled engine oil is recommended. Recommended fuel-oil mixture is 20:1. Mix fuel and oil thoroughly in a separate container before pouring mixture into fuel tank. For cold weather blending, premix the oil with a small amount of gasoline and shake thoroughly until mixture is liquid, then blend with remainder of fuel.

REPAIRS

TIGHTENING TORQUES. Recommended tightening torques are as follows:

Carburetor nuts . . . . 113-147 in.-lbs.
Cooling fan screws . . . . 70-86 in.-lbs.
Crankcase screws–
 6 mm (4 used)** . . . . 70-86 in.-lbs.
 8 mm (8 used)** . . . . . . 156-190 in.-lbs.
Cylinder head nuts–
 SM10 & SM20 . . . . 26-31 ft.-lbs.
 SM11 & SM21 . . . . 23-27 ft.-lbs.
 SM30 & SM40 . . . . 13-16 ft.-lbs.
Engine mounting nuts . . . . 26-31 ft.-lbs.
Engine mount bracket nuts 26-31 ft.-lbs.
Exhaust manifold nuts . . 113-147 in.-lbs.
Exhaust pipe screws . . . . . 78-102 in-lbs.
Flywheel nut . . . . 37-50 ft.-lbs.
Fuel pump screws . . . . 36-51 in-lbs.
Inlet manifold nuts* . . . . . . 70-86 in.-lbs.
Magneto case screws . . . . . 52-78 in.-lbs.
Muffler mounting screws . 78-102 in.-lbs.
Muffler tail pipe screws . . 78-102 in.-lbs.
Recoil starter screws . . . . . 35-51 in.-lbs.
Ring gear screws . . . . 35-51 in.-lbs.
Starting motor mounting screws–
 6 mm (2 used) . . . . 35-51 in.-lbs.
 8 mm (4 used) . . . . 78-102 in.-lbs.
Starting motor housing
 through screws . . . . 35-43 in.-lbs.

*Inlet manifold screws should be torqued in sequence shown in Fig. 4.

**Crankcase screws should be torqued in sequence shown in Fig. 8 or Fig. 8A. On two cylinder models, screws numbered 9, 10, 11 & 12 are 6 mm diameter.

ENGINE R&R. To remove engine from vehicle, remove handle bar from steering shaft and disconnect speedometer drive cable. Remove primary pulley cover, drive belt and instrument panel. Disconnect ground cable, wiring harness, muffler, fuel pump vacuum hose and (on electric starting models) starting motor positive cable. Disconnect wires from spark plugs and fuel line from carburetor. Remove steering shaft bracket, detach steering support arch from chassis and lift arch enough to allow engine to be lifted out. Remove engine mounting nuts and lift engine out toward rear.

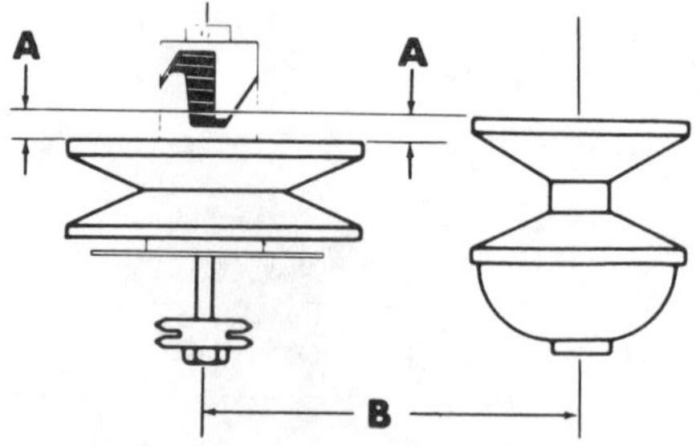

Fig. 7—Inner faces of pulleys must be parallel and offset, shown at (A), should be correct as listed in text. The center-to-center distance (B) between pulleys should be 10-10 5/16-inches.

When installing, locate engine so that pulley faces are exactly parallel and offset the correct amount as shown at (A–Fig. 7). Correct offset is 0.69-0.77 inch for SM10 and SM20 models, 0.16-0.24 inch for all other models. Make certain that fuel line is not pinched between engine mounting bracket and frame. Adjust steering shaft to upper bracket clearance to 0.008-0.020 inch by turning nuts.

DISASSEMBLY AND REASSEMBLY. The cylinder head, cylinder, piston, rings and piston pin bearing can be serviced without removing engine.

CAUTION: Be especially careful to prevent anything from falling into crankcase if crankcase halves are not to be separated.

Flywheel, magneto (or alternator), magneto (fan) case, inlet manifold, primary drive pulley and engine mounting bracket must be removed before separating crankcase halves. Remove the crankcase screws in reverse sequence shown in Fig. 8 or 8A. With screws removed, carefully bump halves apart to prevent distortion.

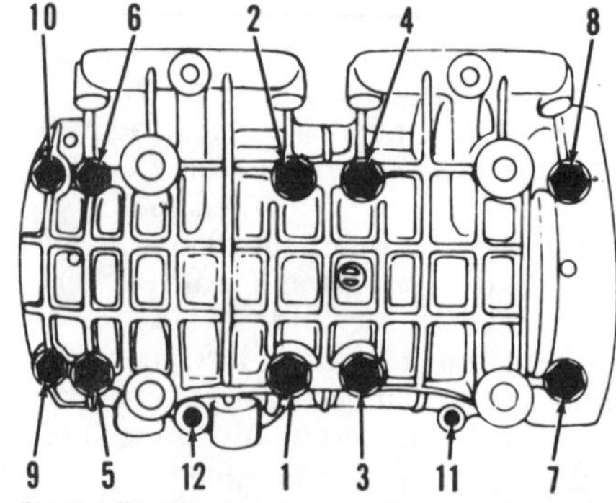

Fig. 8—Tighten crankcase screws on two cylinder models in the order shown. Screws (9, 10, 11 & 12) are smaller than others. Screws (11 & 12) enter from top. Loosen in reverse order to prevent warping crankcase halves.

When assembling, make certain that "O" ring on center seal is correctly positioned and will seal properly. Locate crankshaft, main bearings and seals assembly in lower crankcase half, making certain that all pins (6–Fig. 9) correctly enter holes in main bearings and that locating rings (26 & 27) engage grooves in center seal outer race and right bearing-seal housing. Use sealer on mating surfaces of crankcase halves, carefully install top half of crankcase and tighten retaining screws in sequence shown in Fig. 8 or Fig. 8A. The 8 mm crankcase screws should be tightened to 156-190 inch-pounds torque and 6 mm screws should be tightened to 70-86 inch-pounds torque.

CAUTION: Crankshaft and crankcase will both probably be ruined if locating pins or locating rings are incorrectly located.

Be sure that "O" ring (16–Fig. 9) does not catch between crankcase halves and magneto (fan) housing. Observe tightening torques listed in previous section. Arrow on top of piston should be toward exhaust and mark on side of piston rings should be toward top. Install and tighten exhaust manifold to cylinder before tightening the cylinder and head retaining nuts.

PISTONS, PINS, RINGS AND CYLINDERS. Remove cylinders and piston pin retaining rings, then push pin out of piston.

CAUTION: Do not bend connecting rod or allow anything to fall into crankcase. Do not interchange any used parts between the cylinders when reassembling.

Piston pin should be a snug fit in piston bore and needle bearing should not have perceptible clearance between piston pin and connecting rod bore. If piston pin bearing bore in connecting

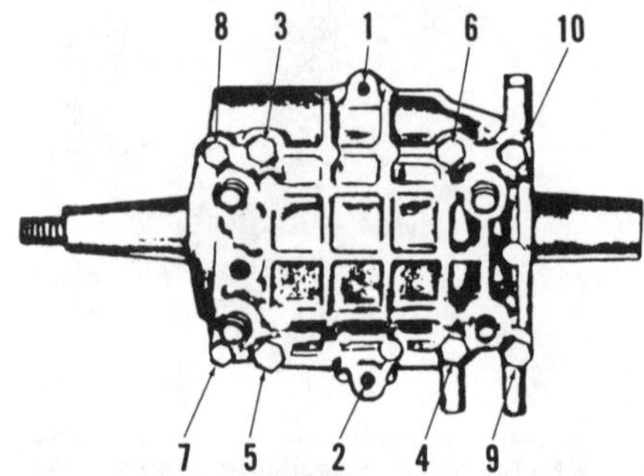

Fig. 8A—Tighten crankcase screws on one cylinder models in the order shown. Loosen screws in reverse order.

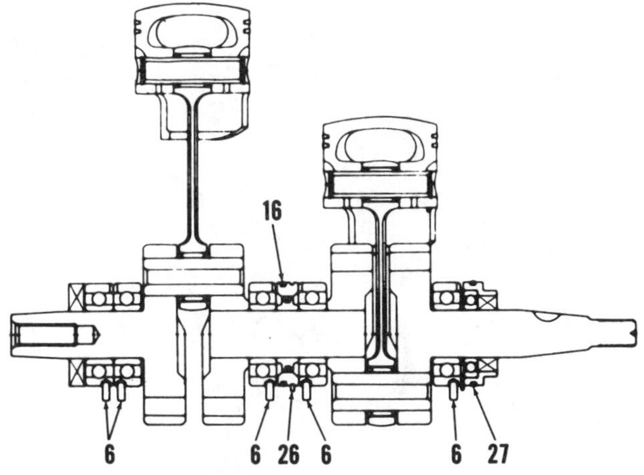

Fig. 9—Drawing of typical two cylinder crankshaft and associated parts showing bearing locating pins (6) and locating rings (26 & 27). Center seal "O" ring is shown at (16). Make certain that bearings are installed on crankshaft correctly so that holes in outer race will align with pins (6).

rod is ridged, the rod should be renewed. Piston pin standard diameter is 16 mm (0.630-inch) for all models except SM30 which is 18 mm (0.866-inch).

Renew or resize cylinder if bore is tapered or out-of-round more than 0.05 mm (0.0020 inch). Refer to the following standard specifications.

SM10

Cylinder Bore
Diameter . . . . 61.000-61.015 mm
2.4016-2.4022 in.
Piston Skirt Diameter 39.5 mm (1.56-in.) from bottom of skirt at right angle to piston pin . . . . 60.900-60.915 mm
2.3976-2.3982 in.
Piston to Cylinder
Clearance . . . . 0.095-0.105 mm
0.0037-0.0041 in.

SM11

Cylinder Bore
Diameter . . . . 59.000-59.015 mm
Piston Skirt Diameter 38.5 mm (1.51-in.) from bottom of skirt at right angles to piston pin . . . . 58.890-58.905 mm
2.3579-2.3585 in.
Piston to Cylinder
Clearance . . . . 0.105-0.115 mm
0.0041-0.0045 in.

SM20

Cylinder Bore
Diameter . . . . 64.000-64.015 mm
2.5197-2.5203 in.
Piston Skirt Diameter 39.5 mm (1.56-in.) from bottom of skirt at right angles to piston pin . . . . 63.875-63.890 mm
2.5148-2.5153 in.
Piston to Cylinder
Clearance . . . . 0.120-0.130 mm
0.0047-0.0051 in.

SM21

Cylinder Bore
Diameter . . . . 64.000-64.015 mm
2.5197-2.5203 in.
Piston Skirt Diameter 39.5 mm (1.56-in.) from bottom of skirt at right angles to piston pin . . . . 63.875-63.890 mm
2.5148-2.5153 in.
Piston to Cylinder
Clearance . . . . 0.120-0.130 mm
0.0047-0.0051 in.

SM30

Cylinder Bore
Diameter . . . . 73.000-73.015 mm
2.8740-2.8746 in.
Piston Skirt Diameter 30.0 mm (1.18-in.) from bottom of skirt at right angles to piston pin . . . . 72.935-72.950 mm
2.8715-2.8720 in.
Piston to Cylinder
Clearance . . . . 0.060-0.070 mm
0.0024-0.0028 in.

SM40

Cylinder Bore
Diameter . . . . 65.000-65.015 mm
2.5591-2.5596 in.
Piston Skirt Diameter 26.0 mm (1.02-in.) from bottom of skirt at right angles to piston pin . . . . 64.935-64.950 mm
2.5565-2.5571 in.
Piston to Cylinder
Clearance . . . . 0.060-0.070 mm
0.0024-0.0028 in.

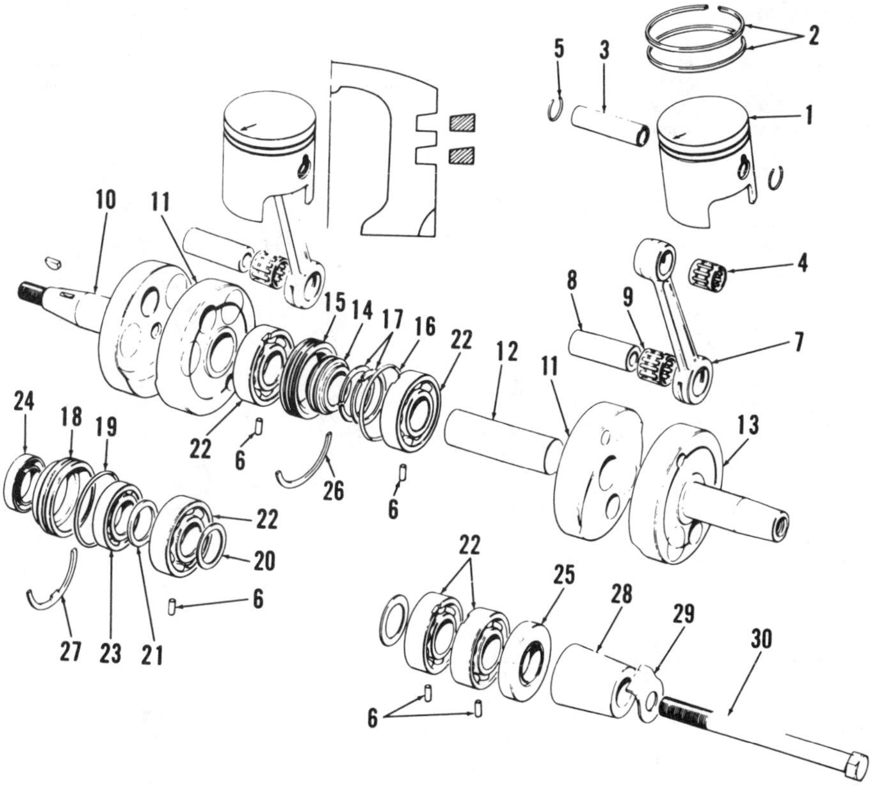

Fig. 10—Exploded view of typical two cylinder crankshaft assembly. Inset shows cross-section of piston and rings with top of grooves and rings angled.

1. Piston
2. Rings
3. Piston pin
4. Pin bearing
5. Retainer
6. Bearing locating pins
7. Connecting rod
8. Crank pin
9. Bearing
10. Magneto end of crankshaft
11. Center counterweights
12. Center main bearing journal
13. Output end of crankshaft
14. Center seal inner race
15. Center seal outer race
16. "O" ring
17. Center seal rings
18. Bearing and seal housing
19. "O" ring
20. Thrust washers (1 mm thick)
21. Thrust washer
22. Main bearings (5 used)
23. Main bearing (smaller)
24. Crankshaft seal
25. Crankshaft seal
26. Seal locating ring
27. Locating ring with tab
28. Collar
29. Lockwasher
30. Screw

Keystone type piston rings are used and must be installed in grooves with angled side toward top of piston. The top of ring is marked.

CAUTION: Use special care when cleaning ring grooves in piston to prevent damaging the grooves.

End gap of rings should be 0.2-0.4 mm (0.0079-0.0157 inch). The locating pins in ring grooves should be toward rear of engine when piston is installed.

CONNECTING RODS, CRANKSHAFT AND BEARINGS. Connecting rod big end bearing can be checked after removing cylinder and piston. Measure side shake of rod at top (piston pin) end of rod. If shake exceeds 3.0 mm (0.120 inch), renew connecting rod, crankpin and/or bearing. Crankshaft is a built-up (pressed together) assembly and must be carefully aligned before installing. Disassembly is not recommended unless experienced with this type of operation and special tools are available. After assembly crankshaft run-out should be checked at center main bearings and at both ends of crankshaft with crankshaft supported on the end main bearings next to counter-weights. Deflection must be less than 0.1 mm (0.0039 inch). Once crankshaft is correctly aligned, use care to prevent crankshaft from being knocked out of alignment while assembling. Spring loaded side of seals (24 & 25 – Fig. 10) should be toward inside.

On two cylinder models, end gaps of seal rings (17) used on center seal should be spaced 180 degress apart. If center main bearings or center seal is disassembled, install "O" rings (16) around outer seal race before pressing the assembly together.

On all models, be sure that dowel pins (6 – Fig. 9) are aligned with holes in main bearing races, before assembling case halves. Incorrect assembly will probably result in damage to crankshaft main bearings and crankcase. Lubricate all bearings and seals during assembly.

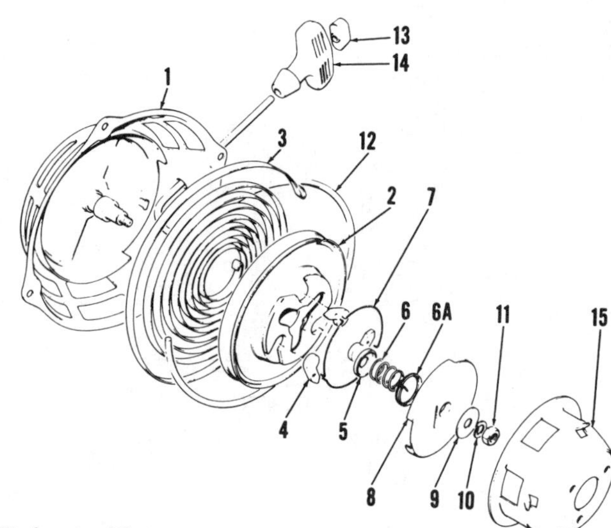

Fig. 12 – Exploded view of typical recoil starter. Recoil spring should be wound into housing, beginning at outside in counter-clockwise direction.

1. Housing
2. Pulley
3. Recoil spring
4. Pawls
5. Spring seat
6. Brake spring
6A. Drive plate spring
7. Link springs
8. Drive plate
9. Brake washer
10. Lockwasher
11. Nut
12. Rope
13. Anchor
14. Handle
15. Starter cup

RECOIL STARTER. Refer to Fig. 12. The starter must be removed and disassembled to renew rope and/or rewind spring. The rewind spring (3) should be wound into housing (1), beginning at outside and in counter-clockwise direction. Pawl springs (7) should engage holes in pawls (4). Preload the rewind spring enough to make certain that handle is pulled against housing when released.

ELECTRIC STARTER. Refer to Fig. 14. Length of brushes (3) is 12 mm (0.47 inch) when new. Renew brushes if less than 5 mm (0.20 inch) long. Standard commutator diameter is 28 mm (1.10 inch). Commutator diameter should not be less than 26 mm (1.02 inch) after resurfacing. The through bolts holding starter together should be tightened to 35-43 inch-pounds torque. The recesses (R) in screw (16) and pinion (15) should be toward end of starter shaft.

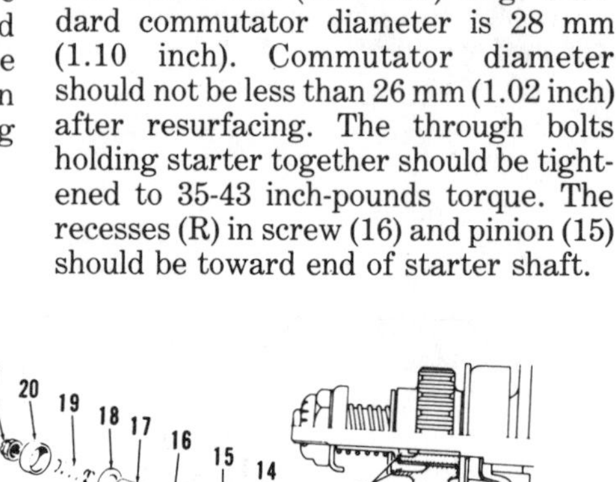

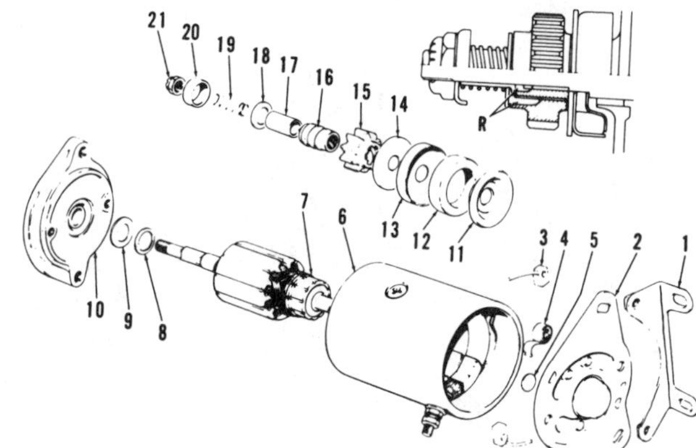

Fig. 14 – Exploded view of electric starter. Inset shows cross-section of pinion drive.

R. Recess
1. Bracket
2. Brush holder and end cover
3. Brushes
4. Brush springs
5. Spacer
6. Housing and field windings
7. Armature
8. Shims
9. Thrust washer
10. End plate
11. Stop plate
12. Cushion
13. Stop cup
14. Washer
15. Pinion
16. Screw
17. Spring sleeve
18. Washer
19. Spring
20. Spring cup
21. Nut

YAMAHA

YAMAHA MOTOR COMPANY
6555 Katella Avenue
Cypress, CA 90630

246 & 292 CC MODELS CONDENSED SERVICE DATA

<table>
<tr><th></th><th colspan="3">S246</th><th>R246</th></tr>
<tr><th>ENGINE MODEL</th><th>1974-1975</th><th>1977-1978</th><th>1979-1981</th><th>1982-1986</th></tr>
<tr><td>Bore – mm</td><td colspan="3">73</td><td>70</td></tr>
<tr><td>Inches</td><td colspan="3">2.874</td><td>2.756</td></tr>
<tr><td>Stroke – mm</td><td colspan="3">59</td><td>64</td></tr>
<tr><td>Inches</td><td colspan="3">2.323</td><td>2.520</td></tr>
<tr><td>No. of Cylinders</td><td colspan="3">1</td><td>1</td></tr>
<tr><td>Displacement – cc</td><td colspan="3">246.94</td><td>246.3</td></tr>
<tr><td>Cubic Inches</td><td colspan="3">15.07</td><td>15.03</td></tr>
<tr><td>Cooling Type</td><td colspan="4">Centrifugal Fan</td></tr>
<tr><td>Carburetor Type</td><td colspan="4">Keihin or Mikuni</td></tr>
<tr><td>Ignition:</td><td></td><td></td><td></td><td></td></tr>
<tr><td>Type</td><td colspan="2">E.T. Magneto</td><td>CDI</td><td>CDI</td></tr>
<tr><td>Point Gap – mm</td><td colspan="2">0.3-0.4</td><td>None</td><td>None</td></tr>
<tr><td>Inch</td><td colspan="2">0.012-0.016</td><td>None</td><td>None</td></tr>
<tr><td>Timing BTDC – mm</td><td colspan="2">1.7-1.9</td><td>1.1-1.3</td><td>1.5-1.7</td></tr>
<tr><td>Inch</td><td colspan="2">0.066-0.074</td><td>0.046-0.054</td><td>0.059-0.067</td></tr>
<tr><td>Spark Plug:</td><td></td><td></td><td></td><td></td></tr>
<tr><td>NGK</td><td>B-7HV</td><td>BR-8HV</td><td>B-8HS</td><td>BR-8HS</td></tr>
<tr><td>Electrode Gap – mm</td><td>0.4</td><td>0.5-0.6</td><td>0.5-0.6</td><td>0.6-0.7</td></tr>
<tr><td>Inch</td><td>0.016</td><td>0.020-0.024</td><td>0.020-0.024</td><td>0.024-0.028</td></tr>
<tr><td>Fuel:Oil Ratio</td><td colspan="4">"Autolube" oil injection and metering system</td></tr>
</table>

<table>
<tr><th>ENGINE MODEL</th><th>Y292</th><th>S292</th><th>SL292</th><th>GYT292</th><th>GP292</th><th>GS292</th></tr>
<tr><td>Bore – mm</td><td colspan="6">73</td></tr>
<tr><td>Inches</td><td colspan="6">2.874</td></tr>
<tr><td>Stroke – mm</td><td colspan="6">70</td></tr>
<tr><td>Inches</td><td colspan="6">2.756</td></tr>
<tr><td>No. of Cylinders</td><td colspan="6">1</td></tr>
<tr><td>Displacement – cc</td><td colspan="6">292.98</td></tr>
<tr><td>Cubic Inches</td><td colspan="6">17.88</td></tr>
<tr><td>Cooling Type</td><td colspan="6">Centrifugal Fan</td></tr>
<tr><td>Carburetor Type</td><td colspan="6">Mikuni or Keihin</td></tr>
<tr><td>Ignition:</td><td></td><td></td><td></td><td></td><td></td><td></td></tr>
<tr><td>Type</td><td colspan="6">Energy Transfer Magneto</td></tr>
<tr><td>Point Gap – mm</td><td colspan="6">0.3-0.4</td></tr>
<tr><td>Inch</td><td colspan="6">0.012-0.016</td></tr>
<tr><td>Timing Advance?</td><td colspan="6">Yes</td></tr>
<tr><td>Timing BTDC – mm</td><td colspan="6">2.3</td></tr>
<tr><td>Inch</td><td colspan="6">0.091</td></tr>
<tr><td>Spark Plug:</td><td></td><td></td><td></td><td></td><td></td><td></td></tr>
<tr><td>NGK</td><td>B6ES</td><td>.....</td><td>B7ES</td><td>B10EN</td><td>BR-8EV</td><td>BR-6ES</td></tr>
<tr><td>Champion</td><td>.....</td><td>N2G</td><td>......</td><td>......</td><td>.....</td><td>.....</td></tr>
<tr><td>Electrode Gap – mm</td><td colspan="6">0.3-0.4</td></tr>
<tr><td>Inch</td><td colspan="6">0.012-0.016</td></tr>
<tr><td>Fuel:Oil Ratio</td><td colspan="6">"Autolube" oil injection and metering system</td></tr>
</table>

MAINTENANCE

SPARK PLUG. Selection of spark plug will depend upon type of service and ambient temperature. Standard plug is given in CONDENSED SERVICE DATA tables. Excessively cold weather and/or light load conditions may require spark plugs of warmer heat range. Hard usage, heavy loads and warm weather may require spark plugs of colder heat range. NGK type B-10EN plug is recommended for 292 models equipped with G.Y.T. kit.

CARBURETOR. One carburetor is used. Idle mixture needle is located on right side, high speed mixture needle on left side.

For Mikuni diaphragm carburetors, initial setting is 3/4 turn open for idle mixture needle; 1 turn open for high speed mixture needle.

For all Keihin carburetors, initial setting for idle mixture is 1¼ turns open from lightly seated if specifications are not listed.

Adjust length of throttle cable so that carburetor throttle reaches wide open position at the same time the control lever contacts handlebar. If carburetor is removed, refer to Lubrication paragraphs for synchronizing the oil injection pump to carburetor opening.

The following lists some standard settings for specific carburetors.

R246-1982 and 1983
Carburetor Model ..... Keihin BD32-28
ID Mark 8R401
Main jet 108
Pilot air screw .... 1¼ turns open
Slow jet 78
Slow air jet 100
Float level .... 13-17 mm
Idle speed .... 1000-1200 rpm

R246-1984 and 1985
Carburetor Model ..... Keihin BD32-28
ID Mark .... 8V6-00 or 80F-00
Main jet 105
Pilot air screw .... 1¼ turns open
Slow jet 78
Slow air jet 100
Float level .... 13-17 mm
Idle speed .... 1000-1200 rpm

S246-1977
Carburetor Model .... Keihin CDX38-34
ID Mark 8F300
Main jet .... #130
Pilot air screw .... 1¼ turns open
Pilot jet .... #50
Fuel level .... 1.5-8.5 mm
Idle speed .... 1300 rpm

S246-1978, 1979, 1980 and 1981
Carburetor Model .... Keihin CDX38-32
ID Mark ..... 8G500, 8G501 or 8G511
Main jet .... #138
Pilot air screw .... 2 turns open
Pilot jet .... #50
Intermediate jet .... #38
Fuel level .... 1.5-8.5 mm
Idle speed .... 1300 rpm

GS292
Carburetor Model ..... Keihin CD34-30 (86700)
Main jet .... #125
Pilot air screw .... 5/8 turn open
Fuel level .... −5 to +2 mm
Idle speed .... 1100 rpm

GP292
Carburetor Model .. Mikuni BN38-34SH (89900)
Main jet .... #140
Pilot air screw .... 1⅜ turns open
Pilot jet .... #72.5
Idle speed .... 1300 rpm

IGNITION AND TIMING. For models with breaker points, gap should be adjusted to provide correct ignition timing. After adjustment, gap should be within range of 0.3-0.4 mm (0.012-0.016 inch). Breaker points should just open when piston is 1.7-1.9 mm (0.066-0.074 inch) Before Top Dead Center for S246 models; 2.3 mm (0.091 inch) BTDC for 292 cc models. Piston should be positioned using a dial indicator. Spark plug hole is angled on some models and adapter (1–Fig. 1) is required or cylinder head must be removed to correctly position piston for checking ignition timing. Ignition must be fully advanced when checking timing. On models with ignition advance, pull advance weight out as shown at (3) when checking.

Later models are equipped with Capacitor Discharge Ignition which is triggered by a pulser coil which is

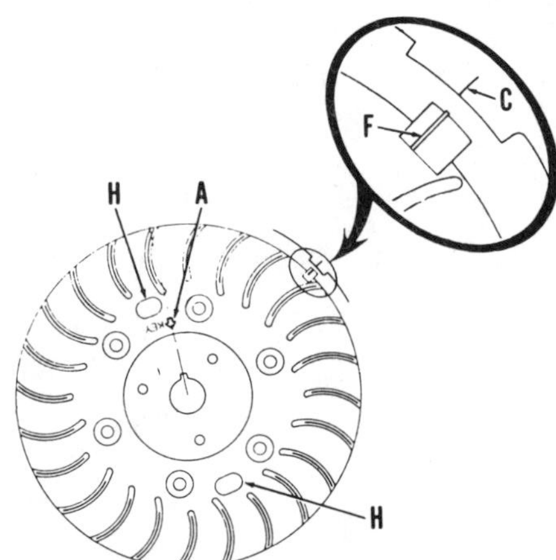

Fig. 2—View of C.D.I. timing marks (C&F). Mark (F) is on fan which should be attached to flywheel with arrow (A) pointing to flywheel keyway.

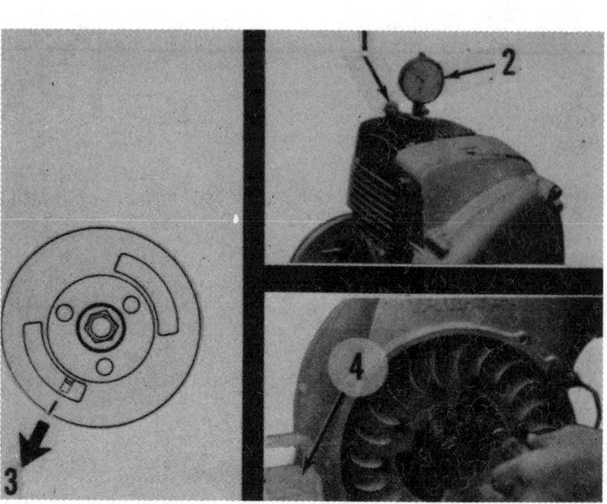

Fig. 1—Ignition breaker points should be adjusted to open when piston is at correct position BTDC. Adapter is shown at (1), dial indicator at (2), and direction to pull the advance weight at (3). Tester (4) should be used to indicate when breaker points just open.

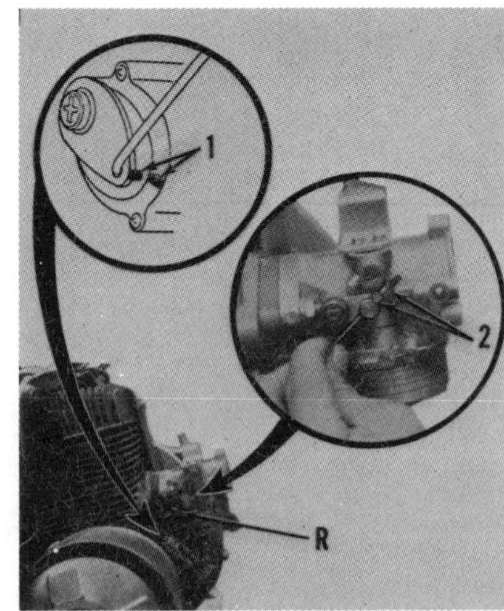

Fig. 3—On all models except R246, marks (1) on pump and lever should align when carburetor throttle is wide open. If incorrect, adjust at nuts (2).

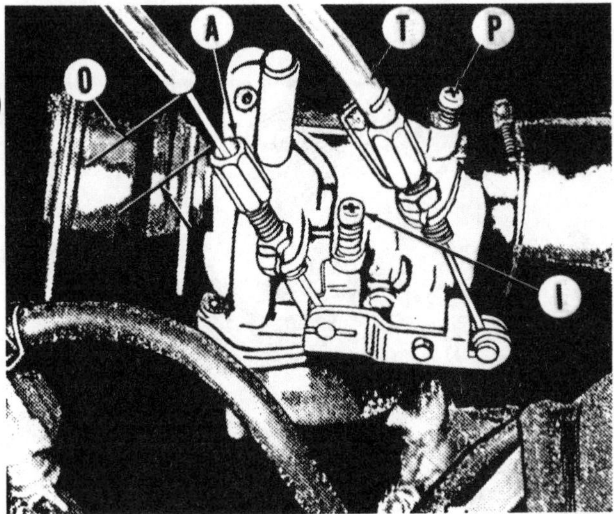

Fig. 4—View of Keihin float type carburetor showing play (O) in oil pump control cable. The oil pump cable must be pulled out of adjuster as far as possible and idler mixture screw (I) must be set correctly to provide 1000-1200 rpm. Pilot air screw is shown at (P) and throttle cable at (T).

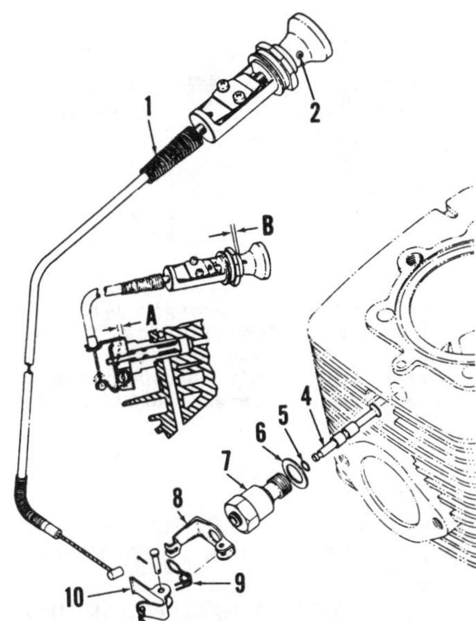

Fig. 7—Exploded view and cross-section of decompressor. Refer to text for adjusting clearances (A & B).

1. Adjustment spring
2. Set screw
4. Valve
5. "O" ring
6. Gasket
7. Valve body
8. Bracket
9. Spring
10. Lever

Fig. 5—Partially exploded view of belt driven oil injection pump used on some models. Pulley (15) and belt (16) are different on "G.Y.T. Kit" to provide more oil.

B. Bleed screw
1. Control rod
2. Adjusting nuts
3. Lever
4. Cover
5. Control shaft
6. Shims
7. Oil pump
8. Oil seal
9. Starter wheel
10. Check ball & spring
11. Drive shaft
12. Bushing
13. Bracket
14. Oil seal
15. Pulley
16. Drive belt
17. Wave washer
18. Washer
19. Snap ring
20. Nozzle
21. Adjusting plate

mounted on ignition stator plate. Ignition timing is checked using a power timing light with engine running at 1000-3000 rpm. Timing mark (C–Fig. 2) on crankcase and (F) on flywheel should be aligned when timing light flashes. Timing mark (F) is located on fan which is bolted to flywheel. If fan is separated from flywheel, be sure to align arrow (A) with keyway in flywheel as shown. Holes (H) are provided so that screws attaching ignition stator plate to crankcase can be loosened and tightened without removing flywheel. To change timing, stop engine, remove rewind starter and loosen stator attaching screws through holes (H). Move stator slightly, then tighten retaining screws. Recheck timing with engine running, using a power timing light. Timing marks should align at piston pistion indicated in CONDENSED SERVICE DATA.

Tighten flywheel nut to 71.5 N·m (53 ft.-lbs.) and the 6 mm cap screws which attach fan to flywheel to 6.9 N·m (60 in.-lbs.) torque. Use Loctite or equivalent on thread of fan to flywheel screws to prevent loosening.

LUBRICATION. A separate oil tank and metering system ("Autolube") is used. The system delivers varying amounts of oil depending upon engine rpm and throttle setting (load).

Oil delivery, on all models except R246, is controlled by rod (R–Fig. 3) attached to carburetor throttle. To check or adjust, open throttle completely and check marks (1). If marks (1) are not exactly aligned adjust length of rod by turning nuts (2).

Oil delivery on R246 model is controlled by cable (C–Fig. 13) attached to pump control cam at one end and carburetor throttle lever at other end. To check adjustment, pull oil pump control cable away from adjuster as shown at (0–Fig. 4). With carburetor at idle and oil pump cable pulled to maximum, distance from end of cable to adjuster should be 24-26 mm. If adjustment is in-

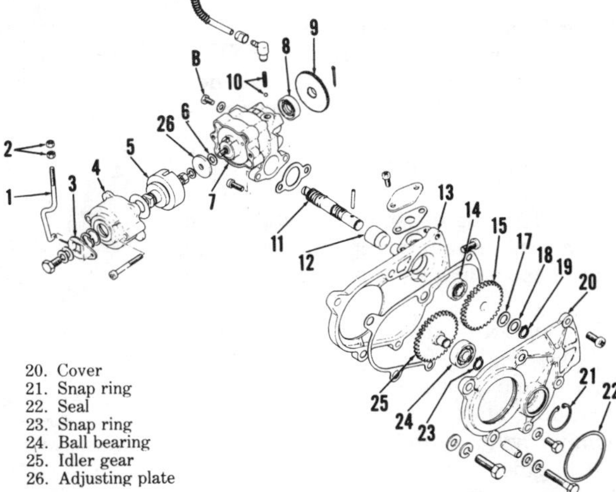

Fig. 6—Partially exploded view of gear driven oil injection pump used on some models. Gear pressed on crankshaft drives idler (25) which drives gear (15). Bleeder screw is shown at (B).

1. Control rod
2. Adjusting nuts
3. Lever
4. Cover
5. Control shaft
6. Shims
7. Oil pump
8. Oil seal
9. Starter wheel
10. Check ball & spring
11. Drive shaft
12. Bushing
13. Housing
14. Seal
15. Gear
17. Wave washer
18. Thrust washer
19. Snap ring
20. Cover
21. Snap ring
22. Seal
23. Snap ring
24. Ball bearing
25. Idler gear
26. Adjusting plate

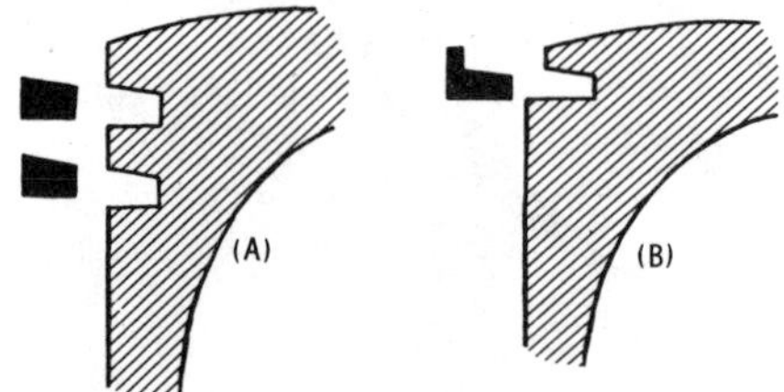

Fig. 8—Cross sectional view of pistons showing piston ring configuration. (A) shows the two Semi-Keystone rings used on some models. (B) shows the L-Type Semi-Keystone ring configuration used on some performance models and kits.

correct, loosen locknut, turn adjuster (A) until distance (0) is correct, then tighten locknut.

Some models are equipped with belt (16–Fig. 5) which drives oil pump. If drive belt is used, inspect condition frequently. Install new belt if condition is questionable to prevent loss of lubrication and subsequent engine damage. Engines equipped with G.Y.T. kit use smaller pulley (15) and shorter belt, which increases oil delivery. Be sure that correct belt is installed. Procedure for adjusting control rod is the same as outlined in previous paragraph regardless of G.Y.T. kit installation.

On all models, minimum and maximum plunger stroke of the oil injection pump is adjusted by varying the number of shims (6–Fig. 5 or Fig. 13). Adding shims will increase stroke. Be sure to mark lever (3–Fig. 5) and pump control shaft (5) to facilitate reassembly. Pump stroke is measured between large washer (adjuster plate) and guide pulley. Pump can be actuated for checking stroke by turning wheel (9) or shaft at this end. Correct minimum stroke is 0.20-0.25 mm for all models. Maximum plunger stroke can be measured after turning control cam to maximum output position. Maximum plunger stroke should be 1.85-2.05 mm for all S246 models; 1.65-1.87 mm for R246 models and all 292 cc models. Oil pump color code is gray on 1974 and 1975 S246 models; green on 1977 through 1981 S246 models and pink on R246 models.

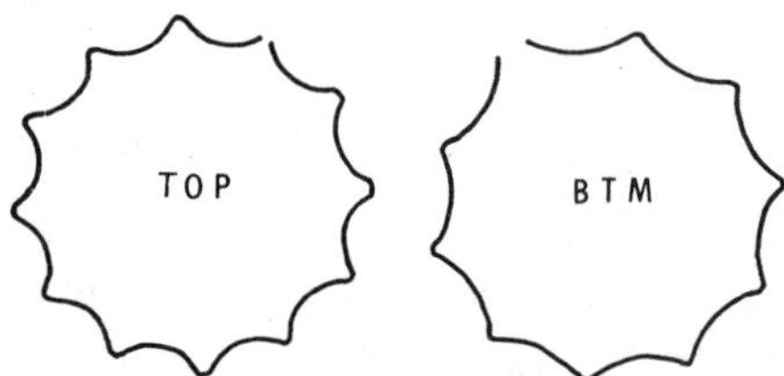

Fig. 9—Cross sectional view of spring-type ring expanders showing means of identification. Note the sharper radius of expander arch on top expander.

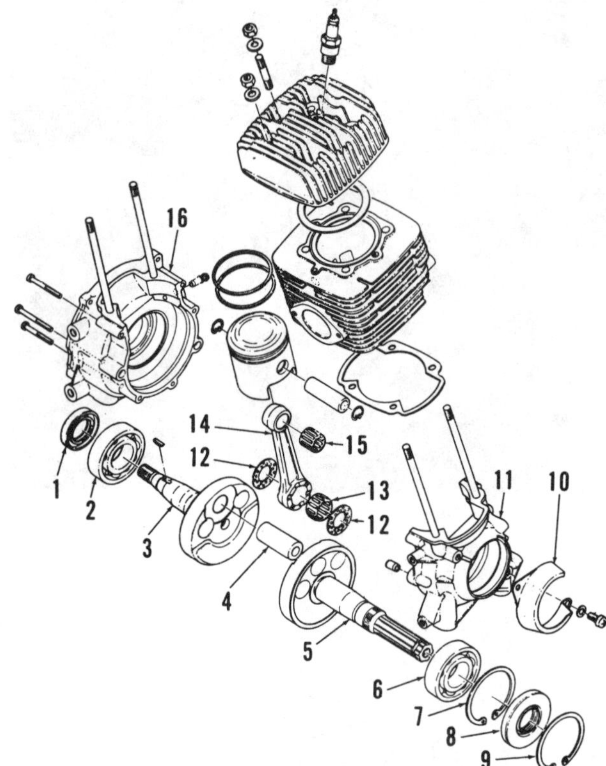

Fig. 10—Exploded view of 292 cc engine. Bearings (2 & 6) are the same. S246 models are similar.

1. Seal
2. Main bearing
3. Crankshaft (magneto end)
4. Crankpin
5. Crankshaft (output end)
6. Main bearing
7. Snap ring
8. Seal
9. Snap ring
10. Shield
11. Crankcase half (output side)
12. Thrust washers
13. Crankpin bearing
14. Connecting rod
15. Piston pin bearing
16. Crankcase half (magneto side)

DECOMPRESSOR. On models so equipped, the decompressor cable should be adjusted so that with control knob pulled out, clearance (A–Fig. 7) between lever (10) and bracket (8) is 1/32-inch. Adjustment is accomplished by turning cable housing spring (1). After clearance (A) is adjusted, push knob in to close decompressor valve and check clearance (B) between knob and housing. Knob must not contact housing and clearance (B) should be 1/16-inch. If incorrect, loosen set screw (2) and relocate knob.

NOTE: The decompressor should only be used to assist starting.

REPAIRS

All Models Except R246

DISASSEMBLY AND REASSEMBLY. The cylinder head, cylinder, piston, rings and piston pin bearing can be serviced without removal of flywheel or disassembling crankcase.

CAUTION: Be especially careful to prevent anything from falling into crankcase, if crankcse halves are not to be separated.

To separate crankcase halves, first remove engine from vehicle. Remove drive pulley, recoil starter, flywheel, magneto stator plate, fan housing, cylinder head, cylinder, piston, oil pump and engine mounting bracket. Remove the seven screws attaching crankcase halves together, then use recommended special tool to separate crankcase halves and to remove crankshaft from main bearings.

CAUTION: The crankshaft can be easily damaged by not using method shown in Fig. 11.

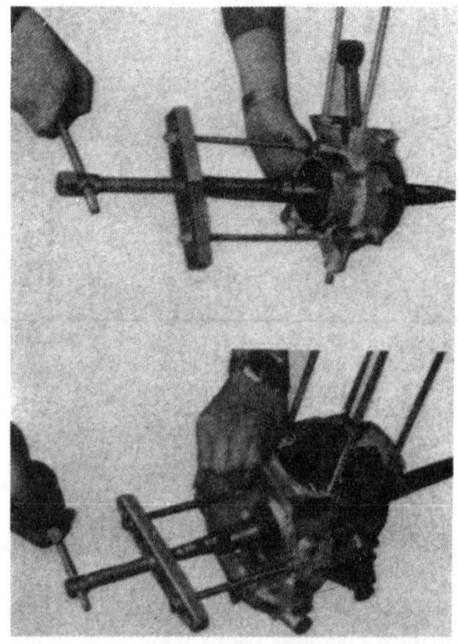

Fig. 11—A puller should be used to withdraw crankshaft from main bearings on all models with vertically split crankcase. The lower view shows use of puller installed on magneto side pushing crankshaft out of main bearing and separating crankcase halves.

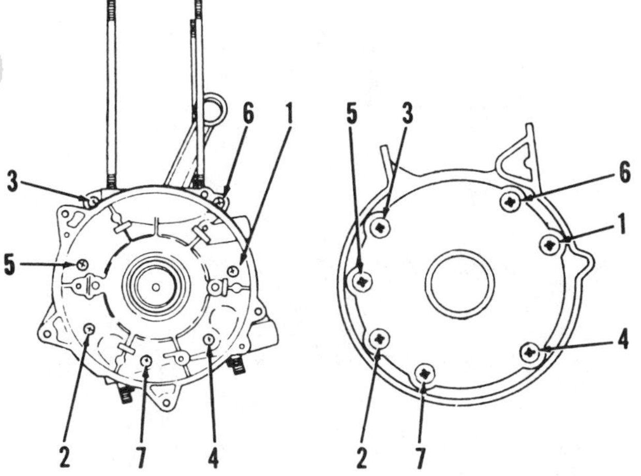

Fig. 12—Views showing tightening sequence for models with vertically split crankcase.

When assembling, the crankshaft and main bearings should be **pulled** into crankcase halves.

CAUTION: Main bearings fit tightly and crankshaft can be easily damaged if improperly installed. Special Yamaha tool is available for pulling crankshaft and bearings into position. Mating surfaces of crankcase halves should be coated with an appropriate sealer such as "YAMAHA BOND No. 5". If special puller is not available for assembling crankshaft and crankcase halves, heat the crankcase halves enough to allow easy installation. Tighten crankcase screws in sequence shown in Fig. 12 to 8.8 N·m (78 in.-lbs.).

When installing cylinder and cylinder head, first tighten the retaining stud nuts to 19.6 N·m (174 in.-lbs.), then to final torque of 24.5 N·m (216 in.-lbs.).

PISTON, PIN, RINGS AND CYLINDER. If cylinder bore taper or out-of-rounds exceeds 0.05 mm (0.002 inch), cylinder should be rebored oversize or renewed and new piston installed. Piston to cylinder clearance should be 0.045-0050 mm (0.0018-0.002 inch) for all models before 1981 (ET250E). Piston to cylinder clearance for 1981 (ET250E) models should be 0.050-0.055 mm (0.0020-0.0022 inch). When checking clearance, measure piston 10 mm (0.4 inch) above bottom of skirt at right angles to piston pin on all models. The piston pin should be a snug thumb press fit in piston. Ring end gap should be 0.3-0.5 mm (0.012-0.020 in). for all 246 cc models, 0.35-0.55 mm (0.014-0.022 in.) for 292 models. The rings are Semi-Keystone type with top angled as shown in Fig. 8. Top ring may be marked "1N" or "1T" and lower ring may be marked "2N" or "2T". Both rings may be equipped with spring-type expanders; refer to Fig. 9 for identification and note that top expander can be identified by the sharper radius of the expander arch. Use extreme care when cleaning ring grooves. All carbon must be removed, but gouges or scratches on lands (especially at bottom) can result in pressure leakage. Oil-based mineral solvents can assist in loosening some hard carbon deposits but degreasing solvents can sometimes remove absorbed oil and harden the deposit. Arrow on top of piston should point toward exhaust side of crankcase when piston is installed.

CRANKSHAFT AND CRANKCASE. The main bearings (2 & 6–Fig. 10) are a tight fit in crankcase bores and on main journals. Refer to DISASSEMBLY AND REASSEMBLY section for use of special tools used for servicing. The crankshaft and connecting rod assembly is a pressed together unit. Service of this unit should be attempted only by qualified personnel with proper equipment for disasssembly, reassembly and checking. Condition of crankpin bearing (13) can be checked by measuring side play (shake) of rod at piston pin end. Desired shake of piston pin end of rod is 0.8-1.0 mm (0.032-0.04 inch). If side shake exceeds 2.0 mm (0.080 inch), crankpin (4), connecting rod (14), thrust washers (12) and/or bearing (13) should be renewed. Side clearance of rod, measured between thrust washer and crankshaft web should be 0.25-0.75 mm (0.010-0.030 in). Crankshaft alignment should be checked by locating crankshaft between lathe centers and measuring deflection of main journals. Deflection should be less than 0.02 mm (0.0008 inch). After assembly, distance between crankshaft webs (shoulder for main bearing inner races) should be 55.95-56.0 mm.

R246 Models

DISASSEMBLY AND REASSEMBLY. The integral cylinder and cylinder head can be removed without separating crankcase halves or removing engine. To separate crankcase halves, first, remove engine from vehicle. Remove drive pulley and oil injection pump gear box from left side of engine. Remove recoil starter, flywheel and magneto stator from right side of engine. Remove cylinder assembly and piston from top, then invert engine and detach engine mounting bracket. Remove screws and separate crankcase halves.

Position crankshaft, main bearings, seals and bearing support in upper crankcase half. Oil bearings and seals. Be sure open side of the nylon bearing support (25–Fig. 13) is toward front. Locate lip of seals and bearing support

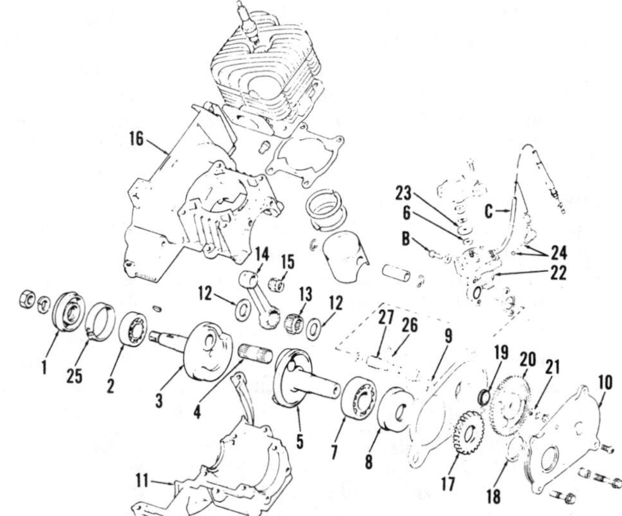

Fig. 13—Exploded view of R246 engine and oil injection pump drive.

C. Injection pump cable
1. Seal
2. Main bearing
3. Crankshaft
4. Crankpin
5. Crankshaft
6. Adjusting shim
7. Main bearing
8. Seal
9. Housing
10. Cover
11. Crankcase lower half
12. Thrust washer
13. Bearing
14. Connecting rod
15. Bearing
16. Crankcase upper half
17. Pump drive gear
18. Seal
19. Seal
20. Driven gear
21. Wave washer
22. Oil pump
23. Adjusting plate
24. Check ball & spring
25. Bearing support
26. Drive pin
27. Wormshaft

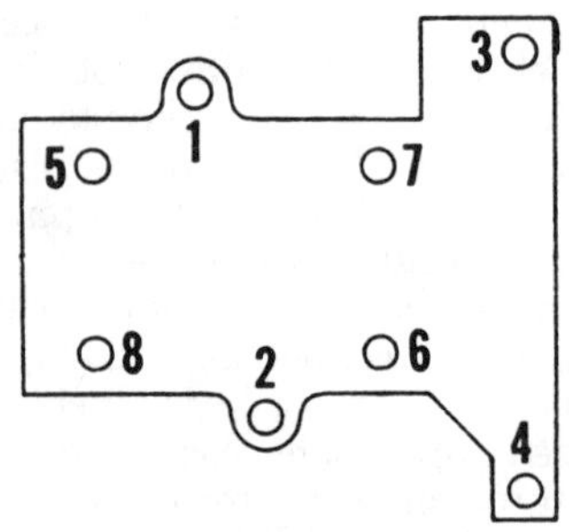

Fig. 14—Tighten crankcase screws in sequence shown on R246 models with horizontally split crankcase.

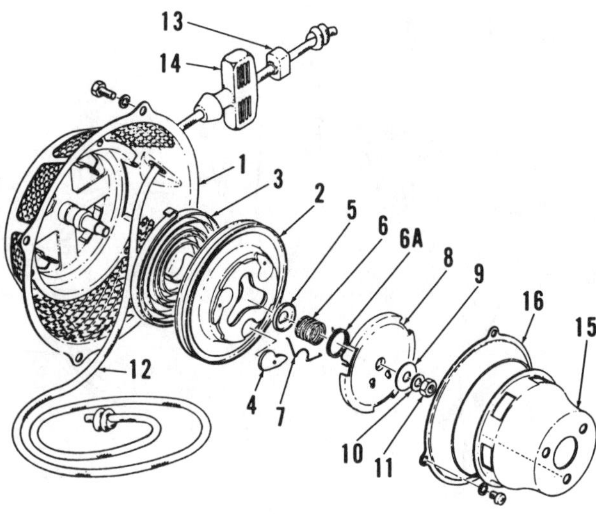

Fig. 15—Exploded view of recoil starter typical of early models. Rewind spring (3) should be wound into housing (1), beginning at outside in counterclockwise direction.

1. Housing
2. Pulley
3. Rewind spring
4. Pawls
5. Spring seat
6. Brake spring
6A. Drive plate spring
7. Link springs
8. Drive plate
9. Brake washer
10. Lockwasher
11. Nut
12. Rope
13. Anchor
14. Handle
15. Starter cup
16. Cover

properly in crankcase. Coat mating surface of crankcase upper half with "YAMAHA BOND No. 4" or equivalent and install lower case half. Install the four crankcase assembly screws and tighten to 14.7 N•m (130 in.-lbs.) torque. The clamp for wires is located under rear screw at flywheel (right) side of crankcase. Attach the engine mounting bracket to bottom of crankcase and tighten the four screws to 19.6 N•m (174 in.-lbs.) initial torque. Use the sequence shown in Fig. 14 and tighten screws (1, 2, 3 & 4) to final torque of 14.7 N•m (130 in.-lbs.); screws (5, 6, 7 & 8) to final torque of 24.5 N•m (217 in.-lbs.). Screws which attach rubber engine mounts should be tightened to 29 N•m (260 in.-lbs.) torque and nuts should be tightened to 13.7 N•m (121.5 in.-lbs.) torque.

Tighten the four screws which attach cylinder to crankcase first to 19.6 N•m (174 in.-lbs.) torque, then to final torque of 24.5 N•m (217 in.-lbs.) using a criss-cross pattern. Tighten flywheel nut to 71.6 N•m (53 ft.-lbs.) and the 6 mm cap screws which attach fan to flywheel to 6.9 N•m (60 in.-lbs.) torque. Use Loctite or equivalent on threads of fan to flywheel screws to prevent loosening.

PISTON, PIN, RINGS AND CYLINDER. The cast iron cylinder bore should not be tapered more than 0.05 mm (0.0020 in.) nor out-of-round more than 0.01 mm (0.0004 in.). Oversize pistons are available and cylinder may be resized to provide correct clearance by qualified machinist using proper resizing equipment. An offset bit and other special precautions are necessary to prevent damaging the upper (combustion chamber) end of cylinder.

Piston skirt diameter should be measured 10 mm from bottom of piston at right angles to piston pin. Clearance between piston skirt and cylinder should be 0.045-0.050 mm (0.0018-0.0020 in.). The top piston ring is Semi-Keystone type, while second ring is plain type. Be careful when cleaning ring grooves. All carbon must be removed from grooves, but nicks, burrs, scratches, etc., in grooves can result in leakage. Oil-based mineral solvents can assist in loosening some hard carbon deposits, but degreasing solvents can sometimes remove absorbed oil and harden the deposit. Ring end gap should be 0.20-0.40 mm (0.0078-0.016 in.). Arrow on piston crown should point toward exhaust when installed on connecting rod.

CRANKSHAFT AND CRANKCASE. Refer to DISASSEMBLY AND REASSEMBLY paragraphs for separating crankcase halves and removing crankshaft. Clean crankcase with mild solvent and dry thoroughly. Check crankcase for cracks, nicks, burrs or other damage that could cause leakage. Inspect oil delivery passages in transfer ports for blockage.

Check main bearings for smooth free rotation. The oil pump drive gear (17–Fig. 13) must be removed before seal (8) or left side main bearing (7) can be removed. If oil pump drive gear is withdrawn from crankshaft, new gear should be pressed on. Manufacturer's marks on main bearings (2 & 7) should be toward outer ends of crankshaft when installed. Lubricate bearings and seals during assembly to ensure adequate initial lubrication. Closed side of seals with manufacturer's identification should be toward outer ends of crankshaft.

Condition of connecting rod crankpin bearing (13) and related parts can be checked by measuring side shake of rod at uppermost (piston pin) end. Side shake should be less than 2 mm (0.079 in.). Side clearance between lower end of connecting rod, thrust washers (12) and crankshaft halves (3 & 5) should be within limits of 0.25-0.75 mm (0.010-0.030 in.). Side clearance can be measured with feeler gage, but should not be adjusted except during assembly of connecting rod and crankshaft. The crankshaft and connecting rod assembly is a pressed together unit and service of this unit should only be attempted by qualified personnel with proper equipment for disassembly, reassembly and checking. Crankshaft alignment should be checked with crankshaft supported at main bearings and measuring deflection at extreme ends of main journals. Deflection should be less than 0.02 mm (0.0008 in.). Assembled width of crankshaft measured between outer sides of crankshaft counterweights should be 55.95-56.00 mm (2.203-2.205 in.).

RECOIL STARTER. Refer to Fig. 15 or Fig. 16. The starter must be re-

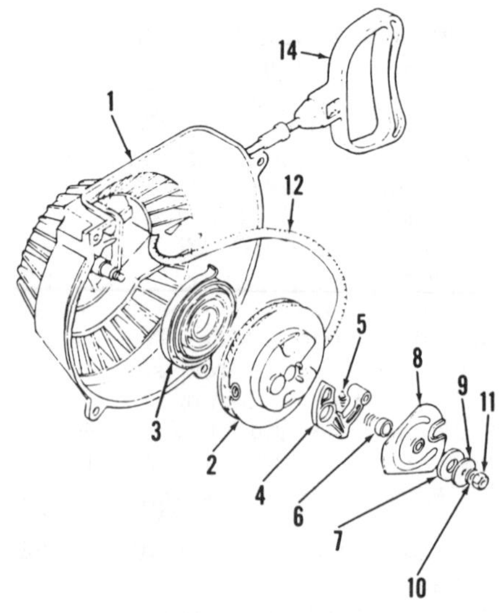

Fig. 16—Exploded view of late type recoil starter.

1. Housing
2. Pulley
3. Rewind spring
4. Drive pawl
5. Return spring
6. Drive plate spring
7. Friction washer
8. Drive plate
9. Thrust washer
10. Lockwasher
11. Nut
12. Rope
14. Handle

moved and disassembled to renew rope and/or rewind spring. The rewind spring (3) should be wound into housing (1), beginning at outside and in counter-clockwise direction. Pawl springs (7–Fig. 15) should engage holes in pawls (4). Preload rewind spring enough (4-5 turns) to make certain that handle in pulled against housing when released. On later (Fig. 16) models, tighten nut (11) to approximately 12.75 N•m (113 in.-lbs.) torque.

SPEED TUNING

292 cc Models

Any change from the original can possibly decrease service life of the engine, can narrow the performance band; and if carelessly done can decrease power and cause extensive engine damage. Normal tuning such as ignition timing, point gap, fuel mixture, lubrication, etc., will become more critical with modification. It should also be noted that gearing changes may be necessary in order to make the fullest use of the modified engine.

The listed specifications include only those modifications made by the factory on their performance models.

CYLINDER PORTS. Fig. 17 shows a schematic view of cylinder ports (not to scale). Refer to table on following page for specification data. All dimensions are in millimeters.

Cylinder liner material is cast iron in all models but the free air SR Kit uses a special cylinder and 8-stud cylinder head.

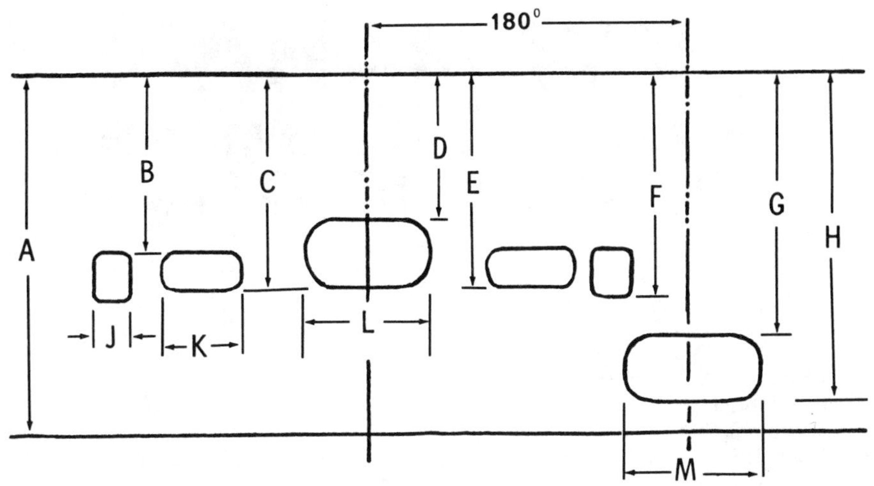

Fig. 17—Schematic view of cylinder port arrangement (not to scale). Refer to tables for measurements.

Model	SL292A	SL292B	GYT292	GP292	SS Kit	SR Kit
A–Cylinder depth	120	120	120	120	120	120
B–Transfer port height	56.5	56.5	56	56	56	56
C–Bottom, Exh. Port.	71	71	71	71	71	72
D–Exhaust Port Height	44.5	44.5	41	41	41	40
E–Bottom, Trfr. Port.	71	71	71	71	71	71
F–Bottom, Fifth Port	78	78	78	78	78	78
G–Inlet Port Height	79	79	78	78	78	78
H–Bottom, Inlet Port	104.5	104.5	106	106	106	106
J–Fifth Port Width	17	17	17	17	17	17
K–Trfr Port Width	24	24	24	24	24	24
L–Exhaust Port Width	47	47	47	49	49	53
M–Intake Port Width	46	46	48	49	49	49

CYLINDER HEAD. All models use 0.5 mm copper cylinder head gasket. Compression ratio (actual) and cylinder head volume are as follows:

Compression Ratio
- SL292A 6.6:1
- SL292B 6.6:1
- GYT292 . . . . 6.2:1
- GP292 . . . . 6.5:1
- SS Kit 6.5:1
- SR Kit 6.6:1

Cylinder Head Volume
- SL292A . . . . 38.5 cc
- SL292B . . . . 38.5 cc
- GYT292 . . . . 38 cc
- GP292 . . . . 34 cc
- SS Kit . . . . 34 cc
- SR Kit . . . . 33.2 cc

PISTON AND RINGS. Standard piston to cylinder clearances (0.045-0.05 mm) are used on all engines. Models SL292A & B use an aluminum piston with two Semi-Keystone type rings as shown in left-hand view, Fig. 8. The GYT292 modified version uses the regular SL piston with only the top ring installed. Model GP292 Standard and all modifications use a one-ring piston with a modified L-Type ring as shown in right-hand view of Fig. 8. No piston modification is performed on factory tuned performance models.

CARBURETORS. The following carburetors are installed on factory standard and performance-tuned models:
- SL-292A & B . . . . Mikuni BN 38-34
- GYT292 . . . . Mikuni BN 44-40
- GP292 & SS Kit . . . . . . Keihin CD 42-38
- SR Kit . . . . Keihin CD 50-43

EXHAUST PIPE. Stock parts are used on all factory standard and performance tuned models; parts numbers are as follows:

- SL292A . . . . 812-14710-01 combined muffler
- SL292B . . . . 822-14710-00 combined muffler
- GYT292 . . . . 812-14710-70 expansion chamber
- GP292 . . . . 823-14710-00 combined muffler
- SS Kit . . . . 823-14710-70 expansion chamber
- SR Kit . . . . 823-14610-70 expansion chamber

YAMAHA
294 cc Two Cylinder Models
CONDENSED SERVICE DATA

Engine Model	E294
Bore-(mm)	56
Inches	2.20
Stroke-(mm)	59.6
Inches	2.35
No. of Cylinders	2
Displacement-(cc)	293.6
Cubic Inches	17.92
Cooling Type	
Carburetor Model	Mikuni B38-32 (1)
Ignition:	
Type	C.D.I.
Timing BTDC–	
Piston position (mm)	1.3-1.5*
Inch	0.051-0.059*
Spark Plug:	
NGK type	BR-9ES
Electrode Gap-(mm)	0.7-0.8
Inch	0.028-0.031
Fuel/Oil Ratio	"Autolube" oil injection

*On 1983-1984 models, ignition timing BTDC is 1.5-1.7 mm (0.059-0.067 in.).

MAINTENANCE

SPARK PLUGS. Spark plugs used should be NGK BR-9ES or equivalent. Electrode gap should be 0.7-0.8mm (0.028-0.031 in.).

CARBURETOR. One Mikuni B38-32 float type carburetor with butterfly throttle is used. Normal setting for the pilot air screw (P–Fig. 1) should be 1½ turns open from lightly seated. Engine idle speed should be 1600 rpm. Main jet standard size is #210, pilot jet standard size is #90 and float height should be 24-26 mm (0.94-1.02 in.). After idle speed is correctly adjusted, throttle cable should have 0.5-1.0 mm (0.02-0.04 in.) free play. If carburetor is removed, refer to LUBRICATION paragraphs for synchronizing the oil injection pump to carburetor opening.

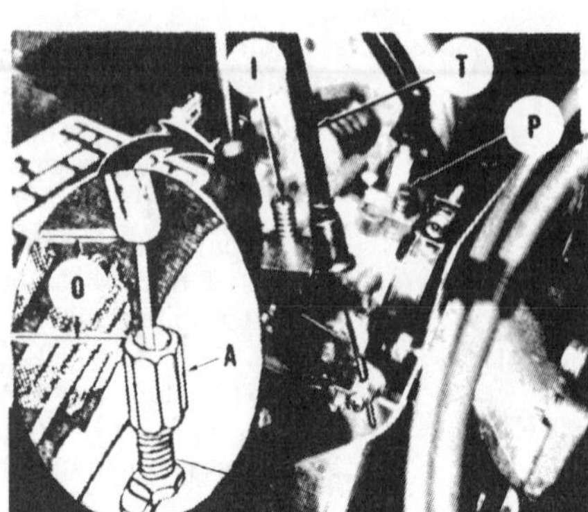

Fig. 1 — View of carburetor showing play (O) in oil pump control cable. The oil pump cable must be pulled out of adjuster as far as possible to check free play. Idle mixture screw (I) must be set correctly to provide 1600 rpm.

IGNITION AND TIMING. All models are equipped with Capacitor Discharge Ignition which is triggered by a pulser coil which is mounted on ignition stator plate. Ignition timing is checked using a power timing light connected to left cylinder high tension lead with engine running at 1000-3000 rpm. Timing mark (C–Fig. 2) on crankcase and (F) on flywheel should be aligned when timing light flashes. Timing mark (F) is located on fan which is bolted to flywheel. If fan is separated from flywheel, be sure to align arrow (A) with keyway in flywheel as shown. Holes (H) are provided so that screws attaching ignition stator plate to crankcase can be loosened and tightened without removing flywheel. To change timing, stop engine, remove rewind starter and loosen stator attaching screws through holes (H). Move stator slightly, then tighten retaining screws. Recheck timing with engine running, using a power timing light. Timing marks should align when piston is positioned at 1.3-1.5 mm (0.051-0.059 in.) BTDC on 1980-1981 model and 1.5-1.7 mm (0.059-0.067 in.) BTDC on 1983-1984 models.

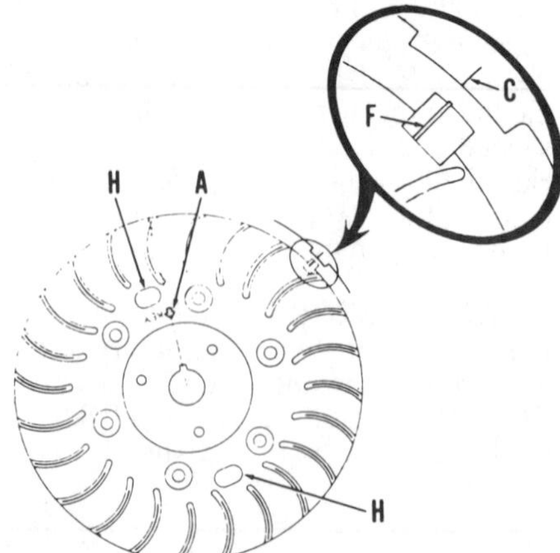

Fig. 2 — View of C.D.I. timing marks (C & F). Mark (F) is on fan which should be attached to flywheel with arrow (A) pointing to flywheel keyway.

Tighten flywheel nut to 71.6 N·m (53 ft.-lbs.) and the 6 mm cap screws which attach fan to flywheel to 6.9 N·m (60 in.-lbs.) torque. Use "Loctite" or equivalent on thread of fan to flywheel screws to prevent loosening.

Ignition components may be checked on vehicle using a suitable ohmmeter. To ensure accurate ohmmeter readings, component temperature should be 20° C (68° F) and all wires to component disconnected.

Ignition coil primary resistance is measured between orange wire and coil ground while secondary resistance is measured between high tension wires and coil ground. On Hitachi CM62-21 ignition coils, primary resistance should be 0.135-0.165 ohms and secondary resistance should be 2800-4200 ohms. On Toyodenso YW-51 ignition coils, primary resistance should be 0.108-0.132 ohms and secondary resistance should be 3200-4800 ohms.

Pulser coil resistance is measured between white/red wire and black (ground) wire. Pulser coil resistance should be 8-10 ohms on 1980-1981 models and 13.6-16.6 ohms on 1983-1984 models.

On 1980-81 models, two charging coils are used and resistance is measured between the black (ground) wire and brown or light blue wire from each coil. Resistance should be 315-385 ohms between brown wire and ground and 13.5-16.5 ohms between light blue wire and ground.

On 1983-1984 models one charging coil is used. Resistance is measured between black (ground) wire and brown wire and should be 531-649 ohms.

The lighting coil is not part of the ignition system, but can be checked with ohmmeter attached to ground and the yellow wire. Correct resistance should be 0.17-0.21 ohms.

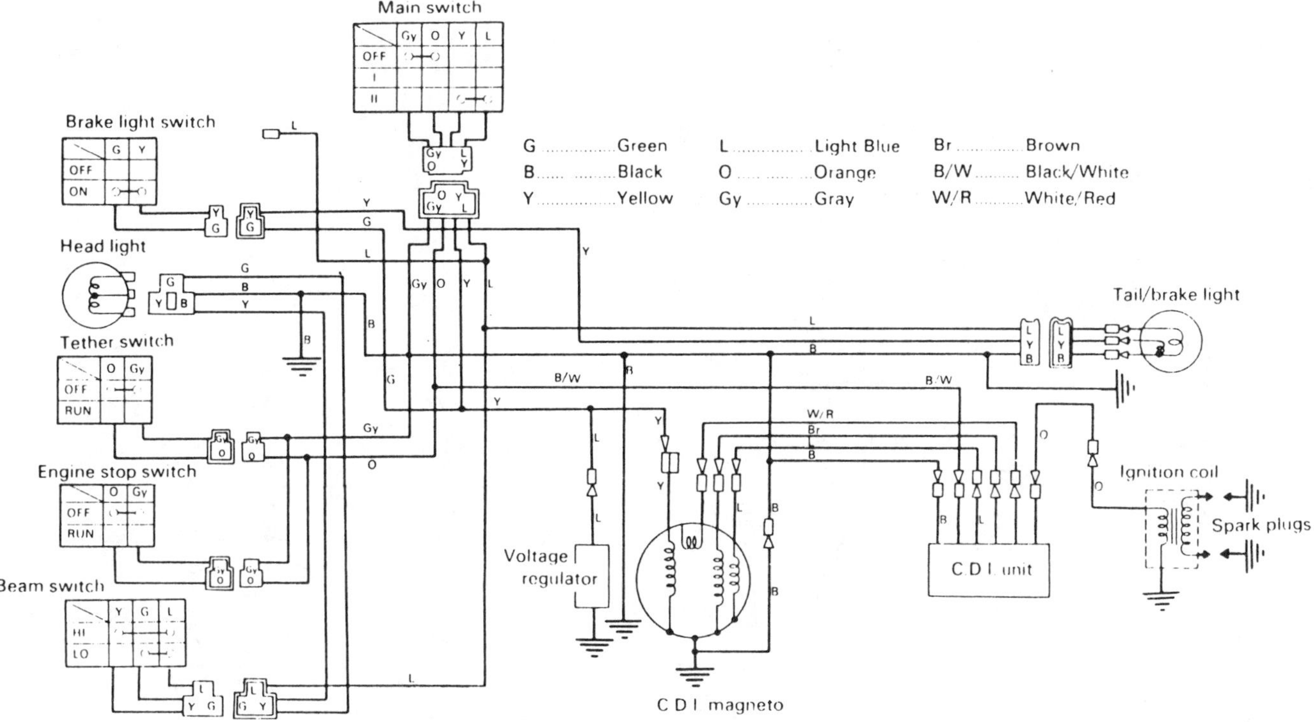

Fig. 3—Wiring diagram typical of early models. Later models are similar.

LUBRICATION. A separate oil tank and metering system ("Autolube") is used. The system delivers varying amounts of oil depending upon engine rpm and throttle setting (load).

Oil delivery is controlled by cable (C–Fig. 5) attached to pump control cam at one end and carburetor throttle lever at other end. To check adjustment, pull oil pump control cable away from adjuster as shown at (O–Fig. 1). With carburetor at idle and oil pump cable pulled to maximum, distance from end of cable to adjuster should be 24-26 mm (0.95-1.02 in.). If adjustment is incorrect, loosen locknut, turn adjuster (A) until distance (O) is correct, then tighten locknut.

Minimum and maximum plunger stroke of the oil injection pump is adjusted by varying the number of shims (6–Fig. 5). Adding shims will increase stroke. Pump stroke is measured between large washer (adjuster plate) and guide pulley. Correct minimum stroke is 0.20-0.25 mm (0.008-0.010 in.) for all models. Maximum plunger stroke can be measured after turning control cam to maximum output position. Maximum plunger stroke should be 1.65-1.87 mm (0.065-0.075 in.). Oil pump color code is blue.

REPAIRS

DISASSEMBLY AND REASSEMBLY. The cylinder heads, cylinders, pistons, rings and piston pin bearings can be serviced without removal of flywheel or disassembling crankcase.

CAUTION: Be especially careful to prevent anything from falling into crankcase, if crankcase halves are not to be separated.

To separate crankcase halves, first remove engine from vehicle. Remove drive pulley and oil injection pump gear box from left side of engine. Remove recoil starter, flywheel and magneto stator from right side of engine. Remove cylinder heads, cylinders and piston from top, then invert engine and detach engine mounting bracket. Remove screws and separate crankcase halves.

Position crankshaft, main bearings, seals and bearing support in upper crankcase half. Oil bearings and seals. Half ring (28–Fig. 5) should be in groove of crankcase and groove in bearing (7). Pins (29) in main bearings (2, 7 and 31) and center labyrinth (30) must properly engage holes in upper crankcase half. Also, be sure that seals (1 and 8) properly engage grooves before assembling lower crankcase half. Coat mating surface of crankcase upper half with "YAMAHA BOND No. 4" or equivalent and install lower case half. Install the ten crankcase assembly screws and tighten to initial torque of 9.8 N·m (87 in.-lbs.) in sequence shown in Fig. 6, then check crankshaft for smooth free rotation. Any bending should be corrected and may be caused by one or more of the pins (29) not correctly engaging holes in upper crankcase half. Tighten crankcase screws in sequence shown in Fig. 6 to final torque of 19.6 N·m (173.6 in.-lbs.). Check crankshaft again for rotation and correct if not smooth and free.

Attach the engine mounting bracket to bottom of crankcase and tighten the four screws to 29.4 N·m (21.7 ft.-lbs.) torque.

When installing cylinder and cylinder head, tighten the retaining stud nuts evenly to final torque of 24.5 N·m (216 in.-lbs.).

Coat gasket surfaces of intake manifold with "Three Bond #50" or equivalent and install new gaskets. Tighten 6 mm intake manifold screws to 9.8 N·m (87 in.-lbs.) torque and 8 mm screws to 10.8 N·m (95 in.-lbs.) torque. Tighten exhaust pipe screws to 9.8 N·m (87 in.-lbs.) torque and air shroud to 5.9 N·m (52 in.-lbs.) torque. Tighten oil pump drive case mounting screws and recoil starter mounting screws to 9.8 N·m (87 in.-lbs.) torque.

Tighten flywheel nut to 71.6 N·m (53 ft.-lbs.) and the 6 mm cap screws which attach fan to flywheel to 6.9 N·m (60 in.-lbs.) torque. Use "Loctite" or equivalent on threads of fan to flywheel screws to prevent loosening and be sure that arrow is aligned with keyway in flywheel as shown in Fig. 2.

PISTON, PIN, RINGS and CYLINDER. If cylinder bore taper exceeds 0.05 mm (0.002 in.) or if out-of-round exceeds 0.001 mm (0.0004 in.), cylinder should be rebored oversize or renewed and new piston installed. Piston to cyl-

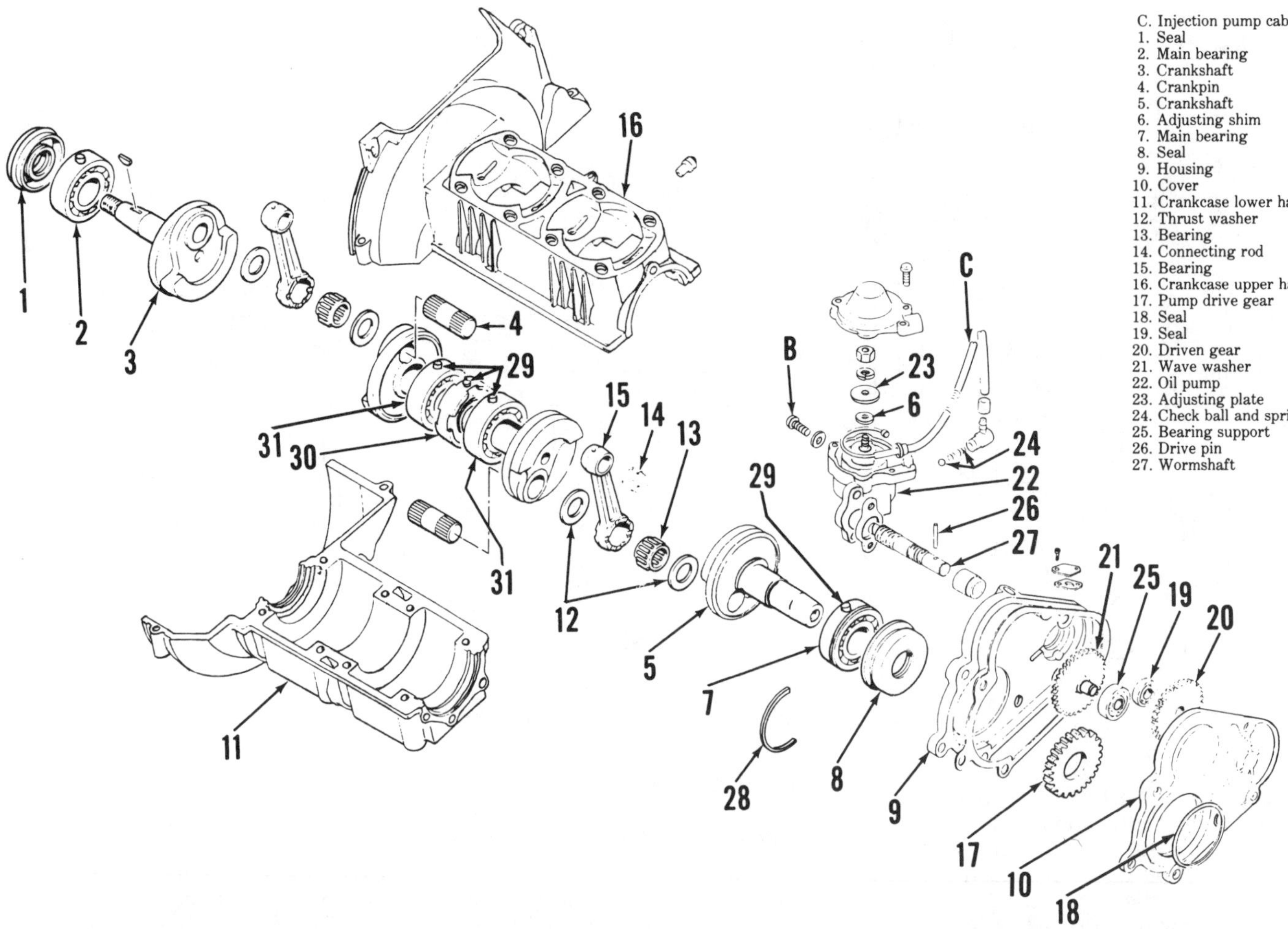

C. Injection pump cable
1. Seal
2. Main bearing
3. Crankshaft
4. Crankpin
5. Crankshaft
6. Adjusting shim
7. Main bearing
8. Seal
9. Housing
10. Cover
11. Crankcase lower half
12. Thrust washer
13. Bearing
14. Connecting rod
15. Bearing
16. Crankcase upper half
17. Pump drive gear
18. Seal
19. Seal
20. Driven gear
21. Wave washer
22. Oil pump
23. Adjusting plate
24. Check ball and spring
25. Bearing support
26. Drive pin
27. Wormshaft

Fig. 5 — Exploded view of crankcase and oil injection pump drive. Parts shown are not E294 model, but are similar.

inder clearance should be 0.040-0.045 mm (0.0016-0.0018 inch). When checking clearance, measure piston 10 mm (0.4 inch) above bottom of skirt at right angles to piston pin on all models. The piston pin should be a snug thumb press fit in piston. Ring end gap should be 0.3-0.5 mm (0.012-0.020 in.) for both rings.

Use extreme care when cleaning ring grooves. All carbon must be removed, but gouges or scratches on lands (especially at bottom) can result in pressure leakage. Oil-based mineral solvents can assist in loosening some hard carbon deposits but degreasing solvents can sometimes remove absorbed oil and harden the deposit. Arrow on piston crown should point toward exhaust side of crankcase and ring end gaps should be toward inlet side.

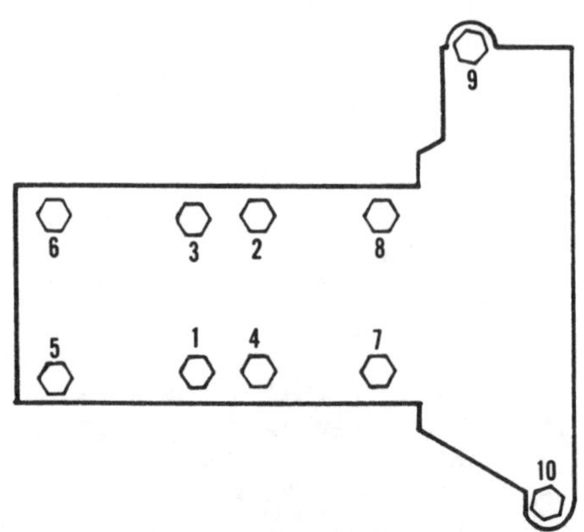

Fig. 6 — Tighten crankcase screws in sequence shown when assembling.

CRANKSHAFT AND CRANKCASE. Refer to **DISASSEMBLY AND REASSEMBLY** paragraphs for separating crankcase halves and removing crankshaft. Clean crankcase with mild solvent and dry thoroughly. Check crankcase for cracks, nicks, burrs or other damage that could cause leakage. Inspect oil delivery passages in transfer ports for blockage.

Check main bearings for smooth free rotation. The oil pump drive gear (17 – Fig. 5) must be removed before seal (8) or left side main bearing (7) can be removed. If oil pump drive gear is withdrawn from crankshaft, new gear should be pressed on. Manufacturer's marks on main bearings (2, 7 and 31) should be toward outer ends of crankshaft when installed. Lubricate bearings and seals during assembly to assure adequate initial lubrication. Closed side of seals with manufacturer's identification should be toward outer ends of crankshaft.

Condition of connecting rod crankpin bearing (13) and related parts can be checked by measuring side shake of rod at uppermost (piston pin) end. Side shake should be less than 2 mm (0.079 in.). Side clearance between lower end of connecting rod, thrust washers (12) and crankshaft thrust surfaces should be within limits of 0.25-0.75 mm (0.010-0.030 in.). Side clearance can be measured with feeler gage, but should not be adjusted except during assembly of connecting rod and crankshaft. The crankshaft and connecting rod assembly is a pressed together unit and service of this unit should only be attempted by qualified personnel with proper equipment for disassembly, reassembly and checking. Crankshaft alignment should be checked with crankshaft supported at outer main bearings (2 & 7) and measuring deflection at extreme ends of main journals and at center bearings (31). Deflection should be less than 0.03 mm (0.0012 in.) at ends; less than 0.04

mm (0.0016 in.) at center main bearings. Assembled width of crankshaft measured between sides of crankshaft counterweights for one cylinder should be 51.95-52.00 mm (2.045-2.047 in.). Assembled width of crankshaft outer sides of the complete crankshaft should be 159.9-160.1 mm (6.295-6.313 in.).

RECOIL STARTER. Refer to Fig. 7. The starter must be removed and disassembled to renew rope and/or rewind spring. The rewind spring (3) should be wound into housing (1), beginning at outside and in counter-clockwise direction. Preload rewind spring enough (4-5 turns) to make certain that handle is pulled against housing when released. Tighten nut (11) to approximately 12.75 N·m (113 in.-lbs.) torque.

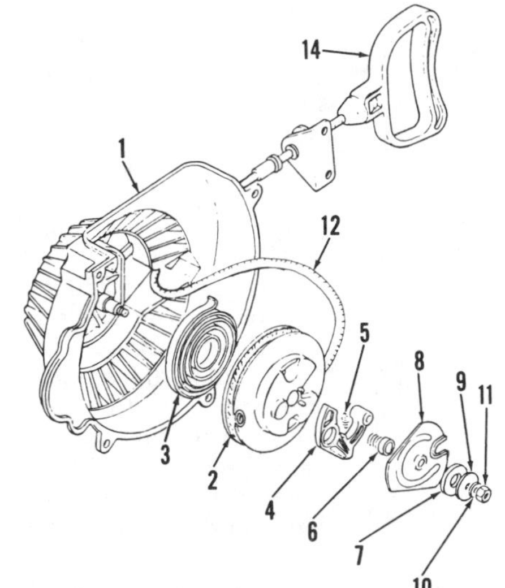

Fig. 7—Exploded view of typical rewind starter.

1. Housing
2. Pulley
3. Rewind spring
4. Drive pawl
5. Return spring
6. Drive plate spring
7. Friction washer
8. Drive plate
9. Thrust washer
10. Lockwasher
11. Nut
12. Rope
14. Handle

YAMAHA

348 cc Models

CONDENSED SERVICE DATA

Engine Model	**801 & 802**
Bore—(mm)	61
Inches	2.402
Stroke—(mm)	59.6
Inches	2.35
No. of Cylinders	2
Displacement—(cc)	348
Cubic Inches	21
Horsepower @ RPM:	
Standard, SL-350	20@6000
Standard, SL-351	23@6000
GYT	35@6750
Cooling Type	Centrifugal Fan
Carburetor Model	Mikuni VM26SC or VM26X†
Number Used	2
Ignition:	
Type	Energy Transfer Magneto
Point Gap	See Text
Timing Advance?	No
Timing BTDC (mm)	1.7-1.9
Inch	0.067-0.075
Spark Plug:	
NGK	B7H, B7HZ
Electrode Gap (mm)	0.5-0.6
Inch	0.020-0.024
Fuel/Oil Ratio	20:1*

†Engines used on Sno-Jet models are equipped with Tillotson carburetors. The carburetor kit installed on some Yamaha models, includes one Keihin diaphragm carburetor and "Y" inlet manifold.

*If not equipped with "Autolube"

MAINTENANCE

SPARK PLUGS. Selection of spark plugs will depend upon type of service, ambient temperature and horsepower of engine. For normal use in original engines, NGK type B7H, B7HZ or equivalent spark plugs can be used. If a GYT Kit is installed, a colder spark plug such as NGK type B9HC is recommended. Excessively cold weather and/or light load conditions may require spark plugs of warmer heat range. Higher horsepower, warm weather and/or hard usage may require spark plugs of colder heat range.

CARBURETORS. Various carburetors have been used. Refer to the appropriate carburetor paragraphs in FUNDAMENTALS section for service. For adjustment of carburetor and "Autolube" linkage, refer to the appropriate following paragraphs.

MIKUNI SLIDE CARBURETORS. Both carburetors must be synchronized and adjusted equally to provide identical throttle opening and mixture for each of the two cylinders. Refer to Fig. 1 and proceed as follows:

Back out the two idle speed stop screws (1) to allow both throttle slides (S) to completely close. Loosen locknuts (2) and turn each adjusting screw (3) until slack is removed from cables.

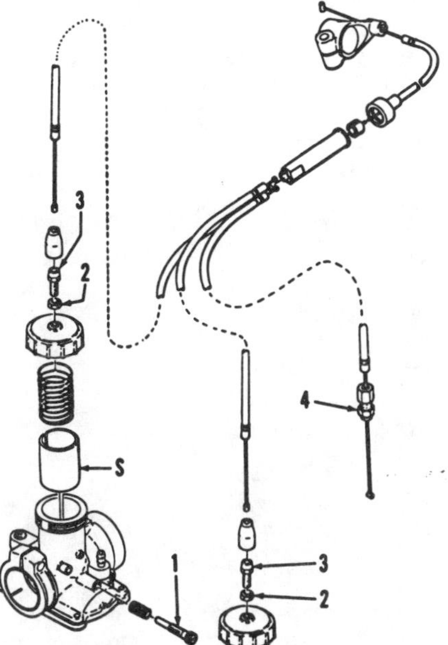

Fig. 1–Schematic view of throttle linkage showing points of adjustment.

2. Locknut
3. Adjusting screw
4. Autolube adjusting screw
S. Throttle slide
1. Idle speed stop screws

Check to see that both throttle slides move out of air horns at the same time when throttle is opened (See Fig. 2). Make minor adjustments as required. With throttle cables adjusted, turn each throttle adjusting screw (1—Fig. 1) in to its stop then back out 3¾ turns to provide the approximate idle setting. NOTE: Some slack (about 1/32 inch) should now exist in throttle cables in idle position.

With throttle linkage set as indicated, check "Autolube" pump cable adjustment with throttle at slow idle position. Guide pin should align with V-mark on adjusting pulley as shown in Fig. 7. Pin should not bottom in pulley slot with throttle at idle or fully open. Adjustment is accomplished by turning cable adjuster (4—Fig. 1), after loosening the lock nut. Be sure to tighten lock nut after adjustment is correct.

KEIHIN DIAPHRAGM CARBURETOR. A carburetor kit is installed on some models and includes one Keihin diaphragm carburetor, "Y" type inlet manifold, crankcase cover plate (fuel pump is built into carburetor) and ignition diode assembly (to eliminate backfiring). Since only one carburetor is used, linkage adjustment is limited to synchronizing the "Autolube" oil injection to the carburetor throttle. The guide pin should align with "V" mark on adjusting pulley as shown in Fig. 7, when carburetor throttle is closed. Pin should not bottom in pulley slot with throttle at idle or completely open. Adjustment is accomplished by turning adjuster on the "Autolube" control cable (similar to 4—Fig. 1), after loosening lock nut. Be sure to tighten lock nut after adjustment is correct.

TILLOTSON DIAPHRAGM CARBURETOR. The throttle cable should be adjusted to permit complete opening and closing of the carburetor throttle valve. On Sno-Jet models originally equipped with Tillotson diaphragm carburetor, engine is lubricated by oil mixed with the fuel and engine is not equipped with "Autolube" oil injection.

FUEL PUMP. On models equipped with Keihin and Tillotson diaphragm carburetors, the fuel pump is integral with the carburetor. On models with Mikuni slide (float type) carburetors, a diaphragm type fuel pump is located on side of crankcase below carburetor at magneto end. The fuel pump is actuated by pressure and vacuum pulsations in crankcase for the magneto end cylinder. The fuel pump is held together by six screws, the one screw which goes into crankcase passage MUST have a fiber washer under the screw head. If engine backfires into crankcase, the fuel pump may be damaged. Silicon stack (diode) part number 806-82390-20 is available to eliminate backfiring. Diaphragm and check valves should be checked carefully. New gaskets should be installed when unit is disassembled. Refer to Fig. 3. Filter should be inspected periodically and cleaned or renewed as required.

IGNITION AND TIMING. Breaker point gap should be adjusted to provide correct engine timing. Use a dial indicator and suitable continuity tester and adjust both sets of points to the exact recommended 1.8 mm piston position before top dead center. Timing for both cylinders must be synchronized to within 0.03 mm of each other. Fig. 4 shows an exploded view of magneto unit.

NOTE: Do not attempt to set breaker points except as described in previous paragraph.

LUBRICATION. On models without "Autolube", the engine is lubricated by SAE 20 (or SAE 30) 2-stroke, air cooled engine oil, mixed with the fuel. Normal ratio is 20:1. On models with "Autolube" a separate oil tank and metering type pump is used. Refer to the "Autolube" section which follows.

"AUTOLUBE". The Yamaha "Autolube" is an automatically metering, engine lubricating system. A separate oil tank and oil pump with metering unit and delivery nozzle is used. SAE 20 oil designed for use in 2-stroke air cooled engines is recommended. In emergencies, SAE 10W/30 automotive oil may be used. The automatic metering system varies the fuel to oil mixture form 16:1 at full throttle to approximately 120:1 at idle, no load.

If the "Autolube" system is drained or the pump unit is renewed, the air should be bled from the system by removing screw (5—Fig. 9) and turning "starter" plate (4) until oil runs freely

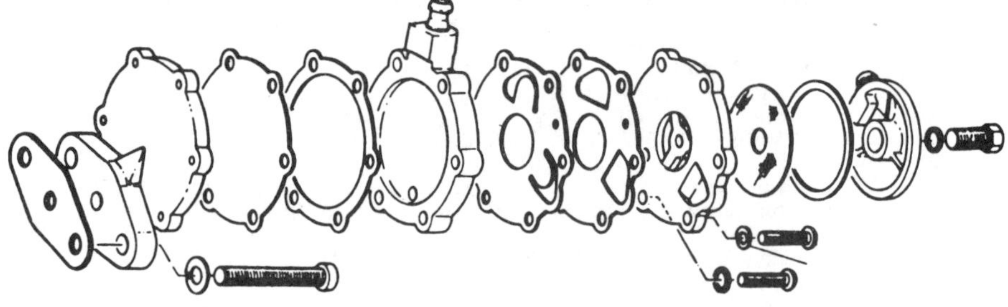

Fig. 3–Exploded view of diaphragm type fuel pump.

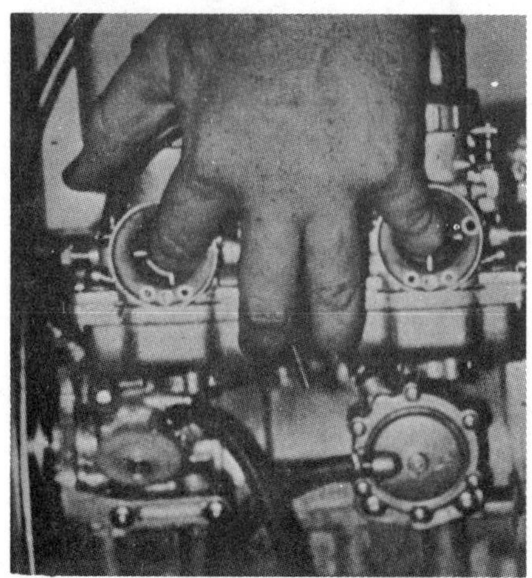

Fig. 2–Feel both throttle slides to be sure they open at the same time when throttle is opened.

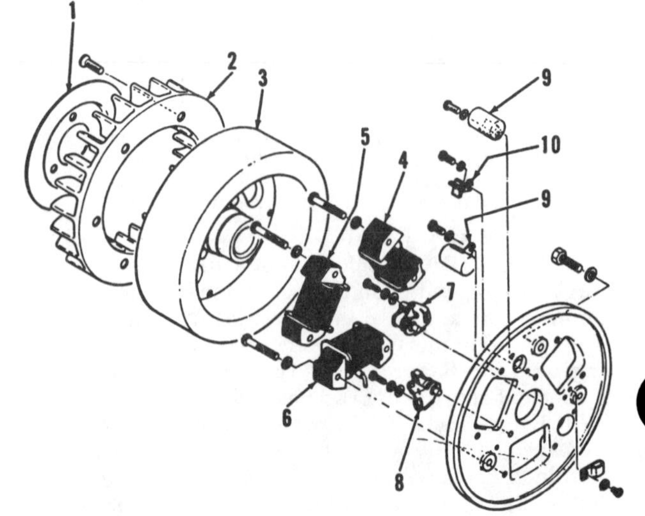

Fig. 4–Exploded view of typical flywheel magneto assembly.

1. Hole cover
2. Fan
3. Flywheel
4. Lighting coil
5. Coil source (R.H.)
6. Coil source (L.H.)
7. Contact points (L.H.)
8. Contact points (R.H.)
9. Condenser
10. Lubricator

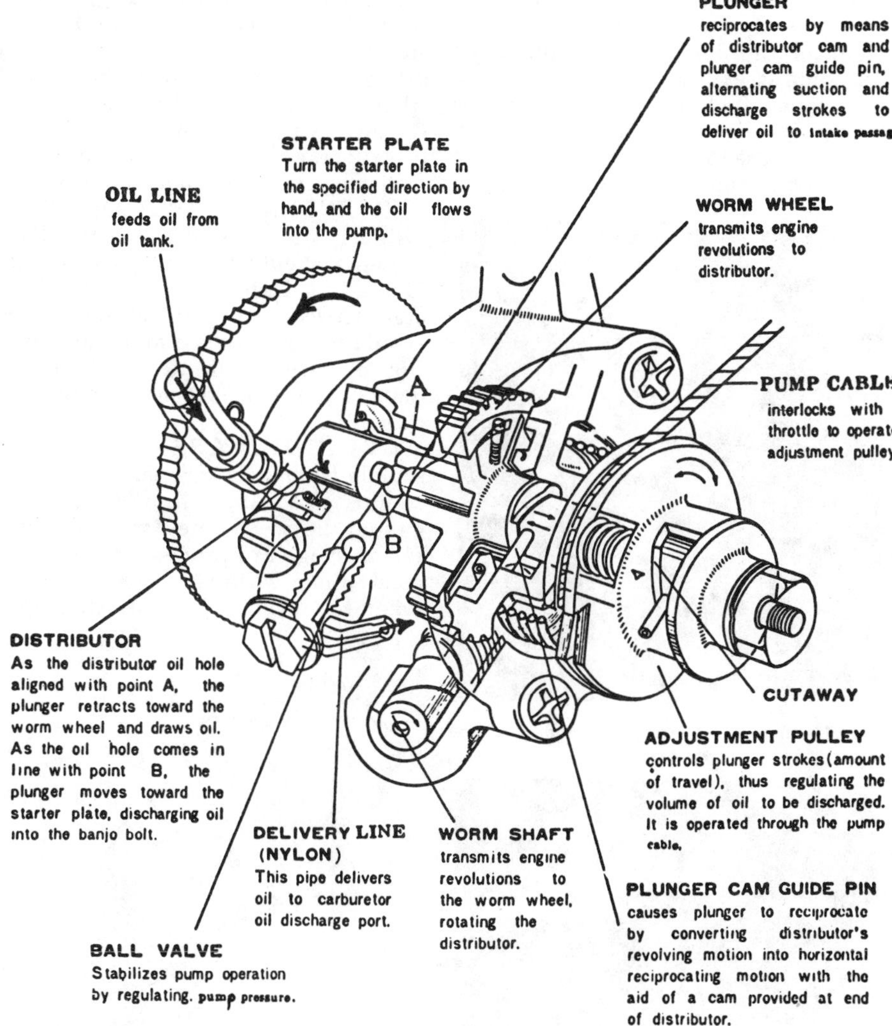
PLUNGER
reciprocates by means of distributor cam and plunger cam guide pin, alternating suction and discharge strokes to deliver oil to intake passage.
STARTER PLATE
Turn the starter plate in the specified direction by hand, and the oil flows into the pump.
OIL LINE
feeds oil from oil tank.
WORM WHEEL
transmits engine revolutions to distributor.
PUMP CABLE
interlocks with throttle to operate adjustment pulley.
A
B
DISTRIBUTOR
As the distributor oil hole aligned with point A, the plunger retracts toward the worm wheel and draws oil. As the oil hole comes in line with point B, the plunger moves toward the starter plate, discharging oil into the banjo bolt.
CUTAWAY
ADJUSTMENT PULLEY
controls plunger strokes (amount of travel), thus regulating the volume of oil to be discharged. It is operated through the pump cable.
DELIVERY LINE (NYLON)
This pipe delivers oil to carburetor oil discharge port.
WORM SHAFT
transmits engine revolutions to the worm wheel, rotating the distributor.
PLUNGER CAM GUIDE PIN
causes plunger to reciprocate by converting distributor's revolving motion into horizontal reciprocating motion with the aid of a cam provided at end of distributor.
BALL VALVE
Stabilizes pump operation by regulating pump pressure.

Fig. 5–Yamaha "Autolube" pump and metering unit typical of all models.

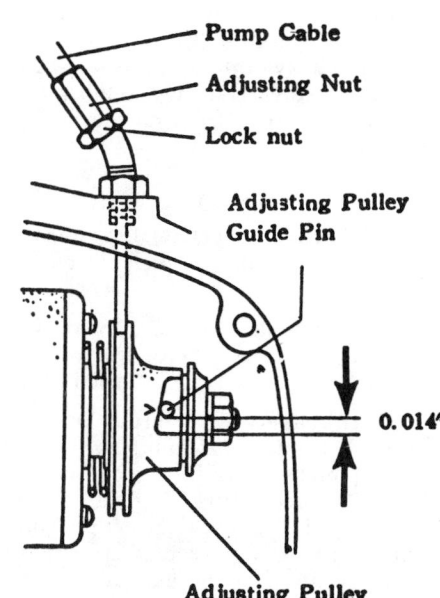

Pump Cable
Adjusting Nut
Lock nut
Adjusting Pulley Guide Pin
0.014"
Adjusting Pulley

Fig. 7–Guide pin and mark on adjusting pulley should be aligned when throttles are closed.

Fig. 8–Worm wheel (Fig. 5) should be installed as shown over pin in distributor shaft.

from the bleed hole, then reinstalling bleed screw.

To adjust the oil metering system, first adjust the engine idle speed. Check minimum plunger stroke by turning starter plate (Fig. 5) until clearance (A—Fig. 6) between adjusting pulley and adjusting plate is at its maximum. Clearance (A) should be 0.22-0.26 MM (0.0086-0.0102 in.) for all models. If clearance is incorrect, add or deduct adjusting washers shown in Fig. 6. Adjust pump cable to align mark on adjusting pulley with guide pin as shown in Fig. 7 with throttle closed. Open throttle fully and make certain guide pin is not touching end of notch. If it is touching, take up slack in throttle cable, and readjust pump cable length.

Fig. 9 shows an exploded view of "Autolube" pump body and associated parts. Only the seals (1 & 2) are available for service. Seal (1) can be renewed by unbolting and removing adjusting plunger cover (3), and seal (2) after removing starter plate (4). No additional disassembly is advisable or recommended.

Adjust pulley
A
Guide pin
Adjust plate
Lock nut
Wave washer
Adjusting washer
Plunger

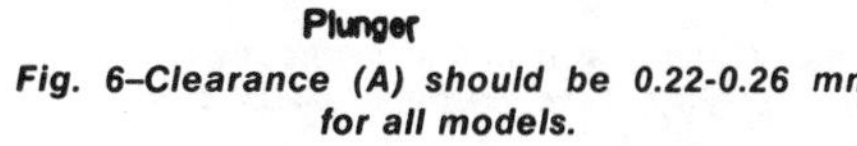

Fig. 6–Clearance (A) should be 0.22-0.26 mm for all models.

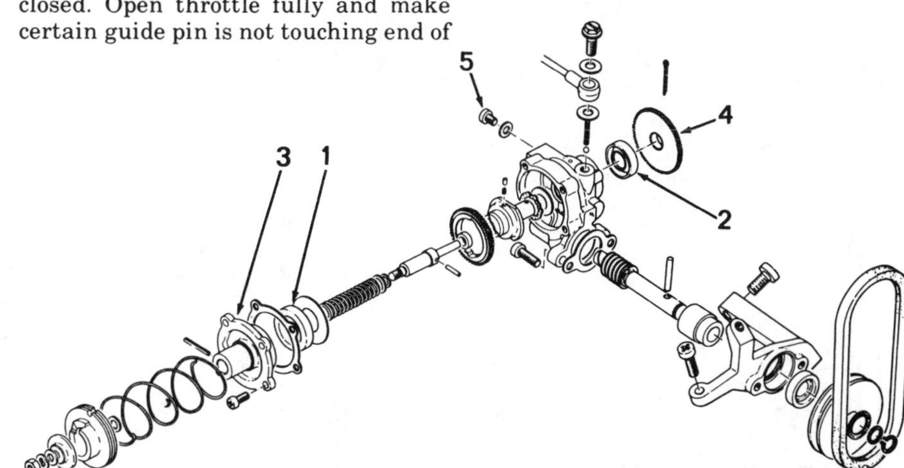
5
3
1
4
2

Fig. 9–Exploded view of "Autolube" pump and metering unit of the type used. Only the seals (1 & 2) are available for service and renewal is accomplished by removing cover (3) or starter plate (4).

The "Autolube" drive belt sheave is machined in hub of Torque Converter primary sheave inner half as shown in Fig. 10. Use care in disassembly and assembly to keep from damaging the belt.

REPAIRS

TIGHTENING TORQUES. Recommended tightening torques are as follows:

Cylinder head	180 in.-lbs.
Crankcase	180 in.-lbs.*
Spark plug	240 in.-lbs.

*Crankcase screws must be very carefully tightened in four stages using the sequence shown in Fig. 11 and the following procedure: Tighten alternately and evenly with no pressure until mating surfaces of crankcase halves contact, to be sure all dowels enter properly. Using Fig. 11 as a guide, tighten to 45 inch pounds, 90 inch pounds, 140 inch pounds; then 180 inch pounds. Loosen screws in reverse order when disassembling crankcase.

CYLINDER REMOVAL. Remove air shroud, spark plug leads, and cylinder head nuts. Remove cylinder head. The cylinder head and piston dome should be decarbonized with a scraper. Be careful not to score combustion chamber or piston. Remove carburetor by unscrewing mixing chamber cap and removing the cable and slide assembly as shown in Fig. 12. Disconnect fuel lines and loosen the clamp ring screw which holds the carburetor to the intake manifold. Remove carburetor from manifold. Disconnect muffler from exhaust flange of cylinder. Remove bolts and nuts holding steering column to steering gate to allow steering column to be moved when cylinder is removed. See Fig. 13. Remove cylinder. It may be necessary to strike the cylinder with a soft mallet to dislodge cylinder from crankcase.

CYLINDER INSPECTION. Check cylinder bore for wear or scoring. Out-of-round should not exceed 0.05 mm (0.002 in.). Differences in bore diameter between top and bottom (taper) should not exceed 0.05 mm (0.002 in.). Pistons are available in 0.25 mm (0.0098 in.) and 0.50 mm (0.0197 in.) oversizes.

CYLINDER ASSEMBLY. Assembly is done by reversing the disassembly procedure. Renew the base gasket between the two surfaces. Piston rings are pinned and end gap must align with pin. Care must be taken to prevent damage to rings, pis-

Fig. 12–Removal of mixing chamber cap and cable assembly.

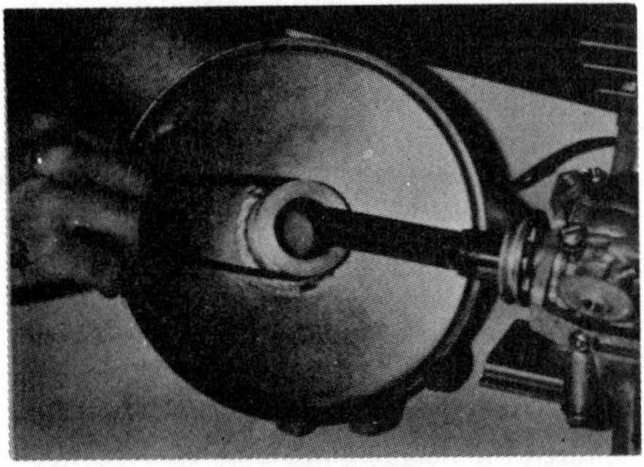

Fig. 10–"Autolube" drive belt runs on sheave machined on Primary Pulley inner face as shown.

Fig. 13–Steering column may have to be moved for cylinder removal.

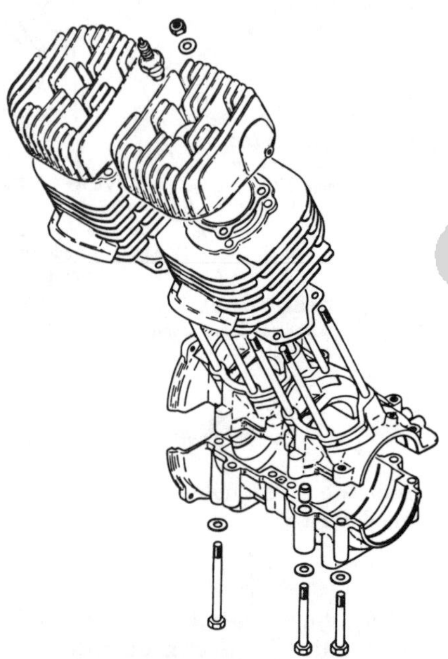

Fig. 14–Crankcase, cylinders and cylinder heads; exploded view.

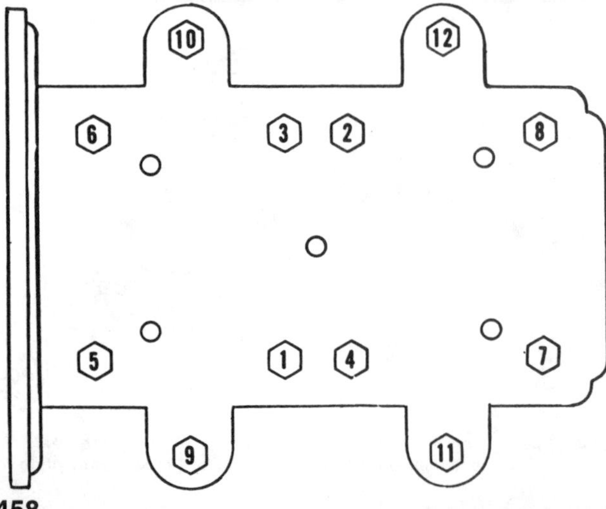

Fig. 11–Tighten crankcase screws in four steps in sequence shown. Refer to text.

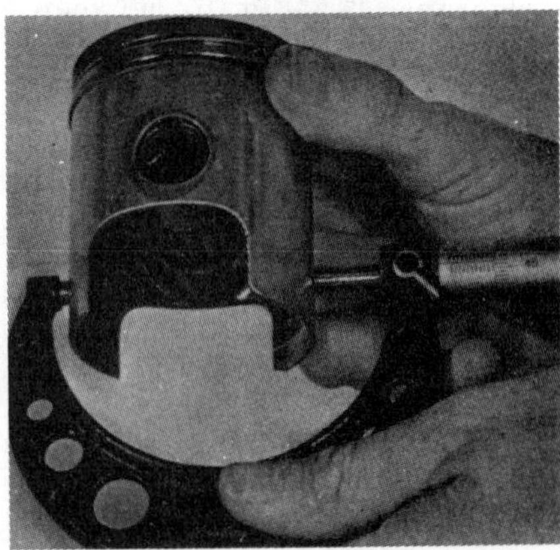

Fig. 15–Largest diameter is checked 10mm (0.4 in.) above bottom of piston skirt.

ton, and cylinder wall. Reinstall cylinder head gasket and cylinder head and torque cylinder head nuts to 15 ft.-lbs. (2.1 kg/m).

PISTON, PIN, AND RINGS. Remove cylinder as outlined in previous section. Remove piston pin clips with long nose pliers and force piston pin from piston with fingers or screwdriver. Remove piston and rings. Decarbonize piston and lightly sand skirt with #400 sandpaper if there is evidence of blowby or scoring. Be sure to clean ring grooves as well as the top of the piston.

Check piston-to-cylinder wall clearance. Largest diameter of piston should be checked (Fig. 15) 10 mm (0.4 in.) above the bottom of the piston skirt. The minimum clearance between the largest piston diameter and smallest cylinder diameter should be between 0.035 mm (0.0014 in.) and 0.040 mm (0.0016 in.).

Check piston pin fit in piston. Pin should fit snugly in piston bore so that it drags when turned. If fit is loose then pin or piston must be renewed. If pin has step wear in center then renew pin and needle bearing.

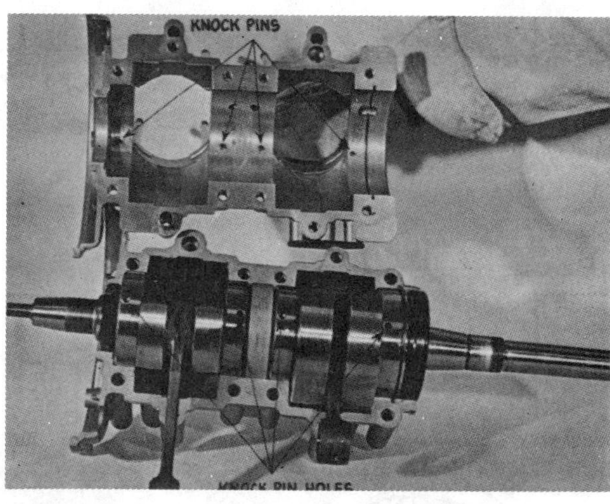

Fig. 18–View of crankcase halves and crankshaft assembly. Note knock pins and corresponding holes.

Clean piston rings and be sure ring grooves in piston are clean. Ring end gap should be 0.15-0.35 mm (0.006-0.014 in.) for both rings. Side clearance of ring in piston groove should be 0.03-0.07 mm (0.001-0.0027 in.).

PISTON ASSEMBLY. Reinstall piston rings on piston. Put needle bearings in connecting rod and place piston over the connecting rod with the arrow on the piston top pointing toward the exhaust port. Align piston pin bore with connecting rod and insert piston pin. Reinstall piston pin clip and check to see that it is in its groove by turning with a screwdriver. Reinstall cylinder as outlined previously.

CRANKCASE AND CRANKSHAFT. Remove cylinder top end, magneto assembly, and primary sheave assembly. Separate crankcase from upper mounting bracket and remove fuel pump. Separate crankcase halves and remove crankshaft assembly (Fig. 18). Do not misplace the two locating dowel pins.

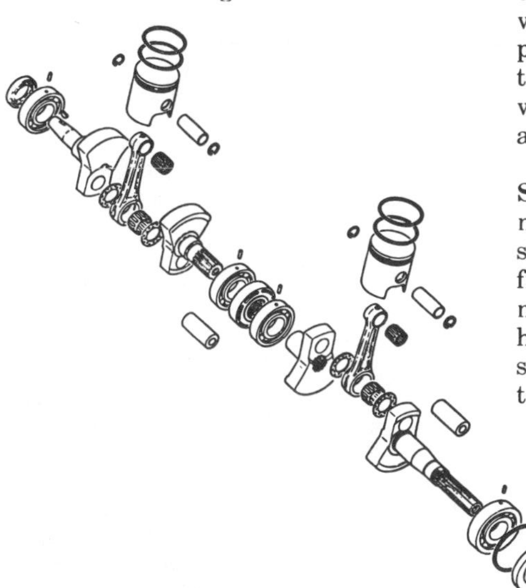

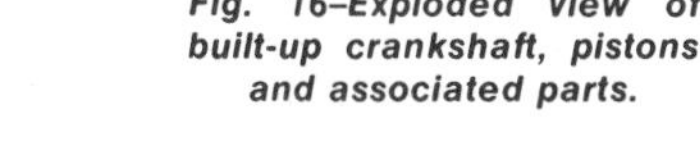

Fig. 16–Exploded view of built-up crankshaft, pistons and associated parts.

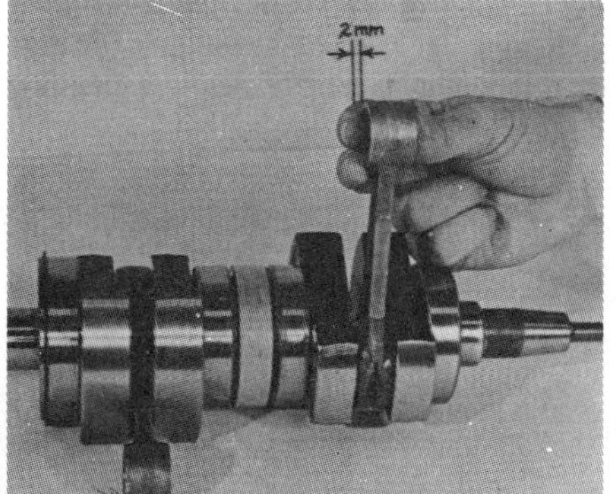

Fig. 17–Determine axial play by moving rod small end with fingers. Play should not exceed 2mm (0.08 in.).

Check wear of the connecting rod big end by measuring the play at the small end of the connecting rod. This axial play should not exceed 2 mm (0.08 in.) as indicated in Fig. 17. Maximum axial play of a new unit should be 0.8-1.0 mm (0.032-0.040 in.). Free play as shown in Fig. 19, should be 0.1-0.3 mm (0.004-0.012 in.).

Crankshaft deflection must be checked before reassembly. The crankshaft is placed between centers or in V blocks (Fig. 20) and using a dial indicator checked for runout. Maximum acceptable tolerance is 0.015 mm (0.0006 in.). Correction is made by tapping the flywheels with a brass hammer and using wedges between the flywheels. As this is a critical operation, it is suggested that should the crankshaft be out of alignment, it should be taken to a shop equipped and experienced in this operation. Once correction has been made, then care should be taken in assembly of the crankcase to prevent the crankshaft from being knocked out of alignment.

CRANKCASE ASSEMBLY. Note lock pin holes and two aligning marks 90° from lock pin hole in outside races of crankshaft bearings. Refer to Fig. 21. The aligning marks should be matched with the sealing surface of the upper crankcase and the knock pin

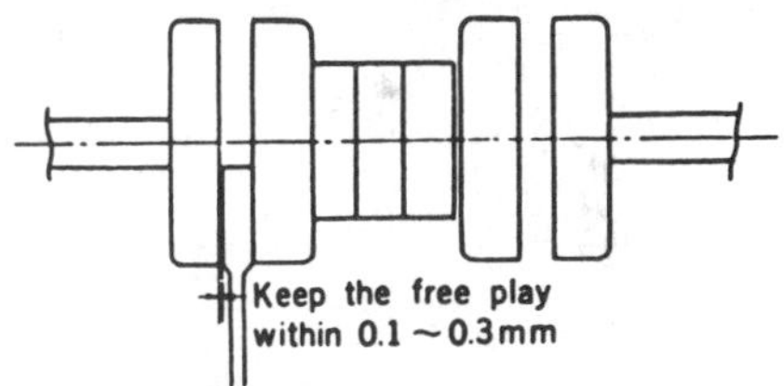

Fig. 19–Check free play as shown.

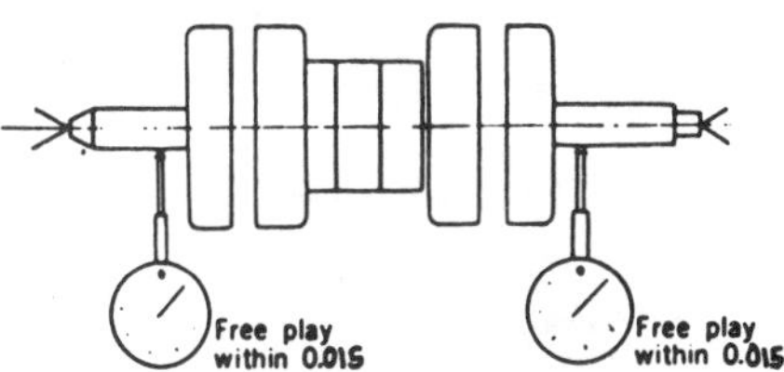

Fig. 20–Crankshaft deflection must be measured before assembly. Adjustment should be done in experienced shop.

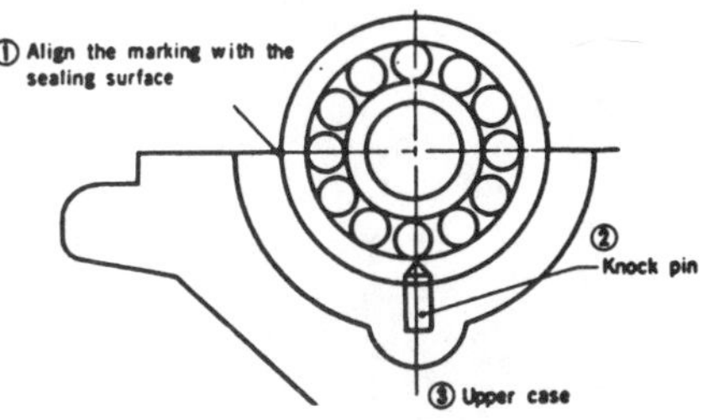

Fig. 21–Align crankshaft bearings with aligning marks and locating holes. See text.

holes with the knock pins of the upper crankcase. The bearing circlip on the sheave end of the crankshaft should be positioned as shown in Fig. 22 and installed so that the oil groove on the upper crankcase half will be between the ends of the circlip. Reinstall oil seals and place crankshaft assembly in upper crankcase half. Thoroughly clean and evenly coat mating surfaces of crankcase with YAMAHA BOND No. 5 or similar sealer. Reinstall lower half and bolts. Tightening sequence is shown in Fig. 11. Use tightening procedure given in TIGHTENING TORQUES paragraph.

STARTER ASSEMBLY. Refer to Fig. 24. The starter assembly must be removed to time the engine. The starter pulley is fastened to the flywheel and the fan case is fastened to the crankcase.

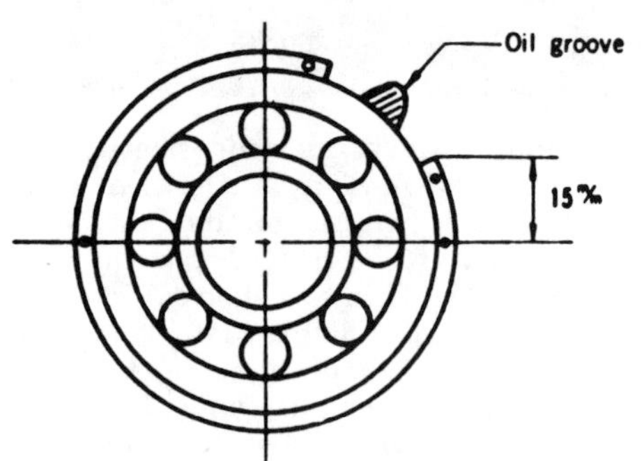

Fig. 22–Oil groove should be between ends of the circlip on the sheave end crankshaft bearing.

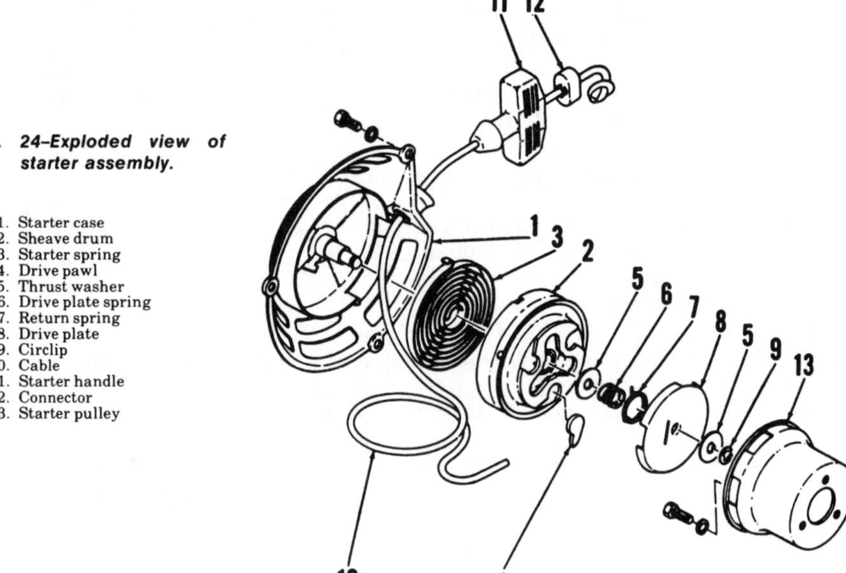

Fig. 24–Exploded view of starter assembly.

1. Starter case
2. Sheave drum
3. Starter spring
4. Drive pawl
5. Thrust washer
6. Drive plate spring
7. Return spring
8. Drive plate
9. Circlip
10. Cable
11. Starter handle
12. Connector
13. Starter pulley

YAMAHA

1975 AND EARLIER 338,396 AND 433cc TWO CYLINDER MODELS

CONDENSED SERVICE DATA

Engine Model	338, 810	396, 811, 813	433 818
Bore—(mm)	60	65	68
Inches	2.36	2.56	2.68
Stroke—(mm)	59.6	59.6	59.6
Inches	2.35	2.35	2.35
No. of Cylinders	2	2	2
Displacement—(cc)	338	396	433
Cubic Inches	20.6	24.1	26.4
Horsepower @ RPM:			
SL, SW, EW	24@5500	28@5500	30@5500
SS, GP	32@6500	36@6000	40@6500
Cooling Type	Cent. Fan	Cent. Fan	Cent. Fan
Carburetor Model	Keihin Diaphragm	Keihin or Mikuni Diaphragm	
Number Used	1 or 2	1 or 2	1 or 2
Ignition:			
Type	Energy Transfer Magneto		
Point Gap	See Text	See Text	See Text
Timing Advance?	No	No	No
Timing BTDC	See Text	See Text	See Text
Spark Plug:			
SL, SW, EW	NGK B7HZ	NGK B7HZ	NGK B7HZ
SS, GP	NGK B9H	NGK B7HZ	Champion N2G
Electrode Gap (mm)	0.5-0.6	0.5-0.6	0.5-0.6
Inch	0.020-0.024	0.020-0.024	0.020-0.024
Fuel/Oil Ratio	20:1*	20:1*	Autolube

*If not equipped with "Autolube".

MAINTENANCE

SPARK PLUGS. Selection of spark plugs will depend upon type of service, ambient temperature and horsepower of engine. Refer to Condensed Service Data for recommended plug for normal use. Excessively cold weather and/or light load conditions may require spark plugs of warmer heat range. Hard usage, heavy loads, warm weather and higher horsepower may require spark plugs of colder heat range.

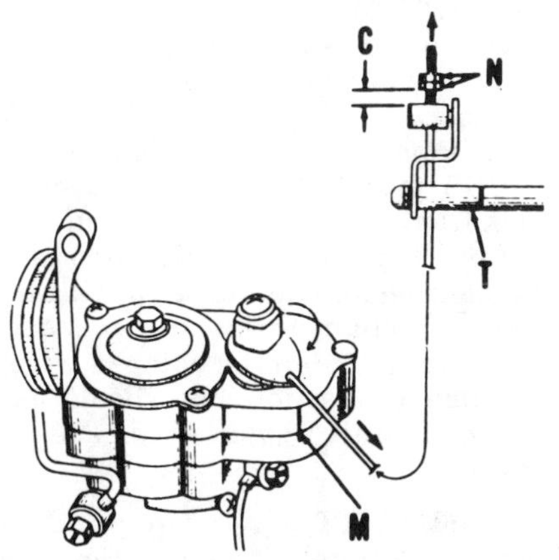

Fig. 1–View showing checking and adjustment points for synchronizing carburetor opening to "Autolube" oil injection. Pump is tilted from normal position to better show the mark. Refer to text for the two methods of checking adjustment.

C. Clearance
M. Mark
N. Nuts
T. Throttle shaft

CARBURETORS. Various carburetors have been used. Refer to the appropriate carburetor paragraphs in FUNDAMENTALS section for carburetor service. For adjustment of carburetors and "Autolube" refer to the appropriate following paragraphs.

ONE (KEIHIN OR MIKUNI DIAPHRAGM) CARBURETOR. The carburetor is installed on a "Y" type inlet manifold and provides the fuel-air mixture to both cylinders. Initial fuel-air mixture setting is as follows:

SL338 (Keihin)—
Idle mixture needle . . . 1⅛ turns out
High speed
mixture needle . . . . . 1¼ turns out
Fuel level (F—Fig. 1A) . . . . . 39 mm
Inlet lever height
(H—Fig. 1A) . . . . 5.7 mm

SW396 (Mikuni)—
Idle mixture needle . . . 1¼ turns out
High speed
mixture needle . . . . . 1⅜ turns out
SW433, EW433 (Mikuni)—
Idle mixture needle . . . 1⅛ turns out
High speed
mixture needle . . . . . 1½ turns out

On all models with one carburetor, linkage adjustment is limited to synchronizing the "Autolube" oil injection to the carburetor throttle. With the carburetor throttle completely open (maximum speed) and the pump control rod pulled to maximum position, clearance (C—Fig. 1) should be 1-1.5 mm (0.04-0.06 inch). Clearance is measured between lower adjusting nut and lever on carburetor. Adjustment is accomplished by turning nuts to obtain correct clearance. The top nut locks the position of lower nut.

Another method is to open throttle completely and check to see if oil pump end of rod is aligned with mark (M). If not relocate nuts (N). It will usually be

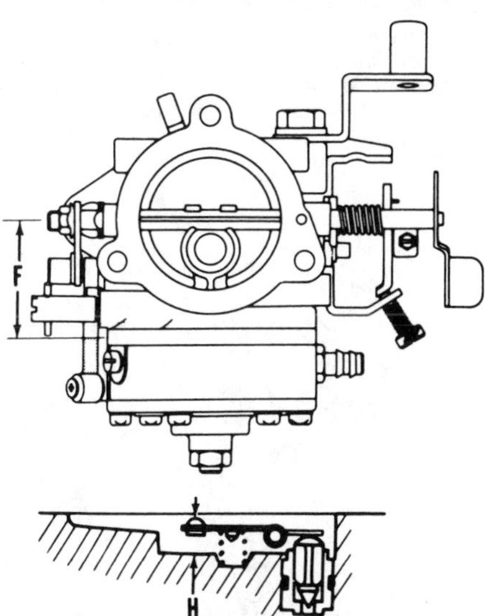

Fig. 1A – Drawing of Keihin diaphragm carburetor. Refer to text for distance (F) between center of carburetor bore and fuel level. Height (H) of fuel inlet needle is listed in text. Refer to FUNDAMENTALS section for method of adjustment.

necessary to remove carburetor cover before mark (M) can be seen.

TWO CARBURETORS. Each carburetor provides fuel-air mixture to one cylinder. Both carburetor throttle valves must be open exactly the same amount in order to properly balance the power output to each cylinder. A carburetor air flow meter (part number 650-806-001) is available from Yamaha for measuring air velocity through carburetors. Synchronization is accomplished by turning the balance screw as shown at (B—Fig. 2). Initial fuel-air mixture setting is as follows:

SS338 (Keihin)—
- Idle mixture needle ... ¾ turn open
- High speed mixture needle ..... ¾ turn open
- Fuel level (F—Fig. 1A) ..... 39 mm
- Inlet lever height (H—Fig. 1A) ....5.7 mm

SS396, GP396 (Keihin)—
- Idle mixture needle .... 1 turn open
- High speed mixture needle ..... ⅞ turn open
- Fuel level (F—Fig. 1A) ..... 39 mm
- Inlet lever height (H—Fig. 1A) ....5.7 mm

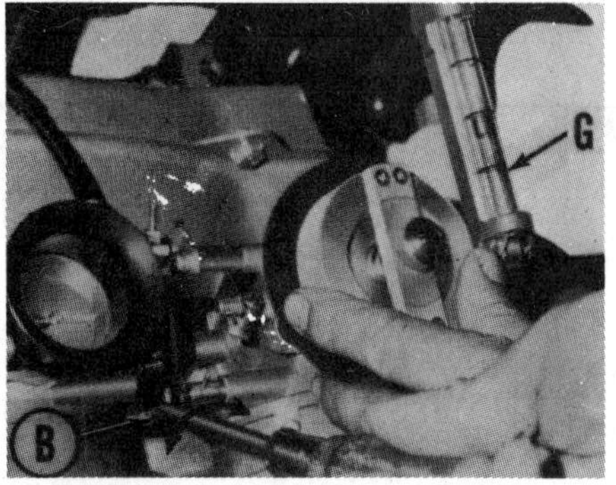

Fig. 2–View showing location of balance screw (B) on models with two Keihin diaphragm carburetors. Air flow meter available from Yamaha is shown at (G).

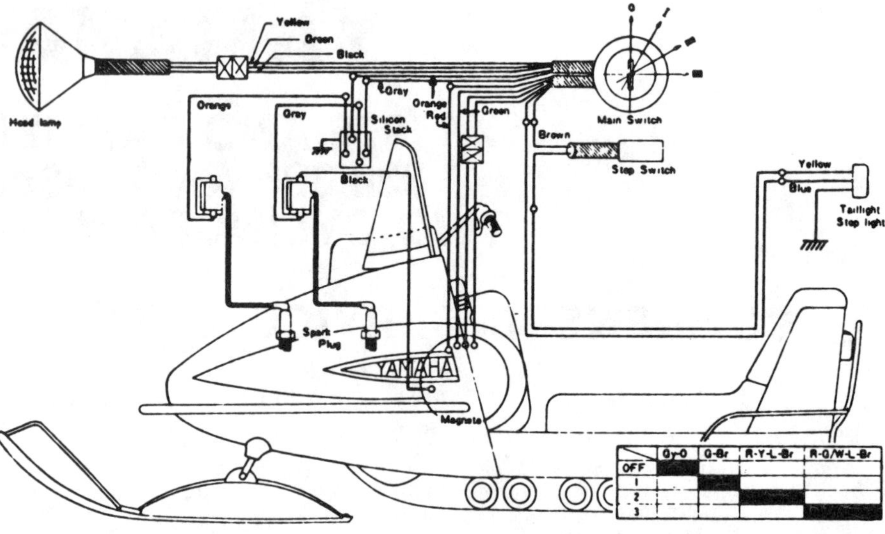

Fig. 5–Typical wiring diagram for manual start models. Main switch connections are shown in insert. Silicone stack shown is not used on all models.

SS433 (Keihin)—
- Idle mixture needle ... ⅞ turn open
- High speed mixture needle ..1-1⅛ turns open
- Fuel level (F—Fig. 1A) ..... 39 mm
- Inlet lever height (H—Fig. 1A) ....5.7 mm

After carburetors have been balanced as described in previous paragraph, check the "Autolube" oil injection linkage. Open the carburetor throttles completely (maximum speed) and pull the pump control rod up. Rod in pump control lever should align with mark (M—Fig. 1) on pump when rod is pulled up. Clearance (C) between lower adjusting nut and carburetor lever should be 1-1.5 mm (0.04-0.06 inch). If incorrect, loosen the top (lock) nut (N) and position the lower nut to provide correct adjustment. Lock the position of lower nut by tightening the top nut.

IGNITION AND TIMING. Breaker point gap should be adjusted to provide ignition timing. Use a dial indicator through spark plug holes to correctly position the crankshaft and a continuity meter (12 volt or less) to indicate breaker points opening.

On all standard production models for 1970 model year, breaker points for right cylinder should just open when piston in right cylinder is 1.6-1.8 mm (0.063-0.071 inch) Before Top Dead Center. Breaker points for left cylinder should just open when piston in left cylinder is 1.8-2.0 mm (0.071-0.079 inch) BTDC.

NOTE: The different static timing will result in ignition occurring at 1.8 mm BTDC for both cylinders with engine running. Breaker point gap should be approximately 0.3-0.4 mm (0.012-0.016 inch), but should be adjusted to provide the correct ignition timing. On limited production SR433 for 1970 and all 1971 and later models ignition timing is set the same for both cylinders (1.8 mm BTDC).

Exploded view of energy transfer magneto assembly is shown in Fig. 4 and typical wiring diagram in Fig. 5. The silicone stack (diodes) is installed on 1970 models to prevent maverick spark from occurring when piston is at Bottom Dead Center. Silicone stack can be checked using a continuity meter (or ohmmeter). Current should flow through common colored wires with one connection but should not have continuity when leads are reversed.

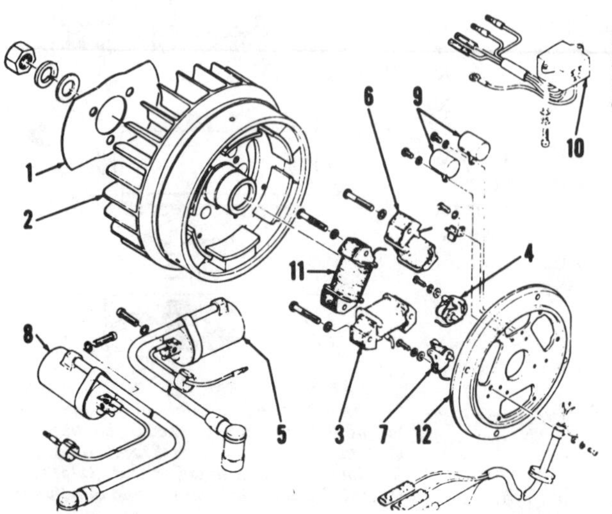

Fig. 4–Exploded view of ignition system components typical of most models. Silicone stack (10) is not used on some models.

1. Hole cover
2. Flywheel
3. Ignition generating coil (Left cyl.)
4. Breaker points (Left cyl.)
5. High tension coil (Left cyl.)
6. Ignition generating coil (Right cyl.)
7. Breaker points (Right cyl.)
8. High tension coil (Right cyl.)
9. Condensers
10. Silicone stack (diodes)
11. Lighting coil
12. Stator plate

LUBRICATION. On models without "Autolube" oil injection, the engine is lubricated by SAE 20 or SAE 30 2-stroke, air cooled engine oil mixed with the fuel. Normal ratio is 20:1. On models with "Autolube", a separate oil tank and metering type oil pump are used. Refer to the "Autolube" section which follows:

"AUTOLUBE" OIL INJECTION. The Yamaha "Autolube" is an engine lubrication system which delivers varying amounts of oil depending upon RPM and throttle setting (load). The oil pump is belt driven from the hub of torque converter primary sheave inner half and the metered pump delivery is controlled by a rod attached to the carburetor throttle. The pump and metering unit draws oil from the tank and delivers it to each cylinder inlet port through nozzles (special banjo fittings). SAE 20 or SAE 30 oil designed for use in air cooled, 2-stroke engines is recommended. In emergencies, SAE 10W/30 automotive oil may be used.

Refer to carburetor paragraphs for checking and adjusting the "Autolube" control linkage. Refer to Fig. 7 for partially exploded view of the pump and metering unit. Internal parts of pump are not available and if damaged, new pump assembly must be installed. Pumps for the different engines are not interchangeable.

If lever (2—Fig. 7) is removed, be sure to mark lever (2) and shaft of the control gear (3) so that the two parts can be correctly reassembled. Hole in lever (2) should align with mark (M) when turned to maximum position. Timing marks (TM) must be aligned when unit is assembled.

Be sure to check condition of pump drive belt frequently on models so equipped, to prevent loss of lubrication because of damaged belt. The drive belt should be renewed if questionable. Oil pump drive belt can be removed after removing torque converter primary (drive) sheave. On some models, it is necessary to install washers between mounting bracket (15—Fig. 7) and crankcase to tighten the belt. Adjust pump control rod as outlined in CARBURETOR paragraphs and bleed air from pump as follows after installing pump on engine. Make certain that oil tank is filled, remove bleed screw (24), open throttle and turn starter plate (22) until air bubbles stop coming out of bleeder hole, then reinstall bleed screw (24) and gasket (25).

REPAIRS

TIGHTENING TORQUES. Recommended tightening torques are as follows:

*Crankcase Halves—
- First torque .... 90 in.-lbs.
- Final torque .... 180 in.-lbs.

Cylinder Head—
- 338 cc Models ...... 156-192 in.-lbs.
- SL396 and SW396 .. 156-192 in.-lbs.
- SS396 and GP396 .. 198-234 in.-lbs.
- 433 cc Models ...... 198-234 in.-lbs.

*The crankcase screws should be loosened in sequence shown in Fig. 9, in order to prevent crankcase distortion. When assembling, first install all screws evenly with no pressure until mating surfaces of crankcase halves are in full contact; tighten all screws evenly to 90 inch-pounds torque; then, retorque screws to final torque of 180 inch-pounds. Make certain that final torque is the same on all 12 screws.

CYLINDER REMOVAL. Remove top air shroud and cylinder head nuts. The cylinder head can be removed and carbon cleaned with no further disassembly. To remove cylinders, remove carburetor and inlet manifold or both carburetors on models so equipped. Disconnect exhaust pipes and oil injection lines from cylinders and remove air shrouds. Remove cylinder and cylinder head retaining stud nuts. Cylinder heads and cylinders can now be lifted off. CAUTION: Be especially careful to prevent anything from falling into crankcase and to prevent piston or connecting rod damage. The pistons, piston pins, piston pin bearings and piston rings can be removed after cylinders are removed.

NOTE: Parts should not be interchanged between cylinders when reassembling. Mark all parts as they are removed to identify parts for installation in correct location.

CYLINDER INSPECTION. Check cylinder bore for wear or scoring. Out-of-round should not exceed 0.05 mm (0.002 inch). Differences in bore diameter between top and bottom (taper) should not exceed 0.05 mm (0.002 inch). The cylinder should be renewed or bored to next larger oversize if out-of-round or taper is excessive. Oversize pistons and rings are available. Piston skirt (right angles to pin and 10 mm from bottom of piston) to cylinder clearance should be 0.04-0.05 mm (0.0016-0.0020 inch).

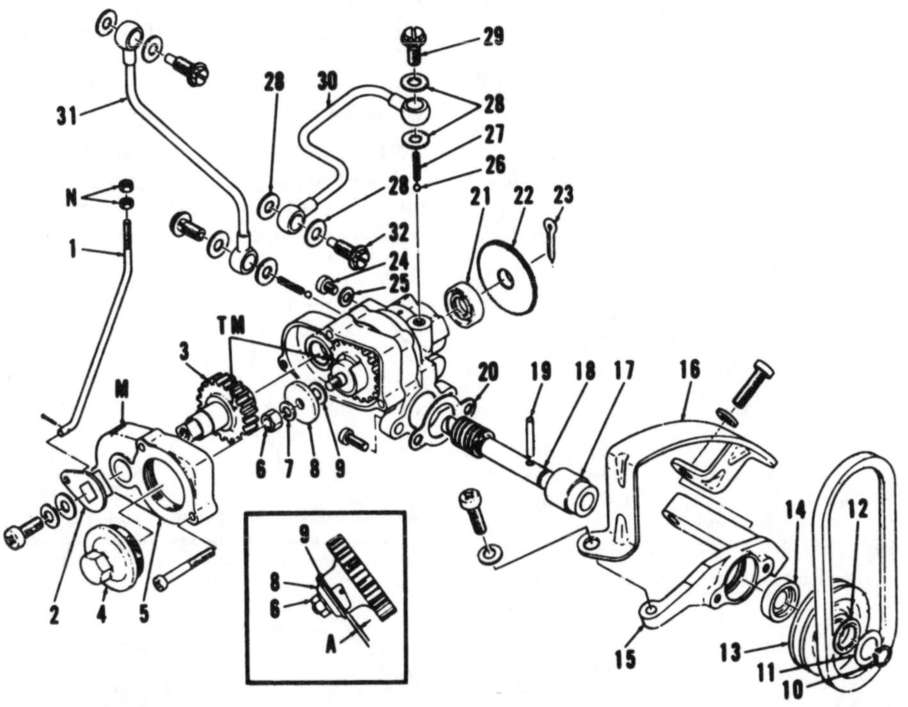

Fig. 7–Partially exploded view of oil injection pump and metering assembly. Internal parts of pump are not available separately. Nuts (N) and mark (M) are also shown in Fig. 1. Pump used on late models is gear driven.

1. Pump control rod
2. Control lever
3. Pump control gear
4. Cap
5. Cover
6. Nut
7. Lock washer
8. Adjusting plate
9. Shims
10. Snap ring
11. Plate
12. Wave washer
13. Pulley
14. Oil seal
15. Mounting bracket
16. Drive cover
17. Bushing
18. Worm shaft
19. Drive pin
20. Gasket
21. Oil seal
22. Starter plate
23. Cotter pin
24. Bleed screw
25. Gasket
26. Check ball (2 used)
27. Spring (2 used)
28. Banjo gaskets
29. Banjo bolt
30. Oil line to left cylinder
31. Oil line to right cylinder
32. Oil injection nozzle

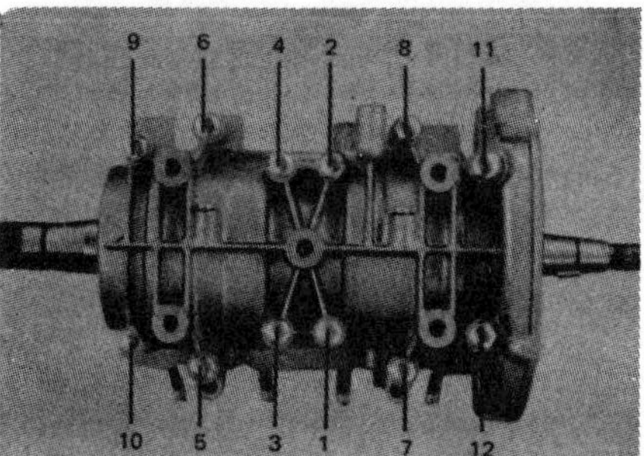

Fig. 9–Crankcase screws should be removed in sequence shown. Disassembling incorrectly may distort crankcase and prevent an air tight seal.

CYLINDER INSTALLATION. Assemble in reverse of disassembly procedure. Remove old gaskets from crankcase and cylinder mating surfaces, then position new gaskets. Piston rings are pinned and end gaps must align with pins when installing cylinders. Some models are equipped with spring-type expanders (Fig. 13). Note that expander for top ring can be identified by the sharper radius of expander arch. Keystone type rings must be correctly installed with tapered side toward top of piston (Refer to Fig. 14). Use caution to prevent damage to rings, pistons and cylinder walls. Reinstall cylinder head and tighten the retaining nuts to torque listed in TIGHTENING TORQUES paragraph.

PISTON, PINS AND RINGS. Remove cylinders as outlined in previous section. Remove piston pin retaining rings and push pin out of piston. CAUTION: Be careful not to bend connecting rod. Remove piston, rings and piston pin bearing.

Piston pin should be a snug fit in piston bore, but it should be possible to install pin with thumb pressure. Ring side clearance in grooves should be 0.03-0.07 mm (0.001-0.0027 inch) and end gap in cylinder bore should be 0.15-0.35 mm (0.006-0.014 inch).

Pistons with "K" stamped after numbers (indicating size) on piston head are for Keystone rings. Keystone rings employ a 7° slope on top side of ring and must be installed with "N" or "T" mark toward top of piston. Number "1" or "2" before the "N" or "T" mark indicates top or second ring. Be sure that ring is installed in correct groove with correct side toward top of piston. Markings "1N, 2N, 1T or 2T" are located near end gap of ring. If rings are oversize the oversize is marked on top of ring across the end gap from previous markings. Some models use only one Keystone ring as shown at (B—Fig. 14). Ring may be 1.5 mm or 2 mm thick. Be sure correct ring is installed. Refer to Fig. 13 for identification of ring expanders used in some models.

Piston to cylinder clearance should be 0.04-0.05 mm (0.0016-0.0020 inch). Clearance should be checked by measuring piston diameter skirt at right angles to piston pin, 10 mm (0.4 inch) above bottom of skirt and cylinder bore diameter, then subtracting.

Refer to piston assembly paragraph for installation of piston to connecting rod. Oversize pistons and rings are available.

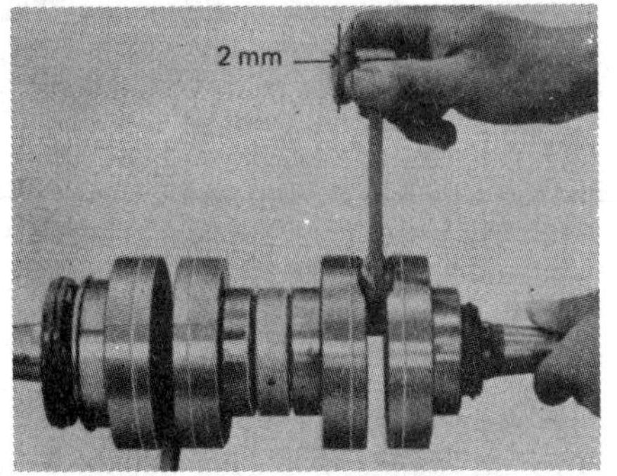

Fig. 10–Determine axial play by moving rod small end with fingers. Play should not exceed 2 mm (0.08 inch).

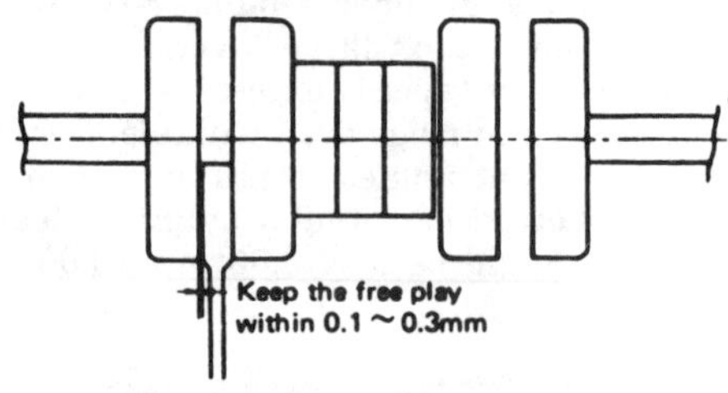

Fig. 11–Check rod side play (clearance) while the crankshaft is being assembled and aligned.

PISTON ASSEMBLY. Install rings on pistons as outlined in previous paragraphs. Position needle bearing in connecting rod bore and locate piston over end of rod with arrow pointing toward exhaust (front) side of engine. Align piston pin bore with connecting rod and install piston pin. Install piston pin retaining rings and make certain that they are correctly seated in grooves. Reinstall cylinder, making certain that ring end gaps are around locating pins and that rings are not broken during assembly.

CRANKCASE AND CRANKSHAFT. Remove cylinder top end, magneto assembly, primary drive sheave assembly and engine mounting plate. Remove screws (1 through 12—Fig. 9) in sequence shown. CAUTION: Loosen each screw slightly until all are loose to prevent distorting crankcase halves. Separate crankcase halves and remove crankshaft. NOTE: Do not lose the hollow dowels between crankcase halves or solid dowels which locate main bearings and center seal.

Check wear of the connecting rod big end by measuring the side play (shake) at small end of rod. This axial play should not exceed 2 mm (0.08 inch) as shown in Fig. 10. Axial play of new unit should be approximately 0.8-1.0 mm (0.032-0.040 inch). Rod side play (clearance) between crankshaft webs should be 0.1-0.3 mm (0.004-0.012 inch). Refer to Fig. 11.

Crankshaft is a built-up (pressed together) assembly and must be carefully aligned before installing. Disassembly is not recommended unless experienced with this type of operation and special tools are available. After assembling, connecting rod side play (clearance) should be 0.1-0.3 mm (0.004-0.012 inch) as shown in Fig. 11. Width (D—Fig. 12) should be 55.95-56.00 mm for all models. Length (E) should be 163.90-164.00 mm for 338 and 396 cc models; 173.90-174.00 mm for 433 cc models. Crankshaft run-out should be less than 0.015 mm (0.0006 inch) when checked at locations (A, B & C) with crankshaft supported in "V" blocks. Once crankshaft is correctly aligned, use care to prevent crankshaft from being knocked out of-alignment while assembling crankcase.

CRANKCASE ASSEMBLY. Install end seals (1 & 15—Fig. 15) around ends of crankshaft next to bearings (2 & 13) with lips toward inside (bear-

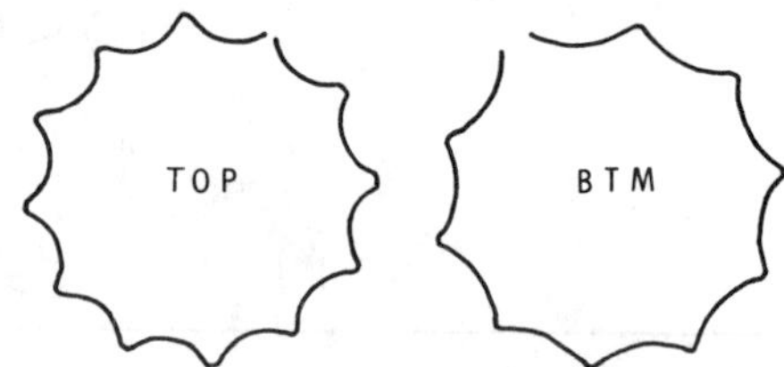

Fig. 13–Cross-sectional view of spring-type ring expanders showing means of identification. Note the sharper radius of expander arch on top expander.

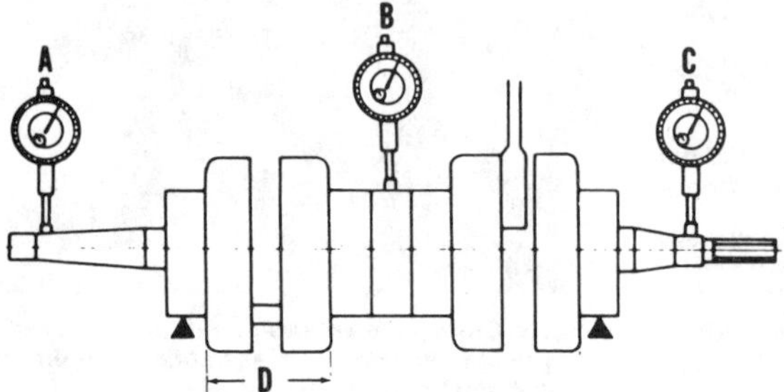

Fig. 12–Crankshaft alignment is very critical and should not be attempted by inexperienced personnel or without proper tools.

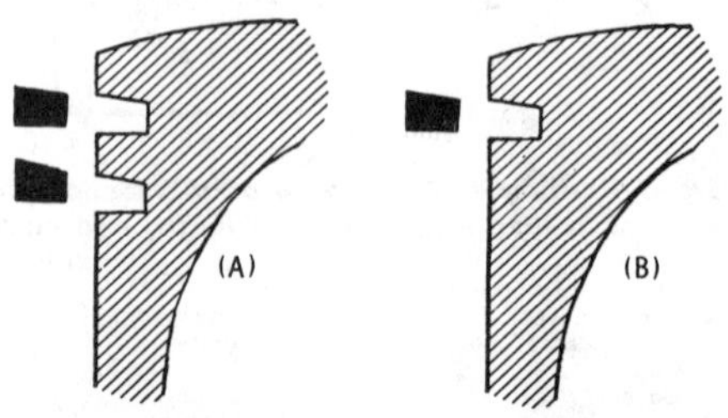

Fig. 14–Cross sectional view of pistons showing piston ring configuration. (A) Two-ring piston. (B) One-ring piston.

ings). Carefully position crankshaft assembly in the upper crankcase half with connecting rods protruding through cylinder holes. Rotate the four main bearings (2, 9 & 13) and the center seal (10) until the hole in outer race engages lock pin (L) located in crankcase bore. Also, two alignment marks are provided 90° from lock pin hole on bearing outer race to help locate hole. Refer to Fig. 16. The alignment marks should be matched with sealing surface of crankcase. CAUTION: The crankcase and crankshaft will both probably be ruined if the lock pins do not correctly engage holes in bearing races and center seal. Thoroughly clean the mating surfaces of crankcase halves and coat surface evenly with YAMAHA BOND No. 5 or equivalent. Refer to TIGHTENING TORQUES paragraph for correct method of installing bolts.

MANUAL STARTER. Refer to Fig. 20. The starter must be removed and disassembled to renew rope and/or rewind spring. The rewind spring (3) should be wound into housing (1), beginning at outside and in counterclockwise direction. Pawl springs (7) should engage holes in pawls. Preload the rewind spring approximately ⅓-turn to make certain that handle is pulled against housing when released.

SPEED TUNING

Any change from the original can possibly decrease service life of the engine, can narrow the performance band; and if carelessly done, can decrease power and cause extensive engine damage. Normal tuning such as ignition timing, point gap, fuel mixture, lubrication, etc., will become more critical with modification. It should also be noted that gearing and clutch changes may be necessary to make full use of the modified engine.

Information on only the 433cc engine is given and only factory modifications are listed for comparison.

CYLINDER PORTS. Fig. 21 shows a schematic view of cylinder ports (not to scale). Refer to accompanying table for specification data. All dimensions are given in mm.

Cylinder liner material is cast iron in all models except SR433B which may be chrome plated, although cast iron liner is used in some modification kits. SR433 uses a special cylinder and 8-stud cylinder head.

CYLINDER HEAD. All models use 0.5 mm copper cylinder head gasket. Compression ratio (actual) and cylinder head volume are as follows:

Compression ratio

SW433	6.5:1
SS433	6.5:1
SR433	7.0:1
GP433	6.5:1
SR433B	7.0:1

Cylinder Head Volume

SW433	30 cc
SS433	28.7 cc
SR433	25.1 cc
GP433	28.7 cc
SR433B	25.5 cc

PISTON AND RINGS. Standard piston to cylinder clearance (0.045-0.5 mm) is used on all engines. SW433 models use two 2.0 mm Keystone rings; other models use one Keystone ring which is 2.0 mm thick on SS433 or 1.5 mm thick on other engines.

CARBURETORS. A single carburetor was installed on SW433 units; other models use two carburetors. Factory application was as follows:

SW433	Mikuni 44-40
SS433	Keihin CD38-32 (2)
SR433	Mikuni BN38-34 (2)
GP433	Keihin CD38-32 (2)
SR433B	Keihin CD42-38 (2)

EXHAUST PIPE. Stock parts are used on all factory standard and performance tuned models; parts numbers are as follows:

SW433	811-14710-02 combined muffler
SS433	813-14610-00 expansion chamber
SR433	820-14610-00 expansion chamber

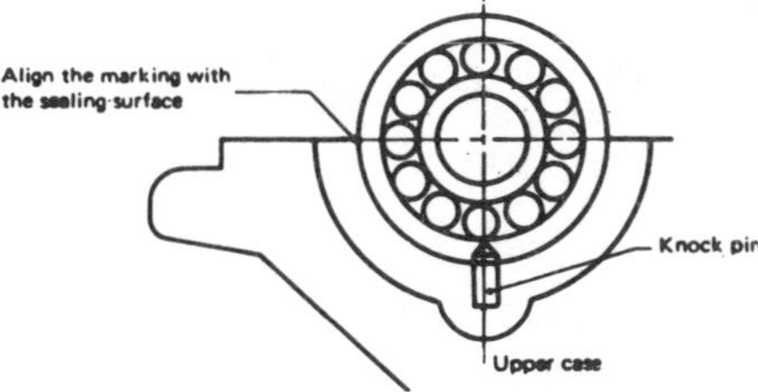

Fig. 16–Align crankshaft bearings with alignment marks and locating holes.

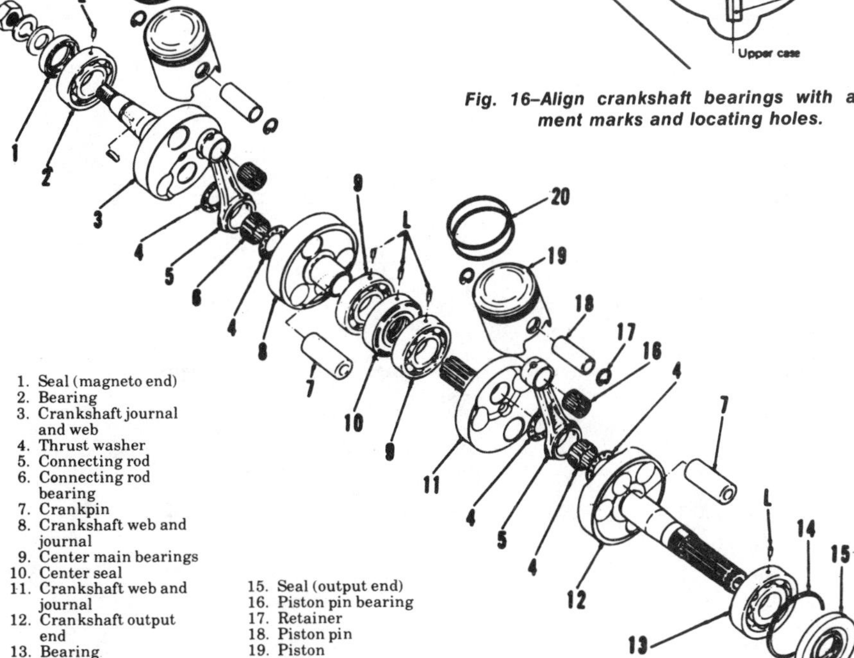

Fig. 15–Exploded view of the crankshaft assembly When installing, make certain that all main bearings (2, 9 & 13) and center seal (10) engage lock pins (L) in crankcase upper half.

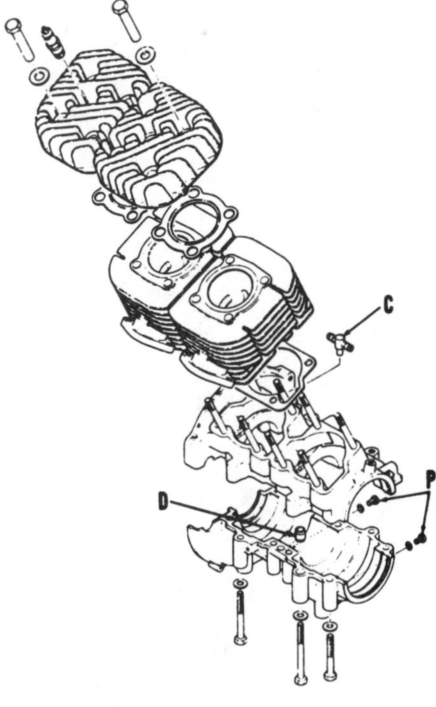

Fig. 17–Exploded view of crankcase and cylinders. Cylinder heads are not interchangeable. Make certain that hollow dowels (D) are in place before joining crankcase halves. Fuel pump impulse fitting is shown at (C) and crankcase drain plugs at (P).

GP433 .... 828-14710-00 combined muffler
SR433B .... 828-14610-00 expansion chamber

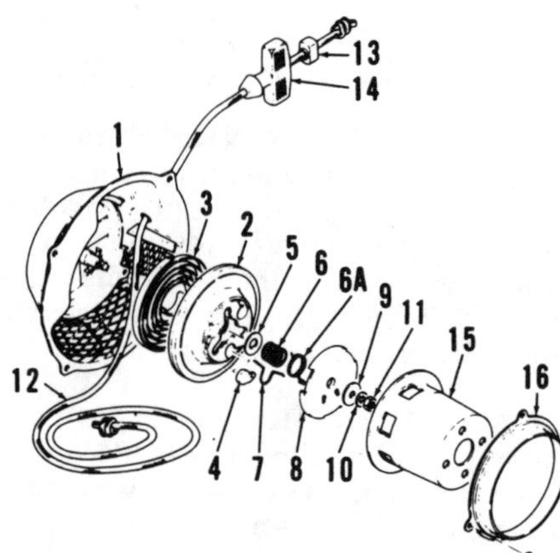
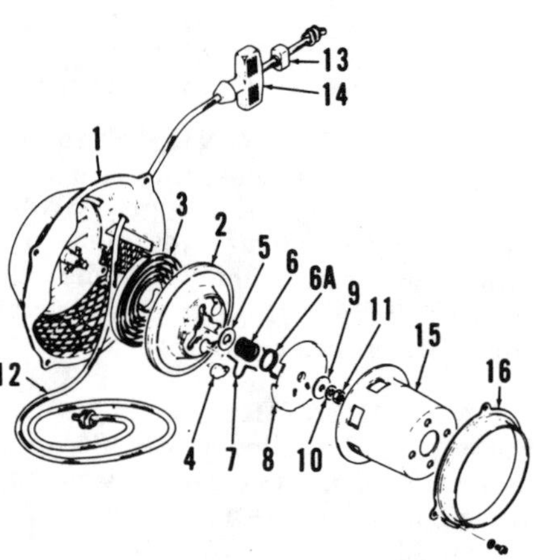

Fig. 20–Exploded view of recoil starter assembly. Three pawls (4) and pawl return springs (7) are used.

1. Housing
2. Pulley
3. Rewind spring
4. Pawls
5. Spring seat
6. Brake spring
6A. Drive plate spring
7. Pawl springs
8. Drive plate
9. Brake washer
10. Lock washer
11. Nut
12. Rope
13. Anchor
14. Handle
15. Starter cup
16. Cover

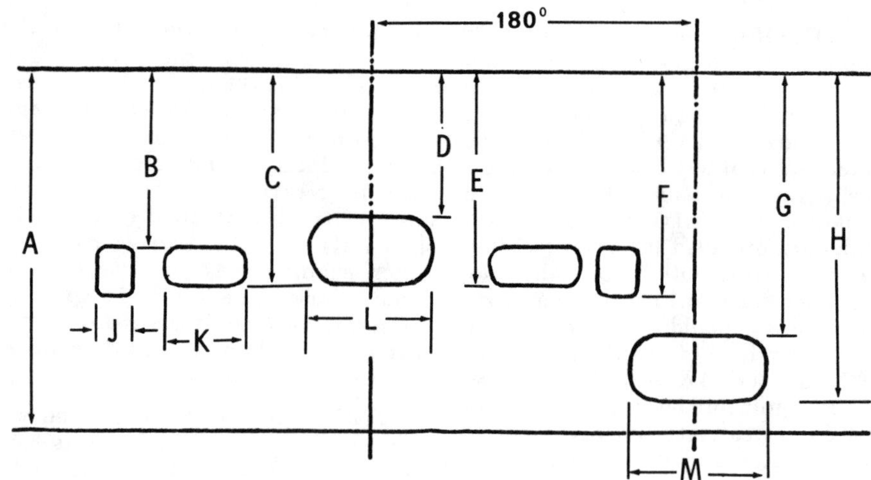

Fig. 21–Schematic view of cylinder port arrangement (not to scale). Refer to accompanying tables for measurements.

Model	SW433	SS433	SR433	GP433	SR433B
A—Cylinder depth	106	106	106	106	106
B—Transfer Port Ht.	48	48	48	48	48
C—Bottom, Exh Port	62	62	62	62	62
D—Exh Port Height	37	35	35	35	33
E—Btm Transfer Port	60	60	60	60	60
F—Btm Fifth Port	63	63	63	63	63
G—Inlet Port Height	72.5	72.5	72.5	72.5	72.5
H—Btm, Inlet Port	98	102	102	102	102
J—Fifth Port Width	15	15	15	15	15
K—Trfr Port Width	23	23	23	23	23
L—Exhaust Port Width	45	45	45	45	46
M—Intake Port Width	40	42	42	42	42

YAMAHA

1976 AND LATER E338, SS338 AND SS433 TWO CYLINDER MODELS

CONDENSED SERVICE DATA

Engine Model	E338	SS338	SS433
Bore-(mm)	60	60	68
Inches	2.362	2.362	2.677
Stroke-(mm)	59.6	59.6	59.6
Inches	2.346	2.346	2.346
No. of Cylinders	2	2	2
Displacement-cc	338	338	433
Cubic Inches	20.63	20.63	26.4
Cooling Type	Free Air*	Free Air	Free Air*
Carburetor Model	Mikuni (B)	Keihin (PW)	Keihin (PW)**
Number Used	1	1	1
Ignition:			
Type	CDI	CDI	CDI
Timing BTDC	1.5-1.7 mm	1.6 mm	1.6 mm
Spark Plug:			
NGK	BR9EV***	BR9EV	BR9EV***
Electrode Gap (mm)	0.5-0.6†	0.5-0.6	0.5-0.6
Inch	0.020-0.024†	0.020-0.024	0.020-0.024
Fuel/Oil Ratio	Autolube	Autolube	Autolube

*Models prior to 1980 use free air cooling. All 1980-85 models are forced air (fan) cooled.

**Engine models prior to 1978 use Keihin (PW) model carburetors. All 1978-1981 models use Keihin (BD) model carburetors.

***Models prior to 1980 use BR9EV. All 1980-1985 models use BR9ES.

†Models prior to 1979 use 0.5-0.6 mm (0.020-0.024 inch) electrode gap. All 1979-1985 models use 0.7-0.8 mm (0.028-0.031 inch) electrode gap.

MAINTENANCE

SPARK PLUG. Selection of spark plug will depend upon type of service and ambient temperature. Standard plug is given in Condensed Service Data table. Excessively cold weather and/or light load conditions may require spark plugs of warmer heat range. Hard usage, heavy loads and warm weather may require spark plugs of colder heat range.

CARBURETOR. A Keihin (PW) type carburetor is used on SS models prior to 1978 and a Keihin (BD) type carburetor is used on 1978-1981 SS models. A Mikuni (B) type carburetor is used on E338 models. Carburetor is installed on a "Y" type intake manifold and provides the fuel/air mixture to both cylinders. Standard idle speed setting is 1,700 rpm on E338 models, 2,000 rpm on SS338 models and 1,500 rpm on SS433 models. Initial fuel/air mixture setting is as follows:

Model	Turns Out
E338:	
1978-1985 models except EC/ET340J models	1
1985 EC/ET340J models	1-3/8
SS338:	
1976-1977 models	1
1978 models	1-1/8
SS433:	
1976-1977 models	1-1/4
1978 models	1-1/2
1979-1981 models	1-5/8

Standard carburetor main jet is as follows:

Model	Main Jet
E338:	
1978 models	220
1979-1984 models	240
1985 EC/ET340J models	135
1985 ET340TJ models	132.5
SS338:	
1976 models	155
1977 models	150
1978 models	140
SS433:	
1976 models	155
1977 models	150
1978 models	152
1979-1981 models	145

If carburetor is removed for overhaul, refer to LUBRICATION section for synchronizing Autolube pump to throttle opening.

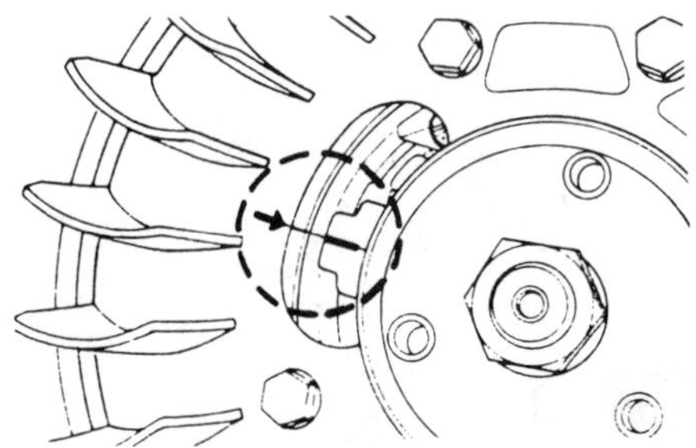

Fig. 1—View showing ignition timing marks located on flywheel and pulser coil used on SS models.

IGNITION AND TIMING. All models are equipped with a Capacitor Discharge Ignition (CDI) which is triggered by a pulser coil that is mounted on ignition stator plate. To check CDI system a special tester must be used. If ignition malfunction is suspected, first check all electrical connections and wires before testing system.

To check ignition timing on SS models built prior to 1980 proceed as follows: Remove recoil starter assembly, then remove left or right cylinder spark plug. Install special Yamaha dial indicator and stand or a suitable equivalent. Rotate flywheel until piston is at TDC, then zero dial indicator face with needle. Turn flywheel counterclockwise until dial indicator reads 1.6 mm (0.063 inch) BTDC on all models. Look through inspection hole in flywheel face and check to see that marks on flywheel and pulser coil are aligned as shown in Fig. 1. If adjustment is needed, reach through inspection hole in flywheel face with a Phillips screwdriver and loosen pulser coil retaining screws. Rotate pulser coil until marks align, then retighten screws. Recheck ignition timing, there should be no difference between left and right cylinder.

On 1980-1981 SS models proceed as follows: Remove recoil starter assembly

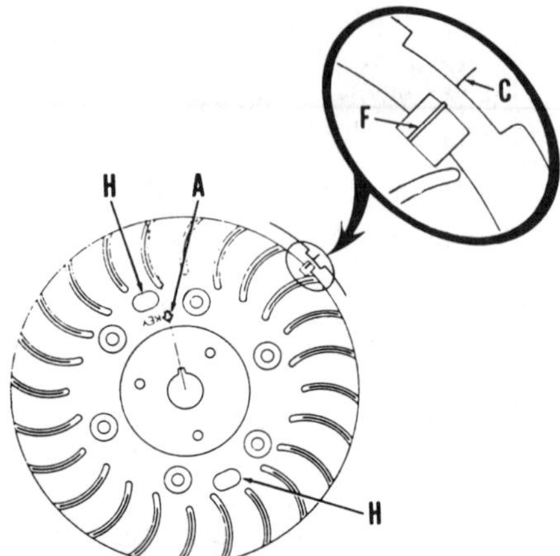

Fig. 2—View of CDI timing marks (C & F) used on E338 models. Mark (F) is on fan which should be attached to flywheel with arrow (A) pointing to flywheel keyway.

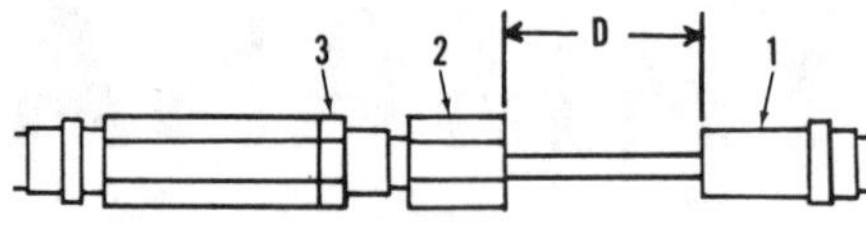

Fig. 3—View showing adjustment of oil pump control cable on models built prior to 1978.

1. Cable outer tube
2. Adjusting nut
3. Locknut
D. Distance

and right side spark plug, then install special Yamaha dial indicator or a suitable equivalent. Rotate flywheel until piston is at TDC, then zero dial indicator face with needle. Rotate flywheel counterclockwise for approximately 3½ needle revolutions, then rotate flywheel clockwise until dial indicator reads 1.6 mm (0.063 inch) BTDC on all models. Look through inspection hole in flywheel face and check to see that marks on flywheel and pulser coil are aligned as shown in Fig. 1. If adjustment is needed, reach through inspection hole in flywheel face with a Phillips screwdriver and loosen pulser coil retaining screws. Rotate pulser coil until marks align, then retighten screws. If adjustment cannot be reached by adjusting pulser coil, then remove flywheel retaining nut and washer. Using a suitable puller withdraw flywheel rotor off crankshaft. Using a Phillips screwdriver, loosen screws securing stator plate and slightly turn plate. Retighten plate securing screws, then reinstall flywheel rotor. Rotate pulser coil until marks align, then retighten screws. Recheck ignition timing, then reassemble in reverse order of disassembly.

On E338 models ignition timing is checked using a power timing light with engine running at idle setting. Timing mark (C–Fig. 2) on crankcase and (F) on flywheel should be aligned when timing light flashes. Timing mark (F) is located on fan which is bolted to flywheel. If fan is separated from flywheel, be sure to align arrow (A) with keyway in flywheel as shown. Holes (H) are provided so that screw attaching ignition stator plate to crankcase can be loosened and tightened without removing flywheel. To change timing, stop engine, remove rewind starter and loosen stator attaching screws through holes (H). Move stator slightly, then tighten retaining screws. Recheck timing with engine running, using a power timing light. Timing marks should align at piston position indicated in CONDENSED SERVICE DATA table.

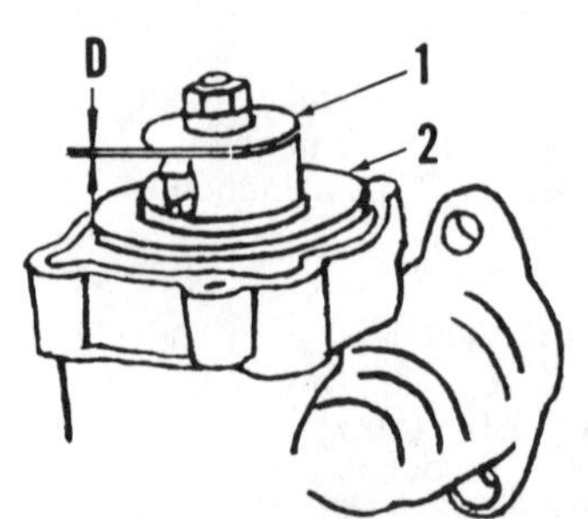

Fig. 4—View showing procedure for measuring "Autolube" pump minimum stroke distance. Distance (D) is measured between adjuster plate (1) and guide pulley (2). Refer to text.

Tighten flywheel nut to 71.6 N·m (53 ft.-lbs.) and the 6 mm cap screws which attach fan to flywheel to 6.9 N·m (60 in.-lbs.) torque. Use "Loctite" or equivalent on thread of fan to flywheel screws to prevent loosening.

LUBRICATION. A separate oil tank and metering system ("Autolube") is used. The system delivers varying amounts of oil depending upon engine rpm and throttle setting (load).

On 1976 and 1977 models, "Autolube" pump is controlled by a cable from throttle lever to the oil pump guide pulley. Check cable adjustment by pulling cable housing (1–Fig. 3) toward throttle lever, then measure distance (D) between end of cable housing and adjuster (2). Measured distance should be 32-34 mm (1.25-1.33 inch). To adjust, loosen locknut (3) and turn adjuster (2) until correct distance (D) is attained, then retighten locknut. To bleed air out of pump, remove bleed screw on back of pump. Turn starter plate clockwise until air bubbles disappear from oil, then reinstall bleeder screw and gasket. Minimum and maximum plunger stroke of oil injection pump is adjusted by varying the number of shims under adjuster plate (1–Fig. 4). Adding shims will increase stroke. To measure minimum pump stroke, turn pump starter plate until pump is at its outermost limit. Pump stroke is measured between adjuster plate (1) and guide pulley (2) as shown in Fig. 4. Correct minimum stroke is 0.1-0.15 mm (0.00390-0.0059 inch). Maximum plunger stroke measurement should be 1.80-1.97 mm (0.0709-0.0776 inch). Increase or decrease number of shims as needed, then recheck pump distance (D). Oil pump color code is yellow on SS338 models and light brown on SS433 models.

On **1978-1985 models** "Autolube" pump is controlled by a cable (C–Fig. 5) attached to pump control cam at one end and carburetor throttle lever at other end. To check adjustment, pull oil pump control cable away from adjuster as shown at (D). With carburetor at idle and oil pump cable pulled to maximum, distance (D) should be 24-26 mm (0.94-1.02 inch). If adjustment is incorrect, loosen locknut (L) and turn adjuster (A) until correct distance (D) is attained, then retighten locknut. Minimum

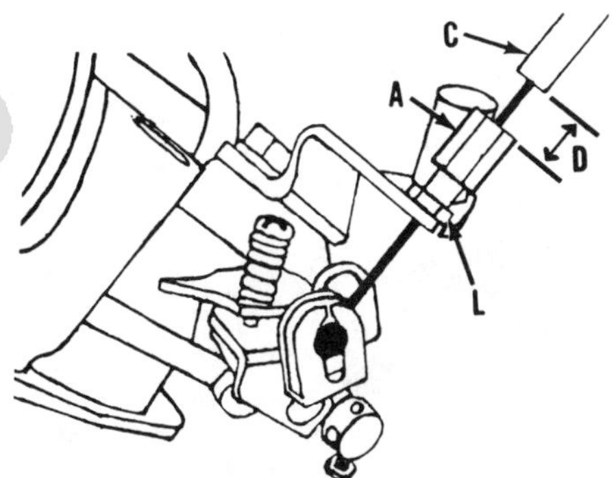

Fig. 5—View showing procedure for adjusting "Autolube" cable (C) on 1978-1985 models. Loosen locknut (L), turn adjuster (A) until correct distance (D) is attained. Refer to text.

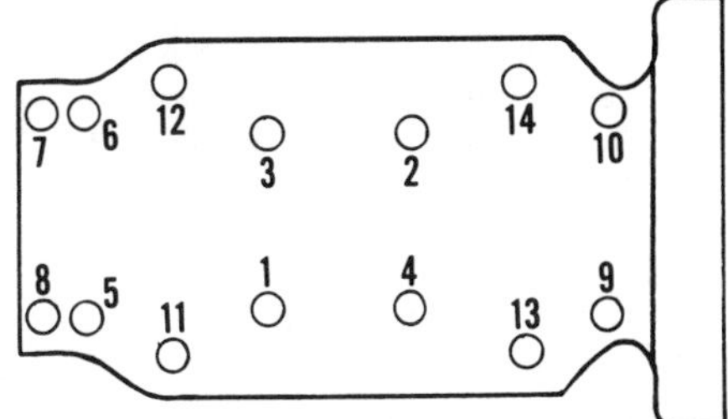

Fig. 6—View showing sequence for tightening crankcase cap screws on SS models.

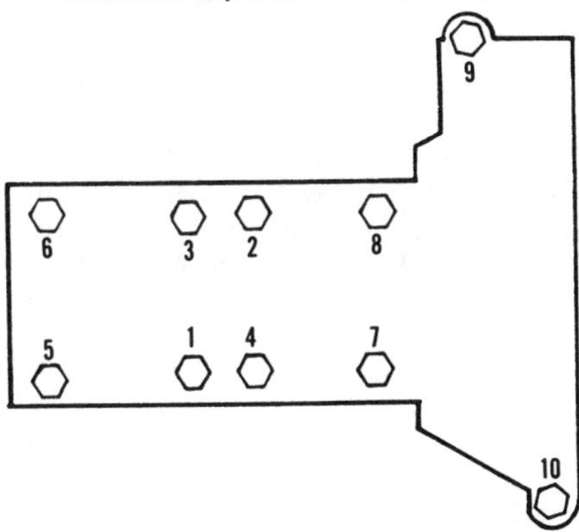

Fig. 7—View showing sequence for tightening crankcase cap screws on E338 models.

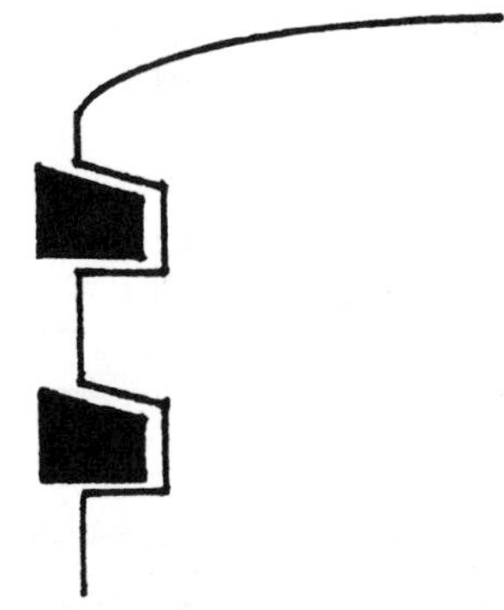

Fig. 8—View showing keystone rings installed correctly in piston ring grooves.

and maximum plunger stroke of oil injection pump is adjusted by varying the number of shims under adjuster plate (1–Fig. 4). Adding shims will increase stroke. To measure minimum pump stroke, turn pump drive gear until pump plunger is at its outermost limit. Pump stroke is measured between adjuster plate (1) and guide pulley (2) as shown in Fig. 4. Correct minimum stroke is 0.20-0.25 mm (0.0079-0.0098 inch). Maximum plunger stroke measurement should be 1.65-1.87 mm (0.0650-0.0736 inch). Increase or decrease number of shims as needed, then recheck pump distance (D). Oil pump color code is dark blue on SS433 models and white on E338 models.

To bleed oil pump, remove bleeder screw located at lower back side of pump. Continue to let engine oil run out bleeder hole until air bubbles disappear, then reinstall bleeder screw and gasket.

To bleed oil pump delivery lines, proceed as follows: Start engine, then pull oil pump control cable at carburetor out until pump plunger is at maximum stroke. Run engine at 2,000 rpm for two minutes. Check and refill oil tank as needed.

REPAIRS

TIGHTENING TORQUES. Recommended tightening torques are as follows:

*Crankcase Halves-
First torque . . . . . 10 N·m (7.5 ft.-lbs.)
Final torque. . . . . 20 N·m (15 ft.-lbs.)
Cylinder Head . . . . . 25 N·m (18 ft.-lbs)

*The crankcase screws should be loosened in sequence shown in Fig. 6 on SS models and Fig. 7 on E338 models starting at largest number and working down to smallest. Loosen screws in ¼-turn increments to prevent distortion of crankcase. When assembling, first install all screws evenly with no pressure until mating surfaces of crankcase halves are in full contact; tighten screws in sequence shown and to the recommended torques as listed above.

CYLINDER REMOVAL. Remove top air shroud, intake manifold, reed valves, exhaust pipes and any other part that will obstruct removal of cylinders. Remove cylinder head securing nuts, then withdraw cylinder head, cylinder and gaskets. Use care when removing cylinder to prevent damage to piston assembly or connecting rod.

CAUTION: Be especially careful to prevent foreign matter from falling into crankcase.

NOTE: Parts should not be interchanged between cylinders when reassembling. Mark all parts as they are removed to identify parts for installation in correct location.

CYLINDER INSPECTION. Check cylinder bore for wear or scoring. Standard cylinder bore is 60.00-60.02 mm (2.362-2.363 inches) on SS338 and E338 models and 68.00-68.02 mm (2.677-2.678 inches) on SS433 models. Cylinder bore should not be out-of-round more than 0.01 mm (0.0004 inch). Differences in bore diameter between top and bottom (taper) should not exceed 0.05 mm (0.002 inch). The cylinder should be renewed or bored to next larger oversize if out-of-round or taper is excessive. Oversize pistons and rings are available. Piston skirt to cylinder clearance should be 0.045-0.050 mm (0.0018-0.0020 inch) measured 17 mm from bottom of piston on SS models and 0.040-0.045 mm (0.0016-0.0018 inch) measured 10 mm from bottom of piston on E338 models.

CYLINDER INSTALLATION. Reassemble in reverse order of disassembly. Remove old gaskets and clean mounting surfaces, then install new gaskets. Piston ring grooves are pinned and ring end gaps must align with pins when installing cylinders. Use caution during installation to prevent damage to rings, pistons and cylinder walls. Tighten cylinder and cylinder head securing nuts to torque listed in TIGHTENING TORQUES paragraph.

PISTON, PINS AND RINGS. Remove cylinders as outlined in a previous paragraph. Clean piston pin bore, then remove pin retaining rings and push pin out of piston. Lift piston off connecting rod and disassemble.

Inspect piston pin and bearing for excessive wear, heat discoloration or any other damage. Inspect piston for excessive wear, cracks, pitting or any other damage. Renew all parts as needed. Piston pin should be a snug fit in piston bore, but it should be possible to install pin with thumb pressure.

Piston ring end gap installed should be 0.35-0.55 mm (0.014-0.022 inch) for top and bottom ring.

To reassemble, first install piston rings on piston. Keystone type rings must be correctly installed with tapered side toward top of piston as shown in Fig. 8. Position needle bearing in connecting rod bore and locate piston over end of rod with arrow pointing toward exhaust (front) side of engine. Lubricate parts with Two-Stroke Engine Oil during reassembly. Align piston pin bore with connecting rod and install piston pin. Install piston pin retaining rings making certain they are correctly seated in grooves. Reinstall cylinder, making certain that ring end gaps are around

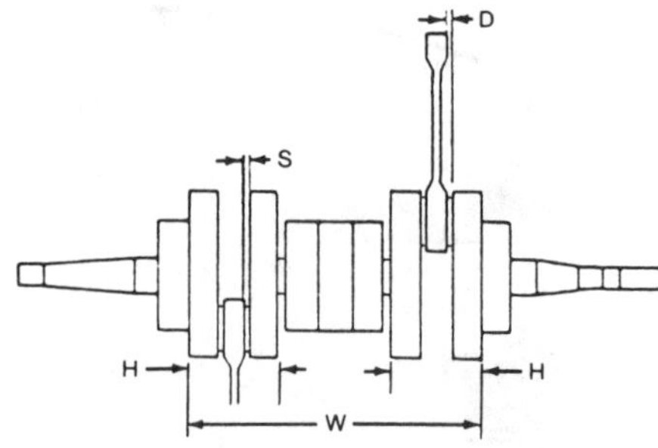

Fig. 9 — View showing position for checking connecting rod axial play (D), side clearance (S) and assembled width (W). Refer to text.

locating pins and rings are not damaged during reassembly.

CRANKCASE AND CRANKSHAFT. To disassemble, remove recoil starter assembly, starter pulley, drive fan pulley and belt on models so equipped. On 1980-1981 models equipped with axial fan, remove cap screws securing cooling fan assembly, then withdraw unit from engine assembly. Using a suitable flywheel holding tool remove flywheel retaining nut, then using a flywheel puller withdraw flywheel assembly. Remove and save key located in crankshaft groove. Remove Phillips head screws retaining stator plate, then withdraw plate assembly. Remove oil pump drive case and pump as an assembly. Disassemble top end of engine as outlined in previous sections. Loosen crankcase screws in sequence as shown in Fig. 6 for SS models and Fig. 7 for E338 models starting at largest number and working down to smallest. Loosen screws in ¼-turn increments to prevent distortion of crankcase. After removing crankcase cap screws lightly strike crankcase with a soft mallet to split upper and lower halves. Separate and lift crankshaft assembly out of crankcase.

Inspect crankcase halves for cracks, pitting, excessive wear or any other damage. Make sure all oil passages are open.

Inspect crankshaft bearings for binding, roughness or any other damage and renew as needed. Using a dial indicator check connecting rod axial play (D – Fig. 9) at top. Axial play should be no more than 2.0 mm (0.079 inch). Check connecting rod side clearance (S) with a feeler gage. Side clearance should be between 0.25-0.75 mm (0.010-0.030 inch). If measurements are not within specifications the crankshaft must be disassembled and defective parts renewed.

NOTE: Crankshaft alignment is very critical, only trained personnel should rebuild crankshaft assemblies.

Assembled width of each crankshaft half (H) should be 52 mm (2.047 inches) for E338 model; 56 mm (2.180 inches) for all SS models. Total width of assembled crankshaft (W) should be 160 mm (6.30 inches) for E338 model; 174 mm (6.85 inches) for SS338 and SS433 models. Crankshaft runout deflection on SS models should be no more than 0.03 mm (0.0012 inch) on left side, 0.04 mm (0.0016 inch) on center (left and right) and 0.05 mm (0.0020 inch) on right side. Crankshaft runout deflection on E338 models should be no more than 0.03 mm (0.0012 inch) on left side, 0.04 mm (0.0016 inch) on center (left and right) and 0.03 mm (0.0012 inch) on right side.

To reassemble crankcase, install crankshaft assembly with new oil seals in upper crankcase half. Be sure bearing pins fit in crankcase pin holes as shown in Fig. 10 and oil seal lip fits in crankcase groove. Apply YAMAHA BOND No. 4 or a suitable equivalent on mating surfaces of crankcase halves. Assemble crankcase halves and install securing cap screws. Tighten cap screws in sequence as shown in Fig. 6 on SS models and Fig. 7 on E338 models. Refer to TIGHTENING TORQUES section for torque specifications. Check crankshaft for freedom of movement and lubricate crankshaft bearings with a good quality Two-Stroke engine oil. Reassemble top end of engine as outlined in previous sections. Reassemble front end of engine in reverse order of disassembly. Refer to IGNITION AND TIMING section for setting engine timing. Refer to LUBRICATION section for adjusting oil pump control cable and bleeding out oil pump.

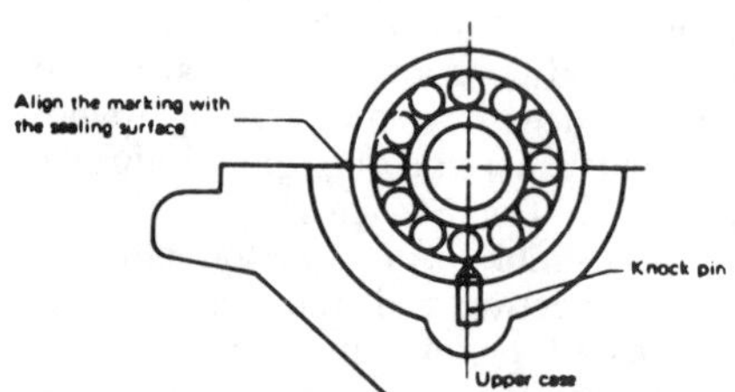

Fig. 10 — Align crankshaft bearings with alignment marks and locating holes.

RECOIL STARTER. Refer to Fig. 11 for a view of a typical early model recoil starter used. Starter must be removed and disassembled to renew rope and/or rewind spring. The rewind spring (3) should be wound into housing (1), beginning at outside and in counterclockwise direction. Pawl springs (7) should engage holes in pawls. Preload rewind spring approximately ⅓-turn to make certain that handle is pulled against housing when released.

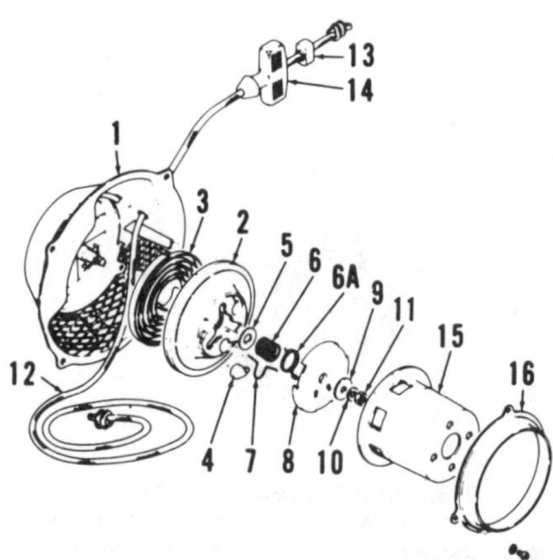

Fig. 11 — Exploded view of recoil starter assembly typical of early models. Three pawls (4) and pawl return springs (7) are used.

1. Housing
2. Pulley
3. Rewind spring
4. Pawls
5. Spring seat
6. Brake spring
6A. Drive plate spring
7. Pawl springs
8. Drive plate
9. Brake washer
10. Lockwasher
11. Nut
12. Rope
13. Anchor
14. Handle
15. Starter cup
16. Cover

For later models, refer to Fig. 12. Starter must be removed and disassembled to renew rope and/or rewind spring. The rewind spring (3) should be wound into housing (1), beginning at outside and in counterclockwise direction. Pawl springs (7) should engage holes in pawls (4). Preload rewind spring enough (4-5 turns) to make certain that handle is pulled against housing when released. Tighten nut (11) to approximately 12.75 N·m (113 in.-lbs.) torque.

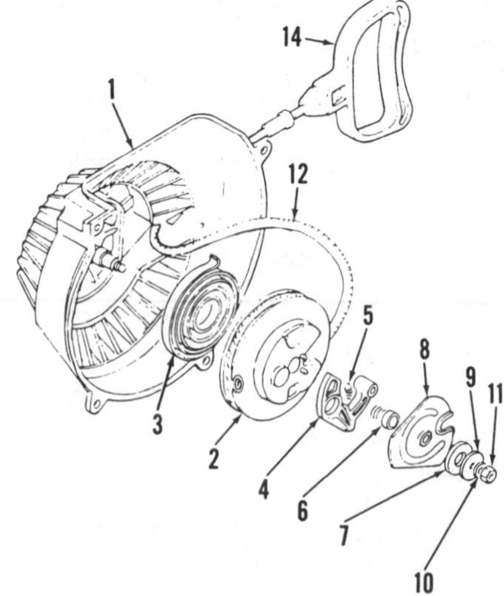

Fig. 12 — Exploded view of late type recoil starter.

1. Housing
2. Pulley
3. Rewind spring
4. Drive pawl
5. Return spring
6. Drive plate spring
7. Friction washer
8. Drive plate
9. Thrust washer
10. Lockwasher
11. Nut
12. Rope
14. Handle

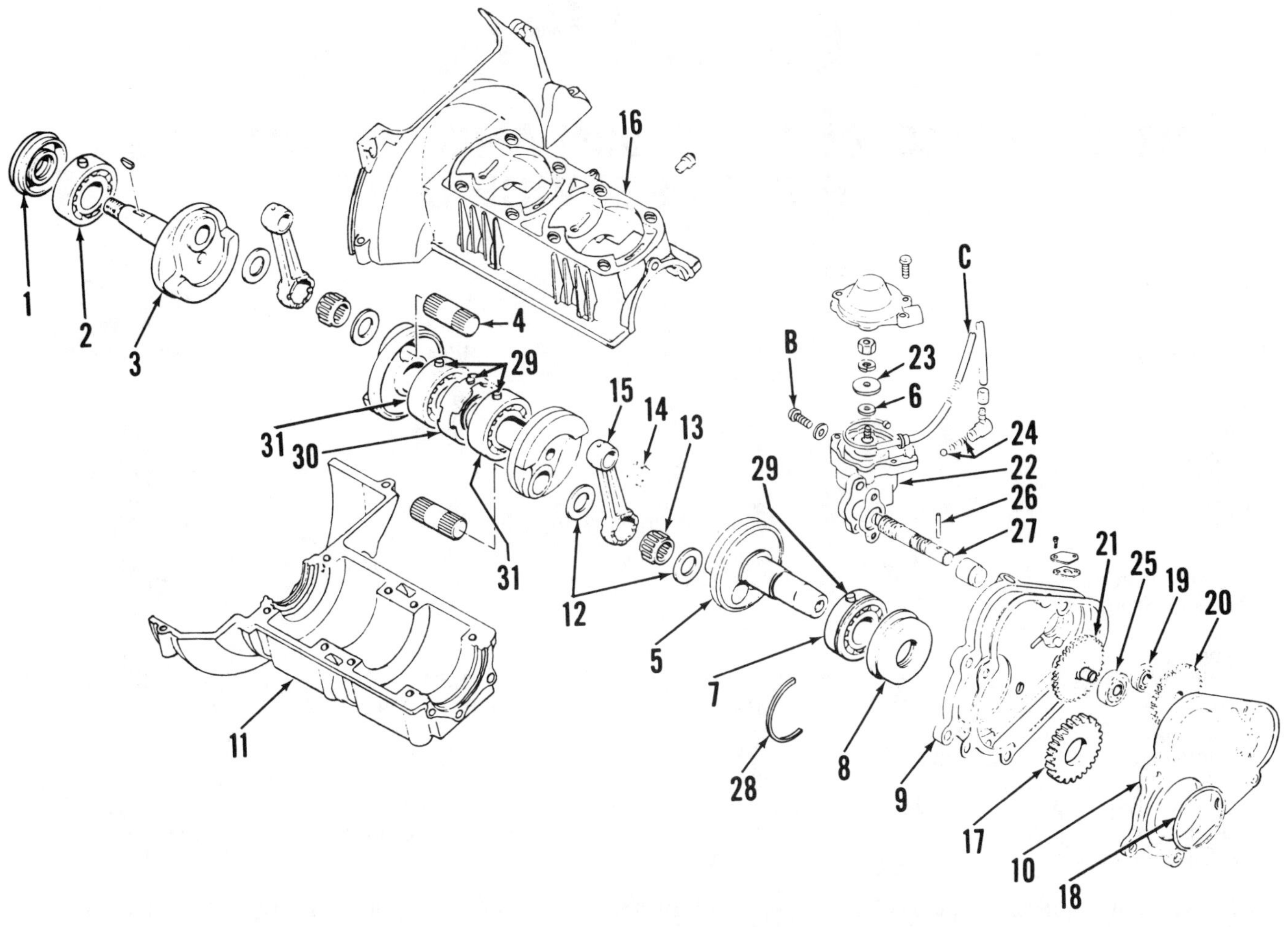

Fig. 13—Exploded view of crankcase and oil injection pump drive. Parts shown are not E338 model, but are similar.

C. Injection pump cable
1. Seal
2. Main bearing
3. Crankshaft
4. Crankpin
5. Crankshaft
6. Adjusting shim
7. Main bearing
8. Seal
9. Housing
10. Cover
11. Crankcase lower half
12. Thrust washer
13. Bearing
14. Connecting rod
15. Bearing
16. Crankcase upper half
17. Pump drive gear
18. Seal
19. Seal
20. Driven gear
21. Wave washer
22. Oil pump
23. Adjusting plate
24. Check ball and spring
25. Bearing support
26. Drive pin
27. Wormshaft

YAMAHA

RT437, RT439, 8U9, 8X6, 80N AND 81K MODELS CONDENSED SERVICE DATA

Engine Model	RT437	RT439	8U9, 8X6 80N, 81K
Bore – mm	66	68.5	73
Inches	2.598	2.697	2.87
Stroke – mm	64	59.6	64
Inches	2.52	2.346	2.52
No. of Cylinders	2	2	2
Displacement – cc	437	439	535
Cubic Inches	26.67	26.79	32.6
Cooling Type	Liquid	Liquid	Liquid
Carburetor Type	Mikuni (B)	Mikuni (VM)*	Mikuni (VM)
Number Used	2	2	2
Ignition:			
Type	CDI	CDI	CDI
Timing BTDC – mm	1.55-1.65	1.3-1.5	1.55-1.65
Inch	0.061-0.065	0.051-0.059	0.061-0.065
Spark Plug:			
Champion	.....	N2G†	.....
NGK	BR9EV	.....	BR9EV
Electrode Gap – mm	0.7-0.8	0.5-0.6	0.7-0.8
Inch	0.028-0.031	0.020-0.024	0.028-0.031
Fuel:Oil Ratio	Autolube	15:1‡	Autolube

*Models prior to 1980 use Mikuni (VM) carburetors. All 1980 models are equipped with Mikuni (B) model carburetors.

†Models prior to 1980 use Champion N2G spark plugs. Electrode gap is 0.5-0.6 mm (0.020-0.024 inch). All 1980 models use NGK BR9ES spark plugs. Electrode gap is 0.7-0.8 mm (0.028-0.031 inch).

‡Fuel and oil must be premixed on models prior to 1980 at a ratio of 15:1. All 1980 models are equipped with "Autolube".

MAINTENANCE

SPARK PLUG. Selection of spark plug will depend upon type of service and ambient temperature. Standard plug is given in CONDENSED SERVICE DATA table. Excessively cold weather and/or light load conditions may require spark plugs of warmer heat range. Hard usage, heavy loads and warm weather may require spark plugs of colder heat range.

CARBURETOR. All models are equipped with two Mikuni carburetors. Carburetors are mounted on individual flanges that are bolted to cylinder assemblies. Mikuni VM36 carburetors are used on 1979 and earlier RT439 models while Mikuni B38-36 carburetors are used on 1980 RT439 models. Mikuni B40-38 carburetors are used on RT437 models. Mikuni VM38 carburetors are used on all 8U9, 8X6, 80N and 81K models.

Standard idle speed setting is 1800 rpm on RT437 models and 1500 rpm on all remaining models. Initial air:fuel mixture screw setting is as follows:

Model	Turns Out
RT437:	
1981	1-3/4
RT439:	
1976-1979	1
1980	2
8U9, 8X6, 80N and 81K:	
1983-1985	1/2

Standard carburetor main jet size is as follows:

Model	Main Jet
RT437:	
1981	145
RT439:	
1976-1979	340
1980	260
8U9, 8X6, 8ON and 81K:	
1983-1985	290

If carburetor is removed for overhaul, refer to LUBRICATION section for synchronizing "Autolube" pump to throttle opening on models so equipped.

IGNITION AND TIMING. All models are equipped with a Capacitor Discharge Ignition (CDI) which is triggered by a pulser coil that is mounted on ignition stator plate. To check CDI system a special tester must be used. If ignition malfunction is suspected, first check all electrical connections and wires before testing system.

To check ignition timing remove right side spark plug and install special Yamaha dial indicator or a suitable equivalent. Rotate flywheel until piston is at TDC, then zero dial indicator face with needle. Rotate flywheel counterclockwise for approximately 3½ needle revolutions, then rotate flywheel clockwise until dial indicator reads 1.55-1.65 mm (0.061-0.065 inch) BTDC on RT437, 8U9, 8X6, 80N and 81K

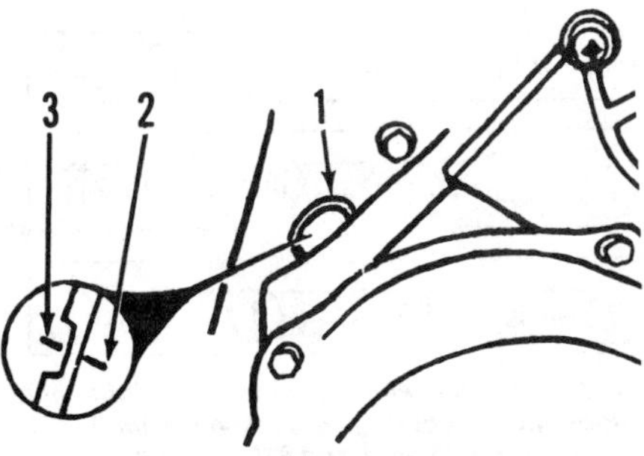

Fig. 1—View showing inspection hole (1) in crankcase cover for checking timing alignment marks on flywheel (2) and stator plate (3).

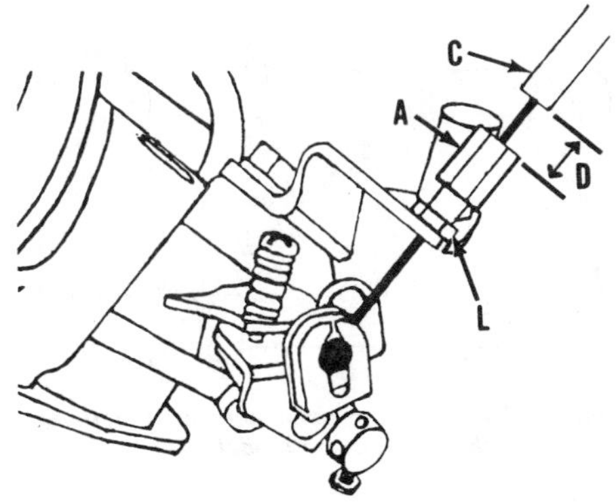

Fig. 2—View showing procedure for adjusting "Autolube" cable (C). Loosen locknut (L), turn adjuster (A) until correct distance (D) is attained. Refer to text.

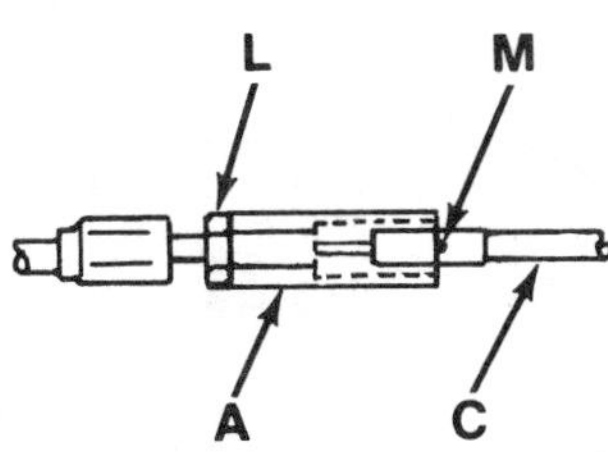

Fig. 3—Adjust oil pump cable free play on Models 8U9, 8X6, 80N and 81K using mark (M) as outlined in text.

models and 1.3-1.5 mm (0.051-0.059 inch) BTDC on RT439 models. Look through crankcase front cover inspection hole (1–Fig. 1) and check to see that marks on flywheel (2) and stator plate (3) are aligned. If marks are aligned then igntiion timing is correct and no adjustment is needed. Should adjustment be needed proceed as follows:

Remove recoil starter assembly, then using a Philips screwdriver reach through holes in flywheel face and loosen screws securing stator plate. Turn stator plate until timing marks are aligned, then retighten screws. Recheck ignition timing, then reassemble in reverse order of disassembly.

LUBRICATION. On all RT439 models built prior to 1980 fuel and oil must be premixed at a ratio of 15:1 before being poured into fuel tank. Manufacturer recommends using Yamalube Two-Stroke Engine Oil or a suitable equivalent.

Models equipped with "Autolube" use a separate oil tank and metering system. The system delivers varying amounts of oil depending upon engine rpm and throttle setting (load).

On RT437 and 1980 RT439 models, oil delivery is controlled by cable (C–Fig. 2) attached to pump control cam at one end and carburetor throttle lever at other end. To check adjustment, pull oil pump control cable away from adjuster as shown at (D). With carburetor at idle and oil pump cable pulled to maximum, distance (D) should be 22-24 mm (0.87-0.95 inch).

On 8U9, 8X6, 80N and 81K models, oil delivery is controlled by a cable attached to pump control cam at one end and throttle grip on handlebar at the other end. To check cable free play locate the cable adjuster and pull cable (C–Fig. 3) away from adjuster (A) until all slack is removed. With slack removed, mark (M) on cable housing should be even with end of adjuster. To adjust cable free play, loosen locknut (L) and rotate adjuster (A) until mark on housing aligns with adjuster end as shown, then tighten locknut.

On all models, minimum and maximum plunger stroke of oil injection pump is adjusted by varying the numer of shims under adjuster plate (1–Fig. 4). Adding shims will increase stroke.

To measure minimum pump stroke, turn pump drive gear until pump plunger is at its outermost limit. Pump stroke is measured between adjuster plate (1) and guide pulley (2) as shown in Fig. 4. Correct minimum stroke is 0.20-0.25 mm (0.0079-0.0098 in.) on 1980 RT439 models, 0.25-0.30 mm (0.0098-0.0118 in.) on RT437 models and 0.50-0.55 mm (0.0197-0.0217 in.) on 8U9, 8X6, 80N and 81K models. Maximum plunger stroke measurement should be 1.67-1.87 mm (0.0657-0.0736 in.) on 1980 RT439 models, 1.72-1.92 mm (0.0677-0.0755 in.) on RT437 models and 2.15-2.27 mm (0.0846-0.0894 in.) on 8U9, 8X6, 80N and 81K models. Increase or decrease number of shims if needed, then recheck pump stroke distance (D). Oil pump color code is yellow on 1980 RT439 models, green on RT437 models, black on 8U9 models and red on 8X6, 80N and 81K models.

Any operation that required draining or repair of oil injection components will make it necessary to fill and bleed system. Check oil reservoir fluid level before proceeding and fill with YAMALUBE 2-Cycle injector oil or a manufacturer approved equivalent. Bleed air from injection pump before running engine. To bleed injection pump, remove bleeder screw located at lower back side of oil pump. With the ignitión switched off, crank engine with rewind starter until air-free oil flows from screw opening. Reinstall bleeder screw and gasket. Start engine and pull oil pump control cable out of adjuster until all slack is removed. With slack removed, oil pump is at maximum discharge position. Increase engine speed to 3000 rpm for 2-3 minutes. Stop engine and refill oil tank if required.

PUMP DRIVE GEARCASE. Models RT437, 8U9, 8X6, 80N and 81K are equipped with a water and oil pump drive gearcase mounted on the flywheel end of engine crankcase. Recommended oil is SAE 75 or 80 oil with an API classification of GL-3 on RT437 models and SAE 80W-90 oil with an API classification of GL-4 on all other models.

The gearcase is filled through dipstick opening on top of gearcase. Oil level should be maintained at upper mark on dipstick. Oil is drained by removing bolt located on bottom of gearcase next to crankcase. Gearcase dry capacity is 35-40 cc (1.18-1.35 oz.).

COOLING SYSTEM. Mixture ratio of antifreeze to water should be 1:1 down to −40 degrees C (−40 degrees F), when ambient temperature drops below −40 degrees C (−40 degrees F) mixture ratio should be 3:2 (60% antifreeze: 40% water).

To drain coolant, first remove radiator cap.

CAUTION: Release coolant pressure slowly, injury could occur if coolant is hot and under pressure.

Remove drain bolts located above exhaust outlets on each cylinder. On RT439 models remove bypass hose located on thermostat housing and point hose downward to drain heat exchanger and water pump. On RT439, 8U9, 8X6, 80N and 81K models remove bypass

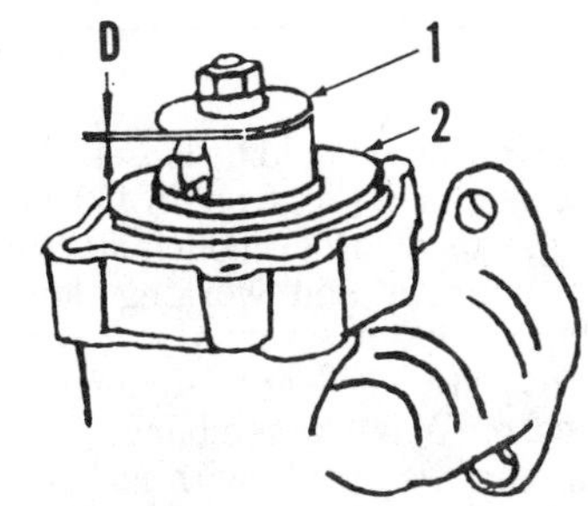

Fig. 4—View showing procedure for measuring "Autolube" pump minimum stroke distance. Distance (D) is measured between adjuster plate (1) and guide pulley (2). Refer to text.

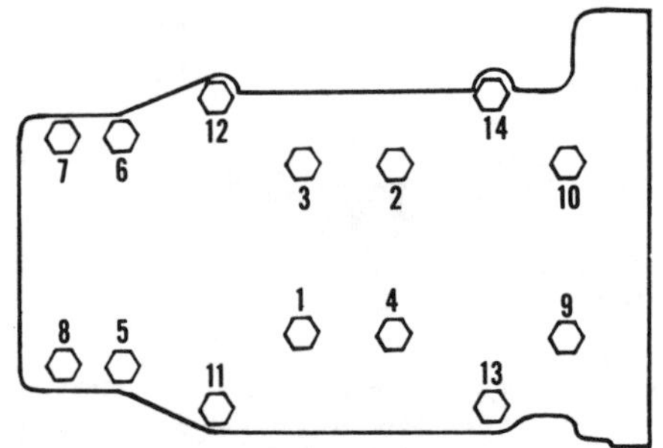

Fig. 5—View showing sequence for tightening crankcase bolts on Model RT439.

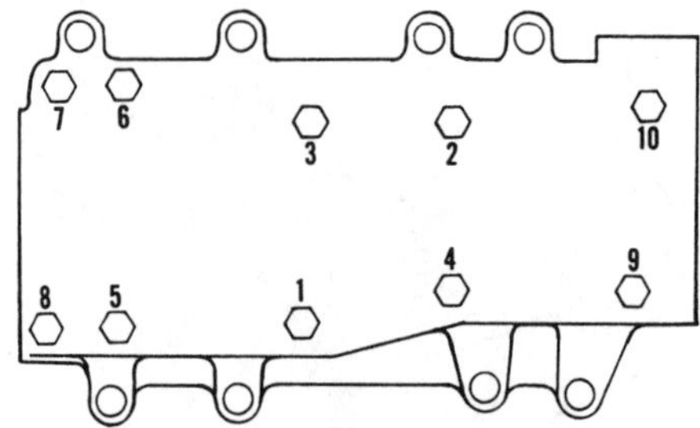

Fig. 6—View showing sequence for tightening crankcase bolts on Model RT437.

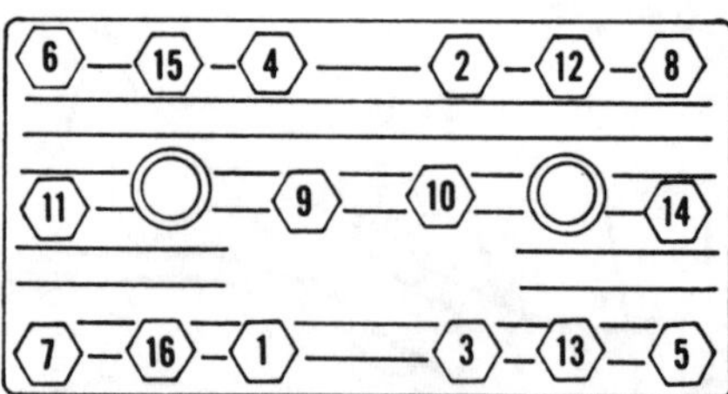

Fig. 7—View showing sequence for tightening cylinder head securing nuts and bolts for RT437, 8U9, 8X6, 80N and 81K models.

hose located under temperature meter block and point hose downward to drain heat exchanger and water pump.

To refill, reinstall bypass hose and cylinder drain bolts. Tighten drain bolts to 28-30 N•m (20.3-21.7 ft.-lbs.). Loosen bleeder bolt located on top of thermostat housing, then pour coolant of correct mixture in radiator until coolant begins to run out bleeder bolt hole. Tighten bleeder bolt. Start and allow engine to warm up, then add coolant in radiator until proper level is attained. When engine is cold check coolant level in reservoir tank and add as needed.

On Model RT439 water pump drive belt deflection should be 4 mm (0.16 inch) when 9 pounds of pressure is applied to center of belt. To adjust, loosen water pump assembly securing cap screws and slide assembly until correct deflection is attained. If belt is damaged or correct adjustment cannot be attained, then drive belt must be renewed.

REPAIRS

TIGHTENING TORQUES. Recommended tightening torques are as follows:

*Crankcase Halves–
First torque . . . . 10 N•m (7 ft.-lbs.)
Final torque . . . . 22 N•m (16 ft.-lbs.)

Cylinder Head–
8 mm bolt . . . . 25 N•m (18 ft.-lbs.)
10 mm nut . . . . 30 N•m (21.5 ft.-lbs.)

*The crankcase should be loosened in sequence shown in Fig. 5 on RT439 models and Fig. 6 on all other models starting at largest number and working down to smallest. Loosen screws in ¼ turn increments to prevent distortion of crankcase. When assembling, first install all screws evenly with no pressure until mating surfaces of crankcase halves are in full contact; tighten screws in sequence shown and to the recommended torques as listed above.

CYLINDER REMOVAL. Remove top air shroud, thermostat housing and "Y" manifold, exhaust pipe and any other part that will obstruct removal of cylinders. Remove cylinder head securing nuts and bolts, then withdraw cylinder head, cylinder and gaskets. Use care when removing cylinder to prevent damage to piston assembly or connecting rod.

CAUTION: Be especially careful to prevent foreign matter from falling into crankcase.

NOTE: Parts should not be interchanged between cylinders when reassembling. Mark all parts as they are removed to identify parts for installation in correct location.

CYLINDER INSPECTION. Check cylinder bore for wear or scoring. Standard cylinder bore is 66 mm (2.59 inch) on RT437 models, 68.5 mm (2.697 inch) on RT437 models and 73 mm (2.87 inch) on 8U9, 8X6, 80N and 81K models. Cylinder bore should not be out-of-round more than 0.01 mm (0.0004 inch). Differences in bore diameter between top and bottom (taper) should not exceed 0.05 mm (0.002 inch). The cylinder must be renewed if out-of-round or taper is excessive. Cylinder bores are hard chromed and cannot be bored. Piston skirt to cylinder clearance should be 0.065-0.070 mm (0.0026-0.0028 inch) measured 10 mm from bottom of piston on RT439 models and 15 mm from bottom of piston on all other models.

CYLINDER INSTALLATION. Reassemble in reverse order of disassembly. Remove old gaskets and clean mounting surfaces, then install new gaskets. Piston ring grooves are pinned and ring end gaps must align with pins when installing cylinders. Use caution during installation to prevent damage to rings, pistons and cylinder walls. Tighten cylinder and cylinder head securing nuts and bolts to torque listed in TIGHTENING TORQUES paragraph. On RT437, 8U9, 8X6, 80N and 81K models, tighten cylinder head bolts and nuts in sequence shown in Fig. 7.

PISTON, PINS AND RINGS. Remove cylinders as outlined in previous section. Clean piston pin bore, then remove pin retaining rings and push pin out of piston. Lift piston off connecting rod and disassemble.

Inspect piston pin and bearing for excessive wear, heat discoloration or any other damage. Inspect piston for excessive wear, cracks, pitting or any other damage. Renew all parts as needed. Piston pin should be a snug fit in piston bore, but it should be possible to install pin with thumb pressure.

Piston ring end gap installed should be 0.35-0.55 mm (0.014-0.022 inch).

To reassemble, first install piston ring on piston. Keystone type ring must be correctly installed with tapered side toward top of piston as shown in Fig. 8. Position needle bearing in connecting rod bore and locate piston over end of rod with ring end gap facing towards intake port side. Lubricate parts with two-stroke engine oil during reassembly. Align piston pin bore with connecting rod and install piston pin. Install piston pin retaining rings making certain they are correctly seated in grooves. Reinstall cylinder, making certain that ring end gaps are around locating pins and rings are not damaged during reassembly.

CRANKCASE AND CRANKSHAFT (Model RT439). To disassemble, remove recoil starter assembly and starter pulley. Remove water pump drive pulley and belt, then remove water pump

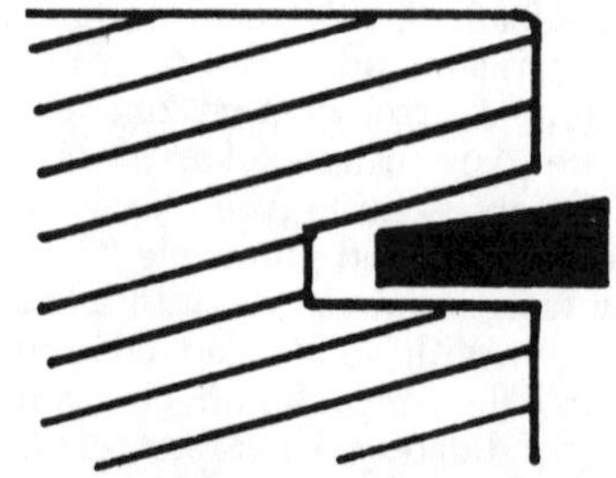
Fig. 8—View showing keystone ring installed correctly in piston ring groove.

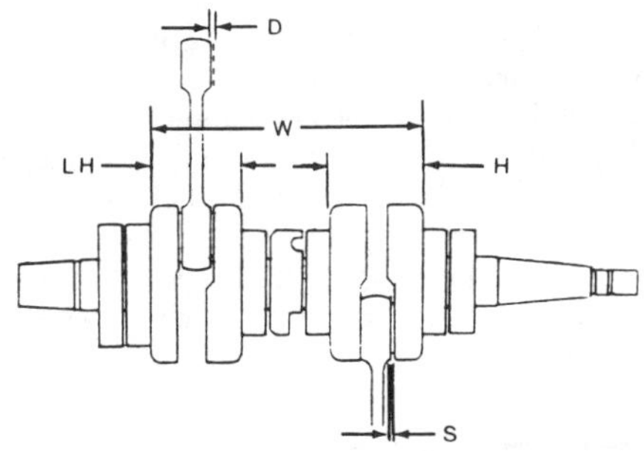

Fig. 9—View showing position for checking connectng rod axial play (D), side clearance (S) and assembled width (W) for Model RT439. Refer to text.

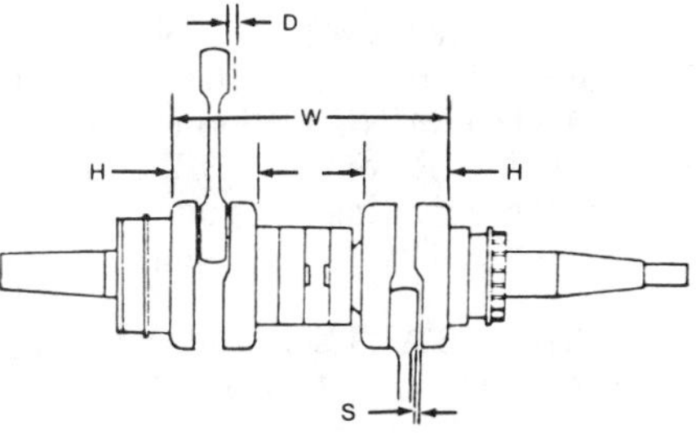

Fig. 10—View showing position for checking connecting rod axial play (D), side clearance (S) and assembled width (W) for RT437, 8U9, 8X6, 80N and 81K models. Refer to text.

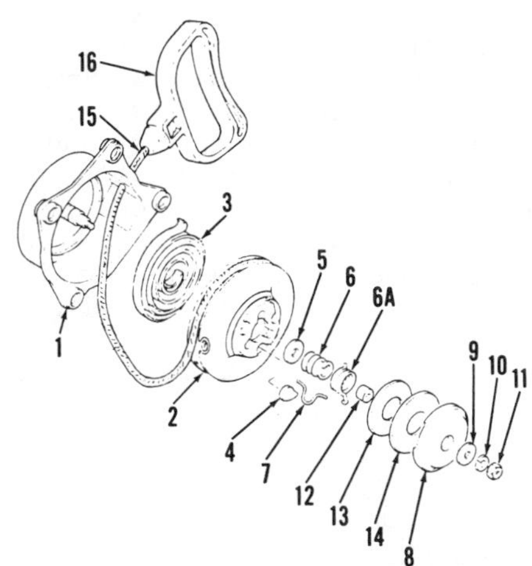

Fig. 11—Exploded view of recoil starter.

1. Housing
2. Pulley
3. Rewind spring
4. Drive pawls
5. Spring seat
6. Brake spring
6A. Drive plate spring
7. Pawl springs
8. Drive plate
9. Flat washer
10. Lockwasher
11. Nut
12. Spacer
13. Washer
14. Washer
15. Rope
16. Handle

assembly securing cap screws and withdraw pump. Remove four cap screws securing crankcase cover and withdraw cover. Using a suitable flywheel holding tool remove flywheel retaining nut, then using a flywheel puller withdraw flywheel assembly. Remove and save key located in crankshaft groove. Remove Phillips head screws retaining stator plate, then withdraw plate assembly. Remove oil pump drive case and pump as an assembly. Disassemble top end of engine as outlined in previous sections. Loosen crankcase cap screws in sequence as shown in Fig. 5 starting at largest number and working down to smallest. Loosen screws in ¼ turn increments to prevent distortion of crankcase. After removing crankcase cap screws lightly strike crankcase with a soft mallet to split upper and lower halves. Separate and lift crankshaft assembly out of crankcase.

Inspect crankcase halves for cracks, pitting, excessive wear or any other damage. Make sure all oil passages are open. Inspect crankshaft bearings for binding, roughness or any other damage and renew as needed. Using a dial indicator check connecting rod axial play (D–Fig. 9) at top. Axial play should be no more than 2.0 mm (0.079 inch). Check connecting rod side clearance (S) with a feeler gage. Side clearance should be between 0.25-0.75 mm (0.010-0.030 inch). If measurements are not within specifications then crankshaft must be disassembled and defective parts renewed.

NOTE: Crankshaft alignment is very critical, only trained personnel should rebuild crankshaft assemblies.

Assembled width of each crankshaft half (H) should be 60 mm (2.362 inches). Total width of assembled crankshaft (W) should be 178 mm (7 inches). Crankshaft runout deflection should be no more than 0.03 mm (0.0012 inch) on left side, 0.04 mm (0.0016 inch) on center (left and right) and 0.05 mm (0.0020 inch) on right side.

To reassemble crankcase, install crankshaft assembly with new oil seals in upper crankcase half. Be sure bearing pins fit in crankcase pin holes and oil seal lip fits in crankcase groove. Apply YAMAHA BOND No. 4 or a suitable equivalent on mating surfaces of crankcase halves. Assemble crankcase halves and install securing cap screws. Tighten cap screws in sequence as shown in Fig. 5. Refer to TIGHTENING TORQUES section for torque specifications. Check crankshaft for freedom of movement and lubricate crankshaft bearings with a good quality two-stroke engine oil. Reassemble top end of engine as outlined in previous sections. Reassemble front end of engine in reverse order of disassembly. Refer to IGNITION AND TIMING section for setting engine timing. Refer to LUBRICATION section for adjusting oil pump control cable and bleeding out oil pump.

CRANKCASE AND CRANKSHAFT (Models RT437, 8U9, 8X6, 80N and 81K). To disassemble, remove recoil starter assembly and starter pulley. Using a suitable flywheel holding tool remove flywheel retaining nut, then using a flywheel puller withdraw flywheel assembly. Remove and save key located in crankshaft groove. Remove Phillips head screws retaining stator plate, then withdraw plate assembly. Remove five cap screws securing gearcase assembly, then using a suitable puller withdraw gearcase, oil pump and water pump impeller as a complete unit. Disassemble top end of engine as outlined in previous sections. Loosen crankcase cap screws in sequence as shown in Fig. 6 starting at largest number and working down to smallest. Loosen screws in ¼ turn increment to prevent distortion of crankcase. After removing crankcase cap screws lightly strike crankcase with a soft mallet to split upper and lower halves. Separate and lift crankshaft assembly out of crankcase.

Inspect crankcase halves for cracks, pitting, excessive wear or any other damage. Make sure all oil passages are open. Inspect crankshaft bearings for binding, roughness or any other damage and renew as needed. Using a dial indicator check connecting rod axial play (D–Fig. 10) at top. Axial play should be no more than 2.0 mm (0.079 inch). Check connecting rod side clearance (S) with a feeler gage. Side clearance should be between 0.25-0.75 mm (0.010-0.030 inch). If measurements are not within specifications then crankshaft must be disassembled and defective parts renewed.

NOTE: Crankshaft alignment is very critical, only trained personnel should rebuild crankshaft assemblies. Crankshaft assembled width (W) should be 200 mm (7.87 inch).

Assembled width of left crankshaft half (LH) should be 63 mm (2.48 inches) and assembled width of right crankcase half (H) should be 60 mm (2.362 inches). Total width of assembled crankshaft (W) should be 200 mm (7.87 inch). Crankshaft runout deflection should be no more than 0.03 mm (0.0012 inch) on left side, 0.04 mm (0.0016 inch) on center (left and right) and 0.05 mm (0.0020 inch) on right side.

To reassemble crankcase, install crankshaft assembly with new oil seals in upper crankcase half. Be sure bearing pins fit in crankcase pin holes and oil seal lip fits in crankcase groove. Apply YAMAHA BOND No. 4 or a suitable equivalent on mating surfaces of crankcase halves. Assemble crankcase halves and install securing cap screws. Tighten cap screws in sequence as shown in Fig. 6. Refer to TIGHTENING TORQUES section for torque specifications. Check crankshaft for freedom of movement and lubricate crankshaft bearings with a good quality two-stroke engine oil. Reassemble top end of engine as outlined in previous sections. Reassemble front end of engine in reverse order of disassembly. Gear case assembly should be filled with 35-40 cc (1.18-1.35 ounces) of API GL-3 SAE 75 or 80 gear oil on RT437 models and API GL-4 SAE 80W-90 gear oil on 8U9, 8X6, 80N and 81K models. Refer to IGNITION AND TIMING section for setting engine timing. Refer to LUBRICATION section for adjusting oil pump control cable and bleeding out oil pump.

RECOIL STARTER. Refer to Fig. 11. The starter must be removed and disassembled to renew rope and/or rewind spring. The rewind spring (3) should be wound into housing (1), beginning at outside and counterclockwise direction. Pawl springs (7) should engage holes in pawls (4). Preload rewind spring enough to make certain that handle is pulled against housing when released.

YAMAHA

SA437, SA535, 80K, 80L, 8VO AND 8Y7 MODELS

CONDENSED SERVICE DATA

Engine Model	SA437	80K, 80L, 8VO	SA535	8Y7
Bore – mm	66	72	73	73
Inches	2.598	2.83	2.874	2.874
Stroke – mm	64	59.6	64	64
Inches	2.52	2.34	2.52	2.52
No. of Cylinders	2	2	2	2
Displacement – cc	437	485	535	535
Cubic Inches	26.67	29.59	32.65	32.65
Cooling Type	Axial Fan	Axial Fan	Axial Fan	Axial Fan
Carburetor Model	Keihin (BD)	Mikuni (B)	Keihin (BD)	Mikuni (B)
Number Used	1	2	1	1
Ignition:				
Type	CDI	CDI	CDI	CDI
Timing BTDC – mm	1.3-1.5	1.5	1.4-1.6	1.5
Inch	0.051-0.059	0.059	0.055-0.063	0.059
Spark Plug:				
NGK	BR9ES	BR9ES	BR9EV*	BR9ES
Electrode Gap – mm	0.7-0.8	0.7-0.8	0.7-0.8	0.7-0.8
Inch	0.028-0.031	0.028-0.031	0.028-0.031	0.028-0.031
Fuel:Oil Ratio	Autolube	Autolube	Autolube	Autolube

*SA535 models prior to 1981 use NGK BR9ES spark plugs.

MAINTENANCE

SPARK PLUG. Selection of spark plug will depend upon type of service and ambient temperature. Standard plug is given in CONDENSED SERVICE DATA table. Excessively cold weather and/or light load conditions may require spark plugs of warmer heat range. Hard usage, heavy loads and warm weather may require spark plugs of colder heat range.

CARBURETOR. One carburetor is used on SA437, SA535 and 8Y7 models. Carburetor is installed on a "Y" type manifold and provides the air:fuel mixture to both cylinders. Two carburetors are used on 80K, 80L and 8VO models. Carburetors are mounted on individual intake manifolds that are bolted to cylinder assemblies. Standard idle speed setting is 1500 rpm on SA437, SA535 and 8Y7 models and 1600 rpm on 80K, 80L and 8VO models. Initial air:fuel mixture screw setting is as follows:

Vehicle Model	Turns Out
Excel V:	
1979-1980 models	2-1/4
PZ480:	
1984-1985 models	1-1/2
SR540:	
1980 models	2-5/8
1981-1982 models	2-1/4
1983-1985 models	2
SS440:	
1980 models	1-1/2
1981-1985 models	2
XL540:	
1985 models	1-1/2

Standard carburetor main jet size is as follows:

Vehicle Model	Main Jet
Excel V:	
1979-1980 models	150
PZ480:	
1984 models	143.8
1985 models	145
SR540:	
1980 models	145
1981-1985 models	150
SS440:	
1980 models	135
1981-1982 models	160
1983-1985 models	155
XL540:	
1985 models	132.5

Float height should be 15 mm (0.59 in.) on Keihin carburetors and 12 mm (0.47 in.) on Mikuni carburetors. To check float height, remove float bowl and invert carburetor. Measure the distance beween bottom of float and outer flange on carburetor body as shown in Fig. 1. Float should be resting lightly on inlet needle when checking height. Carefully bend float arm tang to adjust.

If carburetor is removed for overhaul, refer to LUBRICATION section for synchronizing "Autolube" pump to throttle opening.

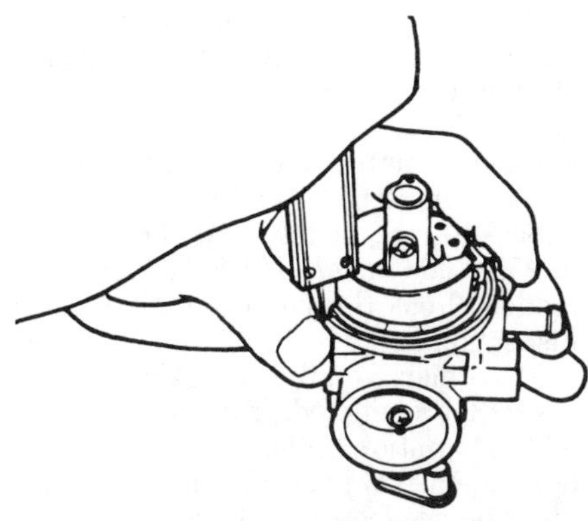

Fig. 1 – Measure float height from bottom of float to outer flange on carburetor body.

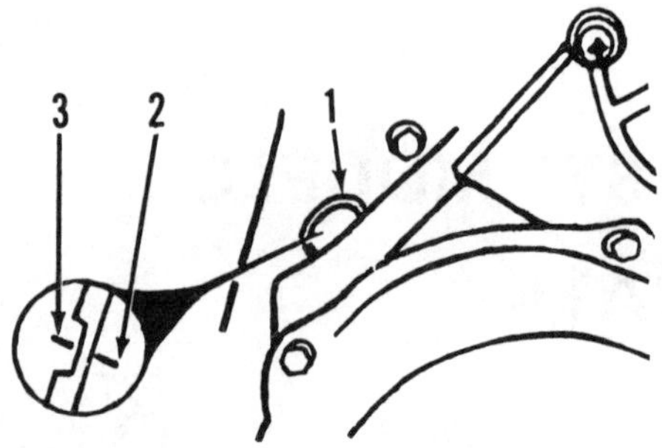

Fig. 2 — View showing inspection hole (1) in cooling fan cover for checking timing alignment marks on flywheel (2) and stator plate (3).

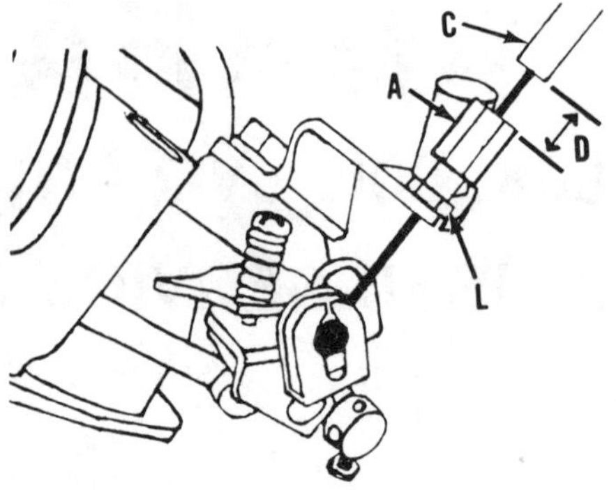

Fig. 3 — View showing procedure for adjusting "Autolube" cable (C). Loosen locknut (L), turn adjuster (A) until correct distance (D) is attained. Refer to text.

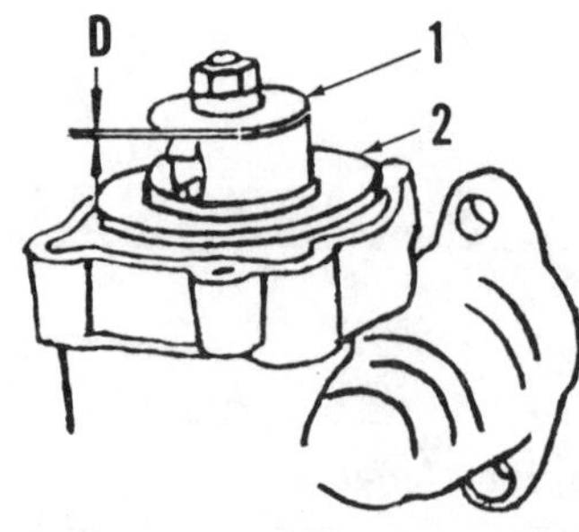

Fig. 4 — View showing procedure for measuring "Autolube" pump minimum stroke distance. Distance (D) is measured between adjuster plate (1) and guide pulley (2). Refer to text.

REED VALVES. All models are equipped with a "V" type reed valve assembly for each cylinder. Remove carburetor(s) and manifold(s) for access to reed valve assemblies.

The reed petals should seat very lightly against the reed block throughout their entire length, with the least possible tension. Tip of reed petal must not stand open more than 1.0 mm (0.04 in.) on 80K, 80L and 8VO models and 0.6 mm (0.024 in.) on all other models. Reed stop opening should be 9.5-9.9 mm (0.37-0.39 in.) on 80K, 80L and 8VO models and 11.8-12.2 mm (0.47-0.48 in.) on all other models. Seating surface of reed block should be smooth and flat. When installing reed and reed stop, make sure beveled corner on reed aligns with beveled corner on stop and that reed petals are centered over the inlet holes in reed block.

IGNITION AND TIMING. All models are equipped with a Capacitor Discharge Ignition (CDI) which is triggered by a pulser coil that is mounted on ignition stator plate. To check CDI system a special tester must be used. If ignition malfunction is suspected, first check all electrical connections and wires before testing system.

To check ignition timing remove right side spark plug and install special Yamaha dial indicator or a suitable equivalent. Rotate flywheel until piston is at TDC, then zero dial indicator face with needle. Rotate flywheel counterclockwise for approximately 3½ needle revolutions, then rotate flywheel clockwise until dial indicator reads 1.3-1.5 mm (0.051-0.059 inch) BTDC on 1980 437 cc models and 1.4-1.6 mm (0.055-0.063 inch) BTDC on all other models. Look through cooling fan cover inspection hole (1 – Fig. 2) and check to see that marks on flywheel (2) and stator plate (3) are aligned. If marks are aligned then ignition timing is correct and no adjustment is needed. Should adjustment be needed proceed as follows:

Remove recoil starter assembly, starter pulley and drive fan pulley. Using a Phillips screwdriver, reach through holes in flywheel face and loosen screws securing stator place. Turn stator plate until timing marks are aligned, then retighten screws. Recheck ignition timing, then reassembly in reverse order of disassembly.

LUBRICATION. A separate oil tank and metering system ("Autolube") is used. The system delivers varying amounts of oil depending upon engine rpm and throttle setting (load).

Oil delivery is controlled by cable (C – Fig. 3) attached to pump control cam at one end and carburetor throttle lever at other end. To check adjustment, pull oil pump control cable away from adjuster as shown at (D). With carburetor at idle and oil pump cable pulled to maximum distance (D) should be 21-23 mm (0.83-0.91 in.) on 80K, 80L and 8VO models and 24-26 mm (0.94-1.02 in.) on all remaining models. If adjustment is incorrect, loosen locknut (L) and turn adjuster (A) until distance (D) is correct, then retighten locknut.

On all models, minimum and maximum plunger stroke of oil injection pump is adjusted by varying the number of shims under adjuster plate (1 – Fig. 4). Adding shims will increase stroke.

To measure minimum pump stroke, turn pump drive gear until pump plunger is at its outermost limit. Pump stroke is measured between adjuster plate (1) and guide pulley (2) as shown in Fig. 3. Correct minimum stroke is 0.15-0.20 mm (0.006-0.008 in.) on PZ480 models and 0.20-0.25 mm (0.0079-0.0098 in.) for all remaining models. Maximum plunger stroke measurement should be 1.56-1.87 mm (0.066-0.074 inch) for 1980-1982 SS440 models, 1.62-1.80 mm (0.064-0.070 in.) on PZ480 models, 1.67-1.87 mm (0.065-0.073 in.) for 1979 Excel V models, 1.65-1.87 mm (0.065-0.074 in.) for 1980 Excel V models, 1980-1982 SR540 and XL540 models. Increase or decrease number of shims as needed, then recheck pump distance (D). Oil pump color code is red on 1980-1982 SS440 models, black on PZ480 models, brown in 1979-1980 Excel V models, pink on 1980-1981 SR540 models, gray on1982 SR540 models and yellow on XL540 models.

REPAIRS

TIGHTENING TORQUES. Recommended tightening torques are as follows:

*Crankcase Halves –
8 mm Bolt
First torque . . . . 9.5 N·m (7 ft.-lbs.)
Final torque . . 20.3 N·m (15 ft.-lbs.)
6 mm Bolt
First torque . . . 4.7 N·m (3.5 ft.-lbs.)
Final torque . . . . 9.5 N·m (7 ft.-lbs.)
Cylinder . . . . 10.8 N·m (8 ft.-lbs.)
Cylinder Head . . . . 24.4 N·m (18 ft.-lbs.)
Intake Manifold . . . . . 9.5 N·m (7 ft. lbs.)

*The crankcase screws should be loosened in sequence shown in Fig. 5 starting at largest number and working down to smallest. Loosen screws in ¼ turn increments to prevent distortion of crankcase. When assembling, first install all screws evenly with no pressure until mating surfaces of crankcase halves are in full contact; tighten screws in sequence shown and to the recommended torques as listed above.

CYLINDER REMOVAL. Remove top air shroud, intake manifold, reed valves and exhaust pipes. Remove cylinder head securing nuts, then withdraw cylinder head and gasket. Remove cylinder securing nuts, then withdraw cylinder and gasket. Use care when removing cylinder to prevent damage to piston assembly or connecting rod.

CAUTION: Be especially careful to prevent foreign matter from falling into crankcase.

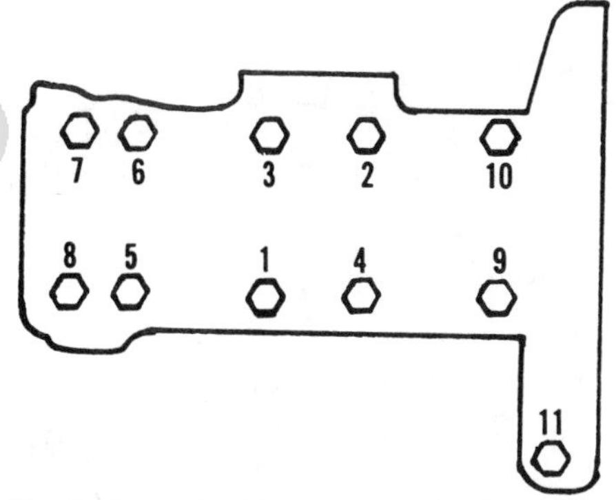

Fig. 5—View showing sequence for tightening crankcase bolts.

NOTE: Parts should not be interchanged between cylinders when reassembling. Mark all parts as they are removed to identify parts for installation in correct location.

CYLINDER INSPECTION. Check cylinder bore for wear or scoring. Standard cylinder bore is 66.00-66.02 mm (2.598-2.599 inches) on 437 cc models, 71.98-72.00 mm (2.834-2.835 in.) on 485 cc models and 73.00-73.02 mm (2.874-2.875 inches) on 535 cc models. Cylinder bore should not be out-of-round more than 0.01 mm (0.0004 inch). Differences in bore diameter between top and bottom (taper) should not exceed 0.05 mm (0.002 inch). The cylinder should be renewed or bored to next larger oversize if out-of-round or taper is excessive. Oversize pistons and rings are available. Piston skirt to cylinder clearance should be 0.045-0.050 mm (0.0018-0.0020 inch) on 437 cc and 485 cc models and 0.055-0.060 mm (0.0022-0.0024 inch) on 535 cc models measured 17 mm from bottom of piston.

CYLINDER INSTALLATION. Reassemble in reverse order of disassembly. Remove old gaskets and clean mounting surfaces, then install new gaskets. Piston ring grooves are pinned and ring end gaps must align with pins when installing cylinders. Use caution during installation to prevent damage to rings, pistons and cylinder walls. Tighten cylinder and cylinder head securing nuts to torque listed in TIGHTENING TORQUES paragraph.

PISTON, PINS AND RINGS. Remove cylinders as outlined in previous section. Clean piston pin bore, then remove pin retaining rings and push pin out of piston. Lift piston off connecting rod and disassemble.

Inspect piston pin and bearing for excessive wear, heat discoloration or any other damage. Inspect piston for excessive wear, cracks, pitting or any other damage. Renew all parts as needed. Piston pin should be a snug fit in piston bore, but it should be possible to install pin with thumb pressure.

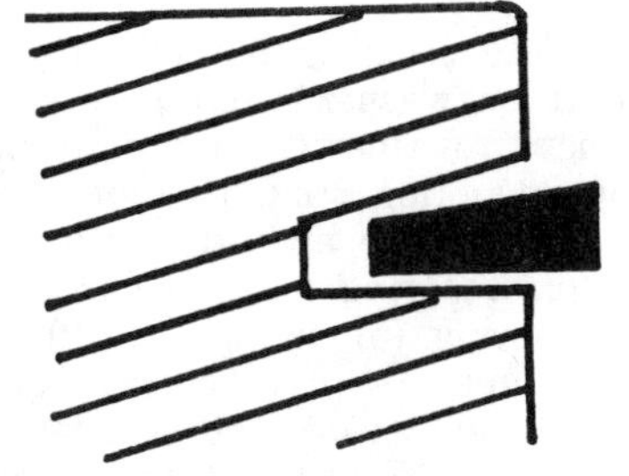

Fig. 6—View showing keystone ring installed correctly in piston ring groove.

Top and bottom piston ring end gap installed should be 0.35-0.55 mm (0.014-0.022 in.) on 80K, 80L and 8VO (PZ480) models, 0.2-0.4 (0.008-0.016 in.) on 8Y7 (XL540) models and 0.3-0.5 mm (0.012-0.020 in.) on all remaining models.

To reassemble, first install piston rings on piston. Keystone type rings must be correctly installed with tapered side toward top of piston as shown in Fig. 6. Position needle bearing in connecting rod bore and locate piston over end of rod with arrow pointing toward exhaust (front) side of engine. Lubricate parts with two-stroke engine oil during reassembly. Align piston pin bore with connecting rod and install piston pin. Install piston pin retaining rings making certain they are correctly seated in grooves. Reinstall cylinder, making certain that ring end gaps are around locating pins and rings are not damaged during assembly.

CRANKCASE AND CRANKSHAFT. To disassemble, remove recoil starter assembly, starter pulley, drive fan pulley and belt. Remove cap screws securing cooling fan assembly, then withdraw unit from engine assembly. Using a suitable flywheel holding tool remove flywheel retaining nut, then using a flywheel puller withdraw flywheel assembly. Remove and save key located in crankshaft groove. Remove Phillips head screws retaining stator plate, then withdraw plate assembly. Remove oil pump drive case and pump as an assembly. Disassemble top end of engine as outlined in previous sections. Loosen crankcase screws in sequence as shown in Fig. 5 starting at largest number and working down to smallest. Loosen screws in 1/4 turn increments to prevent distortion of crankcase. After removing crankcase cap screws lightly strike crankcase with a soft mallet to split upper and lower halves. Separate and lift crankshaft assembly out of crankcase.

Inspect crankcase halves for cracks, pitting, excessive wear or any other damage. Make sure all oil passages are open. Inspect crankshaft bearings for binding, roughness or any other damage and renew as needed. Using a dial indicator check connecting rod axial play (D–Fig. 7) at top. Axial play should be no more than 2.0 mm (0.079 inch). Check connecting rod side clearance (S) with a feeler gage. Side clearance should be between 0.25-0.75 mm (0.010-0.030 inch). If measurements are not within specifications then crankshaft must be disassembled and defective parts renewed.

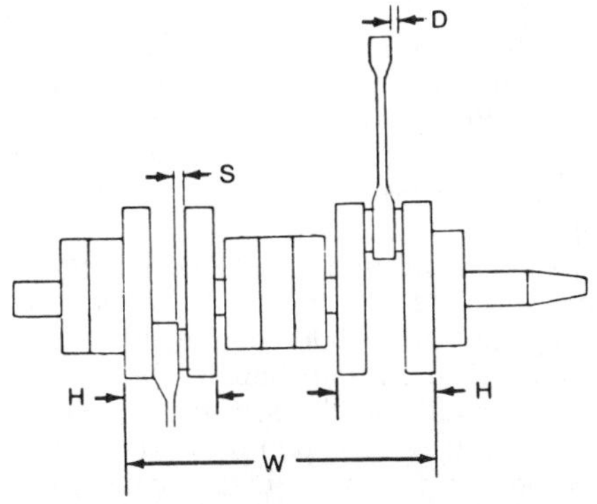

Fig. 7—View showing position for checking connecting rod axial play (D), side clearance (S) and assembled width (W). Refer to text.

NOTE: Crankshaft alignment is very critical, only trained personnel should rebuild crankshaft assemblies.

Assembled width of each crankshaft half (H) should be 56.00-56.05 mm (2.201-2.207 in.) on 80K, 80L and 8VO models and 59.55-60.00 mm (2.360-2.362 in.) on all other models. Total width of assembled crankshaft (W) should be 173.85-174.15 mm (6.845-6.856 in.) on 80K, 80L and 8VO models and 199.75-200.25 mm (7.864-7.884 in.) on all other models. On all models, crankshaft runout deflection should be no more than 0.03 mm (0.0012 inch) on left side, 0.04 mm (0.0016 inch) on center (left and right) and 0.05 mm (0.0020 inch) on right side.

To reassemble crankcase, install crankshaft assembly with new oil seals in upper crankcase half. Be sure bearing pins fit in crankcase pin holes, bearing circlip fits in crankcase groove and oil seal lip fits in crankcase groove. Apply YAMAHA BOND No. 4 or a suitable equivalent on mating surfaces of crankcase halves. Assemble crankcase halves and install securing cap screws. Tighten cap screws in sequence as shown in Fig. 5. Refer to TIGHTENING TORQUES section for torque specifications. Check crankshaft for freedom of movement and lubricate crankshaft bearings with a good quality two-stroke engine oil.

Reassemble top end of engine as outlined in previous sections. Reassemble front end of engine in reverse order of disassembly. Refer to IGNITION AND TIMING section for setting engine timing.

To bleed out oil pump remove bleeder screw located at lower back side of pump. Continue to let engine oil run out bleeder hole until air bubbles disappear, then reinstall bleeder screw and gasket.

To bleed out oil pump delivery lines proceed as follows: Start engine, then pull oil pump control cable at carburetor out until pump plunger is at maximum stroke. Run engine at 2000 rpm for two minutes. Check and refill oil tank as needed. Refer to LUBRICATION section for adjusting oil pump control cable.

RECOIL STARTER. Remove four starter mounting cap screws, then withdraw unit from fan case. Remove drive plate securing nut (11–Fig. 8), then lift lockwasher (10), thrust washer (9), friction washer (7), and drive plate (8) off mounting stud. Unknot starter rope (12) at one end, then withdraw drive plate spring (6), drive pawl (4), return spring (5) and pulley (2) with starter rope. Do not remove rewind spring (3) unless damage is noted. Inspect all parts for excessive wear, cracks or any other damage and renew as needed.

To reassemble, first install rewind spring (3). Be sure loop on outside end of spring is around hook in housing. Install pulley (2) with rope (12) in housing. Feed rope end through housing eye and attach to handle (14). Pulley (2) should be turned four turns counterclockwise to preload rewind spring (3). Complete reassembly of starter with reference to Fig. 8 and torque nut (11) to 9.5 N•m (7 ft.-lbs.) Check starter for proper operation, then reinstall on fan case.

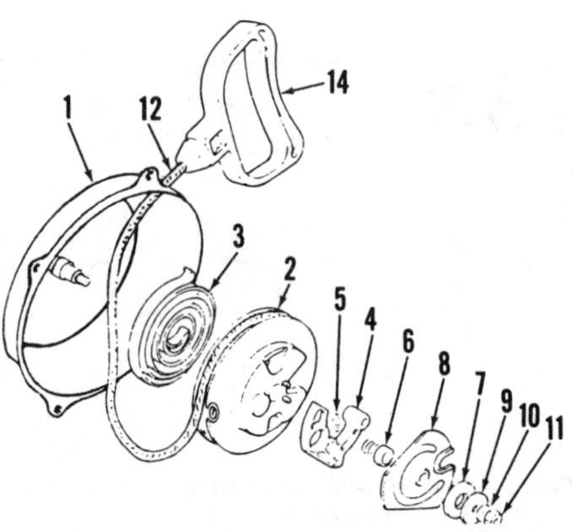

Fig. 8—Exploded view of recoil starter.

1. Housing
2. Pulley
3. Rewind spring
4. Drive pawl
5. Return spring
6. Drive plate spring
7. Friction washer
8. Drive plate
9. Thrust washer
10. Lockwashesr
11. Nut
12. Rope
14. Handle

XENOAH

AIR COOLED MODELS

CONDENSED SERVICE DATA

ENGINE MODEL	G29B	G34B	G40B	G44B
Bore—mm	59.5	64	65	68
Inches	2.36	2.52	2.56	2.677
Stroke—mm	52.6	52.6	59.5	59.5
Inches	2.071	2.071	2.36	2.36
No. of Cylinders	2	2	2	2
Displacement—cc	292	338	394	432
Cubic Inches	17.8	20.6	24.04	26.4
Cooling Type	Axial Fan			
Carburetor Make	*Keihin			
Model	*CD42	*CD42	CD42	*CD42
Number Used	1	1	1	1
Ignition Type	**Energy Transfer			
Make	.....	....	....	....
Point Gap—mm	**0.3-0.4			
Inch	**0.012-0.016			
Timing Advance?	Yes			
Timing Checked at	**Retard			
Setting	**8° BTDC			
Spark Plug:				
NGK	***B7HS			
Electrode Gap—mm	0.55-0.65			
Inch	0.022-0.026			
Fuel:Oil Ratio	20:1			

*Later models use Mikuni BN042 carburetor.

**Later models are equipped with a breakerless capacitor discharge ignition system.

***Spark plug reach is ¾-inch on later models.

MAINTENANCE

CARBURETOR. Early models are equipped with a Keihin CD42 carburetor. Normal initial adjustment is one turn open for idle mixture adjustment needle and 1¼-turns open for load adjustment screw. Both needles must be readjusted for best performance with engine warm and under actual operating conditions. Refer also to the appropriate CARBURETOR SERVICE section elsewhere in this manual.

Later models are equipped with a Mikuni BN042 carburetor as shown in Fig. 1. Carburetor contains two identical diaphragm type fuel pumps which supply fuel to carburetor and return excess fuel to fuel tank. Fuel pump on adjustment needle side of carburetor returns fuel to tank while opposite fuel pump supplies fuel to carburetor. Crankcase pulsations actuate the fuel pump diaphragms. The pulse line fitting is located on outlet side of carburetor.

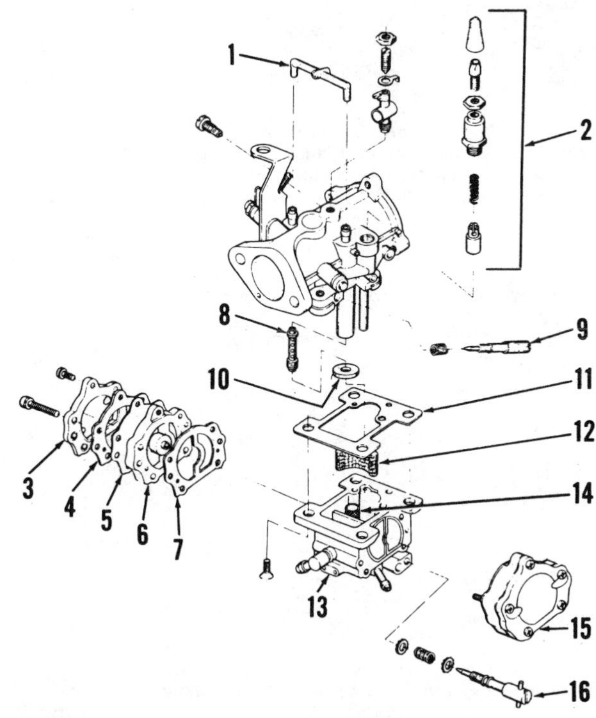

Fig. 1—Exploded view of Mikuni BNO42 carburetor.

1. Air vent tube
2. Starter jet
3. Fuel pump cover
4. Gasket
5. Diaphragm
6. Check valve plate
7. Gasket
8. Main jet & nozzle
9. Idle mixture needle
10. Packing
11. Gasket
12. Filter
13. Fuel bowl
14. Check valve
15. Fuel pump assy.
16. High speed mixture needle

Fuel is pumped past check valve (14—Fig. 1) by fuel pump when engine is running. Check valve prevents fuel from siphoning from carburetor when fuel pump is not operating. Fuel pump fills carburetor fuel bowl with excess fuel overflowing dam around fuel return cavity. Fuel entering fuel return cavity is pumped by fuel return pump to fuel tank. Fuel is drawn from fuel bowl through main jet (8) into carburetor bore. Mixture adjustment is provided by idle (9) and high speed (16) mixture needles.

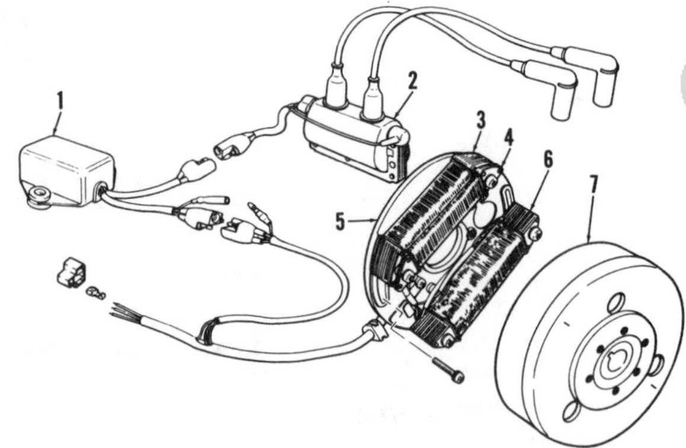

Fig. 4—Exploded view of capacitor discharge ignition system used on later models.

1. Ignition module
2. Ignition coil
3. Exciter coil
4. Pulse coil
5. Stator coil
6. Lighting coil
7. Flywheel

SPARK PLUG. NGK Spark Plugs are standard equipment. The recommendations given in CONDENSED SERVICE DATA tables are for normal operation. A different heat range plug may improve performance under some conditions. Refer to Spark Plug Selection paragraphs of SERVICE FUNDAMENTALS for additional information.

IGNITION AND TIMING. Breaker point gap, on models so equipped should be 0.3-0.4 mm (0.012-0.016 inch). Points can be adjusted after removing recoil starter, fan drive pulley and "V" belt; by working through flywheel windows as shown in Fig. 2. All models with breaker points are equipped with a centrifugal timing advance which provides retarded timing for starting only.

Fig. 2—Breaker points can be adjusted through flywheel timing windows as shown. Timing is correct when timing marks on flywheel align with "F" marks on housing.

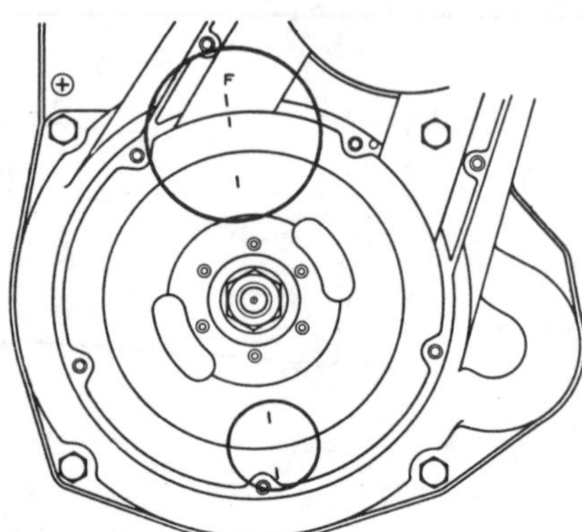

Fig. 3—Timing marks are stamped into flywheel and fan housing to indicate static timing.

On models equipped with breaker point ignition, both cylinders must be timed as nearly as possible alike. It is suggested that point gap and timing be checked on one cylinder; then timing synchronized by varying point gap for the other cylinder if necessary. Static (retarded) timing is correct when points break with flywheel and housing marks aligned as shown in Fig. 3.

Later models are equipped with the breakerless capacitor discharge ignition system shown in Fig. 4. Ignition timing advances electronically to 21 degrees before top dead center at 6000 rpm. Ignition timing should be correct when stator plate timing marks are aligned with crankcase boss as shown in Fig. 5.

If ignition malfunctions and spark plug is not faulty, connect an ohmmeter as follows to check components. Resistance between brown lead and white/red lead of exciter coil should be 250-300 ohms. Resistance between blue lead and white/red lead of pulse coil should be 20-23 ohms. Resistance of primary ignition coil windings should be approximately 0.05 ohms while secondary ignition coil winding resistance should be 640-780 ohms. If module is suspected, replace module with a good module and check ignition operation.

LUBRICATION. The engine is lubricated by oil mixed with the fuel. Good quality regular gasoline and a good two-stroke motor oil should be used. Recommended fuel:oil ratio should be 20:1.

The use of Ethyl, Premium or high octane non-leaded gasolines; or of outboard motor oil is not recommended by the manufacturer.

COOLING FAN AND BELT. The cooling fan drive belt should have ¼-inch free play measured midway between pulleys as shown in Fig. 6. Outer pulley half is notched to accept a holding spanner wrench for removal of shaft nut. To adjust belt tension, remove the nut and outer pulley half; then add or remove adjusting shims located between pulley halves. Be sure not to pinch belt when reinstalling shaft nut. Tighten the nut to a torque of 30 ft.-lbs.

REPAIRS

TIGHTENING TORQUES. Refer to the following table for tightening torques. Measurements are given in ft.-lbs.

Fig. 5—Align stator plate marks with crankcase boss on models with capacitor discharge ignition system.

Fig. 6—Cooling fan drive belt should have ¼-inch free play when depressed with finger as shown.

Cylinder	14-16
Cylinder head	14-16
Crankcase	14-16
Flywheel	45-55
Fan shaft nut	28-32

DISASSEMBLY AND REASSEMBLY. To disassemble the removed engine, first remove ignition coil cover and coils, then remove cylinder shrouds. Remove fan guard, recoil starter and starter pulley. Unbolt and remove fan housing, fan and associated parts as a unit. Remove crankshaft nut using flywheel holding tool and suitable wrench as shown in Fig. 7; then remove flywheel using puller as shown in Fig. 8.

Check armature plate for timing (alignment) marks and mark if necessary, then unbolt and remove magneto plate. Remove manifolds, spark plugs and cylinder heads. Unbolt and remove cylinder units, then remove pistons. Remove plate retaining crankshaft drive-end seal; remove crankcase through-bolts and separate crankcase halves by tapping with a soft hammer.

Piston crowns are marked with an arrow which should be installed toward exhaust side of cylinder. Top piston rings are chromed and all rings are positively located by pins in piston grooves. Crankshaft end play should be 0.00-0.1 mm. End play is controlled by shims located beneath end plate at drive end. Shims are available in thicknesses of 0.1 and 0.3 mm. Tighten crankcase through-bolts using the sequence shown in Fig. 9. All tightening torques are given in tabular form at beginning of REPAIR Section.

Fig. 7—Using the flywheel holding tool to remove crankshaft nut.

Fig. 8—A suitable puller is required for flywheel removal.

7 8

Fig. 9—Tighten the crankcase through-bolts in the sequence shown.

REWIND STARTER. Refer to exploded view of starter in Fig. 10. To disassemble starter, remove starter from engine and pull rope out until it is possible to position rope in notch of rope pulley. Release rope and allow rewind spring to unwind. Remove retaining nut (3) and components (6 through 8). Carefully remove rope pulley so that recoil spring remains in cover. If necessary to remove rewind spring, guard against uncontrolled uncoiling of spring which may cause personal injury.

To assemble starter, install rewind spring in cover so that spring is wound in counter-clockwise direction and outer hook of spring contacts lug of cover. Install rope pulley and rope so that lug of pulley engages with inner hook of recoil spring. Install washer (8), pawls (7), spring (6) and pawl return spring (5). Install retainer cover (4) so that end of return spring (5) protrudes through retainer cover (4) and turn retainer cover one-third turn clockwise to pre-load spring. Install washers and retaining nut. If rope handle was not removed during disassembly, position rope in notch of rope pulley and turn pulley two turns counterclockwise to pre-load recoil spring. If handle was removed, turn rope pulley counterclockwise two or three turns and insert end of rope through rope outlet in cover. Tension on rope should be apparent. Tie a temporary knot to hold rope and install rope handle.

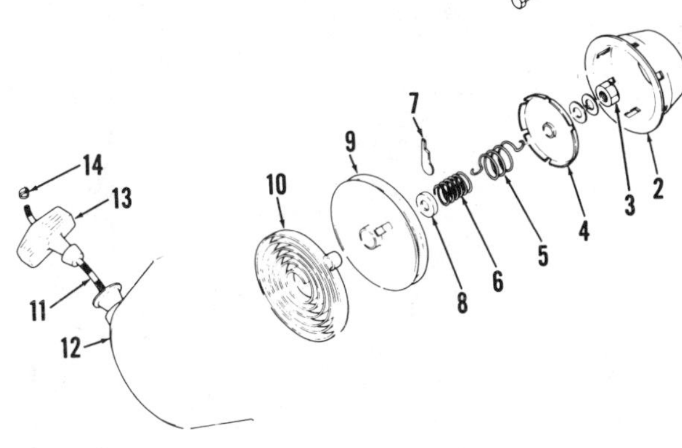

Fig. 10—Exploded view of rewind starter.

2. Starter cup
3. Nut
4. Retainer
5. Return spring
6. Spring
7. Pawls
8. Washer
9. Rope pulley
10. Recoil spring
11. Rope
12. Cover
13. Handle
14. Retainer

XENOAH

LIQUID COOLED MODELS

CONDENSED SERVICE DATA

ENGINE MODEL	G25BWR	G34BWR	G44BWR
Bore—mm	54.8	64	68
Inches	2.157	2.520	2.677
Stroke—mm	52.6	52.6	59.5
Inches	2.071	2.071	2.343
No. of Cylinders	2	2	2
Displacement—cc	248.1	338.4	432.2
Cubic Inches	15.13	20.64	26.36
Cooling Type	Liquid	Liquid	Liquid
Carburetor Make	Mikuni	Mikuni	Mikuni
Model	BNO	BNO38	BNO42
Number Used	.....	2	2
Ignition Type	CD	CD	CD
Timing Advance?	Yes	Yes	Yes
Spark Plug:			
NGK	BUE	BUE	BUE
Fuel:Oil Ratio	20:1	20:1	20:1

MAINTENANCE

CARBURETOR. All models are equipped with Mikuni BNO carburetor shown in Fig. 1. Carburetor contains two identical diaphragm type fuel pumps which supply fuel to carburetor and return excess fuel to fuel tank. Fuel pump on adjustment needle side of carburetor returns fuel to tank while opposite fuel pump supplies fuel to carburetor. Crankcase pulsations actuate the fuel pump diaphragms. The pulse line fitting is located on outlet side of carburetor.

Fuel is pumped past check valve (14—Fig. 1) by fuel pump when engine is running. Check valve prevents fuel from siphoning from carburetor when fuel pump is not operating. Fuel pump fills carburetor fuel bowl with excess fuel overflowing dam around fuel return cavity. Fuel entering fuel return cavity is pumped by fuel return pump to fuel tank. Fuel is drawn from fuel bowl through main jet (8) into carburetor bore. Mixture adjustment is provided by idle (9) and high speed (16) mixture needles.

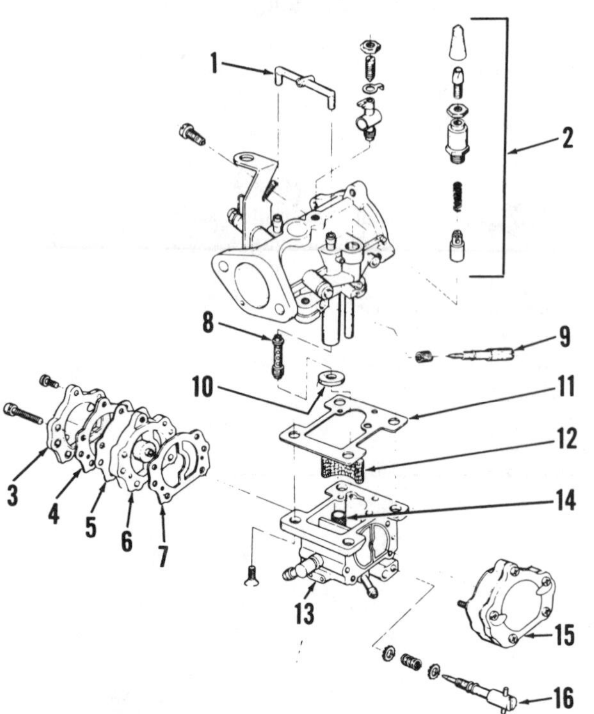

Fig. 1—Exploded view of Mikuni BNO carburetor.

1. Air vent tube
2. Starter jet
3. Fuel pump cover
4. Gasket
5. Diaphragm
6. Check valve plate
7. Gasket
8. Main jet & nozzle
9. Idle mixture needle
10. Packing
11. Gasket
12. Filter
13. Fuel bowl
14. Check valve
15. Fuel pump assy.
16. High speed mixture needle

SPARK PLUG. Recommended spark plug is NGK BUE which is a surface gap type plug. Electrode gap is not adjustable on surface gap plugs.

IGNITION AND TIMING. All models are equipped with the breakerless capacitor discharge ignition system shown in Fig. 2. Ignition timing advances electronically to 21 degrees before top dead center at 6000 rpm. Ignition timing should be correct when stator plate timing marks are aligned with crankcase boss as shown in Fig. 3.

If ignition malfunctions and spark plug is not faulty, connect an ohmmeter as follows to check components. Resistance between brown lead and white/red lead of exciter coil should be 250-300 ohms. Resistance between blue lead and white/red lead of pulse coil should be 20-23 ohms. Resistance of primary ignition coil windings should be approximately 0.05 ohms while secondary ignition coil winding resistance should be 640-780 ohms. If module is suspected, replace module with a good module and check ignition operation.

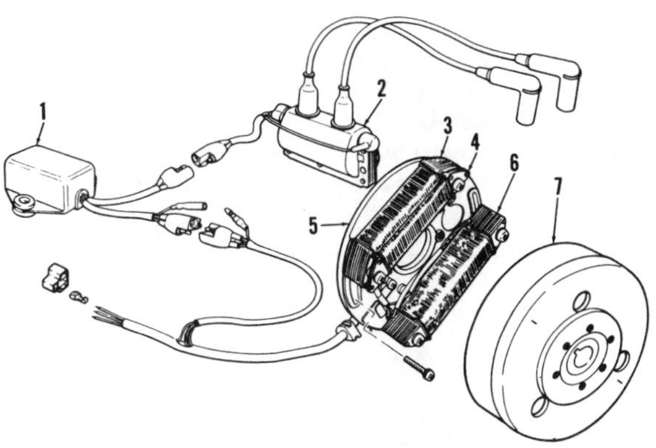

Fig. 2—Exploded view of capacitor discharge ignition system.

1. Ignition module
2. Ignition coil
3. Exciter coil
4. Pulse coil
5. Stator plate
6. Lighting coil
7. Flywheel

WATER PUMP BELT. All models are equipped with a belt driven water pump. Belt tension is adjusted by loosening water pump mounting screws and relocating pump. Water pump belt deflection (D—Fig. 4) should be ¼ inch using finger pressure.

LUBRICATION. The engine is lubricated by oil mixed with the fuel. Good quality regular gasoline and a good quality two-stroke motor oil should be used. Recommended fuel:oil ratio is 20:1.

Fig. 3—Align stator plate marks with crankcase boss.

Fig. 4—Adjust water pump belt tension so deflection (D) is ¼-inch.

REPAIRS

TIGHTENING TORQUES. Refer to the following table for tightening torques. Measurements are given in ft.-lbs.

Cylinder	22
Cylinder head	15
Crankcase	15
Flywheel	50

5 4

3 6

7 8

Fig. 5—Use above sequence when tightening crankcase screws.

Fig. 6—Exploded view of recoil starter.

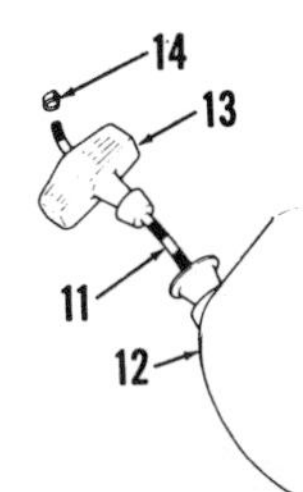

2. Starter cup
3. Nut
4. Retainer
5. Return spring
6. Spring
7. Pawls
8. Washer
9. Rope pulley
10. Recoil spring
11. Rope
12. Cover
13. Handle
14. Retainer

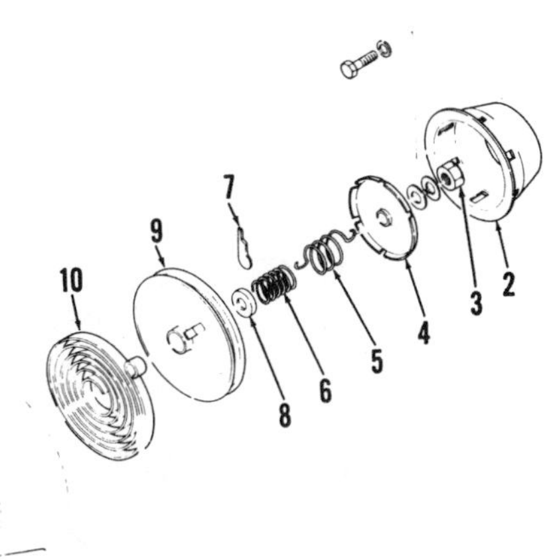

DISASSEMBLY AND REASSEMBLY. To disassemble removed engine, proceed as follows: Remove water pump cover, by-pass hole, radiator hose and water pump assembly. Remove rewind starter assembly, starter pulley and water pump drive pulley. Remove flywheel and ignition stator plate. Remove torque converter drive pulley.

Remove exhaust and inlet manifolds. Remove cylinder head, cylinders and pistons. Remove bearing retainer from output end of crankshaft. Unscrew crankcase screws, separate crankcase halves and remove crankshaft assembly from crankcase half.

To assemble engine, reverse disassembly procedure. Tighten crankcase screws to 15 ft.-lbs. torque using sequence shown in Fig. 5. Crankshaft end play should be 0.002-0.004 inch. Adjust end play by installing shims between bearing retainer shoulder and crankshaft bearing. Install piston on connecting rod with arrow on piston crown pointing towards exhaust side of engine. Piston ring rotation is prevented by locating pins in ring grooves. Be sure piston ring gap is around locating pin when installing cylinder or piston ring may break.

REWIND STARTER. Refer to exploded view of starter in Fig. 6. To disassemble starter, remove starter from engine and pull rope out until it is possible to position rope in notch of rope pulley. Release rope and allow rewind spring to unwind. Remove retaining nut (3) and components (6 through 8). Carefully remove rope pulley so that recoil spring remains in cover. If necessary to remove rewind spring, guard against uncontrolled uncoiling of spring which may cause personal injury.

To assemble starter, install rewind spring in cover so that spring is wound in counter-clockwise direction and outer hook of spring contacts lug of cover. Install rope pulley and rope so that lug of pulley engages with inner hook of recoil spring. Install washer (8), pawls (7), spring (6) and pawl return spring (5). Install retainer cover (4) so that end of return spring (5) protrudes through retainer cover (4) and turn retainer cover one-third turn clockwise to pre-load spring. Install washers and retaining nut. If rope handle was not removed during disassembly, position rope in notch of rope pulley and turn pulley two turns counterclockwise to pre-load recoil spring. If handle was removed, turn rope pulley counterclockwise two or three turns and insert end of rope through rope outlet in cover. Tension on rope should be apparent. Tie a temporary knot to hold rope and install rope handle.

BELT DRIVE CONVERTER UNIT

CONTENTS

CAUTION: Do not run engine with torque converter drive belt removed unless torque converter drive sheave is also removed from engine output shaft.

OPERATION

To understand the operation of the centrifugally actuated variable speed belt drive, it is first necessary to establish certain basic facts about V-belt power transmission.

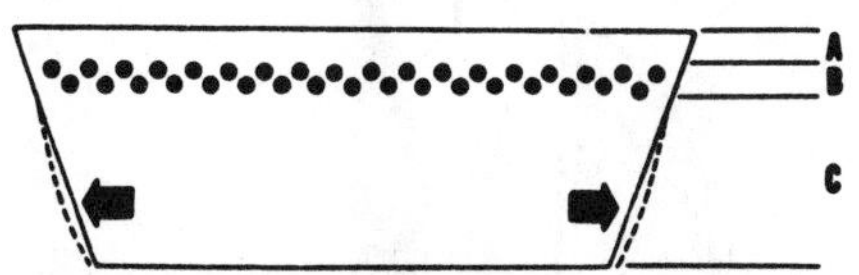

Fig. 1—Cross sectional view of typical V-Belt showing details of construction. The strength (or neutral) section (B) of belt contains cords which establish the operating length of belt. Top section (A) is under tension as belt bends around sheave. Section (C) is under compression, pushing friction sides of belt out as shown by heavy arrows and broken lines. This provides additional gripping pressure to friction faces after belt has entered sheave.

1. Torque is increased and output shaft speed decreased as the relative diameter of the drive sheave DECREASES and/or driven sheave INCREASES.

2. Belt traction is achieved by contact of the sides of the belt in vee of sheave, not by bottom contact.

3. Traction portion of belt expands outward as belt curves around the sheaves, thus increasing contact pressure. Refer to Fig. 1.

If the taper face V-Belt sheaves are properly engineered, the effective diameter of the sheave can be changed while the unit is in operation. By combining two such sheaves in a drive unit, infinitely variable power transmission over a wide operating range can be obtained. Refer to Fig. 2.

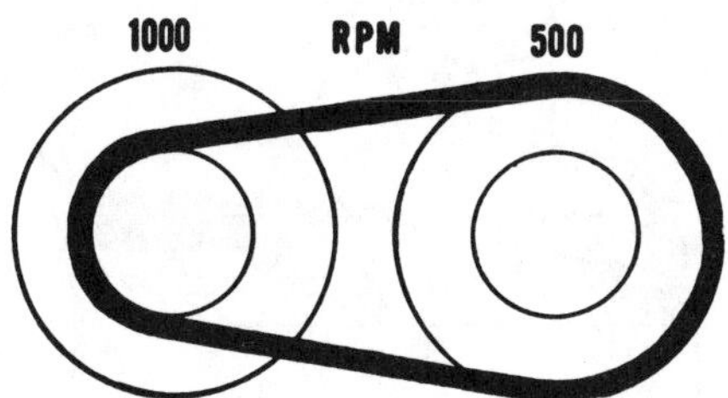

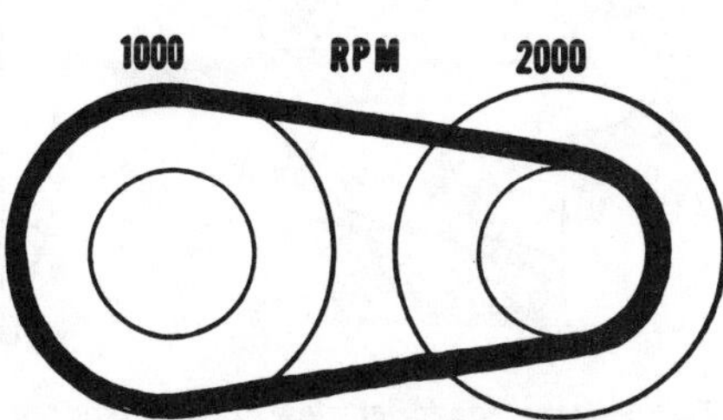

Fig. 2—Schematic view of typical drive unit with fixed distance shaft centers and variable effective diameter of both sheaves. With constant input speed of 1000 rpm, output shaft speed can be infinitely varied from 2:1 underdrive to 1:2 overdrive as shown. In actual design, almost any desired range can be obtained.

In the drive units used on snowmobiles, the drive sheave is spring loaded in the open position as shown in Fig. 3. The driven sheave is spring loaded in the closed position as shown in Fig. 4. The drive sheave (Fig. 3) closes in direction of arrows by centrifugal action of governor weights (W), thus changing drive ratio as changes occur in input shaft (crankshaft) speed.

The drive sheave, driven sheave and belt which make up the torque converter are sold and installed together as an engineered unit in which engine horsepower, final drive (chain) reduction, track area and vehicle weight are considered. Most torque converter units can be overhauled and worn or damaged parts individually renewed. Because of engineering considerations however, substitution of parts or components other than original type should be attempted only when the changes in vehicle operating characteristics are desirable and can be predicted.

Torque converter units used on snowmobiles are built by the vehicle manufacturers or specialty components suppliers. Because the unit may be specially engineered, the vehicle manufacturer usually handles the parts distribution.

Most torque converter units also act as the drive clutch, automatically disconnecting engine and drive train at a pre-determined engine speed. Most drive sheave units use the governor weights as the clutch engaging mechanism as shown in Fig. 3. When engine is at slow idle speed or stopped, the distance between flanges (F & M) is slightly greater than the width of belt (B), and sheave is free to turn around the belt which rests on an idler bearing in bottom of sheave. As engine speed increases, governor weights (W) are thrown outward by centrifugal force, causing belt engagement and transmission of power to the driven sheave. Some early models use a shoe-type centrifugal clutch to connect or disconnect the drive sheave and crankshaft, and flyweights within the sheave vary the drive ratio after clutch is engaged.

On models with belt release clutch, the tension of disengaging spring (R) plus the design of the centrifugal weight mechanism determines the clutch engagement rpm. Spring pressure on driven sheave must be great enough to maintain face contact with belt under all operating conditions, and in units which are primarily speed sensitive, must apply enough pressure to prevent belt slippage throughout the operating range.

The closing thrust of governor weights (W) must be balanced against the combined spring pressure of both sheaves to provide the desired power and speed output curve.

Excessive spring pressure results in additional friction, power loss and shortened belt life. A stronger spring also requires heavier compensating weights and a heavier, bulkier unit results. In selecting a product design, performance, service life and cost are all considered.

All speed sensing models are load-sensitive to some degree. Refer to Fig. 5. When a load is applied, that portion of belt (A) running from driven pulley into drive pulley is under tension and carries the work load. Any slack existing in the belt is accumulated in opposite (B) side of belt and is thrown outward by centrifugal force. The difference in entering angle and entering

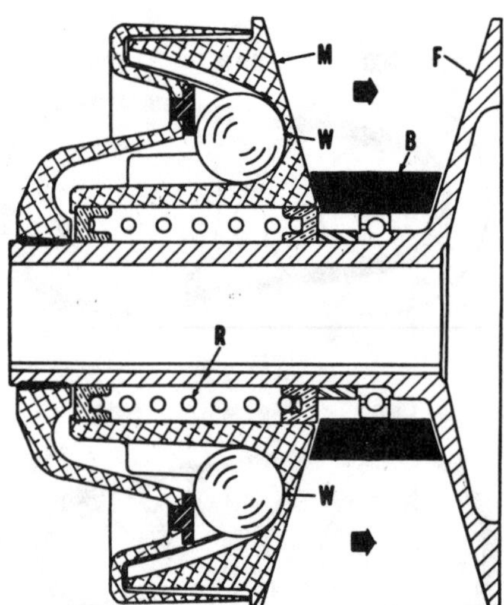

Fig. 3–Cross sectional view of one type variable speed drive (Input) sheave with centrifugal speed control. Moving flange (M) is spring loaded in the open position and centrifugally closed in direction of arrows by governor weights (W).

B. Belt
F. Fixed Flange
M. Moving Flange
R. Reaction Spring
W. Centrifugal Weight

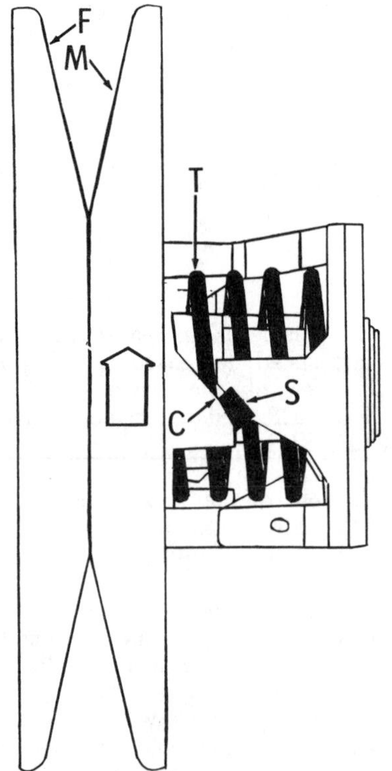

Fig. 4–Cross sectional view of one type of torque sensing variable speed driven (Output) sheave.

C. Spiral cam (ramp)
F. Fixed flange
M. Moving flange
S. Nylon shoe
T. Torsion spring

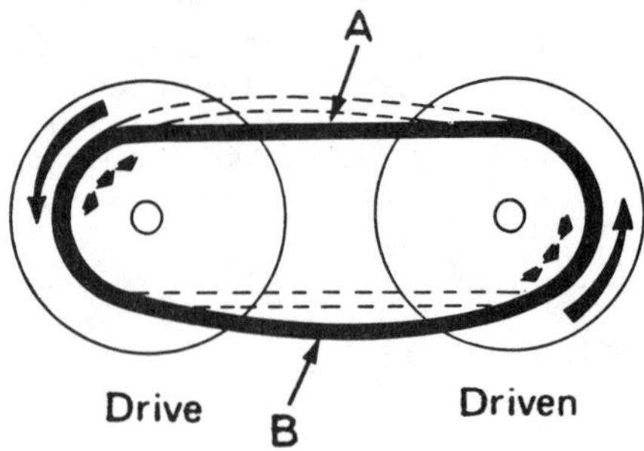

Fig. 5–Schematic cross section of V-Belt drive operating under torque load. One side of belt (A) is under tension and carries the load. All slack is thus accumulated in opposite (B) side of belt which is thrown outward and toward driven pulley by centrifugal and rotative force. The interaction of forces cause the belt to work outward in driven pulley and inward in drive pulley as indicated by arrows, resulting in an inherent torque sensing ability.

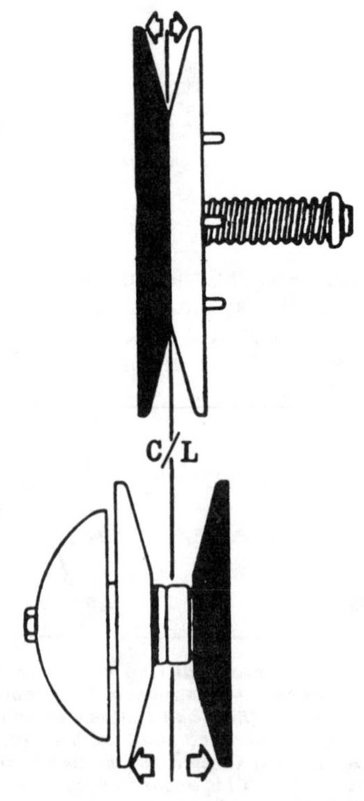

Fig. 6–Fixed sheave flanges (Black) must be placed on opposite sides when variable belt drive (converter) unit is installed, to maintain a common pulley centerline as shown.

tension in the two pulleys combine to cause the belt to work outward in driven pulley groove and inward in drive pulley groove as indicated by arrows, thus slowing the output speed and increasing output torque as increases in load occur.

On many models, a more positive torque sensing mechanism is built into the driven sheave. The mechanism usually takes the form of a helix or ramp (C—Fig. 4) on one flange and a fixed anchor point (S) on the other flange. Rotation of unit in Fig. 4 is in direction indicated by arrow. The fixed flange (F) is attached to output shaft; when torque increases and the belt starts to slip, the moving flange (M) attempts to turn with the belt and the independent rotation is converted to axial thrust by the ramp, creating the desired face pressure and downshift. Less initial spring pressure is thus required to produce the desired operating characteristics.

OPERATIONAL CHECK

The torque converter unit can be shop tested to pin-point possible causes of trouble, but an operational or dynamometer test is recommended if conditions permit. To test the torque converter unit in the shop, proceed as follows:

Remove protective shielding from torque converter unit and block up rear of vehicle or remove drive chain, whichever is easier.

Examine the converter unit as follows: Drive and driven sheaves should be parallel and belt grooves aligned. Friction faces should be smooth and free of oil, grease or rust. Belt should be dry and straight, and free of breaks, cracks or uneven wear; and should ride in bottom of groove in drive sheave and approximately flush with rims of driven sheave, without excessive looseness. If belt wear is uneven, check carefully for improper alignment, incorrect idle speed or malfunctioning clutch engaging mechanism. If offset between sheaves is incorrect or if sheaves are improperly matched, belt may turn over in vee. If belt turns over, check pulley centerline (Fig. 6), offset as given in vehicle section or specific overhaul section, or for improperly mated pulleys.

Start and idle the engine, converter unit should remain stopped or should be easily stopped by lightly applying brake. Stopping converter should not put an apparent load on idling engine. Slowly increase engine speed. Torque converter clutch should engage at just above idle speed and immediately disengage when throttle is released.

If clutch fails to fully disengage, slow idle speed may be too high, compression spring (R—Fig. 3) may be weak or broken, or moving flange (M) may be sticking or binding. Misalignment of sheaves can also cause incomplete belt disengagement.

If engagement speed is too low, compression spring may be too weak (or improperly adjusted if adjustment is provided).

If engagement speed is too high, compression spring may be too strong or improperly adjusted; or engaging mechanism may be sticking or binding.

If engagement action is erratic, engaging mechanism is probably binding.

NOTE: DO NOT stand or allow anyone else to stand in line with drive belt when shielding is removed. Because of the high rotating speed of the units, a broken part or object dropped on the belt or sheaves can be thrown outward with damaging force. Slowly open throttle. Belt should move smoothly outward in drive sheave and inward in driven sheave as speed increases. Drive ratio should change smoothly as engine speed changes. Test the centrifugal action and sheave performance by varying engine speed as required to obtain full movement of sheave faces.

On torque sensing units, check torque sensing mechanism as follows:

Slowly open throttle until belt moves to outside of drive sheave, then maintain this setting by holding throttle steady. Check torque sensing mechanism by applying and releasing the brake. Drive ratio should change smoothly with varying torque load.

Vibration at higher speeds may indicate a bent shaft or imbalance of some component of the torque converter unit.

A dynamometer test of the complete snowmobile is recommended as the preferred method of operational check. Used in conjunction with an accurate tachometer, engagement speed and performance can be accurately checked. Normal engagement speed for family machines is generally in the 2000-3000 rpm range, but speed may be much higher on "hot" performance models. Engagement speed may vary 8-10% from specified but should be relatively stable on a particular machine when operating temperature stabilizes. Wide variation on a particular machine in a series of checks would probably indicate sticking or binding of some element in the governor mechanism.

GENERAL OVERHAUL NOTES

Refer to specific vehicle or unit instructions, if given, for removal or installation procedure. Some drive units are threaded to engine crankshaft but most are keyed and retained to shaft by a cap nut or cap screw. When a cap nut or screw is used, the fastener can usually be loosened by holding the sheave. On models with drive unit sheave threaded to shaft, it is necessary to hold crankshaft from turning when removing the sheave. Most engine manufacturers make available a crankshaft holding tool which is designed to thread into spark plug hole and contact piston; or to hold the flywheel. Do not attempt to hold the crankshaft by inserting a screwdriver or bar into flywheel fan blades or by inserting anything other than the specially designed tool into spark plug hole. One manufacturer recommends feeding a starter rope into spark plug hole to block piston movement. On multicylinder engines use drive end cylinder. Use nothing but nylon or cotton rope. On all models, sheave is turned in normal direction of crankshaft rotation to loosen.

Most engine crankshafts have a machined taper which provides positive alignment and solid mounting of the drive unit. A heat gun (Fig. 7) can be used to assist in hub removal if required. Do not use flame, and do not pry, pound or pull on pulley flange. Expensive parts can be easily damaged by unwise attempts at removal.

When installing the drive unit, make sure that fixed flanges of the two sheaves are on opposite sides as shown in Fig. 6, that mounting shafts of the two sheaves are parallel and that sheave centers are properly aligned. Check offset and belt center distance of the particular unit, if given.

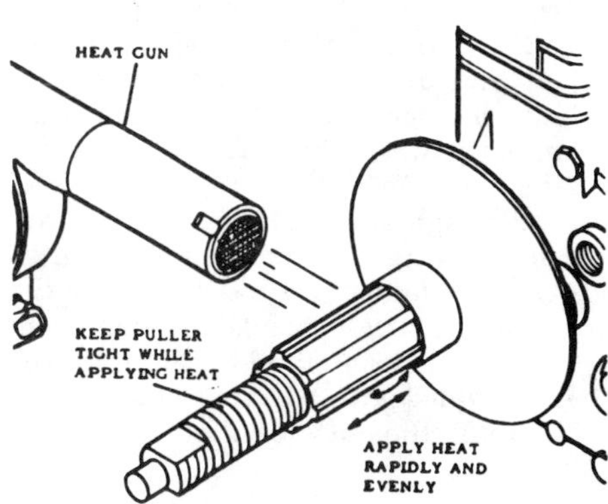

Fig. 7–Using heat to assist in removing torque converter drive hub from crankshaft taper.

It must be remembered that the drive unit is centrifugally controlled and the driven unit responds, therefore belt tension and belt face width have a direct bearing on alignment of sheave centerline. Two sheaves which are in perfect alignment with correct belt tension will move out of alignment if belt becomes too tight or too loose. Belt face wear or a belt of incorrect width can also change alignment and tension even though shaft center distance and offset are as specified.

On most models, the drive belt can be removed with a minimum of disassembly by pulling the belt into bottom of groove of driven pulley then slipping belt off drive pulley. Installation is reverse of removal procedure.

When belt is removed and/or unit is disassembled, inspect all components carefully for wear or other damage. If wear is abnormal, attempt to discover the cause before completing the repairs and returning the vehicle to service. Excessive or uneven wear on sides of vee belt may indicate pulley misalignment, bent pulley half or improperly adjusted idle speed. Examine pulley faces for wear patterns or heat discoloration. Determine and correct the cause of trouble rather than just renew the belt. Sheave parts should fit with a minimum of clearance without binding. Apply a light coating of oil or low temperature grease to sliding parts, but make sure that no excess lubricant will be thrown on belt or sheave faces when unit is in operation. Check for specific overhaul information and disassembly notes in the unit sections or illustrations.

SPEED TUNING

GENERAL

The torque converter unit is involved in any speed tuning decision for two reasons; results and safety.

There is little point in spending time and money modifying and fine-tuning an engine unless the drive train is capable of making the best use of the horsepower gained. The degree of modification of the converter drive and driven units is so inter-related that an exact procedure cannot be outlined. This section, therefore, will attempt to list only the principles which apply and the precautions to be observed.

The high engine speeds associated with performance tuning makes it imperative that care be used in maintaining the balance and trueness of clutch components. Racing drive clutches should be equipped with a scatter shield.

Speed tuning the converter unit generally involves raising the engagement speed, extra attention to dynamic balance of the total unit, careful belt selection, and combating down-shift lag of driven member. The final step in converter tuning is mating the drive unit, belt and driven unit into a carefully balanced package which will transmit engine power to the track in its most effective form.

Although the principles of performance tuning can be documented, so many variables are involved that the actual practice depends on experimentation, experience and a feeling for the job (coupled with a fair amount of luck) that only the outlines of procedure can be given.

DRIVE CLUTCH

Speed tuning an engine usually sacrifices torque at the low end to obtain a power peak in the performance range. The degree of "peakiness" depends on the type of competition involved and determines the tuning of the drive clutch.

In a family machine, the drive clutch should engage smoothly at a relatively low engine speed and upshift smoothly through the power range under all combinations of throttle setting and load. The converter package should automatically shift down as necessary to keep from lugging the engine.

With a "peaky" competition engine, engagement speed must be raised above the stall-out point of engine tuning and total balance of machine, track surface and converter should permit almost instantaneous acceleration to peak horsepower range.

As previously stated, clutch engagement speed can be raised by lightening the centrifugal weights or by strengthening the reaction spring. Clutch and machine manufacturers; and some performance specialists, make heavier springs available. But sometimes the spring is not the whole answer. Centrifugal force increases geometrically as speed increases and any inherent imbalance is correspondingly multiplied. Also, heavy centrifugal weights plus high speed plus a correspondingly strong balance spring in driven unit exert heavy side pressure on drive belt, resulting in increased belt wear and frictional loss of power. For these reasons, weight modification (or selection) is also a widely used modification technique.

A new compensating spring for a competition clutch should be compressed in a vise overnight to pre-set the spring before installation. Weights, weight pins, rollers and similar parts should be installed only in sets and carefully weighed and balanced (using druggists scales or equivalent) before installation. If weights are altered by trimming, balance must be maintained both as to total weight and configuration. Dynamic balance and centrifugal action are both affected by selection of trim point. Refer to Fig. 8. As a general rule, removing weight farthest from pivot point (P), from heavy side of gravity centerline (C), or nearest pulley outer rim will have the greater centrifugal effect. And material nearer pulley rim will "weigh more" from a dynamic balance standpoint than equal weight nearer the hub. Removing weight at shaded area (E) will affect engagement rpm to a greater degree while removal from shaded area (X) will have greater effect on shift pattern. Do not remove material from fulcrum point (F) of kidney weight (right) or from roller contact area of hammer weight (left) when lightening the weights.

Paint, rust, gum or grease must be removed from belt contact surfaces of pulley faces and the surfaces kept clean. Bushing surfaces, pivot pins, rollers and other friction points must

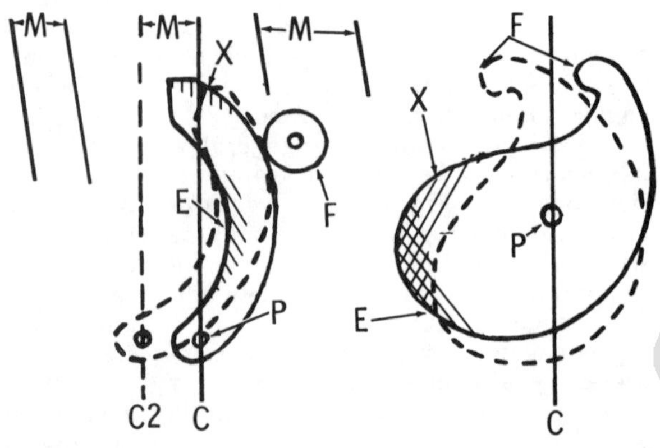

Fig. 8—Cross sectional view of governor centrifugal weights showing: M—Face movement and; Dotted lines—weight movement; to high speed position. Kidney type weight is shown at right while left-hand view shows curved cam-arm type in which pivot (P) moves and fulcrum (F) is fixed. Removing material in shaded area (E) will have greater effect on engagement speed; at shaded area (X) will have greater effect on shift pattern.

C. Gravity centerline
F. Fulcrum point
M. Advance movement
P. Centrifugal pivot

be free of excess clearance or binding. The use and choice of lubricants for friction points depends on the materials involved and to personal choice. The trend is away from conventional oils and greases and toward self-lubricating synthetic materials. Graphite or silicone sprays are sometimes used. If any lubricant is employed, it must be used sparingly and excess removed. Avoid build-up or gum, but parts must be maintained to move freely with minimum friction.

Careless parts modification or fitting can be dangerous. Do not weaken parts beyond safe levels by grinding or other means. Check local and meet regulations regarding scatter shields and guards. Potentially explosive centrifugal force may be generated at competition engine speeds.

DRIVE BELT

Do not use either a brand new or badly worn belt in actual competition. Keep a spare belt (or belts) on hand, but install and run them for one or two hours to "wear in" the belt. An unused belt is stiff and some limbering up is essential for top performance. Any measurable wear from nominal belt width will also lower potential top speed by reducing shift ratio. Some top competitors mark a directional arrow on a "run-in" belt and reinstall to run in the same direction. A reason for marking could not be verified in discussions with belt engineers, but use what works for you.

Some belt manufacturers use a mold release compound which leaves a gummy residue on a new belt. Any such substance should be removed before belt is installed using a suitable non-oily solvent. When not in use, store belts flat. Do not pinch, kink or roll. Do not pile heavy materials on stored belts. A large plastic bag or suitable box which will protect belts from dirt, oil or moisture makes ideal storage when belts are not in use.

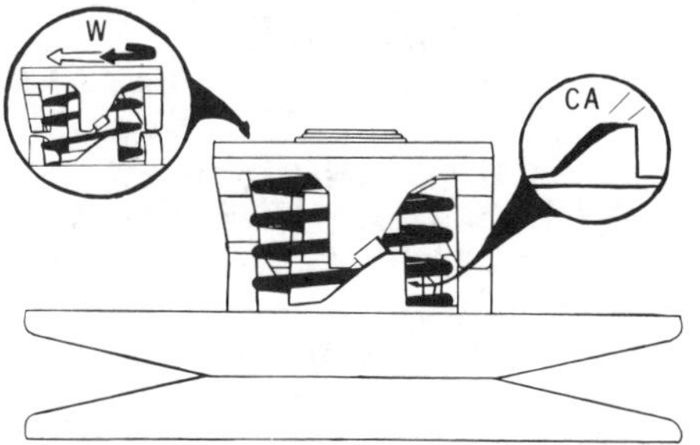

Fig. 9–Cross sectional view of driven pulley. Shift reaction can sometimes be modified by changing ramp cam angle (CA), torque wrap (W); or by installing a heavier or lighter reaction spring.

DRIVEN PULLEY

Driven pulley unit configuration and tuning, coupled with governor weights, determines upshift from power to speed ratio and related downshift under deceleration or power. Parts must move with absolute freedom but should not be excessively loose. The precautions applying to lubricants given in drive clutch section also applies to driven unit.

Modifications which are used to tailor driven unit to engine, drive clutch, and operating conditions are:

1. Installing a stronger (or weaker) torque spring.
2. Increasing (or decreasing) torque spring wrap.
3. Changing reaction cam angle.

A stronger torque spring, increased spring wrap or steeper cam angle will lengthen upshift time, reduce belt slippage and reduce downshift lag. They are not, however, completely interchangeable alternatives. A stronger spring or increased wrap is more effective in slowing upshift. A steeper cam angle or increased wrap is more effective in decreasing deceleration downshift lag. And a shallower cam angle provides a better power downshift if needed for maximum horsepower performance (such as grass racing, small displacement classes, etc.). A common practice is to pre-select spring strength and cam angle, then change the wrap if necessary to adjust for local conditions.

CONVERTER BALANCE

The final step in speed-tuning the converter is balancing the total unit against engine power and field demands. Belt slippage must be avoided as much as possible but unnecessary side pressure on the belt is counterproductive. The finely tuned competition machine will jackrabbit off the starting line and upshift to speed range as fast as available power and track conditions will permit. There must be no hesitation because clutch engagement is too early or because upshift is too fast or too slow.

Clutch engagement speed is controlled by governor weights and clutch reaction spring tension. Upshift is controlled by governor weights, driven pulley spring and cam angle. Downshift is controlled by cam angle and torsion spring wrap.

A tendency to lug off the starting line is combatted by raising clutch engagement speed and/or lengthening upshift time. Ideally, engine should immediately accelerate to peak power range followed by converter upshift as traction permits. Strengthen driven pulley spring or decrease cam angle to eliminate belt slippage. A stronger spring will probably decrease upshift time while a decreased cam angle will possibly increase upshift time. Each change will be a compromise, the problem (and fun) is deciding which compromise to make.

COMET

COMET INDUSTRIES
A DIVISION OF HOFFCO INC.

Models	90C	94C	100	102C	110
Drive Ratio					
Low	....	....	3.62:1	....	3.2:1
High	....	....	1.07:1	....	1.13:1
Belt Width, In.	1¼ in.	1¼ in.	1¼ in.	1¼ in.†	1¼ in.
Drive Sheave Diameter, In.	....	....	7.60	....	7.94
Driven Sheave Diameter, In.	10.71	....	10.71	....	10.71
Engagement RPM (standard)	....	**	3300*	**	Optional

*With standard spring and "C" weights.
**Refer to drive sheave section in John Deere vehicle section.
†1982 John Deere Liquifire models use a 1⅜-inch belt width.

GENERAL

Drive clutch Models 94C and 102C are used on John Deere vehicles. Adjustment of clutch may be done with reference to drive sheave section in John Deere vehicle section.

COMET Model 100 and 110 torque converters are easily adjustable performance oriented units. Model 90 is an economy priced drive unit only, which can be used with original driven units or the Model 100D driven clutch.

Performance characteristics can be tailored to a particular application by changing springs, governor weights, cam ramps and other parts. Normal care should be used to maintain the proper balance between drive and driven units.

ADJUSTMENT

DRIVE SHEAVE. The earlier model 110C Drive Clutch was available with a standard "A" cam arm or optional "B" cam arm and five optional compensating springs which are color coded to designate engagement rate. Using "A" cam arm, relative engagement rpm is as follows:

COLOR CODE	ENGAGEMENT RPM
Pink	3300
White	3900
Yellow	4400
Blue	4900
Silver	5300

The "B" cam arm gives a higher engagement rate of approximately 10% with lighter spring to perhaps 25% with heaviest spring.

The present 100 Series drive clutch has one set of standard "C" centrifugal weights (cam arms) or two optional "D" & "E" centrifugal weight sets; and one standard (Pink) or five optional (Green, Orange, White, or Blue) compensating springs. Engagement speeds using standard or optional springs and weights are as follows:

SPRING COLOR CODE	ENGAGEMENT RPM Weight "C"	Weight "D"	Weight "E"
Green	2300	2700	3500
Orange	2900	3200	3600
Pink	3300	3600	4800
White	4400	5200	6200
Yellow........	4700	5800	6800

Spring tension @ 2⅜ inch compression is: Green – 15 lb.; Orange – 25 lb.; Pink – 45 lb.; White – 75 lb.; Yellow – 10[illegible] lb.; Blue – 120 lb.

Centrifugal weight geometry on 10[illegible] clutch requires that a specified number of spacer washers (W – Fig. 1) be installed with weight kits. Two spacers are used with the "C" weights, which are standard equipment. If "D" weights are installed, remove one of the spacers; if "E" weights are used, assemble the clutch without spacers.

DRIVEN SHEAVE. The torque sensing driven sheave is regularly equipped with a 34° ramp cam (2 – Fig. 2) and standard torque spring (3) which is color coded red. Optionally available is a 45° ramp cam and a weaker spring which is color coded orange. Also present in sliding pulley hub are four numbered torque

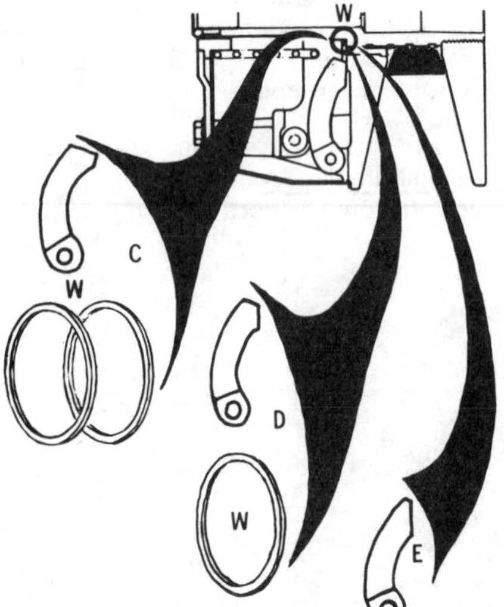

Fig. 1 – Correct spacing of Series 100 drive clutch requires that correct number of spacer washers (W) be installed with available ("C", "D" & "E") cam arms. Refer to text for details.

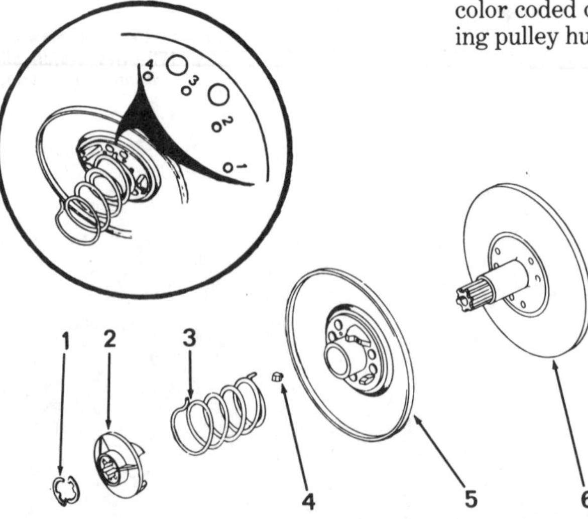

Fig. 2 – Series 100 driven pulley has four marked anchor points for torque spring as shown in inset. Refer to text for adjustment procedure.

1. Retaining ring
2. Cam unit
3. Torque spring
4. Ramp shoe
5. Sliding face
6. Fixed face & hub

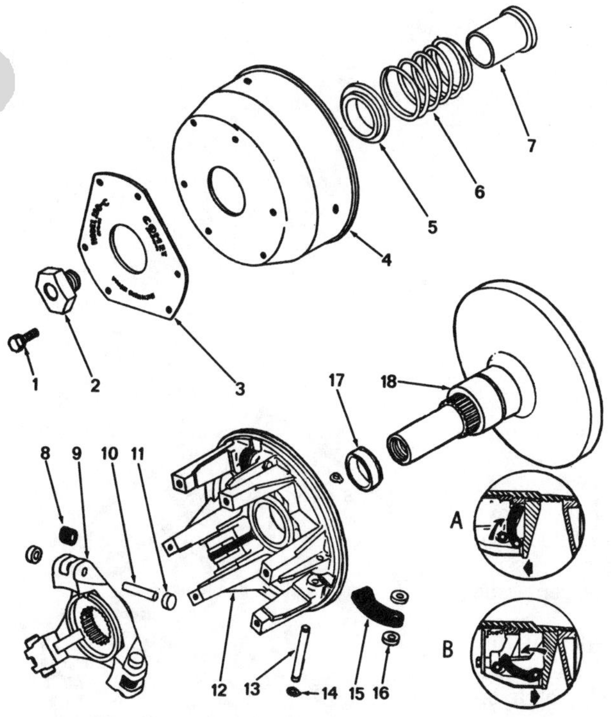

Fig. 3—Exploded view of early Series 110 drive clutch. Inset (A) shows cam weights and roller in disengaged position; Inset (B) in high speed position. Cam weights and rollers are black in exploded view.

1. Cap screw
2. Lock nut
3. Cover plate
4. Cover
5. Guide bushing
6. Reaction spring
7. Spacer sleeve
8. Cam roller
9. Spider
10. Roller shaft
11. Guide button
12. Sliding sheave
13. Weight shaft
14. Snap ring
15. Centrifugal weight
16. Nylon spacer
17. Bushing
18. Fixed sheave

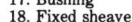

Fig. 5—Use hammer handle or wood dowel to unscrew spider, to keep from damaging pulley posts.

Check pulley faces for wear or misalignment and sliding surfaces for wear, binding or excessive clearance. Ramp shoes (4) can be heated if necessary, for removal. Renew any parts which are worn or questionable. Use a light coating or low temperature grease on sliding hub and ramp cams when reassembling, wiping off any excess to protect belt surfaces. Assemble by reversing the disassembly procedure.

spring anchor holes as shown in Inset—Fig.2. Positioning the spring in a higher numbered hole will increase the wrap and consequent torque load.

Increasing spring tension or torque wrap will increase upshift time but not to the same degree. Torque tension is measured at pulley rim and indicates the force required to move ramp button off of cam ramp by rotating sliding sheave from closed position. Torque tension can be measured by attaching a small C-clamp to pulley rim and measure tension using a fish scale. Normal setting of torque tension is 5-20 lbs. at pulley rim with pulley in closed position. The 45 degree cam or high torque wrap may be used to decrease deceleration downshift for cornering on oval track racing or other purposes. The steep cam and lighter spring minimizes upshift time for fastest acceleration if power and track conditions permit.

OVERHAUL

DRIVEN UNIT. Refer to Fig. 2 for an exploded view. Driven unit can be disassembled by depressing cam unit (2) and extracting split retainer (1). Be sure and note wrap of torque spring (3) and anchor hole location so performance can be duplicated on reassembly.

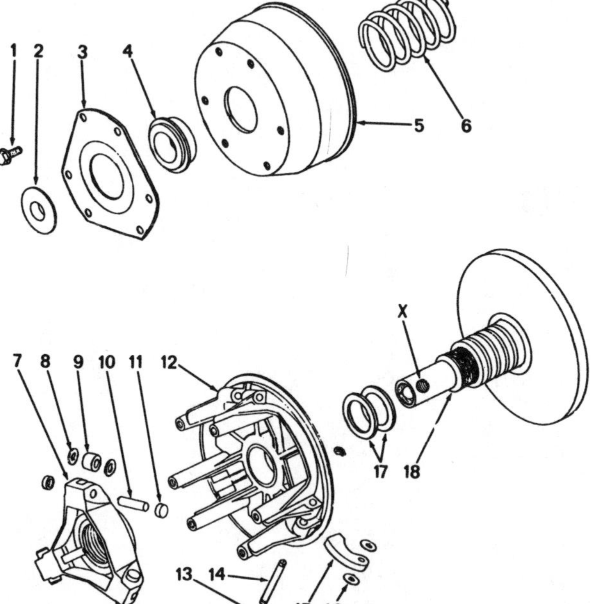

Fig. 4—Exploded view of Series 100 drive clutch showing component parts.

1. Cap screw
2. Pilot washer
3. Cover plate
4. Guide bushing
5. Cover
6. Reaction spring
7. Spider
8. Nylon spacer
9. Cam roller
10. Roller shaft
11. Guide button
12. Sliding sheave
13. Snap ring
14. Weight shaft
15. Centrifugal weight
16. Nylon spacer
17. Spacer washers
18. Fixed sheave
X. Disassembly hole

DRIVE CLUTCH. On the older 110C unit refer to Fig. 3 for exploded view. Place the removed assembly on a clean, solid work surface and remove lock nut (2); then lift off sliding sheave and governor assembly (3 through 16) as a unit. Remove three alternate cover cap screws (1) and loosen the other three. Apply hand pressure to cover plate (3) and remove remainder of screws. Disasemble governor unit. Plastic buttons (11) on roller pin (10) are a tight fit and must be carefully pried off. Do not remove the rollers unless renewal is required of some of the components. Bushing (17) in sliding sheave hub is renewable. Remainder of parts are an easy slip fit and renewal is indicated if clearance exists. Rollers (8), shafts (10), guide buttons (11), snap rings (14), centrifugal weights (15) and spacers (16) are available in sets only and complete set should be installed at renewal. Use a light even coat of low temperature grease on cam weights, rollers and sliding hub when assembling. Assemble by reversing the disassembly procedure, except install spider (9) on splines of fixed sheave (18) before installing cover (4).

To disassemble the late 100C clutch refer to Fig. 4. Place the removed unit on a clean, solid work surface, cover side up. Remove three alternate cover retaining cap screws (1) and loosen the other screws; then apply hand pressure to cover plate (3) while removing the remaining screws. Lift off cover plate (3), cover (5), spring seat (4) and reaction spring (6). Insert an alignment punch or suitable pry bar through hole (X) in pulley shaft. Raise one centrifugal

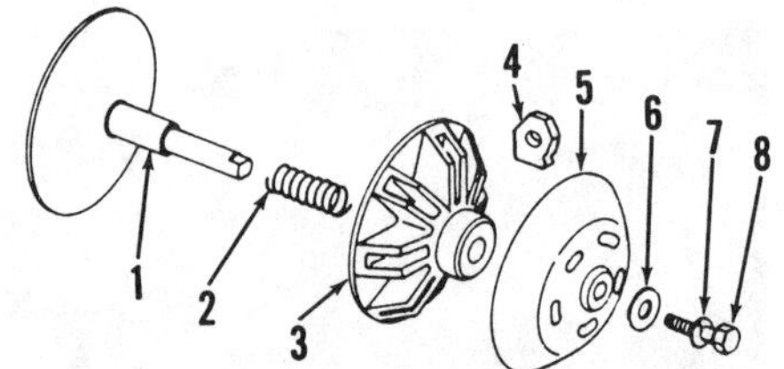

Fig. 6—Exploded view of Model 94C drive sheave.

1. Fixed face hub
2. Spring
3. Moveable face
4. Wedge
5. Cover plate
6. Flat washer
7. Lockwasher
8. Cap screw

Fig. 7—Exploded view of Model 102C drive sheave.

1. Fixed face hub
2. Steel washer
3. Arm
4. Bushing
5. Moveable face hub
6. Bearing
7. Washer
8. Plug
9. Pin
10. Washers
11. Roller
12. Spider
13. Spring
14. Cover plate
15. Washer
16. Washer
17. Lockwasher
18. Cap screw

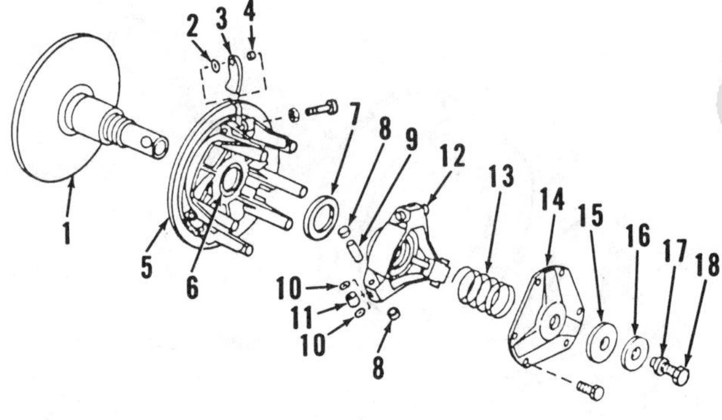

weight for clearance and insert a hammer handle or heavy wood dowel between sliding pulley posts as shown in Fig. 5; and holding hub stationary turn sliding pulley and spider counterclockwise to unscrew spider from clutch hub.

Guide buttons (11) are a tight fit on roller pin (10) and must be pried from position in disassembly. Renew weight shaft snap rings (13) whenever they are removed. All other parts should be an easy slip fit without excessive clearance. Bearing is not renewable in sliding sheave (12).

Spacer washers (17) control spacing of sheave halves and geometry of centrifugal weights (15). Install TWO spacers with Type "C" weight units; ONE spacer with Type "D" weight units; and NO spacers with Type "E" weight units.

Lubricate cam rollers, centrifugal weights and sliding hub when assembling, using a light even coat of low temperature grease. Assemble by reversing the disassembly procedure.

(Model 94C). Refer to Fig. 6 for parts breakdown and identification. Remove cover plate (5) and lift wedges (4) out of slots in moveable face (3), then remove face (3) and spring (2) from fixed face hub (1). Inspect all parts for excessive wear, pitting, or damage and renew as needed.

Reassemble in reverse order of disassembly. Be sure to install wedges in slots on moveable face with notch on wedge up and towards center.

(Model 102C). Refer to Fig. 7 for parts breakdown and identification. Remove cover plate (14) retaining cap screws equally, caution should be used during disassembly as cover plate is under spring pressure. Using a suitable tool and holding fixture turn spider assembly (12) off face hub (1). Complete disassembly with reference to Fig. 7. Inspect all parts for wear, cracks, pitting or any other damage and renew as needed.

Fig. 8—View showing position of alignment identification marks on spider and moveable face hub for Model 102C.

Reassemble in reverse order of disassembly. Refer to Fig. 8 showing location of spider and sheave identification marks. Marks should be aligned during assembly to insure proper balance of sheave assembly.

DRUMMOND

Models	100	200	200HD	400	600
Drive Ratio:					
Low:	3:1	3:1	3:1	3:1	3:1
High:	1:1	1:1	1:1	1:1	1:1
Horsepower (Maximum):					
4-cycle	7	12	....	12	....
2-cycle	12	23	24 up	24	25 up
Drive Sheave Dia. (In.)	5⅝	....	....	7¾	7¾
Driven Sheave Dia.	7⅝	....	....	10½	10½
Belt Width (In.)	⅞	....	....	1 3/16	1⅜
Shaft Centers (Min. In.)	7	....	....	10	10

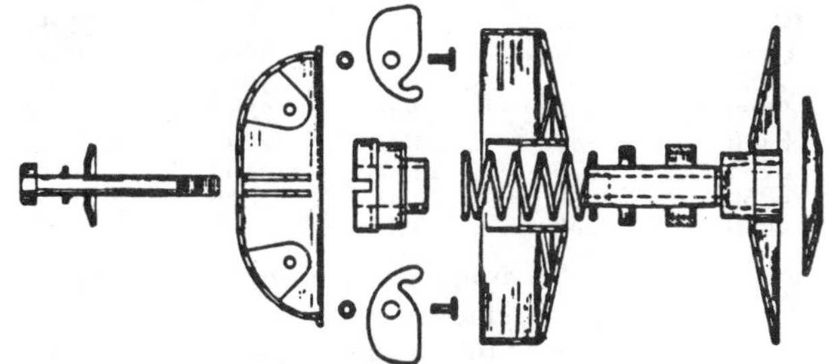

Fig. 1–Exploded view of Drummond Model 200 drive pulley designed for motors up to 23 horsepower.

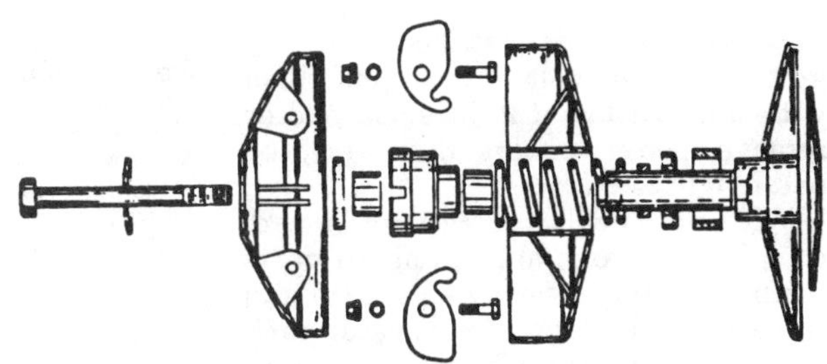

Fig. 2–Exploded view of Drummond Model 200 H. D. drive pulley designed for motors of 24 horsepower and up.

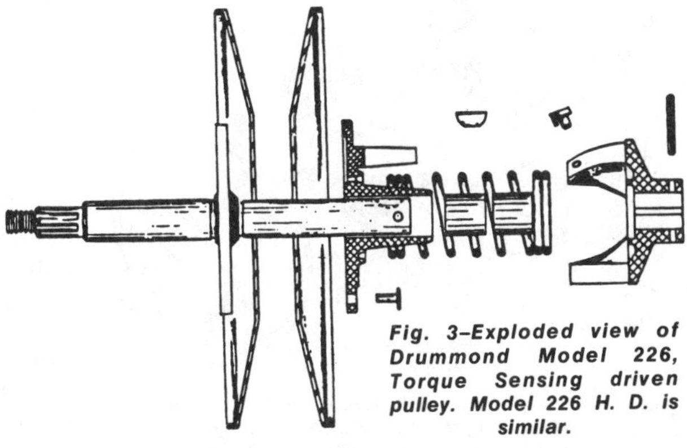

Fig. 3–Exploded view of Drummond Model 226, Torque Sensing driven pulley. Model 226 H. D. is similar.

POWERBLOCK

The POWERBLOCK Clutch is supplied as a drive unit only; or as a partial unit consisting of governor unit, sliding sheave and compensating spring to be installed on an existing fixed flange with one-inch or 1⅛-inch smooth hub. The clutch unit is compatible with most driven units and is widely adjustable to suit performance needs of the combined unit.

ADJUSTMENT

Compensating spring (6—Fig. 2) is available in six different weights which are color coded for identification. Weight blocks (4) may be equipped with threaded caps (C—Fig. 3) and steel weights (W) which may be added or removed and intermatched with the springs to balance the speed change characteristics to the driven unit. Shim spacers (3 & 8—Fig. 2) can also be added or removed as required to match open and closed positions of sheave halves to the width of the belt which is installed.

NOTE: Converter pulley face angle may vary from 26° to 34° (included angle). POWERBLOCK clutch is built with an included angle of 26° but will match satisfactorily with any known unit despite the slight angle difference. The only instance where difficulty has occurred is in maintaining a correct belt centerline through the full shift range. This difficulty can be overcome in part by splitting the difference between high-range and low-range error; or by using the original fixed pulley half and POWERBLOCK partial unit.

MATCHING BELT WIDTH. To match for belt width during installation, install fixed pulley (10—Fig. 2) and idler bearing (9) on engine. Install shoulder washer (7) and sliding half (5), omitting compensating spring (6). Hold sliding pulley (5) in bottomed position (pulley closed) and place the

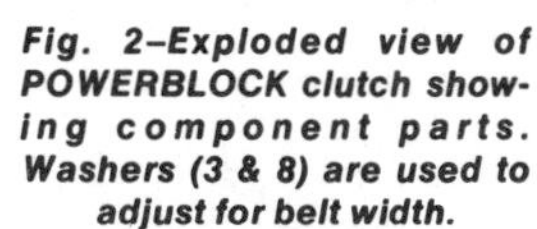

Fig. 1–Assembled view of POWERBLOCK drive clutch.

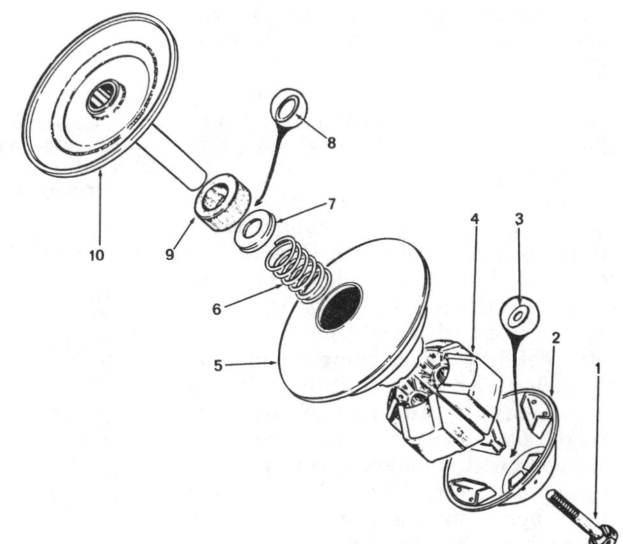

Fig. 2–Exploded view of POWERBLOCK clutch showing component parts. Washers (3 & 8) are used to adjust for belt width.

1. Cap screw
2. Governor cone
3. Spacer washer
4. Weight block
5. Sliding half
6. Reaction spring
7. Shoulder washer
8. Spacer washer
9. Idler bearing
10. Fixed face

belt which will be installed in pulley groove. Top of belt should ride flush with pulley rims; if it does not, add or remove spacer washers (8) until closed belt height is correct.

With closed width correctly adjusted, complete the assembly using all parts including compensating spring (6) and the previously determined spacer pack (8). Temporarily install the same number of outer spacer washers (3) as used in spacer pack (8). Install and snug up retaining cap screw (1). Position the belt in pulley groove making sure it rides on idler bearing (9); then measure the clearance between side of belt and pulley face. Clearance should be 3/32-inch, if it is not, add or remove outer spacers (3) until correct clearance is obtained.

As a final step in assembly, back out the retaining cap screw (1) until screw disengages from crankshaft. Screw should thread into shaft ten full turns to safely retain the clutch; if it does not substitute a longer screw, which should be grade six (four-mark) or stronger. The manufacturer provides cap screws in lengths of 5, 5¼, 5½ and 6 inches in length.

When permanently installing the pulley, coat sliding surfaces of governor cone (2) and sliding pulley (5) (weight block contact surfaces) with powdered or paste graphite and tighten retaining cap screw (1) to a torque of 80-90 ft.-lbs. NOTE: NEVER use grease as a lubricant on governor weights.

GOVERNOR CALIBRATION. When balancing the drive unit against an existing driven pulley, keep in mind the following basic facts about converter performance.

1. Governor centrifugal weights balance against Drive Unit Spring ONLY to determine engagement speed.

2. Governor Centrifugal Weights must balance against the COMBINED strength of BOTH pulley springs determine shift characteristics.

3. It is generally preferable to keep both the weight and spring strength at the lowest practicable level adequate for proper performance.

The six different compensating springs (6—Fig. 2) are color coded, (light to heavy) Chrome, Green, Yellow, Red, Blue and Gold. Up to eight extra steel weight discs (W—Fig. 3) can be added to each weight block (B), the total weight package being retained by threaded cap (C). Weight must be added equally to each of the four weight blocks (B). Standard units are equipped with a yellow spring and two weight discs (W). The following table lists approximate engagement speeds for each of the six springs, variously equipped.

Spring Color	Block Only	Two Weights	Four Wts	Six Wts	Eight Wts
Chrome	2650	2050	1800	1600	1550
Green	3200	2625	2300	2050	1900
Yellow	3400	2750	2450	2200	2050
Red	3775	2850	2550	2450	2225
Blue	4350	3000	2650	2575	2375
Gold	4500	3150	3025	2725	2600

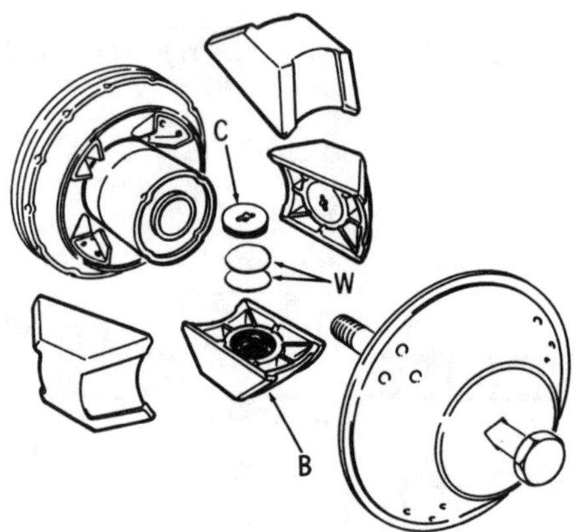

Fig. 3–Weight blocks (B) are built to accept up to eight weight discs (W), retained by threaded cap (C), to adjust engagement speed and reaction.

To summarize, if engagement speed is satisfactory and:

Upshift is too rough or abrupt; install a lighter spring and remove weights.

Pulley heats, upshift is too slow or belt slips; install heavier spring and add weights.

To raise engagement speed, install heavier spring or remove weights.

To lower engagement speed, install lighter spring or add weights.

OVERHAUL NOTES

As belt wear occurs, performance will be improved by re-matching belt width as previously outlined. Melting of the nylon weight blocks is usually caused by belt slippage which should be corrected by increasing tension on driven pulley spring. Maximum allowable wear of fixed pulley hub sliding surface is 0.005.

PRECICO

Fig. 1–Exploded view of Precico drive and driven clutch of the type commonly used.

1. Secondary shaft
2. Fixed flange
3. Moveable flange
4. Moveable hub
5. Bushings
6. Torque spring
7. Ramp shoe
8. Cam hub
9. Bolt
10. Weight unit
11. Bushings
12. Moveable face
13. Reaction spring
14. Spacer
15. Idler
16. Fixed face
17. Drive belt

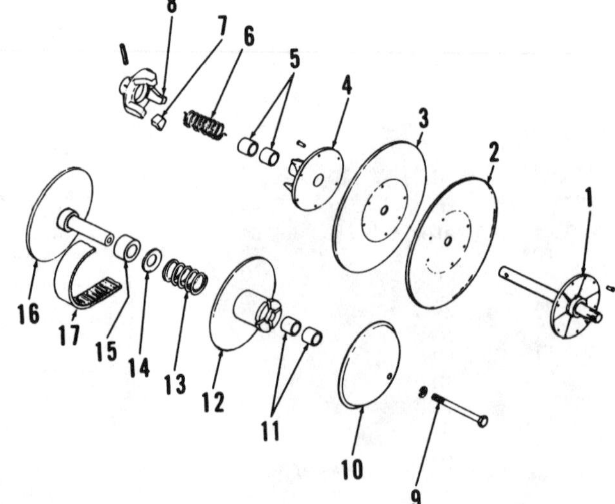

CONVERTER

Precico torque converters are used as original equipment on Ariens, Northway, Skiroule and others. Refer to Fig. for exploded view of torque sensing converter unit. Fig. 2 shows Model 5000 Cam Acuated drive pulley which uses steel cables for centrifugal weights and cam action movement. Specifications are as follows:

Drive Ratio:
- Low 3.3:1
- High 1:1.3

Drive Sheave Diameter (In.) 7¾
Driven Sheave Dia. (In.) 10⅜
Shaft Center Distance (Min. In.) 10½

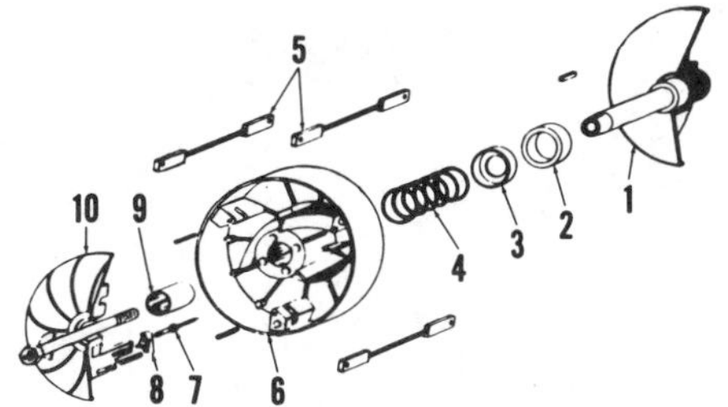

Fig. 2–Exploded view of Model 5000 Cam Actuated Drive Pulley.

1. Fixed face
2. Idler
3. Spring seat
4. Spring
5. Weight unit
6. Moveable face
7. Pop rivet
8. Ramp shoe
9. Bushing
10. Cam cover

ST. LAWRENCE

IDENTIFICATION

ST. LAWRENCE torque converters are available in two series, Standard Duty (up to 22 hp) and Heavy Duty (24 hp and up). Mounting hubs are available for most popular snowmobile engines and the converter unit can be custom designed for a particular application. Designed top speed of drive pulley is 6000 rpm. Drive ratios of standard types are as follows:

Type	Low	High
1000	4:1	1:1.2
2000	3.25:1	1:1.12
3000	4:1	1:1.2
4000	4:1	1:1.2

Part numbers of drive and driven sheaves are key-coded to indicate design characteristics. The key is as follows:

DRIVE PULLEY number consists of five digits:

*....For the first digit, 1—indicates standard unit; 2—indicates 6⅞″ diameter sheave and splined slide; 3—indicates teflon bushing in sliding sheave; 4—indicates splined slide.

.*...The second digit indicates belt width; 2—indicates 15/16″; 3—indicates 1″; 5—indicates 1 3/16″; and 8—indicates 1 7/16″.

..*..The third digit indicates housing type; 0—standard; 2—heavy duty.

...**The last two digits indicate mounting taper in pulley hub. Available tapers are 24, 25 and 30 mm. An E suffix is added for hubs inside threaded to attach to engines with external crankshaft thread.

DRIVEN PULLEY. The driven pulley part number consists of three or four digits:

*...In the first digit 1—indicates integral fixed flange and secondary shaft (Fig. 2); 2—indicates sleeved fixed flange (Fig. 3).

.*..The second digit indicates belt width; 4—15/16″; 5—1″; 6—1 3/16″ or 8—1 7/16″.

..*.The third digit indicates shaft diameter on integral types or sleeve OD on sleeved types: 2—¾″ OD; 3—⅞″ OD; 4—1″ OD; 6—1⅛″ OD and 8—1⅝″ OD.

...*The fourth digit, if used, indicates sleeve inside diameter of sleeved types; 2—¾″ ID; 3—⅞″ ID; 4—1″ ID; 6—1 1/6″ ID and 8—1 3/16″ ID.

OVERHAUL

DRIVE UNIT. To remove the drive unit on standard models, first remove bolt (8—Fig. 1), washer (7), weight unit (6), sliding sheave (5), spring (4), spring seat (3) and idler bearing (2). Insert a ⅜″ diameter steel rod 4 inches long in threaded end of crankshaft, then screw a 9/16-18 NF bolt into threaded end of sheave hub (1). With shaft insert bottomed, bump end of forcing screw with a hammer to release shaft taper. A hot air gun may also be used at this point.

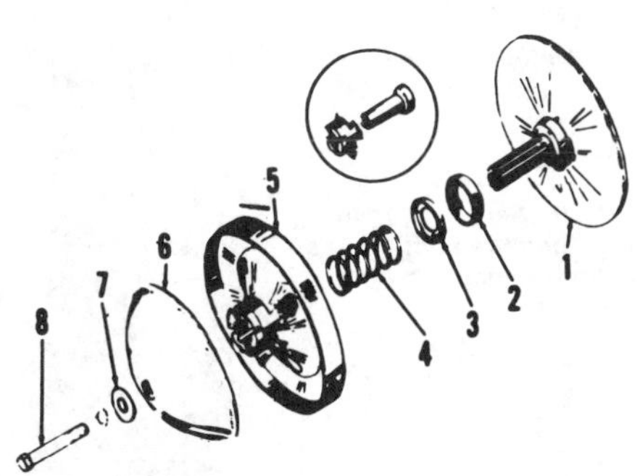

Fig. 1–Exploded view of drive sheave with splined hub. Optional standard hub is shown in inset.

1. Drive hub
2. Idler bearing
3. Spring seat
4. Spring
5. Sliding sheave
6. Weight unit
7. Washer
8. Bolt

When installing unit, be sure taper of hub and crankshaft are clean and free of dirt, burrs or grease. Lubricate sliding hub with low temperature grease and assemble the unit during installation.

DRIVEN UNIT. Refer to Fig. 2 or Fig. 3 for exploded views of driven units. Removal procedure will vary depending on details of machine construction.

Torque spring (4—Fig. 2 or 3—Fig. 3) should normally be pre-tensioned approximately one cam (⅓ turn) as unit is assembled. Pre-tensioning is most easily accomplished by sliding cam hub outward until cams clear, then turning sliding sheave (5—Fig. 2 or 2—Fig. 3).

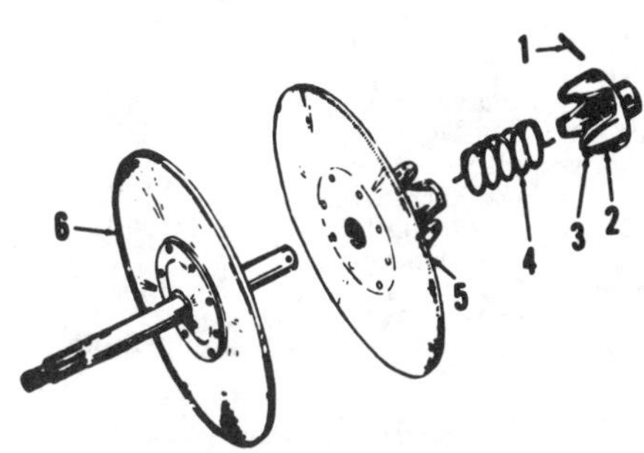

Fig. 2–Exploded view of integral flange driven sheave. Cam hub is pinned to intermediate shaft.

1. Pin
2. Cam hub
3. Ramp shoe
4. Torque spring
5. Sliding sheave
6. Shaft and flange

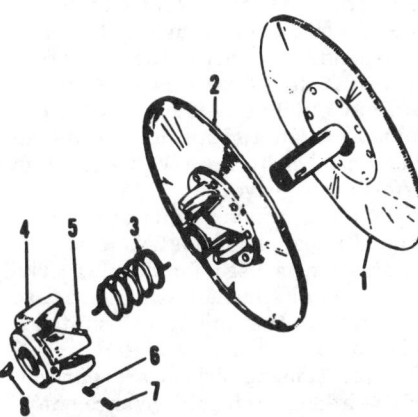

Fig. 3–Exploded view sleeved flange driven sheave. Cam hub is keyed to sleeve hub and locked with set screw.

1. Sleeve and flange
2. Sliding sheave
3. Torque spring
4. Cam hub
5. Ramp shoe
6. Set screw
7. Backup screw
8. Woodruff key

SALSBURY

Models Drive Ratio:	330	500	700	705	770	775	780
Low	2.5:1	3:1	4:1	4:1	3:1	3:1	3.76:1
High	1:1	1:1	1:1	1:1	1:1	1:1	1:1.16
Horsepower (max.):							
4-Cycle (3600 rpm)	5	7	8	10	10	12	12
2-Cycle (5500 rpm)	8	9	15	17	17	19	25
Belt Width (in. nom.)	⅝	1	1	1	1 3/16	1 3/16	1 3/16
Drive Sheave Diameter (in.)	4½	5½	7 7/32	7¼	7 7/32	7 7/32	7 7/32
Drive Sheave Weight (lbs.)	2½	4¾	5½	5½	5½	5½	5¼
Driven Sheave Diameter (in.)	6	7⅜	9⅞	9⅞	9⅞	9⅞	9¼
Driven Sheave Weight (lbs.)	1¾	6¼	9¼	10¾	9¼	10¾	8
Engagement Speeds:							
4-Cycle (3600 rpm)	2000	1600	1400	1400	1600	1400	1600
2-Cycle (5500 rpm)	3100	2300	1900	1900	2300	1900	2300
Nominal Operating Speeds	8500	5500	6000	6000	5500	6000	5500

Drive Ratio:	790	795	850	860	880	910	1190	1195
Low	3:1	3:1	3.42:1	3.93:1	3.2:1	3.14:1	2.88:1	2.88:1
High	1:1.5	1:1.5	0.76:1	1:1	1:13	1:1.28	1:1.27	1:1.27
Horsepower (max.):								
4-Cycle (3600 rpm)	10	12	....	....	....	18	24	24
2-Cycle (5500 rpm)	19	25	....	....	25	32	50	50
Belt Width (in. nom.)	1 3/16	1 3/16	....	....	1 3/16	1¼	1 7/16	1 7/16
Drive Sheave Diameter (in.)	7 7/32	7 7/32	....	....	8⅜	7¾	8 5/16	8 5/16
Drive Sheave Weight (lbs.)	5½	5½	....	....	10½	7½	11	11
Driven Sheave Diameter (in.)	8½	8½	9⅞	11¼	9⅞	9⅞	9⅞	9⅞
Driven Sheave Weight (lbs.)	8	10¾	....	....	9½	8	9¼	11¾
Engagement Speeds:								
4-Cycle (3600 rpm)	1400	1400	....	....	....	....	1500	1500
2-Cycle (5500 rpm)	1900	1900	3500*	3500*	2000	2800	2800	2800
Nominal Operating Speeds	5500	5500	8500*	8500*	5500	5500	5500	5500

*Adjustable.

GENERAL

Salsbury torque converters produced before 1969 were all of the speed sensing type. Beginning with the 1969 model year, torque sensing driven sheaves were made available as an option especially for snowmobile use.

In 1970, the company introduced 7R, 9R and 11R Racing Drive units which corresponded roughly to the 700 series, 900 series and 1100 series in engine application. These drive units were phased out in 1972, being replaced where needed by the 800 series High Performance Drives.

The speed sensing units are recommended for applications where engine compression is used for braking. The toggle weights, when used, increase the ability of the unit to transmit low end torque.

Torque sensing drives are particularly suited to high performance snowmobile use such as racing, etc., but do not effectively transmit reverse torque.

Refer to specification chart for nominal engagement speeds, operating speeds and horsepower recommendations. Performance characteristics can be tailored to a particular operation by changing springs and governor weights or other parts. Normal care should be used in procuring and installing parts, to maintain the proper balance between drive components.

The V-belt should be renewed when wear exceeds ⅛ inch from width given in specification table.

Sheave bores are finished to 0.0005-0.0015 (in.) over nominal size and must be a push fit. If excessive force is required in removing or installing any sheave, correct the cause before proceeding. In the case of difficult removal, check carefully for removal damage at time of overhaul.

ADJUSTMENT. Most drive pulley units have Engagement Speed Modification "Hi-Rev" Kits available which

Fig. 1–On Series 800 drive pulley, engagement speed can be adjusted by loosening jam nuts (A) and turning adjusting screws (B). Refer to text for details.

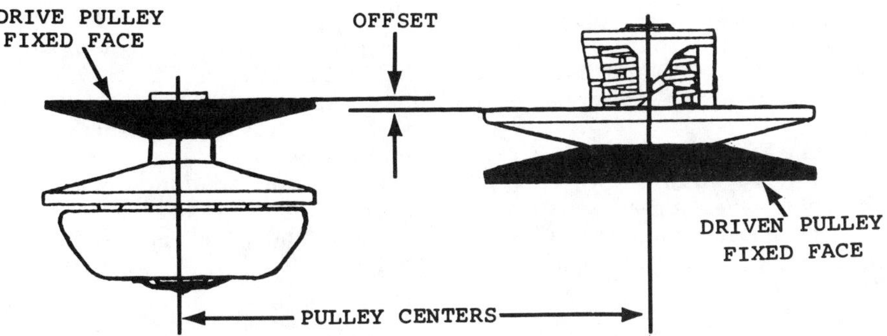

Fig. 2–Correct pulley center distance and offset are both important for proper operation of the unit. Fixed faces must be on opposite sides as shown.

will raise clutch engagement speed from stock to a 3300-4000 rpm range. Some torque sensitive driven pulleys have standard (41°) ramp cam or optional (35°) ramp cam available, plus optional heavier and lighter torque springs.

On 800 Series drive pulley, engagement speed can be adjusted within limits. Refer to Fig. 1 and proceed as follows: Wrap the belt to be used tightly around drive pulley, loosen jam nuts (A) and back out Allen head cap screws (B) until some clearance exists between moving sheave and side of belt. Turn set screws in evenly a little at a time until no clearance exists between sides of belt and either sheave. Tighten jam nuts (A) at this point to provide an engagement speed of approximately 3500 rpm. If a higher clutch engagement speed is desired, back out each screw (B) ONE FULL TURN for each 500 rpm increase desired. Tighten jam nuts securely without moving set screws.

PREVENTIVE MAINTENANCE. The manufacturer recommends that the drive unit be inspected on a periodic basis using the following schedule for normal conditions. The interval between inspection periods should be shortened under adverse conditions.

Every 100 hours or oftener, check engine hold-down bolts (and secondary shaft mountings where applicable) to be sure they are tight. If bolts are loose or if evidence of movement exists, check belt centers and sheave alignment (offset). Refer to Fig. 2. If required, pulleys should be removed, thoroughly cleaned with solvent and working parts relubricated with light oil.

Every 250 hours, disassemble both pulleys. Inspect springs, pivot pins and bearing surfaces and renew any parts that are worn, damaged or questionable. Lubricate bearings and moving surfaces with light oil, being careful that lubricant does not get on belt or pulley flanges. Renew belt if unevenly worn or if worn more than ⅛-inch.

DRIVE SHEAVES. The manufacturer has made available "DRIVE PULLEY DISMOUNT TOOLS" for use in removing pulley from tapered shaft engines. On late units, drive pulley hub is tapped for installation of tool. On other models thread the pilot hole in pulley hub using a ⅞"-14 NC tap and thread to a depth of 1-1¼ inch.

Refer to Figs. 3, 4, 5, & 6 for typical exploded view of Salsbury drive pulleys. Service on governor weights, springs, pivot pins and associated parts can be accomplished after removing ramp plate (6—Fig. 5 or 9—Fig. 6). A press is required for removing drive plate (5—Fig. 3 or 8—Fig. 6). Refer to Fig. 7. Support the sheave in the bed of the press, the supports (P) contacting belt face of moving flange (3). Leave enough room to allow removal of fixed flange (1). Use a suitable bearing plate (A) and press fixed flange (1) and hub downward out of moving flange (3) and drive plate (5). Be sure pins of drive plate enter proper holes in moving flange (3), and hold moving flange in contact with drive plate as unit is assembled.

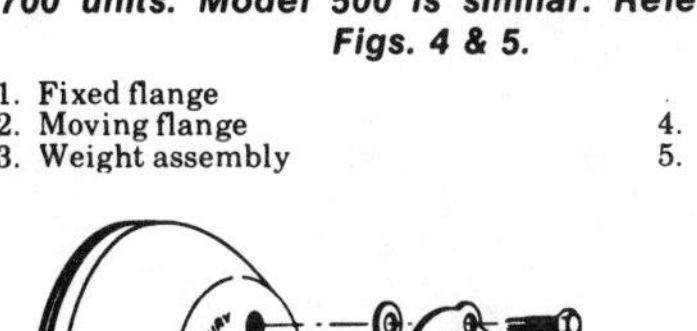

Fig. 3–Sheave faces, drive plate and associated parts typical of that used on all Series 700 units. Model 500 is similar. Refer also to Figs. 4 & 5.

1. Fixed flange
2. Moving flange
3. Weight assembly
4. Roller arm
5. Drive plate

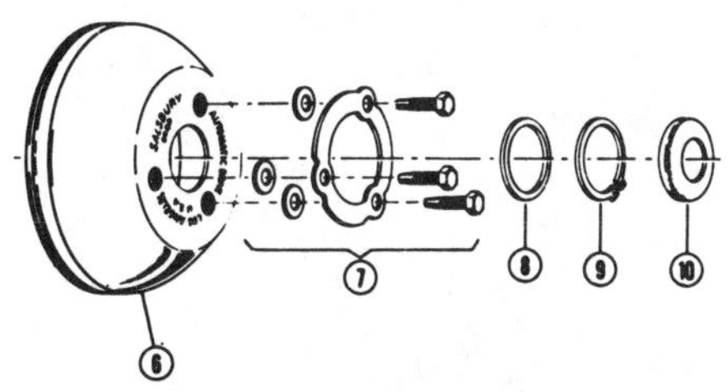

Fig. 5–Ramp plate and associated parts used on Model 780.

6. Ramp plate
7. Lock plate
8. Spacer
9. Snap ring
10. Cup washer

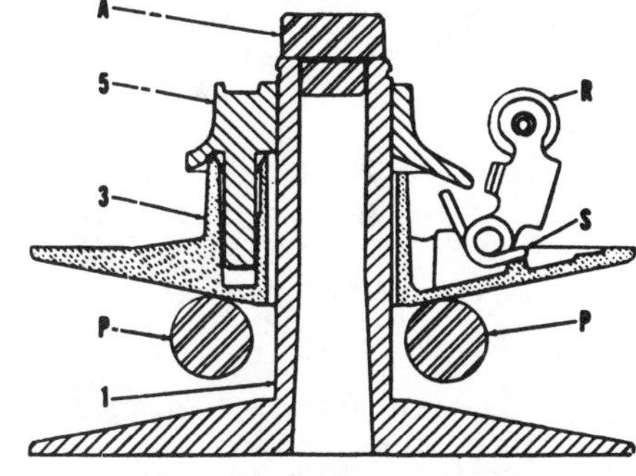

Fig. 7–To disassemble Series 500, 700 or 900 drive sheave, support moving flange in press (P). Use a suitable bearing plate (A) and press fixed flange (1) downward out of drive plate (5).

R. Roller arms
S. Springs

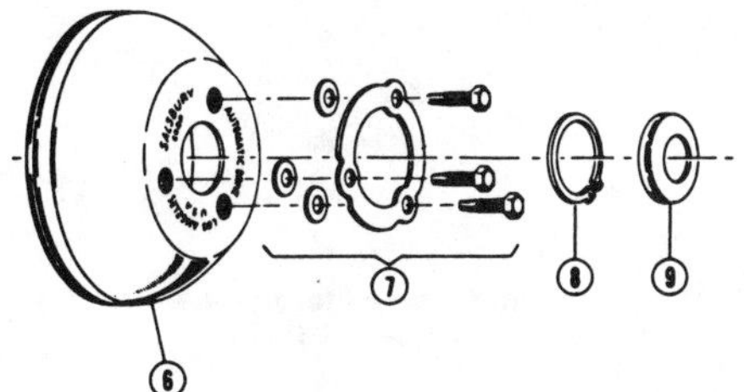

Fig. 4–Ramp plate and associated parts used on all series 700 except 780.

6. Ramp plate
7. Lock plate
8. Snap ring
9. Cup washer

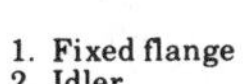

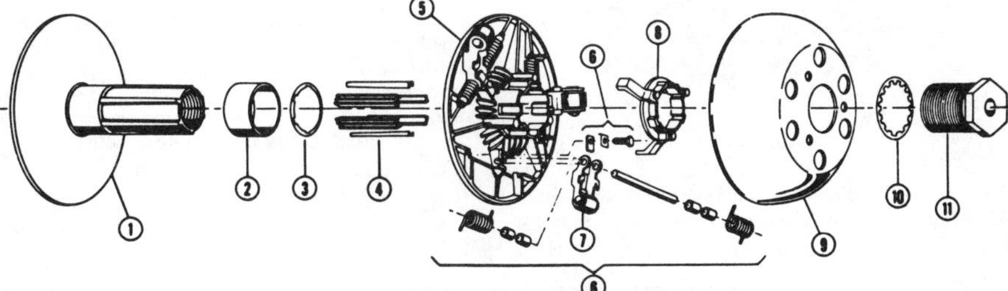

Fig. 6–Exploded view of drive unit used on Model 910.

1. Fixed flange
2. Idler
3. Washer
4. Spline liner
5. Moving face
6. Weight assembly
7. Roller arm
8. Drive plate
9. Ramp plate
10. Lockwasher
11. Nut

Fig. 8 shows disassembly of drive sheave used on early Model 1195. Thread the special Dismount Tool (702926) into bore of sheave hub as shown at (1). Unseat and remove outer snap ring (2). Equally space three wood blocks (3) under edge of ramp plate (4) and tap end of dismount tool (1) until ramp plate slides free of splined fixed sheave hub. Disconnect inner ends of the six roller arm springs from hooks on roller arms, then lift off wave washer (5) and retractor (6). Remove the remaining snap ring and slide moving sheave half from pulley hub. Assemble by reversing the disassembly procedure. Tighten cap screws to a torque of 8-9 ft.-lbs. and bend up lock tabs. Use a sleeve tube just larger than spline diameter to reinstall bell housing on hub splines.

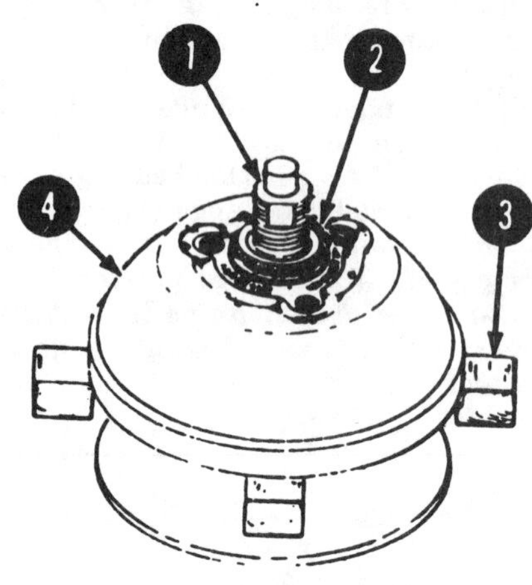

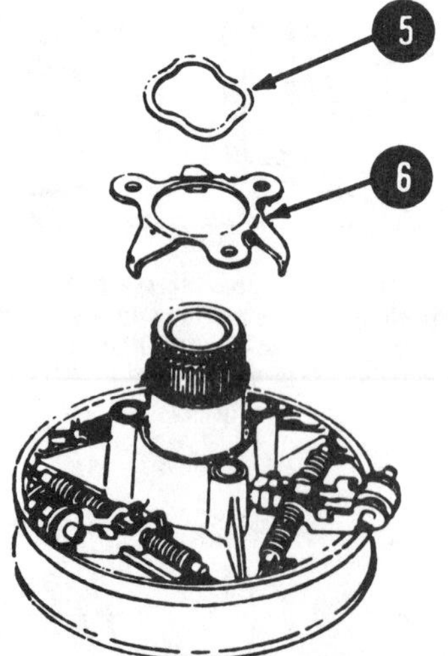

Fig. 8–Views showing disassembly sequence for Model 1195 drive sheave. Refer to text for details.

Fig. 9 shows drive sheave used on Model 880. Bell housing (12) threads onto fixed flange (1) and disassembly is accomplished by unscrewing bell housing.

DRIVEN SHEAVES. Figs. 10 through 13 show views of typical driven sheaves. Speed sensing types are spring loaded and restraint must be applied while removing nuts from through-bolts.

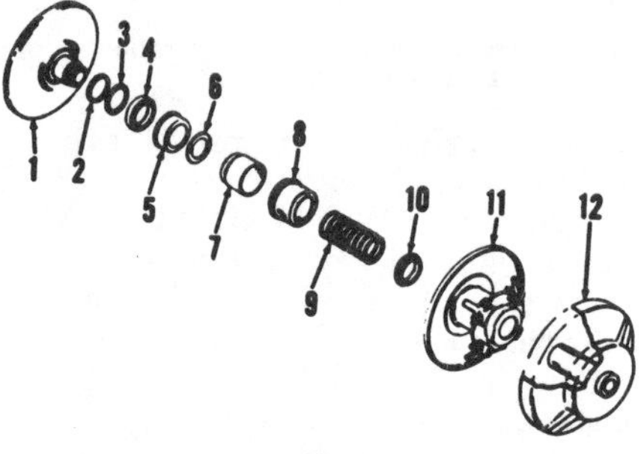

Fig. 9–Exploded view of drive sheave used on Model 880.

1. Fixed flange
2. Spacer
3. Seal
4. Bearing
5. Idler tire
6. Thrust washer
7. Bearing cup
8. Bearing
9. Spring
10. Bearing
11. Moving flange
12. Bell housing

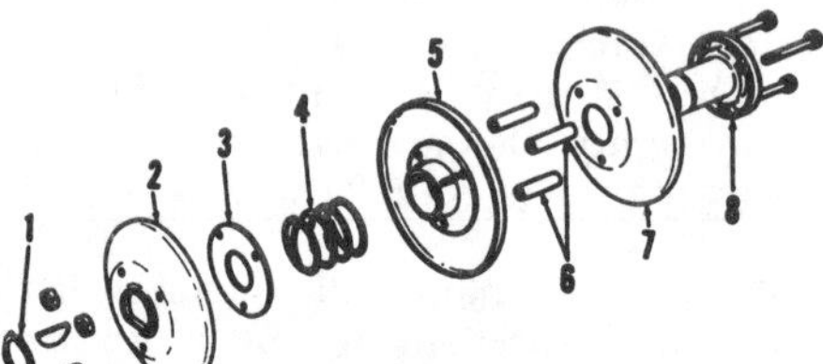

Fig. 10–Exploded view of driven sheave of type used on Models 503 and 504.

1. Snap ring
2. Pressure plate
3. Spring guide
4. Spring
5. Moving flange
6. Spacers
7. Fixed flange
8. Hub

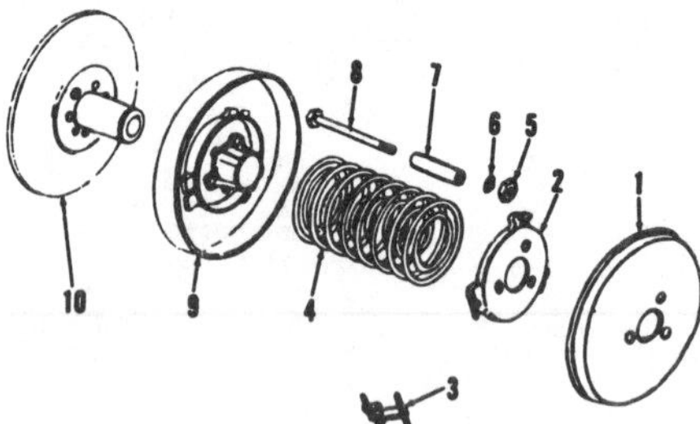

Fig. 11–Exploded view of driven sheave of type used on Series 700 and Model 1195 with centrifugal toggle weights (3). High-speed, modified units are simialr except items 1 and 3 are discarded and a single spring is used instead of double spring (4).

1. Cover plate
2. Spring plate
3. Toggle weights
4. Springs
5. Nuts
6. Washer
7. Spacers
8. Through-bolt
9. Moving flange
10. Fixed flange

Torque sensing models (Fig. 13) are pre-loaded by turning moving sheave half ⅓ turn (one cam) as unit is assembled, making sure ends of tensioning spring engages hub and sheave before unit is tensioned.

Driven pulley dismount tools are available for servicing late units. Part numbers and model applications are as follows:

Part Number	Model
702807	700 Series
702925	880
703079	910
702926	1195

Tools are available from vehicle manufacturers or by contacting SALSBURY Corporation.

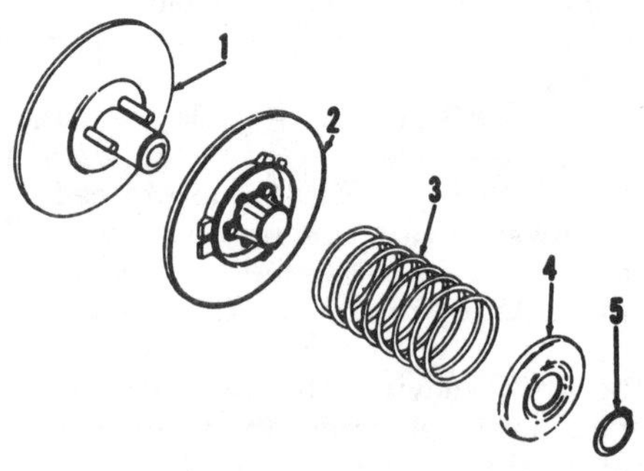

Fig. 12–Exploded view of driven sheave used on Series 880.

1. Fixed flange
2. Moving flange
3. Spring
4. Spring cup
5. Snap ring

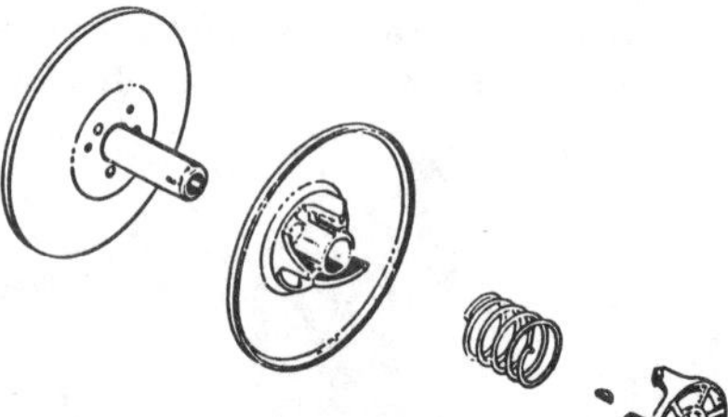

Fig. 13–Exploded view of torque sensing driven sheave with 41° cam. Torque spring must be pretensioned ⅓ turn (one cam) when unit is assembled.

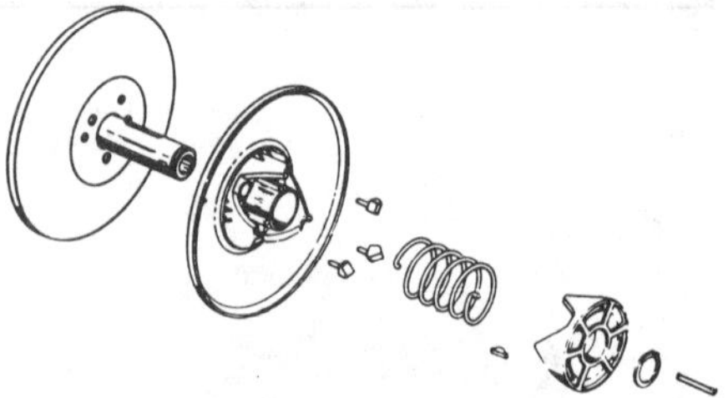

Fig. 14–Exploded view of torque sensing driven sheave with 35° cam.

TRACK DRIVE

CONTENTS

This section covers the drive train from torque converter driven sheave to track drive axle. For convenience only, the brake is also included in this section. The brake is usually installed on the intermediate shaft which carries the torque converter driven sheave.

GENERAL

A roller drive chain is relatively inexpensive, efficient and simple, and for these reasons, commonly used to transmit power from the torque converter to vehicle track.

Several factors must be considered in selecting a roller chain drive, and it is beyond the scope of this manual to attempt to provide engineering data. A working knowledge of the factors affecting drive selection may be useful, however, as a background for the correction of service problems.

The principle dimensions of a roller drive chain are pitch, roller diameter and roller width. Refer to Fig. 1. As a general rule, the shorter the pitch, the higher the permissible operating speed. The larger the sprocket (within practical limits) the more efficient the drive. Sixteen or 17 teeth in the smaller sprocket are generally considered ideal for optimum performance. Horsepower capacity in excess of that provided by a single chain may be obtained by the use of a double chain. The actual drive selected is usually a compromise in which size, cost, performance, dependability and service cost are among the factors considered.

A much simplified series of formulas are given to determine different aspects of snowmobile drive train design. It must be noted that these formulas do not take into consideration track slippage, track area, traction or frictional resistance, most of which are variable factors or dependent upon variables. Neither do they consider the operating characteristics of the engine or torque converter. Performance can only be proven by actual test.

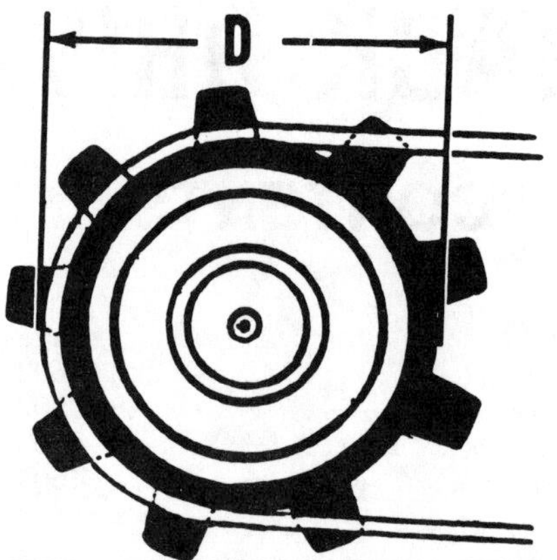

Fig. 2–Track drive sprocket effective diameter can be approximated by measuring the diameter of sprocket where track rides and adding the track thickness as shown at (D).

To determine the number of teeth in one final drive sprocket when the desired rotative speed (RPM) of both shafts are known and one sprocket has been selected:

Multiply the number of teeth in available sprocket by its rotative speed and divide by the rotative speed of other shaft.

To determine horsepower requirement or vehicle speed when the other factor is known:

$$\frac{GVW \times MPH}{1400} = HP$$

$$\frac{HP \times 1400}{GVW} = MPH$$

To determine vehicle speed or track drive axle RPM when the other factor is known:

$$\frac{MPH \times 335}{TSD} = RPM$$

$$\frac{RPM \times TSD}{335} = MPH$$

GVW = Gross Vehicle Weight (With Driver
MPH = Miles Per Hour
TSD = Track Drive Sprocket effective Diameter. See Fig. 2

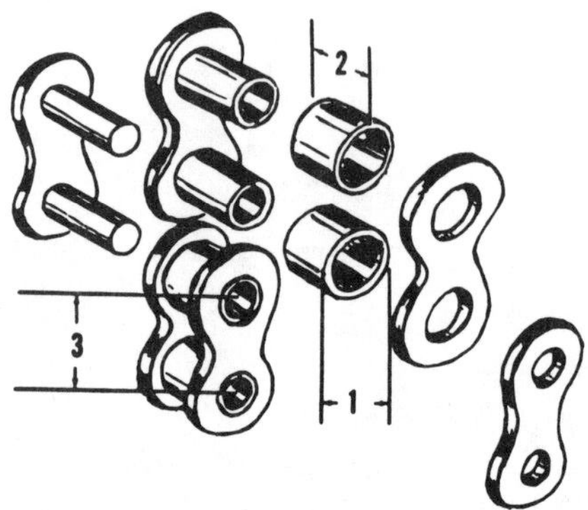

Fig. 1–The principal dimensions of roller chain are (1) Roller Diameter; (2) Roller Width; and (3) Pitch.

CHAIN SERVICE

A roller chain is composed essentially of a number of small bearings which operate under relatively high pressure and speed. The most satisfactory method of providing adequate lubrication is by enclosing the drive in a housing containing an oil supply. Alternate methods are by automatic drip oiling or periodic manual lubrication. If periodic lubrication is required, it is strongly recommended that one of the foaming type aerosol cans of lubricant and cleaner be used. To be effective, the lubricant must enter bearing areas of chain as shown in Fig. 3, and regular oil often does an incomplete job of lubrication.

Sprocket tooth profile is precisely ground to fit the roller diameter and chain pitch. Refer to Fig. 4. When chain and sprocket are new, the chain moves around the sprocket smoothly with a minimum of friction, and the load is evenly distributed over several sprocket teeth. Wear on pins and bushings of a roller chain results in a lengthening or "stretch" of each individual chain pitch as well as a lengthening of the complete chain. The worn chain, therefore, no longer perfectly fits the sprocket. Each roller contacts the sprocket tooth higher up on the bearing area (C) and that tooth bears the total load until the next tooth and roller make contact. Chain wear will

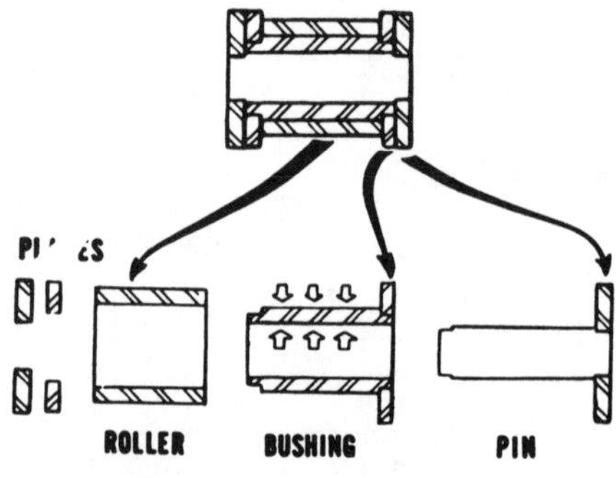

Fig. 3–The lubricant must work between the plates to enter bearing areas (white arrows) on each side of bushing.

therefore quickly result in increased sprocket wear.

As a rule of thumb, the chain should be inspected periodically and renewed whenever chain stretch exceeds 2% (or ¼-inch per foot). Renew #40 chain when a 24 pitch length of chain measures 12¼ inches or #50 chain when a 24 pitch length measures 15 5/16 inches. New length for 24 pitches is 12 and 15 inches respectively. Check sprockets carefully for wear if chain wear is substantially greater than 2%, and renew sprockets if in doubt. Sprocket wear usually shows up as a hooked tooth profile. A good test is to fit the sprocket to a new chain. Wear on sides of sprocket indicates misalignment. If sprockets must be renewed because of wear, always renew the chain. Early failure can be expected if a new chain is mated with worn sprockets or new sprockets with a worn chain.

The load carrying capacity of roller drive chains may be increased by using a heavier (and longer pitch chain) or by using a multi-strand type. The advent of higher horsepower engines in the snowmobile industry has for the most part resulted in the adoption of double (or triple) strand chain as the most practical solution because of the speeds involved.

A roller drive chain should ideally be run with as little slack as possible without being pre-loaded. This is especially important with a high-speed, high-performance drive such as that used on the snowmobile. A rule of thumb is ¼-inch of chain deflection for each 12 inches between shaft centers.

A common form of chain tightener is the eccentric housing shown in Fig. 5. A sliding tightener, rub block or idler sprocket can be used. A rub block must always be installed on the slack side of chain and this is the preferred location for an idler sprocket, although an idler sprocket may be installed on either side.

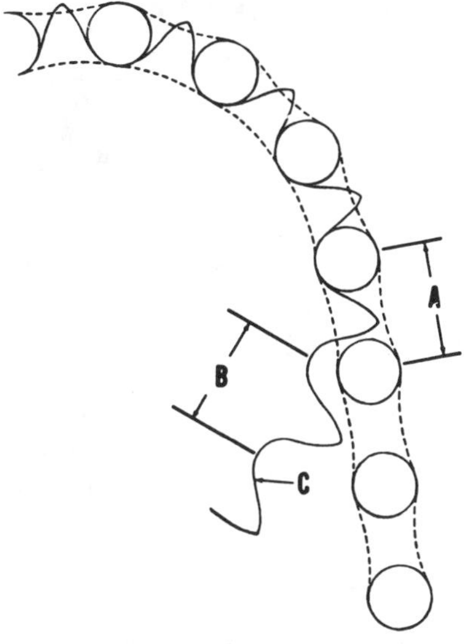

Fig. 4–Chain pitch (A) must exactly equal sprocket pitch (B) to prevent excessive wear on bearing edge of sprocket tooth (C). Refer to text.

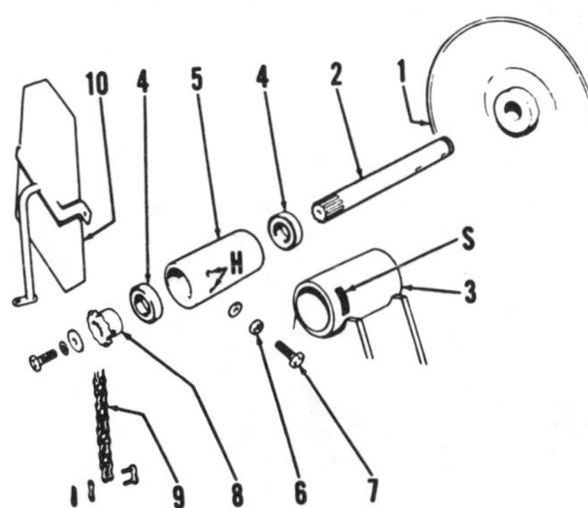

Fig. 5–Exploded view of early type intermediate shaft and associated parts showing eccentric chain tightener typical of that used on many machines. Lock bolt (7) goes through slot (S) into hole (H) in eccentric housing (5). By loosening locknut (6) and pushing down on bolt (7) the distance between sprockets is increased and chain is tightened. Refer to text.

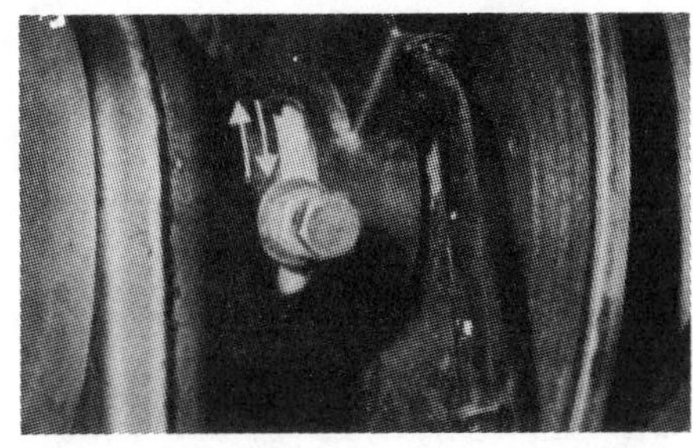

Fig. 6–Assembled view of tightener similar to that shown exploded in Fig. 5. A Ski-Doo Unit is shown.

BEARINGS

Many vehicles use self-aligning, sealed type ball bearings of the general type shown in Figs. 7 and 8. These bearings are an easy slip fit on the shaft. The locking collar and inner bearing race have an eccentric flange as shown. If properly installed, the bearing will not loosen on shaft but can easily be removed if disassembly is indicated. To lock the bearing, be sure eccentric flange is fully engaged as shown in Fig. 8,turn flange in direction of normal shaft rotation as shown in Fig. 7; then set with a punch and hammer using the locking hole provided in flange. Lock by tightening the set screw securely.

NOTE: If locking collar is secured by turning opposite normal shaft rotation, it may loosen after vehicle is returned to service.

When disassembling the bearing, loosen the locking set screw and tap the collar opposite normal shaft rotation to loosen the eccentric flange, then slip bearing and collar from the shaft.

Never immerse a sealed bearing in solvent or cleaning fluid. Outside may be cleaned with a brush and fluid but lubrication may be washed out or dirt washed in if bearing is immersed. Renew the bearing if its condition is questionable.

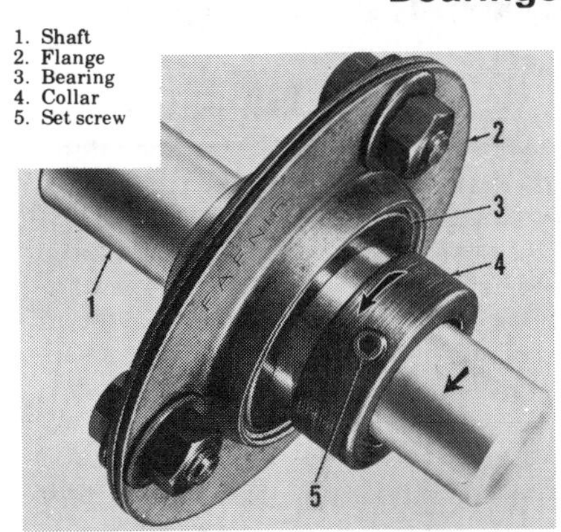

Fig. 7–Assembled view of self aligning, flangette type sealed bearing of the type used on many snowmobile drive shafts. Collar (4) and mating flange of bearing inner race are eccentric and bearing can be firmly locked to shaft by turning the collar. BE SURE to turn collar in normal direction of shaft rotation as indicated by arrows, to prevent subsequent loosening; then tighten set screw (5) securely. To disassemble the unit, loosen set screw then use a punch and hammer to turn the collar opposite normal direction of rotation until collar is loose, then shaft can be withdrawn by hand.

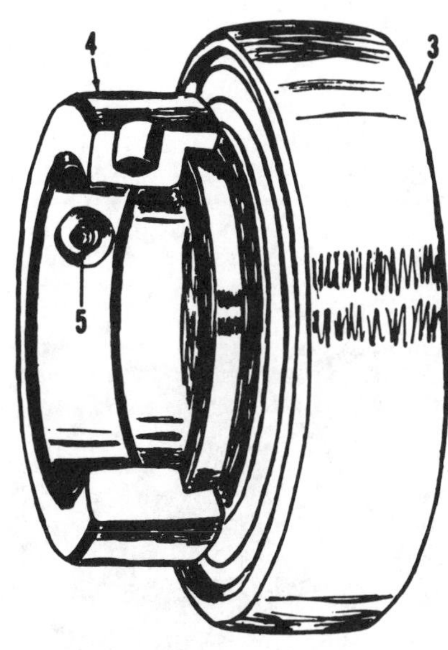

Fig. 8–Cutaway view of locking collar showing eccentric locking flanges. Refer to Fig. 7 for parts identification.

BRAKES

Most snowmobile brakes mount on the intermediate shaft which carries the torque converter driven sheave and final drive sprocket, and are actuated by a cable lever mounted on left handlebar. Disc type, wedge type, band type and shoe type brakes are used. Refer to Figs. 9 through 12.

The principles of brake service are similar for all types. Brake must fully release and fully engage with no interference caused by binding, misalignment or improper adjustment.

On the caliper type disc brakes shown in Fig. 9, cams on actuating lever (8) act through cam pins (6) to clamp the rotating brake disc (3) between the two friction pucks (2). Check the following: Disc (3) should have enough side movement on shaft to allow it to move against and away from the stationary puck, or caliper unit must center on disc if disc is firmly fixed. Contact surfaces of pucks (2) and disc (3) must be absolutely parallel so that full surface contact is accomplished when brakes are applied and no drag exists when brake is released. Cam pins (6) must be free in their bores. Lever (8) should rest with cam pins (6) in bottom of valleys in lever cam as shown in (Insert—Fig. 9A). Castellated nut (9—Fig. 9) provides wear adjustment; lever is repositioned by adjusting the cable.

On wedge type brake (Fig. 10), pulley (4) and band (3) must be perfectly aligned, with equal clearance on both side of friction wedge and throughout the contact length of wedge. Alignment is usually accomplished by moving pulley (4) on shaft, and wear adjustment at anchor end of band (3) or by adjusting the cable.

On the brake shown in Fig. 11, the friction shoe on lever arm (2) contacts the fixed flange outer face of torque converter driven sheave (1). Lever arm must not be bent and shoe should contact evenly when brake is applied. Adjustment is normally accomplished by loosening nuts (C) and repositioning the cable housing anchor.

On all models, the brake cable must move freely in cable housing. The condition of cable can be checked by disconnecting at lower end (B—Fig. 11). Binding can be caused by gum, rust, dirt or kinks in cable or housing. The common method of adjusting a new cable during installation is to thread the two nuts (C) to housing end of threads, then connect lower end (B) with brake in approximate adjustment. Complete the adjustment and/or make further adjustments whenever possible, by using the anchor nuts (C). On most models, actuating lever (5—Fig. 12) can be positioned as desired by loosening clamp (7).

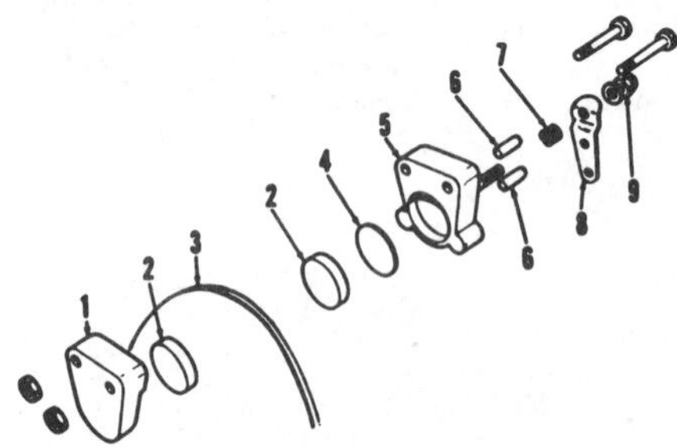

Fig. 9–Exploded view of caliper type disc brake used on many snowmobiles.

1. Body
2. Puck
3. Disc
4. Back-up washer
5. Body
6. Cam pins
7. Spring
8. Cam lever
9. Adjusting nut

Fig. 9A–In released position, push pins should ride in valleys of cam arm as shown in inset.

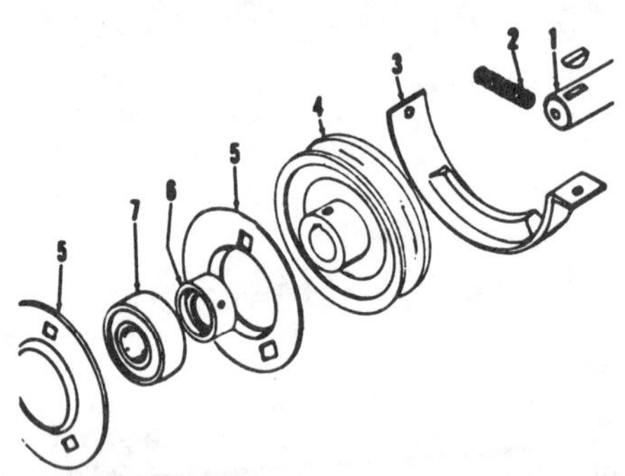

Fig. 10—Exploded view of wedge type shoe brake used on some early models.

1. Intermediate shaft
2. Return spring
3. Band
4. Pulley
5. Flange
6. Collar
7. Bearing

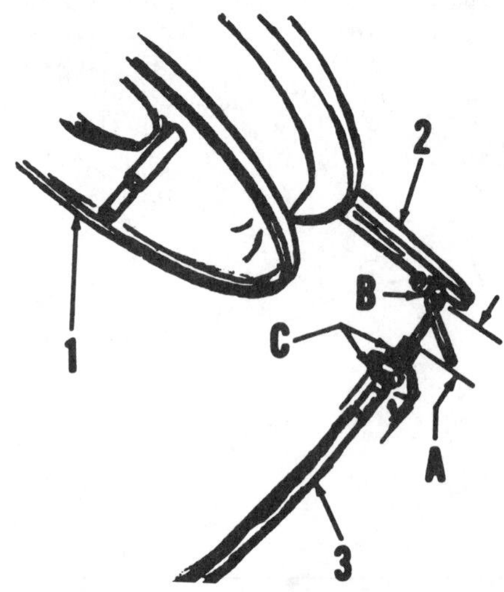

Fig. 11–Some lever type shoe brakes use the driven sheave as a friction face.

1. Driven sheave
2. Brake lever
3. Cable

A. Adjusting distance
B. Cable clamp screw
C. Housing adjustment

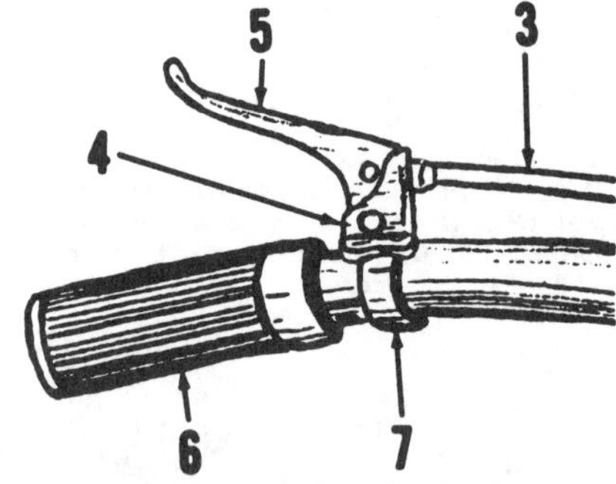

Fig. 12–View of left handlebar showing typical brake actuating mechanism. Hand lever (5) can be conveniently positioned by loosening clamp (7).

TRACK AND SUSPENSION

CONTENTS

GENERAL

The rubber or synthetic composition drive track is used to propel the snowmobile and to provide flotation and cushioning for vehicle and passengers. In common with all field machines, a wide variety of surface conditions is encountered, each of which provides different problems in design, adjustment and maintenance.

Primary support for the front of the machine is provided by the skis as shown in Fig. 1. Secondary front end support (white arrows) is by the curved or upslanting "belly pan" which leads smoothly to the forward portion of the track. The operator, any passengers and approximately half of the machine weight rides directly over the track.

The cushioning track suspension system may be of the "bogie wheel" type shown in Fig. 1 or "slide rail" type shown in Fig. 3. Proponents of bogie wheel suspension claim firmer track contact over uneven surface, therefore improved traction. Proponents of slide rail suspension claim a smoother ride and better high speed stability. Refer to Figs. 4, 5, 6 and 7. Both general types including some hybrids are widely used and individual preference plays a big role in selection.

Although earlier models sometimes used spliced (laced) belts in the track, endless belts or tracks are now widely used (Refer to Fig. 8). Figs. 9 and 10 show the GATES "Poly Trac" and internal drive sprockets which was among the early fully engineered units.

NOTE: Molded, segmented tracks are now reappearing as a service replacement and original equipment item. Refer to OVERHAUL Section which follows.

BOGIE WHEEL. A typical bogie wheel suspension system is shown in Fig. 11 while Fig. 12 shows assembled and exploded views of one bogie frame unit.

Although individual components differ, many units are similar; with front and rear bogie axles spring-suspended from a central support shaft. Most bogie wheels use anti-friction ball or roller bearings and plastic composition or hard rubber tires. Bogie frame can be removed by loosening the track and withdrawing support shaft. Removal is necessary for renewing spring, frame or bearing. Be sure to observe correct method of assembly before unit is removed, for convenience in reassembly.

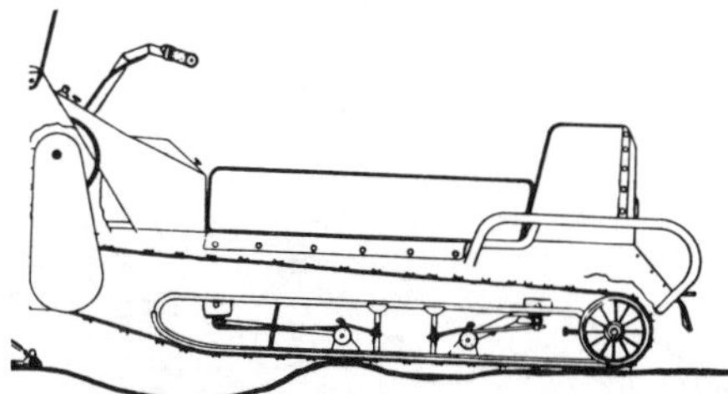

Fig. 7–Slide rail systems can be quickly adjusted for weight distribution and ride.

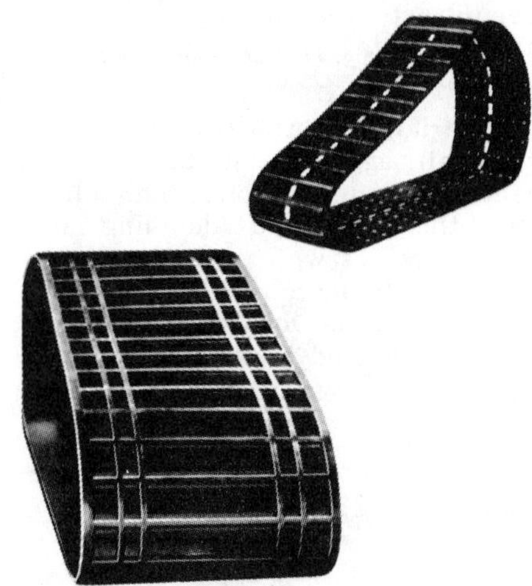

Fig. 8–Endless belts may be of molded construction as shown at bottom, or use metal cleats as shown at top.

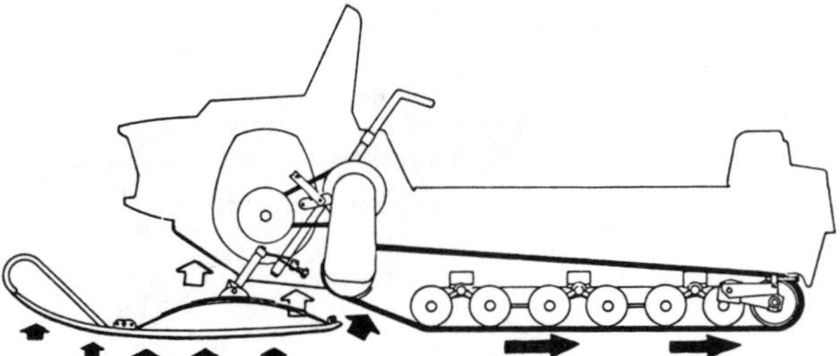

Fig. 1–Primary support for front of sled is provided by skis as shown by black arrows. Secondary support for bucking drifts, etc., by the upslanting belly pan as shown by white arrows. Track slants up at front to provide a continuous surface for traversing deep snow, supports rear of machine and provides traction.

Fig. 9–Cross sectional view of GATES "Poly-Trac" which was among the early fully engineered systems.

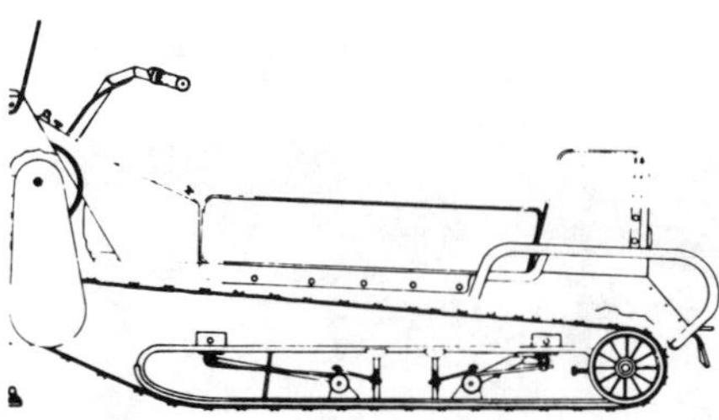

Fig. 3–Cross sectional view of "Slide Rail" suspension showing details of construction.

Fig. 5–More track contact over high spots results in better traction.

Fig. 4–Bogie wheels exert even pressure over uneven surface. See also Fig. 5.

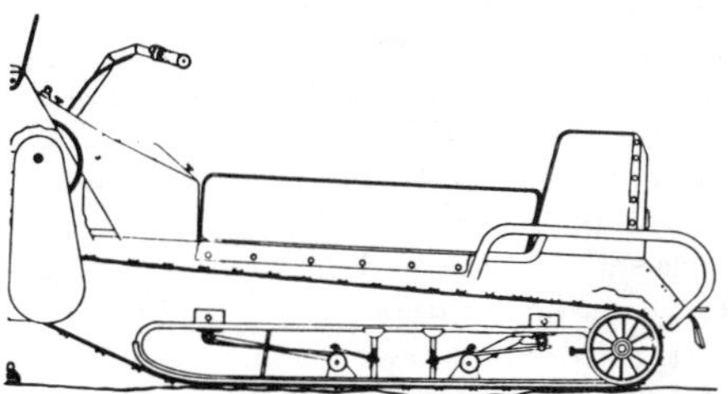

Fig. 6–Slide rails glide over uneven surface, resulting in smoother ride and firmer control. See also Fig. 7.

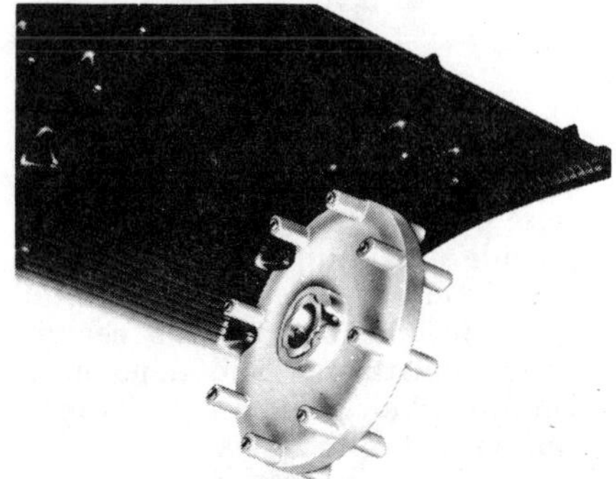

Fig. 10–View of internal drive lugs and drive sprockets used in GATES system.

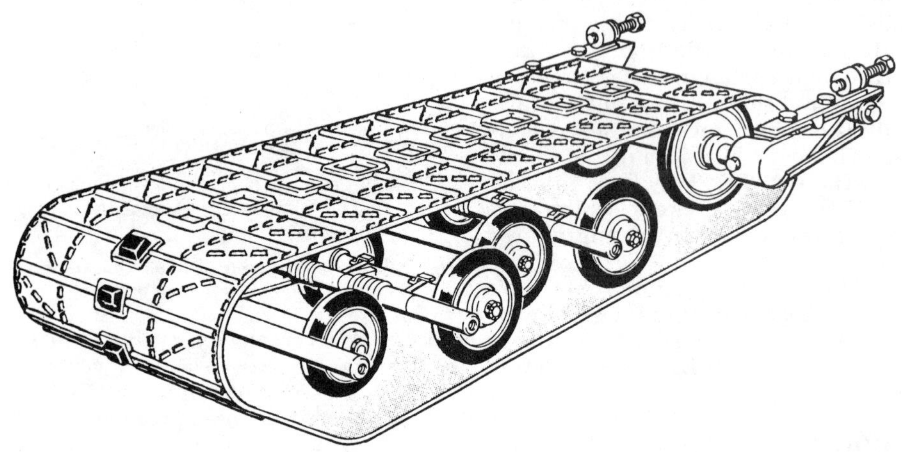

Fig. 11–Assembled view of typical bogie wheel suspension system.

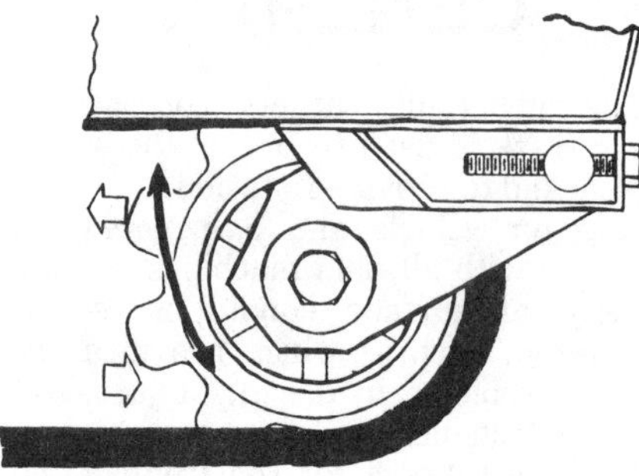

Fig. 13–Typical rear pivoted track idler axle. Arrows show that track loosens under load and tightens when load is removed.

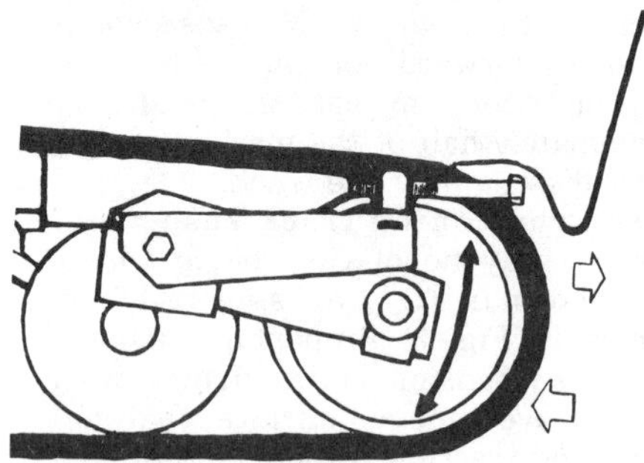

Fig. 14–Front pivoted track idler axle. Track tightens under load and loosens when load is removed as indicated by arrows.

A variation is the trailing unit in which all bogie wheel units are located behind suspension point. This eliminates the "folding up" (doubling back) of front bogies which occasionally occurs with the more conventional bogie system. Another variation is a combination slide and bogie suspension in which one or more sets of wheels are used in conjunction with a rail which may or may not also partially support the track.

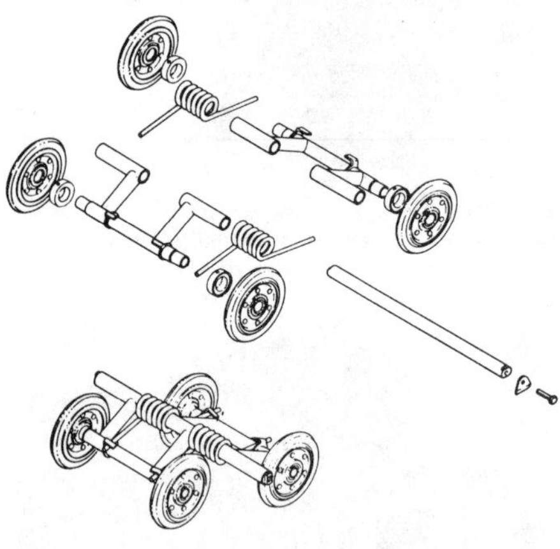

Fig. 12–Exploded view of bogie wheel frame unit showing component parts.

SLIDE RAIL. Slide rail systems are also varied in construction. Most have in common the self-lubricating plastic wear strips (or runners) which evenly support the entire contact surface of track.

As in the case with brake linings or clutch facings, slide shoes should be renewed when worn thin; and before rivets are exposed or shoe worn through at any point. Track and/or suspension damage can quickly occur without the protecting slide shoe. Suspension must be removed for slide renewal.

NOTE: Slide and track wear is minimal as long as parts are maintained in good condition and machine is operated exclusively on clean snow or ice. Rapid wear can occur, however, from use on dirt, gravel or abrasive surfaces. Frequent inspection is recommended when operating in unfavorable conditions.

Fig. 15–One type of suspension mounting showing track adjustment points. Refer also to Figs. 16 and 17.

Fig. 16–Alternate method of suspension mounting. Refer also to Figs. 15 and 17. In each instance, adjustment is made by loosening clamp fasteners (1) and turning adjusting screw (2).

TRACK MAINTENANCE

TENSION ADJUSTMENT. The purpose of track tension adjustment is to provide maximum trouble-free service and performance with minimum wear. The manufacturer's recommended adjustment (and adjustment procedure) when available, is given in the individual vehicle section.

Track should be comfortably snug without tension when vehicle is in operating position; and may be tighter or looser when vehicle is raised or load removed, depending on springing method. Refer to Figs. 13 and 14 for schematic views. In Fig. 13, rear track idler arm pivots from the rear and track loosens as load increases (white arrows). This suspension method is most commonly used. Fig. 14 shows track idler arm pivoted at front and increasing the load causes track to tighten. A track that is too tight will cause excessive wear and will pull hard. A track that is too loose will ride up or slip on drive sprocket and may jump or be thrown off during operation.

NOTE: On some types of track, extreme changes in temperature may affect track length, and therefore track tension. For this reason, adjust or check tension immediately prior to use and in the general area where the machine will be run; and rechecked if considerable temperature change occurs.

Refer to Figs. 15, 16 and 17 for typical adjustment points. Loosen nuts (1) and turn adjusting screws (2) to tighten or loosen track. Both sides must be adjusted alike to permit track to center on drive and idler sprockets.

IMPORTANT: When track tension is adjusted as outlined in individual vehicle sections or by following standard procedure, refer to Fig. 18 and check the track alignment as follows:

Support vehicle on front skis and jack stand (or by placing solid supports under rear corners of frame at points shown by large arrows). With track clear of ground start and run engine at just above clutch engagement speed. With track turning slowly it should remain centered on drive and idler sprockets and in vehicle frame without rubbing on either side. If track runs to left, tighten LEFT track adjustment slightly. If track runs to right, tighten RIGHT side.

If track snakes (runs from side to side) or cannot be centered, check for damage to suspension, sprockets, bogies (or slides) and track; and make any necessary repairs before proceeding with the adjustment.

MINOR REPAIRS. On many models, track inserts are used in drive slots as shown in Figs. 19 and 20. Renew damaged or missing inserts at the earliest opportunity, making sure they are carefully and correctly installed with no rough edges existing which might damage sprockets, bogie wheels or slide shoes. Forming tools for track insert installation are available from most manufacturers using inserted tracks.

Also examine track for cuts or breaks, bent cleats and loose or missing rivets. Pop rivets are used for cleat installation on some models and are very handy for quick repairs. When cuts or breaks expose track fabric, thoroughly clean the area and coat or fill with liquid rubber, latex or flexible plastic to protect the area and keep moisture out.

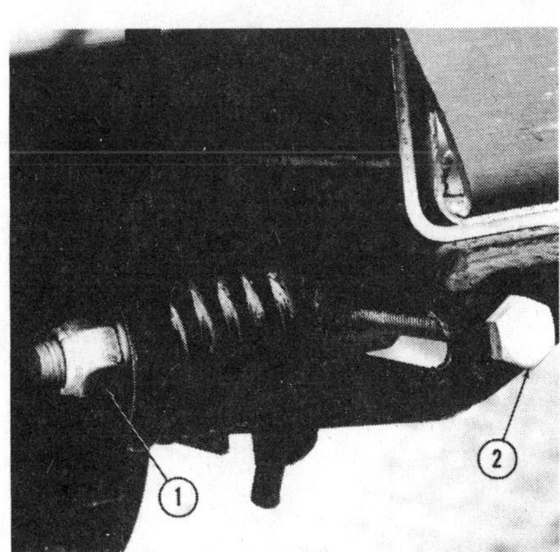

Fig. 17–Third method of suspension mounting. Refer also to Fig. 15 and 16.

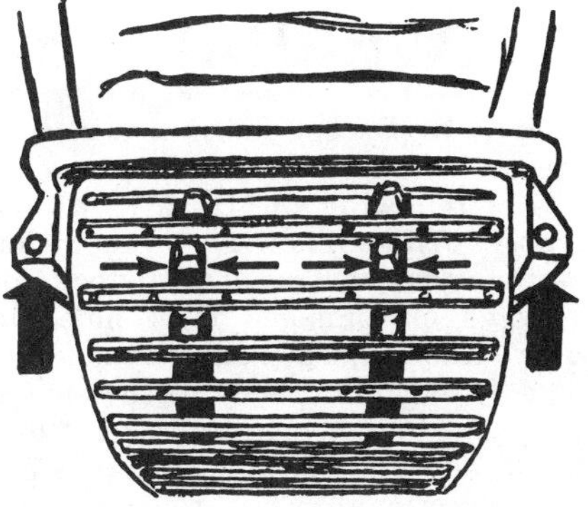
Fig. 18–To check track alignment each time track is adjusted, support rear of machine at points indicated by heavy arrows or by other suitable means. Track must be clear. Run track slowly and check to be sure that track centers on idler sprockets and in track tunnel. When improperly adjusted, track will run toward LOOSE side.

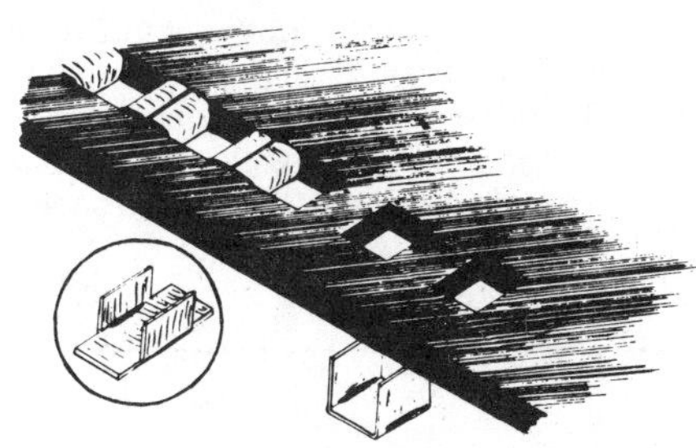
Fig. 19–One type of track insert used to protect drive notches. Widened insert (circled) is used with slide suspension.

PERFORMANCE MODIFICATION. Load distribution plays a significant part in performance, and many manufacturers provide adjustment for varying conditions or individual preference. Increasing pressure on the skis improves steering on hard-packed snow or ice, but may lessen the ability of the machine to break trail in deep fluffy snow. Pressure can be added to the skis by adjustment (on some models) or by the use of riser block as outlined in SKIS AND STEERING Section. Ski pressure can also be added or removed by suspension adjustment or modification as indicated in Fig. 21. Increasing the RELATIVE suspension pressure at FRONT of track LIGHTENS ski pressure as indicated by black arrows. Increasing RELATIVE pressure at REAR of track INCREASES ski pressure as shown by white arrows.

Fig. 20–Second type of track insert used to protect drive notches.

Fig. 21–Relative pressure at front or rear of track affects ski load. Refer to PERFORMANCE MODIFICATION paragraphs.

Some manufacturers provide ride adjustments which can be used to modify performance and the procedure is given in the individual vehicle sections. If provision is not made in vehicle design, the most simple changes can be made by ski alterations but an understanding of the principles of load distribution can be invaluable in correcting difficulties that might arise in performance modification.

Load distribution can be adjusted by altering spring load on all bogies; front bogies only; rear bogies only or rear idler axle. Change can be accomplished by using lighter or heavier springs; changing spring anchor points; shimming; using larger or smaller bogie wheels; or by raising or lowering bogie frame unit.

Plan any modification carefully keeping desired results in mind. Be careful not to "butcher" the machine to the point where it cannot be restored to its original condition if your calculations were in error or if conditions change.

Fig. 22–Two types of FASTRAC segmented track used for replacement and as original equipment.

OVERHAUL

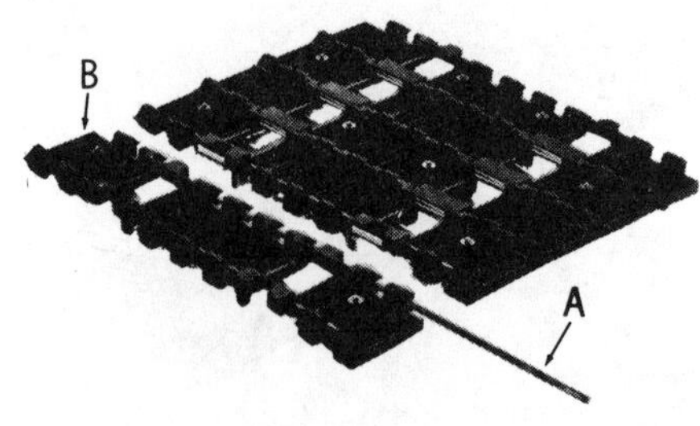

Fig. 23–Individual track segments (B) are joined by a spring steel pin (A).

Traction can be improved on ice or hard packed snow by adding or installing special steel cleats or, in an emergency, short carriage bolts with nuts to outside. Be sure that cleats do not interfere with track carriage or strike track tunnel at high speed. Track material affects traction. Rubber is less "slick" than most synthetic material and provides inherently better traction. Synthetic track materials are tougher and wear longer; and some change less at temperature extremes.

TRACK. Except for minor repairs (previously covered) most repair consists of renewing the track as an assembly. When renewing or repairing riveted type cleated tracks, look for enlarged or damaged rivet holes in belts. Minor enlargement may be overcome by redrilling cleat and increasing rivet size, but in many instances belt should be renewed. Molded tracks are often directional in nature. Look for a directional arrow or other indication or refer to specific vehicle section. Directional arrow indicates direction of track rotation, not direction of machine travel.

On segmented type molded tracks (Figs. 22 & 23) individual sections can be renewed because of accidental damage but would not normally be renewed because of wear. Sections are marked with a directional arrow. Segments are joined using ½-inch spring steel rods (A—Fig. 23) which are a tight interference fit in Polyurethane track material. Provided in the installation kit is a 3/16-inch diameter metal alignment dowel which is first inserted in joint; then hinge rod is installed by tapping with a hammer, driving out alignment dowel as rod is installed. Barbed retaining rings (3—Fig. 24) are installed (points outward) at ends of hinge rod using a center punch (4) or Phillips Head screwdriver as an installation tool.

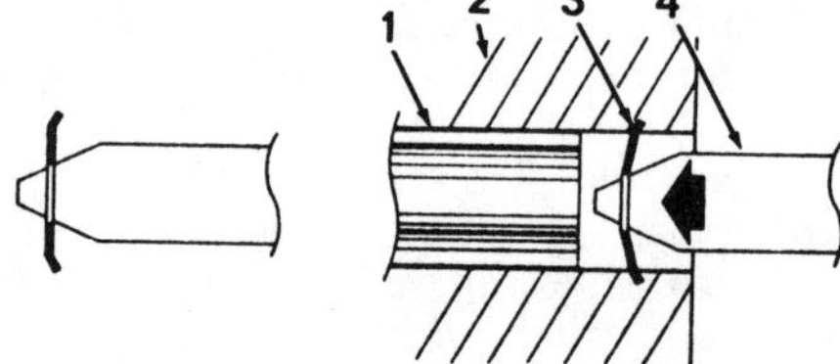

Fig. 24–Hinge rod is retained by barbed retaining rings.

1. Hinge rod
2. Track segment
3. Retaining ring
4. Installing tool

SKIS AND STEERING

CONTENTS

GENERAL

Steering geometry is not merely a matter of connecting two skis to a handlebar. The actual turning moment of the ski depends on relative length of center steering arm and side steering arms, relative location and angle of installation. Fig. 1 shows the actual turning angle of various components as installed but is not meant to imply proper or approved design. Shortening the center steering arm or lengthening the outer arms will cause the skis to turn at a smaller angle relative to handlebar movement while aligning outer arms more nearly with ski centerline will reduce the difference between steering angle of outer and inner ski. It may be concluded from further study that redesign to clear a muffler or engine modification is not the simple matter it might first appear. As a rule of thumb, inner ski should turn a greater distance than outer ski to provide a comfortable feel. Angling ski legs forward as shown in Fig. 2 causes skis to bank into turns as shown in inset.

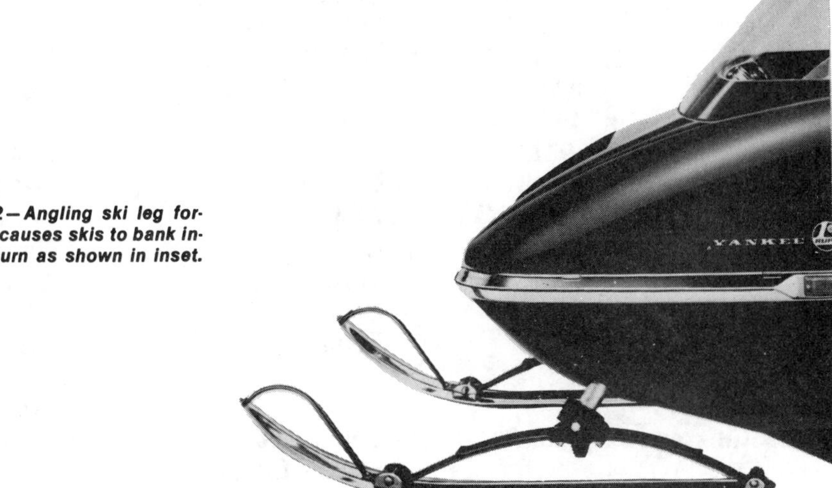

Fig. 2—Angling ski leg forward causes skis to bank into a turn as shown in inset.

Handlebar shaft angle affects handling and balance but is largely a matter of personal choice. Handlebar position is not generally changed in sled modification but consider the effect (or try a sled with similar angle) before making a change.

Additional ski pressure for better control under certain conditions can be obtained by installing a spacer between ski spring leaf and spindle bracket on each side. Longer spring bolts will be required when spacer is installed.

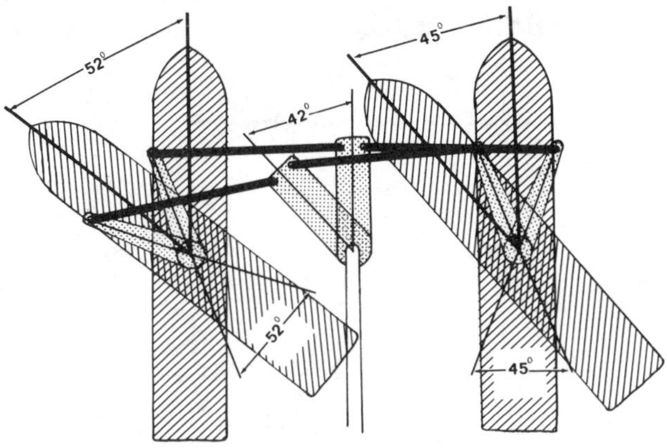

Fig. 1—Things are not always what they seem when it comes to steering geometry. In the illustrated setup, turning handlebar 42 degrees turns outer ski 45 degrees and inner ski 52 degrees. Refer to text for details.

OVERHAUL

Service for the most part consists of renewing bent, broken or damaged parts. Ski alignment specifications are given in vehicle sections. If not given, adjust skis to parallel in straight-ahead position, a slight toe-out being generally preferable to toe-in when all slack is removed from linkage.

METRIC CONVERSION

Cubic meters	= .02832	x Cubic Feet
Cubic meters	x 1.308	= Cubic Yards
Cubic meters	= .765	x Cubic Yards
Liters	x 61.023	= Cubic Inches
Liters	= .01639	x Cubic Inches
Liters	x .26418	= U.S. Gallons
Liters	= 3.7854	x U.S. Gallons
Grams	x 15.4324	= Grains
Grams	= .0648	x Grains
Grams	x .03527	= Ounces, avoirdupois
Grams	= 28.3495	x Ounces, avoirdupois
Kilograms	x 2.2046	= Pounds
Kilograms	= .4536	x Pounds
Kilograms per square centimeter	x 14.2231	= Pounds per square Inch
Kilograms per square centimeter	= .0703	x Pounds per square Inch
Kilograms per cubic meter	x .06243	= Pounds per cubic Foot
Kilograms per cubic meter	= 16.01890	x Pounds per cubic Foot

Metric tons (1,000 kilograms)	x 1.1023	= Tons (2,000 Pounds)
Metric tons (1,000 kilograms)	= .9072	x Tons (2,000 Pounds)
Kilowatts	= 1.3405	x Horsepower
Kilowatts	x .746	= Horsepower
Millimeters	x .03937	= Inches
Millimeters	= 25.400	x Inches
Meters	x 3.2809	= Feet
Meters	= .3048	x Feet
Kilometers	x .621377	= Miles
Kilometers	= 1.6093	x Miles
Square centimeters	x .15500	= Square Inches
Square centimeters	= 6.4515	x Square Inches
Square meters	x 10.76410	= Square Feet
Square meters	= .09290	x Square Feet
Cubic centimeters	x .061025	= Cubic Inches
Cubic centimeters	= 16.3866	x Cubic Inches
Cubic meters	x 35.3156	= Cubic Feet

MM.	INCHES		
1	0.0394	1/32	+
2	0.0787	3/32	−
3	0.1181	1/8	−
4	0.1575	5/32	+
5	0.1969	3/16	+
6	0.2362	1/4	−
7	0.2756	9/32	−
8	0.3150	5/16	+
9	0.3543	11/32	+
10	0.3937	13/32	−
11	0.4331	7/16	−
12	0.4724	15/32	+
13	0.5118	1/2	+
14	0.5512	9/16	−
15	0.5906	19/32	−
16	0.6299	5/8	+
17	0.6693	21/32	+
18	0.7087	23/32	−
19	0.7480	3/4	−
20	0.7874	25/32	+
21	0.8268	13/16	+
22	0.8661	7/8	−
23	0.9055	29/32	−
24	0.9449	15/16	+
25	0.9843	31/32	+
26	1.0236	1 1/32	−
27	1.0630	1 1/16	+
28	1.1024	1 3/32	+
29	1.1417	1 5/32	−
30	1.1811	1 3/16	−
31	1.2205	1 7/32	+
32	1.2598	1 1/4	+
33	1.2992	1 5/16	−
34	1.3386	1 11/32	−
35	1.3780	1 3/8	+
36	1.4173	1 13/32	+
37	1.4567	1 15/32	−
38	1.4961	1 1/2	−
39	1.5354	1 17/32	+
40	1.5748	1 9/16	+
41	1.6142	1 5/8	−
42	1.6535	1 21/32	−
43	1.6929	1 11/16	+
44	1.7323	1 23/32	+
45	1.7717	1 25/32	−
46	1.8110	1 13/16	−
47	1.8504	1 27/32	+
48	1.8898	1 7/8	+
49	1.9291	1 15/16	−
50	1.9685	1 31/32	−
51	2.0079	2.0	+
52	2.0472	2 1/16	−
53	2.0866	2 3/32	−
54	2.1260	2 1/8	+
55	2.1654	2 5/32	+
56	2.2047	2 7/32	−
57	2.2441	2 1/4	−
58	2.2835	2 9/32	+
59	2.3228	2 5/16	+
60	2.3622	2 3/8	−
61	2.4016	2 13/32	−
62	2.4409	2 7/16	+
63	2.4803	2 15/32	+
64	2.5197	2 17/32	−
65	2.5591	2 9/16	−
66	2.5984	2 19/32	+
67	2.6378	2 5/8	+
68	2.6772	2 11/16	−
69	2.7165	2 23/32	−
70	2.7559	2 3/4	+
71	2.7953	2 25/32	+
72	2.8346	2 27/32	−
73	2.8740	2 7/8	−
74	2.9134	2 29/32	+
75	2.9528	2 15/16	+
76	2.9921	3.0	−
77	3.0315	3 1/32	+
78	3.0709	3 1/16	+
79	3.1102	3 1/8	−
80	3.1496	3 5/32	−
81	3.1890	3 3/16	+
82	3.2283	3 7/32	+
83	3.2677	3 9/32	−
84	3.3071	3 5/16	−
85	3.3465	3 11/32	+
86	3.3858	3 3/8	+
87	3.4252	3 7/16	−
88	3.4646	3 15/32	−
89	3.5039	3 1/2	+
90	3.5433	3 17/32	+
91	3.5827	3 19/32	−
92	3.6220	3 5/8	−
93	3.6614	3 21/32	+
94	3.7008	3 11/16	+
95	3.7402	3 3/4	−
96	3.7795	3 25/32	−
97	3.8189	3 13/16	+
98	3.8583	3 27/32	+
99	3.8976	3 29/32	−
100	3.9370	3 15/16	−
101	3.9764	3 31/32	+
102	4.0157	4 1/32	−
103	4.0551	4 1/16	−
104	4.0945	4 3/32	+
105	4.1339	4 1/8	+
106	4.1732	4 3/16	−
107	4.2126	4 7/32	−
108	4.2520	4 1/4	+
109	4.2913	4 9/32	+
110	4.3307	4 11/32	−
111	4.3701	4 3/8	−
112	4.4094	4 13/32	+
113	4.4488	4 7/16	+
114	4.4882	4 1/2	−
115	4.5276	4 17/32	−
116	4.5669	4 9/16	+
117	4.6063	4 19/32	+
118	4.6457	4 21/32	−
119	4.6850	4 11/16	−
120	4.7244	4 23/32	+
121	4.7638	4 3/4	+
122	4.8031	4 13/16	−
123	4.8425	4 27/32	−
124	4.8819	4 7/8	+
125	4.9213	4 29/32	+
126	4.9606	4 31/32	−
127	5.0000	5.0	
128	5.0394	5 1/32	+
129	5.0787	5 3/32	−
130	5.1181	5 1/8	−
131	5.1575	5 5/32	+
132	5.1968	5 3/16	+
133	5.2362	5 1/4	−
134	5.2756	5 9/32	−
135	5.3150	5 5/16	+
136	5.3543	5 11/32	+
137	5.3937	5 13/32	−
138	5.4331	5 7/16	−
139	5.4724	5 15/32	+
140	5.5118	5 1/2	+
141	5.5512	5 9/16	−
142	5.5905	5 19/32	−
143	5.6299	5 5/8	+
144	5.6693	5 21/32	+
145	5.7087	5 23/32	−
146	5.7480	5 3/4	−
147	5.7874	5 25/32	+
148	5.8268	5 13/16	+
149	5.8661	5 7/8	−
150	5.9055	5 29/32	−
151	5.9449	5 15/16	+
152	5.9842	5 31/32	+
153	6.0236	6 1/32	−
154	6.0630	6 1/16	+
155	6.1024	6 3/32	+
156	6.1417	6 5/32	−
157	6.1811	6 3/16	−
158	6.2205	6 7/32	+
159	6.2598	6 1/4	+
160	6.2992	6 5/16	−
161	6.3386	6 11/32	−
162	6.3779	6 3/8	+
163	6.4173	6 13/32	+
164	6.4567	6 15/32	−
165	6.4961	6 1/2	−
166	6.5354	6 17/32	+
167	6.5748	6 9/16	+
168	6.6142	6 5/8	−
169	6.6535	6 21/32	−
170	6.6929	6 11/16	+
171	6.7323	6 23/32	+
172	6.7716	6 25/32	−
173	6.8110	6 13/16	−
174	6.8504	6 27/32	+
175	6.8898	6 7/8	+
176	6.9291	6 15/16	−
177	6.9685	6 31/32	−
178	7.0079	7.0	+
179	7.0472	7 1/16	−
180	7.0866	7 3/32	−
181	7.1260	7 1/8	+
182	7.1653	7 5/32	+
183	7.2047	7 7/32	−
184	7.2441	7 1/4	−
185	7.2835	7 9/32	+
186	7.3228	7 5/16	+
187	7.3622	7 3/8	−
188	7.4016	7 13/32	−
189	7.4409	7 7/16	+
190	7.4803	7 15/32	+
191	7.5197	7 17/32	−
192	7.5590	7 9/16	−
193	7.5984	7 19/32	+
194	7.6378	7 5/8	+
195	7.6772	7 11/16	−
196	7.7165	7 23/32	−
197	7.7559	7 3/4	+
198	7.7953	7 25/32	+
199	7.8346	7 27/32	−
200	7.8740	7 7/8	−
201	7.9134	7 29/32	+
202	7.9527	7 15/16	+
203	7.9921	8.0	−
204	8.0315	8 1/32	+
205	8.0709	8 1/16	+
206	8.1102	8 1/8	−
207	8.1496	8 5/32	−
208	8.1890	8 3/16	+
209	8.2283	8 7/32	+
210	8.2677	8 9/32	−
211	8.3071	8 5/16	−
212	8.3464	8 11/32	+
213	8.3858	8 3/8	+
214	8.4252	8 7/16	−
215	8.4646	8 15/32	−
216	8.5039	8 1/2	+
217	8.5433	8 17/32	+
218	8.5827	8 19/32	−
219	8.6220	8 5/8	−
220	8.6614	8 21/32	+
221	8.7008	8 11/16	+
222	8.7401	8 3/4	−
223	8.7795	8 25/32	−
224	8.8189	8 13/16	+
225	8.8583	8 27/32	+
226	8.8976	8 29/32	−
227	8.9370	8 15/16	−
228	8.9764	8 31/32	+
229	9.0157	9 1/32	−
230	9.0551	9 1/16	−
231	9.0945	9 3/32	+
232	9.1338	9 1/8	+
233	9.1732	9 3/16	−
234	9.2126	9 7/32	−
235	9.2520	9 1/4	+
236	9.2913	9 9/32	+
237	9.3307	9 11/32	−
238	9.3701	9 3/8	−
239	9.4094	9 13/32	+
240	9.4488	7 7/16	+
241	9.4882	9 1/2	−
242	9.5275	9 17/32	−
243	9.5669	9 9/16	+
244	9.6063	9 19/32	+
245	9.6457	9 21/32	−
246	9.6850	9 11/16	−
247	9.7244	9 23/32	+
248	9.7638	9 3/4	+
249	9.8031	9 13/16	−
250	9.8425	9 27/32	−
251	9.8819	9 7/8	+
252	9.9212	9 29/32	+
253	9.9606	9 31/32	−
254	10.0000	10.0	
255	10.0393	10 1/32	+
256	10.0787	10 3/32	−
257	10.1181	10 1/8	−
258	10.1575	10 5/32	+
259	10.1968	10 3/16	+
260	10.2362	10 1/4	−
261	10.2756	10 9/32	−
262	10.3149	10 5/16	+
263	10.3543	10 11/32	+
264	10.3937	10 13/32	−
265	10.4330	10 7/16	−
266	10.4724	10 15/32	+
267	10.5118	10 1/2	+
268	10.5512	10 9/16	−
269	10.5905	10 19/32	−
270	10.6299	10 5/8	+
271	10.6693	10 21/32	+
272	10.7086	10 23/32	−
273	10.7480	10 3/4	−
274	10.7874	10 25/32	+
275	10.8268	10 13/16	+
276	10.8661	10 7/8	−
277	10.9055	10 29/32	−
278	10.9449	10 15/16	+
279	10.9842	10 31/32	+
280	11.0236	11 1/32	−
281	11.0630	11 1/16	+
282	11.1023	11 3/32	+
283	11.1417	11 5/32	−
284	11.1811	11 3/16	−
285	11.2204	11 7/32	+
286	11.2598	11 1/4	+
287	11.2992	11 5/16	−
288	11.3386	11 11/32	−
289	11.3779	11 3/8	+
290	11.4173	11 13/32	+
291	11.4567	11 15/32	−
292	11.4960	11 1/2	−
293	11.5354	11 17/32	+
294	11.5748	11 9/16	+
295	11.6142	11 5/8	−
296	11.6535	11 21/32	−
297	11.6929	11 11/16	+
298	11.7323	11 23/32	+
299	11.7716	11 25/32	−
300	11.8110	11 13/16	−

NOTE. The + or − sign indicates that the decimal equivalent is larger or smaller than the fractional equivalent.

MAINTENANCE LOG

Genuine John Deere Service Literature

For ordering information, call John Deere at 1-800-522-7448.
All major credit cards accepted.

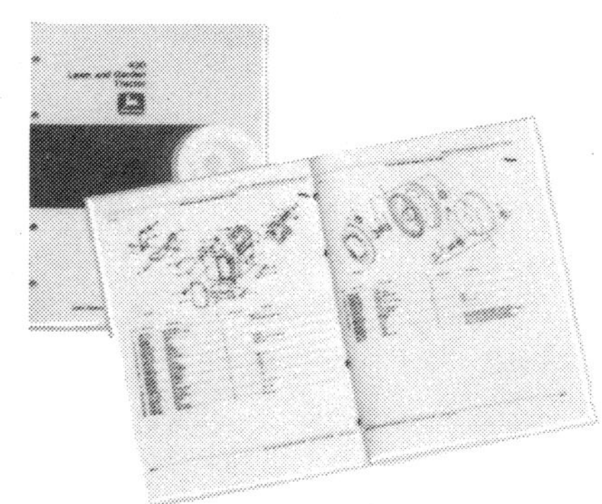

PARTS CATALOG

The parts catalog lists service parts available for your machine with exploded view illustrations to help you identify the correct parts. It is also useful in assembling and disassembling.

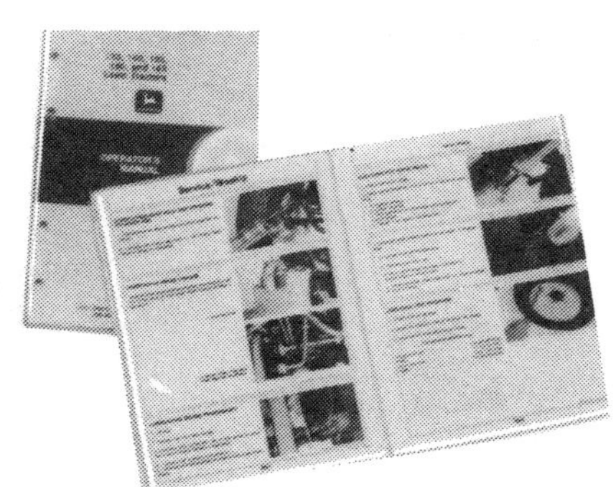

OPERATOR'S MANUAL

The operator's manual provides safety, operating, maintenance, and service information about John Deere machines.

The operator's manual and safety signs on your machine may also be available in other languages.

TECHNICAL AND SERVICE MANUALS

Technical and service manuals are service guides for your machine. Included in the manual are specifications, diagnosis, and adjustments. Also illustrations of assembly and disassembly procedures, hydraulic oil flows, and wiring diagrams.

Component technical manuals are required for some products. These supplemental manuals cover specific components.

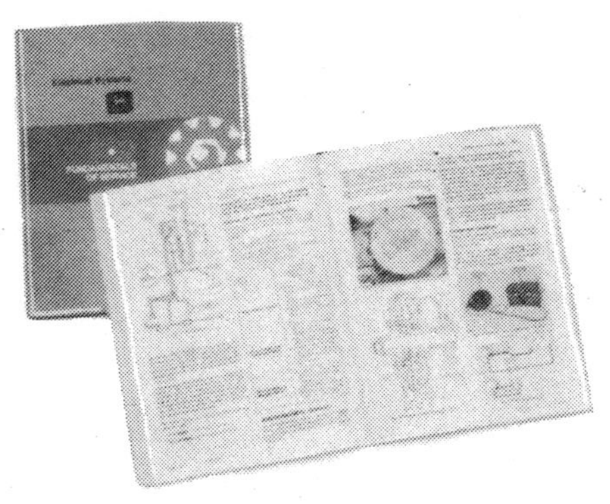

FUNDAMENTALS OF SERVICE MANUALS

These basic manuals cover most makes and types of machines. FOS manuals tell you how to SERVICE machine systems. Each manual starts with basic theory and is fully illustrated with colorful diagrams and photographs. Both the "whys" and "hows" of adjustments and repairs are covered in this reference library.